D1559109

EINSTEIN'S BEETS

Fantagraphics Books
7563 Lake City Way NE
Seattle, Washington 98115

1-800-657-1100
www.fantagraphics.com
Facebook.com/Fantagraphics
@fantagraphics

Editor: Gary Groth
Designer: Keeli McCarthy
Editorial Assistants: Conrad Groth, Paul Maliszewski
Associate Publisher: Eric Reynolds
Publisher: Gary Groth

ISBN: 978-1-60699-976-9

Library of Congress Control Number:

First Fantagraphics Books printing: April 2017

Printed in China

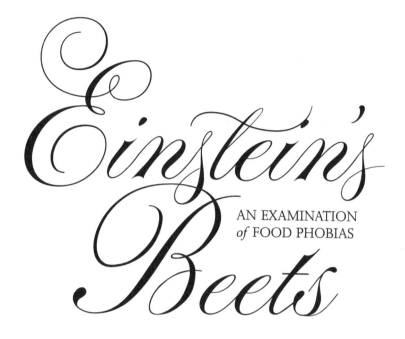

Einstein's Beets

AN EXAMINATION
of FOOD PHOBIAS

ALEXANDER THEROUX

FANTAGRAPHICS BOOKS

I have you fast in my fortress,
And will not let you depart,
But put you down into the dungeon
In the round-tower of my heart.

And there will I keep you forever,
Yes, forever and a day,
'Till the walls shall crumble to ruin,
And moulder in dust away!

Henry W. Longfellow,
"The Children's Hour"

Nothing will give delight.
What once was salt or sweet
Sickens the appetite
Like a corrupted meat
Promiscuous disgust!
How shall I know or choose?
This loathing, like pure lust,
Taints all that I might use.
Like lust, this sick revulsion
Exhausts the flesh and bone,
Turns riot to compulsion,
And feeds itself alone.

    Catherine Davis, "Nausea"

I am gall, I am heartburn: God's most deep decree
Bitter would have me taste: my taste was me."

    Gerard Manley Hopkins, "I Wake and Feel the
    Fell of Dark, Not Day"

In creation there is not only a Yes but also a No; not
only a height but also an abyss; not only clarity but
also obscurity; not only progress and continuation
but also impediment and limitation.

    Karl Barth, *Church Dogmatics*

Complaint: you open doors; what we want to know
is which ones you close.

    John Cage, *A Year From Monday*

What do you despise? By this are you truly known.

    Frank Herbert, *Dune*

CONTENTS

1.

ONE KOMODO DRAGON CUTLET, PLEASE

"NEVER ATE AN EGG IN MY LIFE," boasted the late fat-bellied director Alfred Hitchcock to actor Joseph Cotten. "Never one egg. I suppose eggs are in some of the things I eat, but I never could face a naked egg." "How about caviar?" asked Cotten. It made no difference to Hitchcock who responded, "As far as I am concerned, it is only another kind of egg, or, if you will, *are* eggs." Standing firm, Hitchcock, who dearly loved to eat, nevertheless flatly and emphatically stated what his phobia-food was and had done with it. The director went on rather neurotically—and quite candidly—to try to explain to noted columnist Oriana Fallaci in a movie interview that he gave in 1963, "I'm frightened of eggs, worse than frightened; they revolt me," he declared. "That white round thing without any holes... *Brrr*! And have you ever seen anything more revolting than an egg-yolk breaking and spilling its yellow liquid? Blood is jolly, red. But egg yolk is yellow, revolting. I've never tasted it."

For amusement, try to picture the intransigent ovophobe Hitchcock having to watch the prim, chlorotic, and hypochondriacal President Woodrow Wilson consume his favorite breakfast meal—two raw eggs in grape juice! Raw eggs were a lifelong staple for Norwegian figure skater Sonja Henie, who cracked open the shells and plopped them down like raw oysters. It would have given the rotund English movie director the fantods! Whenever Hitchcock dined out, it was utterly uncomplicated—he preferred to eat nothing but steak, nothing complex, involved, or tricky, as supposedly did the legendary tough guy, John Wayne. No fussifications or pussyfooting for the likes of him, no sirree. Just bring on that damned sirloin, pilgrim!

It is strange how the tastes of men roll out. Canadian Duncan Gillis, the U.S. runner-up to the hammer-throwing champion in the 1912 Summer Olympic Games—he won a silver medal—used to eat a dozen raw eggs for breakfast, *shells and all*, with a little dab of mustard on the shells.

There is no explaining any of it. The motivating factors of food choices, excuses and justifications, are inexplicable and remain impervious to any solid explanations as to why. Personal experience may be one approach. We spend a lifetime improving our taste. "Taste," according to an old French maxim, "is the result of a thousand distastes." While eggs, no delicacy, were not only first tasted—and spat out—by King Louis XV of France and were generally fed to pigs by European farmers, at least according to the writer Inga Saffron in her splendid history, *Caviar,* poet Dante Alighieri considered the plain egg to be "the best food in the world," especially when it was eaten with salt. If it is true that "A question is a trap and an answer is your foot in it," as John Steinbeck remarks in *Travels with Charley: In Search of America*, food is a place on a map you can personally refuse to visit. Let us consider that.

Food preferences become—even if by signaling or signification—virtually our first language. Our own babies by simple reaction, a waving hand, a heaving body, or a sharply turned head immediately tell us what they refuse to eat. The power of food, its centrality to our lives, is immense. We have read in Marcel Proust how by a small cake called a "madeleine" he was able to recapture the past. While that brilliant if neurasthenic novelist subsisted basically on a diet of coffee and croissants, as reportedly he so did, he still reveled over the beauty of food and its hidden essence, although rarely savoring it. He understood food to reveal the hidden essence of reality. It was as if he tasted the connotative cake by the mind and not the palate. Food for Proust was in many instances a vivid way, a vital means, to discover the essence of things beyond their external reality, a significant key to learning beauty and truth.

What more reveals what we are than the food we eat, the fuel by which we move, the resource by which we grow? Who could doubt that what we eat goes a long way in explaining our health, who not believe what foods in facing we choose to refuse, to avoid, to spurn is not equally as significant? In the opinion of Alice Waters of Chez Panisse, "Food is the purest expression of human culture." It is hard to focus on a better index of what a person is like than to know what foods he or she prefers, but even more so, at least regarding crotchets, than to know what food he hates. There is a distinct precinct inside that person's head that is knurled. I defend food aversions and their advocates, however, no matter how odd or pusillanimous they may seem. British wit Frank Muir puts it well, writing, "Nobody can be expected to affect academic detachment about something which he puts into his mouth and swallows."

Anyone who believes that eating choices are uncomplicated, the settled option of one confidant selection of one food over another, should think again. "Most of the energy that we put into our thinking about food, I realized, isn't about food; it's about anxiety," notes John Lanchester in "Shut Up and Eat" (*The New Yorker*, Nov. 3, 2014). "Food makes us anxious. The infinite range of choices and possible self-expressions means that there are so many ways to go wrong. You can make people ill, and you can make yourself look absurd. People feel judged by their food choices, and they are right to feel that, because they are."

It is not merely a matter of strikes and spares, mere whim. Something of the revelation of a soul, a significant tell-tale to a degree, is informed by what in foods as in many things we choose to avoid, select to reject. I tend to side with the Austrian satirist Karl Kraus, who was convinced that every error, no matter how small, even if seemingly limited in importance, can extend to revealing great evils of the world. Degeneracy and corruption is inherent in seemingly small errors. Kraus claimed that he could divine in a missing comma a symptom of that state of the world that could and would allow a world war. It is my belief that every choice of ours, in matters of food especially, reveals—discloses—a significant part of us, although I still personally hold to the ultimate truth spoken by Jesus when, called a crowd to him, he said, "Listen and understand. What goes into someone's mouth does not defile them, but what comes out of their mouth, that is what defiles them." (Matthew 15:10)

We have all come across Ludwig Feuerbach's punning aphorism, "*Man ist was er isst*"—*one is what one eats.* Any given food that we utterly abhor, single out to refuse to eat, equally can signify a great deal. "Food is, anthropologically speaking, our first need," explains French intellectual Roland Barthes in his essay, "Toward a Psychosociology of Contemporary Food Consumption." "It sums up and transmits a situation; it constitutes an [sic] information; it signifies. That is to say that it is not just an indicator of a set of more or less conscious motivations, but that it is a real sign, perhaps the functional unit of a system of communication."

When I began to investigate the matter of food phobias I soon came to see, not without some surprise, that people in general, but especially celebrities, so-called famous people, notables, dearly love to disclose their innermost thoughts and emotions. They will devotedly tell you the sordid truth about their love affairs, pour their hearts out, divulge their deepest secrets. It is uniquely true about what foods they dislike. While a personal matter, such secrets are subtly shared. A sense of complaining can be heard. Whining is often involved, anger, certainly indignation.

Any complaint, let's face it, pledges allegiance to another ideal. I am fascinated by the strong opinion, no matter how oblique or contradictory it may be, for even if wrong-headed or biased, it is a pronounced indication of the self in the same way that, according to Goethe, all writing is confession. Whatever it may be that we personally choose—go out of our way to repudiate—arguably best clarifies, least fudges, crucially pinpoints, sharply insists on, and invariably obtains by way of declaration and protest and in the process sheds the brightest light on who we are and what we dislike. What better than bold defiance clarifies the inner workings of an individual? Just as it is in the literature of small countries that one learns that life is impossible, so by way of a person's food aversions we can come to see how coldly detached he or she can be, not only from common acceptance, general toleration, or mainstream thought, but even himself, for here the mind is often at war with the body.

It is my conjecture, regarding food, that, revealingly, much more than what an individual loves to eat, the aggregating facts of what a person comes to dislike in the matter, remains paramount as the way, at least a way—a very important way—of assessing much of his character. An examination of a person this way is simultaneously a study of one's hungers, one's point of view, one's quirks, and a very revealing catalogue of an individual's tolerance level, as much as an index of hostility. To repudiate anything arguably takes a strong effort, a position assumed, an attitude taken, to deny, disclaim, disavow. Deeper alertness is required, no question about it. If you don't conform in one thing, you must conform in all the others. Any and all self-defenders must be always on guard, spoiling with an alertness that is often grave suspicion. "The thing worse than rebellion is the thing that causes rebellion," said Frederick Douglass, American social reformer, orator, statesman, and close friend of Abraham Lincoln who, having escaped from slavery to became a major leader and conscience of the abolitionist movement, knew more than a little about rebellion.

A hated food can even cause national rebellion. The flashpoint of the savage Indian Mutiny of 1857 was at that very point when soldiers were asked to bite off the paper cartridges to load their rifles that they suddenly realized that all of the ammunition had been greased with animal fat, namely beef and pork, which went against the religious faith of both Hindus and Muslims, respectively. Recently, the Oxford University Press, according to *The Telegraph* (Feb. 11, 2015), banned the use of pig, sausage, or pork-related words in order to avoid offending Muslims. A spokesman for the publishing company went on public record as saying,

OUP's commitment to its mission of academic and educational excellence is absolute. Our materials are sold in nearly 200 countries, and as such, and without compromising our commitment in any way, we encourage some authors of educational materials respectfully to consider cultural differences and sensitivities.

A mere detail about a food may foment resistance. Thomas Love Peacock rated an inn by the state of its mustard pot; if this did not come up to scratch he would stalk out without ordering. (It may also say something about Peacock's love of mustard.) A proud or intransigent soul may simply create a hated food. Custody of the self in both cases is involved. "A monk must never request foods that are not customary to others, lest he give in to the 'disease of vanity,'" wrote the anchorite St. John Cassian. He instructed that a monk choose his foods to moderate the self, which is to say to fight against self-love. What goes deeper than a visceral truth? Or more vividly rides shotgun on our very being, the continuity of our vitality, our health, our very lives? The common ostrich—*Struthio camelus*—lays the largest of all eggs on land—it can take up to 4 hours to hard boil an ostrich egg—but the whale shark actually lays the largest eggs (14 inches in diameter) in the *world*; a single ostrich egg can make an omelet large enough to serve as many as seven people. Can you even conceive the nature of what Alfred Hitchcock's response would be if ever he had to face a breakfast cup holding a hard-boiled *shark* egg? A black scowl, one can easily imagine, in the famous simile of Alfred Lord Tennyson, "as black as the Ash buds in the front of May"!

Food critic Jeffrey Steingarten has gone so far as boldly to pronounce that "intense food preferences, whether phobias or cravings, indicate the most serious of all personal limitations." *The most serious of all personal limitations.* When appointed the food critic of *Vogue* in 1989, he came to see in what was something of an epiphany that he had to become more understanding, more catholic—even more humble—in his tastes, and it was this altering insight that became the subject of his book, *The Man Who Ate Everything and Other Gastronomic Feats, Disputes, and Pleasurable Pursuits*, which is a study of his tastes, strong opinions, and reversals.

A food aversion, at least to some degree, indicates a characteristic of a person, in the same way it may be said that Thomas Edison's "salt test" did. This had to do with the method the inventor followed when hiring people, or so legend has it. (The story may be an urban myth.) If one or more relatively well-qualified candidates were competing for a job with him, Edison would take them to a restaurant. Accordingly, he would then ask them if he might take the liberty of ordering for them, a request to which they cheerfully agreed, and so it was always a steak or hot soup. As Edison distracted them with small talk, he would then watch very carefully as they proceeded. If someone added salt to his steak or soup before tasting it, he failed. If another took a moment to taste his food first before deciding to salt it or not, he passed this very important test. The revealing point was: you either won or lost the job based on whether or not you salted your food before tasting it. It was Edison's subjective reasoning that if you were the type of person who made "assumptions" about the way a food tastes before you even tasted it, deciding therefore to salt it immediately, you lacked the requisite investigative curiosity required for success in much more important undertakings, whereas in Edison's opinion the judicious person is comparatively superior simply because that individual would question those assumptions and preconceptions.

"A human being is primarily a bag for putting food into; the other functions and faculties may be more godlike, but in point of time they come afterwards," wrote George Orwell in his novel, *A Road to Wigan Pier*. He goes on to explain with notable insight how food functions:

> A man dies and is buried, and all his words and actions
> are forgotten, but the food he has eaten lives after him
> in the sound or rotten bones of his children. I think
> it could be plausibly argued that changes of diet are
> more important than changes of dynasty or even of re-
> ligion...Yet it is curious how seldom the all-importance
> of food is recognized. You see statues everywhere
> to politicians, poets, bishops, but none to cooks or
> bacon-curers or market gardeners.

Any person pointing to a food he or she will not eat is, to a degree, a food crank. We are all food cranks. "Everyone has an eating disorder. Almost no one has a normal relationship with food," says novelist Lionel Shriver. Winnie the Pooh liked honey but disliked acorns—"haycorns"—while Piglet felt the opposite. In the E.C. Segar comic strip, Wimpy loved cheeseburgers, as Popeye did spinach. In *Wigan Pier*, Orwell does not speak directly as such to the subject of food aversions, but in the strong, passionate conviction that he brought to all his insights, he perceptibly delineates and comments on the type of people he calls "food cranks," and if the food one has eaten lives on in the bones, why is the food that one rejects less worthy of note? Orwell writes significantly, "The food crank is by definition a person willing to cut himself off from human society in the hopes of adding five years onto the life of his carcase [sic]. That is, a person out of touch with common humanity."

Someone—anyone—dislikes *some* food. I mention honey. It seems safe to say that honey—warm, sweet, soothing—is universally loved. The fact is food writer M.F.K. Fisher *hated* honey. So did *Gourmet* magazine editor, Ruth Reichl, who reveals their mutual—and intense—dislike of honey in an article, "A Sensual Hunger" (December 1999), both finding common ground as well as a source of mutual relaxation in the fact during their first meeting when the editor visited her "heroine" in Glen Ellen, California. A young senior I knew back in college, an active Democrat who was supporting a then-young (and thin) Ted Kennedy, so hated the starboard-leaning Welch brothers, namely Robert W. and James O., makers of Junior Mints, Sugar Babies, Welch's Fudge, Pom Poms, and the thick caramel on a stick known as the Sugar Daddy—the nuclear family of just about every cinema candy concession—that, obsessed, he went to the trouble of personally designing, printing, and handing out flyers (disclosure: I enjoyed drawing some satirical cartoons for the sheets) to all of his fellow students encouraging a wide boy-cott of all of those popular candies because of the Commie-hunting lunacies of the then big noise-making ultraconservative John Birch Society which fanatic R.W. Welch established in Indiana on December 9, 1958.

Food aversions are judgments. What does it cost to express one of them? Nothing. There are those of course who take offense at anything, invariably subjective refusals. An opinion is held and a judgment made, however. It may be a choice, a conscious revulsion or perhaps something instinctive and sen-sual, a semiotic stir, originating in pre-linguistic infant development, the way philosopher Julia Kristeva distinguishes the unconscious from a more con-scious rule-governed system of signs in which words correspond with mean-ing. It is as much about preservation as it is about taste and as much about whim as it is about peevishness. Who was the witty fellow who declared, "Before you judge a man, walk a mile in his shoes. After that who cares?—he is a mile away and you have got his shoes." An ancillary question is what do those aversions then reveal about us? Was playwright George Bernard Shaw correct when he muscularly asserted, "Hate is the coward's revenge for being intimidated"? What exactly is involved in what we will not eat? Are self-deprivation, self-punishment, involved? If so, then exactly what does that tell us of ourselves? Could it be that we are disturbed by what challenges us to be loved? Is chastisement part of it? What is the nature, even the function, of repudiation anyway—an existence assertion? A statement of freedom? A subtle plea for elbow room? For space? A sense of self? A willful *non serviam?* "Hate is the consequence of fear; we fear something before we hate it; a child who fears noises becomes a man who hates noises," wrote Cyril Connolly in *The Unquiet Grave*. There is truth in those aphorisms, surely. Let's face it, no true declaration of intent cannot matter, no strong opinion, not even the tiniest cry for emancipation. A phobic faces a force. The denial of the presence of fear is as false as the presence of fear is a fact.

Refusal gives an ego boost, fills a need "to activate your within," as one insipid television drug commercial puts it about its product. The causes and effects of refusing or repudiating a food vary, of course. Is a revelation made or merely a simple protest? Is something of suppression involved? Self-denial? Weakness? Hatred? In what aspect of it can a sense of threat be detected? Of neurosis? Does such a disapproval cancel something out of the self? What about someone living uncomfortably in this evidence-based society and feeling by dint of that, for ego reasons, the simple go-ahead to tune out, to refuse to conform? Can it then entail something of "cognitive dissonance," rather like the over-deliberate fox who does not like—refuses to desire—the very grapes that he finds he cannot reach? I am suggesting simply that refusal, as such, is a dynamic with a thousand points. Could it be habit, "the ballast that chains the dog to its vomit," as Samuel Beckett remarks in his *Proust*? But disavowal, abrogation, elimination is the opposite of anything like habit—its very correction, no?

St. Francis de Sales in his *Introduction to the Devout Life* assures us, "To give disposes us to receive, so to teach disposes us to learn." It is clear that he is addressing the matter of engagement, of interchange, and how it leads to curious if unforeseen conclusions. One may make the case that any serious working grudge against a given food predisposes one eventually to like it—that in the vigorous passion of rejection one may learn to accept it. There is no question that there exists a capricious attention given to what, often arbitrarily, we choose to spurn or to savor. Food aversions come about by way of self-assertion. Any agreement that is not voluntary is coercive, or at least such is the fervor derived from the rigid logic of the anarchist. If you have not explicitly consented to an authority, then it is your master. The tenet of all authority boils down to control without assent, merciless policing.

Hating a food is a task. This is a matter of confrontation, facing a thing *down*. A hated food is stared at, never ignored. It is about emotion. In *Wind, Sand, and Stars*, Antoine de Saint-Exupéry wrote, "When two people love each other, they do not look at each other, but both look in the same direction." It is the opposite in matters of hostility, where a scowl is sharply pointed at the foe. Alertness in the extreme disallows anything like unfocussed temporizing. Goggle it down!

A food aversion with its crotchety and subjective dismissals can be nothing less than a method of self-control, a ruling over one's dominion, an internalized system of authority, the forceful exercise over the impulse of the will, what St. Thomas Aquinas called the "least natural" part of the personality. A would-be thief ascends to become his own cold Inspector Javert. "A functioning police state needs no police," wrote William Burroughs. The policeman is internalized here, in the spiteful instinct that refuses that one food. What is happening is a kind of puritanical cleansing. A mind by means of its selective pique is literally seeking a naked lunch. I use the word *selective*. When General de Gaulle once complainingly posed the question, "How can you govern a country that produces 258 sorts of cheese?" it was less an observation about variety, in my opinion, than an open-ended lament about the nature of multifarious tastes, as well as implicitly a comment on food aversions.

Taste is identity. Nothing is more private than what we choose to eat—or reject. It is the autistic need for—of—self-assertion. Eating is an orthodoxy that we practice three times a day. Nobody is a blind white fish to such important mind and body decisions as to what specifically we choose to put in or to keep out of our dish. Angles are formed, attitudes shaped, strategies devised. Received notions of what rules to follow as to menu mainly go nowhere. In the twenty-ninth part of his poem, "Like Decorations in a Nigger Cemetery," Wallace Stevens strikes a ringing chord that encourages souls to cast out the spirit that they have inherited and boldly replace it with one of their own, in a profitable and pleasing, rightful exchange that satisfies *you*:

> Choke every ghost with acted violence,
> Stamp down the phosphorescent toes, tear off
> The splitting tissues tight across the bones.
> The heavy bells are tolling rowdy-dow.

Choosing to dislike a food, whether violently or not, may give a person height, autonomy, a sense of selfhood. It should be noted that, significantly, a person's choosing to dislike a given food, almost as a parallel, often has its accompanying or ancillary co-crotchet, with him or her insistently—and perhaps even just as irrationally—madly liking another in as vigorous an extreme, almost as a rightful and balancing lunacy. In his novel, *The Debt to Pleasure*, John Lanchester insightfully writes of the "erotics of dislike," in which by negative revelation one's determined choice of a food that he abhors curiously separates a person from his peers. A rebellious side is expressed—and felt—by what one dislikes. It falls under the heading of existence assertion. One can find madder zeal in a phobic than by anyone pleased, in the same way that *tired* children act crazier, noisier, not the reverse. No truly defiant man is ever a recalcitrant one. To like a given food gives little distinction, notes Lanchester, further stating,

> But dislike hardens the perimeter between the self and
> the world, and brings a clarity to the object isolated in
> its light. Any dislike is in some measure a triumph of
> definition, distinction and discrimination—a triumph
> of life.

Truisms are many on the subject of food aversions. Many opinions go shyly unstated or suspiciously undeclared, for a number of good reasons, but a few are clearly manifest and universal, I daresay, truths few would contest. Most folks hate to eat anything moldy, slimy, smelly, stringy, or brain-connected. They also tend to hate food that is blue, that shines, is viscous, gummy, gelatinous, riddled with gristle, dumbly crumbly, has claws, feet, or eyeballs, or is even remotely penoidal. Fear or hatred of slime—it is known as *blennophobia* or *myxophobia*, a fairly primitive disgust reaction—is high indeed on the repulsion scale, especially with children and adolescents.

I would also throw in anything that your uncle has shot or that has been brought to the house in a paper bag. Capers are irrelevant. Few people, other than Jews, truly savor pickles, a last century food. (A quarter of an aisle in a large grocery store displays them, however, so there must be a larger fan base, but it is one unknown to me. The state of Tennessee eats the most pickles.) I believe I can also safely state that virtually no one, except maybe bunnies and Jews at Passover, enjoy the herb parsley, whose icky, grassy, sodded, turfy, matted, reeded, *sedgy* taste is so immediately off-putting and grim to most of us. Fruitcakes, flat out, are appalling to most of us. American white bread is literally tasteless and abhorrent. "You can travel fifty thousand miles in America without tasting a piece of good bread," lamented Henry Miller in *Tropic of Cancer*. Winter root vegetables, I have noticed, which look wizened, squirmy, and are redolent of deep earth and Hallowe'en, are always a tough sell, especially with kids. As far as I'm concerned, all avocados have the texture of soap.

"Why did you leave Los Angeles?" Peggy Lipton asked singer Lena Horne. Her pointed reply was, "Because living in L.A. people spend their whole morning looking for the perfect avocado." Horne's is clearly a comment, not only on the soullessness of Los Angeles, but also on her attitude to the egg-shaped fruit, which is botanically a large berry. "It's gross, it's got weird texture, and it tastes like butt," wrote one Internet non-fan of the avocado. "Mushy green poop!"

Baldwin apples, not attractive, have unattractive bumps and lumps and for that reason are never displayed in American supermarkets, where glossy, shiny apples are preferred to be shown. We are fastidious about appearances. While Baldwins alone—no other—should be used for apple pies, people don't even know what they are anymore, so neglected have these apples become. They are not great "chawnking" apples. I would avoid buying or eating apples grown in Florida—yes, they grow apples down there, but forget the South for apples in general. Apples need a chill period in order that their buds be set, without which they will not produce. Coolness takes place while trees are dormant for the winter. Temperatures need to be below 45 degrees Fahrenheit for a set number of hours, depending on the cultivar being grown.

I have read of strict, God-fearing Moravians who refused to eat apples because of the negative Biblical connotations having to do with the Edenic fall. It is commonly believed of course that it was an apple that corrupted Adam and Eve in the Garden of Eden, despite the fact that the Hebrew word used in the book of Genesis is *pree*, or fruit. According to Lytton John Musselman, author of *Figs, Dates, Laurel & Myrrh*, his book about Biblical plants, it is highly unlikely such a fruit was an apple. "It was just too hot and dry for apples to grow," explains Musselman. "They need some cold. Through the years, Bible translations from the Hebrew have been done mostly by European Christians who resorted to the names of plants with which they were familiar. The apple was an enormous favorite."

Opinions, opinions, opinions. On the subject of food, they are truly endless. "Fish sauce...for when you want that flavor of cat food and athletic sock...in a good way," says TV chef Alton Brown. Kimchee can bring on deathly salt headaches, not to mention high blood pressure—Koreans suffer from both—and acute stomach ailments. We derive our word for salt from Al-Salt, an ancient agricultural town and administrative center in west-central Jordan, which is close to the Dead Sea. It remains a noble word. Jesus Christ, who surely valued the spice, actually coined the phrase "salt of the earth"—has anyone ever written about the "Son of David" as poet? Our Lord frequently relied on Hebrew poetic structures that are found in the Sacred Scriptures and other ancient Hebrew and Aramaic literature. His use of rhetoric was masterful.

I have some of my own food phobias. Heat in candy, an anomaly to me, seems absurd and does not belong in any confection. I would rather munch dead dung beetles than be subjected to even a small puff of peppermint. Margarine is always a disaster. No adult food involves—or should involve—marshmallows. Cucumbers are best cut paper-thin. Sad to say, most food actually is *improved* by the addition of sugar, no matter how unhealthy. Ham and gelatin, a two-headed monster, make a hideous combination. What other truisms (even if subjective) obtain? Marinades prevent browning, do not tenderize, can burn, and do not penetrate deeply into meat—if you want marinades to penetrate, be sure to add salt. Marmite, liver, offal… the list is long and endless. I have read that the vast amount of food people throw away—one estimate has it that each year 96 billion pounds of food are wasted in the United States (officially 14% of all the food purchased annually!)—speaks not only to our casual, self-incriminating decadence but also constitutes in itself a wholesale kind of food aversion, the inability to process what psychically we refuse to take in. What foulness exceeds waste?

Forget kidneys. The odor of cooking kidneys never departs a house—and I have heard the same thing said about lamb, an animal (and so a product) that for some reason never seems to thrive, or prevail, as a central food delight in the United States as it does in Great Britain, Ireland, and Australia. No, I am one of those who has never been quite rock-ribbed enough to overlook the smell of slow-cooking kidneys. So I confess to being of one mind with Peter Tempelhoff, grand chef at The Greenhouse Restaurant at The Cellars-Hohenort, Western Cape, in South Africa, who despises kidneys. "Kidneys—I just don't get it," he says. "Their pungency says it all… why would you want to eat them if you know what their function is in the body?" Neil Jewell, chef at the Bread & Wine restaurant, Môreson Winery in Franschhoek, South Africa, heartily agrees, saying, "I hate kidneys, they make me go green." And then he adds as a little fillip, "And frozen cauliflower reminds me of phlegm."

Lamb or mutton can exude a horrific smell/aftertaste, an odor hard to describe but one that evokes the reek of old catcher's mitts or discarded handbags. One anti-lamb curmudgeon online, in a fit of descriptive excess, perhaps, responded by creatively listing its offensive smell as, all at once, "Dirt, liver, mold, sour, sweet, green, fermented, sewage, rotting vegetables, fishy (apologies so close to dinner time)."

"Deep in the Amazon rain forest I encountered an indigenous village that invited me to cook with them [cassava root]," wrote Chef Michael Smith, *Food Network* host and cookbook writer. "We did everything under the sun with their staple food… it was all good, until they all started chewing and spitting the mashed cassava. I couldn't handle chewing someone else's already chewed food, even when I discovered it was to kick-start a batch of jungle hooch!" It seems to me that anything mashed bears a danger sign to the suspicious. Food activist Joshna Maharaj cannot bear ambrosia salad. "I threw a Mad Men party once, and wanted to have a full '60s-themed menu," she wrote. "It seems you can't throw a party from that era without the blasted ambrosia salad: Jell-O, Cool Whip, canned fruit, and worst of all—shredded coconut. It was all of it totally disgusting, and I don't like to talk about food like that."

"Noconuts" is a pejorative term frequently used by coconut haters, of which there seems to be a good many. The coconut has been referred to as "The healthy food that's bad for you," loaded with heart-damaging saturated fat and detrimental calories that hide behind its healthy food co-op image. In what seemed a bold claim in a notable study 20 years ago, the Center for Science in the Public Interest stigmatized exotic greases and specifically cited movie theater popcorn as "the Godzilla of snacks," simply because it was often cooked in coconut oil. I once knew an affronted woman who insisted that coconut milk gave her dermatitis. Coconuts can be a food allergen, no question. Surely, the definitive coconut story is Michel Faber's erotic short story, "Explaining Coconuts," in which a group of sex-crazed executives attend a curiously scientific/sexual lecture in steamy Indonesia given by a sensual, highly exotic Miss Soedhono that involves, among other plot lines, her wielding a machete.

I must say, I can barely conceive of the palate that enjoys pizza with (spare me, O Lord!) *pineapple.* No true Italian (of which I am half) possibly could. Oddly enough, it is a semi-popular choice among pizza lovers, even in the most storied pizza emporia, such as Pepe's Pizza in New Haven, Connecticut, "legendary 1925 birthplace of thin-crust New Haven-style pizza, including the popular white clam pie." I have never enjoyed anything in aspic. Then, the taste of margarine has always put me off—it frankly tastes the way it looks, conveying an almost tongue-flattening floor-wax flavor, its semi-solid emulsion, composed mainly of vegetable fats and water, giving it the same gloss, smell, and color—it mimes the consistency of butter and is just as easily spreadable! Margarine was actually a pitiful lard-white when I was growing up, in the late days of World War II. The spread that I recall was a nearly indigestible, greasy, fat substance, as paper-white as Bonomo's "Turkish Taffy." During the war, my mother bought margarine pre-formed as a small plastic-wrapped dirigible of lard-looking white with an odd dot of orange in the middle, like a Japanese flag. Once home, she let us work it, squeeze and knead it, while it was still packaged, into a presentable sunny egg-pale-yellow comestible. I wonder how many families ate that glop during those years of rationing. Hippolyte Mège-Mouriès created margarine in France, in 1869, responding to a challenge by Emperor Napoleon III to create a butter substitute for the armed forces and lower classes. (Margarine overtook butter sales in the United States in 1957.)

I also dislike haggis, Scotch eggs, pork pies, all white bread, sweetbreads, overcooked pasta, salty chips, and I would never buy tuna or even sardines packed in water (or for that matter cheap mushy tuna packed in oil). Dried coconut flakes to me taste like candle wax. Fat-free yogurt, as far as I'm concerned, is an ugly cross between mucilage and sea-foam. I can never again bring myself to drink sweetened *fino* sherry or pale cream sherry, after developing a frightful headache and becoming severely ill after gulping it (unconsecrated) in a sacristy at about age 12 with several other wayward altar boys—was it from that strain of yeast known as *flor* that floats in a layer on top of sherry in the wine barrel? This was perversely repeated when I was a near-starveling graduate student at the University of Virginia, drinking some low-rent Taylor's Cream Sherry, and yet at another time when I heard the echo of sermons in my spinning head based on the memorable if non-sectarian God passage at the end of H.G. Wells' novel, *Mr. Britling Sees It Through*, as well as the ringing if enigmatic line from Wells' *A Modern Utopia*, "Cycle tracks will abound in Utopia"!

I have since read that a *fino* ("refined" in Spanish), the driest and palest of the traditional varieties of Sherry and Montilla-Moriles fortified wine, is always best drunk when comparatively young, and unlike the sweeter varieties of sherry it should be taken soon after the bottle is opened, as exposure to air can cause it to lose its flavor within hours. Personally, I have never done well with white wines, for some reason, which have always left me groggy and groping. Writer and editor George Plimpton would not drink wine. Neither would Hunter Thompson.

I am not certain that I have ever again trusted what was put in a pie after my father in the process of putting us to bed read us aloud (as he held up the lit candle that always precariously accompanied his readings!) the grisly tale of "Nell Cook: The Legend of the Dark Entry," a favorite poem of his which he dramatically loved to declaim—and he did so many nights for us—from the Rev. Richard Harris Barham's *The Ingoldsby Legends*, or whether I ever fully mastered my dread of the extremely pretty but jealous cook who fashioned that poisoned pie ("She bought some nasty Doctor's-stuff, and she put it in a pie"), not only giving me the creeps about pies in general but putting me on full lifetime alert as to the essence of feminine beauty, as well. As her punishment, Nelly was buried *alive* beneath the Dark Entry of Canterbury Cathedral. Sleep well, little Alex! Sweet dreams, and don't let the bedbugs bite!

There is something uncannily inorganic to me about raw celery. I dislike the sulfurous under-taste of slick molasses, which, when growing up in the war years, we resorted to pouring on our pancakes—and for me the same goes for the cloying taste of strawberry ice cream, as saccharine, as obvious, as flattery. I will add I have always felt slighty swindled when finding walnuts in my brownies (and also peanuts in any Szechuan dish): to me they spoil, rather than enhance, the function of chew. Why would someone ruin a perfectly good chocolate brownie by putting nuts in it? I also dislike aggressively overly-fried eggs, staring back bold and hard. Fugitive for me is also the taste, unsavory palate-smack, and flavor of cinnamon. Consider: it is actually *bark*! (Mexicans, strangely enough, enjoy adding cinnamon to meat!)

Christopher Kimball, chief interlocutor of the television show *America's Test Kitchen,* he of the signature yellow bow-ties and owl-beaky eyeglasses—there is a distinctly old hat, fuddy-duddyish, superannuated aspect to the man, as he hovers and gawks over his working cooks like a splenetic chain-store manager—agrees with me and instructed one interviewer, as only Kimball can, in that arch, flammulated way of his, "In this country, the most overused spice is cinnamon. Everyone uses gobs of it, and it ruins everything." It is also Kimball's harebrained view that the most *under*utilized spice in the kitchen is juniper berries! I have read that he suspects spices of any kind, cannot tolerate heat of any level, has little appreciation for anything more ethnic than 1950s farm food, and for some reason dislikes dark restaurants. These may be calumnies, I can't say, but curmudgeons are invariably strenuous haters.

What else do I dislike? I can't stand three-bean salad, pretty much all casseroles, head cheese, Waldorf Salad, menudo, white chocolate, whole wheat pasta with its shredded cardboard and lumbering mouth-feel, egg-salad in any form, especially sandwiches, deviled eggs, or any canned or jellied ham. (On the other hand, I guess paradoxically, I love the taste of deviled ham on fresh-baked, well-buttered, "closed crumb" pumpernickel bread, especially when accompanied with a couple of Foster's "Oil Cans" [the 24 ½ variety]). I have never liked breadsticks. They are literally what Queen Elizabethan II—I am not making this up—feeds her Welsh corgis under the table.

I also draw the line at yellow wax beans, smoked salmon and cream cheese pinwheels (and the thumbprints and slobber usually found on the tray), sweet cloying drinks (as passionately did Raymond Chandler's Philip Marlowe), tossed salads with apple (or any kind of fruit) in it, mince pies of any stripe, store-bought candied fruit, all sorts of contrived verjuices, harsh anchovies—the favorite ("most artful," as he put it) sandwich of novelist Charles Dickens was a parsley, hard-boiled egg, and anchovy combination on a buttered French roll!—and the pablumesque taste of creamed spinach.

I also cannot abide anise-flavored *anything* and so therefore naturally dislike all licorice, five-spice powder, aniseed balls, all black jelly beans, Italian pizzelle, New Mexican bizcochitos, champurrado, or arak, raki, ouzo, flinty Chablis, Pernod, pastis, all anisette liqueurs, Jägermeister, and Sambuca which now comes (an added horror!) in raspberry and banana flavors, all of this, along with the taste of Fennel, an emblem of strength in the language of flowers but to me an herb with a faint reminder of licorice—to me it is merely licorice-flavored celery—and of course the taste of frilly Chervil, the aromatic herb, which has a flavor reminiscent of anise, even though it lists as one of the four traditional French *fines herbes*, her with her perky sisters tarragon, chives, and parsley. Just for the record, I might as well include in my list Sweet Cicely, the perennial herb native to Europe, the feathery leaves of which, used in French dishes combined with tarragon, carry a distinct aniseed flavor, but, served that French way—I once enjoyed it in Lyons in a delicious rhubarb compote—may allow for the only exception I would make to my general proscription.

I believe that I am not much different than the average eater in my aleatoric meanderings, but I also dislike eating eels, can't stand hollandaise sauce whipped to an extreme froth, and dislike terrines in general (layers of *foie gras* and *gelée*, with dessert wine traditionally served alongside *foie gras*?—uh-uh, not for me). I also dislike cheap, flat-tasting insubstantial gummy bears; to me, no middlingly-made gummy bear produced in any country can even remotely approximate the bold, chewy, sparkling brilliance—the fruity and delightful taste—of British wine gums.

I cannot abide fruit-flavored teas. "Have you noticed, by the way, there are no tea-flavored fruits?" asked comedian George Carlin in his satirical collection, *When Will Jesus Bring the Pork Chops*. "Take a clue from nature." To me, Budweiser beer is pure piss. Micturation! At room temperature, it is disgusting. Modern American beer, with its artificial carbonation, in a highly fraudulent way needs to be ice-cold to hide the sharp taste of the excesses of carbonation. When drunk "penguin-shit cold," to borrow a phrase from the creative James Ellroy, almost any beverage tastes good when you are thirsty. Back in the days of the old West beer was never artificially carbonated, as it is now. In those days, the mild natural carbonation required that beer, usually kept in root cellars, need only be cool to be refreshing and tasty. Why is "Bud" America's most popular beer? Aside from the fact that most people are sheep, my theory is that consumers, would-be macho men, love ordering a beer by monosyllable, which to them makes an order crisp, brief, unambiguous, forceful, and manly.

Elizabeth Gunnison Dunn sees the pea in the thimble and wrote in *Esquire* (March 7, 2012),

Gentlemen, the cold is not your beer's friend.
According to Mark Garrison, writing for Slate, this
whole it's-cold-enough-when-the-mountains-turn-
blue thing is just a big conspiracy propagated by
mega-brewers to mask the poor taste of their watery lagers by chilling them to death. In addition
to depressing flavor, cold temperatures also up the
carbonation in beer, giving tasteless stuff a pleasant
tingle. But "there's practically no beer worth drinking
that should be served under 40 degrees Fahrenheit,"
says Garrison (for reference, tap beer comes out at
a chilly 38 degrees). In the case of good craft beers,
the low temperatures just dampen the flavor, causing
you to miss all the things that would open up if a little
warmer. Unfortunately, even bars with serious beer se-
lections rarely serve their brews at the proper temperature, due to the difficulty of varying cooling in a draft
system and unwillingness to contradict a public that
still largely thinks beer should be virtually frozen. But
when you're drinking good beer at home, Garrison
says you should ditch the iced mugs for room-tem-
perature glasses, and let beers sit out of the fridge for a
little while before opening them. For reference, serve
wheat beers, pilsners, and other light beers at 40-45
degrees, dark styles like cask ales and imperial stouts at
50-55 degrees, and ambers and bocks somewhere in
between. Any other warm-beer defenders, or disbelievers, please leave your thoughts in the comments.

I equally revile the smell of just discarded banana peels (an odor that
supposedly nauseated the NASA astronauts)—most pigs won't eat banana
skins raw but will eat them when cooked—and would never eat raw fish in
a restaurant. I have heard it often repeated that it is unwise for anyone to
eat fish on Sunday, Monday, or Tuesday when dining out on Cape Cod—a
good policy to follow—because restaurants usually purchase their fresh fish
on Tuesday for their Wednesday and Thursday menus and again on Thursday
for their Friday and Saturday menus. Let me go on to say that like so many
others I dislike fruitcake; gelatin in every form; aspic, as I've said, and you
might as well throw in acorn jelly. Correct—jelly made from acorns! It is
indeed made and eaten. While acorns are poisonous, their toxins can in fact

be removed by cooking the nuts. In certain areas of Korea, mainly in the mountain regions, acorns grow in huge numbers, and, during times of severe hunger in the past in that country, natives there discovered that acorns could be cooked and powdered to provide a starch. The result is a jelly with a subtle, slightly bitter flavor, which is called *dotorimuk*. (Harvested acorns must always be leached of tannins.) When it is seasoned with soy-based sauces and vegetables, or so I have heard, it becomes a delicious side dish, generally mixed with other ingredients such as slivered carrots and scallions, garlic, sesame oil, red chili pepper powder, and sesame seeds. There are many reports that hungry Confederate soldiers also used smushed acorns in coffee. But me? I will leave that food to any and all "Rebs" and the good, inventive people of Sokcho or Chuncheon, Anyang or Pyeongchang.

A last word on acorns and their reputation, at in Elizabethan times. In *The Tempest*, Prospero threatens Ferdinand with:

> 'Sea-water shalt thou drink; thy food shall be
> The fresh-brook mussels, withered roots and husks
> Wherein the acorn cradled."

It may also give some idea of how low an opinion Shakespeare had of mussels. Could his snipe have been a comment on his audience? Tudor theatre-goers loved their bivalves. Their preferred snacks were mussels, oysters, crabs, cockles, periwinkles and whelks, along with walnuts, raisins, plums, cherries, dried figs, peaches, and prunes, which, also popular in Elizabethan brothels, were thought to cure the pox.

Those are some of my food aversions. But then look at this diverse planet of ours. Hindus object violently to eating beef. Jews will not eat shellfish. Muslims refuse to drink alcohol. Buddhists will not eat any animals. Whereas in France horse meat is part of the human diet—it is lower in fat than beef, yet higher in protein, two selling points—neither the British nor the Americans would never deign to eat dog, while Koreans do; in fact, in China "hornless goat" (dog) is a delicacy, as it once was among the ancient Phoenicians, Greeks, Romans, Aztecs, and, until recently, widely, in the South Pacific. The Chinese, who will not touch milkshakes, eat dogs stewed, fried, minced, and almost always served with lots of chili. Captain James Cook found dog as tasty as English lamb. No one single rule holds for the consumption of food on the planet.

Composer Richard Wagner passionately believed that the virtue of compassion was the only true foundation of morality. He had learned from his mentor, Schopenhauer, that mankind was a species distinguished from other animals solely by our capacities for reason and compassion. It was from such sympathy with all of his fellow creatures that the great musical genius progressed towards his interest in vegetarianism, although he never did strictly become a total vegetarian. In October 1879, Wagner actually wrote an article for the *Bayreuther Blatter* which appeared under the title, "An Open Letter to Herr Ernst von Weber," author of *The Torture-Chambers of Science* (August 14, 1879), writing,

Yesterday I officially became a member of the local Society for the Protection of Animals. Until now I have respected the activities of such societies, but always regretted that their educational contact with the general public has rested chiefly upon a demonstration of the usefulness of animals, and the uselessness of persecuting them. Although it may be useful to speak to the unfeeling populace in this way, I none the less thought it opportune to go a stage further and appeal to their fellow feeling as a basis for ultimately ennobling Christianity. One must begin by drawing people's attention to animals and reminding them of the Brahman's great saying, *Tat twam asi* [That art thou]—even though it will be difficult to make it acceptable to the modern world of Old Testament Judaization. However, a start must be made here,—since the commandment to love thy neighbor is becoming more and more questionable and difficult to observe—particularly in the face of our vivisectionist friends...

Russian peasants in the 18th-century were reluctant to grow or eat potatoes on account of their asexual method of reproduction, believing the tubers (!) to indulge in homosexuality and masturbation. The Maasai of Africa eat virtually no plant foods at all, subsisting on meat, blood, and milk. Many of the Inupiat and the Yupiks of Alaska, the Canadian Inuit and Inuvialuit, Inuit Greenlanders, and the Siberian Yupiks who live on raw fish, game meat, fish roe, and blubber, seldom eat anything remotely green and tend to repudiate any kind of different foods. Curiously, Maasai warriors will not only never drink milk alone, neither will they drink anything in their parents' houses nor eat meat out in the open—they will eat meat only in forests. Some tribes in Nigeria literally forbid men even to *talk* about food, a very odd taboo. There is no end to the many, curious taboos on the Dark Continent. The members of one particular closed society in Africa called *Fang actually* believe that a boy on whose penis his mother's milk has fallen will become impotent.

Nothing that satisfies a people in one area will do so in another. A defining choice seems to be involved. Traveling through the desolate and icy wastes of Baffin Island in northern Canada during the 1880s, the anthropologist Franz Boas proudly wrote to his fiancée, Marie, "I am now truly like an Eskimo... I scarcely eat any European foodstuffs any longer but am living entirely on seal meat." Jesse Williams, a football nose-tackle and star of the 2013 national championship University of Alabama team—he is known as "The Monstar"—was born in Brisbane, Australia, landed in Yuma, Arizona, four years ago, and was greeted by shocking 123-degree temperatures that were so oppressive that the young man complained that "it felt like stepping on the sun." He found the town small and dusty and the food gréasy and stale. It boggled his mind that he could find cheeseburgers more easily than fruit, and for less money. For six months, Williams said, the food there made him sick.

I have mentioned quirks. We enter here the world of the subjective—a subject's personal perspective, feelings, beliefs, desires or discovery, as opposed to those made from an independent, objective, point of view.

Do you remember how in the movie, *The Freshman* (1990) the mafia figure, thuggish Carmine Sabatini (Marlon Brando)—also known as "Jimmy the Toucan"—runs the Fabulous Gourmet Club, an illicit establishment which to avoid the law never holds its exotic feasts in the same place twice, and where at top prices endangered animals are served as the main course? The endearing freshman Clark Kellogg, a dupe, is advised that "for the privilege of eating the very last of a species," a million dollars is charged. Pardon me! I'll take a Komodo dragon cutlet!

The intensity of food aversions astonishes me. I am staggered that so many varieties of it are held—fixed, I would hasten to add—and, while with focus, held with such mesmerizing instability. The *nature* of food aversions fascinates me, as well as the ubiquity of it, the overwhelming ubiquity of it, the almost antic, almost comical ubiquity of it. Is it, are they, heteronormative?

But exactly what constitutes a food aversion? It is a lifelong disgust for a certain food, some say, no matter the rhyme or reason. But suddenly one may simply pop up out of the blue. What are its origins, its causes, its occasions? Who can say? Is it borne of a deep self-consciousness? Linked to weird anti-fantasies? There are all sorts of degrees of hating a food, of course. A lifelong dislike. A week or so of revulsion. Months of an ill response after a bad dinner. Need it always pivot on a bad experience? Is it always pure disgust? Is fear involved? Shame? Are you somehow embarrassed to eat a mess of heavily sauced chicken wings on a first date? Would you be embarrassed to eat sloppy barbecued ribs on a job interview that included lunch? Could the risk of cracking a tooth scare you away from eating pitted fruit?

I once knew a young woman who suffered from anosmia—a lack of functioning olfaction—in other words, an inability to perceive odors. It is a disease she shared with William Wordsworth, singer Stevie Wonder, The Simpsons' Selma Bouvier, and, among others, Mary Baker Eddy, the founder of Christian Science, who shied away from going to restaurants and bizarrely came to dislike and shun most foods, even expressing a hatred for the act of eating itself. While anosmia may be temporary, traumatic anosmia can be permanent.

Anosmia is often due to an inflammation of the nasal mucosa; any blockage of nasal passages or a destruction of one temporal lobe can be caused by chronic meningitis and neurosyphilis that would increase intra-cranial pressure over a long period of time, and in some cases by ciliopathy, which is due to primary ciliary dyskinesia (Kartagener syndrome, Afzelius' syndrome, or Siewert's syndrome). Many patients may experience unilateral anosmia as a result of minor head trauma.

My anosmiac friend, in any case, became acutely self-consciousness about so many foods and in a way evoked uneasy and diffident J. Alfred Prufrock with his question—was it born of a food aversion?—"Do I dare to eat a peach?" I have read and heard many strange twists of interpretation regarding that particular line of poetry. I recall with amusement one college professor fervently claiming that the circumspect 35-year-old Prufrock anxiously imagines himself as being old and rachitic and *worried about the loosening of his teeth!* In Prufrock's time, so the teacher explained, before there was modern dentistry, many people lost some or most of their teeth as they got older; like stiffness of the limbs or shortening of sight, it was thought to be one of the inevitable consequences of aging. Excuse me, this was news? Another owlish academic of dubious distinction, an actual Harvard University-educated commentator for *ClassicNotes* [sic]—I am not making this up—insists with full certitude that the peach in T.S. Eliot's poem stands for "female genitalia." "The peach, through shape and texture," he writes, "has long been a symbol for female genitalia." His penetrating interpretation goes on to state, "Prufrock's anxiety about eating a peach has much to do with his feelings of sexual inadequacy." It may fit in with his nagging worry that his prematurely balding head and endomorphic physique earn him the scorn of women, but I am sure we all agree that the comic and the academic often go hand in hand.

I suppose actual food aversions could include anything from the insubstantial non-diets of emaciated drug fiends and heroine addicts to the endless stories of tasteless food and watery drinks of England so often retailed in the work of playwright Harold Pinter and the Monty Python boys and George Orwell—he called it the "dirty-handkerchief side of life"—to the scandalous preview headline once given by the comical if politically incorrect cartoon broadcaster, vain Tom Tucker on TV's "Family Guy," blasphemously announcing the unseemly and outrageous news headline, "A Pig who refuses to eat Jews. Next." "European folklore explained that Jews did not eat pork because Jews were pigs in disguise," according to Abe Opincar in *Fried Butter*. "Jews forced to convert to Christianity were called Marranos, or swine... In Regensburg, Germany, a carving on the cathedral's exterior depicts Jews sucking a pig's teats...and well into the eighteenth century, one of the gates leading into Frankfurt was decorated with a painted relief showing a Jew sucking shit from a pig's ass."

I believe here I would include the many meals his servants had set out for him, only to have to take them away, ignored and untouched, while a preoccupied Georg Frederick Handel, inspired, composed his glorious *Messiah* over the course of 24 days. He passionately noted, "I did think I did see all heaven before me and the Great God himself." He signed the score, "S.D.G." *Soli Deo Gloria*.

One may even push the case that the civic enforcement of land sitting unused is an example of food aversion. The concept of "adverse possession" was born from the belief that the best interests of society were met when property and land were utilized productively rather than left to sit fallow. This interest was especially noted 600 years ago in relation to food production. During that period, people were starving and lacked the land to produce the food for themselves or others. At the same time, landowners often left farmland sitting unused and unproductive. Adverse possession was thus created to utilize unused land so people could be fed. The rich, who insist that vacant land is not necessarily abandoned land, spit on "squatter's rights" and, because they themselves are not hungry or subject to want, coldly dismiss the idea of adverse possession as nothing but a manipulating scheme to defraud.

Who can explain why Amelia Earhart would only drink buttermilk and never the regular tit-to-table product? Why Queen Elizabeth II dislikes sandwiches cut into basic rectangles and orders scones but never eats them? Why Marilyn Monroe disliked the smell of garlic on humans, but not on food? Why Lady Diana disliked eating game? Why TV's Andrew Zimmern can eat stewed tuna eyes, raw goat testicles, and poisonous toads but cannot eat walnuts? Why Oprah Winfrey who seems to eat just about everything else will not eat hamburgers? (In Texas, bumper stickers and T-shirts sport the slogan, "The only mad cow in America is Oprah.") "Take away this pudding. It has no theme," bitched a crusty Sir Winston Churchill.

Many of those who dislike this or that food are also found to be vague as to the reasons for it and often cannot say why an automatic red light flashes on, with perhaps an added inability even to say how it formed, except that it is a nag that has taken one over like a habit that sits, fat and laughing—as

David Krogh says of cigarettes in his *Smoking: The Artificial Passion*—on one our our cherished assumptions: that we have reasons for doing what we do. In 1928, after catching a cold—she claimed she contracted "Bell's Paralysis"—the poet Elinor Wylie wrote to William Rose Benét (he later became one of her husbands) to tell him that after she "got an earache," "the total destruction or rather metamorphosis of one's sense of taste... suddenly became a collection of poisons such as strychnine and bichloride of mercury," and all foods utterly soured. "You ought to taste an egg, to experience real horror." Or did the problems of this eccentric, high-strung sensuous, extra-emotional, jittery divorceé who often fasted—she claimed she actually "met" the dead poet Shelley—go deeper?

People who are indifferent to eating—especially those who simply do not like to eat, who indeed renounce the whole experience of food and plain, uncomplicated, happy ingestion—are precisely the types who have food aversions, in the same sense that it is not the cigarettes as such that cause your cancer, but rather your own character, at least according to psychologist Hans Eysenck (1916-97). It was the expressed conviction of this right-wing, some-say-maverick, German-Jew—he received "secret" funding from a New York law firm acting on behalf of the tobacco industry—that the very same people who are constitutionally predisposed to take up smoking cigarettes are in fact those who are constitutionally inclined to develop cancer; in other words, it is sociable, impulsive, lively, manic, sensation-seeking types who, often in the grip of "stimulus hunger," also tend to love spicy foods, strong drink, cigarettes, the kick of drugs even, and consistently show a high degree of instability while reacting very strongly to aversive stimuli. It sounds a bit of a dog's dinner to me, a random and vague piling together of elements, but I suppose it offers something to think about.

A person not liking any food *at all*?

Eliza Barclay in her blog The Salt ("What's on Your Plate") offers some remarks on a documented case of such a soul:

> Rob Rhinehart's blog details his two-month experiment consuming mostly Soylent, a concoction he invented to provide all the nutrition and none of the hassle of food. It first attracted the attention of *Vice*, and then *The Washington Post*, which said that his plan just might work. Rhinehart, a 24-year-old electrical engineer in San Francisco, soon found himself inundated with queries from people interested in testing

Soylent. He'd apparently hit on something that resonated with others.

Upon reading that, the inevitable first question arises: What precisely is
so bothersome about eating honest-to-goodness food?

Rhinehart's reply went straight to the heart of the matter. "I resented the
time, money and effort [that] the purchase, preparation, consumption, and
clean-up of food," he complained, "was consuming." Whereas the drink that
he adopted, he claimed, left him feeling satisfied, leaner, and clearer-headed.
In an email to The Salt, he went on to say, "Personally, I've found separating
the social and cultural enjoyment of food from food as 'fuel' has vastly improved my quality of life."

So what is the skinny on meal replacement products? Can what are now
called fortified beverages honestly replace a healthy diverse diet of real food?
Inevitably, getting in on the ground floor, large corporations like Nestle,
Carnation, GNC, and Abbot are peddling liquid meal-replacement products
that come in the form of nutritional high-protein shakes and drinks, bottles
of rich power gulps coming in popular chocolate and vanilla flavors such
as Ensure (with 24 essential vitamins and minerals"), Boost "26 essential
vitamins and minerals"), Carnation Breakfast Essentials, Herbalife Formula
1, and GNC Shakes, to name a few. While nutritionists can be found to
recommend these drinks for the ill and infirm, for invalids, for seniors and
aging folks who have trouble eating food or indeed even swallowing normal
food, even they have reservations about such substitutes for the rest of us.
Such meal replacements may indeed be packed with micronutrients, there is
no question they are missing other beneficial components of real food that
haven't yet been isolated.

There are many people who are so almost paranoically hyper-alert to
foods stigmatized as carcinogens—common foods such as toast, cured or
processed meats, barbecued food, charred grilled meats, raw mushrooms,
caramel (or so I have read), farmed salmon, soda pop, canned tomatoes,
microwave popcorn, potato chips, highly processed white flour, refined sugars, hydrogenated oils, even beef broth, in spite of the fact that it has long
been considered a restorative—that they look upon the very *act* of eating
as an evil temptation. A growing whiff of contagion in GMOs—genetically
modified foods—keeps them suspect. Spoiled grain, bracken ferns have been
held as suspicious, along with butter yellow, a food coloring commonly used
in Europe and the Far East, that has caused liver cancer in animals. So has
safrole, a phenylpropene, a colorless or slightly yellow oily liquid typically

extracted from the root-bark or fruit of sassafras plants. It is a jungle out there, indeed.

Certain foods that are prohibited to a person often fall into the aversionary one way or another, even if, as in Lewis Carroll's *Through the Looking-Glass*, strict social convention, rules of etiquette, and authority are being parodied or not. Remember Alice at the Red Queen's banquet? She misses out on the leg of mutton "because it is impolite to eat a food that you had been introduced to."

> "You look a little shy: let me introduce you to that leg of mutton," said the Red Queen. "Alice—Mutton: Mutton—Alice." The leg of mutton got up in the dish and made a little bow to Alice, and Alice returned the bow, not knowing whether to be frightened or amused.
> "May I give you a slice?" she said...
> "Certainly not," the Red Queen said, very decidedly: "it isn't etiquette to cut any one you've been introduced to. Remove the joint!" And the waiters carried it off, and brought a large plum-pudding in its place.
> "I won't be introduced to the pudding, please," Alice said rather hastily, "or we shall get no dinner at all."
> (*Through the Looking-Glass*, Norton Critical Edition, 200)

Perversely, biographers rarely if ever list "food" in the indices of their chosen subjects. It is an appalling omission, in my opinion, for when the chosen food habits of a subject are pondered with serious attention, the results can be startling, simply by throwing light on a personality in ways that no other commentary quite can. On the other hand, an indexed entry on the topic of "drinking" never fails to appear. It is one of the received formulas of the genre, one I doubt that will ever change. Recently I read a biography of Saul Steinberg in which, among entries on matters personal, the index predictably lists the entry "drinking," but nothing whatsoever on the category of "eating," an odd omission, at least to me, for Steinberg had much to say about food and was something of a food nut. The same goes with, say, Mary Mathews Gedo's insightful *Picasso: Art as Autobiography*, which omits the entire subject of the artist and food. No, the unavoidable fact is that food, eating, a person's attitude toward it, is a serious and highly informative indication of who we are and how we cope in the "kitchen of life," as the writer

Martha Gellhorn used to refer to our daily existence. We all know Harry Truman's caveat, "If you can't stand the heat, stay out of the kitchen."

Quickly, just to address that subject, Picasso ate little and drank less, according to biographer John Richardson in his memoir, *The Sorcerer's Apprentice*. The painter had an antic, pranksterish-type personality, one bordering on the childish, and he loved to act out, often donning goofy hats and scarves and making funny faces. Scraps of things intrigued Picasso (he hoarded debris, flotsam, what we would call yard-sale items and such) and during dinners, for humor, to amuse himself and his guests, he would often fabricate doodads out of corks, cut up napkins, burnt matches, and flower petals. "While eating frogs' legs, he would simulate their croak by drawing the edge of a serrated knife along the edge of his plate, according to Richardson who goes on to say that what he seemed to enjoy more than anything at table while dining was the ceremonial role as host. "Meals seemed to activate his sense of improvisation. He would carve a very thin slice of tongue, hold it up, and announced that he had done a portrait of Villard's domed head."

"What kind of food do you like?" you will rarely hear asked in any interviews. You will *never* hear, "What kind of food do you hate?" Peculiarly, while such a question is biographically revealing, it is never asked in interviews. You can check this out, anytime. Read over the many in-depth *Paris Review* interviews given over the years to find this to be the case. I am not wrong.

It is the case with the cinema, as well, where as a focus it is crucially downplayed. In *Food in the Movies*, Steve Zimmerman writes that "viewing more than eight hundred films—including many from the silent era—only confirmed what I already suspected: historically filmmakers downplayed food's importance and visual appeal. For the most part food was (and still is) ignored or hidden from view so as to be barely visible." He cites many reasons, ranging from expense, food photography problems, the complexity of food—even reheating it—in multiple takes, to its unglamorous aspects regarding close-ups and so forth.

What biographers tend to emphasize of their subjects, regarding food, are the pleasures one took of it rather than any aversions, passing over in the personalities they are examining what would be a revealing characteristic. It characterizes, reveals. What a person avoids is always fascinating. Where it all begins. Its root causes. Its affects. Why it does not go away. How it happens—and why. Custom reinforces what we do in the first place. Define our customs? They are a sort of adjuvant manifesting the helplessness with which we naively define the obscure.

A person may overdose on olives and never want to eat one again. Another may hate someone who loves a certain food, so comes to hate that food as a way of hating them. P. G. Wodehouse turns from food out of romantic disappointment in his poem, "The Gourmet's Love-Song," complaining, "Soup, whitebait, entrées, fricasees,/ They bring me uninvited./ I need them not, for what are these/ To one whose life is blighted?" and to his beloved writes,

> No longer spurn the suit I press,
> Respect my agitation,
> Do change your mind, and answer, 'Yes,'
> And save me from starvation.

Who knows, it may very well be some sort of vertiginous discretionary need in some type-A person, in order to be highlighted in a sparring way, to *avoid* the foods he most enjoys, in the psycho-bizarre way, say, that a guy who secretly dreams of blondes feels it necessary to shun them in order to achieve some sort of psychological balance. It is a type of self-rectifying *bouleversement*. We are faithful to foods, brand-loyal, flavor-loyal, and there is no disputing at all that tastes in and tropes for foods are commonly aligned to family, friendships, religion, country, ethnicity, and national origin. So when we talk of faith, we must perforce talk of infidelity. Dr. Samuel Johnson, for example, a serious drinker who loved brandy, was vocally averse to drinking claret. Boswell notes that Johnson "spoke of great contempt of claret, as so weak a man would be drowned by it before it made him drunk.'" [*see* Boswell April 7, 1779] It is the old battle. We find that to be suitably responsive to one thing, we are automatically driven to ignore or disparage another, in the same way that a simple-minded person believes if he loves the West Coast he must hate the East.

The aesthetic inevitably wars with the ethical, and vice-versa. Søren Kierkegaard wrote in his philosophical masterpiece, *Either/Or: A Fragment of Life*, of that existential dilemma. "I see it all perfectly; there are two possible situations—one can either do this or that," he cynically if realistically wrote. "My honest opinion and my friendly advice is this: do it or do not do it—you will regret both." Some people inveigh against processed food, others against raw.

There are some who object to what novelist Neal Stephenson calls "recombinant cuisine." In his techno-thriller, the spy adventure, *Reamde*, he suggests that culture is in a constant process of hybridization and, as an example, cites food recipes using ingredients that have already been processed.

But is it a sign of decadence or postmodern over-reach? He writes of one of his characters, "Having now lived for a few decades in parts of the United States and Canada where cooking was treated quite seriously, and having actually employed professional chefs, he was fascinated by the midwestern/ middle American phenomenon of recombinant cuisine. Rice Krispie Treats being a prototypical example in that they were made by repurposing other foods that had already been prepared (to wit, breakfast cereal and marshmallows). And of course any recipe that called for a can of cream of mushroom soup fell into the same category. The unifying principle behind all recombinant cuisine seemed to be indifference, if not outright hostility, to the use of anything that a coastal foodie would define as an ingredient....The recombinant food thing was a declaration of mental bankruptcy in the complexity of modern material culture."

"Disgust has elicited little attention in any of the disciples that claim an interest in the emotions: psychology, philosophy, anthropology," writes William Ian Miller in *The Anatomy of Disgust*. In his chapter "Darwin's Disgust," in which he takes note of the fact that the famous English naturalist was the first to study the subject of disgust in its own right, writes,

> It is not hard to guess the likely reason. The problem
> is its lack of decorum. Civilization raised on sensi-
> bilities to disgust show a key component of a social
> control and psychic order, with the consequence that
> it became socially and psychically very difficult for civ-
> ilized people to talk about disgusting things without
> having the excuse of either childhood, adolescence,
> or transgressive joking...To study disgust is to risk
> contamination.

Disgust as such—affadissement—surely evolved to serve the adaptive function of food selection and disease avoidance. It is always a tocsin of fears and caveats, reminding us of infection, invasion, death, the animal nature, body violation, contamination. It varies in degree among cultures, is often inherited, and of course also involves, and widely, religious and secular laws and rituals.

Cognitive neuroscientist Michael S. Gazzaniga notes in his book, *Human: The Science Behind What Makes Us Unique*, "Disgust is the emotion that protects purity." [J.] Haidt suggests that feelings of disgust arose only when hominids became meat eaters. It appears to be a uniquely human emotion. Obviously your dog doesn't feel it. Look what he eats."

niga writes,

Disgust is only one of the four reasons that humans reject food, but we share the other three reasons with other animals: distaste, inappropriateness (a stick), and danger. Disgust implies the knowledge of the origins or the nature of food. Young infants will reject food that is bitter, but disgust doesn't appear until around age five. Haidt and his colleagues suggest that the emotion initially acted as a food rejection system, evidenced by its connection to nausea, concerns with contamination (contact with a disgusting substance), and facial expressions associated with it, which mostly use the nose and mouth. They refer to this as core disgust. "Are you a cautious person or a risk-taker?" an individual is often asked. Caution and risk-taking are not paired opposites, however. The inveterate food aversionist is averse to the latter and a great advocate and avowee of the former, often to the point of monomania, obsession, fixation, and compulsion."

Individual tastes, nevertheless, are incontestably varied and unique. The range of reasons why any person is put off by a certain food can be wide. Certain people are put off by a food's texture, others by its odor or color or possibly even the unpredictable and *varying* look or presentation of a comestible that has been placed in front of them. Yet another eater may be revolted by nothing more than the simple oddity unprepossessing newness of a food, even by its name. Keen on some Spotted Dick? Toad in the Hole? Hellena Fart Juice, manufactured in Warsaw? ("*Fart*" means luck in Polish.) One unvarying truism regarding food aversions—and perhaps, as an absolute, the true measure of its awfulness for an individual—is not only that the person in question finds the particular food disgusting and repugnant but that he or she is equally nauseated and utterly repelled by the simple sight of *another* person eating it. It could apply to anything. Marylanders sweatily cracking crabs with drum mallets? Cockneys spooning up gobbets of jellied eels? Samoans bringing up gouts of *faiai fee* (*masefau*) —octopus in coconut cream—from the third layer of an *umu* or an earth oven? Then who would deny that the mere nap or shape of a food that one hates can matter greatly? (Actress Audrey Hepburn would never wear a wristwatch simply because she could not abide the off-putting sensation of cold or weight against her flesh.) Simply touching a food can disgust someone, the mere thigmotactic response of a tongue to orange juice pulp, say, or someone feeling grit in a clam or dirt in spinach.

It has even been suggested by food critics, extravagantly perhaps, that the very plates that are used at table, and even the music that one may play at dinner, can alter your perceptions of the food's worth, value, taste. G. K. Chesterton would have agreed. He once wrote, "Music with dinner is an insult both to the cook and the violinist." An extremely orthodox Catholic, a convert, he was equally convinced that "modernism" in virtually its every manifestation, political, philosophical, poetical (he utterly reviled T.S. Eliot's "The Hollow Men") was a soul-destroying force, and along with pessimism, determinism, and pragmatism, he included impressionism. All those delicate renderings of Matisse, Monet, Manet, *et alii*? Quite so, for Chesterton impressionism was little more than anti-artistic blasphemy, a declaration of ego, vanity, and crass self-absorption. "It means believing one's immediate impressions at the expense of one's more permanent and positive generalizations," he wrote in his study of William Blake in 1910. "It puts what one notices above what one knows."

Special plates, no music, some music. Lucy Barton, wife of poet Edward Fitzgerald, could take no pleasure at a dinner unless she could dress for it. It is surely an aspect of a kind of food phobia.

There is fear of eating (or swallowing) which is called *phagophobia*, but fear of eating certain food, called *sitophobia* is another thing entirely, a more specific often neurotic concern which can involve anything from the fear of choking to an anxiety of ingesting poison to a waking terror of eating an unhealthy or dirty food, and a kind of phobia may be the seemingly uncomplicated fact—a strange abhorrence—of having to eat in the presence of other people.

What about mere suspicion? Horrid reports? Rumor? Are you aware that the number of insect fragments officially allowed by the FDA in 2013 in a standard jar of peanut butter is 153, the number of rodent hairs 5? Delusional parasitosis, also known as "Ekbom's syndrome," which is a form of psychosis where a victim acquires the strong conviction that he is infested with parasites when of course none are present, has been known to be found in cases of extreme food phobes. Most often imaginary parasites are reported as being "bugs" or insects crawling on or under the skin, a sensation in human experience known as formication, but, as I say, it is not unknown as a response in a beleaguered, disturbed person fleeing a given food.

Suspicion is a fundamental element in food aversions. It may have far deeper roots than mere whim. I roomed with a friend once who was hearing voices—actually hearing "words" in the gurgling of water or steam in the pipes of the building. This I have read and heard, is a typical example of a fairly common and familiar psychological phenomenon called pareidolia," the tendency in a sufferer to "see" or "hear" orderly or meaningful patterns that really are not there in random visual sights or in random hissing, gurgling, murmuring, or crackling sounds—e.g., in seeing faces in tree-trunks or clouds, or discerning the visage of Jesus or the Virgin Mary in a pancake, a wall moisture stain, or a Dunkin' Donuts cruller, or even hearing the otherworldly voices of spirits in radio static, as in the alleged "Electronic Voice Phenomena" that is often attributed to ghosts by credulous or impressionable ghost-hunters with fancy electronic gadgets. I believe pareidolia should maybe encompass certain cases of food aversion. There is an actual experience of onslaught in extreme cases of food aversion, often creating a fortress mentality, where subfusc messages are being telegraphed.

I fancy—just a guess on my part—that a combination of both suspicion as well as the fear of eating/swallowing has added to the growing population of juicearians. We find everywhere nowadays a passionate subculture composed mostly of runners, dieters, and health nuts, who thrill to squeezing fruit for drinks. While fruit and vegetable juices are the most common type of juice, highly nutritious wheat grass is also now big. It is one of very few truly fresh foods available (sprouts are another). The primary benefit of fresh wheatgrass juice—juice derived from the raw, live, soil-grown grain—is the treasured amount of life-force energy that it holds. Right up to the time it is juiced, wheat grass is *alive and growing*, and with any chance, ideally, you are drinking it right after it is juiced. Most of us get our green veggies from food stores, you see, food picked a few days before and refrigerated, thus losing valuable energy the whole time. Lost life force!

I picture these pale, passionate juicearians and nectivores drinking liquids the way tiny iridescent hummingbirds suck, tongues forked distally, each half forming a delicate trough, curved and fibrillating!

How about color? A food's sheen or dullness can repulse someone, and lapidary impressions are often formed by little more than a given color of a food. Does any toddler eat anything that is dark brown or visibly wrinkled? "I eat only white foods: eggs, sugar, shredded bones, the fat of dead animals, rice, veal, coconuts, salt, chicken cooked in white water; fruit mold; turnips; sausages in camphor; pastry; cheese (the white varieties); things like pasta; cotton salad; and certain kinds of fish (skinned)," the oddball composer Erik Satie wrote in *Memoires d'un Amnesique*, documenting his working habits under the heading, "The Musician's Day," adding, "An artist must organize his life."

Some people refuse to eat dark food. Others insist it is healthier than light food, that nutrients reside in the peel and crust, that charcoal-cooked food causes cancer, that meats with bone-in alone taste real, that red food is most salubrious. There are degrees of dislike and loathing, of course. One might distinguish here, for example, regarding white food, between English steak-and-kidney pie, with its flaky crust, and steak-and-kidney pudding, which has a suet crust that tastes, as the New York socialite and 1950s/1960s fashion icon, Slim Keith, a woman whom no food ever seemed to please at all, once proclaimed, "more like a chewy white blanket." Dubbed the original "California Girl," for her golden looks and athleticism, Keith—born Mary Raye Gross—considered a career in opera, before deciding that it was "too demanding." Food aversion is about *specifics*. We are in the world here of fastidiousness, fault-finding, captious, and singular refusal.

It is ironic but apropos to note—because Lady Keith (virtually an antonym to her birth name) was one of those thin, beautiful, fussy, Upper East Side socialites whom Truman Capote referred to as "swans" and with whom he became so overfamiliarly chummy until they had a brutal falling out due to his vicious but apparently accurate short story, "La Côte Basque," published in *Esquire* in 1975, in which he mercilessly lampooned her—that Keith is the only person I have ever heard of who has actually *eaten* swan. It took place on the only legitimate occasion, at least in England, when such a thing is permissible, at the feast of "Swan Upping," for all swans in the UK are the property of Her Majesty, the Queen. This unique celebration is held annually at Fishmonger's Hall in London, a medieval if slightly dotty occasion when four parading chefs, all fitted out in white smocks, carry into a room filled with select guests a cooked swan, borne aloft on a silver platter, when, in the words of Keith (married at the time to Sir Kenneth Keith, her fourth husband), "it is cut up into small, gray pieces that taste exactly like what swans eat—mud." Keith disdainfully and virtuously described it all in her autobiography, *Slim: Memories of a Rich and Imperfect Life,* as a "hateful meal." Still, it makes for a small culinary boast that one—a snob—has eaten it. I imagine she would have eaten sea lion scat if it bore anything like regal connotations.

Those rich, prissy, spoiled Manhattan socialites seem to have been among the fussiest eaters in history, contemptible in the extreme, along with the vain, fad-conscious California women who spend their entire lives hunting perfect diets, those tanned, body-worshipping, trainer-focused sybarites. But then again, as Roberto Bolaño wrote in his novel, *2666*, "There's no place on earth with more dumb girls per square foot than a college in California."

2.

WE ARE WHAT WE EAT

WE ARE WHIMSICAL CREATURES. Who is surprised that tastes vary or opinions are quirky when people are so different, their moods changing from day to day? Our thinking, judgment to judgment, is often saltatory, subjective, whimsical, passionate, illogical. There is no explaining taste, which points directly to the old Latin maxim, "De gustibus non est disputandum," meaning, "In matters of taste, there can be no dispute." The implication is that everyone's personal preferences are merely subjective opinions that cannot be "right" or "wrong," so they should never be argued about as if they were. Think of knives and forks. "In English table manners, the knife is never laid down until the course is finished... the British think they are polite because they never put down their knives; Americans think they are polite, because they do," writes Bee Wilson in *Consider the Fork*. Conductor Leopold Stokowski solved that problem, because he only—always—ate with a spoon. Same with lovely Greta Garbo, by the way, who was once descried in the late 1940s eating lunch at Perino's, an elegant landmark restaurant on Wilshire Boulevard, and instead of using her fork was eating a bowl of spaghetti with only a dessert spoon. This was also the same woman of course who always kissed a man by cupping his head in both hands and seeming very nearly to drink from it! So, whatever happened to George Orwell's often repeated truism, "The secret of a successful restaurant is sharp knives"?

No, taste cannot be disputed. It is all of it non-objective, idiosyncratic, fanciful, intuitive, illusory, and always prejudiced. The late Princess Diana, who from all reports was extremely fussy in most matters, disliked salmon, and also all red meat. Barbra Streisand does not drink coffee. Pitcher Satchel Paige, the first player to be inducted into the Baseball Hall of Fame strictly based upon his play in the Negro leagues, avoided all fried foods ("It angries up the blood"). Manolo Blahnik, Spanish fashion designer and founder of the eponymous high-end shoe brand, is allergic to both wine and vinegar. TV host Howie Mandel reportedly refuses to eat raisins.

A bias need not be hard and fast, it goes without saying, although one's partialities and partisanships, once formed, can invariably become as hard as benchstone. Things change. People grow. Attitudes amend. Minds alter. I recall reading somewhere that Tom Sietsema, the longtime restaurant critic for *The Washington Post*, had a loathing of fennel but then underwent a conversion and now enjoys the herb, an experience he compares to "a person you broke up with and years later reconnect with and see in a new way." The brilliant cartoonist Edward Sorel confided to me in a letter a few Christmases ago, "My only food aversion is fennel—and also wine because it has sulfites." Could it have been that the artist disliked its smell or its glaucous green color—a strangely glaring eye-poke—or was it that the herb is loved by snakes and is often used to treat flatulence by encouraging in the human body the expulsion of intestinal gas, the anethole in it being responsible for the carminative action? Fennel-phobes, incidentally, at least from my experience in talking to a passionate few, insist that they can actually smell the herb a mile away—they are often people with a strong aversion to anise and licorice—and when in an unforeseen circumstance such flavors have subtly worked their way into a meal they say they can never get the taste out of their mouths.

I have encountered all sorts of contentiousness of in the matter of meat. It is the one food category where a major line is drawn. Dilettante Lucius Beebe abhorred over-cooked meat. "One of the minor problems of dining in New Orleans," Beebe once declared, "is to keep the chef from getting his hands on the meat and… trying to cook it. When ordering steak it is well-advised to instruct the waiter to walk briskly through the kitchen holding it within a few feet of the stove." Mormon prophet Joseph Smith who told his followers that meat itself should be eaten "sparingly," and ideally should be taken only in winter, also advised his flock of believers that fruit, vegetables, and herbs are the best of foods, and he added the somewhat eccentric opinion (of which, not unexpectedly, the illiterate religious founder had more than a few) that grains themselves have specific roles: "… wheat for man, and corn for the ox, and oats for the horse…" So, no corn and no oats for humans? Mormon cuisine, by the way, which whether justified or not, has long had a reputation for being worse than plain, hopelessly bland, and, to many individuals, downright awful, stereotypically favors only casseroles and green Jell-O or meat with cream-of-something on mashed potatoes.

Quirks, opinions, odd preferences abound in the widely diverse matter of food. Socionics, in psychology and sociology a theory of information processing and personality types, perhaps alone could provide, not so much the explanation of it all, but offer a resource on where to begin an insightful analysis on the subject. The classic food aversionist—to use terms from Isaiah Berlin's well-known essay, "The Hedgehog and the Fox"—is pretty much a "hedgehog," a type of individual who with a single fixed notion, at least regarding his food crotchet, views the world through the lens of a single defining idea, as opposed to the "fox" who with multiple ideas tends to draw on a wide variety of experiences and for whom the world cannot be boiled down to a single idea. It recalls the idea that Matthew Arnold ponders in his fascinating *Culture and Anarchy* on the hazard of people reducibly, fatally, fixing on one of anything, fully to reject or accept it, to hate or to love it, the result of oversimplifying thinking that "one thing is necessary in life" to correct it. It is an aspect of anti-intellectualism.

There is frankly a kind of *einzelheit* or singlemindedness in people with food aversions, pronounced or otherwise.

I daresay that in the oddball world of food extremism, little can match the pronounced monomania of the radical vegetarian and sun-worshipping nudist from Nuremberg, Germany, August Engelhardt, who at the turn of the last century went off to live on the island of Kabakon in what was then German New Guinea. A maniacal "cocovore"—a person who chooses to subsist solely on coconuts—he went completely native in the Bismarcki Archipelago in order to live out his loony, obsessive, crack-pated fantasy, which was as much about flight as about food. The man, who looked like R.L. Stevenson's Ben Gunn, vigorously worked to establish a colony of coco-vores. Arguably the definitive food aversionist, Engelhardt had concluded by way of a kind of deductive algebra that all—*all*—foods were harmful. Swiss-novelist Christian Kracht's best-selling *Imperium*, a novel about Engelhardt's exploits in the Pacific and his food freakery, gives us a vivid picture of the man's compulsion:

> After having adjudged all other foodstuffs unclean by the process of elimination, Engelhardt had abruptly stumbled upon the fruit of the coconut palm. No the possibility existed; *Cocos nucifera* was, as Engelhardt had realized on his own, the proverbial crown of creation; it was the fruit of Yggdrasil, world tree. It grew at the highest point of the palm, facing the sun and our luminous Lord God; it gave us water, milk, coconut oil, and nutritious pulp; unique in nature, it provided humankind with the element selenium;

from its fibers one wove mats, roofs, and ropes; from its trunk one built furniture and entire houses; from its pit one produced oil, to drive away the darkness and to anoint the skin; even the hollowed-out, empty shell made an excellent vessel from which one could manufacture bowls, spoons, tankards, indeed even buttons; burning the empty shell, finally, was not only superior to burning traditional firewood, but was also an excellent means of keeping away mosquitoes and flies with its smoke; in short, the coconut was perfect. Whosoever subsisted solely on it would become godly, would become immortal."

In the end, a tragic one, inevitably, the mad Engelhardt, who had suffered for decades from a multi-bacillary form of leprosy, proved just how crucially misled the man was in just about every move he made. His badly malnourished body was found on a beach in 1919. He was forty-three years old.

"I hate icy fur on ice cream." "Creamed spinach—*blecch*!" "Soft pears skeeve me!" ("There are only ten minutes in the life of a pear when it is perfect to eat," maintained Ralph Waldo Emerson.) "What I cannot stand is the skin on a cup of old coffee." "I love soggy pie crust, but you never get it on top." "Mushy peas are my definition of hell." "New England cooking is spiceless ratshit." "Rhubarb sucks." "One of my very worst nightmares is cold soup." ("If soup is not hot enough to make a grown man wince, it is undrinkable," pontificates quotation anthologist Terri Guillemets.) "Lobster to me is slimy and disgusting." "Who on earth can bear the taste of salt water taffy?" "The very sight of store-bought meatballs revolts me." "If I see another dish of creamed corn I am going to hurl!"

We have all heard various howls of execration for particular foods that are reviled. Most people leap to express their food dislikes. Our dug-in positions along these lines, pro or con, virtually tell us what we are. Food, what we like, what we have chosen to abhor, is in a very real sense a royal road to the deep self, to the unconscious, to the inner man, whether royal or not. It is the "most familiar and universal medium in our lives," according to Amanda Hesser in her book, *Eat, Memory*. As I say, Feuerbach has told us, "*Der Mensch ist was er isst*"—we are what we eat. It is not a philosophically deep reach, but it speaks to a truth that cannot be ignored in terms of personal identity and the "thisness"—or *haeccitas*—of self.

The Italian editor Carlo Petrini, founder of the International Slow Food Movement–he first came to prominence in the 1980s for taking part in a campaign against McDonald's, the fast-food chain that had opened near the Spanish Steps in Rome—has argued quite convincingly that we ought to think of ourselves less as consumers of what we eat than as actual co-producers who are in fact connected to the food we eat. Fast food fits the modern world. (Americans ordered 9 billion burgers at restaurants in 2014, 30 million more than in 2013.) Pace always seems to be set on high frantic. It was Aldous Huxley who said that speed is the only new vice invented by modern man, which is surely something to think about the next time we are ordering on the run a triple bacon cheeseburger, large fries, and a Coke.

There is a story to Feuerbach's punning apothegm. In a book review of Cita Stelzer's *My Dinner with Churchill*, Bernard Porter, Emeritus Professor of History at the University of Newcastle, wrote "If I remember my [German philosopher and anthropologist Ludwig] Feuerbach rightly, the context here [of that proverb] was the Irish people's supineness in the face of English oppression: they were too filled with '*träges Kartoffelblut*,' he thought, to rise up." If joy is round and tall is handsome and faith is blind, then one may assert that food is friction, fight, ferocity. All wars are fought over land and water, which means food! The guns of power and conquest are fully about hunting, like a nimrod after rabbits. It might be advanced that the brutal half-century occupation by the Soviet Union of Estonia, Lithuania, and Latvia was directly connected to the scrimp fare—potatoes, beets, cabbage, berries—eaten by those weaker nations, leaching any possible strength in them to revolt. The fact is, a person eats an average of 144 thousand pounds of food in a lifetime, and exactly what that food both is and is not surely has to signify. We are what we eat.

Most of us have never managed to taste the best of the world's foods. Quite the opposite. Citizens of the wider world eat—when indeed they are eating at all—mainly the dullest, the cheapest, the most accessible of foods. In many countries it is often the worst food. The ersatz we know—the watered down, the faux, the substitute, the mock, and the mediocre. But who among us has had the luxury of being transported to heaven as we sat down at any of the elegant restaurants of the Savoy or the Connaught, at Claridge's or The Ledbury, or found ourselves being pampered at the St. Regis or the Ritz-Carlton, the Four Seasons or the St. Pierre? How many of us have ever had dessert trolleys spread with delicacies wheeled before us, as is still done at Le Perigord and the Villa Berulia, the Café des Artistes and Belluno's? How many of us, purse-tightening inchlings, have first-hand knowledge of true and majestic excellence in food—the real thing? Special Reserve Ossetra caviar? A filet de daurade royale rôtie à la plancha at Le Cinq? Delicate white shrimp that all South Carolinians insist on for Frogmore stew, a simple boil of shrimp, potatoes, corn, sausage with maybe clams or crab? Fresh steaks from the Argentine—juicy, grass-fed, delicious *Bife de lomo, Asado de tira, Bife de chorizo* ? Or Bulgarian yogurt? Istanbul kebabs? Cashews from the Bengal-Orissa border? An elegant *poulet de Bresse?* Westvleteren Beer XII from Belgium? Jamaican Blue Mountain coffee? Amadei or Teuscher or Richart chocolate? Enstrom's toffee? Trinidad habañero pepper sauce? Oaxacan squash soup? Cabrito from Monterrey, Mexico? A true Spanish manchego? Perfectly cooked Mung Bean Bin Dae Tteok? Swedish raggmunk? A bowl of fresh fat lobsters, still alive and kicking, from Maine?

Who that has dreamed of it has entered an elegant restaurant, say, Arzak in Spain, Osteria Francescena in Modena, Italy, D.O.M. in Brazil, Noma in Copenhagen, to be greeted by the head-waiter with *ancien régime* politeness and a smile? Being seated at a table covered with snowy linen from Garnier-Thiebaut and sparkling candles?

How many of us has had the chance to eat a Densuke watermelon? Or a Yubari melon? Matsutake mushrooms? A Chocopologie bon-bon by Knipschildt with its truffle center? Almas caviar? Actual bird's-nest soup, from China, at $5,000 the pound? A charbroiled Kobe filet? An Australian Wagyu striploin? A *bife de Costilla* from Argentina? What about a cup of Second Flush Darjeeling tea? Or a glass, even a shot, of Ardbeg Galileo, probably the world's best single malt whisky?

Can you be numbered among those who have had a perfect *poulet à l'Estragon,* probably the best chicken recipe in the world, with no stinting of cream and with French (never Russian) tarragon? Or eaten delicate coffee macaroons at Ladurée or enjoyed a *bûche de Noël* at Mulot, patisseries in Paris? Or had the best Iberian ham, like a Pata Negra? Or sat down and eaten a *kabsah* or Saudi Arabian slow-cooked lamb with perfumed rice with forty spices? Or had the delight of enjoying the bite of matchless cheeses like the fragrant Pont l'Eveque or the taste of matchless Saint-Agur, a French blue cheese that melts in your mouth like divine ambrosia, or Etivaz, a proto-Gruyère that is curdled in copper caldrons over spruce fires and is made from the summer milk of cows grazing on violets in the high Alps or Broccio, far and away the best cheese in all of Corsica? ("And that is why Napoleon shall not have it," vociferously declared the Emperor's father in Madam Eugénie Foa's *The Boy Life of Napoleon* [1895], while at the same time giving it to Pauline, his pretty daughter. "Broccio is for good boys and girls; and Napoleon is not good.") Arguably, what we have not eaten, we are not. Most of us on are the bronze team, rarely the gold.

There actually exists *edible gold*. It is commonly flaked and added to drinks and sometimes used as a garnish, and yet oddly enough it is flavorless and, while obviously appeasing the vanity of the consumer, literally adds nothing to a dish but a brainless shininess. Selling from $36,000 to $110,000 per kilogram, it is more than anything else a status symbol for all of the self-serving and egotistical, narcissistic, self-involved, foolishly rapacious and inhuman, piggish and unscrupulous and profane rats and plutocrats, tycoons, diamond and gold billionaires, sheiks, nabobs, oil magnates, barons, merchant princes, and gastrolatrous, self-indulgent Wall Street thieves who live their lives only to gratify and indulge themselves.

It is a truth that it is impossible to live without imagination. To some degree this touches on food aversions, at least regarding the question, as they form or develop, whether fancy in the matter is too weak or too pronounced. We look on a given food with either favor or disdain. We project our feelings; food before us begins to connote, not denote, what in our minds reflects that bias. I have always had a mildly schizophrenic attitude toward rhubarb, for example. Did I like it or hate it—or both? I love rhubarb pie—it is after all called the "pie plant"—and we all know rhubarb lends itself to no end of delicious dowdies, dumplings, crumbles, cakes, cobblers, jams and jellies. Queerly, in a transvestitial way, it is a vegetable used mostly in desserts. Many are its ferocities and fangs, however. When growing up, the kids in our street constantly diddled with rhubarb, yanking it up out of neighbors' gardens, gnashing bites of the stalks. I recall taking big bites out of a tart rhubarb stalk and almost withering from its sourness, an almost electric acridity as bitter as alum. Its harshness has long been recognized as a laxative. Its leaves contain oxalic acid that in extravagant doses could power the rust off an iron girder or bleach a Zambian black hippo white. We are pushed and pulled hither and yon in just about everything we eat, are we not?

Rhubarb is used in sauces, syrups, cocktails, tea, and even on shortcake with great success, but, more often than not, it is combined with fruits in all sorts of medleys. It has great crunch, a tremendous punch, and is a vitamin-C-packed plant. In certain households, years ago mostly, it was served as a "dessert," a bowl served with ruby flesh, now boiled to gray, with lemon-sour pucker along with a cloying sweetness, and yet to many it had all of the texture of a bowl of wet toilet paper. Going back to its etymology, the Romans gave us the word "rhubarb," by taking its name from the Latin *rha barbarum*. Rhubarb flourished along the banks of the river Rha, you see, an ancient name of the Volga. The region was considered foreign by the Romans, a barbarian territory. Thus, rhubarb literally means "from the barbarian, Rha."

I have never quite understood, for example, the concept behind the added-pickle-with-anything syndrome, so popular in America. All fast-food emporia in the country booby trap—sandwich-stack!—their burgers. As far as removing unwanted pickles goes, you cannot. Not all the way. By the time you get to your booth, it is too late. The green infection has spread. In an article, "Peanut Butter Takes On An Unlikely Best Friend," Dwight Garner in the *New York Times* (Oct. 22, 2012) makes a plea for the perfect marriage—a shotgun marriage, as far as I am concerned—of pickles with peanut butter. He writes, "Like Krazy and Ignatz, [James] Carville and [Mary] Matalin, Cupid and Psyche, and Alison Krauss and Robert Plant, the peanut butter and pickle sandwich is one of those unlikely pairings that shouldn't work, but does." He adds, "That's how I've always felt, anyway. I've been happily eating these distinctive little sandwiches for years. The vinegary snap of chilled pickle cuts, like a dash of irony, against the stoic unctuousness of peanut butter. The sandwich is a thrifty and unacknowledged American classic. My father passed them down to me. Peanut butter and pickle sandwiches got him through law school at West Virginia University."

Ah, *there* is the explanation—WVU! Was I somehow expecting to find that Dwight Garner had attended the Culinary School of America? But even Garner goes on to admit that his concoction is not a universal favorite:

> The PB&P has been a minority enthusiasm in America for generations, lingering just under the radar. The sandwiches appeared on lunch-counter menus during the Great Depression and in extension-service cookbooks in the 1930s and '40s in recipes that generally called for a few spoonfuls of pickle relish. A lot of people's grandmothers used to eat them. These days, they're a cult item. Kinsey Millhone, the fictional private investigator in Sue Grafton's alphabet series of mysteries, is probably America's best-known devotee.

What is it about pickles? Where is the cogent explanation that they belong on burgers? People put slices of pickles on hamburgers, on submarine sandwiches, in Chinese food, even (in health spas) on their eyes, to say nothing of going so far as using them—this is sadly true—as ornaments on Christmas trees. There are grilled-cheese-and-pickle sandwiches! May I ask why it is that in the United States just about every food order must automatically come with a pickle? It has become nothing less than a ritualized act. Salty, acid-heavy, wet, sour, crunchy, horrible. I have even seen a recipe for

Kool-Aid pickles, a dubious contrivance made by adding colored fizz-pow-der to the juice of the little beasts with added sugar. As the old New York Yankees skipper, Casey Stengel, used to say, "Include me out."

Subjectivity rules all food aversions.

Gourmand James Beard did not like fresh tuna and felt that it was often dry. Russian gymnast Olga Korbut put ketchup on her pancakes. Chef Jenifer Harvey Lang, the first woman to cook in the kitchen of New York's famous "21" Club, swears that she will never buy sardines packed in water, saying in *Tastings*, "To me, they are worse than having no sardines at all." (Beach Cliff sardines from Maine, packed in soy oil, are the tastiest to her—and also the cheapest!) Italian-Americans buy whole canned tomatoes, while tomato *puree* is favored in Hispanic neighborhoods, and stewed tomatoes are an old American treat. I had a bright classmate in college who avoided tomatoes—in all forms, no matter how presented—like the plague. Spicy foods often contain tomatoes and peppers, which carry acidic lycopene that can be an irritant to some people, by way of throwing off their skin's pH levels and triggering breakouts. (Did you know that the highest concentration of vita-min C in tomatoes is in the jelly-like substance around the seeds?) My friend referred to tomatoes as "Dermatoid chlamydia!"

Novelist Henry Miller insisted that the four cornerstones to good health are garlic, yogurt, honey, and olive oil. Many people will not touch any of them. No tastes—like no people—are the same. Remember Dr. Seuss's crusty Bustard who eats only custard with sauce made of mustard? Then again, al-though Emma Bovary tries to seek peace in a church, she soon ditches that plan after spying an ugly mustard stain on a priest's shirt. (Some would argue that the phrase "ugly mustard stain" is a triple redundancy.) Such are the sort of gustatory antipodes we are talking about.

Believe me, no one can explain the logic of taste—or the nature of ca-veats. Daoist monks ritually practice the avoidance of grains. Pope Francis has entreated us to respect nature and to avoid eating any genetically modify foods. "This is one of the greatest challenges of our time," explained the Pontiff in 2014, "to convert ourselves to a type of development that knows how to respect creation." But then isn't it impossible to taste a genetically modified food from a pure one? Who can explain a palate? I had a Hungarian roommate once, Sandor, who every morning, blithely shaking out a sugar bullet, added a generous helping of sweetness to his *fried eggs*. Charles II, the "Merrie Monarch," ate ambergris with his morning eggs. In Hokkaido, Japan, among some available ice cream flavors are chicken-wing, horseflesh, sea urchin, squid-ink, crab, and pickled plum. Does that sound odd? There are actual ice cream flavors offered in the United States like curry carrot; bacon; "red hot" banana; bleu cheese and caramelized shallot, and sorbets like grapefruit-mustard; soy sauce; and avocado!

Who can explain a palate? In the 18th-century in Salem, Mass. dried tea leaves were boiled and, after the tea was drunk straight, the leaves were then salted and eaten with butter. Frank Sinatra expressly ordered a jar of smooth peanut butter to be placed in every hotel room in which he stayed before a concert. Why—to help his throat? Improve his diction? Simply to munch? (It failed to help him avoid repeatedly mis-pronouncing the name Monique in his recording of that song, where he keeps singing "Monique-a," which is not even a correct pronunciation of Monica!) Chef Jenifer Lang claims—strange statistic—that the majority of people who consume peanut butter are black. Lang's book *Tastings* is an amazing fund of insights and inside facts. George Washington in 1790 in New York City ran up a $200 ice cream bill. The book of Ruth alludes to the practice of using vinegar for flavoring bread: "And Boaz said unto her, 'At mealtimes come thou hither, and eat of the bread, and dip thy morsel in vinegar.'" Chef Lang goes on to explore the whys and wherefores of gout.

Vanilla, which is the world's most popular flavor, scents tea in china, flavors pastry and custards, is found in hand creams, serves to make wax candles exotic, and for centuries was used as the medium of exchange by the Aztecs—a black pod called "*thilxochitl.*"

A memorable fact is that Carson McCullers mentions in her novel, *The Heart is a Lonely Hunter*, that vanilla was employed by many young Southern girls as a perfume. Europeans tend to prefer intensely flavored chocolate with lots of cocoa butter, whereas Americans generally prefer a rougher, slightly ripened chocolate that is "conched" for a very long time and has what is called a "barnyard taste." While the fragrance of the bay leaf is more notice-able than its taste, most people do not realize that bay leaves may be eaten without any toxic effect at all. I know several ingenious cooks—over-inge-nious ones, perhaps—who constantly crumble and eat them. They can also be scattered in a pantry to repel roaches, mice, moths, flies. They are laurel leaves, after all, legendary symbols of victory and achievement.

I have heard Chef Gordon Ramsay dis white truffle oil. (In his opin-ion, however, it is legitimate to use store-bought frozen French fries to shave his truffles over!) I gather it is all a question of what you want in the end, right? No one can truly explain food tastes. Two out of five judges on "Chopped," the reality-based cooking television series created by Michael Krupat, one that pits four chefs against each other competing for the chance to win $10,000,000, hate onions, another one dislikes white pepper, and still another one of them fussily does not like preparations of *chaud froid*, all of which are used in extremely high-end French dishes.

Chika Tillman, one of three owners of the dessert bar ChikaLicious, personally finds oats repulsive but could not keep them out of her restaurant. "Dry, it's like bird food," she claims. "And cooked, it's like somebody chewed it and took it from their mouth." Yet homemade granola was voted in over Ms. Tillman's objections. She tried her best, and dressed it up with yogurt sorbet and cantaloupe *brûlée*, but the oats were too much. It was on the menu for one day.

If George Bernard Shaw was correct in maintaining, "There is no love sincerer than the love of food," I believe I am right is stating there is no greater bias—no more dogged an intransigence—than a solidly confirmed food aversion. Rote is involved, of course. Compulsion. Fixation. An *idée fixe*. Obsession governs much of what we do. Abraham Lincoln, whose understanding took it to be a proclivity, would not sign death warrants against soldiers who ran away. He used to say, "A man is not responsible for his legs." Maybe that is why Shaw was such an inveterate bike-rider. "After one appalling crash," Michael Holroyd wrote of Shaw in *On Wheels*, "he claimed that anyone but a vegetarian would have been killed; and nobody but a teetotaler could have mounted a bicycle again for six months." The reasoning is subjective, the attitude fixed, the position unswerving, the mode fully planted. Seneca (4 BC-65 AD) gave up his vegetarianism to avoid the appearance of sympathizing with Judaism.

There are people who will touch nothing cooked in copper, for example, others who refuse to eat purple food—numbered among whom, one can assume, would be the late actor Peter Sellers who would walk off any movie set if anyone showed up wearing the "unlucky" color purple and Cary Grant who violently opposed the color, especially in women's clothes—still others who are vegetarians, strict vegans, or those who will eat nothing but raw food, gently nourishing themselves on things like raisins, nuts, seeds, and other healthy if comparatively joyless anti-uric substances. Another sub-culture believes that food merely *cooked* is dangerous. Other rabid locavores go tramping around with baskets from one farmer's market to another, health zealots with a determined, beady, vole-like look in their eyes for produce only grown locally. "I respect vegetarians, but I could never fall in love with one," declared the late Nora Ephron. The breezy vanity of love-hunters ready with a long list of inflexible, eliminating notions have always seemed to me arrogant and presumptuous, and, more than anything, imbecilic—but when coming from someone whose face resembled a draft horse's? It seems outright self-destructive! Many vegans also studiously avoid honey as they would any other animal products. (Were you aware that plain honey is used sometimes for antifreeze mixtures and employed in the center of golf balls?)

Believe me, Fussification "R" Us! Film director John Waters hates pickles—"all forms of pickle." Novelist Jonathan Franzen told me that when he was a youngster he "loathed pretty much any vegetable that wasn't corn." Kim Kardashian dislikes sushi. So does pop-singer Taylor Swift. "I have tried so hard to like sushi," she apologetically declared once or twice. "I am the last person on earth who is not cool enough to be able to eat sushi. I can't swallow it." Actress Gwyneth Paltrow apparently hates sugar, or so I have read. She published a cookbook in 2011, *My Father's Daughter*, which is a compilation of easy recipes celebrating family and togetherness, and apparently in the book, uniquely, not a single one of the recipes calls for sugar. Paltrow does not even recommend a sugar substitute, I gather. It proves without a doubt that monomania is often if not always at the root of food aversions.

A good example of an anti-sugar extreme is given by novelist Ann Patchett in a piece, "Let Them Eat Kale" (*Gourmet*, September 1999), where in the course of wittily explaining how members of her family, "being picky," have all chosen what foods they do not want to eat—Richard believes there is something depraved about adults eating dairy ("Mucus," he says), while Ann herself avoids meat—she offers an eye-opening anecdote about a friend of hers who had given up sugar: fruit juice, alcohol, fruit, bread ("which, she says, just converts to sugar"). We are then told just how *completely* resolved her friend became in her resolution:

> "She has given up *carrots*," Patchett exclaims. She asks
> the waiter if there is any sugar in the salad dressing.
> "Carrots?" I ask.
> "Sugar," she says.

Personal convictions about food are one thing, often radical, immoderate, revolutionary, even militant. But then we all find that even in nations there are trends in what people will cherish or put aside, value or disparage. All sorts of conclusions are drawn by what goes down in the process, and there is no end of calumnies leveled by complainers ready to libel what they hate.

Whole countries have been demeaned for having bad food, of course. President Grover Cleveland hated French food. "I must go to dinner," her wrote a friend. "But I wish it was to eat a pickled herring, Swiss cheese, and a chop at Louis' instead of the French stuff I shall find." English cooking has been widely disparaged by everyone from William Hazlitt to James Michener to S.J. Perelman to the narcissistic actor Johnny Depp who, when filming *On Stranger Tides* in London, according to rumor, refused the British food he was offered and petulantly asked for noodles instead. He had been graciously offered sausage and mash, potato and salad, ravioli and chicken curry. But the actor dismissed the food as "just awful." Edmund Wilson, the American literary critic, felt the same way about what he called "lower-class British food, and in his book, *The Forties*, becomes vexed when one lady does not share his disgust. Food in Greece is often judged to be too oily, too salty, too lemony; Indian cuisine too rich, too perfumed; Chinese food too watery and insubstantial. "I don't think anyone eats with very great relish in Spain," novelist William Gaddis wrote to his mother from that country where he had spent much of 1948-49. "All they can grow is [sic] these damned olives, and so, logically (Spanish logic) all they eat is oil."

For classic xenophobic rants surely no one can beat Tobias Smollett, the bawdy Scottish poet and novelist (I hope that I can share a bar-stool with him in heaven), but for xenophobic rants against foreign food—such as his tirade in *Travels Through France* and Italy (1766)—he is at his best:

> A Parisian likes mortified flesh: a native of Legiboli will
> not taste his fish till it is quite putrefied: the civilized
> inhabitants of Kamschatka get drunk with the urine
> of their guests, whom they have already intoxicated:
> the Nova Zemblans make merry on train-oil: the
> Groenlanders [sic] eat in the same dish with their
> dogs: the Caffres, at the Cape of Good Hope, piss
> upon those whom they delight to honour, and feast
> upon a sheep's intestines with their contents, as the
> greatest dainty that can be presented. A true-bred
> Frenchman dips his fingers, imbrowned with snuff,
> into his plate filled with ragout: between every three
> mouthfuls, he produces his snuff-box, and takes a
> fresh pinch, with the most graceful gesticulations; then
> he displays his handkerchief, which may be termed the
> flag of abomination, and in the use of both, scatters
> his favours among those who have the happiness to sit
> near him.

Tallulah Bankhead is contemptuous of German food in the movie, *Lifeboat* (1944), although clearly for strong political reasons. General George

S. Patton hated Italian cooking ("horrid") and particularly loathed seafood. "He was once served a tuna dish at a *luau* and devoured it with relish, but when told afterward what it was, he politely excused himself to go vomit," notes Robert H. Patton in his biography, *The Pattons*. An ethnomaniac, the General had an extended punch list of the many things that put him off; he despised all doctors, Mexicans, babies, infants, parenting in general, Arabs ("bath-robed mendicants"), cats—he once blithely shot several of them for sport—Jews ("lower than animals"), newspaper reporters and the press, the Nuremberg Trials ("pure vengeance"), music (he was tone deaf), and over-weight women. We have noted, oddly enough, that Patton loved—of all things—*fruitcake*. Go figure, right? But then again he stood, almost alone, against the cruel vituperation by the winning side against war criminals, and at the end of World War II George S. Patton stubbornly condemned the "dismemberment" of Nazi Germany, claiming Germans were "the only de-cent people left in Europe"—a distinctly minority viewpoint in 1945, to say the least. The Nazis, Patton unequivocally stated, angrily taking an unbudg-ing position on it, "were no different than Democrats or Republicans."

Boomists seem to fetishize foods, in all ways. They could be of any politi-cal persuasion. It seems that extreme right-wingers and lefties, always polem-ical, can be equally militant and muscular in insisting what foods are healthy. Plato in the *Phaedo* articulates the principle: "Everything arises in this way, opposites from their opposites." To me the random espousal of "health-ism" or "back-to-naturism" by ideologues on the right at one time, and then by liberals or left-wingers at another, is a good example of the always riddling, almost comical "coincidence of opposites" that sets in motion much of the confusion of what or what not to eat.

Writer Rudyard Kipling, a jingoist of the first water and a man who had a love/ hate affair with this country fairly often greatly disparaged American food and in this he was joined by a many a vigorous European. Evelyn Waugh would not touch Indian food. I had an objectionable right-wing suite-mate in my first year of graduate school—he also hated Mexicans—who once told me, "If I come near anything smelling of chipotle, I'm liable to start swing-ing a hatchet." Norman Mailer in his novel, *An American Dream*, describes an uninvitingly crude ethnic scene in the Lower East Side of New York City, writing, "The garbage was out on the landings, the high peppery smell of Puerto Rican cooking, that odor of garlic, pig's viscera and incompatible condiments, a teeming misery." In the movie, *The Guns of Navarone*, Capt. Keith Mallory (Gregory Peck) declares at one point in their adventure that one reason he took his dangerous assignment was because he was sick of the food in Crete. Food critic Jeffrey Steingarten, a powerful voice in food, has written in a less than charitable moment,

I have always considered "Greek cuisine" an oxymoron. Nations are like people. Some are good at cooking while others have a talent for music or baseball or manufacturing memory chips. The Greeks are really good at both pre-Socratic philosophy and white statues. They have not been good cooks since the fifth century B.C., when Siracusa on Sicily was the gastronomic capital of the world. Typical of modern-day Greek cuisine are feta cheese and retsina wine. Any country that pickles its national cheese in brine and adulterates its national wine with pine pitch should order dinner at the local Chinese place and save its energies for other things. The British go to Greece just for the food, which says volumes to me. You would probably think twice before buying an Algerian or Russian television set. I thought for ten years before buying my last Greek meal.

After some soul-searching, he opened his mind up and later revised some of these views, except for feta, okra, retsina, and "that dreaded egg-and-lemon soup."

"The essential flavors of [Mediterranean] cooking—sour, pungent, bitter—cause the mouth to pause... The complex taste of brine-cured olive halts appetite in its tracks," writes food critic John Thorne. "Our mouth, unused to this sensation, meets it with difficulty, even distaste. Our favorite foods, based on meat and dairy, are bland and rich and meant to pass quickly over the tongue. We find our pleasure in the long and blissful slide to the familiar fullness."

A country's cuisine can signify. Back in 1936, did the writer John Dos Passos shift his allegiance from liberalism to the far right due to a poison paella? Franklin Foer in a book review of Alan Ackerman's *Just Words* in *The New Republic*, raises the subject in reference to a hated rivalry:

> At a dinner party in 1948, hosted by the president of Sarah Lawrence College, before they had been introduced to each other, Mary McCarthy strolled into a sunroom and overheard Lillian Hellman denouncing John Dos Passos to a group of students. Hellman accused him of having "sold out" in the Spanish Civil War because "[when] he got to Madrid he didn't like the food." ([Hellman] claims in *An Unfinished Woman* that he did not bring any of his own provisions and ungratefully consumed everyone else's.) Even though McCarthy disliked the rightward turn

in Dos Passos's politics, she despised Hellman's glib
assault on the novelist's honor. A bad paella wasn't
the reason for his disillusionment with the Loyalists,
she insisted; he reversed his allegiance after watching
the communists murder his friends, along with many
other Trotskyists and anarchists.

"If it has got four legs and it is not a chair, if it has got two wings and
it flies but is not an aeroplane, and if it swims and it is not a submarine, the
Cantonese will eat it," an irked His Royal Highness Prince Philip of England
once uncharitably remarked. I remain convinced that Estonia, where I lived
for a while, has no cuisine to recommend it at all. George Gissing who lived
a horrible life, one of his own choosing (married a whore, was convicted of
stealing etc.), wrote a good book about Italy, *By the Ionian Sea*, in which
we find, strangely enough, however, that he hated Italian food. Later, when
he went to Paris to live and to write, he also recorded that he hated French
food. In his *George Gissing: A Life,* Paul Delany finds the writer scribbling in
Paris in 1901, "Now I must go to the centre of France...and vegetate among
things which serve only to remind me that here is not England. Then again,
I had thought night and day of a boiled potato—of a slice of English meat—
of tarts and puddings—of tea cakes; night and day had I looked forward to
ravening on those things."

The British are not fond of cinnamon, olives, or celery. The Japanese
do not like peanut butter—in fact, they dislike butter in general. Westerners
visiting Japan—bad enough that they find us pink, sweaty, and hairy—are
derisively described by some as *batakusai* ("stinking of butter"). Another
slur is *debu* (fatty). Japanese, like the Chinese, dislike milk products, and tend
to regard the cheese and butter Europeans conventionally eat as revoltingly
smelly and off-putting. People who seldom touch animal products, in short,
become extremely sensitive to the kind of body-odor exuded by eaters of
animal fat. The Japanese dislike of American root beer goes beyond unfamil-
iarity. One of the ingredients in traditional root beer is anise, an herb used
in foods across the world, and, although it is used in Japan, as well, there it
is employed for a very different purpose—which is to say, in medicine. Just
as we in the West often flavor our medicine with compounds like menthol,
Japan flavors some of its medicine with anise. So they are not at all prepared
for root beer. On the other hand, try to imagine we Americans sitting down
with delight for a meal of Japanese *nattō*! *Nattō* is a traditional Japanese
food, which made from soybeans, is fermented with *Bacillus subtilis.* It is of
course popular in that country, especially as a breakfast food. As a source of

protein, *nattō* and the soybean paste *miso* formed a vital source of nutrition even back in feudal Japan. Needless to say, with its powerful smell, overpoweringly strong flavor, and somewhat slimy texture, *nattō* for Americans would be less an acquired taste than a bust.

There is a relatively small absence of meat eaten in Japan. (They did not begin eating beef and pork until the Meiji period, which was relatively late in their history.)

Japanese digestive tracts cannot easily cope with red meat. Agricultural chairman Mr. Iwamochi Shizuma, addressing foreign correspondents, stated that, because "everyone knows that Japanese intestines are about one meter longer than those of foreigners, we should all understand that American beef was not suitable for digestion by Japanese." While Japanese cuisine is almost universally regarded as the most beautiful in the world, presentation-wise especially, Westerners are put off by their cold foods, such as sushi and sashimi, which have slick, rubbery textures (seaweed gelatin, raw abalone), and also foods that are coarse (*Daikon oroshi* or grated radish), to say nothing of raw. (How about the stupid American expression, "Cook until half done"—what exactly does that mean?). Still, to the Japanese, used to rice crackers and bean jam, our Western candy is far too rich and overly sweet-smelling for them.

People in countries tend to act in concert, as well. It is as if alarm is transmitted through a series of interconnected roots as a warning the way a worried plant, say, will start to secrete chemicals like jasmonic acid, a hormone, if "word" gets out that, say, a groundhog or rabbit is nibbling it. An anti-pest defense for plants, rabbits find it repulsive. A tree under attack or duress, like being hacked or sawed, even when it begins to lacks water, immediately proceeds to excrete more ethylene than the normal amount of that gas which it ordinarily uses in its metabolism, and when the concentration of ethylene surpasses 0.1 parts per million in the air, trees and plants stop growing. Trees and plants have their own aversions!

Asians, like many if not most people on the planet, are lactose intolerant and avoid milk. *Japanese* Buddhist sects generally accept that Siddhartha *ate* meat and in consequence *do not* practice the habit of vegetarianism, but rather pescetarianism, that is vegetarianism plus fish. The Japanese and Native Americans typically have a higher intolerance to alcohol. At least one-third of the world's population, possibly as much as half, suffer gene-food interactions that make it difficult for them to eat certain foods. Mediterranean people, for example, have a food aversion to fava beans. Eating a small amount of dried fava beans can serve as protective function from malaria, but for them eating green fava beans would often cause nutritional shock and even a toxicity called "favism." Among the Somali people, most clans maintain a strict taboo against the consumption of fish and flatly refuse to intermarry with the any occupational clans that do eat it. One can find very strict taboos on eating fish among many upland pastoralists and agriculturalists—and even some coastal peoples—inhabiting parts of southeastern Egypt, Ethiopia, Eritrea, Kenya, and northern Tanzania. It is sometimes referred to as the "Cushitic fish-taboo," as Cushitic speakers are believed to have been responsible for the introduction of fish-avoidance to East Africa, though not all Cushitic groups avoid fish. One nomadic taunt in Somalia goes, "Speak not to me with a mouth that eats fish." Incidentally, many tribes of the Southwestern United States, including the Navaho, Apache, and Zuñi, have had a long-standing taboo against fish and other water-related animals, including even waterfowl.

Food prohibitions go in all sorts of directions. In the northern part of Kiriwina in New Guinea only fried or roasted foodstuffs may be eaten, while all stewed and boiled foods are banned. For Brazilians it is taboo for those who are ill to consume predatory fish. Many Jamaicans fully believe that eating half an egg will make the child grow into a thief. The Koran forbids the eating of food over which a name other than Allah has been evoked. Some major airlines—this is an interdiction—prohibit two pilots flying together to eat food from the same source within an hour of each other; either they are required to eat at different restaurants, or one of them must wait at least an hour to make certain the other does not get food poisoning or become ill. I spent a long month on my Fulbright to England rooming with a guy, an inflexible fellow, who would fussily cook baked beans *only* with soldier beans and who hated—abhorred—every other single kind of bean. My question was (and is) what kind of a bean can it be that renders every other bean bad? More to the point, aside from the choice of bean, what kind of manner-bereft is it who could be driven to the kind of rigid and obstinate perception that led to that kind of intransigence? Pure food aversion?

An inevitable truth is that our perception accepts a lot of what reasoning declares to be incorrect. Our reason can also be warped in that one of its singular attributes is its endless capacity for questioning and doubt.

On their expedition, Meriwether Lewis and William Clark and their men who carried Harper's Ferry Model 1803 flintlock rifles Cal. 54 (no bayonet), which they used for hunting as well as for protection, were eating nine pounds of meat a day, only meat, depending on it after running out of flour, coffee, etc. The Corps were often desperately hungry, but even in states of such extreme hunger—how ironic!—were often fed up with eating meat meal after meal and often complained about it. It was the opposite with Ernest Hemingway who craved meat. Although he loved the gastronomic delicacies Paris had to offer, he remained all of his life an unapologetic carnivore. When he was a kid, Ernest Hemingway enthusiastically began eating the squirrels that he hunted and the trout that he caught. Later, as a big game hunter, he relished the antelope and other game that he bagged in Africa on safari, having his guides cook them special for him. Papa also had no qualms about tucking into the gigantic marlins that he caught in the open waters between Key West and Cuba. His appetite was huge, and he loved oysters, cheese, and wine by the barrel, but meat he especially craved. "Everyone who has ever eaten meat must know that someone has killed it," proclaimed Papa. "Those who shop to eat should not condemn those who kill to eat."

Hemingway's supermarket was exclusively the great outdoors. He once killed as many as 400 rabbits in a single day, a wretched excess that puts even Elmer Fudd to shame. Papa always loved his dinner meat rare and bloody. Roughness in all phases of his life seemed to snap his flint. In 1953, on safari, he ate steaks of a lion raw—a taboo, by the way, in Kenya—a young male lion in his prime, four or five years old, which he thought firmer than Italian veal, finding the clean pink flesh delicious, "steak tartare without the capers." In December 1955, Hem provided a recipe for a *Sports Illustrated* article entitled "A Christmas Choice of Fair and Fancy Game." Cooking techniques for the novelist were quite basic; his cooking directions were not complicated: "First obtain your lion, add salt, pepper, and fire."

It is a far different world when you are doing "hard traveling." A.B. Guthrie, Jr. in *The Way West* and *The Big Sky* mentions how pioneers coped with their meager goods and food on those wagon trains to Oregon in the mid-1800s. The bulk of their goods was food. Little or no furniture, some implements. Good dishes were always kept "buried safe in the barreled flour." "Better'n apple, I always say corn's better 'n apple," remarked one character of that staple. Beans, rice, cheese, dried pumpkins, onion, and corn meal were common staples for the pioneers. Gammon, coffee, saleratus. "We boil our deer meat, break the bones, so that the marrow boils out of it & it makes a very fine soup," wrote the trekkers in *The Mountains We Have Crossed: Diaries and Letters of the Oregon Mission* (1838). "We have lived on crackers softened in water & molasses." They often ground their wheat in small iron mills and sifted it. Crossing the Great Plains, like Lewis and Clark, they ate salmon and *wapato* (a starchy tuber), and various dried fish that they swapped for nails with Indians. They yearned for quality salt for their meat. That was often a noticeably missing item. Their bacon was mainly what we now call salt pork. A person would haul out a piece and cut off the amount he wanted, replacing—and thus saving—the rest. It was generally required to soak for a time the cuts of pork to dissipate the saltiness before slicing it for frying or cutting into rude chunks for soups or stews. They often ate rice for breakfast, cornmeal mush at noon, and maybe a chunk of bacon and biscuits—or johnnycakes—for dinner. It was not the best age for breakfast outside of New York or Philadelphia or Boston.

I have an image of Herman Melville's hungry Redburn sloshing a stick around the tub of burgoo in that novel just for a taste of mush! Edgar Allan Poe's standard morning breakfast was a pretzel, a crust of bread with salt herring, and two cups of coffee. The singular breakfast for the great 1912 Olympian Jim Thorpe when he was growing up in the wilderness of the Oklahoma Territory was fried squirrel with creamed gravy. How different the classes can be in the matter of prandials. Hugh Lowther, Lord Hastings, the 5th Earl of Lonsdale, famous for his reckless spending—his wild womanising, his love of gambling, horses, hunting and boxing, has endeared him to risk-takers and bon-viveurs the world over ever since—was accustomed to start the day, according to Douglas Sutherland in *The Yellow Earl*, "with a breakfast of mackerel bones cooked in gin." Sutherland explains further,

> He himself ate practically nothing. When this performance was over he would light a cigar and drink, at one gulp, a claret glass of brandy. He would follow this immediately with half a bottle of white wine, and then bid everyone a bright good morning, explaining that he must deal with his correspondence.

W.H. Auden took nothing but orange juice and a chaste cup of coffee. In the last years of his life, the cynical, often gloomy poet Philip Larkin habitually started his day off with three glasses of cheap port. "Well," he confided to his friend Kingsley Amis with a shrug, "you've got to have some fucking reason for getting up in the morning."

I guess my point is, fathom what these supple-minded eaters disliked in food to have chosen such morning repasts.

Who that has read it can forget the great debate in the *Iliad* (Book 19) devoted to the subject of whether or not to eat breakfast where Achilles, arguing with Agamemnon and Odysseus, refuses in a sulk to eat after the death of his eternal friend. Patroclus makes a mockery of feasting. Odysseus pleads,

You want the Greeks to mourn the dead by starving, when hundreds are killed day after day. When would they ever eat? No, we must bury the dead, weep for a day indeed, but harden our hearts. Those who are left alive by this hated conflict must still eat and drink, so as to fight on, without respite.

They sacrifice a boar, and the army eats.

In the *Iliad,* Achilles bitterly craves to carve up the raw flesh of his rival Hector, nemesis of the Greeks, and eat it raw. Tragically, the Trojan warrior is a husband and father. I love the memorable scene on the high wall of Troy when little Astyanax plays with the horse-hair plumes of his father's helmet, while Andromache, his wife, proudly looks on. A loving family—a beautiful marriage—is described in the couple's tender words for each other, and to encounter deep affection of this kind, such a formal bond, the loyalty of a formal union going as far back as early as 1300 B.C. is astounding. On November 18, 2003, four judges on a Massachusetts court, all women, voting in favor of gay marriage (with no public assent), put an end—*after two-and-a-half thousand years*—to the exclusivity of a man/woman union.

No meat for breakfast—never mind squirrel—for Harold Skimpole in Charles Dickens' *Bleak House,* the irresponsible romantic who took a bright disdain for the drudgery of adult life—"I am a child, you know!" he frequently reminds us—and delighted in the innocent pleasures around him, claiming hypocritically, faux-naively, not to understand the complexities of human relationships or society. A rogue, Skimpole sponged off everybody and couldn't have cared less. Give him only conversation, music, mutton, coffee, landscape, fruit in the season, a few sheets of Bristol-board, a little claret, and he asked for no more. His choice for breakfast, as long as someone else was paying for it? "Some men want legs of beef and mutton for breakfast; I don't," he declaimed. "Give me my peach, my cup of coffee, and my claret; I am content. I don't want them for themselves, but they remind me of the sun. There's nothing solar about legs of beef and mutton. Mere animal satisfaction."

Speaking of herring, the erratic Grand chessmaster Bobby Fischer ate salt (or soused) herring when he played Boris Spassky in the Laugardalshöll arena in 1972 in Reykjavík, Iceland, a ploy used badly to unnerve his rival, the chess titleholder. The "Dutch way," notoriously, is to eat herring by lifting the morsel by its tail, holding it over your mouth, and then lurping it down, as inelegant and unsettling a move—it is difficult, frankly, to imagine an uglier one—during a formal chess match as is possible. Fischer's was obviously an antagonistic gesture that would put off just about anybody. The reek alone was bad enough. Soused herring dishes in Northern Germany are traditionally served with potatoes boiled in their skins, French beans, finely sliced fried bacon and onions; it is also common in Germany to eat soused herring with sliced raw onions in a bread roll, in a dish called *Matjesbrötchen.*

I loved to eat the German country breakfast dish called *Bauernfrühstück* in my travels through Germany, a memorably delicious dish that is made with fresh eggs, fried potatoes, leeks, onions, chives, and bacon, all commingled in a pan and fried as an omelette. It was usually accompanied, as I recall, with a side dish of tomatoes or (yes) pickles. It is much tastier than its English counterpart "bubble and squeak." An urban Berlin version is called "*Hoppelpoppel*." Similar dishes are found in other countries, in France, for example, as an omelette *à la paysanne* (with sorrel) and in Spain as a *tortilla de patatas* or in Sweden as *pyttipanna*.

We are what we eat.

We are also what we eat ate.

We are also what we don't eat.

The consumption of horse meat is illegal in California and Illinois. Most people in most states are repulsed by the idea of eating horse meat. The banning of it goes back to the eighth century. Popes Zachary and Gregory III both told Saint Boniface to forbid his missionaries to eat horse meat, as it had a strong correlation to many old Germanic pagan rituals which Christians at the time were earnestly trying to eradicate. Old Germans liked their horse meat, and still do, and until five years ago the United States was the major exporter of restaurant-grade horse meat. It is a popular meat in only a few countries, notably in Central Asia. In South Korea, raw horse meat—cuts from around the neck are favored—is eaten, commonly seasoned with soy sauce and sesame oil. It is a popular delicacy on Jeju Island. In Japanese cuisine, raw horse meat is called *sakura* (桜) or *sakuraniku* (桜肉, *sakura* means cherry blossom, *niku* means meat) because of its pink color. It is mainly served raw as sashimi in thin slices dipped in soy sauce, often with ginger and onions added. From a culinary point of view, horse meat is lean, along the taste and texture of moose or deer. It is dry, sweeter than beef, and improves in flavor by the inclusion of fat when cooking or from a marinade. (Moose meat is also delicious—moose can eat 200 pounds of food a day, and they especially love strands of willow; the best tasting moose is a dry sow, one that has been feeding on chokecherries and wild honey. I once enjoyed a barbecue moose roast in Anchorage, which was delicious.) An equinonoid, Henry Ford loathed horses. It goes without saying, I daresay, that he would have hated horse meat. It is revealing that Ford once proclaimed out loud that he had worked hard to develop the automobile to free man *from the culture of horses*. Think of it. Here is a man who helped change an entire society possibly because he hated the very idea of a particular animal!

It is notable that, despite horses having been bred in England since pre-Roman times, the English language has no widely used term for horse meat, as opposed to four for pig meat (pork, bacon, ham, gammon), three for sheep meat (lamb, hogget and mutton), two for cow meat (beef and veal), and so on. Some English speaking countries, however, have sometimes marketed horse meat under the tidy euphemism "cheval meat" (*cheval* being the French for horse). Note also that the words pork, bacon, mutton, veal, and beef all derive from Anglo-Norman vocabulary, because of the class structure of England after the Norman Conquest in 1066 A. D.: the poor (Anglo-Saxon-speaking Britons) tended the animals, while the rich (French-speaking Normans) ate the meat. The peasants had very little to do with horses. The phrase, "I'm so hungry I could eat a horse" refers to desperation, not taste.

Traveling the world necessitates that one be dubious about what one eats, of course. Salads, unpasteurized milk, ice cream, ice in drinks, shellfish, any uncovered foods, and tap water must be avoided virtually wherever one goes, especially in the Third World, and these may well be listed as legitimate food aversions. But what reasonable creature even at home nowadays would consistently eat smoked and cured meats in any form, lunch meats included? These all have been linked to cancer, disease, gall-bladder pain, heart disease, high blood pressure, and ferocious migraines, plus they are packed with artery-clogging grease! Regulations allow up to 50% [by weight] of fresh pork sausage to be sheer unadulterated fat.

I mention tap water. Many Mexican immigrants in the United States have long avoided drinking it here, consuming instead soft drinks—a slant on a food aversion—having been so used to polluted tap water; the ironic fact is, tap water in this country is fluoridated, giving dental protection, and the teeth of many immigrants, young and old, are quickly rotting.

What about foods made of wood? I am joking, right? Wrong. Take a quick glance at the highly crowded ingredient list for your high-fiber cereal or snack bar, and you will notice an ingredient called "cellulose," which is simply a code word in manufacturing for "wood pulp." Used nowadays to thicken or stabilize our own foods, it is valued for adding fiber and replacing fats and can even be substituted for flour and oil. Have you heard about the Vedda of Sri Lanka [Ceylon], the island in the Indian Ocean? Many folks there are true xylophages, in point of fact, and actually seek out to savor as many as five or six different kinds of rotted wood, which they happily eat after garnishing the pieces with honey, leaves, and fruit!

No more vivid example comes to mind regarding the consumption of crude, unprocessed, untreated, or unrefined food than that grisly scene in Chapter XI of James Fenimore Cooper's *The Last of the Mohicans* where an Indian hunter kills and proceeds to wolf down the raw meat of a deer:

> Notwithstanding the swiftness of their flight, one
> of the Indians had found an opportunity to strike a
> straggling fawn with an arrow, and had borne the

more preferable fragments of the victim, patiently
on his shoulders, to the stopping-place. Without any
aid from the science of cookery, he was immediately
employed, in common with his fellows, in gorging
himself with this digestible sustenance. Magua alone
sat apart, without participating in the revolting meal,
and apparently buried in the deepest thought.

Digestible sustenance?

I side with Magua at this repast, I must say. By the way, Mark Twain selects this particular scene in his essay, "Fenimore Cooper's Literary Offenses," to ridicule not only the, to him, execrable overwriting—the incompetent "surplusage"—of Cooper's literary style but delights in finding gaffe after gaffe in what he dismisses as a poorly described event. (I greatly admire Cooper, the first American writer to recognize the importance of the Indian and the forest in the development of the nation.)

I love the subject of raw food. But is it as benign and as close to the way our ancestors ate? Cooking food had a significant impact on prehistoric man, and scientists believe that it actually helped man develop his large brain. It also significantly increases in the eater the amount of energy that can be absorbed into the body and also reduces the diseases in raw meat. There is no miracle here. This simply means that food can be processed much more efficiently in the gut and so allow extra energy to be used to develop the brain. Several cookbooks, Jacqui Wood's *Tasting the Past* and Jane Renfrew's *Prehistoric Cookery: Recipes & History*, offer accounts of what our prehistoric forebears ate—nettle pudding, wild boar, various oat and barley breads, etc.—and touch on some of the meals that Jean M. Auel in her ice-age epics mentions might have been eaten many thousands of years ago. A recipe for "Neanderthal Stew" in Auel's novel, *The Clan of the Cave Bear*, goes as follows:

Ingredients:

bison (we substituted cow)
wild onion (substituted domestic)
unspecified herbs (chose marjoram, cloves, garlic, and
bay leaf)
thistle stalks (we omitted)
mushrooms
watercress (substituted bamboo shoots)

small immature yams (substituted grocery store yam)
cranberries (substituted canned cranberry sauce with
whole cranberries)
wilted flowers from previous days growth of day lilies
for thickening (substituted potatoes)

I believe that you can find roughly the same thing today in Wyoming or Montana with "sonofabitch stew," prime rodeo fare—often called the cowboy dish of the American West—that in a conglomeration of what I imagine any chef wants to dream up or has on hand in his larder that he wants to throw in the civet usually includes meats and organs from a freshly killed unweaned calf, including the brain, heart, liver, sweetbreads, tongue, pieces of tenderloin, adding especially an item called the "marrow gut," and lots and lots of Louisiana hot sauce. To my mind, for stew, however, nothing on earth beats the taste of "*chakalaka*," a South African vegetable relish that probably originated in the townships of Johannesburg—it is spicy and often includes beans—which is traditionally served there with bread, pap, samp, stews or curries. To balance its fiery flavor, it is sometimes served with *amasi* (thick sour milk).

By the way, I am convinced that it is a stew that Habakkuk made in Judea, which he was told by the angel of the Lord to take to Daniel, then in Babylon in the lion's den. After claiming he was unaware of both the den and Babylon, the Prophet is transported by the angel to the den, where he gives Daniel the food—its ingredients are basic, like "*chakalaka*," essential, rudimentary, and bean-based—to sustain him and is immediately then taken back to "his own place."

Meat and eggs are not usually given to children in Nigeria, simply because parents believe, curiously, that doing so will make the children steal. In October 2011, the use of ketchup was banned in France—except, strangely enough, for use on French fries (variously called there *patates, frites* or *pommes frites*)—in all school and college cafeterias in order to protect the integrity of traditional Gallic cuisine, such as veal or pork stews, cassoulet, boeuf bourguignon. (Were you aware that Worcestershire sauce is basically an anchovy ketchup?) Jews famously love Asian food. Many others do not. The popinjay Lucius Beebe on Polynesian Restaurants: "The food is fabricated from fish heads and boiled newspapers and listed in the bill of fare under names that make Oriental visitors snicker." C. David Heymann in *Bobby and Jackie* describes a scene on a date [their very last!] in February of 1966 at the quaint Russian Tea Room in New York City when Jacqueline Kennedy dined with the eccentric poet, Robert Lowell. As they consulted the menu, the Tea Room owner's name came up—one Sidney Kaye, who was Jewish—and Lowell, looking up, supposedly spouted angrily, "If I'd wanted Jewish food, I'd have gone to a delicatessen!" It seems that on this evidence alone Heymann accused Lowell of being a "virulent anti-Semite."

Persnickety Lowell no doubt would much preferred to have been sitting at Locke-Ober's in Boston, spooning up a bowl of authentic New England clam chowder, followed by a helping of Indian pudding and ice cream.

All of her life, Jackie Kennedy watched her waistline, after being a slightly chubby—self-consciously so—adolescent and teen, but from what her personal family chef, Marta Sgubin, writes in *Cooking for Madam: Recipes and Reminiscences from the Home of Jacqueline Kennedy Onassis,* her boss had few food quirks and—chain-smoking helped—rarely overate. She did not like the look of big vegetables, this in keeping with the late Truman Capote's well-known observation that the defining difference of the rich and the average person was not money but that the rich insisted their vegetables be small. As a matter of fact, Jackie did prefer that almost all her vegetables be cut in a uniform matchstick form. "Madam didn't care so much for shrimp [although she liked mussels and bay scallops]," notes Sgubin who also cooked for JFK, Jr. and Caroline from their earliest years, and later Caroline's three kids, Tatiana, John, and Rose, as well. Tastes varied. "No one in the family likes mayonnaise much," wrote Sgubin. Jackie went on fruit fasts and avoided heavy foods. One of her diets, scrupulously followed, consisted of nothing but a single baked potato, but stuffed with Beluga caviar and sour cream, which she ate once a day. (There are 278 calories in a large baked potato, compared with 539 in a typical large order of fast-food fries.) Although not a martinet, Jackie seems to have had a jittery side —she was a smoker—and, never for a minute hesitating to make her tastes known, was always specific about her wants. "She didn't like to have to deal with cutting her food. She wanted just to be able to pick up a fork and start eating. And I know she didn't want to spend too long at the table. So food shouldn't be complicated to eat." Nevertheless, Jackie was almost always gracious with Sgubin and often generously wrote small thank you notes to her chef.

Many Mexicans who find shrimp repugnant will think nothing—like many people in the world—of eating crickets, fried, boiled, or just plain fresh. Estonians crave blood sausage. New Englanders show little interest in chili, hot sauce, and spiced food in general. (Michelle Stacey's inane assertion in her book *Consumed: Why Americans Hate, Love, and Fear Food* that Puritan "people were put in stocks for having spices in their kitchen" is utter bollocks. For hog theft, drunkenness, slander, blasphemy, gambling, vagrancy, etc., indeed, yes—but for using spices? A pipe dream.) Germans apparently love bananas—"Today they are the highest consumers of bananas per capita, in the world," according to Thomas McCann *in An American Company: The Tragedy of United Fruit.* (Why shouldn't Germans love eating bananas? Although bananas originated in Asia, the first Europeans to eat them were the ancient Greeks and Romans. Bananas were brought to South America by Europeans! By the way, it was in 1876 at the historic Philadelphia Centennial Exposition, with its 167 buildings and 30,000 exhibits on 236 acres, that many Americans were introduced to the exotic banana, sold at the time foil-wrapped for 10 cents each!) It may be noted that having bananas on a ship, incidentally, especially on a private boat or fishing yacht, is considered very bad luck, according to a well-known superstition. It is also, weirdly, considered unlucky to touch the collar of a sailor's suit, to discuss matters of sex, to have a woman aboard—or a cat as a pet—or for a sailor to whistle on a ship, by which act one is encouraging wind strength to increase—also Fletcher Christian is also said to have used a whistle as the signal to begin the mutiny against Captain William Bligh.

I have mentioned previously that I hate the smell of banana peels. On the positive side, however, they can be used to polish silver, to help make a good aphid spray, relieve itchy skin, soothe burns, help remove splinters (bringing them to the fore), fertilize plants, alleviate bug bites, whiten teeth, remove warts, buff leather, shine houseplants, work well as chicken and compost feed, keep roasting chicken breasts moist and juicy (lay on top), and can freshen up the interior of a smoky automobile. True, it is an ill wind that blows nobody any good.

Old clichés are true, apparently. Maxims have it that men dislike raw tomatoes, that women tend to avoid kidneys, innards, liver, and such. (The late French-born wine merchant and gourmet, Andre Simon, on the other hand, once heralded, "A cooked tomato is like a cooked oyster: ruined.") "Pluck" is a comprehensive name for innards, an animal's heart, liver, and lung. Platitudes and banalities are repeatedly endlessly about food. Wilfrid Sheed, the English-born American novelist and essayist, in what seemed a fit of pique blithely dismissed all English food, writing "English cuisine is generally so threadbare that for years there has been a gentleman's agreement in the civilized world to allow the Brits preeminence in the matter of tea—which, after all, comes down to little more than the ability to boil water." "There is no food in Australia. Not as we know it," smugly wrote singer Bette Midler in her book, *A View from a Broad.* "The natives do, of course, on occasion put matter to mouth, but one cannot possibly call what they ingest food." The current contemporary gossip-favorite, from the comic tabloid and TV family, named Kim Kardashian, a monumentally preposterous American reality television star, beefy model, occasional actress, and extra-popular magazine-and-media shuttlecock, happily revealed that she personally finds all Indian food "disgusting." (On one episode of TV's cartoon *Family Guy*, a surprised veterinarian discovered with some disgust that what the item that had been obstructing the dog's wind -pipe was one of baby Stewie's used diapers, Brian's smarmy explanation was, "I thought it was Indian food.") Who can explain anyone's tastes, who explain, who spelunk the human brain to discover exactly what revolts us and why?

"Controlled rot tastes good," Rachel Herz writes in her book, *That's Disgusting*, introducing food like hakarl, the desiccated shark meat eaten in Iceland, or *nattō*, a slimy soybean dish from Japan. In her *New York Times* review of Herz's book, "What We Find Gross and Why," (Jan. 21, 2012). Robin Marantz Henig questions the whole premise of her idea, asking, "Tastes good? Really? It's hard to believe that about casu marzu (Sardinia's "maggot cheese"), which is covered in writhing, wormlike insect larvae. Eating a hunk of fermented sheep's milk coated in live maggots tastes good? Yuck." Henig seems to be a true doubter about the worth, even the validity—the very existence—of "disgusting" food. "Or how about chicha, a popular drink in Ecuador, which a student of Herz's watched as it was made? To prepare the thick beverage, a group of women put handfuls of corn flour in their mouths, chewed it until it 'vaguely resembled the vomit of an infant,' spit it out into a collective milk jug and repeated the process until all the flour was gone. Then the women capped the jug and buried it in the yard to ferment. When a well-aged jug of chicha was unearthed and opened for the grossed-out young woman to taste, it took all her self-control not to gag on the warm, vinegary brew. Too revolting for you? Here's one more, my own personal last straw: the information that in China, 'chefs can serve you monkey brains from a living monkey sitting at your feet with its skull carved open.'" Henig continues, "This is the point at which I wrote, "O.K., that does it," in the margin—and I was only on Page 17. Still to come were descriptions of mucus, semen, blood (both menstrual and non-menstrual), vomit, pus, feces, phlegm; stories about slasher porn, cannibalism, necrophilia; and Herz's attempt to tie it all together with explanations of how disgust evolved, how it protects us, how it works in our brains, and how it keeps us from having to confront our own weaknesses and our own inevitable death."

Paradox can exist here. There are foods that fall under what our traveling friend, Andrew Zimmern, that pompous, loquacious booby who can be found on the television program, "Bizarre Foods," calls, "Zimmern's Law #6:" "The more vile a food looks, the more neutral it tastes." It is a remark I am certain that even die-hard Zimmernites and Zimmernines—to use a

Malayo-Polynesian lexeme, proto-MP *fafine*—must find fully meaningless, for any neutral-tasting food, if not vile, is neither tasty nor truly palatable. His supererogative attempts at showing lordly confidence, solemnly pronouncing about any and every food, are tiresome. *Le goûter des généraux!* It is, most of it, pure twaddle, what I consider prideful stultiloquence. In any case, I wonder how passionately the glib, often flippant Zimmern who, as I say, often talks cheery nonsense and chatty bull, would have enjoyed the freakish magical liquor that is mentioned in Mo Yan's *Red Sorghum* "which male laborers magically produce [called] 'Six-Mile Red' by urinating into the heroine's brewing wine" or tied on a bib gleefully to tuck into the exciting meal awaiting the young protagonist called the kid in Cormac McCarthy's novel, *Blood Meridian*, when he sees what the old hermit offers up:

> He stirred about in the corner and came up with an
> old dark brass kettle, lifted the cover and poked inside
> with one finger. The remains of one of the lank prairie
> hares interred in cold grease and furred with a light
> blue mold. He clamped the lid back on the kettle and
> set it in the flames. Aint much but we'll go shares, he
> said.

Or take another memorable meal, one found in Boccaccio's *Decameron*, where Tancredi, the prince of Salerno, having discovered that his daughter, Ghismonda, is having an affair with one of his valets, one Guiscardo, who is actually a virtuous young man, orders that the poor culprit be strangled, and his heart cut out. He then places the heart in a golden chalice and sends it to his daughter. She unflinchingly raises the bloody organ to her mouth, kisses it, puts it back in the cup, pours poison over it, weeps tears into the chalice drinks it, and dies.

Take out your pie card, Andy!

Disgust is one of "the six basic human emotions" (along with happiness, sadness, anger, fear and surprise) that any healthy adult can experience and recognize, according to Rachel Herz, who began her career as a researcher in the matter of odor and emotional memory. She had been asked to judge the "National Rotten Sneaker Contest" (an annual event—sponsored by the Odor-Eaters brand, of course). Studying disgust as such and its ancillaries—revulsion, abhorrence, loathing, nausea—followed. Does disgust come natural to people? It is Herz's belief that disgust is the only emotion, among living creatures, that is unique to humans, and the only one that has to be learned. "What is disgusting, or not, is in the mind of the beholder," explains

Herz. Disgust is not an automatic reaction, like fear, or so Henig reports in her insightful review. It is rather in Herz's view simply "an unfolding and cognitive emotion." When facing a revolting entity—smell or sight—our disgust response, kicking in, "protects us from creeping dangers that we have to figure out, dangers that are slow in their deadliness, and of which disease, contamination and decomposition are the foremost threats."

If this interests you, as it does not me, go to http://www.wildrecipes.com/, a website that in its excesses and lunacy has to be the absolute nadir of nauseating foods. It may be mentioned here that, at least according to the Institute of Neuroscience and psychology at the University of Glasgow, disgust and anger are similar in their signaling dynamics, just as supposedly surprise and fear are, and so God knows where most food aversions are coming from. As to the fact that disgust has to be learned, you should not be surprised that it starts early. In the original Jacob and Wilhelm Grimm's *Kinder-und Hausmärchen*, the huntsman who was ordered by the Wicked Queen to kill Snow White is, shockingly, told to bring back her lungs and liver (!) as the token of a job well done, although, unwilling to do it, he secretly substitutes the dripping viscera of a young boar. We read, "The cook had to salt these, and the wicked Queen ate them and thought she had eaten the lungs and liver of Snow White." As Anthony Burgess put it, "Walt Disney put some things in, but he also left some out." In a single succinct sentence, the late Joe Brainard brings obloquy down on the food in one of his celebrated "I Remember" series, noting coldly, "I remember liver."

Although not a taboo in a strict sense, "swedes" (Swedish turnip, rutabaga), are seen as a "famine food", and not for general consumption by older German people. This bias has existed from the desolating 1916-17 famine, the so-called *Der Steckrübenwinter* —the "Rutabaga winter"—when Germany in the stark desperation of World War I's endless Western Front, suffered one of its worst winters in living memory, a period when the only food available was often only a Swedish turnip. This deprivation led to a bitter and ongoing distaste for the vegetable, a situation that continues to this day among the older generations, having had either direct experiences from World War II or having endured a childhood growing up with their parents talking about their deprivations and the onset of near starvation. In recent years, these old notions have vanished somewhat as Germans have re-discovered many traditional or local cooking recipes that involve swedes, such as *Steckrübeneintopf.* Waverley Root, American newspaperman and author of many books on food, has written, "The turnip is a capricious vegetable, which seems reluctant to show itself at its best." An aside here: the word for turnip, "*Steckreuben,*" was a code word-signal that Groucho Marx used for his wife, and she used for him, meaning, "You are being a grouch! Stop it!"

But that is nothing new. A string of nomenclatural insults based on food is long and colorful. "*Kraut*" was a disparaging term for a German, especially a German soldier in World War I or World War II. Our English word *cabbage* has the same origin as the word "*boche,*" French slang for rascal but also a racial slur against the Germans during the war. "*Bolillo*" is a slang term used in some parts of Mexico and the United States to refer to Anglos (people of Anglo-Celtic descent) or, more generally, any pale-skinned person, due to the white interior of the bread. A "*mangiafagioli*" or bean-eater is often used as an offensive term, although it is a term commonly—and informally—used for people from Tuscany. Many Estonians good-naturedly refer to Finns as "*mehu,*" "cranberry juice," from the passionate Finnish fondness for that beverage. Early Jewish immigrants on New York's Lower East Side did not hesitate to call their Italian neighbors "*lukshen,*" Yiddish for "noodles," with reference to spaghetti. The traditional outside term for the Inuit, "*Eskimo,*" is a northwest Canadian Cree expression meaning "raw fish eaters." Finally, the To'ono O'odham ("Desert People") of the Sonoran Desert of south east Arizona and northwest Mexico were often referred to as "*Papago*" by outsiders, from a Spanish corruption of Piman Babawïkoa, meaning "eating tepary beans," from their traditional main food staple, a drought-resistant type of bean that manages to grow well in extremely arid conditions. On the subject of words and names, by the way, when do you ever hear references to the "United Mexican States"? Pardon me, but that is indeed the official name of that noble country.

I find intriguing Chinese novelist Mo Yan's slurs against turnips in his novel, *Pow!* Finding the turnip common, the Chinese, along with many people in the West, share a minor disdain for it, although, gastronomically, we have little in common with each other. It is no secret that Chinese eat— and in some cases prefer—cartilage, bones, skin, bowels, and many other (by overseas' standards) inedible bits of an animal, rather than its fleshier pieces of meat. According to Anthony Zhao, chef and cuisine consultant at Ultimate Food Concept, the Chinese are reluctant to eat the meaty chicken breast, which is the main ingredient of the mystic food that to them goes by the simple name *gong bao ji ding* (宮保雞丁), which is to say, chicken fried with chilies and nuts, better known to non-Chinese—like us—as *kung pao* chicken. "Chicken breast in China is usually dry and tasteless," insists Zhao. "People here prefer the meat next to the bones because it has some juice." (The favorite cut of chicken for chef Jacques Pépin is the thigh, which he finds tastes the best.) To many Chinese, *kung pao* chicken is a symbol of poorer times. The prouder people of today are eager to shake off the remnants of their indigent past, which includes turnips.

Charles Fourier, French philosopher and early social theorist, all his life harbored memories dominated by the "tyranny" of schoolteachers and parents in matters of taste. In his day, or so felt Fourier, human beings were living in a world full of strife, chaos, and disorder. He saw how, by the "tyranny" of received notions, authority was used to manipulate human beings. It was his belief that so-called civilized parents and teachers saw children as little idlers, and a driving concern of his was to liberate every human individual, man, woman, and child, in two senses: by education, and by the liberation of all human passion.

He recalled that when eating with his schoolteacher, he was often required to eat turnips, which he loathed. One time he tried to throw his turnip away, only to be discovered by the teacher and forced to eat it, now covered with dust. He was often forced by his father to finish food that he did not like. On one occasion, his father compelled him to eat leeks until he was violently ill. The memory left scars. Later, as an adult, Fourier worked as a traveling salesman, in his spare time writing books of social theory. The foundation of his philosophy was that no one should ever be forced to do anything that went against his inclinations. He dreamed up a utopia—Harmony—in which bread, instead of being the staple food, would be replaced with a mixture of fruit and sugar, more to children's tastes. For him, forcing someone to eat food they could not stand was a form of child abuse.

No, the turnip is not popular. Democritus entirely disapproved of the turnip as a food on the ground that it causes flatulence. A contemporary of his, Diocles, countered by insisting that it was an aphrodisiac. According to Pliny, who devotes whole pages to turnips in his voluminous *Natural History*, "A hot application cures chilblains, besides preventing the feet from being chilled."

The dreaded turnip termite at one point wiped out the entire turnip crop in Dogpatch, the hillbilly hometown where dumb, genial Li'l Abner Yokum and his runty parents Mammy and Pappy live in Al Capp's famous comic strip. You may recall that "presarved turnips"—the fictional town's sole source of support and highest gastronomic delicacy—are virtually the only thing hillbillies there have to eat, except of course for pork chops, far and away Li'l Abner's favorite food. When in the early 1940s termites struck that particular area, which they did almost every year at the beginning of harvest, it was so bad that all of the Dogpatchers decided *en masse* to emigrate to Boston, where they planned to find their way back to financial solvency by picking oranges—in the middle of winter! Li'l Abner's Turnips was a product that was actually sold back in the 1950s. Uncritical in his adventure, *Omoo* (1847) of different Polynesian meals that he is served in Tahiti, Herman Melville could still report that he found the "Indian turnip" unpalatable. One tends to think of turnips as winter fare, a bulbous pale-yellow root that one grudgingly eats when snow and ice are on the ground and the wind is howling. Yet one Saturday morning last June, wandering about the old Haymarket near Boston's North End, Sarah and I bought some freshly harvested turnips, took them home, cooked them, and had a delicious meal. "I like them baked with a brown mustard and brown sugar sauce," an old Down East farmer in Millinocket, Maine once told me, adding, "Mine are big as soccer balls. Good all the way in." "They're so easy to grow," another grumbler told me, "Not so easy to eat."

Turnip wine anybody?

Recipes for turnip wine go back to the early 19th-century, when pioneers and rural folk in general made it, along with tomato wine, verbena wine, even onion wine. I found this one on The Winemaking Homepage. Apparently the process of fermentation gives the final drink a lovely taste. When fermentation has stopped, after you make the wine, you may rack the wine into a jar and store it in a cool area. Wait for the wine to age—about 12 months—before tasting it. It is widely affirmed that turnip leaves contain more calcium than any other vegetable.

Turnip Wine
4½ lbs turnips, without tops
½ lb fresh grape leaves
2 lb light brown sugar
6½ pts water
1½ tsp citric acid
½ tsp pectic enzyme
¼ tsp tannin
1 tsp yeast nutrient
Lalvin RC212 or Red Star Sherry yeast

Scrub turnips and remove small roots and crowns. Chop coarsely and put in pot with water. Bring to boil and cover, continuing to boil until tender. Pour into a nylon straining bag and allow to drip drain (do NOT squeeze). Add sugar to hot liquid and stir until completely dissolved. Add grape leaves to the nylon straining bag with turnip pulp, tie the top, and put in

primary. When liquid has cooled to room temperature, add remaining ingredients except yeast. Cover and set aside for 12-14 hours. Add activated yeast. Ferment 7 days, punching down bag twice daily without squeezing. Drip drain bag of turnip pulp and grape leaves, then discard solids. Rack into secondary, top up if necessary, and attach airlock. Rack, top up and reattach airlock every two weeks for a total of three rackings. Thereafter, rack, top up and reattach airlock every two months until wine clears and no longer deposits sediments. If not clear in 6 months, treat with Amylase or other starch enzyme and wait additional two months. Stabilize, sweeten if desired, wait 10-14 days, and rack into bottles. Age 12 months or more before tasting.
[Unidentified author's own recipe]

Turnip juice, which has twice the amount of vitamin C as oranges or tomatoes, is good for mucous or catarrhal conditions. Turnips are great for the elimination of uric acid from the body, which is good for overweight people and gout sufferers, and they reduce cholesterol. Still, turnips are widely hated. Widely, you ask with exasperation? Aversions are often as shallow and as simplistic as they are common. Hatred may be defined in one way as simply a plain lack of imagination. As Nicias Ballard Cooksey points out in *Helps to Happiness*, "Hatred comes with a persistency worthy of a better cause, yet clamors for possession of the citadel of the soul."

One can find an "I Hate Cilantro" group on the Internet. I knew a guy at MIT who will never go near a food truck. We know that pork is a highly taboo food item in both Islam and Judaism, but are you aware that even Seventh-day Adventists, Rastafarians, and members of the Ethiopian Orthodox church also do not eat pork? (I own and enjoy one of the latter's spiral-bound community cookbooks.) According to Donald Alexander Mackenzie, an aversion to pork has also long existed amongst the Scots, particularly the Highlanders, which he believes stemmed from an ancient taboo. This bias disappeared in the 19th-century. Pigs were held there as unclean in ancient days. Was it also because, as merely meat, it generated lust in the eater? I ask simply because Mrs. Patrick Campbell once reportedly sniped of the vegetarian George Bernard Shaw, "Shaw, one day you will eat a pork chop and then God help all women." Most people who love the taste of lobster, a swill-eating, bottom-feeding crustacean—it will eat anything on the ocean floor—would positively shrink at the thought of eating a grasshopper, a locust, or a witchetty grub. We are inconsistent, stubborn, given to wide swings and gaping generalities, and at the best of times illogical. Take the extremes of binge-eating and bulimia nervosa; both are disorders. An aversionist, following inner mandates, ponders only his own variants. He heeds Archbishop Fénelon's warning, "*Sur-tout ne vous laissez point ensorceler par les attraits diaboliques de la géométrie.*" (Above all, do not permit yourself to be enchanted by the evil charms of geometry). No, food aversions are individual, emotional, instinctive, and personal. We stand against what we need to fight. Are we not often at odds with, or on the opposite side of, the objects of our attention? Our imagination does not duplicate—or add to—reality, except by opposition. The real is the base, true, but it is only the base. What we see is indeed what we *think*, it's true. Strong convictions and persuasions, however, do not fail to breed many fears or stem our anxieties. We need dogmatic comfort whenever we can get it.

The phrase "Don't be afraid" appears 365 times in Scripture, the exact number of days in the year. I cherish that symmetry.

Scriptural wisdom knows what we are, so what we fear.

We fear any number of things.

And?

We are what we eat.

3.

COMIC FOOD, OR "I DON'T TAKE MY WINE IN PILLS"

MUCH IS CHARACTERISTICALLY INVOLVED in what and why people dislike in foods. Many significant factors are in play: smell, sight fright, natural disgust, texture, bad childhood memories, oversensitivity to certain colors, bitter tastes, the unfamiliar, neophobic suspicion, no end of various creepy and often inexplicable subjective associations, and of course plain allergies. The most common allergies are peanuts, shellfish, soy, wheat, milk, and eggs. All the senses play a significant role on this subject. Lorraine Bodger in her *Eater's Digest* has come up with a splendid punch list of "Foods Most Kids Hate:"

> anything you insist is good for them
> anything they haven't tried before
> anything on any diet their parents are on
> rare, bloody meat
> lumpy mashed potatoes
> most fresh green vegetables
> most fresh fruits
> anything you try to slip past them by calling it Cutie
> Fruity Yummy Roll-ups
> anything bitter
> anything soggy
> tuna or chicken salad with something unexpected (like
> chopped celery) in it
> burgers without buns
> soupy yogurt

It is being reported now that finicky eating in children is directly linked to the problem of autism. What is notable is that most food aversions include common, everyday items like coffee, eggs, poultry, beef, green vegetables, milk, and dairy products. The latter will surely not do in the State of Delaware, where milk is the state beverage! (In Ohio, it is tomato juice and, in Florida, orange juice. Curiously, no other states have state beverages.)

The *zeitgeist* is responsible for much in the way of food aversions. It is cool—a cliché—to dislike frog legs in the United States, for example, and few would ever give them a try. Fruit and Vegetable consumption in the United States is surprisingly low, and only getting lower. No State or territory in the US has over 50% of the population consuming fruit more than twice a day, and vegetables three times a day. It is an alarming trend. We imbibe attitudes about food, both good and bad, from popular images; they become as mindlessly accepted as song melodies. I am reminded of the countless movie clichés regarding food. Foods preferences are often linked to such notions. What an iron template was set for so many films set in Hollywood's Merrie Olde England where parodic imitations were given—see actor Charles Laughton—of a dissolute and drum-bellied King Henry VIII with his gross, be-ringed hands rudely tearing into food, invariably a massive chicken drumstick, while tankards go rolling off the table, slabs of meat are being thrown to great big hunting dogs, and ladies of the court wearing snoods and tall head-gear are leering in concerted approval. It has become a cinematic staple, like the repeated scenes of leathery cow punchers all slouched around campfires drinking cowboy coffee—anything burnt, sour, or stale, I gather—and chowing down on baked beans 'n' cornbread, always slurped up by guys holding their spoons like gardening tools, right? "I'll rustle up some coffee" went the cliché in just about every Lone Ranger episode, Gene Autry show, and Roy Rogers movie, about the only occasion in the English language, by the way, when and where one ever heard that odd slang word "rustle" (rush + hustle?), am I correct?

Beans have always seemed a serviceable food in the wild, out camping, and on safari, an almost perfect repast: durable, tasty, filling, nutritious, preservable, and very easy to cook. On Jan. 30, 2011, British explorer Anthony Smith at age 85 and his crew of three set sail on his small raft, *Antiki*, a veritable matchbox, for a hair-raising, storm-tossed, 66-day odyssey across the Atlantic from the Canary Islands to St. Maarten—"Old men ought to be explorers," wrote T. S. Eliot in his "Four Quartets"—stocked only with three dozen tins of baked beans, several bottles of single-malt whisky, pasta, bananas, and "a colossal pumpkin," as Mr. Smith described it in one of his weekly dispatches to the *Telegraph*. Baked beans are also a big food aversion cliché, especially among soldiers, ranch hands, and grumpy, insolent jailbirds. Beans are dull. Proletarian. We find the cliché repeated in old movies, often in prison films and westerns.

"What do I get to eat when I get home?" complains the burly driver Buck (Andy Devine) who lives in Chihuahua and is married to a Mexican woman in the John Ford classic, *Stagecoach* (1939). "Nothing but frijole beans. Beans, beans, beans." It is in that movie that the Ringo Kid (John Wayne) sets a pattern for just about every cowboy movie that followed, not only in what he eats (beans) but in the rustic way he eats them—double-shaking the filled fork with a kind of weighty savoriness before dispatching them. That movie is replete with no end of cowboy platitudes that have since became old chestnuts: the flash of spinning a revolver and rotating a rifle; a mustachioed gambler wearing a Stetson and cape and smoking a stogie; the peremptory call for hot water ("and plenty of it!") by a dipsomaniacal doctor for a baby delivery; the employment of the dudely name "Ringo;" and, as I say, that old cowhand cornball dumb-show of forking up baked beans, all as tired staples as the incessant theme music, "I'm an Old Cowhand," which is played and replayed throughout the entire movie.

Fetishes, icons, and totems in any given culture establish a way of seeing that informs a society's choices. It is the way Hollywood still presents German soldiers as all evil, lounging Roman emperors gobbling grapes, dumb blondes. I suppose the archetype combining food and lust is found in the hedonist, Stepan Oblonsky, in Leo Tolstoy's *Anna Karenina*, Anna's brother and Dolly's husband, a man who is the epitome of decadence, hypocrisy, and self-indulgence—he is a serial adulterer, as well. All bodily appetite, he consumes food like a libidinous Turk, devouring his oysters with an almost fierce sexual appetite, tearing "the quivering oysters from their pearly shells with a silver fork and swallow[ing] them one after another," his eyes "moist and glittering" with gourmandizing greed. No *shchi* or peasant cabbage soup for him! One can find a more innocent parallel in that remarkable cinematic set-piece at the Inn at Upton in director Tony Richardson's film, *Tom Jones*, where a lusty young Tom (Albert Finney) and libidinous Mrs. Waters (Joyce Redman) spend at least five erotic minutes eating, perspiring, at the tavern table, lustily cramming down chicken legs and lobsters, slurping down oysters, and, winking all the while, taking huge, ravenous, face-pushing bites out of juicy fruits as a lewd preface for what is soon to become a carnal night.

On that subject, in Kurt Vonnegut's memoir, *Jailbird*, which for some reason he insists on calling a novel—that predictable and, to me unfunny, author of books so popular among students in the 1960s—he retails an old joke as if it were a new joke that he alone knew. He writes,

We had begun our feast with oysters, so I announced that oysters were not the aphrodisiacs many people imagined them to be. There were boos, and then Sarah Clewes beat me to the punch line of that particular joke. "Walter ate twelve of them the other night,' she said, "and only four of them worked."

Pizza caught on slowly in America—and in Northern Italy!—after World War II. Bagels were never eaten by the general public twenty-five years ago but are now found everywhere. Lobsters, a few hundred years ago employed as crop fertilizer by New England farmers, are now top menu items. No food aversion cannot find an attendant anecdote or example. One recalls, for instance, in Herman Wouk's ethnic novel, *Marjorie Morningstar*, how young Marjorie's raffish seducer, Noel Airman, persuades the young girl to eat a lobster, which was another way of Wouk's layering religion—something of a fretful compulsion with him, always a doctrinaire (and dull) novelist, just as it is now with Philip Roth—into yet another one of his books. Wouk's novel, *The Haj*, is pure racist anti-Palestinian twaddle. It is truly paradoxical and sadly ironic how the attractive heroine of his shamelessly didactic novel, Marjorie Morganstern, after all is said and done ends up as a kosher suburban housewife in a very real sense and actually comes around to the same point-of-view of the avaricious money-lender, Shylock, who in Shakespeare's play, *The Merchant of Venice*—on a religious/culinary level—refuses to dine with the Christian merchant, Bassanio:

> Bassanio: If it please you to dine with us.
> Shylock: Yes, to smell pork; to eat of the habitation
> which your prophet the Nazarite conjured the devil
> into. I will buy with you, sell with you, talk with you,
> walk with you, and so following, but I will not eat
> with you, drink with you, nor pray with you. What
> news on the Rialto?"

Eschewing lobsters, it turns out that the literary character Marjorie is as much a Jewish stereotype as any anti-Semitic formula-figure who ends up spouting unbearable hortatory Yiddishisms like "Enjoy!" and "So sue me!" and "Eat!" which, part of matey, proletarian, immigrant patter, somehow turns all of this slang into rude and pushy intransitive verbs.

Food aversions are about bias. Point of view. Opinion. Belief. Perspective. Saul Bellow in *Jerusalem and Back* recounts one episode how on an airplane to Israel he met an ultra-religious Hasidim who was shocked that he was ordering chicken from the flight menu. The Hasid, scandalized at the thought of a decent Yiddish-speaking Jew like Bellow not ordering a *glatt* kosher meal on the spot offered to send Bellow $15 a week for the rest of his life if he would pledge then and there never to eat non-kosher food again. A detached humanist, a sane and balanced writer, Bellow abstained—from the bet.

Take saffron. Saffron's aroma is often described by connoisseurs as reminiscent of metallic honey with grassy or fodder, forage, and provender notes, while its taste has also been noted as hay- or chaff-like and sweet. Joseph Conrad flatly declared that saffron had no flavor, whereas his fellow novelist, Ford Madox Ford, who collaborated on books with him—notably the novel, *Romance*—gives a highly spirited account of this disagreement in his book, *Joseph Conrad: A Personal Reminiscence*, insisting that saffron was one of the most strongly flavored of all the herbs we know. The two of them heatedly argued the point. As a sailor who had transported whole cargoes of saffron, Conrad felt he had authority behind him. Ford testily replied that he had given saffron to more diseased poultry than ever Conrad had ever carried on ships and, furthermore, had in addition "reproved cooks enough to make ship's crews tremble for failing to add sufficient amounts of saffron into *poule au riz*." Conrad pooh-poohed this—a man who once declared, "I own that I find it impossible to read through a cookery book"—and said saffron was added to rice only to give it agreeable color. Ford judged the color most disagreeable, even offensive. "Conrad's eyes flashed dangerously," wrote Ford, "his teeth white under his drawn-back moustache… Someone changed the conversation to pearls." Ford later wrote that both of them had engaged in only two truly serious arguments in life, stating, "In all our ten thousand conversations down the years, we had quarreled: as to taste of saffron and as to whether one sheep is distinguishable from another." Mind you, this is a classic example of two great novelists discussing a single spice! Such is the power of food preference.

Food aversions are always revealing. One has a fairly good idea by a simple check on the Internet of what are generally considered the most widely disliked foods in the world—lima beans, liver, Brussels sprouts, turnips, avocado, kidneys, beets, eggplant, and, arguably at the top—or bottom—fruitcake, which by the way happened to be one of Franklin D. Roosevelt's favorite foods. Curiously, it was also a favorite, along with chocolate samplers, of General George S. Patton who craved brandied fruitcake—at Christmas he would devour an entire cake all by himself at one sitting, but, then, fearing weight gain, would then leave at once for the hospital to have his stomach pumped. The late artist and illustrator Edward Gorey, with a knowing smirk, always derisively claimed that there were only a very few fruitcakes that existed in the entire world and that folks, parsimoniously re-gifting, simply passed them on in order to be rid of them! Fruitcake, a food arguably designed to be given away rather than eaten, may in fact be the ultimate diet food, *because it is never actually consumed*!

But here, a quick added word on beets and the universal harshing to which they seem to be universally subjected. Although the beet is commonly held to be a rude, fat, worthless, squat, homely scrap vegetable, one must not forget that the surname of the inimitable romantic composer Ludwig Van Beethoven's etymologically means "from a beet garden." Was he actually a peasant? He did look faintly beetish in his squat, short, dumpy way. (Funny how precisely a human can resemble a vegetable. David O. Selznick declared that producer Darryl Zanuck, a man with curly, imprecise, nutty hair, an unruly mustache, and a batch of protruding and missing teeth, looked like "an ear of corn only a maniac would eat.") I still find delicious on a freezing winter night in New England a hearty, gleaming ruby-red *madrilène* of rich, hearty beet and onion, a rich consommé flavored with a spoonful of sour cream.

What about specific food dislikes? The brilliant but fussy pioneer of quantum mechanics, Paul Dirac, refused to eat pickles on the grounds that they were bad for the digestion. He also prohibited his wife from using even a drop of alcohol in her cooking. I know a fellow who flatly refuses to eat meat of any kind, which he finds a nauseating commodity, solely on the grounds that each animal, wastefully, is required to eat twenty-one pounds of grain to produce only one pound of meat. (His proposal is that we should all be eating beans, cats, dogs, possum, and even grilled termites, which are said to contain more than 45 percent protein.) On the other hand, Pythagoras, the Samian sage, in the 6th-century B.C. expressly encouraged people to abstain from eating beans ("*A fabis abstinete*")—this was not a proscription against that particular pulse, as is commonly assumed, incidentally, but rather an admonition against the act of taking part in politics, because it was the common bean back then that people used for casting votes, white symbolizing "*pro*," a colored bean for "*con*"—when electing magistrates and other officials. In his writings, he advised, "Avoid beans as you would matricide." Nor when advocating that his disciples "abstain from beans," was Aristotle referring to their dietary habits of people but rather but to practices of excessive sexual indulgence, which The Master of Those Who Know felt beans fostered. The expression "Spill the beans" referred initially to regurgitation. Poor beans. The legumes have a dim reputation, indeed. Donald Robert Perry Marquis in *The Almost Perfect State* declares, "There will be no beans in The Almost Perfect State."

Although beans well served a good many if not most poor creatures during the Great Depression in the United States in the 1930s who had to subsist on little but navy beans, the repetitious habit created a pronounced aversion to them by many a consumer in the subsequent decades.

The "Pythagorean diet," the sworn abstention from eating meat, fish, and, most notably, beans, goes back very far. Curiously, rumors of Pythagoras' murder revolve around his aversion to beans. According to legend, enemies of the Pythagoreans set fire to Pythagoras' house, sending the poor old man running toward a bean field, where he halted, swearing that he would rather die than enter the field—whereupon his pursuers then slit his throat. Theories have it that the prohibition of beans was to avoid favism, a form of anemia whereby susceptible people may develop hemolytic anemia resulting from an allergy to alkaloids in *Vicia faba* (Faba Beans, Broad beans, Windsor beans), or, strangely enough, by the very act of merely walking through a field where bean plants are in flower. A more likely explanation was due to spooky magical reasons, possibly because beans indicate a potential for life, perhaps even because they resemble the kidneys and genitalia—prevailing still is a belief that both beans and human beings were created from the same material. (Pythagoras, was also the first person to denounce the eating of animal flesh at table, incidentally.)

Regarding this moral stricture of his, several theories have been advanced that (a) he thought that they held the souls of the dead; (b) they resembled testicles (this was Aristotle's theory as to why Pythagoras proscribed them); (c) they were an aphrodisiac. What about farting? We read in Isaiah XVI:11, "My bowels shall sound like a harp." Remember the old schoolboy jingle or roundelay, endlessly repeated?

Beans, beans, the musical fruit,
The more you eat, the more you toot,
The more you toot, the better you feel,
Then you're ready for another meal
Of beans, beans [repeat]

If that seems scandalously trivial, one can go to higher authority to find sanction for this gross emanation, as witness Jonathan Swift's "The Benefit of Farting Explain'd" and Charles James Fox's "An Essay Upon Wind." Benjamin Franklin even wrote a mock letter to "The Royal Academy," which opened explaining why people try to restrain and contain their windy emissions:

It is universally well known, That in digesting our common Food, there is created or produced in the

Bowels of human Creatures, a great Quantity of Wind.
That the permitting this Air to escape and mix with
the Atmosphere, is usually offensive to the Company,
from the fetid Smell that accompanies it. That all well-
bred People therefore, to avoid giving such Offence,
forcibly restrain the Efforts of Nature to discharge that
Wind.

Franklin argued that holding back gas could be painful, even life threatening. If science could improve the smell, maybe people would break wind
freely:

Were it not for the odiously offensive Smell accompanying such Escapes, polite People would probably be
under no more Restraint in discharging such Wind in
Company, than they are in spitting, or in blowing their
Noses.

Empedocles thought it wicked to munch laurel leaves. Hindus of course
shudder at the very thought of eating beef. (All of the McDonald's eateries in
New Delhi, India obligingly—and wisely—fashion their burgers solely out of
mutton, because of that religious restriction.) Mohammedans and Orthodox
Jews, by fiat, regard the flesh of the pig as unclean. Jews, furthermore, are
scripturally prohibited from eating things like lobster and shellfish, because
of the Mosaic Law. (It is a pity because clams, mussels, oysters, shrimp, abalone and mollusks rate as the highest iron foods by nutrient density—28
mg or 155% DV per 100 grams—in the entire world.) Meat, fish, and eggs
revolted Dame Margot Fonteyn, the late famed Prima Ballerina *Assoluta* of
the Royal Ballet, while she was still in her teens. Her favorite meal was reportedly pizza, as well as baked beans on toast. In a recent interview with
The Sun, the actor Nicholas Cage revealed that he chooses what he eats according to the mating habits of the animals in question. "I think fish are very
dignified with sex. So are birds. But pigs, not so much. So I don't eat pig
meat or things like that." This hardly surprises me. Celebrities are fakes, and
actors more or less all mentally ill, no question about it—applause freaks on
the make who in their neediness and desperation are driven into a lifetime of
posing, grabbing gimcrack awards with two hot fists, and painfully craving
public attention, world recognition, and endless acclaim. Come on, get real!
Marlon Brando said, "An actor's a guy who, if you ain't talking about him,
he ain't listening."

Singer Mariah Carey, to maintain her weight, eats only purple foods like plums, grapes, and eggplant three days a week. To lose weight for her film roles Renée Zellweger habitually eats ice cubes as a snack to feel full. Apple co-founder Steve Jobs compulsively ate the same food day after day. At one point, he ate carrots for so long his skin took on an orange hue. (He believed his strict diet reduced body odor, therefore reducing the need for regular bathing.) Maria Callas, the Greek opera star, was rumored to have eaten a tapeworm, *purposely*—to help her lose her ever ballooning weight. Who can ever fully explain the logic of what people will eat or not eat? 84-year-old billionaire Warren Buffet ritually drinks six Coca-Colas a day, accompanied with Utz Potato Stix, declaring, "I checked the actuarial tables, and the lowest death rate is among six-year-olds. So I decided to eat like a six-year-old."

A neighbor of mine refuses to eat any egg that has a yellow yolk, saying "Real eggs—fresh eggs—have *orange* yolks!" Fastidious New York Jews will not look at a "tampered-with" bagel, as a friend of mine puts it. "Bagels should be plain, garlic, seeded, or have any combination of such," he grumbles, carps, and cavils, "all others are just bread. This here cranberry bagel is not just a *shande* [desecration] but an actual sacrilege!" I knew an old Cape Codder who swore against the habit of eating ducks that ate fish, which in his opinion imparted a bitter, off-putting anti-flavor to such ducks and to other fish-eating animals. On the wild sea coast, where they feed on both fish and clams, the flesh of the brass-eye or golden-wing is notoriously bad, whereas their inland counterparts make excellent eating. Pablo Picasso was not a great fan of meat, except for chorizo. The painter's favorite foods were olives and bread; grilled fish; and sheep cheese. Man Ray, the Dada-Surrealist photographer, made a loud point of flatly refusing to eat preserved foods of any kind. Lady Gaga, the pop singer of this generation, has gone on record as saying that she does not like *food at all*, full stop. *Does not like food at all?* Yup. Hard to believe, but some people actually feel that. There is an anti-vision involved in the matter, about which I will have something to say anon. But it is the equivalent in a sense of an individual who has never read a book or who loathes a view of mountains or who flees the vital light of sunshine.

The late Yukio Mishima wrote, "The special quality of hell is to see everything clearly down to the last detail." Who can say, maybe a true dyed-in-the-wool aversionist is privy, in whatever case, to insights that the rest of us simply do not have—a person who sees *too clearly*!

There was a time when nobody at all, or at least very few people, in the world actually *drank water*—or even bathed!—at least for periods such as Renaissance Europe or 18th and 19th-century England. (One person in five never bathes from birth to death, according to Lawrence Wright in *Clean*

and Decent: The Fascinating History of the Bathroom and the W.C. [1960])
Those who did rely on drinking water were mainly primitive tribes, aborigines, Indians, those who lived in ancient times and civilizations going back millennia. It is often asked why people still develop kidney stones but yet seem never anymore to suffer from bladder stones? A highly likely explanation is this is the result of not drinking water. Diabetics incur excessive thirst. (It is called polydipsia.) So do schizophrenics. In the last years of his life, Franz Kafka who was drinking lots of beer, which he loved, more than anything badly craved water by the gallon—pitchers of it were always placed on his dining table, along with the glasses of beer—suffering, as he was, from a constant, plaguing thirst, which was a symptom of his laryngeal tuberculosis, forcing him to take tiny, painful swallows.

Civilized people for decades—centuries—drank mainly alcoholic beverages. Sci-fi novelist Neal Stephenson in his *Salon* interview with Laura Miller is correct in my opinion when he asserted, "Every culture can be defined by what they [sic] drink in order to avoid dying of diarrhea. In China it's tea. In Africa it's milk or animal blood. In Europe it was wine and beer."

But water? It is actually hated and avoided by certain people—and not just winos, rummies, alkys, barflys, and drunks like John Barrymore, Erroll Flynn, and W.C. Fields. I mean *any* water: tap water, well water, designer water, Brita water, restaurant water, ice water, spa water, seltzer water, holy water, flavored water, the purest bottled water. On December 5, 1933, precisely at 7 p.m. that evening when President Franklin D. Roosevelt declared the ratification of the 21st Amendment to the Constitution, which nullified the Eighteenth, making drinking alcohol legal once more, writer and social commentator H.L. Mencken—a man who became nauseous gulping water like a rabid camel and positively loathed the feeling of it sloshing around in his stomach as if in a bus-station commode—comparing its effects, in terms of the suffering that it had caused to the Black Death in Medieval Europe, marked its passing by gulping a glass of water, stating that it was his "first in 13 years."

Philip K. Dick's sci-fi offering *Martian Time-Slip*, which presents a world in which water is a precious commodity and schizophrenia is the norm, is to my mind the definitive toxic-water novel ("The water, unpleasant and tainted, made her cough. We should drain the tank, she thought. Scour it. Adjust the chlorine flow and see how many of the filters are plugged, perhaps all. Couldn't the ditch rider do that?"), a harbinger, although set on the planet Mars, of the lead-heavy water scandal and ecological disaster in Flint, Michigan, in 2015.

Who can forget Squire Matthew Bramble's tirade in the great novel, *Humphrey Clinker*, about the dubious worth of London water?

If I would drink water, I must quaff the mawkish contents of an open aqueduct, exposed to all manner of defilement; or swallow that which comes from the river Thames, impregnated with all the filth of London and Westminster—Human excrement is the least offensive part of the concrete, which is composed of all the drugs, minerals, and poisons used in mechanics and manufacture, enriched with the putrefying carcasses of beasts and men; and mixed with the scourings of all the wash-tubs, kennels, and common sewers within the bills of mortality. This is the agreeable potation, extolled by the Londoners as the finest water in the universe.

Water had always seemed to evoke passion in lunatics. Temperance fanatics and suffragettes like Carrie Nation and Frances Willard demanded that water replace *all* drinks. (Those zealots would have had difficulty getting a koala to drink, however, a marsupial that takes its fluid solely through its one food source, the eucalyptus plant. The very word *koala* in Aboriginal Australian means "no drink.") A favorite instrument of most diet reformers, water was held as a panacea, especially in 19th-century America. One Vincenz Priessnitz (1799-1851), a peasant farmer from Gräfenberg in Austrian Silesia, went from the rustic practice of healing animals and a few ill neighbors by pouring cold water on them to becoming an essential founder of modern hydrotherapy. A major requirement of his regimen was the daily consumption of 20 to 25 glasses of cold water in order to cleanse the system of all impurities and disease-causing materials. Then, Canadian biochemist A.B. Macallum believed that our bodily fluids reproduce the organic environment that surrounded our single-celled ancestors in the primordial seas.

The Chinese consider taking a cold drink to be very unhealthy. But that is only one among many superstitions that they have. They will eat pineapple only after it has been soaked in salt water, because the salt water is said to remove some sort of "taint" in that food. Avoid holding chopsticks at the far end, as that will cause you to move far from your hometown when you marry. Noodles stand for longevity, so never cut them, lest you die young. Eat every last grain of rice in your bowl, lest they become pockmarks or moles on your future husband's face. Never stick chopsticks upright in a rice bowl, for the dead will be offended, because this is the way their food is served – and, upright, they also represent incense burning at a funeral.

Excesses—immoderation—almost always has a comic cast to it, for going to extreme in most matters always leads to Barmyville.

John Lileks in his blog, *The Gallery of Regrettable Food* takes a delightful satirical stand against American "magazine" food—*Family Circle, Better*

Homes & Gardens Cooking Library, Woman's Day, etc. and those small cook books filled with out-of-focus dinner spreads and plates of fat ham, three-bean casseroles, and lavish piles of Christmas cookie. There always seemed to be in the garish photos a pert 1950s-looking housewife with short coiffed hair, always smiling—a young Nancy Reagan clone—wearing a pearl neck-lace and a smile standing behind her clean-cut husband who held a briar pipe looking as pleased as punch. Inveighing against all those now antique "poor-ly photographed foodstuffs and horrid recipes," Lileks goes on to write, "It's a wonder anyone in the 40s, 50s and 60s gained any weight; it's a miracle that people didn't put down their issue of *Life* magazine with a slight quea-sy list to their gut, and decide to sup on a nice bowl of shredded wheat and nothing else. It wasn't that the food was inedible; it was merely dull. Everything was geared for a timid palate fearful of spice. It wasn't non-nu-tritious—no, between the limp boiled vegetables, fat-choked meat cylinders, and pink-whipped-Jell-O dessert, you were bound to find a few calories that would drag you into the next day. It's that the pictures are so hideously unappealing."

There is comic food, surely. What else would you call loony ballpark mustard, made with yellow mustard seeds and a great deal of vinegar and turmeric for that zingo, knock-your-socks-off Day-Glo color? Or flaring Hawaiian Punch (it has less than 2% fruit juice) with foxy faux-flavors like Berry Bonkers, Wild Purple Smash, and Mango Passionfruit Squeeze? A few sweet ketchups that are a hit with kids, like the brands Pure and Simple, Red Wing, and Hunt's No-Salt Added, actually taste like tomato jam! Certain grotesque sundae-style yogurts with fruit at the bottom, such as Dannon, also come with syrup on the top—and Dannon's new "Danimals Crunchers" varieties of yogurt combine nonfat yogurt with crunchy rainbow sprinkles and chocolate candies that kids will love to crunch, mix and munch. Such foods are virtually candy. It would be in order to have Emmett Kelly with his red rubber nose and baggy pants as their spokesman. It is the type of food that you find that seems to fit the characters in certain novels, like those by Nathaniel West or Flannery O'Connor. Charles Portis's *The Dog of the South* (1979), a novel in which much road food figures, is a good example of this. Hapless Ray Midge, the congenial 26-year-old narrator, makes reference to "cold weenies" and "watermelon" and at one points says,

> Melba and I filled up on lime jello [sic]—transparent,
> no bits of fruit in suspension—and peanut-butter
> cookies with corrugations on top where a fork had
> been lightly pressed into them. That was our lunch.

> The doctor talked on and on. He held a spoonful of
> jello [sic] above his bowl but thoughts kept racing
> into his head and he could never quite get it to his
> mouth.

Lileks calls it the "Golden Age of Butter." The "Mom Factor" played a
big role in those old pantry cookbooks, according to Lileks:

> They are not really recipe books. They're ads for food
> companies, with every recipe using the company's
> products, often in unexpected ways. ("Hot day? Kids
> love a frosty Bacon Milkshake!") There's not a single
> edible dish in the entire collection. The pictures in
> the books are ghastly—the Italian dishes look like a
> surgeon got a sneezing fit during an operation, and
> the queasy casseroles look like something on which
> the janitor dumps sawdust. But you have to enjoy
> the spirit behind the books—cheerful postwar perfect
> housewifery is taught in every book. Sure, you'll fall
> short of the ideal. But what's an ideal for if not to
> show up your shortcomings?

I seem to recall that pineapple slices figured in a lot of those photos,
along with deviled eggs, split tomatoes (sometimes with appliqué made
into the hideous simulacrum of a food face!), molded Jell-O, mousse out of
molds, lots of pot roast and corned beef pictures, turkey (with legs wearing
paperettes!), rice-and-creamed peas presentations, consommés, melba toast.

I have mentioned butter. It is a commonplace among chefs, needless to
say, to avoid, indeed condemn, any substitute for butter. British cookery writer
Elizabeth David who was decisive in all her opinions, advice, and instructions
disliked margarine. She had no use for the lame "if you can't find butter, use
margarine," for example. If a cook could not find any butter, her advice was,
create another meal. She did not tolerate the second-rate. "Margarine?" que-
ried Anthony Bourdain in *Kitchen Confidential*. "That's not food. I Can't
Believe It's Not Butter? I can. If you're planning on using margarine in anything, you can stop reading now, because I won't be able to help you." Neither
did Julia Child ever consider cooking with margarine. Child also disliked barbecue, dark restaurants, and casseroles. "Casseroles. I even hate the name, as
it always implies to me some godawful mess," Child wrote to Avis DeVoto on
January 19, 1953, adding with mocking aposeopesis, "The one you described

that [Dorothy de Santillana] ate of pork chops and Bing cherries! Horrid!" Julia Child had many odd food crotchets. Bob Spitz in his biography, *Dearie: The Remarkable Life of Julia Child* cites several. She wouldn't touch kosher salt and shunned the use of white pepper, only black. She had blind prejudices. She was not big for dal, pakoras, or curries. She did not go in for Polynesia-influenced food. The same with Italian cooking in general. ("It really isn't my kind of food.") Arguably, her favorite meal was pan-fried lobster, one of the simplest possible recipes ever to put together, a 20-minute flash-by. Child was willful, opinionated, stubborn, and could be perverse. She baked potatoes in a microwave oven, put red wine in her onion soup, and, inexplicably, preferred Hellman's mayonnaise to Jacques Pepin's superb homemade version, all of which were probably lame devices to flaunt her eccentricity and confound a rival.

One need not go far nor force research to come up with foods that invoke a general and widely-held abhorrence—I mean actual dishes, all real, that are savored in various parts of the world, things like Casu Marzu cheese, a rotten pecorino that happens to be a specialty in Sardinia; Mongolina Boodog, a whole goat filled with hot stones and barbecued; an Asian dish called Balut which is the fertilized fetal eggs of ducks, soft-boiled; whole sheep's head, eyes, ears, and tongues served on a plate; octopus (raw) eaten while still alive; "stinks heads," rotten salmon heads that have been buried until they have aged; jellied moose nose; and fruit bat soup. I am talking about foods that are commonly shunned for a multitude of reasons and just as often with no reason given whatsoever, simply sheer unadulterated dislike.

But it is not complicated. Intention creates meaning. Belief, in the pragmatic view, is the same as action. If our idea of goodness involves avoiding celery, the goodness, for us, amounts to a tendency to avoid it. "The true," wrote William James, "is the name of whatever proves itself to be good in the way of belief." The truth, in short, is just what works. Pragmatism.

An important aspect regarding food dislikes involves the category of what foods people insist on having all the time to the exclusion of all others—in other words, what a person chooses to eat tells us what foods that person despises. Craving a single food exclusively, in other words—monophagia—is a food aversion, arguably one of the most maniacal of the many there are. Although Charlie Chaplin, wealthy enough to afford it, had a full-time Japanese staff that worked in his home for most of his creative life, he always insisted on eating beef at every meal—*demanded* beef even during war times when harder-to-find foods were rationed, which only highlighted his monomania. Karl Kraus, Austrian author and editor of *Die Fackel*, constantly ate his evening dinner at the Café Central, always a very sharp sausage.

A classic example of this syndrome can be found in the Austrian philosopher Ludwig Wittgenstein. In his book, *Ludwig Wittgenstein: A Memoir,* Norman Malcolm wrote of his compulsive subject:

> My wife gave [Wittgenstein] some Swiss cheese and
> rye bread for lunch, which he greatly liked. Thereafter
> he more or less insisted on eating bread and cheese at
> all meals, largely ignoring the various dishes that my
> wife prepared. Wittgenstein declared that it did not
> much matter to him what he ate, so long as it always
> remained the same."

While at the University of Cambridge, although often asked to do so, this highly intense fellow never dined at high table—he explained that all of the communal conversation there sickened him. The daily eating habits of this frequently gloomy, inward-looking, often depressed man were reductively simple, almost paratactic. Myristicaceous mind, mole mode. He was "passionate, profound, intense, and dominating," in the words of his mentor, Bertrand Russell, who quickly hastened to add, "He had a kind of purity which I have never known equaled except by G.E. Moore."

He invariably chose to eat alone and always insisted on eating the same ordinary fare every day, meal after meal, always preferring simple plain food—set forth with regularity—to more varied or elaborate meals given at high table or on social academic occasions. His ongoing option was for an ethical/aesthetic choice of utter simplicity. Allowances were made wherever he went for his idiosyncrasies, which were somewhat insistent. His reputation preceded him.

The almost empty, Trappist-like sparseness of the various rooms that Ludwig Wittgenstein lived in added to his legend, even in his own day. The rooms he occupied constituted basically a cot, a chair, a simple table for writing, and a few books. Extra chairs were piled on the outside landing, if any were needed by him during classes. He also lived in an equally frugal and temperate manner during his vacations in rural and remote parts of Norway and Ireland. Wittgenstein always thriftily dressed down, wearing plain sneakers and a dun, threadbare tweed jacket. It was as if everything was pared down to meet the nakedness of his supreme scruple. Russell noted, "His life was turbulent and troubled, and his personal force was extraordinary. He lived on milk and vegetables, and I used to feel as Mrs. Patrick Campbell did about Shaw: 'God help us if he should ever eat a beefsteak.'"

Whenever he went shopping, Wittgenstein habitually carried his vegetables and fruits in a string bag in order, as he put it, to "let them breathe." He compulsively put his celery in water when serving it for dinner. There was always a darkening extra-attention or dogged focus to his various acts. He insisted that he had to be physically *present* to clarify to colleagues any philosophical point. In a full classroom, as students sat there, he would go pacing up and down sometimes for half an hour, silently, uttering not a single word, peevishly frowning, *thinking*. The prospect of variety in foods seemed to bedevil him, in the inexplicable way, say, insects did. All of his life he was terrified of wasps and bugs, for example. What is it with such tics and geniuses? Albert Einstein developed a dark aversion to mountains. Leonardo DaVinci developed a method of mirror-writing in order to prevent people from stealing his notes. Isaac Asimov was afraid to fly. Stephen King has a neutoric loathing of adverbs. ("I believe the road to hell is paved by adverbs, and I will shout it from the rooftops.") Dylan Thomas was filled with an absolute horror of mice and rats. A.L. Rowse had a savage dislike of being rained on.

Wittgenstein's crotchets were many and varied, and his exacting standards, his almost robotic tropism for order, according to contemporaries, apparently also made the man extremely difficult to work with—for example, he once built and designed a house in Vienna for one of his sisters, Margarethe Stonborough-*Wittgenstein*, between 1926 and 1928, an extremely spare, white, Bauhaus-looking structure—and with over-exacting orders he scrupulously required, among other demands, that all heaters be positioned exactly so as not to spoil the symmetry of the rooms; if they were even only fractionally wrongly placed it would send him into fits of rage. One recalls Nathaniel West in *Miss Lonelyhearts* writing,

> He sat in the window thinking. Man has a tropism
> for order. Keys in one pocket, change in the other.
> Mandolins are tuned G D A E. The physical world has
> a tropism for disorder, entropy. Man against Nature...
> the battle of the centuries. Keys yearn to mix with
> change. Mandolins strive to get out of tune. Every
> order has within it the germ of destruction. All order
> is doomed, yet the battle is worthwhile."

Many a true food phobic shares this psychic need for comforting separation, due discretion, marked boundaries. Trying to curtail one's obsessions may only increase their frequency. Emotional ties—anything healthy along those lines—seem antagonistic to intellectual demands. It was the case with

Wittgenstein—and Einstein. "I want to know how God created this world... I want to know his thoughts, the rest are details," declared Einstein, who sadly ignored both his wives and children. Of Albert Einstein declared Max Born, a friend and rival, both as a physicist and as a humanist, "For all his kindness and sociability, and love of humanity, he was nevertheless totally detached from his environment and the human beings included in it."

It was entirely acceptable that composer Ludwig von Beethoven woke up each morning by taking a cup of coffee—perfectly normal, except that, compulsively, he had to have exactly sixty beans per cup, which he personally counted out. To begin her day, according to Karen Ahn in her blog "Real Brain Food," novelist Patricia Highsmith needed a saucer of sugar every morning with her cigarettes, coffee, and doughnut. As she got older, she became a chronic, confirmed, and hardened drinker and so started her day with vodka instead. Also a compulsive chain smoker, says Ahn, "she only ate American bacon, fried eggs, and cereal at odd times of the day." The eating habits of Swedish film maker Ingmar Bergman were odd, as well. Ahn writes, "According to actress Bibi Andersson, he always ate the same lunch everyday: whipped sour milk with sweet strawberry jam, eaten together with cornflakes." *Peanuts* cartoonist Charles Schulz breakfasted on pancakes pretty much every day. Filmmaker David Lynch, director of *Twin Peaks* (whose main character is a coffee fiend), *Eraserhead* and *Blue Velvet*, had a set habit for seven years: he ate at Bob's Big Boy, a local Southern California restaurant chain, always after the lunch rush. He would order a chocolate shake and 4 to 7 cups of coffee with lots of sugar. He credits the sugar as the impetus behind many of his ideas. Playwright Molière spent the last years of his life eating little but Parmesan cheese.

Scientist and inventor Nikola Tesla, a vegetarian, eventually limited himself to a peculiar diet of only milk, honey, bread, and vegetable juices, according to Marc Seifer, author of *Wizard: The Life and Times of Nikola Tesla*. He ate dinner in New York City at the Waldorf-Astoria Hotel invariably by himself. At any hotel he would insist his room number be divisible by 3. He would telephone the hotel in advance, so that exactly18 clean linen napkins would be stacked for him at his dinner table. While he waited, as Karen Ahn explains, "he would polish the crystal and silver with the napkins. The *maître d'* would serve his food while the electrical genius calculated the cubic contents of the dishes before eating. Not a morsel of food would he eat until he had performed those calculations. He had to do it to enjoy his food."

As he got older, Tesla developed certain other fixations. For example, he would become seriously alarmed about the possibility of contagion by germs and as a result would only eat food that had been boiled. Stranger tropisms even kicked in. He could not stand the company of overweight women, for example, and he hated jewelry of any kind, especially pearls. Later in his life, he developed a penchant for a curious sort of vagabonding. He frequented various parks in New York City, wandering about, often rescuing any injured pigeons he saw to try to nurse them back to health. A Special PBS report on Tesla's life and legacy claimed that when the inventor took up residence at the Hotel New Yorker, "he had the hotel chef prepare a special mix of seed for his pigeons, which he hoped to sell commercially."

Most food aversionists are aberrant. But who isn't—or wasn't—peculiar? Benjamin Franklin began his day, naked, standing before his window for cooling air baths. Charles Dickens, who could never bear to have his hair out of place, always kept a comb handy, running it through his hair hundreds of times a day. T.S. Eliot at times wore green-tinted face powder and lipstick. Friedrich Schiller sought inspiration from the scent of rotting apples. Edgar Allan Poe wrote his works in scroll fashion, on long, continuous strips of paper, attached with sealing wax. Evelyn Waugh so despised the Oxford dean, C.R.M.F. Cruttwell, for calling him when he was a student "a silly suburban sod with an inferiority complex" that for a lifetime he vengefully vilified him specifically by name in as many as four of his novels. Actor Sir John Gielgud despised cats and during one of his performances in a play, *The Vortex*, when one wandered on stage he furiously picked it up and threw it into the audience. Winston Churchill so abhorred anyone whistling, it set up an almost psychiatric disturbance in him. Cole Porter was actually depressed by—grew morbid in the presence of—poor people. Painter Salvador Dalí had a terror of locusts that became so intense that, on one occasion, he threw himself from a window to avoid one of the insects, almost at the cost of his life. Incidentally, does any one of his worshipful biographers ever point out that Teddy Roosevelt carried a vial of morphine at all times in case he ever needed to take his own life?

The mysterious and reclusive Mr. Knott's meals in Samuel Beckett's surrealistic novel, *Watt* (1953), surely memorable, recall—are a virtual parody of—the unvarying Wittgensteinian meal. The all-inclusive dish is cooked for Knott by the odd fellow Watt, now a dutiful manservant, and served "cold, in a bowl, at twelve o'clock noon sharp and at seven p.m. exactly, all the year round." Knott in his house who never complains takes his meals silently and alone and unobserved "with a little plated trowel, such as confectioners and grocers use, and tea-merchants."

Wittily writes Beckett, "On Saturday night a sufficient quantity of food was prepared and cooked to carry Mr. Knott through the week." What is served exactly? The generic meal preposterously consists, *all slopped together* in a crazy bricolage of fish, eggs, game, poultry, meat, cheese, fruit, bread, butter, beverages like milk, coffee, stout, beer iodine, coal, mercury, iron, camomile, mustard, pepper, salt, sugar, among other things, and "worm-powder." Somewhat appalled, we read the comic paragraph:

> All these things, and many others too numerous to mention, were well mixed together in the famous pot and boiled for four hours, until the consistence of a mess, or poss, was obtained, and all the good things to eat, all the good things to drink… were inextricably mingled and transformed into a single good thing that was neither food nor drink, nor physic… and of which the tiniest spoonful at once opened the appetite and closed it, excited and stilled the thirst, compromised and stimulated the body's vital functions, and went pleasantly to the head.

It is, satirically, less a meal than an agglomeration, a salmagundi, with Knott the irresolute garbage disposal. No one who eats food in this way can surely like food, and, all things added up, it may well be Samuel Beckett's character, Knott, who hates food more than anyone mentioned in these pages.

A former Howard Hughes chef says that the late billionaire recluse was, like Wittgenstein, as eccentric about food as he was about his privacy. Garcy G. Reich, who was Hughes' personal chef for nine years—from 1958 to 1967, when the billionaire lived in a small bungalow at the Beverly Hills Hotel—explained that, although his boss' favorite food was tenderloin filet and a beef stroganoff-type dish, he had a mad penchant for fudge. He said that Hughes *existed* at times on fudge, milk and water. Foods he feared more than fancied. The chef said Hughes once sent him a four-page memo on how to pick a can of peaches from the shelf, exactly how to open the can, and which peach to select. Close friends reported that he was also obsessed with the size of peas, one of his rare favorite foods, and used a special fork to sort them by size. These tropisms were obviously signs of mental illness, primarily an obsessive-compulsive disorder. Reich stated that Hughes who stuck to a regimented diet of the same foods, changing the menu about every four months, always insisted that all utensils used in cooking be sterilized. When Hughes moved to Las Vegas, Reich stayed in Los Angeles but continued to cut steaks for the recluse, who had them flown to Nevada. He said Hughes demanded that everything be prepared exactly as he instructed and instantly detected any variation, such as an unwashed cutting board or too much seasoning. Reich said that while Hughes was precise about how his meals were prepared, he did not go so far as to have someone taste his food before he ate it. In 1947, after the US Government rejected his massive H-4 Hercules, Hughes who had suffered a near-fatal aircraft crash in 1946 told his aides that he wanted to screen movies at a film studio near his home. There he stayed in the studio's darkened screening room for more than four months, not leaving once and for sustenance eating only chocolate bars and chicken, drinking milk, and always urinating in the empty milk bottles and containers always kept handy.

According to Minnie Weygandt, who served as Mary Baker Eddy's cook from 1899 to 1907 and who wrote extensively about the food that the enigmatic founder of Christian Science purchased and prepared, Eddy insistently, compulsively, abstemiously consumed the very same breakfast every single day of her life: mush (made of cornmeal), cream, and oranges. Mrs. Eddy was, inexplicably, strangely, particularly fond of salt pork, and in various households where she lived—and there were many (she was married three times)—several pigs were butchered each year specifically in order to preserve salt pork for her in select barrels.

It seems that Mrs. Eddy also had something of a penchant for "mommy food." Although other meals were more substantial—lamb chops, pork chops, chicken or turkey croquettes, tomato or lobster bisque, creamed lobster, oyster stew, and various types of soup such as ham hock soup and mock turtle soup—Eddy asked that virtually all of her food be boiled into what Weygandt describes as a consistency almost that of jelly, even such a dish as the traditional New England boiled dinner, a meal she loved, although it is composed of corned beef and vegetables. Dessert for her was almost always a custard or pudding, and many workers remembered the prevalence of pie at every meal—apple, rhubarb, and mince pie were the most common.

Was this mere fussiness? A neurosis? The result of arrested juvenility? A tropism for order? One of Mrs. Eddy's biographers, Gillian Gill, wrote that, although she was often sickly as a child and appears to have suffered from an eating disorder, reports of hysterical fits may have been exaggerated. Eddy described her problems with food in the first edition of her book, *Science and Health* (1875). She explained that she suffered from chronic indigestion as a child and, hoping to cure it, had embarked on a diet of nothing but water, bread and vegetables, often eating one meal just once a day. "Thus we passed most of our early years, as many can attest, in hunger, pain, weakness, and starvation," she wrote. It would seem that Eddy found much of her ordeal growing up as the linchpin of her vision. It may be noted, significantly, that she also wrote in her autobiography, *Retrospection and Introspection* (1891), that when she was eight she heard a voice call her name, which she interpreted as a religious experience. "For some twelve months, when I was about eight years old, I repeatedly heard a voice, calling me distinctly by name, three times, in an ascending scale."

Food compulsions and fads are common with people with HFA/ASP or "High Functioning Autism" and "Asperger's Syndrome." As we have already noted, Wittgenstein maintained strict, non-alternating routines that persisted to the very end of his life. Ray Monk, one of his biographers, wrote that Wittgenstein and Mrs. Bevan, the wife of the physician seeing him at the time, quickly established the pattern of walking to the local pub at 6 o'clock every evening. "We always ordered two ports," Mrs. Bevan remembered. "One I drank, and the other he poured with great amusement into the Aspidistra plant—this was the only dishonest act I ever knew him to do." Wittgenstein was mad for focus, a demon for exactitude, that variation of honesty. "I am not a hero" is what all would-be heroes know they are required to say when usually they mean the exact opposite, which is not heroic, and one of the worst aspects of false humility—like all lies—is that one loses self-focus. But Wittgenstein was heroic in the very intensity he brought to whatever task loomed before him.

Food fixations in an obstinate and hidebound eater can be said to be the polar *opposite* of a food aversion, even if seemingly a variation of it. Any single food that one has exclusively settled on to the strict exclusion of just about every other in some set way constitutes an outstanding *example* of a food aversion. Obsessives eat the same food day in and day out. Names are even given to them—for example, a Japanese term for people obsessed with ramen noodle soup is *raota*. Is it not arguable that there is always a touch of madness, of insistent lunacy, in anything held that is madly exclusive—what Matthew Arnold called the "one thing necessary"? Such rigid fixations make for the kind of dark rigidification that we tend to associate with obsession. God bless variation! Praise here for the fingers of the human hand, adapted to the grab and the snatch, which are all of a *different length,* used for picking things up—and originally swinging through the trees! An "even hand" would be less versatile.

An infantilization is somehow connected to obsessives and food. Elvis Presley adored bacon. Orson Welles passionately loved hot dogs, although he hated peanuts. (He once declared, "I hate television. I hate it as much as peanuts.") Chairman Mao Zedong constantly craved red pepper, like other Hunanese do; he insistently shook it on eggs, on soup, and once upon a time even on a cat that he devoured when he was starving, skin and bones and grease. Dumpy little J. Wellington Wimpy in E.C. Segar's comic strip, Popeye, the Sailor Man, compulsively ate hamburgers, while Popeye seemed to live on nothing but spinach. In *Popeye the Sailor Meets Sinbad the Sailor*, Wimpy is seen grinding meat or eating burgers almost the entire time— he was always too cheap to pay for them himself. His best-known catchphrase started in 1931 as "Cook me up a hamburger. I'll pay you Thursday;" but in 1932, this then became the famous "I'll gladly pay you Tuesday for a hamburger today."

One can only wonder if Wimpy's obsession for hamburgers would extend to shelling out $120, as he would have to do, for the DB Royale Double Truffle Burger sold at New York City's B Bistro; or $295 for The Serendipity Burger at New York's posh Serendipity 3, which offers Wagyu beef infused with a ten-herb white truffle butter topped with London-made cheddar cheese and a fried quail egg on a buttered roll topped with caviar; or the astonishing price of $777 for the Kobe Beef and Maine Lobster Burger from Le Burger at the Paris Hotel in Las Vegas, a burger which is served with a bottle of Rose Dom Perignon champagne!

Who can explain the lunacies of the private mind and the needs it devises in its search for foods to choose or reject? As George Carlin said, "People who go to Las Vegas, you've got to question their fucking intellect to start with. Traveling hundreds and thousands of miles to essentially give your money to a large corporation is kind of fucking moronic. That's what I'm always getting here is these kind of fucking people with very limited intellects."

Johannes Brahms for breakfast had a Havana cigar and strong coffee. (He carried tins of sardines in his coat pocket and drank off the oil from the tin, peasant-style as he ambled about.) F. Scott Fitzgerald ate canned turtle soup for lunch and Hershey bars for a snack. Babe Ruth drank bourbon-and-ginger ale in the early morning. Actress Reese Witherspoon for meals eats only baby food, according to celebrity gossip. Former Light Heavyweight Champion Lyoto Machida told the Brazilian magazine *Tatame*, "I drink my urine every morning like a natural medicine." Swimmer Michael Phelps who consumed a ridiculous 12,000 calories a day while training for the Beijing Games—that is as much as 10,000 more calories than what the average person should consume—as his daily diet for breakfast eats three fried-egg sandwiches with cheese, lettuce, tomatoes, fried onions, and mayonnaise; then, a five-egg omelet; a bowl of grits; three slices of French toast with powdered sugar; and three chocolate-chip pancakes. Mrs. Hudson, Sherlock Holmes' devoted housekeeper at 221B Baker Street, provides the detective and Dr. Watson with breakfasts of kidneys, kedgeree, ham and eggs, and even chicken curry. The sleuth is certainly no gourmet, nor is he at all inordinately particular.

His "wants," he declares, are "simple: a loaf of bread and a clean collar." His unique occupation made regular meals impossible, and he sometimes fell back on "some cold beef and a glass of beer" or tinned tongue and peaches. Like all workaholics, Holmes often relies on sandwiches. On the trail of a jewel thief, "he cut a slice of beef from the joint upon the sideboard, sandwiched it between two rounds of bread and thrusting this rude meal into his pocket, he started off upon his expedition."

What is it about detectives and sandwiches? Raymond Chandler's private eye, Philip Marlowe, who sticks pretty much to 85-cent dinners and drugstore lunches, gulps endless cups of coffee (his preference is for Huggins Young, an old L.A. brand) and eats diner sandwiches, rarely fresh. We read:

> The coffee was over-strained and the sandwich was as full of flavor as a piece of old shirt. Americans will eat anything if it is toasted and held together with a couple of toothpicks and has lettuce sticking out of the sides, preferably a little wilted. (The Long Goodbye)

and

> Down at the drug-store lunch counter I had time to inhale two cups of coffee and a melted cheese sandwich with two slivers of ersatz bacon embedded in it, like dead fish in the silt at the bottom of a drained pool. (*The Little Sister*)

and

> I got the eggs the way I liked them. The toast had been painted with melted butter past its bloom...I used two drops of Tabasco, swallowed the eggs, drank two cups of coffee and was about to leave the toast for a tip, but I went soft and left a quarter instead. ("The Pencil")

It is a quaint anomaly, having mentioned Popeye, that another cartoon character, Peter Griffin of television's *Family Guy* declares in one episode that he hated "spinach, traffic jams, and the last few years of *M*A*S*H* when Alan Alda took over behind the camera and the show got all dramatic and preachy."

Actor Rod Steiger, a manic depressive—he was married five times and was something of a mad compulsive, from all that I have read—mentioned in a 1969 *Playboy* interview, "I have haunted restaurants all over the world, seeking the definitive beef Wellington and its counterpart, a perfect bottle of vintage French Bordeaux." There is something unbalanced in all obsessives. Repetitive eating habits often indicate a person loves one food too well. There is in the habit of madly fixing on a food either to love or hate an action bordering on disobedience, an obstinate refusal to obey the world's logic. I am here reminded of a characteristic remark once made by the uncompromising Ignatius Loyola, founder of the Jesuits: "To arrive at complete certainty I will believe that the white object I see is black, if that should be the decision of the hierarchical Church." Bullheaded. Implacable. Unswerving. Steady. Unfaltering. Obstinate. Contumacy plays a large role in a person despising a certain food.

According to actress Mia Farrow, comedian Woody Allen had the same tunnel vision, about food, about dress—he always wears a plaid shirt and chinos—even about New York City, a locale on which he is hung-up, in the sense that no other place exists. The all-consuming, compulsive, excessive, pathological, controlling, and besetting needs of a fanatic can make of a habit an obsession. Repetition in just about every phase and aspect of life comforts him, gives him assurance, warmth. His main directorial habit—a tropism for sounding intellectual—is glaringly obvious and repeated through all of his films, the sad subconscious need of the non-college graduate, a deep down drive, to prove himself worthy and to show the world that he is intelligent. It is about habit, yes, but also mistrust and suspicion, doubt, misgivings, wariness, even paranoia. The embarrassment, the paranoia, is *in* the repetition.

What is wonderfully ironic here is that repetition, the same meals repeated over and over, is not a comfort but commonly the cause of food aversions. I realize that repetition is a comfort to some people—even a source of growth, perfection, and creativity. "It is by repetition that myths are created," says Witold Gombrowicz. "I knew by heart all the dialogue of James Dean's films. I could watch *Rebel Without a Cause* a hundred times over," said Elvis Presley, contravening my own opinion; for to me it is positively the stupidest movie ever made. Imagine the anti-hero of the movie, a rugged guy about 17 or 18, bursting into tears simply because his caring parents happen quietly to offer him different *advice?* He blubbers, "You are tearing me apart! You say one thing, he says another, and everybody changes back again!" This is a hero? It is comic puerility. (At exactly the same age, in 1774, Wolfgang Amadeus Mozart had already written his *Missa Brevis* [Mass #6], his Serenade No. 4 or "Colloredo;" Symphonies No. 29 and 30; and his amazing *Litaniae Lauretanae*!) From all that I have read, Woody Allen is obsessive—neurotic, compulsive, beset—in his need for the comfort of repetition. I recall reading that when Allen made *What's New Pussycat?* he went to a restaurant in Paris and ate nothing but sole for sixty consecutive nights. To be frank, however, I have always been highly dubious about the many neuroses that Allen habitually expresses about himself—among a slew of anxieties, for example, he claims to fear peanut butter sticking to the roof of his mouth—because his entire career has been built on that twitchy, neurotic overly-confessional "'fraidy cat" image that he has been using for fifty years, a bit completely plagiarized from comedian Bob Hope.

American physicist Richard Feynman, known for his work in the path integral formulation of quantum mechanics and a Nobel Prize winner in 1965, did this with food, as well. He decided, for example, that he would always have chocolate for dessert so as not to waste time considering anything else. Catallactics—the science of exchange in the free-market system—may explain Feynman's mind-set, in that he felt that in selling his food options he was buying the freedom to think about things more important. It was liberating for him, creating a buoyancy. We like to be free of a thing, shut of it entirely. The concept is cleansing. The Jews and Greeks based their histories on liberation, the former from Egypt, the latter from Persia. The most cherished Christian tenet, its pivot-point, is the Resurrection, with bright promise of life eternal for every individual. To go without, on any level, can offer a distinct joy. Inner resolves sharpen. There is a surprising freedom in downward mobility.

We inhabit, insist on, what personally we need—and love. Several experts tend to believe that in the area of exclusive food preferences, autism may actually be involved, just as many think that in related cases—and with excellent supporting evidence—such behavior is connected to creativity. (With his *Autism and Creativity* Michael Fitzgerald has written the definitive book on the subject.) Dr. Oliver Sacks also ate the same thing every day in order to save his brain for other things. Apparently, he ate lots of sardines. He would not eat chicken, however, and thereby hangs a tale, one which I will tell anon.

Stanley Owsley, born Augustus Owsley Stanley III (January 19, 1935—March 13, 2011) and also known as "Bear"—was an early road manager for the Grateful Dead, an LSD pioneer, and an essential and transitional personality in the development of the San Francisco Bay counter-culture. He was the first private individual to manufacture mass quantities of LSD and was the key distributor in the Haight in the early 1960s. He was a case all by himself in the matter of food and oversimplifying food preferences. He essentially ate only steak and eggs for almost 50 years. No veggies, nor milk. Only ultra-low carbohydrates—fewer than 10 per day. He believed that the natural human diet is a completely carnivorous one, our bodies arranged for a strictly non-carbohydrate diet, and that all vegetables—get this—are toxic! He believed that his body aged much slower than those who ate a more "normal" diet. He was convinced that insulin, released by the pancreas when carbohydrates are ingested, is the cause of increasing damage to human tissue, that, for example, diabetes mellitus is caused by the ingestion of carbohydrates. He received radiation therapy for throat cancer in 2004, a disease that he first attributed to passive exposure to cigarette smoke at concerts, but which he later discovered was almost certainly caused by the infection of his tonsils with HP. He credited his low-carbohydrate diet with starving the tumor of glucose, slowing its growth and preventing its spread enough that it could be successfully treated despite its advanced state at diagnosis.

I have noticed in several visits to Switzerland that many Swiss have an aversion to vegetables and instead go in for dairy products, especially cheeses, which seem to be a substitute.

Can it not be accurately said that, generally speaking, vegetables have always pretty much had to play bridesmaid to the bride of meat, "its attendant lord, one that will do to swell a progress, start a scene or two," as T.S. Eliot might say? William Faulkner's earthy character Lena Grove, an *anima* figure in the novel, *Light in August*—the "good unruffled vegetable Lena," as Faulkner refers to her—in her serene composure, a quiet ineluctable force moving her serenely toward her goal, shows an almost a root-vegetable quality. As a woman she is pure nature, not baffled, neither doubting nor questioning the course of action to take, not torn for a moment by doubts or indecision. Serenely eating cheese and crackers and licking warm sardine oil off her fingers, she is fully at peace as she travels. She lives her life in a scrupulous monotony, born of unswerving convictions, and manages to survive by her blessed, her benign, innocence a protective measure, as does a rutabaga, beet, or a simple carrot.

To Faulkner vegetables were elemental. In another context he wrote, "People need trouble—a little frustration to sharpen the spirit, toughen it. Artists do. I don't mean you need to live in a rat hole or gutter, but you have to learn fortitude, endurance. Only vegetables are happy." Vegetables are commonly the "also-ran." When Gertrude Stein wrote, "A vegetable garden in the beginning looks so promising and then after all little by little it grows nothing but vegetables, nothing, nothing but vegetables"—a sybaritic lament that vegetables are nothing but a poor substitute for meat—is there doubt in anybody's mind she was confessing a disdain for vegetables? Stein wrote in *Tender Buttons*, "Please be the beef, please beef, pleasure is not wailing. Please beef, please be carved clear, please be a case of consideration."

Who can forget the old drunk Boggs in Mark Twain's *Adventures of Huckleberry Finn*, "the best naturedest old fool in Arkansaw—never hurt nobody, drunk nor sober"? Twain describes a sad figure:

> He was drunk, and weaving back and forth in his
> saddle. He was over fifty years old and had a very red
> face. Everyone yelled and laughed and swore at him.
> He swore back, and said he'd get to them and kill
> them soon. He said that'd have to wait, though, be-
> cause he'd come to town to kill old Colonel Sherburn.
> He said that his motto was, 'Eat the meat first, then
> finish up with the sides.'

(The original text went, "Meat first, and spoon vittles to top off on," but Twain decided to change it.) It seems especially to be the preferred position among manly men—"hearties"—that vegetables play second fiddle in a meal.

As we know, however, Huckleberry Finn had his own distinctive opinions about food and just about everything else. Curiously, in the entire novel there is not a single mention of a mother being in his life, that central figure who could have schooled him in traditional ways, cooking included, fixing a meal, etc. and so the poor ne'er-do-well who was forced to learn the basic rules of life and living catch-as-catch-can had to rely in his own resources, which of course he was quite happy to do. (What huge losses we come across in literature, as well as in life. David Copperfield never saw his father, who died six months before his David was born.)

One of Huck's many food quirks in that novel, one that seems slightly feral to me, is that the 13-year-old boy dislikes any supper in which—in a finical or overly cultivated way, it seemed to him—every dish was cooked separately, in other words, meat in one pot, potatoes in another, peas in yet another, etc. ("...everything was cooked by itself," as the 13-year-old puts it.) It is surely an indication that the boy was raised in the worst circumstances, in a shack or a kind of dog-trot cabin or even wildly in the woods. (We cannot forget that he much prefers wild life to the Widow Douglas's prayers and cooking, which drove him earlier to "lit out" and to get into his "old rags and my sugar-hogshead again.") As to the Widow's genteel cooking, young Huck far and away prefers to eat what he calls "slumgullion," a watery meat stew composed of thrown-in ingredients, a portmanteau word, first used in 1890, perhaps from *slum* slime + English dialect *gullion* mud, cesspool. (In *Roughing It*, Mark Twain also employs the word to describe "a cheap drink.") "In a barrel of odds and ends," complains Huck, "things get mixed up, and the juice kind of swaps around, and things go better." It is a quaint theory I have never heard of before and can be said to constitute a kind of melting-pot principle, but I believe that any literary scholar would surely be pushing it some if he or she tried to turn this odd preference into anything like a plea by Huck for a democratic principle or an innocent and praiseworthy pluralism.

As to peevish judgments on vegetables, Owsley was nothing compared to the 19th-century eccentric and autodidact Bronson Alcott, teacher, writer, philosopher, reformer, and food crank from Concord, Mass. A friend of Emerson, Thoreau, and Hawthorne, he was an abolitionist, a transcendentalist, and a man who had theories about just about everything, experimenting wherever he could, including all matters of food. According to one item in Alcott's unique dietary creed was that all vegetable that grew above the ground—"aspiring vegetables"—were wholly edible, but that any and all of the wretched vegetables that grew beneath the earth, like potatoes, with no direct benefit of sunlight were be avoided. (The Jains of India, who neither swat flies nor step on ants, do not eat meat but also avoid eating anything that specifically involves uprooting or injuring a plant.) When Nathaniel Hawthorne brought him ears of corn, Alcott was therefore grateful, and he approved of the grapes grown by Ephraim Wales Bull, his next-door neighbor, who in 1843 began the deliberate process of breeding a grape that could thrive in the cold New England climate. By 1849, having planted 22,000 seedlings, Bull had created a large, sweet variety from a native species, and, although by 1853 the grapes were for sale, within several years, competing growers had begun raising their own crops of Concord grapes, purchased from Bull for $5 per vine. Bull therefore saw little profit from the strain after the initial sales.

I love the anecdote—some attribute it (wrongly) to Abraham Lincoln—when a hearty bibulous drinker is offered grapes at dinner, he declines, saying somewhat sardonically, "Thank you. I don't take my wine in pills."

In May 1843, Alcott purchased a large 90-acre farm in Harvard, Mass. He, Abby, his wife, and their four daughters moved to the farm which he optimistically named "Fruitlands," despite the fact that only ten old apple trees could be found on the property. Optimism was Alcott's middle name. Their goal was to regain access to Eden by finding the correct formula(s!) for perfect living, following specific rules governing agriculture, diet, and reproduction. Calling themselves a "consociate family," they agreed to follow a strict vegetarian diet. They initially began to till the land without use of animal labor, but after some difficulty, they relented and allowed cattle to be "enslaved." As to food, they also banned coffee, tea, alcoholic drinks, and even milk—as well as warm bathwater. As Alcott had published earlier, "Our wine is water—flesh, bread—drugs, fruits."

For clothing, the Fruitland group prohibited all leather, because animals were killed for it, as well as cotton, silk, and wool, because they were products of slave labor. Alcott had high expectations but was often away when the community most needed him, as he attempted to recruit more members. The experimental community was never successful, partly because most of the land was not arable. Alcott lamented, "None of us were prepared to actualize practically the ideal life of which we dreamed. So we fell apart." Other than Abby and their daughters, only one other woman joined, one Ann Page. A rumor had it that Page was asked to leave after eating a fish tail with a neighbor. So the experiment failed, and the Alcotts left Fruitlands. Nor was any member of the family happy with that experience. At one point, Abby May threatened that she and their daughters would move elsewhere, leaving Bronson behind. Louisa May Alcott, who later wrote *Little Women*, was only ten years old at the time of their removing to the Harvard farm, but, later, perceptibly writing of the experience in her *Transcendental Wild Oats* (1873), she clarified, "The band of brothers began by spading garden and field; but a few days of it lessened their ardor amazingly."

I met an old lady, no-nonsense owner of a bed and breakfast in the village of Mallaig on the west coast of the Scottish Highlands when I was roaming that region back in the summer of 1966—probably a descendant of the extremely strict and highly literal Covenanters—who told me that she flat-out refused to eat potatoes simply because the Bible did not mention that plant. My question is, did this strict old *cailleach* who lived on the far west coast of the Highlands also refuse to eat tomatoes, peanuts, pineapple, bell or chili peppers, vanilla, chocolate, or even turkey? I ask because none of these foods are mentioned in Holy Scripture either. Thank God for Jesus (pardon the redundancy!) for the only direct mention of chickens in the Bible (Matthew 23:37). (We know Our Lord ate meat—see Matthew 26:7.) There is no reference to chickens in the Old Testament, none at least that can identify our domestic bird. The many references to "fatted fowl" in these older records, in accordance with the text and the history of the other nations, were pigeons, guineas, ducks, geese and swans.

The common phrase, "eat like a bird," meaning little, is also illogical. Many birds eat twice their weight in food each day. A bird requires more food in proportion to its size than does a human baby.

Quirks, quirks, quirks.

Who can explain them or their causes? Composer Igor Stravinsky always insisted on having jam in his tea. W.H. Auden could not conceive (and would not enjoy) a meal without a serving of potatoes. (As we have already mentioned, he never took desserts.) Dame Edith Sitwell gulped double martinis and cold consommés, which she felt helped lessen the discomfort of her curvature of the spine. MGM mogul Louis B. Mayer in his domineering way thought that any grievance or indisposition could be cured by ingesting his mother's chicken soup, a commodity that was dished out in the studio commissary like Lourdes water. Dylan Thomas madly relished bread and milk but with salt in it, according to his wife Caitlin who stated, "He had to have the salt; he thought that it was the cure for everything, and I had to administer it throughout our marriage." Pee-wee Herman's passion for fried chicken is as strong as Wimpy's for hamburgers. Pop singer David Bowie would eat only raw foods. Actress Sarah Miles supposedly drinks a small cup of her own urine every day, a habit that she has been following for more than thirty years with the claim that it keeps her feeling healthy and vigorous. Madonna takes daily vitamin B12 injections, which I suppose is as rare a food quirk as any. Growing up in California, pop singer Katy Perry and her siblings were not allowed to eat the cereal Lucky Charms, because the term "luck" reminded their credulous Pentecostal parents of Lucifer, and they all had to call deviled eggs "angeled eggs."

Gloria Swanson, the American film actress, best known for her role as Norma Desmond, the fading silent film star in *Sunset Boulevard* (1950), became a vegetarian around 1928 and would thereafter eat nothing but steamed vegetables. An early health food advocate, she was known for carting along her own meals to public functions in a paper bag. It was Swanson who advised actor Dirk Benedict about macrobiotic diets when he was battling prostate cancer at a young age. He who had refused conventional therapies heartily credited this kind of diet and healthy eating with his recovery. In 1975 Swanson traveled the United States in order to help to promote the book, *Sugar Blues,* written by her husband, William Dufty.

Taste aversion has been studied in a great many species, leading with humans. Surveys report that most people have acquired at least one taste aversion, if not more. Many have a long list. Aversions are pronounced, are even cultivated, and have persisted a long time. One can imagine the rather long list of foods that the novelist Somerset Maugham detested when he declared, "To eat well in England you should have breakfast three times a day." Some complaints are specific. The prolific writer, James Michener despised the whole idea of breakfast—and, unsparingly, he went so far as to inform his biographer, John P. Hayes, author of the biography, *James Michener* (2009), that he personally thought the word breakfast was "the 'ugliest' word in the English language"—and on most mornings Michener did nothing more than simply pour himself a glass of unsweetened juice. One can only marvel at the specificity of such localized and furiously uncontained discontentment.

Laboratory experiments have shown that taste aversions are acquired similarly across species. Odor may also play an important role in food aversions. An unfortunate early experience. A particularly bad memory. Unsavory associations. A food can become objectionable to a given person simply because of that individual's having observed another's reactions to a certain food, or because he or she may have linked a previously acceptable food with something else considered sickening—"bait shyness"—or it may be that the food itself for some subjective reason or other may have suggested something unspeakable. Suspicious connections are often made. One thing morphs into another. Color can put people off. The simple, unadorned aspect of the thing. We all have private bells that go off in our heads that others simply do not manage to hear. The nap of a food can matter. Texture looms large in the context of food aversions. Mere skin on a chocolate pudding, for example. A lima bean's dry pall. Awful. Crispiness, on the other hand, is a nearly universally loved texture, even across different cultures. Potato chips, crisps, French fries, pretzels.

Texture is subjective. What we see is what we think, wrote Wallace Stevens in a poem of the same name, adding, ironically, "Another thought, the paramount ado...what we think is never what we see." Nevertheless, our drilling thoughts can easily transform what appears before us, like magic, even if it may require that we transplant ourselves to a solipsistic remove. As Percy Shelley writes,

> I love all waste
> And solitary places; where we taste
> The pleasure of believing what we see.

In Margaret Atwood's peculiar novel, *The Edible Woman* (1969), when the protagonist, Marian McAlpin becomes engaged, her food attitudes undergo a major change. In a bizarre preoccupation, she begins endowing food with human qualities that cause her to identify—to empathize—with it, and she soon finds herself rigidly and almost frantically unable to eat, repelled by the situation of metaphorical cannibalism. More than a hungry woman, she becomes a starving one: she is always hungry but cannot eat. Food appears as a displaced desire: she wants it, but cannot enjoy it, because what she really wants is something else.

There are as many reasons for avoiding foods as people avoiding them. Donald Jeffries, author of The Unreals, told me,

> I don't eat steak. I used to enjoy it as a kid (on the rare occasions my family could afford it), but things changed when I became a teenager. I read something about how the old baseball player Jimmie Foxx, had choked to death on a piece of meat, and for some reason it had an impact on me. So I developed this odd fear of choking to death, and steak seemed to me to be the most likely kind of meat to cause one to choke. I've pretty much avoided it since then, which was a financially fortuitous decision, since I still can't afford it.

The Internet is filled with the cranky, insistent confessions of neurotic, overkeen, and beset people and their odd, off-piste takes on food and its consumption. Rueful anecdotes of choking. Obstruction. Retching Near strangulation. Variations, even, of *Vox faucibus haesit*—voice stuck in the throat. One couple admits to using obscene amounts of olive brine in their martinis. Another confessive-obsessive always has to pour milk on her ice cream in order to consume it like cereal or pablum. One girl reveals that she literally cannot eat ice cream without the use of a plastic spoon. Another woman compulsively has to *spoon* mayonnaise out of the jar in order to eat and enjoy it.

Some avowals are boasts. A man swears that he always eats pumpkin pie-filling on his morning toast. Another man acknowledges that he will not—cannot, I believe—eat sandwiches with his left hand. Some people have an obsessive need to remove their watches and rings, to divest themselves of all jewelry, before they can proceed to eat anything. Another compulsive discloses that she fixatedly wraps *nori* around almost everything she eats. We have all heard of those who cannot stand their foods to touch each other on the plate, a phenomenon that surely reverts to childhood. Another divulges that she can ingest nothing green. What does it all reveal—I mean, aside from the fact that we are all different? One thing for sure, human complexity in the matter of food yields no end of surprises. I knew a fellow who once confessed to me that he hated the fact that windshield wipers go right to left—as if, damnably, he were reading Hebrew books! *Flankism*! He was an artist, a neurotic one to be sure, who also lamented the fact that in printmaking, his field, the image as cut, engraved, or etched, on the plate or block is reversed left and right when it is printed!

Surprises, surprises! The word itself amuses me. Who does not remember with melancholy the tacky phrases that in the 1940s–50s were given to meals, invariably casseroles, such as "Crunchy Cauliflower Surprise!" "Mutton Leg Surprise!" "Gratin Dauphinois Surprise!" "Surprise de Maman!" Ominously, we never knew what those surprises were! God knows what sickening, stomach-turning, odious, and obnoxious tidbits could be found in them! It was a wily person who thought up that "surprise" bit. I recall once finding listed on a menu in a small diner in West Virginia the (serious) specialty entry "baked potato *en foil!*"

Names, alone, can revolt us. "There were some things I didn't like because of the way they sounded," wrote George Carlin. "I just didn't like the name of it. Imagine that? I got away with that shit for a year and a half. Don't sound right to me, Ma. Say that again? Uuuuuugh! I don't like that." Many of us have a kind of "Know-Nothing" mind, suspicious of anything! Carlin goes on to say,

> To this day, there are some things I can't eat because I don't like the way they sound. I still cannot eat... yogurt. I can't eat anything with a Y and a G in it. Squash. "You want some squash?" "Fuck NO!" Sounds like somebody sat on dinner, you know? "How about some wheat germ?" "Germ?!" "Horseradish!" Aaaaagh! "Eggplant." "Well, what is it—an egg or a plant? Tell it to make up its mind and come on back." Something I don't like the sound of: succotash. "What'd you call me, you ****? Look out, hey!" "Hey, hey. Hey, be cool. Hey, be cool. It's lima beans on corn, man." You know, something else doesn't sound very right? Head cheese. Uuuuh. I can't even look at the sign. I'll be down near the baloney. You look at it. Then there are some things that sound too funny to eat. Some things are too humorous to swallow. Guacamole. That sounds like something you yell when you're on fire. GUACAMOLE! Or sounds like something you can't remember the name of. "Where's that little... guacamole I had here?" Something else sounds too funny to eat: garbanzo beans. I mean, that's the first four letters of the word 'garbage' in there. "Hey, did you take out the garbanzo beans?" And, of course, the funniest food:

> kumquats. I don't ever bring 'em home anymore. I sit
> there laughing and they go to waste."

Only a rabid, know-nothing, food aversionist like Carlin could find a way of ingeniously explaining the rationale of both wasting food and at the same time finding the act virtuous. He quipped,

> Leftovers make you feel good twice. First, when you
> put it away, you feel thrifty and intelligent: "I'm saving
> food!" Then a month later when blue hair is growing
> out of the ham, and you throw it away, you feel really
> intelligent: "I'm saving my life!"

A student of mine at Yale from Minnesota—our class was having a student lunch together on blankets out on the grassy grounds in the old quadrangle one late spring—told everybody in passing that she swore she would never again eat so much as even a tidbit of mozzarella cheese after an outbreak of salmonella back in her state in 1989. Alert to all sorts of various food-borne diseases, one can legitimately write off a good many products to avoid illness. Phobias can quickly form. It is all there on record. Thyrotoxicosis, a very dangerous thyroid condition, has contaminated ground meat during gullet trimming, a procedure that harvests muscles from the larynx of cattle. Gastroenteritis, another intestinal disease, has been tracked to buttercream frosting from a local bakery when a careless employee scraped frosting from beaters with his unwashed hands. *Salmonella javiana* comes from cantaloupe fields, *E. coli* from hamburger patties pre-cooked at the producer level, *ciguatera*, a toxic poisoning from eating fish that feed off algae reefs in tropical waters. Certain hapless victims find themselves feeling scalded by iced tea and burnt by ice cream!

Speaking of unholy, the late Hubert Humphrey, senior senator from Minnesota (1911–1978) and 38th vice-president of the United States, was known for the "Hubert Humphrey Special." "My favorite sandwich," said the loquacious, over-hearty politician, "is peanut butter, bologna, cheddar cheese, lettuce, and mayonnaise on toasted bread with lots of catsup on the side." In light of this, how could anybody have ever possibly taken this person seriously? (By the way, were you aware that during the 19th-century, tomato catsup was actually sold as *medicine?*)

So many newly discovered consumables, according to the ingenious British wit Frank Muir in his *An Irreverent and Thoroughly Incomplete Social History of Almost Everything,* were, as a matter of fact, first thought of as medicine: tea, potatoes, coffee, chocolate, butter, boiled cabbage (in Egypt), sugar, and gin. "The attitude, presumably," he logically explains, "was that until a new food or drink had been proved harmless, the safest thing to do was to rub a bit of it on, or pour a spoonful of it down, somebody who was ill anyway."

I have repeated myself here on the subject of pork taboos, but taboos on pork are always very firmly held. Seventh-day Adventists consider the meat of pork taboo, as do many Eastern Orthodox groups. Vedic Brahmins, tantrics, and some Buddhist priests abstain from fungi and all vegetables of the onion family (*Alliaceae*), believing that they excite damaging passions. In Yazidism, the eating of lettuce and butter beans is taboo. Mormons, the founding prophet Joseph Smith in particular—never formally banned or prohibited the drinking of coffee. What Smith inveighed against were what he called "hot drinks," which subsequently came to mean coffee and black tea—but not hot chocolate—for those who hypothesized that God, the Cosmic Drinkmaster, meant to discourage such beverages because they contained caffeine, an addictive substance with negative medical effects. For this reason, some Mormons avoid caffeinated beverages like Coca Cola and Pepsi-Cola, although the Church curiously has no official church doctrine discouraging caffeinated soda pop. Strangely enough, drinking *cold* caffeine is harmless for Mormons! Gov. Mitt Romney who ran for US president in 2012 specifically avoided all hot drinks, no matter what they were—no coffee, no tea, not even hot chocolate. (That surely had to be one of your campaign blunders, Mitt! In Gabriel Garcia Márquez's *A Hundred Years of Solitude*, a priest actually levitates powered by hot chocolate!) You can be quite certain that the Mormons were not that selectively particular with their food proscriptions after the grievous, bitter winter of 1848-49, Brigham Young's very first in the bleak Salt Lake Valley, when after a spring frost large voracious crickets destroyed much of that year's harvest, a portion of which was rescued by the arrival of huge flocks of seagulls, and all his people were facing a condition of near starvation. John G. Turner in his biography *Brigham Young* writes, "Rationing allotted each person a half pound of flour per day, and some Mormons resorted to eating the soft, bulbous root of a sego lily bulbs [the sego lily has since become the state of Utah's floral emblem], wolf meat, and dead cattle from owners who refused to sell them."

The Torah (Leviticus 11:13) explicitly states that the eagle, vulture, and osprey are not to be eaten, although I am told that vulture is often sold as chicken in the shish-kebabs—*suya*—of West Africa. A bird now commonly raised for meat in some areas, the ostrich, is also explicitly banned as food in Leviticus 11:16. Fish without fins or scales are forbidden. (Fish without

fins or scales? May one humbly inquire if indeed any such fish exist?) I believe Jews are also prohibited from drinking and chewing at the same time.
Thorny interdictions in Leviticus, qualifying this and that, call to mind those
intricate Henry Jamesian hierarchies of qualification that, tortuous, windy,
meandering, and seemingly endless, inform sentences that often spool out
half a page or even a page long. The eating of camel is allowed in Islam.
Ethiopian Christians, who will not eat pork, like the Jews are not allowed
to eat camel. In Judaism that slow desert animal is considered "unclean"
and is strictly prohibited in Deuteronomy 14:6-7, despite the fact that it is
in fact a cud chewer. While the foot of every camel is split into two toe-like
structures—who can explain taboos?—that Old Testament passage explicitly
states that the camel does not meet the cloven-hoof criterion.

Is it not strange that although grasshoppers and locusts were specifically
recommended to the Israelites in the dietary laws of Leviticus, one of the
books of Moses, modern Jews avoid them?

"When I was about six years old, I started hating cherry Jell-O. There
was no apparent reason for it. I liked cherry Kool-Aid and shaved ice, and I
was fine with other flavors of Jell-O. But the sight or smell of cherry Jell-O
would instantly make me nauseated," writes David Solot, a Ph.D. student in
organizational psychology at Walden University and a person highly fascinated with the psychology of food aversions. He continues to explain,

> My reaction to it was so bad that my parents used
> to tell people I was allergic to it, just to avoid my
> reaction. They even wrote it down under "allergies"
> on a school form. I just couldn't touch it without
> feeling sick. Perhaps you feel the same way about raw
> tomatoes, yogurt, or eggs. If there's a food that makes
> you feel sick on sight, chances are that your brain is
> enacting a behavior that's been passed down for mil-
> lions of years. It's called taste aversion, and it's one of
> the strongest conditioned reactions in humans. Here's
> how taste aversion works: You and your buddies go
> out for a few drinks. You're young and wild and love
> drinks with the strong coconut flavor of Malibu Rum.
> Things get a little out of hand, and you spend part of
> the night praying to the porcelain god. You recov-
> er, and next weekend go out for drinks again. The
> bartender passes you your favorite drink, but this time
> the smell of coconut immediately makes you want to

vomit. You loved Malibu for years, but now, the very
thought of it makes you sick. What you're experiencing is your brain protecting you from being poisoned.

There is nothing surprising here. The force of memory and association
can often play a large role in what we come to dislike. Both fuse in our minds
like copper and zinc. When Charles Dickens had a fatal stroke at Gad's Hill
in 1870, his older son, Charley, rushed from London to find his 57-year-old
father unconscious; as he sat with his sisters waiting to ascertain his father's
fate, the heavy scent of syringa—lilac—floated through the open windows,
and he could never again bear the scent of those flowers. The force of memory and association is powerful, no question. Was not Ralph Waldo Emerson's
odd remark that he felt no more at the death of his first child than he would
in suffering a financial loss solely a question of confronting memory? As to
food, perhaps we have been forced to eat a hated food when we were young,
or perhaps over-ate something that we relished but then later came to abhor
subconsciously. Misperceptions. Excesses. A predomination of—or confusion among—our senses. Sound, for example. ("I can't stand the sound of
someone crunching celery—or apples! Or ice!") Visual disgust—matters of
texture, say. ("Is that skin on chocolate pudding?") Parents forcing a child to
consume something against one's will. Suspicion, even. The result is always
the same *Mai-più*!

David Solot concludes the segment on CNN on the psychology of food
aversions on "Eatocracy," writing,

> As for my cherry Jell-O aversion, I remembered that
> back in kindergarten I was served room temperature
> cherry Jell-O and whipped cream, all swirled together.
> I got sick to my stomach, and that's when I started
> hating it. By thinking about the cause of my reac-
> tion, I was able to teach myself to enjoy cherry Jell-O
> again. But if I put whipped cream on it, I still get a
> little queasy. A million years of evolution is hard to
> overcome!

He adds, "When we were primitive creatures, we weren't sure what was
safe to eat so we tested things out. If you survived the experience, your brain
had to make sure that you never ever ate that same thing again. So, if you ate
something that made you feel ill, your brain decided 'better safe than sorry,'

and conditioned you to feel sick anytime you saw, smelled or even thought about that same food."

Texture, as I say, plays a substantial role in the world of food aversions. Mashed potatoes. Tapioca. The nap of lima beans. A stiff cauliflower. Cabbage leaves. Octopus. Oysters. Rice pudding. The kinds of food that seem to have been pre-chewed by someone else or spit back on the plate. In A.A. Milne's poem, "Rice Pudding," we all know what is plaguing the little girl questioned,

> "And it's lovely rice pudding for dinner again!
> What is the matter with Mary Jane?"

One blogger wrote, "Just seeing plate of mucky potato mess gives me that lump in the throat. I have even gone so far as to build a 'blinder wall' between myself and the person at the next place setting. Oh yeah, and raw onions. I equate the crunchiness with eating cockroaches." Trolling through the Internet one finds no end of food aversions, a person who despises "fluffy foods," like marshmallows or odd toppings; a person who hates just white foods. "I don't have an aversion per se, but I have issues with most white foods," he wrote. "Rice, pasta, white potatoes, marshmallow, whipped cream, most vanilla-flavored foods, all bland, flavorless."

I mention tapioca. Dario de Angeli, chef at Cube Tasting Kitchen in Parktown North, South Africa, hates tapioca. "Tapioca," he cries. "I don't see the point. It's the consistency of the aftermath of bronchitis without the colour!" Fish eyes, cat sick, frogspawn, eyeball pudding—all are slang synonyms for tapioca, which, let me mention in passing, also happens to be, hands down, statistically, the most hated school pudding in Britain. Loathed by the older generation, and largely unknown by the younger, the fact is the dish has all but faded in obscurity.

Cinnamon rates painfully high in the food hate world. So does—for some reason—tequila. Eggs predominate as a much hated food. So do Lima beans. Split-pea soup. Jell-O. Cilantro. Mayonnaise. It is *amazing* how many people hate mayonnaise. Frédéric Mistral, the beloved poet of Provence— *"Quand le Bon Dieu en vient à douter du monde, il se rappelle qu'il a créé la Provence"* ("When the Good Lord begins to doubt the world, he remembers that he created Provence")—scorned mayonnaise as nothing but mere marmalade, compared to the robust virility of aioli. Although I became quite ill after eating green mayonnaise traveling around the upper reaches of Scotland around Thurso and Scrabster—whether it was wine vinegar, the egg yolks, or the parsley in it I can't say—but passing the "Old Man of Hoy" on my way to the Orkney Islands I was tempted to dive off the boat and end it all. I look somewhat askance on mayonnaise today, although I cannot fully say why.

Food haters love to generalize. It is an absolute in the food-hating world. Another one is the living delight sufferers of various foods and drinks have in confessing their odd aversions, in detail, colorfully, with passion and examples out of number. A soldier friend of mine from Iraq will not even look at bottled water. It is a curious fact, by the way, that the taste of water, mere water, which people randomly describe as being sweet, sour, bitter, salty, flat, or even having no taste, often depends on what food has just been eaten. Many people, for example, find that after the experience of eating pineapples, apples, or even grapefruit, water tastes sour or bitter.

George Carlin, who emphatically declared that he wanted his food "dead, not merely unconscious," had many complaints along visual lines of the foods put in front of him growing up and half the time—the way it is with many if not most kids—he did not know why. "When I was a kid I was known as a fussy eater," he has made clear. "'Fussy eater!' That's what they called it in my house. 'He's a fussy eater.' 'Fussy eater' is a euphemism for 'Big pain in the ass.' I would say, 'I don't like that!' 'Why?' They wanted reasons. Well, you don't always have a reason. 'I don't know. I know I don't like it. And I know that if I ate it, I would like it even less. You like it? You eat it!' Then they would try to corner me with logic. 'How do you know you don't like it if you've never even tried it?' 'It came to me in a dream!'" What Carlin finally figured out in the cognitive way our brains insist on informing us, was that, no matter how irrational, certain foods looked weird. He says,

> I began to realize there were some things I didn't like because of the way they looked. That's a little more rational. The family was glad I had arrived at this new plateau. "I don't like that. That don't look right to me. Did you make that, Ma? Is there a picture of it in the cookbook? I bet it don't look like that!" Some things, let's face it, just don't look right, you know? 'Course, there are some people who'll eat anything; I understand that. That's the other end of the spectrum. Some guys will eat anything. Some of those guys in the Air Force. "I'll eat anything! Whaddya got? What is it? Never mind, just gimme some!" "It's rat's *******, Don!" "Well, it sure makes a hell of a fondue!" Not me, folks. I don't eat anything I don't recognize immediately. If I've got to ask questions, ****

it. I pass, you know? I'm not here to make inquiries. I
come here to goddamn eat! Now gimme something I
recognize! Like a carrot! I can trust a carrot.'"

"Certain things don't look right. Y'ever been going down the buffet
line and suddenly, here's a big pile of yellow ****? Something ya ain't never
seen before! "I don't know what it is. I'm not going to ask, either. But I am
going to look at it. 'Cause other people are eating of it!" And I've noticed
the average pile of yellow **** on the buffet has about five ingredients in it.
But they're all yellow. That means four of them gave up. Now then, there
are some things I don't like the looks of, even though I know what they are.
Sliced tomatoes. I just don't care for the way they look. Looks like a little
pink bicycle tire, you know? Well, I don't eat bicycle tires. Why should I eat
a little pink one? The real trouble with tomatoes—sliced tomatoes, especially—is that they don't look like they're finished developing yet. You know,
looks like they're still in the larva stage. There's thousands of seeds in there
and a whole bunch of jelly-looking stuff, man! It's like that stuff at the end an
egg. "Uuuuuuh! Ugh! Get it off my plate! Ugggggh! It's slimy, ugh!" And
I know it's not the end of an egg; it's the beginning of a chicken! Hen ***!
AAAAAAHHH! Oh, I'm fun in the coffee shop."

Perception certainly carries weight in the food aversion department.
Onions may be perceived as slimy and eye-wateringly offensive. Dried foods
like raisins, prunes, or apricots in their involuted way may impress someone—especially youngsters—as rotten. (Apricots, nevertheless, were Henry
VIII's favorite food.) Mushrooms are seen by many as off-puttingly earthy
and subfusc. "People have a real aversion to things that they think of as
fungus or bacteria," explains Sondra Kronberg, MS RN CDN, a nutritionist who treats patients for food phobia as Founder/Nutritional Director
of Eating Disorder Associates Treatment & Referral Centers and Eating
Wellness Programs. "Mushrooms are technically a fungus," she explains, "so
it makes sense that someone would equate it with germs and growths. Maybe
even sub-consciously they think they'll contract a fungus from the food."
Cheese, Kronberg has found, had a *presence* to patients. "It feels like it is
milk gone bad or it's not wholesome for some people." What we like and
dislike, the whys and wherefores of it all, how they are propped up and reinforced—there is an endless subject. Surely obsessive-compulsive traits figure
in the equation. Memory. Secret fears. Parental complications. Had you been
forced to eat something as a child? Surely the root of many phobias in the
final analysis is almost impossible fully to detect.

Food graphics can play a role in what one dislikes—packaging, for example. It figures significantly in what the brilliant and inventive American cartoonist/ illustrator Ben Katchor finds revolting in foods. "A trip to the local supermarket causes me to lose my appetite, for at least 90% of the products on the shelves are repulsive to me," he once confided to me. "It's not only the idea of adulteration through industrialized processes that nauseates me, but rather the graphic quality of the packaging that turns my stomach." A visual man, Katchor offered some examples.

A box of Kellogg's Special K, with its sickeningly extruded, digitally airbrushed 'K' tipped over a bowl of retouched cereal. The cluttered box-front includes a nail-polish offer and a weight-loss challenge. The mendacious and idiotic attempt at evoking old-time goodness, found on a bag of Pepperidge Farm cookies. Campbell's chunky soups in plastic tubs with snap-open tabs reminiscent of a spackling compound. "Mmm, Mmm. Good to Go!" Zippy, sparkling, and digitally-airbrushed images of all kinds. Plastic squeeze-sacks and shrink-wrapped tuna salads. A pearlescent-white plastic wrap on a cylindrical package of cookies. These are the visual expressions of the poisonous industrial food industry.

"How did this section of the graphic design industry fall into the hands of the most inept practitioners preying upon their clueless clients?" asked Katchor with a gimlet eye for the imagistic chaos.

"The idea of attributing anthropomorphic qualities to canned fruits, vegetables and packaged bread stuffs is deeply disturbing—it crosses the boundaries of the animal and vegetable world. The colors, meant to be eye-catching, make me queasy. Mixing literary sensibilities with food handling, through the naming of products, is also an unfortunate aspect of modern food handling. A name, with an unappealing sound and out-of-control connotations beyond the realm of food, applied to an already disgusting product, is unbearable. The types of paper and plastic used in the packaging are equally disturbing. Why are the owners of these food companies unaware of the intimate connection between the visual and the gustatory?"

Katchor went on to talk about other issues. "As a child, it was difficult for me to eat food produced by any woman other than my mother or grandmother. If I could not see the food preparer, as in a restaurant, it didn't matter. The sight and smell of an unfamiliar woman permeated the silverware, plates, and every particle of food. As I mentioned, I can enjoy almost any dish if it's well prepared. I may never crave it, but I can appreciate its preparation."

A few definitions of terms may be in order. Apositia is just a hefty word for the general dislike of food, as is its twin, asitia. Cibophobia, or fear of food, is a relatively complicated phobia that can rapidly spiral into an obsession. People with this phobia are often mistakenly thought to suffer from anorexia nervosa, a dangerous eating disorder. Anorexia is self-starvation, remember, while bulimia is the compulsion to eat and purge. It may be argued that, compared to anorexics, bulimics hate and fear food to a greater degree simply because they feel less in control of it. The main difference is that those with anorexia fear the effects of food on body image, while those with cibophobia are actually afraid of the food itself. A person can suffer from both disorders, which require proper diagnosis. Highly perishable foods such as mayonnaise and milk, common objects of fear, trigger inordinate responses. People with cibophobia sniff foods, suspiciously examine them, are deeply concerned with expiration dates and the "doneness" of foods. All are to some degree eating disorders, with exaggerated or irrational fears. A refusal to like a given food can add up to a refusal to take nourishment and so approach intense and morbid pathologies with feelings of panic, anxiety, guilt, and terror. I am addressing essentially the subject in general. This is a book about punition—not the buttery French shortbread cookies. I am talking about punishment, the pain, penance, punitive measures, and purgative aspects of food hating.

I will quote here in part from what may be the definitive anorexia story, Jane Rogers's grammatical oddity, "Grateful" (*Granta* 52, Winter 1995):

My mother said you must eat your tea. What did you have for school dinner? Did you eat it all? The food smells gross… I despise food! …When I look at the food and I don't want to eat it I think maybe it keeps better faith with the starving people not to eat it anyway. We're all going to side after all. It's more dignified…

The thing about food is, it decays. I used to think about that when she was telling me about waste. Imagine all the buckets of leftovers from all the houses and schools, poured gloop gloop into tankers and driven and ferried at top speed to all the places where people are hungry. When they arrive: disgusting. Disgusting filthy mixed-up stinking muck, not fit to give to pigs, pour it in the sewers. But (I thought). If you eat it, it's the same. May the Lord make us truly grateful. In that warm stomach. All those chewed bits. Disgusting filthy mixed-up stinking muck. Where does it go? It turns into crap.

Disrespecting food is surely a food aversion in itself, and it is perhaps here that its condition may be—and understood—in its most precise and primary sense. Hunter S. Thompson from all reports had filthy eating habits and raced through just about every meal that he ate—sloppily pigging out, in order to dispense with his food, I gather—but it seems the man lived at high speed. "I would feel real trapped in this life if I didn't know I could commit suicide at any time," he confided to his pal, illustrator Ralph Steadman. In his revealing memoir of his life with the reckless Gonzo journalist, *The Joke's Over*, Steadman wrote,

> He was the messiest, most piggish, food lout I have ever dined with. The plates of unfinished room service orders I have seen over the years in four-star hotels were battlefields with mountains of cold melted cheese, torn hamburgers, decimated salads and tomato ketchup—a massacre on a food trolley. They were battlefield exhibits of the carnage he inflicted on all food and convinced me that he wasn't interested so long as something filled a space in his stomach.

And Hunter's breakfast?

> He ordered two pints of orange juice, two large Bloody Marys. A pint of bitter, coffee, a triple Scotch with ice and a vodka and tonic. He ordered an English breakfast: "Bring every condiment in the house." He smothered his plate in an uneatable layer of mustard, pepper and salt and left it largely untouched. As [journalist] Robert [Chalmers] noted: "Breakfast with Hunter is descending into amphetamine psychosis."

No wonder Thompson ate hand-cream—as is verified by Steadman—to help relieve his occasional sore throat!

Such a display is of course more snouting than eating. I have several times seen this crazed disorder, this mad affliction, take place at pot-walloping oyster and scallop festivals on Cape Cod, at feral, feeding-frenzied barbecues, in restaurants with big, obese butterophagus men and bitey women jackal-devouring stacks of pancakes, perspiring, ingesting their food through blue, gasping, asthmatic wheezes, grabbing syrup-pourers with an owner's reach, avariciously feeding on—and *in*—the food as if in dispatching it greedily to make it vanish without even rapacity's taste or delight. (Elias Canetti in his *Crowds & Power* writes, with utter disdain, of "feast crowds.") "Golluping" his food, as P.G. Wodehouse puts it, was only one of his excesses. Hunter Thompson's was a kind of rage that in a sense recapitulated the mad, violent word-play on his every page, the rude, raw hammering of his raucous, ear-splitting prose. "Gonzo. It confounds reason. That's Gonzo, Ralph," Thompson once told Steadman. *Res ipsa loquitur.*

There are many shared aversions in the food department. President William Howard Taft hated eggs. Curiously, the only breakfast dish that Taft would *not* eat was eggs—he could not abide them. I have read that the fussily gay fashion designer, Michael Kors, an only child, not only dislikes eggs but actually cannot stand to be in the same room with someone eating them. CNN's Larry King? "Eggs—I hate the smell of them." General Robert E. Lee for breakfast ate exactly one soft-boiled egg, and for that purpose a chicken always rode in his chuck wagon to provide that daily comestible, which was prepared by one of Lee's orderlies. In the case of less fastidious U. S. Grant, at dawn he always sat down to cucumbers and vinegar and, who knows, maybe a pull of brandy. The egotistical former US Secretary of State, Henry Kissinger has always been fussy about his eggs, never mind food in general; his vibe bespeaks an enormous eater. His breakfast includes a serving of egg whites, dyed yellow to make them only *look* like yolks. Colonel Tom Parker, Elvis's manager, liked his eggs poached but, depressingly enough, *yolkless.* The hockey-voiced TV personality Guy Fieri (born Guy Ferry), food-ie and game-show host, dislikes eggs—at least, whole eggs—as a component of a dish. However, he does admit to using eggs as an ingredient in other dishes.

In the movie *Big Top Pee-wee*, the comic semi-effeminate fictional pro-tagonist created and portrayed by the American comedian Paul Reubens, surreptitiously throws away in disgust an egg-salad sandwich that his former fiancé, the schoolteacher Winnie, offers him, dopily thinking that it was his favorite food, which as a matter of fact is chicken, as Pee-wee explains, and also cheese sandwiches with pickles, which, as he is hungry, he immediately races off to a general store to buy. Actress Whoopi Goldberg, on the Rosie O'Donnell Show on September 29, 1997, swore that she would never eat an egg. Like Hitchcock, the scraggly-voiced comedienne said that she "would eat things with eggs *in* them," but never eggs, as such.

Strangely, although President Taft loathed eggs, he ate virtually every-thing else and for most of his life weighed more than 300 pounds. When offered the Kent Chair of Constitutional Law at Yale, Taft wittily—and self-deprecatingly—replied that it would be inadequate but that "a Sofa of Law" might be more fitting.

F.B.I. director J. Edgar Hoover could be a tyrant about food, accord-ing to insiders. "His favorite breakfast was a poached egg on toast," writes Curt Gentry in *J. Edgar Hoover: The Man and his Secrets.* "If the yolk was broken, he'd send it back to the kitchen. Yet, even when it was perfect, by his standards, he'd have only one bite, then put the dish on the floor for the dog to finish." No one would find such an idling thing peculiar about a given person unless that same subject also phobically insisted that agents following or attending him never step on his shadow and could go into small, manic, hand-waving conniptions whenever he happened to see in his office un-swatted flies. Ultimately, however, no one could ever fully analyze Hoover's mind. The man was so personally guarded and deeply inverted that one might even question whether he knew himself. He had many selves. Which one did he confide in? You have perhaps heard the joke that the best way to keep a secret in Washington, DC, is only to tell one person at a time. Hoover had many choices.

If Hoover craved poached eggs, it was the opposite with stuffy Major-General Sir Masterman Petherick-Soames, expert on horsewhips, who appears in P.G. Wodehouse's *Mr. Mulliner Speaking,* and when his servant says, "Good morning. Will you have a poached egg?" he sputters brusquely, "I will not have a poached egg. Poached egg, indeed! Poached egg, forsooth! Ha! Tchal! Bah!"

I have never resolved to my satisfaction whether the malicious Daniel Quilp with his ghastly smile and maniacal shell-eating in Dickens' *The Old Curiosity Shop* liked eggs or hated them, when shockingly we read of him, "At breakfast...he ate hard eggs, shell and all, and devoured gigantic prawns with the heads and tails on." Only a great foe of reality could let loose in such a way, no?

Novelist Tom Perrotta in a neurotic essay, "The Squeamish American" in the "Eat, Memory" column of the *New York Times* (October 7, 2007) writes, "I am, I'm sorry to say, a very timid eater. The list of ordinary foods I can't bring myself to consume is long and depressing—milk, raw tomatoes, mushrooms, raisins, tofu, all sorts of fruits and a panoply of nutritious vegetables, not to mention everything that swims in the earth's rivers and oceans." He adds, "I'm the kind of person who goes to Maine despite the fact that lobster is widely available." What does that leave him—PB & J sandwiches? I mention Perrotta here simply because far and away one of the man's biggest food phobias, if not his very biggest, is eggs. "Did I mention that eggs are a problem for me?" he asks. He then treats us to the story of one particular occasion in Paris when a friend of his begins to cook up an omelet, just about the very worst thing, one gathers, that could happen to Perrotta. How pronounced is this almost obsessive dislike in him? "I object to them so strenuously that I don't eat eggplant simply because it contains the word 'egg' in its name. I knew I'd be tested in Europe; I just didn't expect it to happen so soon. It seemed ridiculous, somehow, traveling across an

ocean to find myself staring down at such a familiar and daunting nemesis."
The animadversion here is over an omelet, mind you, not a fire-breathing
dragon, not a fierce monster, not the snake-haired Gorgon. According to his
account, Perrotta actually pauses to give the eggs a try. He confesses,

> I tried, I really did. The first bite went down okay—it
> always does. It's the second one that kills me. I want
> to swallow, but the food just sits there moist and un-
> welcome, and I start to panic: Eggs. My Mouth is full
> of eggs. Smiling at Greg [the cook], I reached for my
> napkin and made a big show of wiping my lips. I did
> this after every bite. My first night in Paris, and I spent
> it with half an omelet in my pocket.

May I mention, in conclusion, that the dauntless Perrotta who admits
to being of Italian extraction actually hates pasta, as well? "As a child," he
writes, "I scandalized my Italian grandmother by regularly bringing a can of
Campbell's chicken noodle soup to her house so I wouldn't have to eat any
of the supposedly-delicious-but-somehow-troubling dishes she'd so lovingly
prepared. I remember the wounded looks she used to give me as I slurped
my industrial noodles and broth while everyone else at the table chowed
down on baked ziti and braciola that tasted like the old country." Oh yes,
indeed, there is a wimp factor in food aversions.

In *Remember to Remember* (1947), in which we find descriptions of
Henry Miller's expatriate days in Paris and opinions (and many wild exaggerations) on subjects ranging from oriental philosophy to exotic recipes,
all with an equal hilarity, zest, and erudition—he rarely wrote a page without rearranging the furniture in your head—he asserts, "The Jews are bad
cooks, despite their great concern for food." Miller loved to frivol with fire,
of course, and had no inhibitions about saying anything he damn well wanted. Still, the common perception about *Tropic of Cancer* is that it is a book
about sex, when the fact is it is much more about good grub. He spends as
much time trying to eat something good as to bonk someone pretty, always
devising complicated plans to wangle invitations to dinner every chance he
gets. Food alone may parallel sex as a subject with as many complications.

All of Torah law seems a muddle of proscription and hair-splitting ped-
antry. Orthodox Jews, for example, can eat edible fat but not suet, the hard
fat formed below the calf's diaphragm, around the kidneys. (Goodbye to
British steamed puddings!) They can eat chicken and goats, but not hogs or
shrimp—or camels, rabbits, oysters, eagles, or lions, which are all denomi-

nated "unclean." They can't eat crabs or catfish but can eat tilapia or carp. They can eat beef hearts, tongue, and the pancreas of cattle, but not the sciatic nerve of the hindquarters, which goes back to Jacob wrestling with a mysterious stranger when he was injured in the nerve of his thigh and had to leave the battle with a limp. Excellent cuts of meat, the hindquarters of slaughtered cattle are sold by Jewish meat packers to Gentile meat packers. The Orthodox Jews, strangely enough, are prohibited in their religion from wearing a mixture of linen and wool in clothing, as it is banned by Mosaic law. All the *tsuris*! Hasidic Jews have fur-lined hats or undented round black felt hats. Phylacteries go on the forehead and the left arm. Biblical passages in the *mezuzah* must be written on parchment.

We have discussed the shellfish caveats. Swordfish, however, also presents a problem, because swordfish are all born with fins and scales, but then, since when swordfish mature they lose their scales, what do you do, call up Jerusalem for a fiat? If in a restaurant a knife that is used to cut a tomato was also used to cut up a side of bacon, that same tomato for all kosher Jews is rendered inedible. It is the same thing with wine vinegar. It has always to be prepared with kosher wines—and who can know?—or it is not acceptable and so unusable. Food proscriptions make the faithful fickle, their taboos making all believers face the dilemma of the "curate's egg," finding in something partly bad something partly good. A probing and inventive shyster, snooping about, can find a loophole in *any* law. The Feast of Passover for Ashkenazi Jews, that is, those of European origin, is a "feast without yeast"—they cannot eat rice, corn, beans, peas, or peanuts, or even make matzo, that is, if the water should touch the flour beforehand. So then how is matzoh made legally? There is the catch, for technicalities—outlets, escape clauses—matter, and entire resolutions can turn on a dime. It is legitimate matzoh if the water is added to flour and all hurriedly kneaded into dough that is quickly baked within 18 minutes—not 17, not 19—so that no leavening has time to take place. "When my cousins from the Lakewood (New Jersey) Yeshiva come to visit us," writes Blue Greenburg in her book, *How to Run a Traditional Jewish Household*, "I buy special milk for them, for, unlike me, they will not drink brand-name milk." No rule doesn't have a regal exception, no law not have a twist.

There are fifteen answers to every five questions—every complication is a *Judenplatz*. Blue Greenburg, who is an Orthodox Jew, has disclosed that not once in her life has she ever tasted shrimp, or marshmallows, or dark chocolate mousse. Forget all of those *milchedig* and *fleischedig* caveats. Suffice it to say that many intricate laws alone involve keeping separate bowls, vessels, utensils. Because ceramic dishes and wooden spoons are porous, profanely, they can often transfer the taste of one food to the taste of another. If a frying pan is used to fry a steak and is then used a few hours later to fry an omelet with cheese, a slight taste of that steak might linger. The act alone of eating dairy after meat, or meat after dairy, poses all sorts of problems. I could go on. Save me some time? Read the book of Exodus.

As to that book, by the way, the antediluvian Hebrew proscription, "Thou shalt not seethe a kid [young goat] in his mother's milk" (Exodus 34:26) is actually—believe it or not—one of the real Ten Commandments, which, with so few people aware of it, may make it the king of food aversions. What people erroneously identify, proclaim, repeat, and follow as the "Ten Commandments" are what Moses reported God first told him on Mt. Sinai (cf. Exodus 20:2–17). The words were never written down. Moses re-climbs the mountain, returning to his people with the "tablets of stone," which are not—and never have been—originally called commandments, but smashes them out of anger and discouragement, upon seeing his people worshiping the golden calf. It is only after Moses' third climb that we read in Scripture: "The Lord said to Moses, 'Chisel out two stone tablets like the first ones, and I will write on them the words that were on the first tablets, which you broke.' (Exodus 34:1–28).

There are only true Ten Commandments, words that are rarely read and never recognized and never printed, although it is the actual Decalogue. The first message or version was "spoken" but never entablatured; the second was a "testimony" (and broken) and the third—alone—were engraved.

Passover brisket recipes often call for Coca-Cola to be used in the marinade with dry red wine, honey, ketchup, and oil. But it has to be Passover Coke! This is bottled during this season using cane sugar instead of the usual corn syrup and can be found in most supermarkets. It is distinguished by a yellow rather than red bottle cap. Pepsi makes a similar product, also with a yellow cap. Yellow-cap Kosher Mountain Dew is available year round! The silent semaphore is intriguing to me. I am certain pulp fiction mysteries could revolve around it

Almost all Orthodox Jews will eat only hard cheeses, such as Swiss or Gouda, those that are rabbinically certified. The situation of cheese, among Jews, is invariably complicated because hard cheese usually involves rennet, an enzyme which splits milk into curds and whey. Although rennet can be made from vegetable or microbial sources, most forms are derived from the stomach linings of animals, and therefore could potentially be non-kosher and so prohibited. The law holds that only rennet made from the stomachs of kosher animals, *if* they have been slaughtered according to the laws of kashrut, is kosher. If a kosher animal is not slaughtered according to the *halakha,* the rennet is therefore not kosher. Rennet is not considered a meat product and does not violate the prohibition of mixing meat and dairy.

No wonder so much marginal food has found acceptance in the Jewish world. Real old Jews from Brownsville, NY, at one time virtually an Eastern European *shtetl,* lived on such delicatessen food like derma, marinated herring, stuffed kishke, eye-burning horseradish, chopped liver, salty gravlax, matzoh-ball soup, stuffed sausage, and homemade dill pickles—followed by desperate trips to the drugstore for bottles of Dr. Brown's celery tonic to cure heartburn!

I can imagine movie-going Jews, whether orthodox or not, wincing with horror while watching *A Night at the Opera* (1935), starring the Marx Brothers—all of the brothers having been born Jewish of course—when hearing the order cheeky Driftwood (Groucho), imperiously gives the waiter when dining out with Mrs. Claypool (Margaret Dumont). The surrealistic exchange goes:

> Driftwood: "All right, we'll have breakfast. Waiter!"
> Waiter: "Yes, sir."
> Driftwood: Have you got any—milk-fed chicken?'
> Waiter: "Yes, sir."
> Driftwood: "Well, squeeze the milk out of one and bring me a glass."

"Poets have been mysteriously silent on the subject of cheese," wrote the English writer and philosopher, G.K. Chesterton, I think wistfully, in a wonderful off-beat remark. (Virgil actually does mentions cheese: Tityrus and Galatea are found together in *Eclogue I* in which that significant pair of pastoral names, suggest "cheese" and "milk." I would also single out John Heywood's witty, philosophical poem, "Of Books and Cheese," as another example.) In his essay, "Cheese," from one of his lesser-known books, *Alarms and Discursions,* Chesterton refers to cheese as "the very soul of song" and the eating of it a "holy act." The simple repast of cheese and bread to him could not be surpassed—bread, notice, never *biscuits,* which the very Catholic Chesterton quirkily dismissed as a substitute for bread. "I asked [the waiter who in a hotel once served him biscuits with cheese] if, when he said his prayers, he was so supercilious as to pray for his daily biscuits," wrote Chesterton. "To eat [cheese] off biscuits is like eating it off slates." He insists in his essay, "The Appetite of Earth," that if the moon were made of cheese it would be inhabited!

Although Chesterton did live long enough, until 1936, in fact, to hear T.S. Eliot disquisit on the subject of cheese, his trenchant remark does rather drive home the fact that entire categories of food, whole food groups, have been ignored by writers down through the years. Food offenses, what puts people off, involve entire regions, education, hygienic principles, all sorts of health regimes, no end of biases and/or the vicissitudes by the way one is brought up, including religion, needless to say. Seventh-day Adventists who believe that whatever they eat and drink should "honor and glorify God and preserve the health of the body, mind, and spirit," for example, are limited to a strictly lacto-ovo vegetarian diet, one that allows milk and eggs, but not animal flesh—they have followed this diet for more than 130 years derived from the health recommendations based on a combination of the Biblical principles of the Levitical laws, the emphasis on self-control promoted by the religion itself, and health and hygiene principles that revert back to as far back as the 19th century.

It is common practice not to serve sour foods during Rosh Hashona, while bitter herbs are eaten at the Passover Seder. Novelist Saul Bellow spoke of an individual being born with a "Litvak tongue," that is, having a penchant for sour-tasting foods like pickled herring, sour cream, sauerkraut, boiled tongue, horseradish, foot jelly, vinegar, rye bread, and I guess I would have to add those dry acid phosphated sodas of yore which gave fountain drinks a sour, less fruity quality, and even powered heady alcoholic cocktails like the "Wet Grave" (acid phosphate with bourbon, dry vermouth, claret syrup, and Peychaud Bitters) and the "Cherry Bourbon Phosphate" (bourbon, cherry juice, Jerry Thomas bitters, soda water.) Howard R. Garis, the author, among other books, of the wonderfully whimsical Uncle Wiggily saga—a solid Christian fellow but a man whose simplistic palate and unilateral taste in food favored sweet things and sweet things only—could not bear to eat anything sour, or bitter, whether it be pickles, sauerbraten, or anything like a vinegar-based food.

Countries are criticized in the matter of food offences. Certain countries, then, produce what is mere cack to other fastidious minds. What one country tends to eat, another country will abhor and condemn.

The United States has been for years ridiculed for its insistent appetite for fast food. Mark Twain was expressly dubious about much of the fare found in Europe. Édouard Manet found Spanish food revolting but badly wanted to study the particular paintings in the Prado and so spent two weeks in Madrid without eating anything at all. In Puerto Rico I saw natives happily buying from food-stalls clams that had been sitting in the broiling sun for hours. I personally find utterly inedible the great gouts of white fat that Estonians euphemistically call pork in that strange, de-gastronomized country. Alan Levy in his book, *The Wiesenthal File,* recounts this anecdote about the angry, revengeful Austrian Nazi hunter, the late Simon Wiesenthal: "When asked point-blank whether indeed he did devour a neo-Nazi a day, Simon bitterly snapped with an icy, 'No, I don't eat pork'"—uttering the punch word "*Schweinefleisch*" in German and somehow making the insult more contemptible.

"Let not him that eateth, despise him that eateth not; and he that eateth not, let him not judge him that eateth," St. Paul wrote in Romans 14: 3. "All things indeed are clean: but is evil for that man who eateth with offence." We must therefore not scandalize our brother by eating what he judges to be offensive, nor should he judge us or be scandalized by what we ourselves eat. "For none of us liveth to himself; and no man dieth to himself." Still, how subjective it all is! It has been charged against St. Paul that he was indifferent to the beauties of nature. On their journey from Perga to Antioch in Pisidia, Paul and Barnabas passed Lake Eğridir, which is one of the most beautiful lakes in the world, yet neither make a single comment about it. What does he say about Athens and art, except that it is a city full of idols? The splendid architecture of Ictinus, Callicrates' temple of Nike, the statues of Athena by Phidias left him cold. (There is also very little said regarding natural beauty in the Old Testament, save for the Psalms.) I make this point only because Paul in his earnest exhortations stresses charity and faith regarding people eating but not food *qua* food, its goodness, its quality, or food as an end in itself. He was a man on a much different mission.

David Koresh, born Vernon Howell ("I am the Son of God"), of the Branch Davidians who were incinerated in his compound at Waco, Texas on April 19, 1993, was paranoid about his followers buying and eating French fries at McDonald's. "All of you gluttons," he snapped at his flock. "If I relax the rules even for a minute, you'll all go out there and eat Babylonian food." One of his followers who later fled the group, Marc Breault, wrote *Inside the Cult* in which he explained the odd food regimen set down by the religious fanatic was a way of arbitrarily controlling his pursuivants. White bread was banned at all times. Brown bread was allowed, as long as it was not combined with corn, avocados, or potatoes. Oranges could never be eaten with raisins. Fruit could not be eaten with vegetables, unless the vegetable was freshly cooked corn or the fruits were lemons, pineapples or avocados. Chocolate ice cream was also on his banned-food list, as were chocolates in general. Koresh believed that the chemistry of an apple changed when cooked. He said nothing about mint chocolate chip ice cream, two pints of which the Oklahoma

City Federal Building bomber Timothy McVeigh requested as the only item for his last meal on June 11, 2001.

On the subject of chocolate, composer Ned Rorem records in his *The Nantucket Diary* for Oct. 11. 1984 that he once commented that few subjects inspired unanimous reaction, confidently adding, "One can safely say that everyone likes Mozart." To which John Simon replied, "I loathe Mozart." Rorem then recalled how surprised he was to hear someone once say, "I really hate Vermont." "Well, at least there's one unanimity," he goes on to say. We accept that one person can hate another as much, say, as Thomas Babington Macauley hated Charles II or Voltaire hated Louis XV, but for someone to hate an object? Strange. Everybody loves chocolate, right? "I can't abide chocolate," said Maggie Paley. It is of course hard to believe that anyone does not like chocolate. But Yoko Ono never liked it. On the final day of her husband, John Lennon's life—the afternoon of December 8, 1980—just before they were about to leave for the Record Plant recording studio, where they wanted to tinker with Yoko Ono's single, "Walking on Thin Ice," she had bought him a chocolate bar, which, uneaten, he had set down on a table at the Dakota, the hotel where they lived. Coming back to the Dakota from the studio, he was shot that night at 10:49 p.m. by Mark David Chapman for whom, earlier, at 5 p.m., he had autographed an album. Mitchell Fink writes in *The Last Days of Dead Celebrities*, "Yoko didn't notice the chocolate she had brought in for her husband until days after his murder. It was still sitting on the table where he had left it. 'I didn't like chocolate at all,' [Yoko] said. "But after John's passing, I thought, 'Should I throw it away? No, that would be wasteful.' So I said to myself, 'Well, okay, I'm going to eat the chocolate, you know. And I did.'"

I would like to believe it was a Hershey Bar. To this day, the Hershey company is controlled by a charitable trust, and its profits fund the best-funded home for orphans and children from broken homes in the world, a spread of 3200 acres, and a refuge to more than 1000 girls and boys of all races and religions.

Robert Benchley in his short essay "The Menace of Buttered Toast" inveighs with highly peculiar fussiness against this common breakfast staple and asserts that Americans "eat too much of it." He not only complains that it too easily becomes soggy but that it should never be dunked in coffee or buttered by children. British author and wit Sidney Smith, a founder of the *Edinburgh Review*, at a banquet table noticed that a lady seated next to him rejected an offer of gravy. "Madam," declared Smith, smiling, "I have been looking for a person who disliked gravy all my life. Let us swear eternal friendship." A noted clerihew assures us that even a great scientist could be like-minded:

> "Sir Humphrey Davy
> Abominated gravy.
> He lived in the odium
> Of having discovered sodium."

There is a pickiness in us, you see, that can abhor even simple toast and gravy. After all, as the precocious and politically conscious 8-year-old vegetarian Lisa Simpson on TV's The Simpsons tries to explain to Homer—she was converted by Buddhism—"Gravy is actually the juice of animals!"

You can feel the fussy, sometimes dainty, occasionally squeamish, but almost always self-upsettlingly exacting and meticulous emotions of the food aversionist—a past master in his localized food grudges of reversing the direction of inference—as he or she presents himself. As the language philosopher Roy Sorensen, described as "the hyper-hip coolster of paradoxical mind-melt," passionately and uniquely exhorts the readers of his probing books, "Think contrapositively, raze hopes, succeed your successor, learn how to conform to confound, and order absence in the absence of order." *Order absence in the absence of order!* There is the fundamental trope, I would suggest, of all complaining forces here, their judgement pivoting on the converse, the inverse, and counterexample. It is, in a very real sense, "organized akrasia." Akrasia in Greek describes in an individual the state of acting against his better judgement. (St. Paul offers the threat of temptation through *akrasia* as a reason for a husband and wife not to deprive each other of sex—1 Corinthians 7:5) From the calm perspective of a "normal" person, a creature rejecting a food is acting against his better judgement. Perception is by definion always skewed. As the Japanese say, *Fugu-jiru kuu baka, kuwanu baka.* "The person who eats globefish soup is a fool; so is he who does not."

Still, perception can buoy a person up. T-bone steak has had a special status in South Africa ever since Archbishop Desmond Tutu, as part of a stalwart campaign to bring his countrymen together around the *braai*, pointed out that the shape of that steak mimics the very shape of Africa itself! There the steak is often served with "monkey gland sauce," a traditional sweet and hot condiment that greatly enhances barbecued meat, chicken, pork, or even Boerewors (farmer's sausage).

Belief determines our judgment always. After her death on July 13, 1954 when the cremated ashes of Frida Kahlo, *la heroína del dolor*, "the heroine of pain," went sliding back out onto a funeral cart from the opening oven doors, a distraught Diego Rivera, some witnesses claim, scooped up a handful and ate them.

4.

M-I-N-C-E, OR VEGETARIAN CRANKS

I LOVE THE SUBJECT of food aversions. So much is said about a person in what he or she—almost always passionately—crucially seeks to avoid in foods or shuns in taste. What could be more informative of a personality? A confession of disgust or disapproval concavely indicates a person's character as much as any one thing arbitrarily rejected or repudiated—a bad blind date, a disliked color, a hated song. What is not revealed by the thorn, the thrust, of any passionately expressed distaste? "Eating is the most intimate and at the same time the most public of biological functions," wrote Guy Davenport in his astute essay, "The Anthology of Table Manners," and it is always a point of view. The sharpness, the force, of strong opinion regarding apositia—aversion to selected foods—irradiates like no other force. Arguably, the frankness alone is refreshing. Clearly foods are rejected because they are seen as either dangerous, inappropriate, disgusting, or distasteful. What are the origins of such feelings? A bad memory? Overdosing? Lack of taste? Some oblique superstition? An overheated imagination? Allergies? Conditioned reflex? Some kind of bait shyness? Odors? Shape? The nap or texture of a food? Sensory qualities? Some unholy association?

Einstein famously hated beets. So does President Barack Obama who has also gone on public record as disliking asparagus, salt and vinegar potato chips, mayonnaise, and soft drinks (he prefers water). Strangely enough, he dislikes ice cream. Disliking beets must be a phobia that infects the entire Obama household. On the "Tonight Show" on January 31, 2012, guest Michelle Obama also confessed, "I don't like beets"—but as a test to try to reform her, host Jay Leno offered her a plate of beets, which she gamely sampled. The moronic, face-pulling jester/rapist Bill Cosby once quipped, "Nobody ever says, 'Can I have your beets?'" (It is an indication of the hypocritical soullessness of Secretary of State Hillary Clinton, an animatronic Chuck E. Cheese, that, when recently asked which foods she disliked, she typically equivocated to be politically correct with the mealy-mouthed remark that *all foods* are basically good! It remains one of the major reasons I would never vote for her—lack of honesty, political pusillanimity, a plastic soul.) The surly psychopath Joe Christmas, served them by Joanna Burden in Faulkner's *Light in August*, grumps, "I hate beets, anyhow."

"Beets made me gag," writes 80-year-old Gael Greene, former food critic of *New York* magazine ("Some people buy emeralds. Some people have children. I am good to my mouth"), looking back, in her sybaritic, tasteless, and for the most part trivially obscene memoir, *Insatiable: Tales from a Life of Delicious Excess*, lists her specific food aversions. "I didn't like to eat olives. I hadn't yet fallen in love with oysters. The worship of caviar escaped me. I had acquired an unDetroiterly [sic] passion for sweetbreads but had not mastered brains."

The dislike of caviar, the iconographic luxury food, is not limited to Greene alone. Actress Naomi Watts hates it. So does Jennifer Aniston, who won't eat it. ("Nope, you can't acquire that taste no matter how many people say that. It's just a shitty taste," the actress told Yahoo.) And remember in the film *High Society*, the lilting lyric in "Who Wants to be A Millionaire?"?

> Who wants a fancy foreign car? I don't
> Who wants to tire of caviar?
> Who wants a marble swimming pool too? I don't
> And I don't 'cause all I want is you.

Elsa Maxwell, the fat Iowa-born professional hostess, impresario—she invented the "scavenger hunt"—gossip columnist, etiquette authority, and press agent, lived a few floors below the Cole Porters at the Waldorf Towers in Manhattan. In his book on Cole Porter, *Red, Hot, and Rich*, David Grafton tells how on one Christmas Eve the Porters graciously sent down to Maxwell, an early if un-telegenic supporter and a voracious eater, a pound of very expensive caviar but were then "chagrined" to hear her say on television not long afterward, "I do hate caviar." Cole supposedly muttered to his wife, "Next time we'll give it to the birds."

"The beet is the most intense of vegetables. The radish, admittedly, is more feverish, but the fire of the radish is a cold fire, the fire of discontent not of passion. Tomatoes are lusty enough, yet there runs through tomatoes an undercurrent of frivolity. Beets are deadly serious," wrote Tom Robbins in *Jitterbug Perfume*, his 1980 novel in which a disquisition on the personalities of vegetables, among other preoccupations just as odd, prominently figures. Robbins gives as much attention to radishes as does Pliny in his *Natural*

History, where the tireless and knowing ancient insists that this vegetable not only counteracts poisons but reduces the size of the spleen and is good for the liver and pains in the loins, adding that any and all lethargic people can benefit by eating them at their hottest, with an implied hint, I gather, that they be slipped into a given dish the way a farmer short-mucks manure by adding straw to it in order to make it more friable when used as fertilizer!

"Slavic peoples get their physical characteristics from potatoes, their smoldering inquietude from radishes, their seriousness from beets." Let me here interject that Robbins has also written that a sense of humor—I gather that his vegetable portraits are meant to be funny—is "superior to any religion so far devised," an opinion rooted in the fact that both of his grandparents were Southern Baptist preachers. When coming across that sort of remark, as occasionally one does, I put it down to a person, or at least a know-it-all, having read too much Mark Twain or Abraham Lincoln, if one may hazard such an unorthodox thought without giving offense:

> The beet is the melancholy vegetable, the one most
> willing to suffer. You can't squeeze blood out of a
> turnip...The beet is the murderer returned to the
> scene of the crime. The beet is what happens when the
> cherry finishes with the carrot. The beet is the ancient
> ancestor of the autumn moon, bearded, buried, all but
> fossilized; the dark green sails of the grounded moon-
> boat stitched with veins of primordial plasma; the kite
> string that once connected the moon to the Earth
> now a muddy whisker drilling desperately for rubies.
> The beet was Rasputin the monk's favorite vegetable.
> You could see it in his eyes.

All of this seems to confirm that there is, at best, a fund of things to ignore in any given author.

I have read that Tom Robbins' culinary biography lists him as being a yearly enthusiastic participant in Seattle's Spam-carving competition, even serving as judge. He apparently also hosts an annual mayonnaise-tasting contest, with as many as 20 international varieties, at his home in La Conner, Washington. This might be the perfect place to cite one of his lines from *Still Life with Woodpecker*: "We are our own dragons as well as our own heroes, and we have to rescue ourselves from ourselves." I guess you could say that food phobias as expressed in their subjective, unpredictable ways may be said to explain everything, except anything.

Robbins also sees a powerful life metaphor in the lowly beet, writing in homiletic fashion in *Jitterbug Perfume*:

> At birth we are red-faced, round, intense, pure. The
> crimson fire of universal consciousness burns in us.
> Gradually, however, we are devoured by our parents,
> gulped by schools, chewed up by peers, swallowed by
> social institutions, wolfed by bad habits, and gnawed
> by age; and by that time we have been digested, cow
> style, in those six stomachs, we emerge a single dis-
> gusting shade of brown. The lesson of the beet, then,
> is this: hold on to your divine blush, your innate rosy
> magic, or end up brown. Once you're brown, you'll
> find that you're blue. As blue as indigo. And you
> know what that means. Indigo. Indigoing. Indigone.

The common march of men, run-of-the-mill types, are not generally big for food aversions. By and large, most of us are breezily accepting and fairly uncritical. Even Superman was a Methodist—well, at least we can say that Clark Kent grew up attending the local Methodist church. Clark also liked football games, peanut-butter-and-jelly sandwiches, the Metropolis Monarchs and the Metropolis Sharks—respectively his favorite baseball team and football team—and, like any honest, open-hearted Midwestern lad, the smell of Kansas in springtime.

But aren't sharp opinions the only ones worth having? One will never know the food aversions of people like Hillary Clinton simply because dullness has no voice. As I say, Einstein hated beets. But he was a man with a brain who unequivocally stated what he hated. He also could not stand *Scrabble*, was bored by science fiction, could not spell (and did not care that he could not), smoked like a chimney, equated monogamy with monotony, never bothered to comb his hair, had a very bad memory, when offered the position refused to become President of Israel, amicably referred to his pet violin as "Lina," loved women, and thoroughly enjoyed any opportunity to go walking about on bare feet. "When I was young," he explained, "I found out that the big toe always ends up making a hole in the sock. So I stopped wearing socks." He was also a fanatical slob, refused to "dress properly"—for anyone—and did not drink, saying jokingly of Prohibition, "So it's all the same to me." He was always an outspoken critic of laws being passed which could not be enforced.

A hatred or contempt for a food involves affirmation, declaration, disclosure, even release. I am convinced that there is a note of conscience-clearing
in it. It might also be asserted that it is a flag of self-hood. It is, needless to
say, flat refusal. The person holding the view, needless to say, can become ferociously obdurate. Anger and contumely can play a distinct part, for certain.
Food-hating and spite go as suitably together as a wet rose and maidenhair
fern. The odium, the rancor of a contrarian for whatever object—whether
born of an allergy, a natural abomination, or a developing antagonism—
may come to serve as much a device for him as a way of seeing, as an acute
form of perspective, an elemental and indemnifying perception that, as a
kind of defiance, becomes a means of interpreting himself. We often use the
language of food to describe something we hate. D.H. Lawrence comes to
mind: "Curse the blasted, jelly-boned swines, the slimy, the belly-wriggling
invertebrates, the miserable sodding rotters, the flaming sods, the sniveling,
dribbling, dithering palsied pulse-less lot that make up England today." It is
amusing to see a hated food take on the dimensions of any bat-winged menace. We are talking here about *individualistes invétereés*.

What is hated is not merely avoided, it is banished. "He who would do
good to another, must do it in minute particulars," wrote the poet William
Blake. "General good is the plea of the scoundrel, hypocrite, and flatterer."
By the same token, fixing on an abhorrent food—isolating it—makes much
the same point. I believe a good deal of narcissism is also entailed in ferreting
out a food to dislike. Something of Occam's Razor is involved in dismissing
a food, in that by asserting, "Entities must not be multiplied unnecessarily,"
the *lex parsimoniae* is invoked by way of the principle of parsimony to draw
the simplest conclusion—conomy, or succinctness, used in logic and prob-
lem-solving always has it that, among competing hypotheses, the one that
makes the fewest assumptions should be selected. "I despise lima beans. I
thus simplify my menu by excluding lima beans. Listen to me!"

Food aversions tend to last—endure, persist, and remain—the way deep
grudges do and are basically of the "kiss-tomorrow-good-bye" ilk, for the
hated object can often be seen as a threat to one's existence and in the extreme may be aligned to something that nightly burns a hole in the sleep of
the victim. I am inclined to believe from all that I have read that almost all
conversions, *détentes*, transmutations, sea changes, and truces are also rather
rare. It is a heno-diabolistic affair. Is it tautological to say that what is desa-
cralized will never again be worshiped?

There adheres a certain snobbery in hating a food. It gives face. Height.
A food aversion is frequently held—cherished—by the affected as a *permis de
sejour* to the differentiating and the discerning. Unpredictable, emphatic, it is

as unique as the shape of your head, your nose, your footprint, your sense of humor (or lack of one). It may be expressed as a joke or a jollity, but also as a snipe pressed through a cold dissatisfaction in a such a structural way that it delights in marking it for eviction. As Gerard Manley Hopkins writes in his poem, "No Worst, There Is None,"

> O, the mind, mind has mountains, cliffs of fall
> Frightful, sheer, no-man-fathomed.

Who is wounded can boast of having feelings, acute perception, sensibility. As the line in the wistful song, "Try to Remember" from *The Fantasticks* goes, "Without a hurt, the heart is hollow." The sharper a gourmand's expressed "disappointment" over a meal, the more astute, attentive, and insightful I suspect he would have you find him. Is he not advertising he is discriminate? Selective? An individual with a sharpened consciousness, judgment, thought, viewpoint? Curmudgeons thrive on what they disdain, preen in their crankiness, are literally defined by what might be called opinion-as-correction, and any food aversion they express, viewed as a safety call, they would defend with the slanting proverb spoken by Cassius in Shakespeare's *Julius Caesar*, "Why, he that cuts off life, cuts off so many years of fearing death."

At the same time, one is inevitably led to ask whether it is a discerning mind, assertively fixing on a food to hate, or merely a fearful, suspicious one. "The nature of consciousness simultaneously is to be what it is not and not to be what it is," as Jean-Paul Sartre put it in *Being and Nothingness*, implying (for our argument) that a well-balanced individual shows an objectivity not found in a food crank. *Zhongyong*, the central theme of Confucian thought, is balance found in disinterestedness, what Ezra Pound called "The Unwobbling Pivot."

Actor Rock Hudson disliked Jell-O. Novelist George Simenon hated Chinese food. So does Japanese novelist Haruki Murakami who cannot even stand "to face a bowl of noodles," according to his wife, Yoko. Patricia Highsmith detested kidneys. So does Daisy Martinez of the Food Network Show, "Viva Daisy." "I have to say that kidneys are my personal Kryptonite. When I made them in culinary school, I had to taste them—after having cooked them—in front of my chef instructor, and I broke out into a cold sweat! They didn't even taste bad, but I was so dead set against them that I was ill for two days afterwards!" Norman Mailer once told me that he harbored a huge dislike of curry. "But don't print that," he laughed and hastened to add, "I will lose all my readers in India." The late Christopher Hitchens disliked biscotti and, amazingly, sought out the chance to say so, a foodstuff that in the eating he thought more trouble than it was worth. "I cannot bear corned beef hash or prunes, even today," wrote novelist James Baldwin two years before he died. When he was a small boy, home-relief workers in Harlem used to deliver cans of hash to him and the large, eleven-member Baldwin family, including his mother and step-father, and although they were all sucking-stone poor and never had enough to eat growing up, the novelist for the rest of his life could never bring himself even to look at these foods, hating and avoiding them the way that bone-picking pianist Glenn Gould quirkily avoided Liszt, Schumann, and Chopin.

I am told that CBS's Katie Couric hates pumpkin pie and virtually any food that has to do with pumpkins, which recalls for me Hans Christian Andersen's fairy tale, "What Happened in the Pie Country," when a long-suffering Princess, who is having a birthday dinner, tries to please all of her guests by graciously offering each of them a piece of pie. The little Prince loftily says, "I can't eat lemon meringue pie. My favorite flavor is orange." Wanting to oblige the Prince, she proceeds to have an orange pie made. When she then offers orange pie to the Butcher's Boy, he flatly refuses it and grumps, "I eat only beef pie." She patiently goes out of her way to have a beef pie made for him. But the Apple Woman's child refuses in turn to eat the beef pie and declares, "I eat nothing but apple pie." The Princess is hurt and bewildered. Pondering her dilemma, the High Chief Pastry Chef ingeniously settles the problem by acting on five magic words that suddenly come to him: "Made Instant Needed Curious Enchanting!"—words that begin with the letters M-I-N-C-E—and devising a mixture of all of their favorite pies creates (drum roll) mince pie!

I have touched on the subject of Chinese food. President Nixon, a culinary primitive, went in for odd food combinations and had a low-brow taste for, among other horrors, low-fat cottage cheese doused with ketchup. In 1972, he visited China in order to open up better relations. On February 21st of that year with a phalanx of television cameras aimed at the center table in Beijing's Great Hall of the People, he and his wife, Pat, sat ready for dinner, with the President's usually glum face—Nick Tosches in his book, *Country,* memorably refers to the devious and corrupt 37th President of the United States as a "large wet cow liver of a human"—incongruously having been brightened, hyperbole here, with pancake makeup, while his zombie of a wife's stiff hard old-gold bouffant glowed in the auditorium's bright light. When their host, Premier Zhou Enlai, unfolded his napkin onto his lap and picked up his—a signal that the banquet was to begin—Nixon clumsily fitted his chopsticks into his hand, plucked a morsel of appetizer from one of the plates, gazed at it quizzically for a moment, put it into his mouth and began to chew, while millions of people around the world watched him eat Chinese food. It was clear that he did not like it, and he later admitted as much. He was served chicken. I began to wonder if that meal, or any meal served to that man, had been superstitiously vetted by his handlers, whether he knew how important cuisine was to the Chinese people, or whether this sad, soulless poop-stick had any understanding at all how food in that ancient society constituted communication itself. One wonders how much of their cuisine Nixon had ever had eaten. Consecotaleophobia, a fear of chopsticks, might have been his problem. A notorious klutz—ineptness in all things mechanical is what prompted aides to install for him that voice-activated recording system that did not require the poor soul to push an on-off button—he may have dreaded poking his eyes out or of spilling food or of bungling such a simple action.

There is an actual Chinese food language. "No conclusive or important business can be transacted, no firm contacts made, no importance marked or asserted, without the sharing of food," we read in E.N. Anderson's *Food in Chinese Culture*,

> The expense, status value, quality, and setting of the
> food communicated more about the critical social dy-
> namics of the situation than language can; much that
> is hard to verbalize, and more that would be impolite
> to verbalize, is communicated by this channel. Such
> use of food is worldwide, as every anthropologist
> knows; but no culture has developed it more than the
> Chinese.

I have pointed out how Chinese hate having chicken represent their cuisine. *Kung pao* chicken is the most culturally divisive dish of China, according to many international cooks. To explain the conundrum, prominent Shanghai chefs were asked to chime into the debate—at their own peril, I gather—including, as CNN notes, "experts Wang Lishi from Shanghai, manager of King Kong Eatery, the home of legendary *kung pao* chicken soup noodles; notable chef Anthony Zhao, cuisine consultant at Ultimate Food Concept and *kung pao* chicken connoisseur; and Corrado Michelazzo, Michelin-star Italian chef at Va Bene Xintiandi, a connoisseur of food who thoroughly enjoys Chinese food." (Do you remember the ethnic joke that the 1970s talk-show host, Dick Cavett, also claimed was the most stolen? "Chinese-German food is wonderful. The only problem is, an hour later you're hungry for power.") According to Anthony Zhao, almost comically, "Chicken in China tastes too much like poultry for us." *Indeed!* "I have to import chicken from Japan for anybody to eat it." It is that starchy, syrupy sauce that Americans use in sweet-and-sour dishes that puts off the Chinese. Dishes like *kung pao* chicken are far too saucy and too intense as they stand. They also badly need a rice accompaniment to be successful. No Chinese would ever eat the dish by itself.

Common among young Chinese people is the deep suspicion that restaurants invariably use intense sauce—yes, such as is used in *kung pao* chicken—as a means to cover the bland taste of old meat. There is a deeper and perhaps more interesting answer to the *kung pao* dilemma. *Kung pao* chicken is a dish that stirs memories and feelings among Chinese that are not always positive. Zhao explains that when the first restaurants opened their doors after that country's economic reforms, they all served simple dishes like *kung pao* chicken. "At the time, chicken was rare and pork was the common staple, so we regarded *kung pao* chicken as special," says Zhao. "But now, eating chicken is the norm, and people's tastes are evolving toward more complicated and sophisticated dishes." According to Zhao, *kung pao* chicken is a symbol of poorer times, at least to many Chinese. Today's proud Chinese are eager to shake off the remnants of their indigent—and embarrassing past.

I know many people who simply dislike the taste—and deleterious effects—of MSG. The FDA (US Food and Drug Administration) has not yet required the separate listing of MSG content on food labels. You may find it, however, or at least its close chemical cousins on the labels of soups and snack foods, hiding behind a variety of aliases, including Kombu extract, Glutavene, Aji-no-moto (on Japanese products), and hydrolyzed vegetable protein, which is plant protein that has been broken down into its constituent amino acids, including glutamic acid.

Another word on the matter of chicken. Rev. Sylvester Graham, the famous American dietary reformer/crank and advocate of vegetarianism, temperance, and anti-masturbation, ascribed cholera to both chicken pies and "excessive lewdness." (He also believed that ketchup and mustard led to insanity and eating meat of any kind to sinful excesses.) It was this slightly over-feverish and God-drenched moonbat who in 1829 invented graham bread, the recipe for which—it was made from unsifted flour and was free from chemical additives such as alum and chlorine—first appeared in *The New Hydropathic Cookbook* in 1855. The use of additives by bakeries was a common practice during the Industrial Revolution. It was done to make bread whiter in color, which made it seem cleaner and commercially appealing. The much darker wheat bread at the time was held to be the fare of country rubes. Refined bread was a status symbol of the middle class because of the "purity and refinement" of its color, with the added selling point that it was purchased, rather than home made.

It was Graham's unswerving belief, however, that firm bread made of coarsely ground whole-wheat flour was more nutritious and healthy than white bread. For this devoted Presbyterian minister, anything stimulating was considered debilitating and possibly immoral. Stimulants for him included not only alcohol, but meat, a warm bath, and sweets. It was during the cholera epidemic of 1832 that he began lecturing widely in public on the subjects of diet and sex, diet and alcohol, diet and illness, and especially on the disease cholera. It would not be known until the 1880s, of course, that cholera was spread by contaminated water, so that the bland diet Graham muscularly recommended—virtually anything that smacked of delight was proscribed, most especially chicken pies—was adopted by many followers. Ralph Waldo Emerson referred to Graham as the "poet of bran bread and pumpkins."

At the Hartford Female Seminary, which she founded in 1823, the American educator Catherine Beecher, older sister of novelist Harriet Beecher Stowe and just as formidable a personage, was a devoted advocate of both Graham flour and the Graham diet. (Younger Harriet picked up the gauntlet of this subject, writing in *Uncle Tom's Cabin* about commercial bread as being "so light that [the loaves] seem to have neither weight nor substance, but with no more sweetness or taste than so much cotton wool.") A passionate experimenter of new and various theories with her girls, the older Beecher concentrated particularly on their health and nutrition and not only weighed all of their food before they ate it but viewed the habit of snacking a distinct vice, writing, "When a tempting article is presented, every person should exercise sufficient self-denial to wait till the proper time for eating arrives." She believed gratifying the palate was a vice. A vigorous anti-suffragist, Beecher felt that women could best influence society as mothers and teachers, and he was convinced that men and women had been placed on this earth for entirely separate reasons, fully accepting the view that it was best that women avoid politics and instead teach their male children to be free thinkers and moral learners which would shape their own political ideas.

This link tenderly identifying women with delicacy strikes me as comic when I recall, in vivid contrast, several stories written by fiber-tough Dorothy L. Sayers, in one of which an insane murderer gleefully turns his victim into an art-deco settee after electroplating the body and in another where there is a search in the wilds of Scotland for the remnants of an old gentleman's stomach!

By the way, if anyone printed the name of this renowned English crime novelist or so much as referred to her without using her cherished middle initial—Sayers, among other things, had difficulty at first in accepting a love-interest in detective stories—she would flip out and have a complete meltdown.

Such is feminine sensibility!

The Battle Creek Sanitarium, which opened on September 5, 1866 as the "Western Health Reform Institute," followed health principles advocated by the Seventh-Day Adventist Church. In 1876, John Harvey Kellogg became superintendent, and his brother, W.K. Kellogg, worked as the bookkeeper of this sanitarium and health spa in the town of Battle Creek, Michigan.. Among the treatments offered at the sanitarium/hospital for various ailments were hot and cold water baths, hydro-therapy with water enemas, electric-current therapy, light therapy using both sunlight and artificial lamps, and a regimen of exercise and massage. No "wellness" treatment went unused or unexamined. It seems that anything cold as Uranus or squirted into your bum or involving some sort of duck-dunking is an evangelical delight.

Patients underwent yogurt enemas, electrical stimulation, cold-air cures, diets consisting of nothing but table grapes (10 to 14 pounds of them a day!) and all sorts of vigorous regimens to stimulate both the body and the mind, with no end of inventive therapies—hydrotherapy, phototherapy, thermotherapy, electrotherapy, and mechanotherapy. Among physiologic tonics used there were douches, sitz baths, "cold mitten frictions," salt glows, towel rubs, wet sheet rubs, wet and dry packings, compresses, and lots and lots of baths taken in all sorts of ways, which included of course full baths as well as an assortment of other kinds, Nauheim baths, electro-hydric baths, shallow and neutral baths, and head dips. There were hot and cold applications that were used to produce "profound reflex effects", including vasodilation and vasoconstriction.

Among the more prominent patients at Battle Creek, were such committed munchers of grain as Mary Todd Lincoln, Amelia Earhart, Warren G. Harding, Johnny Weissmuller, Henry Ford, Sojourner Truth, explorer Richard Halliburton, and, perhaps most notably, cereal pioneer and one-time real-estate mogul, the zippy former farm-implement inventor, C.W. Post himself, a fellow who, having become a fanatical zealot on the subject of the chemistry of digestion, energetically went on to found the highly successful Postum Cereal Company, which also manufactured the still-available-to-day "cereal beverage"—a coffee substitute—Postum.

A dynamic but jittery and impulsive American "go-getter" and self-made millionaire—he was fiercely anti-labor—Post once actually tried to produce rainfall by simultaneously detonating 150 sticks of dynamite hoisted by twenty kites into the arid blue above his Texas ranch. On May 9, 1914, badly despondent over his ongoing stomach issues, a depressed Post ingeniously killed himself in his bed using a rifle, by dexterously pulling the trigger with his big toe.

Both Kellogg brothers were earnest Seventh-Day Adventists, a fundamentalist church emphasizing strict Biblical literalism and clean living, and their religious beliefs had a huge influence on many of their "treatments." The Adventists strongly believed in maintaining the purity of the "body's temple", and forbade the use of caffeine, alcohol and nicotine. They were also strict vegetarians. Talk about food aversions! The Kelloggs came to hate proteins—mainly meat—which they blamed for releasing toxins in our gut and were responsible for *all* our ill health. Cranks can be very scary. Voltaire, despite his sense of the rational, believed that intelligent men should regard infirmity as debasement, and in his novel *Erewhon* (1872) Samuel Butler held it up as a crime, making the preservation of good health a moral obligation.

Dr. John Kellogg, however, took the Adventist faith in the purity of the body to an even further extreme. He was firmly convinced that sex itself was impure and harmful—and most especially the "solitary vice", the "self-pollution" of masturbation, also called "self-abuse." Kellogg had married, but theirs was what is often referred to as a "white marriage." Supposedly the two of them never consummated the union; he and his wife had separate bedrooms, and they adopted all of their children. Kellogg became famous for books of his condemning sex, promoting celibacy, and for luridly describing the evil effects of "onanism", which included everything from epilepsy to violent mood swings to dementia. "Neither plague, nor war, nor small-pox," thundered the reformer in one of his anti-sex books, "have produced results so disastrous to humanity as the pernicious habit of onanism. Such a victim dies literally by his own hand." Among Kellogg's "treatments" proposed to cure masturbation were piercing the foreskin with silver wires to prevent erections and even using carbolic acid to burn the clitoris so it wouldn't be touched! But another part of his anti-sex and anti-masturbation "treatment" came from his traditional Adventist reliance on vegetarianism.

Corn flakes cereal, which is a staple on breakfast tables all over the world, today is marketed as a healthy part of a balanced breakfast. Amazingly enough, the product was originally invented by a fanatically religious doctor as a way to stop people from masturbating. Kellogg had long convinced himself that eating meats and spicy foods increased the desire for sex, and forbade any of them at his sanitarium. Instead, he prescribed a bland tasteless diet containing mostly whole grains and nuts. In this, he was following the earlier lead of Presbyterian religious fanatic Sylvester Graham, who had invented the whole-wheat graham cracker as part of a diet that would reduce people's sexual desire and stop them from both copulating and masturbating. Kellogg now attempted to make his own anti-sex food, by mixing corn meal and oatmeal into dough, adding nuts, and baking them into biscuits, which were then crumbled into pieces. He called it *"granula."* Unfortunately for Kellogg, that name was already being used by another health food fanatic with a similar product, and he threatened to sue—so Kellogg changed the name of his concoction to "granola." The earnest Kellogg encouraged a low-fat, low-protein diet with a major emphasis on whole grains, fiber-rich foods, and most importantly, nuts.

An all-grain diet became, at the turn-of-the-century, something of a fixation and in the morning, at least for many highly driven, energetic entrepreneurs and drum-beaters (or vegetarian cranks, take your pick) an answer to the then standard fried salt-pork and mush people ate at breakfast. ("My favorite breakfast is side pork, herring, and heavy rye bread; sad to say, however, good pickled herring is generally unavailable," writes the non-conformist writer—and bloviating gourmand—Jim Harrison, a novelist who confesses to missing the days of Kit Carson and Jim Bridger.) Apetizo, Orange Meat, Monk's Brew, Malta-Vita, H-O Oats, Puffed Rice and Puffed Wheat, Shredded Wheat Biscuits ("Shot from Guns"), Elijah's Manna Post Toasties, Egg-O-See ("Warm it in a Pan before Serving"), and a bunch of other vigorously-named breakfast foods like Force, Vim, Mighty Man, Strengtho—this was the brain-food (and risibly memorable comic-strip name) of that proponent of physical culture, Bernarr Macfadden—were only some of the yummy-in-the-tummy boxed offerings of granulated wheat, corn, oats, and bran to be put on the table many years ago.

Hearty Bernarr Macfadden of Mill Spring, Missouri—born Bernard Adolphus McFadden—changed both his first and last names to give them a greater appearance of strength, for it was his conviction that "Bernarr" sounded like the roar of a lion, and that "Macfadden" was a far more masculine spelling of his real name. He was not your average, run-of-the-mill joe blow. Macfadden was married four times, had eight kids, buried his money in several secret places in steel boxes in the ground, once made an unsuccessful attempt to found a religion, "Cosmotarianism," a faith-cum-cult that was based on physical culture, claiming that his regimen would enable him to reach the age of 150, and was a passionate advocate not only of fasting but of racism, as well—he held that, because fasting was a practice of self-denial, and passingly difficult, only civilized white men should choose to embrace it.

I wonder how many types or varieties of food aversion have their roots in racism. Many Southern whites still abhor the idea of eating watermelon by hand, fearing black stereotype. I know a sensitive young black woman who turns a gimlet eye on the idea of eating fried chicken. While he was in elementary school, a white teacher warned one of young Langston Hughes' white classmates against eating licorice, for fear that he would end up looking like Langston.

In 1931, during the "Great Depression," a Bernarr Macfadden Penny Restaurant opened at 511 Third Avenue in Manhattan. It offered cracked wheat, Scotch oatmeal, lima bean soup, green pea soup, soaked prunes, seeded raisins, whole wheat bread, butter, raisin coffee, and cereal coffee. Food was sold at low prices and was provided twenty-four hours daily when demand warranted. It was Macfadden's hope to feed the needy and the unemployed. Several others opened as part of a chain where in the words of the pulp-fiction writer Frank Gruber in *The Pulp Jungle*, "you could dine sumptuously for around nine cents per meal. A hamburger steak made of meat-flavored sawdust cost four cents, a good, hard roll was a penny, coffee, two cents (made from dishwater with a dash of chicory), and dessert, two cents. You ate the meal standing up, which was good for your digestion. The food was very filling."

Henry Wadsworth Longfellow would not agree. His noble Indian hero, Hiawatha, who in that famous epic poem in trochaic tetrameter, *The Song of Hiawatha* (1855), undergoes a 7-day fast, finds strength as he wrestles nightly for three days with the symbolic dream-visitor named Mondamin (the corn-spirit) which results in the death of his opponent. His mother Nokomis weeps for her son, "fearing lest his strength should fail him, / Lest his fasting should be fatal," but soon comes to see that the fast, like those of Elijah, Jesus, and Gandhi, paradoxically brings him not only moral strength but a strange power he might otherwise not have had. It may legitimately be asked however if it is biased (racist?) that the poem didactically closes with the approach of a birch canoe to Hiawatha's village bearing "the Priest of Prayer, the Pale-face," the "Black-Robe chief" bringing the word of Jesus Christ, whom Hiawatha welcomes joyously, accepting the Christian message? When Hiawatha bids farewell to Nokomis, the warriors, and the young men, he exhorts them, "But my guests I leave behind me/ Listen to their words of wisdom,/ Listen to the truth they tell you."

Fasting as a spiritual activity, never mind as healthful experience—cleansing our bodies of murderous salts, sugars, grease, and oils—is, like any act of willing abstinence, I suppose, hardly a popular pastime in the United States. It is a calumny to describe fasting as "doing nothing, intelligently," as someone once said. Fasting in a dedicated heart is about humility. It is also healthy. The unavoidable fact is, all of our most common and disabling diseases, including heart disease, asthma, diabetes, arthritis, hypertension, and certain auto-immune conditions are the direct result of glut, surfeit, and surplus, desperate over-eating, in short. They are diseases of excess, not deficiency, of overindulgence and cramming, not lack or dearth. We poor humans are not meant to be bulging with lipid-heavy, hormonally inert, intra-abdominal fat on our stomachs, backs, thighs, necks, cheeks, or bums. Our bodies are designed to be wiry spare, tough, lean, sinewy, or any hypernym you wish to add.

Albert Speer, he of the *Spandau: The Secret Diaries*, who was often given scrimp meals during his long incarceration, especially on the days when hostile Russian guards were in charge, asserts that the sparser the food that he ate, the better it was for him intellectually. He spent 20 years in prison. He wrote, "The monastic orders certainly knew the connection between deprivation and stimulation of the mind." He died of natural causes in 1981, age 76, on a visit to London.

Does not the simple subject of fasting engender—provoke—some of the world's individual free spirits if not greatest misfits and eccentrics? Arnold Ehret was a German health nut, fruitarian, and author of several books on diet, detoxification, fasting, longevity, naturopathy, and vitalism. A friend of mine in college once passed on to me one of his booklets entitled *Ehret's Mucusless Diet*, and I well remember my amusement upon reading the opening sentence: "Every disease, no matter what name it is known by Medical Science, is CONSTIPATION." It was the term Ehret used for any clogging or blockage of the body's internal passages. He claimed to have discovered that the human body is an "air-gas engine" that is powered exclusively by oxygen and that a diet of what he dubbed 'mucusless' foods—the optimum food for human consumption and the key to peak health—fruits, starchless vegetables, and edible green leaves ("herbs"). Ehret maintained human health was determined by the state of the "milieu interior," a term and principle espoused earlier by Louis Pasteur.

Mucus was his *bête noire*. Ehret claimed that pus-and mucus-forming foods were the cause of all human disease, that "*schleimlose*" (slime-free) foods were the key to human health, and that "fasting" (simply eating less) is nature's omnipotent method of cleansing the body from the effects of wrong and too much eating. A Roman Catholic, Ehret also wrote a book about Jesus and in letter to the Pope advanced a theory based on his unswerving belief that Jesus did not die on the cross but rather had been taken down alive and actually revived with herbs and ointments! Ehret believed his proposed diet led to absolute communion with God.

J.H. Kellogg, himself a Seventh Day Adventist, hated animal protein, which he believed promoted masturbation and the proliferation of toxic bacteria in the colon. He was a grain-monger. American health enthusiasts had a great muscular faith in grains. A passionate co-religionist of his, so to speak, was the inimitable Horace Fletcher who earned the nickname "The Great Masticator," by arguing that food should be chewed thirty-two times—or about 100 times per minute—before being swallowed. He declared, "Nature will castigate those who don't masticate." He made elaborate justifications for his claim. He believed chewing reduced one's protein intake. He insisted that *liquids* should be chewed, as well, in order to be properly mixed with saliva! It was Fletcher's argument that the act of mastication increased the amount of strength a person could have while at the same time actually decreasing the amount of food that he consumed. He promised that "Fletcherizing," as the act of chewing came be known, would turn "a pitiable glutton into an intelligent epicurean." A few decades after Fletcher's demise, in 1919, 32 chews became 28. "Now eat your breakfast and chew each mouthful 28 times. Not 20, mind you, or 26, but 28 times," says dapper Mr. Lynn Belvedere (Clifton Webb)—he purports to despise children—to the three young rambunctious boys he is hired to babysit in Walter Lang's film, *Sitting Pretty* (1948)

Advancing all sorts of theories, Fletcher advised against eating before being "Good and Hungry" or while angry or sad. He and his supporters vigorously advocated a low-protein diet as a means to health and well-being. He evinced a special interest in the nature of human excreta. It was his belief that the only true indication of one's nutrition was evidenced by one's excreta, and he advocated teaching children to examine their excreta as a means for disease prevention. If one was in good health and always maintained a proper nutrition, then his excreta, or (ahem) digestive "ash," as Fletcher called it, should be entirely "inoffensive." By inoffensive, Fletcher meant that there was no stench and no evidence of bacterial decomposition, an assertion he makes in spite of the fact that feces is 30% bacteria.

In 1904, Henry James adopted and continued the practice of chewing his food down to a pulp in the interests of reducing his fat and lessening his bouts of gastritis and constipation. He would later blame "Fletcherizing" for half-starving him to death and from bringing on onsets of terrible depression. He followed the regimen for six years. It resulted in symptoms of what the medical experts in his time called "anorexia hysteria," an abhorrence of or an aversion to food, symptomatic of certain mental afflictions. It was his brother William, physician and philosopher, who had sent Henry a copy of Fletcher's early treatise on dietary management, *The New Glutton or Epicure* (1903) with certain passages solicitously marked for Henry to read. I am convinced that the great novelist's attempt to regulate his eating was not only to lose weight but to get control of other aspects of his productive life. But it led nowhere and he only developed a "hatred for the whole act & business of eating." Henry's nervous breakdown in 1910 included a marked increase of a strange and highly persistent stomach crisis and dark bouts of melancholy, although it seems that part of his illness was caused by the fact that the *New York Edition* of his works was selling poorly, that, and his carefully nuanced love for young Hendrik C. Andersen, a 27-year-old Norwegian sculptor whom he met in Rome in 1899 when he was 56 ("I repeat, almost to indiscretion, that I could live with you. Meanwhile I can only try to live without you") as leading nowhere.

As I have said, the main thrust of Rev. Sylvester Graham's teaching was to curb lust and put a stop to sexual shenanigans. For him, an unhealthy diet stimulated excessive sexual desire, which irritated the body and caused disease. He shared with Kellogg an abhorrence of masturbation, which in his mind was not only a catalyst for blindness but stood as the very definition of lack of control and excess. He was also inspired, if I may use the term loosely, by the muscular Christianity of the temperance movement, and he preached loudly and repeatedly that a vegetarian diet was a cure for alcoholism, as well a solution against the unholy drives of sexual urges and carnal temptation. While alcohol had useful medicinal qualities, he admitted, it should never be abused by social drinking. While this minister developed a significant following known as "Grahamites," he was often ridiculed by the media and the public for his unwavering zealotry. According to newspaper records, many women fainted at his lectures when he aired opinions both on sexual relations and the wearing of corsets. Never mind self-abuse, however, these zealots were not big for the pleasures of eating qua eating. They were, in a sense, the Princes of Food Aversions. John Kellogg famously grizzled, "The decline of a nation commences when gourmandizing begins."

One may here pose the question, does vegetarianism seem the natural state of mankind? How elemental is it? The question, an ethical one—a subject that has exercised philosophers for millennia—goes as far back as the ancient Greeks, indeed, back to Adam himself, if, that is, we willingly credit the author of *Paradise Lost* as being correct in his poetic assumptions.

Frankenstein's Monster was a vegetarian. He eats only fruits, acorns, and berries, but never hunks of meat. ("My food is not that of man," soliloquizes the Creature—he is also referred to by words such as "monster," "demon," "devil," "fiend," "wretch," and "it"—"I do not destroy the lamb and the kid to glut my appetite; acorns and berries afford me sufficient nourishment.") The Creature's instinctual vegetarianism confirms not only his rude and basic innocence, his benevolence, but conveys as well many of the same political, social, and ethical attitudes articulated by Mary Shelley's contemporaries, a group whom the astute critic Carol J. Adams in her book, *The Sexual Politics of Meat: A Feminist-Vegetarian Critical Theory*, refers to as "Romantic vegetarians." To Shelley's group, killing animals was murder, "brutalizing those who undertook it and those who benefited from it." Adams explains,

> They argued that once meat eating had redefined
> humanity's moral relationship with animals, the flood-
> gates of immorality were opened, and what resulted
> was the immoral, degenerate world in which they and
> their contemporaries lived. Joseph Ritson thought that
> human slavery might be traced to meat eating while
> Percy Shelley suggested that a vegetarian populace
> would never have "lent their brutal suffrage to the
> proscription-list of Robespierre."

All sorts of positive attributions have been given to vegetarians. George Bernard Shaw, an early, passionate bicyclist and a bold one—his biographer, Michael Holroyd, describes him as often rashly raising his feet to the handlebars and tobogganing down steep places— claimed, after one dreadful cycle crash, that anyone *but a vegetarian* would have been killed.

In *Paradise Lost*, John Milton describes Eve preparing "For dinner savoury fruits, of taste to please/ True appetite." (Book Five) A zealot named John Frank Newton (1770-1827), a radical thinker and vegetarian, in his day not only raised issues about the ethical treatment of animals but in my opinion took his cue from Milton's great epic in the process of writing a truly seminal book called, *The Return to Nature, or a defence of vegetable regimen* (1811), a tract on vegetarianism that has influenced entire generations.

During one reading of *Frankenstein*, Mary Shelley referred to her Creature as "Adam," alluding obviously to the first man in a Paradise—one that he questions regarding his role, indeed his very being—as in her epigraph:

> Did I request thee, Maker, from my clay
> To mould Me man? Did I solicit thee
> From darkness to promote me?"
> (*Paradise Lost*, X. 743-45]

It was in Newton's book that he promoted a new diet, consisting entirely of plant foods and distilled water. It was possibly from Newton's book that the poet Percy Shelley, as well as his wife, Mary—the author of *Frankenstein; or The Modern Prometheus* (1818)—while in Dublin, had adopted the vegetable diet Newton advocated, or possibly from reading original Greek and Roman writers, or both. Shelley soon became a regular visitor to the Newtons' household in London. It was in the pages of Newton's *Return to Nature* that he offered the unique theory that the two symbolic trees in the Garden of Eden represented "the two kinds of foods which Adam and Eve had before them in Paradise, viz. the vegetables and the animals." The consequence of having eaten from the wrong tree brought the very death our first parents had been warned would befall them. The penalty was not immediate death, however, but rather the premature death of disease caused by eating the wrong foods, i.e., meat.

Imagine how horrified Rev. Sylvester Graham would have been with the American novelist F. Scott Fitzgerald. Much of his life, Fitzgerald suffered from an over-secretion of insulin, which resulted in a seriously low blood-sugar level. To compensate for this, Fitzgerald turned away from regular coffee, almost aversion-wise, and began to drink it heavily-sweetened. He developed an inordinate lust for Coca-Cola and fudge, as well. All of it gave him a serious craving for alcohol, and he became a very heavy drinker for the rest of his life. The strange thing is that all the while he turned away from food, the ultimate food aversion. He also loved the pleasures of sex, especially during his hey-day, during the Jazz Age and the so-called Roaring Twenties when he was a national celebrity, the darling of decadence.

English novelist, biographer, and journalist Nancy Mitford expressly hated Coca-Cola. It represented definitive America to her. "I hate everything that has to do with American civilization," Mitford told Art Buchwald who quoted her in one of his early books, *More Caviar*, "your plastics, your skyscrapers, TV, refrigerators, psychoanalysts, and Coca-Cola," to which she added atom bombs, GIs, and American women's fashion ("almost the worst feature of America"). Buchwald fake-naively asked her, "What American do you dislike the most?" She never hesitated for a moment. "Abraham Lincoln," replied Mitford, bitterly. "I detest Abraham Lincoln." She went on to declare, "When I read the book *The Day Lincoln Was Shot* I was so afraid he would go to the wrong theater. What was the name of that beautiful man who shot him?" "John Wilkes Booth," said Buchwald. Mitford says, "Yes. I liked him very much." So much for those passionistas who dislike Coca-Cola.

I have to admit that I also find rabid Coca-Cola drinkers frightening, a passionate group that includes the late Christine Onassis who as a dedicated lifetime addict of the beverage (an expert, she could tell by mere sip of it in which country that particular drink had been bottled), along with Jimmy Durante (who also would never eat candy unless it was cold), Charlize Theron, the Beatles, Taylor Swift, and FDR. When 30-year-old Natasha Harris of Invercargill, New Zealand, died of a heart attack on February 25, 2010, her family suspected that the cause of her death was linked to her extreme fondness for Coca-Cola. Drinking as much as 10 litres (2.5 gallons) a day left the mother of eight with myriad health problems, including rotten teeth, cardiac arrhythmia, and a full-blown addiction. Mexico is the top country for per capita consumption of Coca-Cola, with a 56% growth over the last 10 years and 145% growth over last 20 years. Around the world, 100 million gallons of Coca-Cola are drunk every day.

An individual drinking one 20-ounce bottle of Coca-Cola is consuming 65 grams of sugar (2.43 ounces)—the bottle has more sugar than a large Cinnabon! "Just a spoonful of sugar makes the medicine go down," my ass!

There is a memorable scene in John Steinbeck's *The Wayward Bus* that gave Coca-Cola executives anxiety. At one point in the novel at a bus-stop lunchroom at Breed's store, the smarmily ardent Ernest Horton, a traveling salesman, attracted to her legs, says to the blonde, Camille Oaks, "Now, let's have a couple of cups of coffee." He pauses and adds, "You rather have a Coke?'

"No. Coffee. Cokes make me fat."...
"Got any coke?" another character asks.
"No," says the proprietor. "Few bottles of Pepsi-Cola.
Haven't had any coke for a month. It's the same stuff.
You can't tell them apart."

Consider this. In a brief exchange, the Coca-Cola brand—in an exchange of almost comic ineptitude—is not only (a) ignorantly pluralized but (b) referred to in lower-case, while at the same time, along with all sorts of trademark violations and no brand loyalty to Coca-Cola, its rival Pepsi-Cola is mentioned (correctly), added to which is the blasphemy that both tastes the same!

It is a serious matter, coffee, and to those who drink it the *summum bonum*. (After oil, coffee is the second largest item of international commerce in the world.) Writer Jack Dunphy, Truman Capote's partner, once said that, in all of their years together, he and Capote, *un pensée sauvage*, had only one serious argument—over Jack's favorite coffee, Medaglia d'Oro. "Oh, I was such a nuisance about it," recalled Dunphy. "I had to have it." Gioia Diliberto in a *People* magazine article (Oct. 15, 1984, vol. 22, no. 16) explains, "At the time both men were living in Connecticut, and Capote spent the entire day going from shop to shop in search of the elusive brand. When he came home without it, Dunphy snapped, 'What! You couldn't get it?' For Capote that was much too much. 'Truman was so angry,' Dunphy later recalled, "I think he threw some books at me." Capote had a great many pet peeves and long list of major hates, among which included the act of sightseeing; Miami ("an empty, heat-heavy atrocity"); Bob Dylan; Joyce Carol Oates ("A joke monster who ought to be beheaded in a public auditorium or in Shea stadium or in a field with hundreds of thousands watching"); Hollywood ("Better Death in Venice than life in Hollywood"); the entire state of California ("It's a scientific fact that if you stay in California you lose one point of your IQ every year"); the Guggenheim Grant committee ("boneheads"); Rudolf Nureyev; book critics; and all academicians—except victimized Newton Arvin, a professor and close personal friend. He was never a truly fussy eater, although, liking the best, he cultivated a few favorite foods which included hamburgers, pasta and potato salad. Truman liked to eat early. One thing he disliked was soy, which has been called by some a "gay" food. James Rutz, chairman of Megashift Ministries and founder-chairman of Open Church Ministries—is the author of *Megashift: Igniting Spiritual Power*—boldly oraculated in 2006 that soy, which contains substantial amounts of estrogens, is making kids gay. He writes, "Estrogens are female hormones. If you're a woman, you're flooding your system with a substance it can't handle in surplus. If you're a man, you're suppressing your masculinity and stimulating your 'female side,' physically and mentally." Rutz rants,

> Soy is feminizing, and commonly leads to a decrease in the size of the penis, sexual confusion and homosexuality. That's why most of the medical (not socio-spiritual) blame for today's rise in homosexuality must fall upon the rise in soy formula and other soy products. (Most babies are bottle-fed during some part of their infancy, and one-fourth of them are getting soy milk!) Homosexuals often argue that their homosexuality is inborn because 'I can't remember a time when I wasn't homosexual.' No, homosexuality is always deviant. But now many of them can truthfully say that they can't remember a time when excess estrogen wasn't influencing them.

It may be worth mentioning in this context that the small, toothless, ubiquitous, odiferous, Bohemian 1940s vagrant of Greenwich Village, little Joe Gould, a.k.a. "Professor Sea Gull," who supposedly spent much of his life writing and rewriting "An Oral History of Our Time," a compilation of strange if original opinions on food, false teeth, the zipper as a sign of the decay of civilization, insanity, Indian languages, etc., asserted in one of his blotted notebooks—he always carried them around with him everywhere—that the typewriter had an emasculating effect on literature. He wrote, "William Shakespeare didn't sit around pecking on a dirty, damned, ninety-five dollar doohickey, and Joe Gould doesn't either."

Among some of the more verifiable truths of Shakespeare, whose temperament we can discern by reading: he did not like lawyers, loved to invent words, was fascinated by butchery, had a strong affection for his father, deeply experienced the agonies of jealousy, disdained the name Richard, and, among other things—for our purposes—preferred drinking to eating.

While Abraham Lincoln loved the taste of coffee—back in his day, when soldiers in the field drank ersatz coffee made of everything from chicory to roasted dry brown bread crusts, rye grain soaked in rum, acorns, barley, beans, beets, bran, chestnuts, corn meal, cotton seeds, dandelion, okra seeds, sweet potatoes, peas, rice, dried peas, peanuts, persimmons, sorghum molasses, sugar cane seeds, and even watermelon seeds and wheat berries parched, dried, browned or roasted, anything for a hot drink infusion (they often preferred to chew on whole beans while they marched)—one could never be certain what was being served under the designation "coffee," even in some of the better hotels. One time a hotel waiter brought over to Lincoln the drink that he had he ordered. After tasting it and finding it less than perfect, however, never mind unidentifiable, Old Abe said to the waiter, no doubt with a wink, "If this is coffee, please bring me some tea. But if this is tea, please bring me some coffee."

Maybe the President should have ordered fruit juice—but then again he did. Are you aware that, botanically, coffee *is* actually fruit juice?

Henry David Thoreau, austere, shunned every single beverage except water and particularly reviled coffee—and tea. Always something of a puritan, he wrote, "Think of dashing the hopes of a morning with a cup of warm coffee, or of an evening with a dish of tea! Ah, how low I fall when I am tempted by them." Journalist Kathryn Schulz in her excoriatingly dismissive essay of Thoreau, "Pond Scum" (*The New Yorker*, Oct. 19, 2015), regards the Concord philosopher as a peevish, obstinate, hypocritical, cruel, and contradictory skinflint, writing,

I cannot idolize anyone who opposes coffee (especially if the objection is that it erodes great civilizations; had the man not heard of the Enlightenment?), but Thoreau never met an appetite too innocuous to denounce. He condemned those who gathered cranberries for jam ("So butchers rake the tongues of bison out of the prairie grass") and regarded salt as "that grossest of groceries"; if he did without it, he boasted, he could also drink less water. He advised his readers to eat just one meal a day, partly to avoid having to earn additional money for food but also because the act of eating bordered, for him, on an ethical transgression. "The fruits eaten temperately need not make us ashamed of our appetites," he wrote, as if our appetites were otherwise disgraceful. No slouch at public shaming, Thoreau did his part to sustain that irrational equation, so robust in America, between eating habits and moral worth.

Food was bad, drink was bad, even shelter was suspect, and Thoreau advised keeping it to a minimum. "I used to see a large box by the railroad," he wrote in *Walden*, "six feet long by three wide, in which the laborers locked up their tools at night": drill a few air holes, he argued, and one of these would make a fine home. ("I am far from jesting," he added, unnecessarily. Thoreau regarded humor as he regarded salt, and did without.)

Charles William Eliot of Harvard (1834-1926) who served as the university's president for 40 years, was very prudish, very correct, and throughout life remained a true Boston Brahmin. During his long tenure, Eliot opposed college football as a lout's game and tried unsuccessfully to abolish it. In 1905, *The New York Times* reported that the venerable president had called it "a fight whose strategy and ethics are those of war," that violation of rules cannot be prevented, that "the weaker man is considered the legitimate prey of the stronger" and that "no sport is wholesome in which ungenerous or mean acts which easily escape detection contribute to victory." Eliot, for whom rowing and tennis were the only truly clean sports, also made public objections to other contact sports like baseball, basketball, and hockey. Fair play was everything to him, as it was at the time to any true gentleman. "Well, this year I'm told the team did well because one pitcher had a fine curve ball. I understand that a curve ball is thrown with a deliberate attempt to deceive," he declared. "Surely this is not an ability we should want to foster at Harvard." Cheating was guile, underhandedness foul, and what we call "gamesmanship" utterly beneath contempt. Rectitude was all. Later in life, a contrite Eliot expressed to a faculty colleague that he "used beer and wine when in company, but with no ardor, and neither ever produced any perceptible effect on me." It is a sign of his staid and upright nature that he regarded *coffee* as something of an opiate; he once startled a suddenly surprised acquaintance by wistfully confessing after a social event over which he had presided, "I made a bad speech last night. I was garrulous and diffuse. In fact I was intoxicated—I had taken a cup of coffee."

Donald Trump, the boorish and insult-spewing political neophyte who, as of this writing, has completely taken over the Republican Party as the leading candidate for president, does not drink coffee (or tea or alcohol). "I always scrape the toppings off my pizza—and I never eat the dough," the billionaire has stated. I have read that the actress Drew Barrymore is allergic to coffee—and garlic. The late novelist David Foster Wallace, in his need to study or write, would often superadd a tea bag to a cup of coffee, needing an extra infusion of caffeine, so may one therefore conclude that he liked the taste of neither beverage? (Malays actually eat the *leaves* of the coffee plant because they contain more caffeine than the beans!) "I have measured out my life with coffee spoons," reflects T.S. Eliot's poetic character J. Alfred Prufrock, which gives us a small measure of his regret for the beverage.

Caffeine, a basic prurine alkaloid, is by survey the most widely used psychoactive drug in the world. Depending on the strength and brew, 6 oz. of coffee can contain between 30 to 180 mg. of caffeine, whereas 360 ml. of cola contains between 30 to 60 mg. David Wallace suffered many dietary prohibitions due to his manic depressive condition. Taking the drug "Nardil" at one point, the young writer learned that he could no longer drink coffee or alcohol—or in fact eat hot dogs, any smoky cheeses, aged or fermented foods, or liver. The poor guy, in despair, later hanged himself at the age of 46 on September 12, 2008.

It was not rebellious colonial Bostonians alone who objected to tea. William Cobbett, the 18th-century English pamphleteer, farmer, and journalist who at times wrote under the pseudonym "Peter Porcupine"—he was also against paper money, taxes on imported grain, and, among other things, "fat and lazy and laughing and singing negroes"—wrote in *Cottage Economy* (1821), "I view tea drinking as a destroyer of health, an enfeebler of the frame, an engenderer of effeminacy and laziness, a debaucher of youth, and a maker of misery for old age."

A singular food-craving is only a step away from a food aversion. Although after much struggle, Dorothy Day, the saintly co-founder of *The*

Catholic Worker, managed to break a long nicotine habit from cigarettes, having been a heavy chain-smoker for most of her life, she was less successful with a life-long caffeine addiction, however, and it was her habit never to travel anywhere without a jar of instant coffee in her handbag. St. Teresa of Avila is supposed to have fed her nuns steak when they were sad or weakened by melancholy. I have heard reported the same needs about singer Taylor Swift and Pop-Tarts and comic Jerry Seinfeld and peanut butter. The one thing necessary is by nature always *exclusionary.*

When back in the 1980s host Bryant Gumbel on the *Today Show* used to place his full, fat, perspiring hand over the mouth of his coffee cup—sebum alert!—and then drink from it, I cannot tell you how much it put me off my own coffee, every time. I don't know which was worse, that indecor, or the unctuous way he finished with a guest and said, as always he did, "Thank you so very much."

I love one special coffee story. It touches on the notorious Ruth Snyder murder case. A Queens housewife, Snyder was executed at Sing Sing prison for the murder of her husband, Albert. In 1925, coincident with a love affair with one Henry Judd Gray, a married corset salesman, she began to plan the murder of her husband, enlisting the help of Gray, though he appeared to be very reluctant. Her distaste for her husband apparently began when he insisted on hanging a picture of his late fiancée, Jessie Guishard, on the wall of their first home, and also named his boat after her. Guishard, whom Albert described to Ruth as "the finest woman I have ever met," had been dead for 10 years. On January 12, 1928, after a scandalous trial, both criminals Snyder and Gray were hastily dispatched in the electric chair. Warden Lawes saw to it that they were given no opiates or sedatives. They ate somewhat heartily of a last dinner of roast chicken, soup, coffee, celery, and mashed potatoes. Gray, in ordering his meal, had underlined his written request for "good coffee." As he handed the chit to the guard, Gray declared, "And I mean good coffee."

I wonder what Gray would have thought of the drink Berliners after World War I called *Blümchenkaffee,* that is, "coffee of the little flowers," a term used because the flower patterns on the bottom of the cups in which it was served were visible through the weak, diluted liquid. I remember back in college a few friends and I formed a breakfast group called the Runagates Club, named after a John Buchan book, which met very early in the morning, before classes, when in my old '53 Chevy we drove down to the various beaches—this was back in Maine in the early 1960s—where we had cups of coffee and smoked joints, a lovely combination, but on special days, which was most of the time, we drank bottles of white wine. Have you heard of civet coffee, also known in Indonesia as *Kopi Luwak*? I had the occasion to drink it in Bangkok and found it spanking hot and delicious. It is an unusual luxury type of coffee produced by harvesting coffee beans from the dung of the Asian palm civet cat. Civet coffee is currently the most expensive type of coffee in the world! A small cat-like animal (it belong to the same suborder, but not the same family) native to several regions of Asia, including China and Southeast Asia, it weighs about seven pounds, is two feet long, predominantly eats fruits and insects. The thing is, one of the palm civet's favorite foods is the coffee bean, which is, ultimately, how and why civet coffee exists. Civets eat the beans, pass them in their dung or feces in the form of largely undigested clumps, and civet coffee collectors then collect the dung, wash and dry it, and then parcel it for sale. The civets can eat and process any form of coffee, so there is not a specific taste or type of coffee produced by this method: arabica, robusta, and other coffee plants could be processed in the same manner. All coffee connoisseurs, however, agree that civet coffee lacks the bitterness of coffee, has a characteristically rich aroma, and is admirably thick. Medical researchers have confirmed that when properly washed civet coffee is safe for human consumption, despite the odd, somewhat disturbing manner of its cultivation.

Most civet coffee production is centered in Sumatra, Indonesia, and most production is effected by using caged civets thriving on farms. This coffee is typically available for several hundred dollars per pound. There are also synthetic civet coffees (attempting to imitate the civet's digestive process without using the animal itself), which are available for a fraction of the cost, as well as authentic civet coffees (made using dung painstakingly collected from wild animals living in their natural environment) available at far higher prices. There are also several other related products. Weasel coffee is a Vietnamese-to-English translation of the same product, which is more likely to be a synthetic form. In addition, *Kopi Muncak* is a related product, which is made in a similar fashion, except by collecting the dung of the muncak, a small species of deer also found in Southeast Asia.

One last note on the singular subject of coffee. At certain periods in his life in New York City when he realized he had been drinking too much, the witty and, one has to admit, resourceful reporter, Gene Fowler, used to pay for high colonics with—coffee! He would directly telephone a certain Dr. Nagel, the house physician for both the well-known Pennsylvania Hotel and the Hotel Vanderbilt and tell him to "get ready for another exploration of the Cave of the Winds—put on the coffee pot." This was followed by vitamin injections, steam baths, and bed rest. His writing buddy, Ring Lardner, often did the same, but insisted for his own coffee enemas that the doctor, instead of using Maxwell House—Fowler's select brand—use Arbuckle's brand to which he was more partial. Is coffee now a food aversion for you?

The Buddha died eating tainted food. The *suttas* tell us that he felt ill immediately after eating the Sukaramaddava. No one knows exactly what he had been eating, except that it was meat and had been served by Chundha the goldsmith. In his last hours at the scene of his final Nirvana at Kusinagara, holy Siddartha blessed Chundha, feeling that the man might reproach himself for serving that unfortunate meal, assuring him that, as it was the last offering given to Buddha before his passing, it was blessed and he would receive his reward in some future life. From what we know, the onset of Buddha's illness was quick, although he began traveling. While eating, he suspected that something was wrong with the food and gently suggested that his host have the food buried, out of compassion for others. Soon afterward, he suffered severe stomach pain and passed blood from his rectum. We can reasonably assume that the illness started while he was having his meal, making him think there was something wrong with the unfamiliar delicacy. Theravada Buddhist tradition has adhered to the assumption that the Buddha passed away during the night of the full moon in the lunar month of Visakha (which falls sometime in May to June). But the timing contradicts information given in the *suttas*, which states that the Buddha died soon after the rainy-season retreat, most likely during the autumn or mid-winter, that is, November to January. Is it possible that the moon could have devoured Buddha? I pose that question because weird, dome-bald, be-mustachioed George Gurdjieff, the crown prince of baloney, claimed, because the moon exerted a pull on all things, not merely drawing the tides or driving biological cycles, that we ourselves are "food for the moon." Due to the fact that our bodies are largely made of water and just as the moon pulls on water to create the ocean tides, he reasoned, our bodies move in similar but more complicated ways through hydraulic principles. I wonder if any of this signifies regarding hunger and ocean-going, because food is far more ritualized and enjoyed at sea, no?

Lepidopterist and novelist Vladimir Nabokov—in a fit of zeal? madness? respect for his prey?—once actually tried snacking on butterflies, which he said tasted "vile," like a combination, he added, of "almonds and perhaps green cheese." I imagine this was a scientific experiment for the novelist, but in pursuit of what? (One gathers that he had a delicate stomach, once suffering a bad case of food poisoning from eating Virginia ham in Cambridge, and, in 1947, traveling in New Hampshire, becoming ill by the smell of fried clams drifting in from a Howard Johnson's.) While the late Iraqi dictator Saddam Hussein was in captivity, he enjoyed Kellogg's Raisin Bran Crunch and dismissed his other option: "No Froot Loops!" Was this murderous madman with the forked eyes—a man who with a mere blink sent men to be beheaded—honestly concerned about his *sugar intake*; worried that the rainbow-colored crumbs would look silly in his beard; or personally irked that no matter what color Fruit Loop you ate—which is the case—they all taste the same?

According to reports, novelist V.S. Naipaul has always been a fussy loon about food—even an arrogant supremo. "I have all the shyness of the very vain," he once wrote with a bewildering and paradoxical candor. There is a scene in *An Area of Darkness*—in Kashmir—where, a confirmed vegetarian, Naipaul throws a shit-fit after being served soup he felt "might" have meat in it. He goes haywire. That moment is worth reading as an extreme example of food-fanaticism. There was no one specific dish that he hated, but meat—beef especially ("I hate sinew")—he abominated. A crotchety man, he actually admitted both fearing and hating Trinidad, the place where *he was born*, and even loathed being called a West Indian novelist.

I have always had the feeling that V.S. Naipaul never touched "poor food," the beans-and-rice dishes that poor people in Trinidad ate. He is a native Trinidadian, but he was also a ruthless and inveterate snob. Here one recalls a scene in Paul Theroux's non-fiction work, *Sir Vidia's Shadow*, in which Naipaul found himself displeased and angry after a Q & A gathering in the Netherlands, when he handed back his speaking fee and departed the country:

> "What went wrong?" [asked Theroux]
> "Does it matter when one is dealing with nonsense?" Vidia told me.
> I had had enjoyable experiences in Holland where most people speak fluent English and are intellectually curious and widely traveled.
> "The Dutch," he said. "Potato eaters."
> The famous image in the Van Gogh painting said everything about the culture, he believed: "ugly, moronic, famished peasants in a greasy kitchen, hunched over a basin of spuds, and cramming them into their mouths."

There can be found an account of a similar scene in that same chapter called "Tainted Vegetables" where Naipaul gets into an argument with Dame Drue Heinz, patroness of the arts and part of the Heinz food fortune, who dared question him when he objected to being served vegetables with an implement that had come into contact with a meat dish, saying, "Those vegetables are tainted." If you find irksome Naipaul's disgust of poor people's food or consider him arrogant, what about the wide swath involved in gourmand James Beard's universal dismissal of one people's entire cuisine as he sweeps it from the world? Beard rarely appeared in print without a certain kind of plexed artistry. He bumptiously writes, "I've always felt that food in the Caribbean is perhaps the worst in the world." Eating rice, Friedrich Nietzsche was convinced, caused one to become addicted to opium, while the epicure Jean Brillat-Savarin warned that consuming it made people weak, craven, and timid. As to rice, I would venture to say that stand-up comic Mitch Hedberg is no great fan of it. "I like rice," he pronounced. "Rice is great if you're hungry and want 2000 of something."

Who can forget that point in Conrad's *Heart of Darkness* when Charles Marlow records less with sardonic humor than a kind of disgust approaching malevolence the specific food he detests but the cannibals in the Congo had carted along to eat?

They had brought along a provision of hippo-meat which went rotten and made the mystery of the wilderness stink in my nostrils. Phoo! I can sniff it now.

On the other side of the spectrum, it is also revealing that an overfastidiousness for food, daintiness, hyper-discrimination, can be seen—subjectively interpreted—as an aspect of vaingloriousness. It seems that among St. Ignatius Loyola's besetting passions in his youth were not only an inordinate craving for fame, a tendency to pugnacity, and a strain of what might be called "machismo," something that the Thomas Carlyle chalked up to sensuality and, indeed, to gluttony. The Scot might not have been far off the mark when accusing Loyola of these vices of pride, greed for power, and a lust for fame when that energetic, willful, and driven fellow decided to become the Catholic Church's leading champion against the Protestant revolt, with Carlyle in the process—and in high dudgeon—rhetorically exaggerating in a decidedly negative way Loyola's supposed youthful craving for "sauces."

Gluttony—and Europe's flourishing lust for spices as well as gold, not to mention sugar, herrings, and whale oil—grew with the great Renaissance voyages of discovery. The particularities of food politics became linked with the spice wars between the East Indian trading companies of the 17th- and 18th centuries. The aptly named Pierre Poivre, a French horticulturist born in Lyon and missionary to China and Cochinchina, in the 1750's stole spice plants, such as nutmeg and clove, from Dutch Indochina for the *gloire* and prosperity of French Africa; indeed, he is mainly remembered for introducing to Mauritius and Reunion such spices and other commodities, which at the time, as I say, were controlled by the Dutch, who had a virtual monopoly on these spices in the East Indies. Poivre's intriguing book, *The Voyages of a Philosopher*, was read with interest by Thomas Jefferson, incidentally. It was Poivre's description of mountain rice cultivated in what is now Vietnam in fact that caught Jefferson's attention. Speaking of the third president of the United States, it is him that we can also thank for introducing ice cream, waffles, and macaroni to the USA.

It was in Loyola's odd jump from "sauces" to piety and asceticism that Carlyle felt that the man showed no true repentance or humility, but rather displayed a vile continuing pride and self-assertion, what Nietzsche (or Friedrich's proto-Nazi sister) would later call the "*Wille zu Macht*," seeking glory by setting himself up as the Church's chosen hit-man against the Protestant revolt against the Pope and Virgin. It fell out that Loyola had heard rumors that there had lately been a revolt against the authority of the Church and Virgin and so, in Carlyle's view, megalomaniacally decided to take on the job of quashing that rebellion himself. It was to Carlyle a new expression of or outlet for his own continuing inner drive for sensuality, self-will, and self-assertion now that he could no longer indulge his former appetites for sex and "sauces." Snobbishly, those who went in for sauces were fastidious and over-advantaged and pious fops, according to the hearty, rough-hewn, no-nonsense, down-to-earth Carlyle. The greater part of Carlyle's essay, "Jesuitism," was devoted not so much to attacking or ridiculing Loyola, and even specifically the Jesuit Order, as to using "Jesuitism" as a metaphor for self-gratification, vain tampering, and of course any attempt to prop up a religion, whether Catholic or Protestant, that had lost its original inner spiritual vitality, for political or social purposes. Carlyle felt that the 16th-and 17th century Protestant Reformation and Puritan movement had arisen as a protest against a late-mediaeval Catholicism that had grown decadent and inwardly empty, that had lost the true vitality it still enjoyed in Dante's time or with the 12th-century Abbott Sampson of his *Past and Present*. Catholicism, he felt, had lost its true vigor, ready to pass on after fulfilling its original mission, by the beginning of the 16th-century, and the Counter-Reformation of the Council of Trent and Loyola's Jesuit order was a futile attempt artificially to resuscitate what was really now a dead body. A food obsession, Carlyle felt, had transmogrified into theological adventurism, a willful and equally arrogant obsession.

Talking someone out of a food aversion, anyone, incidentally—daring even to mount coherent and logical reasons against it—is fruitless, pointless, useless. As Dr. Johnson said, when in 1770 the playwright Thomas Sheridan opened an Academy of Oratory in Bath, "Sir, it is burning a candle at Dover to show light at Calais." Food obsessives are almost all True Believers.

It is interesting this link with food and prissiness or degeneration. Max Nordau associated vegetarianism with other "decadent" late 19th-century European tendencies in his widely-read, controversial *Entartung* (1892; *Degeneration*, English translation, 1895). Dutch Marxist historian Jan Marius Romein presented vegetarianism as a component of the "*kleine ge-loven*" (little religions) in his study of *fin de siècle* Europe—he also included, along with vegetarianism, temperance, nudism, and homeopathy—which he interpreted as expressing "the bad conscience of a ruling class that was no longer convinced of its divine right to rule but not yet under sufficient threat to take full stock of its shortcomings."

It is a theme classically illustrated, moreover, in George Orwell's famous complaint in his novel, *The Road to Wigan Pier* (1936) that Socialism—let it substitute for the kind of fixation that Carlyle held against Loyola—"drew with magnetic force every fruit-juice drinker, nudist, sandal-wearer, sex-ma-niac, Quaker, 'Nature Cure' quack, pacifist and feminist in England," while at the same time attracting all sorts of exacting or snotty marginals like "veg-etarians with wilting beards," the "outer-suburban creeping Jesus" addicted to yoga, and "that dreary tribe of high-minded women and sandal-wearers and bearded fruit-juice drinkers who come flocking towards the smell of 'progress' like bluebottles to a dead cat."

A fussy or persnickety food-hater can and often invariably does prove to be a perfectionist about the foods that he demands. Carlyle himself, for example, who was extremely dainty about his own food, madly loved milk, according to James Anthony Froude in his *Thomas Carlyle: A History of the First Forty Years of His Life, 1795-1835*, describing his and Jane Welsh Carlyle's life together at their farm at Craigenputtock during that couple's first years of their marriage. Indeed, milk he loved. On the other hand, the fractious and cross-grained Scottish historian expressly disliked any small del-icacies and exotic sauces, which he determined were foppish, and overly-con-sidered, and also disparaged in *On the Choice of Books* (1866)

> flimsy, desultory readers, who fly from foolish book
> to foolish book, and get good of none, and mischief
> of all—are not these as foolish, unhealthy eaters, who
> mistake their superficial false desire after spiceries and
> confectioneries for their real appetite, of which even
> they are not destitute, though it lies far deeper, far
> quieter, after solid nutritive food?

He nevertheless expected cleanliness and perfect cookery of common things, "and if the porridge was smoked, or the bread heavy, or the butter less than perfect, or a plate or a dish ill-washed, he was entirely intolerable." Froude observes, making the noteworthy comment, "Thus the imperfections of Scotch farm servant girls had to be supplemented by Mrs. Carlyle herself. Among her other accomplishments, she had to learn to milk cows, in case the byre-woman should be out of the way, for fresh milk was the most essential article of Carlyle's diet."

I have long been aware of Carlyle's dismissal of the French as "a nation of pastry-cooks and dancing-masters" and of his scorn for indulgent Parisians "eating, everlasting eating," as typical of the so-called the "European Counter-Enlightenment," which in turn I also see as a kind of soured, hardened, darkened offshoot of late-18th- and early-19th- century German Romanticism. If you wanted a one-sentence summary of Sir Isaiah Berlin's *The Roots of Romanticism*, it would be that 18th-century German intellectuals saw the French in the very same way, an obvious stereotype that comprehensively underlies the whole 19th and early 20th-century German chauvinist dichotomy of profoundly spiritual Germanic *Kultur* versus shallow, materialistic Anglo-French *Zivilisation*. There is a kind of cultural food aversionism here, in fact. It is an old, old story of the splenetic German (and more general East-Central European) resentment against the Anglo-French Enlightenment—and the ultimate *fons et origo*, too, of the inflexible right-wing strain of Baltic culture, which in turn is why I have become so fascinated with the cultural conflicts of Weimar Germany.

It is in the particular, not the universal, however, where we find food aversion becomes most memorably concrete.

In a television interview in 2002, Larry King directly asked Julia Child if there were any foods that she hated. She replied, "Cilantro and arugula I don't like at all. They're both green herbs, they have kind of a dead taste to me." "So you would never order it [sic]?" Mr. King asked. "Never," responded the late great chef. "I would pick it out if I saw it and throw it on the floor." Dried herbs always put her off, which I have often found bewildering. When her epistolary friend from Cambridge, Avis DeVoto, wife of the critic, novelist, and historian Bernard DeVoto, once mailed her a packet of dried chives, Child was horrified by them and wrote back in response, "Tastes like hay with onion flavor." Another time DeVoto declared that she liked the taste and use of Accent seasoning. "I don't use it at all as I sort of hate the idea," Child wrote back. "But I am sure it is useful in the USA where vegetables have probably lost some of their freshness from being shipped under refrigeration for days and days."

Cilantro is not a popular herb. There are legions of cilantro haters. Cellist Yo-Yo Ma hates it. Julia Child, as I say, loathed it. So does Ina Garten, host of the Food Network program, Barefoot Contessa. Cilantrophobes compare the taste of this annual, also called "Chinese parsley," to hand-lotion, bug-infested bedclothes, chemical cleaning agents, hand sanitizer. Card-carrying protesters of the plant (all parts of which are edible) make loud public appearances. Jeffrey Steingarten writes of being acquainted with a respected and powerful editor of cookbooks—he does not name her—"who grew so nauseated by the flavor of cilantro that she brought a pair of tweezers to Mexican and Indian restaurants and pinched out every last scrap of it before she would take a bite." He adds, "I have heard the complaint so often that cilantro tastes like dish-soap that I only wonder why a dish soap has not been made of it!" Among other food Steingarten hates include kimchi, anchovies, and any—and all—*blue food*!

Dish-soap as a comestible plays a small role in at least one fellow's gastronomic life, by the way. During World War II, comedian Redd Foxx—born Fred Sanford—has admitted that he dodged the draft by eating half a bar of soap before his physical, a trick that resulted in heart palpitations.

Mollie Katzen, godmother of vegetarian cuisine and author of *The Moosewood Cookbook*, dislikes capers on anything. "Sagebrush is a very fair fuel, but as a vegetable it is a distinguished failure," wrote Mark Twain in *Roughing It.* "Nothing can abide the taste of it but the jackass and his illegitimate child the mule." As to disliking vegetables, Ferran Adrià, chef of the now defunct Spanish restaurant, El Bulli, and a man who hails from Barcelona, dislikes bell peppers. Crowned the "chef of the future" by *Gourmet* in October 1999 for his many gastronomic concoctions, he is not hesitant to speak his mind. He deigned to clarify that one aversion in an *Esquire* magazine (January 2011) interview, "Yes, I can tell you why God did not want me to like bell peppers. It is necessary that there is something I do not like."

To detest only *one* thing in life? One thing *alone*? I would have to call that an absolute miracle. I must say, I find the theological detail, especially personalized, a bit affected, but when were chefs not vain?

I have mentioned some of Julia Child's food aversions. Julie Powell, a would-be acolyte of Julia Child's (although Child moodily dismissed her as nothing but a stuntist) who tried cooking her way through *Mastering the Art of French Cooking* and writing about the experience in her best-seller, *Julie & Julia: 365 Days, 524 Recipes, 1 Tiny Apartment Kitchen,* initially doubted whether it was the right project for her and whines to her husband. "I'd be exhausted all the time. I'd get fat. We'd have to eat brains. And eggs. I don't eat eggs, Eric. You know I don't eat eggs." Powell goes on to confess—and rather stridently—to other food dislikes. "… I didn't eat beans, ever," she writes. "… and I didn't eat coconut or nuts or jam, not ever." "Much of what I read made no sense to me, but I could see the recipes were full of stuff I didn't like, mushrooms and olives and spinach." It is as if Powell exaggerates what foods she dislikes to make more dramatic her conversion to the safari she undertakes.

We have already mentioned the less than humble Ferran Adrià, he of the liquid nitrogen flans and culinary foams. Gastronomes used to fawn over him as if he had come down from Mount Parnassus, surrounded by bright light. Fans would pilgrimage to his three-star restaurant on Spain's Costa Brava and line up merely merely to see him, never mind shake his hand, or, a fantasy hard to realize, hope to be one of the lucky ones to eat at one of his tables, for his restaurant, El Bulli, where vision met fusion and led to illusion—it was *open for business only about six months of the year, from mid-June to mid-December—would receive over 2 million reservation requests each year, when only 8,000 were available per season.* Voltaire was not wrong when he declared in *La Pucelle d'Orleans,* "*L'illusion est le premier plaisir.*"

Chefs, among the least modest people on the planet—the French word comes from Latin *caput,* meaning "head," and is cognate to the English "chief"—are people who cook professionally for other people and are hired to work, for money, like any other menial. Today, however, the average executive chef struts about like the Lord of the Admiralty. I have referred earlier to the parading chefs in Fishmongers Hall in London. I once worked one summer in Kennebunkport, Maine for an ill-tempered chef for whom we dishwashers and dogsbodies had a muttering dislike and whom we called the "Green Hornet," a nasty piece of work who, tersely oracular and dismissively cut and dried, ran the small hotel restaurant the way *SS Obergruppenführer* Reinhard Heydrich ran the city of Prague. (In the secret SD, incidentally, Heydrich a truly pro-active malevolent who was a master of cunning and intrigue, went by the covert designation "C," which was the traditional cover name given to the head of the British SIS—he was a rabid reader of spy novels—and "it cannot have escaped his notice that amongst old Nazis," as Callum Macdonald writes in his book, *The Killing of Reinhard Heydrich,* "Hitler was known as '*Der Chef*' [the Boss], or 'C.'") In any case, at our summer hotel the Green Hornet thought he was God, in spite of the fact that he was a crotchety, labile, rancorous, dish-throwing, hissing and spitting near-dwarf who resembled to a T wizened little Louie Dumbrowsky, the runty, cigar-chomping sweetshop-owner and in real life the father of Leo Gorcey of the Bowery Boys movies.

I would put it down as a solid and ungainsayable truism: only a true-born, natural, confirmed compatibilist can get along with the average chef, at least in my opinion, and I only wonder why anyone would try.

"What is it that you most dislike?" novelist Danielle Steel was asked by *Vanity Fair* (July 2012) on their "Proust Questionnaire." Her reply—a succinct one—was "Dishonesty, meanness. Vegetables." She apparently had to pause after the first two universal dislikes to separate concepts from complaints, but feebly to dismiss an entire food group this large—and the most healthful one of them all, to boot—surely says more about this low-brow writer than it does about the corn, peas, cauliflower, radishes, beets, broccoli, celery, spinach, peppers, etc. she lumps together to hate. To her they are nothing more than dumb inventory. In a 1989 episode of "Married—With Children" called "Can't Dance, Don't Ask Me Why," Al Bundy tells his pretty but dim daughter, Kelly, who has been forced to go to dancing school, "There are two things the Bundys don't do—we don't eat vegetables and we don't tap [dance]." I am sure that even Kelly Bundy would find the novels of Danielle Steel worthless.

Can radishes be that bad? William Jennings Bryan, a glutton, kept them in his pocket for pick-me-ups. It is the one vegetable, in my opinion, that anybody can grow, starting with children. Fraggles, those small anthropomorphic creatures, typically 18 inches tall in the TV puppet show, "Fraggle Rock," that came in a variety of colors and had fur-tuft tipped tails, lived *mainly* on radishes and so-called "Doozer sticks," ground-up radishes and the material with which the Doozers build their homes! Fraggles lived a generally carefree life, spending most of their time (they had only a thirty-minute work week, my kind of employment) playing, exploring, and generally enjoying themselves.

Veggies can put people off, however. I knew a pretty young Southern girl who hated ramps so much that she refused ever to date any boys who ate them, the raw ones—boys and plants, both!—smelling much stronger than leeks. Ramps, which are a wild onion, have a garlicky smell (Old English *hramsa* means "wild garlic"), grow in patches, with tangled roots, and sprout beautiful flat broad leaves, which in the South are eaten as a spring delicacy. They need to be scrupulously washed before eating. "Ramp breath" can be the result. Ramps, which have a uniquely pungent flavor, can be used raw or cooked in any recipe calling for scallions or leeks, but are traditionally used in salads, shredded over pasta, and often added to soups, egg dishes, casseroles, rice dishes, and potato dishes. A jelly is even made from it.

A produce wholesaler, Joseph Solomon, the father of food critic, the inventively self-named Mimi Sheraton—she was actually born Miriam Solomon but earnestly tried all of her life by association to capitalize on the elegant hotel name—actively hated vegetables. A produce dealer who hates vegetables? So says his daughter, not that she ever confessed that she did. In her memoir, *Eating My Words: An Appetite for Life*, she discusses the Brooklyn of her early adulthood as the daughter of a produce wholesaler, who, as I say, unpredictably enough, despised his own products. From her surname, one would conclude that she had a fancy pedigree and was classy, but from stories of her early life in Brooklyn she sounds as if she were raised on the hip in a grubby *shtetl*. On November 15, 2010, in an interview with a person named Aaron Kagan on a highly peculiar blog with the rather peculiar name, *The Jew & the Carrot: Jews, Food, and Contemporary Issues*, Sheraton said,

> When the big family gathered around the table, especially on Passover, and everybody had too much wine and told too many stories [which were among my favorite memories]. There was one story in *My Mother's Kitchen* from when my grandmother was alive. She used to buy a live carp and keep it swimming in the bathtub until she was going to kill it to make gefilte fish, and I had a cousin who thought the fish was getting too cold. He ran hot water into the bathtub, and of course the fish rolled over on its side and was cooked long before it got to be "gefilted."

The first marriage of Ms. Solomon was to a William Schlifman, a two-pack couple, who also went under the name Sheraton. Did she marry again? To someone with an Italian name? I ask only because she has a son, Marc Falcone, who is a partner in the litigation department at Paul, Weiss, Rifkind, Wharton & Garrison, which bewilders me, but I must say no one really has a clue about the many aliases and names in that family. They all seem to have tried on whatever name was available—grabbing it out of thin air—that would hide their origins. It reminds me of the ploy of corrupt companies when a customer is ordering something on-line, using the fine print of seeking a further charge, hiding behind another pay wall.

"Life is too short for self-hatred and celery sticks," stated Marilyn Wann, an American author and an activist in the Fat Acceptance Movement who lives in San Francisco and proudly identifies herself as a member of the "fat pride" community. (I wonder if she is aware that celery was given as a prize to winners in the sports arenas of ancient Greece.) "Basically," says Wann, "we want to be treated with respect, the same as everyone else." At 5'4" and

about 285 pounds, she proudly identifies as a fat person. With her magazine
Fat!So?, first released in summer of 1994, and the publication of a book of
the same name in 1998, she has played a role in trying to convince the public
that fat people deserve equal opportunity in society, regardless of size. She
has not only valiantly served on the National Association to Advance Fat
Acceptance (NAAFA) board but has also swum with the Padded Lilies fat
synchronized swim team and performed with Big Moves modern ensemble
and its hip-hop troupe, the Phat Fly Girls. Wann has also engaged in militant
street actions with the Bod Squad Cheerleaders, a fat pride group. She promotes the idea that it is possible to be "fat and fit." The crux of the issue is
summed up by the "Fat!So? Manifesto:"

> So there's nothing wrong with being fat. Just like
> there's nothing wrong with being short or tall, or
> black or brown. These are facts of identity that cannot
> and should not be changed. They are birthright.
> They're beyond aesthetics. They provide the diversity
> we need to survive.

I would claim that the definitive story here is "Fat Girl," a Brendan Gill
fiction that appeared in the *New Yorker* (Sept 26, 1970), about Jeanne, a
lovely, sweet "big, soft bolster of a girl, with no sharp edges" who loves to
eat anything, everything, and is murdered by a fanatic lover. Her "fate was in
every way characteristic of her; she died as she did because, up to the very last
moment of her life, she was kind, lazy, and accommodating: a fat girl content
with her lot, who pleased herself and pleased others." The fact is, Jeanne is
adorable, and the story glorifies her sexy indolence. "She managed to convey
without the least taint of vanity the impression that she believed herself to be
a remarkable physical specimen."

Is it possible that women chefs (cheves?) actually hate vegetables in the
way that women, all women, are said—or is it a calumny—to dislike the
Three Stooges? To be fair, men of course also have their hates, like sleepovers,
cottage cheese, bathroom products, emotional outbursts, bad novels, *Cosmo*
quizzes, and talking on the phone. As to the matter of the name for women
chefs—after all, we have "waiter" and "waitress"—what about "cheffetes" or
"chefesses"?

Female chefs seem to be given much less attention in the restaurant
industry than men. Is it basically a boy's club? Only ten percent of jockeys
are women, and it is even less with race-car drivers, boxers, wrestlers, garage
mechanics, and scientists. Exactly what is wrong with having two X chromo-

somes? What is the nature of the bias? Is it all about quotas? Or is it envy? The need for dominance? Does it all revert to sexism? "I can almost always tell when a pianist is a woman," Canadian classical pianist Glenn Gould once remarked and went on to explain,

> Women generally have much less control over the up-
> per arm, so they come down with their forearms, ham-
> mer-like. And it also shows in their rhythmic thinking
> of the work. There is generally less spinal momentum
> in a woman's playing because they tend to be more
> committed, more directly acting upon the keys, rather
> than feeling above the instrument.

So, what does that mean—women chefs should be pulverizing pieces of meat harder or less so? It is difficult to fathom how anything like a "sword-in-the-stone" moment can be instanced by the way a woman strikes piano keys, which makes me wonder if Gould had not entered some wormhole, although a man who insisted on playing his music on the same ancient, battered chair and who lived on cocktails of antidepressants and anxiety-suppressing pills that were, ironically, more harmful to him than helpful—he died shortly after his 50th birthday, on October 4, 1982—maybe was, as once described, "wilfully idiotic."

5.

LIBERACE'S STICKY BUNS, OR HOW GAY IS YOUR FOOD?

JUDY GARLAND ATE NO BREAKFAST CEREAL in thirty years, and orange juice, which she studiously avoided, gave her hives—surely an off-putting food aversion in that, although born in Grand Rapids, Minnesota, she grew up in sunny California. In the course of her life, she never seemed to understand food and alternately ballooned or went matchstick-thin, sometimes in the course of the same month. During her studio days, Judy's daily menu and chosen foods were restricted by directors, agents, and bosses, particularly that gluttonous, overbearing pig of a tycoon, pushy L.B. Mayer, head of the entire MGM studio, who exploited and abused her for decades with dieting-by-drugs, while he himself mumped everything in sight. (Among his favorite desserts was honey poured over a bowl of fresh strawberries.) It is pitifully revealing that in *The Harvey Girls* (1946), a musical film celebrating the well-known western restaurant chain, Garland not only appears rail-thin—the movie begins with her riding on a train heading west and nearly starving—but, a thematic gaffe, not a single scene in the movie shows food ever being cooked or served, almost a metaphor of the star's dilemma.

The movies as a medium of food aversion—it is an intriguing sociological subject! I found the same nutty oddity in *Mildred Pierce* (1945) in which, though the lead character, an energetic entrepreneur (Joan Crawford), opens a chain of "Mildred's" restaurants throughout Southern California, we never see the act of food being cooked not so much as a burnt burger! Could it be that in a sexist way Hollywood down-played the anti-corporate power of a woman, while it went out of its way to puff the skills of the male entrepreneur, Fred Harvey? Were you aware, by the way, that Harvey (1835-1901) was a British immigrant, whose first restaurant in the Topeka, Kansas depot—table linen from Belfast, silver from Sheffield—specialized by menu in sage-fed Mexican quail, antelope fillets, and the best steaks and chops?

While the character James Bond was a good cook—he famously insisted on large portions of food (and his favorite meal was breakfast)—his creator Ian Fleming was supposedly a dastardly one. "Ian Fleming's cooking always tasted to me like armpits," declared Nöel Coward, whom we may assume also disliked outdoor cuisine, at least regarding a remark made to a fully bearded fellow at a party, "Is that a beard or are you eating a muskrat?" "She gave me rice when she knows I hate rice," painter Mark Rothko complained to a friend, after his long-suffering wife, Mell, served him a meal to help him on his low-fat diet. "Eating rice cakes is like chewing on a foam coffee cup, only less filling," writes humorist Dave Barry.

As to James Bond being handy in the kitchen, I am certain a good book could be written about many surprisingly unlikely but talented chefs. According to the artist Lee Krasner, Jackson Pollock—otherwise a disheveled, rancorous, and desperate alcoholic—had gifts that way. "He was fastidious about his baking—marvelous bread and pies. He also made great spaghetti sauce." (It was Linda Lee Porter's—composer Cole's wife—insistent but civilized conviction that strong drink destroyed a person's ability to enjoy fine cuisine, and she firmly set a two-cocktail limit before dinner, which her husband obeyed.) Actor Danny Kaye was reputedly (and boastfully) something of a gourmet chef. "I'm a cookbook reader and I cook almost anything—Italian, Chinese, barbecuing. I even make my own noodles," he bragged. He made sausages, special sauces, exotic desserts. The theater and demonstration kitchen under the library at the Culinary Institute of America in Hyde Park, New York is named for him, and in fact his work as a chef earned him the *"Les Meilleurs Ouvriers de France"* culinary award. I believe Kaye is the only non-professional chef to have achieved this honor.

Novelist George Orwell was full of opinions about cooking. So was Willa Cather. Poet Sylvia Plath, who loved to cook, was passionate about collecting recipes. From all reports, Truman Capote was capable in the kitchen, although he never fully threw himself into it—"Oh, I adore to cook. It makes me feel so mindless in a worthwhile way," he said—having learned the basics of baking and broiling after settling down in Sicily with his partner, Jack Dunphy. The diminutive writer was particularly fond of desserts, whipping up cookies and gooey cakes to satisfy his sugar cravings. Among amateur chefs are Jack London, Scarlett Johansson, Jean Cocteau, Virgil Thomson, Boy George, Al Capone, Jessica Biel, Morley Safer, Saul Bellow, Gunter Grass, Anthony Burgess, Jane Bowles, Emma Stone, Sheryl Crow, Ted Nugent, Fidel Castro—he expertly made cilantro-peppered *ceviche* and particularly loved vegetable soup—John Cage, Vincent Price, Naomi Judd,

Robert Mitchum, Emily Dickinson, Johnny Mathis, and the Biblical prophet Ezekiel.

Gourmand James Beard could not stand the taste of chicken livers. He also hated the taste of wild rice—actually loathed it, and as far back as the early 1960s he declared, "And the bias remains with me still." Beard could really get wound up about food. He was glad and big and full of what I would call forthputtingness. "I feel it [wild rice] is far overrated and appeals to people largely because it is expensive. It has no delicacy but rather a crude and overpoweringly strong flavor, and the more I think about it, the more I believe it is fit only for the birds, for whom it was meant anyway." This, from one of the fussiest, fattest, crankiest eaters who ever lived, a finger-sucking wastrel who spent a lifetime pursuing exotic, expensive foods and thought nothing of lavishing a fortune on lark's-tongues or crossing a world to find the perfect blanquette de veau or ballotine of pheasant or gratin Savoyard. A native Oregonian and something of a provincial, despite having traveled widely in his life, Beard had a pronounced regional bias. Although born in turn-of-the-century Portland, Oregon, a semi-rustic dorp back in 1903, he gave off urban airs, and nothing like, say, the traditions of New England were going to sway him. He had a gay man's snarky fussitude, the kind of preciosity that liked to break ikons and at the same time exalt his matchless palate.

I have seen Beard interviewed several times. There was a distinct sadness, a low sort of humming melancholy to the man. A certain *tristesse* adhibits to the wretchedness of big powerful men. A heft seemed to drag at him. Joylessness in a chef also somehow carries the weight of a further irony. "Actually, the true gourmet, like the true artist, is one of the unhappiest creatures that exist," we read in *La Bonne Table* by Ludwig Bemelsman, the Austro-Hungarian-born American writer and illustrator of children's books and an internationally known gourmet himself. "His trouble comes from so seldom finding what he constantly seeks: perfection."

"Mother"—Elizabeth, the hotelier, James Beard's dragon of a mother whose insufferable hauteur and ass-kicking and rigid pronunciamenti formed her son's many opinions for life—"taught me to detest beans done with molasses and brown sugar," he wrote in *Delights and Prejudices.* It turns out that she once spitefully brought along a can of beans to an outdoor picnic for him alone as a didactic humiliation after the young but temeritous boy had once dared to voice a preference for canned beans over her own perfect recipe. Cranberry sauce was another of Beard's dislikes. "We were never a cranberry family, thank heavens," he wrote, weirdly, as if randomly liking one particular food or another committed one to a policy about it, something like devotion. "To me, the berry's rather bitter tang is an offense to the palate, an abomination in any menu. And why the cranberry has become so generally accepted with turkey as to become a gastronomic cliché I will never be able to understand."

The fact is, Beard cultivated an anti-East Coast prejudice, which proves, among other things, that food aversions, at least in some instances, are often little more than sectionalistic biases, pro and con. Alistair Cooke is another classic example—on the very same subject, by the way. Cooke, the British media historian who wrote about America, peevishly (and inanely) wrote,

It has been an unchallengeable American doctrine that cranberry sauce, a pink goo with overtones of sugared tomatoes, is a delectable necessity of the Thanksgiving board and that turkey is uneatable without it. There are some things in every country that you must be born to endure; and another hundred years of general satisfaction with Americans and America could not reconcile this expatriate to cranberry sauce, peanut butter, and drum majorettes.

There was something lost about the older James Beard, who, to some degree having been infantilized by his mother, never got his head out of the past and suffered from "Where are the days of yesteryear?" syndrome. In many ways his reality was lost in pointless reveries of looking backward. "Young man, everything is honeycombed with childishness," writes Witold Gombrowiz in *Ferdydurke*, a novel eloquent on the subject of one being imprisoned by the past: "All around there was arising a jungle of absurd reflexes, a desert of senseless actions." John Thorne says, "Like many people with perfect sensual memory, [Beard's] adult life was hounded by the feast of his childhood, an acuity of flavor that nothing in later years could even hope to match. His cooking changed with the times, but not his heart."

I notice that I repeat the word "bias" in writing about James Beard. But, after all, bias is the subject of this book. If it is not normal, it is to be expected, even if it cannot be explained. Christ particularly loved—went out of his way to make it clear —the apostle John. St. Peter had a special deep affection for Mark and Petronilla, as had St. Paul for Timothy and St. Thecla. St. Gregory of Nazianzen often boasted of his matchless friendship with St. Basil and wrote, "It seemed as though we two had but one soul." One need not to look to metaphysics or resort to the fields of socionics or depth psychology to explain why, often inexplicably, one finds that through his/her discrimination one human or object is preferred over another.

Actress Angelina Jolie apparently hates Thanksgiving and "wants no part in rewriting history like so many other Americans," a friend of hers has gone on record as saying. "To celebrate what the white settlers did to the native Indians, the domination of one culture over another, just isn't her style. She definitely doesn't want to teach her multi-cultural family how to celebrate a story of murder." Apparently Ms. Jolie—from all that I have read of her, the Queen of Earnestness—dislikes turkey as much as she does the official holiday and the entire concept of convening. (I doubt that she has much to fear for the continuance of such things. Convivial dinners seem more and more to be virtually disappearing as an American tradition and with their eclipse any gathering sense of festivity and exchange, of community and sacrament. It is already considered pretty much a crime to salute people by calling out "Merry Christmas" anymore, while sacred Nativity displays have been officially banned in public—having been replaced by anemic strings of tawdry, silver-tin-foil letters spelling out that eunuch of all messages, "Season's Greetings," a sign that is invariably held up on either end by a cross-eyed cartoon elf or two with a posse at hand of idiotic plastic snowmen, all of this thanks to craven, anti-Christian pusillanimists, peevish Milquetoasts, and gutless ACLU loons who cannot abide the holy name of Jesus. "Those who forget God, the single assurance of our safety however that word may be defined, can be recognized in the fact that they make irrational responses to irrational fears," wrote Marilynne Robinson in her essay, "Fear," *The New York Review of Books* (September 24, 2015).

No PETA members of course will be numbered in the pro-turkey line-up, either, a group that includes Paul McCartney, Natalie Portman, Forest Whittaker, Mike Tyson, Woody Harrelson, Marisa Tomei, Joaquin Phoenix, Alicia Silverstone, Shania Twain, and Avril Lavigne. How sad that actors, the stupidest, least informed citizens in the country, are always quoted the most.

In his essay "Eating with the Pilgrims," the to-me always unfunny and tedious writer Calvin Trillin argues that, because historians cannot agree on what the Pilgrims ate on the first Thanksgiving, there is no reason for turkey—which he abhors—to have become the default meal for the holiday. (Have you heard the one about the three-year-old's response to her Christmas dinner? "I don't like the turkey, but I like the bread he ate") As for Trillin's lunatic choice of a holiday substitute, this man suggests as his lead offering the dish called spaghetti carbonara, a particular meal to which, if anyone can find an American link, I'll leave to poverty-headed Mr. Trillin's lame explanations, frankly not worthy enough to report here.

Thanksgiving was the late Christopher Hitchens' favorite holiday, just as it was Franklin D. Roosevelt's, Pres. Barack Obama's, TV anchorman Willard Scott's, Pee-wee Herman's, actor Jimmy Stewart's, and of course Abraham Lincoln's, who on October 3, 1863 was the first to proclaim it a holiday. For the late, determined, and dependably robust atheist Hitchens, it would signify of course that this annual November holiday would be one fully unencumbered by any formal religious obligations. Ironically, the gastronomic side of Thanksgiving made no headway with Hitchens, either, for in his essay, "The Turkey Has Landed" (*The Wall Street Journal*, Nov. 23, 2005), he explicitly stated that he could not stand eating turkey or pumpkin pie, caviling and complaining about such a day where one "forces down, at an odd hour of the afternoon, the sort of food that even the least discriminating diner in a restaurant would never order by choice." (Eating a meal without smoking cigarettes, by the way—I am not exaggerating—was a meaningless act to Hitchens, as he declared in print more than once.) But suddenly comes from Hitchens a bold defense of this feast day, for—in what is a rare manifestation of sentiment in the cynical, often black-hearted journalist—this Brit who at the late age of 57 became an American citizen, adds,

> Never mind all that... I have become one of those to whom Thanksgiving is a festival to be welcomed, and not dreaded. I once grabbed a plate of what was quite possibly turkey, but which certainly invoked processed cranberry and pumpkin in a U.S. army position in the desert on the frontier of Iraq. *It was the worst meal—by far the worst meal—I have ever eaten.* [my italics] But in all directions from the chow hall, I could see Americans of every conceivable stripe and confession, cheerfully asserting their connection, in awful heat, with a fall of long ago. And this is a holiday that in no way could divide them. May this always be so, and may one give some modest thanks for it.

Before we crown Hitchens with an olive wreath, one may be reminded here of the surprisingly petulant and juvenile anti-Christmas column, "Bah, Humbug," that he wrote for *Slate* (Dec. 20, 2005), where with gleeful malice he took up the cudgels to bludgeon the holy day for its "collectivization of gaiety and the compulsory infliction of joy," spitefully referred to all Christian "enthusiasts" as "stupid," and dismissed out of hand any and all propaganda of a day bloated with "paganism and corruption," including the Nativity itself, the significance of which, here and elsewhere, he has always found hollow, inane, purposeless, and trivial.

In a memorable essay on food memories, the brilliant French chef, author, and painter Jacques Pépin—a more poetic, larger-souled fellow than Mr. Trillin ever was—makes no apology for eating turkey on Thanksgiving

Day; as a matter of fact, it is one of the highlights of his holiday. He gracefully explains,

> There is a sweetness and gentleness to the fall. I love
> the fragrant smell of apple tarts, making cider, roasting
> a duck with sweet potatoes, the bursting yellow and
> red of the maple trees, the tanginess of the Concord
> grapes, and, finally, the turkey of Thanksgiving, my
> favorite holiday.

As to turkey, finally, I wonder how serious a culinary condemnation composer Richard Rodgers and lyricist Lorenz Hart were actually making—or if it was a criticism at all—when in the introductory verse of their "The Lady is a Tramp" for their 1937 musical, *Babes in Arms*, they wrote,

> I've wined and dined on Mulligan stew
> And never wished for turkey
> As I hitched and hiked and grifted, too,
> From Maine to Albuquerque.

Did you know there are no turkeys in Turkey? Much confusion is attendant on this whole linguistic story. Early eaters thought that the fowl that we know came from India, which is why Hindustan means the "Land of Turkeys." Europeans, you see, confused the fat creatures we eat on Thanksgiving with the guinea fowl imported through Turkey, the country. In Turkey, their name for their country is Turkiye, while their word for the bird—which does not exist there—is the word "*hindi*." Who can explain? The Turkish name for Egypt is *Misr*, which means corn. Go figure.

Back for a moment to James Beard and his ornate fussiness about food. Fussiness surely figures in food phobias. Don't children famously hate to have their vegetables touch on a plate, spitefully refusing to eat one or both of them? I hated when a little boy to have my mother cut up my food. Toddlers begin to experience at the age of two what pediatricians call "food neophobia," a fear of new foods. Then look at all the Old Testament quirks. Jehovah refuses polluted offerings. (Malachi 1:7). Daniel refuses the King Nebuchadnezzar's pagan food. (Daniel 1:9) The Hebrews refused to eat bread made with human dung (Ezekiel 4:12). King Saul, who in something of a blue funk—he was known for them—refuses to eat *anything*, because the Philistines made war against him, and he feels God has "deserted him." (1 Samuel 28:15)

Speaking of Ezekiel, one may recall that the prophet actually devours a *scroll*. In Ezekiel 3:3, we read, "And he [Jehovah] said to me, 'Son of man, eat what is before you, eat this scroll; then go and speak to the people of Israel.' So I opened my mouth, and he gave me the scroll to eat. So I ate it, and it tasted as sweet as honey in my mouth." Although the scroll the Prophet eats contains God's bitter judgments against Israel, it tastes as sweet as honey to him, only because, dutifully, responsibly, selflessly, the God-fearing man is serving the Lord.

I am convinced Ezekiel was kitchen bound. His book, full of bizarre visions and puzzling revelations, is rich in food imagery, everything from cooking pots to the food of mourners to the subject of priests eating offerings. I imagine that the man cooked a lot. There is no mention of him having offspring, only that his wife died rather young, propitious circumstances for that likelihood.

I was going to say no wonder Jews are referred to as the "People of the Book," but scroll-eating appears in the New Testament, as well (an angel standing on the sea gives St. John a scroll to eat in the book of Revelation 10:9, another beacon of prophesy) — until I am suddenly struck by what is arguably the strangest fact of all regarding these many oddball food caveats and proscriptions, and that is our very deepest theological beliefs were set in stone—two thousand years ago!—*by minor agricultural societies of the eastern Mediterranean!*

I remember reading that Crazy Horse, the brave chief of the Oglala Lakota—it was only one of his many eccentricities—would never smoke a pipe if the tobacco had been packed down in the bowl with a stick, as was commonly done by most Indians back then; unless his tobacco was pressed down *with thumb* by *all smokers* quaffing the pipe, this great foe of General Custer would not touch it. Other idiosyncrasies of his hardened into habits. Before battle, for example, Crazy Horse always threw a handful of dust over himself and his pony and never went forward without wearing a single hawk feather, along with a very small stone behind his ear.

As I have mentioned, Beard was gay, and one cannot truly discount a certain overfastidiousness or stickling need in him to queen it about tastes and cooking techniques. Simon Doonan's *Gay Men Don't Get Fat* is another book of wittily subjective and slightly over-considered opinions, a fund of campy advice and Corinthian fastidiousness that playfully breaks down culinary options into two categories: gay food and straight food. Doonan, who has been the impish wit behind the eye-catching and irreverent window displays of Barney's luxury department stores for almost 25 years, is also a cookbook author. He is a tiny, smiling, leprechaunish chap with a nose longer than Cosima Wagner's, big eyeglasses, which he waves about, and a penchant for screamingly loud floral shirts as loud as Baked Alaska, supposedly the archetypal queer food.

"Mix it up," Doonan advised Jeff Gordinier (who is straight) over lunch in a *New York Times* interview (Jan. 3, 2012) regarding the balanced diet of both so-called gay and straight foods. "It's the savviest way to stay svelte. Think of it, if you must, as bisexual eating," he declared. "Gay men don't stay trim because they only eat gay food. I don't live on macarons and lettuce." Still, heavy meat dishes like thick steaks, full chops, even jumbo burritos are no-no's for him. Weighty, hefty, and ponderous do not make up the Doonan template. "Meatloaf, that's a whole lot of hetero to digest," informed the gay author who is also completely put off by fat. He is full of lavendrical observations, his mind fruitcaked with no end of quotable aperçu. "Brisket is the Super Bowl of hetero cuisine. The thought of it gives me the vapors." "A Caesar salad's pretty heterosexual. They whip a lot of egg into it." "You must be on guard when you see a *panini* coming toward you," he darkly warns us, "because they can cram an enormous amount of meat and cheese in there." And so forth.

Salads, by the way, were the favorite food of anthropologist Margaret Mead, author of the 1928 classic, *Coming of Age in Samoa,* a woman who was often quoted for her remark, "People don't eat nutrition, they eat food." Her go-to salad began with her beating oil, vinegar, lemon juice, mustard, salt, and pepper in a bowl, and then throwing in capers, pimiento, fresh dill, tomatoes, and greens, a standard meal that was accompanied by French bread, Gorgonzola, Camembert, Liederkranz, or blue cheese. (Ironically, she found Samoan food "starchy.") Is not the exclusive daily focus on one food or foods an aspect of food aversion?

I ask that because, to take but one example, the late racist Israeli politician Ariel Sharon, born Ariel Scheinerman of Russian subbotniks, a 350-pound hippo and proto-foodie known as "The Bulldozer," was apparently fixated almost exclusively on eating chicken. A complete pig of a man, a merciless glutton, he ate with his hands and could dispatch three chickens at a single sitting. An especially endearing meal of his, called "Beit Jala Chicken," was slathered in a blanket of thick white paste that was composed of garlic, potato, lemon oil, and lemon, a gloppy emulsified mess rather like a mayonnaise with the texture of whipped cream. He would bolt down a dozen or more halva cookies at interviews, but it was chicken he gobbled like a frenzied raccoon. Chew-toy food he craved. He lusted after deep-fried turkey testicles ("hot nuts") rolled in bread batter, a bit gummy, like spine or brain, with a grassy smell and a gamey undertone of glands, the kind of offal-intensive taste fancied by rabid meat mutts and rustic peasants who love to bite crispy, crunchy, fast-delivering grease.

So, are salads gay? Although Mead was married three times, she had a very close relationship with Professor Ruth Benedict, an instructor of hers at Columbia and a major influence on her life. In her memoir about her parents, *With a Daughter's Eye*, Mary Catherine Bateson implies that the relationship between Benedict and Mead was partly sexual. While Mead never openly identified herself as lesbian or bisexual, the details of her relationship with Benedict have led to that conclusion. In her writings, in fact, Mead proposed that it was not rare to find an individual's sexual interest may evolve throughout life. She spent her last years in a close personal and professional collaboration with anthropologist, Rhoda Metraux, with whom she lived from 1955 until her death in 1978. Letters between the two, published in 2006 with the permission of Mead's daughter, clearly express a romantic relationship.

Gay interest in cooking, homosexual fascination for things culinary, was a popular archetype back in the '30s, '40s, '50s. Remember Rock Hudson in the movie, *Pillow Talk* (1959), trying to convince, mockingly and with great relish, the very straight and virginal Doris Day over the telephone that his alter-ego in the movie sounds a little...gay? "There are some men who just are very devoted to their mothers," Hudson gleefully but not too subtly clarifies for her, "you know, the type that likes to collect cooking recipes, exchange bits of gossip..." Day's reaction? In a splendidly homophobic over-reaction, filled with social alarm, she gulps, does a double-take for the camera, and looks bewildered, surprised, and shocked.

Without putting too fine a point on it, back in the 50s the observation "He cooks" pretty much means "He's a twinkie." The received picture is of a male wearing a damson apron, reaching for a pinch of cumin while mincing over to a kitchen counter to check a detail in a cookbook, softly mouing "I like long fat thick noodles—nobody likes a soggy noodle, right?" Real racy stuff! When you eat the food someone makes for you, *you are eating their love*! Anyone for zucchini?

In Dawn Powell's novel, *The Happy Island* (1938), almost all of the characters are either gay or bisexual, happily switching partners with abandon amid bouts of coke-sniffing and food feasting. Powell personally referred to gays as "fairies," a term she used mainly with affection." Very revealing is her diary entry for March 2, 1936, quoted from Tim Page's *Dawn Powell*:

> John Mosher, unattractive to women, silent in the
> house, finds balm in getting the pale silent young man

> in borrowed evening clothes away from Dwight. He
> has him in his house where he encourages him to go
> on with his cooking, gets him his Escoffier, Brillat-
> Savant [sic], Sabatini, Moneta, brings him home little
> gadgets, egg slicers, canapés, entertains, proud of his
> pompano in fig leaves, his duck *a la presse*. John talks,
> educating him culturally; Dopey listens, says salad too
> wet... John encourages Dopey to write cookbook
> a la Brillat-Savarin, but week after week Dopey gets
> gloomier. Presently sees manuscript. "Cooking is the
> art of making something to eat. Everybody likes to
> eat. People mostly put too much water on in cooking
> vegetables." John's heart sank. You ought to get out
> more.

Comically, the serious art of cooking in *Pillow Talk* devolves into a joke. We drop headlong from the sublime to the laughably trivial. The gay mind is prone to bathos. In Matthew Arnold's words, we all have a "natural taste for the bathos" and are in a great rush to mistake it for a "relish for the sublime." On the other hand, with gays, bathos is often intentional and bathetic chit-chat (hint, hint), often given with the precious bijou of a wink. Food and cooking is—or surely can rate—high in the domain of kitsch, and remains one of its main refuges.

Simon Doonan who thrives on twee exaggeration, wild overstatement, and campy pronouncements claims to be put off by the fattening traps sprung by avocado and guacamole. "Burritos are clearly the hate crime of the gay food world," observes Alexander Abad-Santos in "How Gay is Your Food?" in the blog "The Wire"," "and bring together Doonan's unholy trinity of meat, cheese, and avocado (along with that dodge-worthy sour cream). Then again," he adds, "we've seen that combination on cheeseburgers." Doonan fully agrees that baked chips are inherently gay, but then who is going to be taking the time to settle into a snack of baked chips when there is a mound of irresistible guacamole staring at you?

Let me hasten to add that by no means do I carry a brief against gays or gay food, if such indeed exists, and I have many times told people that my favorite dinner guests would unquestionably include, among others, sparkling Oscar Wilde, Henry James, Frederick Rolfe, Erik Blore, Edward Everett Horton, Clifton Webb, Cole Porter, Monty Woolley, Truman Capote, and the always cynically ironic comedian/actor Paul Lynde, matchless companions specifically chosen to share my table, not for anything particularly scandalous or *réclame* about them, but strictly for the sublime wit of their great company, conversation, gossip, blague!

Other invitees welcome to my dream table would surely include Juvenal, John the Baptist, William Shakespeare, Christopher Marlowe, Charles Lamb, Sir Philip Sidney, H.H. Munro, Richard Wagner, Jonathan Swift, St. Paul, Charles Dickens, Gerard Manley Hopkins, Ludwig Wittgenstein, Henry David Thoreau, Dr. Samuel Johnson, Henry Fielding, Alexander Pope, Leonardo DaVinci, Patricia Highsmith, Charles Doughty, Thomas Jefferson, W.C. Fields, Abraham Lincoln, Tecumseh, Eugene Debs, and, among others, historian James Henry Breasted.

I wonder how Doonan would have gauged the food diet, gender-wise, of the literary Bloomsbury Group where burly Ralph Partridge was in love with the lesbian Dora Carrington who had fallen passionately in love with homosexual Lytton Strachey who was greatly attracted to heterosexual Ralph. Talk about the happy island—this was nothing less than a race of hedonistic musical chairs! Beyond that, isn't Doonan himself stereotyping his own subculture, pontificating about gay tastes as if there were only *one* gay point-of-view? According to the poet W.H. Auden, one even needs to know what a gay person's particular sexual preference is—what he or she does in bed—if you wanted to understand him or his work.

When Gordinier asked Doonan about almonds, he condescendingly acknowledged that he was not averse to the occasional nut, if it were the right one. [The right nut? I feel the need here to point out that such filigree distinctions are glaringly one of the many compulsions of a "Food Douche," that is, a person who fully believes that he knows the best place to get any one specific item of food and that all the places that *you* know all suck. Gays are big FDs—and a good many people from Manhattan.] "I'll do an almond. Or two. Not a fistful. You know when you get those mixed nuts on a plane? If I'm sitting next to a straight guy, he'll basically take the little container and heave it into his mouth... I'm a big believer in dried fruit. Figs. Dates. Raisins. You have to be careful with the dried apricots because they really do make you gassy." There is no question that Doonan with a lordly, sniffing preeminence tends to give straight cuisine less than high marks, finding much of it a bit too common and indeed slightly rebarbative. Interpreting Doonan, Gordinier goes on to write,

> Straight food, according to the Doonan rubric,
> tends to be leaden, full of protein, and thick with
> fat. Consider the grub he grew up with in England.
> "British food used to be so straight when I was a kid,"

he said. "Haggis. Horrible stews. Boiled greens that
were gray. Now they've gayed it up, and British food
is incredible." The way he sees it, gay food is lighter and brighter. It feels art-directed, not just tossed
together and deep-fried, with an attention to aesthetic
and dietary detail. "Gay foods are more decorative;
they're more frivolous," he said. "The macaron craze
is the ne plus ultra of gay fooderie. I can't believe any
red-blooded straight guy can even walk into a macaron shop. If you wanted to ruin a politician's career,
just publish a picture of him shopping for macarons."

Where the prescient Doonan self-pointedly adjudges as if by a far greater
power than we can contradict that the taste of "straights" runs solely to the
leaden, the fat, and the odious—we all indulge in generalities now and again
but need we make whole books of them?—I am inclined to look on his bias,
no matter how comic, with what Noël Coward, after reading Mary Renault's
The Charioteer (1953), a tale of two blooming young "tulips" during World
War II, called a "shimmering lack of understanding of the subject." The gay
Coward impatiently carps,

> I do, do wish well-intentioned ladies would not write
> books about homosexuality. This one is turgid, unreal
> and so ghastly earnest. It takes the hero—soi-disant—
> three hundred pages to reconcile himself to being
> queer as a coot, and his soul-searching and deep, deep
> introspection is truly awful.... I'm sure the poor wom-
> an meant well, but I wish she'd stick to recreating the
> glory that was Greece and not fuck about with dear
> old modern homos.

Gay subtext, not food, is behind the often-quoted exchange in the
movie *Spartacus* (1961) when Crassus (Laurence Olivier) quizzes Antonius
(Tony Curtis) on the latter's taste in food—specifically, how the extremely
able-bodied slave feels about gastropods and mollusks. "Do you consider the
eating of oysters to be moral and the eating of snails to be immoral?" Crassus
probingly asks, and he then rather unsubtly points out that "taste is not the
same as appetite, and therefore not a question of morals." When Antonius
replies such an assertion "could be argued so, master," Crassus shares what

was surely among the worst-kept secrets of the ancient world: "My taste," he says, "includes both snails... and oysters."

A quick gloss here on that reference to gay foods being more decorative is, pardon the pun, a great dish. The gay, campy, Corinthian-minded pianist Liberace—Wladziu Valentino Liberace—always fussily insisted that only white raisins be used in his well-known recipe for sticky buns, which has often been anthologized. He would not look at red-flame raisins! A dried fruit more popular in the 1970s than it is today, white raisins for fussy Lee specifically had to be soaked in rum just prior to being baked. A fellow who was not exactly known for his restraint, Liberace kept seven (count them!) dining areas in his house, each with a different theme. He always went all the way! The Liberace Museum now sells copies of his 1970 cookbook, *Liberace Cooks*, from their website for $12.95. Way back in high school Lee inaugurated a cooking class, which he says became very popular with his fellow students, preparing foods, learning different cuts of meat, and so forth. Liberace was widely known for his special fruitcakes, as symbolic of him as his candelabras—forgive the false plural: strictly speaking, the Latin word *candelabrum* is singular, with *candelabra* as its legitimate plural——the secret ingredients for which he was given by his devoted Polish mother who took the trouble to soak the nuts and fruits in brandy. Liberace's fruitcakes. Sticky buns. Nuts and fruits. (I have duly provided the nouns, reader—you can have your own fun with the verbs, all right?). *Confidential* magazine, which always referred to the florid pianist as "Dimples," highlighted the pianist's penchant for cooking in high school. Back in September 27, 1956, a vituperative columnist for the *Daily Mirror* named Sir William Neil Connor, who was known under the pseudonym of "Cassandra," penned an acid portrait of Liberace, describing the American pianist as

> ... the summit of sex—the pinnacle of masculine, feminine, and neuter. Everything that he, she, and it can ever want... a deadly, winking, sniggering, snuggling, chromium-plated, scent-impregnated, luminous, quivering, giggling, fruit-flavoured, mincing, ice-covered heap of mother love.

for which the pianist took the columnist to court for libel. In those days, Liberace wore a loud perfume, which was the occasion of Connor's descriptive assault, as the Associated Press reported. Liberace claimed he was using the strong scent to overcome the smell of an antiseptic he had been administered for a bee sting! To the British press, it was merely another sign that the man had long gone over the bridge to Pimpleton—you know, was a bit light in loafers. But that this was not glaringly obvious is a joke. The entire waking world knew he was a Fanny Bellhop. "One windy night we arrived at this premiere and we were getting out of the car and Liberace got out first," television actress Betty White recalled. "I held out my hand because I thought he was going to help me out of the car. But he was holding his hair."

The first time that Liberace performed in Allentown, Pennsylvania, he ate out at Hess Brothers, a department store restaurant, and later he claimed repeatedly that he fell head over heels for one of their "specials," their strawberry pie. It was so typical of Liberacean kitschiness. Every Christmas thereafter, Liberace would never fail to order a large amount of Hess pies and have them directly shipped to all his friends as holiday presents. Sadly, the department store is with us no longer—it went belly up in 1996—but thanks to *findadeath.com* I did manage to find both this wonderful pie story—and the exclusive pie recipe:

> Hess's Strawberry Pie
> 8 cups whole fresh strawberries, stems removed
> 10 to 12 additional strawberries with stems attached,
> for garnish
> 1 cup confectioners' sugar
> 1 cup sugar
> 3 Tbsps. Cornstarch
> 1 cup water
> 12 drops red food coloring
> 1 cup whipping cream
> 1/4 cup confectioners' sugar
> 1 tsp. vanilla
> 1 9-inch baked pie crust
>
> Wash and stem the strawberries. Mix 6 cups of them
> with confectioners' sugar. Let stand for one hour.
> Cook remaining 2 cups berries with water until tender
> and rub through a sieve. Mix granulated sugar and
> cornstarch and add to the strained strawberry juice.
> Cook until clear. Add food coloring. Let mixture
> cool slightly, stirring occasionally. Arrange whole
> strawberries, stem side down in the pie shell. Mound
> the berries in the center of the pie. Pour the cooked

strawberry mixture evenly over the strawberries in the
pie shell. Refrigerate until cold.

Pour whipping cream into cold mixing bowl. Beat
cream at medium-high speed until it begins to thicken.
On low speed, add confectioners' sugar and vanilla.
Continue to beat until stiff, but fluffy. Whipped cream
may be used as a decorating tool. Just pipe it onto the
pie up to two hours before serving it. Garnish with
whole strawberries, still attached to their stems. Keep
refrigerated until ready to serve.

Liberace treasured those cooking classes at East Milwaukee High, although word has it that he was often ridiculed for it, and enjoyed cooking
dinner at night when he was refining his act and playing under the, to me,
comic name "Walter Busterkeys." In 1941, when Liberace's parents got divorced, he sulkingly blamed his father, to whom he would not speak for
many years. Both of his parents remarried, and Frances Liberace Casadonte,
his mother, became the owner of an ice cream shop where her illustrious son
loved to tuck into huge sundaes with whipped cream and cherries. It was
Lucullus who supposedly first introduced cherries to the west, something for
which Liberace would have been grateful, as he ate the fruit by the handful.

At one point Liberace even *taught* a cooking class. He kept separate
dining rooms in his mansion, one for buffets, others for cookouts—he had a
canopied cook-nook facing his garden—midnight suppers, banquets, watching TV (one-dish meals were popular fare there), and dining in the kitch-
en. Main dinners were served in his formal dining room. He loved fish. He
craved bacon and butter and used both in his heralded guacamole. He got
up at noon and called lunch breakfast.

But back to Simon Doonan whose irrepressible delight in lilting and
ornate pontifications knows no end. His list of favorite foods is specific and,
one gets the impression, fussily selected. He loves sushi, sashimi, crudo, seafood tartare, ceviche, black bean soup, and field greens. Any light, stylized
fare on stunning, perhaps over-worked plates are fine. But no spicy mayo
anything on rolls, or supermarket sushi, or any roll with more than three
ingredients or one fried object. I have never come across anyone who had
complicated issues with rolls, as such, except A.P. Herbert, English humorist,
novelist, playwright and law reform activist whose ditty "Bacon and Eggs," a
celebration of the English breakfast, includes the lines:

> But gross Europeans who constantly munch
> Too little at breakfast, too freely at lunch
> Sit sated in cafés, incapable souls,
> And go to the devil on coffee and rolls—
> Coffee and rolls,
> Windy wet rolls;
> At coffee
> I'm scoffy,
> I execrate rolls!"

Doonan is apparently very strict with himself as to diet. "I never eat between meals. I tap dance between meals. I clog. I baton twirl. But eating? Not so much." "A little choccie [chocolate] before lunch can put a skip in your walk… and, as you may have guessed," he hastens to add, "I am a big fan of skipping." In his opinion, French fries are "very heterosexual." Basically, for Doonan, heavy foods are hetero, light foods are homo. Mexican food? The ultimate in straight cuisine. Sushi? Its opposite. "Japanese food—that is some seriously gay food," pronounced Doonan. "I've been to restaurants in Japan where they bring out a watermelon in its entirety and they open it up and inside it's full of ice and one little pink piece of sushi in the middle. Basically, you're taking sloppy bits of fish and making them into these exquisite little bonbons, and that seems inordinately gay to me."

We all know about the "French Paradox"—wine-drinkers in France never have heart attacks. Doonan has happily gone on record as scandalously saying that "gay men are basically French women with penises…[but be careful] regarding alcohol: Booze is catastrophically disinhibiting. Two glasses of gin and most people will eat everything in sight." He loves to correct false myths. "Quiche Lorraine is, and has always been, straight food wickedly packaged as gay," he says. He was once asked if there are any gay Passover foods? He replied, "Bitter herbs are somewhat gay. Matzo balls are as straight as Moshe Dayan."

Are we to understand that every individual with, um, Scythian inclinations are all sold on *all* French cuisine as much they are, say, of designer underwear, Judy Garland, gym selfies, Broadway show tunes, yappy little dogs, the color lavender, taking off their shirts, skipping, and eating "choccie"?

Gordinier notes that Doonan uninhibitedly used the word "lesbian" to describe certain earthy, healthful foods. "Organic olive oil, thick porridge, heaping helpings of wheat germ," he said. "A crusty loaf of whole-grain bread is both ferociously lesbian and wildly heterosexual." They came to dessert. Doonan looked at a rich cappuccino mousse with Oreo-cookie crust and whipped cream. "Desserts now have a very gay sensibility," he explained. "If you're looking for a basic apple pie, you're going to be out of luck." He scanned the menu. "There's a fresh-baked pie of the day. See, I want to know what that is. I might succumb to it. Because I've been quite abstemious." I'd consider gay the Irish dessert Yellowman, a toffee-like sweet of treacle, butter, vinegar, and brown sugar.

Comedian Joan Rivers always said, "I think gay men are the best cooks." Rivers was asked by *Gourmet* magazine, "What was the worst meal you ever had?" She replied, "Oh god, it's all about color. The worst was an all-white meal. It was cod, and mashed potatoes and cauliflower on a white plate! It was served to me by a friend, as a joke. It was July Fourth and we all did a red white and blue theme. I got the white meal." The magazine asked, "Is there one thing you refuse to eat?" Rivers was a flaming liberal. "No. I am the hostess' delight. I will say, 'I like seconds of the haggis! Gimme some more kimchi! Blood sausage? Delicious!' I look forward to airplane meals. I really will eat anything." The crude comedian said, "I'm not a picky eater. If I were in the Donner party, I would ask for seconds."

Strangely enough, for a Jewish person, Rivers (born Joan Molinsky) was not big for Asian food. Before she died, she wrote in the introduction to a cookbook, *Eating Delancey: A Celebration of Jewish Food* and among other tidbits she wrote, "I'm not happy at a Chinese restaurant. I want kreplach! Jewish food makes Italian food seem like Lean Cuisine." On the other hand, she did say, "My last meal would be everything Italian—lasagna, noodles, cheeses, cannolis." (N.B.: in Italy, you spell *lasagne* with an *e*, because it is several layers of dough.)

The kitchen was not Joan Rivers' favorite place. "I'm no cook," she once quipped. "When I want lemon on chicken, I spray it with Pledge." A favorite joke of hers was, "What does a Jewish woman make for dinner? Reservations."

The idea of food being exclusively gay or LGBT, a term in use since the 1990s, can certainly be argued one way or another. Ornateness, bordering on showy, elaborate, and florid seems to be a common denominator in much *soi-disant* gay food. Gay actor Neil Patrick Harris told *Bon Appetit*— he speaks of "wine pairings," "fancy bread carts," and "boutique-y" restaurants—that his husband, David, serves great dinners. He loves floral drinks such as "pineapple rum-based Tikis" and a cocktail he has concocted called a French Manhattan" ("two ounce of rye whiskey with half an ounce of Chambord, some Angostura bitters, cherry bitters, and a maraschino cherry"). "I'm super adventurous," says Harris, and recounts dining out at Park, an Asian restaurant in Montreal where they serve "acupunctured snapper."

"It's snapper that has been caught and then killed in a way that is very calm—the fishermen insert needles so that the trauma of death is avoided, and the cut is really tender." Could anyone possibly devise a gayer statement?

American novelist, reporter and war correspondent, William Vollmann believes that there are vast differences of taste and varying approaches to the whole idea of eating. "I am a happy heterosexual male," explained the daring novelist to a crowd in New York City last year while promoting, *The Book of Dolores*, a bold and un-self-consciously shocking collection of self-portraits, a study of his female alter ego named "Dolores," a persona that he has assumed in real life as both a literary strategy and a means of sexual exploration in order to investigate womanhood. It is his conviction that in order best to imagine his character, he had to become Dolores. "As to the transgendered taste of food," he told me,

> I myself have been known to stuff delicious food into
> my mouth and bolt it like a greedy animal. Dolores,
> however, worries about messing up her makeup,
> dropping food on her dress, and other errors, which
> I might commit in her shoes. Hence, that girl eats in
> small bites. This certainly makes the food taste a little
> different. When I played with hormones, I felt great
> changes in mood, sensibility, and even cognition,
> but particularly in taste. However, you could try the
> experiment. Get some [he gives a brand name here]
> cream or the like at the supermarket and rub a few
> gobs of it on your chest for a few weeks. (Be warned:
> you may get breast cancer, and after you stop, your
> risk will be as great as a woman's for a year or more.)
> But you will feel different within a day or two. Perhaps
> your sense of taste will alter. (If you decide to publish
> this, Alex, best to blank out the brand, so you and I
> don't get get sued by angry bearded gourmets whose
> basketball-sized boobs are killing them.)

While I must say that I have no personal interest myself in investigating the trials of womanhood from within, I find it intrepid of Bill bravely to go to such extremes in his exploration of "t-girls," as he calls them, and in an experiment both epistemological and physiological, to be willing to make himself, as he says, "a bit vulnerable and ridiculous and pathetic in the attempt to show my sincerity."

Simon Doonan must have undergone some kind of change after October 2008, when in an article about "lush, flamboyantly attired, and hospitable" Palm Beach, Florida for *Travel and Leisure* he wrote, "Food is king in Palm Beach… In P.B. you will find a relentless emphasis on simple 1950s digestible fare. Yes, it's true that the majority of your fellow diners will all be *d'un certain âge*. Look upon this as a bonus. I do—to enter any restaurant at 56 and bring the median age crashing down is a sweet thing. There are the more grandiose, chandelier-festooned eateries, where the women wear tiaras. My personal favorite, however, is on South Dixie Highway in West Palm Beach—La Sirena. Jonny [his husband] and I always share the yellowtail snapper for two, followed by a *torta mattina* for him and a *torta caprese* for me. Our game plan is fairly transparent: we minimize our entrée carbs so that we can pig out on the house-made desserts. As you leave, please remember to generously tip the blond valet who boldly indicates available parking spaces to new arrivals with the aid of a large flashlight. We like her." Pig out on the house-made desserts?

Poet W.H. Auden never ate desserts. Neither does Japanese novelist Haruki Murakami, who, something of a foodie, discloses the very spare, Spartan diet that he undertook for his long-distance running program in his book, *What I Talk About When I Talk About Running*, explaining, "I began to eat mostly vegetables, with fish as my main source of protein. I never liked meat much anyway, and this aversion became even more pronounced. I cut back on rice and alcohol and began using all natural ingredients. Sweets weren't a problem since I never much cared for them." Celebrity chef Enrique Olvera, a true kitchen auteur, owner of Cosme in NYC, and one of the great experts on Mexican cuisine, is not big for desserts. "They say sugar is worse for you than cocaine. I am going to take dessert off the menu at Pujol [his restaurant in Mexico City, considered one of the best in Latin America].

The late movie actor, Paul Newman, avoided all desserts. Popcorn was his sweet, so to speak. After he died, his daughter, Nell, went on the Internet to say that he did, after all, secretly enjoy a favorite orange chocolate angel food cake, ever since identified—and rather widely, I gather—as "The Paul Newman Chocolate Cake." It is light as air, low in fat, tasty, and very easy to make, according to Nell Newman, who uses organic ingredients when she makes it. People online claim that it is delicious. I am surprised that Newman did not like macaroons, especially because he was Jewish, and Jewish people are famously partial to macaroons. Although macaroons were first made by monks in the 9th-century, Italian Jews later came to adopt the cookie as their own because it has no flour or leavening (macaroons are leavened only by egg whites), and so it is one food that may be eaten during the eight-day observation of Passover. It was introduced to other European Jews and became popular as a year-round sweet. Over time, coconut was added to the ground almonds and, in certain other recipes, replaced them. Potato starch is also sometimes included in various macaroon recipes, to give them more body. A Jewish acquaintance of mine from some years ago, while she flat-out considered macaroons as absolutely the single worst food on earth, nevertheless—go figure—found the French *macaron* delicious.

What is the difference? The macaron is a sweet meringue-based confectionery made with egg whites, icing sugar, granulated sugar, ground almond, and food coloring and is commonly filled with ganache, buttercream, or jam filling and sandwiched between two cookies.

A person named Jesse Taylor in a particular blog that I happened to come across commented in October 2012, at the height of the Mitt Romney/Barack Obama battle for the Presidency, how fussily Romney ate muffins—if that is even the right verb. "He does it like a weirdo," writes Taylor. It appears, like a good Bain & Company capitalist, he approached the dessert with a muffin strategy. Taylor goes on to say,

> For most eaters, a muffin is consumed unthinkingly, in big messy bites, [with them] pawing last crumbs off the wrapper because, well, they taste good. For Mr. Romney, however, a muffin is an analytical challenge—a risk to be weighed. Indeed, eating muffins the Romney way takes discipline: He consumes the top, and only the top, to better avoid the unhealthy butter that supposedly flows downward during baking, according to an account by one of his biographers... Besides the fact that we are 99% sure the 'butter at the bottom' thing is bullshit (as experienced bakers, obviously), why does Mitt Romney, trying to save calories, reflect on how he would manage the nation? Michelle Obama has been trying to do that for years, and she is apparently a horrible Amazonian hell beast. After reading all six pages of this article, it is clear: Mitt Romney's muffin waste goes to show that, like the rest of us, he does mildly irrational things for no reason that in no way qualify him to be president. Take that and be comforted.

Worthy of a reader's attention are the singular passages in Shakespeare where any and all the associations of the word "candy" are sickening, invariably linked to the obsequious and slavering fawning of a dog. (Anthony Burgess in his *Shakespeare* asserts, "Will was given more to nausea than to appetite at the thought of rich feeding.") What is "candied" is always pejorative. We read, "No, let the candied tongue lick absurd pomp, /And crook the pregnant hinges of the knee/Where thrift may follow fawning" (*Hamlet*, III.iii.223); "Will the cold brook, candied with ice, caudle thy morning taste" (*Timon of Athens*, IV.iii.223); "Why, what a candy deal of courtesy/ This fawning greyhound then did proffer me" (*1 Henry IV*, I, iii.246-247).

It is hard to believe that simple jelly beans can figure in a subversive, antagonistic way as a threatening food, but there is a notable instance of such. "'Repent, Harlequin!' Said the Ticktockman" is a 1965 short story by sci-fi writer Harlan Ellison. It is nonlinear in that the narrative begins in the middle, then moves to the beginning, then the end, without the use of flashbacks including a paragraph about jelly beans which is almost entirely one run-on sentence. I see it as the "definitive jelly-bean" work of literature. It is a futuristic tale of a man named Everett C. Marm who, disguised as the anarchical Harlequin, engages in whimsical rebellion against the "Ticktockman." Everett is in a romantic relationship with a girl named Pretty Alice, who is, among other complaints of hers, exasperated by the fact that he is never on time, frustratingly always late. In this neo-Orwellian story, being late is not merely a working offense or a misdemeanor but constitutes a crime, in fact, one that carries a very hefty penalty, in that a proportionate amount of time is "revoked" from one's life. The ultimate consequence is to run out of time and be "turned off." This is done by the severe and forbidding Master Timekeeper, or Ticktockman, who in dispatching people utilizes a device called a "cardioplate" to stop a person's heart once his time has run out.

The rebellious, indeed subversive Harlequin maniacally disrupts the rote of the totalitarian work schedule of his robotic, enslaved society he lives in with methods such as distracting factory-workers from their tasks by throwing into their midst thousands of multicolored jelly beans, forcing the Ticktockman to pull people off their normal jobs to seek him out for punishment:

> Jelly beans! Millions and billions of purples and yellows and greens and licorice and grape and raspberry and mint and round and smooth and crunchy outside and soft-mealy inside and sugary and bouncing jouncing tumbling clittering clattering skittering fell on

the heads and shoulders and hardhats and carapaces
of the Timkin workers, tinkling on the sidewalk and
bouncing away and rolling about underfoot... jelly for
god's sake beans! This madness! Where did he get the
money to buy a hundred and fifty thousand dollars'
worth of jelly beans?

Overfussified desserts or treats can put people off. "People who dip sweetly tart strawberries into liquefied chocolate, wait for it to cool, and then eat the whole thing ought to be placed in mental institutions," wrote George Carlin in *When Will Jesus Bring the Pork Chops?*. "What you should do is this: Drink the chocolate before it cools, then put the strawberries on your kids' cereal. And while we're at it folks, nuts have no business in ice cream. Ice cream should be creamy. Nuts interrupt the creamy idea. Chunks of nuts don't belong in ice cream. Put 'em in a little bowl by themselves; put 'em in a candy bar; stick 'em up your nose for all I care, but leave my ice cream alone. And, in general, please folks, stop fucking with my desserts!"

Before we leave behind the subject of desserts, the British novelist and non-fiction writer Sheffield-born Geoff Nicholson, author of *Bleeding London* and *The Lost Art of Walking*, told me that, while he very much enjoys Indian food, he simply cannot abide the taste of Indian desserts. He explained to me, "I grew up in a 'typical' working class home in northern England in the late fifties and sixties. My parents despised exotic food (which generally meant foreign food). Garlic was regarded as an abomination, olive oil was something you put in your ear if you had earache, *bleu* cheese was disgusting because it supposedly had worms in it. I didn't share these prejudices and wanted to try things, but my parents were absolutely certain I wouldn't like them. At the same time we ate foods like pig's trotters and black pudding, all of which I still love and which I'm well aware many people can't stomach."

But Nicholson's affection for the complete foreign menu went only so far. He went on to tell me,

When I left home I trained myself as an omnivore,
partly by going to cheap 'foreign' restaurants; Greek,
Chinese, and especially Indian. I embraced most
Indian food (or at least a British version of it), but
there's one thing I cannot eat—Indian desserts. I
can't say I've tasted every single variety, but I've tasted
plenty and every one has been cloying, nauseatingly
sweet, texturally unpleasant, and more often that

not infused with cardamom. You want names? *Gulab
Jamun*—spongy dough balls made using milk powder,
and soaked in rose scented syrup. *Ras Malai*—sugary
cheese dumplings in clotted cream sauce (with cardamom). You'd think *Kulfi*, which is often described as
Indian ice cream, would be OK, but it's made with
evaporated and condensed milk, white bread and
cardamom! *Malpua*—sugar soaked pancakes with
cardamon. You see where I'm going with this? There's
also the all too well-named *Barfi*. I'm sure it's my
failing but I just can't eat this stuff. When I say can't,
I suppose that isn't literally true. Put a gun at my head
and I'd eat anything. But given the choice between a
bullet and a selection of Indian desserts I'd definitely
have to think twice.

I wonder what Nicholson would think about a super-sweet dessert served
in Cuba that is known as *tocino del cielo*, or heavenly bacon—a light and
tender custard which is made with egg yolks, sugar and water but is lighter
than a traditional flan or creme caramel but which smacks more of candy.
Then there is a Cuban Mango Mousse made with honey, heavy cream, and
lime-juice and some of the cloying milk shakes there like *tamerindo, zapote,
nispero, plátano*, and *piña*, all too sweet for my taste. Then of course there
is Akutaq or agutak also known as Eskimo ice cream—the word comes from
Yupik and means "something mixed"—which is a common food in western
Alaska, consisting of whipped fat mixed with berries, with optional additions
such as fish and sugar, but I have tasted it in the Kenai peninsula where it was
served with edible greens, seal oil, reindeer fat, and snow!

We compromise constantly on our walk through life, often settle for the
match of average, are obliging. It almost always leads to the rise and eventual
success of greedy, lying, and incompetent political candidates. Who of us has
not witnessed how when a political candidate gets through that seemingly
endless, expensive, and clownish obstacle course of running in a presidential
primary, he or she turns out to be the most mediocre, ironed-flat, overly
compromised nincompoop of the entire lot, the very butter-and-egg man (or
woman) we come to loathe, a person glaringly lacking the one ingredient of
which the country is always most needful: authenticity?

Are gays the arbiters of taste? "French women only think they know
everything. Actually, it's the gays who know everything," Doonan told a reporter from the New York Post. "Being the outsider automatically gives you

a more creative, more intuitive view on life and style and magic." He adds helpfully, "Being gay is an insane, fabulous gift. It's the ultimate Whitman's Sampler." Here, but wait, isn't that the cheapest, most low-brow of all chocolates on the market. What is to be Doonan's next book, *Gay Men Don't Mind Contradiction and Inconsistency*?

Chef Anthony Bourdain says "enough" with the processed cheese, cheap ground meat, and—indeed—bacon. "I love bacon as much as the next guy, but do I need a bacon tattoo?" he asks. Are his ambivalent squawks an example of his Jewish heritage emerging—his mother was born Gladys Sacksman—after a late dormancy? "I think we're maybe a little overenthusiastic on bacon. It's only cured pork—there are other forms of cured pork, many of them wonderful." "I hate bacon," snaps Jeanette MacDonald in the movie, *Rose Marie* (1936), stuck out in the wilderness by a campfire with Nelson Eddy, but, hungry and tempted, she devours a helping of beans and bacon, a better meal than cooked rattlesnake. Fanny Lemira Camp, the mother of the American safety-razor magnate King C. Gillette was a rabid recipe-collector and cook—she collaborated with Hugo Zieman to write, *The White House Cookbook*, which was first published in 1887—and once in a sudden fit of experimental zeal prepared a dinner of rattlesnake meat which the entire family abhorred. People say it tastes like chicken.

Who was it that said, "If there never was a chicken, everything would taste like nothing"? Jewish comedian Jackie Mason in one of his bits on stage inveighs against people who will order exotic meats like ostrich or rattlesnake and then claim it tastes like chicken. "Meanwhile," says the sputtering Mason, "an entire chicken is only five bucks, but some pretentious shmucks would rather eat something that 'tastes like chicken;' for $40 a serving." Pretentiousness is the cause of it all, surely. Mason goes on to say, "Food critics and restaurants have convinced us that we ought to pay big money for bitter-flavored European salad vegetables with exotic names like arugula, radicchio, escarole, fennel, and kale. The pricing was determined by a simple method: the more unpleasant it tasted, the more it cost."

Speaking of chicken and the so-called gay aversion to heavy meats, in 2010, Evo Morales, Bolivia's president, caused controversy when he implied that eating chicken could not only cause male pattern baldness but also *makes* men gay. At the World People's Summit in Cochabamba, he claimed that chicken, when pumped full of female hormones, makes men "stray from being men." Colombia model Natalia Paris claims girls between the ages of 7 and 10 are starting to develop sooner because hormones in poultry make everything in the body accelerate, turning them gay.

Fennel, by the way, the hardy perennial herb, may soon turn out to be unavailable, that is, if Nestlé, the Swiss giant, gets its way, for the world's largest food corporation is presently seeking to nail the exclusive patent for the use of *Nigella sativa* —it is called "black seed," "black cumin," or "fennel flower" in English and known as *habbat al-barakah* in Arabic—to prevent food allergies, claiming property over the plant seed and extract whenever they are used as a food ingredient or drug. In what seems to many to be an act of bio-piracy, Nestlé, claiming to own it, has been filing patent claims around the world to try and take control over the natural cure of the fennel flower and turn it into a costly private drug. In a paper published in 2012, Nestlé scientists claimed to "discover" what much of the world has known for millennia: that Nigella sativa extract could be used for "nutritional interventions in humans with food allergy." But instead of creating an artificial substitute or fighting to make sure the remedy was widely available, Nestlé is attempting to create a Nigella sativa monopoly and ultimately to gain traction to sue anyone using it without its permission. Nestlé has filed patent applications—which are currently pending—around the world.

Gooey chocolate fudge cake, finally, I'm told, is a homosexual icon. If the term positive feedback describes situations where an effect accentuates its cause, I can easily picture some gay guy forking into this fudgy dessert and saying to his jealous partner, "Well, one of us has to be the Top!"

6.

IRON JELLO

POVERTY CAN OVERCOME anyone's food aversions. Eating is not solely about choice or fussy delectation but obviously often rather a matter of simply staying alive. Hunger is a stern corrective. I have referred to mystery and Western pulp fiction author, Frank Gruber—he wrote for *Black Mask* magazine—and the meals he took in Macfadden's Penny Restaurants when he was a struggling writer. There was no shortage of such food emporia back in the 1950s, little corner hot spots selling hamburgers or hot dogs served either from greasy grills or yanked from aluminum meat humidifiers (often kept under a damp towel) in a mist of steam and condensation—someone rang a bell—on slightly moist buns under a sign that shouted, "Buy 'em by the Bag!" which was as much a desperate threat as an exclamation of value.

When Ignatius J. Reilly, the lazy, misanthropic anti-hero of John Kennedy Toole's *A Confederacy of Dunces* innocently inquires of a New Orleans street vendor what the ingredients of weenies are, the unexpected response is, "Rubber, cereal, tripe. Who knows? I wouldn't touch one of them myself." Unfazed, the obese Reilly who is always hungry—he favors junk food, "plenty bakery cakes," and endless bottles of Dr. Nut Cola, always "frosty cold"—not only wolfs them down by the dozens in the novel but eventually ends up selling them from a street cart.

I remember buying hot dogs with great snap in the bite—*perky* franks—in little soft, steamed, sometimes wilted buns and gray, fist-sized burgers at Joe & Nemo's on Summer Street in Boston, another "Buy 'em by the Bag" shop, located only in that city, with plastic squeeze bottles that squirted a bilious orange blend of mutsup. There were several of Joe & Nemo's in various parts of the city, little steamy corner spots that seemed always to be crowded with short, busy working-class hustlers standing up and wolfing them down with double fists. People often opted for the "all-around," a fat furter always served with mustard, onions, relish, and horseradish. A long-time worker in the chain, one Ed Insogna, explained to David Kruh in his book on Boston's notorious old Scollay Square, *Always Something Doing*,

> We steamed the rolls and cooked the dogs in water.
> We did not boil the dogs. Never! The skin breaks
> and that releases the flavor in to the water and the
> dogs don't taste as good. That was part of the secret.
> People could buy the dogs [uncooked, to take home]
> and they would come back and say, 'they don't taste
> the same.' That was probably why."

By the early 1960s, Kruh explains, there were twenty-seven restaurants serving over a million hot dogs a year throughout the greater Boston area and Florida, as well. The last Joe & Nemo's hot dog was served in June 1963.

All Joe & Nemo's hot dogs, as I say, had snap and were disgustingly delicious, but were I suspect not much different than the kind of cartridges referred to by the witty H.L. Mencken, who believed all hot dogs were composed "of all the sweepings from the abattoir floor." At least back then none of us were driven to resort to the gastronomic extremes faced by the country bumpkin Eddie (Randy Quaid) in *National Lampoon's Vacation* (1983) when, cooking for the traveling Griswalds in Coolidge, Kansas where they have all stopped to visit Ellen's cousins, he says to Clark, "I don't know why they call this stuff Hamburger Helper. It does just fine by itself, huh? I like it better than tuna helper myself, don't you, Clark?"

Taste, goodness, enjoyment had little to do with it. "I had 'tomato soup' at the Automat on Broadway at least once a day," writes Gruber. "You got a bowl intended for soup, went over to the hot water nozzle and filled up your bowl. You sidled along to where you got the hot soup and picked up a couple of glassine bags of crackers (free), supposedly to go with the soup. You then sought out a free table, sat down, and crumbled the crackers into the hot water. Every table was provided with a bottle of ketchup. You emptied about half of the ketchup into the hot water and cracker mixture. Presto—tomato soup! Cost? Nothing." I have already mentioned little Joe Gould, the Greenwich Village eccentric. Ketchup was actually a staple for him. "While having a sandwich," Joseph Mitchell writes in his classic *Joe Gould's Secret* (1965), "Gould customarily empties a bottle or two of ketchup on his plate and eats it with a spoon. The countermen in the Jefferson Diner, on Village Square, which is one of his hangouts, gather up the ketchup bottles and hide them the moment he puts his head in the door. 'I don't particularly like the confounded stuff,' he says, 'but I make it a practice to eat all I can get. It's the only grub I know of that's free of charge."

Gould always explained that he was out of joint with the rest of the human race because he did not want to own—to possess—anything. He smoked street butts and fed pigeons crumbs and died in 1957, at age 68, in the Pilgrim State Hospital on Long Island, NY, of arteriosclerosis and senility. No one has ever found the fat book that he claimed to have been writing all his life.

An anorectic, Virginia Woolf, liked sausages but little more. She cooked occasionally toward the end of her life—she dismissed her servants and had a habit of turning sausages in a pan with a pen holder. She once or twice baked a pie of potatoes and peas and boasted of it. I will have more to say about her—desperate—food aversions later. She was a snob and detested her help whom she thought all stupid and vulgar. "I bought my fish & meat in the High Street," she noted when living with her husband, Leonard, at Richmond, "a degrading but rather amusing business. I dislike the sight of women shopping. They take it so seriously." Woolf, who has been accused of being unable to delineate in her novels an accurate portrait of a servant, hated confronting them—the tension between her and her cook of 18 years, Nellie Boxall, was famous—and sought to avoid talking to them by leaving them sharp notes. The servants "with their talk-talk-talk," their toing and froing and wonder "expressed in loud laughter" fiercely jangled Woolf's always thin nerves and got into her writing like the smell of boiled cabbage into the curtains. "If she failed to write about them convincingly, it wasn't so much she couldn't enter into their minds, as that she was afraid of them getting into hers," notes Rosemary Hill in her review of *The Mrs Woolf and the Servants: The Hidden Heart of Domestic Service* by Alison Light.

Woolf had never been tutored in housework. The job of cleaning rooms was prescribed as therapy for her while recovering from several nervous severe breakdowns she had suffered during her fragile life ("It's really rather fun and makes a wonderful difference"), while her cooking classes were silly, with one of them spoiled when she baked her wedding ring into a suet pudding. A diary entry: "I make bread. I cook mushrooms. I wander in & out of the kitchen." When war broke out, she became more self-sufficient. She spent the morning of her suicide helping with the dusting. She gave no access to her servants of her frailty.

How ironic it is that Woolf, who treated her servants like prats and looked down with disdain on shoppers, shabbily feigns a professional touch as she describes for her readers that lovely dish of *boeuf en daube* that Mrs. Ramsay's Swiss maid, Mildred, spends three long days preparing for the famous dinner party in *To the Lighthouse*, the one time in any of her novels that Woolf—precariously?—allows herself to indulge in a domestic scene involving the preparation and presentation of food. We encounter true triangulation here. In the novel, the *meal* is so delicious that Mrs. Ramsay cannot help but falsely take the credit for it. "'It is a French recipe of my grandmother's,' said Mrs Ramsay, speaking with a ring of great pleasure in her voice," writes Woolf. Consider the irony of Woolf writing, as if with true expertise, "And she must take great care, Mrs. Ramsay thought, diving into the soft mass, to choose a specially [sic] tender piece for William Bankes. And she peered into the dish, with its shiny walls and its confusion of savoury brown and yellow meats and its bay leaves and its wine…" Where Woolf dunderheadly spits the bit—and Simon Schama highlights the striking anomalies of the scene in an amusing essay in *Scribble, Scribble*—is revealed in the pointless, altogether fretful elaborations the truly ignorant non-cook Mrs. Ramsay makes, dodging about and crying that "everything depended upon being served up to the precise moment when they were ready. The beef, the bay leaf, and the wine—all must be done to a turn. To keep it waiting was out of the question." Like Mrs. Ramsay, had Woolf ever done any cooking at all, even food at its most basic (like a *daube*!), she would surely have known that a *daube* is a stew and needs never be on time—it can sit there forever, the longer it simmers the better. The great secret—and the whole success of the dish turns on this—cooking it slowly and as long as possible, for days even.

Mark Zuckerberg, co-founder of Facebook, claims that he will only eat meat that he kills himself. Apparently, he likes to challenge himself with a new and interesting proposal each year, and 2011 had to do with avoiding store-bought meat. After the birth of her child, the actress Jessica Alba became a sturdy advocate against processed foods and so she no longer eats white, enriched food, something of a curious semi-anomaly in that her surname in Spanish means "white."

Pop star Madonna's irrational food fads and increasingly bizarre attempts to hold back time—via surgery, exercise and exploring just about every therapy going—by all accounts certainly helped to doom her marriage with Guy Ritchie. (Perhaps this is the most apposite place in the book to quote what is probably humorist James Thurber's most scarifying remark, "The most dangerous food is wedding cake.") Alison Boshoff in her exposé, "The Mad World of Madonna," subtitled "Grains for every meal, rice milk, no TV, and sleeping in a plastic suit covered in £500 cream," explains to some degree how the 5'4" American singer/tycoon/foodie Madonna adopted a macrobiotic diet in the early 1990s and lived almost fanatically loyal to a whole set of culinary overelaborations, eating as a vegetarian and compulsively dining on quinoa grains and organic vegetable dumplings and rice milk. Writes Boshoff, "She told her chefs what was permitted: she chose the precise blend of Colombian coffee and tutted over the exact provenance of air-freighted Canadian blueberries."

Meat for Madonna was, needless to say, a primal taboo in their married lives. "How could anyone expect [her then husband Guy] Ritchie, a macho man who is fond of the pub and likes to shoot pheasant, to dine contentedly every night? It now emerges that apparently every aspect of life at the Ritchie residence in London was dictated by the lady of the house… Guy, then, has allegedly had to endure a life that… included no TV, no newspapers, and no welcome for his 'London' friends—sustained on a diet, which would make a Hollywood starlet feel faint. For instance, gossips claim that his elegant Christmas meal was minus chipolata sausages last year because she would not hear of processed meat crossing the threshold. He had to drink his tea every day with rice milk, as dairy is banned. Meat is only very occasionally present on the menu. The only exception to this was at their country estate, Ashcombe House, in Wiltshire, where Guy was allowed (*nota bene*) to serve a full breakfast to shooting parties, even including such fat-filled items as steak-and-kidney pie. Madonna thought this kind of food so foul that she would leave the room in disgust when it arrived and sip reproachfully at her bowl of Japanese miso soup."

The forever dependably classy Madonna summed up her food life, saying, "I'm a vegetarian. I used to not eat anything that could take a shit. Now I eat fish. I changed it to not eating anything that walks on earth."

The great American chess Grandmaster Bobby Fischer, who, for most of his life, was predominantly a vegetarian, was a genuine food eccentric. Food poisoning was one his main phobias. He commonly demanded that restaurants juice the fruits and vegetables he ordered in front of him. Some of his fussiness was religious. He became interested in 1967 in the Church of God, a Christian Protestant fundamentalist sect, which believes the truths of the Bible to be literal, and its members not only avoid certain meats, but alcohol and even pasteurized milk. Something of a health nut, Fischer loved watching the fitness guru, Jack LaLanne, do exercises on television and was converted to Christianity by the television ministries of Herbert Armstrong and Garner Ted Armstrong. After going to live in Iceland in 2005, he came to dislike Icelandic bottled water, which he believed made him very ill. Brad Darrach in *Bobby Fischer vs. the Rest of the World* wrote in 1974 that he "still has a deathly fear of maraschino cherries." Paranoia, however, which ruled, indeed overruled, much of Fischer's life, figured in many of his public disputes, opinions, quirks, expressed antagonisms, and odd but consuming hostilities. In the end, the chess genius very much wanted to become a Catholic, but before that he quickly died of renal kidney failure at the age of 64 on January 17, 2008. His very last words were "Nothing is as healing as the human touch."

Geniuses, I find, all somehow seem to avoid meat, although I have noticed, as well, that like many vegetarians they miss the taste—or is it the memory?—of it. "I am a vegetarian for moral reasons," Professor Douglas Hofstadter told me. Pulitzer Prize-winning author of the masterpiece, *Gödel, Escher, Bach: An Eternal Golden Braid*, an analysis on the fundamental notion of meaning and communication which has been described as "a metaphorical fugue on minds and machines in the spirit of Lewis Carroll"—through illustration and analysis, the book discusses how self-reference and formal rules allow systems to acquire meaning despite being made of "meaningless" elements—he explained, "I still would enjoy the taste of a Wendy's Spicy Chicken sandwich (with onions!) or a hamburger (well done, with onions!) or bacon (e.g., a BLT), but I wouldn't want to eat any of them." He confided to me, "I don't much like tofu, unfortunately, but in some dishes it's reasonably good."

Mary Tyler Moore early became a confirmed vegetarian. She learned of the cannibalism of the legendary Donner Party when she was a young girl and was shocked that "those starving wretched souls ate the flesh of their dead companions." She writes in her autobiography, *After All,*

> I have come to feel the same revulsion I experienced at the Donner Pass at the thought of eating animals. My proximity to the sheep, cattle, and geese who are now my neighbors in the country is what has finally turned me into a vegetarian. I talk to these animals when I walk… Don't we now have enough tasty things to eat from the garden and all the delicious ways to prepare them?

Strangely enough, St. Francis of Assisi, the legendary 14th-century patron saint of nature and of all God's creations—he was born Giovanni di Pietro di Bernardone—never thought of becoming a vegetarian. He was a wealthy young man (his father, Pietro, was a silk merchant) before he chose to become "God's tatterdemalion." But even as a friar he enjoyed pig's foot stew and a good meat dinner. As to his incorporative love of animals, he did not like ants, which he felt worked too long and hard, and, notably, never stopped to utter any praise, nor did he particularly care for mice or ever bother to claim any spiritual brotherhood with them. (Field mice had once badly plagued and tormented him in a hermitage cell during a protracted illness.) If friar Francis had a positive bias for anything, it was toward birds, emphasis on moor-hens, robins, hawks—he had a favorite hawk named "La Verna"— and sweet cowled larks, earth-colored like monks and humble, which always sang. He was fascinated by fire and, among his friars, would never allow one to be roughly extinguished.

How St. Francis—tough, daring Italian Johnny Bernardone—would have been offended by prissy gourmands and the likes of hedonists such as James Beard, Lucius Beebe, and A.J. Liebling, who spent their entire lives pompously priding themselves on fey and fussy arcana like knowing that in France a whole fish is always served with its head to the left (a tradition, which customers expect), that partridge is commonly served without the head, while woodcock is always brought to table with the head intact, and that the thinner the tablecloth in a French restaurant, the better the food— the stress being on excellent food, you see, not décor. In such instances, does one possibly need more solid proof that in such extremes the concept of food and eating is possibly an erotic surrogate? They are comic versions of the Reverend Dr. Gaster, an individual who appears in Thomas Love Peacock's first novel, *Headlong Hall*, whose principal talent is offering disquisitions on the art of stuffing a turkey. (He also allows that no Christmas party could ever be complete without him.) The hedonists listed above, with their vain need constantly to be tucking into costly and rare dinners, an orgy of the unfamiliar—in their gluttonous lusting after exotica like matsutake mush-rooms, kobe beef, three different kinds of saffron, etc.— are classic examples of people engaging in what chef Alton Brown refers to as the "pornification of food." Brown disdains foodies, stating, "At best, love is the gasoline. It is not the car."

A serious Christian, Brown told Ana Maria Cox in an interview in *The New York Times Magazine* (September 6, 2015), not without dismay, "I do believe that there is a spiritual act in breaking bread and sitting down and be-ing thankful. The pornification of food takes away the importance of sharing it with one another and instead focuses only on the food."

"Foodies" in a very real sense are sinners, glaring offenders against the First Commandment, in their vain, unappeasably rapacious, self-cherish-ing extremes of hedonism not much different than Baal-worshipers. Walter Pater's idea that our finest moments come to us through the sensory pulses of aesthetic appreciation, basically art for art's sake, is in essence idolatrous, ungodly, and basically pagan. Atheism in the final analysis is materialism. Susan Sontag was never more correct than recognizing how polarities limit and imprison us. "In upstate New York, a transplant from Israel started raising a new breed of duck, supposedly torturing them benignly (was that possible?) by using light and music to wake them up so they'd eat and fatten their livers," writes Gael Greene in her book, *Insatiable*, itself a tedious compendium of pointless self-indulgence and vulgarly shallow epicureanism. The motto of Paul Levy's *The Official Foodie Handbook* is "Be Modern, Worship Food." Levy—he coined the word "foodie" (and some say, exemplified the concept)—defines a foodie as "all palate, with a vestigial person attached." In their biting profligacy, I think of a "foodie" as a cross between an out-and-out savage and a mental defective.

As I write the words "foodie" and "palate," forgive me if they call to my mind an image of the actor Eugene Pallette, the 300-pound-plus gravelly-voiced human dirigible who, being offered a plate of hors d'oeuvres in *My Man Godfrey* memorably squawked, "Food with toothpicks in it? Tell your sister to get her behind out here so we can eat!" A true glutton, the man was convinced in 1946 that there was going to be a "world blow-up" by atom bombs, and he received considerable publicity when he went and set up a "mountain fortress" on a 3,500-acre ranch near Imnaha, Oregon, as a hideaway from universal catastrophe and stocked with a sizable herd of prize cattle, enormous supplies of food, and its own canning plant! Charged by cantankerous director Otto Preminger to be a Nazi, Pallette, who supposedly loathed Hollywood Jews, was a right-wing zealot and a loudly ferocious anti-Communist. Of no small irony, or coincidence, was that in many of his films Pallette, bulking huge, would often be found growling at some poor creature with, "What's eating you?" (cf. *Topper*)

It is a commonplace to compliment the French and their cuisine about anything and everything. Not everyone is aboard, however—quite the opposite. Thomas Carlyle who did complain, describing a trip to Paris, that the French seemed to devote all their time to "eating, everlasting eating," also referred to the French as "a nation of pastry-cooks and dancing-masters." I have mentioned he found delicate sauces fastidious. The crusty old Ecclefechan believed that Scottish grub like haggis, kippers, hard biscuits, and thick, woolly oatmeal in the morning were much better than any French sauces. What would a greedy gourmand like the ravenous and insatiate A.J. Libeling have thought of Alexandre Dumas who in his *Dictionary Cuisine* famously lists crow as a comestible, along with pheasant and guinea hen? Frankly, Liebling knew, simply because, having cultivated snobbish attitudes throughout his life, so insecure was he and so unthinkably fat, he felt that knowing such outré facts was not only a means of impressing people with his familiarity with exotic foods but also of proving apodictically that he had lived in Paris and of course knew all its very best restaurants, in spite of the fact, such was his appetite and urgency, that as Damon Runyon in the hilarious short story, "A Piece of Pie," said of his less than elegant character, Nicely-Nicely Jones, he ate "under the handicap of modern civilization, which required that an eater use a knife and fork while in the old days eating with the hands was a popular custom and much faster." Liebling quotes Dumas as saying that at least seven hours of sustained simmering are required when cooking crow and explains one must give "constant attention to the 'scum' that forms on the surface of the water level." Liebling read cookbooks all the time. A fat man's only conversation is of food.

Henri de Toulouse-Lautrec, while he did not serve crow, did dish out heron. The artist who saved his lavish hedonism mainly for food and drink served his guests, along with heron, meals of squirrel, calf's liver with prunes, and skate wings in black butter. One can still see in the Musée Lautrec in Albi some of the menus that he drew up (and often illustrated) for some of the notorious dinner parties that he threw. He was so fond of his own cooking he rarely went out to eat at restaurants. He particularly loved American cocktails, in all styles, and actually concocted several new ones of his own – and for him the more explosive, the better.

Andrew Zimmern, traveling host of the Travel Channel's "Bizarre Foods" and a fellow who is apparently an indiscriminate pantophage—the man will eat anything, pig snout, reptile hash, roasted bats, crickets and caterpillars, no end of gristle, bull's pizzles, sea squirts, camel kidneys, Cambodian tarantulas, purple blood puddings, the eyes of various kinds of animals, decaying codfish, the foulest headcheese, etc.—was asked by interviewer Mike Barish, "Is there anything that you won't eat, either because you just don't like the taste or texture? Is there anything that you were more than willing to try and after the fact said, 'Okay, good. I tried it and I never want it again'?" It was a splendid question. Out-of-shape, cueball-domed, drum-bellied Zimmern's surprising answer was—"Walnuts." He explained, "I've tried them a million ways. They just don't agree with me. They got a bad aftertaste. It's soapy! I eat every other nut on the planet. [But] I hate [walnuts]. I can't stand them."

That bouncy, beaver-tooth-grinning Zimmern can get testy, or worse, shows by the thousand-yard stare he often gives the camera when something goes wrong. I suspect he has one of those thixotropic personalities, stable at rest but becoming fluid when agitated. Several times I have noticed him the object of a zealous, harmless walnut-purveyor. Distinct unease registers, a muttered exchange or two (and *brouille*). In one particular TV episode I happen to recall, one filmed in China, I must say I was somewhat shocked to see how Zimmern scolded a woman there, his host, chastising her—actually publicly bullyragging the poor thing—for simply handing him to eat a piece of walnut-leather, food that she had claimed did not taste like walnuts. She made a feeble attempt to explain, but his frown silenced her in mid-sentence. To quote the always memorable writer Saki, Zimmern "went pale as a beet-root that has suddenly heard bad news." He almost inflated with anger—went bonkers!

Allow me to point out here that this preoccupation—munching on elephant meat, tiger paws, eland tongues, ibex lips, etc.—is not new, not as a crowing interest, in any case, if not as an act.

Not at all.

Think of Mungo Park. Burton and Speke; men in the Burke and Wills expedition in Australia; intrepid Charles Doughty, whose odyssey in Arabia was perilous in the extreme, daily faced ghastly fare: porcupine, wild goat, ostrich. ("The hunters eat the bird's breast, which is dry meat; the fat is precious, one of their small coffee cups full is valued at half a *mejidy* [Turkish crown].")

Alluding to goats and goat meat, this is the place to record some remarks of my friend, Thor Hanson, author of *Seeds*—a masterpiece—who had a forgettable eating experience in rural Uganda. He explained to me,

> Boiled goat meat! I had to find a way to dump it. If I could just sidle over to the shrubs or tall grass, one casual tilt would empty the whole bowl—all I needed was a split second when no one was looking. But for a Peace Corps volunteer in Uganda, those split seconds were few and far between. People from all over the valley stopped by my table in a steady stream, shaking hands and smiling with approval at the steaming bowl of goat in front of me. While I wouldn't say I was the life of the annual village Christmas Party, I was certainly at the center of it.

> The constant attention and conversation at least offered me a polite alternative to eating, and I'd managed to get by so far with only a few spoonfuls of broth. Even that much had coated my mouth with a greasy rancidness that previous experience told me would last for days. What was it that made boiled goat so bad? The roasted variety tasted fine, and I had

no trouble tucking into all sorts of more exotic local fare, from fried grasshoppers to home-distilled banana whiskey. Perhaps they saved only the oldest, toughest 'billies' for boiling, or perhaps it was the recipe—a skinned and quartered carcass simmered indefinitely in cooking oil and river water. Whatever the reason, my aversion to the entrée didn't alter the fact that I needed to end that party with an empty bowl. It was a special occasion, and anything less would be an affront.

My mind raced back to various childhood schemes— lining up steamed peas beneath a butter knife, or tossing blanched carrots into the fireplace inside a wadded paper napkin. In the end, I chanced on something far simpler. Rising to greet a delegation of elders, I moved around the group to shake hands with each of them, murmuring greetings, and gripping my elbow as a sign of respect. When they finally walked off to join the buffet line, I realized I was now standing two tables away from where I'd started. So I sat down quickly, right in front of an empty bowl. Later, before the dancing started, I carried it over to the dishwashing area like a trophy.

Dr. Francis Buckland, a 19th-century English surgeon and zoologist, claimed that he had eaten his way through the entire animal kingdom, adding—expertly!—that the lowly mole tasted nastiest of all. (Afterwards he told Lady Lundhurst that there was one thing even worse than a mole, and that was a bluebottle fly.) This was a fascination that Buckland got from his father, whose own residence, the Deanery, offered such rare delights as mice in batter, squirrel pie, horse's tongue, and ostrich. After a celebrated "Eland Dinner" held in 1859 at the London Tavern, the unconventional surgeon zealously formed the Acclimatization Society, the official aims of which were, among other things, to foster the search for a completely new food – a typically decadent if scientific quest. In 1862, a hundred guests convened at the club to sample Japanese sea slug, kangaroo, guan birds, flutter-headed curassow, and Honduras turkey. This repast was offered as a modest menu—for the irrepressible Buckland, always precipitate, had his eye on capybara for a future meal! Dr. Buckland's London home, at number 37 Albany Street, was famous for its menagerie and its varied menus, which included over the years boiled elephant trunk, rhinoceros pie, porpoise heads and—I imagine because he had undergone the torture, others should—deliciously stewed mole!

Shall we stop here and say grace, invoking in this case Ninkilim, the goddess of field mice and all God's teeming creatures?

Zimmern is, I gather, not in a club or in any sense of the term clubbable. He eats with a crude insouciance, often sitting side-saddle at a table, poking and shuffling at his portions of food as, with shrugs, he offers meandering *obiter dicta* about this and that, often flapping at his helpings out of sheer indifference, as if bored with all the barking plenitude. He rarely employs his knife at table but slouchingly uses his all-purpose fork to shear, shape, and cut his food. He gives the impression that his hunt for exotic foods is the result of some kind of stratigraphic excavation, but in fact he is always accompanied by local interlocutors *who eat the same foods*!

Scalp-bald, beaky, and voracious, he has the head of a California condor, except that flabby body is that of a manatee—his tumblehome cheeks often jiggle when he fades backwards in a mime of a glorious appreciation—and he actually grazes like one of those sea cows which can consume a hundred pounds of weeds, grass, and seaweed in a single day. "Fat is not an evil word," he repeats, and he eats fat, lardo, grease, butter, etc. with abandon. I have noticed that Zimmern will often walk about with a sort of glazed stare, a look that may indicate in a person who assumes it the process of digesting information, but in the case of Zimmern it has the element of the goofiness of a clown. His severely hairless head, those gleaming pop eyes of his, and a visibly weak mouth give him the scary look of Donatello's unprepossessing statue of the skeptical and mistrustful prophet, Habakkuk, at the *Museo dell' Opera del Duomo* in Florence, except that Zimmern is much by far porkishly fatter and, needless to say, far, far less ascetic. I must say that the man is protean in his looks, at one point resembling a kind of smudged and semi-ogling Richard Diebenkorn-figure and yet in another light egg-headed Ernst Stavro Blofeld from the movie, *You Only Live Twice*.

He makes with lame jokes like a lot of Jewish comedians, does double-takes, can become a considerable show off, and yet the would-be machismo he hopes to reveal in daring to eat odd things is registered by all sorts of dramatic shrugs, twee head-wags, and no end of feigned insouciance. He scoots about the world, large and in charge, always with breezy confidence—*chutzpah*—as busy as a fart in a mitten, as old Cape Codders like to say. I watched Zimmern slackly gobble up a tagine in Morocco in his typical way, slouching, one hand lazily sawing the helping before him with a probing fork as he took slow, slovenly bites from it like a dull, inattentive peasant. It is mortifying to think of what he has done to the American image abroad.

I can also report that Zimmern cannot stand eating oatmeal. "I hate oatmeal—it's a texture thing," he stated, literally gagging on a spoonful of it on one of his shows in Portland, Oregon. "I hate well-done beef," I heard him once blurt out during another one of his shows. He solemnly claims that there are five things that he will not eat but—why? —will publicly name only two, walnuts and oatmeal.

Okay, kids, "One of these things does not belong," as they say on television's Sesame Street—can you guess? Andrew Zimmern. Well-done beef. Coyness. Oatmeal. Kitttenishness. Good taste. Walnuts.

I have watched Zimmern's show a few times and cannot help but notice that he is not only morbidly corpulent, slob-fleshed, and totally unathletic, but also quite visibly unhealthy—a sackbut, in fact, which is hardly a running endorsement for gobbling out of-the-way foods or endorsing them. His muscleless body, those fat rolls, that coconutoidal head, all sublineally telegraphing something of sapped depletion and a kind of despoiled vacancy, contrive to reveal of Mr. Mastication less of a human body than a walking food coma. His torso, which is unquestionably oval, seems curiously the right shape for him. The sad fact is that on his show he is much of the time sitting down with or eating next to hard-working, farm-strong, often poor—many very poor—workers and athletic laborers, raw and muscular peasants, and the visual anomaly is ludicrous. He tours the wide world in his rumpled way, noshing and ingratiatingly glad-handing anyone who offers him a free nibble or sample, all sorts of bewildered street-vendors, stall peasants, and obliging fat ladies in booths who, although they often look on him with a kind of shock as some kind of stranded, never-before-seen, almost inflated sea creature, are still willing to offer him tidbits or little tastes of this or that.

I have never had the pleasure of seeing Zimmern cook. Would this not be something of an anomaly? What he glaringly does not do is as surely revealing as what he does. I rate the fact, for example, that during one year the great Joe DiMaggio struck out only seven times—a mere *seven*—as easily brilliant an achievement, if not a greater one, than his probably never-to-be-broken legendary 56-game hitting streak in 1941. Yet very few people know of that former statistic of the "Dago's," while everyone celebrates the latter, whether Yankee fans or not.

Zimmern is a crass, unthinkably loud, toothy New Yorker with clown eyes, fully unselfconscious and pink as a shrimp, who goes sauntering about fat-assedly in enormous ballooning XXXL shorts, which make him look like an enormous thumb-sucking baby. It is an ugly picture. I am talking Medusa ugly. He is more often than not a fashion horror who wears do-rags on his head in tropical climes and on more formal days will often squeeze into voluminous, billowing guayabera shirts, floppy, end-of-the rack, groin-relieving floods, and big chubby, often orange (yes) shoes. Zimmern is—how to put it?—circumferentially challenged, and, as I say, he loves, sports almost idiotically (in the sense that in foreign countries he seems completely oblivious to ridicule) those great baggy shorts that are at least "rotund accessible." I have also noticed that he often wears his collar up in a prissy, posturing way, a ludicrous affectation that I recall having seen only worn by actress Dorothy Malone and old, rickety, bleary-eyed shockjock Don Imus, the equivalent of wearing a coat or cape slung carelessly over one's shoulders, in the way of fey Leonard Bernstein, a pretension that the narcissistic conductor borrowed from his mentor, orchestra conductor Serge Koussevitsky.

There is something in Zimmern's cartoon eyes that gives the impression that he is guying everybody he meets and doesn't mean a word of what he says or thinks or feels or eats or refuses to eat. It is a pop-eyed version of a fellow who has the crazy face of a Thurber character, empty of all but eyes and mouth. Zimmern makes no secret of the fact that he cannot bear the taste or texture of a good many strange or foreign fruits, spiky or otherwise, several of which I have seen him wretch up after sampling just a mere bite. Take Noni, for example, an oval green fruit of the Morinda citrifolia tree which is mainly indigenous to Southeast Asia, Australasia, and the Caribbean. It bears what is called "cheese fruit" and is traditionally used in Polynesian cultures to treat menstrual cramps, bowel irregularities, diabetes, liver diseases, and urinary tract infections. It has a nubbly look and has many seeds and an extremely pungent odor when ripening, and hence it is also called "starvation fruit," and even "vomit fruit." Despite its strong smell and bitter taste, the fruit is nevertheless eaten as a famine food in the Pacific. I found it almost pathetic to have to watch Zimmern in Honolulu hopelessly bailing on taking even a small sip of Noni juice, as he wussishly sampled a dab of it of his pinkie finger. "You couldn't pay me enough to do what you just did," said the intrepid food adventurer, wincing, as a woman, his host, happily polished off a glass of it. She looked at him. He kept standing there, goggling, a rude *enfoire*.

But I question even Zimmern's taste in general, his penchants, predilections, inclinations, partiality. His favorite meal—"The Best Thing I Ever Made" he boasts on the Internet—is, shockingly, just a meal as plain-as-dick's-hatband, a recipe of gloppy Chinese chicken wings, "the most heavenly piece of comfort food you'll ever taste," according to Zimmern, who, when I consider this, seriously makes me wonder if at some point in his life he ate too many paint chips. It reminds me of Elvis Presley's taste. Elvis could have collected anything—*owned* anything—on the face of the earth, but what did he collect? Rare vases? Old Masters paintings? Chinese lacquered furniture? Rare books? Nope. *Sheriff's belt buckles!*

Give me a real food-eating pioneer! Reindeer hunters in Lapland and Siberia are, compared to Zimmern, far braver, who eat the half-digested mush from the stomachs of the deer—a rich source of vitamins—just as it was done in ancient times during the Palaeolithic, according to Sir Leonard Woolley and Jacquetta Hawkes, a period when hungry men ate most of their meat raw.

I also have some serious doubts about Zimmern and his sense of daring. I mean, who wouldn't be delighted to find himself eating high-end hand-cut Wagyu or Matsuzaka beef alone at a single-seat table in Tokyo served by two or three kowtowing Japanese chefs or rare Chinese Lantern shrimp in Beijing or a nine-course white truffle dinner served at elegant restaurants in Paris or Lyons or Dijon? In a posh five-star restaurant Zimmern is in heaven, of course, energetically cramming down fragrant, mouth-watering foods like a crossbill on spruce seeds or a nuthatch on pine. But what about some of those southern delicacies from Guizhou province mentioned in the Lonely Planet book on China like live rat embryos which is a dish nicknamed the "three squeals" because the embryo squeals when you pick it up with your chopsticks, once more when you dip it in soy sauce, and finally when you put it in your mouth? No, no, it is a much different story when it comes to truly disgusting things like Ethiopian *injera* or Icelandic *hákarl* or Korean baby mice wine or Mexican *escamoles* (the eggs of giant black Liometopum ants) or *casu marzu* from Sardinia, when any viewer can see Zimmern taste—pinchbite—*casu marzu*, taking nothing more than the merest, the tiniest *soupçon when the camera cuts immediately away!*

Most ant species are edible, tasting mildly sour, due to ants secreting an acid when threatened, giving them a vinegar-like flavor. Down in South America ants are roasted with salt and commonly eaten at fiestas. The queen ants are generally preferred, having big juicy bums (more fat). In many folk cultures, queen ants are reported to boost one's libido. Ant larvae are also fairly scrumptious. These can often be found in clumps under rocks, or on top of anthills when they are being moved or kept warm. I remember once eating chocolate covered ants in Greenwich Village on a high school trip. Years later, I ate ants with the house guacamole at The Black Ant restaurant on Second Ave. in New York City, a collation served with *sal de hormiga*, or salt with ground-up chicatanas—large, winged leaf-cutter ants, creatures that are harvested in the Mexican region of Oaxaca, a taste described by

Silvia Killingsworth in a "Table for Two" feature in *The New Yorker* (August 24, 2015) as being "somewhere between nutty and buttery, with a chemical tang, and lend the salt a bit of umami."

Ant eaters, the passionate few, are surely among those who need a selmelier, a culinary professional who specializes in salt's uses in cooking and pairing with foods and wines!

A "tell" is clearly revealed when Zimmern puts a particular food into his mouth that he does not like, in fact abhors. You will always see him when confronting such repulsive food simply because his eyes are always adventuring toward the smallest piece possible. A transparently lame trick of his to which he repeatedly resorts whenever he has to taste something he personally finds nauseating—it is obvious to any fool—is to chew the food at the very front of his mouth. You know, keeping at a spit-out-able exit. Out on the perimeter. This is pretty weak. It is in the rear where the bitter *taste buds* are found, of course, the very *back* of one's tongue. (Taste is also the weakest of our five senses.) Watch for this trick the next time you see him perform. As Texas rhythm and blues singer Delbert McClinton puts it in a lyric, "It ain't what you eat, but the way how you chew it." So for all of his bravado, that is how Zimmern copes with much of the revolting food he feigns to eat, when he does eat it—and a likely reason why he does not become ill, I gather. "I have never gotten sick on a trip," he boasted in a long interview with Will Harris (wharris@bullz-eye.com). "It's not like I'm doing some safe dieting!" Zimmern has more than once defensively explained. "I'm in some of the most bacteriologically compromised places, eating some of the most pathogenically different foods for a Westerner, but I think what it is, is that over time, you either develop antibodies for some of this stuff or you don't."

Much about Zimmern is a fraud. "I could eat about seven more bats," he muttered to a group of skeptical natives in Samoa, then hastily bum-bustled off camera away from their dirty campfire. Seven more bats? Total bullshit! On camera, the guy, I wanted to say ate—but he scarcely nipped!—nothing more than a dime-sized piece of bat! Face it, half the time he is merely trying to keep the brand! It was in Samoa that in a dramatic show, all wind-up and no pitch, he ate one grub—one! "Earthy and filthy and fabulous," he sputtered, just mailing it in. It is as if he is completely unaware that TV watchers can see him not eat something! As ESPN broadcaster Keith Olbermann would sarcastically say, "The world's out here, pal!"

All of Zimmern is not faked, of course. He loves to eat, gobbles for free, envisions himself a daredevil, has become famous, is widely recognized by the public, and signs autographs. He is hearty and matey, very much the populist American, windy as Drake Passage, loud, extremely *tutoiement* with every fruit peddler and market-stall vendor and sweaty cook. *Zimmern Being Dinnered* could be a painting—a genre, even! He sits there like a pasha, being waited on, tossing select gobbets into his mouth with the flash of a snipe, complacent, shining-pated, flash-lit.

He lacks what the French call "mesure." He always overdoes it, constantly piling bananas on bananas, as they say in show business. In his philosophical essay, "On Bullshit" (2005), Harry G. Frankfurt, defining the concept, analyses his subject strictly in terms of communication. He points out that bullshit can be neither true nor false; hence, the bull-shitter is someone whose principal aim—when uttering bullshit—is to affect the listener or reader with words, communicating an *impression* something is being done or has been done, words that are neither true nor false, however, and so they obscure the facts of the matter being discussed. Bullshit is Barnumism!

But let me be honest and say right up front that my enjoyment of this guy and his dumb show of chasing-around-the-world-in-order-to-eat-vile-food—in public, on television, pulling faces—recapitulates exactly the one-word reply made by the sexually ambiguous creature, Alexander Woollcott, when comedian Groucho Marx asked the fat, cantankerous drama critic straight out, "When you were in France during the War, did you get laid?" and Aleck said, "Infinitesimally." And let me ask: is not the inevitable day coming, and very soon, when our friend and frenetic food-sampling guru, The Portable Zimmern, does take a trip—that inevitable one-way trip—to one of the less-than-exotic far territories of Ischemia and Tabatznik or the regional festering outposts of Anondontia, Morgellonsville, or doom-dark atolls like Trypanosomiasis, *Clonorchiasis, Anisakiasis, Angina-Diphyllobothriosis?*

The word is that Zimmern already does have medical problems with his hips and his lower back. Going on nothing more than that, "Dr." W.H. Auden, by his own unique medical evaluation, would characterize him as an overreacher, a trespasser on the hunt, a walking zealot for gain, someone who self-defeatingly undermines his own purpose by trying to do more than is possible.

As I say, although I have seen him do the front-of-the-mouth "chew" many times, which is basically a lip-nip, I have witnessed the timorous Zimmern—and not without embarrassment for him—gutlessly bail straight out when it came to certain questionable foods. I watched him in Thailand, for example, dubiously turning away from a piece of durian ("It needs a toe tag," he whined), a particular fruit, if I may say so, that I myself have eaten several times without a qualm—OK, maybe with a slight and very understandable hesitation, that is, until I heard in my mind the encouraging echo of one of my dear father's favorite redresses to his children whenever any one of us chose stubbornly to oppose him with a weak or captious argument, "That is the swift decision of one who sees only half the truth," my father would reply—and while I myself cannot say that I fully enjoyed the uncommon experience of eating even a small piece of durian, I must say I did manage to find in the taste of it, despite its unprepossessing fetidity of its odor, a very slight tang, a small encouraging bang, of moderate palatability. Sampling a can of *surströmming* (sour herring) in Sweden, with a rubber-necking crowd of natives around watching his every move, Zimmern, with a very squeamish couple of fingers, took a farthing-sized piece of the dripping fish and sampled nothing but a jot of it, all the while making a bigger argy-bargy about it than Maria Callas singing Tosca at her most dramatic. He does a lot with humming and pop eyes. He declared that it was "like licking the inside of an ammonia can."

Some say fermented, I say festering. It is not for me, none of it. I well remember the almost physical pain I felt when reading Günter Grass's *The Tin Drum* and being shocked at how bullying children played such cruel tricks on the mentally-deficient hunchbacked dwarf named Oskar Matzerath, the anti-hero of the novel, making him drink frog-and-urine-soup. His mother died after a surfeit of eels and sardine oil! But Zimmern is being paid to eat such stuff, is he not?

I have also seen Zimmern literally gag in Alaska trying to down a spoonful of spoiled salmon eggs, the small, glistening, golden, so-called "stink eggs," while sorely offending the several old Tlingit folk sitting at the table next to him who had frankly taken pride in serving the food to him. No, the man gets a D- with bad fruit, which in interviews he says is "the worst of all to deal with." I have seen him choke on custard apple in Jamaica, claiming it was too grainy, but having made only the feeblest attempt to take even a small bite. He simply walks away from the camera to spit it out. His record is not that great. I would say that he is batting a weak .205. He has vividly gagged on, among other things, mullet roe in Florida, 14-day old tofu, Spam, rancid goat meat, worms, and cookie dough. An iron stomach should eat anything! Do the job or don't. I say cut the man's pay! Franchement!

What is Zimmern's trademark look of disgust? Simple. His face—asymmetrical to start with—literally falls, his eyes like a hare's, flush with his head and very bright, turn dull and go miffed in a piggly-wigglyish way, all the while that head, obovate as a moon-melon, is sweat-shining gall and a bit of angry panic. The sourball effect of it all is as if he is having a vicarious feud with the universe, a foretaste of a megacosm exploding. The better to chronicle his face I would quote Graham Greene's facial description of Gustav Escobar, a character in his novel *The Honorary Consul*: "His face, brick-red as laterite, resembled a clearing which had been hacked out of the bush and his nose reared like the horse of a conquistador." So we know that it is total horseshit —"Salmon eggs look delicious!"—when Zimmern with that cheerleaderly exhortation of his, that sprightly and slightly inane incitement, his brand mantra, so to speak, trumpets at the end of every episode of every show, "If it looks good, eat it!" It conjures up for me nothing but a handful of gimme and a mouthful of much obliged.

But it is not only bad fruit that he abhors, not by a long shot. I have noticed that he was unable to keep down *hongeo* (rotten skate fish) and *hákarl* (fermented shark meat) and "stinky tofu," a brinish concoction made of fermented milk, vegetables, and meat, as well as dried shrimp, amaranth greens, mustard greens and bamboo shoots, and Chinese herb, which can take as long as several months to "cook." Sean French in his witty essay, "First Catch Your Puffin," in *Granta 52*, although he flatly states that *surströmming* "smells quite startlingly of shit," does accurately point out, "Much of the pleasure of food is a flirtation with the process of decay."

We prefer to use the term "fermented" —you can say fumed, pothered, curdled, yeasted, soured, or rancidized, if you want—which by the way describes many foods we love or are at least familiar with, such as kefir, salami, kimchi, sauerkraut, miso, injera, tempeh, fish sauce. How about coffee and pickles, tea and chocolate? Sourdough bread is fermented with the help of wild yeasts. French goes on to confess, not without logic, "The richness of fresh milk makes me gag, but when it rots, it becomes cheese, which I love." As to eating foods like *surströmming* or *kiviak* or *rakfisk* or *gravlax* (it means "buried salmon") or *lutefisk* and such foods—for me?—I myself would much prefer to have to consume a meal of Blue Jello, the jiggly treat supposedly made from collagen found inside the bones of Smurfs!

Don't laugh. I remember in my travels seeing signs in London advertising "Iron Jello," although later no one believed me whenever I mentioned that fact. Friends insisted what I had seen were ads for vitamin tablets called iron jelloids (Vitamin B/Ferrous Fumarate). I was resigned to their view over time until one night on the late show when watching *The Demi-Paradise*, a comedy from 1943 starring Laurence Olivier as a Soviet inventor who travels to England to have his revolutionary propeller manufactured, I noticed in a pan across Piccadilly the flash of an electric sign that read—yup—"Iron Jello." I was vindicated.

Although Zimmern in his act is steadily blabbing, and brashly, sending out a great circadian wind of nonsense mostly, he is relatively inarticulate, with a limited vocabulary—he rarely does much better than "buttery," "smoky," "tart," "frickin' great," "yummy," "funky," "fantaaaaastic," "awwwwsome," "sweet," "very nice," "I'm blown away," and, when wildly carried away, re-sorting to "insaaaane," his harebrained go-to word for the highest acclaim and praise—and in all seriousness he will use the geekwad word "diapery" when tasting various sweepings, gubbins, and lights, ("collateral" food) like tripe, kidney, liver, spleen, and other innards. That is Zimmern's umbrella word for a fundament food. Diapery. He overuses the word, needless to say. He is not one to reach for *le mot juste*. We are not talking John Ruskin here, OK? Sampling blood sausage in Vancouver, Zimmern insincerely blubs, "There is nothing Band-Aid-ey about this." Now *there* is an insight. Diapery. Bandaidey. Only on-the-go television barkers would use such lazy, ridiculous, numptyesque words as high tokens of praise. I remember a book that my parents read to me and my brothers growing up, *The Adventures in Wallypug Land* by G.E. Farrow, and in it I particularly recall A. Fish, Esq.'s comic but scholarly lecture on the "Unreasonableness of Misunderstandability"! How Zimmernanian a title—and how well it applies to this munching picaro!

It is comical how so many off-hand or random remarks (*obiter dicta*) have been so often quoted as profound by admiring boobs that they have im-pressed a culture, trivial assertions or declarations such as "This is the place" (Brigham Young); "Be sure you're right, then go ahead" (Davy Crockett); "Here I stand, I cannot do otherwise" (Martin Luther); "I shall return" (Douglas MacArthur); even the astonishingly bland and hugely unmemo-rable "You can't handle the truth" (the irate Col. Jessup in the movie, *A Few Good Men*), each one a commonplace remark, flat, unmemorable, and uninteresting, that creates by its very presence the insufficiency it documents. How about *Quotations from Chairman Mao Tse-Tung*, published from 1964 to about 1976, known in the West as "The Little Red Book," one of the most printed books in history? It is not only extremely dull and unrelievedly boring, it is entirely unmemorable ("The world is yours, as well as ours, but in the last analysis it is yours," etc.) Among equally bland remarks one might easily include General Pershing's boast, "Lafayette, we are here!" when he led the first contingent of American soldiers into France in World War I. It is literally incredible. What should be immediately forgotten is memorized. "Pin down an American and he utters a quotation," said Ezra Pound.

A smarmy head-break and that stage-managed turn-away or physical pivot—Zimmern's toast-of-the-town gestures of praise—are supposed to in-dicate to any attendant chef, line-cook, shack hand, long-suffering stall-meis-ter, or poor, non-English-speaking rustic *adscriptus glebae* in a conical coolie hat who happened to hand him a bunching onion or a leaf of edible burdock, "You've knocked my socks off!" It is sad if not amazing how idiotically un-conscious this caracoling zany is of the untranslatability to total strangers of his hammy slang—cant and jargon that is embarrassing, since not a soul in Bali, Guanzhou, Mongolia, Tobago, Kampala, Apia, or Pago Pago has a clue to what those asinine words mean. What poor slob in the far-flung purlieus of Marrakesh or Mae Hong Son or Mogadishu could possibly understand "Gorrrrr-jus," "That's a keeper!" "Get outta town!" "You gotta be kidding me!" "This is *smiiiile* food!" "Yikes! "Wow!" "Fantaaastic!" or "*Unnnnn*-believable"?

His is of course the standard combination of flummery and twaddle, puffery and palaver. Platitudes "R" Us. I do not believe that the man knows a single foreign language—what, "ooh la la"?—which, given his particular line of work, traveling to the far ends of the earth to pop sushi and sardines, is in itself if not outright mortifying, at least culturally discomforting. A distinctly under-medicated "wow," almost a whisper, is his cover-word when he has no reaction or is extremely tired. There is a lot of the carnival shill about Zimmern, much fustian. A cynical friend of mine, a chef, shrugs and declaims, "If he ever took an Ex-Lax, he would disappear." But is his job, in any sense, anything like a real job anyway—tasting weird food?

I who can confessedly manage to see the crooked timber of self-interest in the most altruistic intentions find in Zimmern far less a portrait of itinerant pea-and-thimble man, a wandering mountebank like Mark Twain's the King and the Duke, than a study of the nature and limits of an individual self.

To me, Zimmern's ugly and peremptorily snatched nips of food while standing up is the direct opposite in every way of Francesca Bassington's chaste repast of China tea and small cress sandwiches taken with her brother, Henry, in the drawing-room of their house in Blue Street, described by Saki in *The Unbearable Bassington* as follows:

> The meal was of that elegant proportion which, while ministering sympathetically to the desires of the moment, is happily reminiscent of a satisfactory luncheon and blessedly expectant of an elaborate dinner to come.

Zimmern is great for bunkum. He loves coming up with unique cross-tasting perceptions, explaining in bright eureka moments how fresh squid tastes like strawberries or how scampi tastes like celery leaves or how "reeeaaal gooood" calamari tastes like grass. "It's like licking the ocean floor!" he exuberantly tells a poor bewildered foreign chef about some ragged ocean tidbit or other, hoping (pathetically in vain) that he has spontaneously managed to come up with a compliment, when the fact is he usually lays an egg. They look at him confused. He is friendly, give him that. He kisses cooks, bear hugs them, squibbles their cheeks, pours on the banana oil. At times he positively iridesces. He is unfailingly and continuously obsequious, however, which is the vice of all scammers. He bows, he scrapes, he shines, he "makes a leg," as they put it in the 18th-century, he virtually genuflects. Kowtows! Oh yes, he hard-steps with all his might on the charm pedal. At times you could lube a car with the oiliness and snaky insinuation of his demeanor. Zimmern with his shameless chutzpah is capable of doling out more pure unadulterated flattery than Plutarch.

All in all, there is a parallel regarding Zimmern of what the historian John A. Garraty once wrote of the loud-mouthed, populist boomer, William Jennings Bryan, the "Boy Orator of the Platte": "He preferred baggy clothes, a full stomach, and the easy, undemanding companionship of small minds."

We have noted that gourmand and cookbook writer James Beard was a fussy eater with strong opinions. On the subject of his food aversions, there is a limitless fund of declarations on his part. He pronounced that the United States produced the "worst hams, veal, and lamb in the world." He hated even the concept of eating raw clams, stating that "cherrystones, Little Necks, and other types of New England clams are better left in the sea than eaten uncooked," while at the same time he refused to bother to marinate venison. "Mother," said Beard, "felt that venison which had to be marinated and cooked a long time in wine and spices wasn't worth the trouble, and I am inclined to agree." Beard perfectly abhorred "Swedish meat balls," stating, "No cook in Sweden would ever have connected the frightful, overcooked, over-seasoned, coarse-textured balls of meat I have had served to me at buffets as 'Swedish.'" "Cornichons, the gherkins that are served with all sorts of charcuterie in France," he also scorned, stating that they "are for the most part one of the big mistakes the French make in eating. So acrid, usually, and so lacking in flavor, they destroy the palate for accompanying food and wine." Making candy at home, for Beard, is stupid. "How tired and really unsavory homemade candy generally is! Marshmallows and bonbons and taffy and brittles—all of them should be dispensed with," he wrote and added, rather Grinch-like, "I hold similar views about Christmas cookies."

James Beard preferred tea to coffee, "no matter how well coffee is made." Punches, of any sort, were too common for him. "I take a dim view of all punches. I know they are a necessary evil," he wrote, "but I myself do not wish to absorb any more of the evil than is required to be polite. I may have had to dispense a thousand different punch recipes in my day, but I haven't had to drink them, by God!" (No problem, Jim. Let us all imbibe what you refuse but—for money—smilingly endorse.) Beard even went so far as to express a continuing dislike of the well-known, some people would even say storied Parisian restaurant, Maxim's, the bistro founded in 1893, which is made reference to not only in Franz Lehár's operetta *The Merry Widow* and Georges Feydeau's play, *La Dame de Chez Maxim*'s 1899), but also Jean Renoir's 1937 film *Grand Illusion*, and the movie, *Gigi*, among others. "The décor, the charm, and the ambiance of Maxim's still dominate the food, I'm afraid," he declared. "It is not a great restaurant, nor will it ever be, since it can survive on its own legend."

If Beard disliked Christmas cookies—and, remember, King Friday XIII on TV's "Mister Rogers' Neighborhood" hated fortune cookies—would-be humorist P. J. O'Rourke in his secular grumpiness made a fiercer, much more general complaint about the sacred holiday and its foods. He may have been thinking of his hometown of Toledo, Ohio when he cantankerously wrote, "There is a remarkable breakdown of taste and intelligence at Christmastime. Mature, responsible grown men wear neckties made out of holly leaves and drink alcoholic beverages with raw egg yolks and cottage cheese in them." Cottage cheese? Was that big in Toledo?

Curiously enough, cottage cheese was what Patricia Nixon, the wife of President Nixon, virtually subsisted on. On the night of the Inaugural of her husband on January 20, 1969 while everyone was ordering for a festive dinner—steaks, mainly—Pat ordered cottage cheese, an item considered so low, so negligible, in the White House that not a trace of it existed there. The chefs had to send someone out that night on the cold streets of Washington, D.C. to find it.

I would like to note here, as an echo of gay Mr. Beard and his high-striding, dominant, yet independent English mother, Elizabeth, who owned and operated the Gladstone Hotel in Portland, Oregon and who significantly hovered over his entire life until she died, that she was indisputably that chef's major cooking influence. You will find parents and food aversions oddly co-ordinate in these pages and frankly come across the words "mother" and "grandmother" quite frequently in this book. "He who feeds you, controls you" was one of the memorable pronouncements of the military captain Thomas Sankara, the assassinated Burkinabé Marxist revolutionary, Pan-Africanist theorist, and President of Burkina Faso from 1983 to 1987. A charismatic and iconic figure of revolution, he is still commonly referred to as "Africa's Ché Guevara." Who among us would deny that food is a distinct force?

James Beard was only one of a number who grew up deep within the gravity-pull of his mother. She was born Elizabeth Jones, raised in the countryside of Wiltshire around 1868, and was adopted by a childless aunt and uncle who lived in London. At 16, eager to see the world, she jumped at an opportunity to tour the US as a governess for a Canadian family. At the end of two years, they all happened to be in Portland, Oregon when the family was suddenly called back to Toronto. Elizabeth decided to remain in Portland, found a job, saved her money, and went to live in New York where she made lifelong friends. She moved back to Portland and continued to travel now and then. She was married twice—her first husband died after only a year of marriage, and her second marriage to John Beard (James' father) took place in 1899. A plucky businesswoman, gourmand and general connoisseur, she owned and successfully ran a hotel called the "Gladstone" in downtown Portland, sagaciously overseeing all the food served to her guests that was cooked by her loyal Chinese chef, Let. She painstakingly made sure that only the freshest, highest quality, and seasonal foods were served to her guests, shopping for the best hams, beef, and produce. Beard, the so-called "Dean of American Cookery," declared of his domineering mother, "Mother had an uncanny sense of food and the talent to show others how to prepare it. She loved to cook, eat and talk food more than almost anyone else I have known. At the turn of the century she had an international approach to food that would have been considered revolutionary in the last ten years. When women were still subordinate and modest, Mother was forceful and fearless. She swept through a room or down a street with an air of determination and authority, and she met men on their own terms."

Her son went on to adopt many of his mother's recipes and proudly served them throughout his life. Oysters. Broiled scallops. Cold scallop salad. Ginger cod cakes. Fricassee of chicken. Braised lamb Provençal. Coconut cream cake. His mother's clam chowder was a flagship dish for him. He used Tabasco for a good many of his recipes, which originated with his mother. Tabasco was introduced as a mass-market product in the 1890s in both America and in England. Weirdly, in the twenty-plus cookbooks that Beard published when he was alive, the highly quirky and, I am told, often irascible, ill-tempered Beard never published—refused to publish—his mother's rare shortcake recipe, which relies on a clever secret ingredient: hard-boiled egg yolks. Lucky for us, he saw fit one night to share it with his friend, Larry Forgione, as the two were relaxing and talking food at Beard's townhouse. As Forgione tells it, Beard believed "there can be no dessert better, only fancier."

I am not at all suprised to hear of Beard queening it. Next to poets, actors, and college basketball coaches, chefs have to be among the vainest, fussiest, most intolerant, and egotistical oddballs alive.

A chubby little mama's boy who most of his life was addicted to warm, loafy, fattening comfort foods like baked macaroni, cheeseburgers, donuts, pizza, and French fries, President Bill ("Slick Willie") Clinton now claims to be allergic to chocolate, flour, and dairy products—he is from all reports severely milk intolerant—although I recall seeing many photographs of the guy stuffing his face with ice cream every chance he got, and at campaign dinners chowing down like a Michigan lumberjack. Like all textbook narcissists, however, Clinton proved to prefer the option of looking good as opposed to gluttonizing, and so in 2010—he claimed it was on behalf of his daughter's wedding—he gave up eating meat, cheese, fish, and of course all dairy foods. As to Clinton and his chocolate problem, our friend Jeffrey Steingarten frankly—and astutely—notes, "I have always considered people who believe that chocolate is a poison to be twisted beyond redemption."

Actress Joan Fontaine (*Rebecca, Suspicion*, etc.) was allergic to chocolate. "I have a strange allergy," she wrote in her autobiography, *No Bed of Roses*, "Chocolate makes me sneeze, peppermint makes me sneeze, and, most of all, I sneeze when I'm bored." The Marquise de Sévigné in her *Letters* (1725) condemns chocolate in a blast of unique and original racism! "The Marquise de Poëtlogon took too much chocolate, being pregnant last year," she wrote, "that she was brought to bed of a little boy who was as black as the devil." Christopher Columbus who was the first European to taste chocolate, on his fourth (and last) voyage to the New World, was himself not at all impressed with it, although others were. It has been observed that far more exciting and worthy treasures on board his galleons meant the humble cocoa beans were ignored. It was left to his fellow explorer, the Spanish Conquistador Don Hernándo Cortés, to first realize the commercial value of cocoa beans, which he brought back to Spain in 1528, whereupon slowly, very gradually, the custom of drinking—of using—chocolate spread across Europe, reaching England in the 1650s.

Beautiful Grace Kelly—Princess Grace of Monaco—for example, rarely if ever took sugar or touched white bread throughout her entire life. Andy Rooney, the late curmudgeonly pundit on CBS's "Sixty Minutes," coldly snapped on one of his grumpier segments that he hated chocolate-chip cookies. He was also dubious about the art of food presentation, as a good many philistines are, complaining with that fussy whine of his that he loved to employ to make a point, "I don't like food that's too carefully arranged; it makes me think that [the chef is] spending too much time arranging and not enough time cooking. If I wanted a picture I'd buy a painting." During the filming of *The Gold Rush* (1924), the comic Charlie Chaplin in one of the movie's most famous scenes, starving, hungrily cooks his shoe and eats it.

"Striving for perfection," writes Lita Grey Chaplin in *My Life With Chaplin* (1966),

> He cooked the enormous black shoe in a tureen,
> stirred it, brought it out, placed it on a dish, garnished
> it and began delicately to carve it as Mack [Swain]
> watched in fascination. This fascination, I learned later,
> was tinged with true revulsion. Poor Mack had strug-
> gled with the shoe-eating scene for five consecutive
> days a couple of months earlier. The shoe and the laces
> were made of licorice, which he—and Charlie, too for
> that matter—abhorred. So for five days, in retake after
> retake, he'd been kept on a steady diet of Licorice, and
> for days after was too queasy to eat. So was Charlie.
> And they both were going to be sick again.

All through Chaplin's body of work, informing his comedy, is the pros-pect of hunger, an inevitable subject for a tramp, particularly for someone who grew up in stark poverty and hardship and felt the social stringency of having no money. (He had been sent to a workhouse twice before the age of nine.)

An early bias can become a lifetime bias.

Singer Sammy Davis, Jr., in one of his many shape-changing modes, quite seriously thought of himself as a gourmand. One of his many crack-pated money-making and egotistical ventures involved forming, with the financial input of several Cleveland food partners of his, the SDJ Food Corporation. It involved selling barbecue sauces, spices, and other sauces. Sammy was officially listed as Chairman of the Board. The venture ultimately proved to be a bubble. "Friends snickered behind Sammy's back that he had become obsessive with cooking Italian food for one reason: Frank cooked Italian," observes Wil Haygood in his biography of the singer, *In Black and White*, highlighting how embarrassingly and sadly obsequious Davis was to Sinatra all his life. There were some boundaries, however. "John Souza tried to implore Sammy to explore grilling food—chops on the grill. 'He [Sammy] would say, 'I don't do charcoal. I don't like charcoal.'" In every way, it was a psychological dead-end for Sammy and in fact constituted a food aversion. Haygood insightfully explains the anger behind the phobia, clarifying, "In the days of vaudeville, negro performers used to carry around little sacks of charcoal. They'd use it to 'black' their faces up darker—just like white per-formers. So the hell with charcoal."

Beryl Reid in *So Much Love: An Autobiography* (1984) when writing of her early years as a struggling actress notes, "This season on Poverty Row was the time I used to live almost entirely on baked beans—probably the reason I can't abide them now. To me they smell of feet." The eccentric father of the writer Djuna Barnes who believed that, because chickens ate pebbles to aid their digestion, a few pebbles in the diet of his children might be equally salubrious. Samuel Butler famously asserted that life was an affair of being spoiled in one way or another, but I truly wonder if one of the things he had in mind was nibbling pebbles!?

I have mentioned Bill Clinton and his slightly eerie, thought-provoking, almost smothering-mother-love of ice cream. The portly aesthete Oscar Wilde disliked ice cream. When visiting the United States in 1882, he was introduced to this new American craze. It was in the city of Indianapolis that his hosts gave him his first taste of ice cream. He remained unimpressed. "Mr. Wilde promptly placed the small of his back in the seat of his chair and spooned in the ice cream with the languor of a debilitated duck," wrote a *Saturday Review* reporter, adding with understatement, "Perhaps ice cream disagrees with him." The old Victorian comic song, "The Man That Couldn't Get Warm," a classic, touches on the dangers of eating a cold ice:

> You that are fond, in spite of price, of pastry, creams,
> and jellies nice,
> Be careful how you take an ice, whenever you are
> warm.
> A merchant once from India came, Shivery Shakey was
> his name;
> A pastry-cook did him entice to take a cooling, lus-
> cious ice.
> The wheather, hot enough to kill, kept tempting him
> to eat, until
> It gave his corpus such a chill, he never again got
> warm.
>
> CHORUS: Shivery Shakey, oh dear, oh! crimini jimini,
> isn't it cold?
> Shivery Shakey, oh dear, oh! the man that couldn't get
> warm.
>
> Close to a blazing fire he got, and took to drinking
> brandy hot;

He sent for doctors, such a lot, the man that couldn't get warm.

They recommended chamois leather, flannel shoes, and india-rubber,

Mustard chillies, and cayenne, but nothing seemed to warm the man;

And when the doctors took their fees, it chilled their blood near twelve degrees,

It even made their fingers freeze, the man that couldn't get warm.

Shivery Shakey & c.

The room was hot enough to bake, and yet this man with cold did ache;

It made the servants shiver and shake, the man that couldn't get warm.

The nursery maids, the scullion, the cook, even John, the coachman, shook,

And all kept crying, night and morning: we really must give master warning.

What's worse, his wife began to pout, and left the house, quite chilled, no doubt,

For he even froze the gardener out, the man that couldn't get warm.

Shivery Shakey & c.

Then he, with grief filled to the brim, resolved to go abroad by steam;

But not a ship would move with him, the man that couldn't get warm.

He went to the engine room, I'am told, and gave the stoker sudden cold,

Condensed the steam, and stopped the wheels, and gave the passengers the chills.

The vessel, ice-bound, even so, the captain, shaking from top to toe,

Declared, on shore again must go the man that couldn't get warm.

Shivery Shakey & c.

Next morning this poor man was drowned; in a hot
bath he was found,
The water frozen all around, the man that couldn't
get warm.
The jury proved it in a trice, he died from indigested
ice;
And then the foreman, Patrick Price, the verdict gave
with this advice:
Och, ate ice creams, whene'er you will, but only take
them when you're ill;
And first of all, take off the chill, and swallow your ices
warm.

Shivery Shakey & c.

It is difficult somehow to picture anyone developing a food aversion to
drinking. James Joyce would never drink red wine—he derisively called it
"beefsteak." It is interesting that Joyce placed red wine on the tasting menu
as a *food,* even if it was one he rejected. There is the persistent and pervasive
belief that wine suitably belongs in that category, especially among vintners
and chefs. Indeed, beyond that, in the modern world it is now considered a
health food.

Wine *is* food—or so Brillat-Savarin argued. It held a high privilege with
the great man who believed that to serve elegantly prepared food for one's
guests was to take charge of their happiness. He understood that, like dishes, wine lightly amplified the body, in his words made it "brilliant," but did
not, should not, alter it—did not "mute" it. The position he took, regarding wine, stood in direct opposition to that of the decadent poet Charles
Baudelaire who found in wine a "path of deviance," that it was, in short, a
drug." To the great French epicure and gastronome, who revolutionized the
whole concept of eating, wine is an *anti-*drug.

Roland Barthes in his introduction to *Physiologie du gout; ou Méditations
de Gastronomie Transcendante; ouvrage théorique, historique et à l'ordre du
jour, dédié aux Gastronomes parisiens, par un Professeur, membre de plusieurs
sociétés littéraires et savants* (*The Physiology of Taste*)—the great book, since
1825, has never been out of print—heartily agrees and asserts,

> Wine is not at all a conductor of ecstasy. The reason
> for this is clear: wine is a part of food, and food, for BS
> [*sic*] is itself essentially convivial, therefore wine can-
> not derive from a solitary protocol. One drinks while
> one eats, and one always eats with others; a narrow
> sociality oversees the pleasures of food.

One recalls Hans Castorp likes wine, but in *The Magic Mountain* he rather oddly sends back a bottle of Bordeaux—a Gruaud Larose, in this case—to have it warmed. It is there in the restaurant of the International Sanitarium Berghof at Davos, Switzerland by the way, and certainly worth pointing as a comforting anodyne in a book on food aversion, that Thomas Mann has his young protagonist make that hand-washing gesture, so familiar to us— was this the first time it was recorded in print?—made in bright expectancy of a good meal: "Hans Castorp clasped his freshly washed hands and rubbed them together in agreeable anticipation—a habit of his when he sat down to table, perhaps because his ancestors had said grace before meat [*sic*]," although I myself have never before heard that such an ikon was ever aligned to saying grace. A calumny against American blacks is their reputedly low taste for "Ripple," a brand name that has become an eponym for cheap, flavored fortified wines—usually made of grape, citrus wine, and sugar—that typically have an alcohol content between 13% to 20% by volume (ABV). I know African-Americans who refer to *all* wine as "gin."

"These unscrupulous 'Orientals' concocted 'nigger gin,' a peculiarly vile beverage compounded to act upon the Negro in a most vicious manner, producing outbursts that led to rape," wrote Henry Ford in *The Dearborn Independent*. (It is no surprise that Adolf Hitler fervently and respectfully kept Henry Ford's picture on his wall. Ford is the sole American mentioned in *Mein Kampf.*)

Mark Twain, something of a xenophobe despite the fact that he traveled widely and often, disliked almost all "European" food and made no bones about it. He ironically once devised a recipe for "English Pie" and has left us his tongue-in-cheek recipe for it, more than hinting at the awfulness of the food:

> ...Take a sufficiency of water and flour and construct
> a bullet-proof dough. Work this into the form of a
> disk, with edges turned up some three fourths of an
> inch. Toughen and kiln-dry for a couple days in a
> mild but unvarying temperature. Construct a cover
> for this "formidable creation", in the same way and

of the same material. Filled with stewed dried apples.
Aggravate with cloves, lemon peel and citron, and add
two portions of New Orleans sugar. Then solder on
the lid and sit in a safe place until it petrifies. Serve
cold at breakfast and invite your enemies.

In an amazingly hostile polemic in "The Staff of Life" in *Remember to Remember*, a book that I have already mentioned, the iconoclastic and often profane novelist Henry Miller indignantly excoriated the American lack of taste ("Americans eat without pleasure. They eat because the bell rings three times a day") and its food in general, particularly the country's spongy white bread which he describes as "good for nothing except perhaps to fill a hole." The bread's flaccid, over-processed artificiality completely disgusted him. Miller wrote,

Bread: prime symbol. Try and find a good loaf. You
can travel fifty thousand miles in America without
once tasting a piece of good bread. They are dying of
inanition, but they go on eating bread without substance, bread without flavor, bread without vitamins,
bread without life.

"We make a manure which we eat before we have time to eliminate it… Every time I fling the stale bread over the cliff I beg forgiveness of the birds for offering them our American bread." Miller wrote sarcastically that a plate of false teeth meant more to an American than a loaf of good bread. The diet-to-disorder-to-disability for the writer went something like this: poor bread, bad teeth, indigestion, constipation, halitosis, sexual starvation, disease and accident, the operating table, artificial limbs, spectacles, baldness, kidney and bladder trouble, neurosis, psychosis, schizophrenia, war and famine. Miller's criticism is dark, and of course the man always swung wide. "Has anyone ever had a good stew in an American restaurant?" asked Miller. "Here a stew means a couple of spoonfuls of superannuated meat swimming in a tiny pool of grease and bilge with bloated potatoes as a garniture." (Actor John Barrymore who shared Miller's mistrust of stews once stated, "I would like to find a stew that will give me heartburn immediately, instead of at three o' clock in the morning.")

Miller could truly rant. American pie is "filled with gangrene and arsenic," he complained. "The crust looks like scurf and is scurf, usually of the finest rancid grease made by the Criscomaniacs of America." There were

other howls of his. "Nothing on God's earth is more uninviting, more anemic, than the American salad. At its best it is like refined puke." Miller actually cringes that Europeans might one day have to taste our cookery. "I
would sooner feed them [Europeans] buzzards than the leftovers from the
American table," he writes. "Hardly any American over twenty-one," he
concludes, "whether he works hard or takes it easy, is without eyeglasses.
Almost every American suffers from hemorrhoids. Practically every American
over forty has a bad heart. Cancer, syphilis, arthritis, tuberculosis, schizophrenia are so prevalent that we accept them as part of the bargain—i.e., the
American way of life."

One can only wonder what Miller would have thought of the death-deal-
ing galaxy of America's chemical-rich, bad-for-me, zit-making, lardy, bad fad
sad desserts, like the endless stream of brands like Table Talk Pies, Suzy Qs,
Mallomars, Yodels, Sunny Doodles, and Raspberry Zingers, just to name a
few, that we have been bolting down decade after decade with such uncommon regularity and such unguilty bliss that they have become household
names.

In a *New York Times* article, lamenting the closing down on November
16, 2012 of the Hostess Brands factory in Irving, Texas, makers of Twinkies,
Sno-Balls, Ring Dings, Ho-Hos, Funny Bones, and other sweet treats—they
also make Wonder Bread (bleccch!)—reporter Dan Barry referred to their
famously indestructible Twinkie as "a loofah sponge you can eat!" He adds,
"Though the bankrupt company attributes its closing to a strike by a union
with a mouthful of a name—the Bakery, Confectionery, Tobacco Workers
and Grain Millers International—the truth is that the bad-snack market has
been in decline for years."

It seems consumers nowadays want to know what kind of ingredients
they are ingesting, as well they should. A capacity to look for what to avoid
in foods, sagely to scrutinize the potential trash you are putting into your
system is like being able at will to turn a 6-4-3 double-play, referred to in
baseball as "the pitcher's best friend." The Hostess Brand had been in a
death spiral for years, decades, in fact, before the company went bankrupt
and was shuttered in 2012. Corporate buyers hustled quickly in. Even before
Hostess folded, however, Americans had turned to its several rivals' snacks
and goodies, while ingredient costs and labor expenses were climbing. *Junk*
food is correct. But no one can deny it is seductive.

I recall when two of my young nephews were visiting me from England
many years ago, and I bought the two of them Twinkies, a snack-food unavailable to them abroad. I am here to say that nothing could match their
spontaneous elation when biting into them—they emitted the loudest, over-

whelming exclamation of gleeful diphthongs I ever heard: "*Ai, Ae, Au, Ei, Eu, Oe, Yi, Oi, Ui.*" It was the same with me when at the age of six I bit into my first honey-dipped doughnut, and my heart swelled like the first time, years later, when I heard—live, up close—Luciano Pavarotti sing at full voice, Franz Lehár's "*Tu che m'hai preso il cuo.*"

Wonder Bread is a horror in its own right, and the wide animus held against it for years for its indefensible gumminess and gruesome over-processed lack of nutrition, not unfounded, in fact too often ignored—and for almost century—caused the Hostess Brand to fold in November 2012, due to lack of sales. It is a comestible (!) often listed very high in the wide spectrum of food aversions. Why would a person who is even remotely sane choose to buy, never mind eat, a scentless, impermeable, sponge-like junk food, whiter than a cadaver, that has to have been fortified, supplemented, with additives previously taken from it, a bread, in the words of Michael Pollan, that "scarcely waits to be chewed before transforming itself into glucose"? (I would ask the same question about Budweiser beer, incomprehensibly the best-selling brew nationwide thanks strictly to the positively huge amounts of capital spent on advertising the product, in spite of the fact that the drink is so bland and flavorless that the St. Louis company, as of this writing, is being sued and taken to court for literally having watered it down.) Susan Seligson in her book, *Going With the Grain*, an informal study of breads around the world, focuses in one highly revealing chapter on Wonder Bread, after having visited in 2002 the "world's largest bakery" in Biddeford, Maine.

"It emits no familiar smell," Seligson points out sarcastically. "But don't go calling it a factory." (The plant has since moved to Mexico.) It is less a bread, in fact, than a sad, de-enriched ghastly white smushball of calcium peroxide, buffering salts, and seamless crumb. It has no aroma. It is bleach-white and bland beyond words, recalling for me one of the witty ditties from the early English comedy, *Gammer Gurton's Needle* (1533), anti-bread in theme, which goes in part:

> I love no roast but a nut-brown toast,
> and a crab [apple] laid in a fire;
> A little bread shall do me stead,
> much bread I do not desire...

(Although the singer has a weak stomach, rhyming, "I cannot eat but little meat/My stomach is not good"), he never loses his passion for booze ("I stuff my skin so full within/of jolly good ale and old").

The process of making Wonder Bread necessitates that it be chemically altered, in Seligson's words, "to make it taste moister than it actually is, spongy as a genuine sponge, fortified with sweeteners, and so uniform it allows no light to shine through anywhere." The company's aggressive, gong-banging campaign going back to the 1930s that "it builds strong bodies twelve ways," by way of added nutrients, building body cells, appetite, brain, blood, energy, growth, bones, and teeth, is a calumny of deception. It was nonsense, of course. The same could be said for just about any food in existence. "How can a nation be called great if its bread tastes like Kleenex?" asked Julia Child without mincing words. Curiously—she was daring, unconventional, racy, opinionated, and often happily flouted custom, the norm, and tradition—the *hors d'oeuvres* she most often served to her guests were common cheesy Goldfish snack crackers which can be found in any corner supermarket!

"The supermarket bread taste is vapid, neutral," writes Dan Wing, a Vermont physician in his book, *The Bread Builders.* "There is not really a taste of wheat, and only a little of caramel (unless caramel was added to the dough as in commercial 'wheat' bread)." Wing observes,

> The crumb is soft because the walls of the gas cells are
> thin and flexible—squeeze it a little too much between
> your fingers and it collapses, never to spring back. Put
> it into a bowl of soup and it instantly dissolves. Bite
> it and you can see a little rim of collapse in the crumb
> where your teeth have… crushed it. Chew it and it
> is gone—a moist plug of paste that slides down the
> throat on its own moisture, having failed to stimulate
> a flow of saliva in its short stay in your mouth.

So are there healthier breads? If you aren't diagnosed with celiac disease or gluten intolerance, keep in mind that gluten-free doesn't necessarily mean healthy, either—and gluten-free baked goods like bread, cookies, and crackers often are jam-packed with more refined flours, artificial ingredients, and sugar than traditional baked goods. Plus, they can cost up to twice as much as you would normally spend. Writer Arthur Koestler loathed "cellophane-wrapped bread" even if it was half-decent, so you can imagine what he would think of packaged supermarket breads. From the man who wrote, "Nothing is sadder than the death of an allusion"?

I love the stabbing irony of the last paragraph of Denis Johnson's novel, *Resuscitation of a Hanged Man,* in which intense, melancholy young Leonard English, after recovering from a suicide attempt, faces a fate he settles for:

> English felt hungry every minute. Baloney sandwiches
> on Wonder Bread with Campbell's soup for lunch.
> Cereal and reconstituted milk for breakfast, one piece
> of white toast. Potatoes and ground-beef gravy for
> supper, Wonder Bread on the side. "This is the stuff,"
> English said, shaking his piece of bread at the man
> across from him. It flopped back and forth like a pan-
> cake. "I really like this stuff," he said. And he did. He
> liked being hungry and in prison.

And this was after—not the cause of—his suicide attempt! It must be true. God tempers the wind to the shorn lamb.

The Wonder Bread wrapper, that contrived bubble-burst logo of red, blue, and yellow balloons, going back to 1921, was the inspiration of one Elmer Cline, vice president of merchandising for the Taggart Baking Company of Indianapolis, the original producers of the bread, who, in Seligson's words, "was spellbound by a sky blooming in primary colors at an international balloon race." The sales pitch has it that the "visionary" Cline was filled with "wonder" by the scene of hundreds of balloons creating a kaleidoscope of color resulting in the iconic red, yellow and blue balloons featured on the Wonder Bread logo, one that was designed by commercial artist Drew Miller while he was on staff at a Chicago ad agency. The insidious but hardly subtle fact is this freak food is aimed at kids.

Clown food is to real food what all the chattering numbskulls on the cable networks are to real news. Fast-food emporia offer mascots and per-forming shills like Big Boy, Speedee the Chef, Ronald McDonald—Ronald McDonald is considered the second most recognizable character in the world, after Santa Claus, and just ahead of Mickey Mouse—Rat Hamster, Noid, Grimace the Mutated Prune, the King (big creep factor), the Hamburgler, even the cartoon Colonel Sanders of KFC with that dopey goatee, child-mo-lesting grin, and Oompa Loompa hairdo, all tugging at the legs of kids while these restaurants with their shouting colors present play-rooms and dumbo nurseries bright with Muzak and three-ring décor replete with slides, chutes, rocking horses, and plastic jungle-jims. I honestly wonder how many victims of the "fast-food" generations will later in life be sorely plagued with Capgras Syndrome, credulously convinced that people are hiding their identities be-hind masks!

"Obesity is generally viewed as a failure of personal resolve, with no ac-knowledgement of the genuine conspiracy in this historical scheme," notes Barbara Kingsolver in *Animal, Vegetable, Miracle*. But she sees the nature of the corruption exactly, where and how the exploitation works. "People actually did sit in strategy meetings discussing ways to get all these surplus calories into people who neither needed nor wished to consume them." She writes,

> Children have been targeted especially; food companies spend over $10 billion a year selling food brands to kids, and it isn't broccoli they're pushing. Overweight children are a demographic in many ways similar to minors addicted to cigarettes, with one notable exception: their parents are usually their suppliers. We all subsidize the cheap calories with our tax dollars, the strategists make a fortune, and the overweight consumers get blamed for the violation. The perfect crime.

The very brand names that are used to grab kids are comic, circus-like words made to seduce the young: Pop Tarts, Twizzlers, Screaming Yellow Zonkers, Beef Jerky, Prawn Crackers, Funions, Bunny Tracks Ice Cream, Crunch-and-Munch, Rold Gold Pretzels, Cheez Snax, Fruity Booty, Fish Nibblers, Mr. Krisper's Rice Chips, Pop Chips, Moon Pies, Chipwiches, Pork Rinds, Donettes, Cup Cakes, Yummies, Jolt Cola, Bac-Os, Reddi-Wip, Kool-Aid, Easy Cheese, Spaghetti-O's, Potato Buds. The blazes of garish orange, the flash color for American kids, has the shouting symbolism of circus all over it—Tang, Velveeta, Cheese Doodles, Twinkies, Shake'N' Bake, Cheez-Its, Doritos, Cup-a- Soup, Pringles, Ore-Ida Tater Tots, Wheaties, Minute-Maid, Slim-Jims, Pam, Sanka, and Jiffy Pop with its inane jingle:

> Jiffy Pop, Jiffy Pop, the magic treat
> As much fun to make as it is to eat.

Fun, see? *Funnnn!* There are no truer words than John Thorne's who writes, "The next step toward the truly crass requires that the food also be as easy as possible to make. There is no more edifying spectacle in vulgar American cuisine than when greed gets down in the mud and wrestles with sloth—and no recipe succeeds better than one that satiates the first and still indulges the second." There are all sorts of hired hoopoes and hucksters who are being paid big money to think up all these zany names, by the way. They beckon the young like heat to a pone cake. It starts early. Were you aware that that distinctive smell one experiences opening a box of crayons comes from stearic acid—which is the formal name for processed beef fat?

Turning our own kids into ovoids! Butter tubs! Man balloons! We are the dummies, we are the consumers, we are the consumed, we *are* the food we eat. "You gotta tell them, Soylent Green is people!" It was the Victorian poet Gerard Manley Hopkins, writing of "God's deep decree," who with a raw glare saw into the nature—the "*thisness*"—of that truth in his dark, Plutonian but majestic sonnet, "I Wake and Feel the Fell of Dark, Not Day," which ends,

> "I am gall, I am heartburn. God's most deep decree
> Bitter would have me taste: my taste was me;
> Bones built in me, flesh filled, blood brimmed the
> curse.
>
> Selfyeast of spirit a dull dough sours. I see
> The lost are like this, and their scourge to be
> As I am mine, their sweating selves, but worse.

Presently there are people, psychological unfortunates, eating three meals a day from CVS. I walk through their stores and see sixteen flavors of Oreo cookies, and I wonder: *my God, am I in Cuckooland?* But even infants yearn for sweets. It is not our genes that tell us what foods we find tasty or repulsive; it is an undisputed fact that we all come into this valley of tears with a delight if not craving for sweets (a tiny baby can easily distinguish various sugars among fructose, glucose, lactose, and sucrose) and something of an aversion to bitterness, and after only four months develop a fondness for salt. Curiously, only sweet and bitter are inborn, whereas salt is an acquired taste. Baby food manufacturers well know that they can sell more of the stuff if they salt it. Why? The fact is it is the mothers, the spotlight consumers who buy it and best respond to the taste. It is a craving, a yearning born of need. Doctors insist that babies do not need salt and lament the fact that hooking them or toddlers at such an early age predisposes them to high blood-pressure. (Salt is hygroscopic, meaning it absorbs water, which is why one cannot drink seawater—it will dehydrate you.)

A good many of us are born with digestion issues, sensitivities to taste or odor, various allergies. Everything else that we take in our mouths is learned, by the same truth and in the same way that Rodgers and Hammerstein have assured us by way of music that one has to be taught to hate. "You've got to be taught from year to year/It's got to be drummed in your dear little ear," as Lieutenant Joe Cable sings in the hit musical, *South Pacific*. "You've got to be carefully taught." This is where the food corporations go a-hunting, all suited up and loaded for bear. It has nothing to do with any values of health, only greed and self-interest.

I cringe when I consider that, traditionally, immigrants arriving at Ellis Island were served *ice cream* as part of their very first American meal. Confused, many of them attempted to spread it on their bread. The metaphorical implications of that—a seduction beginning at the shoreline—is too rich.

Junk food typically contains high levels of fat, salt, sugar and numerous food additives such as monosodium glutamate and tartrazine (also called E102). For example, E102 is a synthetic lemon yellow dye used as a food coloring derived from coal tar. It is the liquid by-product of the distillation of coal to make coke and coal gas. Rich in additives, junk food is lacking in proteins, vitamins and fiber. It is popular with suppliers because it is relatively cheap to manufacture, has a long shelf life—a packet of Slim-Jims, the modern pemmican, can sit in your cupboard for as long as eight months—and may not even require refrigeration. It is also popular with consumers because it is easy to purchase, requires little or no preparation, is convenient to consume and has lots of flavor. Consumption of junk food is associated with obesity, heart disease, diabetes and dental cavities. There is also concern about the targeting of marketing at children. These are the kinds of bad foods, along with heavily sugared and addictive soft drinks, that are transforming American kids into great waddling unperambulatable Tons o' Funs! What a contrast to the children I saw in the desolate Langa and Khayelitsha townships in Cape Town, South Africa in 2013—the name of the latter is Xhosa for "New Town"!—stark naked, shoeless, their plump little beer-barrel "corporations" as a result of their daily hunger giving them the look of being quaintly top-heavy as they bumbled along the dirt paths in a state of unstable equilibrium.

What about our obese kids? There are nine calories in a gram of fat, more than 4000 calories in a pound (454 grams) of fat. A pound of fat has the same as the volume of a pound of butter. Jack Sprat's hefty wife who could eat no lean—and, remember, both she and her husband had distinct food aversions—has nothing on them. We are developing little porkers. An "Extreme Gulp" drink sold at a 7-Eleven convenience store has twice as much liquid as the average human stomach can *hold*! Paradoxically, overweight kids are always undernourished, at the risk of diabetes, high cholesterol and high blood pressure. Obesity also badly takes a toll on a youngster's psychological development. Social problems arise, causing low self-esteem, which can later develop into eating disorders. Clearly, there is less brainpower in their parents than the kids they enable. Do these parents ever count up the money they throw away by sheer stupidity? A pound of potato chips costs 200 times more than a pound of potatoes! Movie popcorn costs more per ounce than a filet mignon! A McDonald's meal costs almost as much as a small turkey with stuffing that would feed a family for a week!

In a quest to reinvent its image, the McDonald's chain is on a health kick, or so it claims. The perverse reality is that some of their new so-called "nutrient-enhanced" meals are actually no different than junk food, say some health experts. One of their new crispy chicken Caesar kale salads—leafy green kale having lately become a trendy super food, being a vegetable chock-full of vitamins—has more calories, fat, and sodium than a Double Big Mac! It is diabolical—you have to have evil genius to devise such a thing, no? I mean, the connivance of it all!

Fat children are mockery's punching bag. I remember well how in both secondary school and high school overweight classmates of mine suffered ignominious pain day after day, becoming the objects of scorn. Novelist Lionel Shriver, who lost her older brother to complications of obesity and addressed the subject in her novel, *Big Brother,* several years ago, recently wrote,

> What traits do we instinctively ascribe to the obese? Laziness, sloth and gluttony. Indulgence, indiscipline and lack of self-respect. If not outright stupidity, at least irrational self-destruction. We once assumed they were jolly; now we assume they're miserable. However heavyweights might incline us to pity, that sympathy evaporates the moment they encroach on our space—crowding our bus seats, spilling over our airline armrests. Notorious for commanding more than their share of resources, they're apt to draw glares in NHS [National Health Service] waiting-rooms. So they're selfish, too. That's a shocking amount of information—much of it bound to be false—to glean from a glance.

Americans consume 54.8 gallons of soft drinks per person each year! Big Gulps, the legendary drink from 7-Elevens, are matched with Frozen Fanta Cherry Ices and Mello Yellos at Burger King and gut-busting 32-ounce killer Cokes and Pepsis at McDonalds, which are one and a half times bigger than the largest cup at outlets in Japan. Fizzies! Rip Its! Hubba Bubbas! Hey kids, line up, grab 'em with both hands! Guzzle away to your heart's content! Say hello to these gigantic cups of carbonated corn syrup—and fret not! Corn is a vegetable, right?

Cranky Bernard DeVoto in his whimsical jeremiad, *The Hour* (1948), "a cocktail manifesto," is convinced that our lust for sugary drinks—adults, not merely children—begins at the soda fountain:

> Americans are too indulgent to their children; they give them too much money to spend on sweets. I don't suppose the stuff does them any immediate harm, but it does give them false values. Chocolate, maple syrup, two dozen other goos; the whole catalogue of pops, tonics, phosphates, and trademarked soft drinks that would corrode any plumbing except a growing child's—they may seem innocent but they aren't.

An ice cream soda can set a child's feet in the path that ends in grenadine, and when you see someone drinking drambuie, crème de menthe, Old Tom gin, or all three stirred together and topped with a maraschino cherry, you must remember he got that way from pineapple milkshakes long ago. Pity him if you like but treat him as you would a carrier of typhoid. For if the Republic ever comes crashing down, the ruin will have been wrought by this lust for sweet drinks.

Sweetness seduces us, and as to cuisine, the passion has been with us for millennia. One of the causes of the fall of ancient Rome, among decadence, military emperors, and the excesses and expenses of far flung military adventures, was due to the lead poisoning of its citizens. Their underground pipes were lead, their cooking utensils were lead, and the food they consumed and wine they drank was all lead-sweetened. (See Edward Gibbon.) Most Romans, then, consumed sugar of lead, a sweet-tasting but highly poisonous chemical known to chemists as lead acetate. At the time it was common to use lead-lined pots and cooking vessels to boil down various foods such as crushed fruits and grapes and old wine that had soured. Soured ("oxidized") wine contains acetic acid, and, as any high school chemistry student can tell you, acetic acid plus lead metal goes into making lead acetate. The Roman gourmet and lover of Marcus Gavius Apicius, whose *De Re Coquinaria* is the world's oldest existing cookbook—he lived sometime in the 1st century A.D., during the reign of Tiberius—contains scores of recipes that include sugar of lead among the ingredients.

Sugar of lead—it has also gone under the names lead diacetate, plumbous acetate, salt of Saturn, and Goulard's powder—is a white crystalline chemical compound with a very sweetish taste. The ancient Romans, who had few sweeteners besides honey, would boil must (freshly squeezed grapes) in lead pots or kettles in order to produce a reduced sugar syrup called *defrutum* (half the original volume) which was concentrated again into *sapa* (one third the original volume), or two-thirds the original volume, called *carenum*. Such popular syrups, conventionally used in ancient cooking, was generally used both to sweeten wine and to sweeten and preserve fruit, although they were also employed in and as all sorts of infusions. These fragrant, saccharine, and pleasant, but sometimes cloying sugar syrups kept almost forever, with flavors not just sweet, but much more complex, with slight bitter undertones.

Defrutum, carenum, and *sapa* in Ancient Greek cuisine were referred to as both *siraion* (Greek: σίραιον) and *epsima* (Greek: ἔψημα) The word *siraion* (σίραιον) means the young wine in caskets, as it is fermenting, while *epsima* (ἔψημα) means what is boiled. *Defrutum* was used as a food preservative in provisions ear-marked for Roman troops, as well, especially soldiers located in far-flung places like Judaea, and it was also given to food animals such as pigs, cows, and ducks to improve the taste of their flesh. *Defrutum* was mixed with *garum* to make *enogarum* and as such was one of old Rome's most popular condiments, ubiquitous. Quinces and melons, among other fruits, were preserved in *defrutum* and honey through the winter, and some Roman women used *defrutum* or *sapa* as a cosmetic.

Lead acetate is no longer used in the production of sweeteners in most parts of the world because of its recognized toxicity. A toxicological examination of the remains of Pope Clement II, who died in October 1047, was conducted in the mid-20th century and confirmed centuries-old rumors that he had been poisoned with lead sugar. In 1787, the painter Albert Christoph Dies swallowed, by accident, approximately 0.75 ounces (21 g) of lead acetate. His recovery from this poison was slow and incomplete. Although the use of lead (II) acetate as a sweetener was already illegal even back in his day, the Romantic composer Ludwig von Beethoven may have died of lead poisoning caused by wines adulterated with lead acetate.

Americans, it seems, might as well be eating sugar of lead, slurping it up with ham-fat ladles! What can you say about a country where you can buy fried butter on a stick—a quarter-pound stick, deep-fried, sweetened with cinnamon and sugar? It is a popular item at the annual Iowa State Fair. How about a Wisconsin State Fair midway favorite, a Krispy Kreme Donut Cheeseburger, a spliced donut filled with beef, cheese, and pieces of chocolate covered bacon?! The legendary array of fried foods at the Texas State Fair—if you will excuse the expression—-surely takes the cake. On the midway you can order such takeaway items as chicken-on-a-waffle, fried upside-down cake, chicken-fried-loaded baked potato, deep fried pig's ears, deep fried brisket, deep fried pumpkin spice Oreos, deep fried mac and cheese, and deep batter-fried Thai *sriracha* balls, and fried milk-and-cookies on a stick!

"Think about it!" as rocker Jerry Lee Lewis would truculently say.

Oprah Winfrey, who has influenced millions on her television talk show, has repeatedly boasted to her slavish nation that her favorite foods, hands down, are sour-cream potatoes, Ding Dongs, and fried chicken! I do not believe a food exists that she does not like, except maybe retsina, as she reports that she loathes the smell of fuel (In 1992, she weighed 240 pounds.) Lawrence Durrell in *The Greek Islands*—and he loved the country—cordially dismisses resonated wine as "pure turpentine which has been strained through the socks of a bishop."

No wonder we suffer from oxidative stress. Oxidative stress in the extreme is actually thought to be involved in the baleful onset of cancer, Parkinson's disease, Alzheimer's disease, atherosclerosis, heart failure, myocardial infarction, Sickle Cell Disease, vitiligo, autism, and chronic fatigue syndrome. I remember many a morning when I was smoking cigarettes and eating poorly, mainly in my graduate school days, I would wake in an untamed, farouche stupor only to find my face the visual counterpart of the sound of a Mongolian death gong! Was that feral, undomesticated creature looking back at me from the addled mirror a pituiatry thymocentric? Some lunatic Morgellon with delusional beliefs? A barbarous pirate?

Who would deny that we are out of control? I suggest this was one of the reasons that the great if pessimistic English historian, Thomas Babington Macauley, who was opposed to popular government—he had a low opinion of Thomas Jefferson—predicted that the American Republic would be laid waste by barbarians in the 20th-century, "torn by the Scylla of dictatorship on the one hand, or the Charybdis of anarchy on the other," in the sarcastic words that President FDR quoted to mock him. Macauley distrusted popular trends and a populace that indulged themselves in them. In 1857 he wrote to an American friend, Henry S. Randall,

> I cannot help foreboding the worst. It is quite plain
> that your government will never be able to restrain a
> distressed and discontented majority... The day will
> come when... a multitude of people, none of whom
> has had more than half a breakfast, or expects to have   ~
> more than half a dinner.... will do things, which will

> prevent prosperity from returning, that you will act
> like people who should in a year of scarcity devour
> all the seed corn... Your Constitution is all sail and
> no anchor... Either some Caesar or Napoleon will
> seize the reins of government with a strong hand; or
> your republic will be... laid waste by barbarians in the
> Twentieth Century as the Roman Empire was in the
> fifth.

American kids, balloon-headed and riddled with salt, are all walking around on flapping feet with a bellyful of frosted chocolate and donut sludge. Today, about one in three American kids and teens is overweight or obese. The prevalence of obesity in children more than tripled from 1971 to 2011. Kids not only cannot do a pushup but will topple in a high wind! Can you find them in libraries? (No public libraries are open full-time anymore.) Can you find them on ball fields? (No youngsters bother playing sandlot baseball anymore.) Can you find them doing homework? (Not when the alternative is video games.) So where can they be found? Eating! Where? You name it. Ribomac's! Chickateria! Coneburger! Eggo-Baco-Tako! LunchMunchCrunch! Pizzariba, where Daffy Duck was given his surprise party! Planet of the Grapes! Pita Pan! Lard Have Mercy! Custard's Last Stand! Then deal with the fact that, as studies show, the average American, kids included, watches six hours of television per day—almost a full working day exposed to trash, slick relentless advertising, sex talk, imbecilic shows, tendentious news networks—and you can see why China will conquer us, oh, if I am asked to guess, I would say sometime around the year 2051.

As Brendan Behan writes in the closing lines of *The Hostage*, "There's no place on earth like the world."

The Twinkie, which was created during the Depression, contains as many as 39 ingredients. One of them, perhaps among the mildest, is the preservative sorbic acid. Added to this is cellulose gum, Polysorbate 60, and calcium sulfate, which as ingredients—ready?—are also used in shampoo, sheet rock, and rocket fuel. Should it therefore come as a surprise that Twinkies sends kids into tailspins—or even depression, perhaps fat comas? The junk-food was cited as a defense for murder, called the "Twinkie Defense," an almost comic catchall term that was coined by many reporters during their coverage of the trial in 1979 of defendant Dan White for the murders of San Francisco city supervisor Harvey Milk and Mayor George Moscone. White's defense was that he suffered diminished capacity as a result of depression stemming from a change in diet from healthy food to Twinkies and other sugary foods. Upon examination, one might assert that the Twinkie is barely a food. Ettlinger found that the vitamins, artificial colors, and flavorings in Twinkies come from petroleum. "Five ingredients come from rocks," writes Kate Thorp with some astonishment in her review of Steve Ettlinger's definitive book, *Twinkie Deconstructed*, in which he addresses the subject to demonstrate where our processed food ingredients come from. "This got my attention," writes Thorp, adding "However, it only got worse when I discovered that the ingredients come from phosphate mines in Idaho, gypsum mines in Oklahoma, and oil fields in China. Okay, so now I was wondering if I was watching a real news story—come to find out, I was... I started to wonder how this tasty treat made from gas and rocks can be so light and airy. In comes Mr. Ettlinger again. Apparently, it's limestone that makes Twinkies light. And that tasty cream center—it's got to be milk, right? No. It's made of shortening; there is absolutely no cream in the cream."

Half the time you never know what you are getting for what you have bought. In June 2014 the Supreme Court, no less, ruled against the Coca-Cola Company for flogging a fraudulent juice blend, charging that the company's practices "allegedly mislead and trick consumers, all to the injury of competitors." The blend, sold under Coca-Cola's Minute Maid brand, is made almost entirely from common apple and grape juice, and yet it is called "Pomegranate Blueberry." The Justices said Coca-Cola can be sued for false advertising by labeling as "Pomegranate Blueberry Flavored Blend of five juices" a drink containing just 0.3% pomegranate juice! It was a rare 8-0 ruling—Justice Stephen Breyer recused himself—and is said soon to have a broader impact on the clash between free enterprise and false advertising.

Mysterious doings—where the protagonist herself questions frauds and inexplicable tricks—emerge in Edith Wharton's eerie short story, "Pomegranate Seed," a tale of fearful jealousy, the title of which, an oblique reference, alludes to the Greek myth in which Persephone, goddess of fertility, is abducted and taken to Hades, where she breaks her vow of abstinence by eating some pomegranate seeds. There is not a single reference to the fruit in the story.

Dubious and deceptive nutrition claims on products prevent you from making sound decisions when shopping. "Lite" means exactly nothing, whereas "Light" refers only to taste and color. Foods high in fat bear labels stating that it is low in cholesterol—a "cholesterol free" food. Potato chip companies avoid using the toxic word "fried" and adopt instead the more healthful-sounding term "toasted." "Cheese foods" have replaced the word cheese. A ploy explained by the sinister euphemism "vanishing caloric density" allows vincibly ignorant consumers eating "constructed foods" to believe that the cheese puffs that melt in your mouth have no calories in them. The term "low-salt" we read on snack foods is cheerfully employed as a green light for eaters only to scarf down more. The smarmy slogan, "as good as homemade," is as false as asserting that all frozen pizzas tastes different than the box they come in! The late comedian George Carlin, speaking for us all, no doubt, is duly skeptical about the word "homemade" on packages and various supermarket products. "Folks, take my word for this," he advises, "any food company operating out of a ninety-acre processing plant is functionally incapable of producing anything homemade. I don't care if the CEO is living in the basement, wearing an apron, and cooking on a hot plate. It's not gonna happen." Carlin comes right to the point and declares with a zing,

> Homemade is a myth. You want to know some things
> that are homemade? Crystal meth. Crack cocaine. A
> pipe bomb full of nails. Now we're talking homemade.

So exactly what does "less" and "reduced" and "diet" actually indicate when highlighted on a yogurt or olive oil or ice cream? Zip. Nada. One can also find the reassuring phrase "undeclared ingredients"—ponder the lunatic hubris in listing it—in many meat and pharmaceutical products. (Were you aware that for the so-called food "ethnic markets" (brand-speak for blacks and Hispanics) that the Kool-Aid, among other products, that is sold all through Latin America has more sugar than that sold in the USA?) As one nutritionist puts it, "Part of the reason [frozen diet entrées] are all under 200 calories is that they are the portion-size for a rat."

Are you not heartened to find on products the American Heart Association's heart-check logo with the flaming torch that assures consumers that the product you are buying is good for your health? (On its bright website this non-profit organization urges, "Donate now and help save lives.") Any serious person gets a solid working sense of how corrupt this organization is when he discovers that there on the supermarket shelf a bottle of Welch's Grape Juice proudly bearing the AHA logo despite the glaring fact that one 8-ounce serving has 36 grams of sugar, more than a standard-size Snickers bar! Also, try this one on it has now been medically proven that a good many dietary supplements and aids—herbal pills, green tea extracts, health powders, vitamins, minerals, probiotics, fish oils, and many so-called "fat-burning" products, even a lot of prescription drugs—now account for nearly 20 percent of drug-related liver injuries that turn up in hospitals. Dr. Herbert L. Bonkovsky, the director of the liver, digestive and metabolic disorders laboratory at Carolinas Health Care System in Charlotte, N.C., is reported as saying in the *New York Times* (December 22, 2013), "It's really the Wild West. When people buy these dietary supplements, it's anybody's guess as to what they're getting."

Health deaths!

The ultimate oxymoron.

We are manipulated on a thousand fronts. Were you aware, for example, that there are 200 ingredients on the list of government-approved additives for wine? That bottled wine today is a far cry from pure grapes? That wine manufacturers are not required to list their ingredients (which can include animal proteins, oak chips, sulfurs, yeasts, enzymes, preservatives, and Mega Purple, a brand of concentrated wine color) on the side label? Today, wine is pervaded, permeated, and infused with things like nitrogen, diammonium phosphate, magnesium sulfate, yeast hulls, thiamine, folic acid, niacin, and calcium pantothenate. The ploy is all about sales. "Thermovinification, a hot maceration technique that can produce wine in a few hours rather than a few weeks or months, is used in many wine-producing regions," writes Alice Feiring in *Naked Wine*, a book that makes a plea for making natural wine. "Stupefyingly, in a world favoring slow food, few seem to mind fast wine."

But PHOs are food additives—maybe the worst of them! Why have not all partially hydrogenated oils, the primary dietary source of artificial trans fat in processed food—"plasticized" fats—been banned in the United States by the FDA? The answer is simple: it is not good for business. (Denmark, which was the first country to ban them, did so back in 2003!) The use of PHOs is strictly for junk food manufacturers who want a shelf-stable that will not liquefy and leak out of their processed foods. (Freeze dried eggs can be shelf stable for as long as 25 years!) Trans fats, which are usually made from genetically modified soybean oil, are far and away the perfect junk food ingredient simply because, while they taste fatty, they are also ambient, that is they can be stored in a sealed container at room or ambient temperature. We are being poisoned not only by the toxicity of trans fats but also by heavy metals, mercury, sodium nitrite, MSG, aspartame, even artificial food colorings.

Many other countries scrupulously refuse to poison their citizens. Farm-raised salmon is banned in Australia and New Zealand, for example. No one in the European Union can buy genetically-engineered papaya. All processed foods containing artificial food colors and dyes are banned in Norway, Finland, France, Great Britain, and Austria. Bread with potassium bromate is banned in Canada, China, and the EU. The UK does not allow BHA in infant foods.

Here, anything goes. There is corporate corruption everywhere. The profit motif is the bottom line. When one sees the politique of so many cagey business-weasels at work, one can well understand why we are told in James 4:4 that anyone who chooses to be a friend of the world becomes an enemy of God. Where are the altruistic men and women that this country gave us a century ago?

John Dewey, for example, the American philosopher and psychologist, was also an educational reformer and liberal who was shocked by the plight of the urban poor, their lack of adequate nutrition, the pervasiveness of class and race-based structural inequalities, and the crying need for education to liberate them from these conditions. His writings on school gardening alone—he had six children—are fascinating. He saw school gardening as a natural extension of the study of the nature movement, a late-nineteenth, early-twentieth century program of the examination of natural history in education. He was deeply concerned about "food justice." His ambition was to redress the procedural unfairness in how food is produced and distributed in this country, in the same way that environmental justice seeks to address environmental health. Food access is food sovereignty, and Dewey yearned for us to grow and enjoy healthy food, allowing for a sovereignty which fosters a community's prerogative to determine the structure of its own agricultural and food systems. Nowadays, hapless American youngsters seem to be left to every last exploiting predator to turn them fat.

Part of the problem is with all the garbled facts coming down you never know which information is right and which is wrong.

I have always thought it bizarre, for example, that the Russo-Greek-Armenian guru and pseudo-philosophizing quack, G.I. Gurdjieff, who visited the United States nine times, starting in 1924, mocked us with his self-indulgent partying character named Mr. Bellybutton and condemned out of hand America's strange and destructive eating habits—canned foods, processed slop, even frozen and genetically altered foods, the cause, he felt, of all of our digestive disorders—and yet was himself a fanatical drug-taker and abuser of alcohol, a mad drunk, to say nothing of other loony interests of his like in experimenting with medically unsound radium water and magnetic treatments. He was an extremely heavy user of many psychoactive substances. Coffee and cigarettes were a daily fixture in his life throughout his long teaching career, excesses which have been documented by biographers, journalists and students. The official medical cause of his death was cirrhosis of the liver and liver cancer.

A sharp indictment of corporate sleaze ("When in doubt, add sugar") can be found in Michael Moss's essay in the *New York Times* (February 20, 2013) entitled "The Extraordinary Science of Addictive Junk Food," a shocking exposé on competing greed in which he explains how major corporations with their eyes solely on sales figures like Kraft, General Mills, Nabisco, Proctor & Gamble, Coca-Cola, and Mars—all desperately fighting for "stomach share," the amount of digestive space that any one company's brand can grab from the competition—reveal themselves to be hopelessly corrupt and utterly conscienceless. Companies hire well-paid shills to become their advocates and spokesmen, contriving to buy off with cash former whistleblowers who once opposed them. (Carl Sandburg once confided to James Thurber, who had inquired if in his books on Lincoln he had ever intentionally omitted any facts, that indeed he had and that one of them was Ol' Abe's excuse for hiring the cantankerous asthmatic Edwin Stanton as Secretary of War: "I would rather have him in the inside pissing out than on the outside pissing in.") The sordid and disreputable hirelings all take on the profile of the kind of corner-cutting villains who appear in the plays of Henrik Ibsen. Moss sought out a functionary named Howard Moskowitz, a food industry "optimizer" who number-crunched ways to help seduce consumers and boost sales by reforming Prego spaghetti sauce, a product in which, it turns out, the largest ingredient after tomatoes is sugar. His "gift" to the American people was helping to re-engineer Prego spaghetti sauce in order to maximize the sensory intensity of its sweetness to hit the optimum peak or "bliss point." The company followed his directions and met with great success. A mere half-cup of Prego Traditional now has the equivalent of more than than two teaspoons of white sugar, as much as two-plus Oreo cookies, while delivering one-third of the daily sodium recommended for a majority of American adults. "There's no moral issue for me," Moskowitz flimsily explained. "I was struggling to survive and didn't have the luxury of being a moral creature. As a researcher, I was ahead of my time." The goal is to pump into foods more sugar, more fat, and more salt and to make consumers love it! There's no moral issue for me!

This is what gonzo reporter Hunter S. Thompson presciently called "rat fucking," what contemporary novelist Tom Wolfe referred to as "behavioral sink." Under the leadership of like-minded Stephen Sanger, the CEO of General Mills, which has overtaken not just the cereal aisle but other sections of the grocery store, the company's Yoplait brand, in Moss's words, "transformed traditional unsweetened yogurt into a veritable dessert. It now has twice as much sugar per serving as General Mills' marshmallow cereal, Lucky Charms." But because of yogurt's well-tended image as a wholesome snack, sales of Yoplait went soaring, with annual revenue topping $500 million." Emboldened by this, the company came out with a yogurt variation for kids that comes in a squeezable tube which they called "Go-Gurt." Right off, it racked up $100 million in sales. "Don't talk to me about nutrition," Sanger reportedly said. "Talk to me about taste." These people are true devils.

You think that you are eating well. But as P.G. Wodehouse wittily writes in his novel, *Very Good, Jeeves!* "Unseen in the background, Fate was quietly slipping lead into the boxing-glove." Corporations are not at all serious about health. It is solely about profit, with decisions being made strictly in relation to the bottom-line, with all the scrums in the boardroom having to do with monetizing the products, like the Kool-Aid folks debating whether to keep Sharkleberry Fin flavor or to discontinue the Great Bluedini flavor for fear their little consumers might confuse it with windshield-washer fluid; or the Swanson people coming up with "Hungry-Man" dinners (total fat: 45.0 g) and while claiming to add taste and flavor making it only fattier and saltier; or the Dr Pepper Snapple Group advertising the seafood magic of bottles of Clamato while at the same time managing to keep it 99% clam-juice free. It all recalls for me what H.G. Wells's Mr. Polly murmured when the ironmonger opposite took no notice of his morning hello, being far too busy arranging his shop, "Zealacious commerciality."

In the end, you honestly have to concede that in a frightening way it takes a kind of evil genius for the McDonald's Corporation ingeniously—devilishly!—to have come up with a simple fruit-and-yogurt parfait whose calories add up to more than 50 percent sugar. Did you know that McDonald's salads contain up to 60% more fat than their burgers? The huge McDonalds conglomerate now has over 33,000 restaurants in 119 countries (14,000 franchises in the United states alone), serving as many as 47 million customers a day. McDonald's sells as many as 75 hamburgers every second of every day. "Identimeals" go to 47 million customers daily! In 2012 McDonalds' earnings exceeded almost $7 billion in revenues. The primary preoccupation of Madison Avenue is all too simple: *sell, sell, sell!*

Fast food has become very expensive. I recall when I was teaching at Yale how the local McDonald's right next to the University—it was a popular hang-out—would immediately fill up to bulging with young black high school students all shouting and ordering Big Macs and Quarter Pounders with big killer soft drinks, and you knew many if not most of them were poor. Don't kids go home to *eat* anymore? Are there any homes anymore, with bright kitchens, or dining rooms, with tables, around which families sit? *Are there families anymore?* (St. Paul asked the very same thing of rude, obstreperous, loud, and selfish supper-goers in Corinthians 11:22: "Don't you have homes to eat and drink in?") Are all American parents, unemulously slouched on their sofas, watching plasma TV sets the size of Nebraska, too lazy to go into their kitchens nowadays and make a few sandwiches? "The price gap between junk food and real food only seems to be widening," chef Alton Brown pointed out recently (*New York Times Magazine*, September 6, 2015), underlining the irony that it is now cheaper (and healthier) to buy food at a supermarket than at a fast-food restaurant. "We have designed our system to force people into nutritional slavery."

I cannot help but find an apt (and frightening) analogy to these fast-food conglomerates in the film, *The Third Man* (1949) regarding crookedness and profiteering. "Have you ever seen any of your victims?" asks the scandalized Holly Martins of the corrupt thief Harry Lime in a famous scene. During the war Lime had been stealing penicillin from military hospitals, diluting it, and selling it on the black market, leading to many deaths. Martins and Lime are seen high up on a Ferris wheel in post-war Vienna, meeting after five years or so. They were once old school friends, and Lime had promised Martins a job, except that he has since discovered to his disgust that Lime's racket was so odious. Looking down from their height on the tiny figures of the many people below, Lime replies, "Victims? Don't be melodramatic. Look down there. Tell me. Would you really feel any pity if one of those dots stopped moving forever? If I offered you twenty thousand pounds for every dot that stopped, would you really, old man, tell me to keep my money, or would you calculate how many dots you could afford to spare? Free of income tax, old man. Free of income tax—the only way you can save money nowadays."

The cynical Lime, without missing a hitch, adds portentously, "Nobody thinks in terms of human beings. Governments don't. Why should we? They talk about the people and the proletariat, I talk about the suckers and the mugs—it's the same thing. They have their five-year plans, so have I." Martins melancholily asserts, "You used to believe in God." The cynical Lime is utterly indifferent. "Oh, I still do believe in God, old man. I believe in God and mercy and all that. But the dead are happier dead. They don't miss much here, poor devils."

Notice how throughout the scene the skeptical and spiritually congested Harry Lime, needing antacid tablets—he repeatedly asks Martins for some—suffers from heartburn, which I see as indication of his moral turpitude, an occlusion of soul, for seeing people as suckers, mugs, dogs, poor devils. It is a kind of godless anti-communion that the selfish malefactor seeks to allay his personal pain. The illnesses of the needful people that Lime has bilked of their medicine he has duly contracted. No one, including film critics, in the many discussions and analyses of this celebrated film ever chooses to discuss the tablets or bother with their significance, but I consider it a symbol of his corruption that is used metonymically in the film. It is a curious nexus:

greed, corruption, and the ramifications of exploitation, for Lime who is shown to be ill from his many dodges is brought low and inevitably pays the ultimate penalty.

Supermarkets are the insidious locations where we find these, not foods, but food-like substances. How are they laid out? "Processed food products dominate the center aisles of [most supermarkets] while the cases of ostensibly fresh food—dairy, produce, meat, and fish—line the walls," observes Pollan. "If you keep to the edges of the store you'll be that much more likely to wind up with real food in your shopping cart." You will become, otherwise, just another dopey, non-examining consumer and gullible pea-brained mark and, looking for the kind of trash food an old roommate of mine craved—he drank 24 Pepsi-Colas a day—go whistling off to the nearest Piggly-Wiggly at every chance very like Pinocchio did to Pleasure Island only to be diddled and daddled. My roommate's food whims? Peanut butter and a Sara Lee's Soft & Smooth Whole Grain White Bread, the ingredients of which are:

> Enriched bleached flour [wheat flour, malted barley flour, niacin, iron, thiamin mononitrate (vitamin B1), riboflavin (vitamin B2), folic acid], water, whole grains [whole wheat flour, brown rice flour (rice flour, rice bran), high fructose corn syrup, whey, wheat gluten, yeast, cellulose. Contains 2% or less of each of the following: honey, calcium sulphate, vegetable oil (soybean and/or cottonseed oils), salt, butter (cream, salt), dough conditioners (may contain one or more of the following: mono- and diglycerides, ethoxylated mono- and diglycerides, ascorbic acid, enzymes, azodicarbonamide, guar gum, calcium propionate (preservative), distilled vinegar, yeasts nutrients (monocalcium phosphate, calcium sulfate, ammonium sulfate), corn starch, natural flavor, beta carotene (color), vitamin D, soy lecithin, soy flour."

It is not as if the US government is helping, either. "Very simply, we subsidize high-fructose corn syrup in this country, but not carrots," laments Pollan in *The Omnivore's Dilemma: A Natural History of Four Meals*. "While the surgeon general is raising alarms over the epidemic of obesity, the president is signing farm bills designed to keep the river of cheap corn flowing, guaranteeing that the cheapest calories in the supermarket will continue to be the unhealthiest."

It appears that just about every food in the supermarket contains high fructose corn syrup. Breakstone cottage cheese. Contadina Tomato Paste. Robitussin cough syrup. Jim Beam Steak Sauce. Ben & Jerry's Cherry Garcia Ice Cream. Claussen Pickles. Cool Whip. Nabisco Wheat Thins. B&M Original Baked Beans. The very first ingredient listed on bottled barbecue sauces is high-fructose corn syrup. HFCS is about six times sweeter than table sugar (which consists of fructose, the sweetest of all sugars, and glucose, another simple sugar). The very first ingredient in the popular best-selling American infant formula, Enfamil, a Mead Johnson product, by the way, is—corn syrup solids! Baby food! Yum! Yum! Yum!

Corn syrup! America's main food ingredient! There is virtually no food that it mercifully skips. It reminds me of a sign that I once saw in front of a Church of Christ: "If you are looking for a sign, this is it!"

Baby food is all sugar-ridden! One teaspoon of granulated sugar equals 4 grams of sugar. Put another way, 16 grams of sugar in a product is equal to about 4 teaspoons of granulated sugar. Virtually no baby snack isn't candy! Plum Organics "Plum Berry & barley" organic baby food has 10 grams of sugar in a 3.5 ounce squeeze packet, while Earth's Best "Organic Fruit Yogurt Smoothies" (USDA Organic)—a Sesame Street "Healthy Habits for Life" logo can be found on the package—has 15 grams of sugar in a 4.2 ounce squeeze packet. One packet of these, in short, has more than *three teaspoons of sugar*! Such foods are bordering on the criminal!

Sugar seduces. How insidiously, you ask? Are you aware that nowadays even our vegetables and fruits are becoming less bitter? One diabolical trend in order to satisfy America's craving for sweetness is that food manufacturers have for awhile now been reducing bitterness in foods, trying to make sweet food like broccoli, grapefruits, and tomatoes, raising fears among nutritionists that naturally and normally acrid, biting, or unsweetened fruits and vegetables are becoming the "junk foods of the fresh produce aisle," according to Jennifer McLagan in *Bitter: A Taste of the World's Most Dangerous Flavour*. Supermarkets, for example, are already perversely advertising milder Brussels sprouts as "kid friendly." She writes,

> On the face of it, reducing bitterness in foods sounds
> like a great idea. Wouldn't it be nice if broccoli were
> always mild and sweet? But there is a catch. The
> same chemicals that make fruit and veg bitter also
> imbue them with many of their health benefits. When

scientists talk about the healthiness of green tea, dark chocolate, red wine or broccoli, much of what they are talking about is due to bitter chemicals called phytonutrients.

We have all evolved to savor sweet ingredients—they give us energy, delight us, taste good. A balance of tastes is required for our health. Anything salty contains sodium, which is necessary for our bodies to function well. "Bitter, on the other hand, suggests toxicity," explains Jennifer McLagan, "which is why our natural reaction is to want to spit it out. Bitter phytonutrients act as a natural pesticide, protecting plants against all kinds of enemies, from bacteria to insects and cows. Thousands of these nutrients have been identified so far, giving the bitter tang to familiar foodstuffs such as Brussels sprouts and coffee." She goes on to say, "But despite phytonutrients being toxic in large doses, a growing body of evidence suggests that small doses can confer a host of health benefits. The elusive white grapefruit is a prime example. Its most prominent phytonutrient is ultra-bitter naringin, which turns out to have anti-ulcer and anti-inflammatory properties." McLagan points out that "thirty years ago, Florida, the grapefruit capital of North America, produced 27 million boxes of white and 23 million boxes of the colored varieties. Today, however, they ship more than twice as many red and pink grapefruit as they do whites ones." (It would not have mattered to Jim Davis's cartoon cat, Garfield. He hated grapefruit—he even declared that the only thing he hated more than grapefruit was *hating* grapefruit.)

It turns out that grapefruit is the harbinger of a wider problem, for the trend upon examination affects much in fresh produce, from cauliflower to potatoes, tomatoes, and juices. "Naringin can also inhibit the growth of breast cancer cells, and induces cervical cancer cells to commit suicide. The sweeter pink and red varieties have substantially less of the stuff. The mechanism at work is known as *hormesis*—simply put, it's the idea that what doesn't kill you makes you stronger. The reason bitter phytonutrients are cancer-preventing is that they can destroy cells," writes McLagen. That the food industry is seeking to strip some foods of the very chemicals that make them good for us is more than ironic. A paradox is involved. The fact is we all *need* bitter foods! "They are healthy because they are toxic," notes epidemiologist Adam Drewnowski. One study found that eating a diet rich in *quercetin*, which is found in green tea, broccoli, and red wine, might help in protecting us from the fierce ravages of lung cancer, especially in heavy smokers. Many vegetables include glucosinolates, which may have anti-cancer benefits. It has been well established that even cooking vegetables and fruits can diminish the amount of vitamins. It is grotesque—upsidedownland! Jed Fahey, a molecular scientist at Johns Hopkins School of Medicine in Baltimore, Maryland, writes, "Eating fruits and vegetables without phytochemicals would in many ways be analogous to drinking the empty calories of a can of soda."

"People who eat white bread have no dreams," professed queenly Diana Vreeland in *Vogue* magazine—from which the vitamins have been actually removed! Vreeland would surely have been among the last people alive who would have known that in the Middle Ages refined white bread was used almost exclusively by the Church and the surplus sold to the nobility, while the poor people ate dark bread, thus establishing a tradition for a very long time of associating white bread (also white rice, white sugar) with wealth and status.

It was strictly from snobbery that Vreeland found white bread common and not to be chewed but eschewed. Many another agreed. One of Henry Miller's funniest essays has as its satirical object the American loaf of white bread, what the poet Karl Shapiro disdainfully referred to as "the poisonous loaf of cleanliness wrapped in cellophane, the manufacture of which is a heavy industry like steel." Diana Vreeland who lunched every day at her desk on only a glass of scotch and a peanut butter-and-marmalade sandwich, sitting there like a Swine Queen ordering all of her underlings about with silken devoirs and bullying yaps, would eat that mixture exclusively on whole wheat bread. She who excoriated white bread sniffed, "How common, you know, flour and water. That's what white bread is made of, and that's what we use to make library paste of." Americans love white bread and generally eat white flour bright enough to blind us, never mind that it is poached of all vitamins. The late Shah of Iran, Reza Pahlavi, never the soul of wisdom or of pity, frankly, with uncharacteristic foresight actually forbade the consumption of white flour in his country. The only place one could purchase it in Iran at the time was—yup—at the U.S. Embassy commissary.

What about the shrimp that we consume in this country? It comes mainly from the Far East and not only has been farm-raised and spawned in soups of filth and disease but *less than 2 percent* of that gets inspected by U.S. regulatory agencies. Say that out loud! "I have never seen a food writer mention this, but all shrimp imported into the United States must first be washed in chlorine bleach to kill bugs. What this does for the taste, I do not know, but I think we should be told," writes British journalist Charles Clover in *The End of the Line: How Overfishing Is Changing the World and What We Eat.* As I say, almost all of our imported farmed shrimp comes to us scooped up from an almost incomprehensible stew of contaminants, which include, according to Marianne Cufone, director of the fish program at the nonprofit

Food and Water Watch, "antibiotics, residues from chemicals used to clean pens, filth like mouse hair, rat hair, and pieces of insects." And that list does not include Salmonella and E. coli, both of which have been detected in imported shrimp, which is so dirty that it accounts for 26 to 35 percent of all shipments of imported seafood that get rejected due to filth. Two samples of farm-raised (as opposed to wild) shrimp from India and Thailand tested positive for nitrofuranzone, an antibiotic that is a known carcinogen, at levels 28 and 29 times higher than those allowed by the FDA. Another antibiotic, chloramphenical, was detected at levels 150 times the legal limit. It has been banned in food production in the United States because of possible severe side effects such as aplastic anemia and leukemia. We still haven't a qualm about eating imported shrimp. Not only do we all saunter out of big croaking, door-busting food warehouses like Costco and BJ's with great walloping bags of such compromised shrimp, whatever the size—jumbo, jeroboam jumbo, jehosophat jeroboam jumbo—all flash frozen white, but are serenely content scarfing up large platters of it, unquestioned! As Raymond Chandler once observed, "It is not a fragrant world."

At least water of some kind still flows in South East Asia—no thanks to the tub- thumping sanctimonious evangelist, Rev. Billy Graham, a double-dealing millenialist crackpot and unapologetic Republican tool for half a century. It was this vain, so-called Christian born of rustic doctrinaires who blithely suggested to then President Richard M. Nixon, a toad who was not above going along with such a plan, that, if the negotiations known as the "Paris Peace Talks," begun in 1968, proved to fail, the United States should seriously consider the destruction of Vietnam's *entire* irrigation infrastructure, although such a criminal act would kill more than a million civilians. Alexander Cockburn wrote in *CounterPunch* in March 12, 2002,

> Back in April, 1989 a Graham memo to Nixon was made public. It took the form of a secret letter from Graham, dated April 15, 1969, drafted after Graham met in Bangkok with missionaries from Vietnam. These men of God said that if the peace talks in Paris were to fail, Nixon should step up the war and bomb the dikes. Such an act, Graham wrote excitedly, "could overnight destroy the economy of North Vietnam." Graham lent his imprimatur to this recommendation. Thus the preacher was advocating a policy to the US Commander in Chief that on Nixon's own estimate would have killed a million people. The German high

commissioner in occupied Holland, Seyss-Inquart, was
sentenced to death at Nuremberg for breaching dikes
in Holland in World War Two. (His execution did
not deter the USAF from destroying the Toksan dam
in North Korea, in 1953, thus deliberately wrecking
the system that irrigated 75 per cent of North Korea's
rice farms.) This disclosure of Graham as an aspirant
war criminal did not excite any commotion when
it became public in 1989, twenty years after it was
written. I recall finding a small story in the *Syracuse
Herald-Journal.*

Aldous Huxley was not wrong when he wrote, "Morality is always the product of terror; its chains and strait-waistcoats are fashioned by those who dare not trust others, because they dare not trust themselves, to walk in liberty."

But do not the biggest national loudmouths eventually and inevitably always prove they are talking out of their asses?

I see the obese talk-show host Rush Limbaugh, right-wing loon and aficionado of the counterfactual, as the embodiment of America's insane eating habits, and, beyond that, as an example of those who eat white bread and have no dreams—they are related, to some degree. His less than conventional mind is a midway carnival shill's. His thought is never outside the box but from inside the refrigerator. He no more stands for the real America than the jumped-up Confederate states stood for anything more than an outlaw band that preyed on the South and the southern people, for as Abraham Lincoln said, the term "seceded states" was a *misnomer*. The Union remained unbroken. Those eleven Southern states had not seceded, because they could not. To me, Limbaugh is the living embodiment of our laziness, our stupidity, our anti-intellectualism, and our bad diet. He is a buffoon whose sole interest all along has been simply to buck-rake, never to lead, but instead of wearing a goofy hat, big flapping clown shoes, and a red rubber nose-ball his motley is low-brow and irrational right-wing-ism. St. Gabriel, patron saint of broadcasters, must be cringing up in heaven looking down upon at what he sees with this guy. El Rushbo is a steadfast and obdurate climate-change denier, although he actually lives in Palm Beach, Florida, ground-zero when it comes to the pending cataclysm of ocean inundation, a catastrophe thought by scientists in the areas of the southern part of that state to be rising by century's end to a ten-to-thirty foot range, ten times the rate of average global sea level rise. Water will be pouring in to the landmass from above and even below! As someone has pointed out, "The water comes from six sides in Florida." I can easily see Limbaugh in my mind's eye being carried out on the crest of a giant green sea swell, snorting to clear his nostrils, bellowing and roaring like a bewildered elephant seal!

As the ultimate American food-coma psycho, Limbaugh is also a niddering chicken-hawk, who avoided the draft during the Vietnam War by cowardly claiming to have a pilonoidal cyst on his ass, the very place where he has spent most of his life as a comical bully-ragging majordomo. How did such a *bruggioli* ever manage to wangle a national show? I would cite a passing remark of Dr. Samuel Johnson's for the simplest and best explanation: "He was dull in a new way, and that made many people think him great." So we ask how can such an obvious imbecile run a viable show for three hours a day? The answer is by blabbing. A talker by definition is not a listener. Limbaugh invites no guests, dares no combat, allows no rebuttal, encourages no debate, elicits no opposite point of view. (I have waking dreams of him debating Noam Chomsky and getting julienned like a jumbo yellow carrot!) No, Limbaugh pays attention only to himself, lost in the mazes of his own nonsense.

"I am pretty much one-dimensional," he told Maureen Dowd in one of his very rare honest and accurately insightful moments, as she reported in "At Dinner with Rush Limbaugh," a column that ran in the *New York Times* on March 24, 1993. The two of them for that occasion were dining at the "21" Club, but it very well could have been at the Phât Phúc Noodle Bar because Limbaugh has no taste or in fact much affinity with what he calls "the arts and croissant crowd." "I don't go to movies," he acknowledged. "I've been to a couple of plays. I basically work. I don't watch television. I watch the news and the NFL, that's it." What else can a raging anti-intellectual, poorly read Boob McNutt do but frankly admit that he *is* lunch-meat? "To the uneducated, an A is just three sticks," as we read in *Winnie-the-Pooh.*

A momo like Limbaugh, one with his walloping girth, cannot possibly disguise what he is, so he must be candid. "One of the reasons of my success is that I'm totally concerned with me," he confessed. "Sometimes I have a date and somebody'll want to watch a movie so I'll say, 'All right, let's go to the video store.' And I go in there and I buy some videos. That way, you don't have to take 'em back... I don't walk. I just despise it. I don't like shopping. I hate window-shopping. I don't browse. One thing I like about New York is that they bring it to you. You call 'em up and they bring it to you. You don't have to go find it, shop for it, look for it, if you don't want to. I love that," declares this spokesman for the Fruited Plain, as he refers to the United States of America, a country as I say whose military service he cowardly dodged. He puffs cigars, embiggens every year, predicts absolutely nothing correctly, consistently praises the phony and belittles the noble, and claims to like—even play—sports but walks like a hippo and has a golf-swing shiver like a dolphin farting. He says he stays away from museums "until I can find a golf cart in one."

Shamelessness does not even describe Limbaugh. Although he boasts about his ever-soaring income, he has been unapologetically shilling commercials day in and day out for 28 years, picking up all the spare change he can, like a common tinker, and, while still claiming to be a strong political voice, hawking everything from loan companies to mattresses, cigars, house gutters, girdles, credit unions, venetian blinds, insurance chains, fat supplements, vitamins, golf supplies, heating & cooling firms, Hillsdale College, auto glass, SUVs, state lotteries, pajamagrams, testosterone products, and tax form services, although I have read that as many as forty-eight of the top 50 network advertisers and major national ad agencies have excluded Limbaugh from doing their ads anymore, finding him a distinct liability.

I am reminded of Limbaugh in the Hieronymus Bosch painting "*Gula*" [gluttony] in the *Seven Deadly Sins* wheel (c. 1500), less so by that tubby central figure selfishly tucking into a wet hambone than by the grasping fat boy at his knee—the crazy little pinguid—in gross black clogs and be-shitten clothes. Curiously enough, in *Le Ménagier De Paris*, a French medieval guidebook from 1393, which is written in the (fictional) voice of an elderly husband addressing his younger wife—it is filled with helpful recipes—included in the definition of gluttony is the extended vice of wanton, unscrupulous, and unprincipled speech!

A more desolate man-balloon, a sadder capon, is truly hard to picture than Rush Limbaugh, the social foundling from Missouri Central High School. Since 1993, he has been married four times, which confirms that he is not good at it, as I suspect most fat, desperately vain, personality-less suisexuals probably are not. He sits there alone in his hermetic studio, spouting right-wing propaganda bloated with exaggeration, afraid to have guests on of any kind, never mind opposite thinkers, with the concomitant need to praise himself at every turn. There is no question that he was bullied all through his school years and mocked by girls, who engendered a textbook mysogynist. As to food, he avoids grocery stores because, as he boasts, "I can order food from D'Agostino's on my computer and have it delivered." He mocks anyone who heads for the country on weekends, even though he appears to do little of anything in the city. "I like to vege," he says, unsurprisingly. A sluggard, he literally refuses to walk on a golf course and will never play the game—say on rainy days when vehicles will leave grooves—without being wheeled around in golf cart.

Of the seven famous characteristics of a "living thing"—(1) movement, (2) respiration, (3) sensitivity, (4) growth, (5) excretion, (6) nutrition, and (7) reproduction—I would have to declare that Limbaugh is completely missing, respectively, numbers 1, 3, 4, 6, and 7. Children ("chirrun") he abhors and mocks at every turn. In his childishness and immaturity, surely no one is more temperamentally unsuited to fatherhood, being also a spite-master with an intense serial interest only in himself. "I'm a little long here," he compulsively repeats on his show, acknowledging less a time break, a segué into a commercial, than a laughably optimistic but ultimately sad would-be priapism—another of his pipe-dreams—a semi-sexual quip I have always assigned to an incipient case of medomalacuphobia, a fear of detumescence. Talk about the substance of things to be hoped for, the evidence of things not seen! Swollen only in his girth, ego, and conceit, Limbaugh is the very definition of flaccid. It would be a mistake to call the man self-loving, however, for he has no "interior paramour," to borrow a phrase from Wallace Stevens. You can hear it confessed in the sad, feeble, mournful extravagance of his endless bombast, hollow as a cenotaph. He is also fractious, grumpy, and disgruntled. One would think to have made all that money on a knack for nothing more than skewing news, he would be grateful.

What is it about media people and petulance? After the brilliant pastry chef Nick Malgieri took the expert trouble to make an Old Viennese apple strudel on her show and began cutting it to serve her, crabby Martha Stewart, hovering as if on skis, rudely barked, *I don't like the ends!* Cavilling over shape, cuts, favorite pieces, sections, even shares, portions, bits, quotas, and percentages—making a big argy-bargy about it at table—is another hideous aspect of food aversion, usually by low-rent mediocrities who have no consideration for their dining companions.

7.

GULPY, GURGLY, PLOBBY, SQUISHY

"AMERICANS AS A GENERAL RULE," noted the English journalist Alex Atkinson in his witty and often excoriatingly satirical 1959 travel book, *USA for Beginners: By Rocking-Chair Across America*, "like their food big, and preferably taste-less. To take a simple instance, if they detect the slightest flavour of bread in a loaf they will take it out at once and bury it three hundred yards from the nearest dwelling, and report the baker to the Department of Sanitation. I had tried tinned apricots in mutton stew, tomato sauce on trifle (with pis-tachio nuts), strawberry jam with a double-decker sandwich of home-cured pork and crayfish, and lamb chops swimming in chocolate sauce. The great thing about Americans, leaving aside their plumbing for a moment, is that they are not afraid of the food," he writes, even if he is not very subtle in implying that many if not most cooks or chefs in this country have spent too much time biking without a helmet. (Wait, could I have read that correct-ly? An Englishman criticizing *American* plumbing?) Americans eat sorghum and broom corn. Cauliflowers are called Brussels sprouts. Tomatoes are too big. We over-lard everything, in his opinion, and eat from enormous plates the size of pizza trays. Servings are all out of proportion. He was served a steak in Texas so enormous that he tried to jettison it after a week. "Each night when I got back to my hotel, I'd have it sent up to my room. Then I'd sit down and try to hack another five inches off it. On the last evening, admitting defeat, I wrapped up the remaining three-quarters of a pound in a towel, and hid it in the wardrobe. Then I checked out. When I got to Dallas it was waiting for me, with a note from the management. 'Sir,' said the note, 'you never finished your chop.'"

"Oddly, outside of urban centers, it is difficult to find a first-rate steak in the West, except in Nebraska and Kansas," writes Jim Harrison in his *The Raw and the Cooked. In the entire West?* May I ask what kind of jackass would make such a cavalier, such an outrageous remark? This fat obsessive with his penchant for truffle-sniffing and caviar-spooning and venison-snogging was a far greater food snob than Orson Welles or Danny Kaye ever was—a real kitchen queen—but what is seriously painful to see is an inveterate food-snob trying to fob himself off as a tough ol' Montana hand. "I can think of only one truly great one," he writes regarding American wine, "the 1968 Heitz Martha's Vineyard." Only *one* truly great American wine? He would have you believe, on the one hand, that he is a tough old cowhand, but then he talks about Périgourdian duck legs, soft-shelled crab *meunière*, and cobia marinated in Mozambiquean piripiri and skewered with peppers and mushrooms! We come across sentences of his like, "I just tasted my *estouffade*—really quite good, though it occurred to me that I had forgotten to blanch the salt pork" and "I have a passion for *tête de veau* (the tongue, cheeks, brains, and neck meat of a calf)" and "I'm on my second glass (a twelve-ouncer) of Gigondas, a Côtes du-Rhone I favor."

Can you imagine eating a meal with this pain-in-the-ass? A tremendous food bully for whom (his words) "only more approaches enough"—the definitive slogan of a food hog—tells us, "Once on a food tour of the south with my friend, de la Valdene, we had strictly limited our food budget to a thousand dollars a day but went well over this limitation every day for a week," writes this so-called man of the people. "Just because you are full doesn't mean you lose interest in food." Never mind eating a meal with the guy, how about going on a long *trip* with him and having to listen all day and night to all of these ultracrepidarian opinions of his? It is obvious he knows everything. Giving him advice would be like giving a fish a bath. The guy should be keelhauled. And what about the guy breezily appropriating—baldly plagiarizing—his book title, *The Raw and the Cooked*, from Claude Levi-Strauss's *Le Cru et Le Cuit*?

I wonder if Harrison would deign to join the for-the-moment non-fastidious Gael Greene in a pull of Gallo plonk. "Even blind, I recognized Gallo Hearty Burgundy at once," she writes at one point in *Insatiable*. "It was a cross between Beaujolais nouveau and strawberry Jell-O in a jug, and Americans, including me, adored it. 'I know this is just a little California jug wine,' I whispered to the vaunted expert Frank Schoonmaker on my right, 'but I like it.'"

Our British visitor, Mrs. Frances Trollope, back in her day had more complaints about Americans and food than does Atkinson. She was disgusted to see that Americans ate in perfect silence, like bumpkins, but always with astonishing rapidity, with hungry men zeroing in on bowls like voracious goldfinches after flowering teasel, an indication to her—proof—of pure greed. It was with total disdain that she saw how we rushed and hurried in *everything* that we did, which she found unspeakably crude. Yet Fanny herself was forever impatiently bustling about, especially when she arrived in the New World, pursuing one new scheme after another. Is it not vulgar by definition? "Hurry mars and defeats even the most ordinary expression of the feminine character," stated Thomas De Quincey, a remark supposedly made in reference to Dorothy Wordsworth, the poet's energetic, slightly peculiar, and repressed sister, a woman on whom at least for a while the writer had something of an—unrequited—crush. "Any sign of haste is non-U [not upper class]," archly declared the writer Nancy Mitford, who was dubious even about air-mailing a letter and about whom I will have more to relate. But the point is, the act of scarfing up food is more than anything *the* social crudity!

Let me quickly mention that the Wordsworths came in for their own abuse as to their personal eating habits. It was Mary Russell Mitford, English author, dramatist, and wit, who coyly reported in her *Recollections of a Literary Life* (1852) that among the many "absurdities" of the poet Wordsworth was that he never dined. Back in that day, I gather, formal dining had its own set of rubrics. "To be sure fourteen people must eat," went one rule of society, a concept that apparently "shocked" the Wordsworths, living over there in the Ullswater area. A friend of Mitford's named Mrs. Holland, a gossip, wrote to her, "The Wordsworths never dine, you know; they hate such doings; when they are hungry, they go to the cupboard and eat."

This was about the convivial habit of sitting down, around a table, with friends, and in traditional *agape* being civilized in sharing one's food, as opposed to the barbaric, almost Gutnish refusal to eat with friends.

Other Americaphobes like Stendahl, Charles Baudelaire, Charles Dickens, Captain Marryat, William Cobbett, and Knut Hamsun all reviled us in print as rude and unappeasable slobs and barbarians as we hunched over our bowls, attacking our food with knives, slurping our bowls empty with grunts, "eating as a horse bolts his chopped hay," as Charles Lamb would say. Charles Dickens reproved the same vulgarity and in his American travels came to develop an even greater loathing for our national habit of openly spitting; our unbearably over-heated rooms—closed to fresh air to the point of suffocation—and the thieving fact that all publishers in this country freely pirated his books without so much as a qualm or payment.

Fanny Trollope had often heard it boasted that America was a country in which man's noblest aspirations were realized but, to her dismay, and at first hand, she found quite the opposite to be true. Her first book, *Domestic Manners of the Americans* (1832), an account of her stay here, was so venomous that it succeeded in angering the general populace in this country probably more than any other book written by a foreign observer before or since.

On these obviously biased shores it earned her the dubious nickname "Old Madam Vinegar." As she sat at table in the acrid smoke of early 19th-century America, sitting cheek-to-jowl in tourist homes among gatherings of louts, farm rubes, trenchermen in overalls from the Midwest, and grabby jonathans—*bourrant leurs visages*—yanking slabs of bread from plates like great skua kleptoparasitically snatching pieces of gull from each other, dispatching meals of Indian corn pudding and fried pork, it was all the poor disgusted Englishwoman could do to keep from screaming out loud! She was *extremely* unforgiving about our table manners:

> The total want of all the usual courtesies of the table,
> the voracious rapidity with which the viands were
> seized and devoured; the strange uncouth phrases
> and pronunciation; the loathsome spitting, from the
> contamination of which it was absolutely impossible
> to protect our dresses; the frightful manner of feeding
> with their knives, till the whole blade seemed to enter
> into the mouth; and the still more frightful manner of
> cleaning the teeth afterward with a pocket knife, soon
> forced us to feel that we were not surrounded by the
> generals, colonels, and majors of the Old World; and
> that the dinner hour was to be any thing rather than
> an hour of enjoyment.

St. Paul complains in Corinthians 11:20-22 about the very same things in pot luck dinners of old ("for as you eat, each of you goes ahead without waiting for anybody else. One remains hungry, another gets drunk") that angry Mrs. Trollope did of crass vulgarians at mid-19th-century tables. American rudeness, gluttony, class divisions, refusal to share, and bad manners infuriated her.

There was little that peevish Fanny Trollope witnessed in the few years she spent here from 1827 to 1831 that she approved of, as the general coarseness of our society, a word she could barely bring herself to use in describing us, was overwhelming—the abuses of slavery, misogyny, boasting, hyper-nationalism, over-familiarity of address, the homely buildings, crude evangelism, drunkards and tobacco, all the strange fashions, the boarding-house habits, and general oafishness. To her, we were all basically crude and unacculturated scissorbills. It got so bad for her as she sojourned among what she called the "I'm-as-good-as-you" population here, rustic nincompoops, that she questioned the very notion of equality. One can hear more fury than frustration when, separating theory from fact, she concluded that:

> the theory of equality may be very daintily discussed
> by English gentlemen in a London dining-room, when
> the servant, having placed a fresh bottle of cool wine
> on the table, respectfully shuts the door, and leaves
> them to their walnuts and their wisdom; but it will be
> found less palatable when it presents itself in the shape
> of a hard, greasy paw, and is claimed in accents that
> breathe less of freedom than of onions and whiskey.

Dining in antebellum America had to be horrible experience for anyone. Bad manners, hasty eating, forking or grabbing food—the so-called "boarding-house reach"—impossibly greasy food, dirty tablecloths, no napkins, slouching at table, and the habit of spitting was ubiquitous. Charles Dickens was appalled at the illiberal and vulgar use of spitting and spittoons. It revolted William M. Thackera, sorely putting him off his food simply to witness the accepted habit of Americans crudely eating with their knives alone, shoveling in food with rude abandon. He observed with disgust, "I saw five of them at supper the other night with their knives down their throats. It was awful." In his very last novel, *The Ways of the Hour* (1850), Fenimore Cooper complains how at tavern-dinners the din of a "rattling of knives, forks, and spoons, and the clatter of plates" is as hideous as people eating with "railroad speed." He declares, "'Haste' forbids 'taste.'" Served food was also often burnt. Cooper blames newfangled stoves!

"On an evil day, some Yankee invented an article termed a 'cooking-stove,' and since its appearance everything like good cookery has vanished from the common American table. There is plenty spoiled; abundance abused. Of made dishes, with the exception of two or three of very simple characters, there never were any; and these have been burned to cinders by the making processes of the 'cook-stoves.'"

American table habits left a lot to be desired. Thoreau wrote, "The gross feeder is a man in the larva state; and there are whole nations in that condition, nations without fancy or imagination, whose vast abdomens betray them." As all food was placed on the table at the same time back then, the person who ate the quickest (or had the longest arms and farthest reach), snatched the most. Spices were unavailable, vegetables overcooked, meat often dicey. During meals, coffee and tea, water or cocoa were gulped in large quantities. Cheap whiskey was the most popular alcoholic beverage, especially in the South and the Far West, and led to much drunkenness. In *The American Democrat* (1838) James Fenimore Cooper was able to write,

> The Americans are the grossest feeders of any civilized nation known. As a nation, their food is heavy, coarse, and indigestible, while it is taken in the least artificial forms that cookery will allow. The predominance of grease in the American kitchen, coupled with the habits of hearty eating, and the constant expectoration, are the causes of the diseases of the stomach, which are so common in America.

Although Charles Dickens was feted by the elite and treated like a king on his two trips to the United States in 1842 and 1867, he mocked Americans for our vulgarities and felt that we not only overate but ate unhealthily. He was also put off that in many places "an awful gong" proclaimed the serving of dinner. Wined and dined by worshippers of his books, he chose to see generously laden tables as merely excessive; there was always, he whined, an "unusual amount of poultry at the table and at supper at least two mighty bowls of hot stewed oysters." Too much chicken! And meat? "No breakfast was without a deformed beefsteak with a great flat bone in the center [the T-bone steak was unknown in Europe] swimming in hot butter." He wrote,

There was... a canal boat in Pennsylvania: At about six o'clock all the small tables were put together to form one long table, and everybody sat down to tea, coffee, bread, butter, salmon, shad, liver, steak, potatoes, ham, chops, black-puddings and sausages... the gentlemen thrust the broad-bladed knives and the two-pronged forks farther down their throats that I ever saw the same weapons go before except in the hands of a skillful juggler. [The next morning, at breakfast] everybody sat down to tea, coffee, bread, butter, salmon, shad, liver, steak, potatoes, pickles, ham, chops, black-puddings, and sausages all over again... Dinner was breakfast again without the tea and coffee; and supper and breakfast were identical.

One is forced to ask oneself if the bald crudities that so repelled Dickens as he witnessed Americans gorging themselves or disgusted prim Fanny Trollope watching people eating in silence, feeding with crude speed, smacking their lips and then bolting from table without so much as a by-your-leave was any less barbaric than the fact that many Americans nowadays rarely sit down to eat together. Much of what we eat nowadays is a cagmag of processed mouth-feel. The plates that we use, which are the size of manhole covers, make us badly overeat, as well. Servings are often double-size. Do we not also turn just about every event in this country as an occasion to eat? We never *stop* eating! I know someone whose chubby little daughter literally sees the Toyota symbol on their family automobile as a fat kid with his mouth open! Strangely enough, I myself see it in the eyes of a peacock's feathers. (Look sometime!)

I am not suggesting that Americans in general, instead of eating cheese-burgers, should be dining at the posh Ledbury in London or at Le Bernadin in New York or at Narisawa in Tokyo and sitting down to tables with fresh linen and sparkling candles and enjoying legendary repasts of *Tartare de saumon et maquereau fumé à l'aneth* or *truite meunière aux amandes, pommes de terre à l'anglaise* or *aiguillette de foie gras d'oie en chaud-froid aux noix et raisins, glaceé au vieux Madère* (a slice of cooked *foie gras* stuffed with nuts and currants that have been soaked in 10-year-old Madeira). Quite the opposite, dear reader. My plea is that simply that we should all be eating real food.

But not *foie gras*. Thousands of ducks die in agony every year on *foie gras* factory farms even before many of them can be slaughtered, their organs bursting from being force-fed grain. Experts have found that force-fed ducks also die of throat injuries, liver failure, aspiration pneumonia (which occurs when the grain is forced down into the ducks' lungs), and heat stress because they cannot reach drinking water—all direct results of the savagery of force-feeding, and this just to feed rich pricks all over the world! Foie gras production is so cruel that in at least fifteen countries it has been completely banned, including Australia, Germany, and the U.K. France, quite shamefully, is still its biggest exporter, followed by Hungary, Bulgaria and—yes—the United States, where to this day it is sanctioned. Talk about food aversion!

"I contend that most of what we are consuming today is no longer, strictly speaking, food at all," wrote Michael Pollan in 2008. One lament, among others, is that in the United States we are now swamped with many imitation foods that have been allowed to be peddled thanks strictly to corrupt legislation. What happened was the FDA repealed the 1938 rule concerning imitation foods, and the regulatory door was thrown open. A revised imitation rule held that, in Pollan's words, "as long as an imitation product was not 'nutritionally inferior' to the natural food it sought to impersonate—as long as it had the same quantities of recognized nutrients—the imitation could be marketed without using the dreaded 'I' [imitation] word." Any and all existing regulatory barriers to the marketing of such faux-foods were removed. "Fats in things like sour cream and yogurt could now be replaced with hydrogenated oils or guar gum or carrageenan, bacon bits could be replaced with soy protein, the cream in 'whipped cream' and 'coffee creamer' could be replaced with corn starch," we read. "Fake foods were engineered to be nutritionally equivalent to the real article."

It recalls for me Henry James's short story, "The Real Thing," where, for painters, the best, true-to-life models proved to be credible "*stand-ins*," never examples of the real thing. (Were you aware that in Cézanne's painting, *Still Life with Plaster Cast*, the unidentifiable food in the image, which some art historians refer to as apples and onions, was not modeled on real food? Cézanne painted too slowly to use food before it went rotten and resorted instead to plastic foods.)

American scientists are presently developing "nonfood" items that are said to approximate in taste real food but cannot be absorbed by the human body. The concept of "nonfood" is that compulsive, obsessive eaters will be able to devour large portions of their favorite dishes without putting on a gram.

A sort of faux-food already exists, of course—the infamous "Prison Loaf," which also goes under the name Nutraloaf and no end of other cynically caustic appellations such as "disciplinary loaf," "food loaf," "confinement loaf," "seg[regation] loaf," or "special management meal." (One of the early prognostications of the Russian-born chemist and science fiction writer Isaac Asimov, along with cellphones, microwave ovens, electric coffee-makers and driverless cars, was artificial meat.) Nutraloaf is a grim, truly unappetizing food that is most commonly served in United States prisons to inmates, usually the worst of the worst, child rapists, mass murderers, recidivist perverts, and other born losers who have assaulted, maimed, and killed prison guards or fellow prisoners. Significantly *intended* to taste bad, it is a glop, similar to meatloaf in texture but with a wider variety of ingredients, that is beyond bland, tasteless, weak, flavorless, insipid, and a manufactured commodity intentionally made unpleasant, as I say, and yet prison wardens insist Nutraloaf still provides enough nutrition to keep prisoners healthy without requiring utensils to be issued.

Although Nutraloaf is now being fed to prisoners, its use is controversial. It was mentioned by the U.S. Supreme Court in 1978 in Hutto v. Finney, while ruling that conditions in the Arkansas penal system constituted cruel and unusual punishment. There inmates were fed a thing called "*grue*," which has been described as "a substance created by mashing meat, potatoes, syrup, margarine, vegetables, eggs, and seasoning into a paste and then baking the mixture in a pan." It is little but butt mud, a kind of savorless and offensive skilligalee or slushtub, as awful as burgoo or loblolly, a cake of what old sailors once called duff (a northern form of *dough*), a flour pudding boiled or steamed in a cloth bag, except it would not be as tasty as that seafare. It has been described by Jeff Ruby, a Chicago dining critic who bravely ate it, as:

> a thick orange lump of spite with the density and taste
> of a dumbbell, [which] could only be the object of
> Beelzebub's culinary desires. Packed with protein, fat,
> carbohydrates, and 1,110 calories, Nutraloaf contains
> everything from carrots and cabbage to kidney beans
> and potatoes, plus shadowy ingredients such as "dairy
> blend" and "mechanically separated poultry." You
> purée everything into a paste, shape it into a loaf, and
> bake it for 50 to 70 minutes at 375 degrees. Eat two a
> day and, boom, all your daily nutrients, right there...
> But the funny thing about Nutraloaf is the taste. It's
> not awful, nor is it especially good. I kept trying to de-
> tect any individual element—carrot? egg?—and failing.
> Nutraloaf tastes blank, as though someone physically
> removed all hints of flavor. "That's the goal," says
> Mike Anderson, Aramark's district manager. "Not
> to make it taste bad but to make it taste neutral." By
> those standards, Nutraloaf is a culinary triumph; any
> recipe that renders all 13 of its ingredients completely
> mute is some kind of miracle.

The majority decision delivered by Justice John Paul Stevens upheld an order from the 8th Circuit Court that the loathsome "grue" diet be discontinued. The standards of the American Correctional Association, which formally accredits prisons, discourage the use of food as a *disciplinary* measure, although it should be noted that adherence to the organization's food standards is in fact voluntary. It was the courts' judgment that denying prisoners food as punishment is unconstitutional, but, ironically, because the loaf is generally considered nutritionally complete, it is at times justified as a "dietary adjustment" rather than a denial of proper meals. Lawsuits regarding Nutraloaf have taken place in several states, including Illinois, Maryland, Nebraska, New York, Pennsylvania, Washington, and West Virginia. In March 2008, prisoners brought their case before the Vermont Supreme Court, arguing that since Vermont state law does not allow food to be used as punishment, Nutraloaf must be removed from the menu. The Vermont Supreme Court held that a Nutraloaf and water diet constitutes punishment, as it was designed to be unappetizing, on the border of revolting, and as such compelled their conclusion. In April 2010, the tough and unyielding martinet sheriff of Arizona, Joe Arpaio of Maricopa County, a hero of the far right, won a federal judgment in favor of the constitutionality of Nutraloaf. *Nutra* could very well be neuter, a rectangular blank of featureless protein and fat, void of interest.

We cannot get away from fat. A 2000-calories daily diet should include no more than 30 percent of calories from fat (about 67 grams). Yet even the seemingly most innocuous foods in this country are riddled with fat. One half a cup of Contadina Alfredo Sauce contains 34 grams of fat, 20 of them saturated. Only one-fourth of a cup of Quaker 100% natural cereal contains 6 grams of fat. Nissin Chicken Cup O Noodle soup has 14 grams of fat, 1700 milligrams of sodium. Häagen-Dazs ice cream gives you 26 grams of fat in only three-quarters of a cup. When one of my brothers who was in the Peace Corps in Western Samoa on several visits home reported on their diet, I could scarcely believe the fat content, a cuisine of roasted whole pig; palusami, a parcel of rich coconut cream wrapped in taro leaves and baked (the dish is eaten in its entirety, including the leaves); and taro, the starchy root vegetable, roasted, baked, or boiled, that is considered a staple in African, Oceanic and Asian culture. A traditional Samoan meal, along with these staples, may also consist further of pork kidneys, liver, and heart; eel; mutton fat; and various fruits, all cooked over a fire. A Paleo diet also is heavy on breadfruit, bananas, papayas, mangoes, cassava, coconuts, of course, chicken, pork, canned corned beef (*pisupo*), and seafood. Needless to say, we are talking about tons of fat, fructose, seed oils, various sugars, and carbohydrates. Many sociologists describe Samoans as having what is known as "thrifty genes," conditioning them in crisis to be able to survive a famine, an endomorphic people who naturally manage to store a great deal of body fat efficiently. In modern times, with food in abundance, they eat more than what their bodies require, so they get fatter. There is also there a mentality that fat equals wealth while skinny equals lowly farm laborer (poor).

Samoans eat food—"mutton flaps"—that New Zealanders utterly despise and disdainfully either throw away or scatter to the birds or feed to their dogs. (Picasso vigorously used to rub mutton fat onto his bronzes to improve their patina.) This fat, artery-clogging cut of meat, called *sipi* in the Pacific world, is regularly shipped from New Zealand to Tonga, Fiji, Samoa, and other islands. Lu Sipi, *palusami* with mutton flaps, is a highly popular Samoan dish. Folks there love canned corned beef especially, a certain meat, a *pisupo*, that "swept Samoa like wild fire," writes Nelson Eustis in *Aggie Grey of Samoa,* his insightful portrait of that island and of one of its celebrated natives, the restaurateur of the title. What is a *pisupo*? While it is obvious that the word itself comes from pea soup, it now exclusively means corned beef or bully beef. Let Eustis himself explain this linguistic puzzle. "In the early days, when the first shipment of miraculous food arrived in cans," he writes, "it so happened that it comprised only pea soup. A Samoan word had to be given to the foreign import and this was pisupo, simply pronounced pea-soupo." He goes on to say,

> So when any other foodstuffs appeared in cans, no
> matter what their contents were, all were called pisu-
> po. The thing is, Samoans did not like pea soup or any
> of the other cans—with the exception of corned beef
> from New Zealand. This they loved. It swept Samoa
> like wildfire. Everybody liked this new pisupo, and the
> name has stuck ever since.

Taro root, which has the consistency of Play-Doh and the flavor of mucilage, is a perennial, tropical plant popular in the Pacific culture that is actually inedible when raw and even considered toxic due to the presence in it of calcium oxalate crystals, which are highly insoluble and contribute to kidney stones. The toxin is minimized by cooking it with a pinch of baking soda and may also be significantly reduced by steeping the root in cold-water overnight. One never really thinks of gastronomic delight in regard to the Pacific islands. "The real, native South Seas food is lousy. You can't eat it," proclaimed the well-traveled Victor J. ("Trader Vic") Bergeron. But as to Samoan food in general? Yoicks! Taro root is not only starchy like breadfruit and green bananas but also high in complex carbohydrates like most tubers and incidentally contains more calories, gram for gram, with 142 calories per 100 grams, than a potato which has 93 calories per 100 grams, although it has a low Glycemic Index, while a leek, on the other hand, registers as little as 2.32, the lowest level of sugar in any vegetable. *Vegetables with sugar levels?*—good grief! By the way, fat woman are adored in Samoa.

Nothing compares to man's illogicality—never sell mankind short when it comes to oddities or low contrivances, born of greed and gain, to make things worse whenever better is expected of him. Thick-wittedness is our natural birthright. I am talking about the modern methods that manufacturers are now using, by replacing whole foods with junk food that is filled with additives, antioxidants, and fat, to make our foods even more dangerous to eat. I find a lack of logic in the passage of the Gospels just below—one not unrelated to food—that never ceases to amaze me. Our expectations will brook no challenge, with no corruption too vile in response. When we fail to get what we want, we become impatient and seek to force the matter, seeking to circumvent whatever good might otherwise be ours.

When Jesus spoke in the synagogue at Nazareth (Luke 4:21-30), he was facing a group of people who, because he was speaking in his—and their—hometown, expected special favor. "But the truth is, there were many widows in Israel in the time of Elijah, when the heaven was shut up three years and six months, and there was a severe famine over all the land," Christ replies, disappointing them, "yet Elijah was sent to none of them except to a [non-Israelite] widow at Zarepkath in Sidon." Jesus's point is that when Israel rejected God's messenger of redemption, God sent him to the Gentiles—and so it will be again if they refuse to accept Jesus. There would be no indulgence given to Jews, in short. It fell out that, in spite of his explanation, the lesson was never learned but in fact got only worse, for again the Jews rejected him. When they heard this, all in the synagogue were filled with rage. They rose immediately and drove him out of the town to the brow of the hill on which their town was built so that they might hurl him off a cliff. Their fury resulted from his condemnation of Israel and his favorable attitude toward the Gentiles. In other words, being unappeased, they sought to murder him. It would appear, given mankind's shortcomings, that every time we have the chance to improve—what seems to happen? We only make it worse. As Henry James, Sr. once said, "Nothing is my last word on anything."

A grotesque cycle in food "construction" recapitulates a kind of simple-minded eternal recurrence. It involves an almost Hawthornian-like tampering with nature. Food products might now be sent to us by way of the contrivances of some mad Rappaccini, radioactive in his poisonous garden—and we have become inured to them. Do you think that the chicken we eat tastes like it once did? Or the beef or the pork that we consume? (Grass-fed beef, which is now considered rare exotica, is almost impossible to find in a supermarket. Or try to find a Poulet de Bresse, the best-tasting chickens in the world). What of the eggs that we crack in a skillet? I remember in junior high school writing a paper on young Charles Darwin and alluding to the bizarre fact that he once blithely boasted to a schoolfellow that he could vary the color of flowers by watering them with colored fluids, and I remember finding *that* unholy. Whole foods nowadays have been replaced by fortified junk foods, replete with additives, corn in hideous forms, and truly offensive substances. For example, to make dairy products low fat, the fat is removed, but then to try to preserve the creamy texture of the real thing, say, in skim-milk, powdered milk is added, but that, you see, contains oxidized cholesterol, which many scientists say is worse for your arteries than ordinary cholesterol, so food makers try to compensate by adding antioxidants to the product.

Tampering with nature—the horrors of it—was the predominating theme of Nathaniel Hawthorne's entire work: the unnatural acts that twist a person's soul. It recalls for me a morbid story, "Green Magic" by Jack Vance, originally published in 1963, about a magician and pursuer of secret lore with a deep yearning for eternal health, strength, and beauty who embarks on a study of green magic but finds to his great sorrow that it has refined and etherealized his nature to the extent that he is no longer able to enjoy ordinary earthly pleasures—including earthly food and wine—which he comes to find abhorrent. In the end, the magician seeks to be divested of his knowledge and powers and to be restored to mundane, mediocre, normal humanity. Vance vividly writes,

> Howard Fair plunged into the enjoyment of these
> pleasures. He forced himself to drink quantities of
> expensive wines, brandies, liqueurs, even though they
> offended his palate. Hunger overcame his nausea,
> he forced himself to the consumption of what he
> thought of as fried animal tissue, the hypertrophied
> sexual organs of plants. He experimented with erotic
> sensations, but found that beautiful women no longer
> seemed different from the plain ones, and that he
> could barely steel himself to the untidy contacts. He
> bought libraries of erudite books, glanced through
> them with contempt. He tried to amuse himself with
> his old magics; they seemed ridiculous. He forced
> himself to enjoy these pleasures for a month; then he
> fled the city and established a crystal bubble on a crag
> in the Andes. To nourish himself, he contrived a thick
> liquid, which, while by no means as exhilarating as the
> substances of the green realm, was innocent of organic
> contamination.

There are now something like seventeen thousand new—not foods—but food-like *substitutes* available to us every year. "Thousands of plant and animal varieties have fallen out of commerce in the last century as industrial agriculture has focused its attentions on a small handful of high-yielding (and usually patented) varieties, with qualities that suited them to things like mechanical harvesting and processing," Pollan laments. "Half of all the broccoli grown commercially in America today is a single variety—Marathon—notable for its high yield... A century ago, the typical Iowa farm raised more than a dozen different plant and animal species: cattle, chickens, corn, hogs, apple, hay, oats, potatoes, cherries, wheat plums, grapes, and pears. Now it raised only two: corn and soybeans." In olden days in this country, there were no hybrid vegetables, only true varieties, succulent, bursting with flavor, like sweet "Early Evergreen;" the solid but delicious "Golden Bantam," which originated in Massachusetts and is loaded with eight to ten rows of plump, golden kernels; "Country Gentleman," with its kernels growing every which way; tightly-husked sweet white "Silver Queen;" brilliant white "Stanwell's Evergreen," a crossing of Menomony Soft Corn and Northern Sugar Corn, which was considered the "King of all Sweet Corn," most of them a thing of the past. I am not even bringing up here the creepy subject of genetic engineering or food modification or transgenic technology such as the creation of herbicide-resistant fruits and vegetables winningly called "frankenfoods."

Talk about food aversions. Do you know what food activist Michael Pollan recommends? "Eat food. Not too much. Mostly plants." While noble advice, it is hardly an original concept. John Evelyn, author of the informative 17th-century diary by which we know him best today, must be credited with two other equally important works, his *Terra: a Discourse of the Earth Relating to the Culture and the Improvement of it, to Vegetation and the Propagation of Plants (1675)* and his *Acetaria: A Discourse of Sallets* [Salads] (1699) which, along with marshaling many coherent arguments against "flesh-devourers," vigorously promote his belief in the worth of a strictly vegetarian diet. Unfortunately, according to the usual perversity of literary enterprise, these remain among those books which, representing some profounder truth, maddeningly remain oddball volumes, neglected by people who seek truth in contemporary iterations, the Moderns being more credible than the Ancients.

Evelyn explains that carnivores become "heavy, dull, inactive, and much more stupid [than those who] feed more on plants." He compares "the short lives of most carnivorous animals, compared with grass feeders, and the ruminating kind; as the Hart, Camel, and the longævous Elephant, and other feeders on roots and vegetables." While our gardens are refreshing, perfumed, and rich with endless varieties of fruits and vegetables, the slums or "shambles"—picture crowded London in 1676—are "covered with gore and stench" and the "insults of the summer-fly." Evelyn blames the history of all our wars and excessive violence on the insistent and inordinate eating of meat by humans, being persuaded that "more blood has been shed between Christians through addiction to sanguinary food than by any other cause."

Meat-based diets are in the crosshairs of modern-day data keepers. Aside from the moral stigma advanced by ethicists to eating animals. We all know that the grotesque misallotment of grain to cows is shocking. It takes 25 times more energy to produce one calorie of beef than a single calorie of corn. As much as 400 gallons of water is used to fashion a quarter-pound hamburger. The meat industry emits more greenhouse gases than all forms of transport. The likelihood of premature death from any cause is 75 percent higher in heavy meat eaters.

It is his theological contention that Noah and his sons were permitted to eat flesh (Genesis 9:3-5) as a punishment, "namely, for the hardness of their hearts, and to satisfy a murmuring generation." Jewish theology is not as harsh. Previous to the Flood, according to the *Talelai Oros* and other Jewish writings, mankind thrived as vegetarians. After the "generation of the Flood," given the ferocity and turbulence, frenzy and depravity, of that wayward generation, God allowed compromises to be made for man's moral weaknesses, and Noah and his family were permitted to eat anything, except other people. If man was still struggling with basic moral issues (what to kill and why), or so goes Jewish legend, why then burden him with additional prohibitions on lesser, arguable issues? So after the Flood, Jewish theology— more intricately legalistic than the innocent, if compulsive, diary scribbler John Evelyn ever was—explains that Yahweh lowered the standards of morality expected of mankind simply because it was weak. Lamentably, it appears, customs and habits fall out and form that way, but such food—meat—is not and never was our natural diet. Evelyn writes,

> Certain it is, Almighty God ordaining herbs and fruit for the food of man, speaks not a word concerning flesh for two thousand years; and when after, by the Mosaic Constitution, there were distinctions and prohibitions about the legal uncleanness of animals, plants, of what kind soever, were left free and indifferent for everyone to choose what best he liked. And what if it was held indecent and unbecoming the excellency of man's nature, before sin entered, and grew enormously wicked, that any creature should be put to death and pain for him who had such infinite store of the most delicious and nourishing fruit to delight, and the tree of life to sustain him? Doubtless there was no need of it. Infants sought the mother's nipple as soon as born; and when grown, and able to feed themselves,

ran naturally to fruit, and still will choose to eat it
rather than flesh and certainly might so persist to do,
did not Custom prevail, even against the very dictates
of nature.

I love John Evelyn. His books bore the motto, *Omnia explorate; meliora retinete* ("Test everything; keep the best") from 1 Thessalonians 5:21. Paul's letters were written before any other Christian texts, by the way, even the Holy Gospels. And the earliest Christian text of all is—indeed—1 Thessalonians.

In a sense, man does eat grass.

A memorable passage from Thomas Middleton's earliest known work, the zany, idiosyncratic *The Wisdom of Solomon Paraphrased* (1597), in which among other things he investigates the power of language, we read,

Is grass man's meat? No, it is cattle's food.
But man doth eat the cattle, which eats grass
And feeds his carcass with their nursed-up blood,
Length'ning the lives, which in a moment pass.
Grass is good food, if it be joined with grace
Else sweeter food may take a sourer place.

There are 120,000 edible plants worldwide. Pollan mentions only a few of the 30 plants most commonly used, and his next book should highlight the sad fact that only about a thousand of them end up in our modern markets. I wonder how many people go out nowadays to harvest wild young green dandelion leaves, chicoria, which my maternal Italian grandmother, Angelina, knife in hand, taking us to a park or even a local cemetery when we were kids, taught us how to pick. If ever we stood around idly, not working, she would laugh at us pityingly and call us a "*polenta*" (cornmeal mush), urging us to get cracking. It is the young dentated leaves of the plant that are the jewels of Spring; served with a tad of oil and vinegar, they are crisp, peppery, succulent, rich in iron, and loaded with calcium—they have far more protein per serving than spinach, and no naturally occurring food on earth is higher in vitamin A. Typically, human beings never value what they can have for free. If dandelion leaves were sold in supermarket produce sections, they would soon be commanding the highest prices. Our views are all about perspective. An artichoke, after all, is a thistle, watercress a weed. Red and green mixed together yields a Christmas brown.

As Henry David Thoreau wisely wrote, "All voting is a sort of gaming, like checkers and backgammon, a playing with right and wrong; its obligation never exceeds that of expediency." No, it is all about point-of-view, and angles, aspects, and attitudes matter. I also thoroughly enjoy eating litchi tomatoes, sea kale, nasturtiums, and garlic scapes—one of the most neglected of nature's delicacies (most people throw them out!)—which are the curly flower stalks of the hard neck garlic plant and can be snipped off for salads or stir fries about a month before the garlic bulbs are ready to dig up. As to this species of onion genus, the pyramid builders confidently fed it to the toiling slaves to increase their strength (a fact inscribed on the Great Pyramid of Cheops), and the only actual Egyptian slave revolt, in fact, was fomented unpropitiously by a lack of garlic, after an overflowing Nile had destroyed that year's crop.

Nature offers such edible delights as Quince, St. Anthony's Turnip, Sweet Autumn Clematis, Screwpine, Queensland Silver Wattle, Blue Lotus, Day Lilies, which are slightly sweet with a mild vegetable flavor, like lettuce or melon, the Chinese Perfume plant, and even blue Spiderwort, the flowers of which—amazingly—open only one day a year. (The Biblical "lilies of the field" were actually red anemones, still growing wild and in abundance in Galilee.) What Pollan does not mention, however, is that there is also a plethora of *inedible* plants and flowers flourishing on this earth and waiting to bring us down with a bite. Mexican poppy, Salvia, Horse Nettle, Wavyleaf Basket Grass, Lupine, Waxy Privet, Earth Smoke, Mulberry Weed, Rattlebox (Crotolaria spectabilis)—it is highly toxic, from the top to the bottom, including its cute little yellow rabbitbells—Tahitian Bridal Veil, Hairy Crabweed, Harlequin Glory- bower, Hog Weed, and, yes, among others, Mistletoe!

May we not find it significant in the whimsical portrait-head painting, *The Spring*, by the imaginative mannerist painter Guiseppe Arcimboldo, a composition of fruits, vegetables, and flowers, that, while from the hat to the neck every part of the portrait, even lips and nose, is composed of flowers, the body is strictly composed of *plants*? (In his lavish *The Winter*, the human that we visualize is composed mostly of the *roots* of the trees.) It is amusing to recall that on a bet in the Catherine Wheel Pub in Kensington, London, the two wild and highly capricious poets, Roy Campbell and Dylan Thomas, comrades, dedicated Bohemians, and pyrotechnical drinkers both, together wolfed down a whole bunch of daffodils—flowers, leaves, and stems—in celebration of St. David's Day. I suspect that the two indiscriminate roisterers had the good sense to have avoided eating the bulbs, which can cause vomiting, excessive salivation, diarrhea, convulsions, bad tremors, and heart problems.

This might be the place to mention, regarding the bitter leek, that it is the part of an ancient custom that, following a long tradition on St. David's Day, March 1, the most recently recruited subaltern of the Royal Welch Fusiliers stands up and, while a drummer plays a continuous roll until it is completely consumed, eats a raw leek. The junior officer is then handed a loving cup for the toast, "*y Dewi Sant!*" All of those present who have not as a comrade "eaten a leek" with the Regiment, including guests, are then expected to proceed to do the same before the party withdraws.

Many plants, we know, are toxic. Some of them can cause blindness, permanent scarring. Others can deliver a severe case of phyto-dermatitis. Butterweed is laced with pyrrolizidine, which is an alkaloid that, if you eat it, can damage your liver. The sap of honey-vine can damage your eyes and, if consumed, stop your heart. I love the deeper paradoxes of the plant/human exchange. We inhale mostly nitrogen (78% of the air we breathe), followed by oxygen and argon, but exhale carbon dioxide, which may be mentioned in passing is a greenhouse gas and a pollutant. "We don't want it, and the fact that plants like it only diminishes its stature—after all they enjoy ammonia and horse manure, too," wittily notes Bob Berman in *Strange Universe*. "Carbon dioxide, which we exhale, is the gaseous equivalent of urine." Lobsters are bottom-feeding scavengers, so how explain their delicious meat? As I once wrote in another context, in the muddied palate of Botticelli sat "*The Birth of Venus.*"

"Eat plants!" Michael Pollan urges us. Many of our loveliest and most useful plants are poisonous, however—the Christmas poinsettia, oleander, daffodil, scilla, lily-of-the-valley, hyacinth, and larkspur. Many plants have cyanide in them. A poison can emerge only in times of drought or when the plant has been trampled or disturbed. (Plant poisons are usually at highest concentration in the lowest stems near the ground.) Your senses must work in concert. If a plant looks like a mint and smells like a mint, it is a mint and is edible. But it must do both. If it looks like a mint, but does not smell like a mint, do not eat it. Likewise, if it smells like a mint but does not look like one, do not eat it. This same rule applies to garlic and onions. If it looks like a garlic and smells like a garlic, it is garlic. If it looks like and onion and smells like an onion it is an onion. But both elements must be present. You can find a plant, which before blossoming looks just like garlic, even has a bulb, but no garlic odor. It can make you very sick, if not kill you. It is a weird world. Foraging is a dicey business.

Boy Scouts and Girl Scouts all know what to avoid in poisonous plants, an aspect of scouting taught early. Eating Canada moonseed, which can be mistaken for wild grapes, can be fatal. Nightshade resembles a potato plant, and its berries are poisonous. Water hemlock looks like a huge wild carrot plant, but all parts are extremely poisonous. These are all 911 emergencies

There is a plant in central Florida, which only takes one pea-size seed to kill you, though it will take several painful days to do so, and there is no antidote; yet it is edible after cooking. There are truisms without number. White sap is a huge warning sign that a plant is not edible. (As for white berries, 99.9999 percent of those are indeed toxic. Do not eat them.) All mustards are edible. Mallows are all edible in some way, except cotton (excluding refined cottonseed oil.) It will vary which part of the mallow is edible, but other than cotton, mallows pass.

What forager for a taxonomy of plants and vegetables and their worth, medical and otherwise, could possibly outdo Pliny who in his *Natural History* (Books XX to XXIII) rehearses the values, pluses and minuses, of the spectrum of plants, many we have never heard of, like navews, hibiscum, gingidion, elecampane, squill, caesapon, orache, and spignal, just to name a few. I wonder if Michael Pollan or Euell Gibbons or Henry Thoreau ever heard of Hydrocotyle, which the Chinese call *chi-hsueh-ts'ao* or the "Elixir of Life." It can be found only in Asia and Africa, and its leaves give off an oleaginous substance, vellarine, having the odor and bitter taste of resin, gum, sugar, salt, alkaline sulphate, and tannin. Li Ching-Yuen, the Chinese herbalist, who died in 1933 in the city then called Peking, drank an infusion of it daily and not only married twenty-four times but lived to the age of 256!

The andromeda with its sage-green leaves and urn-shaped flowers grouped in nodding umbels—he was addicted to scent, and in a subtle but intoxicating way it smells like honey—was Henry David Thoreau's favorite flower. While toxic if consumed, an aromatic tea can nevertheless be made of its tender leaves and short tips if boiled—they should be first soaked in water in direct sunlight. I look forward to having a hot cup of andromeda tea every May 6th at nine o'clock in the morning, the hour when in 1862 this Man of Concord gently passed from earth. Two days before, when his good friend, Edmund Hosmer, said he saw a spring robin, Thoreau whispered, "Yes, this is a beautiful world. But I shall see a fairer."

To see a fairer world requires the kind of self-examining faith that Henry Thoreau showed by his questing self. "At least he was asking questions," I would try to persuade my students at Harvard, regarding T.S. Eliot's poem, whenever they callowly ridiculed the unmanly diffidence of slightly fey, self-conscious J. Alfred Prufrock. The food phobic in admitting his or her abhorrences takes a major step in the direction of truth. No man, according to Christ, can examine his soul unless he knows the negative and inferior aspects of himself and bravely faces and acknowledges them, the essential step toward transcendence and redemption.

It may said to be an inspection close to what French mathematician Pierre de Fermat referred to as the "Principle of Least Action," a variational principal where, in a minimized action, the solution requires finding the path that has the least change from nearby paths, a way found by imagining all possible trajectories that your wily system can conceivably take, computing the action (a functional of the trajectory) for each of these trajectories, and selecting one that makes the action locally stationary (traditionally called "least"). True trajectories are those that have least action, in this case, that action that allows for the least dodges and delusions!

8.

WHITE BREAD FOR ZEROES

OLD TOBIAS VENNER in his *Via Rectas* (1620) joined with Mark Twain in his detestation of bread. He wrote, "Bread made only of the branny part of the meal, which the poorest sort of people use, especially in time of dearth and necessity, giveth a very bad and excremental nourishment to the body: it is well called *panis canicarius*, because it is more fit for dogs than for men." Bran to him was linked to poverty, but peasant breads also irked T. Adolphus Trollope, older brother of novelist Anthony Trollope, who wrote in *A Summer in Brittany* (1840), "You no longer see a goodly array of flitches of bacon in the cottages of the peasants. Many of them do not ever get the black bread of the sarazin [buckwheat]. They make a sort of cake, called 'galette,' by pouring into a hot frying pan a portion of their sort of gruel made of sarazin meal. This assures almost the consistency of leather, and is in appearance the nastiest food which can be conceived." Vulgar comic Alan King, known for his unfunny anal-retentive jokes, came down against bran himself, riffing. "You do live longer with bran, but you spend the last fifteen years on the toilet."

It was the branny, grainy part of flour that specifically pleased others, however. *Harper's Bazaar* (and later *Vogue*) editor Diana Vreeland, as I have mentioned, loved her peanut-butter-and-marmalade sandwich only on whole-wheat bread. Tall, loud, brash, opinionated, and as homely as an empty glass of buttermilk, Vreeland was eccentric and always coming out with grand pronouncements. She adored India, loved freesias, claimed to be obsessively searching for the perfect color of red which she arguably found in a favorite nail polish, for her nails were always stoplight-red, matching her huge mouth, which was always open. She looked like a cigar-store Indian with a nose more sharply hooked than Cochise's. Her dyed hair, slicked back with lacquer, was so relentlessly black that it shone navy blue. Curiously, she always insisted that a "good hairline" was a hallmark of elegance. She could

barge about, but her characteristic walk was a kind of pelvic-thrust carica-
ture of a model's runway walk. In her day, working, she always sported a
black sweater, a black Mainbocher skirt, and funny little black T-strap pumps
and, according to Truman Capote, had "a voice similar to the Duchess of
Windsor imitating Jimmy Durante—or vice-versa."

Vreeland was frankly not a food person at all. One of her many quirks
was insisting the coffee she drank had to be cold. "You're not supposed to
put anything really hot in your stomach," she declared. Any coffee ice cream
that she ordered had to be like soup, according to Eleanor Dwight, because
according to the great fashion magazine editor one is not supposed to eat
anything too cold. She could be found knocking back a couple of scotches
before she undertook any project. "Reed [her husband] taught me that if I
have that scotch," she said, "it would get me through until the evening." At
all social events, Vreeland always drank vodka straight, with a piece of lemon peel. Fruits she absolutely adored—could not get enough of! She once
clucked, "The Civil War was nothing compared to the smell of a San Diego
orange."

All in all, she was one of those stagey, over-the-top drama queens like
so many other Manhattan editors, socialites, and foulard-wearing actresses,
all half-nuts, like Kay Thompson, Carol Channing, and Gloria Vanderbilt
who, madly looking for attention as they flounced around the city wearing
cat-shaped diamante eyeglasses on signature chains—they were all homely,
pushy, and loud—doled out scads of unasked-for and largely inane advice
nobody ever heeded. I rarely think of any of these women without seeing
Barbara Stanwyck on film chastising a bellhop.

When Vreeland in her autobiography, *DV*, gets around to the subject
of eating and boldly says by way of confession, "Besides, food is something
I know nothing about. I'm the first to admit it"—no truer words were ever
spoken—one has a difficult time taking her seriously on just about any other
subject she brings up, but especially in her dogmatic pontifications about
food:

> Toast should be brown and black. Asparagus should
> be sexy and almost fluid... Alligator pears can never be
> ripe enough—they should be black. What *you* throw
> in the garbage can, *I* eat! The best raspberries, too, are
> the black ones, and they should be *tiny*—the tinier and
> *the blacker*, the better! Strawberries should be *very* big
> and should have *very* long stems attached so that you
> can pull them out easily. Yvonne, my maid, used to

choose them individually for me at Fraser-Morris. Very
splendid. God know what they cost today.

It is clear that in her yakking she is talking through her hat, and in an ugly and rather snobbish way decadently inverting the general values, aesthetic and otherwise, in all matters of taste.

Something of a philistine, Vreeland, for example, expressly disliked Chinese food, Thai food, Mexican food, Russian food, you name it. "I loathe native food," she theatrically goes on to proclaim in *DV*, by which the silly woman of course meant foods that were not predominantly American or recognizable to her. "This comes as a surprise to some people. For some reason—having to do with aesthetics, I imagine—they expect me to adore raw fish, which I detest. There are a few places I've been in the world, like Hong Kong, Japan, and Russia, where my every meal has been boiled chicken and rice—period. With boiled chicken and rice, you're never wrong—you're always sustained, and it's very good. If ever there's anything native around, it's boiled chicken and rice for me." A less intrepid traveler never existed, yet the lady was considered by the general public—laughably—a cosmopolite! A peculiar list of eccentric declarations follow. "Chutney is marvelous—I'm mad about it. To me, it's very imperial. It's very much the empire, Victoria, the maharajahs... the great days. Lettuce is divine, although I'm not sure it's really food. The consommé at Maxim's. That, to me, is food. It has every bone, from every animal, every vegetable... it's the best nourishment in the world." *Lettuce is divine.* Surely among the lamest remarks in food history. What a short reach about a nothing food by a true vulgarian.

It is the snob aspect, notice, the British *raj* in India, that endears her to chutney, which is truly pitiful. In my opinion, the greatest chutney in the world, the nonpareil, by the way, is not British at all but South African, a fruity condiment my wife Sarah and I enjoyed so much in Cape Town that we took several bottles back with us—Mrs. H.S. Ball's Extra Hot Chutney (Ekstra Sterk Blatjang), the ingredients of which as listed on the identifiable 8-sided bottle are, quote, "sugar, water, vinegar, dried fruit, peaches, apricots, maize, starch, salt, Worcestershire sauce, molasses, onion powder, garlic powder, chili," but I suspect that the exotic taste of it might be a bit too "native" for the fussy Vreeland. Apparently, one food that Vreeland did fanatically crave at every turn was shepherd's pie—"all she ate," according to Jackie Kennedy's chef, Marta Sgubin, who was asked to make it on each visit Vreeland made to Jackie's house. It seemed that she lusted after the mashed potatoes!

What is it about serious Scotch drinkers that makes them all seem off their dot? They have always seemed a bit odd to me, to a one. The breakfast of choice for Walt Disney, according to his biographers, was donuts dunked in Scotch. Do you find that strange? A nervous man, illustrator Norman Rockwell always drank Coca-Cola for breakfast and liked scotch. The analyst Erik Erikson, who was on staff at Riggs and whom the occasionally depressed Rockwell consulted, is said to have told the artist that he painted his happiness, but did not live it.

Vreeland's nuttily euphoric and breezy pronouncement that "lettuce is divine" may come as news to many world travelers who have gotten dangerously ill from eating that vegetable, in spite the fact that bunnies and wild hares love it. ("*Flayrah*" in the Lapine Glossary of Richard Adams' novel *Watership Down* is the word for "unusually good food, e.g., lettuce.") Punk singer Patti Smith, mindful of "starving artists," in her memoir *Just Kids* offers her recipe for lettuce soup, which remind me of W.B. Yeats's explanation in 1899 of the source of his poetry: "I made it out of a mouthful of air." In any case, the recipe goes as follows:

> Boil water.
> Throw in a few bouillon cubes, vegetable-flavored for
> vegetarians, chicken-flavored if you're in need of some
> protein.
> Maybe throw in some salt or pepper. Preferably sea
> salt.
> Take your head of lettuce, cut it up into quarters, and
> throw it into the boiling water.
> Immediately turn off the stove, and your lettuce soup
> is ready to be served! Bon appetit!"

I had a sour, not particularly likeable character in my novel *Darconville's Cat* define lettuce as the "eunuch of vegetables," although I suppose I could have said the same thing about celery. ("If God had created celery [sic!], it would only have two stalks, because that's the most that almost any recipe ever calls for," according to skint blog foodie.com) Lettuce, along with basil, mushrooms, and celery all contain high levels of chemicals that are known to cause cancer when fed to experimental animals. For no good reason that he offers, the English actor and writer John Cleese in his autobiography *So, Anyway...* declares, "There are, in fact, only three comestibles that I do not allow to pass my lips: celery, sea-urchin and raw human flesh"—three items,

I gather, he more or less equates. Two in that short list I can accept, but I cannot quite understand celery having that kind of repulsive power.

Cancer in plants? you ask. Indeed. "Safrole" is a known carcinogen that is present in many plants eaten that are eaten in various parts of the world. Oil in sassafras which was used in 'natural' sarsaparilla root beer in the USA is about 75% percent safrole. Black pepper contains small amounts of safrole and large amounts of the related compound piperine. In Dr. Richard Dawood's *Traveler's Health* he writes rather alarmingly, "Hydrazines are found in many mushrooms including the most commonly grown commercial mushrooms (Agaricus bisporus); they cause lung tumors in mice." Dawood goes on to add,

> Fucoumarins are potent light-activated carcinogens
> and are present in high levels in celery, parsnips, figs,
> and parsley. The level in celery can increase about
> a hundredfold if the plant is bruised or diseased.
> Pyrrolizidines are known to cause liver and lung dam-
> age and tumors in animals and man. They are found
> particularly in herb teas such as comfrey tea and in the
> bush teas brewed in parts of the Caribbean.

A word more on lettuce and cancer. Were you aware that Bravo, a cigarette brand introduced in 1968, the only clinically tested non-nicotine smoking product in the world today, ditched tobacco as a filler to make their cigarette from the leaves of lettuce? The faux cigarettes are processed and treated with enzymes and flavored pleasantly with organic herbal extracts. Bravo smokes are more expensive than tobacco cigarettes, however. Exploiting addicts is the goal here. *The Heavy Smoker's Super Saver Survival Kit* put out by Bravo in 2013 magnanimously offers a would-be quitter: 14 packs of non-addictive Bravo smokes, plus a diary with three how-to methods for quitting. The cost? A mere $98. Step right up, ladies and gentlemen, come on, now, close in, step up front, tell you what I'm gonna do!

Hey, but people can get ill on popcorn. Ever hear of "popcorn lung"? In 2007 a worker got a whopping $7.2 million settlement after suffering high levels of diacetyl, an artificial flavoring that is used to give popcorn its buttery taste. His diagnosis was bronchiolitis obliterans, a rare and serious disease of the lungs. He said he ate two bags of microwaved popcorn every day for about 10 years. At low levels, diacetyl contributes a slipperiness to the feel of an alcoholic beverage in the mouth. It also adds an aroma to cultured cream, cultured butter, and cultured buttermilk. Oh yes, it is also used in mosquito repellent and is highly effective against the fruit fly! The microwaving cannot have helped. Perhaps that is why Julia Child dismissed the machine, saying, "It's good for drying out the newspaper when it's been left in the rain." Copper cookware, molds, artful knives, and elegant pans at Dehillerin's in Paris were what impressed Julia, not a three-button hit and a hum!

As to European food, well, Europe is a vast place. I love foreign cuisines almost to a fault. But, I found it, let us say, less than enchanting in the Baltics and to much criticism dared to say so in my book *Estonia* where I described their food as "something of an oxymoron," pointing out it is heavily dependent on the seasons and simple peasant food. Estonians eat mainly potatoes, cabbage, pork, dairy products, and black bread. The elemental turnip was a staple, and when I write that I think of Albert Goldbarth's lilting poem "Music and Vegetables," in which, looking back on his grandparents who came from Eastern Europe, he writes,

> They gnawed at shtetl turnups, keened,
> They brewed potatoes for schnapps and yelped
> whoopee.

I believe what I could least abide most of all was the gross Estonian appetite for the sanguinous. "Blood is also huge in Estonian food," I pointed out. "At Christmas, sausages are made from fresh blood and festively wrapped in pig's intestines. God rest ye merry, gentlemen, let nothing [!] you dismay! *Terimaks!* A favorite food of theirs is *verikäkk*, which is essentially balls of pork blood—*blecch!*—rolled in flour and eggs with added bits of pig's fat thrown in for taste. Sometimes blood balls are coated in chili jam and/or rolled in anything from wheat grain to chopped peanuts to cilantro, then sliced, fried, and served." I will add I felt not much different about their pork fetish. I wrote a kind of summation in my travel book:

> Cold pork is a huge favorite with them. Cold pork:
> I began to feel those two words summed up my
> aversion to the Baltics. But pork at any temperature
> is a favorite. An Estonian consumes 71 kilograms of
> meat per person per year, half of which is pork. Pig
> parts of all sorts arrayed in metal trays in the torgs of
> Tartu reminded me of a passage in Mo Yan's story,
> "Bull," where the young narrator bubbles over when
> he sees his favorite cuts: "I took a long look at the
> pigs—it was true that there wasn't much meat on

either of them, but those four flesh ears would have made for good snacking. To me, the ears were the best part of a pig's head—no fat, not much grease, and tiny little bones with a nice crunch. They were best with cucumbers—the thorny ones with flowers—and some mashed garlic and sesame oil." An Estonian will devour knobs of pure fat. I once set out hungrily and ended up mistakenly mistakenly buying a roll of meat (rubiroll), which while it looked delectable in the market turned out when I got home to be nothing but a raw knob of inedible fat, flecked with tidbits of dead carrot—not a trace of meat! Are you surprised that the name for ham in that country is sink? A favorite comestible of theirs is *kats* which is made by boiling pig's feet into a gelatin and then poured into a mold. As Brendan Behan exclaimed of the prison food in *Borstal Boy*, "Jesus judge the food that could be worse." Another jellied meat thing in Estonia is called sylt or sult, a sort of Meat Jell-O. Who eats this stuff and why? To fight the cold in winter? To stave off cutting winds? To expiate past sins?

I have alluded above to the notable Eastern European penchant for potatoes and schnapps, surely an odd beverage. But are you aware that wine in early 19th-century America was commonly made from *frosted* potatoes—crushed, bruised, boiled with hops and common white ginger? You swished it all about, waited three days, added yeast to the mix, to ferment the liquor, then threw in sugar. That was brave, centuries ago, when early American beverages went under such names as "Bang" and "Bogus" and "Patent Gas Beer" and "Rumbooze" and "Kill Devil."

Potatoes meant something to us. Jacquot d'Arc, the maiden Jehanne's father, grew potatoes. It was in her father's potato fields in 1424, at the age of 13, that St. Joan of Arc first heard voices of Sts. Catherine and Margaret and Michael the Archangel. She was loved by my French father, our family. We always commemorated her birthday on January 6th, also the feast of the Epiphany.

In an interview, Graham Greene told Anthony Burgess, "I don't like [sausages made of] all meat, on French lines. I like a bit of bread in them." Sausages, more often than not, can be flat and flaccid, the Nelson Eddy (or Kevin Costner) of meats, with their flat declarative delivery and huge fat content. A succulent German-style bratwurst with that wonderful snap of a natural pork-casing, one that is made with the best meat and the balanced seasoning of fresh garlic, seasoned with white pepper, nutmeg, ginger, and traditional spices, just as they are made in Berlin or Nuremburg, is a great deal different than the common stale "banger" that one finds in an English pub or wrinkled chipolata or those rock-hard salametti that could perfectly suffice for use as a burglar's cosh to bash in someone's head. The Bauhaus group—Gropius, Moholy-Nagy, Breuer, Feininger, etc.—by the way, all tried keeping scoutmaster clean and pure with vegetarian food, including liberal amounts of garlic, I have read.

Curiously, Graham Greene's preference for sausages with "a bit of bread in them" reminds me of an idiosyncratic remark of Francis Bacon's in his utopian *New Atlantis* when he refers to a bread found on the mythical island of Bensalem that is able to sustain life "without any other meat," a food that also allows its eaters to "live very long." Diet was the key to the prolongation of life, an obsession with Bacon—it was a Renaissance fascination—and what was healthy for humans inflamed his imagination, although he was scornful of other ingredients used to lengthen life such as ambergris, vipers' flesh, stag marrow, and "the fume of youth breathed from a young virgin." In 1625 Bacon died after catching a terrible cold while supposedly stuffing a chicken with snow in an early experiment in refrigeration.

Stuffing a chicken with snow would have proven no weirder than stuffing it with the best recipe, or so seemed to be the late food writer Laurie Colwin's decided opinion in her article, "Stuffing: A Confession" (*Gourmet*, November 1987), writing, "It was years before I could come out and say how much I hated stuffing. Everyone in the world but me it seemed was fired by an elemental urge to fill up bird cavities with this and that." She goes on to complain,

> At Thanksgiving, friends would proudly confide their
> stuffing recipe, many of which I personally found
> nauseating: dried bread, prunes, oysters, and water
> chestnuts, for example. Prunes and oysters! If such a
> dish were set before you at a restaurant you would flee
> in horror and dismay, but, when it comes to stuffing,
> anything goes.

People get to make up disgusting combinations and then stuff their poor turkeys with them. Holiday after holiday, I would push my portion around in my plate. After all, you cannot say to those near and dear to you, "I think your stuffing tastes like sawdust flavored with sage and has the consistency of lumpy library paste."

Such is the nature of food aversion, whether an American tradition or otherwise. It turns out, however, that in what Colwin then quite suddenly saw as something of an epiphany, she abruptly changed her mind, explaining, "One night while drowsily meditating on the issue of stuffing, it came to me: corn bread and prosciutto. Yes, that was it! The perfect stuffing." Apparently, this sudden reversal, a recipe of her own devising, solved Colwin's eternal (and arbitrary?) argument against stuffing.

My brother Paul, by the way, is living proof of my idea that one very valid test of a food aversion may not be that you happen to find a particular item of food disgusting or repellent but that you are bothered, repelled, or even sickened by the sight of *someone else* eating food. This was a view—an example of the I/Thou relationship evaporating altogether—that was shared by Charles Darwin, Laurence Sterne, Anton Chekhov, and novelist Marcel Proust, among many others, some of whom at times were driven to wear ear-plugs in order to stifle their disgust in hearing someone chewing or chomping food. The muncher is as bad as the munchee. Dr. Samuel Johnson is surely Test Case #1. He literally *grolched* his food. "The author of *The Rambler* used to make inarticulate animal noises as he ate. Was this the music quite proper to be preceded by grace?" asked the essayist Charles Lamb. Yet Lamb himself, an oddball by every account, in the words of a contemporary, one J.J. Morgan, had "a particular kind of rabbit-like delight in munching salad without oil or vinegar—after dinner [!]—a steady contemplative browsing on them." *Crunch, crunch, crunch!*

It can be unbearable to hear someone chewing, like Faye Greener eating gingersnaps in Nathaniel West's novel, *The Day of the Locust.* Munching, chomping, nibbling, gnawing, champing! My brother Paul has repeatedly told me how he becomes nauseated by the mere sight of a person chewing fat or gristle, for example—and this from a person who in his world-wide travels, granted, mainly by railroad train ("Send a fluffier pillow to Pullman #41, a bottle of J &B, ice, and a wake-up call for 9:30 a.m.") has eaten, or so he claims, owls, sparrows, crocodile tail (considered the best cut), turtles, snakes, sheep brains, shark fin, beaver, and even whale sashimi. Dear Paul who is also compulsively and self-admiringly forever the steadfast, brave, and unwavering hero of his own books, both fiction and non-fiction—the sole bold, talented, and hypersensitive man of courage and vision born in an otherwise loud and noisy family of flat, cartoon-like, one-dimensional losers—is at best an untrustworthy narrator. I am always amazed at the spectrum of such exotic smorgasbords, incidentally. British adventurer Bear Grylls in his far-flung, world-traveling tramps and adventures has eaten yaks' eyeballs, goats' testicles, live snakes, and giant scorpions!

A good example of such might be a Westerner's reaction to the potentially offensive loud, sucking noises made by noodle-eaters in Japan. Every person in Japan, from little kids to old men and women, slurps noodles. It is a practical skill that has been adapted to allow one to eat the noodles while they remain scalding hot. Paul could not stand the hawking noises made by a given Chinese when he sat over a bowl, eating, slurping, hawking. I, who sometimes grow furious just listening to someone chew, could understand. Lord Byron, admittedly something of a misogynist, claimed that he got sick watching a woman eat. There is something to the idea of being revolted at another person's chomping way at a food that we may find disgusting, a double horror in the making. What about a revolting someone *looking back at you* as you revoltingly look at him? In the H.G. Wells story, "The Truth About Pyecraft," we are given a glimpse of the fattest member of the narrator's London club (and a bore), an "uneasy jelly of substance," a tubby fellow with "a great rolling front of chins and abdomins [sic]" who "sits at one of the little club tables in the huge bay by the fire, stuffing. What is he stuffing? I glance judiciously and catch him biting at a round of hot buttered teacake, with his eyes on me. Confound him!—with his eyes on me!"

Disbelievers may laugh, but in how many early Charlie Chaplin movies—*The Count* is one—are we not also repulsed when the Little Tramp sits down to one of his meals sucking up spaghetti or cracking eggs with a hammer or trapping black flies in his pocket or frantically attacking a harmless watermelon? That psychotic "eating machine" scene in the didactic movie, *Modern Times*, in which we see only the actor's head being fed by a crazy Rube Goldbergesque invention, evokes a sort of piggery. Chaplin's extremely ugly mouth does not help at all. Then we have that witty exchange in P.G.Wodehouse's novel, *The Code of the Woosters* (1938):

> "Have you ever seen Spode eat asparagus?"
> "No."
> "Revolting. It alters one's whole conception of Man as
> Nature's last word."

We have referred above to Charles Lamb's comments on Dr. Samuel Johnson's eating habits. That was merely the beginning of The Great Lexicographer's oddities regarding food. He had noisy eating habits, indeed, characterized by breathing noises, sniffling, barking, whistling. It sent out a turbulence that was almost impossible to bear while dining out with him. He suffered from all sorts of tics, antics, obsessions, and compulsions. Biographer James Boswell tells us that "he made various sounds with his mouth, sometimes as if ruminating, or what is called chewing the cud, sometimes giving a half whistle, sometimes making his tongue play backwards, from the roof of his mouth, as if clucking like a hen, sometimes protruding it against his upper gums in front... he used to blow out his breath like a whale."

Recalling Dr. Johnson's remark, "He who makes a beast of himself gets rid of the pain of being a man"—and Hunter Thompson quotes the line in the preface to his *Fear and Loathing in Las Vegas*—we read of Johnson at table in the *Encyclopedia Britannica*, 11th edition (Vol. XV):

> Being often very hungry when he sat down to his meals, he contracted a habit of eating with ravenous greediness. Even to the end of his life, and even at the tables of the great, the sight of food affected him as it affects wild beasts and birds of prey. His taste in cookery, formed in subterranean ordinaries and à la mode beef shops, was far from delicate. Whenever he was so fortunate as to have near him a hare that had been kept too long, or a meat pie made with rancid butter, he gorged himself with such violence that his veins swelled and the moisture broke out on his forehead.

Spastic movements made him look outlandish, as did talking to himself, but even his appearance was zany: slovenly dress, a wig too small for his head, stockings that dragged around his ankles. Boswell describes his long fingernails, saying, "He would not cut his claws, not make a tiger a cat to anybody." Johnson's wide mouth was almost constantly opening and shutting, as if he were chewing his cud. He also had a strange method of twirling his fingers and twisting his hands, his body in a continual agitation, seesawing up and down, his feet never still.

How extraordinary a genius, yet how strange an eater. He manifested so many quirks and crotchets in the matter of eating. He hated to be asked twice if he wanted a food. Hester Thrale asserted that he once got the idea that eating an apple would make him drunk. He was glad to obtain, by pawning his best coat, the means of dining on tripe at a cook shop underground, where he could wipe his hands, after his greasy meal, on the back of a Newfoundland dog! But did he enjoy food as much as critics say, or was food merely a practical means for him to sleep? It seems he dispatched food unmeticulously. Boswell records him saying, "For my part, now, I consider supper as a turn-pike through which one must pass, in order to get to bed."

Speaking was an older Dr. Johnson, age 68, addressing cheery Oliver Edwards, a solicitor at Barnard's Inn and only a passing acquaintance. Once a great big-bodied eater, the sexagenarian lexicographer, in whom the gustatorial fires had now been somewhat banked, is a bit disingenuous here when, unconvincingly, he continues to say, "I never felt any difference upon myself from eating one thing rather than another, not from one kind of weather rather than another. There are people, I believe, who feel a difference; but I am not one of them."

It was the Edwards alluded to here, by the way, who has gone down in Johnsonian history for having uttered the "deathless remark:" "You are a philosopher, Dr. Johnson. I have tried too in my time to be a philosopher; but, I don't know how, cheerfulness was always breaking in."

Anxiety is a watchword in the way we disapprove of another's eating habits. In Mrs. Gaskell's novel, *Cranford*, a town that is in possession of and ruled by the Amazons—women, idiosyncratic, trying to preserve their lifestyles—all sorts of comic crotchets emerge. One passage goes,

> When oranges came in, a curious proceeding was gone through. Miss Jenkyns did not like to cut the fruit; for, as she observed, the juice all ran out nobody knew where; sucking (only I think she used some more recondite word) was in fact the only way of enjoying oranges; but then there was the unpleasant association with a ceremony frequently gone through by little babies; and so, after dessert, in orange season, Miss Jenkyns and Miss Matty used to rise up, possess themselves each of an orange in silence, and withdraw to the privacy of their own rooms, to indulge in sucking oranges.

And another:

> Small pieces of butter grieve others. They cannot attend to conversation, because of the annoyance occasioned by the habit, which some people have of invariably taking more butter than they want. Have you not seen the anxious look (almost mesmeric), which such persons fix on the article? They would feel

> it a relief if they might bury it out of their sight, by
> popping it into their own mouths, and swallowing it
> down; and they are really made happy if the person on
> whose plate it lies unused, suddenly breaks off a piece
> of toast (which he does not want at all) and eats up his
> butter. They think that this is not waste.

Watching a rabid eater's habits cannot be fun. Repellent apparently were the eating habits of Alexander Pope, the matchless 18th-century poet, for in biographer Prof. Maynard Mack's assessment in *Alexander Pope: A Life*, the diminutive fellow is recorded as often having "promiscuously stuffing himself" in lavish meals of oysters, trout, thrush, grouse, peacock, gull, pike. Crippled at birth by a tubercular infection which resulted in a severe spinal curvature—one side was badly contracted—only four-and-a-half feet tall, he was forced to wear a fur doublet under a shirt of a coarse linen as well as a bodice or corset of stiff canvas and needed the aid of female attendance. Mack adds, however, "... while plain living was and had to be his practice owing to the weakness of his constitution, this was punctuated from time to time by excesses, especially dining with congenial friends."

And in *Blandings Castle*, Wodehouse offers us in a blackly comic way a rich onomatopoeiac account of a noisy group of eaters as, "A sort of gulpy, gurgly, plobby, squishy, wofflesome sound, like a thousand eager men drinking soup in a foreign restaurant." Look closely and you will find that many of the richly evocative names that Wodehouse came up with in his novels and stories over the years reflect the author's fascination with food—inherently saucy—and, while they are unique, taken together that wonderful gallery of bumbling twits and daffy upper-class toffs with their comic lack of character and empty-headed zaniness, all doing nothing for a living while living well and yet having nothing to worry about, in their shallowness and fey, poofy, one-of-a-kind identifiability do seem to be objects or products: J. Chichester Clam, Lady Julia Fish, Rev. Rupert "Beefy" Bingham, Cyril Bassington-Bassington, Eustace Oates, Clarence "Hash" Todhunter, Esmond Haddock, D'Arcy "Stilton" Cheesewright, Roderick Pyke, Reggie "Kipper" Herring, Claude "Catsmeat" Potter-Pirbright, private detective Claude "Mustard" Pott, Freddy Widgeon, even Joe the Dip. We also come across stories in Wodehouse's *Young Men in Spats* (1936) where all of the Drones Club members are identifyingly divided, seemingly at random, into Eggs, Beans, and Crumpets, and we can hear chirpy raconteur, Mr. Mulliner, hold his audience spellbound with "fish stories" about his nephews, including the engaging Archie, a sock collector who can mimic a hen laying an egg. Lest we forget, incidentally, Mr. Pelham Grenville Wodehouse always affectionately signed his personal letters "Plummie" or "Plum" (abbreviating "Pelham") to most of his family and friends.

Wodehouse was largely a carnivore, although he did once make a solemn vow in 1927 to abstain from eating meat, because, as he wrote, "I saw a lamb being killed in a field," but his general resolves never lasted long. "Any sort of dietary limitation in his fiction is usually seen as a cruel and unusual form of torture," Sophie Ratcliffe asserts in her book, *Wodehouse: a Life in Letters*, "—see, for example, Madeline Bassett's unsuccessful attempt to convert Gussie Fink-Nottle to vegetarian ideals in *Stiff Upper Lip, Jeeves* (1963) which results in his eloping with the cook." I am certain that in the early 1940s in the city of war-engaged Berlin, while he and his wife, Ethel, were staying at the prestigious Adlon, the favored hotel of the Nazis—a place where Hitler's speeches were broadcast nightly to the entire dining room— the two of them contentedly (and blindly?) went along with "*Eintopf* Day" (or one-pot day), when a simple vegetable stew was the only dish on the menu.

Vladimir Nabokov scholar Professor Yuri Leving from Dalhousie University once confided to me, "I remember once going for a job interview at a prestigious college in cold, snowy Minnesota. It was so frigid and unwelcoming that I knew that I would never go back there again regardless of the outcome. After picking me up at the airport, the local professor, a bear of a man, invited me to a restaurant. When he ordered a beer and a pig's leg, my Kosher sensitivity was on the brink of a collapse! Yet, once this specialist on the Russian avant-garde had begun to fiercely gnaw on the pig's flesh in front of me, while I was gently working my way throughout a dish graced with parsley and guacamole, I could hardly resist vomiting. In short, I hate both pork and swine." It must have been very cold there, given Leving's origins. "I was raised in the Soviet Union of the 1980s when it was easier not to have any aversion to food simply because our rations were too sparse to allow for any fastidiousness. The latter was a prerogative of either the bourgeoisie or the stupid. The patient buyers could not be deterred by the bluish sight of poultry ('shot with a machine-gun at close range,' as my Russian friend used to say) and when it would miraculously appear on the shelves of the food stores' meat department, where the long lines of willing buyers resembled spaghetti. Surprisingly, we knew what spaghetti was (though the Soviets call it '*makarony*.') Our first pizza, however, did not arrive until some time during Perestroika. Only once after I had emigrated to the West was I able to confirm that our Perestroika pizza had a very distant culinary relationship with its Mediterranean cousin. The lack of product was one thing; the quality and the all-encompassing culture of cheating within the centralized socialist distribution system was quite another. My mother loved one particular anecdote about a Soviet salesperson who, before leaving work, left a note for the incoming shift, reading, 'Masha, do not dilute the sour cream, I have already done this!' Most of the food that we had in childhood did not come pre-packaged, and the sour cream was no exception. I remember my disgust as a kid at the very thought of a white substance being stored in a huge open vat that slowly would make its way into a refillable glass jar, the type which Soviet housewives carried around just in case that some deficit product might become available. As a 'Pioneer Camper' (something like your Boy Scout), I hated the jellied kasha, though as inventive members of the Young Communist League, we took a particular pleasure in driving the aluminum forks into its hardened sleek surface. As an adult, my food choices have become less eclectic and more gourmet-oriented. I've learned to appreciate vegetarian dishes and fish, although the mere look of a medley of live lobsters in an aquarium still terrifies me each and every time that I enter a Canadian grocery. I cannot imagine how anybody in their right mind can consume these docile, crawling creatures with bound tentacles. Finally, East or West, for me it is not so much the taste of a dish—it is the culture of eating that matters."

Czech food generally disappointed novelist John Banville, whose *Prague Pictures* is his non-fiction portrait of a city which he visited in the depths of the Cold War. He is bewildered by, among other foods, that country's "inexplicable but almost universal enthusiasm for... dumplings." He writes sarcastically, "These delicacies can be anything from the size of a stout marble—what in my childhood we called a knuckler—to that of a worn-out, soggy tennis ball, with which they share something of their texture, and possibly of their taste. The Czech species [of dumpling]," he writes, "comes in a wide variety of strains, from the very common *houskové knedlíky*, or bread dumplings, through the *bramborové knedlíky*, potato dumplings, often temptingly served alongside a smoking midden of white sauerkraut, to the relatively rare—rare in my experience, anyway—ovocné knedlíky, or fruit dumplings. Perhaps the dumpling's most striking characteristic is its extreme viscosity. It sits there on the plate, pale, tumorous and hot, daring you to take your knife to it, and, when you do, clinging to the steel with a kind of gummy amorousness, the wound makes a sucking, smacking sound and closes on itself as soon as the blade has passed through."

Sogginess is a hazard in Czech cuisine, which may also be said of some Baltic and Hungarian cookery. I have heard it charged against *Túrós palacsinta, a cheese pancake dish, and Túrós csusza, an Hungarian savory curd cheese noodle dish, and in this country things like bread pudding.* A minor theme in the nonsensical and comically unrealistic American spy film, *Across the Pacific* (1942), starring Humphrey Bogart and Mary Astor, is that of a tainted bread pudding being served aboard a Japanese merchant ship, a poisoning plot not unaligned to, given the war, the understandably prejudiced—and blatantly racist—language where Bogart spitefully refers to "Japs" and actually mutters the line, "They all look alike." "They make perfect servants," chimes in Sydney Greenstreet, playing the evil Dr. Lorenz, a spy who is determined to blow up the Panama Canal. Along with the theme of the tainted bread pudding, it should be noted that not one of the characters in the movie ever reaches the Pacific Ocean, never mind crosses it, for that matter. Young director John Huston left the production literally mid-scene to join the Armed Forces, leaving command of the movie in the inexperienced hands of young director Vincent Sherman.

Banville rather petulantly declares that Czech cuisine is "no better than that of Bavaria, which statement is, as anyone who knows Bavaria will confirm is a ringing denunciation." He goes on to say, "I have eaten badly in many parts of the world" and, as if to prove it, recalls "a macaroni studded with gobbets of cow's kidney that was served to me by a resentful cook— her name was Miss Grub, honestly it was—" when he was visiting a friend's house in London. The cooks in Prague pleased him no better, for he expresses distaste in everything from their "accompaniments" to "sauerkraut, three shades of glistening grey" to one dish whose description he snobbishly quotes straight from a menu: "'Filled chicken brest [sic] with banana in almond sauce with cream and griotce.' Serves me right for an English language menu. *Griotce*, by the way, is a cherry liqueur; I have never, so far as I know, tasted it."

Secretary of State John Kerry dislikes celery. Pop singer Taylor Swift hates mashed potatoes. Mandy Moore dislikes frosted animal crackers. Britney Spears loathes meatloaf and "all lumpy stuff." Actress Anna Chlumsky admits that egg salad puts her off. Actor Patrick Stewart is repulsed by cooked mushrooms, grousing, "They're slimy and old-tasting." Chef Alice Waters of the Chez Panisse restaurant does not like jam. "People always give me jam," she complains, "and I never use it, so it remains in my fridge." Maybe Waters should have used her imagination and taken a page right out of Charles Baudelaire, who always took his *hashish* in his confiture, that is, he chose not to smoke it by way of a pipe or reefer but consumed it as a green jam!

Chicken-haters can be found in abundance. An uncle of mine once reported to me, "I won't eat any part of a chicken that has a job"—meaning the interior "lights," I presume, gizzard, heart, lungs, etc. He never descended into particulars. It befuddled me, as I was only a kid. What part of a normal chicken going about its business, when alive, does *not* have a job? But in their enigmatic way, you see, all food aversionists fetishize what they repudiate, just as a person may do with a food that he compulsively likes. As the old pedophile who lusts after young Chris, *Family Guy's* Mr. Herbert asks his niece, "If I gave you a sandwich, do you think you could get Chris to fart on it?" Mrs. Hester Thrale, Dr. Samuel Johnson's close friend, detested roast goose, writing in her *Anecdotes* (1826), "I was saying to a friend one day that I did not like goose; one smells it so while it is roasting." Sigmund Freud, Austrian neurologist and father of psychiatry, harbored a lifelong dislike specifically for chicken and for cauliflower. What about human beings? Strictly speaking, Freud may have had an aversion about *himself*! He was personally not very charismatic, for example, and actually once confessed of himself that he lacked that "indefinite something which attracts people." He did however like Mark Twain's books, Mozart operas, playing records, and antiquities in general, things like old statues, and he also took a strange delight out of receiving mail and was one of the first people in Vienna to have a telephone installed.

Actor George Hamilton in *Don't Mind If I Do* recounts how, when visiting LBJ's ranch—he was then dating Lynda Bird—he heard the President ask his cook, Zephyr, what was for dinner and when she told him, he angrily squawked, "I lived through the Depression. I don't want any more goddamn *chicken!*"

Jonathan Miller, well-known British stage director and sometime physician, never overcame his dislike of boiled chicken. "I could impersonate chickens. I was a chicken," he writes in his funny essay, "Among Chickens." "I said to people, I will imitate a chicken for you, and this pleased them. I don't know why. It did. Therefore, I became extremely observant of the minute dialect of chickens." Miller offers printed variations of his chicken-speak: "*Buk, buk, buk, buk, buk, buk... BACAGH.*" His father, a doctor, actually raised a small flock of chickens for fun. Young Miller grew up eating no end of chicken, boiled chicken. He describes repetitious boyhood lunches and of too often having had to eat "rather glum meals of boiled chicken, not one of the chickens we kept, but another chicken, a chicken which looked as though it had never said a single '*bacagh*' in its entire life and had been simply tipped into hot water and come out with that awful goose-pimpled appearance that boiled chickens have. We ate the same meal every day. Boiled chicken, year in, year out."

Henrietta Nesbitt, for a long while the main cook during President FDR's administration whose notoriously bland cuisine and notoriously dull preparations often caused various presidential invitees to pass up formal White House dinners, constantly served up chicken in different guises as the war wore on, simply because chicken did not require issued meat-ration coupons, and the whole Roosevelt family began to dislike it. "You tell Mrs. Roosevelt I'll get rid of Mary Campbell [his private cook] when she gets rid of Nesbitt," cried the Chief Executive when Eleanor wanted Campbell let go, as J.B. West reported in *Upstairs at the White House*. Hating foods is an amusing and endless caucus race, a sort of nutty and outrageous pavane. The subject hums. Jump in anywhere you want and begin dancing.

Alphonse Daudet disliked grouse. Edmond de Goncourt wrote in his *Diary* (April 3, 1878) of his host and the proffered repast: "He gave us a very choice, very tasty dinner, a real gourmet's dinner, including some grouse whose scented flesh [Alphonse] Daudet compared to an old courtesan's flesh marinated in a bidet." "After a few mouthfuls of the average chicken à la Kiev or boeuf Stroganoff—two of my unfavourites—your appetite will be fully satisfied," wrote the curmudgeonly (and alcoholic) Kingsley Amis in his essay, "The Boozing Man's Diet," in *Everyday Drinking*. I gather Amis also disliked fondue. "Neufchâtel will help you to force it down," he writes next to the entry. Amis was fussy about his drinks, needless to say. "The point about white Burgundies," he wrote in *The Green Man* (1970), "is that I hate them myself... so closely resembling a blend of cold chalk soup and alum cordial with an additive or two to bring it to the color of children's pee." "The only kind of seafood I trust is the fish stick, a totally featureless fish that doesn't have eyeballs or fins," declared humorist Dave Barry who liked snails no better. "Escargot is French for 'fat crawling bag of phlegm'." But has he ever asked what make up the ingredients of a fish stick? It is unlikely that Barry will be found ordering the leathery body of the sea cucumber, called *trepang* in Indonesia—"trepanging" is actually the Anglicisation of the act of harvesting sea cucumbers—which is considered a delicacy, or the gonads of the green sea urchin, periwinkles, or lethargic mollusks called chiton which are all edible in various parts of the world.

I allude above to Mrs. Nesbitt. The virtually inedible food that she cooked for FDR—he often dined off a simple, solitary tray in his study—was her way of saying that she disliked food, and maybe even the very nature of pleasure or even celebration. It was a policy that had been abetted perhaps by Ms. Eleanor Roosevelt herself, who was abstemious and something of a cheeseparer, a woman not only suspicious of what she considered indulgence but also a person, as often found to be the case with folks having a marked sense of duty, with an aversion to pleasure. We know that she suffered from her husband's attraction to other women, and she may have set a puritan standard for him in food as with women. True, the war was on in the early 1940s, but, even prior to that time, knowing guests visiting the Roosevelt White House expected very little in the way of great dining. They often ate something beforehand to stem the tide. It was well known that FDR loved white asparagus, for example, but Nesbitt rarely if ever served it. She told him it was unavailable, when in fact it could be bought in cans, sometimes even fresh, at any grocery store. It was the same with cocktails. Eleanor, something of a puritan, was often vexed that her husband, who was full of bonhomie, enjoyed more than a half-hour drinking with guests. Franklin's deep love and affection for Lucy Mercer may well be attributed to the existence of these two tough old birds, Henrietta Nesbitt and his long-suffering but rather exacting wife, Eleanor, for Lucy became for him an obliging, gentle, affectionate, warm, soft, sympathetic, truly indulgent and compassionate alternative. Eleanor was alone when the President succumbed to a cerebral hemorrhage on that April afternoon in Warm Springs, Georgia.

Dry, short, tut-mouthed Calvin Coolidge who quirkily referred to every meal as "supper," whether breakfast, lunch, dinner, or a formal state affair—for ages down in the Deep South lunch was called "dinner" and dinner called "supper"—was very finicky about chicken and believed that no chicken could truly taste good unless it had been raised just outside his kitchen door. (Today to most Vermonters, "dinner" is eaten at noon and "supper" whatever you eat after work.) So Coolidge went and had a chicken yard built right in back of the White House, where he proceeded to keep a small noisy flock of his favorite Vermont chickens. It is all to be found in Poppy Cannon's gossipy *The President's Cookbook*. To Coolidge, from then on, only the chickens from this special coop of his, when prepared for the White House table, were to be eaten, for all of them carried the mysterious flavor—whatever it was—hat he loved. Investigation later revealed that Coolidge's chicken-yard had been built smack, right on top of President Teddy Roosevelt's mint bed.

Coolidge generally breakfasted (or supped, as it were) on hot cereal prepared in the White House kitchen by combining three parts whole wheat and one part whole rye, cooked in its unground state. The lean little Yankee was provincial and fond only of the pickles of his native Vermont. One of his cherished boasts, asserted in his soft, quacking New England patois, was "No Coolidge ever went West." He was a strange, unreachable quat of a fellow. After child actor, the young Jackie Coogan met Coolidge in 1924, he described him as 'the dullest asshole I ever met."

Writer Susan Sontag, who adored lists, compiled her likes and dislikes, and, among specific foods she disliked, were anchovies; the taste of licorice; baked beans, ketchup ("a goy food"), meatloaf, Coca-Cola, and "all German food." (She did like cinnamon, sushi, maple sugar candy, pizza, raw peas, and sturgeon.) She also hated cats, umbrellas, washing her hair, Robert Frost, hirsute men, freckles, television, painted nails, football games, cigars, paperback books, flat pillows, standing up, and taking photos.

"To taste is to know," to paraphrase somewhat Italo Calvino in *Under the Jaguar Sun,* where he makes a cognitive short circuit of the Italian words *sapore* ("flavor") and *sapere* ("knowledge") in an attempt to explain that the sense of taste, transcending strict definitions, has much wider philosophical implications regarding the whole concept of man's curiosity.

Taste is unpredictable. A century ago, Maine Indians, who lived on what they hunted and trapped, maintained what can be considered a variation of food aversions, for they had a distinct chain of (a) favorite tastes, (b) favorite animals to eat, and (c) favorite parts to eat of those animals. Moose, deer, and caribou led the list of tastiest animals preferred by the Penobscot, the Abnaki, and Mohawks. These were followed by beaver, bear, muskrat, hare, porcupine, and partridge. Muskrat remains a favorite local delicacy in southeast Michigan, where it helped early European settlers ward off starvation during the lean years of the War of 1812. It is typically parboiled with vegetables and fried with onions. Aside from beaver and muskrat, the most valuable pelts in early America were those of the fisher and pine marten or arboreal weasel, which white trappers referred to as "sable." The lips and tongue of the moose were especially highly prized among Indians and seen as true delicacies. They ate corn, berries, grouse, wild turkey, of course, rabbit and hare—hares have red meat, rabbits white—but it was larger game they preferred. In Joseph Conrad's *Last Essays,* the "gloomy Pole" (as described by Nabokov) includes an essay "Cookery," which served as a preface to his wife Jessie's cookbook, *A Handbook of Cookery for a Small House.* In that preface Conrad attributes the violence of the "North American Indians" to their bad food, poor cooking, and "perpetual indigestion" and uniquely assigns their savagery to their being "prey to raging dyspepsia."

Indian food preferences can be found in Parkman, Thoreau, and accounts of the Jesuit martyrs of North America, brave and godly men like Frs. Isaac Jogues, Jean de Brébeuf, René Goupil, and Noël Chabanal. Cannibalism existed. The savage Mohawks, the most easterly tribe of the Iroquois Confederacy, which sided with the English—both peoples despised and greatly feared each other—were often wild in their cannibal forays, and some scholars say they favored the flesh of the white man because of the salt in his diet, endowing it with a delicate saline taste. ("It is not for me. I tried human flesh, and it is too salty for my taste," boomed the notorious, fanatical bully, Major General Idi Amin Dada, President of Uganda in the 1970s.)

Still, it is thanks to the American Indian that we have beans, squash, artichokes, sunflower seed, maple sugar, acorn meal, lye, hominy, popcorn, persimmon bread, nut oil, turkey, deer, bison, and pemmican.

The Iroquois, composed of six nations Mohawk, Oneida, Onondaga, Cayuga, and Seneca were regarded as the most notorious for their cruelty regarding the eating of human flesh and the torture of war prisoners. In the Algonquin tongue the word Mohawk (borrowed from the Narragansett "*mohowaùuck*," meaning "they eat [animate] things") actually means "flesh-eater." The mere sight of a small band of Mohawks put fear even into neighboring tribes, but they were not alone in engaging in cannibalism and torture. There is proof that the Huron, Neutral, and Algonquin tribes were guilty, as well. It is an historical fact that the Indians of northeastern America have consumed the flesh of fellow humans, in rituals, out of hatred, even insanity, and certainly in desperate cases of overriding hunger, especially during winters when they were on the cusp of starvation—but almost never as a common part of their diet.

Why not bison? The white man slaughtered as many as 80 million bison that once roamed the grasslands of North America in massive herds when buffalo hunting became the chief industry of the plains by commercial hunting within a scant 30 years, cutting out their tongues and stripping their hides. History records that as many as 50,000 to 100,000 animals were slaughtered every day, depending on the season. Bison or buffalo hunters commonly left behind carcasses that slowly decayed into giant piles of bones, making the prairie so white, or so some said, that it looked as if it were covered in snow even during the summer months. The extermination of the American buffalo was part of a diabolical plot by the U.S. Government to control the Native American population, of course. Government initiatives, both local and federal, were intentionally undertaken to starve the Plains Indians by eliminating the buffalo, as herds were the basis of the survival of the tribes. Without the sustaining buffalo to feed and clothe them, Native Americans were forced to leave or starve to death.

Many menstruation taboos existed among Indians. The Mohawk prohibited women from pounding maize and touching food during this time for them. Southwestern Indians forbade salt during menstruation. In the Cayuga, the Delaware, and cultures of the Northwest Coast, menstruating women were not allowed to touch or eat meat. Delaware girls were not allowed to do any cooking during their periods; if they did, no one would dare eat for fear of abdominal pains. Creek culture forced women to live fully apart during menstruation as well as eat from separate dishes and utensils rather than the communal bowl. Their women were not allowed to cook for men. If a woman did, she was liable to be accused of any misfortunes that befell the tribe. Among the Ten'a of Alaska, no women of child-bearing age was allowed to eat mink or otter. The meat of the otter was considered very powerful, meant for older men, and a violation of the taboo would keep the animal away and inflict misfortune on the man who caught it. Young girls at puberty in the Northwest Coast cultures were expressly forbidden to eat meat. No unmarried girls were allowed to eat lynx. "There are certain parts of the flesh of deer and moose that Indian women are never allowed to partake of, nor can they eat the head, heart and paws of a bear," wrote the trapper Martin Hunter in *Canadian Wilds* (1907), one of my favorite books. Was this stricture a way of braves keeping meat for themselves, or did they feel it instilled bad passions? (I should point out here that Apache Indians never hunted the bear, believing that the animal might contain the spirit of a great warrior who had passed on. To this day, whenever Eskimos kill a polar bear, they place its skull on a rock with the eyes facing inland, so that its spirit and its power will remain among the animals they hunt. The bear's eyes are always kept away from the sea, so that its spirit cannot wander off into nothingness.) Status might be expressed in special foods made and served only to chiefs, hunters, warriors, elders, or men. Among the Kwakiutl of the Northwest Coast, and all other tribes of this area, organ meats, including the heart and liver of the sea lion, were reserved for elders, who are almost always respected. Among the Kwakiutl, pectoral and anal fins of fish as well as tails and salmon-heads were also given to older tribal members.

Up in Alaska I have eaten a bowl of *akootuk*, the aromatic "ice cream" of the Arctic, boiled from the suet of caribou, to which seal oil is added, some snow and wild berries folded in, a pinch or two of sugar and then the frothy snow-white soufflé frozen. It tastes much the same as frozen custard.

Nevertheless, there are dangers associated with the indiscriminate eating of certain animal parts. While polar bears feed mainly on freshly-killed seal and so are generally free of taint, a person by eating their liver can be fatally poisoned from acute hypervitaminosis A, for the bear's liver contains extremely high levels of retinol, the form of vitamin A found in members of the animal kingdom. While some vitamins dissolve in water, vitamin A, along with vitamins D, E, and K, dissolve only in fat, meaning that any excesses of vitamin A do not exit the body in urine but collect instead in the body's filtration organ, the liver. It seems to stand as that "distinguished suspicious thing," always. Eskimos have always avoided livers, not even giving it to their dogs, and Arctic explorers learned to leave it alone.

While there was a long and sacred tradition of these taboos in old American Indian life, they were aligned to rituals for men and braves that in some sense coordinated with the food prohibitions set for women. Beaver bones were never thrown to the dogs, Martin Hunter points out, but carefully collected and sunk in lakes or rivers, returned to the elements from which they were taken. A bear that was killed by an Indian was always addressed as cousin and a prayer of sorts given him by the hunter as a pardon asked for the necessity of taking his life. The bones, especially the skull, were always hung up at the exact spot where he fell, journeys from camp often being taken with the express purpose of carrying out this sacred duty. Norwegian explorer Roald Amundsen on his Antarctic expedition (1910–12) to discover the South Pole in December 1911, however, without a qualm, ate most of his sled dogs for fresh meat, just as he had planned to do, beginning with his own favorite. His rival, explorer Robert Scott, who was bested by Amundsen going due South, froze to death with some of his men on the ill-fated *Terra Nova* expedition after living chiefly on the flesh of seals.

In a Karen Russell story, "Dougbert Shackleton's Rules for Antarctic Tailgating," the narrator offers lots of advice, ghastronomic [sic] included, for anyone hopping down to the South Pole and the discourse touches on a few food aversions. "You may have heard of pemmican, the Spam of Antarctica? A big favorite with the early polar explorers? Pemmican consists of a repugnant arithmetic of dried beef + beef fat. We don't eat that dog food on my ship," he says, adding,

> Dehydrated foods, nonperishables—these are
> Antarctic tailgating staples. Apocalypse food is ap-
> propriate for the Antarctic tailgate, the sort of stuff
> you'd find in a Cold War bunker: jerky, canned tuna,
> powdered milk, soups in envelopes. If you're a health
> nut, don't tailgate in the Antarctic. You can always put
> balsamic vinaigrette on salted meat and sort of pretend
> it's a salad… Quick and easy cooking is a must for the
> Antarctic tailgater. Here is a family recipe that will give
> your Antarctic tailgate some "regional flavor":
> 1. Whale meat.
> 2. Fire
> Salt to taste and all that.

On their noble expedition, Lewis and Clark and the Corps captured and ate countless small and exotic animals and birds such as hawk, coyote, fox, crow, eagle, gopher, muskrat, seal, whale blubber, turtle, mussels, crab, salmon, and trout and occasionally familiar and unfamiliar varieties of fruits, vegetables, mushrooms, seeds, and nuts that were found to be edible. However, they ate their dogs, as well. Writing on January 3, 1806, Clark entered into his journal, "Our party from necessity have been obliged to subsist some length of time on dogs, have now become extremely fond of their flesh; it is worthy of remark that while we lived principally on the flesh of this animal we were much more healthy, strong and more fleshy than we have been since we left the buffalo country. As for my own part, I have not become reconciled to the taste of this animal as yet." The main culprit was diet. For the most part their fruit and vegetable intake was insignificant, and the beef jerky they made was probably contaminated with bacteria. With the germ theory of disease still unknown, Clark could do little but blame the murky, muddy water. He wrote in his journal on June 21, 1804, "The water we Drink or the Common water of the missourie at this time, contains half a Comm Wine Glass of ooze or mud to every pint."

I mention turtle. Frank T. Bullen in his whaling classic, *The Cruise of the Cachalot*, in which he offers accounts of eating standard ship fare such as "salt horse" and "plum duff" is maybe at his most memorable describing a most unforgettable meal ever served to hungry men. He writes,

> A large turtle was obtained for twenty-five cents and handed over to the cook to be dealt with, particular instructions being given him as to the apportionment of the meat. At eight bells there was a gathering of the men in front of the poop, and a summons for the captain... Just then I caught sight of the kid's contents, and could hardly restrain my indignation. For in a dirty heap, the sight of which might have pleased an esquimaux, but was certainly enough to disgust any civilized man, lay the calipee, or undershell of the turtle, hacked into irregular blocks. It had been simply boiled, and flung into the kid, an unclean, disgusting heap of shell, with pieces of dirty flesh attached in ragged lumps.

It seems almost as much a taboo in the killing of that poor beast, never mind how it is served, as it is nowadays to hear described, several times, the unconscionable butchery of so many sperm whales. Incidentally, in his travel book *North America*, Anthony Trollope writes about American food fascinations, like canvas-back ducks and terrapin, and while he expresses a distinct appreciation for the former ("fully deserves all the reputation it has acquired") he cannot say the same for turtle, which he found charmless:

> It is held in great repute, and the guest is expected as a matter of course to be helped twice. The man who did not eat twice of terrapin would be held in small repute, as the Londoner is held who at a city banquet does not partake of both thick and thin turtle. I must however confess that the terrapin for me had no surpassing charms.

Taboos, whether temporary or situational, had to do with rites of passage, life cycle events, and various traditions, which probably could be traced to either theology or matters of health or both. (The single sentence in the book of Exodus that we have discussed before as one of the actual Ten Commandments, for example—"You are not to boil a kid in the milk of its mother," possibly a proscription against cruelty or possibly a mere superstition—became the basis for a large portion of Jewish dietary laws for thousands of years about keeping all meat and fowl separate from all milk and milk-based foods, even to the complication of maintaining two sets of dishes and kitchen implements.) Salt taboos were strangely strong among many Indian tribes. The western tribes observed this prohibition during pregnancy, birth, boys and girls' puberty rites, menstruation, boy's initiations, vision quests, and mourning periods. Boys in the Oneida tribe were prohibited from eating salt or anything hot after their young voices changed. These taboos were seldom found or included all together in one tribe, but it was rare not to have at least one in each culture. Of course, taboos in all cultures can be found connected to traditions. Salting one's food at a dinner party to which you were invited in Egypt is considered to be a huge insult. Bringing chocolates, quality chocolates, or high-end pastry as a gift is also a must there. In Spain, all food is eaten with utensils, including fruit. If you are invited to a Brazilian house for dinner, you should gracefully arrive at least 30 minutes late, for a large party at least an hour late, whereas in other countries such a thing would be considered rude.

The Gabrielino Indians—so called because of their proximity to San Gabriel Mission, established in California in 1771—considered bears, rattlesnakes, and owls highly taboo. Other food restrictions occurred by ceremony. New mothers fasted and only drank warm water. New fathers fasted at the birth of the child, and were not permitted to fish or hunt. Hunters fasted during the hunting party, and they were not expected to eat their own catch.

There were special foods and drink prepared only for initiation ceremonies for boys and girls at puberty.

In the old days, it was taboo for the Navajo to eat any foods that had been burned, especially breads. Another taboo food for them was chicken. This is no longer the case. Chicken is nowadays an integral part of their diet. The meat of chicken is so popular that commercial fast-food chicken establishments have actually sprung up on Navajo reservations. A concurrent increased incidence of gall-bladder disease is attributed to this change in diet. I have studied Navajo some, a tough language that is extremely verb-heavy and full of tones, glottal stops, voiceless consonants, and no separate words corresponding to the adjectives of our own English grammar. Verbs serve/include all adjectival functions.

So, "*Naa'ahóóhai séłt'é*" is how one would say, "I cooked *chicken.*" It may be argued that one must be stone-cold sober not to confuse even the basic words of the Navajo—or *Dine* (pronounced *di-nay*), as they prefer to call themselves—like mescal (agave*)* *ná-ta ná-ta ná-ta* and potatoes (wild) ĭlh-tsú si-tsí n-nĭ pi-ji-né *ná-ma-si* and *corn na-tán na-tán na-tán.*

Chickens are thought unclean by high-caste Indian Hindus because they will eat anything they scratch up. Buddhists are repelled by domestic fowl because they eat living insects, mites, and bugs. No true Brahmin feels clean after touching a chicken, but, if he does so, he will immediately bathe. In Tibet chickens are detested for their claws, which are also found on vultures that pluck at corpses.

According to a Jicarilla Apache legend, diseases come from snakes and bears. Might this refer to the fever caused by snake-bite or infection from a bear attack? During their medicine feast or ceremony to cure this, bread baked in the ashes is a taboo food. Apaches did not eat reptiles or fish. They also avoided bacon or pork, because pigs ate those forbidden foods. A Windigo legend is thought to have evolved as a taboo against cannibalism, which might be a temptation to peoples in lands where food was scarce. While religious practices varied from group to group, it was common that the eating of the totemic animal was considered taboo, either by the entire clan represented by it, or the individual with the personal animal totem. Not all tribes believed in totem animals, however. Gluttony was taboo, a restriction that supported sharing, and was taught from the earliest age among all North American tribes. Among the tribes in the Iroquois Confederacy—the Mohawk, Oneida, Onondaga, Cayuga and Seneca—the children were warned that eating too many maize cakes soaked in maple syrup would provoke a visit from the bogeyman, "Longnose." Indians were sagacious, I find, and respectful of nature. I find exaggerated Joseph Conrad's assertion,

"The Noble Red Men were great warriors, great
orators, great masters of outdoor pursuits; but the
domestic life of their wigwams was clouded by the
morose irritability which follows the consumption
of ill-cooked food. The gluttony of their indigestible
feasts was a direct incentive to counsels of unreason-
able violence."

As to bogeymen and cannibalism, in *A Taste for Women* [the original title
was *Aimez-vous les Femmes*], a film written by Roman Polanski, a secret sect
of cannibals who owns a vegetarian restaurant, used as a cover, meet once
a month with nefarious plans, one of which is to dine on a beautiful young
woman as their main course during a full-moon sacrifice. Ed Sanders writes
in *Sharon Tate*, "Gleefully, Polanski has even gone so far as to work out the
recipe for anyone interested in preparing such a dish for his own table."

Savagery, Charles Darwin saw, was everywhere in Patagonia back in the
1830s. During hard winters, natives had no hesitation in killing and eating
their women. In his discourses, Darwin repeats a conversation that the captain of a sailing ship had with a boy from Tierra del Fuego. Why, the captain
wanted to know, did the Fuegians not eat dogs? "Dog catch otter," the boy
replied with a simple shrug, "women good for nothing; men very hungry."

"Elegance is refusal," pronounced glib, often harebrained Diana
Vreeland. It fits the mode of the prancing ego, of course. But what exactly
did she mean? (She would have been the last to be able to explain or clarify.) Unforgiveness is chic? Coldness is cool? One should never seek to make
amends? Maintain a chaste, uncluttered apartment? Join nothing? Are we
talking about flat-out denial? Turning down a proposition? Playing hard to
get? Giving up something for Lent? Furtive unavailability? Withholding affection from a person who loves you? One wonders how seriously such a quip
should be taken, especially from a dubious fashionista who commented in
1946 that "[T]he bikini is the most important thing since the atom bomb."
(During the bleak days of World War II—what, using fantasy as a panacea for
gloom?—Vreeland also induced women to trade their shoe ration coupons
for ballet slippers!)

Disliking a food has its own distinction, offering a definite panache. A
negative chic attaches to refusing something outright. The act of *spurning*
acquires a kind of power. It gives advantage, dominance. A mysterious side
of it solicits guesses as to your motive, for you reveal a sharpness, suggesting,
acuity, bravado, judgment. "Poems are about what you don't mean, as well
as what you do mean," insisted Robert Frost.

Refusal is the cry of its own occasion, not grim reality, but reality grimly seen. Any determined position, indicating firmness, *shows* style. Refusal, magnificently, offers its own seal of approval: disapproval.

9.

HEARST, HEBREWS, AND HYDROPHOBES

WHAT ONE CHOOSES to eat and/or prefers to ignore—or abhor—often depends on what is available, especially in matters of survival, considerations often not within the purview of the unlucky. Of the 132 Pilgrims and crew who left England for the New World on the *Mayflower* in 1620, only fifty-three of them survived the first winter. Corn to the them was a bonanza, or what Jimmy Durante in the movie, *What? No Beer* (1933) called a "bonzana." The constantly carping Hebrew tribes, wandering in the Sinai desert, that wedge-shaped peninsula that lies between Egypt and Canaan, and running out of food, were in no condition to turn up their noses at what God sent them to eat: quail, as well as a starch that they called, for want of a better term, "*mahn-hu*"—Biblical scholar Thomas Cahill translates this vague word as "whaddayacallit"—which almost all English Bibles transliterate as "manna." It was in all probability the white edible insect secretions that they found on the branches of some rare Sinai plants. Considering this period in the Bible, the Hebrews had a drink to match the manna that was just as gross. Do you recall how, after descending Mt. Sinai bearing the Ten Commandments, Moses was scandalized by the blasphemous idol that Aaron and the people had scandalously set up? What was the result in terms of a beverage? It was not exactly Louis Roederer Cristal. As a matter of plain fact, Moses melted down the idol, ground it to powder, and ingeniously mixing it with water, actually proceeded to force the Children of Israel to drink the vile mixture (Exodus 32:19-20)! A wretched excess? The Hebrews of old ate human flesh. Moses and other prophets predicted that if the Israelites forsook God, they would fall into such degradation as to cannibalize their own children. These harrowing prophecies were actually fulfilled after the siege of Samaria, during the reign of King Jehoram (2 Kings 6:28-29), a period dated to 849-842 B.C. Cannibalism was a manifestation of the physical horror, which accompanied the spiritual horror of apostasy.

I like this symmetry. In H.G. Wells's *The Time Machine,* the Eloi are clothed and fed by the Morlocks, and in return, the Morlocks eat the Eloi.

Was that any worse than offering human sacrifice? Did the Israelites really engage in such? We do know that they had adopted forms of pagan worship and had even sacrificed their sons and daughters in the fire (2 Kings 17:17). There is also that direct reference in Hosea 13:2 ("They offer human sacrifice and kiss the calf-idols"), part of the reason the Prophet cites for the Lord being angry with his sinful people, for their wicked acts of prostitution, infidelity, and despair.

What about God himself—had he not food aversions? For example, what possible brief had Yahweh against *leavened* bread?

A querulous Bertrand Russell writes in his *Autobiography,*

> What a queer work the Bible is…When Moses begs to see God, God allows him to see his 'hind parts.' [i.e., "Then I will take My hand away and you shall see My back, but My face shall not be seen"] There is a terrible fuss, thunder, and whirlwind and all the paraphernalia, and then all God has to say is that he wants the Jews to eat *unleavened* bread at the Passover—he says this over and over again, like an old gentleman in his dotage. Queer book.

The first mention of leaven appears in Exodus 12–13, in commemoration of Israel's Exodus at the feast of Unleavened Bread. Unleavened bread is referred to as the "bread of affliction" in Deuteronomy 16:3, for it symbolizes the haste in which Israel fled their captivity in Egypt. Because it was the Lord who brought Israel out of Egypt, not a work of the people, it became significant for the Hebrews to remember the event by eating unleavened bread as a symbol of their powerlessness. During Passover, *chametz*—bread and other food made with leaven—is forbidden to eat, according to Jewish religious law. Leaven is another word for yeast, a naturally occurring fungus. In ancient times, they were ignorant of this. What they did know is that if one kneaded flour and water and left it in a cool place, that dough would rise. They also knew that one could save a small amount of dough each time bread was made, that could be added to the next batch, a reserve that is now called a "starter." It was a good way to preserve yeast that made good bread, as opposed to leaving out the dough every night in the hope that it would catch a good wild yeast versus a bad one.

God is exacting nothing less than obedience of the recalcitrant Hebrews, asking what in essence we likewise demand by way of loyalty to ourselves in the matter of what personally we choose to eat or not eat, the alternative being disobedience, having chosen in disobeying Yahweh the downward spiral of increasing sin and degradation, and shame and weakness in disappointing ourselves.

So, we see that Jehovah himself levied food proscriptions. In the book of Hosea (3:1), it may be noted, even the seemingly unscriptural and exotic comestible, "sacred raisin cake" is held up as decadent by the Lord, food that fallen-away Israelites had eaten, who have turned to other gods. Remember, too, that Solomon—the king is said (along with Agur and Lemuel) to have written the book of Proverbs, around the time of the 10th-century B.C.— offered his own food caveats. They were sweeping proscriptions, including the highest and the lowest. Regarding rulers and kings, we read in 23:3, "Do not crave his delicacies for that food is deceptive." Nor did Solomon hesitate to cover small particulars, for in 23:6 he adjures his people, "Do not eat the food of a stingy man, do not crave his wise delicacies."

Today, savage *Israel* is itself the stingy man.

It is now official Israeli government policy to restrict the amount of all food going into Gaza, a ruthless but entirely deliberate policy whereby the dietary needs of the Gazan people are chillingly calculated to keep the population alive at a near-starvation level. A witless Dov Weisglass, a senior advisor to the corrupt Prime Minister Ehud Olmert, joked that they were "putting the Palestinians on a diet, but not to make them die of hunger." In 2012 it was revealed that in early 2008 Israeli authorities drew up what can only be considered a satanic document calculating the minimum caloric intake necessary for Palestinians to avoid malnutrition so Israel could limit the amount of foodstuffs allowed into Gaza without causing outright starvation. As an act, it has the calculating touch of Dr. Mengele. Immanuel Kant was right in his assertion, "From the crooked timber of humanity not a straight thing is made."

A few truly scandalous truths—aside from the fact that the crimes are committed with the connivance of the United States government—are that 10% of children under five experienced stunted growth due to prolonged malnutrition due to Israel's blockade and siege of Gaza. A full 58.6% of Gaza's schoolchildren are anemic, as are more than 68% of children aged nine to 12 months and nearly 37% of pregnant women. According to UNICEF, more than 90% of the water from Gaza's only aquifer is unsafe for human consumption due to pollution, while repairs to Gaza's sewage and water infrastructure cannot be carried out because of Israeli restrictions on the entry of building materials and equipment. As of July 6, 2014, Israel limited fishing in Gaza's territorial waters to just three nautical miles off the coast, barring all Palestinian fishermen from reaching fertile fishing grounds further out, in full violation of the terms of the Oslo Accords, which stipulated a fishing limit of 20 nautical miles. Bias and bigotry by the U.S. government against the Palestinians is an ongoing scandal. A recent survey of *New York Times'* online articles shows that, while the *New York Times* covered 140% of Israeli deaths in the headline, first paragraph, or featured photo caption, it only covered 37% of Palestinian deaths in the same way.

In 1951, Elizabeth Bishop suffered an allergic reaction to the fruit of the cashew tree in Brazil and became very ill. It was how the poet bonded with the woman who was to become her lover for years, Lota de Macedo Soares, who nursed her back to health and encouraged her to stay and live together in the house that she was building in the mountain resort of Petrópolis. The late Asian actor and martial arts expert, Bruce Lee, avoided refined flour, dairy food, Chinese food, baked foods, and all biscuits and cakes, which he described as being "empty calories." It is worth mentioning that today many people attribute irritable bowel syndrome to the excess consumption of refined flours. Lee's philosophy was not to consume calories that did not provide some benefit to the body. The writer Shirley Jackson hated cocoa. "Cocoa," she exclaimed in *The Bird's Nest* (1954). "Cocoa. Damn miserable puny stuff, fit for kittens and unwashed boys. Did Shakespeare drink cocoa?" G.K. Chesterton felt the same way. In his poem, "The Song of Right and Wrong," he wrote,

> Tea, although an Oriental,
> Is a gentleman at least;
> Cocoa is a cad and a coward,
> Cocoa is a vulgar beast.

James Bond, Agent 007, hated tea, which he believes caused the collapse of the British Empire, although his absolutely favorite meal is breakfast, specifically scrambled eggs with bacon and/or sausages. (Bond will eat them any time, day or night, with vodka and tonic or Champagne.) When in London, Bond maintained a simple routine. Sitting down to read the *Times*, he breakfasts on two large cups of "very strong coffee, from De Bry in New Oxford Street" brewed in a Chemex coffee maker and an egg served in a dark blue egg cup with a gold ring round the top, boiled for three and a third minutes. In *Live and Let Die*, we find that there is added whole wheat toast, Jersey butter, and a choice of Tiptree 'Little Scarlet' strawberry jam,

Cooper's Vintage Oxford marmalade, and Norwegian Heather Honey from Fortnum and Mason, served on blue Minton china. (Who does not find ludicrous Bond's effete insistence on food vehicles, and things like the proper dishes and plates?) Breakfast is always prepared by May, Bond's elderly Scottish housekeeper, who cultivates a friend that supplies her with speckled brown eggs from French Marans hens. Agent 007's diet can vary according to wherever he finds himself in the world. Although a typical hotel breakfast would normally consist of coffee and eggs, maybe with bacon, Bond's first breakfast in Istanbul in *From Russia, With Love* is quite remarkably different: "The yoghourt, in a blue china bowl, was deep yellow and with the consistency of thick cream. The green figs, ready peeled, were bursting with ripeness, and the Turkish coffee was jet black and with the burned taste that showed it had been freshly ground."

It is well known how much Bond loved gin, especially in martinis. It is fascinating how specific tastes, regarding food and drink, rule. T. S. Eliot attributed his inspiration to gin. Philip Larkin said that, along with listening to jazz, gin was "the best remedy for a day's work I know." It was the drink of 18th-century rookeries and 19th-century royalty. The diabolist Aleister Crowley claimed to have invented a gin cocktail called the "Kubla Khan No. 2" which involved the addition of laudanum, a drug to which he was both dedicated and addicted.

Food aversions? I never thought you would ask. On assignment, James Bond will eat *langouste* in France, *tagliatelle verdi* in Italy, and stone crabs and melted butter in the United States, but this highly opinionated and ornate man could be persnickety and remained contemptuous of the cream and wine sauces in French cuisine which he felt were designed to hide the poor quality of the meat. Bond's favorite foods when off duty include grilled sole, *oeufs en cocotte* (eggs and *crème fraîche* to you and me) and cold roast beef with potato salad. So crème fraîche turned out to be acceptable in the cream department. Why be consistent, right?

Many fail to see that James Bond, despite his dislike of tea, was jingoistic and stereotypically British in his food preferences, as many of his countrymen quite frankly are—even in pronunciation of foreign words; they truly dislike enunciating, articulating, vocalizing words they see as irritatingly odd. I have heard many an English person unbudgingly and inflexibly say "*dewbonnet*" for Dubonnet and "*pitza*" for pizza and "*pass-ter*" for pasta and "*take-o*" for taco. I believe that the English out of disdainful snobbery actually go out of their way to mis-pronounce certain foreign words, smugly to do it incorrectly as a snub. Why would a BBC reporter pronounce the word "Nicaragua" as "*nick-ur-agg-you-uh*"? Then there's the really dim-witted one: "*jag-yoo-arr*". What else can one expect from a country where Cholmondeley is pronounced "*chumley*" and Woolfhardisworthy becomes "*woolzee*" and the surname Menzies, by some glossal prestidigitation beyond me, becomes "*min-gus*"?

In his cozy Blimpism, never mind spite, Bond would have to go some to match his countryman, Tobias Smollett, for sheer vitriol, as witness the attack against French food in *The Expedition of Humphrey Clinker* (1771):

> As to the repast, it was made up of a parcel of kick-shaws. Contrived by a French cook, without one substantial article adapted to the satisfaction of an English appetite. The pottage was little better than bread soaked in dishwashings, luke-warm. The ragouts looked as if they had been once eaten and half digested: the fricasses were involved in a nasty yellow poultice; and the rotis were scorched and stinking, for the honour of the fumet [the smell of well-hung game]. The dessert consisted of faded fruit and iced froth, a good emblem of our landlady's character; the table beer was sour, the water foul, and the wine vapid.

Arbitrariness plays heavily in the matter of food aversions. So does conditioning, which is also known as the "Garcia effect" (after the psychologist Dr. John Garcia), an example of Pavlovian conditioning. Conditioned taste aversion is the result of a subject associating the taste of a certain food with symptoms caused by a spoiled or poisonous substance. Generally, taste aversion is caused after ingestion of the food causes nausea, sickness, or vomiting. The ability to develop a taste aversion is considered an adaptive trait or survival mechanism that trains the body to avoid poisonous substances (e.g., poisonous berries) before they can cause harm. Normal connections are made in the mind to avoiding further poisoning. A conditioned taste aversion can occur when one's sickness is merely coincidental and not related to the food (for example, a subject who gets a cold or the flu shortly after eating an apple might develop an aversion to the taste of apples). This concept, while obvious, does touch on classical conditioning because it contradicts some of its core findings in the Russian physiologist Ivan Pavlov's dog experiments.

You will recall that Pavlov consistently had to pair the unconditioned stimulus with the conditioned stimulus many times in order to generate the conditioned response, while with conditioned taste aversion it usually only takes one instance to generate the conditioned response. Garcia discovered through experiment that if a rat became nauseated after being presented with a new taste, even if the illness occurred several hours later, it would avoid that taste, contradicting the belief that, for conditioning to occur, the unconditioned response (in this case, sickness) must immediately follow the conditioned stimulus-to-be (the taste). This has also been called the "Sauce-Béarnaise Syndrome," a term used by psychologist Martin Seligman, who once at dinner ordered a filet mignon steak with sauce *béarnaise* and later became violently ill. After a single instance of retching due to the sauce, he could never again taste it without feeling like vomiting. Such experiments hardly touch on matters of deep complexity. A "learned" food aversion is the direct result of a person coming to hate a particular food because those around him when he was a kid (parents and other family members or other outside stimuli or experiences) would refuse to eat that or certain other foods on their plate, and so he learns that the food is bad, the matter relating to his brain responding negatively to certain foods when eaten, smelled, or seen.

Jack LaLanne, the TV exercise buff and founder of the modern fitness movement—he died in 2011 at the age of 96 from pneumonia—was very fussy about what he ate. He expressly never drank coffee. "I also use no milk of any kind," he said. "And anything that comes from a cow I don't eat." (Doctors believe nowadays that as many as 1 in 7 people cannot digest milk.) The anarchist John Brown, the intransigent fellow responsible for the insurrection at Harper's Ferry, always quirkily insisted that those around him drink tea instead of coffee. Novelist Franz Kafka, a teetotaler, would never touch coffee, tea, or, strange as it may seem, even chocolate, and he insisted on only the freshest vegetarian food. Christopher Wallace, the long-philtrumed, Republican-biased Fox Network reporter, in an interview told *Playboy* magazine (Jan. 2012) that he has never drunk a cup of coffee. It is the same with NBC meteorologist Bill Karins. On the other hand, the beverage of choice for the Swedish investigative journalist, Mikael Blomkvist in the three highly popular "Millennium" novels by Stieg Larsson, *The Girl with the Dragon Tattoo, The Girl Who Played With Fire,* and *The Girl Who Kicked the Hornet's Nest* is coffee, coffee, coffee—there are, in all seriousness, at least 240 references in the book to cups of coffee being drunk!

Abraham Lincoln who stood 6'4" always abstemiously ate a very spare breakfast of one egg and toast, but he needed his black coffee in the morning. Catherine the Great of Russia could not begin her day until she gulped five cups of strong black coffee. A deeply addictive personality, the queen also craved nicotine and always had snuff all over her clothes. With all the lovers and liaisons that she had—"She was quite a gorl [sic]," a pretty Kremlin tour-guide wearing a large "Flower Power" button told me in 1969—coffee must have boosted, not sapped, her energy. (Catherine supposedly could wiggle her ears!) Voltaire drank as much as 50 cups of coffee a day, always mixing it with chocolate, crediting it for the inspiration (and stimulation) of his deepest thoughts. Ludwig Beethoven always insisted on drinking coffee brewed with exactly 60 beans, no more, no less, and he would never drink coffee that he had not made himself. Thomas Jefferson called coffee the "favorite drink of the civilized world." The Dane Søren Kierkegaard, according to his biographer, Joakim Garff, would eccentrically pour sugar into a dry coffee cup up until it was piled to the rim, then he would pour the liquid coffee onto it which slowly dissolved into the white pyramid, and then as a culimantion of the event would gulp the entire cup at one go.

Ben Franklin loved to drink coffee because it "excited cheerfulness," a theme shared by J.S. Bach who actually wrote a comic opera about the beverage, called "The Coffee Cantata" (a.k.a. *Schweigt stille, plaudert nicht*), a humorous one-act operetta (*Cantata BWV* 211) about a stern father's attempt to check his daughter's indulgence in the much loved Saxon habit of coffee drinking, which seems to him a corrupt taste, although he says nothing of its seductive smell. A composition on the morality of the place of coffee in daily life, it is a rather rare example by that composer of such a secular work. (The libretto suggests that certain people in 18th-century Germany viewed coffee drinking as a bad habit.) The plot is simple:

> Lieschen (so goes the plot) loves her coffee, but her father, Schlendrian, a killjoy—his name means "stick in the mud"—demands that his daughter give up her coffee habit so that she can get married. She seemingly agrees to do so but later decides instead to find another coffee addict who'll agree to marry her. Lieschen literally sings a love song to her coffee: "*Ei! Wie schmeckt der Kaffee süße.*" All happily reconcile when Schlendrian lovingly gives in and agrees to have a guaranteed three cups of coffee a day written into her marriage contract, and the cantata ends happily with the father, daughter, and narrator all coming together to sing a vital song expounding the benefits of coffee drinking, which essentializes the moral of the story, "drinking coffee is natural," the witty *Die Katze Läßt Das Mausen Nicht.*

And we know that Honoré de Balzac, often writing for long days at a stretch, gulped gallons of coffee a day. The novelist exuberantly wrote,

> This coffee falls into your stomach, and straightway there is a general commotion. Ideas quick-march into motion like battalions of a grand army to its legendary fighting ground, and the battle rages. Memories charge in, bright flags on high; the cavalry of metaphor deploys with a magnificent gallop; the artillery of logic rushes up with clattering wagons and cartridges; on imagination's orders, sharpshooters sight and fire; forms and shapes and characters rear up; the paper is spread with ink—for the nightly labor begins and ends with torrents of this black water, as a battle opens and concludes with black powder. (translated by Robert Onopa)

"Coffee is a great power in my life," Balzac wrote. "I have observed its effects on an epic scale." The French novelist thought people who drank tea pale, sickly, garrulous, immeasurably boring, and preachy.

Frederick the Great, the Prussian king, came to hate coffee, coming to condemn the increase in coffee consumption in his country as "disgusting" and urging his subjects to drink beer instead. Let me explain. It turned out that the early 18th-century enthusiasm in Western Europe for coffee amongst the middle classes, which was huge and growing, was also affecting Prussia's economy. The monarch wanted to block imports of green coffee as Prussia's wealth was being drained by the huge sums of money going to foreign exporters. Also, the right to sell coffee was intended to be restricted to four distillers but the fashion for drinking coffee had become so widespread that the law was being flouted and coffee beans illegally roasted. (Coffee beans are not actually beans—they are in fact fruit pits.) In any case, Frederick employed coffee smellers, men who stalked the streets sniffing for the outlawed aroma of home roasting. However, such was the public outcry that eventually he was forced to change his mind. It was much of this controversy that prompted Bach's musical satire, the "*Kaffee-Kantate*."

Smell, in my opinion, is of all the senses the least praised in English and American literature, especially poetry. Is it not a romantic subject? Is it vulgar subject? A hundred years ago, the zoologist Gustav Jaeger declared that the nose is the seat of the soul. Smell, the oldest of our senses, leads directly to the brain, its sensations going arrow-straight into the amygdala and olfactory cortex, both parts of the limbic system, without pausing at the thalamus along the way. Smell is also hardwired to the brain's emotional centers. When you smell something, the sensation rushes, practically unfiltered, into the frontal lobes. What truer, what sharper, report can be given of a food that one suddenly loves or quickly comes to hate? Enthusiams delight, but a food that we detest registers sharper than an écailler.

A lifelong vegetarian and peevish foodie, Mahatma Gandhi decided to forego not only sweets, condiments, and spices, but took cocoa in place of tea and coffee, which he considered to be injurious to one's health. He lived mainly on nuts, fruits, and goat's milk—he brought his own goat on his travels. At a fruitarian luncheon at Grosvenor House in London 1920, he nibbled kale like a crank. Gandhi told any and all of his followers who grew discouraged by fasting—amazingly!—to chew their water! The late Dr. Noah Fabricant, who back in the late 1960s made a close study of drugs, pointed out that Gandhi, suffering from high blood pressure, for years took Rauwolfia serpentina, an old Indian tranquilizer made from snake root that was used in Asia to fight hypertension, schizophrenia, even to diminish sexual ardor for those who wished it. (Alexander the Great administered this very plant to his wounded general, Ptolemy I Soter, who had been shot by a poisoned arrow.) The Mahatma's favorite meal was probably aloo dum, a meal of potato, curry, and peas, but toward the end of his life he was eating little more than purslane, a succulent eaten throughout much of Europe, the Middle East, Asia, and Mexico, but in the United States is considered little more than a weed. It has a slightly sour, salty taste and may be eaten as a leaf vegetable, as its stems, leaves and flower buds are all edible. It is often used fresh in salads and even steamed and stir-fried or cooked as spinach is, and because of its mucilaginous quality it also is quite suitable for soups and stews. Australian Aborigines actually use the seeds of purslane to make their seedcakes.

But back to coffee, a fulmination against something as simple as coffee can be found in *The Women's Petition Against Coffee* (1674), where we read, "Trifle away their time, scald their chops, and spend their money, all for a little base, black, thick, nasty, bitter, stinking, nauseous puddle water."

President Harry S. Truman told writer John Hersey, "I'll take a strip of bacon, a scrambled egg, a piece of toast, and a glass of milk. No coffee. I don't crave coffee. It hurts the peculiar talent I have for lying down and dropping right off to sleep in two minutes." John Greenleaf Whittier disliked coffee. So does actress Sharon Stone. King Charles II was another anti-coffee tyrant who in 1675 issued "A Proclamation for the Suppression of Coffee Houses," banning all coffee shops. (The chemical name alone for caffeine—1,3,7-trimethylzantihine—is, I suppose, as good a reason as any to avoid drinking coffee.) Actor Ray Milland, who starred in the *The Lost Weekend* (1945), the hugely unsettling portrayal of a desperate alcoholic, actually disliked Champagne and wrote in his autobiography, *Wide-Eyed in Babylon* (1974), "It gives me terrible heartburn and an even worse hangover." Anglo-French writer and wit Hilaire Belloc dismissed the beverage, exclaiming, "Of Champagne I know nothing. Besides which, Champagne is not a wine but a drug." The poetaster/writer Elaine (Brimberg) Dundy claimed to hate champagne. In her book *The Dud Avocado* (1958) she writes, "I hate champagne more than anything in the world next to Seven-Up."

Dundy surely would have had a hard time meeting the dogmatic food standards of the fastidious poet, Lord Byron, something of a misogynist, who once famously said, "A woman should never be seen eating or drinking, unless it was lobster salad and champagne, the only true feminine and becoming viands." As to fussiness, Truman Capote preciously insisted that he would not drink anything out of a glass that was not perfectly plain crystal. If it had a glass pattern or even a simple gold border, Capote flatly refused to take it. Remember the toothless old tramp Davies in Harold Pinter's play *The Caretaker* (1960), the nutball "going down to Sidcup to get his papers" who adjusts aspects of the story of his life according to the people he is trying to impress, influence, or manipulate? He mightily snaps at one point, "I can't drink Guinness from a thick mug. I only like it out of a thin glass."

Extremism in the matter of food aversions is no surprise. Lunacy often speaks directly to the subject. Franz Kafka's short story "The Hunger Artist," written in 1922, may be the text-book example. The victim all his life of a cruel domineering father, Hermann, a gross ill-tempered domestic tyrant in that Jewish family, Kafka wrote fiction in spite of the fact that his day job, his *Brotberuf* ("bread job"), was working as a lawyer for an insurance company. It was his literary efforts that brought out his father's scorn which, ironically, in various transmogrifications, became the theme of his son's writing—arguably he never wrote about anything else. The short story is simple. A professional performance artist in a cage fasts in public both as entertainment and clearly as an act of masochism, while groups of curious spectators ogle him (until they become bored) and have been doing so for many years. The act he performs in its shamelessness and clown-like peculiarity—his drive to command attention, without any talent—frankly serves the same function as that of three Jewish food zanies on television who, with exhausting regularity, never seem to go away, Anthony Bourdain on "No Reservations," Andrew Zimmern on "Bizarre Foods," and Adam Richman on "Man versus Food," strangely enough, none of whom show the slightest discernible talent. I personally think of them, respectively, as "Mr. Sardonicus," "The Human Crocodile," and "Swillbowl." I find it hard to explain the mortifying need in anyone to make a numbskull of himself, never mind the lack of shame involved or the vulgarity. What *is* it with Jewish boys and the food circuit? Easy money? Love of fame? An exhibitionist's need for attention? No other options? Wrong! They do it for the *free food*!

Despite the attention he draws, the Hunger Artist grows dissatisfied and feels misunderstood. He is as often despised as he is pitied. As George Orwell wrote in *Down and Out in Paris and London*, "It is fatal to look hungry. It makes people want to kick you." If a spectator, observing his apparent melancholy, tries to console him, he angrily erupts in fury, shaking the bars of his cage. A humiliating spell in a circus then follows, but public interest wanes. In the end, the protagonist explains that he should not be admired for what he does and gives as his sole reason: "I couldn't find the food I liked. If I had found it, believe me, I should have made no fuss and stuffed myself like you or anyone else."

Those are the last words he speaks. So the Hunger Artist is a—maybe the ultimate—food aversionist. In the end, he is ignominiously buried with the straw of his cage and is then replaced by a panther, which gives the public more delight. What does it all signify? Alienated man? Jewish paranoia? A misunderstood artist? Is it a portrait of degradation? A moral fable against food? Is it an allegory, and if so of what?

Morbid writers like Dostoevsky, Baudelaire, Celine, and Kafka tended toward the shadowy and the shade, like vines and other plants that exhibit negative phototropism and grow toward dark solid objects, like trees.

I feel that the theme of the tale is black self-assertion, that in the subtext of all that spite, sulking, and starvation, all of the muffled anger and abject humiliation—under the stubborn illogicality and public self-destructiveness of the Hunger Artist's theatricality—we are to discern Kafka's own metaphorical attempt by way of fiction of dramatically trying to snatch back the moral initiative—an identity-assertion—from his censorious father. The unnamed protagonist, like his creator marginalized by society, undertakes his performance by manipulation, by determination, by victimization, just as Kafka in exercising his craft—writing the story—acts to counteract his father's dominance. Both figures no matter how grotesque seek to wrest some semblance of his self-hood as they to try to survive. The Hunger Artist controls the one thing that he can. It is the reason Kirillov in Dostoevsky's *The Possessed* commits suicide to exercise his freedom, to express his self-will, to prove his autonomy.

The irony is that in the very process of his performance the Hunger Artist repudiates—literally persecutes—himself. Paradoxically, it is contradictory self- abnegation, his disconfirmation, the positive negation of his performance of starving that allows to him both to "selve" and to survive. The French philosopher Jean-Paul Sartre controversially contended that "the Jews had survived because of their persecution, for which, therefore, they should thank God." Self-repudiation is what Kafka is all about, as well. All of his work taken together thematically recapitulates the weird, self-conscious, ambivalent life that he himself led, revealing repeatedly that he tended to view himself as much as an irrelevant, repulsive bug as a neurotic solipsist. He suffered from a case, at least to some degree, of anthropophobia, a fear of people in society. He hated his looks, which were strange and indeed somewhat feral or vulpine. A medium-level schizophrenic who was tortured by sexual desire, voyeurism, and a need for incessant womanizing, he never married—he much preferred pornography and visiting brothels. He had an identity problem, to say the least. Revealingly, he never once used the word "Jew" in his fiction, never made any of his characters Jewish, and as a matter of fact never learned Hebrew. He never completed a single one of his full-length novels, burned 90% of his own work, and on his death-bed gave explicit instructions to his literary executor, Max Brod—who disobeyed him—that all of his manuscripts be "burned unread." But let us not overlook the story's dominating metaphor and, crucially, its central theme: the repudiation of food. Self-cancellation. Willful starvation. Denial and assertion at the same time—just like bulimia. A nervous, anxiety-ridden, self-disapproving Jew, Kafka himself was thought to have had a serious eating disorder. Dr. Manfred M. Fichter of the Psychic Clinic of the University of Munich presented "evidence for the hypothesis that he suffered from an atypical anorexia nervosa."

The Hunger Artist's choice to refrain from food constitutes for him what amounts to a penance for the guilt he feels, the same culpability that in real life the author Kafka feels in writing the story is an "answer" to his mean-spirited father's abuse. Afraid to confront him, the story is more than anything a parable of evasion, simply because the author and subject cannot confront the real issue troubling them. I have often thought that in extreme cases the food a person selects to dislike might very well be an objective correlative of his or her guilt, the projection of an inner demon. Jorge Luis Borges, the characters for whose stories are often found wandering about in geometric madness and along "black nightmarish halls and along deep stairways of dizzyness," once pointed out that we do not fear the darkness because of the "boogie man" but rather create the "boogie man" to explain our fear of the darkness.

Winston Churchill loved champagne, particularly bottles of Pol Roger, his preference. He did not particularly like beer. Churchill's drinking revealed his international side more. He liked French wines in general, as well as Cognac, and Scotch whiskey (Johnnie Walker Black Label)—"the main basic standing refreshment of the white officer in the East," as he called it. Did that somehow reflect his imperialism? It was the whiskey and brandy that made people suspect him of being a drunk—he often started at breakfast—but he almost always drank them heavily diluted—really no more than a "mouthwash," was how his private secretary described it; and it was Churchill's preferred belief that drinking of any sort not only made him more clubbable but "quickened his intellect." Were you aware that alcoholic beverages have all of the 13 minerals necessary for human life? Maybe that is why we read in Wodehouse's *The Inimitable Jeeves* (1923), "Uncle George discovered that alcohol was a food well in advance of modern medical thought."

The astute reporter Gene Fowler, novelist, screenwriter, and biographer, as well, was once taken to a new bistro in Greenwich Village where he was to be wined and dined by several friends as prelude to showing him something of the city as well as a locale in his search for news. This was around 1918. Fowler had been recently appointed to work for the *Daily Mirror*, a Hearst newspaper. An owner of the bistro named Count Bruno, after specially serving a bottle of Piper-Heidsieck *brut* to Fowler's group, stood by looking for approval, according to H. Allen Smith in *The Life and Legend of Gene Fowler*, and then actually sought it. An indifferent Fowler simply shrugged and famously declared, "All wine tastes like cider to me." A huge melee followed when Count Bruno asked one of the party's members to dance, which irked Fowler, who supposedly said, "Only nances dance." Born Eugene Devlan in Denver, Colorado—Fowler took his stepfather's surname when his mother remarried—hugely disliked meat, as well, only yet another quirky aversion of Fowler's in the food department. It turns out that, in looking to a vocation, he had had a false start in taxidermy, something that he never got over, and he later claimed, loudly, that it gave him a permanent distaste for red meat.

I have alluded to William Randolph Hearst above. At the castle at San Simeon, the meals served were generally quite plain. Spare Ribs. Hominy. Omelets. Pastry. Lentil soup. Roast beef. Ringneck pheasant. Gravy. Mashed Potatoes. Buttered String Beans. Apricot tartlets. All American and identifiable. Although food was served on *actual Old Willow* English China, only casual silverware was used, even though—go figure—the room itself was filled with fine antique silver *objets*. *Hearst himself* preferred plain cooking and had a special passion for well-aged beef, which he would not touch until it had hung for 12 weeks. The newspaper mogul thought of himself as a gourmand to a degree—apparently he loved plain Welsh Rabbit—but he could not cook worth a damn. Hearst's son wrote about his father,

> He would be in the kitchen either grabbing a snack of
> cold meat and cheese for himself, or making a Welsh
> rarebit [sic] for all comers. The latter dish he made
> with pride and some beer, but whatever the recipe, I
> know it was a favorite of all those who were fortunate
> enough to partake of it.

The fifty-four-foot table in the main dining room of the castle could accommodate as many as 40 guests who sat in tall, upholstered chairs, on the walls above which hung tapestries, pennants, guidons. (Prince Albert, Victoria's husband, once proclaimed, "Things always taste so much better in small houses"—and was probably correct.) All the meals Hearst had served were for the most part far more relaxed than their refined and (faux-?) elegant, eclectic surroundings. Paradoxically, the napkins were of paper, and sauce bottles and other condiments were set out in the bottles they came in. This was not an economizing feature, but rather a sentimental one. Such informalities reminded the very sentimental Hearst of the early days in the 1870s and 1880s when he came out to this very spot with his mother and father where they picnicked in the open. These were detailed memorials and reminders of his youth.

Hearst disapproved of drinking alcohol. There were no elaborate French fripperies during meals at San Simeon, no cascades or epergnes or ice swans or anything like *le trou Normand* (or Norman hole), that all-important digestive that is taken in the midst of a Normandy meal—it can be a sorbet, a light beverage, a neutral food, or even a fiery Calvados—to settle what has gone before and to prepare what is to come after, to avoid heartburn, indigestion, and to stimulate the appetite. Actual menus from back in those days are can still be found on display

Hearst was not fussy. He was importunate and demanding—and greedy. His own father once notoriously said of his extravagant only son who grew up to be the portly, unappeasable man, prototype of the intransigent anti-hero of the movie Citizen Kane: "I notice that when my boy, Bill, wants cake, he wants cake; and he wants it now." I believe that he meant that literally, as well as figuratively. He also loved luscious filled pastries—unlike Marilyn Monroe, who hated pastries—and especially big, sweet, gooey cakes, of the frosting-thick variety that at wedding receptions one always see a bride mis-shoving into the mouth of her groom, which as far as nuptial traditions go is as iconic as the most popularly played requests nowadays—Etta James' "At Last," The Carpenters' "We've Only Just Begin," and The Marcels' "Blue Moon."

Dis donc, because I have mentioned Marilyn Monroe, along with pastries and the smell of garlic—on humans, not food—she also disliked olives and, among other things, director George Cukor, zoos, spaghetti, heavy clothes, complicated movie scripts, and people she generally referred to as 'users.' However, she dearly loved red roses, blue delphiniums, steak, caviar, puppies, Abraham Lincoln, and one special song above all others: "I've Got a Crush on You." She could apparently cook an extremely authentic, and very tasty, bouillabaisse.

William Randolph Hearst drank mainly water. He took comfort in water, in its purity, its permanence, the peace it brought the heart. He once wrote a poem about it, called "Song of the River," which goes in part,

> So why prize life
> Or why fear death,
> Or dread what is to be?
> The river ran its allotted span
> Till it reached the silent sea.
> Then the water harked back to the mountaintop
> To begin its course once more.

There are those who hate water. Hydrophobes. To me, it constitutes a food aversion, frankly, a rather grievous one. Who can deny it? I know several people who actually refuse to drink water. "It is for them Shakers and Mormons, tall-hatted teetotalers," a neighbor of mine, an ex-cop, once told me. "People who sip." I think he meant gay people. Maybe not. Another was an otherwise seemingly level-headed woman—an assistant professor at Yale, she resembled a thundering bass, wore big black rubber galoshes, even in summer, and was always whistling Shostakovich—who for some reason or other frequently would announce to her colleagues that she never drank tap water. She could be seen everywhere in buildings, twitching usually, lugging her bottles around. I would also see her walking through the quads, buzzingly busy, large and in charge, looking like a sodawaterwallah in steamy Bangalore hawking her wares at trainstops. She also refused to eat citrus fruits, potatoes, raisins, and iceberg lettuce, warning us that they contained heavy—poisonous—levels of fluoride. "Cryolite! It is actually a fluoride-based pesticide!" It is actually the uncommon mineral, sodium aluminum fluoride. "A pesticide? It is an insecticide," she would howl, "a venom that is used to give fireworks a yellow color!"

She reminded me of General Jack D. Ripper in the movie, *Dr. Strangelove* ("Mandrake, have you ever seen a Commie drink a glass of water?"), that bullish, cigar- chomping, paranoid Russkophobe who looked for every chance to rail against the dangers of Communist pollution. One of his rants goes,

> Do you realize that in addition to fluoridating water,
> why, there are studies underway to fluoridate salt,
> flour, fruit juices, soup, sugar, milk, ice cream? Ice
> cream, Mandrake? Children's ice cream!... You know
> when fluoridation began? 1946. 1946, Mandrake.
> How does that coincide with your post war Commie
> conspiracy, huh? It's incredibly obvious, isn't it? A
> foreign substance is introduced into our precious
> bodily fluids without the knowledge of the individual,
> and certainly without any choice. That's the way your
> hard-core Commie works. I first became aware of it,
> Mandrake, during the physical act of love... Yes, a pro-
> found sense of fatigue, a feeling of emptiness followed.
> Luckily, I was able to interpret these feelings correctly.
> Loss of essence. I can assure you it has not recurred,
> Mandrake. Women, er, women sense my power, and
> they seek the life essence. I do not avoid women,
> Mandrake... but I do deny them my essence.

Marcella Hazan in her memoir, *Amarcord*, notes that her paternal grandmother, Nonna Polini, never drank water. "Water, the old lady said, *'fa infradicire i pali'* (will rot a fence post)." As a boy, I was not allowed to drink water after 6 p.m., an attempted remedy against my habitual bed-wetting. (My only consolation was that New York Yankee slugger Mickey Mantle wet the bed until he was 12 years old.) Trolls, those supernatural beings of Norse mythology, do not drink water, are afraid of water, and in fact, hate getting wet. A troll is usually hungry all the time. They typically wolf down anything that does not require hard chewing. According to myth, trolls like to eat humans. When they get the chance to catch a human, they immediately rip off the person's head and throw it away. They do not like the taste of human brains. They behave exactly like human beings; their appearances vary, most of them are notoriously ugly, slow-witted, unhelpful, and not at all friendly.

Poets have for centuries despised any and all hydrophiles. One of Horace's most famous *dicta* can be found in his *Epistles* (I.19): "No poems can please for long nor can live which are written by water-drinkers." Charles Baudelaire suspiciously wrote, "A man who drinks only water has a secret to hide from his fellow men." We all know what W.C. Fields thought of water. "I never drink water because of the disgusting things that fish do in it," he pontificated. (One day when Groucho Marx was visiting Fields, the curmudgeonly comedian took him up to his attic to show him $50,000 worth of liquor in boxes. "Don't you know prohibition is over?" asked Groucho. Fields replied, "Well, it may come back.") Fields, who hated the 18th Amendment and all it stood for, went on to declare in another context, "Once during prohibition, I was forced to live on nothing but food and water." Hilaire Belloc described water as "The mere beverage of the beast." And in his *Selected Prejudices:Second Series*, H.L. Mencken, who was more than a determined and devoted tippler, loathed the idea of water as a drink—he once dolefully referred to marriage as "the end of hope"—wrote,

> All the great villainies of history, from the murder of
> Abel onward, have been perpetrated by sober men,
> and chiefly by teetotalers. But all the charming and
> beautiful things, from the Song of Songs to bouilla-
> baisse, and from the nine Beethoven symphonies to
> the Martini cocktail, have been given to humanity by
> men who, when the hour came, turned from tap water
> to something with color in it, and more in it than
> mere oxygen and hydrogen.

The colonists on the *Mayflower* drank no water. They drank beer. No one in 1620 ever drank water, except as a last desperate resort, as it was believed to be injurious to one's health and often fatal. In England, beer was the preferred drink for the whole family, even children. The Pilgrims were surprised that their children were so healthy when they drank water instead of beer. Milk was not considered a very good option to drink either; it was usually made into butter or cheese or cooked to make tasty grain porridge. Porridges? Writer William Trevor mentions knowing a fellow who always spoke of porridge in the plural, saying, "I'd rather have salt on them than sugar." On their 66-day voyage, the Pilgrims survived on salt meat, hard biscuits, and dried peas. As far as anything like a treat went, it is likely there may have been "burgoo," oatmeal sweetened with molasses, or "doughboys," dumplings of wet flour boiled in pork fat, or best of all "plum duff," a suet pudding containing raisins or prunes. Curiously enough, the Pilgrims had almost no interest in fish as food.

It was their captain, Christopher Jones, a man who had grown up in the port town of Harwich, England, who went a long way to helping the hungry and soon-to-be-no-longer-fussy Pilgrims to change their minds about eating fish. But he was not the first. It was the intrepid Indian Samoset, having boldly strode into their camp, who not only introduced them to their Indian neighbors but more importantly taught the group how to live off the land—and to fish

Samoset was the first Indian to greet the Pilgrims at Plymouth and came *four months* after they arrived, when half their number had died from sickness and exposure to the cold. He was a sagamore (subordinate chief) of an Eastern Abenaki tribe that resided at the time in what is now Monhegan Island, Maine, and he had come to visit the Wampanoag chieftain, Massasoit. (Wampanoag, a Native American tribe still living on Cape Cod and environs, means "The people of the first light.") An English fishing camp had been established up north to harvest from the bountiful area now called the Gulf of Maine, and Samoset had learned what little English he knew from fishermen who came to fish off Monhegan Island. He knew most of the ship captains by name. He spoke to the beleaguered colonists in English, saying, "Welcome, Englishmen! I am Samoset. Do you have any beer?" After spending that night with the Pilgrims, he left to return with five others, who brought deerskins to trade.

In a very real sense—a theological sense—the Pilgrims were the "sheep of God's feeding." It was with shouts of joy that they spied land on Cape Cod on that chill November day in 1620 when William Brewster, an elder, leader, and preacher of the Scrooby group, humbly suggested at that very same moment that a song of gladness and humble thanks be offered to God, so on the deck of the *Mayflower* all chanted the words of Psalm 100, which goes in part:

> Know that Jehovah he God is
> It is He that made us, not we
> His folk and sheep of his feeding

They *themselves* were exemplary food.

The inimitable Phil Harris, that brash, florid-faced, boozing band leader with the crocodile grin on radio's Jack Benny Program was known for his snappy one-liners–and he was always putting down water. As I say, W.C. Fields' life-long distaste, indeed huge dislike, for something so simple—and elemental—as water was well advertised. "My abhorrence and loathing for water fructificated in my receptive adolescent brain," wrote the notorious curmudgeon in one of his autobiographical snippets, demonstrating his characteristically Micawbersque reliance on wild circumlocution. "In retrospect the sufferings of the Noah family, the Johnstown flood, and other nefarious pranks water had played kaleidoscoped through my immature brain." Fields made a career out of sniping at the element ("Water rusts pipes," "Say anything you like about me, except that I drink water," "You can't trust water: even a straight stick turns crooked in it," etc.) but, again, his most widely quoted remark on the subject, offering his rationale, which went, "I never drink water because of the disgusting things that fish do in it," was in the original much more comical, to say nothing about being more precise: "Fish fuck in it."

A person on the Internet wrote, "I used to be fine just drinking plain water, but after I tried the water with some Crystal Light, I can never go back. Now water just tastes terrible by itself."

It is sad to hear of such a decline, water always having been a sacred element, symbol of life and renewal. Christ uses it constantly in his Parables. During the days of Jesus, in fact, when true believers often had to meet in safe houses, one coded signal was following a man with a jug of water through various towns. Christ resorted to such measures not to evade the Roman political authorities, but to elude the Jewish high priesthood, then held by the Annas family, of whom the Talmud records, "A plague on the House of Annas: a plague on their spying."

Water fountains—what we used to call "bubblers" when I was growing up—have pretty much disappeared from all public spaces. Have you noticed? Celebrity morons and deluded pillocks have made the act of drinking signature bottled water more than a fad; it is now nothing less than a nationwide obsession. Just plain water? Forget it. Same with tap water. But isn't it just about all just plain water? Coca-Cola's "Super Pure" Dasani bottled water—lovely phrasing—is nothing more than filtered tap water, which has to put it up there in the gullibility pantheon with Pet Rocks. Drinkers of common "Adam's ale" and nothing more have been marginalized as unsophisticates, yokels, rustics, and rubes who are culturally nowhere. When he was Vice President of the United States, the sour ball and satanic creep Dick Cheney—"I think that in fact was one of the approved techniques," the VP said, smiling, regarding the Saudi Arabian prisoner, Abu Zubaydah, who at the Guantanamo Bay detention camp was water-boarded and then kept in a coffin-sized box for 266 hours, and in an even smaller box (21 inches wide, 2.5 feet deep, 2.5 feet high) for 29 hours—always insisted on having provided in his room 4 to 6 bottles of water, those along with two bottles of "sparkling water (Calistoga or Perrier)" if his wife had accompanied him. "He also required that 'All televisions [in his hotel rooms] be tuned to FOX News...' lest he accidently see other sources of news and information," according to Peter Gleick, who in his book, *Bottled and Sold: The Story Behind Our Obsession with Bottled Water,* has catalogued all the neuroses and nervy—farcical—demands in this department.

Jennifer Aniston, of TV's "Friends," drinks Smart Water. Secretary of State John Kerry at every venue sends out his command for bottled water "uncarbonated. Poland Spring preferred. No Evian." Sarah Palin fussily demands two bottles of "unopened still water" with "bendable straws" plus a special kind of private jet on top of her $75,000-plus speaker fee, writes Gleick. Singer Mary J. Blige will drink nothing unless it is Fiji water—"absolutely, positively must be FIJI" at room temperature. When they were married, as part of the flight arrangements in 2004 for Tiger Woods and his then wife, Elin Nordegren, the contract specified: "Mr. Tiger Woods drinks liter bottles of Evian cold... Ms. Nordegren drinks Fiji room temperature..." Gleick writes that "Christina Aguilera wants Arrowhead, along with L'Occitane vanilla-scented candles with matches, 4 black bath towels, and Veuve Clicquot champagne." Do these people think they are fucking kings and queens? In 2008, the rock group Pearl Jam preferred for their bottled water "ETHOS water, no Aquafina, Dasani, or Evian." Madonna mainly insists on having bottles of special Kabbalah water at her photo shoots and appearances." There is an odd exchange in James Salter's strangely beautiful novel, *A Sport and a Pastime,* that goes,

> "They always tell you drink wine to be safe."
> "Yes, but I drink the water."
> "Everywhere, so do I," he says. "You know where the cleanest water in the world is?"
> "No."
> "The Yale swimming pool," he says. His voice is fading. "Anyway, that's what they always told us."

The honor of having the best tasting municpal water on earth in 2013, according to the Berkeley Springs International Water Testing in Berkeley Springs, West Virginia, goes to Emporia, Kansas; Independence, Missouri; and Greenwood, British Columbia, Canada, in that order. It seems that every time I have visited Rome someone feels compelled to tell me—is it chauvinism?—"*Roma ha la migliore acqua sulla terra, caro amico—non guardare altrove, Ecco la fontana di Bandusia!*" (Rome has the best water on earth, dear friend—look nowhere else! Behold, the Bandusian fountains!) I have always relished the pure natural spring water in my corner of West Barnstable, Mass.; there is a perpetual geyser of it flowing only a few jogs from my house. It is vibrant, sparkling, rocky, a constant flow of water tasting of the essence of green virgin forest with a subtle tinge of sharp grapefruit. I also detect the scent of fresh watercress in it, a viridescence of glacial coldness deepening colors, opening the eyes, and clearing the head with the song of godly ringing bells.

There is in the sudden need for water, its detailed urgency, something that touches on the perverse and becomes akin to hating it. Pontius Pilate washed his hands in a basin, in expiation. "When Pilate saw that he was getting nowhere, but that instead an uproar was starting, he took water and washed his hands in front of the crowd. 'I am innocent of this man's blood,' he said; "it is your responsibility!" (Matthew 27:24). Some stories hold that bodies of water consistently rejected his corpse. The irony is that Jesus in his purity stood before him as the true personification of salvation by water, for he had often said, "Whosoever drinketh of this water that I shall give him shall never thirst; but the water that I shall give him shall be in him a well of water springing up into everlasting life" (John 4:14). The water to which he refers is his Gospel, which is the knowledge of how to "grow" into "everlasting life." Christ went on to tell us that he further personifies that water by saying, "If any man thirst, let him come unto me, and drink, (John 7:37)." In other words he is saying to any believer that thirsts for spiritual knowledge, "I am that water," which means of course that he is the way, the only way, to salvation, and is therefore the Messiah. (Note. Revelations 7:15–17—"The Lamb. . . shall lead them unto living fountains of waters.") No consensus has been reached on the subject of where exactly where Doubting Pilate was born or the circumstances of his death. The only direct evidence we have for the 5th procurator of Judea, a second-rate posting, is one limestone block and a few small coins. He was of the Samnite tribe. No one knows what his first name was. Origen believed his wife, Claudia Procula, was the first Gentile to believe in Christ's teaching. He stayed in Judea 10 years, left almost no traces behind him. Some say he committed suicide, others that he was executed by the Roman Emperor, Tiberius.

Strangely, the Hebrew word for "prophet," *nabi*, is derived from a verb signifying "to bubble forth" like a fountain; the word means one who announces or pours forth the declarations of God. The English word comes from the classical Greek word *prophetes* (πρωφέτες), which signifies one who speaks for another, especially one who speaks for a god, and so interprets his will to man; hence its essential meaning is "an interpreter," in a modern sense "one who predicts."

Are all weak and guilty bureaucrats hydrophiles? In Shakespeare's *Macbeth*, Lady Macbeth compulsively washes her raw claws in an attempt to cleanse an imagined stain, an act clearly representing her guilty conscience regarding crimes she had committed and induced her husband to commit. "I had an irresistible passion for water," wrote Rudolf Hoess, SS-Obersturmbannführer and Nazi commandant of the Auschwitz death camp in a personal testimony that he was forced to write by the Allied command before he was hanged by the Poles as a war criminal in 1947. "I had to constantly wash and bathe. I would take any opportunity to wash or bathe in a tub or stream that flowed through our garden [where I grew up]."

10.

KING YOLK OF EGGVILLE

IT IS HARDLY A DEEP INSIGHT to observe at this juncture that in a good many, if not most instances, not only is fussiness the *sine qua non* of food aversions but that the individual turning away a particular food item as revolting (or turning up his nose at it) is often also a faultfinder, a griper, a grouser, a growler, a grumbler, a grump, a kicker, a malcontent, a moaner, a sorehead, a sourpuss, a whiner, and, not to put to fine a point on it, something of an inveterate—literally—bellyacher.

The controlling image you want here is one, maybe two, defensive hands of a person, alarmingly high and flat: *thrusting away.* It is Disquiet or Consternation raised in protest, warding off advance of whatever kind.

I have already mentioned Bernard DeVoto, the curmudgeonly historian, and his quirky polemic, *The Hour,* in which he engages in a lot of score-settling with not only drinking fads but the social ills they engendered. More than anything, his book is a disquisition on what a cocktail should—and should not—be. In his opinion, there are two and really only two adult beverages that are worth caring about: straight whiskey (rye, bourbon or scotch) and martinis made with gin and dry vermouth. He abhors the use of fruit juice in any drink that attempts to call itself a cocktail. Sweetness, of any kind, in a cocktail utterly revolts him. Any martini made of *sweet* vermouth in his words constitutes "a grievous betrayal of trust; the bottles should not even be kept on neighboring shelves, still less brought near the martini pitcher. Indeed, sweet vermouth should not be kept on any shelf in my house or yours." An intense man and something of a martinet, full of High Seriousness, he looked down on people who put either olives or pickled onions in their martinis and castigates those who mix them beforehand to keep in the refrigerator until cocktail time. Martinis must always be prepared just before serving, he insists, and any leftover in a pitcher should be thrown out once the first round has been poured. He writes, "You can no more keep a martini in the refrigerator than you can keep a kiss there." He attacks the very notion of mixed drinks, in short. "Whisky and vermouth cannot meet as friends and the Manhattan is an offense against piety."

DeVoto's eccentric peeves are pronounced. The word *vodka* is not to be found in the book, for one thing. He makes no mention of wine or beer. Nothing about popular summer drinks such as gin-and-tonics or Tom Collinses. Aside from the martini, to him all mixed drinks were abominations: "Put it this way. Maybe you like a good Burgundy, or a Pouilly, or a Champagne. How would you like it mixed with root beer and Veg-8?" Rum was his *bête noire*. It is frankly difficult to imagine a serious intellectual, never mind a Pulitzer Prize-winning scholar, consumed with what may legitimately seem to many complete trivia—I mean, the man wrote the solid *Across the Wide Missouri* and edited *The Journals of Lewis and Clark*—but I suspect much of his wrath masked the deeper anger of a critic who was notorious for hastily wedging works that he never fully understood into an easy anti-American category. (But then again the Pulitzer Prize, an eminently silly award, has often been handed out as the result of pull and political log-rolling, and that to some of the biggest frauds and fools alive.)

DeVoto who despised rum and could get up a full head of steam on the subject—he was a past-master of the personal crotchet in his stubbornness, whimsicality, and foolishness—writes,

> "Let us candidly admit that there are shameful blemishes on the American past, of which by far the worst is rum" and adds, "In both cheapness and effectiveness it proved the best liquor for Indian traders to debauch their customers with. People without taste buds can enjoy it now, though the head that follows it is enormous, and such sentimentalists as the sea-dogs of small sailing craft can believe they do. But mainly it is drunk as all sweet liquors are, in a regressive fantasy, a sad hope of regaining childhood's joy at the soda fountain."

A great big wind blowing, right? As Horace notes, "*Montes parturient, nascetur ridiculus mus.*"

Fancy DeVoto's thoughts on Red Sox slugger Ted Williams' habit of mixing lemonade and beer together, "an old fisherman's drink," according to Claudia Williams in *Ted Williams, My Father*. (Ted also loved Tabasco, a staple with him. Claudia writes, "Asked once how much he enjoyed Tabasco,

Dad shook the bottle into a tablespoon until it was full to the brim and downed the sauce with pleasure.")

A preposterous doctrinaire, DeVoto believed that the "hour to drink" should begin specifically at 6 p.m when "all lamps should be shaded and only a few of them lit, for if the body is in shadow the soul will the sooner turn toward the sun." At his club, he writes, "I take my drink to a chair so big that one's head cannot be seen above its back, by a window that faces a cross-town street." He solemnly advises that one not drink alone, but at the same time he holds disdain for large, loud parties, and he contributes a scathing animadversion against "cute" bars in suburban households where one often finds kitschy utensils shaped like nude women's torsos and tacky wall placards that broadcast: "To the Bar. Check your Morals" or "Danger: Men Drinking." It is clear that busy, little Benny DeVoto had lots of time on his hands.

Drinks, who imbibes what—and what kind—what they represent, and why and where they are consumed, well, there's a subject.

Prince Charles of England does not like coffee and never has—he always drinks lapsang souchang tea. He hugely dislikes chocolate pudding, according to Ingrid Seward in *Royal Style*, her book on taste and style among the British Royal Family, but does eat chocolate Bath Olivers. (To the Royals, all fruit is dessert, and to them everything else is referred to as *pudding*.) He likes chicken vol-au-vent, but rarely eats any other kind of meat. "When I ate raw squid in Japan," stated Charles, surely a fellow who needs an iron stomach to do all of his official traveling, "it tasted like chopped up garden hose. We ate very strange food in the Far East: things like octopus. But the sight of all those suckers was rather revolting. I wouldn't like the idea of sheep's eyes... maybe if I could swallow them in one go! It is probably the thought of having to chew them that puts me off. But I'm quite prepared to try anything once." It is well-known among the inner circles of Highgate that Charles likes cold food best. (Diana did not.) In contrast, the late Emperor Hirohito of Japan, a Divine Being to many, on the other hand, had to be served everything tepid, as he could not bear to eat very hot food of any kind.

"All this pleasure inspires me with the same nausea I feel at the sight of rich plum cake or sweetmeats; I prefer the driest bread of common life," wrote the co-founder of the *Edinburgh Review*, Sydney Smith (1771-1845), whose creed was common sense but who was also apparently something of a killjoy in matters of dramatic desserts, although the man did have his enthusiasms, once having declared, "My idea of heaven is eating *pate de fois gras* to the sound of trumpets." I wonder if the Royals would enjoy going out to eat at School Dinners, a London restaurant near St. Paul's Cathedral, where customers—out of sentiment and nostalgia cheerfully pay to eat the same dull, dreary fare that in former times, during their callow youth, they ate day in and day out, in public (or boarding) schools, porridge, wet, sludgy, overcooked Brussels sprouts, spotted dick and custard, bangers and mash, and overcooked pieces of salmon the shade of fuchsia called Hollywood Sunset in nail polish.

"If there is one food associated with personal dislikes in the Anglo-Saxon world, it is the Brussels sprout," confidently writes Bee Wilson, a Brit, in *First Bite: How We Learn to Eat*. She explains,

> Many people assume they have no choice in this matter—they just can't stand them. Are they right? In an article singing the praises of Brussels sprouts, the great chef Yotam Ottolenghi noted that there was a 'genetic explanation for why people either love or loathe' these little green brassicas. Ottolenghi argued that being a sprout hater was likely a consequence of having a certain gene—TAS2R38—which "makes a protein that reacts with a chemical called PTC to create the sensation of bitterness." Could this really be true? Is there a molecular basis to our hatred—or otherwise—of green vegetables?

Certainly some people taste certain flavors more acutely than others, whether the asperity of them or the electricity.

Odd food approaches may apply to most people, although a good many of us have all sorts of quirks. Actor Paul Newman, eating in public restaurants, often compulsively squired off his salad to the bathroom to wash off any inferior salad dressing, only to return to mix up his own at the table—always oil cut with a dash of water. Boxer Rocky Marciano ate only once a day. So did Michael Jackson who ate turkey burgers, Chinese food, a lot of vegetables, and he tried to stay away from red meat. Actor Danny Kaye instead of orange juice always began breakfast by ingesting a tall glass of cider vinegar with two tablespoons of honey. Eating once a day is often a sort of mendicant rule for people whose intent is to tame food, deny themselves to a degree, refuse to be either co-opted or dominated by appetite.

A big attraction—a seductive aspect—of food is flavor, needless to say. Flavor in a sense actually connaturalizes us to its authority and can dominate us in very subtle ways. One-meal-a-day eaters, at least many of them, refuse to be governed, controlled, or ruled by the waving lures of food.

Flavor actually consists of several different sensory modalities. It is not simply the taste in your mouth but also the way the food smells in your nose, the way it looks on your plate, the way it feels in your mouth. Food aversions pivot crucially on so many varying aspects. Neil DeGrasse Tyson, an American astrophysicist and science communicator, appeared as a host for NOVA Science NOW on the subject of "The Science of Picky Eaters," which aired on PBS on July 21, 2009. Setting out, Tyson was looking to find out why, despite eating the very same foods, so many people respond differently to them. The answer, he discovered with some surprise, may lie in their genes. People differ in their ability to taste. What makes a dish taste good to some people makes it taste terrible to others. Our caveman ancestors had to use all of their senses to find the nutrients needed to survive in a hostile environment. It is pretty much an old story. Sweet foods provide a lot of energy. Who is surprised to learn that most people strongly prefer sweet? Bitter is a warning—a protective sense in way, explained Bob Margolskee from the Monell Chemical Senses Center. "It is a signal for something potentially poisonous," said. "A plant put out a compound so people won't eat it." Our bitter taste buds honor and respect that fact in a plant. Little new there.

Our taste buds, the long slender leaf-like shapes on the tip of our tongues are taste cells which enable us to detect five basic flavors: sweet, salty, bitter, sour, and "umami," the Japanese word for the savory taste in meat and cheese. (This word, coined in 1908, is still relatively new to the English-speaking world.) When the hundreds of tiny taste receptors on the outside of each taste cell—they are actually proteins, made by our genes—bind with the foods we eat, it opens a chemical pathway into the cell that leads right up the highway to the brain, and that is what we call taste. "Biologists have discovered that, out of thousands of genes in our DNA, there is one that determines if we like the taste of some healthy greens or if we can't stand them," noted DeGrasse. "And that single gene was discovered by geneticist Dennis Drayna. He found it by testing how strongly people react to the taste of PTC, a compound a lot like the chemical found naturally in vegetables like cauliflower and broccoli. While some people hate the taste of PTC, others can't taste it at all." There is a biogenetic argument, in short, for what influences our food choices, just as our senses work together to create our perception of flavor.

While laws seem stable, it is human taste that remains variable, shifty, slippery, unsteady, vacillating, temperamental, ticklish, uncertain, suspicious, spasmodic, mercurial, capricious, and fitful!

Who can be found that does not like at least one main thing? Novelist Sinclair Lewis loathed alcohol and refused to keep any company with drinkers. Steven Tyler, the epicene lead-singer of the rock group, Aerosmith, on a Japanese tour completely destroyed a backstage area in indignation that a promoter had placed turkey roll on the buffet table. "I explicitly said, 'No turkey roll!'" screamed the petulant rock star. In Baden Baden, the reek of garlic on the breath of her "friend" (some say lover), Jimmy Donohue, caused the querulous Wallis Simpson, the Duchess of York, to screech at him about that "repellent commodity." His drunken response was furiously to kick her shin under the table, an impulsive act—"We've had enough of you, Jimmy," screamed the Duke, "Get out!"—that ended their friendship forever. There was never any bread on the Windsor's lavish tables. It was not allowed. They considered it a commodity strictly for the poor, and so *verboten*.

We are talking about bread.

Such an attitude here seems almost blasphemy.

A hatred of bread—for Christ, another symbol of life—- comes close to being a Scriptural offense, does it not, something almost dogmatically sinful? After he was abducted on May 11, 1960 and clandestinely brought back to Israel by secret agents for a public show trial and eventual execution, it was discovered that the Nazi commandant and legendary anti-Semite, Adolf Eichmann, hated bread. It was a food, singular in the attention he gave it—such is the food aversionist—that he grew to abhor. After he was abducted by Israeli commandos, the fact was not forgotten. In order to torment the ex-SS-Obersturmbannführer, therefore, his cruel, vengeful, and abusive military captors, with a savagery typical of them, constantly fed bread to their notorious prisoner day after day, almost exclusively, which they saw to it he was forced to eat. They took delight in his misery. It was an eye-for-an-eye. A question I would ask: would it not have been more in keeping with the Hebraic need for revenge, the kind we are forced to witness throughout the entire Old Testament, to have served that old demon, instead, the red lentil stew—or "pottage of lentils," as the King James version has it—cited in Genesis (25:29–34), which the invidious and wily Esau, the eldest son of the Biblical patriarch, Isaac, deviously sold to his cunning younger brother, Jacob ("Israel") in exchange for his birthright? It is the oldest recipe in Scripture:

> 3 tablespoons olive oil
> 1 large or 2 medium onions, chopped
> 3 medium carrots, chopped
> 2 stalk celery (diced)

2 cloves garlic (minced)

1 teaspoon ground cumin or paprika

8 cups chicken broth, beef broth, or water

2 cups red lentils, washed and drained

1 bay leaf

salt and pepper

1 tablespoon all-purpose flour dissolved in 2 tablespoons water

1. Heat the oil in a large, heavy saucepan over medium
heat. Stir in the onions, carrots, celery, and garlic and
sauté until softened (5 to 10 minutes). Stir in the
cumin or paprika.

2. Add the broth, lentils, bay leaf, salt, and pepper.
Bring to a boil, cover, reduce the heat to low, and
simmer until the lentils are very tender (about 30
minutes).

3. Puree the soup. Return to the pot, add the flour
mixture, and simmer until thickened. Serve warm.

Disparaging someone by way of bread seems a blasphemy. "He's white bread." "You're an absolute bagel!" The unmitigated cynic Jaques in *As You Like It*—the only purely contemplative character in Shakespeare, moreso than deliberating Hamlet—speaks of a fool he met with a brain "dry as the remainder biscuit after a voyage." A fellow who ponders things but does nothing. Jaques' whole occupation is to titillate his mind; he is completely indifferent to his body and his fortunes. Hazlitt describes him as "the prince of philosophical idlers; his only passion is thought; he sets no value upon anything but as it serves as food for reflection." Bread imagery figures throughout Shakespeare's history plays, suitably linking that staple food of the poor with toiling men and the workaday world by way of the Sermon on the Mount and the Lord's Prayer. Richard III, Falstaff, Prince Hal, Henry V all cite its substance.

Body-builder and sex-athlete Bernarr Macfadden, to whom we have already referred, was also fanatically opposed to the consumption of bread, which he not only defined as the "staff of death" but zealously banned from all of his money-making "healthatoriums." In Gillian Flynn's fictional trifle, *The Grownup*, the mere scent of bread for one of her aura-prone, vibration-aware female characters smells of despair. She explains, "That was just her scent, of a desperate soul." Athletes in general who tend to eat huge, satisfying meals can also be very picky about their choices. New England Patriots' quarterback, Tom Brady, the greatest quarterback in NFL history, is a good example. At 38, he appears to be in perfect shape, as is his super-model wife, Giselle Bundchen. His diet may be among the most healthful on earth. Allen Campbell, his progressive modern personal chef, on Boston.com breaks down the diet he supervises for the athlete and his family, explaining that "80 percent of what they [Tom and Giselle] eat is vegetables. [I buy] the freshest vegetables. If it's not organic, I don't use it. And whole grains: brown rice, quinoa, millet, beans. The other 20 percent is lean meats: grass-fed organic steak, duck every now and then, and chicken. As for fish, I mostly cook wild salmon."

What is proscribed for the Brady diet?

No white sugar. No white flour. No MSG. I'll use raw olive oil, but I never cook with olive oil. I only cook with coconut oil. Fats like canola oil turn into trans fats... I use Himalayan pink salt as the sodium. I never use iodized salt. [Tom] doesn't eat nightshades, because they're not anti-inflam-matory. So no tomatoes, peppers, mushrooms, or eggplants. Tomatoes trick-le in every now and then, but just maybe once a month. I'm very cautious about tomatoes. They cause inflammation. What else? No coffee. No caf-feine. No fungus. No dairy...The kids eat fruit. Tom, not so much. He will eat bananas in a smoothie. But otherwise, he prefers not to eat fruits...For snacks, I make fruit rolls from bananas, pineapple, and spirulina. Spirulina is an alga. It's a super fruit. I dehydrate it. I dehydrate a lot of things. I have three dehydrators in their kitchen. I also make raw granola and raw chocolate chip cookies.

I make mention above that Chef Campbell favors the Brady family with servings of wild salmon. Let me make a gloss on that. Known as the finest purveyor of seafood and caviar in the world, Rod Browne Mitchell, of the Browne Trading Company, a man famously intolerant of imperfection and one of the true living experts on seafood, is quoted in *Art Culinaire* (Spring 1997) as saying, "Farm raised salmon is probably superior tasting to the wild. Fish like cod or halibut, however, are better wild."

Food crotchets are never quite predictable. "I don't like calamari. I do not like pomegranates, because to consume them properly you have to eat them in a bathtub," caricaturist Al Hirschfeld told *Gourmet* magazine (February 1996). Audrey Hepburn hated Danish pastry. It may seem strange, but it is the case. In the film *Breakfast at Tiffany's*, the actress pleaded with film director Blake Edwards, regarding that famous morning scene when stylishly dressed and standing in front of Tiffany's window, that she be allowed to eat ice cream instead of a cheese Danish. Edwards insisted that Hepburn do as she was told, ordering, "Eat the Danish!" Could one part of Hepburn's excuse been the particular kind of Danish offered her? "American Danish can be doughy, heavy, sticky, tasting of prunes and is usually wrapped in cellophane," wrote R. W. Apple, Jr. in "The Danish Worth an Ocean Voyage" in *New York Times* (November 22, 1978), "whereas Danish Danish is light, crisp, buttery and often tastes of marzipan or raisins; it is seldom wrapped in anything but loving care."

Surprisingly, chef Emeril Lagasse told *Playboy* magazine (February 1999) that he does not eat pastry—at all! Samuel Gridley Howe, 19th-century advocate for the blind and husband of poet Julia Ward Howe, author of the "Battle Hymn of the Republic," was a health advocate and would never eat pastry, coconut cakes, fried foods, or ham. A stiff-necked Boston Brahmin and equally censorious husband, he vigorously opposed the idea of women working or speaking in public or writing poetry. He became something of as teetotaler in his later life.

Travel writer Jan Morris hates grape jelly, particularly as it appears, ubiquitously and unappetizingly, in the questionable form of those nasty little plastic peel-back gel-cubes that are commonly found on one's breakfast plate in virtually all American restaurants and diners. "Addict as I was of bitter orange marmalade with my toast"—one of the traditional staples of a standard English breakfast—"I was dismayed to discover that nearly everywhere [in the USA] all that was available was something called grape jelly, sealed in cellophane," wrote Morris with some disgust and, as she went on, no small bias. "I had never tasted it before... They [the grape jelly packets] seemed to represent all that I distrusted about America: synthetic, over-sweet, slobby of texture, artificially colored, and unavoidable." Still, like Paddington the lovable bear, Morris loves marmalade—world-wide sales of this British conserve have badly fallen off in the past decade, however—but I wonder if, for all her deep cerebrations on food, Ms. Morris has ever considered what Americans may think of the questionable British habit of eating cold baked beans for breakfast (or kippers!).

Was she not aware that George Orwell describes a jar of marmalade in *The Road to Wigan Pier* (1936) as "an unspeakable mess of stickiness and dust"? The comestible epitomized for the writer the plight of the English unemployed, the poor, hard-working classes after World War I, and to no small degree symbolized for him the idea that the class system should be quickly overthrown. (Memorable in the novel is the dwelling for single miners described as overcrowded and dirty and how the owner, who never washes his hands but butters the bread his borders eat, always leaves on each cut slice a large black thumbprint). One may also inquire of Ms. Morris, as an alternative to her jelly problem, if she ever took the effort to make her own marmalade. "*Bought* marmalade? Oh dear, I call that very feeble," wrote Julian Fellowes in his *Gosford Park: The Shooting Script*, and we hear the same sentiment echoed in a squawk by the Dowager Countess Violet (Maggie Smith) on television's *Downton Abbey*. I will mention as an aside here that Anacreon, the Greek lyric poet (582-485 BC), who wrote chiefly in praise of love and wine is said to have died at the age of 85, ironically, as the result of choking on a grape stone, or so says Pliny the Elder. Was it the result of his gluttonizing on grapes or distastefully rushing them down?

I was briefly acquainted with a Jewish guy back in graduate school, a haunted and unhappy but well-read history buff, who refused to eat—was entirely revolted by—marmalade, as it was specifically the promise of free bread and marmalade that was cynically offered by the Nazi military officials to all the Polish Jews gathered in the summer of 1942 at the Umschlagplatz, the square in the Warsaw Ghetto in German-occupied Poland as part of "Operation Reinhard," only to be herded onto crowded freight cars that were destined for "resettlement" at Treblinka, the most terrifying of all the concentration camps. It turns out that an uncle of this particular college acquaintance of mine had fought in the 1944 uprising in that city, and he had bitterly lived to tell his impressionable nephew about his hatred and horrors of the experience, not excluding the mere mention of that fruit preserve.

I am ironically, paradoxically, reminded in the hateful trickery of the Nazis, oddly enough, in the wonderful but didactic children's book, Madge A. Bigham's *Sonny Elephant* (1930) which Miss Steeves read aloud to us in second grade, as we all sat prim but excited in our little seats. In the story, the innocent young elephant makes friends with the wily gray monkey, and the gray monkey leads him into trouble by telling him about a story of free food, which proves to be bait for an elephant trap. It turns out that Sonny's parents are also trapped, and they are trained by the small elephant man's son to perform their tricks on the Caliph's feast day. There is more than a touch of the sinister "Operation Reinhard" in that book, I fear.

There is also a message here being told to children regarding free food. The shortcut invariably offers a downfall in the Aesopian and/or fabulous world. Dr. Urbino, a character in Gabriel García Márquez's *Love in the Time of Cholera*, is served a dish that has been cooked by a callous, somewhat indifferent new housekeeper. The knowing doctor pushes the dish back completely uneaten and declares, "This dish has been cooked without love."

Adolf Eichmann. Attila the Hun. Bernarr Macfadden. They were driven men and monomaniacs. But the strange focus of hating bread seems to be an offense against life itself. As to that food aversion, there was the breadless old harridan, overwhelmed with kids, who lived in a shoe who took a whip to them.

> There was an old woman who lived in a shoe,
> She had so many children, she didn't know what to
> do;
> She gave them some broth without any bread,
> She whipped them all soundly, and put them to bed.

Mother Goose Rhymes are 60% about food aversions—or at least deal with appetites being thwarted. The senses matter greatly to children—no bedtime story revolving around a child being wet, hungry, cold, etc. can possibly fail. Being hungry is surely a major motif throughout, and having that hunger thwarted its ancillary theme. Think of Jack Sprat and his wife. The farmer's wife who savagely cut off the tails of the three blind mice gives off more than an aura of kitchen menace. Without a penny, Simple Simon never tasted a pie. After Mother Hubbard could not find a bone for her dog in the cupboard, it was all over, and though she subsequently went on to buy the creature some bread, tripe, fruit, he ignored her. I recall when I was a child my mother reciting to me and my brothers, "In marble walls as white as milk," while trying to spoon an egg into me ("…lined with a skin as soft as silk, / within a fountain crystal clear, / a golden apple doth appear; / no doors there are to this stronghold, / yet thieves break in and steal the gold"), but I must add it never made me want it. Also, remember, those who like pease porridge hot will not eat it cold. Fairy tales often codify our deepest fears and, in that, awaken in children many a dream from the collective unconscious. In some cultures, hunger is actually considered an emotion.

Attila the Hun never ate bread in his entire life. It was fare fully repugnant to him, considered the food of peasants, and unfit for a fighting man. He ate only raw meat and drank mares' milk. Raw meat was methodically tenderized by the Huns by being placed between the thighs of the horsemen and the sides of their horses and carried that way. Roman delicacies and strange dishes were abhorrent to Attila, who, legend has it, also never hid his anger or dislike of the Romans who apparently added to his already murderous personality by mocking both his manners and the ferocious, primitive look of the barbarous youth. The "Scourge of God" is described in the *History of Byzantium* by Priscus, the 5th-century Greek historian and Roman diplomat, as short, swarthy, broad-shouldered with a flat nose and a sparse beard. Historian C.V. Wedgwood writes, "The monkish chroniclers of later times enlarged on the ugliness, strangeness, and violence of this heathen people and their terrible king."

It is surely revealing, regarding the diet of the Huns, to know that, according to scholar Robert N. Webb, it was regular practice for these tribes not only to kill off the old men of their tribes but also to eat their bodies! They were barbarians from the steppes of Asia and wild and primitive as the woods. When Attila was born he was snatched from his mother's arms only minutes after his birth, according to Webb, and his father, Mundzuk, king of the Huns, stood by as a waiting warrior slashed the baby's small cheeks with a sword, whereupon the boy was handed back to his mother. It was the Hunnish belief that each and every male child must feel a wound before being permitted to receive nourishing milk from his mother, on the assumption that the feeling of pain, tasted early, would make him a bold and fierce warrior. Attila would drink only from a wooden cup, affected the coarse and simple dress of a herdsman-warrior, scorned every nicety, always wore his sword unadorned—unlike many of his fierce warriors who used gold and silver goblets, the loot of the imperial provinces, and had gems on their belts and sword hilts—and supposedly never smiled.

I suspect that Virginia Woolf disliked jelly, held it to be a common preserve or confit. "One has to secrete a jelly in which to slip quotations down people's throats—and one always secretes too much jelly," she wrote. It stands in such contrast to those vital, free-spirited, sumptuous scenes in Leo Tolstoy's descriptions of jam-making in the novel, *Anna Karenina*, which evoke that splendid world where a well-laid tea table was always filled with several varieties. In Ivan Bunin's memorable story "Sukhodol," so many different kinds of jam are offered at a fancy tea that it is impossible for the guests to taste them all. Woolf could never have been so lighthearted, never mind about jams or jellies, but about food in general. She was plagued by food demons. We have already described how nervous, how madly jittery she was. That seems to have been her main mode of approach. There is no question that Woolf's food aversion was a strategy of protest. Struggling with mental illness, even decades before she sadly walked into the River Ouse in 1941 to drown, she reverted in her despair to the harshest extremes of anorexia and deplored food itself as dirty and damaging. She suffered from a bad body image and spoke of the "sordid mouth and sordid belly demanding food," all repulsive matter in her mind, which must be excreted in a disgusting fashion. The only course for her was to refuse to eat. I remember a phrase of hers from *Mrs. Dalloway*: "...her soul rusted with that grievance sticking in it"

Writer Graham Greene, who disliked tomatoes, comments on it in his story, "Cheap in August," where he points out with disgust that Americans in Jamaica with vulgar indiscrimination seem to eat them with everything. Incidentally, President Ronald Reagan—hating tomatoes—went 70 years without ever eating a single one, and I have this on the direct authority of his wife, Nancy, who personally told me so at a partry one evening at Gloria Vanderbilt's. How ironic that it was during the Reagan administration ketchup was regarded as a vegetable! This sad if farcical judgment which was actually proposed by US Department of Agriculture (USDA) Food and Nutrition Service regulations early in Reagan's presidency, intended to provide more "flexibility" in meal-planning to local school lunch administrators coping with National School Lunch Plan subsidy cuts enacted by the Omnibus Regulation Acts of 1980 and 1981. Imagine, not small waifs in Maine or hungry little Native American kids in South Dakota, but fat, indulged, corrupt smooth-skinned, millionaire Republican Senators themselves dining out—in best bib and tucker—on ketchup sandwiches!

I have an astute and knowledgeable friend, Alec, who smokes pipes, collects exotic tobaccos, and feels perfectly fine about smoking. "Nicotine? The hell with it. *Tomatoes* contain nicotine!" he says. Alec is correct. Tomatoes, belonging to the Solanceae family, are found to possess a nicotine alkaloid called tomatine. There is a 7.1 nanogram of nicotine in a single gram of tomato. Findings show that nicotine levels decrease as a tomato ripens. We have pointed out that star quarterback Tom Brady follows his chef's advice about tomatoes: "So no tomatoes, peppers, mushrooms, or eggplants... I'm very cautious about tomatoes. They cause inflammation."

"I hate tomatoes in spaghetti sauce [!]" actor Danny Aiello told an interviewer recently. "I can't stand anything chunky [in it]. And no onions. My mother made me a sauce, the best, it was smooth. It had the consistency of ketchup. I hate anything that looks solid in sauce." (We will discuss comfort food and mothers anon.) "You've probably noticed that modern super-market tomatoes are inedible," wrote the humorist Dave Barry. "This is because they are not bred for human consumption. They are bred to be shipped long distances via truck, which requires that they have the same juicy tenderness as croquet balls. Even as you read these words, top vegetable scientists are field-testing the Tomato of Tomorrow, which can withstand direct mortar fire and cannot be penetrated by any known kitchen implement except the Veg-O-Matic Home Laser Slicer (Not Sold in Stores)."

The anti-tomato faction may be missing something. Tomatoes contain lycopene (from the Latin word *lycopersicum* [lit. "wolf's peach," from its red color similar to deadly nightshade as a mythic summons for wolves and werewolves] for the tomato species name), a powerful antioxidant. Its bright red carotene and carotenoid pigment and phytochemical can be found not only in tomatoes but in other red fruits and vegetables, such as carrots, red bell peppers, watermelons, plums, and papayas (but not strawberries or cherries). One study involving 47,000 men over ninety revealed that the subjects who ate at least four servings each week of tomato-based foods such as pizza or pasta sauce cut their risk of prostate cancer by 20 percent. Ten servings or more reduced the risk by almost half. But, here, let us not disparage strawberries. A fact is strawberries have more vitamin C than an orange!

Married to slugger Joe DiMaggio for nine months, Marilyn Monroe complained to her lover at the time, Hans Jørgen Lembourn, who later wrote *Diary of a Lover of Marilyn Monroe,* that the "Yankee Clipper" was "only interested in poker and baseball and TV—and spaghetti." Monroe came to despise that single food, even many years after divorcing the sports legend. (He had also managed to turn the poor thing into a confirmed alliumphobiac, as he often smelled of garlic.) Once in a motel in New Jersey, just after they arrived, she was hungry. "The luggage can wait," she said. She pouted. "I'm hungry. Bring whatever you can find in the restaurant. Just not spaghetti." The sexy actress had eaten enough of that stuff, more than enough, during her second marriage, even if it did last only 9 months. Was eating pasta a damned religion? In Joyce Carol Oates' novel about Marilyn Monroe, *Blonde,* her disapproving Italian mother-in-law complains to her son, the "Ex-Athlete,"

> In the kitchen it was true she tried hard. She meant well but she was clumsy. It was easier to take things from her and do them yourself. So she'd get jumpy and nervous, if you came near. She'd let pasta boil to a mush if you didn't watch her every second, and she was always dropping things, like the big knife. She couldn't do a risotto; her mind was always drifting off. She tasted something, she didn't know what she was tasting. 'Is it too salty? Does it need salt?' She thought onions and garlic were the same thing! She thought olive oil was the same as melted margarine! She said, "People make pasta? I mean—not just in a store?" Your aunt gives her a marinated hard-boiled egg out of the refrigerator and she says, "Oh is this to eat? I mean—standing up?"

Notice that Marilyn Monroe refers to "spaghetti," as doubtless DiMaggio always did, while Joyce Carol Oates perfunctorily writes of pasta. The food was not always called pasta, the sort of semi-snobbish but of course now widely accepted and liltingly generic term that we use today. Back in the Middle Ages, the many and various forms of noodles—flat, thin, tubular, bent, inverted, curved, thick, round, etc—went under the all-encompassing word, "*maccheroni*." In her travel book *Italian Days* Barbara Grizzuti Harrison notes, "Pasta was not a word we ever heard in Italian Bensonhurst; my brother calls it a designer name for 'macaronies,' and he has a point."

A "*mangiamaccheroni*" was Neapolitan slang for a person who bought pasta from street vendors and ate it with their fingers. Street kids eating spaghetti with their fingers on the streets—holding plates and, head full back, dropping whole fingerfuls of it down their gullets—were a featured image in cheap postcards and old prints of the late 19th and early 20th century. It was not much better—the reputation of pasta—in late 18th-century England when Dr. Samuel Johnson pejoratively defined vermicelli as "a paste rolled and broken in the form of worms."

Consider, beyond that, the phrase is always "spaghetti and meatballs"—you never hear the phrase "pasta and meatballs," right? A *meatball* has always had goofy connotations, also being an Italo-American term for a stupid, clumsy, or dull person. I have heard it used as well for a fat person; a ridiculous pitch in baseball; and a general "loser." Meatballs are rarely if ever eaten in polite society, for one thing. For another, there has always been something odd or *déclassé* about meatballs as a food, "something not quite *comme il faut*," explains John Thorne in *Outlaw Cook*, who with a kind of gentle and loving pity refers to it as "a food with a permanent culinary refugee status stamped on its passport" and observes,

> They [meatballs] confuse us by being vulgar and delicate all at once, and a little defiant besides. Originally made mostly of sinew and gristle and the least bits of meat and fat, meatballs were willed into existence by determined eaters whom fate had denied any right to meat, but who themselves determined otherwise... Meatballs are a dish of the aspiring poor and the displaced genteel—and especially, the food of artists, students, dreamers, and other malcontents who have taught themselves to wear their poverty with a flourish. In the meatball they find an insouciance that matches their own. What is a meatball, after all, if not a triumph of quick wit over brute reality?"

We have mentioned Ernest Hemingway earlier as craving meat. When he was older and much grumpier, he often bitched about the interminable amount of times that his fourth wife, Mary Welsh, served him spaghetti at their house, Finca Vigia, in San Francisco de Paula, at least according to Norberto Fuentes in *Hemingway in Cuba*. I have no doubt that Hemingway had eaten a whopping great deal of Italian food during his European years, certainly Spanish food in the 1930s, French food in Paris, and so on, but it is a good bet that he had grown tired of such ethnic cuisines over the years. On the other hand, how positive can one be about old Papa's taste in good food when you learn with some shock that, toward the end, his favorite sandwich consisted of merely olives, mayonnaise, and thick onion slices? Photographer Alfred Eisenstadt saw him devour a bowl of raw onions, a favorite meal of his. (Mussolini also gobbled dishes of raw garlic. "I couldn't go anywhere near him after that," his wife Rachele confided to the family cook. "At night I let him sleep alone and took refuge in one of the children's rooms.")

Papa wrote in his big-game hunting memoir, *The Green Hills of Africa*, "I did not mind killing anything, any animal, if I killed it cleanly, they all had to die, and my interference in the nightly and the seasonal killing that went on all the time was very minute and I had no guilty feeling at all." Were his diminished food options at the end of his life possibly an emergence of those guilty feelings he claimed never to have?

Forget Papa on spaghetti. What odd aversion for it prompted the almost psychotic salvo against pasta by Patrick Leigh Fermor in his "An Apology for Gluttons" (*Horizon*, January 1963)? It is one of the great rants by Britain's greatest travel writer—he walked the length of Europe, lived to the age of 91, although he smoked 80 to 100 cigarettes a day —and is a splendid example of a polemic where classic wit meets hyperbole, to say nothing of cultural insight. "The most convincing example of the influence of food in national character is Italy. Look at Italian art. Pasta wrecked it!" declares Fermor, who saw it as torpid food. "Some say it was imported from the Orient by Marco Polo. Others that an old woman discovered it in Naples in the time of the Holy Roman Emperor, Frederick II of Hohenstaufen, the *Stupor Mundi*, in the words of 13th-century chronicler, Matthew Paris. Cimabue and Giotto and Duccio lived on dried fish and polenta and beans and black bread and olives. And you can't picture Dante eating spaghetti, or Amico di Sandro wolfing ravioli down. They lived on hardtack from the *trecento* to the Renaissance, you mark my words."

> Then pasta ascuitta came. It must have taken a century
> or two to conquer Italy, spreading from the south

like a clammy and many-tentacled monster, smothering Italy's genius on its northward journey, and strangling its artists like the serpents of Laocoön. Thousands of seething dripping tongues of macaroni squirming and coiling up the Apennines, gathering volume every mile, engulfing towns and provinces and slowly subduing the whole peninsula. The North held out heroically for a while—there is no pasta in those banquets of Veronese—and the last stand was at Venice. The rest of the country lay inert under its warm and slippery bonds—slippery, perhaps, but still unbroken today—while Tiepolo held out, and Longhi and Guardi and Canaletto, the last lonely frontiersman of a fallen Empire.

Such asceticism was too good to last, according to Fermor, continuing a lament as keen in his disappointment as if over the fall of Rome.

But one day some treacherous dauber must have swallowed a streaming green yard or two of tagliatelle—the end of the enemy's foremost tentacle, you might say—and, hotfoot, the rest of the huge, victorious monster came coiling into the Veneto and reared itself for the kill. And then, wallop! A billion boiling tons of pasta fell on the town, and the proud city, the sea's bride, with her towers and domes and bridges and monuments and canals, went under. The piazzas were a tragic squirming tangle of spaghetti and lasagne, the lagoon ran red with tomato sauce. Italy's genius was dead, laid low by her own gluttony...not only Italy's painting, but Italian thought and poetry and literature...and even Italian architecture. Everything was turned into macaroni.

A last observation on Italian food. We instinctively but erroneously associate Italy—and all Italians—with food like tomatoes, pizza, and songs like "Come Back to Sorrento," "Lazy Mary,"and "Eh Cumpari." We have these, for the most part, half-assed and received images mainly from the areas of Southern Italy, which back then constituted the largest immigrations. Most immigrants came from the areas of Calabria, Puglia, Sicily, and Campania. In

Boston's North End, for example, one finds mainly Avelinese, in New Orleans Siciliani, and around New Haven most Italians came mainly from Amalfi. There is, strictly speaking, no pan-Italian identity. Northern Italians who are often called "*Polentani*" because their food interests are focused mainly on a polenta-risotto-related cuisine. "Certain Gucci-Pucci-Armani Italians have told me that they have never eaten spaghetti and meatballs," writes Jim Harrison in *The Raw and the Cooked*, adding with something of a broad-brush exaggeration, "Tuscans look down on the Calabrese and Neapolitans in the same way that New Yorkers regard poor white southerners." But about spaghetti-and-meatballs he is essentially correct. He goes on to say, "These Cerruti aristocrats [sic] tell me that the dish is an American perversion of Italian cuisine." Of course regional differences involve regional tastes. It is true, many Northern Italians were never much interested in anchovies (popular with Sicilians) or pesto sauce (popular with Ligurians) or pizza (popular with Neapolitans), nor were they familiar with a lot of the slang or corrupt expressions that by way of dialect crept into (Southern) Italo-America usage, like the vulgar "Cend'an" (*cento anno*) or "pasta fazool" (*pasta e fagioli*) or the utterly misapplied and inauthentic word "gravy"—good God!—for *salsa*, the indiscriminate use of which would have personally made my (maternal) Italian grandparents, Alessandro and Angelina (neé Calesa) Dittami—respectively from northern Piacenza and Chiaveri—utterly cringe.

An anti-garlic slur—a food aversion that embodies an anti-Italian slander or slight—occurs in the movie, *It's a Wonderful Life*. Fearful that his Building and Loan will be forced to shutter, George Bailey appeals to flint-hearted Henry Potter, Bedford Falls' richest resident and largest shareholder in the company. Potter denies George's plea, mocking him in the process for "playing nursemaid to a bunch of garlic-eaters"—a reference to Guiseppe Martini, whose family had been helped by George's Building and Loan get a new house. At the time, this was a crude anti-Italian smear and encapsulated an opinion shared by many Americans. The movie was released in 1946; just at the close of World War II, when US officials had made 600,000 Italian "resident aliens" carry on their person proper identification cards, while placing hundreds in internment camps. The irony is that the film was directed by Frank Capra, who was born in Sicily but at age 6 moved to Los Angeles.

It goes without saying that regarding food Italians, just like people from any other country, follow their own bliss. My Italian grandmother would never serve tortellini in sauce, but always and only in *brodo*. "Italian food in New York means Mama Leone's with its monstrous gross loads of spaghetti, and not the pasta-less refinements of Bologna and Milan," wrote Anthony Burgess. It is a vulgar cliché, like Chico Marx's dopey accent, the go-to

Hollywood gangster-name "Rico," those ripped wife-beater t-shirts, and the idea that every living Italian on the planet is mad for pizza, subs, and spaghetti and tomato sauce. Burgess points out, "The Milanese [among many others] scorn the tomato, preferring a patrician white diet."

After World War II, under the occupation of Japan, Americans, particularly G.I.'s, living in Japan, came under strict food laws, as levied by Gen. Douglas MacArthur and SCAP (Supreme Commander for the Allied Powers). "Indigenous" (i.e., Japanese) food could only be eaten if it was bought in shops, taken home, and cooked by buyers themselves, for they were not allowed to enter Japanese restaurants. It was done under MacArthur's orders, not only as a sanitary precaution (dysentery was rife in the early days), but also to forestall any charge of exploitation of the occupied people, who were poor, hungry, and short of food. Japanese were not allowed to go into soldier's PXs or any US commissary. (Nor could they attend G.I. movies, carry G.I. money or shop at foreign traders' stores or even in the Imperial Arcade.) Many soldiers, facing Japanese food, were not particularly interested in trying it, out of bias, suspicion, and plain distaste. A fear of unfamiliar tastes—geumophobia—pervaded their thinking. Country singer Loretta Lynn, who had to eat so many of them so often on the road in her earlier show-business life, has come to hate sandwiches—of all sorts, just name one and it will disgust her. The very idea of them, their whole frame of reference to them, puts her off. Sandwiches in any shape or size, regardless of content! It is never inconsequential to see how childhood, the way one is brought up, effects later attitudes adults have toward food. Actress Katharine Hepburn was given an allowance by her domineering father not only as a child but even as an adult and celebrated movie star; he paternalistically doled out to her her very own money, money that she herself had earned, up until the day he died. It is manifestly clear that he trained his daughter well. With her New England good-sense and a touch of frugality, even parsimony, Hepburn claimed never to have eaten in a restaurant in over sixty years—"too expensive," she declared even in later life. "Can't bear to pay the prices. Can't bear to see anybody be dumb enough to pay the prices," she told *Esquire* magazine (December 1983). One might add here that it was a well-known fact that Hepburn also suffered from a paralyzing fear of, and sort of snobbish distaste for, being observed. A big eater, she admitted to having a special fondness for Viennese chocolate, red meat and vegetables, and, as she said, "the second joint of a chicken leg." A woman who took eight showers a day, brushed her teeth with soap, wrote letters with no punctuation, thought freckled people funny-looking (she was one herself), believed marriage was not a natural institution, and never owned a dress or wore stockings, jewelry, or perfume, she had strict rules that in later life became the advice she gave to everyone.

Among some of the lead exhortations were: eat cooked fruit with your dinner, always avoid eating out, always please yourself—and don't put too much flour in your brownies. Her brownie recipe is well-known and often reprinted: lots of butter, lots of sugar, but only a *very tiny bit of flour*—apparently her one secret to the making of great brownies. She had a hard chin. I have always thought of Hepburn as a late Victorian or early Edwardian poseur, one of those lordly ladies with something of a chilling presence and an assumed grandeur, a dramatic need for isolation, and a penchant for visiting only close female friends for a late afternoon *thé complet*, which provided the perfect occasion for her to snap out her many opinions.

Gigantic meals virtually constituted a Victorian and Edwardian art form. At the famous John Greenleaf Whittier dinner given in Boston at the Brunswick Hotel on December 17, 1877 with William Howells, Ralph Waldo Emerson, Henry Wadsworth Longfellow, and Whittier of course, among the invited guests—Mark Twain was a featured speaker and supposedly gave scandalous parodies of the notable poets—the menu began with oysters on the half shell and proceeded with the phalanx of a dozen wines through two kinds of fish, *capon a l'anglaise* with rice and cauliflower, saddle of mutton, filet of beef, squabs, terrapin, broiled partridges on toast, and canvasback ducks, to *charlotte russe, gelee au champagne, gateaux varies*, and fruit. The coffee arrived some three hours after the oysters.

Victorian food was heavy and dull, at least according to the waspish, red-haired, balding, always dependably hovering Christopher Kimball of television's The Food Network. Disillusioned with the classic old Fannie Farmer cookbook/*vade mecum*, a book in its popularity that for more than half a century was to American housewives what *Goodnight, Moon* is to infants today, he tears down one of her most ambitious 12-course menus, a major dinner that he somewhat satirically sought to duplicate. The filling for her vigorous rissoles he judges "bland." The lobster *á l'Américaine* he flatly declares "a bit ham-handed." Fannie's venison he feels was accompanied by "lackluster" potatoes Lyonnaise. Her salmon recipe was "pedestrian;" the deep-fried artichokes, "heavy and pedestrian;" the goose stuffing "soft and boring." Even Fannie's grand finale of cakes Kimball he finds disappointing and "uninspired"—this from a cook who arguably may have single-handedly turned us into a nation of sugar junkies! With each course, Kimball becomes more critical and even fussier, sharply elbowing his way through her measured and treasured recipes until at last, dissing poor Fannie altogether, he proceeds to finish the feast with featured recipes from *The Epicurean*, an encyclopedic cookbook of over 1,000 pages written in 1894 by the French chef of Delmonico's Charles Ranhofer, with his own gourmandish pomposity.

Still, I agree, the mere act of reading a good many of those venerable 19th-century dinners—with their stacks of meats and game, heavy sauces, and buttery cakes—could make one ponder becoming a vegetarian!

Granted, Fannie went too heavy on heavy cream, offered a chapter in her cookbook, since dropped, queerly entitled "Filled Things," and did offer mystifying "receipts" such as "Barbecued Lima Beans" and "Cannelon of Beef," an atypical meatloaf in fact that frankly cost no more to prepare than regular meatloaf but tastes rather good. (I once bothered successfully to make it.) Fannie, a red-haired woman who had polio—she attended my high-school in Medford, Massachusetts—was concerned about her readers' budgets, as was Lydia Maria Child, the American Mrs. Beeton, who was born in Medford, where her house still stands. In her 1829 *The American Frugal Housewife* ("For Those Who Are Not Ashamed of Economy"), an improvised cookbook as well as a book on housekeeping, she encourages virtuous abnegation and in her pages advises her shoppers to use the cheapest cuts of meat: "calf's liver at 2-cents a pound." "Avoid green fruit pies ('dear pies,' as she calls them)," she writes, "because they take so much expensive Havana [!] sugar."

Fannie Farmer's recipes could be equally stark. Her recipe for succotash, for example, is "as brief as is blasphemous," according to the insightful John Thorne in *Simple Cooking*—"Succotash: cut hot boiled corn from the cob; add equal quantity of hot boiled shelled beans; season with butter and salt; reheat before serving"—and he goes on to put the boot in: "There is so much wrong here that it takes the breath away, but the revealing flaw is calling for the kernels to be cut from boiling-hot cobs: even cooks with hands heat-hardened from wood-burning stoves would balk at that. What I suspect is that this is a *pro forma* disguise that fooled nobody: Yankee families were treated to last night's left-over corn on the cob as this night's succotash, congratulating themselves on their frugality even as they gnawed away."

So I will yield to King Yolk of Eggville (my name for the fussy, ever-hovering, red-headed, snit-prone, bow-tied Christopher Kimball) whose dunderheadedly (and weird, oddly foreshortened) sad single hum—"*Mmm*"—is, embarrassingly, his sole response to whatever food he happens to like on TV's America's Test Kitchen, a strictly Z-type appreciation that in its feebleness surely must stand at the furthest platonic remove from that of Major Lance's, the American R&B singer, whose cool "flavorgasms" we remember from his 1964 Okeh hit, "Um, Um, Um, Um, Um, Um." (Language is by no means the first gift of the Test Kitchen chefs who universally resort to "*nice* and brown," "*nice* and crisp," "*nice* and thick," etc. to describe just about anything.) How ironic those dim little effusions from a man who at other times attempts to sound like Diderot! *Il lui fourre son chaque discours avec pompeux conseils et faits.* Who can say, maybe that muffled "hmm" represents orgasmic delight. After all, he is the man who once declared, "There is something about pleasure I find annoying."

I do have to agree with Kimaball that the old stand-by cookbook compiled by Fannie Farmer, "the mother of level measurements," does have some questionable recipes—the 1918 edition was the last edition of the classic completely authored by Mrs. Farmer herself—especially when one takes into account such recipes as "Calf's Head á La Terrapin ("cut meat from cheek in small cubes"), Cocoa Flummery, Pigeon Compote, Sweetbread and Mushroom Timbales, Salmon Loaf with Cheese, Carrot Ring (two pounds of mashed carrots with a surround of Brussels sprouts), Tomato Jelly Salad, an aspic that can be made with anchovy paste." She also furiously boiled coffee and called donuts "fried cakes." But I have always admired her and have written about her myself years ago in the *New York Times.* Farmer suffered from polio and was wheel-chair-bound the last seven years of her life. She went to Medford High School in Massachusetts, of which I am also a proud alumni, and taught at Harvard University, which for five years I myself did, but, more than that, Fannie was an early nutritionist who cared deeply for the sick and convalescent, believing that she would be remembered chiefly for her work in that field as opposed to her work in household cookery. Farmer understood perhaps better than anyone else at the time the value of appearance, taste, and presentation of sickroom food to ill and wasted people with poor appetites; she ranked these qualities over cost and nutritional value in importance.

Might it not be argued that Fannie Farmer was the first American cook of note? Why not? I wouldn't contest it. We all come out of a small, local world. I am certain that Saul Steinberg was serious when he argued that the first "large scale American painter" was Tom Sawyer when he painted that fence white in Hannibal, Mo.—"emblematic of the culture" noted biographer Deirdre Bair, writing "for me [Steinberg] believed that the premier school of American painting was not 'the Academy,' but rather 'the do-it-yourself House Painter school.'"

I suppose Kimball is due some credit for even looking in the direction of the old *Boston Cooking-School Cook Book.* Cooks and chefs whom one assumes are not shy in the ego department clearly do not read each others' cook books and all things considered remind me of the endlessly droning talking heads on cable—or "constituent" —television like the pathetic, pitiful, parochial Fox and MSNBC Networks who end up grotesquely talking only to themselves. Cooks ignoring each other? It is absolutely true. They are all competitive, combative, and weak on charity. They are as floral, as ornate, and as narcissistic as poets, with nobody vainer—and often with little reason. Ignoring each other is their forte. John Thorne writes,

> In all of Marcella Hazan's Italy there is no whisper of Guiliano Bugialli; in his Italy there is no hint of her—nor of Ada Boni, Elizabeth David, or Pellegrino Artusi. Generally, what these writers are saying to us is not 'here is Italian cooking as I have experienced it' (since part of that experience must have included the reading of cookbooks), but the very different statement of "I am Italian cuisine"—as if it had just welled up inside of them in some kind of spontaneous generation.

Are not all of these solipsists and unilateralists in one degree or another just plain food aversionists themselves? Writing about tians—the terrine named for the vegetable peasant dish in which it is served—Thorne highlights the ludicrous fact that from cookbook to cookbook it is alternately described as round (Elizabeth David), square (Roy Andries de Groot), rectangular (Julia Child), and oval (Mirielle Johnston)! He finds nonsensical the common cookbook exhortation, "eat with seasons," asking, "Are there any benighted souls left who have yet to learn that sweet corn, tomatoes, green, peas, and asparagus are best when just picked—ideally from one's own garden?" I suspect that spouting nonsense may be a cookbook hazard.

As to some oddball examples, consider some available today, like *Cooking with a Serial Killer, The Iguana Cookbook, Bad Bananas: a Story Cookbook, Cooking with Poo* ("*Poo*" means crab in Thai), *The Dead Celebrity Cookbook, Cooking for Cats, The Bacon Freak Cookbook* ("Bacon is Meat Candy"), *Any Bitch Can Cook, Ruby Ann's Down Home Trailer Park Cookbook, Cooking with Your Evil Twin, The Testicle Cookbook*, and *White Trash Cooking*.

There is a Nancy Drew Cookbook! Debuting in 1973, *The Nancy Drew Cookbook* mixed in a dash of mystery with a pinch of thematic recipes. Nearly half of the 111 recipes incorporate part of titles from the first fifty volumes of the Nancy Drew Mystery Stories—including the sinister *Double Jinx Salad*, the warm and toasty *Ski Jump Hot Chocolate*, and the mysterious *Haunted Showboat Pralines*. Remember, Nancy was a gourmet cook, among her other super-girl qualities. She was nothing less than a prodigy! At sixteen she had studied psychology in school and also spoke French. Along with being a fine painter, she was a skilled driver and was even adept at riding a motor boat. She was an excellent outdoorswoman, a sure shot, an excellent swimmer, a superb oarsman, an expert seamstress, and a fine bridge player. Nancy brilliantly played tennis and golf, and rode like a cowboy, danced like Irene Castle and, as someone said, "could administer first aid like the Mayo brothers."

Such impossible perfectionism must surely remain an *anti-example* to young girls. What was Stratemeyer thinking in offering us such a heroine? Such strained credibility—it approaches the marches of insufferability, really. I recall an instance of Drew's characteristic unbelievability when in one of the books she has (expertly!) frosted a cake with chocolate icing but then with the saintly restraint of the perfect girl is too good—too much in control—to *lick the spoon!* (I found the same ludicrous bullshit in the tendentious movie, *Marathon Man* when Babe Levy [Dustin Hoffman] in a final face-off with the melodramatically evil Nazi Christian Szell [Laurence Olivier], after taking possession of Szell's briefcase filled with stolen diamonds, walks him at gunpoint to a water-treatment plant in Central Park, where Levy demands that Szell eat the diamonds which he refuses to do and so ends up angrily throwing fistful after fistful of diamonds at Szell, which all fall through the grating platform into the splashing water below, a climax in which moviegoers are almost comically—and almost insultingly—asked to believe that his retribution is so pure and above greed that the Jewish hero would happily throw away a rare fortune of diamonds. Conveniently, Szell fatally falls on his own knife-blade, and, triumphantly, Levy walks out of Central Park throwing his gun into the reservoir and never looks back. *Suuuure—everyday!*)

Then there is Caroline Blackwood's sardonic *Darling You Shouldn't Have Gone to So Much Trouble,* which is, surprisingly, a cookbook. It was compiled by the jittery, alcoholic heiress who on a lark wrote to various celebrated friends of hers soliciting recipes of the comic and easy sort. The book is full of witty, often spiteful stories about people and replete with daft, surrealist dishes, contemptuous presentations, and "cheat" recipes and shortcut offerings, because of course the truly wealthy never lower themselves to cook. ("Cans must be opened and hidden before the guests arrive.") It is actually a snide, insolent, anti-working class, food-hating manifesto, mocking the housewife and her common toil. "Dishes that require her presence in the kitchen—that require her loving surveillance in case they burn, curdle, shrink or shrivel, or go wrong in some other unspeakable way, we cannot recommend," Blackwood snobbishly writes. Among some of the offerings she inveigled other British snobs to contribute are Roald Dahl's "Norwegian

Cauliflower;" Quentin Crisp's "Tibetan Workhouse Soup" ("boiled in an unwashed saucepan"), Marianne Faithfull's "Different Sweet/Sour Pork;" Lucian Freud's "Tomato Soup *au Naturel*," and painter Francis Bacon's "Thick, Fat Genuine Mayonnaise," which goes:

> Break the yolk of an egg on to a flat plate. Throw away the white. Use about 6 oz. to ½ pint of good olive oil to the yolk of egg. Stir vigorously. As soon as the yolk and oil begin to emulsify, the oil can be added more rapidly. This makes the best mayonnaise. If possible don't add vinegar, lemon, or mustard, just very little salt. The easiest way to separate an egg is to break it in your hand, let the white trickle through your fingers, and pull away the membraneous [sic]strings. If you use a large shallow dish, it doesn't matter so much if you pour in more oil than you intended since you simply tip the dish so that the oil slides away from the emulsion and you can scoop up as little as you like and carry on mixing (a large fork is best). Although a food processor and some some very fast blenders make perfect mayonnaise with a whole egg, for the hard-made sort even a touch of white means disaster.

Blackwood's peculiar book is cynical at bottom, showing she did not care much for anything or anyone, including, if not especially, herself. Anita Brookner reviewed the cookbook with contempt, writing, "This is corrupt food, food intended to impress, to deceive, even intended to inspire fear and loathing."

One of my favorite cookbooks is by Sir Kenelm Digby, the polymath who is credited with being the first person to note the importance of "vital air," or oxygen, to the sustenance of plants. His cookbook, *The Closet of the Eminently Learned Sir Kenelme Digbie Knight Opened,* was actually published by a close servant, from his notes, in 1669, several years after Digby's death. It is currently considered an excellent source of period recipes, particularly for beverages such as mead. By the way, Digby is also considered the father of the modern wine bottle. During the 1630s, Digby owned a glassworks and manufactured wine bottles, which were globular in shape with a high, tapered neck, a collar, and a punt. His manufacturing technique involved a coal furnace, made hotter than usual by the inclusion of a wind tunnel, and a higher ratio of sand to potash and lime than was customary. Digby's technique produced wine bottles, which were stronger and more stable than most of their day, and which due to their translucent green or brown color protected the contents from light. Today, brown bottles are favored by most reputable beer brewers for that reason.

"The more toppings a man has on his pizza, I believe the more manly he is. ... A manly man don't [sic] want it piled high with vegetables! He would call that a sissy pizza," bumptiously declared Herman Cain, briefly one of the Republican candidates for the presidential nomination in 2011, in an interview with *GQ* magazine. The remark, the grammar, and the several loony sentiments may give one a small idea how and why the head of Godfather Pizza (CEO from 1986-1996)—a womanizing, sexist, ill-educated black man who never held a single elected office—was a political rocket that briefly rose and flamed out so quickly in his comic if pathetic run for the job that it was little more than a joke.

A few summers ago, my wife Sarah and I ordered a Godfather's pizza when driving through Nebraska, for true Italian food not exactly Naples. I have to say it was insipid and unappealing at bite one. The cheese was sour, the crust hard at the edges and cardboard in texture. I was reminded of the scene in Vergil's *Aeneid* (Book 7) when, after finally reaching the shores of Latium, ruled by King Latinus, Aeneas and his crew sit down to tuck into what, I must say, sounds like pizzas or what could pass for them! "They sit beneath a tree and eat the wheaten cakes on which their meal is set." While all the Trojans are eating the cakes that they had been using as plates—trenchers, in fact—Ascanius laughs and cries: "Look, we are eating our tables!" As you may recall, that curious remark fulfills the dire prophecy of Celaeno, one of the Harpies, that the Trojans would not succeed in founding the city, their new Troy, until hunger had reduced them to gnawing their tables—a dark prophecy that had long terrified them. It is Aeneas who immediately recognizes the sign, however, and assures his companions that this place is their destined homeland. (Aeneas remembers another occasion, one we know nothing about, when Anchises, his father, had also told him that it was only when hunger had forced them to eat their tables on an unknown shore that they would be able to build their city.) It is not an end to their misfortunes, however. Aeneas is wrong. Their past misdeeds—like killing someone else's cattle and trying to drive off the rightful owners—have followed them into the new world.

Vergil's description of the "table-eating"—which to a degree echoed my own bout with Godfather's pizza—is ominously descriptive, as there is a touch of the frenzied and uncontrolled in the men:

Consumptis hic forte aliis, ut vetere morsus
Exiguam in Cererem penuria adegit edendi,
Et violare manu malusque audacibus orbem
Fatalis crusti patulis nec parcere quadric:
"heus, etiam mensas consumimus?" inquit Iulus.

They turned upon the thin cakes with their teeth;
they dared profane and crack and gnaw the fated
circles of their crusts with hand and jaw; they did
not spare the quartered surfaces of their flat loaves.
"We have consumed our tables after all,"
Iulus laughed.

(translation by Allen Mandelbaum)

The language suggests profanation, a Bacchae-like intemperance, and to any astute reader of the classics it brings to mind, as Virgil expected, the violation of Odysseus's men killing the "Oxen of the Sun" in that Greek epic, recalling the harpy Celaeno's prophecy, the polluted feast, and her terrifying words.

Our unique food preferences, while camouflaging one of our most elemental drives at the same time, define us by way of those very choices. What better states a human direction than what we choose to put in or—often with a hectoring bark—not to put in our mouths? The options here fit perfectly the role of signs as part of social life, of social psychology, and hence of general psychology. It plays into a semiology (from the Greek *semeîon*, 'sign') that stands as analogy, metaphor, and symbolism all at once. What may seem but a mask of arbitrary volition disguises a fixed face that is quite sharp, and a deeper truth, something emblematic of a bias that, upon examination, is fixed to our very self. "There's Jack—he hates Chinese food!" It is our "thing." One savors it and favors it and belabors it and owns what becomes part of our ipseity or particularity, in the same way that the big loud car stereo seems to represent the bulk of the owner's net worth. While it does impart in a prideful way a walking sense of being distinct from others, in the positive way that anyone's ego is reinforced by any defining fact, it can dominate us at its most extreme and make us feel bleakly different, like a bedwetter at variance with others. How odd that a food that one singles out to snipe can so imperil—even command—our self-absorption.

Although it may seem obvious, I find that a highlightable note on food aversions is that we hate food only for ourselves, that is, on our own account.

Does that sound foolishly redundant? My point is simply that it is honest to that degree and never done in behalf of others, in the way, say, that we may vote liberal to seem kind or smoke cigars to appear more manly or buy a Prius to want to seem "green." Our actions are curvilinear or oblique more often than not, like a knight's move in chess. "If women didn't exist, all the money in the world would have no meaning," wealthy shipping magnate Aristotle Onassis once strangely remarked, yet who would have ascribed to him such a romantic, almost troubadour-like notion, never mind point to it as his primary drive in amassing a fortune, his reason to be make billions?

Confessions tell us truth. It is what I have always valued in reading Charles Baudelaire who with his disinfecting insight and gloomy introversion—brave, ever immune to humiliation, unstable, melancholic, naïve, murderous, bold, terrifyingly candid—dared to revolutionize modern literature by being the first to write in his own voice without the pretext of a mask and leave us a record of inward transactions that were as daring as they were disturbing.

Food aversions, superimposed on us, illogically in many case, reach into the subject of biography. They bear complex histories, come to us by way of no end of battle-awful predicaments that are noisome, offensive, immobilizing, double-dealing. Ghastly poisons are made manifest to us as food. At least in our neurasthenia that is the way we see them, for who would deny that a crotchet against any particular food is borne of a private turmoil within us? Whatever the cause, its roots, the spoor it can be traced to, the intransigence is almost always writ large.

When an unnamed character is pestered by a character known as "Sam-I-Am," to sample a dish of green eggs and ham in Dr. Seuss's *Green Eggs and Ham*—he serves as the story's narrator but could stand for any dyed-in-the-wool food aversionist (although he is converted in the end)—the unnamed character flatly refuses, responding, "I do not like green eggs and ham!" He will flat out not eat them—he makes it clear. It is an archetypal manifesto of food refusal. He is resolute, inflexible, determined, resolved, steadfast, adamant, unshakeable, and unmoving!

> I could not, would not, on a boat!
> I will not, will not with a goat.
> I will not eat them in the rain.
> I will not eat them on a train.
> Not in the dark! Not in a tree!
> Not in a car! You let me be!
> I do not like them in a box.

I do not like them with a fox.
I will not eat them in a house.
I do not like them with a mouse.

Our iterations against whatever food is in question are, in the extreme, invariably the stammering by-product of a personal and complicated psychomachia involving that tenuous agreement with the mind and reality. The painful sensation of what we, how we, when we respond to what is unbearable in these instances can reach to repudiating what is blessed in the universe. I believe that in a Freudian way, it repudiates parentage itself on one level, invites our refusal—born often from deepest childhood memories—to have inscribed on us another's conviction, orders, that by way of bullying and totalitarian fiats loomed as threats, both unsupple and unsubtle. We must often exaggerate our dislikes to make certain they register, to be convinced they are heard. We badly need them to be felt. "I will not eat that" is a variation of Bartleby the Scrivener's *non serviam*. Atrocious experiences with food, which often go back to our earliest days are emblazoned on our consciousness like paint-blazes on a trail. How bad must one thing be that we are driven to spend a lifetime repudiating it, depicting it in our minds not only as discrediting us but virtually refuting us almost in the way that shame and humiliation do. Don Quixote fought such battles. We re-describe ourselves in every refusal of whatever unspeakable food we push away. Unspeakable melancholy fixes on trying to delineate the causes of it and the void it has instilled in us. An aesthetic of melancholy is constructed. Aversions literalize the withdrawal of ourselves from their brutal insistence. "It will vex a dog to see a pudding creep" goes a well-known apothegm, meaning that even a common cur would be revolted in seeing skin form on the top of a pudding. These are deep threats. It is sheer nightmare to ingest—to have to ingest— any vile, impersonating foods that in our hearts for no matter what reason we have denominated alien. Our impression is they suck! No alien object is more alien than the object we must eat against our wishes, in one imagined but nevertheless real, brutal, de-eroticizing gulp. It is fatal in its exactitude. Starvation in contrast is a blessing. Death itself would be preferred.

We fight not to worry, seek to catbriar any fears that threaten us. Does silage effect—produce—mediocre cheese? Why does chocolate become covered with an ugly white film after a few days? Doesn't hard sausage taste of decomposition? Why do all darkened vegetables seem so hideously revolting? Do chicken livers perspire? Parallelepipedal slices of cheese are all chalky, aren't they?

The suspicion of an anorexiant, pitting a lack of faith in food's value or goodness, is the direct opposite of the glutton's food worship, his table idolatry, which is more about the misguided direction of his soul than about the contents of his cupboard. Each fights the discipline of moderation. In Dante's *Inferno*, the "great worm" Cerberus guards the gluttons, who are forced to lie and loll in a vile, disgusting slush that has been produced by ceaseless, foul, icy rain. (Virgil obtains safe passage past the monster by filling its three mouths with mud). Is spite the converse snare?

Radical food phobics remind me of olive trees. Strange trees—short, squat, gnarled, and twisted—with dry misshapen trunks, snapping, fissuring, and cleaving with age and twisting and warping with heat, they yet have delicately tinted pale-green leaves. Their fruit is curiously full of oil, not juice. The species is fire-resistant, indestructible, deathless. They are immune to severe droughts, killing rosts, brutal heat, and show a marked preference for calcareous soils, flourishing best on limestone slopes and bitter crags. Suffering seems only to embolden them. (Think of Christ's agony in the garden: we get the name "Gethsemane" from the Hebrew words "*gat shem-anim*" or olive press.) As a matter of fact, where severe cold has damaged or killed an olive tree, the rootstock can survive by producing new shoots, which in turn become new trees; thus, olive trees can regenerate themselves. They grow slowly, can live for millennia, but, being cranky, seldom bear fruit two years in succession, and in many cases, in fact, a sizeable harvest occurs only every sixth or seventh season.

The food phobic is a true enantiodromiac (Greek, "running opposite"), an individual by self-assertion insisting on a principle of equilibrium, *his own*, proving by his position, no matter how extreme, that he must resist the system he faces in order to restore balance. A correction is inevitable, with the superabundance of any force inevitably producing its antithesis. It is a bold Heraclitean truth, where a dynamic motion that is set in spin has been generated notably by disparity and conflict. When things reach to their extreme, they inevitably turn into their opposite.

Still, we have the right to our impressions. We are entitled to our choices. Authority over ourselves allows us to march boldly past all predictable colors thrown at us in this brief life, while singing with Jenny Jenkins,

> *I'll buy me a foldy-roldy, tildy-toldy*
> *Seek-a-double, use-a-cozza roll to find me*

Roll, Jenny Jenkins, roll!

11.

WHY THE BRITISH ARE PECKISH

Auberon Waugh, a son of novelist Evelyn Waugh, in his memoir about his family, *Will This Do?* as a late teenager had the luck to be able to spend with a male friend of his about eight months in Florence, Italy. With the aid of some people of influence, they got to stay at a pleasant lodging in that lovely city where for a modest rent a huge lunch was provided everyday, as well, "usually piles of spaghetti followed by [sic] meat balls." So generous was their landlady/owner that they could not eat all the food she gave them and so they would "wrap up large amounts of it in newspaper and hide them in a cupboard for later distribution through the streets of Florence." "Seeing our plates empty, she would give us more and more of this revolting food until the cupboard almost collapsed under the weight of the greasy bundles." Revolting food. It was not the quality of the food that they so disliked, notice, it was the *commonness* of it. This, mind you, from a callow British 17-year-old spending time in Italy living on a free stipend of $600 a week—in 1957, no small sum—"quite literally doing nothing," a person having been raised on the kind of slop typically served in the refectories of British public schools! Waughs, of course, all of them, were notorious snobs and would have had a long punch-list of complaints even if they had been given front row seats in the Heavenly Kingdom itself. I believe that British food snobbery, wherever it appears—often in novels—is more often than not a form of indirection, dissembling, if you will, mainly blameshifting, as a way of defending national pride.

"There was greasy toad in an equally greasy hole, and a bacon and egg pie so dry and powdery that it was like eating a crumbling 17th-century wattle and daub cottage," wrote David Nobbs on the grim food he and his fellow students at Bickley Hall were forced to eat during the war years.

I remember sentences from Evelyn Waugh's *Brideshead Revisited* in which, among other things, there is an unfeeling scene of monstrous indifference when a duck is strangled in a duck press: "We ate to the music of the press—the crunch of the bones, the drip of blood and marrow, the tap of the spoon basting the thin slices of breast." This is the occasion where Waugh recounts a meal with Charles Ryder and Rex Mottram, who is engaged to Julia Flyte. Rex is suspect in a number of ways—he is Canadian, ambitious, a self-made man—but he and Charles want the same thing, to be accepted into the family circle at Brideshead, and their status as outsiders is cunningly portrayed in the scene of this meal. As they converse, we hear statements and encounter attitudes that are all at once arrogant, condescending, haughty, ostentatious, overbearing, insecure, rude, and patronizing all at once: "You know, the food here isn't half bad; someone ought to take this place up and make something of it" and "The sole was so simple and unobtrusive that Rex failed to notice it" and one contesting exchange that is particularly memorable for its snobbish ugliness: "I like a bit of chopped onion with mine," said Rex. "Chap-who-knew told me it brought out the flavour." "Try it without first," I said. "And tell me more news of myself."

British public (i. e., private to Americans) schools come in for a lot of abuse regarding what John Lanchester in *The Debt to Pleasure*, refers to as "stodge," a grim fare of "inept nursery food, hostile saturated fats and and intentful carbohydrates. (There is a sinister genius in the very name Brown Windsor Soup.)" We have referred earlier to Lanchester who in the novel cited laments public-school food. His vivid and somewhat shockingly un-prepossessing descriptions of noisy. sharp-elbowed schoolboys at greasy tres-tle-tables having to gobble down "unabashed gristle floating in a mud-colored sauce whose texture and temperature were powerfully reminiscent of mu-cus" echoes accounts that one has read elsewhere in Cyril Connolly, George Orwell, and no end of tidy English autobiographies and memoirs.

"There is an erotics to dislike," Lanchester explains, pointing out how a food aversion can give us definition by separating us from what is outside us, setting a person apart from the world "in a way," as he says, "that mere banal liking cannot." He quotes epicure and gastronome Brillat-Savarin who stated rather obviously, "Gourmandism is an act of judgment, by which we give preference to those things which are agreeable to our taste over those which are not." To like something is to want to eat it and in doing so to submit to the world, to adapt, to conform, in short, in Lanchester's dramatic words: "to like something is to succumb, in a small but contentful way to death." The "erotics of dislike" he speaks of, on the other hand, can be a negative revelation of such strength, he suggests, that it often hardens in a discerning young individual the already burgeoning suspicion that one's aesthetic (in what he calls an "artists's nature") separates one from one's alleged fellow men. It is a rebellious, Promethean side in one that dares to dislike. Liking a given something gives little distinction.

But dislike hardens the perimeter between the self and the world, and brings a clarity to the object isolated in its light. Any dislike is in some measure a triumph of definition, distinction and discrimination—a triumph of life.

An epiphany comes to Lanchester's protagonist, Tarquin, in *The Debt to Pleasure* who sees in the "defining moment" of his development a newly acknowledged luxury that he can be different to follow his taste, choosing

> France rather than England, art rather than society,
> separation rather than immersion, doubt and exile
> rather than yeomanly certainty, *gigot á quarante gous-*
> *ses d'ail* rather than roast lamb with mint sauce. "Two
> roads diverged in a wood, and I, I took the one less
> traveled by / and that has made all the" [important
> word coming up] "difference."

The British, long plagued by belittling comparisons, tend to have an invidious—often paranoid—view of French food. The history of their divergent tastes bristles with tension. Waddesdon Manor in Buckinghamshire, built for Ferdinand de Rothschild in 1874-1889 and constructed in the tradition of the châteaux in the Loire Valley, is a good example of untranslatable taste. It was bequeathed to the British National Trust, along with all its art and objects by James A. de Rothschild in 1957, and although the furniture, tapestries, carved wooden paneling, etc. was refined and valuable, the manor itself was generally deemed "hideous." "*Le Goût Rothschild*," describes a detailed, elaborate style of interior decoration, which had its origins in France and Germany during the 19th- century. The decorative interior elements of "Rothschild taste," which from a modern perspective inevitably has a distinct pejorative connotation to it, include lavish use of extravagant heavy textile fabrics (like brocade, damask, and velvet), the use of gilt, elaborate stucco ceilings, and rare, valuable (and often antique) wooden paneling and parquet flooring. French food, which is characterized, not only by regional variations, but cream sauces, braises of beef, wine, bacon, onions and carrots, liberal use of cheeses, all sorts of fresh produce like apples, berries, haricot verts, leeks, mushrooms, and various squash and stone fruits, flaky pastries and desserts, and of course intricate preparations and an array of great wines, has set a standard that has been praised as a cultural nonpareil throughout the world.

I experienced more than my share of dodgy British food, living there off and on as I did in the 1960s. Beyond my comprehension was the idea of someone eating pork pies out of plain volition. I would happily throw in Scotch eggs, jellied eels, pork pies, calves feet, crubeens, oxtails, sea-snails (or whelks), greasy sausages, eel pie, stale Cornish pasties, baps and buddies, jam and cream sandwiches, and haggis, a savory pudding containing sheep's pluck (heart, liver, and lungs) minced with onion, oatmeal, suet, spices, and salt, mixed with stock and traditionally encased in the animal's stomach, a Scottish food, by the way, not a British, although historians insist that it came to Scotland in a longship from Scandinavia. I learned to drink tea and love it when I was living there, because I agree with the late comedian Fred Allen who said, "English coffee tastes like water that has been squeezed out of a wet sleeve." Brussels sprouts in Britain are cooked down to a virtual soup— Brits insistently boil their veggies to mush—which bleaches them even of their color (Dickens refers to "the national dread of colour" in *Our Mutual Friend*), and I found their porridge, pottage, or gruel to be almost always stodgy. At Oxford University, Charles L. Dodgson (writer Lewis Carroll), a formal steward of the common room, was in the words of critic Michael Sadler "the most prolific malcontent ... ever on the *qui vive* for negligence on the part of the college servants or minor inconveniences affecting his own comfortable life... He not only complained that too much milk was always being sent up with his breakfast"—was he to be charged for it?—"but also specifically 'negatived' cauliflower because it was always badly cooked." I daresay, the author of the *Alice* books meant *overcooked*!

"The English fear, not emotion, but reason; they mistrust, not poetry, but intellect; Nature they love, and to Hell with art," wrote British journalist Dilys Powell in her well-known essay on Alexander Pope, and I suspect in that wide category of art she would certainly include English cookery.

Back in the late 1960s in London, the hamburgers in the Golden Egg and Wimpy chains were as hard as pucks and served in brittle, over-crisped buns, shaped like a half-closed hand, that were all as dry as a Bedouin's sandal. No American could identify—never mind eat—one of them. Mushy peas or Brussels sprouts are to a British meal what diamonds are to Manhattan's 47th St., a commodity virtually defining the place. I recall seeing fried snails served with porridge to which a bunch of green herbs (I forget which kind) had been added. I daresay anyone's taste buds would be sorely tried if he or she had been brought up from an early age on kedgeree or a staple of hard vinegar on crisp chips. How different than the Mos burger in Japan—

short for "Mountain Ocean Sun"—which, considered the best burger sold anywhere in the world, is, according to British writer, Christopher Ross in *Mishima's Sword,* born of the Japanese genius for *kaizen,* "continuous refinement."

Which is not to say that food snobbery in England doesn't exist. At the very beginning of John Galsworthy's novel *The White Monkey,* we find tidy Sir Lawrence Mont, Ninth Baronet, on a mid-October afternoon in 1922 haughtily passing the Remove Club, that, to him, antediluvian home of Liberalism. We read that he "set his fine nose toward the east wind, and moved his thin legs with speed. Political by birth rather than by nature, he reviewed the revolution which had restored his Party to power with a detachment not devoid of humour." His privileged thought is about food. He thinks, "Some sweating into shoes, there! No more confectioned dishes. A woodcock—without trimmings, for a change!"

As to British insularity and their attitude toward France, including cookery, one recalls the derogatory jape, "The wogs begin at Calais!"

Back in 1969 when I was given a Fulbright Grant to England, I was living in London in Mecklenburgh House, near Russell Square, the halls always reeked with the revolting school-food odors of stale fish, mushy cabbage, Brussels sprouts, gluey potato soups, and a fetor of chicken-stock scum that disembogued into every room. (Yale Commons always smelled of mushroom-barley soup.) English journalist William Connor's dislike of turkey was legendary. "The turkey has practically no taste," he wrote in the *Daily Mirror* on December 24, 1953, "except a dry, fibrous flavor reminiscent of a mixture of warmed-up plaster of Paris and horsehair. The texture is like wet sawdust and the whole vast, feathered swindle has the piquancy of a boiled mattress." Nothing can quite match in eloquence, however, his description of cabbage as cooked (!) in the English manner against which he fulminated in his column (using the *nom-de-plume*) "Cassandra" in the *Daily Mirror* (June 30, 1950):

> Boiled cabbage *à l'Anglaise* is something compared
> with which steamed coarse newsprint bought from
> bankrupt Finnish salvage dealers and heated over
> smoky oil stoves is an exquisite delicacy. Boiled British
> cabbage is something lower than ex-Army blankets
> stolen by dispossessed Goanese doss-housekeepers
> who used them to cover busted-down hen houses in
> the slum district of Karachi, found them useless, threw
> them in anger into the Indus, where they were recov-

ered by convicted beachcombers with grappling irons,
who cut them in strips with shears and stewed them
in sheep-dip before they were sold to dying beggars.
Boiled Cabbage!"

All cooked vegetables at Mecklenburgh House were not merely boiled but boiled down to what was more or less a viscous, liquid state. One could easily tell from half a block away from the building that broccoli or cauliflower or Brussels sprouts was being served for lunch or dinner or that some kind of stew was on the boil. I am not now and have never been a fussy eater but must confess that I almost always passed on such stuff, wondering whether such food was reliable or not, while my young British colleagues gleefully slurped it all up as if it were a *crayfish velouté* served at posh Alain Ducasse at The Dorchester. "Skim off the scum." That phrase. It is one of those memorable phrases that you somehow manage to come across in just about every published cookbook, and, while "scum," as such, does indeed appear to be the one cooking by-product for which no one has ever truly and honestly found a secondary use—as Michael Tucker wittily observes in his *I Never Forget a Meal*, "I have yet to see, 'Set scum aside for that little risotto tomorrow'"—British kitchens do seem to have a lot of the stuff on hand from what they broadly refer to as cooking. *La ragougnasse*! Could this be one of the reasons why so many folks in the UK are always hungry? The British—or the "Islanders," as James McNeill Whistler, the American-born, British-based artist and a mocker, always referred to the British—seem always peckish.

Vladimir Nabokov who matriculated at Trinity College, Cambridge from 1919 to 1922, seems to have the same response to an academic British refectory as I did. We read in his "The University Poem:"

The naked benches stretched along
the naked tables; there we sat,
in the black cowls of brothers' capes,
and ate the over-seasoned soups
made out of pallid vegetables.

At that time, the Russian novelist in his spare time was writing light verse ("I sit, I fit together rhymes") both in English and his native tongue, some of which he translated—it was a lifetime snipe of his, sexism at its most extreme, that a good translation of any work could only be done by a man, never a woman —and playing lots of tennis. He was oddly spoiled and incompetent.

Nabokov never acquired the skill – or cared – to use a typewriter and never learned to drive a car.

As to British eating, it was not long before I learned the drill. Across the pond, there is no such thing as iced tea. (Tea is only drunk hot.) In my day, you could not buy a decent ice cream cone in London. They do not use HP sauce—our A1—on steak, but rather with a full breakfast (or "fry-up") where, along with eggs and back bacon, they also fancy servings of fried bread, tomatoes, baked beans, mushrooms, often kippers, and a variety of side dishes, not excluding at times pilchards, herring, or leftover vegetables from the main meal of the day before. What a line-up! Was that any worse, however, than what peripatetic Henry David Thoreau found waiting on his table one morning, as described in his sand-gritty chapter "The Wellfleet Oysterman" in his memorable travel book, *Cape Cod* (1865): "At breakfast we had eels, [stale] buttermilk cake, cold bread, green beans, doughnuts, and tea"?

A British breakfast for the gentry was once another thing entirely. At a typical Edwardian country house breakfast around 1910, if you were "week-ending," you would find the wealthy guests "coming down at intervals to tables, all lit by rows of spirit lamps, that offered a tempting grouping of all sorts of food," as Harold Nicolson notes in *Small Talk*, "fat hams, tongues, galantines, cold grouse, pheasant, partridge, ptarmigan"—no Edwardian meal was complete without ptarmigan—"and a delicate little rectangle of pressed beef from the shop of Mr. Benoist." On another table stood fruits, jugs of cold water and lemonade, and the next with porridge utensils, and on yet another table pots of coffee and of tea (with yellow ribbon indicating Chinese and red for Indian). Nicolson's portrait of snobbery and culinary, sartorial, and social excesses ends: "Nor, when all is said and done, can one forgive the Edwardians for their fundamental illusion. For it never dawned on them that intelligence was of any value."

Only truly improper Edwardians in country houses breakfasted in their rooms. Old tried and tired rituals were followed time in and time out. Food was usually eaten cold. "To want the food to be hot seems to have been a 19th-century refinement," according to Mark Girouard in *A Country House Companion*. Nicolson, again, in *Small Talk* gives us an inside view, writing,

> Edwardian breakfasts were in no sense a hurried proceeding. The porridge was disposed of negligently, people walking about and watching the rain descend upon the Italian garden. Then would come whiting and omelette and devilled kidneys and little fishy mess-

es in shells. And then tongue and ham and a slice of
Ptarmigan. And then scones and honey and marmalade. And then a little melon, and a nectarine or two,
and just one or two of those delicious raspberries. The
men at that stage would drift (I employ the accepted
term) to the smoking-room. The women would idle in
the saloon watching the rain descend upon the Italian
garden.

Solid meals presented as such do not seem to please the British as things
like finger buffets, fork suppers, sausage roll do's, canapés or *vol-au-vent*,
"life with the crusts off," as English wit Alan Bennett puts it. I recall attending a good many of these little events, when I often left feeling a bit
peckish. Eating habits depend on all sorts of memories, good and bad, and
grow in all sorts of bizarre directions, of course. On the British talk-show,
A Taste of My Life, Bennett told host Nigel Slater that, growing up, he had
always been shy of eating in public—something that he shared with concert
pianist Glenn Gould, incidentally—a hang-up stemming from his mother's
insistence, mortifying him, "on smuggling in their own bread and butter
while eating at a fish-and-chip shop." His boyish fear was that they would
be arrested. He also admitted that until he got to Oxford University, he had
never "eaten out at night."

Rules—procedure—is quite important in Great Britain. I was once cor-
rected for eating a scone with honey, because apparently in England scones
must be eaten only with clotted cream and strawberry jam. But it gets even
more refined. To eat a real scone correctly (with or without currants), one
must properly cut it in half, you see, and spread the jam on each half, top it
off with the cream, and enjoy it with a cup of tea. No other method is permitted or forgivable. This in a country where people seem to despise pasta
(they like quick-cooking Quaker macaroni, "ready in seven minutes"); gobble jellied eels and winkles, a form of sea snail; eat bacon roly-polies which
is a pastry filled with bacon, onion, sometimes suet; crave a ghastly, sticky,
dark brown food paste called Marmite ("Love it or hate it")—the processing
of which is top secret—love a sweet/savory suet pastry called a Bedfordshire
Clanger; and where most of the children are fond of tinned luncheon-meat,
fried, and indeed regard luncheon-meat curry as a treat! No, food in the UK
can be grim. The further you are from England, as Lewis Carroll's Carpenter
stated, the nearer you are to France.

Oh, there are all sorts of British provincial dishes, many of them comfort foods that joyously ring the bells of locals! Blaad, Bedfordshire clan-

gers, Parkin, Fadge, Scouse, Covach, Soor Plooms, Parmo (a cutlet in breadcrumbs) Claggum, Rag Pudding, Berwick Cockles, Snoodle, Clod, Buckings, Solloghan, Water Souchy—a dish consisting of small fish stewed and served in a little water—Oon, Rumbled Thumps, Haps, and Yarg, a semi-hard cow's milk cheese made in Cornwall.

How about their Cullen skink? Fizzy Vimto? Black pudding? Bird's Custard Powder? Jammie Dodgers' biscuits? Batchelor's Marrowfat Peas? Tiptree Green Fig Jam? Haribo's Licorice Wheels? Cameron's Banger Rolls? Curate's Pudding? Quosh Squash Mix? Tommy Moloney's White Pudding? Bulmer's Woodpecker Cider? Stargazy pie, a Cornish dish made from pil-chards, eggs and potatoes baked within a pastry crust, the main feature of which is that a bunch of sightless fish heads poke like spears through the top of the crust and appear to gaze upward? Then what about their delicious slices of "butter pie" in Britain? Remember the song, "Uncle Albert" by the Beatles and those wonderful lyrical lines,

> Admiral Halsey notified me,
> he had to have a berth or he couldn't get to sea.
> I had another look, and I had a cup of tea and a butter
> pie.

Being invited to tea in England—afternoon tea, that is—you will find ham, tongue, cucumber, fish paste, smoked salmon, mustard and cress, scones (with clotted cream and jam), and usually cakes and pastries, such as Battenberg cake, fruit cake or Victoria sponge. I always saw a plate of ginger-snaps. High tea there, also known as "meat tea," an evening meal or dinner of the working classes—a hot dish, followed by cakes and bread, butter and jam, and occasionally ham salad or cold cuts of meat—is eaten later, typically eaten between 5 pm and 7 pm, and is something else entirely. Americans find their tastes and their combinations odd. Mushy peas go with fish and chips on which they sprinkle vinegar. The parson's nose is the tail of a chicken. Their rump steak is our sirloin steak, and so on and so forth.

And one must not forget anchovy paste!

There is that whimsical exchange between Bertie and Jeeves in P.G. Wodehouse's novel, *Joy in the Morning* (1946), in which, incidentally, there is a good deal said about the craft of fishing, which goes,

> "Only a tin of anchovy paste, sir."
> My heart sank a bit. Anchovy paste is a slender reed
> on which to lead in a major crisis. Still, it was fish

within the meaning of the act, and no doubt contained its quota of phosphorus.

"Go and wade into it."

"Very good, sir."

"Don't spare the stuff. Dig it out with a spoon," I
said, and dismissed him with a moody gesture.

To the noble Lion of Common Sense and Unicorn of Fancy as the stalwart heraldic symbols of the United Kingdom, I must admit that I have often
thought that to them should be added the Dodo—flightless, goofy, slug-
gardly, obsolete—as a symbol of their cooking incompetence. No, regarding
food, I tend to agree with Henry Miller's remark in *The Cosmological Eye* on
the English and England, "It is a sort of fish-world which is completely alien
to me."

The British positively love huge tins of shortbread cookies. Their biscuit tins are presented, gift-wide, in all shapes and sizes: Royalty keepsakes,
chests, bookshelves, cars, lunchboxes, etc. and the assortments vary. I have
mentioned above several of Vladimir Nabokov's many crotchets. In his short
story, "Lance," in the process of fictionally attacking the many hackneyed clichés of popular, vulgar magazines he goes out of his way—somewhat surprisingly, perhaps arbitrarily—explicitly to disapprove of these cookies. Nabokov
(metafictionally intruding into his narrative) singles out to spurn especially
the platitudes in science fiction, finding in them among the worst, most art-
less aspects of all cheap reading matter. He writes,

They are like those "assorted" cookies that differ from
one another only in shape and shade, whereby their
shrewd makers ensnare the salivating consumer in a
mad Pavlovian world where, at no extra cost, variations in simple visual values influence and gradually
replace flavor, which thus goes the way of talent and
truth.

One must assume Nabokov hated shortbread cookies, butter cookies,
Christmas cookies, tea cookies, hob nob cookies, ginger snap cookies. He
was famous for listing his gripes, but I've never found mention of cookies.

I will add that I came to like their Lancashire hot pot, Cornish pasties, Bulmer's Woodpecker Cider, ginger biscuits, Tiptree blackberry jam
with toast and brioches, handy Oxo vegetable cubes, Guinness Brown
Sauce, Rowntree's Fruit Pastilles, Beefy Bovrite, McVitie's Plain Chocolate

Digestives, Duerrs Fine Cut Seville Orange Marmalade, Fortt's Original Bath Olivers, but, most of all, wine gums, the best little sweets in the world. Lamb in Britain is superb, their roast beef (grass fed) being much tastier than ours, and they have delicious mutton, which seems to be almost uneatable in the United States. I savored (and tried to keep handy) lots of bags of fruit pastilles, lemon humbugs, dolly mixtures, boiled sweets, malt balls, black jacks, licorice allsorts, jelly babies, wheels, chocolate buttons, pear drops, and sherbet fountains, and I enjoyed their Aero Bars, Fun Dip, and Cadbury Wispas.

I also thoroughly loved all British custard tarts, both the small ones in cups you could find in the old Lyons Corner Houses which have long vanished—my favorite was located near Charing Cross Station—or larger ones, like those big delicious-looking pies being served in Pieter Brueghel's canvas *Peasant Wedding*, which I believe are medieval cheesecake custards or a variation of what I believe was called *vladen* in the Middle Ages. America has no equivalent of these British tarts, a tidy, small circular wodge of dry pastry around the rim, its wobbly custard center sprinkled with nutmeg on top, and—I love the moist under-crust of a pie—that soggy fillip of pastry at the bottom. It all went swimmingly with a cup of tea.

In his essay "In Defense of British Cooking," by the way, George Orwell claims that he could never find in other countries crumpets, Devonshire cream, dark plum cake, saffron buns, kippers, and Yorkshire pudding.

No, I promise, there is an England I love, believe me. Shakespeare's England. Milton's England. Spenser's England. The rollicking days of Chaucer. The Albion of poets and novelists. The England of bleak, inky skies; of J.M.W. Turner light; of steam or yellow mist; of rural Maldon, Ashurst Wood, and Dorset; of driven partridges; of dark hammering rain; of lighted cheerful pubs and old stone churches like miniature cathedrals serving so few; of each tiny village tightly buttoned into its private life. I became content, even after those bad meals at London House, by making up for them later by eating what Brits call a "butter shag," a few restorative slices of fresh bread and butter. I can happily add here that in general dairy has always been fresher in England than anywhere else on earth, let's face it, and unlike everywhere else you can have a wide choice of much better cheeses simply because the British are neither fanatical nor brainlessly paranoid about pasteurizing absolutely everything. (Everyone knows that the best cheeses are made with unpasteurized milk.) My question? Will bloaters ever be served in the USA? Or brawn? Or buisson of crayfish? Or blackbirds in a pie? Or baps and buddies? Bangers and mash? Bubble and squeak? And that is only the B's!

There is much antagonism brought against British food by many of its greatest writers, from Tobias Smollett to Quentin Crisp, from Jonathan Swift to Alan Bennett, from P.G. Wodehouse to Anthony Burgess.

The drama critic Kenneth Tynan gloomily stated, "Distaste, disdain, revulsion—the nouns of withdrawal, of contact rejected or scorned—these evoke the characteristic behaviour of only one country. They are the nouns of England." Much of that man's life of course was filled with obloquy, and after all he did write, "A bedwetter, I soiled my mother, and she punished me by refusing to feed me." "I would not growl over most of the dishes one is offered in British households," wrote fey, feline-loving Beverley Nichols, not a lover of English cookery, in his *Cats' A.B.C.* "but I would certainly growl over caviare." Nichols is here defending any cat's right to growl whenever it wants, a habit he feels should be adopted to "greatly enliven human dinner parties," as well. The eccentric author in this small book advocates, among other things, always leaving a small piece uneaten on one's plate as a sign of grace and also stresses the crucial importance of seating arrangements at table—that there are certain places where one wishes to dine—suggesting in its vital importance that one's appetite may turn on such a thing. "Many of us have probably attended dinner parties in Paris where there have been frightful froideurs about procedure, when some obscure but legitimate count has threatened to leave the room because he has been placed in an inferior position to an equally obscure, but bastard, marquis." A food aversion may play into any number of quirks or quodlibets.

There is no shortage on the subject of British eccentrics and food, trust me. British essayist Charles Lamb was a Swiss Army knife of food aversions—from the fundamental (vegetable, veal) to the relatively insignificant ("Butter ill-melted—that commonest of kitchen failures—puts me beside my tenor.") In one of his controversial essays, "Grace Before Meat," Lamb wrote,

> I am no Quaker at my food. I confess I am not
> indifferent to the kinds of it. Those unctuous mor-
> sels of deer flesh were not made to be received with
> dispassionate services. I hate a man who swallows it,
> affecting not to know what he is eating. I suspect his
> taste in higher matters. I shrink instinctively from one
> who professes to like minced veal. There is a physiog-
> nomical character in the tastes for food. C——holds
> that a man cannot have a pure mind, who refuses ap-
> ple-dumplings. I am not certain but he is right. With

the decay of my first innocence, I confess a less and
less relish daily for those innocuous cates [delicacies].
The whole vegetable tribes haved lost their gust to me.
Only I stick to asparagus, which still seem to inspire
gentle thoughts.

Lamb took perverse delight in being profane. It was thought by many that he was mentally unstable. (He had spent some time in a mad house in Hoxton.) He was poorly groomed, seldom shaved, drank excessively, abominably stammered, and was described as having odd eyes. He abjured good manners. Spiritual to a degree, he hated organized religion and looked for any occasion to undermine it. He gasped and sputtered when he spoke, was melancholic, and fidgeted, quibbled, and quacked. Flagrant acts of infantile wickedness recommended themselves to him. He once pulled Wordsworth's nose with impunity, saying, "Now, you old lake poet, you rascally poet, why do you call Voltaire dull?" Robert Lynd in his essay on Lamb, observed,

He used to like to force his way into the Misses
Norris's school at Goddard House, and make discipline impossible, teaching the girls a new version of
the Church catechism. He also took great pleasure in
teaching a small girl to say the Lord's Prayer backwards. Devoted though he was to children, he did not
hesitate to propose a toast of the 'm-m-much ca-ca-
lumniated good King Herod' on one occasion, and in
the same mood he wrote approvingly of the Massacre
of the Innocents.

In the attention given to the ritual of eating, especially in thanking God, Lamb found wretched excess. "We sit too long at our meals, or are too curious in the study of them," he wrote. Saying grace at table particularly irked him. To him, the act added "hypocrisy to injustice." He refused to grasp why the blessing of food should have "a particular expression of thanksgiving annexed to it," and went on to inquire in "Grace Before Meat," "Why have we none for books, those spiritual repasts, a grace before Milton—a grace before Shakespeare—a devotional exercise proper to be said before reading the *Fairy Queen*?" He grizzled, "Gluttony and surfeiting are no proper occasion for thanksgiving. When Jeshuron [a poetic name for both the land and the people of Israel] waxed fat, we read that he kicked. Virgil knew the harpy-nature better, when he put into the mouth of Caelano [one of the Harpies] anything but a blessing… When I see a citizen in his bib and tucker, I cannot imagine it a surplice."

Why is English cookery reputedly so bad? Surely no one can say with any final authority, if it is indeed true in the first place. Say it is a mystery, just like their fall foliage—why is fall scenery so dull in old Albion? A sad fact is autumn leaves in that country never appear in the bright colors of, say, New England in the fall. The deep October forests there—the general scenery—are curiously flat, subdued, and oddly muted, which is something of a puzzle or conundrum. Could it be because of the relative dampness there, the fog, the rain, the smoke? Am I mistaken—is it their eccentricity—or do the English always seem to come in on a slant? How about their stubborn refusal, for example, to pronounce any foreign words accurately—as I have said, they say "*pitza*" for "pizza and "*Dew-bonnet*" for Dubonnet. The Swiss diplomat Carl Jacob Burckhardt claims that he had once heard Adolf Hitler say, "It is a great sorrow to me that I have never met an Englishman who speaks German well enough for me to feel at ease with him." There is a willfulness to the British that seems born of their insularity. They seem always to find *one way*, approve it, and never vary. What else explains the stupidity of their treatment of the Colonies in the 1770s?

While a major consumer, the United Kingdom remains only a very minor producer of wine, with English and Welsh wine sales combined accounting for just 1% of the domestic market. At the inn of the Golden Cross, young David Copperfield in Charles Dickens's novel tentatively samples a wine that "had more English crumbs in it than were to be expected in a foreign wine," and all the while seems not to reckon that there was a good local alternative to drink.

The British love to use warmers to keep the food warm for as long as they can, as well, I mean for *days*, which cannot be good. They tend to boil everything when they cook. Meat served in the British army, which was notoriously bad, was almost always boiled. In the late 1870s, boiled meat was referred to as "Harriet Lane," this being the name of a woman hacked to pieces by the savage murderer, Henry Wainwright, a brushmaker who murdered his mistress and then buried her body in a warehouse he owned. Brits rarely deign to employ spices or any vivid succulent flavoring in their cookery. Cauliflower cheese, anybody? Baked beans and tomatoes and toast for breakfast? Fish and chips in a newspaper wrapper? Compare their tame offerings, for example, with certain audacious and elaborate French dishes such as *jarret de porc* (back of a pig's knee), *oeufs brouilles* (befogged eggs), *joue de boeuf* (bull's cheek), and *ris de veau* (calf's thyroid). Fruits that grow well in warm weather (citrus, peppers, etc.) are of course harder to find fresh in

Great Britain. Alas, England has long had a bad cooking reputation. Spartan is a watchword there regarding food. Speaking of Spartans and food, remember the notorious "black broth" soldiers there took to prove their toughness? It was composed of pork stock, vinegar, and salt. No, boldness in the kitchen is not an English virtue. "My, I get so depressed after a poor meal; that's why I can never stay in England for more than a week," wrote Julia Child to Avis DeVoto on January 30, 1953.

When he was a youngster, novelist J.G. Ballard had spent time in a Japanese prison camp, when in early 1943 they began to intern Allied civilians. Ballard was sent to the Lunghua Civilian Assembly Center along with his parents and younger sister. He spent over two years, the remainder of World War II, in that internment camp. The wartime food they were fed was deplorable. "The Japs could hardly feed *themselves*," Ballard told Martin Amis in his book of essays, *Visiting Mrs. Nabokov.* "Why should they bother about an enclave of Allied detainees? These are the realities. We ate cracked wheat, warehouse scrapings, weevils. You'd shift the weevils to the sides and eat them last. I often had three rings of them on the edge of my plate." Amis asked, "What did they taste of?" He replied, "They don't taste of anything, funnily enough. Absolutely nothing. We had to eat them for the protein."

I mention all of this simply because, returning to England from Shanghai, while living with his grandparents, the young Ballard attended the Leys School in Cambridge, England, a co-educational school noted for its academic excellence that is still flourishing. Ballard described the school to Amis, saying the school was "just like camp, only the food was worse."

John Cleese in his autobiography, *So, Anyway...* writes of his parents' taste for generic British food as presented. He writes,

> The highest praise for food (other than hotness)
> [from them] was "plain." There was a hint of xeno-
> phobia here: the unspoken purpose behind English
> cooking was that the results should not damage you.
> Vegetables had to be boiled to death, because good-
> ness knows what could be hiding in there, ready to
> pounce on you; meat and fish were more demonstra-
> bly dead, and so safer, but they still required the *coup
> de grace*. The sight of someone eating a steak *tartare*
> would have occasioned a call to the Samaritans.

"British food" jokes, many insist, are a relic of WWII and are a bit silly now, even strained. There were the deprivations of two consecutive world wars, when people learned to live with less—almost nothing—took a tre-mendous toll on its citizens—boiled meat, oatmeal in the morning, canned Spam (if they were lucky)—after which it was very difficult to go back to a fully developed cuisine. It was a desperate time back then when folks had to plant seeds and grow vegetables in flowerpots, random tubs, even around the moat surrounding the Tower of London. There was no butter, no meat, no sugar, no eggs. War forced people to eat mock meals and create dubi-ous preparations like "Beet the Cold," "Sheep's Head Broth," "Pigs Feet in Jelly," "Carrots on a Stick" (instead of ice cream) and "Eggs None for Breakfast," a platter of tinned apricots cooked in bacon fat and dressed out to look like eggs on toast! No, the British memory cannot soon forget the Second World War and the servings one faced day in and day out of whale-meat, snoek, Woolton pie, monkfish, and other dubious conversions that they were forced to put on the table in the 1940s. Even those lean years of strain, austerity, cheese-paring, and belt-tightening that followed the war when food was still rationed and the palate was rarely rewarded will not soon be forgotten. A more significant fact to be considered, perhaps, is that a good many British homes did not have stoves until the first quarter of the 20th-century. Traditionalists, the people forbore and stayed with their open fireplaces, and consequently British food in the main was boiled, stewed or something that could be put on a fork and toasted over the fire.

The war years were grim in Old Blighty. Rationing was introduced at the beginning of 1940. The first nine months of 1942 were the worst for depri-vations. Eggs, cheese, onions, oranges, luxury fruits and vegetables were vir-tually unobtainable. For more than six years no tropical fruit was seen in England. Housewives had to queue for even essential foods. The English ate dehydrated mutton and whatever corned beef could be scared up—meat rations were stretched with oats—and lived mainly on potatoes, carrots, sprouts, turnips, artichokes, and thin watercress. Lemons and bananas were treasured objects. An acute shortage of fish was the result of closed fishing grounds, which were now used for mine sweeping. "Condensing food was the key to keeping Britain fed," notes Lizzie Collingham in her compre-hensive *The Taste for War*. Custard powder and starchy things like rice and tapioca could be had at intervals without "points." The taste of dried banana powder, dried coffee, and processed cheese were reportedly unspeakable. Collingham writes,

> The British stubbornly continued to use egg powder
> to make omelettes and scrambled eggs. "The two
> words which still make my blood run cold are DRIED

EGG," wrote Jill Beattie, who was at a boarding
school during the war. "The very worst breakfast...
was a two-inch block of hard scrambled egg oozing
with water which saturated the half slice of so-called
toast beneath it—and the TASTE—ugh!"

William Trevor's less than savory reveries about food in the Irish boarding school that he attended inform several sections of *Excursions in the Real World*. In mid-morning, he writes, all gathered for

a tumbleful of soup. It was a yellowish colour, with
globules of grease floating on the surface. Chunks of
potato and turnip sank to the bottom, and an excess of
barley made the mixture difficult to consume: you had
to open your mouth as wide as you could and tip the
tumbler into it, feeling sick while you do.

"We used to get food parcels from the United States, which for some reason always took the form of cling peaches," wrote Jonathan Miller in his witty essay, "Among Chickens," which addresses many of his boyhood food memories. "I don't know what the Americans thought we were suffering from—massive cling peaches deficiency presumably," he writes. "For children in immediate post-World War II Britain, disliking food was hardly a choice," my good friend, Peter Gwynne, scientist and *Newsweek* columnist on science explained to me:

Rationing of already scarce resources meant that
youngsters always ate what was put before them, good
or bad (and probably bad more often than good in
my case; my mother readily admitted that she hated
cooking). Certainly lacking from my family's diet was
any variety of cuisines. My maiden aunt, Doris, expressed a view held by many Britons at the time when,
confronted by a plate of spaghetti Bolognese, she said:
"I won't eat any of that foreign stuff."

Peter went on to clarify his own tastes:

More than sixty years later, I have a stronger recall
of foods that I enjoyed in childhood than those I

disliked. My family expressed skepticism about the lunch of cold fried fish with salad that my Church of England primary school served on occasional Fridays, but it always delighted me. So did the stuffed hearts that my mother cooked—well, in both senses of the word—as a Sunday roast, the mention of which appalls my American wife.

Any particular aversions he might have developed? I asked Peter.

Dislikes? Well, tripe represented a food that, on the infrequent times my mother served it, guaranteed failure to join the "clean plate club." I imagine that it's quite tasty when cooked properly, but I've never had the gumption to try it. Equally inedible was a lunch concoction that contained eggs and unidentifiable ingredients in a somewhat oily sauce served at my secondary school. They called it curry, but any resemblance to Indian food was entirely circumstantial. By late 1966, when I arrived in the United States, I had become more catholic about food. Nevertheless, some of the old prejudices remained. I could accept the huge portions. But hamburgers have rarely struck me as appetizing. The McDonalds variety, in particular, is exceeded in tastelessness only by those that I try to cook myself. Two other foods seemed, well, strange. Corn, for example. As far as I knew, it was something that farmers fed to pigs. It took decades before I tried it and liked it. Then there was iced tea. Was it really different from stewed tea left in the teapot so long that it had become naturally cold? Eventually I found out that it was. But I still have difficulty with iced coffee.

Porridge often served as a standard breakfast before either of the great wars. I always had to laugh that in Robert Louis Stevenson's *Kidnapped* when young David Balfour, an orphan, goes to the ominous House of Shaws in Cramond, his devious uncle, Ebenezer, bitter that he has in his mind been cheated by David's father out of that house, serves what amounts to an all-day breakfast from a large pot of porridge which is reheated not only for lunch but also for dinner that same day! The orphans in Dickens' *Oliver Twist* are given nothing but a scrimp three-meal-a-day diet of thin gruel, a thinner version of cereal, boiled in water or milk. Dr. Samuel Johnson mocked the Scots for eating the very same food that their horses did.

A transition—an apt one—beckons. Meat rationing had begun in England on March 11, 1940, belt-tightening prevailed, and British troops were being sent abroad, to France, Denmark, and Norway. In view of the desperation at the time, a Mr. Branson, to whom I much prefer to ascribe patriotism than sheer lunacy, wrote the following letter to *The Times* of London on May 2, 1940:

> In view of the publicity you have accorded to Mrs. Barrow's letter, I hope that you will spare me space to say, as an advocate for the consumption of grass-mowings, that I have eaten them regularly for over three years, and off many lawns. The sample I am eating at present comes off a golf green on Mitcham Common. I have never suffered from urticaria or any of the symptoms Mrs. Barrow mentions. Nor did any of the many of my horses to which I have fed grass-mowings, freshly cut and cleaned from stones, &c. For my consumption I also wash them well.
>
> Yours faithfully, J.R.B. Branson

[A typical meal *chez* Branson: Lawn mowings mixed with lettuce leaves, sultanas, currants, rolled oats, sugar, and chopped rose-petals, with uncut rose-petals sprinkled over the whole.]

May one ask, what was a meal Branson typically served, *lawnmower sauce & leaf clippings as a peppery garnish?* (Almost all varieties of breakfast cereals, come to think of it, are made of grass.)

Most of the food even back in 19th-century Britain came in by way of horse-drawn barge, so ordinary folk, even the middle classes, were forced to eat a cuisine primarily based on canned goods (mushy peas), preserved meats (pressed pies), local sea food (whelks, eels, periwinkles), and root vegetables that did not need refrigeration (e.g. potatoes, swedes) which explains the basic chips. As far as eating meat went, people—children included—ate mainly mutton. It was a working-class favorite, as was bacon. Preference was given to cheese over butter, fish over meat, simply because they were cheaper. Smoking and salting helped preserve everything. Oysters were a popular food in Victorian times because they could be pickled to keep several weeks and salted so as to taste reasonably fresh. "Poverty and oysters always seem to go together," said the astute cockney Sam Weller in *The Pickwick Papers*, remarking of Whitechapel, where by the 1850s oyster beds had been virtually depleted, "... the poorer a place is, the greater call there seems to be for oysters."

I must go back several centuries to find my nomination for the indisputable *locus classicus* on the grimness of English food. I would point to the relentless, immoderate grousing contained in a June 8th letter from London to Dr. Lewis by the splenetic patriarch Matthew Bramble in Tobias Smollett's comic epistolary novel, *Humphrey Clinker*. Old Bramble writes,

> The bread I eat in London is a deleterius paste, mixed up with chalk, alum, and bone ashes; insipid to the taste, and destructive to the constitution... The same monstrous depravity appears in their veal, which is bleached by repeated bleedings, and other villainous arts, till there is not a drop of juice left in the body, and the poor animal is paralytic before he dies; so void of all taste, nourishment, and savour, that a man might dine as comfortably on a white fricassee of kid-skin gloves; or chip hats from Leghorn... It was but yesterday that I saw a dirty barrow-bunter in the street cleaning her dusty fruit with her own spittle... cherries rolled and moistened between the filthy and perhaps ulcerated chops of a St. Giles huckster.

Bramble rants about Londoners boiling their greens "with brass half-pence in order to improve their colour" and attacks the pork as "an abominable carnivorous animal, fed with horse-flesh and distillers' grains" and weighs in against oysters "kept in slime-pits occasionally overflowed by the sea." Strawberries are nothing but "pallid, contaminated mash... soiled and tossed by greasy paws through twenty baskets crusted with dirt," while the very worst milk ever drunk is "the produce of faded cabbage leaves and sour draff, lowered with hot water, frothed with bruised snails, carried through the streets in open pails, exposed to foul rinsings discharged from doors and windows, spittle, snot, and tobacco-quids from foot passengers."

Are not canned goods almost definitively abhorrent as to quality, taste, and freshness of food? Not necessarily. I say that by way of recalling Harlan Ellison's fanciful and extravagant post-apocalyptic sci-fi short story with the Dadaistic title, "I Have No Mouth, and I Must Scream." In this exotic story, set at a time after the destruction of civilization, paradoxically, canned goods are preferred to the disgusting meals served to the survivors who live together and try to seek out the "ice caves" where it is rumored the canned good are stored. Needless to say, the confounding fact of having no can-opener figures in the plot!

I mention potatoes. There were potatoes around in Shakespeare's boyhood, but they were rarely to be seen and very expensive. The Bard never mentions them. Neither does he mention forks, tobacco, or for that matter—out of self-conscious pique for his own lack of education?—the name of any of the venerable Oxford colleges or schools, not even *once*. His was apparently an entirely limited world as to produce. Versatile as it is, as much as three-quarters of a potato is water, and no doubt it stood bland as a bubble for the Elizabethans when it was brought over to the British Isles in 1586 by Thomas Hariot from Sir Walter Raleigh's lands in Roanoke, Virginia. (Could it possibly have been potatoes that he used as experimental substitutes—lighter and far more easily handed ovoids—when asked by Raleigh to find the most efficient way to stack cannonballs on the deck of a ship?)

The Bard never mentions carrots either, save one time when making a pun on the Latin word "caret." Vegetables back in Elizabethan days consisted of little but cabbage, leeks, and onions—no cauliflower, so spinach, no sprouts. Turnips and cabbages in his plays appear only once each. Staples for the Elizabethans were salt meat, salt fish, and wholemeal bread. In the 16th-century the winter diet seemed to be a murderous ally of the winter weather and depleted vegetable gardens. Mid-winter tables were ghastly. In consequence, there was a common deficiency of Vitamin C, with the result of a general affliction of scurvy in the populace.

It is somewhat surprising, Shakespeare's neglect of carrots. The plant appears to have been introduced into Europe via Spain by the Moors back in the 8th-century. The antiquary John Aubrey (1626–1697) in his little masterpiece, *"Schediasmata: Brief Lives"* (a favorite work of mine) does note, "Carrots were first sown at Beckington in Somersetshire. Some very old Man there [in 1668] did remember their first bringing hither." No English farmers knew their origins were in the Middle East. But how many of us today realize that the Cuban Sandwich, the English Muffin, German Chocolate Cake, Garlic Bread, the Fortune Cookie, and the Chimichanga—as Brandon Specktor points out in "Six Foods You'd Never Guess Were American" in *Reader's Digest* (Nov. 2015)—have their origins, not abroad, but respectively in Florida, New York, Massachusetts, Michigan, California, and Arizona?

I have always found British Christmas food—its mince pies, its stodgy puddings, its ominous cakes—often teeth-achingly rich and overpoweringly saccharine. As George Orwell once observed, you almost never find British food being served in restaurants, even in his day. You can find no end of international food in restaurants in the larger cities, Indian, Burmese, Chinese, Italian, Greek, and French, but generally speaking one comes across solid British food only in a British home. It is often repeated that "proper English food" is "diverse," you know, the old boast (calumny?) that Britain has absorbed the food of many other cultures. What has happened, however, is that

Britain has borrowed the food of many other countries and basically fobbed it off as its own national cuisine, which is, at least in the middlingly chiding if not reproachful words of Londoner Henry Hitchings in his book, *Sorry! The English and Their Manners*, "a blend of imperialism, insensitivity, incuriosity, and fear, passed off as justifiable caution." Are you aware that "Chicken Tikka Masala" is officially considered the third national dish of (drum roll) Jolly Old England?

Why does this come as such a big surprise?

There has never been an English royal house! William the Conqueror was a Norman, King Arthur a pure Celt, and the Tudor dynasty was a royal house of *Welsh* origin, descended from Prince Rhys ap Tewdwr. The House of Stewart (latterly gallicised to Stuart), was European, Charles II had not a drop of English in his purple blood, the Hanoverians were fat Germans, and Queen Victoria, who was the granddaughter of George II and an ancestor of most major European royal houses, was more German than Kaiser Wilhelm (whose mother was English)! If you really want to push it, Thomas à Becket was French, the Brontës Irish, the Rossettis Italian, and Adam Smith, David Hume, Robert Louis Stevenson, and Thomas Carlyle were all from Scotland, David Lloyd-George from Wales, and Sir Winston Churchill's mother, Jenny Jerome, part Iroquois Indian, was born in Brooklyn, N.Y.!

But how essentially sad and benighted is a dopey country with a national dish essentially consisting of one food?

British food, borrowed as it is, may be an improvement on Irish cuisine, which for centuries was based on the potato which arrived in the 16th-century, initially as a garden crop, and soon became the the dominant feature of the rural economy and main food of the poor, one that was supplemented with buttermilk. Potatoes, which were served in all sorts of ways, were also used to feed to pigs, to fatten them prior to their slaughter at the approach of the cold winter months. Baleful accounts of the starvation they faced in mid-19th century due to the potato blight are hair-raising. The desperate Irish poor became turnip-eaters, at best, devoured mangel-wurzel, a large, coarse reddish-orange beet grown as fodder for cattle, turnip-tops, sand-eels, seaweed, and lived month in and month out on rotten "boxty," potatoes scraped, reduced to pulp, dropped into a cloth, squeezed as dry as possible, and then flattened into cakes and baked on tongs over hot coals. That was fare for the lucky ones. A million people are said to have died of hunger in Ireland in the late 1840s, a quarter of the nation.

I would say that witty Flann O'Brien's scathingly satirical work, *An Béal Bocht* (1941), which was translated as *The Poor Mouth*, is the definitive potato novel. What brought down national wrath on the unwitting author's head was his suggestion that his unimaginative and indolent countrymen lived on a subsistence of little but potatoes and rainwater. He writes,

> —There's no fear for you, my soul! said Martin sadly, because there'll be a spud of mine for you while we've pigs at home and a pot boiling for them. You there, he said to me, over with you and get a big spud from the pigs' pot in my own wee cabin... I set off with a will and did not halt until I had procured the biggest potato in the pot and had brought it back to the place of famine. The man on the ground devoured the potato greedily and when he had swallowed the meal, I noticed that he had recovered remarkably from his ill-health. He sat up.—That was the tasty eating and I'm full up of thanks, said he, but you see I'm not so pleased to be begging from ye or to be leaving the pigs short.

Toward the end of the book, we are treated to the sententious chestnut—possible O'Brien at his most captious—"He who is threatened throughout his life with misery and is short of potatoes, does not understand easily what happiness is nor the management and correct handling of wealth either."

It seems almost a blasphemy under any circumstances to denigrate the common potato, which, functioning as the planet's most versatile vegetable, served as a staple for Peruvian cuisine to the battle-proof food supply of the Thirty Years' War to food for the entire Irish nation for a century.

Bridget Jones' Diary—well, at least regarding 32-year-old and single Bridget's cooking—does not do a lot for the reputation of British food, what with her caper berry gravy ("I have to say, this really is the most incredible shit") and "We have blue soup to start, orange pudding to end, and, well, for a main course you have, uh, congealed green gunge" and "Well done, Bridge, four hours of careful cooking and a feast of blue soup, omelette and marmalade. I think that deserves a toast, don't you? To Bridget, who cannot cook, but who [sic] we love." It is all summed up in the pithy, "Make coffee, consider grapefruit. Defrost chocolate croissant."

I spent much of three months wandering around Ireland back in 1966 and, despite the occasional meal of tripe soup, snaffles mousse, winkle omelets, pâté and egg aspic, pressed ox tongue, calves' brains in puff pastry, and jellied eels, cannot attest to all of the food being *bête et mechant*. I can recall having had lovely meals, for example, for mere shillings, of snipe pudding;

skate with black butter; a tasty dish called "rabbit rabble," a casserole of jointed rabbit with steamed potatoes; and in the Dublin suburb of Castle Knock enjoying a delicious "Dublin Coddle," a rich dish of green bacon, pork sausages, onion, and waxy potatoes. The desserts there I remember as fairly flat, but I must say I love Orange Fool and Guinness Cake.

Despite the elegant repasts and grand gastronomic feasts with which Charles Dickens regales us in his books, the great Boz was neither a big nor a fastidious eater, often serving up a chop or a piece of mutton to guests at his house on Doughty St. in London. His wife, Catherine, however, who to his great grief grew into a portly and somewhat indolent woman, did publish a slim, 60-page cookbook called *What Shall We Have for Dinner?* under the Restoration-sounding pseudonym, Lady Maria Clutterbuck, with a preface spoofing her husband's "great gastronomical experience." It is such dishes that one comes across here that makes one wonder why Dickens, who from all evidence was a tasteful diner, ever ate anything served from his wife's kitchen, given things like "potato balls," "Italian cream," "Pig's Jaw," "Lamb's Head," "Lark Pie," and other such delights as "Water Cresses" (which makes forty appearances in the book!), "more meals than one would have thought possible with bloaters," in the words of one unsympathetic reviewer, Margaret Lane.

Catherine's was a short book, published in 1851, which ran to five editions up until 1860. There are no surviving first editions, but a second edition of it was published. We all know of the sulfurous, scandalous public break-up of the Dickens' marriage. It is perhaps no surprise that there is not a single mention of the book by her husband in any of his correspondence. Catherine referred to her menus as "Bills of Fare" and generally offered what to cook for between "two to eighteen persons." Their baby, Dora, had died in infancy in April of the very year of publication, and it is conjectured that compiling her small cookbook provided a suitable distraction for the grieving mother. Catherine was buried in the same grave as her daughter Dora 19 years later. The novelist always ate modestly; a favorite dish was leg of mutton stuffed with oysters; and from all reports his weakness was toasted cheese. During banquets, Dickens diluted his champagne with water and drank beef tea at intervals between those killing dramatic public readings of his that eventually brought him low. Critic Penelope Vogler in an incisive article in *The Guardian* notes, "Jane Carlyle waspishly writes that the Dickens' dinner parties with their 'quantities of artificial flowers' and 'overloaded desserts' were too grand for a 'literary man.' She works herself to a pitch of excitement because 'the very candles rose each out of an artificial rose!' Good God!"

Novelist Anthony Burgess goes out of his way to denigrate Catherine Dickens' cookbook, noting that the heavy, heart-squeezing foods that this plump, heavy-jowled woman offered, great feasts of suet dumplings, mashed turnips and things like huge raspberry-jam sandwiches for puddings, are "paraded to surfeit with no allaying greens." Vogler herself shows most of the spreads to be rich, writing, "A typical dinner is a five-act drama, in which Catherine carefully orchestrates taste (turbot with lobster sauce and cucumbers in one course), textures (crisp little mushroom patties; emollient oyster curry and a mousse-like grenadine of veal), and colour (spinach and beetroot salad to enliven a roast saddle of mutton)." Ah mutton. I recall to this day from my hungry graduate-school days at U.Va.—we loved 18th century literature and virtually lived to quote Alexander Pope, John Gay, Thomas Parnell—the lines from Jonathan Swift's delightfully tempting "Cooking Poem: How Shall I Dine"

> Gently blow and stir the fire,
> Lay the mutton down to roast,
> Dress it nicely I desire,
> In the dripping put a toast,
> That I hunger may remove:
> Mutton is the meat I love.
>
> On the dresser see it lie,
> Oh! the charming white and red!
> Finer meat ne'er met my eye,
> On the sweetest grass it fed:
> Let the jack go swiftly round,
> Let me have it nicely browned.
>
> On the table spread the cloth,
> Let the knives be sharp and clean:
> Pickles get and salad both,
> Let them each be fresh and green:
> With small beer, good ale, and wine,
> O ye gods! how I shall dine."

British mutton was not for everybody, of course. Recall that troll's memorable complaint about it in J. R. R. Tolkien's *The Hobbit*: "Mutton yesterday, mutton today, and blimey, if it don't look like mutton again tomorrer."

R. W. Apple, Jr. in his essay, "Much Ado About Mutton, but Not in These Parts" (March 29, 2006), points out,

> Americans don't eat much lamb, let alone mutton. We consume on average only slightly more than a pound a year for each adult, compared with 50 pounds of pork and 65 pounds of beef. New Zealanders eat 40 pounds of lamb apiece every year and Greeks eat 31... there was in fact a time when mutton was common on American tables. The 1918 edition of Fannie Farmer's immensely influential cookbook, for example, gave instructions for preparing leg, saddle, chops and curry of mutton, although it also noted that "many object to the strong flavor of mutton."... "Gamy" is a term of opprobrium on this side of the Atlantic, and mutton is decidedly gamy. Even Elizabeth David, although a mutton maven from way back, admonishes readers in her *Mediterranean Food* (1950) to "make sure it has no smell of grease." Erica Rosa of the Livestock Marketing Information Center in Lakewood, Colo., near Denver, traces the decline of mutton in the United States to the canned mutton sent overseas to help feed G.I.'s during World War II. They hated it, she said, and "when they came home they said they never wanted to see lamb or mutton on the table again." Poor cooking techniques and inadequate distribution have also hurt, she said.

I would point to *The Wind in the Willows*, that little epic of lovely tidy meals, as the best defense of British cookery, with its richly-filled picnic baskets generously shared by Toad, Mole, Ratty, Badger, and their compadres, there in those wonderful yellow fields and scent-bright meadows and in their cozy, tiny, fitted-out underground homes, where they all have access to hot food, dry clothes, and a loving fraternity. Think of all those hot coffee pots, baskets full of nuts, and jars of honey! Ratty's springtime picnic on a gorgeous Sunday afternoon with a "fat, wicker luncheon-basket," the idea of a delicious meal of cold tongue, cold ham, potted meat, ginger beer, lemonade, soda water, pickled gherkins, and warm French rolls, is a truly transporting experience. "'O stop, stop' cried the Mole in ecstasies, 'This is too much!'"

12.

EVER EAT A PINE TREE?

Intellectuals like to think of themselves as iconoclasts, but if one takes a look through history, one finds it rarely to be the case. Too often, respected thinkers are those who usually conform and choose to serve power interests. Subservience! Subservience! It is no different with "safe" writers, timid or money-grubbing drudges drudges and hacks who in their books not only tell people what they want to hear, but are afraid to write anything original or assume a unique voice or try a different form or use a strange word or dare to employ rare metaphor or exercise counter or innovative ideas. Speaking for myself, I do not crave the world's approval of what I write. From all I have seen of life, Mark Twain was right about the human race. Praise—even generosity—is a form of patronage and condescension. It appeared so to Kant.

What Kant insisted on was the privilege—uncompromisingly—of a person best being himself. The concept of human freedom intoxicated the man. To relinquish one's freedom made that person, *pro tanto*, a barbarian. To Kant it was not only a paternalistic government that was the greatest conceivable despotism for destroying all freedom, it was anything at all that made inroads on the will. Will to Kant was autonomy. Any sort of determinism remained incompatible with freedom and morality. To choose to dislike a food is in every way the exercise of a freedom of self. If you should be scorned or vilified for it, bugger it—and bugger it if you are inordinately praised for it—or even pitied. To be pitied was perhaps worse than being ridiculed, ignored, or insulted. The inborn liberty of choice, to Kant, was sacred.

Man should not even agree to identify with or be part of nature, if in being so he is therefore determined by it. The sacredness of autonomy is understood by Americans. We should never be consensus humans bleakly leading consensus lives to live as directed by consensus authorities. We must seek self-reliance, avoid heteronomy, refused be pushed and pulled about by external forces. What alone is worth possessing is our personal unfettered will. Any restrained man is an imprisoned one. It is not easy. This is a failed world, to start with. In my opinion, Twain was correct in finding human beings the lowest creatures, not the highest. "Man is the only Slave. And he is the only animal who enslaves," he wrote. Our species, to me, has flunked. History, bunk, *is* written by the winners. Truth rarely emerges. Righteous people are calumniated. To me it is a miracle people obey laws. We are savages, at bottom.

I have described food aversionists as being complicated types, personality deficients—or, perhaps better, personalities that recognize fuller, darker dimensions of the self. To me this is a type described in several books by C.P. Snow who wrote in *The Masters*, "I want a man who knows something about himself. And is appalled. And has to forgive himself to get along." There is an echo of this in his *The Conscience of the Rich*, in which we read, "To know what goodness means, perhaps one needs to have lain awake at night, hating ones own nature." It would be folly to try to identity a single generic type of food crank, so wide is the spectrum of possibilities, for I would say they incorporate so many kinds of people, ranging from weak, fussy, and pusillanimous types to unbudging realists to highly individualistic heroic Prometheans. At their worst I cannot imagine that in their loony ranting and raving extravagances they could possibly recapitulate some of the barmies in today's sports, especially coaches. Why do crazy, cross-eyed, ranting, college basketball coaches immediately come to mind, those spitting, spiteful, useless, arm-waving, screeching, intemperate, towel-biting, immature, out-of-control, obscenely overpaid shitheads and scam-artists?

Vladimir Nabokov in his *Nikolai Gogol* was correct when he wrote, "Impressions do not make good writers. Good writers make them up themselves in their youth and then use them as if they had been really original." It is not unlike that with food aversions. They have no empirical foundations half the time, or so I am convinced. They are made up, fabricated, developed, projected, and in the process of course given credence to and fully believed. We select to dislike what we choose to want to banish from the realm of our inner being! It does not mean that all our impressions are stored up or even used at all, as if reality mattered. Robert Frost who is not strictly a literary poet was born in San Francisco and lived there until the age of 10, when at his father's death in 1885 the family moved to Lawrence, Mass. where the boy worked in a local mill. There his paternal grandfather was an overseer. At 36, he sailed with his family to England, where his first two volumes of poems were published. Yet in the course of his very full lifetime Frost never wrote a single poem about his childhood or of San Francisco, and there appears not a word of a mill throughout his entire poetry. Furthermore, not one poem of his has an English setting. He also said that he never read a book through before he was 14. (His favorite volume was *Tom Brown's School Days*, and this he never finished because he could not bear to feel that it was the end.) We are creatures of thorn and thumb-nosing, selection and spite, attitude and aversion.

To this very day, in certain places, being a vegetarian is tantamount to being cuckoo or a commie or an over-considered fop, a choice—the fabrication—of a human hothouse flower, a congenital fussball.

Vegetarians of course all avoid meat. A true and seasoned co-religionist has not only clearer skin but sweeter breath than a carnivore, and there is a distinct protuberant root look to them, a thin pale, anti-proteinaceous cast to face, body, and limbs which no doubt prompted the memorable witticism of the old humorist Finley Peter Dunne, who said, "Most vegetarians look so much like the food they eat that they can be classified as cannibals." The food gadabout, Anthony Bourdain, filled with disdain, dislikes vegans and such and peevishly insists that vegetarianism is a luxury strictly for the pampered. "Being a vegan is a first-world phenomenon, completely self-indulgent," he told *Playboy* (November 2011). There is an aspect of proletarian truth to what Bourdain says, an attitude, if skewed, that it could be argued is even worthy of the saintly soul, but with his blanket position of assigning vegetarians the role of sybarites, he ignores far more than he should acknowledge and, with immiserating oversimplification, reduces all chaste plant-eaters to simpering asses and prigs.

There is an insightful conviction among certain impatient folks that vegetarians like to be taken as exceptional, noteworthy, or remarkable for their judiciousness and refinement in what they eat. Alton Brown, one among many, becomes impatient with such a notion. Kim Severson in "Alton Brown, Showman of Food TV, Pulls Back the Curtain" (Sept. 26, 2016) quotes him:

> "Unless you have a medical bracelet that says celiac, shut up and eat the food," [Brown] said. "We want to be so special. We not only want to be special for our cooking, we want to be special for our eating. There are times when vegetarians should shut up and eat the pork chop."

A salient fact to recognize is that, along with the pure need to pursue good health, a piety—a humility, self-control—adhibits to vegetarianism. Many great minds, geniuses, were vegetarians, including Henry David Thoreau, Albert Einstein (toward the end of his life), Mahatma Gandhi,

Benjamin Franklin, Leo Tolstoy, G. B. Shaw, Jane Goodall, Sir Isaac Newton, Rosa Parks, Upton Sinclair, Leonardo da Vinci, Mary Shelley, Nikola Tesla, Thomas Alva Edison, and Steve Jobs.

Actor Clint Eastwood is a grumpy vegan. "I take vitamins daily, but just the bare essentials, not what you'd call supplements. I try to stick to a vegan diet heavy on fruit, vegetables, tofu, and other soy products," he explains. "As to the tolerance of non-meat-eaters, their reputed gentleness, and the considerate and compassionate understanding vegetables impart, recall what that breathy hambone actor wrote in June 2014, "I voted against that incompetent, lying, flip-flopping, insincere, double-talking, radical socialist, terrorist-excusing, bleeding-heart, narcissistic, scientific and economic moron [President Obama] currently in the White House!" A pity the doltish mannerbereft Eastwood was not our resident economist at the time, him with all of that intellectual bandwidth.

Some illustrious meat-eaters, I mean those other than the usual workaday types—"If we aren't supposed to eat animals, then why are they made out of meat?" asked Jo Brand—do have certain rather pronounced quibbles, however. Frank Sinatra, according to Bill Zehme, "had a violent hatred of the smell of roasting lamb." When asked why he had come to South Africa, Cecil Rhodes acknowledged his love of adventure. But, with a wink, he confided to a friend, "The real fact is that I could no longer stand English eternal cold mutton." Queen Christina of Sweden developed quite serious aversions to certain foods—the sight of pork in any form, for example, made her actively ill. Also, she could not bear the smell of beer or wine. What of those whose dislike of vegetables is as strong as their revulsion of meat? Lachanophobia—the fear of vegetables—may throw as much light on a person's set of mental disturbances, may indicate how dented a person's psyche can be, as any intransigent meat-hater. Asked if he liked vegetables, the Regency rake Beau [George Bryan] Brummell replied, "I don't know. I have never eaten them... No, that is not quite true. I once ate a pea."

The dandy also could not abide cabbage. A serious intention to marry one Lady Mary, although a woman nobly born, was brief and ended abruptly. "What could I do but cut the connection?" Bram straightforwardly observed to an intimate. "I discovered that Lady Mary actually ate cabbage."

Slick, smarmy, overweening Hollywood producer Robert Evans, who feebly boasted to his third wife, Ali McGraw, that he "never ate a meal south of Forty-second Street"—less a reminder, no doubt, that he was not even close to being high-born than that he was snobbishly determined always to go first class in life—was a master of disguise and deflection. Not surprisingly, he was actually born Robert J. Shapera, the son of a Jewish dentist named Archie Shapera and a housewife, Florida. Sycophancy goes both ways. Tubby little Bob Kraft, owner of the New England Patriots football team, is for no good reason I see always referred to by craven, obsequious, and forelock-tugging reporters in the media, both print and electronic, as "Mr. Kraft," never Bob, simply because he is a multi-billionaire. Snobbery is always about belonging, a job mainly for those who never belong, lackeys.

I tend to agree with G.K. Chesterton regarding people like self-cherishing Robert Evans, whose church, in too many cases, is their own body, the altar their precious gullet: "There is more simplicity in the man who eats caviar on impulse than in the man who eats Grape-Nuts on principle."

We know Anthony Bourdain finds vegetarians, at least many of them, simpering idlers and snobs who have the luxury fussily to choose what they want to eat on a planet filled with starving people, but when he declares in *Kitchen Confidential,* "Vegetarians, and their Hezbollah-like splinter faction, the vegans ... are the enemy of everything good and decent in the human spirit," it is total bullshit. And exactly why is Hezbollah any worse than the thuggish and merciless Israeli government that has had its foot on the neck of the oppressed Palestinian people for the last fifty years? In 1997, Hezbollah formed the Lebanese Brigades to fight the illegal and corrupt Israeli Occupation of the West Bank and Gaza whose goal is genocide. But surely no stupider hyper-moralizing about food could possibly be found than the simple-minded quackery of that schmaltzy versifier Shel Silverstein, with the following bollocks so maudlin as to make me want to stop up his gob with an enormous hairy turnip:

> Thanksgiving dinner's sad and thankless.
> Christmas dinner's dark and blue.
> When you stop and try to see it
> From the turkey's point of view.
> Sunday dinner isn't sunny.
> Easter feasts are just bad luck.
> When you see it from the viewpoint
> Of a chicken or a duck.
> Oh how I once loved tuna salad
> Pork and lobsters, lamb chops too
> Till I stopped and looked at dinner
> From the dinner's point of view.

You nail three major Christian feasts right there, Shel. But of course we all know that turkeys, chickens, and ducks just *love* it when being served up in matzoh ball soups, roasts, grilled kebabs, dumplings, and goulash during Hanukkah, Rash Hashanah, Purim, and Yom Kippur, right?

Guy Fieri. Paula Deen. Andrew Zimmern. These are the TV food gurus we are stuck with in this dopey age. They pinpoint the late great journalist William Bolitho's dismissive views on the media: "General jackdaw culture, very little more than a collection of charming miscomprehensions, un-targeted enthusiasms, and a general habit of skimming." Such boob-tube folk are little more than hucksters, carnival pitchmen who usually stay out of the heavy sand. Cats, dogs, wolves, and foxes, along with pea-and-thimble men, all walk upon their toes. Although a hard marker, Bolitho was surely right about the state of human dumbness and gullibility. In his autobiography, *I Write as I Please*, Walter Duranty wrote that Bolitho said to him: "Don't forget…that the majority of people and the majority of opinions are nearly always wrong about everything, not always, but nearly always, and if you ever are in doubt and can't make up your mind, and have to make it up, there are long odds in favor of your being right if you take the opposite view from the majority."

Mind you, Bolitho, who died of a burst appendix in Avignon on June 2, 1930, never even heard of television. Television, however, metastasizes all of the stupidity to which he sadly referred. I will recall here what the French writer, Jean Malaquais ("There are no heroes in American life, just celebrities, and they are immediately transferred to television"), once said to Norman Mailer on the French-German cultural television network, ARTE, in November of 1994, causing at the same time what is said to have been a serious rift in their long friendship, after Malaquais became convinced that Mailer had capitulated in becoming less a writer than a celebrity: "Television is un-Christian, untrue, distorting, decelebrating."

The moral dimension of vegetarianism has been stressed by many of our world's thinkers and philosophers. John Wesley, the English theologian who founded Methodism, once declared. "Thanks be to God, since I gave up flesh and wine, I have been delivered from all physical ills." Emmanuel Swedenborg crusaded against meat eating because "eating the flesh of animals, considered in itself, is something profane." Leo Tolstoy who was a vegetarian in the last 25 years of his life, although he did eat dairy products and eggs, declared, "Vegetarianism serves as a criterion by which we know that the pursuit of moral perfection on the part of man is genuine and sincere."

The 18th-century Bath physician George Cheyne in a series of books, notably *The English Malady* (1733), expressed grave warnings on how indulgence and corpulence inevitably produced derangements of the digestive and nervous systems, impairing both health and a person's mental stability. It is what Roy Porter in his splendid book, *Flesh in the Age of Reason*, describes as "an expression of a Mystical Christian Platonism trained at the emancipation of the spirit," the premise for Cheyne's call for moderation being the idea that "the flesh was indeed the spirit's prison house."

"Excessive flesh encumbered the spirit; burning it off emancipated it," Porter reiterates, and goes on to explain the nature of Cheyne's views on human intake and the vegetarian diet:

> Following the teachings of the German mystic Jakob Boehme, he imagined prelapsarian bodies innocently feeding on "Paradisiacal Fruits." After the Fall, the flesh of the newly carnivorous humans had been subjected to the laws of corruption of matter. Addressing "*Expiation, Purification*, and *progressive Perfection*," his works aimed at recovering the purity of the prelapsarian body. So, through keeping the "pipes" of the body clear of "peccant Humours," vegetarian diet also relieved fallen humanity from "the present *load of corruption*" and soothed the "mortal Distemper" which had afflicted sons of Adam ever since the Fall. The ritual of weighing the soul was an iconographic topos familiar to Christianity from the ceremony of the weighing of sins at the Last Judgement.

Mohandas Gandhi who frequently had bizarre nightmares of goats bleeding in his stomach became a vegetarian and ate dates, nuts, fruits, and whole-meal bread but still resolved never to take in more than five items in one meal. He held that it was necessary to be vegetarian in order to create a non-violent society. He experimented with meat eating in his youth, then gave up the consumption of meat to please his mother. Later, in England as a young student, he read a pamphlet by Henry Salt entitled "A Plea for Vegetarianism" which completely convinced him. "From that day forward," Gandhi says in his *Autobiography*, "I may claim to have become a vegetarian by choice"– and the spread of vegetarianism "henceforward became my mission." He ate no eggs and refused cow's milk because it "stirred the passions." At one time, suffering from an attack of dysentery and advised to drink milk, he refused because of a "vow against it." His wife convinced him to drink goat's milk (instead of cow's milk), but he regretted doing so later because, as he said, "The ideal of truth requires that vows taken should be fulfilled in the letter as well as in the spirit. I have killed the soul of my vow by adhering to its outer form only, and that is what galls me."

"Ever eat a pine tree?" asked outdoorsman Euell Gibbons, the proponent of natural diets during the 1960s who wrote *Stalking the Wild Asparagus.* "Many parts are edible." While he recommended eating Grape Nuts cereal over eating pine trees—the taste of the wheat reminded him of "wild hickory nuts"—it was his pine-tree question that caught the public's imagination and fueled his celebrity status. On many a *Tonight Show*, host Johnny Carson joked about sending Gibbons a "lumber-gram." Commonly mistaken for a scientist or a survivalist, Gibbons was nothing more than an advocate for folks eating nutritious but neglected plants. As a naturalist, he was not a patch on other truly inspired teachers of wood-lore knowledge like Mors Kochanski, Frank Kingdom-Ward, John McPherson, John Muir, Sigurd F. Olson, and, one of my heroes, Ellsworth Jaeger, wide traveler, exponent of Indian lore, and author of *Wildwood Wisdom*, one of America's great neglected classics. Gibbons typically prepared plants not in the wild, but in his small kitchen in Maine with an abundant use of spices, butter, oil, and garnishes. He wrote to capitalize on the ecology movement, then in high fettle. Several of his books discuss what he laughably called "wild parties:" *soirées* where guests were served dishes prepared from plants gathered in the wild. Among his favorite recommendations were lamb's quarters, rose hips, young dandelion shoots, stinging nettle, and cat-o-nine tails. He often exclaimed against wastrels and the brainless decadence of Americans dimly over-looking good available food, exasperatedly pointing out that gardeners throw away the tastier, more nutrient-rich crops when they pull such weeds as purslane and amaranth out from among their spinach plants.

People eat mud. At the Santuario church in Chimayó, New Mexico, a shrine and National Historic Landmark, pious visitors enter an inner room called *el pocito* (the little well), which contains a small round pit, the source of "holy dirt" (*tierra bendita*), often in hopes of a miraculous cure for themselves or someone who could not make the trip. I keep in my library several vials of that dirt, which I filled there on a visit back in 1991. Devoted Christians will eat the dirt, or curative clay, in a commemorative way. In the city of Esquipulas in Guatemala, where the Basilica is famous for its *Tierra del Santo* (Holy Earth), and also the "Black Christ" (a dark wooden image)—both central points of Catholic pilgrimage—the clay there is revered by the faithful as a spiritual or medicinal curative. Pilgrims rub themselves with it, and sometimes eat it with reverence after it has been cleaned and pressed into small cakes. In Persia, an edible yellowish clay called *tin najahi*, much prized by gourmets, was sold in many counties. Muslim physicians swore by it, prescribing it for nausea and to combat the effects of greasy foods. A 10th-century classic, called *Kitab al-abniya* by Muwaffasq al-Din Harawi, is the oldest book to list different kinds of edible earth. To eat dirt, even metaphorically, is a reminder of one's mortality. It is spiritually nourishing.

In his poem, "The Church Porch," George Herbert writes, "Look on meat, think it dirt, then eat a bit/And say with all, *Earth to earth I commit.*" I cannot truly identify eating a fresh beet from my garden without tasting a speck of dirt in it. "Food tastes better when it's got dirt in it," asserts the street vendor of rice with chickpeas, Mevlut, in Orhan Pamuk's novel, *A Strangeness in My Mind*, "a truth commonly acknowledged by anyone in Istanbul who makes a habit of consuming street food."

All orchids are edible, but some not palatable. Vanilla *planifolia* is considered the world's only edible, fruit-bearing orchid (and the planet's second most expensive spice, eclipsed only by saffron). Orchids! Their color, their scent, their extravagant architecture. I can picture Oscar Wilde ordering a colorful bowl of them at the Café Royal, Voisin's, or Paillard's, lounging at table with callow Bosie. The colors, the shapes, even the etymology (nudge, nudge) of the flowers suited them. Both adored the species of flowering plants and could have had their choice of splendiferous blooms—among them, the fabulous *Coelogyne rochusseni*; the speckled *Gastrochilus*; the tropical *Oncidium*; the *Vanda coerulea*, one of the truly rare blue orchids and a rare example of the color blue found in nature; the luminously white *Barkeria*; the emerald-green *Ida Locusta*, found only in Peru. Orchids have been described as tasting like a combo of cucumber and endive, and the same is said of tulips. Wonderful, sparkling bites and mouthfuls of smooth, gracile leaves.

Ah, sweet botanicals! There are so many! Daylilies taste like sweet lettuce, and lilacs which are infused into sorbets and puddings add a delicate flavor. Nasturtiums, Snapdragons, Violas, Bachelor's Buttons, Marigold blooms and petals, Clover, Cornflowers, Chrysanthemums, Wild mustard, curled dock, Lamb's Quarters, Purslane, Violets, Sheep Sorrel, Bleddo. The leaves, flowers, and stems of Begonias. All are edible—and nowadays the rage of haute cuisine. Sorrel, Chickweed, Alexanders, Wild garlic, Red algae—Carragheen or Irish moss. Even dulse, or dillisk, Popweed or bladder wrack, boiled gently and served as a vegetable. Roots are edible—Bulrush, Pond Lily, Turk's Cap Lily, Prairie Turnip, Cat Tail, Arrowhead, Indian Cucumber. The nuts and seeds of White oak, Blackjack oak, Swamp White oak, Post oak, Chestnut oak, Black Walnut, Chestnut, Mockernut, Water Chinquapin, Chia, Hog Peanut, Wild Rice, Beech, Butternut, and Piñon Pine are all edible.

Gibbons was an extreme vegetarian. He loved wild foods. Strangely enough, he also had a bad smoking habit and, as his writings reflect—to some people, in a rather scandalous way—indeed, he often indiscriminately added saturated fats (bacon grease, butter, egg yolks) to his vegetables. It was not as unusual to smoke cigarettes or to add high amounts of saturated fat to foods back then. These risk factors combined with his hard life and lack of exercise in his later years (arthritis pain limited his movement) undoubtedly contributed to his death.

Eating wood!

Does doing so seem an unlikely proposition?

Yet just such a circumstance was the occasion, however unlikely, of being the "best meal" writer Elizabeth Gilbert claimed she ever had. Traveling about with her then boyfriend in Luang Prabang in Northern Laos back in 2006, the two of them stopped to eat outside of an old French hotel one night, an event recounted in a later article "Don't Mess with Perfect." The meal was unique. She writes, "It was a slow-cooked potage of buffalo meat and vegetables with the oddest and most surprising ingredient—a sizable chunk of *wood*, like a small piece of kindling, boiled right into the mix." It turns out that the wood was a chip of bark from a local tree whose flesh was permeated by a strong mentholated oil. I have previously mentioned how much I dislike peppermint. In my opinion, just a *trace* of mint in a food, a savory, or even in candy, ruins the taste in the way a spot of yolk can ruin egg-whites for beating, or, say, a baby's brief cat-nap can prevent a sleep of longer duration. No, thumbs down on mint. You can imagine therefore how this taste-test would have gone down with me. Gilbert who offers all of this with the kind of easy hyperbole that seems to be in its galling overstatement among the worst kind of lie goes on further to explain,

> We were instructed to suck on the wood when our stew was finished... and so we did. The long-boiled wood released a spicy explosion into our mouths— something sort of peppermint, sort of cinnamony, sort of pine-pitchy, that was the single most breathtaking (literally) flavor I have encountered anywhere in the world. Then I splashed some of the fizzy, cold rice wine into my still-astonished mouth and the spicy pep-permint-cinnamon-pine-pitch sensation only doubled. I swear to the heavens I saw stars. At that moment I thought, Well, that's finished—I can now stop looking for the best meal on earth, because I've just had it.

Wood with peppermint? Tree bark oil? Excuse me, but this is being offered with almost time-stopping magnification as "the best meal on earth"?
Best meal on earth, *anywhere in the world*? Swear to God? Is it not revealing
that Gilbert and her friend, on the basis of one particular meal, decide to
to stay on in Luang Prabang "forever," never again to come back to the
United States, except that both of them do come back—to New Jersey, of all
places, "which is kind of exotic," she parenthetically adds in the very same
paragraph? It has to be one of the most anticlimactic sentences ever written.
On the subject of food aversions, arguably, this is certainly unique—a person
discovering the best meal on earth, which necessitates, philosophically, any
further need whatsoever to expect it to happen again! I mean, why hunt
further? Why eat ever again?

It was the "time and hassle" of eating, as I have pointed out earlier, that gave 25-year-old software engineer Rob Rhinehart what Hunter
S. Thompson would call a "king-bitch dog fucker of an idea." It became
Rhinehart's singular eureka moment to do away with food altogether. He
began to think that food was an inefficient way of getting what he needed to
survive," writes Lizzie Widdicombe in "The End of Food." What would be
the result if, instead of eating, an individual went straight to the raw chemical
elements of food itself? He figured we need amino acids and lipids, but not
milk itself; carbohydrates, not bread, fruits and vegetables, which are however mostly water. So he came up with a product by experimentation and
research named Soylent, a food substitute intended to supply all of a human
body's daily nutritional needs, a kind of slurry—a thick, tan liquid that is
yeasty, grainy, and fairly sweet composed of fish oil, whey protein, oat flour,
canola oil, rice protein, maltodextrin, and raw chemical powders—that can
be taken in simple, daily, everything-your-body-needs gulps. A commercial
version, created through a "crowdfunding" campaign and venture capital
group that has raised over $3,500,000—funding that paid for additional
research and modification of the formula—is presently being commercially
marketed.

On the web one can find many varieties of such created concoctions as
Soy Hemp, Eggman's Sizzurp, Canadian People Chow, and Super Food that
remind us of samplers of Cream of Wheat and Ralston Purina and Metamucil.

Hey, eating wood may seem preferable! Pine cone nuts, shelled, in fact
are edible, best roasted, the needles from the tree can be boiled to use in
making tea, and even the cones, when they are not toxic (which some however can be) traditionally used to be shaved by severely hungry Indians to
concoct a woodland tea. The tough cones are quite efficacious as a rump-
swab, as any enterprising camper knows. A pine cone when cut length-wise,

by the way, curiously resembles the hand of Christ, which, according to legend, was a sign of his blessing on the tree that sheltered the Virgin Mary when with alarm she was fleeing the murderous troops of Herod with her family. This phenomenon was often used as a pictorial lesson by the North American Jesuits, the "blackrobes," when preaching to the Mohawks and Abnak. 'Neeshch'ii is the Navajo word for pine cone, but they are referring to the pinyon.

A bronze pine cone, incidentally, once stood in the atrium of old St. Peter's Basilica, the ancient church built by Constantine the Great in the 4th-century A.D. that preceded the present basilica designed by Michelangelo, Bramante, Maderno, and Bernini by a thousand years. "It is perhaps some relic of an ancient Roman bath," offers Alfred Werner in "The Vatican" (*Horizon*, January 1962) to explain that cone. He was only partly right. It may have stood in a Roman bath as an emblem, but Christians often took pagan symbols—our Christmas day was once the Roman Saturnalia—to adopt them as sacramentals. The bronze cone, part of Vatican treasure and one of the few remaining objects of what was for so long the most venerated church in Christendom, stands today in the Vatican palace courtyard. I believe that the pictorial lesson of the North American Jesuits is linked to this symbol.

The consumption of wood is sadly not always a festive or offbeat phenomenon. More than a decade after a famine killed 500,000 to a million people in North Korea, recent news from that benighted country suggests it is once again on the brink of mass starvation. Good Friends, a Buddhist human-rights group in South Korea, say that in rural areas there families are again adding tree-bark and grass to their diet and foraging for food in the wild. Reports say that in South Pyongyan province in west-central North Korea, people are already dying of starvation, while listless farmers ignore official calls to plant this year's rice. For years, the World Food Programme (WFP) has called upon nations for urgent help to avert a "serious tragedy."

To bring up starvation in a book on food aversions surely raises an unbearable irony even if it does highlight the topic. During the Nazi siege of Leningrad, which lasted 900 days from September 1941 to January 1944, people were driven to eat cats, sawdust, wallpaper, shoes, even their own dead babies. During the siege, nearly a third of the population—800,000 people—starved to death, roughly one person in three, many of them outside in the streets. Vicksburg citizens were starving during that siege in 1863, as General Ulysses S. Grant sought to undermine that strategic city of the Confederacy sitting high on the bluffs of the Mississippi River. Its beleaguered citizens were eating mule beef, bread made with pea-flour, and in the end were scoffing up slop, which was just marginally better than "living on air." Hunger reduced wealthy planters to slave and humans to animal. One Dora Richards Miller, a diarist whose stark entries have come down to us, confided to a page, "I am so tired of corn-bread, which I never liked, that I eat it with tears in my eyes." Rats to eat eventually reached a dollar apiece, although demand for them outpaced supply. In their desperation, folks soaked hard tack in water over night to soften it, then fried it in any grease thay had at hand. More than 300,000 people starved in Darfur and the Sudan, never mind a million made homeless in a conflict between rebels and Arab militias.

Another quick word on Euell Gibbons and breakfast cereals. He happened to choose the correct ones, but American children generally do not. Michael Pollan, whom the 2006 *New York Times Book Review* described as a "liberal foodie intellectual," considers the cereal aisle to be among the most treacherous places in a supermarket, and perhaps with good reason. Cereal labels with their deviously disguised and boasting labels are quick to cite, to market, whole grain content, but are far less likely to highlight dangerously high levels of sugar or genetically engineered ingredients. Pollan points out that Lucky Charms cereal lists whole grains as the top ingredient, but—check it out—several different forms of sugar follow.

Sugars on cereal boxes, notice, are listed in the plural, which includes not only the sucrose from sugar cane (listed as "sugar" among the ingredients) but also sugars that are naturally present in the food, such as lactose in the milk, the fructose in the fruit, and the glucose, maltose, and fructose in any corn sweetener that may be present, according to Robert Wolke in *What Einstein Told His Cook 2.* What about the elegant fairy words that are listed like "evaporated cane juice"? Only more perfidy. Wolke says it is nothing but "a sneaky expression used by 'health-food' purveyors to avoid the dreaded s-word on their labels." He wisely advises,

> To check your cereals (or other manufactured foods)
> for sugar content, look at the Nutrition Facts table
> and divide the number of grams of sugars (or other
> manufactured food) per serving and multiply by 100.
> You'll find, for example, that Kellogg's Raisin Bran is
> 30 percent sugar [!] by weight and Multi-Bran Chex is
> 21 percent sugar.

Many of these cereals which taste like doll stuffing make no pretense of being anything better than harsh sugar infusions; even the cartoonish names, shamelessly exploitative, do not even try to disguise their lyrical addictiveness! Cocoa Pebbles, Smacks, Frosted Mini-Wheats, Quangaroos, Wackies,

Sir Grapefellow, Kaboom, Frankenberry, the redundantly hard-selling Cap'n Crunch Peanut Butter Crunch Cereal, Cocoa Krispies, and Count Chocula ("artificial chocolate flavor frosted cereal with chocolate flavor marsh-mallows"). I remember several cereals back in the 1970s named "Fruity Freakies," "Quispies," and "Grins & Smiles & Giggles and Laughs." A new cereal today unashamedly called Kellogg's Krave and advertised as "The Cereal with Chocolate-Flavored Center"—the seductive word "chocolate" is repeated for our benefit as many as 5 times on the front of the box ("made with real chocolate," "crispy multi-grain cereal outside, smooth chocolate in-side," etc.)—contains 3g of fat but 11g of sugar, which is a gruesome 22.2% more than the average covering all cereal nutrition facts. One of Pollan's more solid admonitory Food Rules: "Never buy any cereal that makes your milk turn a different color."

New tricks, new logos, new slants, new jingles, appear everyday from cereal manufacturers who are, after all, in the seduction business. I have lived to see the death of my childhood friends, the Arthur Rackhamesque Snap, Crackle, and Pop! In their protean zeal, a diffident Kellogg's in 1949 replaced the endearing jug-eared, long-nosed little creatures who had first appeared in 1933—"reimagined them with younger and more proportional features," as they would have it—only to give us three soulless artlessly-drawn mod-ern versions of the great originals that are nothing but saucer-eyed generic copies of cute boys who all look the same. If you are interested in the fail-ures of image-fiddling, compare the elegantly statuesque lady holding high the flaming torch in the original Columbia Pictures logo with the deficient, "updated" version that replaced her in 1992, a pie-faced homemaker with a lame, out-of-proportion right arm that looks as though it were added as an afterthought.

I have mentioned previously that Prince Siddhartha, the Buddha, died soon after eating a local dish called "pig's delight." Scholars have long de-bated whether it was pork or rather a particular food that pigs liked, such as truffles, roots, or mushrooms. The late Irish playwright Brendan Behan, who indiscriminately loved food and drink of any kind, actually came to detest American hot dogs. So did William Zinsser who wrote in his *The Lunacy Boom* (1970), "I've often wondered what goes into a hot dog. Now I know and I wish I didn't." The odor alone of hot dogs made the actress Ethel Barrymore dreadfully sick, bringing on ghastly reactions, and whenever she took her children out to Coney Island, she always made sure to carry hand-kerchiefs saturated with Atkinson's White Rose and breathed through them.

James Beard comes down heavy on the dreadfulness of frankfurters, in any case those that are made nowadays. "In my day they still had skin, and what's more they had flavor," he wrote with some anger. "They snapped crisply when you bit into them, and exuded a delicious trickle of juice. And the buns they were served in tasted as though they had really been made from flour and yeast, not cotton." *Cotton?* That would be a plus from my experience! The last time I watched the Red Sox at Fenway Park four wieners cost $21—this for a few rubbery ingots of processed ground-up pork, maybe beef, probably six years stale, hydrolyzed skim milk protein concentrate, corn syrup, dextrose, potassium lacate, autolyzed yeast, sodium nitrite and erythorbate, and maybe a few obliging insects, or rodent hairs, all of it liquidized, ammoniaized, and loaded with filler and chemicals—and the government declares that the full contents of the damn stuff need not be disclosed? Speaking of Boston, I think of those boiled hot dogs (and dense damp meatloaf) served up by Don Gately, former thief and Demerol addict, in David Foster Wallace's *Infinite Jest*. Weenies. Red-Hots. Footlongs. Tube Steak. Coney Island chicken. Flaunters, Grandstanders. Call them what you will. It is all mystery meat. There's a "whodunit" in every bite.

Every American hot dog—guaranteed—is packed with hydrolyzed vegetable protein (HVP), a sneaky ingredient-label euphemism for MSG and not only one of most common soy-based food "fillers" used in this country but liberally used in literally thousands of processed food products—hot dogs, veggie burgers, gravy mixes, soups, sauces, chilis, stews, snack foods, dips, dressings, you name it. Thank HVP for that bulliony chicken-mush mouthfeel when next time you're shoving a foot-long-with- everything into your pie hole! (Actor Robert Mitchum who loved chili, claiming the hot stuff could cure all ills, always shaved chocolate into his recipe!)

Do not be consoled that by way of some commercial double-speak ("We have to answer to a higher authority") holy heaven is protecting you from all the mysterious crap squeezed into a frank. The monstrous, almost-comic-if-it-were-not-blasphemous claim that kosher hot dogs are better for you—whistling up the Creator of the Universe (a lying one to boot!) to endorse disgusting hot dogs—is total bullshit (salmonella has often been found in kosher meats, as well). And price? Hebrew National charges 87 cents per hot dog, as contrasted to the less expensive 25 cents per hot dog charged by Oscar Mayer. Hebrew National's hot dog ingredient list:

> Beef, Water, Contains 2% or Less of: Salt, Sodium
> Lactate, Spice, Hydrolyzed Soy Protein, Paprika,
> Sodium Diacetate, Garlic Powder, Sodium
> Erythorbate, Sodium Nitrite, Flavorings.

is virtually the same as Oscar Mayer's:

> Beef, Water, Contains Less than 2% of Salt, Corn
> Syrup, Dextrose, Sodium Lactate, Sodium Phosphates,
> Sodium Diacetate, Ascorbic Acid (Vitamin C),
> Extractives of Paprika, Dried Garlic, Spice, Sodium
> Nitrite.

Let me here helpfully remind you of several other apposite Pollan Food Rules: "Do not buy anything with more then five ingredients." "Do not buy any foods that you have seen marketed on television." And finally "Do not buy anything that your third-grader cannot pronounce the ingredients of."

I am convinced the hot dog explains why the Dalai Lama became a vegetarian. Remember the old Weenie/Tibetan Buddhism joke? The Dalai Lama walks up to a street vendor who is selling hot dogs and says, "I want one with everything." The vendor hands him one and says, "Four bucks." The Dalai Lama gives him a $5 bill and waits to receive his change—but the vendor ignores him. The Dalai Lama finally asks, "Where's my change?" The hot-dog vendor replies, "Change only comes from within." The change came from within precisely when the Holy High Lama in his Gelug sadly came to learn the wiener's full ingredients.

Consumer advocate and one-time presidential candidate, Ralph Nader, whose concerned and hands-on parents were of Lebanese extraction, grew up in Winsted, Conn. without ever tasting a single hot dog. In his memoir, *The Seventeen Traditions*, he explains how his mother not only did not like fatty foods but taught her children to eat purely healthy fare, and she stressed that her family eat only fresh food. Nader writes, "She never fed us hot dogs, not because she knew they were bad, but because she just didn't know what was in them. She believed in serving a healthful variety of simple foods, and didn't like to fuss over food." Movie director John Huston when growing up suffered from chronic nephritis, or "Bright's Disease," which at one time was considered to be a terminal illness, and he had to stick to the blandest of diets, no red meat, no eggs, no condiments, no salt. George Orwell's hero George Bowling, in the novel *Coming Up for Air* (1939), is entirely pessimistic about the food that he eats: beer, pie that is colder than beer, coffee, and—in Orwell's own words—"the kind of tasteless stuff that comes out of cartons and tubes." The first frankfurter that Bowling bites into brings him down to earth with a terrible bump—in fact it actually shocks him. The horrible food that Winston Smith eats in the canteen at the Ministry of Truth in *1984* (1949) can only be erased by Victory Gin, an oily drink that tastes like nitric acid but which, unfortunately, is the only beverage that is available in that weird totalitarian world. And of course the great poet Percy Shelley loathed meat, writing,

> It is only by softening and disguising dead flesh by
> culinary preparation that it is rendered susceptible
> of mastication or digestion; and that the sight of its
> bloody juices and raw horror does not excite intolera-
> ble loathing and disgust.

Perhaps this the place to mention that the late novelist and essayist Susan Sontag who grew up in Arizona somewhat anemic and who also badly suffered as a child from migraine headaches and asthma once confided to a young friend of hers, Sigrid Nunez, author of *Sempre Susan*, that she actually recalled the daily habit of drinking glasses of *blood* that her mother brought home from the butcher!

Novelist Pat Conroy's Chicago-born father always insisted that the Superdawg restaurant in his home town served the best red hots. "When my father was dying in 1998, to please him," Pat said. "I called Superdawg and was surprised that it was still in business. A most pleasant woman told me to dress the red hots with relish, mustard, onion, and hot peppers with a pickle on the side. 'If you put ketchup on it, just throw it in the trash,' she added."

John Steinbeck in *Travels with Charley* stated, "I don't greatly care for venison or bear or moose or elk except for the livers." As to liver haters? There are many, many. Curmudgeonly Andy Rooney of CBS news unambiguously declared, "I know I dislike liver, and I don't want to try another piece, ever!" Keith Snow, founder of Harvest Eating, "I am absolutely opposed to liver, and also to anchovies—the smell of either of them can almost make me sick. One night, while I was a line cook at a country club the executive chef had liver and onions as a special. I threatened to quit and refused to cook it. He complied and changed the dish!" Actor Tom Cruise has gone on record as hating only one food: liver. In one episode on the television sitcom, "Happy Days," Richie wants to publish a story about Arthur Fonzarelli's secret fear, although it nearly wrecks their friendship. What was the "Fonz's" weakness, what he feared more than anything would be disclosed? He hated liver! Of the many things that wealthy heiress Daphne Guinness hated at St. Mary's in Wantage, a boarding school she attended when growing up, what was the one thing that she singled out that she most despised? Homework? Loneliness? No. "There was the food: liver, with veins coming out—really horrible," she told Rebecca Mead ("Precarious Beauty," *The New*

Yorker Sept. 26, 2011). It was one of her most loathsome memories. Finally, remember the formal cause of the gippy tummy that young Alfred Kralik, played by Jimmy Stewart, was suffering from at the beginning of the splendid movie, *The Shop Around the Corner*? Precisely—goose liver. He had eaten too much of that rich food the night before.

The narrator of the Chinese novelist Mo Yan's *Pow!* is a young fellow, Luo Xiaotong, whose love of meat as a boy was so obsessive that it actually calls out to him in a sort of preternatural way, begging to be eaten. He is referred to as a "carnivorous genius" and "the world's most gluttonous boy." Just watching him stuff his face, one man says, "is better than embracing my wife in bed." I love the novel for its many cogent and unique observations on food, digressions on all sorts of exotic munchables. It is filled with wild descriptions of things like a shrimp paste "so salty it nearly made you jump in the air." "The author lingers on meals in which devoted attendees gorge on 'delicacies' such as donkey lips, cow anuses, camel tongues and horse testicles,'" writes Dwight Garner in his *New York Times Book Review*, "A Meaty Tale, Carnivorous and Twisted."

> It is the sort of book in which little girls have the ability to belch like sumo wrestlers. The plot of *Pow!* glides, like fat on a griddle, in two directions. We listen to the story of the boy's troubled childhood. After his father abandoned his mother for a sexy wine merchant named Wild Mule, the boy's miserly mother began withholding meat from him, nearly driving him insane with longing. At the same time the novel chronicles the corruption and greed in a town where the farmers have left the fields to raise meat animals or become butchers. Capitalism has gained a toehold, and the new bosses (some of them former peasants) are mostly as bad as the old ones. It is an era, one man declares, of "primitive accumulation." Butchered meat is fraudulently injected with water to increase its weight; formaldehyde is applied to keep it fresh. Still, most of the citizens seem to agree with our narrator, who maintains, "I'd rather eat unhealthy meat than healthy turnips." There is an annual Carnivore Festival, and a Meat Appreciation Parade. Fireworks explode over these events, tattooing the sky red with the Chinese character for meat.

I am prompted to recall when reading through Mo Yan's pages of some of those legendary Italian *brut de décoffrage* meals, such as the peasant dishes of *pollo alla scapariello* (shoemaker's style), *coniglio alla boscaiulo* (wood-cutter's style), *porco alla cacciatore* (hunter's style), and *capra alla mugnaia* (miller's style), all of which are often—and should be—served with a chunk of rustic bread or a bit of pasta on the side. Many folks love *la cucina bruta*, others do not, put off by the "heft" of such food, strong exotica such as raw mackerel flavored vinegar; bitter chocolate sorbet; *penne* with tuna roe; *farinata ligure*; succotash and scrapple; minestrone and ratatouille; real horse-bread; *lampredotto*; *fagioli giubbalunga*; *scroccadenti*; *sfrappole*; rooster stew, and so on. I have a friend who, head-buttingly stubborn, will eat nothing but Romagna cuisine, rough, primitive, barbaric in its perfection.

"I've eaten crocodile in Holland; barbied kangaroo at Uluru; and mountain oysters in Cody, Wyoming," wrote Simon Schama in *Scribble, Scribble*, "but tongue...has always tasted my gag reflex... Lamb's tongues are a particular problem—like pigs' tongues, so I'm told—these being pretty much the same size as our own, a confusing subject and object of mastication, one stands a fair chance of biting the former rather than the latter."

Then there is mutton.

In her cubist novel, *Tender Buttons*, the mannered, always conflicted, and word-mad Gertrude Stein seems to inveigh against that meat (who can fully know?), writing in her usual jibbery-jabbery way,

> A letter which can wither, a learning which can suffer and an outrage which is simultaneous is principal. Student, students are merciful and recognized they chew something. Hate rests that is solid and sparse and all in a shape and largely very largely. Interleaved and successive and a sample of smell all this makes a certainty a shade.

Elvis Presley loathed under-cooked meat. "Any meat that Elvis ate had to be almost burnt," said one of his closest aides, Marty Lacker. "He didn't like to see any red or any blood. He'd gag at the sight of a pink hamburger. Or he'd throw it away or throw it at somebody."

President John F. Kennedy could not tolerate barbecue, much as he liked it—it invariably upset his stomach. What the late president most liked to eat was simply New England clam chowder and Locke-Ober's roast beef hash. Moira Hodgson, a food critic for the *New York Observer*, under-rates barbecue, saying, "I have never quite understood the mystique that surrounds this dish which so often consists of charred, dry, and fatty meat slathered in a sauce that tastes mostly of ketchup." Calvin Trillin, showing an odd prejudice, is suspicious of white people cooking barbecue. "Going to a white-run barbecue is, I think, like going to a gentile internist: it might turn out all right, but you haven't made any attempt to take advantage of the percentages." You gotta love it. Trillin, a Jew—born Trilinsky—insults everyone but his own kind. Racism in three prejudicial octaves: Jews are better doctors than Christians; blacks are better barbecuers than whites, which is to say, Jews are smarter than Christians, and blacks belong in the kitchen. To paraphrase Prime Minister Lloyd George somewhat, "When they circumcised Calvin Trillin, they threw away the wrong bit."

"In five things America excels modern England—fish, architecture, jokes, drinks, and children's clothes," wrote the poet Rupert Brooke in 1913. *Fish?* I manage to miss that point. He also believed that drinking a lot of water between meals was one of the chief causes of American good health. An emotional crisis in 1912 led to his nervous collapse, and as part of his recuperation, he toured the United States and Canada to write travel diaries for the *Westminster Gazette*.

Jeffrey Steingarten cannot stand swordfish. "This is a favorite among the feed-to-succeed set, who like it grilled to the consistency of running shoes and believe it is good for them," he writes. "A friend of mine eats swordfish five times a week and denies that he has any food phobias. Who's kidding whom? Returning obsessively to a few foods is the same as being phobic toward all the rest. This may explain the Comfort Food Craze. But the goal of the arts, culinary or otherwise, is not to increase our comfort. That is the goal of an easy chair."

The take-no-prisoners Steingarten has never been shy about his personal food phobias, even while as a sensitive fellow he struggled—and succeeded —explaining them to himself, later to revise many of his opinions. The long list of foods that he initially said he would not eat, even if he were starving on a desert island, was so extensive that he considered himself unfit to become a food critic. I believe a person who has no food aversions can have no taste. By this standard Steingarten singularly qualifies for—well, food editor for *Vogue* magazine isn't bad, is it? (On Bastille Day, 1994, in recognition of his writings on French gastronomy, he was made a Chevalier in the Order of Merit by the Republic of France.) It may be asked now, are there any foods that Steingarten will not touch? "None," or so he asserts in his fascinating book *The Man Who Ate Everything and Other Gastronomic Feats, Disputes, and Pleasurable Pursuits*, "except maybe insects. Many cultures find insects highly nutritious and love their crunchy texture. The pre-Hispanic Aztecs roasted worms in a variety of ways and made pressed caviar from mosquito eggs. This proves that no innate human programming keeps me from eating them, too. Objectively, I must look as foolish as those Kalahari Bushmen who face famine every few years because they refuse to eat three-quarters of the 223 animal species around them. I will deal with this phobia when I have polished off the easy ones."

More than 2 billion people, or roughly one-third of the entire global population, are entomophages. Crickets are the most popular of edible insects: a single cup of cricket flour has 70 grams of protein, about as much as 9 ounces of beef. Munching exoskeletons may seem a grim prospect, but a piece in *Audubon* magazine (Sept./Oct. 2014) notes that many food companies "are easing Westerners into the practice by hiding the six-legged base ingredients in energy bars, chips, and cookies."

"Six-legged meat" has become the popular, slightly winking euphemism for the nutritional potential of insects, which are now being eaten in many quarters of the world, as the global meat supply is badly strained by booming population demands. Much of the developing world *already* eats insects. Forget beef, pork, and chicken. Insects, which are comparatively easy to raise, produce relatively little waste, require very little water, are relatively disease free, and can live in extremely dense quarters without stress. They are not only high in protein and low in fat but are also cold-blooded, so need less feed, and best of all they are abundant.

Steingarten also bountifully offers a full list of foods that he dislikes under "Foods I Wouldn't Touch Even If I Were Starving on a Desert Island Until Absolutely Everything Else Runs Out." He begins with kimchi, noting,

> Kimchi, the national pickle of Korea. Cabbage, ginger, garlic, and red peppers—I love them all, but not when they are fermented together for many months to become kimchi. Nearly forty-one million South Koreans eat kimchi three times a day. They say 'kimchi' instead of 'cheese' when someone is taking their picture. I say, 'Hold the kimchi.'

He dislikes Greek food, swordfish, okra, and many forms of yogurt. He adds, "Anything featuring dill"—and, before he forgets, throws in lard, adding, "The very word causes my throat to constrict and beads of sweat to appear on my forehead." He singles out for special opprobrium desserts found in Indian restaurants. "The taste and texture of face creams belong in the boudoir, not on the plate," he writes. Nor does he exclude candy. "During my own praline period, which lasted for three years," he writes, "I would order any dessert on the menu containing caramelized hazelnuts and ignore the rest. I grew so obsessive that I almost missed out on the *crème brûlée* craze then sweeping the country. After my praline period had ebbed, I slid into a *crème brûlée* fixation, from which I forcibly wrenched myself only six months ago."

Tang, as such, in its various morphs and manifestations seems to irk Steingarten the most. It was used by earlier NASA manned space flights, but in 2013 astronaut Buzz Aldrin said, "Tang sucks." Steingarten hates anchovies. "I met my first anchovy on a pizza in 1962," he said, "and it was seven years before I mustered the courage to go near another. I am known to cross the street whenever I see an anchovy coming. Why would anybody consciously choose to eat a tiny, oil-soaked, leathery maroon strip of rank and briny flesh?" I detect something of a tang element in other foodstuffs that he abhors: "Miso, mocha, chutney, raw sea urchins, and falafel (those hard, dry, fried little balls of ground chickpeas unaccountably enjoyed in Middle Eastern countries)."

Regarding Steingarten and hazelnuts, one may mention here a highly curious historical anti-food aversion. The Elizabethans had, more than a fondness, an actual craving for hazelnuts—also called filberts or cobnuts. Archaeologists in their excavations found layers of them and other fruit seeds in theaters of the era, middens in places, in the foundations and under the ingressi (wooden stairs leading to the galleries), and why? First off, hazelnuts were the popcorn of English Renaissance drama. They also coincidentally protected playgoers against the bubonic plague, because the flea that spread the disease was repelled by the odor of nuts.

Or at least so I have read. One hears a lot of hooey in both the prescriptive and proscriptive matter of nuts and seeds. There are people who still maintain that one may achieve *invisibility* for a time by eating fern seed!

Then there is Steingarten's ancillary list of "Foods I Might Eat If I Were Starving on a Desert Island But Only If the Refrigerator Were Filled With Nothing But Chutney, Sea Urchins, and Falafel." Clams, he leaps to condemn. "I feel a mild horror about what goes on in the wet darkness between the shells of all bivalves, but clams are the only ones I dislike. Is it their rubbery consistency or their rank subterranean taste, or is the horror deeper than I know?" He goes on to attack blue food, adding "not counting plums and berries." His explanation is quite simple, as he is the first to admit. "This may be a rational aversion, because I am fairly sure that God meant the color blue mainly for food that has gone bad." Other aversions? "Cranberries, kidneys, okra, millet, coffee ice cream, refried beans, and many forms of yogurt."

It seems for their force these food aversions would be resolutely held, but then in 1989 Steingarten suddenly had a change of heart. In what might called an epiphany, he suddenly saw himself as an opinionated prig and saw his food biases in the light of what they were, intransigent, especially in light of the fact that he wanted to be a fair—and disinterested—food critic. "For I, like everybody I knew, suffered from a set of powerful, arbitrary, and debilitating attractions and aversions at mealtime. I feared that I could be no more objective than an art critic who detests the color yellow or suffers from red-green color blindness." A new-found humility found him contrite, and he began to eat the foods he had earlier reviled. He explains,

> In just six months, I succeeded in purging myself of nearly all repulsions and preferences, in becoming a more perfect omnivore. This became apparent one day in Paris, France—a city to which my arduous professional duties frequently take me. I was trying a nice new restaurant, and when the waiter brought the menu, I found myself in a state unlike any I had ever attained—call it Zen-like if you wish. Everything on the menu, every appetizer, hot and cold, every salad, every fish and bird and piece of meat, was terrifically alluring, but none more than the others. I had absolutely no way of choosing. Though blissful at the prospect of eating, I was unable to order dinner. I was reminded of the medieval church parable of the ass equidistant between two bales of hay, who, because animals lack free will, starves to death. A man, supposedly, would not." He became almost embarrassed over his own vanity and cautions himself. "Just because you have become a perfect omnivore does not mean that you must flaunt it. Intoxicated with my own accomplishment, I began to misbehave, especially at dinner parties. When seated next to an especially finicky eater, I would often amuse myself by going straight for the jugular. Sometimes I began slyly by staring slightly too long at the food remaining on her plate and then inquiring whether she would like to borrow my fork. Sometimes I would launch a direct assault by asking how long she had had her terror of bread. Sometimes I tricked her by striking up an abstract conversation

about allergies. And then I would sit back and compla-
cently listen to her neurotic jumble of excuses and explanations: advice from a personal trainer, intolerance
to wheat gluten, a pathetic faith in Dean Ornish, the
exquisite—even painful—sensitivity of her taste buds,
hints of childhood abuse. And then I would tell her
the truth. I believe that it is the height of compassion
and generosity to practice this brand of tough love on
dinner-party neighbors who are less omnivorous than
oneself. But the perfect omnivore must always keep
in mind that, for one to remain omnivorous, it is an
absolute necessity to get invited back.

Every taste is king in its own domain and must rule by its own laws seems
to be one unalterable law Steingarten is making, or as the great Curnonsky
used to say, "*La cuisine, c'est quand les choses ont le goût de ce qu'elles sont*"
(Good cooking is when things taste like what they are). Maurice Edmond
Sailland, better known by his pen name Curnonsky (based on *Cur non?* Why
not?)—editor of the popular cooking magazine, *Cuisine et Vins de France*—
was the most celebrated writer on food in France in the 20th century and
was dubbed the Prince of Gastronomy." I suspect that Jeffrey L. Steingarten
might be his avatar.

A quick digression here on what were once food aversions but for the
trending and whimsical public are no longer. How many different foods,
now relished—and indeed now very expensive—in former times used to be
discarded as virtual garbage? Grappa, garlic scapes, lobster, even edible offal.
For that matter, parts of fruits and vegetables like broccoli leaves and onion
skin are still thrown away although they contain health benefits—and we
can easily include them in our diet, or so say nutritionists. Chard stems, for
example, are packed with glutamine, antioxidants and phenolic compounds:
the stems are as edible as the leaves. Orange peel, probably the most common of all identifiable peels, is a true powerhouse of fiber, flavonoids, and
vitamins. Anecdotal evidence has revealed that an active chemical in orange
peels (d-limonene) helps relieve heartburn and indigestion. The good concentration of vitamin C helps boost the immune system and can help ward
off respiratory infections. It is said that the priciest food in the world is not
Beluga caviar or Kobe beef—no, the most expensive food in the world is
what spoils before you eat it!

Talk about food aversions in the literal sense? The USDA estimates that
40 percent of food, or 80 billion pounds, produced in this country goes

uneaten every year—is tossed out—amounting to a loss of $161.6 billion annually. We live here in the richest nation in the history of the world in terms of food production, yet as many as one in six Americans is going hungry. Talk about a disturbing statistic! A glaring and ongoing scandal is that grocery stores catering to wealthy shoppers discard billions of pounds of wholesome food in the United States because of very minor cosmetic flaws—ugly and/ or blemished produce is thrown out as food scrap—while, in low-income neighborhoods across the country, 48 million Americans lack reliable access to affordable, nutritious food! Think about it: almost *half of the food in the United States is wasted*, according to the US Department of Agriculture. That means that $30 to $40 of every $100 spent at the grocery store is thrown out. Discarded. Wasted. Jettisoned. Scrapped. Simply thrown away just like it never was!

I am not talking about "Freeganism." Have you heard this odd term? It is the practice of reclaiming and eating food that has been discarded. (The word "freegan" is a portmanteau of "free" and "vegan.") Freegans and freeganism are often seen as part of a wider "anti-consumerist ideology, and freegans zealously employ a range of alternative living strategies based on limited participation in the conventional economy and minimal consumption of resources. Freegans, as one rosy-eyed critic says, "embrace community, generosity, social concern, freedom, cooperation, and sharing in opposition to a society based on materialism, moral apathy, competition, conformity, and greed." Dumpster divers and bindlestiff scroungers are not all vegans, but the basic ideology of veganism is inherent in freeganism. Freeganism, as a matter of fact, started in the mid-1990s, out of the antiglobalization and environmentalist movements. The movement also has elements of "Diggers," an anarchist street theater group based in Haight-Ashbury in San Francisco in the 1960s that gave away rescued food but that today is still often associated with the witchy female pursuivants of the Manson Gang.

But back to what once went on the scrap heap. Grappa started off as a by-product in the Italian winemaking trade, a rough drink made with what was available, potent enough to get farmers through the cold winter months. It was good at warming you up, but not particularly tasty, similar to the grain alcohols of the Midwestern United States. Grappa largely remained a drink of the poor workmen and farmers until the 1960s. It now averages about $65 per bottle. A bottle of Grappa Gioiello Chestnut Honery Nonino costs $110. Private vineyard issues and certain rare bottle stocks sell for even more.

Garlic scapes for years were considered little more than a by-product of the garlic plant. They were usually trimmed off in early or middle summer, simply to ensure that all of the plants' energy went into the forming plump bulbs underground. Today, however scapes are harvested not only for that reason but also to meet growing demand for them as a much-sought-after ingredient.

Lobsters used to be prison food, fodder for slaves and indentured servants and were often fed to pigs, cows, goats, and cats, while Native Americans used them as fertilizer and fish-bait. The crustaceans acquired a stigma, and, according to American observer John Rowan, became "signs of poverty and degradation." Stewards and servants from Massachusetts once got so fed up with eating lobster every day that they took their masters to court, and judges often resolved in their favor, ruling the servants would only have to eat lobster three times a week. It was only in the late 19th-century that a second look was taken at the crustaceans. Lobsters, like crabs and shrimp, are in fact crustaceans and not, strictly speaking, shellfish. They do not have shells, as such, even though that is the term we use for them. Their "shells" are properly carapaces; hard carapaces have joints for movement and, while they grow with the creature, are periodically sloughed off, that is, shed and regrown. When cooked, crustaceans turn color, of course—shrimp from a translucent white-bluish-gray to pink or orange and white, and lobsters from blue-black-scarlet to bright orange-red. What's interesting is almost all eaters and cooks throw away the carapaces, or shells, if you will, whereas it is much more savvy to use them simply because as a resolve they actually can yield more flavor. Cheap because you have already bought lobsters for their meat, all the shells make a good foundation for broth. We are so used casually to throw them away when eating a steamed lobster or shrimp cocktail. Habits are often a vice. After making your first lobster or shrimp broth, using these shells, you will to hate yourself when you think of the hundreds of dollars you have thrown into the garbage over past years.

We are of course inured to what we discard in the way of foods by what we are conditioned to dislike and so adjust ourselves to rigid positions, holding them inflexibly to us like life-saving ballast.

In the space of six weeks during the winter of 1918 whilst living in Switzerland, Vaslav Nijinsky wrote his "diaries," a rambling string of sentiments in a "stream of consciousness," with no dates, that were strongly influenced by the later writings of Leo Tolstoy, especially his book *The Kingdom of God is Within You*. Nijinsky was far from alone in his preoccupation with vegetarianism and hatred of meat, as there were many "Tolstoyans" including Gandhi, who named his South African ashram "Tolstoy Farm." Nijinsky's refusal to eat meat was linked to his sex drive, which, out of guilt, he sought to suppress. "At every opportunity I tell my wife [Romola], it is bad to eat meat," wrote the highly neurotic ballet dancer, "My wife understands me but does not want to eat only vegetables, thinking that it is only a whim of mine. I wished her good when I asked her not to eat sausage at night, knowing its action. She says, 'What is good for you is not good for me.'" Another entry goes:

> The Spaniards spill the blood of bulls and therefore like murder. They are terrible people because they murder bulls. Even the Church and the Pope cannot put an end to this slaughter. The Spaniards think that a bull is a beast. The toreador weeps before killing the bull. I know that many toreadors whose stomachs the bull has split. I hated this slaughter, but I was not understood. [Serge] Diaghilev said with Z. [Diaghilev's friend] that a bullfight is a magnificent art. I know they will both say I am mad and one cannot be offended with me, because Diaghilev always used that trick… I do not like eating meat because I have seen lambs and pigs killed. I saw and felt their pain. They felt the approaching death. I left in order not to see their death. I could not bear it. I cried like a child. I ran up a hill and could not breathe. I felt that I was choking. I felt the death of the lamb. I chose a mountain, where there were no people. I was afraid of being ridiculed.

"I was called to lunch at half past twelve. I wanted to eat. I did not lunch as I saw meat," writes Nijinsky, continuing,

> My wife wanted to eat it. I left the soup, which was made out of meat, my wife became angry. She thought I disliked the food. I dislike meat because I know how the animals are killed and how they cry. I wanted to show her that marriage is non-existent if people are of different opinions. I threw the wedding ring on the table, then took it and put it on again. My wife was terribly nervous. I threw the ring once more, because I felt that she was wanting meat. I love animals and could not therefore eat their flesh, knowing that if I did, another animal would have to be killed. I only eat when I am hungry. My wife is sorry for me and thinks

> that I must eat. I like bread and butter and cheese and
> eggs. I eat very little for my constitution, and I feel
> better since I have not eaten meat. I know that doc-
> tors will say all this is nonsense—that meat is neces-
> sary. But it is not: it arouses lecherous feelings. Those
> feelings have disappeared since I have not eaten meat.

The very *act* of eating became an issue for Nijinsky. "I do not know what I need, but I want to write. I will go ahead and eat and will eat with appetite, if God wills it. I do not want to eat, because I love him. God wants me to eat. I do not want to upset my servants. If they are upset, I will die of hunger."

Associative distaste has long been a trope with food phobias: grappa with stark poverty, meat with animal slaughter, foods like lobsters, parsnips, and scapes with trash fare, the snobbish refusal (often leading to pellagra) by die-hard white provincials even to consider eating or drinking "potlik-ker," so associated is it, even today, with the diet of poor black folks, and so forth. Many French citizens are still made uneasy by hearing such mundane terms as *eau de Vichy*, *vichyssoise*, Vichy pastilles, even the cooking style called "Vichy" where certain foods, like carrots, for example, are cooked with a small amount of water, butter, sugar, and sprinkled lightly with minced pars-ley, for to this day the word *Vichy* evokes the repellent collusionist French regime in France that colluded with the Nazis during World War II. We tend to discern only what determines what we want, so any diagnosis is on a tilt. As Stephen Crane wrote in *The Blue Hotel*, "Every sin is a result of collaboration."

13.

MYSTIC REFUSALS

I have often wondered what is indicated in suicides, or extreme or prodigious fasters, of the act of starving oneself to death. It is obviously the ultimate gesture of deprivation. Eratosthenes. Anaxagoras of Clazomenae. Emperor Wu of Liang. St. Maximilian Kolbe. Pope John XIV. Robert O'Hara Burke. Pavel Filonov. Kurt Gödel. Romola Nijinsky's mother, upon being widowed, starved herself to death. Singer Karen Carpenter, an anorectic who suffered from a psychological disturbance, refused to eat anything. Most common in females, anorexia nervosa is characterized by extreme loss of weight and a refusal to gain pounds, with the person involved having a distorted body image. Although generally associated with believing oneself to be overweight, a distorted body image could refer to a fear of *being* itself. *Anorexia mirabilis* literally means "miraculous lack of appetite." This refers predominantly to women and young girls of the Middle Ages who in God's name starved themselves, often to the point of death. This phenomenon, also known by the name *inedia prodigiosa* ("prodigious fasting"), was frequently coupled with other ascetic practices, such as lifelong virginity, flagellant behavior, the donning of hairshirts, sleeping on beds of thorns, and other assorted self-mutilations. Pope Leo I, also called the "Great," called fasting the "food of virtue," writing that "from abstinence there arise chaste thoughts, just decisions, salutary counsels." It was largely a practice of Catholic women known as "miraculous maids." Margaret of Cortona and Angela of Foligno are two who come to mind. According to legend, the Portuguese mystic, Alexandrina Maria da Costa, lived exclusively on the Eucharist from 1942 to 1955. St. Catherine of Siena, who once famously declared that "a full belly does not make for a chaste spirit" (*The Dialogue of Divine Providence*, 125), referred to her inability to eat as an infirmity, yet she also believed fasting to be a soul-saving means of penance, not only for her own sins but for all the sins of her family and those of the Roman Catholic Church, as well.

As a form of asceticism and with the purpose of purifying themselves and their world from sin, such fasting women believed that through prayer, self-denial, and even self-torture, they could achieve perfect unity with God, and that giving in to their human needs was indeed selfish, greedy, and gluttonous

Most of us seek to be fed. In a sense, it is our most essential sojourn as wayfarers on our life's journey. In our desperation, we would even give up our freedom for food, as Dostoevsky points out in "The Grand Inquisitor" in *The Brothers Karamazov*, where we read, "In the end, they will lay their freedom at our feet and say to us, 'Make us your slaves, but feed us.'" In our search for food we greatly fear that we will come up empty, feeding on the wind (see Hosea 12). It is a story that we find evocatively told in *The Confessions of St. Augustine*, almost as a moral fable. The Augustinian pilgrimage is portrayed as a metaphor for the need of true and actual satiety, leading one to God. He himself was a gorger, and readily admitted it. "I stole from my parents' cellar and table, sometimes just because I was a glutton." He tells us, "I lived to indulge my mood." "I felt no desire whatever for the Living Bread, not because I had plenty, but because the more I went without it, the more I seemed to loathe it. My soul was weak and puny." He felt unsatisfied and echoed the words of the Prodigal Son: "I wandered so far from your presence that I was not even able to eat the husks that I feed the swine" (Luke 15:16). An inner debate, causing Augustine turmoil, was that, although we live at a platonic remove from truth, we find in ourselves a pressing need for actual truth, with no removes. "As a beggar, I yearned to be filled by him in the midst of those who eat and are satisfied," he wrote out of deep humility, seeking peace. When he does find God, he says, "How good it felt to be done with the delectable trifles of life."

In his famous poetic passage in book 27, the God-consoled Augustine arrestingly sang out in all humility,

> Late have I loved you, O Beauty ever ancient, ever
> new, late have I loved you! You were within me, but I
> was outside, and it was there that I searched for you.
> In my unloveliness I plunged into the lovely things,
> which you created. You were with me, but I was not
> with you. Created things kept me from you; yet if they
> had not been in you they would have not been at all.
> You called, you shouted, and you broke through my

deafness. You flashed, you shone, and you dispelled
my blindness. You breathed your fragrance on me; I
drew in breath and now I pant for you. I have tasted
you, now I hunger and thirst for more. You touched
me, and I burned for your peace.

He writes in aposeopesis to God, "You gave out such a delightful fragrance, and I drew it in and came breathing hard after you. I tasted, and it made me hunger and thirst." The Lord becomes for him the "food that never perishes. (cf. Psalms 74:21) He is the God of Hosts—sacramental bread. "Restore us again, O God of Hosts; cause thy face to shine, and we shall be saved," sings the Psalmist (80:7). For Jesus Christ assured us as he did Augustine, "I am the living bread that came down from heaven. Whoever eats this bread will live forever. This bread is my flesh, which I will give for the life of the world." (John 6:51) He is the promised bread of the Presence (Lev. 21:6, 8)

As a young Trappist novice, I became fascinated with St. John Cassian on the Desert Fathers and pondered the ascetic life and "perfection of the heart" of many of those isolatos, reading hour after hour during *lectio divina* of the strange and storied accounts of anchorites like Pachorius, John Climacus, Benedict of Nursia, St. Helen of Babylon, and the great St. Anthony of Thebes, the father of all monks, mystics, cenobites and seekers who took to heart James 4:4, "The world's friendship means enmity with God." I daresay that few if anyone in the modern world reads John Cassian anymore, especially on such subjects as the methods of prayer, the forms and shapes of vainglory, the Psalms recited among the Egyptians, what makes a true renunciant, how to fight the habit of gluttony, the proof of prayers being heard, what to eat in the desert to sustain life, even botanical subjects like the mysterious Middle Eastern plant called "charlock" (prepared with salt and steeped in water), which he actually considered to be a luxurous "temptation" —an anchorite's daily fare was sparse, as he longed to be "free to feed on the word of God without distraction by appetite"—or would ever trifle with such arcana as even bothering to look into the "Sayings of the Fathers" (*Apophthegmata Patrum*, originally in Coptic, the language of the Desert Fathers).

Over the course of my life I have read many books by and about saintly Charles de Foucauld, a man who lived a life of holy solitude in a hermitage among the Tuaregs in Tamanghasset in southern Algeria, a region in the central part of Sahara and the Ahaggar Mountains (the Hoggar). In my early idealistic reveries, I actually dreamt of living the very same way he lived. I came to despise authority and developed into an anarchist in the very monastery where I had given my soul to God. (Anarchy consists, not in chaos or disorder, but in rejecting a centralized authority or ultimate arbiter.) It was inculcated in me by an officious Prior named Fr. Owen Hoey who early one morning invited me into his office, had me kneel at his desk, a customary procedure between novice-master and novice, and, after several sententious remarks about monastic life and a few perfunctory questions about my well-being, quietly pointed out for me that I had shown myself to be "bumptious" the day before in not waiting like the other novices to be told (by a hand sign) to begin mowing the lawn at the guest house. It seems I had been headstrong in my peremptory action in doing what in his eyes constituted an act of willful disobedience by refusing to wait for direction and energetically—but presumptuously—jumping off the truck to begin mowing the grass. I later wept on my knees in private but chose anarchy, as opposed to hierarchy thereafter, in spite of the fact that, to me, still, the true monk is the noblest man on the face of the earth.

There is a wonderfully apt if overly sentimental modern echo of the "distraction of appetite," in J.D. Salinger's story, "Franny," while we are also shown—in vivid contrast—crass overindulgence. We find lovely, questing Franny Glass with all her Salingeresque hypercriticality and warm humanism disturbed and distracted at lunch in a fancy restaurant sitting before a glass of milk, from which she takes a few tiny sips, and a chicken sandwich that goes untouched, while her obnoxious date, Lane, boasting about his Flaubert paper for which he received a grade A, is tucking into a large order of snails, frog's legs, and salad. Franny eats nothing, feels faint, and becomes progressively more uncomfortable talking to Lane. She is in possession of a small book titled *The Way of a Pilgrim*, which recounts the story of a Russian wanderer who learns the power of "praying without ceasing." The "Jesus Prayer" involves internalizing the prayer, "Lord Jesus Christ, Son of God, have mercy on me, a sinner," to a point where, repeated, it becomes an unconscious mantra, almost like a heartbeat, that can lead to mystical truths. The particular prayer means a great deal to Franny and in a very simple way reveals her to be a seeker, a quester. On the other hand, Lane is focused on keeping their timetable for a party and football game. It is clear that her spirituality is in her temperance. She is "other," as critic Janet Malcolm notes in her essay "Salinger's Cigarettes," "the misfit... unable to eat the food normal people eat."

Who anymore, for that matter, struggles against the "flesh"—or would even think of using that phrase anymore—or actively resorts to the remedies of spiritual fasting or self-denial? It seems a kind of antediluvian madness even to be asking such questions to man in the modern world, when, say, even Christmas now is no longer celebrated as a holy day. One has to be removed to meditate, pray, cloistered from the temptations of foolishness and farce by which most men live today. The anchorite lives alone with his prayers. Ἀναχωρεο (*anachoreo*) means to withdraw. T.E. Lawrence understood this who for a while lived among people who accepted the spirit of denial and in *The Seven Pillars of Wisdom* wrote, "The desert Arab found no joy like the joy of voluntarily holding back. He found luxury in abnegation, renunciation, self-restraint. He made nakedness of the mind as sensuous as nakedness of the body. He saved his own soul, perhaps, and without danger, but in a hard selfishness. His desert was made a spiritual ice-house, in which was preserved intact but unimproved for all ages a vision of the unity of God... This faith of the desert was impossible in the towns. It was at once too strange, too impalpable for export and common use."

I once visited the tomb in Surrey, England of Christine Carpenter, the Anchoress of Shere. A young girl, she left her anchor-hold once but then wrote a letter—one in her behalf (she probably could not write, females not being educated), requesting of the Bishop of Winchester that she be re-enclosed. We do not know why she left or how long she led an extra-mural life, only (so goes a document) "now with God's help changed in heart, wishing to return to her former abode and calling, she has humbly petitioned us that she may be treated mercifully by the Apostolic See." The letter asked that she be permitted to return to her cell, "lest by wandering any longer about the world she be exposed to the bites of the rapacious wolf and, which heaven forbid, her blood be required at your hands." In the 14th-century church, the hagioscope or "squint" through which she received her food still exists. I love visiting abbeys; I had badly wanted to visit the original old monastery at Monte Cassino; sadly, it was destroyed in 1944 by Allied bombing, even if it was rebuilt after the war.

Monks of the old school usually ate—and very lightly—at the ninth hour of the day, counting the hours of the day from sunrise. The "ninth hour" (*nona hora*) was 3 p.m., an hour (and office) monks call "*none*," not at noon, the fossil word we still use today (noon is cognate to Latin for the number 9). They adopted the Jewish custom of praying at certain hours, and the daily timetable drawn up for prayer, centering their lives, also dictated when the monks ate, meager food like dry bread, green herbs, black radishes, lentils, an olive or two, water. Vegetables were sometimes salted in brine to preserve them for future use. It was reasoned it was better that one should eat every day, but only a little, so as not to be satisfied. It was customary to keep the canonical fasts of Wednesday and Friday, set days of complete abstinence from food, in memory of the Passion of Christ, but on other days a meal in the evening, usually after Communion, was the norm. Prayer and self-denial are the tried recourses of the saint. French philosopher, Christian mystic, and political activist Simone Weil—Albert Camus described her as "the only great spirit of our times"—is remembered to have attended daily Mass at Corpus Christi Church in Harlem in New York City, where the then Columbia student and future Trappist monk, Thomas Merton, was later received into the Roman Catholic Church. A Jew who became a Christian convert, Weil who chose to suffer in imitation of Christ daily refused to eat more food than did her fellow countrymen in occupied France or the victims in the Nazi concentration camps.

Precocious, she learned ancient Greek as a teenager, and even some Sanskrit. She attended the Lycee Henri IV and, studying philosophy, graduated from the École Normale Supérieure, where she sought keys to spirituality as well as ways to discover a wisdom of transcendence, almost as if taking fully to heart the insightful remark of A.N. Whitehead, "The essence of education is that it be religious." She never married, had no children, and led a selfless but altruistic life, defending workers and taking up not only their causes but also the problems of the unemployed. She sided with the left in the Spanish Civil War, worked as a laborer to understand the working class, and was at times a Marxist, pacifist, and a trade unionist.

When at the end of her life in London Weil was diagnosed with her fatal illness, to the great frustration of doctors and her friends, she chose to eat sparsely and only sporadically. She became an impossible patient. She told the doctors that she would eat no more than ordinary French people under Nazi occupation were eating. She ate virtually nothing, no hypernutremia for her—no vitamins, no calories, no protein. One of the doctors called her the "most difficult patient I have ever seen. "Religion is a form of nourishment," Weil said. "We must give up everything which is not grace and not even desire grace." She declared, "We only possess what we renounce. May God grant that I become nothing. We must become nothing. We must go down to the vegetative level. It is then that God becomes bread." Ultimately, they tried tube-feeding her in an attempt to save her, but it was all in vain. She died alone in London, on August 24, 1943, at the age of 34, mourned only by a handful of friends.

Renouncing food may be moral, as much a food aversion as a moral stance in a very real way. The satisfaction of our bodily needs is not in itself a sin, but it may become so whenever a moral issue is involved. Tempting our Savior in the desert in Milton's *Paradise Lost*, Satan asks Christ, "If food were now before thee set wouldst thou not eat?" and Jesus replies, "Thereafter as I like the giver." The rich repast is the offering of the Devil. Christ's exemplary victory is a victory of temperance, the triumph of reason over desire.

The punishing regimes of labor that she assumed during the war took a heavy toll on her, which led to that diagnosis of consumption. The coroner's report indicated that "the deceased did kill and slay herself by refusing to eat whilst the balance of her mind was disturbed." The cause of her painful death, nevertheless, remains a subject of debate for many to this day. Some claim that her refusal to eat came from her desire to express some form of solidarity toward the suffering victims of the war. Others are convinced that Weil's willful self-starvation was the act of an extreme neurotic after intensely studying the work of Schopenhauer. In his chapters on saintly asceticism and salvation in Christianity, the German philosopher simply described self-starvation as a preferred—and chosen—method of self-denial. However, Simone Pétrement, the first and perhaps foremost of Weil's biographers, considers that the coroner's report was simply mistaken. Illness seemed to speak to her in ways many cannot understand. But are we not given to understand that the development of Hans Castorp's disease in Thomas Mann's *The Magic Mountain* is the prerequisite for his growing self-awareness? It was in the process of undergoing an illness that St. Francis came to a sudden understanding of God with a concomitant drive to follow him.

Basing her view on letters written by the personnel of the sanatorium at which the convalescent Simone Weil was treated, Simone Pétrement affirms that Weil asked for food on several different occasions while she was hospitalized and at times even took in a little bit of nourishment a few days before her death. It is the contention of Pétrement that it was in fact Weil's poor health, her run-down, desperate condition that eventually made the woman unable to eat.

It may have been what is called a "perversion of virtue," a term coined by Thomas Joiner, a professor of psychology at Florida State University and a specialist in the study of suicidal behavior, where a person by way of a disturbed rationale develops the unswerving conviction that his or her life is more valuable when she is dead—where, in an act of violent mercy, absence is triumph.

Weil's concept of "*malheur*" goes beyond simple suffering, although it certainly includes it. Only certain souls are capable of truly experiencing affliction; these are precisely those souls which are least deserving of it—those that are most prone or open to spiritual realization. Affliction for her was suffering that transcended both body and mind; such physical and mental anguish scourges the very soul. It is associated with both necessity and with chance and fraught with necessity because it is hard-wired into existence itself and imposed upon the sufferer with the full force of the inescapable. Yet it is also subject to chance, inasmuch as chance is an inescapable part of the nature of existence. The element of chance is essential to the nature of affliction; in other words, one's personal afflictions do not usually—let alone always—follow from one's sins, as Christian theology has it but are rather visited upon a person for no special or extraordinary reason. The person who has known unalloyed joy, even if only for a moment…is the only person for whom affliction is something devastating. At the same time, he is the only person who has not deserved the punishment. For him, in the final analysis, it is no punishment; it is simply God holding his hand and pressing rather hard. For, if he remains constant to faith, what he will discover buried deep under the sound of his own lamentations is the pearl of the silence of God. She listened for silences. It was part of her mystical engagement with God and his infinite mystery. Thoreau wrote in his *Journals* (January 1852), "The longest silence is the most pertinent question most pertinently put. Emphatically silent. The most important question, whose answers concern us more than any, are never put in any other way."

A major revelation of Weil's she traced to an epiphany that she had in 1938 while reciting a poem by 17th-century poet George Herbert entitled "Love (III)," a dramatic monologue spoken by Jesus on the cross, "after which," she explained, "Christ himself came down and took possession of me." All of her writings thereafter became more mystical and spiritual.

Weil had a desert mind. Unlike the brilliant but atheistic philosopher, Bertrand Russell, who somewhat hesitantly confessed in his *Autobiography* that he could only find true internal peace in the presence of moving water, she found comfort and took solace in the company of the poor. This was her anchor to windward. She fully participated in the French general strike of 1933 that had been called to protest against wide unemployment and wage cuts, personally working all the while for charitable causes. The following year she took a twelve-month leave from her teaching position in order to take a job, incognito, as a laborer in several factories, one of them owned by Renault, believing that the experience would allow her to connect with humanity. God came first with Weil, however, who was a seeker of truth and not merely a syndicalist activist. This is important to see in relation to her spiritual life.

Just as Ludwig Wittgenstein, sought to cast off all encumbrances that imposed an insupportable burden on his attitude to the outside world, seeking to shed all things, big or small, that he found to be petty or ludicrous, as his friend and later architectural collaborator, Paul Engelmann explained,

Simone Weil chose extreme abnegation as a penance, as a way to serve Christ and poverty.

Average people were foreigners to the poor, Weil felt, and truly to feel their need, to empathize with them, to suffer with and for them, one needed to "renounce all compensations," food among them. It was an aspect of John the Baptist's exhortation for man to repent, to "change one's mind" (μετανόια).

Suffering, to Weil, ennobled a person. Indulgence, eating if you will, cooperates with a kind of pride of the self and in doing so refuses affliction, participating in a kind of willfulness. Her *Gravity and Grace*, a compliation of notebooks that she left behind, echoes in a very real way the Calvinistic thoughts raised by severe Father Mapple in his fulminating sermon delivered in Melville's *Moby-Dick*. When we obey ourselves, we automatically disobey God. It is only when we disobey ourselves that we can obey God. Citing Jonah, the minister says, "But all the things that God would have us do are hard for us to do—remember that—and hence, he oftener commands us than endeavors to persuade. And if we obey God, we must disobey ourselves; and it is in this disobeying ourselves, wherein the hardness of obeying God consists." A woman truly Christian in her mansuetude, Weil's essential life, born of her faith, goodness, and need, was her prayer life, and she believed with St. Thomas Aquinas, that she learned more by prayer than by study, for in her opinion it was through prayer and fasting in God's name that alone will bring a person joy. Sacrifice to her was the very linchpin of love. The harsh truth is that on this earth we all have to participate in Christ's crucifixion. The cross is the gift that God gives his friends.

Eating has been seen by some, falsely of course, as an unholy form of ego, of self-assertion, of vanity. Was that how Weil saw it? We live in a valley of tears, she felt, because God is not here. I say this because it was *absence itself* for her that became the key image for her theodicy, her metaphysics, her cosmology. It was her firm belief that God created everything by an act of self-delimitation—in other words, because God is conceived as a kind of utter fullness, a perfect being, no creature could exist except where God was not. Creation occurred when God withdrew in part. We inhabit "not-God-space," a state of becoming that in Weil's view ought to make us humble. True humility meant everything to Weil and became for her a *kenosis* (emptiness) that precedes the corrective filling of Christ's holy incarnation (cf. Athanasius). We are all born in a sort of damnation, not so much owing to Original Sin, as to the fact that, being created at all, we are in creation precisely what God is not, i.e., we are the *opposite* of what is holy. We have to earn our value by prayer and self-denial. Simone Weil often fasted. What did she live on? Mere light? The darkness of night? Maybe she ate electricity? It brings to my mind some magical lines from "Insomnia" by Marina Tsvetayeva who in her own terrible pain roamed the streets at night,

> The lights are like threads of golden beads,
> in my mouth is the taste of the night leaf.
> Liberate me from the bonds of day,
> my friends, understand: I'm nothing but your dream.

[Translated by Elaine Feinstein]

This notion of creation is a cornerstone of Weil's theodicy, for if creation is conceived this way (as necessarily containing evil within itself), then there is no problem regarding the entrance of evil into a perfect world. Nor does this constitute a delimitation of God's omnipotence. It is not that God could not create a perfect world, merely that the act of "creation" implies in its very essence the impossibility of perfection. It is pure Jansenism, a theological movement that began and flourished in France, emphasizing original sin, human depravity, the necessity of divine grace, and predestination. The notion of the necessity of evil, however, does not mean that we are originally and continually doomed. On the contrary, Weil assures us, a paradox is involved: "Evil is the form which God's mercy takes in this world." It was her belief that evil, and its sad consequence, affliction, served to drive us out of ourselves and *towards* God. "The extreme affliction which overtakes human beings does not create human misery, it merely reveals it," she wrote. Specifically, affliction drives us to what Weil referred to as "de-creation," a state which is not death, but rather closer to "extinction" (nirvana) in the Buddhist tradition—the willed dissolution of the subjective ego in attaining realization of the true nature of the universe.

It was brave souls like Simone Weil who, fully embracing spiritual truth, fought the kind of moronic authority that made the world so topsy-turvy, so hypocritical, so false. Who was it that said a true gaffe suddenly occurs when in rare instances politicians are caught telling the truth? "For our law has in it a turn of humour or touch of fancy which Nero or Herod never happened to think of: that of actually punishing homeless people for not sleeping at home," wrote G.K. Chesterton. Weil was in the world, not of it. "Only he who has measured the dominion of force, and knows how *not* to respect it, is capable of love and justice."

Speaking of religion, one cannot ignore TV's *Star Trek*, which is a modern forgery of faith, if you will—I don't get it myself—with a very large congregation. I will ignore as much clatrappery as I can and concentrate on its quirky, Kirk-y food side.

The Vulcans of *Star Trek* fame cannot eat barbecue. It is part of their abstemious culture. "We all know what Vulcans are all about—ultra logical, emotionless, intellectual, non-indulgent, cool under pressure. Their food is generally bland, too," writes Adam Kuban in a fairly comprehensive blog called *A Primer to Star Trek Food and Drink* in May 2009, "and from what I can remember in all my years of watching Trek shows and movies," he adds, "there has not really been a standout dish that is mentioned again and again in the way Romulan ale is."

"Any Trek fan worth his or her salt (included in Starfleet emergency rations, by the way) knows that Romulan ale is one of the most widely referenced food-and-beverage items in the franchise. It is an ultra-potent blue drink that reportedly results in instant drunkeness. Its proper Romulan name may be 'kali-fal.'"

Vulcans also do not drink alcoholic beverages. There have been exceptions to this on a number of Star Trek episodes. On several occasions, Spock has been known to partake. On what is the definitive blog, Spocklives.com, we learn that in the episode, "The Enterprise Incident," he shares a glass of Romulan Ale with the female Romulan commander. In "Requiem for Methuselah," he requests Terran Brandy and in the film, *The Undiscovered Country*, he can also be seen drinking Romulan Ale at a formal dinner with the Klingons. There is apparently also a beverage called Vulcan Port, although there is some debate among Trekkies as to whether this wine is exported from Vulcan, where the speculation is it is used in ceremonial practices, or the name is simply applied to it. It may even be non-alcoholic. The novelization for "The Voyage Home" suggests that Vulcans are immune to the effects of alcohol, but become intoxicated upon consuming chocolate. Kuban writes,

> Science fiction often holds a mirror up to contemporary culture, critiquing its practices, politics, and mores. It is also the case with Romulan ale. Because of the United Federation of Planets' standoff with the Romulan Empire, the drink is illegal within the Federation, very much in the way Cuban cigars are banned and unavailable in the U.S. But like the captains of industry of today, captains of starships indulge in this vice.

At one time, Kuban says, a dedicated fan could go out and actually purchase six packs of Romulan Ale, traveling to one of the venues like the Star Trek Experience in Las Vegas, which is now of the past and long gone.

As James Tiberius Kirk says in "The Undiscovered Country," the routine violation of the embargo is "one of the advantages of being a thousand light years from Federation headquarters."

Are you aware that there is an *Official Star Trek Cooking Manual?* It is supposedly counted—or so I have read—as the rarest of all the Star Trek paperback books. This so-called recipe book, one assumes, was transported to the present time by a diligent amanuensis. There are notable Trekkies, experts in the information department, among them, Dour Drexler, Dorothy Duder, Harry Doddema, Dan Carlson, and, as I have mentioned, the zealot, Adam Kuban whom we have already met. Kuban observes,

> As Memory Alpha notes, "The introduction includes what is purportedly a food synthesizer algorithm for Dr. McCoy's favorite dish; in fact, it is FORTRAN source code for a program that prints the message, 'CHICKEN 3.14159 SKEPTIC.'"

Is Kuban serious? It means Mock Chicken Pi(e)—get it? One can peruse the many Star Trek sites to scope out entire food systems.

"Memory Alpha," by the way, is a collaborative project to create the most definitive, accurate, and accessible encyclopedia and reference for everything related to Star Trek. The English-language Memory Alpha started in November 2003 and currently consists of as many as—count them—34,990 articles. If this is your first visit, please read an introduction to Memory Alpha. Lotsa fun, huh?

A major difference between Star Trek and Star Wars people (I am emphatically neither) is that the Star Trek characters actually *eat food*. In all six Star Wars movies, I believe that the characters attempt to eat nothing but one floating pear and Aunt Beroo's blue milk. I should perhaps mention here, as I failed to do before, that there are several recipes out there for Earth-bound Romulan ale. The simplest involves mixing equal amounts of vodka, rum, and blue curaçao, but this one sounds a bit tastier: equal parts vodka, triple sec, blue curaçao, and lemonade.

Strangely, blue is the *least* common color in the food that human beings eat. The word "blueberry" was the original scent of the blue-colored Magic Scents Crayons that were introduced by Binney & Smith Inc. in 1994. The crayons were given mostly *food* scents. Numerous reports were soon coming in that children were actually eating the food-scented crayons. The food scents were retired and replaced with non-food scents. The scent for the color blue became "new car." Leave it to Madison Avenue to find any hole to get in under the tent, right?

Most Vulcans are vegetarians, of course. They are a nonviolent species, which is reflected by their eating habits. It may be summed up best with a quote from *The Logic of Surak* (as presented in Diane Duane's *Spock's World*), which states: "Ideally, do no harm... As far as possible, do not kill. Can you return life to what you kill?" This philosophy would most likely imply that Vulcans are not just simply vegetarians, but vegan. A Vulcan would see no logic in raising an animal to consume its eggs, as that could be considered taking a life.

As we read on Spocklives.com, "The first time that Vulcan vegetarianism is established within *Star Trek* 'canon' is in the episode 'All Our Yesterdays,' when after consuming meat Mr. Spock states, 'I'm behaving disgracefully. I have eaten animal flesh, and I've enjoyed it. What is wrong with me?'" Perhaps his slip was due to being 5000 years in the past, which would be before the Vulcan "Time of Awakening" or simply because there was nothing else available at the time. The Vulcan repertoire regarding food may be regarded as chaste and, if you will, a bit over-considered. "A little digging shows that Vulcans are absolutely prissy when it comes to food and drink," writes Kuban, and further elucidates,

> First of all, alcohol reportedly has no effect on them (even though they do produce spirits on the planet Vulcan). According to Memory Alpha, "Vulcans have a superior metabolism to Humans. Caffeine and sapotoxins have little effect on them. They are also capable of surviving for long durations without food or sleep." Some Romulan foods are: "Jumbo Romulan mollusk," a delicacy that appears to be served over rice, with perhaps scrambled egg. "Osol Twist," A very tart candy first mentioned in *Deep Space 9* episode "Image in the Sand," and, among others, "Viinerine," a military staple, it first appears in *TNG* episode, "Face of the Enemy."

It may be noted here, in the "faux" or near-meat department, that some Vulcans have been known to eat what is called "replicated" meat, because, according to Spocklives.com, "it is only patterned after real meat and thus did not require violence to obtain as it is considered artificial. Likewise, some Vulcans may also consume seafood. However, both of these facts are debatable, as some have argued that in order to make replicated meat, they must first dematerialize and store actual meat compounds. It must also be pointed out that because Jumbo Vulcan Mollusks are available does not mean that Vulcans themselves eat them. Vulcans may consume meat only in dire circumstances where to do so is the only logical course of action. It is also interesting to note that it is customary for guests of a Vulcan home to prepare meals for their hosts." All these are important distinctions in the ST world.

It is well known that Vulcans do not like to touch their food with their hands, if at all possible, although Spock can actually be seen eating meat with his hands in "All Our Yesterdays." A popular Vulcan dish is plomeek soup, first seen in "Amok Time." Kuban remarks on this, explaining,

> This means that Vulcans would hate (if they could hate—emotionless, remember?) Buffalo wings, pizza, hot dogs, hamburgers, and sandwiches of all kinds. And barbecue would make them spaz—again, if they could spaz. (Then again, maybe trongs would help them?)

Kuban's list of Vulcan foods goes as follows:

> Brandy: Alcohol supposedly does not affect Vulcans, so Vulcan brandy may be used for ceremonial purposes or for export only
> Gespar: Some sort of breakfast food
> Jumbo mollusk: Related to the Romulan jumbo mollusk
> Mocha: You'd never guess that this was a coffeelike beverage, would you?
> Plomeek soup (Plomeek broth): A bland breakfast soup. In the original series (TOS), Spock threw a bowl of it at Nurse Chapel while he was going through his *pon farr* (crazy, horny mating period)
> Plomeek tea
> Pok tar
> Vulcan port: Again, Vulcans are supposedly immune to the effects of alcohol... You know, I really love Memory Alpha. It's so geeky and thorough. Its entry

on Vulcan port goes into AOC/DOC territory,
noting that a port wine is techinally from the Douro
Valley in Portugal and hence Vulcan port probably "is
a colloquialism, which suggests that the production of
Vulcan port, and the production of Vulcan alcoholic
beverages in general, are an imported practice not
native to Vulcan culture"
Redspice: Helped make a dish so tasty that Chief Miles
O'Brien (DS9) asked for the recipe
Vulcan spice tea: Seems like it was Captain Janeway's
(Voyager) version of Earl Grey
Vulcan tea

What about Klingon food? Fear not, Kuban goes out of his way to discuss the food of Klingons. Klingon bloodwine, for example. "Along with *gagh*, this is probably one of the best known Klingon foodstuff," he writes, and goes on further to elucidate,

Served warm, it's an alcoholic beverage that you
probably don't have the cojones (or whatever they
call them in Klingon) to consume. Jonathan Archer
(Enterprise) was the first human to give it a go.
According to Memory Alpha, Lieutenant Commander
Worf 'liked his young and sweet,' which sounds kinda
dirty. Also, according to Memory Alpha, the *Star Trek
Cookbook* seems to suggest it's made with fermented
blood and sugar. Recipes: If you want to go really nuts
and make an Earth-bound version, here's a recipe for
fermenting your own Klingon bloodwine that uses
10 to 15 packs of unsweetened Cherry Kool-Aid.
Wow. Sounds almost as potent as the actual stuff from
Qo'noS. If you're too much of a *bIHnuch* for brewing
your own, the Klingon Imperial Diplomatic Corps has
a number of cocktail-based Bloodwine recipes.

Kuban gives us an important footnote: "Update: Eugen Beer of Coldmud points out that *buy' ngop*, which would translate to 'That's good news!' literally means in Klingon, "The plates are full.""
Other Klingon food and drink that Kuban lists:

Bahgol: A warm tealike beverage. Well, not too different from humans...

Bregit lung: Spoke too soon. Bregit lung is not actually a respiratory organ but a dish of reptilian animals. Commander Riker (TNG) professes to like it. (Of course, Riker would—didn't he try to impress a Klingon female in one episode with his love of gagh?) Bregit lung is often eaten with grapok sauce

Gagh: A Klingon delicacy—live serpent worms. Allegedly, the actual taste of gagh is revolting and it is eaten solely for the unique sensation of the gagh spasming in one's mouth and stomach in their death throes.

Gladst: Finally, some vegetable matter. I was beginning to get worried about Klingons' regularity

Klingon martini: Neat. It's a bit of cultural fusion—vermouth, gin, and a dash of bloodwine

Pipius claw: Looks like chicken feet. I doubt it tastes like chicken, though

Racht: A big bowl of live worms

Raktajino: The rare Klingon foodstuff that humans enjoy. Probably because it's a coffeelike beverage

Rokeg blood pie

Targ: A type of Klingon herding animal. Eating heart of targ is believed to instill courage in a warrior, and the milk of the creature is apparently consumed as well

Zilm'kach: Some fruit to round things out

14.

WE CANNOT SMELL SALTINESS

The cantankerous English novelist, Evelyn Waugh, suffered few things very long that he did not like. Augustine Courtauld told the story of how on some Arctic expedition or other Waugh apparently disgraced himself at a time that rations ran short when, in a fit of pique, he pushed an entire sleigh-load of pemmican over a glacier, stating flatly that he "would rather die of starvation quickly than eke out a life on such a revolting substance." Pemmican, a concentrated mixture of fat and protein and a food commonly eaten in the Yukon, is a creation of the native peoples of North America; it was widely adopted as a high-energy food by gold-miners—characters chewing frozen pemmican appear in many of the poems of Robert W. Service—hunters involved in the fur trade, and even, notably, by Arctic and Antarctic explorers such as Britain's Robert Falcon Scott and Norway's Roald Amundsen. "Frankly, it's like chewing on a soft beef-flavored candle," said one critic. (The word comes from the Cree word *pimîhkân*, which itself is derived from the word *pimî*, "fat, grease.") The specific ingredients typically used were usually whatever was available, the meat often being bison, moose, elk, or deer. Fruits such as cranberries and saskatoon berries were often superadded, pressed into the meat. Cherries, currants, choke-berries and wild blueberries were also used, but almost exclusively in ceremonial and "wedding pemmican." Sioux pemmican back in Francis Parkman's day (cf. *The Oregon Trail Journal*) was composed of sun-dried buffalo meat packed in fat, flavored with pounded wild cherries, and kept in rawhide bags for storage.

A modern brand, Pemmican Traditional Beef Jerky is still sold. Ingredients: Beef, Water, Sugar, Salt, Garlic Powder, Maltodextrin, Monosodium Glutamate, Black Pepper Powder, Apple Cider Vinegar, Sodium Tripolyphosphate, Sodium Erythorbate, Citric Acid, Sodium Nitrite. It must be heady fare, as directions state: "For fresher tasting jerky, please consume within 3 days of opening." The one time I got looped in high school was drinking with some friends at the Irish-American Club in Everett, Mass., knocking back dime beers—"dimies"—and snapping off bites of Slim Jims (one ingredient, I recall, was "mechanically separated chicken"), and the ingested salt floored me. As to balsamic vinegar, chef Aaron Bashy hates cooking with it. "It's one of my pet peeves," he says. "Sometimes I think it's overused and can taint the color of a dish." When Bashy does use it, he simmers it with garlic or star anise—anything to sweeten it so he can use it as a drizzle like he does on the double stuffed pork chops. He also notes that many times aged red wine vinegar can be substituted for balsamic, because it offers a similar impact without the tannic flavor dimension. It has no sodium.

Table salt and other salts are used with almost criminal abandon in fast food and processed food. We wolf brininess in chemical gulps: olives, cheese, salami, anchovies. Our processed and pre-packaged meals could have been prepared by Huixtocihuatl, the Aztec goddess of salt! Sodium, like a sponge, soaks up water in the bloodstream, forcing our kidneys to retain more and more fluids. If you take in more than 2,300 mg. of salt per day, you may ex-perience water retention, high blood pressure, and bad headaches. Over-use of anything, of course—semicolons, antibiotics, buying lottery tickets, salt—cannot be good. Count the times in the film *Naughty Marietta* that card-board-voiced Nelson Eddy addresses Jeanette MacDonald as "blue eyes" or that Cary Grant in *Suspicion* calls Joan Fontaine "monkey face." I mean, *repeatedly*! Time out of number. It is an actual assault—and unrestrained. You want to scream.

We cannot smell "saltiness," however. That is one of its odd, anomalous features about the spice. It can be subtly subversive, even in the way we put on weight. That is why a good cook while working must always taste a dish. One single extra teaspoon of salt can ruin a sauce or a soup faster than a dog can lick a dish—adding a pinch of sugar is not an anodyne—and di-saster stories from the excesses of salt inform many of what might be called "infamy narratives," with half our population keeling over from high blood pressure, hypertension, and heart attacks. One such narrative on salt might have reached the stage back in 1956. Poet Robert Graves wanted Benjamin Britten to collaborate with Jerome Robbins and himself on a musical about the Queen of Sheba, and part of the plot—a bunny-hopping rebus—involved a feast of over-salted food in honor of Lot's wife, the only water pitcher being in Solomon's bed-chamber, where Sheba's increasing thirst would eventually lead the poor seductee—I believe the right adverb here is—thither. It was all arranged. Reportedly, however, singer Lena Horne who was being sought out to play the lead eventually bailed, as she "didn't dig the lyrics," and the whole thing was consigned to the land of Lethe.

Salt is one of the four things the tongue can taste (with sweet, sour, and bitter). I know people who eat *See Moi*, Chinese plums soaked in brine, then dried, probably the saltiest preserve known to man, and then lick the empty bag. I have seen magazine photos of little stores in Hawaii—I have never visited the place nor have I ever been invited there—with big glass jars of rock salt plum, salty white *li hing mui*, red ginger and other scalding salty treats. It is surely an unenviable statistic that the residents of Hawaii are the largest consumers of Spam per capita in the United States. Chains of the Hawaiian Burger King restaurants actually began serving Spam in 2007, in order to compete with the local McDonald's chains there. In Hawaii, Spam is so popular that it is sometimes referred to—derisively? —as "The Hawaiian Steak." One popular Spam dish in Hawaii is Spam *musubi*, where cooked Spam is combined with rice and nori seaweed. Is this one reason why Hawaiians are so fat?

Outside the United States, the largest consumer of Spam is South Korea, where it is considered not only a luxury item but often given as a significant gift on occasions of importance when one wishes to pay special honor and proper respect. It even comes in decorated gift boxes! In the *New York Times* ("In South Korea, Spam is the Stuff Gifts are Made Of," January 26, 2014), Choe Sang-Hunjan writes, "Spam's journey from surplus pork shoulder in Minnesota to the center of the South Korean dining table, began at a time of privation—hitching a ride with the American military during the Korean War and becoming a longed-for luxury in the desperate years afterward, when American troops stayed to keep the peace."

Spam, nevertheless, may have been the occasion of art. "Spam, blackouts and Nissan huts" was Evelyn Waugh's self-conscious and mildly disparaging explanation to Graham Greene (who didn't like the book) for writing what I feel is his masterpiece, *Brideshead Revisited*, during the six months between December 1943 and June 1944, following a minor parachute accident. Waugh said, "It was a bleak period of present privation and threatening disaster—the period of soya beans and Basic English—and in consequence the book is infused with a kind of gluttony, for food and wine, for the splendours of the recent past, and for rhetorical and ornamental language which now, with a full stomach, I find distasteful." It was a time of rationing and great shortage and very few Brits were eating "soup of *oseille*, a sole simply cooked in white wine sauce, a *Caneton à la presse*, a lemon soufflé." The novel, a lush one, is filled with detailed descriptions of sumptuous meals. But it was the hatred of soybeans that drove Waugh to write *Brideshead Revisited*.

A vegetarian, Adolf Hitler hated meat. Abstemious, he virtually existed on gruel, linseed mush, muesli, soups. He ate eggs. "I was greatly relieved to find that we didn't all have to follow the Führer's diet," Gertrude ("Traudl") Junge explained in her unique memoir, *Hitler's Last Secretary*.

> "I'd have had to be very ill, I'm sure, to subsist on gruel, linseed mush, muesli and vegetable juice on my own free will." She explained, "During meals, Hitler himself often mentioned his difficulty in getting decent vegetarian dishes. He had a delicate stomach, although later I came to believe that much of his illness was nervous or imaginary."

What Hitler mainly ate, in fact, was the diet food of the then well-known Zabel sanatorium, a nursing home right there in Berchtesgaden. Hitler loved fried eggs, creamed potatoes, baked potatoes, and vegetables of the general sort. He preferred a special crisp-bread over white or black bread. He enjoyed drinking Fachinger mineral water with his meals. Occasionally, he took apple-peel tea or sometimes a cup of caraway tea—"never anything else," said Ms. Junge—and he always ate a piece of baked apple cake with it, perhaps a biscuit or two.

Private, even covert, Hitler was circumspect about his food. "He thought he could only digest fresh fruit and vegetables, but did not want to eat any produce that came from a market garden that he did not know," wrote Junge. As to the linseed oil she mentioned, Hitler had a peculiar passion for it. It was his habit to eat it especially on baked potatoes with curd cheese when he would pour the unrefined oil over them, which is also called flaxseed-oil, the same kind that painters use. It is an edible oil, but, because of its strong flavor and odor, it has always played virtually no role at all in human nutrition in the United States, although it is marketed as a nutritional supplement in many parts and places in Europe, where it is traditionally eaten with potatoes and bland quark, what Americans call cottage cheese. It is regarded as a delicacy due to its hearty taste, which spices the nature of bland quark.

I have read that the last meal that the Fuhrer ate was a pasta dish. He famously loved almost all pastries. In the afternoon, he liked cocoa with apple pie. He adopted a strict vegetarian diet some time in the late 1930s or early 1940s and almost always ate sparely thereafter due in part to gastrointestinal problems he had. (German psychoanalyst, Erich Fromm, believed that Hitler's vegetarianism was actually a means of atoning for the death of his half-niece, Geli Raubal, as well as a means of proving to himself and others that he was incapable of killing.) Lilli, another cook at the Berghof, often baked a Hitler favorite, cheesecake, which later was forwarded to him regularly when he was in Berlin. Dione Lucas, a chef at a Hamburg hotel patronized by Hitler, claimed that her stuffed squab was a big favorite of his. In his book, *The Mind of Adolf Hitler*, Walter C. Langer writes:

> If he (Hitler) does not eat meat, drink alcoholic beverages, or smoke, it is not due to the fact that he has some kind of inhibition or does it because he believes it will improve his health. He abstains from these because he is following the example of the great German, Richard Wagner, or because he has discovered that it increases his energy and endurance to such a degree that he can give much more of himself to the creation of the new German Reich.

However, Alexander Cockburn observes:

> Nazi leaders were noted for their love of their pets and for certain animals, notably apex predators like the wolf and the lion. Hitler, a vegetarian and hater of hunting, adored dogs and spent some of his final hours in the company of Blondi, whom he would take for walks outside the bunker at some danger to himself. He had a particular enthusiasm for birds and most of all for wolves. [...] Goebbels said, famously, "The only real friend one has in the end is the dog... The more I get to know the human species, the more I care for my Benno." Goebbels also agreed with Hitler that "meat eating is a perversion in our human nature," and that Christianity was a "symptom of decay," since it did not urge vegetarianism. [...] On the one hand, monsters of cruelty towards their fellow humans; on the other, kind to animals and zealous in their interest. In their very fine essay on such contradictions, Arnold Arluke and Boria Sax offer three observations. One, as just noted, many Nazi leaders harboured affection towards animals but antipathy to humans. Hitler was given films by a maharaja, which displayed animals killing people. The Fuehrer watched with equanimity. Another film showed humans killing

animals. Hitler covered his eyes and begged to be told when the slaughter was over.

The breakfasts Hitler ate, which were prepared in the cavernous kitchen by the Austrian Ms. Constanze Manziarly, his cook/dietician at the Berghof and during his final days in Berlin before he died on April 30, 1945, followed the balanced diet of raw vegetables and fruit of the Swiss physician, Maximilian Bircher-Benner, who is best known for the invention of muesli cereal, which was basically the regimen adopted by John Harvey Kellogg in the United States, another theorist fascinated by the subject of what constitutes a healthy diet. Manziarly mysteriously disappeared into Russian hands wearing a Wehrmacht jacket after being seen by several witnesses ominously being taken towards a U-Bahn tunnel by two Russian soldiers. According to Traudl Junge, Manziarly reportedly called out to her, "They want to see my papers." The woman disappeared and was never seen again after that.

Speaking of raw vegetables, incidentally, one of the more eccentric ideas of the notorious Heinrich Himmler, the commandant who formed the *Einsatzgruppen* and built extermination camps, a man who fancied himself a visionary nutritionist, was his preposterous plan to distribute onions and other raw vegetables to the victims in Nazi concentration camps, "an initiative," according to Nikolaus Wachsmann in his classic *KL: A History of the Nazi Concentration Camps,* "that would have caused more misery for inmates suffering from intestinal infections." Can onions dissolve blood clots? A chemical in onions called carraganen is supposedly a powerful anti-coagulant and might conceivably transform heart surgery, or asserts a character in Bruce Chatwin's book of essays, *What Am I Doing Here.*

At meals on the Berghof, he loved to talk about the horrors of the abattoir. Ms. Junge describes his quirky delight in jokingly trying to put people off their food, when in a light-hearted mood all were dining at "Wolf's Lair" in the Obersaltzburg. Once he told of an abattoir that he had visited in Germany and how he proudly he was to have stayed to watch while all of the others left. He said,

> It was a fully modernized factory seeing the job right
> through from pig to sausage, including processing the
> bones, bristles and skin. Everything was so clean and
> neat, with pretty girls in high gumboots standing up
> to their calves in fresh blood. I run no such risks. I can
> happily watch carrots and potatoes being pulled up,
> eggs collected from the henhouse and cows milked.

We tend to forget—indeed, refuse to believe—that Adolf Hitler had his charms, such as they were, and much prefer to see the man as the devil. Can nothing whatsoever be said in the defense of someone who loved Alsatian dogs, his mother, pastry cream, young girls, sculpture (Anton Breker was his favorite sculptor), the novels of Karl May, his favorite author—oddly, Christian values play an important role in May's works—the symphonies of Anton Bruckner, the "Big Top" and virtually anything to do with circus performances? (He compulsively sent ornate boxes of expensive chocolates to several female acrobats, whose names he noted to remember, and ballerinas.) It is well-known, it may be added, that he not only loved Walt Disney's animated film, *Snow White*, but in sketches and doodles drew pictures of the rollicking little dwarves with innocent delight. Friendship mattered greatly to him. He genuinely admired Benito Mussolini, revered Karl Donitz, loved Albert Speer as a son, and had a soft spot for his devoted chauffeur, Erick Kempka. He worshipped Frederick the Great. He may have even had a child, at least according to Leslie Charteris.

I suspect that such sweetness in someone who at the same time could undergo an insane vasovagal response when, for example, seeing a Jew wooing an Aryan German girl has its coordinates; no doubt the two went hand in hand. Hitler also never used cologne; refused to let anyone see him naked or bathing; often wore ugly neckties; had impeccable handwriting; loathed snow; tended badly to sunburn; preferred cold rooms; hated vases with flowers; chose to stay out of glare and invasive sunlight; thrilled at seeing raging fires in all forms, in fireplaces, on battlefields; cared almost nothing about literature; was a fanatical ikonophile—he once flew into a frenzy of rage on a drive through Munich when he discovered razed his favorite old movie house, the "Fern Andra," named after voluptuous Vernal Edna Andrews from Watseka, Illinois, an American actress from German silent films of the 1910s, a woman whom he no doubt thrilled to in his youth—and in architecture craved giantism and monumentality. He obsessed over buildings, and was especially attracted to arched passageways, domes, curvilinear lines, and, generally, the baroque and ostentatious. In the opinion of Reich architect, Albert Speer, Hitler "wore his mustache in order to divert attention from his excessively large, ill-proportioned nose."

Strangely, there was a starved, hollowed-out look about Hitler. The interior of his mouth in photographs—you rarely see his teeth—almost always looks as empty as his capacity for mercy. There is always a link, to my way of thinking, between the fussy or abstemious eater and frayed—or potentially frazzled, guilty, eroding or unraveling—nerves. Once again, food aversions say a great deal about an individual's personality. In his solipsistic way, the

Fuhrer was as lonely and isolated as Milton's Satan. His smile was strictly for children, women, and dogs, which is why the well-known Trappist monk, Thomas Merton, in the only instance where I have ever encountered such a thing, could actually compassionately pray for the repose of the Fuhrer's soul. In his poem, "A Prayer for Robert Lax," Merton makes an entreaty,

> Lax, when you say your prayers, pray for me to be a
> good priest.
> Pray for all priests to be good, and pray for the salva-
> tion of all
> people, nuns, business men, Hitler, everybody.

In a 1966 television episode of *The Saint* series entitled "Little Girl Lost," Simon Templar, while vacationing in Ireland, comes to the aid of a pretty young girl, being pursued by two thugs, who identifies herself as Hitler's daughter. Hitler was also a beautiful whistler. "While I played, he'd recline and whistle the melody, tremolo. How he enjoyed the [Hasty] Pudding Club scores," wrote Ernst ("Putzi") Hanfstaengl, an early friend, who helped finance both the publication of Hitler's *Mein Kampf* and the NSDAP's official newspaper, the *Völkischer Beobachter*. Adolf Hitler in fact was the godfather of Putzi's son, Egon. Putzi wrote both Brownshirt and Hitler Youth marches, both patterned after his own Harvard football songs, and, he later claimed, he devised the chant "*Sieg Heil*" (Hail victory!) which to him recapitulated a typical cheerleader's cry during a football game. Putzi Hanfstaengl's presence at his 25th Harvard reunion in 1934 created a huge furor, following vociferous and repeated complaints from various Jewish alumni and anti-Nazi student groups. His controversial arrival in New York was met by 1,500 angry protesters, and two students were arrested at Harvard Commencement after chaining themselves to benches and disrupting the entire ceremony with howls of "Down with Hanfstaengl!" and "Down with Hitler!" Months after the reunion, pressured by many outraged colleagues and alumni, then Harvard President James F. Conant rejected a donation of $1,000 from Hanfstaengl.

"Do you know what lipstick is made of?" the Fuhrer once asked Eva Braun when she appeared at table. Hitler, who at times resorted to mocking light banter, according to Junge, began laughing with the ladies and listed the ingredients of lipstick. "If you only knew that in Paris, of all places, lipsticks are made of the fat skimmed off sewage, I'm sure no woman would paint her lips anymore." And what was transpiring while Hitler sat there idly fretting about fish-scales and cochineal in women's lipsticks and hugging puppies? Forty million human beings died in Europe during World War II, more than half of them innocent civilians.

Melissa d'Arabian, the Season Five winner of "The Next Food Network Star" and host of "Ten Dollar Dinners" frankly explained to Katie Workman, the Editor-in-Chief of Cookstr.com, "The World's #1 Collection of Cookbook Recipes Online," some of her food aversions:

> I used to have two things I didn't eat—goat cheese
> and lamb. I just didn't like the taste, which is odd,
> because I love really strong flavors usually. Give me
> a stinky cheese and knife and I'm happy. Well, my
> husband is from a small village in Provence where goat
> cheese and lamb are flagship items. He has converted
> me on the lamb front. I'll eat it now but goat cheese—
> not yet. He is so set on the notion that if I could only
> taste the right goat cheese, I would love it. We have
> an agreement: I try goat cheese for him once a year.
> Seven years, seven tries, and so far—I still don't like it.

As for herself, Katie Workman uncompromisingly states, "Red meat is just not for me; the taste, the texture—it's all unappealing to me. I didn't like it even as a kid, and stopped eating it altogether when I was 12. Strangely, I don't mind cooking it for others, but other than bacon, which is closer to potato chips than meat in my mind, red meat is off the list." But she does eat lamb. Not so actress Jennifer Lawrence, star of *The Hunger Games*. During an interview in a taqueria with Jim Windolf for *Vanity Fair* (Feb. 2013), the management thoughtfully sent over to their table a comp of lamb meatballs. Lawrence cringed and whispered, so the waitress could not hear, "I can't stand it. I don't eat lamb. I think it tastes like feet."

Artist Edward Gorey, whom we have previously quoted touching on the matter of fruitcakes, pleaded with everyone for the longest time to avoid eating veal, so that no one was surprised to learn after he died that he had willed his money and any proceeds from sales of his work to animal charities, specifically to the Animal Rescue League; the Xerces Society for Invertebrate Conservation, and Bat Conservation International. Animal welfare protestors have long complained about the terrible lives and excessive cruelty that young calves have to endure, penned up indoors in veal crates, often with wobbly, precarious floors, suffering the immeasurable agony of restricted movement, tortured by prolonged sensory, social, and exploratory deprivation; and utterly susceptible to high amounts of stress, disease, and pain.

"I'm not a fan of how chickens are raised in this country on a factory level; I'm not a fan of commercial beef processing in this country," chef Alton Brown has gone on record as saying. "I get most of my meat from farmers around my area. I am lucky because I can afford it, and I live in a region [Marietta, Georgia] where lots of things are raised. My fondest wish would be that our adopting and truly accepting some analogs, as I say, would allow us to change the way we produce our animals." He adds, wisely, "My problem is not with killing animals; my problem is letting them live terrible lives up until the time we kill them."

Horrors abound with poultry. The Broad Breasted White is now commercially the most widely used breed of domesticated turkey. We eat only one or two varieties nowadays of the many there are, special breeds that are bred—"grown"—locked in huge sunless, grass-less pens, quickly overfed, slaughtered. They can barely stand up, cannot breed, are basically food balls bio-wrenched with genetic tomfoolery into large, ungainly, overweight (due to excess muscle) meat-balloons, and yet, although they suffer from heart disease, respiratory failure, and damage of the joints, as many as 40 million will be eaten this Thanksgiving. It is a kind of commodity food, and yet heavily cultivating only one breed of any species is flirting with danger. Patrick Martins notably writes in *The Carnivore's Manifesto*, "Because of the reliance on a single strain of the Broad Breasted White [turkey], entire flocks, and even the species itself, are one novel pathogen away from being wiped off the American dinner table."

In one particular advertisement, singer k.d. lang flatly declares, "Meat stinks." Needless to say, ranchers in lang's hometown of Consort, Canada— or anywhere—did not agree. A sign at the edge of her small town reading "Consort: Home of k.d. lang," after her anti-meat comments, was spray-painted to read, "Eat Beef Dyke." But did Lang hate only beef? I suspect her loathing for flesh ran the entire gamut from goldfish to 'gators to goats. But what is beef, after all? What we impound is a mixture of no end of what animals feed on. Go to the driving wheel. As Margaret Visser points out in *Much Depends on Dinner*, "Meat *is* largely corn. So is milk. American livestock and poultry is fed and fattened on corn and cornstalks." Fancy trying to convince k.d. lang that the steak in front of her is only an altered variation of corn on the cob. I wonder how she would feel about the richly vivid passage from chapter nine in the novel *Tarzan of the Apes* where the Apeman, eating a boar, "tore his food from the quivering flanks of his prey and his gleaming teeth sank into the succulent flesh," after which he chases to the Mbonga the ebony warrior (who slew the boar with an arrow) and pauses to deliberate seriously whether or not literally to eat him!

Regarding both Lang and Tarzan, as the witty British comedian John Cleese once logically inquired, "If God did not intend us to eat animals, then why did he make them out of meat?"

I will not even mention the meat pie Titus plans to serve Tamora in Shakespeare's *Titus Andronicus*—blood and bones ground into a paste—or in Euripides' grim play, *The Bacchae*, in which the gory tale is recounted that once every two years the women of ancient Greece on a mid-winter night go into the mountains, wildly dance in the snow, and as an edifying climax tear apart goats and bulls in a frenzy and eat their bleeding flesh, still warm, sharing in communion the raw power of Dionysus himself. Does that sound so savage? It is reported in Acts of the Apostles 7:54, by Luke the Evangelist that Jewish mobs gnashed upon St. Stephen with their teeth! *Does* eating meat aggravate and inflame the passions? Satchel Paige, the great right-handed pitcher of the American Negro League thought so. One may ask how gastronomically (or theatrically) significant it was that Edmund Kean, the 19th-century Shakespearean actor, sat down and typically ate a big meal of beef when he was about to play a murderer and also a meal of pork before going on stage in the role of a tyrant. (He was also said to enjoy a dish of mutton before playing the role of a lover!)

Who does not associate the "funeral baked meats" in *Hamlet* with illicit passion and profanation? Remember how Hamlet wants to know if Horatio, like himself, thinks that having a funeral and a wedding so close together is grotesque, indeed corrupt. "Indeed, my lord, it followed hard upon," replies Horatio, meaning the wedding came too quickly after the funeral. Hamlet makes a bitter joke, saying, "Thrift, thrift, Horatio! The funeral baked meats / Did coldly furnish forth the marriage tables" (I.ii.180–181). There is not only the suggestion that the King and Queen were trying to save money by serving left-over funeral food at the wedding but that the playwright is implying cold meat itself is a metaphor for the lewd two in their cold coupling.

The crews of the distinguished British explorer, navigator, cartographer, and captain in the Royal Navy, Captain James Cook, hated the taste of walrus meat and almost mutinied over having to eat it. During his explorations in the desolate Antarctic, he would order his men to shoot seals, sea lions, and walruses for sustenance. The men, however, rebelled at the walrus, "finding it tough, chewy, and indigestible, and their refusal to eat it brought on a notable confrontation with Captain Cook," notes Frank McLynn in his biography, *Captain Cook*. What should be noted is that Cook, a godly man who came from a working-class family thought it "morally inappropriate," unholy even, to be fastidious about food, a matter in this secular age of ours rarely considered—not just wasting food, but turning one's nose up at it. It is no small consideration in a book about food aversions and its aspects.

I have often wondered whether Nathaniel Hawthorne avoided meat. "There is something lacking—a good deal lacking," Melville candidly wrote in February 1851 to his friend, Evert Duyckinck, regarding Hawthorne, "to the plump sphericity of the man. What is that? He doesn't patronize the butcher—he needs roast-beef, done rare." What exactly was the message the more rough-sided Melville was conveying, that his fellow author boldly needed a more vigorous diet, specifically animal flesh? Was he suggesting that Hawthorne was too soft and to a certain degree too pusillanimous and that he needed to adopt a sturdier, more durable, even a wilder attitude in his writing? I have never seen pictures of Nathaniel Hawthorne when he did not appear smart, alert, well profiled and looking hale, hearty, and handsome.

Poet W.H. Auden who enjoyed eating such *outré* things as tongue, tripe, brains, and, among other things, Polish sausage, paradoxically—and inconsistently?—ascribed the eating of beefsteak as a taste of the lower orders. "It is madly non-U!" he declared, using one of the snobbish in-terms that the English writer Nancy Mitford created to distinguish between the widely differing habits of the upper (U) and lower (non-U) class habits. Auden had strong opinions. He had to have potatoes with dinner. Going to bed, always at 9 p.m., it was often with a bottle of wine—California Pinot Noir was his favorite—and a plate of boiled potatoes. Not unlike the novelist James Joyce who came to abhor red wine (he sneeringly dismissed it as "beefsteak!"), Auden disliked Chianti wine, declaring, "Chianti tastes like red ink." A bit of a curmudgeon, he was a bristling fund of precise and forked dislikes.

I have mentioned that Auden disliked desserts, something that he shared, by the way, with the late, vain, fastidious General Douglas MacArthur, of whom William Manchester wrote in *American Caesar*, "He never touched pastries or cake." Auden abhorred every kind of sweet, simple pies and cakes included. "Glad the ham arrived," he wrote to his partner, Chester, in 1949 who was living in Paris at the time, "which should be followed soon by the package intended for Thanksgiving because it contains canned pumpkin which I sincerely hope will be all consumed before I arrive." According to Dorothy J. Farnan in *Auden in Love*, the poet "did not approve of the rage for health foods or organically grown vegetables, believing such theories to represent a false primitivism." (Yet he had his own unique theories, one being that you can cure yourself of any and all allergies by—with conscious love in your heart—forgiving your enemies and ridding yourself of all grievances.) Auden also hated the French, loathed the poems of Edna St. Vincent Millay, disliked Racine, never ate later than 7 p.m. (doing so would give you bad dreams), rarely flushed the toilet, wore second-hand clothes and bedroom slippers in the street, loved to drink Champagne, never ate sweets or took salt with his eggs, and flatly refused to answer a ringing telephone or a persistent doorbell before one o'clock in the afternoon. He also believed, uniquely, that Othello was stupid and Iago the most honest man in the play, and that pretty much any given man on the street could play Hamlet, because it was not about acting but a succession of disquisitions—on the one hand this, on the other that—about decisions.

English television chef Tamasin Day-Lewis has shared memories of her actor brother, Daniel, with Britain's *Daily Mail* recently, recalling how the pair of them used secretly to hide their least favorite food from their parents in order to avoid eating it. She engagingly reminisced,

> Grown-ups were a mysterious race to us, but we discovered a world of our own where our imaginations ranged, solidarity ruled and a sense of being fellow conspirators disobeying the rules gave us excitement in an otherwise often dull, monotonous and strict upbringing. Surreptitiously hiding the food we hated in our pockets (in my case corned beef hash, which reminded me of cat-food and in Dan's the dreaded fish pie with anchovy essence) before flushing it down the loo

In her book, *Bettered by a Dead Crustacean*, the prolific lesbian/atheist author Kelli Jae Baeli writes, "I've never seen Salisbury steak on a restaurant menu. It's only in frozen dinners. Is there something we should know about that? What is Salisbury steak anyway? And where do they hunt or harvest the salisburies?"

Meat haters abound. Horace. Plutarch. Alexander Pope. Gustave Mahler. Paul McCartney. St. John Chrysostom. Kate Bush. Gandhi. Leo Tolstoy. Henry David Thoreau. Jane Goodall. Susan B. Anthony. Thomas A. Edison. Meat Loaf (yes, indeed!). Charles Darwin. G.B. Shaw. Mary Shelley. Louisa May Alcott. Vincent Van Gogh. Cesar Chavez. Voltaire. Johnny Appleseed. Singer Sinead O'Connor. Ian Wright, of Globe Trekker fame. Heavy drinking novelist Kingsley Amis, who hated everything in the meat department from beef and chicken to paté ("I sometimes feel that more lousy dishes are presented under the banner of paté than any other"). Amis described the opening of Kafka's "Metamorphosis," where as we all know the anti-hero or protagonist wakes up one day with the horrid realization that he has been hideously transmogrified into a bug, as the best literary representation of a hangover. I believe the only time that I have ever seriously considered abstaining from eating meat was after listening, against my better judgment, to the radio talk-show host, Rush Limbaugh, talking at some length about various cuts of meat, with that disarmingly smug, bready, profondo, over-eater's voice of his. I must add, however, that this is one subject El Blimpo, with his eater's great girth, would actually know something about.

Can't you see Limbaugh's zeal in having memorized bovine graphs of the major cuts of beef: chuck, fore shank, short plate, rib, sirloin? Listen to the theme song of his show—it *defines* lumbering! Limbaugh chose the piece, a sub-textual—subconscious—confession, I suspect, that he sees *himself* as a pachyderm. I see him as an enormous mammal in the fatness of his dermal armor plates, that immense body clanking, as he lumbers to graze on the shrub Serico-compopsis, said to be the favorite food of rhinos. Big ass blew in from Missouri, big ass blew right out again!

There is another way of hating meat or, to put it another way, derogating the human—and the humane—condition, and that is, showing it in its most reduced form, a carcass. British painter Francis Bacon painted carcasses. He understood that, being no different than beasts, everyone lives off of everything else. He saw even the crucifixion of Jesus Christ that way. A distinct theme of food aversion permeates the paintings of this Irish-born iconoclast. With his sinister gift, Bacon's blood-curdling images of flayed animal carcasses and gouts of raw meat depending on hooks were no different than the bloody meal of chops and trotters he was sharing with his biographer, Michael Peppiatt, when he said, "Life's just like that. We're all on our way to becoming dead meat. And when you go in that restaurant... you see the whole cycle of life and the way everyone lives off everything else. And that's all there is." He is telling us that we ourselves are—and end up—spoiled and overripe meat.

Bacon allowed a series of rare interviews with David Sylvester in 1963, 1966, and 1979. The painter explained,

> "I've always been very moved by pictures about
> slaughterhouses and meat, and to me they belong very
> much to the whole thing of the crucifixion. There've
> been extraordinary photographs, which have been
> done of animals just being taken up before they were
> slaughtered; and the smell of death... I know for
> religious people, for Christians, the crucifixion has a
> totally different significance. But as a nonbeliever, it

was just an act of man's behaviour, a way of behaviour
to another."

He was fascinated by the sight of raw meat. The raw, bleeding flesh of the *abattoir* and the butcher's slab was a sight affecting him like almost nothing else and it was to become his personal metaphor of death. Bacon's feelings about cuts and carcasses—about the butchered torsos of animals, gouts of meat, and tortured and mutilated human flesh—while perhaps ambivalent, discloses the painter's loathing for the elemental, the reduced and most basic nature of life. On the one hand, while such harsh fantasies fascinated him by their "seductive beauty," on the other, they grimly served as a solemn and punishing reminder of his own mortality. We are slabs. His painting, *Figure with Meat* (1954), is modeled aslant on the Pope Innocent X portrait by Diego Velázquez; however, in the Bacon painting the Pope is shown as a dire, gruesome figure and placed between two bisected halves of a cow. The fresh meat recalls the lavish arrangements of fruits, meats and confections in 17th-century *vanitas* paintings, which traditionally carried subtle moralizing messages about the impermanence of life and the spiritual dangers of sensual pleasures. There is mockery, of course, in the immanent concept that we are all nothing but carcasses, and by way of biomorphic—and secular—surrealism he reveals cadavers promise no resurrection.

Any sight of food in his art shows signs of being overripe or spoiled, presenting corruption. The painter offers nothing at all in the way of salvation, merely the power of carnal sensuality, as well as a decadence that renders (such an apt Baconian word!) an existential view of damnation. *"We're all on our way to becoming dead meat. And when you go in that restaurant... you see the whole cycle of life and the way everyone lives off everything else. And that's all there is."*

"As I cut back on sugar and salt, I became more perceptive (and disgusted by) meat and fish that is a little "off" or chemically "enhanced," William Vollmann, the novelist, explained to me regarding his food aversions. He explained,

> When my daughter was young, I used to take her to
> a certain fast food chain for the burgers, which she
> loved and I used to [like them as well]. Then I began
> to taste "pink slime." After two or three repetitions, I
> used to take her elsewhere. [I hate] the foul aftertaste
> of much farmed salmon, the organ meat rancidity in
> low quality meatloaf, day-old sushi, etc. are all vile,

but not so much as lima beans, which if politeness
demands I will eat. (The best liver I ever had was in
Yemen, when they slaughtered the lamb in front of
me—in a gas station—and served it 15 minutes later).

The story of meat is a tale of dramatic and opposing opinions, often ferocious, partisan arguments. Aristotle believed that meat eating was the source of cold black bile and that it infected human beings with what he called "*malaina cholos*," the "deadly melancholy." Meat is too expensive and wastes grain, which is better used for healthy consumption. Worse than anything, the act of eating meat is savage and cruel to animals. But certain select animals, right? Remember how in E.B. White's *Charlotte's Web* poor Wilbur, once the runt of the litter and saved only by the whim of a girl, is fattened up and ready for slaughter? It raises the "meat paradox," our odd passion for eating the animals that we also love. (Americans eat the equivalent of 21,000 entire animals in a lifetime!)

A further irony is that, weirdly, arbitrarily, we tend to eat only those food animals such as pigs, cows, and chickens that are known to be mentally inferior to those like dolphins, horses, cats, and dogs, which we don't typically eat. Then there is the argument that meat also makes a person smell bad. Actor Larry Hagman told *Playboy*, "I'd been a vegetarian on and off for years, and I knew somehow it made me feel better. My shit didn't smell. My body odor went down. I went to China last year and Maj [his wife] and I suddenly realized, standing in the midst of these Chinese, that they didn't smell. And of course it was because they eat very little meat." Others insist that eating meat creates unhealthy passion, which leads to anger.

And what about meat-eating affecting a person's looks?

Food revenges itself on people, and each and every country in the world has its own gastronomic devils with which to pitchfork its pigs. "The Germans are the worst, for sheer bulk," declares Patrick Leigh Fermor, of fond memory, here regarding his anti-pasta rant. He sadistically writes,

> What miles of liver sausage, what oceans of beer and
> quagmires of those colossal bellies! How appalling
> they look from behind; the terrible creases of fat three
> deep across solid and shaven napes! Necks wreathed in
> smiles, the stigmata of damnation; and delusive smiles,
> for when they turn round there is nothing but a blank
> stare and a jigsaw of fencing scars.

The British in the18th-century were ravenous for beef and tucked into red meat with gay abandon. I love the raw passage in *The London Spy* in 1757 making cruel if robust play with [William] "Pitt's Militia" (a predecessor of the Home Guard we know today) parading in Westminster Palace Yard, describing them as "so many Greasie Cooks, Tun-Bellied Lick-Spiggots, and fat wheezing Butchers, sweating in their Buff Doublets, under the Command of some fiery-fac'd Brewer, whose Gudgel-Gut was hoop'd in with a Golden sash."

One inevitably calls to mind the portraits in museums of all those gouty, jowly English dignitaries and landed squires, their faces flushed brick red—John Singleton Copley's *Portrait of Cornwallis* (circa 1795) is a classic example—who seemed, to a man, to be suffering from a case of vascular rosacea. In all likelihood they were mostly unrepentant rip-roaring carnivores, inveterate beef-eaters, who had all spent a lifetime extravagantly dining out on great haunches of venison, beef, and mutton and towering tankards of ale. Speaking of the English, Leigh Fermor is no kinder to them—or the Mexicans, or the Spanish—acidly writing,

> The outward effects of food are a sure guide. In
> England they are very noticeable. Prosperous
> Edwardians had an unmistakable ptarmigan sheen.
> There was beef and claret in the faces of the squirear-
> chy, cabbage and strong Indian tea among non-con-
> formists, and limpid blue eyes in the Navy, due to
> Plymouth gin, and so on. Above all, a general look of
> low spirits that tells its own tale. Direct results are still
> more striking. Curry induces instability of temper and
> fosters discord; hot Mexican food leads to cruelty, just
> as surely as blubber, the staple of the Eskimos, spells
> torpid indifference. The rancid oil they cook with in
> Spain tastes as though it came straight out of a sanctu-
> ary lamp; no wonder the country is prone to bigotry.

He has words for the French, as well:

> France, you will agree, is the place where the instinct
> has been most successfully harnessed and exploited.
> But this preeminence exacts a cruel price. The liver!
> That is their Achilles heel! It is a national scourge,
> brought on by those delicious sauces, by all those

truffles and chopped mushrooms, peeping through the
liquid beige. Every Frenchman over fifty writhes under
its torments. He is a chained Prometheus, a victim of
the tribal inventiveness. Only it's no vulture that pecks
at the weak spot but the phantom and vengeful beaks
of an army of geese from Strasbourg.

Wretched excess is the culprit. It is not that meat alone will wreak havoc. Again, remember, too much of anything—the Greek ideal (μηδὲν ἄγαν), echoed in the Romans with *ne quid nimis*—brings us down. We seem to be getting further and further from moderation by the day, however. I wonder how a recent in-vitro experiment with faux-hamburger will play in the future. Does replicated meat shock you? Skeeve you? An "engineered" meat, an *in-vitro* hamburger, is presently being experimented with and indeed constructed in Maastricht, the Netherlands, from a particular type of cell that has been removed from cow shoulder obtained at a slaughterhouse, tiny bits of beef-muscle tissue now being grown in a laboratory. On August 5, 2013 in London, such a burger was made into a patty, fried, and then eaten in a demonstration to provide an example, at least in one view, of the future of food. The project, which took two years to complete at a cost of $325,000, was undertaken by Dr. Mark Post, a Dutch researcher at Maastricht. The "cultured" meat was produced using stem cells—basic cells that can turn into tissue-specific cells—that were "then multiplied in a nutrient solution and placed into small petri dishes, where they became muscle cells and slowly formed tiny strips of muscle fiber," according to Henry Fountain in his seminal article "A Lab-Grown Burger Gets a Taste Test." The burger, he writes,

consists of about 20,000 thin strips of cultured muscle
tissue. Dr. Post, who has conducted some informal
taste tests, said that even without any fat, the tissue
"tastes reasonably good." For the London event he
plans to add only salt and pepper. But the meat is produced with materials—including fetal calf serum, used
as a medium in which to grow the cells—that eventually would have to be replaced by similar materials of
non-animal origin. And the burger was created at phenomenal cost—250,000 euros, or about $325,000,
provided by a donor who so far has remained anonymous. Large-scale manufacturing of cultured meat
that could sit side-by-side with conventional meat in a

supermarket and compete with it in price is at the very
least a long way off.

Three people who ate the burger claimed that it was dry and somewhat lacking in flavor. One of the tasters, Josh Schonwald, a Chicago-based author of a book on the future of food, declared, "The bite feels like a conventional hamburger," adding that the meat tasted "like an animal-protein cake." No alarming reports were made of a pseudobezoar suddenly appearing in anyone's gullet! The semi-futuristic event had been arranged by a public relations firm and was broadcast live on the web in hopes that such projects with in-vitro meat, a serious science, deserved additional financing and research. Proponents of the idea, including Dr. Post, enthusiastically proclaimed that lab-made meat as such could eventually provide high-quality protein for the planet's growing population, while also avoiding most of the environmental and animal-welfare issues related to conventional livestock production.

American agribusiness has for a decade, however, been thumping the tub over foods that imitate meat with things like fake chicken, ersatz pork, mock duck, mimic beef, and copycat burgers, all ingeniously fashioned from ingeniously engineered plant-based proteins that come from yellow peas, mustard seeds, carmelina, which is a weed or oil plant with seeds often called "false flax." Beyond Meat© offers "chicken-free strips." Morning Star© offers a line of ground meat substitutes called "Crumbles." But why oh why do people who abhor it need something that looks and tastes like meat? Exactly what kind of schizo-psychosis is a-borning?

We come here to what may even be called a "theology of meat." Some significant Christian thinkers have seriously considered the ethics of the matter. St. Thomas Aquinas addressed the matter of killing living things in his *Summa Theologica* and concluded to his satisfaction that it does not apply to trees (because they "have no sense") or animals (because they "have no fellowship with us"). His argument is that we are better than animals, so therefore we can eat them. Some say that he did not read his Bible carefully. What Genesis 1:29–30 states is, "I give you green plants for food." God's first set of instructions tells us what we should eat. He does change his mind after the Flood, but animals were and are never just fodder. They are included in God's covenant (this is repeated five times), and humans are told—warned—never to eat or to drink the blood of an animal, "for the blood is the life." (Orthodox Jewish wives, to be comfortably certain, traditionally fry or broil their steaks gray-brown, even black—"done to death," as the phrase goes.) The partisan arguments we are looking at, regarding food aversions, apply even to the ways and means by which all meat is cooked, for even cooking methods—indeed, eating methods as well ("The hunger gratified by cooked meat eaten with a knife and fork is a different hunger from that which bolts down raw meat with the aid of hand nail, and tooth," as Karl Marx wrote in his *Grundrisse*) as an extension of various social biases, have cultural connotations.

Claude Lévi-Strauss explores means of cooking in his essay, "The Culinary Triangle," and, among other considerations, he says that while the boiling of meat is not completely natural in that it uses a receptacle to hold water, it is by far the most preferred way to cook because in the process neither meat nor juices are lost. In most cultures, this method represents the way most women cook for small closed groups, or families. It is suggested by noted archaeologists Jacquetta Hawkes and Sir Leonard Woolley in their comprehensive *Prehistory and the Beginnings of Civilization*, that boiled food was actually unknown before the invention of pottery. Native American women, even as late as the 19th-century, predominantly went in for stone boiling, heating and then dropping—infusing—hot stones into a pot or receptacle to cook soups and stews. An amazing fact to consider, as far as the acts of fire-making and cooking go, although it seems hard to believe, is that in the Neolithic warmth, protection, and even the hardening of wooden implements all preceded cooking among its uses.

Asia in prehistorical times discovered fire before Europe did and Europe long before the continent of Africa, where there are no extant signs of fires (and no true cave-dwellings) before late Acheulian sites of the last interglacial period. Among modern primitives, all possess fire-making appliances except the Andaman Islanders who have lost or have never known the art of fire making.

Roasting, on the other hand, is of course a natural method of cooking because it uses no receptacle and is done by directly exposing the meat to the fire, in what Lévi-Strauss calls an "unmediated conjunction." Boiling is however doubly mediated by both the water in which it is immersed and by the receptacle that holds the water and the food. Man, according to the French ethnologist, is a structure-making animal, and his cooking methods follow suit. There is an affinity of the roasted with the raw, he goes on to explain, which in many if not most cultures is the method associated with men and the way meat is most commonly offered to guests—"exo-cuisine," he calls it, as opposed to "endo-cuisine," as prepared for domestic use. It is basically the epic battle between Spit and Pot, fast roasting as opposed to slow braising.

Both involve cooking, thankfully. Earlier cultures were not always so dainty. In a telling detail that Joan Smith cites in her essay, "People Eaters," Juvenal condemns the Egyptians, "not just for eating their fallen enemy but for failing to turn him into a stew, perhaps unconsciously contrasting their rapacious appetites with the Romans' highly sophisticated culinary practices."

Broadly speaking, the two different methods—with smoking and grilling linked to roasting—distinguish between "culture" and "nature." A contrast here has also been raised between the democratic and the aristocratic. Denis Diderot and Jean-Baptiste le Rond d'Alembert, co-authors of the *Encyclopédie* (1750), greatly favored the boiled in meats and foods, writing, "Boiled meat is one of the most succulent and nourishing foods known to man... One could say that boiled meat is to other dishes as bread is to other kinds of nourishment." Whereas in his *Physiologie du goût* (1825), Jean Anthelme Brillat-Savarin, the French gourmet, wrote, "We professors never eat boiled meat out of respect for principles, and because we have pronounced ex cathedra this incontestable truth: boiled meat is flesh without its juice... This truth is beginning to become accepted, and boiled meat has disappeared in truly elegant dinners; it has been replaced by a roast filet, a turbot, or a matelote."

What about that eating meat that has gone off or "eerie," as they say in England—often with game like pheasant or guinea hen? Durian surely has its carnal parallel in raw fermented meat. In an interview in the Spring 2012 issue of *Meatpaper*, an American quarterly devoted to the subject of meat, one Mike Grogan, a living aficionado of "high meat"—which is basically fermented, congealed, green, often rotten meat—confessed that he loves it, in various shapes and sizes, although he admits "it can have a real harsh, acrid quality to it." He explains,

> I had some beef pancreas one time. I did not like it fresh, and I could not get myself to like it high. It was squishy and gooey and flavorless. Smell is not always a big deal. I've got some deer brain right now that I'm probably going to try soon. The brain's about a month and a half old... Shrimp is very good high, but it will stink. If you open a container of high shrimp in a large room with good air circulation, it's rough on everybody. It got to the point, where people told me, "Look, you can't bring your food in here anymore." I had to eat my lunch in the car.

Food crank J.I. Rodale—he was born Jerome Irving Cohen on the Lower Side in New York City—hated all cooked food. It was an extreme crotchet and constituted a kind of food phobia. It was not his only quirk.

He not only described peas as seeds but declared the same thing of eggs—he claimed that they are "seeds!" So when you cook them, you "destroy their living powers." (Does that mean if you plant an egg, it will grow?) According to reporter Edward Jay Epstein, the fact that Lee Harvey Oswald had been seen sipping from a bottle of Coca-Cola on the second-floor lunchroom of the now infamous Texas School Book Depository struck a responsive chord in Rodale, apparently something of an assassination maven, and led to his sudden surmise, "Oswald was not responsible for his action: his brain was confused because he was a sugar drunkard." Rodale unhesitatingly concluded, "What is called for now is a full-scale investigation of sugar consumption and crime." In *The Organic Front*, Rodale asserts that when a person eats an ear of corn—typewriter-style, that is—this is a very good thing simply because in doing so you "exercise the front teeth," because, as he explains, "most foods are usually eaten on the right side or left side." (Q: Has any human being ever *tried* eating an ear of corn with side teeth?) The man was a grade-A, fur-lined, arm-waving, light-bulb-eyed nature fanatic! Cooking anything was his *bête noir*. Pasteurized milk, you see, was "cooked" milk and the worst thing for you, robbing it of vitamins. Cooked food is dead food! Take wine. Cook it and you can't get drunk on it, and why—because you have killed its potency. Rodale commented,

> It is ridiculous to cook [vegetables]. They are so easy to take raw and any child will agree that in cooking something is lost... Don't overlook the fact that peas are seeds... when you cook them, that living quality is destroyed. Its germinating power is annihilated. You are then eating a dead food. It is ironic to see people eating cooked peas, followed by then taking vitamin pills. The vitamins are in the peas. Cooking destroys part of them.

Mr. Rodale's own health? He died from a stroke at 72, capsizing in public on *The Dick Cavett Show* in 1971. After just finishing his interview, he looked suddenly peculiar. Cavett leaned over to ask, "Are we boring you, Mr. Rodale?" Two interns rushed onto the stage to try to revive him but were unsuccessful. He had just bragged in the interview, "I am in such good health that I fell down a long flight of stairs yesterday and I laughed all the way," adding, "I have decided to live to be a hundred" and "I never felt better in my life." He had also previously boasted, "I'm going to live to be 100, unless I'm run down by some sugar-crazed taxi driver."

There are militant others who abhor cooked food, people like RAFers (short for "Raw Animal Foodists") or RPDers ("Raw Palao Dieter") who find that food that is heated is tampered with. Novices usually begin eating dishes like beef carpaccio, steak-tartare, raw-meat kitfo, raw oysters, and so forth. Such raw animal-food is fairly basic. A major step is to move on to raw organ-meats, especially the high-fat ones, and to consume the meat raw at room temperature. Serious RAFers and RPDers go for standard organ-meats like raw adrenals, brains, marrow, suet, thyroid, grass-fed liver, raw wild boar meat, goat meat, wild hare, mutton (which they say is far better than lamb and cheaper, as well), although I have heard many RAFers say they draw the line at eating raw chicken, which for sheer grimness, I don't know, I imagine would be like chewing a balloon or sucking on a just-caught haddock. Organ meats are much cheaper in price than muscle-meats, remember. Cooked diets, they say, can also often lead to deterioration of one's glandular system.

I wonder what RAFers would do with some of the street foods that I came across when I was in South Africa, munchables popular among blacks and so-called "coloreds." One was called "Smilies" which is sheep's head charred on the *braii* or *chisa nyama* (Zulu for barbecue) and sold with a liter of Coca-Cola and a large loaf of bread—the brains and eyeballs are said to be particularly tasty—a name that beguilingly derives from the grisly grin of death that the elate head sports after the lips have been burnt off, revealing a smiling set of teeth. Another is the head and feet of chickens, which are eaten mainly in the Townships in all nine provinces and that are known as "Walkie Talkies:" here, the feet along with the head, intestine, hearts and giblets, and "chicken dust," are submerged in hot water, so that the outer layer of the skin can be removed by peeling it off, and all is covered in seasonings and then grilled.I was buying from a stall a dish with meat, gravy, and porridge known as "mealie-meal." "*Le mpupu yimbi,*" a Zulu standing nearby told me, "The mealie meal is bad." He toothily laughed. "*Letani uhlaka nitate lomuntu ofiler nimuse endhlini yabafile,*" he said, pointing to me. "Bring the stretcher and take this dead boy to the mortuary!"

Nelson Mandela, the South African anti-apartheid revolutionary hero, in his autobiography, *Long Walk to Freedom,* as a prisoner at Robben Island, Pollsmoor Prison, and Victor Verster Prison for 27 years, explains how he virtually lived on nothing but mealies all that time, receiving boiled mealies for lunch, along with phuzamandla, a yeast and powder made from mealies. Dinner consisted of mealie pap porridge, "sometimes with the odd carrot or piece of cabbage or beetroot thrown in." The brave, fearless, and indomitable leader writes,

> Breakfast consisted of mealie pap porridge, cereal made from maize or corn... [it] was delivered to us in the courtyard in old metal oil drums. We would help ourselves to pap using simple metal bowls. We each received a mug of what was described as coffee, but which was in fact ground-up maize, baked until it was black, and then brewed with hot water... In the midst of breakast, the guards would yell "*Val in! Val in*" ("Fall in! Fall in!"), and we would stand outside our cells for inspection.

They eat lion meat in Africa. But so do we here. One can buy exotic meats on the Internet: bear, zebra, coyote, etc. For exotic, try bush meat, monkey and bat, so popular in Sierra Leone, Liberia, and Guinea, that it became the direct cause of spreading the lethal Ebola Virus in 2015. A petition created by Cheryl Semcer, a New Jersey animal lover, on Change.org ("The world's petition platform") elicits signatures to ban the consumption of lion meat. Outraged when she discovered that a multicultural fusion restaurant called Taste & See in Wichita, Kansas, planned to serve African lion meat as part of an exotic game dinner, Semcer demanded that the USDA ban the sale of lion meat in America. Taste & See chef Jason Febres, deluged with protests, proceeded to take lion off the menu, although his customers were still able to enjoy kangaroo, alpaca, and water buffalo, among other variety meats. On Big Cat Rescue, a non-profit educational sanctuary, one can see that there remains a trend for exotic meats, "It turns out that the Wichita establishment wasn't the only restaurant in this country that was catering with cat," the blog notes, continuing,

> Spoto's The Steak Joint in Dunedin, Fla., about 20 miles northwest of Tampa, had lion on the menu for a while, although diners there now will have to be content with such poor substitutes as black bear, yak, and Burmese python. Dave's Pizza and Burgers in Colonie, N.Y., just outside Albany (the same proprietor previously ran Albany's Burger Centric), was serving a lion burger (for $75!) alongside burgers made from alligator, rattlesnake, llama, goat, and other such creatures, but he has bowed to pressure from critics both local and national and scratched it off the list (it still appears on his online menu).

I had a good friend, Ed, an African-American auto mechanic, back when I was teaching at Longwood College in Prince Edward County, Virginia. He grilled alligator steaks outdoors on a big hollowed-out metal barrel, basting the meat with bacon fat. I loved the taste, something like fish, of a coarse-grain sort. Said Ed, "Best taste from 'gators three-feet long, meat taken from the tail."

In 2012, Boca Tacos y Tequila in Tucson, Arizona, announced plans to serve lion tacos for one night only, if enough customers signed up by advance order. Instead of orders, the place was deluged with angry telephone calls and emails, and the plan was jettisoned. The African lion is not an endangered species, so it is perfectly legal to raise and butcher lions in this country and sell their meat for food (it reportedly tastes like particularly chewy pork). Exactly where the lion meat comes from that does get sold in this country remains a bit of a mystery, though. One past source, ExoticMeatMarkets.com, which peddles bobcat, beaver, coyote, eland, nutria, and reindeer as well as foie gras, frogs' legs, wild turkey, and ibérico pork, has a large photograph of a lion on the order page of its website, but nary a morsel of the regal feline is to be found anywhere for sale. The company had previously reported, "Our African lions are raised in the state of Illinois."

There may or may not be a connection, but the website for Czimer's Game & Seafood in Homer Glen, Illinois, about 20 miles southwest of Chicago, does have a listing for African lion—at prices ranging from $9.95 a pound for pre-made 1/3-pound burgers (Dave's in New York State was going to make a killing) to $24.95 a pound for "tender loins"—although a parenthesis notes "not available." In 2003, interestingly, Czimer's proprietor Richard Czimer was sentenced to six months in federal prison, a $5,000 fine, 300 hours of community service, and required to make restitution payments of $116,000 to the Fish and Wildlife Foundation's Save the Tiger Fund for his role in an exotic animal trafficking operation.

It reminds me of a restaurant called The New Deal that at one time existed in downtown New York's Greenwich Village, on 12th or 13th Street. The place did good business in the late 1980s, early 1990s, I believe, and on the menu was offered all sorts of exotic meats—e.g., elephant, hippopotamus, camel, gnu, eland, and wildebeest steaks, possibly lion meat, as well, although I cannot specifically say. A friend of mine and I ate there a couple of times and, largely out of sheer curiosity, on a whim, she ordered—a set of?!— duck testicles as an appetizer, on which without effort I cheerfully passed. As I recall, it was something of an expensive restaurant—it used to be listed in Zagat's Restaurant Guide for New York. I have not heard anything about it in years, and it is quite likely to have gone out of business.

As far as eating lion meat goes, in *Tarzan the Untamed*, one of the books in the highly popular Tarzan series, author Edgar Rice Burroughs depicted in its pages the lost city of Xuja, a desert valley apparently located in the African Sahel. It is a place that is inhabited by dominant warrior madmen who not only worship monkeys and parrots but who also breed lions for their meat, to which they are virtually addicted. This tribal people are completely insane as a consequence of long in-breeding. (It was this novel of Burroughs, published in 1920, that became highly controversial in Germany, stemming from the author's blanket portrayal of Germans as stereotypical, irredeemable, and unrelenting villains.) The Xuja speak a language that sounds vaguely, tantalizingly familiar to the Smith-Oldwicks, a European couple who become captives of the Xujans. The couple feels as if they had heard something like this language once before, but they cannot place it. What exactly was this language? Could Burroughs have been trying to suggest that the Xujans spoke a somewhat altered or corrupted form of Egyptian, Punic, Babylonian, or Greek? If Punic, could it have reminded them of Hebrew that they had once heard on a visit to a synagogue? Remember, the Carthaginians were transplanted Phoenicians from ancient Lebanon.

Chris Cosentino, a winner of Top Chef Masters, is one American chef that is noted for his offal dishes, a fare in places now considered haute cuisine. He is a chef-partner at Incanto, which *Forbes Traveler* calls "perhaps America's most adventurous nose-to-tail restaurant … On offer are lamb's necks, pig trotters and a five-course nose-to-tail tasting menu perhaps including venison kidneys and chocolate-blood panna cotta."

Cosentino is presently writing a cookbook on offal cookery and runs an offal-themed website called OffalGood.com, his "educational and inspirational tool for those who are interested in learning and cooking with offal." Brains, incidentally, contain 4 ½ times more cholesterol than eggs.

Destruction breeds creation. While one person may hate a particular food, another will delight in it. So it is with offal. Those who hate a particular thing are not wrong. Curiously, a fire sparks in the censoring mind, and a man striving to make something of continuing refusal, stridently follows his own funny fate, wherever it leads, elsewhere. Let him go his way, holding high his lantern, poking over scrabble and gravel. There is something primitive but weirdly admirable in stark, unbudging refusal; equally can be found a daring and intrepid new adventure. That map in our mind, while confusing to others, yet mandates we follow it. Søren Kierkegaard put it memorably in a gnomic paradox: "Life must be understood backwards … but it must be lived forwards."

Reading Joseph Conrad's letters recently, I found that a self-discipline that he imposed on himself, while writing, included a policy of giving up meat and, at certain times, actually foregoing eating. There is the commonly held belief that the creative intelligence is most alert when in a state of deprivation, of stark fasting, especially from what is considered by some passion-producing meat. Perhaps Conrad's renunciation took place during the period when he was writing that scene in *Heart of Darkness*, where Marlow explains how he had enlisted certain odd-fellow members of his crew. "Fine fellows—cannibals—in their place. They were men one could work with, and I am grateful to them. And, after all, they did not eat each other before my face." In the novella, the singular cannibal preference for hippo meat must have consoled the intrepid Marlow, to some comforting degree.

As to what human flesh tastes like, many accounts vary, from Piers Paul Reid's *Alive* to Kenneth Roberts' *Boon Island* to William Buehler Seabrook's *Jungle Ways* (1931), which in the opinion of critic Brian Palmer in *Slate* (June 4, 2012) "provided the world's most detailed written description of the taste of human flesh." Seabrook noted that, in raw form, human meat looks like beef, but slightly less red, with pale yellow fat. When roasted, the meat turned grayish, as would lamb or veal, and smelled like cooked beef. As for the taste, Seabrook wrote, "It was so nearly like good, fully developed veal that I think no person with a palate of ordinary, normal sensitiveness could distinguish it from veal." I have read elsewhere that human flesh tastes like banana and that when facing the extremes of such a crisis the palms of the hands, cut in very thin strips and sun-dried, should be eaten first and taste best.

At least this was the working method, the option, by which the sixteen young men of the remaining 45-members of the Uruguayan Rugby Team managed to survive, faced with the unthinkable, there on the mountain for ten excruciating weeks, after their plane had crashed on October 12, 1972 into an extremely remote, snow-peaked section of the Andes. Different parts of the human body have been favored in different and varying circumstances in cannibal literature. Heart, thigh, upper arm, lips. The taste of infant meat, which supposedly tastes like fish, has been highly valued. It has been recorded that women's breasts are scrumptious. But maybe there is a message in the outraged response to Gustave Courbet's bold *The Bathers*. When the painting was exhibited in 1853, one critic exclaimed of the great flaccid nude whose back and striding thighs fill most of the picture, "Crocodiles would not eat them."

Seabrook's account may be questioned for he was not allowed by the Guero tribe in West Africa to eat flesh or partake in their native traditions.

"In his autobiography," Palmer notes, "Seabrook claims to have obtained the body of a recently deceased hospital patient in France and then cooked it on a spit."

Poet Phyllis McGinley particularly disliked ham, disparagingly referring to it as the South's "pet cuisine" in her poem, "Notes for a Southern Roadmap" which runs in part:

> Ham
> Ham,
> Not lamb or bacon
> But ham in Raleigh
> And ham in Macon.
> Ham for plutocrats,
> Ham for pore folk,
> Ham in Paducah and ham in Norfolk;
> In Memphis, ham, and in Chapel Hill,
> Chattanooga,
> And Charlottesville,
> Ham for the Missy,
> Ham for the Colonel,
> And for the traveler, Ham Eternal,
> Oh, patriotically I implore,
> Look away, Dixieland, from the smokehouse door.

In vivid counterpoint, one cannot fail to mention here Chef Sean Brock, of the Husk restaurant in Nashville, whose almost intimate affection for this meat had him say, "I have taken naps on country ham."

Dr. Evelyn Handler (*neé* Sass), born on May 5, 1933 in Budapest, one of four daughters of Donald and Ilona Sass, Orthodox Jews who moved their family to New York in 1940, was appointed president of Brandeis University in Waltham, Mass. in 1980 and was an innovator. As president, she wanted as much as possible for Brandeis to be less provincial in its policies and have a more pluralistic campus. (When growing up, Handler's mother kept a kosher household, but in her adulthood she herself did not.) She immediately set about raising money to begin renovating dorms, invigorating the sports program, and diversifying the student body, which was about 70 percent Jewish, with recruiting efforts and subtler initiatives to underscore Brandeis's non-sectarian foundational principles. She struck a nerve, however, when she instructed the university food service in 1987 to "internationalize" the student cafeteria by adding both pork and shellfish to the menu." It set off a storm of protest. The eating of non-kosher beef and the mixing of meat and dairy dishes is considered as blasphemous a violation of Jewish law as the eating of pork, crabs, and scallops. Although the dining halls at Brandeis were mainly non-kosher, such foods are considered, glaringly, among the most "*trefah*" or non-kosher foods forbidden under Jewish dietary law, avoided even by many non- observant Jews. Both foods are also staples in the diet of many, if not most, Asian-Americans—a demographic that Handler sought to attract. In the ensuing uproar, known on campus as the "trefah war," extreme religious students on the far right accused Dr. Handler of blatantly trying to "de-Judaize" Brandeis. A sulfurous scandal boiled up. What aggravated the situation was that the menu change occurred just about the very same time that the Hebrew word *emet* (truth) was dropped from the university logo and a change in the school's calendar replaced all references to Jewish holidays with the wording "no university exercises."

Amid protests, Handler, who by all accounts was hired because of her reputation as a formidable and strong-willed executive, held her ground, designating only one dining area as trefah-free. Well-aware, surely, that this very conflict reflected the same bitter tensions that are presently found in Israel among secular and religious Jews about preserving Jewish identity in a non-Jewish world, she refused to give in to the close-minded sectarians and held out.

The storm grew worse, however. Support unraveled. Several trustees turned on the university president. A major donor withdrew financial support. Her best efforts proved to be in vain in the end. Due to all the negative publicity and the boisterous and parochial opposition from blindly sectarian alumni and prospective donors, Brandeis University partially backed down. A new edict was issued. Pork chops and shrimp were not to be served in the college dining-hall where kosher food was offered. The word "*emet*" was returned to the university's logo, and all of Jewish holidays were given mention on the university calendar. In a 1989 interview with the *New York Times*, Handler lamented, "I think there are a number of students who would like to see Brandeis become a sectarian institution." In the same interview, she attributed the dispute to a rise in Jewish religious fundamentalism. The enmity and bitterness stirred by the controversy was considered a major factor in her decision a year later to resign out of pure frustration over the backlash of what was seen as her maladroit attempts to change the university's image. She later confided to friends and family she had concluded that the old guard was not prepared to make the changes it had hired her to make.

I have always found it passingly ironic, and paradoxical, for the large Jewish population in New York City that cheesecake, of the many confections there are, is the traditional steakhouse dessert, "perfect punctuation to a meal of meat," as John Thorne observes, writing how "those with an intense craving for the well-marbled (and well-salted) sirloin have a compensating lack of interest in sweets. They want only a final, tasty, unctuous mouthful to round off their meal." Although meat can be eaten soon after most dairy meals, observant Jews may wait as long as up to six hours after eating meat before taking any dairy.

The late Elijah Mohammed, a complete fraud born Elijah Robert Poole in Sandersville, Ga. who became a religious leader of the Nation of Islam, outlawed pork for black people, but, according to Eldridge Cleaver in *Soul on Ice*, it had nothing to do with dietary laws. "Blacks eat chitterlings from necessity… [but the fact is] the people in the ghetto want steaks. *Beef steaks*," he wrote, adding, "The emphasis on Soul Food is counter-revolutionary black bourgeois ideology." Eating chitterlings is low, like "going slumming" to advantaged blacks, Cleaver insisted, and the so-called popular taste for "soul food" is nothing but jive. He wrote,

> The point is that when you get all those blacks cooped
> up in the ghetto with beef steaks on their minds…
> then something's got to give. The system has made
> allowances for the ghettoites to obtain a little pig, *but*
> *there are no provisions for the elite to give up beef.*

The white man—"Whitey"—in a sense was pork to Cleaver. The political activist who became an early leader of the Black Panther Party, was also a convicted rapist with intent to murder and spent seven years in Folsom and San Quentin. While in prison, he was given a copy of Marx's *Communist Manifesto*, a book that justified all of his feelings of rebellion and hatred. He memorably wrote in his bitter poem (in part) "To a White Girl," involving the concept of outlawed food,

> I hate you
> because you are white.
> Your white meat
> is nightmare food.

Speaking of pork, the famous old septuagenarian pedestrian, Edward Payson Weston—in 1909 he walked alone from Manhattan to San Francisco, 3,895 miles, in 104 days—personally abjured it. He did eat beef and mutton, but he refused to have any of it fried. Fried food was anathema to him. He liked soup but never any canned foods. Other dislikes of his were exotic dishes with sauces. As to alcoholic beverages, he restricted himself to wine, Bass Ale, and Guinness. Oddly, never American beer—he didn't like the taste. A true eccentric, he started each day with a cold bath and after a long day of walking he always rubbed his feet with whiskey and wore a red flannel nightshirt to bed as a preventative against rheumatism.

The poet Heather McHugh wrote me, saying,

> I was said, from an early age, to be suffering from "an imagination." In my childhood that meant I fostered aversions to foods with names I thought taxonomically suspect, such as "eggplant," and "cheese food." I was skeptical about Miracle Whip and Wonder Bread, and remain so today, though I've come to love eggplant in any of its forms. Cracker Jacks escaped my withering disdain, despite the manifest failure of the thing itself to resemble Melba Toast or playing cards. (Some foods benefited from the toys or "fortunes" tucked inside their wrappers. Auguries of puberty.)

Was she a vegetarian, I asked?
McHugh replied,

> As an adult, my imagination attaches rather to the reality than to the name. In my middle and later years, I found myself more and more repelled by foods whose source-animals suffer miserable lives as parts of a food industry rather than as fellow creatures on a farm where they can see plants and sunlight, mingle with other animals, have room to breathe and move; and where, when death comes, it comes in a more merciful fashion than we afford to any sentience from which we avert our eyes, or our imaginations. It takes imagination, said Valery, to see what is.

It is of course under the easy grace of euphemistic names that allow us guiltlessly to eat meat. As actor Peter Ustinov noted in his autobiography, *Dear Me*, "You don't eat cow, but beef. You don't eat calf, but veal. You don't eat pig, but ham, bacon, or pork. You don't eat deer, but venison.

Cold-blooded fish are among the few living entities that retain their identity in death."

15.

DO YOU BELIEVE IN COD? OR,

NO KIPPER EVER TASTES AS GOOD AS IT SMELLS

Elvis Presley loathed and would never touch fish, which reminded him—even the smell of it—of childhood poverty. That included catfish, which Southern boys tend to enjoy. He demanded his wife, Priscilla, never eat fish around him. Elvis's cook Mary Jenkins who wrote *Elvis: The Way I Knew Him* informs us that Priscilla loved tuna salad but that the only time she made it was when Elvis was either on tour, away from home, or asleep. Elvis hated the smell of fish. (Jenkins' book contains only three recipes of the many foods he liked: vegetable soup, corn bread, and macaroni salad.) The great sex-symbol of music also disliked olives and had a real aversion for almost any and all pastries. Peter the Great, Tsar of Russia, never once ate fish, convinced of the bad effects it would have on him. "I've never really wanted to go to Japan—simply because I don't like eating fish. And I know that's very popular out there in Africa," the pert pop-singer Britney Spears, not a geographer, told a reporter a few years ago. Beautiful Marilyn Monroe was among such skeptics, abominating the very smell of sea food, as well. She told photographer Jock Carroll in 1952, "I can't eat fish."

There are a good many fish haters out there. I was once served (from a jar) a farrago of gelatinous white trawl called "gefilte fish," a popular Shabbat food, which tasted to me, I'm afraid to report, like the dark backroom of an *abattoir* smells. It is a concoction apparently made to avoid *borer*, one of the 39 activities that is prohibited on the Sabbath as outlined in Code of Jewish Law. (*Borer*, literally "selection/ choosing," occurs when one picks the bones out of the fish, taking "the chaff from within the food.") "I regret to say there's a certain peculiar oil in bluefish that invariably poisoned me—I can't see what's so darned funny about me being poisoned," croaks the thersitical drunk Wallace Beery to Lionel Barrymore in director Clarence Brown's film of Eugene O'Neill's play, *Ah, Wilderness!* (1935). "I remember that we ordered fish sticks (for Henry haddock was the only fish that existed)," wrote Elizabeth Coatsworth in *Especially Maine*, a sort of memoir-cum-anthology of her husband, writer Henry Beston, author of the now revered nature memoir, *The Outermost House*.

How weird that one of the writers so legendarily associated with the maritime areas of Cape Cod and Maine would be so fastidious as to eliminate as worthwhile food every last living fish in the sea but *one*!

I have mentioned that the intrepid God-fearing Pilgrims who came to the New World, the 102 daring souls sailing on the *Mayflower*, had virtually no interest in eating fish or any other sea-catch as food and only reluctantly, out of necessity, starvation, desperate need, had to abandon their tastes for traditional English food. They had planned to *labor* at fishing, of course, but their intention was to fish, wherever they had decided to put down roots, for mercantile reasons. It turned out, sad to report, they soon discovered after they had landed that they had brought the wrong-sized hooks—too large for the kind of fish to be caught in the waters of Plymouth Bay.

A diet of clams, oysters, mussels, and seafood in general might have done them good. Oystercatchers, for example, are incredibly long-lived, with the present record-holder dying at age 35. I have read that some reach 40! Or is it simply that the birds are happily monogamous?

The smell of fish agitated Dutch Renaissance theologian, Desiderius Erasmus, to no end. In his highly opinionated work, *Ichthyophagia*, a peppery colloquy between a competing butcher and a fishmonger—and one of Rabelais' favorite books—Erasmus passionately wrote, "Fish is the only thing on which salt loses its flavor… Fish corrupts even salt itself."

Conductor Arturo Toscanini, who as a young student was fed so much fish in various forms at the Royal School of Music in Parma, Italy, that he developed a violent distaste for it, cooked in whatever way, that an aversion for fish would stay with him throughout his entire life. The maestro would not only never touch fish, he was known actually to flee from a house wherever it was being cooked and he had merely sniffed its presence. "His wife, Carla, once served some canapés of fish without telling him [what was in them]," explained Howard Taubman in *The Maestro*. "He took a bite and spat it out." He stated, "I am a peasant, like Verdi." The Toscanini family diet, when he was growing up a boy in Emilia-Romagna, basically consisted of bread and soup and nothing more. Toscanini was satisfied to keep things there. He said, "That is why I like soup and bread all my life."

One may judge oneself what Raymond Chandler's plain-fare-eating Los Angeles private detective Philip Marlowe thought about fish for dinner when we read in *Farewell, My Lovely*, "The fish smell from the Mansion House coffee shop was strong enough to build a garage on." He should have lived in Gloucester, Massachusetts, ground zero for the fishing industry for hundreds of years, specifically close to the venerable old Gorton-Pew fishery—Pee-Yoo!

Novelist Pat Conroy, whom we have met, has written that his mother hated fish and so in order to meet their Roman Catholic obligation on Fridays growing up, always served frozen fish-sticks to her large family. "My youngest brother thought that fish were rectangular in shape," he wrote. It is comic, but no doubt such is the case with many Midwesterners or in-landers. *Hey, visit a museum*!

There is sacredness to fish. The *icthus* (Greek for fish) from the Greek (ἰχθύς, "fish"), which is a symbol consisting of two intersecting arcs, the ends of the right side extending beyond the meeting point so as to resemble the profile of a fish, was also an acronym in very early Christianity for Ἰησοῦς Χριστός, Θεοῦ Υἱός, Σωτήρ", (Iēsous Christos, Theou Yios, Sōtēr), which translates as "Jesus Christ, Son of God, Saviour." There is only one passage in the whole of the New Testament where it is specifically and explicitly said that Jesus ate meat (Luke 24:41–43), and that meat was fish. Jesus distributes loaves and fish in Matthew 14:13–21. Fish, of course, have been often employed as a spiritual metaphor. Rupert Brooke's fantasy poem, "Heaven," for example, addressing the rewards of faith, offers us a whimsical world of dreaming, cerebral, reflective fish who "ponder deep wisdom, dark or clear,/ Each secret fishy hope or fear" and speculate on their own transcendent—"fishy"—eternity. There is a spiritual allusion in John Greenleaf Whittier's long poem, "Snow-Bound"—it is taken from the quaint simplicity of *Chalkley's Journal* (Thomas Chalkley was probably the most influential Quaker minister in colonial America during the 18th-century)—when and where a hard-pressed skipper in a precarious boat on a stormy sea, starving to death, is suddenly sent a salvific school of porpoise:

> "Take, eat," he said, and "be content;
> These fishes in my stead are sent
> By Him who have the tangled ram
> To spare the child of Abraham."

I believe that, after fruit, fish still persists as the favorite subject for still-lifes—like Manet's earlier painting *Fish (Still Life)*. Courbet's *The Trout* (1873), which probably stands as the best example, is dramatically depicted mid-flop. The silvery fish appears to have been freshly caught, gasping for breath on a riverbank. The oil-on-canvas is worked with heavy, rough brushstrokes. One critic offers, "The application of paint paired with the helplessness of the subject could suggest the frustration the Artist was experiencing at the time with the judiciary system."

What about an entire *people* hating fish? The Jews of Iraq abstain from eating fish because the Hebrew word for fish is *dag*, which sounds like *dagah*, the Hebrew word meaning "worry, anxiety." The name *quenelle* comes from a dish of elongated fish balls, which are said to resemble a suppository. Hence, the phrase "

Did the epic poet Homer hate fish?

One only asks because fish was conspicuously not present at the banquet scenes or heroic feasts of the *Iliad* (Plato discusses this)—nor was it ever used, or considered, as a suitable animal for sacrificial rituals—paradoxically so, because the Greeks were huge consumers and lovers of fish. No cookbooks survive from ancient Athens, the largest and richest classical city, and the Athenians' own contribution to the history of cookery was confined to their cakes. An *opsophagos* is someone with a distinct predilection for fish. (*Opsony*—a term now obsolete—in its basic meaning describes any food eaten with bread [plural *opsonia*.]) James Davidson in his book *Courtesans and Fishcakes*, writing of the passions of classical Athens, explains that the word *opsarion* refers to cooked fish, differing from the general word for fish, *icthus*, an early Christian symbol/anagram, as we have seen. The word *opsarion* occurs only five times in the Gospel of John and nowhere else in the New Testament. In the famous Miracle of the Loaves and Fishes, the fish that Christ multiplied and had distributed were of course—perhaps obvious to say—cooked fish, indeed incontestably the more palatable.

By the way, who ever makes note of, never mind gives credit to—one of the most enigmatic allusions in the Gospels—the *boy* mentioned in John 6:9 from whom the loaves and fishes were *taken*? ("Here is a boy with five small barley loaves and two small fish, but how far will they go among so many?") I wonder, was he subsequently given the twelve baskets full of food left over, as a tip?

"Most native [African] tribes refuse to eat fish, the Tongas being a noted exception," wrote Dudley Kidd of Africa in his comprehensive if outdated classic, *The Essential Kafir*. The American showman and theatrical shill Billy Rose—William S. Rosenberg—always flatly refused to eat fish. Actor Rod Steiger is another who has gone on record as abhorring all fish, declaring, "I will not eat that goddam trash." Judith Jones, the legendary editor who has helped shape modern cookbook publishing, confesses in her book, *The Tenth Muse: My Life in Food*, that over the course of her lifetime she has had a bit of difficulty with scallops, which she refers to as "my old nemesis." The waspish fussifier Christopher Kimball of television's America's Test Kitchen has stated, "I'd prefer to be shot than cook shad roe." Frankly, I would prefer to be shot than have to cook with that peevish, cold, and disapproving Vespa hornet staring over my shoulder and looking as if he were about to sting me! "Fish is the only food that is considered spoiled once it smells like what it is," pronounced P. J. O'Rourke, which shows clearly where he stands on the subject.

But are not most foodies a tribe of cheese-paring and pedantic flints and mutts? What else was Jesus getting at when He railed at religious phonies tithing even the tiniest spices from their herb gardens, crying,

> Woe to you, teachers of the law and Pharisees, you
> hypocrites! You give a tenth of your spices—mint, dill
> and cumin. But you have neglected the more import-
> ant matters of the law—justice, mercy and faithfulness.
> You should have practiced the latter, without neglect-
> ing the former.

It is amazing how all encompassing some people's dislikes can be—how widely and, if I may say so, irrationally sweeping—and how entire categories are banished from sight. As I say, Vladimir Nabokov grumpily once listed "the Orient"—speaking of generalizations—as being among things of no interest to him. (Charles Darwin felt the same way about Australia but may at least be credited with having visited and to a degree examined the place.) In his novel, *Molloy* (1951), Samuel Beckett writes, "I don't like animals. It's a strange thing, I don't like men and I don't like animals. As for God, he is beginning to disgust me." Beckett also writes in *Watt*: "For if there were two things that Watt disliked, one was the moon, and the other was the sun." Later: "And if there were two things that Watt loathed, one was the earth, and the other was the sky." Nothing like the all-encompassing to avoid the specific, right?

Prejudice against fish and fish-eaters were rampant in 19th-century New England. It was considered among many Brahmins, except for the chowders they loved, low scrubby fare for all help and below-stairs Irish. Abundance alone of fish connoted trash. Even lobsters were fed to chickens, and prisoners in jail were forced to eat lobster three times a week. "Fish-eating was associated with poverty and Roman Catholicism. Fish were undomesticated at a time when wild food was not preferred fare," observes food historian Sandra Oliver in her *Saltwater Foodways*, her compendium on what New Englanders ate a century ago. Fish was eaten and produced by people with whom many old Yankees did not wish to identify."

We have all been assured that fish is brainfood—and healthfood. I have been hearing encomia on the salvific value of sardines all my life. The character of novelist P.G. Wodehouse's character, Jeeves, the chipper, trouble-prone dimwit valet who is oddly practical and impeccable, are frankly elusive and unfathomable. Attempts to explain the powers, which always prevail, are futile. Yet Bertie Wooster's best theory is that his servant's intelligence is the result of eating tremendous amounts of fish, despite Jeeves' persistent, polite denials.

Julia Child would not countenance oily fish in a bouillabaisse. An authentic Marseille bouillabaisse along with bony rockfish, for her, had to include *rascasse* ("scorpionfish" in English), despite the fact that, like sculpin, it is rarely eaten in any form other than in a bouillabaisse. It also must officially include *congre* (European conger) and *grondin* (sea robin). According to the *Michelin Guide Vert*, the four essential elements of any true bouillabaisse are the presence of *rascasse* (or scorpionfish), the freshness of the fish; olive oil, and an excellent saffron. Quirks seem to apply to the making of a bouillabaisse. Some connoisseurs insist it is impossible to make authentic bouillabaisse without fish from the Mediterranean. It is said it needs *both* oily and white fish and that any true bouillabaisse should never be made for fewer than eight people. Traditionally, a bouillabaisse is eaten in two courses. First the broth is poured in bowls with some *sauce rouille* spread on the *croutes*. Afterwards, the fish platter is served, often with thinly sliced buttered potatoes.

A *rascasse*—the word may derive from a Provençal word for "moth," perhaps because the fish's skin is speckled like a moth's wings—is hard to find in the United States. (It is also Provençal slang for a stingy person.)

I knew a petulant head chef in Maine (a co-worker and I used to refer to him as "The Green Hornet") who, watching someone create a bouillabaisse, would begin shouting and then go into a complete conniption, stomping his feet, if he noticed the ingredients were being added all at once. *"Cuisine brut!"* he would scream if he saw anyone—a sloven, in his mind—do that, or even add salt. The best method is first to boil the broth, and then, while adding the different kinds of fish one by one, each time the broth comes to a boil, gently lower the heat. One can see a *rascasse*, by the way—one of the world's ugliest-looking fish—just above the subject's ear in Guiseppe Arcimboldo's imaginative fish-face portrait called, *"The Water,"* a painting that is sometimes also called "The Admiral." He painted it in 1566, and it presently hangs in Vienna at the Ausstellungskatalog des Kunsthistorischen Museum.

I love cod, haddock, snook, salmon, mackerel, giant perch or barramundi, marlin, and tuna—dog tooth, albacore, and black skipjack, the flesh of which is very red when used on sashimi. Cape Codders love fish. More than once I have used cod—and several times even mako shark—in a bouillabaisse. Mako is often sold as swordfish, but I try to use the real thing. Neither blue shark nor white shark is in demand as food, and the same goes with salmon shark and trigger shark, and neither is generally eaten. At least I have never thrown in barracuda, fearing *ciguatera*, a food-borne illness caused by eating certain reef fish whose flesh is contaminated with toxins that come from dinoflagellates that live in tropic and subtropic waters. I love sardines. ("I loathe sardines. I simply loathe them," declared the painter Francis Bacon.) Of course for me lobster is king. Sir Philip Sassoon, however, likened Lobster Newburg to a "puree of white kid gloves."

H.P. Lovecraft, author of horror tales and a general oddball, also hated fish and all seafood. An allergy to it led to rather mad and ongoing assaults against it, fulminations, as is made clear in many of stories. He told a friend, "I have hated fish and feared the sea and everything connected with it since I was two years old." While the very sight or smell of fish always made Lovecraft physically ill, he yet worked this anxiety and disgust into his fiction, where a pronounced obsession with the sea surfaces in such scary tales of his about Cthulhu, Dagon, and the Deep Ones, where he focused on marine and aquatic demons or monsters, icthyoid and batrachian. He referred to these creatures as "night gaunts" in "The Shadow of Innsmouth" and "The Doom That Came to Sarnath." His deep-seated fear was apparently not a terror of the ocean but rather of the mysteries and its menaces that lurked beneath its surface.

In Lovecraft's story "The Horror at Martin's Beach," for example, which he wrote in 1922, an unseen sea-monster tricks sunbathers on a resort beach into grasping a long rope that extends into the water. Hideously, the bathers find themselves unable to release it; inexorably, all are drawn like fish on a line, screaming and weeping, beneath the waves. The strange thing to note about this author, whose central thesis was that the universe is fundamentally inimical to the interests of humankind, is that his strange fixation on—his all-consuming attraction to—the vast mysterious ocean, led to poetic remarks about it like, "But more wonderful than the lore of old men and the lore of books is the secret lore of the ocean" and "Blue, green, gray, white, or black; smooth, ruffled, or mountainous, that ocean is not silent" and "Ocean is more ancient than the mountains, and freighted with the memories and the dreams of Time."

Lovecraft's brilliantly weird tale, "The Colour Out of Space," tells the story of the narrator's attempts to uncover the secrets behind a shunned place referred to by the locals of Arkham as the "blasted heath." It is the story of an ecological disaster in which, while crops come in unnaturally large and abundantly, they prove to be inedible. It is said that a meteorite has poisoned the soil. Over the following year, the problem begins spreading to the surrounding vegetation and local animals, warping them in unusual ways. Any plant life around the farmhouse becomes "slightly luminous in the dark." People are isolated, go mad, lock themselves in rooms, and even the vegetation begins eroding into a gray powder, while the water from the wells becomes tainted. The livestock begins turning gray and dying, and, like the crops, their meat is tasteless and inedible. Finally, the horror destroys the last surviving resident.

Art Buchwald, the late syndicated columnist and satirist, in his somewhat maudlin memoir, *Leaving Home*, recounts how when as a toddler, after his mother died, he was sent away with his sisters to a small boarding house for sick children in Flushing, New York. It was a dreary place run by Seventh-Day Adventists. The boy lived there with a family until he reached the age of five. I have always found Buchwald tiresomely unfunny, a hard view that was ameliorated when I read with some surprise and sadness of some of the misery that he went through at such an early age. "My strongest impression of the home was the strict religious upbringing I received," bitterly wrote Buchwald, who was somewhat self-consciously a Jew and deeply resentful of the dogmatic caveats that he met with there. "The nurses were God's messengers on what constituted sin and what didn't," he complained. "I am talking about serious sin now. They practiced their religion faithfully, and they expected us to do the same. Eating meat, fish, and eggs was a sin." Later he goes on to say,

> I have spent almost as much time on the Seventh-Day Adventists in my analysis as I have on my mother. I am willing to bet that this place was as responsible for many of my hang-ups. I conjured up all forms of sin from my childhood. I once had a bull with four horns attack me in a dream because [later in life] I had eaten steak for dinner that night. To this day, I can't eat fish with scales on them. I have made my peace with shellfish and meat, but there is still a tiny Seventh-Day

Adventist inside of me screaming to get out every time
I make a pass at a tuna fish sandwich.

It is curious to see how, when people explain their food phobias, they often feel an extra-astringent need to attach them to deeper, scarier, more threatening reasons than simply plain distaste. Why does Buchwald's disgust or fear of scale fish have to attach to Seventh-Day Adventism particularly? Obviously, because it makes the aversion more dramatic and, of course, if phobias indict us, why not engage in a bit of blame-shifting, no? It is almost comic that Buchwald was perfectly prepared to proceed through life eating meat, pork, and shellfish, since it is obvious the man liked those foods. He never became a vegetarian. How much baggage did Buchwald have to carry from those early year? A good deal, it seems. He reminds me of the regretful old man in E.A. Robinson's poem, "The Pity of Leaves," who suffers from the brown, thin leaves that skip by with a freezing whisper and even mock him, for

Now and then
They stopped, and stayed there—just to let him know
How dead they were.

This may be said to be the primal scream of the food aversionist, complaint reverberating through the lonely corridors of one's bias, like the dead, remembered leaves that plague Robinson's old man on those cold November moors.

Fish fears? I have mentioned deeper, scarier reasons than mere distaste in food phobia. After a Nazi flotilla sailed up the fjords in Norway on April 9, 1940, one of the troopships, the heavy cruiser *Blücher*, was sunk by a shot from the Oscarsborg Fortress, thus saving the Norwegian King and government from being taken prisoner. The people of nearby Oslo refused to eat mackerel from the fjord for a long time afterward, however, suspecting the fish were nibbling on German soldiers!

Another brief word on Buchwald's personal scenario. I certainly do not believe one can deny that in the world of food phobes a small percentage cannot be found whose aversions grow from personality disorders, a bizarre transferal, say, table-turning, or a passive aggression dodge of the "Look what you've done to me" or "You didn't treat me well" sort. Food aversion in extreme cases may very well be a plea for attention, a need to show off or seem like an alert and discerning eater, even a small suicidality borne of split-off feelings that grow out of suspicion one personally does not want to, or cannot, feel. It is not strictly anger in Buchwald's case of blaming evangelicals for his many "hang ups," although he clearly feels the need to rinse out his guilt, citing a memory of "sin" for his hated foods. Spite—opposition, defiant disorder, as much a medical condition as a personality quirk—we will consider later, considering the willfulness of Dostoevsky's Underground Man and Melville's Bartleby and their furious, often spiteful intransigence as a defense mechanism. The same could be said of paranoid Jews like K. in Kafka's *The Trial* and Joey in Witold Gombrowicz's *Ferdydurke* and profane Alex Portnoy in Roth's *Portnoy's Complaint*. Sylvia Plath wrote, "I munch on chagrins."

Food aversionists in their dogged insistence, implacable energy, and stubborn willfulness are madly self-propelled—like jets. They need no help for what they believe and are, as a matter of fact, usually invigorated by opposition. Rockets in space carry an oxidizer to ignite their engines, often in the form of liquid oxygen, in order to burn their engine fuel. That is the essential difference between rockets and jets; the latter get oxygen from the pure air. They forcefully "selve."

One could also cite Henry David Thoreau, a master of intransigence and, at times, a rigid and obdurate Yankee, pigheaded, and unaccommodating. Critics charge that in his crotchety essay, "Resistance to Civil Government," a polemic popularly known as "Civil Disobedience," the Concord native comes across as an anarchist concerned merely with himself, a man of an unhealthy individuality, a humorless and irksome popinjay who was at best vain and wanting in compassion. What did his going to jail involve, they ask, and was his ambition in the matter to prove his outsider status, a figure of spite and refusal basically focused on his own self-sufficiency?

Thoreau in being characteristically willful was being wild. "In wildness is the preservation of the world," he wrote in "Walking," his memorable essay which was first published in the *Atlantic Monthly* in June 1862. One of his most famous remarks, it is an apothegm which is crucially misquoted, where one mistakenly substitutes the word "wilderness" for "wildness." By understanding the word *wildness* in the way in which Thoreau took it is to live a life that is willful, deliberate, and free from the civic forces that are often at variance with our true nature.

A person who intransigently—uncompromisingly—refuses a food is often, and pejoratively, described as willful. In a Thoreauvian way, however, he or she is as wild, in a positive sense, as he or she is stubbornly headstrong. But is not willfulness a *cri de coeur* in a victim saying, "I count"? Such a man repudiates orthodoxy as a premise for living his own life. "Orthodoxy means not thinking—not needing to think. Orthodoxy is unconsciousness," wrote

Orwell in *Nineteen Eighty-Four*. Thoreau's concept of wildness in fact grew out of his 1853 reading of Richard Trench's *The Study of Words*, in which we read, "'Wild' is the participle past of 'to will;' a 'wild' horse is a 'willed' or self-willed horse, one that has never been tamed or taught to submit its will to the will of another; and so with a man." No etymological idea could possibly have spoken more directly to Thoreau or found a more sympathetic pursuivant. Fast upon reading the passage, Thoreau noted in his journals,

> A wild man is a willed man. Well, then, a man of will
> who does what he wills or wishes, a man of hope and
> of the future tensed [sic], for not only the obstinate
> is willed, but far more the constant and persevering.
> The obstinate man, properly speaking, is one who will
> not. The perseverance of the saints is positive willed-
> ness [sic], not a mere passive willingness. The fates are
> wild, for they will; and the Almighty is wild above all.

The obstinate man, properly speaking, is one who will not. True. By our intransigence, you will know us. By what we refuse to eat, by what we refuse to do, in the way we refuse to bend, speaks directly to one who may seem— even be—obstinate, but it also recapitulates in the mind of Henry Thoreau, even if in a small or trivial way, a sense of the constant and the persevering. "Guard the good treasure entrusted to you, with the help of the Holy Spirit living in us." (1 Timothy 1:14)

The splendid writer Paul Maliszewski told me that when he was a kid he ate a lot of liverwurst sandwiches, which had something of a baleful effect on him.

> What makes me feel sick anymore is thinking about
> all the liverwurst sandwiches I had for lunch when I
> was a kid. I liked liverwurst best on Saltine crackers.
> My mother made them like a tower, an alternating
> pile of crackers and liverwurst, the beige paste like a
> mortar spread between bricks, squeezing out the sides,
> stuck into the tiny Saltine holes. I must have had those
> sandwiches every day for several years. I took other
> stuff for lunch, too—carrot spears, celery sticks, maybe
> some chips, I don't know. I had a lunchbox then: hel-
> mets of the National Football League. Milk I'd buy a
> little carton of from the cafeteria. I can't fathom eating

a liverwurst sandwich today. My lip curls, my nose wrinkles, my stomach suffers at the thought.

But it is whole fish—the corpses—that Maliszewski has studiously avoided for a lifetime. Back in 2012 he wrote to me, saying,

> When I was young, the smell of fish made me want to retch. There was a seafood market near our house where we went every week, my mother, brother, and I. It was in an elbow-shaped strip mall, though something about the place made it seem older, as if the market had been established a hundred years before and then the shopping center grew around it. They had a lot of fish, four or five refrigerated cases. Red plastic lobsters were caught in nets strung across the windows. Packets of spices for sale, jars of cocktail sauce. I don't know what my mother bought. I have this memory that she and my father were big into red snapper for a while. My brother and I survived on hamburgers mostly, hamburgers and hot dogs. My mother looked at all the fish before deciding what to buy. From my viewpoint, of course, she could never decide quickly enough, the smell was so overpowering, thick and, I want to say, multidimensional. There is in that fish smell the smaller smells of brine and algae, but there is something more, too, a sort of sliminess, a movement, a life. What truly unnerved me, though, was seeing the whole fish stacked on beds of ice, their bodies keeling to one side, laid out like pointed planks, and their eyes, fogged over, empty, glaucomal eyes staring fixedly through the glass back at me.

He went on to confess,

> I eat fish now. Or I will, anyway; I can, from time to time. I prefer tuna to salmon, generally, but both are fine. Fish markets remain hard for me—I still avoid the whole fish, avoid even looking in their direction—but I'll go to the market in our neighborhood and pick us up something for dinner.

In her witty memoir, *Eileen*, the wife of Irish dramatist Sean O'Casey, recounts her early schooling and excoriates the unappetizing food that was served to the students by the strict, no-nonsense Sisters of Charity at their Hyde Park establishment in London, particularly the steamed fish, served whole. "I could manage it as a rule except when it was cod—a full-sized fish, all of it, dumped on the serving plate, head, tail and an eye that, dead and dreary though it was, seemed to be fixing me." Eileen Carey Casey goes on to explain in detail,

> I could never get the cod down. Its sauce, thin and watery with a bit of green parsley, did not help. All I could do was to sit, with tears trickling into the sauce, while I tried and tried to swallow a portion so large that I felt there must be some special spite against me. Now and then, if it was not too sloppy, I would sweep the whole thing into paper ready on my lap, roll it up, and push it into the elastic of my knickers to throw away later. That was the plan, but though I went prepared every time, I was not very clever and succeeded only once or twice. Failure was the end, for if you could not eat everything before you they would take it away, talking about the waste of God's food. Then at tea-time back it would be, the same old cod, cold now and jellied, and served to you by yourself at a side-table. Not that you were starved; they did allow you one piece of bread and a drink—cocoa, usually—but no biscuit, no jam, no golden syrup. Afterwards, if you still refused the cod, it disappeared. As far as I know, it returned only once; there were no refrigerators and it would not have been safe to keep it longer. Some things I did look forward to: plum-duff particularly, with plenty of large sultanas; and on one Irish feast-day, colcannon, which meant cabbage and potato and onion fried up, rather like bubble-and-squeak, in a big enamel dish. It was a treat then; I loathe it now."

Bob Callahan in his *Who Shot JFK?: A Guide to the Major Conspiracy Theories*, suggests (comically?) that the fervent anti-war journalist, Alexander Cockburn, mocked in the pages of *The Nation* Ms. Ellen Ray, the publisher of Jim Garrison's 1988 memoirs, *On the Trail of the Assassins*, for being a blind Kennedy worshipper and for having a pro-Irish bias in regard to Oliver Stone's film, *JFK,* dating back to the days of the Irish Potato Famine (*an Gorta Mór,* the "great hunger"), because of his own, Cockburn's—I am not making this up—"well-known *distaste for potato salad.*" [my italics]. An Irish-American writer, Cockburn was brought up in Ireland but had lived and worked in the United States since 1972 and then in 2009 became a United States citizen.

One rarely reads an autobiography or memoir without coming across in its pages at least somewhere a reflection on the stark horrors of one particular food or other served to the subject at home or in school refectory, because, for literary value, it is standard—and highly dramatic—fare. (Only in the indices of biographies are food compulsions or aversions curiously omitted, as I have previously pointed out, while alcoholic drinking is always indexed.) It is with lots of ballyhoo that Gardner McKay in his memoir, *Journey without a Map,* that the traveler, writer, and actor boasts in his chapter, "How to Eat a Piranha Before It Eats You," how on the Marowijne River in British Guyana they caught piranha, but the crux of the piece—he neither caught it nor cooked it himself—is that our "explorer" did not like it. His minions did all of the work. McKay writes, "Boy cleaned it and cut it open like a book and laid it on a grate of green sticks, skin high, a foot above the flames of a hardwood fire. He cooked it for a couple of hours. It didn't taste good..." The intrepid McKay boasts—gingerly—that he tried sampling one or two pieces of anteater, as well. His dainty verdict? "They were too tough to chew." My only question is: who could not comfortably sit back in his boat, let hired guides do all the work, and proceed to nibble (or not!) dinner?

On the other hand, many a hearty fish eater weighs in on his virtue. The contemporary Icelandic novelist, Sjón, in his book, *The Whispering Muse,* boasts of the great influence of fish consumption—"the healthiest diet available to man"—on all of Nordic civilization. In a great crowing chest-flexing lecture, the main character in the book chauvinistically attributes Nordic "prowess in every field" to fish-eating, pointing to their "extraordinary vigor, stamina, courage," even their height—"the Nordic type is generally taller and more powerfully built than the German," he asserts—and explains in a huzzaing bit of odontology, "Our teeth bear witness to this. They resemble neither the teeth of carnivores nor those of herbivores but are, on the contrary, designed to chew the sustenance provided by the sea."

With a spate of books on the subject of overfishing and unregulated fishing, ecotarians are now reminding us daily that with the destruction of marine habitats and all sorts of ocean pollution—the chemicals, sewage and waste, the antibiotics, the colorants, are appalling—fishermen have adapted to dwindling catches by shifting their attention to dogfish, then hagfish, as cod declined. There is no question that out-of-control pollution, unregulated fishing practices, and climate change have affected what ends up on our plate. It is now bottom-feeding fish, once ignored never mind despised, that we are now eating. Groundfish are fish that live on, in, or near the bottom of the body of water they inhabit. Some typical saltwater groundfish species are sole, flounder, and halibut. Bottom-feeding fish include flatfish (halibut, flounder, plaice, sole), eels, ling cod, haddock, bass, grouper, bream (snapper) and some species of catfish and shark, whereas bottom-feeding invertebrates include things like shellfish, crabs, crayfish, sea anemones, starfish, snails, bristle-worms, and sea cucumbers." Statistics are horrifying. Fish stocks have been dwindling for decades. A 2015 study found that between 1970 and 2012, global fish populations decreased by about 50 percent. Sixty percent of the world's fish species are fully exploited, and over a third of commercial fish stocks in the United States have been savagely over-fished. The once-teeming cod population in New England crashed years ago. Despite conservation efforts and periodic if quixotic reports of a comeback, cod for decades now are far below the number required for a sustainable fishery. The US Commerce Department declared a disaster in the Northeast ground-fishing industry for the 2013 fishing year as fish stocks fail to rebuild. After 50 years of heavy harvesting in the late 20th century, the Canadian cod fishery collapsed in the early 1990s. A new study has predicted that for the first time a major population of Atlantic cod, near Newfoundland, Canada, will essentially go extinct within twenty years, despite the most desperate attempts to manage it. "This is the most shocking and disturbing news I've ever heard about a marine fish population," says fisheries biologist Jeffrey Hutchings of Dalhousie University in Halifax. Where blue fin tuna were once large, with mature individuals growing to 20-feet in length, most now are a third that size. The huge demand in China for shark-fin has reduced global populations of the biggest species to as little as one percent of natural levels. At Tokyo's Tsukiji Fish Market in January 2012 a blue fin tuna caught off the northern coast of Japan fetched a record 56.49 million yen, or $736,000, at the first auction of the year. Divided up, the nearly 600-pound tuna costs $1,238 per pound! Wild tuna only breed at around 11 years old, so the result is that the crowds of juvenile tuna that are kept in cages never get the chance to breed and have to be fed huge quantities of other fish.

Taras Grescoe in his highly alarming book, *Bottomfeeder*, sounds the tocsin by pointing out how consumers over the years have been forced to eat fish that were once considered beneath contempt by just about everybody, fit only for alley cats, dim crustacean species from lower and lower down the food chain. There are 30,000 varieties of fish on the planet, and in the United States with its miles of seacoasts, its gulfs, lakes, and rivers, a greater variety than in any country. The main question is: what are the depletion amounts of these fish, never mind the variety? It has become a worldwide crisis. As large predatory fish are slowly disappearing from world-wide fish catches— the great fish like cod, swordfish, sea bass, shark, marlin, snook, mackerel, and tuna—the lower orders of fish that were at one time ignored by consumers have now multiplied. It is an ominous sign and a bleak indication of the state of fishing. "Fishermen in the Gulf of Maine have switched from pelagic species to lobster, which are now flourishing," writes Tim Escott in his book review, "The Last Survivors: Jellyfish." (*The Guardian* August 1, 2008). This is bad news: lobsters have multiplied because the kelp beds in which they breed have grown into rampant forests. Once upon a time kelp was kept in check by sea urchins. Urchins multiplied when the cod disappeared, and then they in turn were wiped out by hustling fishermen who sold them to the Japan, a nation that regards urchins as a delicacy. As the larger predators are caught or removed, the bottom-feeders, the algae and the salps, proliferate. Grescoe's thesis is chilling: "The lobster boom may be a tiny blip on the slippery slope to oceans filled with jellyfish, bacteria, and slime." It is, all of it, a black disaster on the planet.

Fish is brain food and a matter for human health. "Brain size is limited by the availability of docosahexaenoic acid (DHA, one of the fatty acids found in omega-3 supplements), without which it is impossible for the body to build brain cell membranes," explains Grescoe. "The only place this acid is abundant in the food chain is in fish from the world's ocean, lakes, and rivers… Without fish, we might still be microcephalic apes, swinging through the trees." The human brain is composed of 60 percent fat, and so who would deny that the kinds of fat that we eat determine what our brain cells are made of? Grescoe who has the facts at hand points out, "Thanks to half a century of consuming cheap vegetable oils, the average cell membrane of an American is now only 20 percent omega-3-based fats. In cultures where fish is still a staple, such as Japan, the average cell membrane is 40 percent omega-3-based."

How many decades will pass—three, four, five?—when we will never see great fish displayed or sold anymore in supermarkets, when they disappear utterly? Gray sole and skate, common catches off the New England coast, no longer appear artfully arranged in fish cases. Atlantic cod will no longer be sold if it is caught by trawlers, which drag nets across the ocean floor, a much-used method. Things disappear, often. Mutton. Carrier pigeons, now extinct. Rum punches. We seldom ever see quinces used to make marmalade anymore.

"Shrimp? After reading the descriptions of how it is farmed in India, China, and Thailand I couldn't even think about eating one, my stomach turns. Anyone reading this book will never set foot in a Red Lobster again," writes Lloyd Alter for Treehugger.com on the subject of bottom-feeding fish. "And good old Cap'n Highliner fish sticks? They could be caught in Chile, sent to Hong Kong, shipped to China for processing, sent by container to Vancouver, trucked across Canada to Nova Scotia, cut up and breaded and refrozen, and then shipped across the country to be sold in a Wal-Mart in San Diego! It is shocking. Alter adds, "But that doesn't mean that there isn't anything to eat; sardines and anchovies can be delicious, pollock and halibut are healthy, and you are doing the world a favor by eating carp or jellyfish, they are in surplus." Jellyfish anyone? Escott joins in. "Prawns were once my favorite dish," he confesses,

> but I haven't eaten them for more than 15 years. I have seen the destruction prawn farms in east Africa and Madagascar have brought to the mangrove ecosystems, and the havoc caused by trawling the ocean bed for shrimp. Many other species are on my forbidden list because, like many divers and naturalists, I have witnessed the decline in marine habitats that overfishing has wrought. Whenever mainstream authors delve into the oceans I am excited and encouraged, hoping the dire news about overfishing will spread.

"I have gotten very sick eating shrimp, several times," novelist Stephen Dixon told me, adding that he has sworn off them for life. "The first time was in a Japanese restaurant in Manhattan—a noodle dish, back in 1965. I was with my girlfriend who also ate the same shrimp but didn't get sick. The second time was at a roadside stand in Massachusetts: this was fried shrimp. 1974. I was with a different girlfriend at the time. She also ate shrimp and didn't get sick." He adds,

> The last time both my wife, Anne, and I got sick from some take-out soup from a Chinese restaurant in Baltimore near our apartment. 1982. We'd just had our first child. Anne wisely stuck her finger down her

throat and threw up and felt better right after that and
even watched a movie on the TV soon after. I have
a horror about voluntarily throwing up, so I didn't,
despite Anne encouraging me to, and was sick for the
next 7 days. The soup, of course, had shrimp in it.
That was the last time I ever ate anything with shrimp
in it. You'd think I would have learned after the first
two times. A similar scene takes place in my last novel,
His Wife Leaves Him.

Australian comedian Barry Humphries, a.k.a. the vainglorious celebrity Dame Edna Everage, had a lovely top-forty hit in 1965 with "Chunder Down Under In The Old Pacific Sea," which begins,

I was down by Manly Pier, drinkin' tubes of ice cold
beer
with a bucket full of prawns upon me knee
when I swallowed the last prawn,
I had a Technicolor yawn
and I chundered in the old Pacific Sea

There is a parallel in regard to the world's increasing need to turn to bottom-feeding fish of a similar degradation in the lumber industry. Back in Colonial days, white pine—tall, glorious, the "whales of the forest"—were harvested by many nations for masts on ships. It was the great treasure tree across the snow belt of the Great Lakes, then northwest to the Yukon. "Prior to 1845, no spruce was cut for market," wrote Lew Dietz in *The Allagash*, his brilliant book on that river in Maine. "The few who began to consider the idea [of harvesting spruce for lumber] were dismissed as a bit mad, at best addle-pated." Spruce for ages was considered a weed tree, not at all comparable to pine trees, the jewels of the forest. It is the same with oak wood. At one time, oak wood was held in very low esteem. Oak furniture in the antique shops, even in mid 20th-century, was frequently given away, set out front to be taken away.

"We used to pile up any and all oak furniture out in front of our shop—chairs, tables, large desks—with an appended sign that read 'Free,'" the populist Cape Cod "mermaid" painter Ralph Cahoon told me about early days in Chatham when he and his wife, Martha, ran a small antique shop. "These items would sit there for weeks. Nobody wanted them. Oak. Now they cost a fortune."

The need for nutrients, which at least bottom-feeding fish supply, is all important. It explains the Inuit Paradox, which allows a people who both gorge on blubber and rarely see a vegetable to remain healthy—maybe healthier than most. Conditioned by glacial temperatures, stark landscapes, and cold protracted winters, the traditional diet of the Inupiat and Yupiks of Alaska is extremely low on plant food, empty of agricultural and dairy products, and pitiful in the carbohydrate department. In the far reaches people subsist on what they hunt and fish. Coastal people mostly exploit the sea, while those living inland take advantage of caribou feeding on tundra mosses, lichens, and plants too tough for humans to stomach (though predigested vegetation in the animals' paunches became dinner as well). All of a caribou is eaten; its eyes are an Eskimo treat. The half-digested mosses in its stomach are known as "tundra salad." Snowgeese eggs are highly prized. Folks do what they can. The main nutritional challenge is avoiding starvation in late winter if primary meat sources become too scarce. Such foods in no way make up a "balanced" diet most of us grew up with and resemble nothing we know like the mix of grains, fruits, vegetables, meat, eggs, and dairy reflected of conventional food-pyramid diagrams. Grasses, tubers, roots, stems, berries, fireweed and seaweed (*kuanniq* or edible seaweed) are also collected and preserved, depending on the season and the location. Still, how can such a narrow diet possibly be adequate for health? How did people get along on little else but fat and animal protein? What the diet of the Far North illustrates, says Harold Draper, a biochemist and expert in Eskimo nutrition, is that there are no essential foods—only essential nutrients.

Seaweed, now called a sea vegetable by some, is one of the world's most sustainable crop and is now being farmed. As Dana Goodyear notes in "A New Leaf," it requires "neither fresh water nor fertilizer... it absorbs dissolved nitrogen, phosphorus, and carbon dioxide directly from the sea—its footprint is negative—and proliferating at a terrific rate," growing as much as three-quarters of an inch a day, reaching to ten-foot plants. Entrepreneurs recognize in dulse and kelp a great source of human food, biofuel, and animal food, and such food may soon be replacing fish on our tables before half a century is out. Frighteningly, Goodyear reminds us that some scientists predict virtually fishless oceans by 2050!

While the expanse of the seas is vast, it is being depleted, and while arcane and mysterious, it has been abused, misused, dredged, overfished, and circumscribed by reckless exploitation. The paradox is that while it remains enigmatically a *mare ignota,* of much is ruined. In other words, what we're familiar with, we have estranged. Curiously, the imbalances in the ways we have used the planet are astonishing. "The ocean covers seventy percent of the earth and produces less than two percent of our food," observes Goodyear. "To grow the rest, we use almost forty percent of the world's land and nearly three-quarters of our fresh waters."

Seaweed, incidentally—the succulent variety of it—is sold and eaten in Wales under the name of "rock laver," and I am told that it goes down very well, when fried with bacon. The most common variety that is eaten is purple laver, an edible, littoral red alga, usually a brownish colour although it boils down to a dark green pulp when prepared. It is unusual among seaweeds because its fronds are only one cell thick. The high iodine content in the seaweed gives this "lettuce" its distinctive flavor, a bit in common with olives and oysters and clams. By the way, laverbread (*bara lafwr* or *bara lawr* in Welsh) is a traditional Welsh dish. To make the bread, the seaweed is boiled for several hours, then minced or pureed, and the gelatinous paste is usually rolled or coated in oatmeal prior to frying. Traditionally eaten as part of a Welsh breakfast, often with cockles, it can also be used to make a sauce to accompany lamb or crab, and it is even used to make a laver soup (Welsh: *cawl lafwr*). Actor Richard Burton has gone on record as describing laverbread as the "Welshman's caviar." Rock laver is also eaten across the Bristol Channel in North Devon, especially around the Exmoor coast around Lynmouth, Combe Martin, and Ilfracombe.

Since the 1860s, when the Seventh-Day Adventist church was formed, wholeness and health have been stressed as godly. Adventists are known for presenting a "health message" that recommends vegetarianism and expects adherence to the kosher laws of Leviticus 11, of which possibly Art Buchwald was ignorant. (A simpleton in his humor, which was always broad and silly, the guy never managed to graduate from either high school or college.) Obedience to church laws meant abstinence from pork, shellfish, and other foods proscribed as "unclean." The church discourages its members from all use of alcohol, tobacco, or illegal drugs. In addition, some Adventists also avoid coffee, tea, dark colas, and other beverages containing caffeine. The pioneers of the Adventist Church, proselytizers, had much to do with the widespread acceptance of cold breakfast cereals into the Western diet. The modern commercial concept of "cereal food" in fact originated among Adventists. John Harvey Kellogg was one of the early founders of Adventist health work. His development of breakfast cereals as a health food led to the founding of Kellogg's by his brother William. In both Australia and New Zealand, the church-owned Sanitarium Health Food Company is still a leading manufacturer of health and vegetarian-related products, most prominently Australia's national breakfast cereal, Weet-Bix. (Weetabix in Britain.)

It may be pointed out that research funded by the US National Institutes of Health has shown that the average Adventist in California lives as much as 4 to 10 years longer than the average Californian. The research, as cited by the cover story of the November 2005 issue of *National Geographic*, asserts that Adventists live longer essentially because they do not smoke cigarettes or drink alcohol, take a healthful day of rest each and every week, and always try to maintain a healthy, low-fat vegetarian diet that is rich in nuts and beans and vegetables.

An estimated 35% of Seventh-Day Adventists practice vegetarianism, according to a 2002 worldwide survey of local church leaders. The cohesiveness of Adventists' social networks has also been put forward as an explanation of their extended lifespan. Since Dan Buettner's 2005 National Geographic story about Adventist longevity, his book, *The Blue Zones: Lessons for Living Longer from the People Who've Lived the Longest*, named the area of Loma Linda, California a "blue zone" because of the large concentration of Seventh-day Adventists. He cites the Adventist emphasis on health, diet, and Sabbath-keeping as primary factors for Adventist longevity.

The novelist Carlos Ruiz Zafon can be numbered among the group of strident anti-pescatorians. "While serious authors are well aware that good childhood traumas require a deep Freudian bent if they are to be reviewed or mentioned in the *New York Review of Books* and other fine publications," the Spanish novelist wrote to me in the autumn of 2012,

> I'm afraid mine are far less worthy of the Merchant-Ivory biopic treatment. Take fish, for instance. With all due respect to the grand chefs of the world and to the fact that probably most of humanity and certainly 99% of self-aware gourmands consider it the finest of delicacies, I just find it repugnant. I cannot eat fish. Or even smell it. And don't get me started on anchovies, the single most repulsive substance in the universe that was not excreted by a mammal. Since early childhood I have been unable to stand, let alone swallow, a single piece of fish. If it swims, has scales, and has the IQ of a Facebook enthusiast, I won't eat it. Period. I can deal with shellfish, although on a highly compromised level. I can do lobster to be polite. I've been known to ingest shrimp, although never by choice. But give me a sea bass, a sardine, a trout or any of their cousins, and I will draw the line.

> The roots of my phobia, like many food phobias
> I presume, originate in school. [Zafon grew up in
> Barcelona, Spain.] Like many kids, I was forced to
> eat the most repugnant pieces of fish known to man
> in medieval sessions of culinary torture. By the time I
> was 10 years old, I was rendered unable to deal with
> anything fishy for life. For many years the finest chefs
> and restaurateurs wanted to cure me of my phobia.
> They offered the most exquisite delicacies from under
> the water, swearing it was all in my mind, not in my
> palate. I agree. It is in my mind. And there it remains.
> I'm sure I'm missing the world, yet I am resigned by
> now. It could be worse. Some people don't like jazz,
> or Mozart. That would really worry me. But anchovies
> and any kind of fish, well...

In any case, Zafon's experiences with lobster are far exceeded by that of the British politician, Sir Philip Sassoon, for whom lobster Newburgh went down, grimly, "like a pureé of white kid gloves." Who can forget the scene in the movie, *Carefree* (1938) where Ralph Bellamy tells Ginger Rogers, "I know something that's positively vile. Lobster with gobs of mayonnaise"?

"I am not allowed to touch shellfish—no prawns, langoustes or lobster," Greta Garbo told a friend, Sven Broman, in Klosters in 1985. "I have a very peculiar stomach department. I haven't got enough things to digest food with—if you don't have hydrochloric acid or whatever it is, then the stomach goes on strike. I don't know what the hell is wrong with me, but down we are." The Sphinx loved soup and virtually lived on "Bieler Broth," which was a simple soup composed of one pound of string beans, two pounds of zucchini, a handful of curly parsley, enough water to cover the veggies, and then all of it pureed using the water you cooked it in to the consistency you desire. (The only book that Greta Garbo ever endorsed, in fact, was Henry G. Bieler's *Food Is Your Best Medicine*, which advocated the treatment of disease with foods.) Bieler was a recognized pioneer in alternative medicine, who used non-pharmaceutical, diet-based therapies to cure or control various diseases and ailments which included asthma, diabetes, and cancer. His main interest was restoring the liver as a way to health. He found all drugs harmful and advised his patients to avoid them. Garbo was "ferocious" about the punctuality and content of meals, said actress Dana Wynter. The beauty did not eat lunch. She was a fussy eater, loved spaghetti, could not cook well, and was at least to a certain degree something of a gourmand. She loved poached eggs and Postum.

"I will haf a nikolaijecek," she told director Billy Wilder's wife, referring to a drink supposedly made by placing a small slice of lemon on the tongue, dissolving sugar on the same spot, and then washing it down with a light brandy, or so Norman Zierold states in his biography, *Garbo,* but I have found no record or reference to this drink anywhere else on earth.

Garbo delighted in talking about food. She devoured strawberry ice cream. She drank whiskey, and "Cutty Sark" was her favorite brand of whiskey while she lived in New York. She adored waffles with jam. She loved lingonberry jam, her favorite Swedish delicacy. Swedish food excited her. She loved *spraaten*—fish, like sardines. "I can't eat much nowadays, hardly anything at all," she told Broman. "But you can't imagine how much I miss Swedish food sometimes—salmon pudding—that was my favourite dish, and stewed bilberries and herrings and schnapps. Does *Skåne* [a kind of aquavit] still exist? And string beans... I haven't eaten vegetables for two years." After Hollywood, when living in New York City, she bought meat at the Mid-City Food Market or Green Valley Foods on First Avenue. At the Dover Deli, she would buy lox, sturgeon, and Nova Scotia salmon. More expensive fare was purchased at a gourmet emporium on Madison Avenue or at Nyborg & Nelson, a Swedish deli on Fiftieth and Second. According to the proprietor of her favorite produce store, Garbo loved zucchini and artichokes and was "crazy about" persimmons. She said,

> I always buy fresh vegetables. They're everywhere and it doesn't take brains to fix them. They don't taste like anything and they just sit there, [but] I'll tell you a little secret: buy sour cream. They sell it in buckets. All you do is take a great big heap of sour cream and put it on a vegetable with salt and it's delicious...more fun than with margarine. So get your sour cream, and get going...

I remember reading that Garbo said that in her dreams she often saw the faces of people she knew on oranges.

Garbo's taste for sour food is intriguing—Scandinavians tend to like it—as is any link of beauty to astringence. Who can explain the grotesque attraction of the exquisitely beautiful Jane Birkin, possibly the prettiest woman who ever lived, to the frog-faced sleazeball and pornocrat, Serge Gainsbourg? I have read of a modern trend among chefs nowadays to favor elegant dishes with souring agents like sumac, tamarind, pomegranate molasses, lime, vinegar, and wild and bitter herbs.

Donn Fendler, the young author of the celebrated *Lost on a Mountain in Maine*, an autobiographical account of his having been lost on Mt. Katahdin for 9 days in July 1939—with no shoes, no compass, no food, no shelter—hated fish. He saw many trout in brooks as he wandered over the massive dark boulders and the dense brush of that dangerous area, while he was being virtually eaten alive by midges, black flies, and what the Indians call "no-see-ums," but the boy was never tempted to eat a fish, not that he could have caught one. I can say that I had the great good luck to be able to visit him in Newport, Maine when he was a handsome 86-year-old man—no small thrill for me, as my father had read Fendler's book to me and my brothers back when we were very young boys—and he told me, "I still hate fish."

Lost on the dangerous mountain, he said, "I thought if I saw a Boy Scout I'd ask him for a doughnut and a drink of milk. I thought so hard of doughnuts that sometimes I could smell them." Milk especially tempted him. "Just before I went off to sleep, I thought of a glass of milk—a big, cold glass with white foamy milk in it. Boy, the juice just ran down the corners of my mouth thinking of it! Anybody who doesn't like milk is crazy." But no fish, never fish.

"Fish, to taste right, must swim three times—in water, in butter, and in wine," according to an old Polish proverb. What about oil—it doesn't count? I have a Greek friend, Nikos Biniaris, who will never eat fish unless it has come in contact with the very best olive oil. During the Renaissance, let me add here, it was the fat of pigs that was the main fat used in cooking. Although olive oil was produced in large quantities in southern Europe during that period, it was not generally used for cooking—possibly because of the fact that cooking in vegetable oil was associated with the Jews, who did not use pork fat for religious reasons.

Nancy Kinchela, chef at The Saxon Boutique Hotel in Sandhurst, South Africa, says, "I hate kippers—the smell, the taste… to wake up and have to look forward to having kippers for breakfast would destroy my day." Although kippers were once a staple of the British diet, however, it seems to be no longer the case. They are hard to find nowadays, there is that. Then when they are served, people do not like dealing with the bones. There are solutions to cooking and eating the clean, easy and smell-free way. Boil the water, put the kippers into the jug, cover them with water, set the timer for 7 minutes, then pour the water out of the jug—and presto, no smell. Also, the bone-proof way of eating kippers is to place the fish bone-side up on the plate, grab the back bone by the tail and pull it away from the fish, slide your knife under the rest of the bones that are left, to release them from the flesh, using a knife and fork pull the flesh away from the skin, then eat and enjoy them. Try kippers with horseradish sauce, for the tartness of the sauce counteracts the oiliness of the fish. Others take a more conventional route and eat their fish with bread or toast. It is said that kippers of old were a much stronger taste than those we have today. An English writer—Evelyn Waugh in *Vile Bodies*, I believe—declared, "No kipper ever tastes as good as it smells."

Ringo Starr both wrote and sang the lead of "Octopus's Garden," recorded for the Beatles' Abbey Road album in 1969—it was only the second song he had written. A friend had lent him a boat when he was in Sardinia with his family and at sea the captain happened to serve octopus for lunch. Ringo refused to eat it!

"The four most over-rated things in life are champagne, lobster, anal sex, and picnics," wrote Christopher Hitchens, so chalk off lobster for him. (But wait! The value of noisy, pushy, social-climbing English writers moving to the United States to live, to pontificate, to purvey their trashcan-lid banging polemics for added cash-flow is not over-rated?) Although novelist Stephen King grew up eating lobster, part of the beast still gives him a frisson. In an informal interview in Pasadena, Calif. in 1989, he said, "Some kid told me that if you bought a lobster and cracked open the tail, there's a nerve dangling down its back, and if you eat that, you'd be paralyzed. I know it's not true, but I can't bring myself to eat that black thread." Have you heard the term the "lobster shift"? It supposedly has its origins in an old wives' tale that designated lobster meat as being very hard to digest and that anyone who overindulged was kept up much of the night. It then became a term for anyone who had the late night or midnight shift on a job. R. Crumb, the matchless underground illustrator and cartoonist, once mentioned to me in a letter that he greatly dislikes and refuses to eat any and all crustaceans, nor does he drink alcohol. There is a plethora of fish-haters. Sleek black fashion model, beautiful and tempestuous Naomi Campbell, has gone on record as saying that she is allergic to tuna fish. Oscar Wilde particularly hated cod and quirkily offered his explanation for loathing it by pointing to Rudyard Kipling's adventure novel about cod fishing, *Captains Courageous*, a novel that he immensely disliked.

I think of Elvis, re-reading *Moby-Dick*, when I come to the chapter on the Try Pots Hotel where everything in the place has something to do with fish. Chowder is the *only* item on the menu, Mrs. Hussey, the landlady, wears a homemade necklace of cod vertebrae, and even the account books of the establishment are bound in sharkskin. It would have been Elvis' nightmare. Just about every breakfast, dinner, and supper on 18th-century Cape Cod, according to Samuel Eliot Morison in *The Maritime History of Massachusetts, 1783–1860*, consisted of boiled fish and shellfish, perhaps along with some beans, brown bread (of home grown "rye and injun" and pie. Notice, incidentally, that Mrs. Hussey's chowder includes "small juicy clams, scarcely bigger than hazel nuts, mixed with pounded ship biscuit, and salted pork cut up into little flakes; the whole enriched with butter, and plentifully seasoned with pepper and salt," but, significantly, leaves out the chunks of potato that today as a staple of the dish ennobles traditional New England chowders. We know that Herman Melville planted his own potatoes in Pittsfield, Mass.—he often alluded to such plantings in various of his letters to Evert Duyckinck, Nathaniel Hawthorne, and others—so he must have eaten them. So what is behind that glaring omission in Mrs. Hussey's recipe?

I wonder if Elvis could have been persuaded by, even been sold on, Melville's hearty endorsement in the chapter in *Moby-Dick*, "The Whale as a Dish," stating, "Porpoises, indeed, are to this day considered fine eating. The meat is made into balls about the size of billiard balls." In *A Pattern of Islands*, Sir Arthur Grimble refused to try it, even cured and salted, in Polynesia. He wrote, "I could not bring myself to eat it. I never did grow fat in the Gilbert Islands."

It is said that Henry David Thoreau never again ate chowder quite comfortably after the ominous date of April 30, 1844. It was on that spring day in Concord that, with his companion Edward Hoar, while cooking fish chowder on a dried-out tree stump that they set the woods on fire, accidentally but thoroughly. It was a very windy day, and a spark from their makeshift fire leapt to the extremely dry grass around them. They tried to put out the flames with their feet, panicking, and then tried banging at it with a board, all in vain, and then they ran for help. "The first farmer whom I met driving a team, after leaving the woods, inquired the cause of the smoke. I told him. 'Well,' said he, 'it is none of my stuff,' and drove along," wrote Thoreau a few years later. "The next I met was the owner in his field, with whom I returned at once to the woods, running all the way. I had already run two miles." Over 300 acres of forest were burned black, causing over $2000 in damages (nearly $160,000 in today's money). Thoreau was 27 at the time, rather old to be that irresponsible. He had been viewed by many townspeople even before that as something of a ne'er-do-well in the first place and a Bohemian eccentric. The *Concord Freeman* reported on May 3, 1844: "The fire, we understand, was communicated to the woods through the thoughtlessness of two of our citizens, who kindled it in a pine stump, near the Pond, for the purpose of making a chowder. As everything around them was as combustible as a fire-ship, the terrible flames quickly spread and long hours elapsed before they could be subdued. It is to be hoped that this unfortunate result of sheer carelessness, will be borne in mind by those who may visit the woods in future for recreation." Chowder! Curious and ironic, is it not, that our word chowder comes from *chaudière* [French for cauldron] and that from an Old English outgrowth of the Latin *caldarius* meaning "pertaining to warmth"?

For years thereafter, Thoreau was considered by the locals to be a fool, the town drongo. He was seen as a wastrel, certainly, judged to be something of an irresponsible half-wit, and for a time, old Yankee memories being what they are, the young man had to endure the ignominy of being called vile names. He said, "Some of the [land]owners, however, bore their loss like men, but other some declared behind my back that I was a 'damned rascal;' and a flibbertigibbet or two, who crowed like the old cock, shouted some reminiscences of 'burnt woods' from safe recesses for some years after.". Oddly, Thoreau felt remarkably guilt-free of a crime. A sort of arrogance even kicked in. A few years later he made an entry in his *Journal*,

> I have set fire to the forest, but I have done no wrong
> therein, and now it is as if the lightning had done it.
> These flames are but consuming their natural food."
> (It had never troubled me from that day to this more
> than if the lightning had done it. The trivial fishing
> was all that disturbed me and disturbs me still.)

Thoreau heeded little he chose to ignore. "A man is rich in proportion to the number of things which he can afford to let alone," he wrote in *Walden*. It is an apothegm that seemed to include for him—among social preoccupations like marriage, voting, Sunday worship, hunting, bar-hopping, the drudgery of daily job, etc.—sex. ("The generative energy, which, when are loose, dissipates and makes us unclean, when we are continent invigorates and inspires us.") I could not conjure a more classic example of a text-book aversionist personality. Thoreau was as removed as Elijah, fed by ravens. Does pure freedom begin in sociophobia?

"He was bred to no profession; he never married; he lived alone; he never went to church; he never voted; he refused to pay a tax to the state; he ate no flesh, he drank no wine; he never knew the use of tobacco and, though a naturalist, he used neither trap nor gun. It cost him nothing to say No," said Ralph Waldo Emerson at Thoreau's funeral. "He had a beautiful soul." I will humbly correct Emerson here only on one crucial point. Thoreau ate fish, occasionally did eat salt pork, and once as a simple experiment actually dug in and devoured a fresh woodchuck, enjoying the meat, as he said, "notwith-standing its musky flavor," although even this nature-lover expressed doubt that it would become an item for the village butcher.

Oscar Wilde also disliked cod. According to biographer Hesketh Pearson, Wilde was lunching with Lord Alfred Douglas, his adored "Bosie," at a sec-ond-rate restaurant in Torquay. "A nice piece of cod?" the waiter suggested. "I hardly think cod is a very nice fish, is it?" exclaimed the haughty poet and playwright. "Oh, no doubt the cod is a splendid swimmer, admirable for swimming purposes, but not for eating." I have mentioned Wilde and Rudyard Kipling's *Captains Courageous*, which describes a young boy's ad-ventures among the cod fishers off the Banks of Newfoundland. It wasn't Wilde at his wittiest perhaps but he surely was being candid when he said, "I really don't know why an author should write a book about codfishing... but perhaps," he added ruminatively, "it is because I never eat cod."

The American journalist and later Ambassador to Finland Carl T. Rowan in his memoir, *South of Freedom*, a stirring account of growing up in the racist South and of the difficulties for Negroes in general in the mid-20th-century, writes of the poverty he and others faced and of his hard-working father who labored stacking lumber ten hours a day for a sal-ary of two dollars a day and, among other things, of the cheap jack-salmon that his father used to buy at the Piggly Wiggly supermarket for 10-cents a pound and bring home to the family. "In those days, fish became almost as unpopular around my house as white salt-pork (known to McMinnville [his home town in Tennessee] Negroes as 'Hoover's ham'), and I vowed that some day I would ban from my table anything that had bones or scales and couldn't clean itself."

Playwright Jerome Kass has gone on record as having the very same pho-bia. He has declared, "I would not eat fish because I was seriously afraid of fish bones, a paranoia inherited from my father, who was sure that he would choke on a bone and die if he ever ate fish." (Bone fears figure highly in hat-ers of fish.) Film director John Waters avoids swordfish, fussily finding it too trendy to eat nowadays in restaurants "Have you ever been in a restaurant where swordfish isn't on the menu?" he asked. "Yuppies have made sword-fish the next endangered species." I gather availability can both start and kill a trend, reminding me of something that Hunter Thompson once said, "Crack is ruining the drug culture."

As to growing up poor and black, fish was the last worry many families had. On the occasion of the very last full speech that he ever gave, on Feb 16, 1965, to a small group in the Corn Hill Methodist Church in Rochester, New York, the brave and much missed Malcolm X explained, "Our food came from the welfare. They were stamped 'not to be sold.' I got so many things from the store called 'not to be sold,' I thought that was a store some place. [much laughter] This was the condition the black man was in, and that's till 1939."

Bottom-feeding fish like bass, tilapia, halibut, flounder, plaice, sole, eels, even cod, haddock, bass, grouper, carp, bream (snapper)—which in many restaurants are now replacing larger, better-tasting fish—are our only options as the result of world-wide overfishing. Oils, PCBs, red tide, harmful algal blooms, water with increased nutrient-loading from human activities, all serve to infect the quality of the sea. It is the kind of pollution that makes musician Frank Zappa so down on virtually anything—food or forces—with which we come in contact: "Dioxin in toilet paper, dioxin in tampons, dioxin in water filters, dioxin in coffee filters, dioxin in tea bags, dioxin in vegetables because of the runoff from paper plants."

> I don't mind eels
> Except at meals.
> And the way they feels

as Ogden Nash wrote seems to make sense.

But do we not actually come in *contact* with music, Frank? It is surely the reason why the free-thinking intellectual, atheist, and naturalist Ludovico Settembrini states in The Magic Mountain, "There is something suspicious about music, gentlemen. I insist that she is, by her nature, equivocal. I shall not be going too far in saying at once that she is politically suspect."

Moe Howard had an intense dislike for shellfish. In the longest of the short films of the Three Stooges, entitled, "*A Pain in the Pullman*"—a movie in which at one point in the same upper berth of a train Moe nudges Larry awake, only to tell him "Wake up and go to sleep!"—all three find themselves in a drawing room with a lovely table set with all kinds of delicacies. "At one point Curly picked up the hard-shelled Dungeness crab," Moe later reflected in his book, *Moe Howard and the Three Stooges.* "We, of course, were not supposed to know what it was. Larry thought it was a tarantula, Curly figured it to be a rag, and I concluded that it must be something to eat or it wouldn't be on the table with crackers and sauce. As the scene progressed, Curly fitfully tried to open the crab shell and bent the tines of his fork. I took the fork from Curly, tossed a napkin on the floor, and asked him to pick it up. When Curly bent over, I hit him on the head with the crab, breaking the shell into a million pieces. Then Curly scooped out some of the meat, tasted

it, and made a face. He threw the meat away and proceeded to eat the shell."
He goes on to add, regarding crustaceans,

> I have to tell you, if there's one thing to which I have
> an aversion, it's shellfish, and I couldn't bring my-
> self—even for a film—to put that claw in my mouth.
> Preston Black, the director, asked me to just lick the
> claw, but I couldn't. He finally had the prop man
> duplicate the claw out of sugar and food coloring and
> had me nibble on it as though I was enjoying it. I was
> still very wary during the scene. I was afraid they had
> coated the real shell with sugar and that that awful
> claw was underneath. I chewed that claw during the
> scene, but if you'll notice, I did it very gingerly. In the
> meantime, Curly was still chewing on the shell, which
> was cutting the inside of his mouth. Finally, our star
> comes back to his room and kicks us out, and we three
> climb into our upper berth to go to sleep.

Queen Elizabeth, an ostraconophobe, does not like shellfish, for example, clams, oysters, or crabs, although she does make an exception when
it comes to lobster. Onetime palace chef Darren McGrady has reported
that potatoes are not on her menu, stating, "They are never served when
she dines alone." Soup is also out. A former aide of hers says, "She just
doesn't care for it." Other pet peeves of the Queen, according to US magazine (January 27, 2014), are babies at dinner, men in shorts, long sermons,
three-piece suits ("only fit for servants"), the word "pregnant"—she prefers
"in a family way"—and the sound of clinking ice cubes. "She's served ball-
shape ice in her cold drinks, because they make less noise," says one of her
aides. The Queen's favorite tea is a special blend of China and Indian tea, a
mixture, notably, available to anybody who stops in at Fortnum & Mason.
The Royal family will eat nothing tinned or frozen. They never eat between
meals, by the way, and the idea of the stupid American word *brunch*—the
very concept of it—is entirely unknown to them. They eat four times a day—
breakfast, lunch, tea, and dinner, although their main meal is taken at night.
Cheese is never served at dinner, even privately. Game is never on the menu,
as the Queen feels some guests may not enjoy it. You will never find Royals
being fastidious in a public way; good manners would never allow it. I think
of President Harry S. Truman here, who was not a picky eater. He preferred
plain, traditional farm food like roast beef and fried chicken. He stated suc-

cinctly of his food preferences, "Never notice what's put before me. Learned in the army to eat what could be obtained and like it. In my outfit when a man kicked about the food, he was given a chance to improve it. That soon cured the kickers, and they took what was put before them and liked it."

The best dish the Pilgrims could offer wanderers into their rude and impoverished early colony in the 1620s was "a lobster or a piece of fish without bread or anything else but a cup of fair spring water," according to Governor Bradford's *Journals*. The fish they caught were mainly herring or alewives, fish greasy enough to cook without benefit of butter. Clams, along with cornbread, some parsnips, carrots, and onions, served their meager diet. They felt deprived living on this fare, greatly missing beef, wheat bread, and beer, staples they loved and sorely missed. Unfortunately, no cattle were in the colony, nor any domestic animals at all, except a few chickens. A great *dislike* of seafood meals, ironic when you think of it, became commonplace among them. It should be noted that the Puritan separatists—the notable "Pilgrims" of 1620—were a peaceful people not only obedient and God-fearing but extremely tolerant of others, accepting their fate as God's will; they should not be confused, as too often they are, with the illiberal, narrow-minded, domineering Puritans of the Massachusetts Bay Company, the many thousands of English non-conformists who sailed to New England over the next decades, spreading to lands north of Plymouth, a group of dour, autocratic, undemocratic theocrats who demanded religious conformity. (All of the Pilgrims were Puritans, but very few Puritans—the later immigrants who flocked to the New World with all sorts of get-rich schemes—were the Pilgrims we now revere.) It was these people who began to quell any dissension from their rigid orthodoxy and sent into exile anyone who disagreed with them, Roger Williams, Anne Hutchinson, and Rev. John Wheelwright. Still, it is odd to think of such wayfarers disliking seafood, which was so abundant.

Strangeness, I suppose, is the thrown shadow of food aversions. I have earlier alluded to gritty dwarfish Daniel Quilp, he of the notorious shell-crunching breakfast habit who appears in Charles Dickens' *The Old Curiosity Shop*. Quilp is truly primitive. It was all cracks, crunches, and little snaps in the Quilp household, and it is something of a miracle that Betsy, the poor, beleaguered wife of that freakishly malicious hunchbacked deformed dwarf moneylender, went and married the man, never mind put up with him, as she became the favorite object of his cruelty. Tough little Quilp's favorite term for those he speaks to is "dog." This splenetic, dirty, stubble-chinned, misshapen nut-ball who was full of violence ("I'll beat you with an iron rod, I'll scratch you with a rusty nail, I'll pinch your eyes, if you talk to me—I will") comically brought that violence to the groaning table. Dickens wittily observed,

> He chewed tobacco and water-cresses at the same time
> and with extraordinary greediness drank boiling tea
> without winking, bit his fork and spoon till they bent
> again, and in short performed so many horrifying and
> uncommon acts that the women were nearly fright-
> ened out of their wits, and began to doubt if he were
> really a human creature.

Although one's flesh is made to creep when Quilp kisses Little Nell. ("'Ah!' said the dwarf, smacking his lips, 'what a nice kiss that was—just upon the rosy part.'") even as a young reader I felt a deep lesson was revealed in that Betsy appeared to love that weirdo, in spite of everything—she was always genuinely worried when he disappeared for any long period—which incorporates cruelty, crippledom, ugliness, eavesdropping, sarcasm, and, needless to say, grotesque food habits.

I have mentioned comix illustrator, R. Crumb, hating shellfish. Writing to me of his food phobias in a letter of July 8, 2011, he told me, "I can't eat lobster. The sight of someone eating a lobster or crab makes me want to gag." He frankly admits, "I am not adventurous when it comes to food. I don't like to try exotic dishes, unlike my wife, Aline, who will try anything. She would eat toasted larvae with the pygmies if she happened to be visiting with them. Mostly I like the plain American food I grew up on, meat and potatoes, spaghetti, rice pudding. I like bread and butter, fried eggs and coffee, pancakes with maple syrup, chicken a la king, roast beef with mashed potatoes and gravy, canned or frozen peas... brownies, ice cream, cookies, potato chips. I like Mexican food, burritos, rice and beans... I don't like a lot of raw vegetables. I eat greens sparingly. I like fresh tomatoes with mayonnaise. I don't like apples... I can eat a lot of food at one sitting. I can really PIG out sometimes. But I'm fortunate in that I don't gain weight. I've weighed around 140 lbs. since I was about 30. I can't drink any alcohol. It doesn't agree with me at all. I don't enjoy the sensation caused by it. Sometimes I drink Coca-Cola. I mostly drink water with meals. In the morning I have black tea or coffee. My taste for sweets has declined with age... I like oatmeal and Cream of Wheat, with milk and sugar. Mmm. Yum, yum."

Given R. Crumb's dislike of apples, he might consider through the happy medium of transmigration becoming an apple tree instead—by literally *sprouting* into a memorial tree! Indeed? A company, A Bios, makes a biodegradable cinerary urn, which contains a seed—"100% biodegradable, made of coconut shell, compacted peat, and cellulose"—designed to convert you into a tree after life. It has two parts, a top capsule for the seed, and a bottom part for the ashes of your loved one (or you!), a structure that allows the seed to germinate separate from the human ashes and their high acidity. Once the urn starts to biodegrade, the seed roots are already strong enough to contact them, and then the entire set becomes part of the sub-soil. Commodiously, the seed absorbs the nutrients in your ashes, and in a real sense you bloom.

"It changes the way people see death, converting the 'end of life'"— so goes one advertisement—"into a transformation and a return to life through nature. [It is] a smart, sustainable, and ecologically friendly way to approach what's, probably, one of the most important moments in human life." Fascinating to report, after due deliberation and the nature of one's appetite, if one should choose as a memorial tree one that bears fruit, your family can end up eating *you*!

Sour television celebrity Bryant Gumbel has often gone on record as saying that he hates cheese. James Joyce disliked cheese, as well, stating, "A corpse is meat gone bad. Well, and what's cheese? Corpse of milk." So does poet Heather McHugh who hastened to add in once writing me, also "cheese food." I recall a junior high-school friend who aversely referred to the overly floury cheese in our lunchroom baked macaroni as "lava." ("School cafeterias have so stigmatized macaroni and cheese that it's hard to convince anyone that it can be a good meal," writes Miriam Ungerer in *Good Cheap Food*.) I wonder if Ernest Hemingway happened to be expressing a personal disdain for this food—or for his character's taste—when in his novel, *A Farewell to Arms*, he has his hero, Lt. Frederic Henry, blown up (but not killed) while eating a piece of cheese. During the Allied landings on the beaches of war-torn France in 1944, the pungent odor given off by nearby Norman cheese dairies resembled the odor of corpses to American soldiers who were threading through the countryside and in consequence prompted some of them to destroy those dairies. I remember during one of my food shopping sojourns in Paris, after sampling the edible white rind of a *Fromager d'Affinois* in an expensive *fromagerie* on the Ile de la Cité, innocently asking, "How can you tell when a cheese is actually rotten?" I managed to set an odd precedent in that one friendly exchange. Subsequent visits found me amicably buttonholed by the obliging, generous *vendeur*; I was offered many samples, including small eye-watering tastes of Taleggio, Pont l'Eveque, Abbaye de Citeaux, Brescianella, and one day a memorable chunk of Epoisses (although Brillat-Savarin himself classed it as the "king of all cheeses," it is banned in Paris from being carried on public transportation).

Do you happen to recall reading in *Uncle Wiggily on the Farm* about the enigmatic Magoosielum? "The only thing that will drive away a Magoosielum is pineapple cheese, and Baby Bunty has none of that." Cheese can play havoc with people. "No goat, blue, or overripe cheese," wrote the actress Jennifer Aniston on a Mexican hotel rider in 2011. (She apparently likes Uniekaas, Piave, and—although she is of Greek extraction—French feta.) The fastidious Mitt Romney, running for President all through year 2011, was subject to a lot of bad food on the road. His unfailing food-rule is always to take the cheese off of his pizza before he eats it. May one inquire: what else is pizza *but* cheese? "Don't eat cheese," ordered Courtney Love, punk Hole singer and and wife of the late rocker, Kurt Cobain, in one of what I gather are many of her hysterical rants. "There are a million things to eat that are not cheese," she snarled in a 1993 interview for a zine called *Rollerderby*, stating,

> No cheese... People I tell this to lose ten, 30 pounds. STOP CHEESE. You know why the Orientals are not fat? 'Cause they look on cheese as this gross, Western habit—it's like sour milk LARD. They don't want anything to fucking do with cheese. If you're gonna eat cheese, take it out on a picnic, cut it up carefully, and really taste it—with wine or something. Don't melt it on shit.

Cheese, as we know it, does not go over big in India. Paneer, or "*Chhena*," as it is called in the eastern areas, an unaged, acid-set, non-melting farmer's or curd cheese made by curdling heated milk with lemon juice, vinegar, or any other food acids, remains the most common type of cheese that is used in traditional South Asian cuisines. "'What is that smell?'" asks a bedwildered character in Kiran Desai's novel *The Inheritance of Loss* (2006), set in the Himalayas.

> "Cheese."
> "*Kya cheez?*" said a fellow from Meerut.
> They had never heard of cheese. They looked unconvinced. It smelled far too suspicious and one of them reported that he thought it smelled of bomb-making materials. '*Gas maar raha hai*,' said the Meerut boy.
> "What did he say?" asked Father Booty.
> "Something is whacking gas. Something is firing gas."

A Swiss priest, Father Booty has plans for inspiring cheese-making across the Himalayas. "We live in India, thank you very much," he is told. "We don't want any cheese and the last thing we need is chocolate cigars."

Understand, not all celebrities hate cheese. After one of her European shopping sprees back in the 1980s, Imelda Marcos discovered to her horror that the plane she had boarded upon leaving Rome had no cheese on board, and that autocratic bitch with a few choice barks immediately ordered the jet plane back to the airport in order to correct that oversight. This is a good example of what might called "fashion gluttony." The First Lady of the Philippines, queen of that poor country, owned at least 35 rare mink coats, 1,200 designer gowns, 1000 handbags, no less than 2,700 pairs of shoes (size 8½), 700 mostly black brassieres (34B), enormous suitcases filled with girdles (size 40 and 42), 1,700 handbags, 45 large standing racks of expensive fur coats, and a vast cache of expensive jewelry. According to her friends, her dresses were worn only once, and some had taken as long as a year to embroider by hand. Overeating and hoarding are not at all unrelated as to the greed principle.

Although I have quoted earlier G.K. Chesterton's remark that poets have been strangely silent of the subject of cheese, his opinion remains fairly airtight; it is entirely possible that there are too many kinds with which to deal. In any case, Hugh Kenner once had the great good luck to dine with T.S. Eliot at the elegant Garrick Club in London and in his masterful book, *The Pound Era*, reveals one aspect of Eliot—"a great joker," Kenner points out—that is rarely seen when Ol' Possum discusses the topic of cheese. Kenner writes, "After jugged hare at the Club ('Now there is jugged hare. That is a very English dish. Do you want to be English; or do you want to be safe?'); after the jugged hare and the evasions, he addressed his mind to the next theme. "Now; will you have a sweet; or... cheese?" He continues,

> Even one not conversant with his letter to the *Times* on the declining estate of Stilton [November 29, 1935, p. 15] would have understood that the countersign was cheese. "Why, cheese," said his guest; too lightly; one does not crash in upon the mysteries. There was a touch of reproof in his solicitude: "Are you sure? You can have ice cream, you know." (At the Garrick!)
>
> No, cheese. To which, "Very well. I fancy... a fine Stilton." And as the waiter left for the Stilton, Eliot

imparted the day's most momentous confidence: "Never commit yourself to a cheese without having first... examined it."

The Stilton stood encumbered with a swaddling band, girded about with a cincture, scooped out on top like a crater of the moon. It was placed in front of the Critic. ("Analysis and comparison," he had written some 40 years earlier, "Analysis and comparison, methodically, with sensitiveness, intelligence, curiosity, intensity of passion and infinite knowledge: all these are necessary to the great critic.") With the side of his knife blade he commenced tapping the circumference of the cheese, rotating it, his head cocked in a listening posture. It is not possible to swear that he was listening. He then tapped the inner walls of the crater. He then dug about with the point of his knife amid the fragments contained by the crater. He then said, "Rather past its prime. I am afraid I cannot recommend it."

He was not always so. That was one of his Garrick personae. An acquaintance reports that at dinner in Eliot's home "an ordinary Cheddar" was "served without ceremony."

The Stilton vanished. After awing silence the cheese board arrived, an assortment of some half-dozen, a few of them identifiably cheeses only in context. One resembled sponge cake spattered with chocolate sauce. Another, a pockmarked toadstool-yellow, exuded green flecks. Analysis and comparison: he took up again his knife, and each of these candidates he tapped, he prodded, he sounded. At length he segregated a ruddy specimen. "That is a rather fine Red Cheshire... which you might enjoy." It was accepted; the decision was not enquired into, nor the intonation of you assessed.

His attention was now bent on the toadstool-yellow specimen. This he tapped. This he prodded. This he poked. This he scraped. He then summoned the waiter.

"What is that?"

Apologetic ignorance of the waiter.

"Could we find out?"

Disappearance of the waiter. Two other waiters appear.

"?"

"_____."

He assumed, at this silence, a mask of Holmesian
exaltation:

"Aha! An Anonymous Cheese!"

He then took the Anonymous Cheese beneath his left
hand, and the knife in his right hand, the thumb along
the back of the blade as though to pare an apple. He
then achieved with aplomb the impossible feat of peeling off a long slice. He ate this, attentively. He then
transferred the Anonymous Cheese to the plate before
him, and with no further memorable words proceeded
without assistance to consume the entire Anonymous
Cheese.

That was November 19, 1956. Joyce was dead, Lewis
blind, Pound imprisoned; the author of *The Waste
Land* not really changed, unless in the intensity of his
preference for the anonymous.

Although in the *Times* letter of 1935 to which Kenner alludes above,
Eliot seriously plumped for the formation of "A Society for the Preservation
of English Cheeses," the poet's manner was often unmistakenly facetious.
A flavor of irony hung about his manner and much that he said. As I say,
Kenner considered him to be a great joker. Eliot's ostentatious gravity was
itself often a parody of it, whereby he caricatured a venerable tradition of
English culture, as, for example, when he declined I. A. Richards' invitation
to visit with him in Peking in 1929 on the grounds that he did "not care to
visit any country which has no native cheese."

The British of course eat their cheese after their dessert, whereas the
French have it before meals. Brits never have cheese after dinner; it is only
served after lunch, even with a so-called "Ploughman's Lunch" which consists of bread, butter, sliced onion, and wedges of cheese. At dinner the
British have what they call savories. There is cheese in the savories, of course.
Because they like port after meals, you see, one could not very well drink
port after a sweet, could one? I should mention here, regarding the almost
Asiatic fuss with Eliot and the Stilton at the Garrick, that, traditionally, Stilton
cheese is always to be sliced, never scooped. In *Their Noble Lordships*, Simon

Winchester observes, "Argument at dinner over whether you are a slicer or a scooper is still considered an excellent choice of topics by some aristocrats."

Were you aware that the single food people around the whole world most crave is cheese? That comes from official international statistics. I wonder what that says about the human palate and, for that matter, what, by the same token, it does not enjoy. Does this mean that the world as we know it is essentially a cow and goat culture? I suggest that the world-wide popularity of cheese is due to its very high salt factor. *Umami*—the word for "savory, pleasant" in Japanese—is actually the taste of L-glutamine $C5H10N2O3$. The optimum umami taste depends also on the amount of salt. Umami taste is common to foods that contain high levels of L-glutamate IMP and GMP, most notably in fish, shellfish, cured meats, vegetables, (mushrooms, ripe tomatoes, celery, etc.) or green tea and fermented and aged products, especially cheese. (A person's first encounter with umami is probably breast milk. It contains roughly the same amount of umami as warm broths.) When aged cheese is added to pasta, it is the umami in the cheese that exaggerates the umami of the pasta. The standard short list for the tastes our tongues register are: salty, sweet, sour and bitter. Umami—the piquant taste often associated with MSG—was added to this list merely seven years ago, and there have been no additions since then, not until 2016, that is. There has now come into view a sixth primary taste—and it may explain why we love carbs, according to Jessica Hamzelou in *The Daily News* (Sept. 2, 2016). What the five tastes listed above miss is a major component of our diets, according to Professor Juyun Lim at Oregon State University in Corvallis, who explains, "Every culture has a major source of complex carbohydrate. The idea that we cannot taste what we're eating doesn't make sense." Hamzelou writes,

> Her team tested this by giving a range of different carbohydrate solutions to volunteers—who it turned out were able to detect a starch-like taste in solutions that contained long or shorter carbohydrate chains. "They called the taste 'starchy'," says Lim. "Asians would say it was rice-like, while Caucasians described it as bread-like or pasta-like. It's like eating flour."

What is the unique new taste suddenly discovered deserving of its own category? Starch. The evidence points to the fact that carbohydrate-rich foods—"starchy"—may now be considered a flavor in its own right.

16.

THE OVERKILL FACTOR

James Roosevelt in his autobiography/memoir, *Affectionately, F.D.R.,* mentions an English nurse or nanny that the family had when growing up—she goes unnamed in the book—whom he refers to as "Old Battleaxe." "We would eat with her occasionally, and I, unfortunately, was fascinated with her habit of slathering her meat with a thick layer of English mustard—the 'hot' variety. I could not keep myself from staring, and this enraged her. 'Keep on gawking,' she threatened me one day, 'and I'll make you eat the whole of this mustard pot.' True to her word, she carried out her threat. "One day the harridan did make me eat the contents of the mustard pot, spoonful by spoonful. I was miserably ill, and to this day I cannot abide even mild mustard—not even on a hot dog at the ball game. I am certain that the experience led to the chronic stomach ailment from which I have suffered most of my life." Roosevelt was indisposed with ulcers throughout all of his adult years.

A quick word on mustard. Apparently the only comestible the Indians did not like in early days was English mustard, "whereat they made many a sour face," we read in the account of Samuel Purchas in *Purchas, His Pilgrimes* (1625). Captain Benjamin Gosnold was aboard *Concord* in 1602 when fifty Native Americans in nine canoes paid a visit to Elisabeth Isle, "stout and lusty men with their bows and arrows; amongst them there seemed to be one of authority, because the rest made an inclining respect unto him." Stepping forth, he hugged an Indian chief, and when they "all sat down in manner like greyhounds upon their heels," he gave the chief a straw hat and a pair of knives. On the seventh day, after "going to dinner about noon," Gosnold wrote, "they sat with us and did eat of our bacaleure [fish] and mustard, drank of our beer, but the mustard nipping them in their noses they could not endure: it was a sport to behold their faces made being bitten therewith." The old explorers could laugh.

Always fastidious in his tastes, Lord Curzon—the illustrious George Nathaniel Curzon, 1st Marquess Curzon of Kedleston—loathed the unremitting tapioca and rice pudding ("which we detested and which we used to drop into our caps when she was not looking and carry away and hide in chinks in the wall where she was not likely to discover them") dispensed by Miss Paraman, the governess under whose sadistic regime and system of terrorism he and his siblings suffered throughout their childhood. By his own account, Paraman beat them unmercifully in her attempts to reinforce her fierce and crushing discipline, tied them for endless hours to chairs in uncomfortable positions and shut them up in darkness with their hands holding a pole, mockingly dressed them in red petticoats with conical caps with the words "Liar," "Sneak," and "Coward," and often forced them to parade in silence around the town to show themselves to the villagers. In later life, Curzon described Ellen Mary Paraman as a "fiend," a person "representing a class of governess and method of tuition (in entire dependence of the parents)," no longer allowed or approved, lamenting that "With children who are constantly with their parents such a system would be incapable of concealment." "In her savage moments she was a brutal and vindictive tyrant," Curzon wrote later, "and I have often thought since that she must have been insane."

Curzon was not only lacking in self-confidence but sensitive, too, about his appearance, particularly the abnormal breadth of his head that throughout life required that all of his hats be specially made, as Kenneth Rose notes in his biography, *Curzon, Superior Person*. A spinal injury when he was in his teens, incurred while horseback riding, left Curzon in lifelong pain, often resulting in insomnia, and it required him to wear a metal corset, contributing to an unfortunate impression of stiffness and arrogance. It has been reported that the death of his first wife, Mary Victoria Leiter, after only nine years of marriage—she was the daughter of a co-founder of what is now Marshall Field—was the greatest personal loss of his life.

Was it these reversals or the tyranny in the nursery, his Spartan upbringing, that stimulated Curzon's life-long combative qualities and encouraged the obsessional side of his nature, despite his being well-born and well-placed, that led the man to grow up to become so intractably snobbish and crotchety in his later years, also parsimonious and scornful of the help? It seems that he could never forget all the horrors of food! Angrily, he complained to his second wife, Grace, even when he was a grown man, that on a "chill horrible day" the kitchen maid served him everything that he detested and perversely "proposed mayonnaise of lobster and cold rabbit pie for lunch." "At every meal since you left," he told her virtually in whining schoolboy tones, "I have swallowed (or refused to swallow) the horrid little mould of jelly or yellow blancmange with a bisected apricot or pear swimming at its base."

Young Dwight Moody, long before he became an evangelist, found no sympathy from his strict mother, a woman who chose to instill in him discipline and temperance, when he complained that for 19 consecutive meals his only food had been cornmeal and milk. The imprint of an early trauma, whether related to food or not, will never be forgotten. "When I was at summer camp in New Hampshire when I was eight I choked on a bean in a boiled green bean pod," Stephen Dixon told me, which began a long spell of apprehension. "I wasn't able to eat green beans again till I decided to overcome my fear of them when I was past thirty. It worked. From that moment on I liked green beans again, especially the way that they're cooked in Chinese restaurants." It is amazing how one early trauma can lead to a lifetime of anxiety. In a *People* magazine interview (January 26,1981), Truman Capote told journalist Andrea Chambers, "Once, when I was 5, I got lost during Mardi Gras, and they took me to the police station. I was there all night before my mother came. I was terrified. I was never interested in Mardi Gras after that." I am reminded here of an old friend of mine, Jim Scoppa, who once told me that, years ago, coming home from grammar school to an empty house and finding himself terribly hungry, he found only a box of raisins and proceeded to wolf down the entire contents—there was nothing else to eat—and that, in consequence, for the rest of his life he could not bear even the sight of raisins.

"Well, I guess I have got down to the raisins," was a pet phrase of Abe Lincoln's whenever he felt he had reached the end of a subject or made a final conclusion. When people asked what that meant, as they usually did, the explanation he gave for that quaint little phrase, one of only an endless fund of extra-vivid, even crude anecdotes that the President had, was of a small girl who after eating a large bowl of raisins became ill. It was only after regurgitating the whole mess that, upon looking, she could find relief enough to say she "got down to the raisins." This is the Overkill Factor. In his book *The Eleventh House*, Hudson Strode—writer, gardener, gourmet, world traveler, and biographer of Jefferson Davis, president of the Confederacy—explains how in Paris he once ordered *champignons provençale*, not realizing that virtually everything *provençale* was cooked in heavy garlic. He added with disgust, "I have never been able to abide the taste of garlic since." It became a watershed event. Strode is hardly alone in his acute scorodophobia. Many venerable Bostonians, of the Brahmin sort, still peevishly look down on items like crow garlic as a Mediterranean onion for peasants, meant for the lowly. Poets Robert Browning and his invalid wife, Elizabeth Barrett, who lived in Italy for 15 years, in Pisa and then in Florence, could not abide the taste of garlic or olive oil. The Italian chef and cooking teacher Marcella Hazan, who would not suffer fools who were afraid of salt or butter or even the small effort it took to find quality ingredients, was quick to condemn the overuse of garlic in much of what passed for Italian food in the United States.

May I make a quick aside here? British cuisine generally uses little or no garlic, and many citizens in the UK have long held it in disesteem. The aesthete John Ruskin considered alliums to be one of the strongest of class barriers. Lexicographer Dr. Samuel Johnson prejudicially felt that garlic was a low-brow condiment and complained that navvies and ditch diggers badly reeked of it. John Evelyn in *Acetaria: a discourse on sallets* (1699) wrote,

> Garlic, allium...altho' both by Spaniards and Italians, and the more Southern people, familiarly eaten with almost everything... we absolutely forbid its entrance into our salleting [salad-making], by reason of its intolerable rankness, and which it so detested of old that the eating of it was (as we read) part of the punishment for such as had committed the horrid'st crimes. To be sure, 'tis not fit for ladies' palates, nor those who court them, farther than to permit a light touch on the dish with a clove thereof.

Garlic, face it, was just not something that quality folk in later centuries or that vigorous eaters with good taste enjoyed, certainly not in that country. The zealous cookbook editor, Judith Jones, to whom we have already referred, begins her memoir, *The Tenth Muse: My Life in Food*, with a revealing anecdote about how when she was a young girl her mother detested anything like a bulb of garlic so much that she prohibited it from household use. Jones observes,

> To her, garlic represented everything alien and vulgar. It smelled bad, and people who handled it or ate it smelled bad. Moreover, it covered up the natural flavor of honest food—and that was suspect... Not only was garlic banned, onions were permitted only when a lamb stew was being prepared, for which two or three well-boiled small white onions per person were deemed appropriate.

Johan Wolfgang von Goethe, Louis XV, the Roman poet Horace, King Alfonso XI of Castile, Shakespeare (In *A Midsummer Night's Dream*, Act IV Scene 2, Bottom instructs the actor, "And most dear actors, eat no onion, nor garlic, for we are to utter sweet breath, and I do not doubt but to hear them say, 'it is a sweet comedy'") and Thomas Nash all hated garlic. Dracula hates garlic. So do mosquitos! *Cancer* hates garlic! (It serves to kill brain cancer cells.) Historian Ammianus Marcellinus wrote that in the second century, emperor Marcus Aurelius contemptuously referred to Jews as "garlic eaters" after traveling through Palestine, hating their noisiness and stench. He spoke of "malodorous Jews" (*foetentium judaeorum*), finding them disgusting, smelly, and rebellious. The belief that Jewish bodies exude a foul odor, the so-called "Foeter Judaicus," was common among medieval Europeans. Cleopatra herself said of the victorious Romans: "*...their thick breaths, rank of gross diet.*" In *The Canterbury Tales*, garlic is used in the description of the coarse and "lecherous" Summoner. Actor Michael Caine stated that he hated the smell of garlic as he associated it with his service in the Korean war where North Korean and Chinese troops would munch it as a snack. Actor David Cassidy of *The Partridge Family* fame is allergic to garlic, by his own account. Many actors and people in show business will not take the chance of eating the odorous species of onion. Nevertheless, there are always strong exceptions. Lady Caroline Blackwood craved the taste of garlic so much that, according to her daughter Ivana Lowell, "she brought her own [cloves] to restaurants, claiming that they [chefs] never put enough in [to the food]."

Raccoons, while omnivorous, also hate garlic, as well. They dislike tomatoes or anything else in the Nightshade family, and leave these plants alone, along with squashes like pumpkins, cucumbers, oriental poppies, globe thistle, and "Kentucky Wonder" pole beans. They not only have delicate palates, so shun spicy foods, but also have sensitive feet and avoid walking on prickly plants. On this subject I have stumbled on what might be a universal truth: all animals seem to love *peanut butter*!

According to Pliny, both garlic and onions were invoked as deities by the Egyptians at the taking of oaths. They are to many people harsh and palate-shocking plants, asperous and unrelenting—credulous Pliny actually believed garlic strong enough to demagnetize lodestones—and one Islamic myth has it that when Satan stepped out of the Garden of Eden after the Fall of Adam and Eve, garlic sprang up from the very spot where he placed his left foot and onions sprang up from where he placed his right. The inhabitants of Pelusium, in Lower Egypt (who worshiped the onion), are said to have had an aversion to both onions and garlic as food. In India, the priestly caste, the Brahmins, were forbidden to eat garlic. The prophet Mohammed said, "If you eat garlic don't come to the place of worship: Whosoever ate from this plant (i.e. garlic) should not enter the mosque" (*Quran*: Vol. 1:812).

Joltin' JoeDiMaggio, the New York Yankee slugger, eager to assimilate into the American mainstream, although he appeared in most instances to be a robust Italian—his parents were first-generation immigrants from Ísola delle Fémmine, on the northern coast of Sicily, where many of his relatives were fishermen—was known to have one steadfast request, ironically enough, when it came to food: no garlic. Was the crude if brainlessly affectionate nickname "Dago" that his teammates gave him, the oafish humor of joshing close friends, just a bit too much for him to take?

Overkill can wipe out a food for you. "I have had such an overdose of [Sherlock] Holmes," wrote A. Conan Doyle, "that I feel towards him as I do to *paté de fois gras*, of which I once ate too much, so that the name of it gives me a sickly feeling to this day." (It is often served with garlic.) Soviet poet Vladimir Mayakovsky in his neo-Whitmanian autobiography of 1928, *I Myself*, felt the driving need to mention how in 1906 when he was 13 in the old town of Baghdati, now Georgia, he ate something he could never bear to eat again. This is his brief entry: "Bought and ate four buns with candied peel. Went rowing with what was left on Patriarch's Pond. Since then can't bear buns with candied peel." "When I was a young boy growing up on our farm [in Batavia, New York], we were quite poor and ate a lot of buckwheat," the novelist John Gardner wrote, "and truthfully I haven't much liked it since."

John Thorne ascribes his dislike of frozen vegetables to having suffered early doses of being fed them. "Until recently, there were only two standard frozen vegetable mixtures—carrot cubes and peas, and baby limas and corn—both equally horrible. I'm no fan of frozen vegetables of any persuasion, but what makes these mixes especially awful is that each combines a quick, with a slow-cooking vegetable, all subtleties sacrificed for a flat-flavored compromise. But it was standard American fare, and regularly, all during my childhood, I received a salutary dosage. I didn't care to look succotash in the face after that for many, many years."

It was no different with Ernest Hemingway who, having earlier in life over-glutted on eating yams or sweet potatoes, could never again bear the sight of them. "There are articles of food, like the sweet potato, that I can no longer eat," he wrote in *The Toronto Star Weekly* (November 24, 1923), in a youthful piece that was clearly a Thanksgiving article called "Wild Gastronomic Adventures of a Gourmet," "because I once made a pig of myself about them. There are other things, like spaghetti, that I cannot eat so well, now that my hand is losing its cunning." I believe by that cryptic remark that he simply found the act of twirling spaghetti around a fork not only too messily complicated, but in the end just not worth all the effort.

As to sweet potatoes, who that has heard her pronouncement can forget Julia Child's terse if not glacial comment on the subject of sweet potatoes with marshmallows: "I rather like marshmallows"?

It was due to an obsession with eating meat that Jean Nidetch became a co-founder of the Weight Watchers organization. It is the classic "worm-turns" story about food. Born Jean Evelyn Slutsky in Brooklyn, New York, to David Slutsky, a cab driver, and Mae Slutsky, a manicurist, Nidetch was grossly overweight. She had experimented with numerous fad diets before, in 1961, following a regimen prescribed by a diet clinic sponsored by the New York City Board of Health. After losing 20 pounds, and finding her resolve weakening, she contacted several overweight friends and founded a support group, which developed into weekly classes, and incorporated on May 15, 1963, into the Weight Watchers organization. In 1978, Weight Watchers was sold to the H. J. Heinz Company. And now you know the rest of the story.

Historian Bernard De Voto who hated asparagus, artichokes, "and even the commoner vegetables," as his wife, Ava, told Julia Child in a letter, would eat "lamb in no form because he spent a year on a sheep ranch in Idaho where they fed the help on fresh killed mutton twice a day." During the Renaissance, many folks swore by phallic asparagus and the shoots it sent up as an aphrodisiac, so the Roman Catholic Church banned it from convents. In 2014, chubby Mike Wilbon, an ESPN commentator and former sportswriter and columnist for the *Washington Post*, explained on one of his broadcasts that over the course of fifty-plus years he has never eaten asparagus, Brussels sprouts, or a single raspberry. It takes all kinds.

Food blogger Ted Luoma abominates all white food and traces it back to being forced by his father—"cajoled is too soft a word"—to drink white milk. "I don't know what his obsession was because I loved chocolate milk, but I guess at six or seven, I was his experiment in Nazi parenting." He says,

> My dad was the White Milk Enforcer. Numerous times, he would wrestle me in the kitchen to pour that evil beverage down my throat. He would literally pour it down my throat after he pried my mouth open. My hatred for that ivory abomination ran so deeply that he usually ended up pouring two glasses onto my face only for it to soak us. After the fight was wrestled out of me I would finally submit so that I could brush my teeth and take a shower.

Luoma confesses that there are "some innocuous white foods like eggs, potatoes and rice," but insists "I sincerely abhor mayonnaise, cream cheese, white milk (or milk in general)… you get the picture. There are exceptions to the rule, like when you need to use mayonnaise for tuna salad or cream cheese for a velvety peanut butter pie, but when I cook with these ingredients I have my cleansing ritual. There's nothing worse than leaving a milk ring on the counter with the milk cap… I still have to scrub down like I'm about to perform an appendectomy after their use."

I have alluded earlier to James Baldwin's food aversion to prunes and corned-beef hash. His account of the subject is an example of a classic case of "overkill." In his autobiographical essay, "Here Be Dragons," the Harlem author explains why that revulsion lasted all his life, writing,

> I hit the streets when I was about six or seven, like most black kids of my generation, running errands, doing odd jobs. This was in the black world—my turf—which means that I felt protected. I think that I really was, though poverty is poverty, and we were, if I may say so, among the truly needy, in spite of the tins of corned beef we got from home relief every week, along with prunes. (Catsup had not yet become a vegetable; indeed, I don't think we had ever heard of it.) My mother fried corned beef, she boiled it, she baked it, she put potatoes in it, she put rice in it, she disguised it in corn bread, she boiled it in soup (!), she wrapped it in cloth, she beat it with a hammer, she banged it against the wall, she threw it onto the ceiling. Finally, she gave up, for nothing could make us eat it anymore, and the tins reproachfully piled up on the shelf above the bathtub—along with the prunes, which we also couldn't eat anymore. While I won't speak for my brothers and sisters, I can't bear corned-beef hash or prunes even today.

The Irish writer and poet, Paul Muldoon, gave me a vivid account on the subject of badly overindulging and regret.

> When I was a child I had a particular fondness for a confection known as clove rock. It was a hard candy or boiled sweet, so called because it was made of syrup

heated to a temperature of 160 degrees centigrade.
Flavored with clove oil as it cooled, molded into
chalky red and white stubs, clove rock was thought
to relieve toothache and generally numb the palate.
In the small country store my father ran in Eglish [a
name for the town that is a corruption of the original
Gaelic name, *An Eaglais*, meaning "church"], County
Tyrone, in the early 1950s, there was always at least
one jar of clove rock. Indeed, one such finds its way
into a poem of mine entitled "The Right Arm." The
main reason it is enshrined there has to do with an
experience I had a bit later, in the early 1960s, in
McAvinchey's shop in Armagh City. I bought a pound
of clove rock and ate it like there was no tomorrow.
As I should have, there being nothing like a future for
clove rock and myself.

Punk novelist Chuck Palahniuk cannot stand the taste of butterscotch.
"I hate butterscotch, because we once took cases of this Israeli butterscotch
pudding and ate it all," he wrote. "It was the only dessert we had for the first
fifteen years of my life." "I stay away from mayonnaise," NBC 's Late Night
show host Jimmy Fallon told *Bon Appetit* magazine in June 2008, in spite of
the fact that mayonnaise is the largest selling sauce in the United States—yes,
although used as a condiment, it is defined as a sauce. Fallon goes on to explain that his detestation of mayonnaise began when he was young. "It goes
all the way back to when I was a kid. I must have thought it was cool to stick
my head between metal bars on our back-porch banister. I couldn't get my
head out, so my grandfather suggested rubbing mayonnaise all over my head
to lube it up so that they could slide it out. It is 90 degrees out, my head is
covered with mayonnaise, and I'm crying hysterically. My head finally just
slipped out. I'll never enjoy a tuna fish sandwich like everyone else."

"I once got drunk—wasted—guzzling a bottle of Southern Comfort
back in 1981 going up on a bus to the Andover/Exeter football game," confessed Ming Tsai, a former student of mine at the pretentious New England
prep school Phillips Andover Academy, where I managed to teach for three
(seemingly endless!) years and now the well-known American restaurateur,
television personality, and celebrity chef of East-West cuisine, "and to this
day I cannot bear even to smell the stuff." "Was it the spices in it?" I asked
him, regarding the sweet American liqueur made from neutral spirits with
fruit, spice and whiskey flavorings. He shook his head and groaned, "It's

the memory." He laughed and said, "Now I like good wine, cognac, champagne." Ming told me that when he was a young boy—he often helped his parents, Stephen and Iris, with their family restaurant, Mandarin Kitchen in Dayton, Ohio—he developed a huge dislike of cilantro, mushrooms, and even beets but eventually came around to liking them. "I cannot eat nattō, though," he told me and then went on to explain,

> The first thing that one notices after opening a pack of nattō, fermented soybeans, is the reeking, almost overpowering smell, something akin to but far more nose-pinching than, "high" venison or certain pungent and semi-malodorous cheeses like Gorgonzola, Roquefort, Limburger, and other blues that notoriously reek, never mind soft, washed-rind and smear-ripened Reblochon, a soft smear-ripened cheese found in the Alps made from raw cow's milk—it has not been available in the United States since 2004 due to the enforcement of laws concerning the pasteurization of soft and semi-soft cheese—which smells like a urine-soaked sock. Stirring the nattō produces lots of sticky strings. Oppressive! Durian is too putrid-smelling for me. I've eaten many insects in the world, scorpions, beetles, snakes, even pig-brain sashimi, and traveled to Taiwan every other summer from the time I was born to age 12 and ever since of course I have tasted and tried many things, but I honestly have to confess that there I draw the line.

Traveling the world, Ming found a diet common to most people on the planet. I was surprised to hear that, for I do not recall being impressed by Ming as a daring or bold person. Remarkably, 80% of the world eats insects. Folks commonly wash, flour, and fry them. Other odder creatures, like spiders or roaches, have to be gutted—"field-dressed," I believe, is the proper euphemistic term to be used here—detoxified and defanged. There are entomophages in Guinea who eat also eat flies. (As one happy frog said to another, "Time's sure fun when you're having flies!") Paul Rozin, professor of psychology at the University of Pennsylvania and an expert on the emotion of disgust, focuses on psychological, cultural, and biological determinants of human food choices. He is hardly original when he points out that most of us follow commonly received and accepted notions of what are widely considered off-putting foods. Disgust, which has its own facial expressions, may be most widely displayed in the matter of disliked *foods*. Rozin speaks of the "contamination response."

Simply, and it is hardly a surprise, there are acquired likes and dislikes of food. Most people like steak, not snake. (Perhaps this is the place to mention that in 2013, the state of Montana legalized salvaging road kill!) Paul Rozin is quoted in *Gourmet* (January 2000) stating that he himself will try just about anything, locusts, ground cactus-moth larvae, spleen, spinal cord, testicles, and even worms, but adds, however, "I don't really like soft-boiled eggs."

I have a recollection in writing about mayonnaise of the fatal stroke that killed the Scottish novelist Robert Louis Stevenson on December 3, 1894. He had been preparing mayonnaise for a salad, standing around with guests on the wide veranda of his imposing wooden house named "Vailima," that he had built for his family in Western Samoa. The writer was never healthy and probably suffered from undiagnosed TB. He was almost always incorporeally thin, never healthy, and all of his life apparently had a greige look to him, unfinished, unbleached, undyed. Just before the "thundering apoplexy" hit him, he had grabbed his head, sank to his knees, and cried out, "Do I look strange?" When she was only a child of four, novelist Edith Wharton's brother, Frederic, a boisterous youth of twenty, antically forced her to swallow a glassful of claret, an event—and a terrible memory—that was so upsetting to the small sensitive girl that she remained completely unable to bear the taste of wine for the rest of her life. Writer and publisher Caresse Crosby, wife of the mad Harry Crosby, in her autobiography, *The Passionate Years*, details an unforgettable horror she had experienced during a day at Miss Chapin's Boarding School when a forgotten roast beef sandwich went bad inside of her desk and had become so putrid that in her preternatural disgust she dared not lift the cover for days lest someone else get a whiff of the horrid rotting cache, which she eventually got up the courage to whisk away and throw into a gutter. "That sandwich looms as the greatest horror of my adolescence," she wrote, adding, "To this day I prefer a toothache to a bad smell and a stone to a roast-beef sandwich."

A long poem by Puerto Rican poet Judith Ortiz Cofer entitled "Beans: An Apologia for Not Loving to Cook" is an animadversion against not only the legume but a brief against cooking itself. Beans represent for her the "oppression of women at the stove in Puerto Rico and watching the women in my family getting up early in the morning to cook for others." An "old 1970s feminist" (her words), Cofer writes that her memory turns, not happily, "on the cloying smell of boiling beans/ in a house of women waiting,

waiting for wars, affairs, periods/ of grieving, the rains, el mal tiempo, to end, the phrase/ used both for inclement weather and to abbreviate the aftermath/ of personal tragedies." It has all grown into a major polemic with her. "Beans," she writes, "I grew to hate them/ Red kidney beans whose name echoes of blood, and are shaped/ like inner organs, I hated them in their jaw breaking rawness/ and I hated them as they yielded to the fire." Cofer recalls her childhood,

> The women waited in turns by the stove
> rapt by the alchemy of unmaking. The mothers turned
> hard
> at the stove, resisting our calls with the ultimate threat
> of burned beans. The vigil made them statues, rivulets
> of sweat coursing down their faces, pooling at their
> collarbones.
> They turned hard away from our demands for atten-
> tion and love,
> their eyes and hands making sure beans would not
> burn
> and rice would not stick, unaware of our longing
> for our mothers' spirits to return back to the soft sac
> that once held us, safely tucked among their inner
> organs,
> smelling the beans they cooked for others,
> through their pores.

In one comic piece of his self-exposé of foibles and worries, *A Certain Lucas*, Julio Cortázar satirically refers to an invented sport called "Swimming in a Pool of Gray Grits" or chickpea mush ("*Nadando en la piscina de go-fio*"). It makes reference in an exaggerated way to a childhood memory of over-eating finely ground chick-pea flour mixed with sugar which he explains in a footnote was "the delight of Argentine children of my time." He writes, "These grits are a grayish powder that come in little paper bags, which children raise to their mouths with results that tend to end in suffocation. When I was in the fourth grade in Banfield (Southern Rail Line) [a suburb south of Buenos Aires] we would eat so much gray grits during recess that out of thirty pupils only twenty-two of us finished the year."

Cortázar's memory of "gray grits," although stressing over-indulgence in a way Proust did not of his madeleine, does touch on the fact I pointed out earlier that it was as if they had tasted their confections with the mind and not the palate. That mind and body are involved is indisputable, but to what degree? Gilbert Ryle in *The Concept of the Mind* argues that mind is part of the body's activity. Others say the mind is a product of the body. (What of the complementary truth that the body—the way we live in it—is also a product of the mind?) A thorny but intriguing and certainly applicable question arises, regarding causation, in the matter of what we come to like or dislike in a food. Can one say that mind and body are "indissociable complementarities"? American philosopher John Searle argues that they are in fact different levels of description of the same set of phenomena. While the philosopher René Descartes favored a strict separation of the two in 17th-century France, the "positivistic" movement in turn reduced mind to body, leading both Jacob Moleschott, the Dutch physiologist and writer on dietetics and the scientific racist Karl Vogt, a polygenist, among others, to conclude that thinking was a secretion of the brain in the same way that gall is a secretion of the liver! Plato believed that mind and body were united, separated at death, Aristotle that the mind is a property exhibited by the body, one among many. Immanuel Kant and Thomas Huxley weighed in on this with further discernments on the soul.

Like Kant, Prof. Noam Chomsky points to the mind's inherent programming, asking not only to what extent our mental creations are limited by the innate functioning of our brain/nervous system—call them our "factory settings"—but also to what extent they are our own creations.

Overkill. The bane of excess. I have mentioned that the British neurologist and writer Oliver Sacks would not eat chicken. The story has its origin, like many food phobias, in a past disaster. Early in his medical career, he was doing scientific work with invertebrates at the Laboratory of Human Nutrition, studying how the compound TOCP (triorthocresyl phosphate), a slow-acting poison, insidiously affected the nerves. Worms and frogs refused the TOCP; he found chickens would gobble anything. Misjudging the various doses he administered to his little flock, however, he inadvertently managed to kill them all. He writes regretfully of its effect in his autobiography, *On the Move*: "The end, for me and my research, was seeing my favorite hen—she had no name, but number 4304, was an animal of unusually docile and sweet disposition—sink to the ground on her paralyzed legs, chirping piteously." Sacks wistfully confesses in the book that he developed a "horror" of chickens thereafter.

All sorts of theories have come down to us to explain what controls the "machine," as Hamlet describes his body to Ophelia ("Thine evermore, most dear lady, whilst this machine is to him [referring to himself]"). To the late 18th-century French physiologist, Pierre Jean George Cabanis, a noted materialist who linked biology with psychology, all of our intellectual processes evolve from what he called "sensibility" (a popular reference in his day and the theme of many novels of that period) which is a directing property of the nervous system. Sensibility, by which Cabanis meant the ability to have sensations—they were the source of all intelligence, he believed—are a property of the nervous system. He tried to show how a materialist conception of the human organism can throw light on our mental and moral life. Like René Descartes, he insisted on the union of the mind and body, but unlike the French philosopher he was no dualist, re-adopting a broadly materialist approach, which gave a central role to sensation. The soul is not an entity, it was his argument, but rather a human faculty, and thought is the function of the brain. Just as the stomach and intestines receive food and then digest it— our large intestine, the gut, contains over 100 trillion bacteria—so the brain receives sense impressions, digests them, and has as its organic secretion, thought. It is known that Pierre Cabanis belonged to the "vitalist school" of the German chemist and physician Georg Stahl who hypothesized that all matter had a vital force, or a "soul" of sort, and in his posthumous letter to Claude Fauriel on first causes, actually a book-length work, *Lettre à Fauriel sur les causes premières* (1824), the consequences of this significant influence, forming into an opinion, became clear. The concept of "life" is added to the organism; for over-lording the universally diffused sensibility, there is a vital, living, and productive power to which we append the name of "nature." It is impossible to avoid ascribing both intelligence and will to this universal power, a living power, immaterial and immortal, that prevails over us.

I raise these deeper issues here simply because one would like to know in the matter of food aversions if it is the material world or the world of ideas that govern taste, if they both do, and which precedes which, or are both simultaneous? So much is involved in the debate. Intentionality. Consciousness. Ontological subjectivity. Rationality. Social bias. Can one assert with full certitude, for example, that the mind must first detest what the body in consequence must follow? And would that also be accomplished without conflict or any psychic resistance? Or does the body inform the mind what it has empirically—by taste, sight, touch—come to abhor and therefore both must avoid? Other questions are apposite as to what degree one holds sway over the other. What of habit, does it help or hurt? Solidify or wound by duration? Can the mind be said to be a prisoner of the senses, because, as Aristotle tells us, nothing is in the mind that has not come through the senses? Is the body a donkey that the intelligent mind should dominate (as Paul Bragg claims in *The Miracle of Fasting*, one of my favorite books)? How does our sensibility enter into what we like or do not like, choose or reject? Are the many judgments that we make of given foods conscious or unconscious? Formed by memory? Selected or rejected out of as or expectation? Shaped by habit? How exactly are judgments formed? Maintained? Are they derived from (and consistent with) more general physical laws? Are they subject, for example, to unconscious as well as conscious psychological phenomena? Physiological under layers?

What of other mental differences between various people, arising from their inherited physical constitution in interaction with environmental factors? What about the relativity of things we like and dislike flung in the face of acquired characteristics? We read in Proverbs 15:17, "Better a meal of herbs where love is, than a fattened calf with hatred." It could all of it figure in a person hating parsnips.

Immanuel Kant was correct. Our minds never come into direct contact with ultimate reality. The reality we perceive and "understand" is at least a stop or two removed from things in themselves (*Ding-an-sich*). Knowledge stems originally from experience rather than reason. Experience, too, is frankly different from reality, because it consists of sense impressions or perceptions of things, not of the things-in-themselves. What we perceive in space and time, what we deduce—what flavors we hate, colors we fear, textures we abhor, etc.—are only the perceptible aspects of things, the face they show us, what Kant calls "phenomena." We are experiencing how the world appears to us, not how it is! Yes, indeed, there is a real world out there supplying us with those appearances, what is called the "noumenal" world, in which a thing is just what it is, not what it appears, that is, the world of the thing-in-itself. We cannot know it, however. So maybe appearances are indeed reality. It is fully in the phenomenal world that James Roosevelt lives with his nightmares of mustard, Jim Scoppa with his disgust for raisins, and Julio Cortázar with his gray grits.

Harpo Marx explains in his autobiography, *Harpo Speaks* (1961) that when he was a 12-year-old boy he was hired by a lusty delicatessen owner, "a crazy dame," who immediately took him downstairs to the storeroom and tried to seduce him, grabbing his hand and pressing it to her all over her body. It created a trauma for him, one that he sought to erase. "My hand, I felt, had been tainted. It was nasty, filthy, dirty. I had to wash it, immediately. The only facility in the storeroom was a big, open pickle barrel. So I washed my hand in the pickle juice and ran upstairs and through the store and never went near the joint again." There were ramifications, of course. Harpo concludes—no small admission for a Jewish boy, and in his case a particularly voracious one—"For years I couldn't eat pickles."

Remember when Jane Eyre arrives at Lowood in that novel and, along with the other girls, is served burnt porridge for breakfast? It is so alarmingly disgusting to all that nobody could eat it. There was also that dark period during the young Jane's period of homeless wandering, when a woman and a little girl tending a pig give her a bowl of cold, congealed porridge that the pig would not eat. It is a vivid and indeed memorable example of the humiliation and subjection of a person, especially an innocent, being *forced* to eat anything, but especially something so grim. It is Mr. Brocklehurst's opinion that, if the girls are served inedible porridge, they should either eat it and be grateful anyway and "mortify the flesh" or as an alternative go hungry and creatively make use of the opportunity to "mortify the flesh." So when Jane is forced to take and eat the cold, hard porridge and be grateful for it, she is doomed to a kind of overkill that is slavishness. This is Victorian heartlessness.

A textbook case of the Overkill Factor, one nevertheless that led to fame and notoriety for him, is Andy Warhol and his Campbell's Soup can, the artist's first famous subject and the one by which he is still mainly identified. The work, referred to as *32 Campbell's Soup Cans* was produced in 1962 and consists of thirty-two canvases, each measuring 20" x 16" and with each showing a painting of the canned soup varieties the company offered at the time. 1962—so long ago, the very year that JFK (that is correct) began bombing South Vietnam, leading to a force build-up there of 400,000 troops in late 1966, early 1967. Warhol's individual paintings were produced by a printmaking method he used, a semi-mechanized screen process employed by using a non-painterly style. The painting's reliance on themes from popular culture helped to usher in "pop art" as a major art movement in this country. It turns out that when growing up, after eating so much of it, he came to hate it, going to far as to mock it in conversation. Tony Scherman and David Dalton in their book, *Pop: The Genius of Andy Warhol,* give one account of the painting's origin by quoting an explanation by advertising friend of the artist, John Mann, who knew Warhol back in 1961:

> As I recall, he said, "I hate grocery shopping." As it
> turned out, Mrs. Warhola [his mother] often asked
> Andy to run across the street for groceries. "So Muriel
> [Latow, a gallery owner] mentally took him inside the
> A & P, down the aisles. It was all very languid and flip
> on Andy's part. Before long, they got to Campbell's
> soup and Andy said he hated that, too. He said that
> his mother made it every day for lunch and after all

those years, it was like, "Oh, Mom—again?" Which
particular Campbell's soups, Latow asked, did Andy
dislike? All of them, he said. In that case, suggested
Latow, why not run over, buy one of each, and paint
them all? According to [Ted, a commercial art assis-
tant] Carey, "The next day Andy went out to the supermarket... and he [bought] a case of all the soups."
But, in fact, Warhol, as was his practice, painted the
cans not from life but from existing images: a magazine ad, a piece of Campbell's corporate stationery
that he obtained, and the studio photographs of Ed
Wallowitch.

Exploiting the subject, Warhol created something of a "pop" trend by
shamelessly coming out with all sorts of variations of that soup can, fabricat-
ing realistic images of it, pencil drawings, all sorts of prints, even a dented,
damaged variation in the early Sixties called *Crushed Campbell's Soup Can
(Beef Noodle)* and one with a ripped label called *Small Torn Campbell's Soup
Can (Pepper Pot)* and then in the late 1970s reproducing images of the same
can in all sorts of different lurid and pastel hues, even inverting and reversing
the image, all peddled with far more frequency than ever his mother served
him hot bowls of it.

"Once when I was a kid, I was mad on cherries... found a silver mejidie
[Turkish medal] and pinched it, bought a basket o' cherries... began eating
it... till I was all swollen out," said the wild, charismatic Zorba in Nikos
Kazantzakis's novel, *Zorba the Greek*. "My stomach began to ache and I was
sick... thoroughly sick, and from that day to this I've never wanted a cherry.
I couldn't bear the sight of them. I was saved. I could say no to any cherry. I
don't need you anymore and I did this same thing later with wine and tobacco. I still drink and smoke, but at any second, if I want to, whoop! I can cut
it out. I'm not ruled by passion. It's the same with my country. I thought too
much about it, so I stuffed myself up to the neck with it, spewed it up and it
has never troubled me since."

In all likelihood, Katharine Mansfield has probably written the best indictment of cherries in her short story, "The Modern Soul," where she has a
crack-pated old German musician explain to a young girl,

Cherries... there is nothing like cherries for producing free saliva after trombone playing, especially after
Grieg's *Ich Liebe Dich*... Or perhaps you do not care

to eat the worms. All cherries contain worms. Once I made a very interesting experiment with a colleague of mine at the university. We bit into four pounds of the best cherries and did not find one specimen without a worm.

During those three hellish days at Gettysburg, General Robert E. Lee was badly suffering from a severe case of diarrhea after having eaten too many cherries, an indisposition—given his ill-considered and ultimately amateurishly fatal decision for the Confederacy to attack from the front (and relatively below) on July 3, 1863—that cost his army a victory that day, an incredible mismaneuver and unstrategic folly that became, as it turned out, the turning-point of the entire war that led to the full and final defeat of the South.

An acquaintance of mine who suffers from gout came to excoriate cherries, even in fact the mere mention of them, having overdosed on them in a fit of zeal after reading a Boston University study which found that eating about 30 pieces of the sweet fruit within 48 hours of a gout attack could possibly cut the risk of recurrence of that painful arthritic condition by 35 percent. (Anthocyanins, an antioxidant pigment which seem to stabilize the free radical molecules responsible for causing inflammation and cell and tissue damage, are found in cherries and other red and purple fruits and vegetables.) A common story regarding the baleful effect of this fruit refers to President Zachary Taylor who in July 1850 sickened and suddenly died of *cholera morbus* after eating a bowl of cherries and then chugging down an entire pitcher of ice-cold milk, an error doubly compounded in a city like Washington D.C., where the extremely poor sanitation of that marshy locale at that period in history made it perilous to consume raw fruit or dairy products during the sweltering summer months. Mary Todd Lincoln's father was carried off by the same illness at the young age of 59 a few months earlier.

Surfeiting on any food can be a killer. William Thackeray, who continually overate and drank too much, was all his life addicted to spicy peppers, the eating of which played havoc with his digestive system, and then at the young age of 52 the novelist died from a stroke, almost certainly caused by his eating habits. Also, a letter that Wolfgang Amadeus Mozart wrote shortly before his death, which contained a reference to eating a lot of chops, was compared, by a certain Dr. J.Hirschmann, to his symptoms, and the physician concluded that the composer died from trichinosis, a disease caused by worms found in undercooked pork.

Wild cherries, richly red and tempting in the trees, were a big 19th-century delight for young and old. In 1854 Thoreau competed for them with the cedar waxwings, which drew them to the trees. One of young John Greenleaf Whittier's neighbors in Haverhill, Mass., a Miss Chase, had a cherry tree that she jealously guarded, Samuel T. Pickard tells us in his *Whittier-Land* (1906), a fond memoir of the poet. To show the extent of the popularity of the youngster in his home town even before he grew up to became a poet, he tells the story of how one day Miss Chase happened to see a boy up in the branches of her precious tree, and she issued upon the scene with dire threats. When she caught sight of the culprit's face, however, she instantly changed her tone. "Oh, is it you, Greenleaf? Take all the cherries you want!"

What did Thomas Lux see in his refrigerator "lit-from-within red, heart red, sexual red, wet neon red, shining red in their liquid, exotic, aloof, slumming in such company"? It was a jar of maraschino cherries, the single food he never ate. He writes in his poem, "Refrigerator, 1957,"

> Maraschino cherries, maraschino,
> the only foreign word I knew. Not once
> did I see these cherries employed: not
> in a drink, nor on top
> of a glob of ice cream,
> or just pop one in your mouth. Not once.
> The same jar there through an entire
> childhood of dull dinners—bald meat,
> pocked peas and, see above,
> boiled potatoes.

> He concludes, noting,
> They were beautiful
> and, if I never ate one,
> it was because I knew it might be missed
> or because I knew it would not be replaced
> and because you do not eat
> that which rips your heart with joy.

Unforgettable is the vomiting scene of cherries in John Updike's *The Witches of Eastwick*. Felicia Alden, the Christian wife of newspaper editor, Clyde Alden, is not a witch but is somehow able to sense that the horny tycoon, Daryl Van Horne, is up to no good. Her gossip against her sexy neighbors becomes the occasion of her death when they unknowingly cast a spell against her and in front of her husband she begins in a grotesque scene to vomit cherry pits. Because he cannot bear to watch his wife's illness progress, Clyde beats Felicia with a fire poker, killing her. Many filmgoers say, "I still won't eat cherries to this very day." For that matter, I used to love *rumtopf,* a mixture of various kinds of fruit, high-strength rum and sugar—popular in Germany and Denmark—which is poured into a large stoneware pot (the eponymous rum pot) and then matured for several months until the fruit becomes very soft and completely saturated with rum. The exudations of Felicia in both book and film, in their gaseous, glaucous spills evoking a similar sheen and color, killed that for me forever. Is there any reader of Wilson's novel, *I Thought of Daisy,* who does not recall Wilson's description of a girl's feet as being like "moist cream cheeses"? I have to confess that I rarely partake of cream cheese without fighting an image of that.

I have already regaled you with my Ancient Marineresque tale of how in high school I got looped drinking beer and eating Slim Jims and became so sick I had to be carried home by two pals while several other friends at the bar, as I was carted away unceremoniously, might well have shouted that valediction once so familiar in the old days of whaling, "A greasy voyage!" To this very day, I cannot even bear to look at one of those old-fashioned, industrially fermented, over-salted sausages greasier than pig tallow, ultimately nothing but unforgivably ropey meat sticks fabricated from blinking old steers with partially ossified vertebrae (and no doubt small reason to live) and as rigid as electrical flex-wire. The sodium nitrite that binds the water molecules in the meat leaves little water available for microbial activity, thereby preventing spoilage, all of it cosmetically added in order to combine with myoglobin in the animal muscle to keep it from turning pewter gray! Yikes! Antibiotically, that NaNO3 inhibits botulism. Toxicologically, 6 grams of the stuff—roughly the equivalent of 1,400 murderous Slim Jims to be had in any bar—can kill you, as one Patrick Di Justo clearly explains in a *Wired* magazine breakdown of that particular item of junk food.

So go easy on it, champ. A single Slim Jim shockingly provides more than one-sixth of the sodium your body needs daily. It is a killer comestible. Salt! I had a similar but far less dramatic reaction once—nausea, in my case—after eating several inexpertly-made *torrone semifreddo,* that rich Italian nougat made with honey, egg whites, sugar, and nuts. It must have been a tinctured batch cooked up by some crazy *strega.* Witches hate—and fear—salt. It is excoriated in their covens. Want to detect a crone? Sprinkle salt under her seat cushion and she will howl! Demons, devils, and fiends also detest salt. If you spill some, pitch it over your left shoulder (where spirits gather), and any curse will instantly vanish. Pure and strong, salt seals covenants, reinforces vows, bonds friends, and counteracts curses, maledictions, evil oaths,

I have alluded to the subject of whaling. One of my favorite books on the subject, *Cap'n George Fred* (1928), a memoir by the legendary Vineyarder Captain G.F. Tilton—he began his sailing life as a 14-year-old stowaway—gives a disheartening account of the scrimp fare allowed on the whaling ships of the late 19th-century. "We lived on smoked herring," he writes, and "beef that was saltier than Lot's wife that had to be soaked on a 'steep-tub' overnight before it was cooked. Saltpetre would eat all the fat off it, and it was pretty tough eating." No butter, no spices, no frills, rude hard- or soft-tack for bread. And those ships would head out on voyages that took years. There is food. Edibles. These are normal munchables. Then there are vittles, stodge, peckage, aliment, tommy, cibo, orts, broma, impasta, vivers. But Tilton's fare was *provender*—whaling slang—workingman's grub "as dead as Tom White's father."

In one of their long-running magic shows in Las Vegas of Penn and Teller, Penn Jillette dexterously juggles apples, among other objects. He eats 100 needles that he plucks from an apple; then he eats a length of thread; and then he eats the apple. The trick ultimately peaks when he pulls out of his mouth several yards of meticulously threaded needles. "After juggling with apples for 11 years, I don't ever eat apples outside of the show," Jillette has often complained. I am here reminded of how the actor Keith Reddin in the Murray and Boretz play, *Room Service*, in one memorable scene had to gulp down an entire pitcher of milk. Who can be surprised that he now despises milk? I daresay he probably abhors the play, as well.

Chef and restaurateur Donatella Arpaia, a judge on the Food Network's "The Next Iron Chef," falls into this category of what turned her off from childhood. It is this kind of phobia that endures. "I just cannot take the smell of lamb," she says. "I have had a distaste for it since I was a child. My mother would make lamb every Easter, and she would tell me it was something else to make me taste it! I have such a deep, offensive reaction, it just turns me off." When in the 1940s James Beard, then a struggling chef, started up in New York City his catering service, Hors, d'Oeuvres, Inc, he with others began making his own Vichyssoise, which sold for $2.00 a pint. "We made it by the vat," Beard explained; alas, they soon became ill at the mere thought of Vichyssoise. Beard in several cookbooks is not shy about making that clear. "Alas," he wrote, "here is another dish I will never be able to enjoy again. Even the sight of it can send me running from a room." Beard went on to note that, while rationing in Europe during and after World War II was widespread, the most abundant vegetable in those days was eggplant.

It was served in all sorts of ways, stuffed, fried, grilled, baked, cut up for salads. "Some of my friends, especially in Provence, said they would sooner starve than face another eggplant," Beard wrote, "I know exactly what they meant."

Writer and professor Edward Burns wrote to me to confess, "The only food I don't like is eggplant (even as *caviar d'aubergine*), a dislike that comes from my mother's cooking." Billy Graham once recalled how, when he was a boy of about 12 or 13, his father, William, a hard-nosed Scottish Presbyterian, made sure that his children would grow up to become staunch, godly, life-long teetotalers by buying a case of beer—Graham recounts this story as if his father were not only sane but a man of virtue—and then brutally forcing the future evangelist and his sister Katherine to gulp down bottles of the stuff until they became good and sick, which created such an aversion in them that both avoided alcohol and drugs for the rest of their lives. I daresay it also made his son to grow up with an inflexible and almost sclerotic stubbornness and in my opinion a concept of spirituality that basically conceives of God as little more than an unyielding stalwart of the Good Old Republican Party.

Bill Sievers, the handsome but muddy-faced U. S. Marine in David Douglas Duncan's memorable photograph of that brave soldier's face, did not like to speak of Korea, but a friend of his, Tom Justice from Waco, Texas, once asked him why a Southern boy such as he did not eat grits. Sievers explained to Justice that in the military he ate grits three meals a day for months on end, and vowed that if he ever got home, he would never eat grits again. Arriving homer, he kept his vow. In the deep American South, "grits" in many places still comes under the category of poor food. It is "a pale, lumpy, tasteless kind of porridge," in the words of the Harlem-born novelist James Baldwin in his book, *No Name in the Street*, "which the Southerner in-sists is a delicacy but which I believe they ingest as punishment for their sins."

One of my uncles, an aerial gunner on a B-17 during World War II, would not allow cabbage in his house. He had been shot down over Hanover, Germany, was wounded, and spent the rest of the war in a prison camp. The Germans kept feeding the prisoners some horrid cabbage soup, nearly every day. He became so sick of it that thereafter the smell of cabbage always nauseated him. The great Jamaican runner, Usain Bolt, the "World's Fastest Human," was asked by CNN interviewer Piers Morgan on December 5, 2012, inquiring about a rumor, "What about yams? Are they the secret to your success?" Bolt wagged a finger and replied, "I don't eat yams anymore. I had too much of them when I was young." In his memoir *The Eleventh House*, Hudson Strode, the witty but opinionated writer, gardener, and world-traveler from Alabama, writes that after once eating a Champignons

Provençal cooked in heavy garlic, the classic mushroom dish from Escoffier, "I have never been able to abide the taste of garlic since." A college friend of mine, Henry Bernatonis, hates Green Giant cooking bags. "These were the old boil-in-plastic bags of garbage. They were cheap, tasted like dog shit, but my mother couldn't cook. I cannot bear to look at peas, never mind these bags, even today." Riding his horse, "Old Tom," the young lawyer Abraham Lincoln often rode up to thirty miles a day traveling the legal circuit of the fourteen-county Eighth Circuit of central Illinois. Meals were often catch-as-catch-can, according to David Herbert Donald in his *Lincoln*. At one rest stop where the proprietor had run out of meat and bread, Lincoln grabbed a plate and announced cheerfully, "Well, in the absence of anything to eat, I will jump into this cabbage." Please note well that the President's irresolute and tepid willingness to eat cabbage is an alternative to eating food!

Abe Lincoln, although abstemious, a man with simple tastes, was particularly fond of bacon. For lunch, one of his secretaries John Hay reported, he "took a little lunch—a biscuit, a glass of milk in winter, some fruit or grapes in summer," but he goes on to add, "He ate less than anyone I know. Lunch was usually eaten irregularly...He almost always dined in a spartan fashion... He would rather nibble fruit. His wife Mary tried everything to make Abe eat but was frustrated time and time again to see the finest foods left all but untouched on his plate." One of the few entrees that always tempted the President was fricassee, according to one White House chef, the Czech François Rysavy, in his *A Treasury of White House Cooking*. "Lincoln liked the chicken cut up in small pieces, fried with seasonings of nutmeg and mace and served with a gravy made of the chicken drippings. He said that his wife, Mary set a table at the White House, which included such food as aspic of tongue, *paté de foie gras*, turkey stuffed with truffles, and all sorts of wild game, such as venison, pheasant, or canvasback duck. But all too often the President merely picked at his food."

Overdosing in any food can be a killer, even if that particular food may be considered a luxury and on the high end of popularity. Take best-selling author Stephen King. He was raised in West Durham, Maine by his struggling mother, Ruth, after his father, Donald, walked out on the family when the writer was but two years old. "They ate a lot of lobster while Steve was growing up—back then it was considered to be poor man's food," wrote Lisa Rogak in *Haunted Heart: The Life and Times of Stephen King*. "A family would often keep a pot of stew on the stove for several days, reheating it when necessary and adding more lobster meat, potatoes, onions, and carrots when the pot ran low. Though it provided necessary sustenance, many families were embarrassed at having to rely on it. King said of his mother, "If the minister visited, she took it off the stove and put it behind the door, as if he wouldn't be able to smell it, but the smell was all through the house and got in your clothes, your hair." Later, King met Tabitha Spruce from Old Town, Maine in 1968 when they were both writing students in Orono, and they got married three years later.

"Also like Steve, Tabby wouldn't care if she never saw another lobster in her life," explains Rogak. "As a teenager, she worked at a tourist seafood restaurant near Bangor called Lobsterland and often ran the lobster press, where all of the lobster left over from customers' plates was gathered and dumped so it could appear on new plates the next day as lobster salad or lobster roll. She grew to detest the way the stale seafood smell permeated her skin, hair, and clothes, but it was the only work open to her at the time." After Tabby graduated from the University of Maine in June 1971 with a degree in history, often attending classes while she was pregnant, jobs were hard to come by and the only position she could find was working as a lowly Dunkin' Donuts tweenie. More overkill. In time, Steve and Tabby viewed the smell of doughnuts the same way that they viewed lobster. "It was a nice aroma at first, you know, all fresh and sugary," claimed Steven, "but it got pretty goddamned cloying after a while. I haven't been able to look at a doughnut in the face ever since."

Maybe not a donut, but Stephen King, compelled, always eats a big slice of cheesecake before sitting down to write.

17.

MILK, OR, MY LISTENING SKIN RESPONDS

WITH A CREEPING UNDERNEATH IT

Revulsions of food that go back to one's childhood can involve all sorts of subjective trauma, the result of sights and sounds and tastes that queered the pitch, as it were. Country music TV and radio host Ralph Emery to this day admits to not being particularly fond of pork. But he openly despises chicken. A self-styled "picky eater," he explains in his autobiography, *Memories*, "I refuse to eat chicken." It is a bias that goes back as far as when Emery was growing up poor in the piney backwoods of McEwan, Tennessee when he witnessed chickens being slaughtered. "This obsession is rooted in memories of my grandmother taking a pathetic and squawking bird by its head, then twirling it like a lariat," he writes significantly. "Momentarily, she would be left holding only the chicken's head, it would run around the barnyard, propelled by the bird's nervous system. A chicken, newly without its head, will run all over the place, splattering everything in its path with speckles of crimson. My grandmother's decapitated fowl would eventually quiver onto its side, emitting a final flow of blood from its lifeless body. At that point, Grandmother Fuqua [he was raised by his grandparents] would mechanically retrieve the bird and dip it into a kettle of boiling water. The brewing liquid loosened feathers and released a foul stench. It was a filthy and fatal procedure and affects my appetite for chicken today."

You might want to earmark the fact, my well-meaning and earnest organic friends and devoted free-range chicken consumers, that, according to an official 2004 study by the Agricultural Research Service of the USDA, as well as one by the *Journal of Food Protection*, approximately the same percentage (about 20 to 25%) of certified organic and free-range chickens as well as conventionally raised chickens tested positive for salmonella, campylobacter, and shigella.

Air-cooling chickens is a method that helps inhibit the spread of bacteria by keeping all of the chickens independent from each other, and not only saves 30,000 gallons of chlorinated water every day but produces a better-tasting chicken. With no water added, the air-chilled method keeps the "real" chicken flavor and juices. No water is absorbed, so you get the natural flavor of chicken. Conventionally-raised chickens are typically dunked in iced, chlorinated water, which is used to bring down the chicken's temperature after it has been slaughtered, making them spongy and less flavorful. Compare this to air-chilled chickens, which have all been eviscerated, sprayed with chlorinated water inside and out, and then rapidly cooled in cold air chambers in an effort to keep bacteria to a minimum. They also cook quicker than conventionally produced chickens because their meat lacks additional fluids. In the U.S. today, only a handful of smaller plants use the air-chilling process.

A measure of Emery's gastronomic intelligence—or general IQ—may be determined by an anecdote that he blithely offers in the same book. "I remember my grandma Fuqua would give me a teaspoon of coal oil (kerosene) and sugar when I had a cold," he writes. "It wasn't as bad as it sounds, when administered by a single dose. But it was really nauseating after I bragged to my buddies that I could drink a whole gallon of coal oil without ever taking the container from my lips. They said I couldn't. I said, 'Stand aside.' I downed what might have been a pint of coal oil. I put it away in seconds. I threw up for hours."

Growing up on Long Island, the African-American novelist Colson Whitehead to make some money scooped ice cream for three summers at Big Olaf's emporium on Sag Harbor's Long Wharf in the 1980s. "The perk of the job was all the ice cream you could eat, and ice cream was all I ate," he writes in a small polemical essay, "I Scream." He helpfully provides as he writes a small list of his favorite treats: "chocolate in a plastic cup with rainbow sprinkles, chocolate shakes, chocolate ice cream sodas, chocolate twist dispensed by a lever into wavy, brown, short-lived peaks." (Does this rather curiously one-sided and monochromatic list not indicate what in part may be the cause of his pending—and predictable—aversion?) The result of course was inevitable, as who would not have guessed, simply because failing to follow the ancient Roman ideal of nothing to excess, he overindulged in what, almost by algebra, he would very soon come to abhor. Excess is the mother of all execrations, is it not? Whitehead ruefully goes on to explain,

> I was nauseated at the end of each day, but I persisted,
> never suspecting that I was conditioning myself to

hate that which I so ardently desired. My metabolism
is such that I did not suffer any physical effects from
my gluttony. I was cursed in other ways: my aversion
to ice cream spread quickly to most sweets, and then
to all desserts. Birthday parties and weddings force me
to share my tales of Olafian woe with my incredulous
companions, who shake their heads before asking
if they can have my plate. Take it, take it all. Most
people mistake the terrified expression on my face in
our wedding photos as a sign of regret. In fact, my
face records the horror at the knowledge that I must
eat cake at some point or, in the post-cutting photos,
utter revulsion over the spongy clump of frosted hell
scraping through my gut.

We have all experienced the "dessert fascists" he speaks of, aficionados
of sweets who insist on offering one spoonfuls of ice cream or cake, excitedly
cooing, "You have to try this" or "Trust me, you'll like it." He concludes
with the bumptiousness of a normal food aversionist, "Say what you will
about ice cream haters—pity us, condemn us, take us off your guest list—but
we don't need anyone's validation. We are content in ourselves, and at the
feast of life, we happily dine alone."

Tucker Carlson, bow-tied political news correspondent for the right-
wing TV Fox News Channel and conservative commentator, hates baked
beans. Working at the B & M baked bean factory in Portland to help defray
college expenses, he did all sorts of jobs there, mixing ingredients at the
pot-saucing station, scraping charred beans from the inside of ovens, extract-
ing hot cans of brown bread. "One day toward the end of my short career at
the plant, a supervisor sent me to a storeroom on the third floor," he writes
in a melancholy essay, "Bean There:"

Inside there was a pile of hundreds of bean cans, all
of them full. Apparently, some of these cans had bad
seams. It was impossible to know which ones were
defective, but the company wasn't taking any chances. Leaky seams meant spoiled product, maybe even
botulism. You couldn't just throw them away, for fear
that someone would retrieve them from the trash, eat
them, get sick and sue. They had to be destroyed. My
job was simple: puncture every can.

Carlson proceeded to do so with a special spiked tool with inevitable results. "A plume of fermented beans [would] burst forth like a geyser. The liquid was brown and bubbling and smelled like sewer gas. It hit me directly in the face, spraying into my eyes and mouth, and running down the inside of my collar. I felt like screaming, but there were people watching, so I just kept whacking cans. My uniform stuck to me for the rest of the night." There were perks to the job, needless to say. At one point, he was buying cases on the cheap of dented pork-free beans in sauce for three dollars a pop. "Taste changes over time, though," he significantly writes. "I worked there in 1989. I haven't had a baked bean since."

"There is no dignity in the bean," wrote Charles Dudley Warner, the American essayist, novelist, and friend of Mark Twain, with whom he co-authored the novel, *The Gilded Age: A Tale of Today.* Warner was also an inveterate gardener who harbored what might be called a case of "vegetable racism." "Corn, which in my garden grows alongside the bean and, so far as I can see, with no affectation of superiority, is, however, the child of song. It waves in all literature. But mix it with beans, and its high tone is gone. Succotash is vulgar. It is the bean in it."

Lupini beans, yellow legume seeds, now primarily eaten as a pickled snack food, are said never to fill you up because of a curse they received from the Virgin Mary when they hurtfully pricked her legs on the flight to Egypt. Superstition plays well into food aversions. Spilling wine or olive oil prognosticates bad luck among credulous Italians, just as can sweeping at night, finding an open safety pin, descending a ladder, dreaming of old wood, dropping scissors, or buying a new broom in August, to name merely a few from a very long list. I have heard that eating chicken at night on New Year's Eve will surely bring poverty for the coming year!

What foods we avoid, as a convex matter, we greet, in the concave. The only drink that Philadelphia Flyers goalie, Pelle Lindbergh, a Swede, would take during intermissions was a Swedish beverage called "Pripps." Not only must it be that specific drink, but he could drink it only if it had exactly two ice cubes in it; if it was given to him by a specific trainer; and he would only take it from the trainer with his right hand. He was killed after a party in an auto accident, driving drunk. He lingered one day and died on November 11, 1985, age 26.

A nephew of mine told me when he was twenty-three years old a charming story that fits in here. "When I was about 10, my mother who cared about health somehow got it into her head that potassium could only be found in bananas," he said. "So one day she cut up a banana and stuffed pieces of it into my mouth, no doubt thinking she was filling me with vitamins, but I only got nauseous—even panicky—and from that day on, I could never manage to eat one again." His anecdote brought to mind the book, *No Surrender*, the amazing account of the intrepid Japanese soldier, Second Lieutenant Hiroo Onoda, who emerged from the Philippine jungle in 1974 after a thirty-year ordeal dodging the American Army in the deluded if patriotic belief that World War II was still being waged. During those furtive decades, he was driven surreptitiously to kill any available cows that he came across, which he desperately cut up with a machete and roasted in order to survive—the dubious meat or its preparation often sickened him, impeding his breathing and overheating him, so he began to drink the milk of green coconuts as a vegetable substitute—but he explained that bananas were his principal staple food. "I cut off only the stem, sliced the bananas, skin and all, into rings about a quarter inch think, and then washed them thoroughly in water," he wrote. "That way the green bananas lost much of their bitterness. Then I boiled them with dried meat in coconut milk. The result tasted like overcooked sweet potatoes. It was not good. But I ate this most of the time."

There is resonance for all of us in Lieutenant Onoda's resourceful and imaginative methods of coping, instructive as well as being a fact of simple curiosity, that the banana cannot reproduce itself without the help of man. A single banana has no seeds on it. (It also grows upside down, not on a tree—it is an herb—does not grow on branches, has no woody tissue, and is not a fruit but a berry.) Because the domesticated banana plant functions by way of asexual reproduction, workers must help it produce more seeds in order to propagate. Wild bananas originally did have larger seeds, but because people specifically produced it in order to have smaller seeds, so it would be easier for consumption, more palatable, it now has smaller seeds. Those smaller seeds make it harder for the banana plant to reproduce itself.

Notre Dame football coach, Knute Rockne, back in 1927 counseled his players not to eat bananas, or so it was reported in *Time* magazine. Coach Rockne sent in a letter to the editor, reading in part, "The article should have read 'unripe bananas,' as I have no objection to the fruit when it is ripe. I have some very good friends in the banana business, and I would not care to say something about their business which is not true." Rockne cagily stemmed that rumor.

Memorable are the delicious banana breakfasts that British captain Geoffrey "Pirate" Prentice serves to his hung-over soldiers in Thomas Pynchon's *Gravity's Rainbow*, luxurious frappes and glacées made from the homegrown, rooftop bananas that he has cultivated on his rooftop. It is quite an amazing display of culinary imagination. Among the captain's repertoire are:

banana omelets, banana st pas la sandwiches, banana
casseroles, mashed bananas molded into the shape of
a British lion rampant, blended with eggs into batter
for French toast, squeezed out a pastry nozzle across
the quivering creamy reaches of a banana blancmange
to spell out the words C'est magnifique, mais ce n'est
pas le guerre (attributed to a French observer during
the Charge of the Light Brigade) which Pirate has
appropriated as his motto... tall cruets of pale banana
syrup to pour oozing over banana waffles, a giant
glazed crock where diced bananas have been fermenting since the summer with wild honey and muscat
raisins, up out of which, this winter morning, one
now dips foam mugsfull of banana mead... banana
croissants and banana kreplach, and banana oatmeal
and banana jam and banana bread, and bananas flamed
in ancient brandy Pirate brought back last year from
a cellar in the Pyrenees also containing a clandestine
radio transmitter...

Food aversions rarely flare in matters of distress, or so they say. It might
be a truism. Onoda's account proves that. With people lost at sea and stranded on boats for weeks, likewise. Then one thinks of what the trapped citizens
of beleaguered Leningrad had to face during the 900-day-long Nazi siege
of that city in 1941. Starving, they had to resort to desperate measures and
ate anything that came to hand—'yeast soup' from fermented sawdust, join-
ers' glue boiled and jellified, toothpaste, leather, cough mixture, and cold
cream. They licked the dried paste off the wallpaper. Rumors of cannibalism
abounded. Amputated limbs disappeared from hospital theaters. No agony
or torment can compare to that of extreme starvation, nor the extreme measures taken to ward it off, a situation for which, sadly, history has provided
example after example. "*Cummerspeck*" (literally, grief and bacon) is Yiddish
slang for weight gained from mindless overeating due to grief. There were
many instances of Holocaust survivors who developed food problems from
overeating after years of starvation and deprivation, and it was the case with
many war survivors in general.

Audrey Hepburn, born in Brussels, Belgium in 1929, while she was fashion model-thin, had strong memories of a food-deprived fatherless childhood during the war, suffered the opposite problem, for although she was
starving she flirted with anorexia. During the war in the city of Arnhem,

she imagined for herself a fantasy life in order to survive. In her mind, she took the measure of blocking out her need for food and water, because food became scarce and was running out. She became painfully anorexic. The paradox was something she understood.

> I guess I began to resent food around this time. That's a strange thing to say about food—"I resent it." You eat it, don't eat it, like it, dislike it. But resent it? I actually got angry with it for being so difficult to come by and tasting so awful. I decided to master food; I told myself I didn't need it. I could sense it caused my mother great pain not to provide my brothers and me with the well-balanced and beautifully served meals she was used to, so I felt I could eliminate her problem by denying I missed the good things we used to eat. Of course, I took it to an extreme. I forced myself to eliminate the need for food. I closed my eyes to the fact that I was starving.

It was nothing less than tragic. "Jan (her brother) was the most hungry," Audrey painfully recalled. "That was clear. He'd sometimes hold his stomach and cry for food. I couldn't stand another minute of it. I suppose Mother was hungry too, but she was too sad to notice. I, on the other hand, was sure I wasn't hungry. I had that one beaten. The only thing I knew was that I had to take care of them, so I devised this outlandish plan to make money."

In the light of such deprivation, it is somehow loathsome to hear William Grimes, a former restaurant critic of the *New York Times*, archly refer to such common dishes as hash, macaroni and cheese, rice pudding, and the like as "slob food." It is close to contemptible, under any consideration.

As I say, the personal food attitudes of many people, chefs included—revulsions and reveries—were incubated in childhood, borne of those early years when we first encounter them in their many morphs. Chef David Waltuck of Chanterelle remembers eating one too many celery stalks with cream cheese and paprika when he was young. Fresh celery is the "devil's weed" to *Guardian* restaurant critic Marina O'Loughlin. Angela Hartnett, Chef Patron for Murano restaurant and the York & Albany pub in London, cannot stand coriander and desiccated coconut. Floyd Cardoz of Tabla, disliking the sight of them, has refused to eat bananas since the age of 10. When he was named executive chef a while back, banana desserts were actually banned from his kitchen. "Growing up in India, the only fruit we'd have year-round is bananas," he complained. "Banana fritters, bananas in cream, bananas, bananas, bananas." It was just too much for him to take.

I myself never wanted to eat another banana after first watching Andy Warhol's first sound film, *Harlot* (1964), a pointless and inane scatological vehicle for the drag queen and member of the Factory, Mario Montez—the director preferred to call dressing as a woman "going into costume"—who in this dopey movie grotesquely fellates one banana after another. (As a "very religious" Roman Catholic Puerto Rican, Montez, according to Warhol in his book, *POPism*, thought that, although being in drag was a sin, if God really and truly hated such a thing, He would have struck him dead.) Mark Ladner of Lupa shares a loathing for bananas but for a different reason. "It might be from all that banana Bubblicious I ate in the '70s," he said. The opinions of these chefs are recorded by Oliver Schwaner-Albright in in his bright article in the *New York Times*, "I'm the Boss, And I Say No Lentils."

We eat with memory, of course. Who would deny it? The mind concentrates intensely on what it has received to feel, to think, to know, to savor. There is a balancing pause that takes place. "Would 'mother's cooking' still taste so wonderful if we ate it for the first time and not, as it were, commemoratively?" asks art expert and culture maven, Bernard Berenson, in his published diaries of 1947–1958, *Sunset and Twilight*. One entry on September 7, 1954, after taking in what he felt was an immoderate repast the day before, the 89-year-old writes,

> Perhaps I indulged too much (for my poor stomach)
> in mushrooms at luncheon. I like their smooth texture
> and earthy taste, and I eat them (ever so rarely) be-
> cause they recall soups made with mushrooms that as a
> very little boy I used to enjoy so much in Lithuania."
> [He was born in Vilna in 1865]

In 1866, visiting the Hawaiian Islands, Mark Twain felt pretty much the same way, writing, "Bananas are worth about a bit a dozen—enough for that rather overrated fruit." He had problems with other fruits in the Pineapple State. "Mangoes and guavas are plenty. I do not like them. The limes are excellent, but not very plenty. Most of the apples brought to this market are imported from Oregon. Those I have eaten were as good as bad turnips." Many readers of Twain are unaware that in 1884 he was at work on a novel about Hawaii, part of which was to focus on the leper colony on the island of Molokai. He never finished this book, for unclear reasons, although seventeen pages of the novel are still extant. Oh, and it is with sharp disgust that lovely Rosalind Reynolds (played by Esther Williams), kidnapped and flown to a Pacific island by a mooning Lt. Lawrence Y. Kingslee (Peter Lawford) in *On an Island with You* (1948), refuses his offer of food with a rancorous, "I hate bananas!"

One must not fail to mention, regarding bananas, the ramifications of their stomach-filling effect in J.D. Salinger's short story, "A Perfect Day for Bananafish," when Seymour Glass, honeymooning in Florida with his shallow new wife Muriel, whom he calls "Miss Spiritual Tramp of 1948," while wearing his bathrobe chats with little 4-year-old Sybil Carpenter on the beach about the tragic breed of fish who swim through a hole in a cave in order to eat the bananas there, only to gorge themselves until, becoming so fat, they cannot exit the hole:

> "Miss Carpenter. Please. I know my business," the young man said. "You just keep your eyes open for any bananafish. This is a perfect day for bananafish."
>
> "I don't see any," Sybil said.
>
> "That's understandable. Their habits are very peculiar." He kept pushing the float. The water was not quite up to his chest. "They lead a very tragic life," he said. "You know what they do, Sybil?"
>
> She shook her head.
>
> "Well, they swim into a hole where there's a lot of bananas. They're very ordinary-looking fish when they swim in. But once they get in, they behave like pigs. Why, I've known some bananafish to swim into a banana hole and eat as many as seventy-eight bananas." He edged the float and its passenger a foot closer to the horizon. "Naturally, after that they're so fat they can't get out of the hole again. Can't fit through the door."
>
> "Not too far out," Sybil said. "What happens to them?"
>
> "What happens to who?"
>
> "The bananafish."
>
> "Oh, you mean after they eat so many bananas they can't get out of the banana hole?"
>
> "Yes," said Sybil.
>
> "Well, I hate to tell you, Sybil. They die."
>
> "Why?" asked Sybil.

"Well, they get banana fever. It's a terrible disease."

I understand that bananafish were ordinary looking, not curved like bananas but straight, to negotiate what we commonly think of as a round hole. There are no straight bananas, right? I once heard it from no less an authority than Tiny Tim with his ukulele back in 1970 when he sang in concert "I've Never Seen a Straight Banana" in the Albert Hall in London. It is an old novelty song from 1926—popular with buskers—written by Ted Waite and popularized in 1927 by Fred Waring and His Pennsylvanians who had the hit recording, which went:

> I've seen lots of funny things in my time
> But there's one thing I've been trying hard to get
> For years and years and years I've kept on searching
> But I haven't had the luck to see one yet
> Although I haven't seen one you all know the thing I
> mean
> And now I'm going to tell you what it is I haven't
> seen
>
> I have never, never, never, never
> I've never seen a straight banana
> I've searched quite a bit
> But I must admit
> They're even curved when they are served in my
> banana splits
> I have seen them by the car loads on the Delaware and
> Tijuana
>
> But I have never, never, never, never
> I've never seen a straight banana
>
> [spoken]
> Oh how much I've been yearning to see that straight
> banana, though unfortunately I've had no luck... in
> fact...
> I recall when I was in Alaska
> I have seen the sun at twelve-o'clock at night.
> I've seen the waterfalls at old Niagara
> I confess it is a most impressive sight.

I'd love to see a certain thing
But if it's not to be,
I'd like to meet somebody else
Who saw what I can't see.
I've never, never, never, never
I've never seen a straight banana.

Though there are things I hate
Millions I have ate.
But doggone me I've yet to see
Bananas that are straight
I have traveled far to find one.
From the Argentine to the Havana.

But I've never, never, never, never
I've never seen a straight banana.
No I've never, never, never, never
I've never seen a straight banana!

Salinger himself in real life, in what often seems to be in an unhinged way, was a bit of a frenzied obsessive about many things, especially food. He was a true "foodie." He once confided to Lillian Ross, "A man must have aunts and cousins, must buy carrots and turnips, must have a barn and woodshed, must go to market and to the blacksmith's shop, must saunter and sleep and be inferior and silly." Writers, he believed, had trouble meeting such needs, and he referred to Flaubert and Kafka, negatively, as "two other born non-buyers of carrots and turnips." Young Joyce Maynard who at 18 went to live with the strange, older, reclusive 53-year-old writer for nine months in Cornish, N.H. in the early 1970s, later lamented in her memoir, *Looking Back* (1973), a book he took as a betrayal and for which he never forgave her for writing, that by his fiat they lived on little but a diet of raw peas and cucumbers.

In another book, *At Home in the World*, Salinger, as depicted by Maynard, emerges as a peevish curmudgeon, dedicated to the practice of homeopathic medicine and so obsessed with the other strictures of his diet, mainly raw fruits, vegetables and nuts, that he forced himself to throw up whenever he ate something bad. One rigid regime seemed to follow another. She writes,

> We had a very set routine—the things that we did and
> the foods that we ate—and the times that we did these
> things. We were very early risers. The first thing we
> did was have a bowl of frozen Birds Eye Tiny Tender
> Peas, not cooked, but with warm water poured over
> them so they'd defrost a little bit, so they were just
> cool... [Salinger] was a believer in raw food; he was
> actually way ahead of his time in many ways.

Another Salinger dinner favorite was lamb patties—undercooked. "I started to sneak food. I borrowed the car and went to the supermarket," confesses Maynard, "and then... ate three yogurts in a row, followed by a bag of popcorn or half a pack of Fig Newtons. And, though I knew by this time how to make myself throw up (a skill the man had taught me), I couldn't get rid of everything I took in. I ceased to be so thin. Maybe I was a normal weight, but I felt gross, unlovable and ashamed."

One would normally conclude that Jerry Salinger would have found fast food unspeakably bad and done everything to avoid it—but you would be wrong. In 2011 there emerged a packet of newly discovered letters (50 letters, 4 postcards) that were written to one of his old friends from the 1930s, an Englishman named Donald Hartog. In the pieces, Salinger alludes to coach trips they made to Nantucket, Niagara Falls, and the Grand Canyon and in the process of doing so shows that his tastes were utterly unfussy and mainstream. He even confidently states that he thought Burger King burgers were better than those from other chains!

Fast food betrays in a sense an aspect of leveling, the same way that the flat income tax in Russia where everybody is obliged to pay 13% of their income is a false equality and clearly unfair. There is a touch of cult and an air of whiggery to the devotees and menu-memorizing pursuivants of fast food ("but what is Whiggery?/ A leveling, rancorous, rational sort of mind/ That never looked out of the eye of a saint/ Or out of drunkard's eye," wrote W.B. Yeats in "The Seven Sages") and to all those large-scale, clown-endorsed, sloganeering juggernauts with standardized food and standardized ingredients and standardized cooking and standardized production methods. No wonder they have drawn criticism and concerns, ranging from claims of negative health effects to alleged animal cruelty to cases of worker exploitation to cultural degradation by way of shifts in people's eating patterns away from traditional foods.

I find places—any places—where people, usually jumped-up loonies, willingly line up for anything somewhat frightening *in and of itself.* It is what has always put me off about that growing multitude (about 5,000) in Bethsaida who had gathered around Jesus to be fed. Notice that initially Jesus Christ "withdrew by boat privately to a solitary place," but the crowd followed, and so, relenting, he fed them because they had all gathered for a free meal. There was also that day in Nazareth when, in the local synagogue, Jesus read a text from Isaiah, commenting on his own Messiah-ship, ironically promising the locals there—his neighbors—that they would get no special consideration from God, infuriating the large assembly who had assumed they were favorites and so, gathering against him, sought to kill him. It is right there in the Holy Book, all of it. Traditionally, Christians presumed that the Sermon on the Mount was given by Jesus to a great, devoted multitude seated on the grass. On close inspection, however, this is not the case. Most were hungry, others curious, and no doubt it was an aggregate of many idlers. The truth of the matter can be deduced by considering what immediately precedes the sermon itself:

> And there followed him great multitudes of people
> from Galilee, and from Decapolis, and from Jerusalem,
> and from Judaea, and from beyond Jordan. And
> seeing the multitudes, he went up into a mountain:
> and when he was set, his disciples came unto him:
> And he opened his mouth, and taught them, saying.."
> (Matthew 4:25–5:2)

In actual fact, Jesus went atop the mountain to get *away* from the crowd rather than to teach them. When his disciples came to join him atop the mountain, he taught them, but not the multitude he had left below.

Canadian novelist Robertson Davies loved meatballs, but as he wrote in his entry, "On Meatballs," in *The Papers of Samuel Marchbanks*, there was "only the True Meat Ball," a crucial distinction, at least for him, that he fussily drew between "[meatballs] prepared in an open pan and tasting of meat [and] the False Meat Ball, prepared in a pressure cooker and loathsomely studded with raisins." Davies went on to clarify for the unenlightened, "The pressure cooker is all very well in its way, but there are some dishes with which it cannot cope, and the meat ball is one of them." False Meat Balls to him gave off a taste, which he imagined "a particularly forgiving Anglican missionary would have in the mouth of a cannibal."

Davies who cared deeply about food suffered much of his life from what the British call a "gippy" tummy—"troubled by my tripes," as he put it, writing in October 1989 to the famous physiologist Horace W. Davenport, an educator at the University of Michigan who had laid a foundation for more effective ulcer treatments by revealing how gastric acid works in digestion without consuming the stomach itself. Dr. Davenport's textbook, "*The ABC of Acid-Base Chemistry*," taught an entire generation of medical doctors about how the body regulates acids and alkalines, and of their highly delicate interplay in the bloodstream. "Sometimes I used to wonder if I had not eaten more barium meals than Christmas dinners," wrote Davies. "For a time I was in the hands of a man who liked to dig into my arsehole with a tiny scoop, to secure what he called 'a bolus of stool,' which he then tested with litmus. It was always acid, as I could have told him, for at the very thought of him my whole digestive tract turned sour."

It was Davies' fascination with another of Dr. Davenport's text-books, namely *Doctor Dock*, that led to several exchanges between the two about a man who ate so many bananas in the course of a cure that he got impossibly stopped up with, well, what Davies called "Banana shit."

Regarding food, it is almost amusing to encounter fixed fury. Chef and cookbook author Marcella Hazan truly hated cinnamon, ketchup, all frozen foods ("cemeteries of food"), cranberry sauce, coffee cake, Champagne, and goat cheese on pizza. Victor, her husband, despised chicken almost as if he feared it and all of his life refused to eat a fowl of any stripe, no matter how it was cooked.

Can one call hatred what is intemperate?

An ungainsayable truism in the matter of food aversion does support Hippocrates' theory that "everything in excess is opposed to nature." Moderation, in most cases, has to be learned, often painfully. To prefer things in measure, sadly, is not natural to man. Hollywood actor Burt Reynolds, no seer, hedonistic in his high-flying days, after a history of bankruptcy, wastrelism, tax troubles, and alimony payments, did live wistfully into his poorer old age wisely to reflect,

> There isn't anything, no matter how good it is, or how good it tastes, or how much fun it is, where too much is good for you. It can destroy you. And you have to learn. It's a hard lesson. But you have to learn to back off and do as good as you can in your chosen profession. And don't screw it up. And the best way to screw it up is having too much of a good thing.

But moderation impinges on freedom.

The food phobic is neither left-brained, obvious, or cogent.

Logic is a meddler, a buttinski, a math snool, a second-guessing priest of juddering ratiocination with authority and no power, unable to attack, an unforgiving slave of obligation with no allegiance to any single subject. It discovers nothing of the reports it makes with the drone of a robot. Nor has reason bounty. It is a skinflint with alligator arms that never picks up a check, a horizontal fall. Its demands will have been—future perfect, imperfect result—always part of its terror. The food phobic needs self-rule, lift and height, the freshness of wind, and declares with St. Prerogative, "*Et non potest impediri.*" (I will not be hindered.)

The phobic's brute ownership of passionately insisting on his right to refusal provides him his only personal sanctuary.

Jeanette Winterson in her memoir, *Why Be Happy When You Could Be Normal* writes, "I realized something important: whatever is on the outside can be taken away at any time. Only what is inside you is safe."

18.

AWW, SHUCKS!

Word-master and linguist Willard Espy hated oysters. "As a kid I was drowned in them. We seemed to have them for every meal. Even oyster pie. I cannot stand the sight of the damned things." Who can forget the classic short subject *Dutiful but Dumb* (1941) in which Curly, funniest of the Three Stooges, orders an oyster stew only to find in the middle of the bowl a defiant bivalve with a splash snapping up each and every cracker that he pops in it? Pulling out a revolver he wildly fires bullets at it about twenty times, getting the attention of the Vulgarian guards—three guys named Click, Clack and Cluck, paparazzi-like photographers in a foreign country working for *Whack* magazine —who promptly capture the Stooges and carry them off, upside down, on the bayonets of their guns. I remember reading in *The Enchanted Places*, Christopher Robin's memoir of his very strict and censorius father, A.A. Milne, which revealed a good deal about the son's many grievances, high among which was his deep and abiding loathing for fish-paste sandwiches, wafer-thin crust-less triangles that despite the fact that he hated them he was always being given at tea time.

Young Jack London at age 6 once got roundly shinwacked, stopping to sip some beer while bringing a pail of it to his step-father, a daily chore that he was given to bring the man some refreshment while he was in the midst of plowing fields—and the boy became violently ill. Later in a life of great familiarity with alcohol, London's preference was never beer. What about oysters?

> One day, after I had been eating them for about five
> years, the question was asked [Did I like them?] No as
> a matter of fact, I didn't. I'd much rather have a nice
> thick crust of bread and perhaps a tomato.

The subject of oysters is intriguing. It is a particular food—would it be the sliminess of them?—that is strangely and utterly abhorrent to many, although the caustic English writer, Saki (H.H. Munro) once had the effrontery (cf. John Lennon on Jesus) to remark, "I think oysters are more beautiful than any religion." He added, "They not only forgive our unkindness to them, they justify it, they incite us to go on being perfectly horrid to them. Once they arrive at the supper-table they seem to enter thoroughly into the spirit of the thing. There's nothing in Christianity or Buddhism that quite matches the sympathetic unselfishness of an oyster." King George I of England was fond of oysters, but always refused to eat them—go figure—until they had begun to spoil. (Could His Majesty have been misunderstood due to his inability to speak English?) Ambrose Bierce in his *The Devil's Dictionary* cynically defined them as "a slimy, gobby shellfish which civilization gives men the hardihood to eat without removing its entrails! The shells are sometimes given to the poor." William Makepeace Thackeray once actually compared eating an American oyster to "swallowing a baby." When the painter Salvador Dali was offered his first raw oyster to eat, he visibly shuddered and exclaimed with disgust, "I'd as soon eat a piece of Mae West!" All of this negativity, mind you, despite the indisputable fact that oysters, cooked or raw, are usually listed as #1 on every aphrodisiac potency poll, although no one ever seems to mention the physical passivity of this tasty delicacy.

A cousin of mine at a Christmas family feast a few years ago, where delicious piles of Wellfleet oysters were served, cheekily whispered to me, with a wink, as I began shucking them, "If you check out one of these things under a microscope it looks like the traffic pattern of Manhattan at rush hour."

Novelist Norman Mailer loved good Wellfleet oysters and, examining the empty shells, personally enjoyed the sport of finding faces in them, in relief. It intrigued him. At one of Mailer's favorite restaurants, Michael Shay's in Provincetown, waitresses often boxed a pile that he had selected to take home. "He cleaned them and then put them out on his deck to bleach," writes J. Michael Lennon in *Norman Mailer: A Double Life*. "On each shell he saw the suggestion of a Greek warrior, or a long-dead beauty. He had Norris [his wife] touch up the features with paint and photograph them. He thought they might make an interesting book."

At the end of his life, oysters—almost an obsession—were virtually all Mailer ever ate. He was a foodie to a degree and was fussy about what he put in his mouth. A man who badly needed attention, his desperate need for love may be partially explained by the oddity of having been married six times. Impossible to count were the many extra-marital affairs he had that lasted to the end of his life. He was a mama's boy, born into a privileged and effete middle-class world, forcing him by default to aspire to become a more manly man, an alpha male (boxing, head-butting, stabbing a wife, writing about killers, etc.) I happen to know that the novelist disliked plastic for some reason, in any form, packages so wrapped from noodles to vegetables, salad dressing to cheese, meat to soda pop in a plastic bottle. Microwaving anything wrapped in plastic sent Mailer up a tree. The concept of corporate hustling, of fast food, of any short-cuts, irked him. I visited with the man several times at his home in Provincetown when I liked to bring him a box or two of almond toffee coated with Belgian milk chocolate or dark chocolate and roasted hazelnuts made by the Trappistine nuns of Mount Saint Mary's Abbey in Wrentham, Mass. which he came to crave.

Dwayne Raymond, author of *Mornings with Mailer*, used to cook for him and witnessed something of the precisian in him, the occasional cranky fussbudget he could be. "There was a long period of time when he favored having only a grapefruit for lunch. It had to be a white grapefruit, however, never pink," writes Raymond. "He preferred it cut a certain way; halved, scored around the sides to separate the flesh from the skin then sliced into at least nine precise 'V' sections. The slices would float freely in a pool of juice in the 'skin cup,' so at the end, one was rewarded with a satisfying drink."

Raymond saw certain aspects of Norman Mailer on the food side that most people never had the chance to see in his lifetime. "He considered the cutting of grapefruit, or a particular way of cooking fish, beef, mushrooms, soup and broccoli with as much vigor as he approached concepts of man's place in the universe. Few know he deliberated, while lying in bed chasing an increasingly elusive capacity to sleep, how to intermingle flavors. Habitually he would tell me he had mused about blends of tastes, puzzles consisting of seasonings, in dark hours of the morning and forced himself to remember to tell me in the light of the next day."

Oysters seemed to engender nothing but disgust in young Marcel, the narrator of Marcel Proust's *Remembrance of Things Past*. When we find him dining with Mme. Villeparisis and his grandmother at the dining-room of the Grand-Hotel in Balbec, the narrator shows himself a distinct ostrophobe—put off by that seafood—but then later in the resort restaurant at Doncières with Saint-Loup, the ideal nobleman and military man, along with his fellow officers, among men, it seems by the description that Marcel has eaten oysters there. Has perhaps the cultured painter, Elstir, whose renditions of sea and sky, by the way, echoing the novel's theme of the mutability of human life—a character supposedly modeled on James McNeill Whistler—hoping to broaden his outlook, in the interim, taught Marcel to try them? Franc Schuerewegen in his splendid essay, "Monsieur Marcel's Gay Oysters," in the anthology *French Food* (2001) analyzes a gay subtext for this seeming change or contradiction.

"I don't fish, cook, dance, endorse books, sign declarations, eat oysters, go to analysts, or take part in any demonstrations," professed the lordly novelist Vladimir Nabokov who cultivated a long list of private peeves that in his rather low-brow way he, a supremo, presumed it high-brow always to keep on bright display. ("What is your position in the world of letters, Mr. Nabokov?" he was once asked. His humble reply: "The view is pretty good from up here.") A vain, patronizing man, he badly needed to matter. "I loathe such things as jazz; the white-hosed moron torturing a black bull, rayed with red; abstractionist bric-a-brac; primitivist folk masks, progressive schools; music in supermarkets, swimming pools; brutes, bores, class-conscious philistines, Freud, Marx, fake thinkers, puffed-up poets, frauds and sharks. I also loathe go-go gangs, jungle music, and science fiction with its gals and goons, suspense and suspensories. I don't get drunk or go to church." This stuffed-shirt was not a "class-conscious philistine," right? With a winking condescension, Nabokov always concluded his taxonomies by saying, "I'm a mild old gentleman, very kind."

When in the musical *Roberta* (1935) John Kent (Randolph Scott) says to Huckleberry Haines (Fred Astaire), "You don't appreciate her. I know she seems a little hard and sophisticated, but underneath she's a pearl." Haines replies, "And a pearl, so I'm told, is the result of a chronic irritation on an oyster." I bother to mention the fact in my treatise here because in this musical the entire suave cast makes manifest in their stylishness the elegance of sophisticated oyster eaters. When Ginger Rogers rests her pretty head on Fred Astaire's shoulder as they elegantly dance "Smoke Gets in Your Eyes," it is surely one of the high watermarks of dancing in movies, as far as I am concerned, and as one of the truly glistening moment of defining beauty and elegance of the entire 1930s it makes the whole movie worthwhile. Pearly King and Queen, in the shuck and click of graceful movement, open to perfection just like an oyster and with a similar lure of luminescence, white, pure, classy, stylish, clear, and true, also flow thin with liquid beauty. I herewith toast them with a glass of sparkling white wine. I will add, as to refinement, that in *Roberta* Astaire pronounces the word *debut* correctly—a rare thing in any context—not "debout" as with the French word "standing upright," nor the ugly "day-byoo." Such style seems to have long flown.

In the film *Yankee Doodle Dandy*, James Cagney, playing George M. Cohan, correctly refers to vaudeville as "voh-de-ville"—in *The West Point Story* he also properly pronounces the word poems "poyems," not the usual dopey 'pomes"—just as in the film *Casablanca* Humphrey Bogart classily gives the drink the French "bore-bun" instead of the more common and slovenly "burrbun." E.M. Forster in his novel *Howard's End* inveighs against the "clipped" words and "formless sentences" of what he called the new "language of hurry." I remember with particular horror a fat, banana-nosed lawyer in ballooning purple shorts and wearing a wide Mexican sombrero on the beachside portico of the Princess Hotel in Acapulco, howling to his wife, "Heyyy, Gafnit, look, *booooola-baize*!" But at times it can be a tough call. Was novelist Joseph Conrad right or wrong when driving around the Kentish lanes at a belting pace with his son, Borys, to refer to the model car he was driving as a "Cadiyac"?

Sobakevich, the fat landowner in Nikolai Gogol's *Dead Souls*, who with a hacking fork and knife eats turkeys the size of a calves, gigantic pastries, and half a saddle of mutton in a few bites, is nevertheless another individual who cannot stand oysters. A huge glutton with a face as round "as a Moldavian pumpkin called *gorlyanki* from which balalaikas are made in Russia" who consumes food by the slab—devouring a whole sturgeon "in a little over a quarter of an hour," right down to the tail, is one of his boasts—he eats anything, all of it "fare fit for some uncouth giant," in the words of Vladimir Nabokov, who adds that his "prandial metre is the Homeric one." Still and all, Sobakevich shuns oysters—and also turnips. Gogol writes, "Such delicacies as oysters and frog's legs are revolting to the crude palate of Sobakevich, and the idea of diet is incomprehensible; he describes it as curing people of hunger. As a man obsessed by solid flesh, he can think of nothing more worthless than a steamed turnip." Eating only solid food—lunks, chunks, hunks—fat Sobakevich's food aversions extend to food lacking in consistency, for it is the case with him that anything soft, insipid, or slimy is, to him, food "it is already eaten." Gruesome!

Gogol, at least in his classic Russian excesses, is a fascinating study on the subject of food aversions. In his writings, he shows himself to be obsessed with food, which in the eyes of many over-heated critics, at least regarding the semiotics of eating, show not only his lack of interest in sex but a deep, sublimated desire for his mother. (Gogol never married, and his work is devoid of any sexual passion.) All of his novels and tales are replete with descriptions of dinners, dishes, scenes of tables groaning with salmon, pork, cheesecake, pickles, fish head pie, tripe served with the borscht, pelmeni, radishes cooked in honey, pumpkins, dumplings, blini, and hot, steaming soups. Much of his satire, many of his metaphors, most of his attention revolves around food, which is often the hobby-horse of many of his characters. In *Dead Souls*, critic Marc Slonim counted eighty-six varieties of food. It is therefore somewhat surprising to learn that at the end of his short life—he died at 42—Gogol, becoming scrupulous, began to question the ethics of his work in general and self-indulgence in particular, a complete reversal of his former self coordinate with a heightening religious consciousness and search for God. Rebuking himself for what he saw as his own lavish excesses and pages of self-gratification, he sought direction under the guidance of the zealous starets, or monk, one Fr. Matvei Konstantinovsky, who became his mentor. In consequence, "Gogol began to refuse food during the Butter Festival (the Russian Maslenitsa, or Shrovetide), an entire week of merry-making and indulgence when Russians traditionally gorge themselves before the start of Lenten Fast," writes Darra Goldstein in her definitive article on Gogol and food, "The Hunger Artist: Feasting and Fasting with Gogol" in *The Global Gourmet*, June 2008. In an attempt to cleanse body and soul, he enacted a voluntary penance, a kind of spiritual anorexia, denying himself, praying, and following ascetic practices. His appetite vanished. With a sense of sinfulness for all of his imaginative work, he burned some of his manuscripts, which contained most of the second part of *Dead Souls*, and even went on a pilgrimage to Jerusalem.

What makes anything valuable is simply that someone desires it—so went the guileful reasoning of greedy, self-indulgent Sobakevich as the mercantile premise for his selling dead souls. Of that venal character, Gogol observed just about the worst thing a Russian novelist could say about one of his own creations: "No soul whatever seemed to be present in that body." (Sobakevich's name derives from the Russian word for dog, sobaka.) Gogol became convinced that his stomach was malformed and upside-down and complained to a friend, Mikhail Pogodin, "My hemorrhoidal illness has spread to my stomach." He began to tremble, fearing his soul was in jeopardy. It was against his own body, its insatiable demands, that Gogol now turned. He renounced the pleasures of the flesh and began to fast. "He ate less and less: a few spoonfuls of kasha or borscht, a piece of holy bread, a glass of water. His legs could hardly carry him, and still he called himself a gluttonous pig," wrote biographer Henri Troyat. Novelist Ken Kalfus in a 92nd Street Y lecture gives us a vivid account of Gogol's end:

> The doctors were called in. Their attempts to save him from self-starvation were well-meaning, brutal and absurdly inept. The suffering man was told to rub his stomach with alcohol, drink cherry-laurel water and take rhubarb pills to relieve constipation. He refused, instead multiplying the icons to which he genuflected. They tried mesmerism. After that failed, "Gogol was

seized bodily and thrust into a tub of hot water, while a servant poured hot water over his head. Then he was put naked into his bed and Dr. Klimentov applied a half dozen leeches to his nose." They forced a cup of bouillon down his throat. They inserted a soap suppository.

Struggling with the Devil, as Gogol described it, he took to bed, flatly refusing all food offered him, and died in great pain. Simon Karlinsky in his biography *The Sexual Labyrinth of Nikolai Gogol* argues with some persuasion that Gogol, whose fear of and distaste for women—images of them re-appear in his work grotesquely compared to food (buns, doughtnuts plums, sour cream) —was a closeted, fiercely repressed homosexual. He associated food with Satan. In his story, "The Fair at Sorochintsey," Satan appears as an old woman selling bagels.

William E. Gladstone, Prime Minister of England, loathed oysters. So did actress Joan Fontaine, who once took to bed for three days after eating only one of them on the half-shell. Actress Shelley Winters, who loved to eat just about anything, hated Oysters Rockefeller and unequivocally stated, "They're awful—raw caviar and raw oysters." The fey singer Prince not only hated white fish—an excerpt from his song, "Animal Kingdom" goes, "It's why I don't eat red meat or white fish/ Don't give me no blue cheese/ We're all members of the animal kingdom/ Leave your brothers and sisters in the sea—but would also never eat oysters. Nor does comic filmmaker Woody Allen, who in an often-quoted remark said, "I will not eat oysters. I want my food dead—not sick, not wounded—dead." Novelist Stephen King told *Bon Appetit* magazine (July 2013), "I'm not a fan of anything slippery or slimy. I don't eat oysters. It's horrible, the way they slither down your throat alive." Nor would the late comedian George Carlin truck with oysters. In one of his routines, he ranted,

And oysters. I cannot eat oysters—or clams—not for the reason you mention, which is "Uuuuuuh!" but because when I look at an oyster, I think, "Hey! Somebody lives in there! That's somebody's little house! I'm not going to break in on somebody just to eat them." Come on! We've got laws against that. That's "breaking and eating," I believe. Don't get me wrong. If an oyster slips and falls out of his shell, I'll eat that *********** in a minute! I got no mercy

on a clumsy mollusk. But I'm not going in after somebody. Hey, he might be making a pearl. He might
have just brought home a Heathkit and cleaned off
the tabletop. Not my job to mess with an [echo effect]
oyster's... oyster's... oyster's!

It was no different as to lobsters and crabs with Carlin. Shellfish or crustaceans (not the same!) made him uneasy. "Lobsters and crabs; they don't
look like food to me either. Anything that's crawling toward me, sideways,
with big pincers, you know? Hey, that don't make me hungry! In fact, my
instinct is, 'Step on that ****! Step on that big thing, before he gets to the
children!' They look like they mean business. Frog's legs. I can never order
them. I keep wondering, what did they do with the rest of the frog? What do
they do? Do they give them little dollies and send them back out onto the
street to beg? You know? Try to return them to a normal life? The trouble is,
the 'Dollies for Froggies' program is underfunded. Boy, they're doing something with them. You never see it on the menu: 'Frog Torso.'"

The French refuse to eat oysters with milk. While they will consume
the gizzards, lungs, and brains, including the limbs, right down to the jelly inside the hooves of an animal—they enjoy *ris de veau* (a calf's thyroid)
and *jarret de porc* (back of a pig's knee)—it is no go with oysters in milk.
Aucun moyen ne comment. I have earlier referred to the finicky attitude over
food and general snobbery of V.S. Naipaul in matters of what he would and
would not eat. In his early novel, *A House for Mr. Biswas*—were these his own
tastes?—he has the main character, sick of vegetarian food, boldly try eating
oysters with hot sauce. After overdosing on the little creatures (he eats 26 of
them), the poor novice becomes severely ill. Naipaul writes, "The raw, fresh
smell of oysters was now upsetting him. His stomach was full and heavy, but
unsatisfied. The pepper sauce had blistered his lips. Then the pains began."

Actress Jennifer Lawrence, star of the film *The Hunger Games*, in an interview in 2012, singles out oysters as the one outstanding food she would
not touch. Yet, ironically, of the many there are, there is no food that could
possibly be cleaner or, in the sense of being self-contained, purer than an
oyster. It seems to matter little nevertheless to those who are so revulsed by
them, and the group is not small. T.E. Lawrence, the celebrated Lawrence
of Arabia, wrote in a letter (January 4, 1929) to Ernest Thurtle, "I will
eat anything except oysters and parsnips." Screen actor Charles Laughton,
a great big walloping fat man and a huge eater, utterly detested oysters. He
declared, "I only ever ate one once at Scott's Fish Restaurant in London,
and I swear it flipped when it went down." Heiress Gloria Vanderbilt told

me that she has always disliked oysters. She also hates calves brains, identified as *cevette de veau* on menus in restaurants, and dislikes "sweetbreads," which are listed as *ris de veau*. Neither will she eat caramel custard, and she fussily added, "Soft-shell crabs have to be very, very small." She shook her head. "Otherwise—no!" As to custards in general, curmudgeonly Ambrose Bierce despised any and all custards. His creative definition of one? "A detestable substance produced by a malevolent conspiracy of the hen, the cow, and the cook."

"I was eating, with my sister Pat and my mother, in Oscar's Fish Restaurant on the East Side of New York. 1972," Stephen Dixon told me, sharing a reminiscence. "I remember: we'd come from seeing my father in Mt. Sinai Hospital. We shared a dozen oysters. The oyster which I chewed—I realize that one is not supposed to do so—and swallowed, because I didn't want to spit it out at the table, was foul, and had tasted foul the moment it entered my mouth." He continued,

> My sister and mother urged me to go into the men's room and stick my hand down my throat and throw up the oyster. I could not, for reasons mentioned, though did go into the men's room to wash out the foul taste in my mouth. I went to bed that night thinking I had poisoned myself. Nothing happened. I fell asleep and woke up well and swore off eating any raw meat of any kind for the rest of my life. In Maine, in 1985, my wife and some of our friends collected mussels on the shore of the beach house our friends were renting. They boiled them for dinner that night. I refused to eat them. I didn't trust the mussels. They all got sick from the mussels. I took care of Anne that night and the next day, as well. She continued to eat mussels at restaurants and those she picked off the rocks in Blue Hill Bay and never got sick from them again. I continue [to this day] to avoid all shellfish except sautéed scallops. For no good reason I trust them if they're sufficiently overcooked.

Raw oysters, just like raw meat or lively raw milk cheeses, can be dicey in the food department and can test high for the dangerous listeria monocytogenes. Sarah and I happily buy our oysters by the dozen on Cape Cod at a "special place" for 66 cents apiece, but nowadays oysters are all so relatively small that you never get the sense of any great taste when eating them. (Cape Codders are notoriously mum and mean-spirited about the source of where lobsters can be pulled out, where best to go clamming, where to purchase the meatiest oysters, etc., a habit which I despise, but I do not want to implicate our vendor here, either.) Roy Blount pronounced, "I prefer my oysters fried; that way I know my oysters died."

Oyster purists insist that raw molluscs be eaten pure, in an unadorned state. No lemon. No Tabasco. No leek butter. No cocktail sauce. No white wine. No wine vinegar. No shallots. No sausages. No astringent tart flavors or fey *mignonette granité*. Nothing. An oyster-borne typhoid fever that started on Long Island but that spread killed 150 in the winter of 1924-25, with as many as 1,500 people taken sick. The esoteric modern dancer Isadora Duncan, nevertheless, credited the oyster (by way of her mother) for the spirited performances that, barefoot and barely be-draped, she later brought to the stage with bravura, stating, "Before I was born my mother was in great agony of spirit and in a tragic situation. She could take no food except iced oysters and champagne. If people ask me when I began to dance, I reply 'In my mother's womb, probably as a result of the oysters and champagne—the food of Aphrodite.'"

"Are there really foods that we don't like, or just foods that we haven't liked yet?" asked a former *New York Times'* restaurant critic, Frank Bruni in "A Taste You Hate? Just Wait" in the "Dining and Wine" section (February 24, 2014). He offers both beets and oysters as a personal example.

> Suddenly, what had once seemed slimy now seemed silky, and a shade of crimson previously lurid to my eyes was positively gem-like. I began to lust for beets, no doubt partly because chefs were serving them with cheeses like Cabrales. You could crumble Cabrales on Brillo and I'd have seconds. There was a lesson here, and I heeded it, reconsidering other foods that I had tried and rejected as a grown-up and had consigned, perhaps foolishly, to the compost heap of history. Oysters, for example. For a long, sad stretch of time, they did nothing for me. I find that mystifying today, at the age of 49, when I could have an oyster omelet for breakfast, an oyster sandwich for lunch and an oyster roast for dinner. My only gripe would be the absence of oyster gelato for dessert... No cauliflower for him. No broccoli for her. This Mary won't have

even a little lamb. That Larry won't touch skate. All
of them assume that their predilections are as rooted
as redwoods, as fixed as eye color. And all of them are
wrong, because appetite isn't just or even mainly physiological. It's psychological. Emotional. It's a function
of expectation, emulation, adaptation.

There is certainly nothing new in Bruni's observation, "Our attitudes toward, and responses to, certain foods can be altered enormously by the con-
texts in which we encounter them, the number of other people we see eating
them, the way they do or don't dovetail with the diets we mean to maintain."

Jo March's cooking in Louisa May Alcott's *Little Women*—and, remember, she is the novel's heroine—is famously ghastly. She burns the toast, her
potatoes are all under-cooked, the asparagus disintegrates at the top ends
while the lower stalks stay hard, the blancmange is lumpy, and her little pots
of fruit and cream are so bad her sister Amy takes a mouthful, chokes, covers
her face, and flees. Open a jar of olives! As to that particular fruit—it is not
a vegetable, by the way—it is likely that the grumpy essayist William Hazlitt
disliked them, when we find in his writings that he crossly compares them
with an author he abhors. "There are people who cannot taste olives—and
I cannot much relish Ben Jonson, though I have taken some pains to do it,
and went to the task with every sort of good will. I do not deny his power
or his merit; far from it, but it is to me of a repulsive and unamiable kind."
Of olives, Elizabeth David has gone on record as insisting smaller ones taste
better.

The English virtually do not know what olives are. Koreans hate olives.
The French have almost stopped growing them. Italians are now importing
vast quantities of olives from Greece and Morocco, today the biggest producer of olives, followed by Greece and Spain. Strange, no? The olive is one
of the plants most often cited in western literature. In the *Odyssey*, the hero
crawls beneath two shoots of olive that grow from a single stock, and in the
Iliad (xvii, 53 ff) we find a metaphoric description of a lone olive tree in the
mountains by a spring. It was one of the few foods that the Roman poet
Horace ate in his own chaste diet, which he describes as very simple: "As for
me, olives, endives, and smooth mallows provide sustenance." The olive tree
and olives which are mentioned over 30 times in the Bible, in both the New
and Old Testaments, were not only sacred for the oil burnt in lamps and one
of the rare fruits promised to the Jews in Canaan, but olive wood was used
to build the Temple of Solomon. It was an olive leaf that a dove brought
back to ancient Noah to demonstrate that the deluge was over. No, the olive

is ageless. Lawrence Durrell in *Prospero's Cell* wrote that olives have "a taste older than meat, older than wine. A taste as old as cold water."

Frank Sinatra who believed that all dairy products caused phlegm—the bane of any singer—swore off using any milk and cream for years. He also would never touch soft drinks, as the carbonation caused gas and bloating. FDR hated to have cream put in his coffee. Singer Lionel Ritchie and actor Billy Bob Thornton suffer from bad allergies to dairy products. The pompous, self-cherishing gourmand and bon vivant Mr. Lucius Beebe—he was also a noted photographer, railroad historian, journalist, infuriatingly fussy and difficult diner (or a "Leona," after the so-called "Queen of Mean" Leona Helmsley, as they say in the restaurant business) and syndicated columnist—along with hating children whether tethered or on the loose, confiscatory taxes, going second class, and the gullible American public, frequently went on record as utterly despising milk, except with "a liberal infusion of proof spirits." (We shall be speaking more of Beebe anon.) Punk singer Iggy Pop is allergic to milk. "Cream … is the very head and flower of milk," sourly wrote Tobias Venner in his *Via Recta of 1620*, "but it is somewhat of a gross nourishment, and by reason of the unctuosity of it, quickly cloyeth the stomach, relaxeth and weakeneth the retentive faculty thereof, and is easily converted into phlegm, and vaporous fumes."

One also recalls how much Violet (Ann Sothern), secretary to Ross Hunter, hated milk in the movie, *Will Success Spoil Rock Hunter?* (1957). James Beard in his memoir *Delights and Prejudices* (1964) unequivocally states, "My earliest hate was milk." The curmudgeonly gourmand goes on to say, "I loathed milk, cold or hot. It simply couldn't be made attractive to me as a drink. And if occasionally a zealous adult with standard notions about growing children forced me to drink a glass, I promptly became sick. It has never failed to be an effective emetic for me, and I am still revolted when I see people drinking milk with a good meal."

The writer Okakura Kakuzo, a Japanese Buddhist and scholar, author of *The Book of Tea*, found the western habit of consuming milk, which is taken from the "interior of a cow," as well as butter and cheese, a nauseating practice. (He also found dancing morally repugnant "where men and partly disrobed ladies embraced intimately in public, whirling their bodies around and stamping to the sound of loud and strident music until all hours of the morning.") I suspect he would not have dined with Samuel Pepys, whose love of dishes of cow's udder was irrepressible.

Agatha Christie has gone on record as positively detesting "the taste and smell of hot milk." She abhorred every kind of alcoholic drink and alcohol itself, "except in cooking." Among other food dislikes of hers were marmalade, oysters, and all lukewarm foods. (She loved food and had a very good appetite, by the way.) This famous mystery writer, who was selectively and rather eccentrically phobic, had in various interviews also stated that she particularly hated cigarette smoke, all crowds, any and all protracted talking, noise, and—yes—"the feet of birds, indeed the feel of a bird altogether." The feet of birds? *Hello?* Food aversions. What about the skin of custards, killer viruses, the eyes of murderous sharks? When it comes to the matter of foods, nothing at all is predictable, everything quite unpredictable. There can even be found in Thomas Pynchon's novel, *Gravity's Rainbow*, an attack on a British candy: wine-gums. I mention this only because it happens to be my favorite candy. I not only love wine-gums, but personally claimed in print ["American Candy," *Harper's* (February 1982)] that it was far and away the best candy on the planet. A Pynchon character says, "The other day I had one of these things they call 'wine jellies.' That's their idea of candy, Mom! Figure out a way to feed that to Hitler 'n' I betcha the war'd be over tomorrow."

On the subject of sweets, incidentally, Henry Ford quite queerly feared that the sharp crystals of granulated sugar would cause internal bleeding in his stomach! Had he nothing else to preoccupy him?

By the way, a posthumous essay by the late eccentric French writer Georges Perec was published in *Granta 52*, and it consists of nothing more than a detailed record of his food and drink intake during 1974. The editors, who state that he cannot have enjoyed fish all that much—in that, after 365 days of eating, he lists only 41 fish dishes that he consumed—glaringly fail to take note of one item that is never mentioned at all—candy. There is something wrong there, no?

Milk is far from everybody's delight. "Milk drinker!" was baseball manager Casey Stengel's dismissive—and disgusted—descriptive phrase for any guys, his own players included, who refused to drink alcohol and, by extension, it was his word for anyone who in his opinion was a wuss. Actor George Brent (*Dark Victory, Jezebel*) loathed milk. In the dumb movie, *Will Success Spoil Rock Hunter?* (1957), as the result of a two-timing boyfriend who is a milkman, Violet (Joan Blondell) hates milk. Was it not Max Apple in *I Love Gootie* who writes, "Milk is fine. If you want to wake up the worms that are lying in your intestines just waiting to torture you"? "Oh dear I cannot drink goat's milk, never, never," said Gertrude Stein, who owned a goat, whom she named "Bizerte," because she acquired the animal on the day of that big war offensive in November 1942, as well as a treasured white poodle, "Basket." Stein wrote, "They always say look at him you would take him for a sheep." In any case, Stein had no trouble with cow's milk, which she drank with no small avidity. How about the gruesome habit of drinking a combination of Pepsi-Cola and milk together? It was none other than Laverne DeFazio's favorite drink on the '70s TV sitcom, *Laverne and Shirley*! No one repudiated milk drinking, of course, more than the bibulous comedian and movie curmudgeon, W.C. Fields. "My illness is due to my doctor's insistence that I drink milk, a whitish fluid they force down helpless babies," Fields famously remarked.

Who can forget in *Never Give A Sucker An Even Break* (1941), his last movie, one that he wrote under his comic pen name, Otis Criblecoblis, when, landing in the nest-like dwelling of the beautiful Ouliotta Delight and her ghastly mother, Mrs. Hemoglobin, a woman whom he later courts, he downs several snorts of 100-proof goat milk—"Nanny goat's milk," clarifies Fields, who, lighting a cigar, finds in the proximity of his liquid breath a two-foot flame leaps out! Transcendentalist Bronson Alcott of Concord, Mass., eccentric founder of the commune "Fruitlands," scorned all humans for the consumption of milk—he excoriated all of the communists at Brook Farm for drinking it—simply because he believed that milk belonged to the calf itself, in the same way that wool was the rightful property of sheep.

Weird Norman Bates in *Psycho* (1956) psychotically cannot utter the word "bathroom" in front of his female visitor—are not all Momma's Boys characteristically subjected to cloacal fears?— and twitchily proceeds to offer Marion Crane a repast of "sandwiches and milk." It is specifically what his overbearing mother, as her son was growing up—which he of course never fully or finally managed to do—would have offered the poor, raddled, demented boy whose hideous disconnects are endless and whose dependencies on mommy cannot end even in death. There was also lovely Sarah Brown, the dedicated Salvation Army soldier in the hit musical *Guys and Dolls* (1955), who orders milk in Havana, much to gambler Sky Masterson's dismay, until through a leisurely trick he seduces her into drinking several alcohol-laced *dulce de leches*. One may also remember, in that same musical, tough Harry the Horse telling wise-guy fellow gambler, Nathan Detroit, "Just because Big Julie drinks milk, don't get the wrong idea." (All devoted readers of Rex Stout's Nero Wolfe stories know that tough guys do drink milk—was it not the favorite drink of that tough detective?) I also love that scene in *That Touch of Mink* (1962), when Cary Grant cannot get to sleep and cheerful Doris Day helpfully suggests, "Try buttermilk," how the sophisticated Grant dryly, archly, replies, "I'm not that eager to get to sleep."

Perpetual sleep may be what Johnnie (Cary Grant) has in mind when playing the possibly murderous husband in *Suspicion* (1941) and walking slowly (and what seems fatefully) up the long staircase he brings his wife,

Lina (Joan Fontaine), a glass of milk before bed, which she is too afraid to drink. It all ends well, but I have always felt that the ambiguous plot top-heavily by far pointed to her death.

On another episode on the Travel Channel, we find Andrew Zimmern, again ("If it looks good, eat it!") wandering through Chile, where he stops to drink a glass of warm donkey milk—straight from the teat, no less, you know, while wearing like a shield that cold, staring, shit-eating cockiness that promulgates his "only-real-men-do-this" bit. "All things in delicate equitable showers," as Walt Whitman says, right? I could not take it. I cannot take *him*. An onlooking peasant, grinning, unconvincingly proceeds to hold up three fingers, slyly to indicate—Zimmern smirkily divines this—that one gulp could power three great fucks. "Liquid Viagra," Baby Huey Zimmern mutters and walks out of the shot. It all seems so staged, so continuously, theatrically, arranged. But as to the tit-to-table milk? Our babies Shenandoah and Shiloh love it, but not me. I like chocolate milk, curiously enough, but white milk? I've personally got the "Milk 'Em in the Morning, Feed 'Em, Milk 'Em in the Evening Blues."

As to Zimmern, I gotta say that His Moose-ishness makes me think of the Maasai by way of *lucus a non lucendo*. While as I have said, he looks like an adult Baby Huey (or, well, at least a *gnoccho*)—he wobbles about and jiggles around with a swinging gut suggesting denial-state fatness—the sleek Maasai, tall, trim, and elegantly spare as any Giacomettian figure, appear as fluid as water in their graceful movements and are so beautifully built. They are not only known for their endurance and bravery but resemble tall, slim lustrous girls, at least to me, for do they not often move and stand like them in almost effeminate, half-draped attitudes? To see a handsome, tall, glistening tribal warrior proudly polishing the tip of his hunting spear with animal fat is surely to behold two distinctive works of art. Tallness alone has beauty. No, Zimmern lends himself much more to parody than to provender.

I have mentioned earlier that Maasai warriors do not drink milk alone, nor will they ever drink anything in their parents' houses or eat meat out in the open, rather only in forests—three tribal taboos. "Baba, will you drink milk?" is among the Maasai the traditional offer of hospitality to you. You may be given rancid cheesecake made from sour milk, cattle's blood and a dash of urine if you enter their manyatta, the cigar-shaped mud hovels that they live in. Milk is sacred to the Masaai. In many of their rituals, milk is drunk, sprinkled from a gourd, or spat from the mouth to give a blessing, as Igor and Valerie de Garine explain in *Drinking: Anthropological Approaches*. (The authors' analyses of the milk production of African pastoral peoples is brilliant.) The Maasai rarely take milk and meat together, however. Before a woman of the Maasai retires, she always makes certain that her milk gourds (different sizes and different shapes have different names) are placed on her bed, clean and ready for the morning milking. The first quantity of drawn milk is sacrificially thrown from the gourd into the sky. The Maasai then make supplications, "God give us a good dawn!" "Let our heads live long!" "Give us always wet heads!" (Dry heads are dead). A young would-be elder who has not yet performed the ritual of *enduruj* (a taboo which forbids him to have sex with circumcised women or to eat or drink in their presence) is never allowed to take a drink of milk in front of any women. When he does drink his milk, all women have to go out of the hut. When he has finished drinking, he calls her back. The Maasai drink milk once in the morning and once in the evening. They say, "We go to drink milk (*emaapeti aok kule*)," even if it is tea with milk, thin porridge or thick porridge.

Milk also remains a repulsive, off-putting drink to many people in the consuming world. Actress Gertrude Lawrence confesses in her autobiography, *A Star Danced*, that she simply could not stand it that, much as she loved him, her husband, Richard Aldrich, habitually drank a glass of cold milk every morning. (Fancy what her comment would be upon learning that John F. Kennedy, according to Ted Sorenson, "drank vast quantities of milk.") Alcoholic Van Heflin in *Johnny Eager* (1941) at one point after hours of boozing is given a glass of milk by Robert Taylor and, after several revolting glugs, mutters, "It is hardly a nectar of the gods." Regarding JFK and his efforts to convince Americans to drink milk, he commented in February 1962, "I am certainly enjoying being with you newsmen this evening. None of you know how tough it is to have to drink milk three times a day." When the French photographer Eugène Atget developed stomach problems late in life and was advised to take only milk, bread, tea, and sugar for his midday meal—he believed all other foods were toxic—with a convert's zeal he broadcast this food list as the sole salutary form of nutrition, only one of the man's quixotic habits, but it was one that badly weakened him. He spent his last years a semi-recluse, sitting on piles and piles of astonishing photographs. ("Orthorexia nervosa" is the general label designated to those people who are concerned about eating healthy foods. Characterized by disordered eating, fueled by a desire for "clean" or "healthy" foods, those diagnosed with the condition are overly preoccupied with the nutritional makeup of what they eat.)

It has often struck me that many of the current American health and dietary concerns of the last few decades—e.g., alarming tocsins blown over the consumption of red meat, sugar, or smoking—while in large part reality-based and passingly legitimate also reflect an unwitting post-1970s

American cultural resuscitation of the late 19th- and early 20th-century German and Austrian *Lebensreform* ("Life-Reform") movement, a middle-class German attempt to palliate the ills of modern life deriving from the growth of cities and industry through alternative life-styles such as natural and herbal medicine, vegetarianism, nudism, self-sufficient back-to-the-land rural communes, and abstinence from red meat, alcohol, and tobacco to restore themselves to a healthier, more natural existence. Some *Lebensreform* groups and advocates were liberal, but others overlapped with the vigorous anti-modern, reactionary, grass roots, "*Voelkisch*" movement often seen as a precursor of Nazism, and some *Lebensreform* advocates who came to California in the early 20th-century are also said even to have influenced or inspired the later hippie movement, "natural living," and communal lifestyle.

The Chinese associate milk with excreta, of course. Indeed, there are a good many people who, shunning all dairy products as unhealthy, begin their punch-list with milk. It looms to many a worried mind as a prevalent food taboo. I have to say that whenever I see it drunk in quantities—the way, for example, that in the war movie *The Young Lions*, when going off to the service and saying goodbye to his wife, Hope Lange, on the front steps in an early morning street scene, Montgomery Clift, meeting the milk-man, takes a loud gulp of milk from a bottle, while the pie-faced milkman in an inexplicable cinematic moment boasts that he himself drinks "two quarts a day"—I feel vaguely nauseous and must admit, to quote a line from Edwin Arlington's poem "Merlin," my "listening skin responds with a creeping underneath it." A memorable Abbott and Costello movie, by the way, delightfully shows us fat, goofy Lou, nervously scarfing pickles on a park bench—he has been incompetently wooing a pretty girl—and continues with his usual fluttering discombobulation, here dipping the pickles in milk. *Aaaarghhh!* Needless to say, the mumbling comedian becomes suddenly ill!

It may be noted finally that the commonest act of the so-called evil eye— the Italian *malocchio*—is to turn good milk sour, although many other and widely varied curses are called down in its name. "The *malocchio* is a milky thing," writes Anthony Burgess in his essay, "Evil Eye," noting,

> The eyes of those who see too much, like Homer and
> Milton and James Joyce, are turned into miniature
> saucers of milk. Oedipus, who had looked on his
> mother with desire, tore out his eyes rather than let
> the gods make them lactiform. In the Balkans, milk
> has everything to do with the evil eye. Its posses-
> sors are those who, having been weaned, go back to

their mothers' breasts. This they learn of the dual,
or [Austrian-born British psychoanalyst] Melanie
Kleinian, mother—the one who comforts them with
milk and the one who strikes them when they bite.
But the malocchio tradition only exists in ectolactic
communities, steady static societies which till the fields
and keep cows.

Snobbish English writer Nancy Mitford, a xenophobe, belittled Greek food, American food—although never once bothered to visit the United States—and even French food, writing in the *Sunday Times* (August 6, 1961), "The French consider that horses are useful. When the soil is wet, they produce manure and can eventually be eaten, none of which can be said of the tractor." The most hate mail that she ever received was in response to her article in 1962, "The Other Island," a hatchet piece in which she not only vilified her neighboring country of Ireland as a rude, brainless outback "where they wash your hair backwards," pronounce the word boutique as "bowtike," and "scrape manure off their trousers with knives," but annoyingly explained, "A typical Irish dinner would be: cream flavoured with lobster, cream with bits of veal in it, green peas and cream, cream cheese, cream flavoured with strawberries." One wonders how lovely blancmange failed to make an appearance in her memorable list.

Blancmange, that sweet dessert unknown in this country but served in England, is white mush that is commonly made with milk or cream and sugar thickened with gelatin and, as I recall, was widely mocked and frankly despised, at least when I was living there—a sentient, table-sized, extragalactic blancmange pudding figures as a flying object in several Monty Python sketches from the 1970s—and Terence Scully, a food scholar, has proposed the alternative etymology of "*bland mangier*," reflecting its often mild and "dainty" (in his context meaning fairly refined) taste and popularity as a dish for the ill. Imagine a recipe that begins "Break an ounce of isinglass into very small pieces," the first ingredient of blancmange, a substance obtained from the dried swim bladders of fish which is a form of collagen used in blancmange before the inexpensive production of gelatin. Blancmange does not exist in France, either as a word or as a sweet. Are you surprised? For that matter, moreover, neither do the words *bon viveur, savoir-faire,* or *object de vertu*. It is amazing how vocabulary does not cross the Channel. The farcical word "epergne" can be found in no legitimate French dictionary—it is called a *surtout* in that country, a word oddly meaning a frock coat in England. "*Pot-pourri* is a medley of tunes, not musty dried rose leaves in a bowl; a *porte-manteau* is a coat hanger and a *chiffon* is a duster; what we call chiffon is [to them] *mousseline de soie*," noted Mitford in her "Paris Column" in the *Sunday Times* (Feb. 1, 1953). She ridiculed other peculiar maladaptions by the English. "Raconteur, which in England connotes wit, in France means one who insists upon telling long dull stories," she explained. "'Cul-de-sac' has not been used [in France] since the eighteenth century; a street with no exit is an *impasse*. *Bijou* is not an adjective. Nobody has ever heard a French audience shout '*encore*!'"

Beyond that, there are a good many food-related French words that have no specific English translations at all, certain words that you will rarely hear an English person rely on to explain anything, a few of them being *casson-ade, gibier, patte, ravier, tartine, panade, bouffer* (to wolf down food), and écoeurant, something that is too rich or too sweet that borders on the cusp of nauseating. There is something symmetrical in the not unrelated fact that there are also many American ingredients rarely used in France, foods such as corn, sweet potatoes, molasses, brown sugar, pine nuts, pecans, avocados, limes, American wines, and bourbon, as Madeleine Kamman observes in her highly educational cookbook, *The Making of a Cook*.

The pickle, we'll agree, stands as the #1 candidate in all bad-food-combination stories (see above) as well as the standard freako-outlandish go-to food item of every pregnancy-craving in the case of all mothers-to-be, whether in movies, books, or real-life. When in *Susan Slept Here* (1954), a fatuous film directed by the dependably stupid and talentless vulgarian Frank Tashlin, in which an old, wrinkled, hair-dyed Dick Powell (actual age 50), playing Mark, preposterously marries a nubile Debbie Reynolds (actual age 20)—it is the only feature film in Hollywood history ever to be narrated by an Academy Award!—and when Susan is found at one point eating strawberries and pickles, Mark's friends of course assume she is pregnant. Susan eventually confesses to Mark that she just happens to like that combination, silly! After having an Oscar statuette introduce itself and invite us into Mark's apartment, you believe that you have reached an all-time low—that is, until you hear Dick Powell, the successful *screenwriter*, *seriously* utter the thudding line, "I don't sleep good."

If you have any questions about where Hollywood taste lies, this movie was nominated for an Academy Award! Oscar being anthropomorphosed hardly surprises me. Is he not the only friend in Hollywood people truly seek? "Nobody really knows anybody here," said actor Rod Steiger in a *Playboy* (July 1969) interview. "Above all, Hollywood is a community of lonely people searching for even the most basic kind of stimulation in their otherwise mundane lives."

Strawberries and pickles. I have a serious suspicion that in the end combinations of disparate foods lurk in the imagination of many as the source of their food aversions, an unholy bringing together of swinish inequities, which reminds me of Noël Coward's comment after watching the cinematic abortion, brutal with alterations and omissions made in 1949 by MGM of his 1929 operetta, *Bitter Sweet*—"a tenth rate endeavor"—when he said that watching actors Jeanette McDonald ("insane coquetting") and Nelson Eddy ("stocky, flabby heaviness") was "like watching an affair between a mad racing horse and a rawhide suitcase." I believe I can assert with full confidence that a worse gastronomic trifecta cannot be found anywhere other than in Edward Gorey's *The Loathsome Couple*, where we read, "They sat down to a meal of cornflakes and treacle, turnip sandwiches, and artificial grape soda."

Sugar haters today, however, fight a losing battle. One 12-ounce glass of soda alone contains up to ten teaspoons of sugar. An ironic fact is Americans are actually getting fatter, however, on low-fat, high-carbohydrate diets, confidently gobbling food-like substances with the misguided notion that over-processed food is healthy. In her book, *Pandora's Lunchbox*, Melanie Warner, who broadly defines processed food as the kind of things one cannot make at home, maintains that the human body literally cannot handle—physically cannot healthily receive—the stuff. Foodstuffs that claim to be healthy, like breakfast cereals, low-fat frozen meals, energy bars, and vitamin-packed snack foods are not only not healthy but through lab-created fiber, chemical alteration, genetic modification, artificial flavors, all transformed so that they can come in consistent shapes and sizes and that mold cannot touch, can last for a year or years on shelves! It is scary. Even snacks like pita chips, onion-flavored rings, and cereal bars, which pretend to wear the halo of good health, are revealed to be as bad for you as Doritos or Snickers. "When corn oil and chips and sugary breakfast cereals can all boast being good for your heart, health claims have become hopelessly corrupt," writes Pollan in his *In Defense of Food*. "The American Heart Association currently bestows (for a fee) its heart-healthy seal of approval on Lucky Charms, Cocoa Puffs, and Trix cereals, Yoo-Hoo Lite chocolate drink, and Healthy Choice's Premium Caramel Swirl Ice Cream Sandwich—this at a time when scientists are coming to recognize that dietary sugar probably plays a more important role in heart disease than dietary fat." Scandalized by the "Western diet," Pollan goes on to say,

> Only the power of the sugar lobby in Washington can explain the fact that the official U.S. recommendation for the maximum permissible level of free sugars in

the diet is an eye-popping 25 percent of daily calories. To give you some idea of how permissive that is, the World Health Organization recommends that no more than 10 percent of daily calories come from added sugars, a benchmark that the U.S. sugar lobby has worked furiously to dismantle.

Nathan Pritiken (1915–1985), the American nutritionist and longevity research pioneer, hated sugar. Diagnosed with heart disease in the 1950s, he engaged in a low-fat diet that was high in unrefined carbohydrates, a regime that became known as The Pritikin Program for Diet and Exercise. In the early 1980s, he began to suffer severe pain and complications related to what was a decades-long fight with leukemia. He was a porcupine of warnings, a-sprout with caveats. "Don't eat sugar" was only the beginning. Don't eat salt. Don't eat fat. Don't drink coffee, or tea. Don't eat hot dogs. Do not eat any cheese, hamburgers, peanut butter, crackers, pies, pastries, honey, syrup, avocados, nuts or olives. Avoid cholesterol like the plague. Eat toast without butter, salads without oil, no chicken livers, egg-yolks. Lunch for him consisted of water-sautéed vegetables tucked into an egg-white omelet, and maybe a whole-wheat muffin. A fanatic, he was probably one of the greatest food haters that ever lived, despite his concern—his almost Ahabian concern—for good health. He ran four to five miles daily. He was never ill. Suddenly he became sick. This peevish man, practically a cadaver, saw that his diet did not work for him in terms of longevity and, despairing when he lost control of his own vigorous body, the 69-year-old guru of low-cholesterol diets decided life without health was not worth fighting for. The chemotherapy he had been undergoing to treat his resurgent leukemia failed. When he died, it was discovered at the autopsy that his veins were amazingly unoccluded. Studying the body, Dr. Steven Inkeles, the medical examiner of the Pritikin Center, said that he was astounded at the superb condition of Pritikin's heart. Said the doctor, "He had the arteries of a pre-adolescent boy."

A paradox played out here. In what virtually constitutes an Aesopian fable, the studiously exacting man who had paid such extreme attention to his body unfortunately had at the same time ignored his *soul*. He failed to heed the Greek ideal (μέδέν αγάν), which is also the Latin ideal (*ne quid nimis*), which also invokes the Christian ideal: temperance. Pritikin had not the trace of a spiritual life. He committed suicide: sending his family out to dinner, he took up a scalpel and, severing both of his brachial arteries, he bled to death in his hospital bed.

I cannot help but think of the writer James Agee when the subject of cholesterol and bad diets is raised. He was fat and loved to eat and suffered two serious heart attacks in his life, the second one fatal. Still, he went on chain-smoking and drinking hard until he died, age 45, in a taxicab on his way to a doctor's appointment. As for food, let one quotation suffice—cited by his biographer Laurence Bergreen—as his small but tidy *apologia pro cibus*. "Let the doctors prescribe their low-fat, 1200 calorie a day diet, he [Agee] would continue, 'fiercely to enjoy what I eat.'" "Fruits bore me sick," Agee complained. Salads, he said, "leave me cold." The writer much preferred to scarf down high-cholesterol cheese. "I abominate health foods," he declared. As for fish, "Between Fridays and the Coast of Maine, I've had enough sea-food to carry me well past the grave..." At one point Agee portentously remarked, "The mere attempt to examine my own confusion would consume volumes." As to Agatha Christie, or at least mystery writers in general, it is perhaps worth noting that fictional detectives never seem to have very distinguished food tastes—for all the many personal details touching on them in so many novels (art collecting, hobbies, favorite music, brands of whiskey, finances, etc.), food invariably goes unmentioned—simply because the poor bastards are always smoking, pipes, cigarettes, Philip Marlowe with his Camels, Philo Vance with his Regies, Lord Peter Wimsey with his Whifflets, Jules Maigret, like Sherlock Holmes, with his pipe—he keeps a rack of fifteen of them in his office at the Judiciare on the Quai des Orfèvres beside the Seine and is rarely seen without one clamped between his teeth, his hands thrust deep into his coat pockets—Sam Spade who chain-smokes, and so on and so forth. At least they were real cigarettes. What book on food aversions can ignore what had to be the worse fags on earth—Brendan Behan's. He wrote, "The Bible was a consolation to a fellow alone in the old cell. The lovely thin paper with a bit of mattress stuffing in it, if you could get a match, was as good a smoke as I ever tasted."

Both Leslie Charteris and his detective character, Simon Templar, called "The Saint," heartily relished the good life, enjoying as often as possible the best of foods and wine. (Charteris actually wrote a column for *Gourmet* for several years.) Too, monocled, Lord Peter Wimsey, the well-educated creation of Dorothy L. Sayers, a true gentleman and Eton graduate, was an expert on food (especially wine), as well as a man excelling at playing the piano (Bach especially). We never really see him at table, dining in full array. Where food is concerned, Georges Simenon's Jules Maigret, the fictional French police detective, is also a gourmet, with favorite dishes of his including *pintadeau en croute and fricandeau á l'oseille*.

As to detectives and food, Sherlock Holmes' diet, if one can even speak of it, was of the sparest. He seemed to shun all foods in favor of the strongest tobacco at least fifty percent of the time. When he finally did eat, did he choose animal proteins—a side of cold beef, bacon, oysters, a brace of partridges—with cups of tea and the occasional bit of bread? Watson frequently makes note of Holmes' erratic eating habits. The detective is often described as starving himself at times of intense intellectual activity, such as during "The Adventure of the Norwood Builder," wherein, according to Watson, "[Holmes] had no breakfast for himself, for it was one of his peculiarities that in his more intense moments he would permit himself no food, and I have known him to presume upon his iron strength until he has fainted from pure inanition." Throughout the many episodes recorded of him, he never seems to eat. He is obviously quite thin. Had he an eating disorder of a kind, or is it really just like Sherlock says in the series that eating distracts him while working? What about drugs? In any case, Holmes in his linearity fits the kind of intense, brooding, slightly over-fervent type of food niggard. They are none of them *menefreghisti*—they are never carefree, don't-give-a-damn types but people who live in what I like to call the world of the question mark.

Nero Wolfe, Rex Stout's world famous detective, would be the polar opposite of Sherlock Holmes in terms of the gastronomic. He views much of life through the prism of food. Wolfe cannot bear to see a meal rushed. Regularly scheduled mealtimes for lunch and dinner are part of Wolfe's daily routine. He also has a rule, sometimes bent but very rarely overtly broken, against discussing business at the table. He knows enough about fine cuisine to lecture on American cooking to Les Quinze Maîtres (a group of the 15 finest chefs in the world) in *Too Many Cooks* and to dine with the "Ten for Aristology" (a group of epicures) in the story, "Poison à la Carte." Wolfe has a personal chef, Fritz Brenner, and does not enjoy visiting restaurants—with the occasional exception of Rusterman's, owned for a time by Wolfe's best friend, Marco Vukcic. In *The Red Box* (chapter 11), Wolfe states, "I know nothing of restaurants; short of compulsion, I would not eat in one were Vatel himself the chef." All his gustatory requirements are met in the privacy of his sacred brownstone or scarfheim!

A tubby private eye—he is a moose and weighs between 310 and 390 pounds—Wolfe is both a gourmand and a gourmet, enjoying generous helpings of Fritz Brenner's cuisine three times a day. Fritz is an exceptionally talented Swiss cook who prepares and serves all of Wolfe's meals, except those that Wolfe occasionally takes at Rusterman's restaurant. We frequently hear Archie Goodwin, the narrator of the stories and Wolfe's energetic live-in assistant, typist, and dedicated foot-soldier, describing the detective as weighing "a seventh of a ton"—a vivid if caricaturing detail, but one soberly intended to indicate unusual obesity at the time of the first book (1934), especially through the use of the word "ton," which is why the detective, in Goodwin's periphrastic words, "limits his physical movements to what he regards as the irreducible essentials." So enormous is Wolfe that from necessity he restricts even the scope of his visible reactions; Goodwin says, for example, "He shook his head, moving it a full half-inch right and left, which was for him [Wolfe] a frenzy of negation."

Fritz also acts as the household's majordomo and butler. His living quarters are in the basement of Wolfe's famous brownstone, where he keeps 289 cookbooks, the head of a wild boar he shot in the Vosges, and commemorative busts of Escoffier and Brillat-Savarin, as well as a cooking vessel thought to have been used by Julius Caesar's chef. Archie and Fritz get along well enough, and Archie often spends time in the kitchen, as he puts it, "chinning" with Fritz. Fritz's relationship with Wolfe is generally one of respect and admiration, except for those occasions when they quarrel over a recipe. The notoriously finicky Wolfe has even gone so far as to refuse to eat one of Fritz's dishes, when the chef to season starlings uses tarragon and saffron instead of sage. Starlings, yes—Nero Wolfe has a Roman Emperor's gluttony!

Shad roe is a particular favorite of the detective's, prepared as it is in a number of different ways. Goodwin himself enjoys his food but lacks Wolfe's discerning palate. He laments in *The Final Deduction* (chapter 9) that "Every spring I get so fed up with shad roe that I wish to heaven fish would figure out some other way. Whales have." Shad roe is frequently the first course, followed by another of Wolfe's favorite dishes, roasted or braised duck. Archie Goodwin also complains that there is never corned beef or rye bread on Wolfe's table—are we to conclude he dislikes them or scarfs them?—and so he sometimes dodges out to grab a corned beef sandwich at a nearby diner. But in "Cordially Invited to Meet Death," a young woman gives Wolfe a lesson in preparing a dish of corned beef hash. A contradiction: in *Plot It Yourself*, Archie goes to the diner to eat "fried chicken like my Aunt Margie used to make it back in Ohio," because Fritz does not fry chicken. But in *The Golden Spiders*, Fritz serenely proceeds to prepare fried chicken for Wolfe, Archie, Saul, Orrie, and Fred.

Wolfe displays an oenophile's knowledge of wine and brandy, but it is only implied that he drinks either of them. In *And Be a Villain* (chapter 17), he issues a dinner invitation and regrets having done so on short notice: "There will not be time to chamber a claret properly, but we can have the chill off." Continuing the invitation, Wolfe says of a certain brandy, "I hope this won't shock you, but the way to do it is to sip it with bites of Fritz's apple pie."

Upon leaving Nero Wolfe's luxurious brownstone on West 35th Street in downtown Manhattan brings us smack into another New Yorker.

The illustrator Saul Steinberg, famous for his brilliant if idiosyncratic *New Yorker* drawings, wonderfully imaginative cartoons, delicate and spidery, and those many lovely magazine covers, disliked American food in all its forms. He insisted that most of it was governed by the taste of children—spaghetti, pizza, hot dogs, hamburgers. "Speak into the clown's mouth," as my friend Chuck Timlin, used to quote sarcastically as every so often we squired his happy kids to local fast-food emporia for a treat in Wallingford, Ct. It was Steinberg's opinion that the only good meal that one could get, nationwide, was breakfast, with its solid, predictable fare: eggs, bacon, omelets, pancakes, hot coffee, orange juice. Sitting down at a table replete with breakfast provender, Steinberg was always merry as a marriage bell. It represented pure happiness to him, a substantial table of food he understood. He would notice everything! In his opinion, the nicest waitresses (he was at heart a womanizer) were in the Midwest.

A natty dresser and highly fastidious man—highly alert to smells especially—Steinberg was widely traveled but, according to his biographer Dierdre Bair, he dismissed outright the food of Milan, Odessa, England, Turkey, and Spain. He felt disgust seeing a person drink beer directly from a bottle, so offended that such a thing would make him leave a chosen hotel. Whenever and wherever he traveled, Steinberg usually ate breakfast three times a day. It will come as no surprise that he especially loved eating in diners, for the booths, the service, the quaintness, the informality. "Diners, cars, girls" defined the America that he first encountered.

Diners are also Charles Bukowski country. A heavy drinker, the "Buke" was, like most dipsos, never much of an eater, and he took in food mainly because he had to do so to live. His rumpled and battered alter ego, Henry Chinaski in the novel, *Pulp*, bleakly reflects, "Teeth. What goddamned things they were. We had to eat. And eat and eat again. We were all disgusting, doomed to our dirty little tasks. Eating and farting and scratching and smiling and celebrating holidays." Bukowski—and Chinaski—lived in and loved cafes and diners. There are few better evocations of a respite from the cold, painful confusion of life than his mysterious poem, "Nirvana," the skeltonics of a lost young man who on a bus stop finds peace in the sanctuary of a cafe in North Carolina. It is something of a moral fable set in a food context ("He ordered and the/ food arrived/ the meal was/ particularly/ good/ and the/ coffee.") An unaffected waitress, a crazy fry-cook, and a laughing dishwasher in that small place all become endearing to him. It is in essence an anti-food aversion story.

> he wanted to stay
> in that cafe
> forever.
> the curious feeling
> swam through him
> that everything
> was
> beautiful
> there,
> that it would always
> stay beautiful
> there.

Joy is fleeting, however, for such are the terms of life. The young man has to board the bus again, and then that brief shining moment disappears, the strikingly blessed instance, the warmth and comfort that has brought him home, so to speak. Because we are never told where the young man comes from or where he is bound—it is revealed only that he is "on the way to somewhere"—what we can say is that, wherever it is that he is going, which could be anywhere, it is not the place he should be. We hear only tires at the end of the poem, moving away from Nirvana.

No—rejection as reply—sits at the grammatical center of food aversion. It is the watchword, epitomizing its essential core and prerogative, demanding steadfastness and commitment. One must obey its full resolve. Adam and Eve refused to do so. So also did Eurydice, wife of Orpheus. A vivid example is Lot's wife; by looking back at the "evil cities," she betrayed her secret longing for corruption, was deemed unworthy to be saved, and turned into a pillar of salt. When Leo Tolstoy and his brother were children, they would pretend that any fond wish that they made would come true only if they could stand in a corner and *not* think of a white bear.

The habit of saying *no*, incidentally, according to many therapists, is conducive to a person's psychological well-being. *No* is a boundary, a partition, a dividing line that allows an individual space. It is a location that has its own aesthetic. Where an obligation can be quickly slain, freedom may ensue. I have often considered that the deepest dream of a human being is to be able to fly.

19.

ANDY WARHOL EATS A CHEESEBURGER

Speaking of marginal men, there was the artist Andy Warhol. Andy Warhol ate hamburgers. We can see him do so in a movie. There is a short film of him actually doing nothing but sitting at a table opening up a bag and eating a "Whopper" from Burger King. Standing on the table is a bottle of Heinz tomato ketchup. Whether he enjoyed them is anybody's guess. This peculiar little *jeu* was shot by Danish filmmaker, Jorgen Leth, for his art movie, *66 Scenes from America* (1981), in which he stitched together a series of lengthy shots as a visual postcard of a journey across America. There are no ads or intros, outros or whatever. Here, the thin, twitchy, be-wigged, rumpled-potato-nosed artist sits self-consciously forward in jacket and tie, with terrible rubbery skin and wispy hair. (I have read in several places that a good deal depended on which particular toupee he was wearing—the messy one was supposed to indicate that he was in a bad mood and was not to be approached.) Watching the film for the first time, I couldn't help but think to myself here is the worthless, half-baked, and unfinished man like poor sinful Ephraim described in Hosea 7:8 as "a flat cake not turned over."

Throughout the whole process, the artist is looking stiff, awkward, and diffident, as always, maintaining a formal pose, then twitchily shakes out an almost microscopic dollop of ketchup, into which he delicately dips the burger, twice—hating ketchup?—in the course of eating it, although at one point—hating bread?—he peels off half of the burger bun and wraps the rest of the meat in a single side of the bun. It is as if he does not enjoy eating a lot of bread or a lot of ketchup. There is something robotic about it all. ("I don't believe in style; I want to be a machine," he once said.) He fiddles with a napkin throughout, as if it were a prop he was never accustomed to using. Throughout the entire scene, which takes exactly 4 minutes and 28 seconds to record, Warhol's eyes shift about nervously. At the end of the short film, he simply sits there, pale, silently, almost duncically, for almost two minutes, and then he mutters in the way of a gratuitous post-announcement quip, "My name is Andy Warhol, and, ah, I've just finished eating a hamburger." One may recall here that Gore Vidal once said, "Andy Warhol is the only genius I've ever known with an IQ of 60."

He was a bundle of food quirks. He adored Sara Lee Pound Cake. He was a fanatic for peppermint Life Savers. The scum that formed on cocoa when it cooled repelled him. He was color sensitive and extraordinarily acute to sounds and smells. He refers to "the banana smell of dry cleaners." "I also love the smell of each fruit that gets into the rough wood of the crates and into the tissue-paper wrappings," he preciously declared. "I really do live for the future, because when I'm eating a box of candy, I can't wait to taste the last piece. I don't even taste any of the other pieces. I just want to finish and throw the box away and not have to have it on my mind anymore." "My favorite simultaneous action is talking while eating. I think of it as a sign of class. The rich have many advantages over the poor, but the most important one, as far as I'm concerned, is knowing how to talk and eat at the same time. I think they learn it in finishing school. It's very important if you go out to dinner a lot. At dinner you're expected to eat—because if you don't it's an insult to the hostess—and you're expected to talk—because if you don't it's an insult to the other guests. The rich somehow manage to work it out but I just can't do it. They are never caught with an open mouth full of food but that's what happens to me. It's always my turn to talk just when I've filled my mouth with mashed potatoes. The rich, on the other hand, seem to take turns automatically; one talks while the other chews; then one chews while the other talks."

"I can't tolerate eating leftovers," asserted dainty Warhol. "Food is my great extravagance. I really spoil myself, but then I try to compensate by scrupulously saving all of my food leftovers and bringing them into the office or leaving them in the street and recycling them there. My conscience won't let me throw anything out, even when I don't want it for myself. He adds,

> As I said, I really spoil myself in the food area, so my
> leftovers are often grand—my hairdresser's cat eats
> paté at least twice a week. The leftovers usually turn
> out to be meat, because I'll buy a huge piece of meat,
> cook it up for dinner, and then right before it's done
> I'll break down and have what I wanted for dinner in
> the first place—bread and jam. I'm only kidding my-
> self when I go through the motions of cooking pro-
> tein: all I ever really want is sugar... At the end of my

time, when I die, I don't want to leave any leftovers. And I don't want to be a leftover."

God did not want any leftovers, either, remember (cf. Leviticus 7:15), so here is a memorable nexus of agreement, God and A. Warhol!

Sterility in food pleased Warhol, as did the plastic, faux, relatively anti-human, antiseptic locations he favored to do anything in any circumstances, if we can believe what he often said about living. ("Actually, I jade very quickly.") "I really like to eat alone. I want to start a chain of restaurants for other people who are like me called 'ANDY-MATS—The Restaurant for the Lonely Person.' You get your food and then you take your tray into a booth and watch television." It was the antiseptic quality of them he liked. He liked empty American lunchrooms. "Today," he wrote in 1975, "my favorite kind of atmosphere is the airport atmosphere... The atmosphere is great, it's the idea of flying that I question. Airports and airplanes have my favorite kind of food, my favorite kind of bathroom, my favorite kind of non-servile service, my favorite peppermint Life Savers, my favorite kinds of entertainment, my favorite kind of lack of responsibility for your own direction, my favorite shops, my favorite graphics—my favorite everything." For all of these assertions of his, you would be mistaken to think that in any sense he celebrated life. Although Warhol appeared to be a social butterfly—he made every possible effort to look so—he very likely suffered from a condition called alexithymia, the emotional lack of awareness, crippling social detachment, and bent personality deficiency that repels rather than invites people in.

He yearned for infertility, barrenness, anti-life, the manufactured, the fake and the faux. What was arid, bare, barren, bleak, deserted, insincere, manufactured, unnatural, and desolate invariably pleased Warhol. He had a gloomily dead, leaden voice and a morbid, almost zombiesque stare, even at the best of times. He *cultivated* artificiality. "I am a deeply superficial person," he liked to tell interviewers, something he often repeated in that flat, reportorial, inhuman, rote voice of his, deflavored of all emotion. "I love Los Angeles. I love Hollywood. They're beautiful. Everybody's plastic, but I love plastic. I want to be plastic." So it was with his food choices. They were aversions, disinfected, dry, effete, empty, fallow, fruitless, futile, gaunt, germ-free, hygienic, impotent, infecund, infertile, pasteurized, septic, sterilized, unfruitful, uninfected, unprolific, vain, wasted, without issue. He preferred vacuuming his rooms to food. He once confessed, "Cleaning is more important than eating to me."

I find it difficult to think of food and the vulgar, cultural backwater of Los Angeles—dumb actors, pushy agents, fat producers, all yammering at a garden party—without recalling Harry Kurnitz's cold remark, "Lunch Hollywood-style—a hot dog and vintage wine" or hearing Hoagy Carmichael's "In the Cool, Cool, Cool of the Evening" (lyrics by Johnny Mercer) and the stanza,

> Sue wants a barbeque.
> Sam wants to boil a ham.
> Grace votes for bouillabaise stew.
> Jake wants a weenie bake,
> steak and a layer cake.
> He'll get a tummy ache, too.

Warhol purported to be a true democrat, claiming to find comfort in this country's diner-like egalitarianism. He once declared, "What's great about this country is that America started the tradition where the richest consumers buy essentially the same things as the poorest. You can be watching TV and see Coca-Cola, and you know that the President drinks Coke, Liz Taylor drinks Coke, and just think, you can drink Coke, too. A Coke is a Coke and no amount of money can get you a better Coke than the one the bum on the corner is drinking. All the Cokes are the same and all the Cokes are good. Liz Taylor knows it, the President knows it, the bum knows it, and you know it." He surely felt the same thing about a Burger King "Big Whopper." He explained in *The Philosophy of Andy Warhol*, "The idea of America is so wonderful because the more equal something is, the more *American* it is [my italics]. For example, a lot of places give you special treatment when you're famous, but that's not really America." Shallow, marginal, donkey-like people in Warhol's movies always appear positively in the same way that, inversely, religious people in the books of Salman Rushdie, for example, are always negatively portrayed—you can depend on it, although both the painter and the writer were both tawdrily alert to the algorithmic fame-friendship protocols that could best serve them and bring them the most attention, always working the rope-line, so to speak, and banking on what is known as the "Gore Vidal Law" which holds that "Everyone who is famous knows everyone else."

In spite of the fact that Warhol and his attendant group of divas, drug-addicts, and deviants all lived in a virtual hot house of decadent exclusivity and national notoriety—with every one of them desperate for attention—in The Factory in Manhattan, Warhol wrote, "Ghetto space is wrong for America. It's wrong for people who are the same type to go and live together. There shouldn't be any huddling together in the same groups with the same food.

In America it's got to mix 'n' mingle. If I were President, I'd make people mix 'n' mingle more." The needy and narcissistic in-crowd at the heart of the Warhol group, all avid to be celebrities and deeply competitive, were more rivals than they were friends. You see reflections of this sort of sunny shallowness in those candid present-day *Vanity Fair* photo-shoots of posh Manhattan parties, where sexy young debs chat with fat producers, actors pose with rich fashion ladies, all grinning like mad cats to be seen, and over in a corner, always, horse-faced Fran Lebowitz, in her big tux, sits on a sofa glumly alone. (Such inanely vapid occasions always reinforced for me Oscar Wilde's sentiment, "Fashion is a form of ugliness so intolerable that we have to alter it every six months.") I am certain that Warhol would have agreed with the often standoffish Saul Steinberg who did many drawings of people not only talking past each other but usually on the lookout for other people more interesting—a habit leading to the slang phrase "He was 'better dealin' me"—and he once wrote that "true friendship, which is a provincial art, does not exist in New York. It is more a matter of seeing each other at parties and other daily, dissolute, alcoholic activities."

What do you get when you put a chocolate bar between two pieces of white bread? Andy Warhol called it "cake." Can one assert that Warhol validated Cesare Lombroso's idea in *The Man of Genius* (1889) that artistic brilliance is a form of hereditary insanity? I never saw Andy as anything like a genius, more like an inspired goose, close to Vasily Grossman's description of a person in *Life and Fate*: "He was endowed with the extraordinary powers of endurance characteristic of madmen and simpletons." Warhol was not a mystery at all. He was vain, selfish, greedy, ambitious, fey, energetic, shy, basically a voyeur—not at all the kind of enigmatic character that Mr. Edmund Ludlow said of the complex heroine of *The Portrait of a Lady*, "Isabel's written in a foreign tongue. I can't make her out." I believe that Warhol for gay New York City was right out of central casting.

I mention omelets. Tolstoy loved them and on his estate, according to legend, an omelet was constantly being prepared in the kitchen in case the great novelist called for that favorite dish. (I have heard the same said of spitted chickens being always on deck for the Emperor Napoleon, who was so busy that his cooks never knew when he would stop work and settle down to eat.) The late filmmaker and pop-writer Nora Ephron, to go from the sublime to the ridiculous in writers, inveighed against the tastelessness of only egg-white omelets. "The people who eat them think they are doing something virtuous when they are instead merely misinformed." So how could she like something as odious as cabbage strudel? The phrase to me is a glaring oxymoron. "Cabbage strudel is on a long list of things I loved to eat that used to be here [in New York City] and then weren't, starting with frozen custard," she wrote in "The Lost Strudel" as an op-ed piece in the *New York Times* in 2005. Ephron explains,

> This delectable treat vanished when I was 5 years old, when my family moved to California, and my life has been a series of little heartbreaks ever since... [it] looks like apple strudel, but it's not a dessert; it's more like a pirozhok, the meat-stuffed turnover that was a specialty of the Russian Tea Room, which also vanished. It's served with soup, or with a main course like pot roast or roast pheasant (not that I have ever cooked a roast pheasant, but no question cabbage strudel would be delicious with it). It has a buttery, flaky, crispy strudel crust made of phyllo (the art of which I plan to master in my next life, when I will also read Proust past the first chapter), with a moist filling of sautéed cabbage that's simultaneously sweet, savory and completely unexpected, like all good things.

I suspect the infusion of sautéed cabbage explains the secret why in Mindy's Nathan Detroit in the musical *Guys and Dolls* bawls out, "I hate strudel."

Cabbage is considered to be a low food. Greta Garbo in *Joyless Street* (1925) plays the terribly hungry Grete [sic] who, living in the poor part of an Austrian town called Melchiorgasse, in one extended heartbreaking scene leaves a grim meal of cabbage soup and goes to stand in line all night, along with other women in ragged shawls, effortfully, weakly, leaning against a building for support, in order to purchase frozen meat. In his autobiographical novel, *Tar: A Midwest Childhood* (1926), a transparently fictionalized account of his own growing up poor in the farming town of Camden, Ohio, Sherwood Andersen writes rather shamefacedly, "Corn meal mush or cabbage soup will do at a pinch, but you don't want to ask a guest to sit down to it. If you're poor and hard up, you don't want the whole town to know and be talking."

When the American journalist and novelist Gene Fowler went out to Hollywood in the 1930s to write film-scripts, a self-betrayal of which he felt ashamed and which he more or less compared to kissing the Devil's Fundament, the day he moved in with his #5 Royal typewriter to the working studio assigned him, he mounted on the mantel-piece the head of a cabbage, "as a symbol of front-office intellect," noted his biographer, H. Allen Smith, and then got ready for work. There is a slang expression used in Italy, "*cavoli riscaldati*"—reheated cabbage—which is used to describe an attempt on someone's part to revive a dead love affair. The idea is that trying to do so is not only unworkable and messy but probably hopeless. It is predominantly smelly cabbage that the impoverished Bucket family is driven to eat in Roald Dahl's *Charlie and the Chocolate Factory*, "thin cabbagey meals three times a day," except on Sunday when second helpings of cabbage are allowed, that is until Charlie finds the "Golden Ticket." Notice that the despised food is the antonym of chocolate. No, cabbage has been used the world over as a deplored and ignominious symbol.

In the city of Bukhara, Marco Polo ate *kush-kush*, a local dish made out of cabbage, lamb's eyes, and garlic. That was on his voyage to China (where he spent 17 years) when, after describing his party's arrival in the ancient city, he strangely—and casually—remarked, "And here, from our inability to proceed further, we remained three years." That mysterious sentence truly perplexed me when as a schoolboy I was excitedly doing a 8th-grade term paper on the great Venetian. Was the delay due to his learning the Mongol language? To linger there to study old volumes? (Bukhara was the center of the book trade at the time.) Or was Polo waiting out a period of trouble or social unrest in the western khanates? He loved food. My pedantic little paper was on the subject of pasta! There is a Creole corn mush also called "kush kush" which also goes under the name *couche-couche*. ("Mush," one of the more well-known universal derogatories for any disliked food—it probably traces back to French word *marche*—is no longer used in dog-sled racing, such as the famous 1,049 mile Iditarod Race from Anchorage to Nome. Drivers nowadays bark out to their Huskies "gee" for right and "haw" for left and "Arhra, Arhra" for something like "Get your asses moving!")

Militant zucchini haters abound. It doesn't matter what form it takes, they loathe it—zucchini bread, zucchini crudo, "green fries," chocolate zucchini cake, and so on and so forth. John Thorne banishes zucchini as having "the nutritious value, flavor, and texture of rained-on newspaper." He writes,

> The zucchini hasn't been popular in this country long enough to have acquired a sufficient hate literature, though you'd think more people would be suspicious of a vegetable whose only virtue is that any fool can grow one. One? The whole problem with zucchini is that you can't grow just one; the amateur's first blush of pride in the vulgar fecundity of this squash soon

enough turns to terror. Its much touted versatility is
just a polite way of saying that it constantly intrudes
where it isn't wanted, a vegetable form of that blandly
grating familiarity, "Have a nice day."

A driven and dedicated cook, Thorne is actually a tenacious food detective with an overwhelming cognitive gene. Rethinking—re-jiggering—recipes in order to perfect them is his singular gift, along with an inexhaustible need to explore, to study, to maximize flavors and tastes, "If someone tells me that this is the way something must be done, I take no pleasure in doing it unless I can somehow prove them wrong," he writes in *Mouth Wide Open*. I have often repeated that, if ever I committed a crime, the most feared, hang-tough individual I would not want pursuing me would be the dogged and implacable St. Paul of Tarsus, relentless, persistent, and dead-set on his goal; how many times, when hatefully driven out of a city, did the holy zealot turn right around and head straight back in order to continue proselytizing? I would place the intense, hyper-diligent Thorne in this unique but frankly slightly scary category. A New England realist who takes no prisoners, he has never been coy about his dislikes. He disdains cold breakfast cereals ("Breakfast cereal is terrible stuff... Apart from a brief flirtation with granola in the sixties, I haven't touched a bowl of it for almost twenty years"); sponge cake ("It tastes like its namesake without the redeeming scrubbing power"); commercial baking powder ("The good old Royal brand was a mixture of cream of tartar and baking soda"); graham crackers ("There's no such thing as a graham cracker, only the graham cookie"); cooked tomatoes; vichyssoise ("It isn't potato soup at all, just a buttery-bland mouthful of weightless-seeming luxury for rich folk to start their gorging on"); commercial cold cuts in a sandwich; kiwi fruit ("An insipid expensive fruit with a phony, cutesy name—I say it's a Chinese gooseberry and I say the hell with it"); chili powder (Thorne grinds his own dried chile pods); Golden Delicious apples; blood sausage ("the only offal-related food that I'm completely unable to eat"); water-packed canned tuna. Thorne, who as an original compulsively goes against the common way of thinking, also finds, for example, that the traditional and long-held iconographic match of tomatoes with lettuce actually work against each other in a salad. "I want to write that they taste too much the same; that's what my tongue tells me, even if my brain says that they have nothing in common at all," he explains. "All I know is that their flavors don't work well together without a host of intermediaries or some chef's trick to pull the thing off. Even Greek salad is better without any lettuce..."

Thorne is delightfully opinionated, and witty pronouncements worthy of Oscar Wilde or Saki or Philip Larkin flow out of his golden pen like water coursing off a spillway. Among some of my favorites are "Real macaroni and cheese is unkempt;" "Eat johnnycake plain with butter; even the best maple syrup overpowers it;" "Apples go on living after they're picked. After all, they want to be a tree;" "Clotted cream is to cream what the Missouri is to rivers—too thick to pour but too soft to slice;" "No soup was ever so good as when a little corn cake was broken into it;" "Chocolate is out of place in a cheesecake because its cocoa-butter richness drowns out all the sour notes of the cheese;" "Perfect dishes do appear now and again… but perfect recipes never;" "There are sexual overtones to salted anchovies;" "One of the best ways to learn more about a dish is to get a bunch of recipes arguing with each other;" "One definition of a pessimist is someone forced to spend too much time in the company of optimists;" "Frozen fried chicken tastes as if it were made for some alternate-universe fowl that resembles the original only in skeletal structure, which can be a source of amusement if you're in a certain kind of mood." God bless Thorne!

Fads, taboos, and prejudices in food can be found in every period of history, born of religious differences, dietary theories, social class, geography, and, indeed, tradition. The *Encyclopedia of the Renaissance and the Reformation* sheds fascinating light on the subject. "Melons, cucumbers, and other watery fruits were disparaged on health grounds, and broad beans were disliked because the peeled bean was thought to resemble a human embryo," it is reported. (Ironically, it was precisely melons and cucumbers—along with fish—that the Hebrews wandering in the desert most missed looking back to Egypt.) Snobbery of course often played a role:

> Other foods, such as brown (rye) bread, were stigmatized because of their class associations. Indeed, awareness of food as a social indicator seems to have sharpened during the Renaissance; several Italian cities tried to codify the various foods appropriate to the different social classes, while English sumptuary laws laid down the precise number of courses that should be served to various dignitaries (six for a peer of the realm but nine for a cardinal). Sharper, particular disapprovals were reserved for novelties from the New World; the potato was despised merely for its unprepossessing appearance and like corn (maize) considered fit for only the lowest classes of peasant, while the tomato

was inveighed against by moralists, who were convinced that it incited lust (and may even have been the
forbidden fruit in the Garden of Eden). One import to
fare better was the turkey, which quickly found acceptance as an alternative to goose or peacock.

I have pointed out that sufferers from favism, many who can be found
in the Mediterranean basin, where the broad bean originated, in fact, cannot
manage to make in their bodies the enzyme glucose-6-phosphate dehydro-
genase, which simply means that the circulation of sugar in their bodies is different, and red blood cells are destroyed as a result. Very often, the condition
can be found in regions where there is also malaria. Greek and Romans associate broad beans with bad luck, even death. Was it because they were used
as a food for the dead, such as during the annual Lemuria festival, a religious
feast in ancient Rome during which participants performed various rites to
exorcise the malevolent and fearful ghosts of the dead from their homes? As I
have mentioned, the Pythagorean code prohibited the consumption or even
the touching of any sort of bean. While in ancient Greece and Rome, broad
beans were used in voting (a white bean cast meant a yes vote, while a black
bean indicated no)—even today, the word *koukia* (κουκιά: fava beans) is used
unofficially, as slang, referring to the votes—the attendant priests of Jupiter
in ancient Rome were forbidden to touch broad beans or even mention the
word *faba*.

Cultural experts reckon that we are born with a natural sweet tooth,
that by means of evolution we have been taught—it has been conveyed to us
over millennia—to avoid and abstain from bitter foods. There are the standard foods that appear on every list of hated foods in the west. Lima beans.
Gizzards. Head cheese. Cabbage. I have also seen commonly listed here:
casseroles, licorice flavor—star anise in or on anything—cold fried foods,
frozen bananas, super-hot foods, anything that swims, okra, and lunch meat
of any description. I knew a Boston Brahmin who would eat spaghetti only if
the pasta and the sauce were served in entirely separate bowls. And the smell
of spinach cooking. "I took no more pleasure in spinach-eating than I would
have obtained from devouring a hooked rug," wrote Kenneth Roberts in
Good Maine Food. (Later when he learned to steam it, he grew to like it.) The
great trial lawyer Clarence Darrow carried a lifetime dislike of the vegetable,
saying, "I don't like spinach, and I'm glad I don't, because, if I liked it, I'd
eat it, and I just hate it." Who can forget little Shirley Temple in *Poor Little
Rich Girl* (1936) singing (at her very cutest),

Noooo spinach!

Take away that awful greenery.

Nooo spinach!

Give us lots of jelly beanery

We positively refuse to budge

We like lollipops and we like fudge

But *nooooo* spinach!

Spinach, stay away from my doooor"

The song elicited its counterpart in the 1939 movie, *Naughty But Nice*— no doubt a cinematic response—with a song sung by Zerla Manion (Ann Sheridan), an upbeat ditty entitled "Hooray for Spinach."

Salvador Dali loathed the vegetable. He exclaimed, "I detest spinach because of its utterly amorphous character... the only good, noble and edible thing to be found in that sordid nourishment is the sand." In *How to Eat Like a Child* the writer Delia Ephron, wrote, "On the subject of spinach: divide into little piles. Rearrange again into new piles. After five of six maneuvers, sit back and say you are full." Arthur the cartoon aardvark's little sister, D. W., a fussy eater, not only will not eat anything with eyes but also hates liver and—particularly—spinach. (She also despises vegetables, fish, fruit, and meat!) It is curious that most everybody considers spinach to be an iron-rich food. Thank cartoonist Elzie C. Segar, Popeye the Sailorman's creator, for this, after years of showing his sailor hero, after gulping whole cans of it—his favorite maneuver—but you should know that a hamburger contains about the same amount of iron as an equal weight of spinach. So how and why is it that spinach, on the one hand, made Popeye powerful, while, on the other hand, hamburgers made Wimpy wimpy? Spinach has always been a revolting food for many kids because of the sour oxalic acid that it contains. Try anytime to get a small child to eat rhubarb, which packs a mouth-puckering load of oxalic acid! A deer will not eat rhubarb. It is nevertheless eaten raw in Alaska among the Inuit and in Afghanistan, although it is rarely eaten at all in Italy, in Spain, or in France, despite the fact that the French imported it in 1724.

Did you know that rhubarb is generally considered a vegetable, but that a US court decided in 1947 that because it was used here as a fruit, it was to be counted as a fruit for the purposes of regulations and duties? A side effect was a reduction on imported rhubarb tariffs, as tariffs were higher for vegetables than fruits!

One of CNN's newscasters, Anderson Cooper—he grew up the pampered son of heiress Gloria Vanderbilt—has not the slightest qualm about confessing his very strange food habits to the public. He revealed that he really does not care that much about food in general, to begin with, but has recently argued with comedian Jerry Seinfeld about his extremely picky food habits. On his talk show, Cooper, in what I gathered was something of an adventure for him, daringly tried tasting both coffee and spinach—hard to believe—for the very first time ever. It comes as no surprise that he was not a big fan of either. "I like just plain things," the wooden-faced Cooper replied. "I don't like fancy mixing of stuff." Later, Cooper and Seinfeld went out to the street to a local waffle cart down by Cooper's studio. He told Seinfeld that he had never eaten a waffle. "I don't understand the point," he said. "Texture!" Seinfeld exasperatedly responded, as if he were in an episode of his sitcom. "The point is texture!" "But there's pancakes and pancakes are good enough!" Cooper protested. Seinfeld insisted that waffles were crispy. "Why do you need crispy?" Cooper asked. "For the experience of eating!" Seinfeld squawked in high exasperation, adding, "You are really weird!" The two guys returned to the studio, where Cooper actually admitted that he is "like a seven-year-old" when it comes to his eating habits. He claimed during a cooking segment that he did not "see the point" of couscous ("There's already rice!") or eggs.

In that stiff, robotic manner of his that Cooper manages to reveal making even the simplest point, what therapists call "lack of affect," Cooper then proceeded to list some of his other highly idiosyncratic food preferences: he hates all hot beverages and admits that he has never tried most green vegetables. *Most?* Does he mean such odd things as peas, snap beans, broccoli, lettuce? One can only imagine what this strange, finicky guy would do when faced with salsify, cardoons, chayote (or mirliton), or nopales or cactus paddles! "It just seems so watery," complained Cooper before precariously taking a sip of coffee as if he were imbibing liquid lava. "Really?" he asked with wide-eyed astonishment. "That's what people drink everyday? I don't see the point in that." Then he tried some spinach, which he dispiritedly described as "gross" and "slithery." Growing up without eating green vegetables is barbaric, never mind unhealthy. Does it not reflect on his mother and father? What did this person eat growing up, éclairs? Cheesecake? Blueberry pancakes? Baked Alaska?

It is rather clear that there are many six-year-olds who have more refined tastes than does the rigid Cooper. Just take a look at the guy. He is bamboo stiff with a frozen face and has one of the driest looking bodies on the planet, sexless, with not a sign of dewiness. No one on earth has a skin more eleukotic, fish-belly white, and without so much as a trace of gloss. His stiff crinkled hair with that odd quiff is an unearthly white and sheenless, his face, badly lined, seems almost mechanical or programmed, so to speak, characterless even as he laughs, with no easy passage from one expression to the next. He also compulsively giggles. You can see immediately that Cooper's is a classic case of arrested juvenility. He is a mere boy. Could he have been traumatized, wrenched, or rigidified by his mother's quartet of marriages—or "bus accidents," as actor John Barrymore referred to marriage—along with her many well-publicized and widely published (by herself—*It Seemed Important at the Time: A Romance Memoir*) affairs with a flock of different men?

Another buzz-killing weezer—or "straight arrow," as we used to call the type in high school—is Fox News Network reporter Chris Wallace, the dreary, long-philtrumed son of CBS's Mike Wallace. "I've never had a full cup of coffee," admitted Wallace in a *Playboy* magazine interview, adding, as if for balance in trying to co-categorize the two, "Drugs never interested me. I am probably the only person in the history of Harvard in the 1960s who never took drugs."

We all know the slimy, slithery, jelly-like categories are unpopular—oysters, eels, tripe, clams. A British survey recently listed the "Top Most Hated Foods," which are here quoted in order: Tripe, Snails, Oysters—here, all true Cape Codders can only think, "The more for me!"—Black Pudding, Squid, Crabsticks, Sago, Junket, Kidneys, Cockles, Tapioca, Haggis, Mussels, Tofu, Spam, Aspic, Oxtail, Rabbit, Semolina, Peanut Butter, Olives, Black Pudding, Liver, and Anchovies. A Fussy Food Nation report also featured kippers, blue cheese, beetroot, sardines, Brussels sprouts, avocado, pate, prawns, and mushrooms. Tripe leads the list, notice.

Sir Thomas Beecham famously believed that everything was worth a go, bar Morris dancing and incest. Had he not had a meal of tripe? I remember one rainy night in Rotherhithe, where I found that I had ended up after a 20-mile walk, I sat down in a small corner restaurant and, feeling daring, cavalierly ordered a bowl of tripe stew and within minutes soon understood why nearly 30% of people in Britain who have tried tripe once will never do so again. I recall, significantly, right off, the spoon being too big. There was more than a hint in the stew of the farmyard and a distinct echo of death. Admittedly, regarding tripe, one should have it cooked by someone who knows what he is doing, which I gather that night was not my luck.

In a memorable account of one of her lunches with the novelist Colette, the American literary journalist and bookseller Adrienne Monnier in her memoir, *The Very Rich Hours of Adrienne Monnier*, mentions that, as soon as the two of them were seated, snails were offered—*escargots de Bourgogne*. Contrary to her declared love for the food and wine of her native Burgundy, the writer revulsed. "Ah, no!" exclaimed Colette, who, by the way, was a vegetarian, "it's the only thing I've never been able to eat. I have tried to enjoy them, but nothing goes down except the juice." Whereupon Monnier confesses, "In my corner I exult, for I have a horror of snails, and I have never wanted to put one of them in my mouth."

"Snails are snails, for God's sake: maggoty, warty little pellets sliming their way across the garden," wrote Oliver Thring, a food blogger at *The Guardian*. He vigorously goes on to say, "And fresh oysters don't taste bad, just salty. But it's a slopping, snotty, slippery, squelchy thing, and it's alive."

I must say Damon Runyon makes tripe sound appetizing to some degree when his rowdy narrator in the story, "Blonde Mink," begins, "Now of course there are many different ways of cooking tripe but personally I prefer it stewed with tomatoes and mushrooms and a bit of garlic and in fact I am partaking of a portion in this form in Mindy's restaurant one evening when a personality by the name of Julie the Starker sits down at my table," and so on.

I have made reference to black pudding. Many people hate puddings of any kind. A skin that can quickly develop on a pudding's surface badly puts off many eaters. I have mentioned that I like egg custards, and I must add that I love virtually every sort of British pudding, boiled, steamed or baked— jam roly-poly, tipsy cake, spotted dick, many of their lovely rich flummeries. "Eton Mess" is another simple dessert which I love to make, with sweet sherry and heavy cream. Have you tasted *quindem* (or *quinden*) pie? It is a popular coconut treat made in Brazil with lots of egg yolks, coconut, sugar, butter, and baked in a water bath, a dish that can be concocted in one large custard ring. Custard has a negative image. "Whatever is funny is subversive," wrote George Orwell, "every joke is ultimately a custard pie... a dirty joke is a sort of mental rebellion." "Well, don't stand there, Miss Preen. You look like a frozen custard," Monty Woolley acting the fastidious Sheridan Whiteside brays at his nurse, played by homely but lovable Mary Wickes, in *The Man Who Came To Dinner*. Great Britain is a pudding-loving country, at least so it was when I spent lots of time there years ago. So I was surprised to see black pudding listed in a *Daily Mail* survey in 2013 as one of Britain's most hated foods, thrown in with the likes of snails, tripe, oysters, squid, anchovies, liver, cockles, kidneys, olives, avocado, and goat's cheese.

Vegetarians certainly have their detractors. "Vegetarianism isn't simply distaste for animal products. It's a way of life: faddish, cranky, and holier-than-thou," wrote Harriet van Horn in the *New York Post* (June 23, 1978). "Vegetarians are the enemy of everything good and decent in the human spirit, and an affront to all I stand for, the pure enjoyment of food. The body, these waterheads imagine, is a temple that should not be polluted by animal protein. It's healthier, they insist, though every vegetarian waiter I've worked with is brought down by any rumor of a cold. Oh, I'll accommodate them, I'll rummage around for something to feed them, for a 'vegetarian plate,' if called on to do so. Fourteen dollars for a few slices of grilled eggplant and zucchini suits my food cost fine." J.B. Morton in *By the Way* agreed: "Vegetarians have wicked shifty eyes, and laugh in a cold and calculating manner. They pinch little children, steal stamps, drink water, favor beards…wheeze, squeak, drawl and maunder."

Sir James Barrie was once sitting next to George Bernard Shaw at a dinner party. The vegetarian Shaw had been provided with a special dish of salad greens and dressing. Eyeing the unpleasant-looking concoction, Barrie whispered to Shaw, "Sir, have you just finished or are you just starting?" In an exercise at the Iowa Workshop, a young Flannery O'Connor compared the experience of tasting celery to "sucking warm water out of a dish rag." "I detest diet foods," Julia Child is quoted in *Gourmet* (Feb. 1995), "You can get cake down to 230 calories a slice with flour, egg whites, and vegetable oil, but why would you want to eat it?" Always unselfconsciously frank about weenies and joy-killers and gastronomic Malvolios, she went on to complain,

> Why not eat a piece of something good? I can't
> stand anything touted by the health mavens. There is
> nothing like a good piece of American bacon. I don't
> like low salt, diet bacon. I am often disappointed in
> our beef today. And it becomes harder to get a decent
> piece of beef, beautifully marbled. Instead we get what
> we call 'diet beef,' lean and without taste. And isn't it
> difficult to get a good chicken? I remember in France,
> we would cook a Bresse chicken hanging by a string
> in the oven, with mushrooms and potatoes below to
> catch to catch the fat drippings. Today we have so-
> called fresh chickens that aren't fresh at all. They have
> been frozen, defrosted, and frozen again.

But it is far, far worse than that. What about the unwholesome trash that chickens nowadays are given to eat? Birds are fed not only soy and corn mix but often bulked up with "feather meal" (ground-up chicken feathers) and other animal by-products left over from slaughter, same species meat, skin, manure, even unhealthy amounts of grains, as well as bakery scraps like stale commercial leftovers, which therefore allows producers to describe their feed as "vegetarian." (In a recent study analyzing feather-meal, researchers at Johns Hopkins found, along with the residue of arsenic and caffeine as well as the active ingredients of Benadryl, Tylenol, and Prozac—fed to birds to alter their mood—also coffee pulp and green tea powder, used to keep the chickens awake so that they can spend more time eating.) Again, raised in the most unnatural circumstances on the most unnatural diets—certainly chickens, but in fact most of the food animals in the United States are no longer raised on farms at all, but instead come from hopelessly crowded factory farms, denominated "large confined animal feeding operations" (CAFOs)—birds are dipped upside down in electrically charged baths which stun them, a machine then cuts their throats, they are bled, plunged into hot water, plucked, and chilled in cold baths (where bacterial contamination can spread), to absorb up to 14 percent of their body weight in water, further plumping up their weight to leave them with a spongy, washed-out flavor. During processing, they are also "enhanced" (read: injected) with a solution of chicken broth, salt, and flavorings. Chickens are drugged to grow so large so quickly that their legs and organs can't keep up, making heart attacks, organ failure, and crippling leg deformities common. Many become crippled under their own weight and eventually die because they can't reach the water nozzles. When they are only 6 or 7 weeks old, they are crammed into cages and trucked to slaughter. They have no federal legal protection. Birds are exempt from the Humane Slaughter Act.

There seems to be no end to the chicane involved with chickens. I have mentioned chicken feathers. A chicken's feathers actually consist of 97% protein, and University of Georgia researchers have lately found a way of turning them into a fine white powder that is claimed to be easy to digest. A panel that tasted cookies made from this powder have described them as "pretty good to eat."

Terms in the poultry industry are not regulated, nor are standards enforced. A label or tag of "hormone-free" is empty reassurance, because the USDA does not allow the use of hormones or steroids in poultry production, but loopholes are rife, allowing companies to inject the eggs—not the chickens—with antibiotics and to feed birds that grotesque feather-meal that is laced with residual antibiotics from treated birds. Nor is the facile word "natural" meaningful, despite the fact that it is ubiquitous on food labels. The sad truth is the USDA has applied that term strictly for fresh meat, stipulating only that no synthetic substances have been added to the cut. Producers may therefore raise their chickens under the vilest conditions, feeding them contaminated diets, and yet all the while claim on their packaging they are "natural."

The only proof of rigorous enforcement is when a given package bears the USDA Organic seal. As we have said, the famous gastronome and epicure Jean Antheme Brillat-Savarin declared, "Tell me what you eat, and I will tell you what you are"—one of the world's most often misquoted apothegms—but Michael Pollan in his *In Defense of Food: An Eater's Manifesto*, with stutter-stepping wisdom wittily puts it, "You are what what you eat eats."

It may be noted here, on the subject of someone disliking eggs, that an egg was specifically the only thing that novelist Saul Bellow's conservative and by-all-accounts grumpy father, Abraham, could find to eat when visiting the unorthodox household of his son who did not "keep kosher." Kosher—*pareve*—is a world of food aversions. In despair, reduced to pondering what amounted for an orthodox Jew to a non-menu, facing foods that did not conform to the dietary laws of kashrut, Abe Bellow would cry, "Cook me an egg in the shell!" Treif derived from the Hebrew word *teref* means torn and originally referred to non-kosher meat only. In Exodus 22:30 it is written "Do not eat meat from an animal torn in the field." Thus Jews were forbidden to eat meat from an animal that was torn or mortally wounded. Over time the meaning of the term treif expanded from one category of non-kosher meat to anything non-kosher. The kosher certification has been given to such products not only to crackers, cheese, fruit but also to Sealtest milk, Clorox, Folger's Coffee, Reynolds Wrap, Dr. Pepper, Glad Sandwich Bags (!), Grape-Nut Flakes cereal, and Evian water.

Kosher often seems to be a term that is completely arbitrary, randomly applied, and the use of it subjective. Salt is one of the few items that does not require rabbinical supervision, for example. The phrase "kosher salt" in fact means nothing; it is called that simply because in so-called "kosher" salt the crystal size and shape are best for koshering meat and chicken. Were you aware that there are now 86,000 kosher-certified products—only 50,000 in 1996—in this country? A recent survey showed that only 21% of the 10 million Americans who buy kosher do so for religious reasons, they rest are under the pathetic delusion that they are eating healthier food! Any arbitrary meaning assigned to a word I suppose needs to be accepted in the speech community that uses that language, but much of it often seems contrived and phony. Who knows? I once heard an obese man in a yarmulke loudly bitching that he couldn't get a decent pepperoni kosher pizza with extra mozzarella when he was visiting Israel!

As to food aversions, various groups in this country from Kosher Fraud, Inc. to the World Union of Deists, including many outraged litigants, claim that the whole kosher apparat is nothing but a scam. They accuse rabbis of greedily selling the "right" to companies to display their particular kosher marking, each one shamelessly hustling and hawking his own "brand" like a

Seventh Avenue garmento! An ancillary accusation is that each item bearing a kosher mark offered to customers costs us, all of us, the general public, additional money. The individual amounts are usually small, but the aggregate take is huge. "Just one full-time mashgiach, or kashrut supervisor, runs between $40,000 and $50,000 per year!" or so goes the complaint on the website, "The Kosher Scam." "Common sense tells us that those kashrut supervisors who get paid decent salaries and also have full job benefits along with 401K plans all have money flowing in from somewhere. Add to this that *The Wall Street Journal* reports in its April 18, 2011 edition that companies 'pay from $2,000 to tens of thousands of dollars annually' to the rabbis to declare their products kosher and to allow their kosher seal to be placed on the products' packaging! It becomes very obvious that the take is huge! Reality tells us the source of their cash-flow is the pockets of consumers, the over whelming majority of whom don't even believe in this ancient Jewish superstition!"

Few Americans are aware of the "Kosher Tax" that is silently levied against every United States citizen, whether Jewish or not, but there are those who do refer to the ploy as the "Kosher Nostra" and refuse to buy any product that has a kosher symbol. "Major food companies throughout America pay a Jewish Tax amounting to hundreds of millions of dollars per year in order to receive protection," writes the teratoid Ernesto Cienfuegos, Editor-in-Chief of *La Voz de Aztlan* and author of a particularly harsh online rant that traces this financial corruption directly to the heart of the Israeli government and its leaders. "This hidden tax gets passed, of course, to all non-Jewish consumers of the products. The scam is to coerce the companies to pay up or suffer the consequences of a Jewish boycott. Jewish consumers have learned not to buy any kitchen product that does not have the (U), the (K), and other similar markings. Another shocker was learning who is actually behind these sophisticated 'Kosher Nostra Scams.'" Cienfuegos explains the source of the conspiratorial roots. He writes,

> It turns out that the perpetrators of these elaborate extortion schemes are actually Rabbinical Councils that are set up, not just in the U.S. but in other western countries as well. For example, the largest payola operation in the U.S. is run by those who license the (U) symbol. The (U) symbol provides protection for many products sold here in Aztlan and in the United States. This symbol is managed by the The Union of Orthodox Jewish Congregations with headquarters

at 333 Seventh Avenue in New York City. The scam
works like a well-oiled machine and is now generating
vast amounts of funds, some of which are being utilized by the Union of Orthodox Rabbis to support the
Ariel Sharon Zionist government in Israel. The website of the Union of Orthodox Jewish Congregations
is full of pro-Israel and anti-Palestinian propaganda. (It is especially galling when one stops to think
that the United States gives Israel $20 billion every
year—outright grants, not loans—which from 1949
is somewhere in excess of $5 trillion, or $16k per
American—to say nothing of the incalculable amounts
of foreign aid we hand out to Egypt, Jordan, Syria,
etc. as virtual bribes lest they should attack Israel.)

Many complaintants are anti-Semites. Others are level-headed and legitimate, however—and also correct. A more logical criticism was registered by
a woman named Susan Bolles who, more or less crying "*ne sois pas si bête*,"
approached the problem into Rense.com with a calculator in hand:

I had to do the math. I had hoped to find out that
it really was a fairly insignificant tax. But, this is what
the numbers say. If the average kosher tax on a Birds
Eye frozen food is .0000065 And if you purchase
an average of 35 U or K items per week The total
paid for the kosher tax over a year for one person is:
0.01183 That's a pretty small number. But... there
are 281,500,000 people living in the United States
according to the 2000 census figures with a median
age of 35.3 years old. So if you multiply the number
of people by the tax, well, its starting to add up to a
lot of money. $3,330,145 total paid per year for the
kosher tax. I wouldn't call that insignificant. Take it a
step further, and if this has been paid for the last 35.3
years-median age of an American, that adds up to:
117,554,118.50, and that's a lot of money. I think it's
not really fair that the consumer should pay for the
services of a religious organization to monitor food
production. If anything, the organization should be
providing the service for free.

By the way, Bolles does not even mention the $10.2 million of American tax money that is sent in aid to Israel every single day. (On September 14, 2016 Pres. Obama just signed a new 10-year $38 billion aid package to Israel.) It is impolitic in the United States to mention such statistics in an article, never mind a book, given the huge power of the Israeli lobby (AIPAC) in Washington, DC, and the obsequious influence of the U.S. press, most of it cravenly intimidated but many bought off and paid for. Fact: one tenth of 1 percent of the world's population lives in Israel; 25 percent of world stories in the *New York Times* in 2012 mentioned that country.

You might be surprised to learn, furthermore, that not a single organization exists today that uniformly governs the more than 900 or so "official agencies" that certify Hebrew foods as kosher. There must be tens of thousands of them world-wide in Canada, Brazil, Mexico, Lithuania, Australia, China, France, just about everywhere. The thing is, any dork in town can do it! Just change your name to Myron Klotz or Hyman Pekkar or Heshie Circumcisionofsky, draw up a logo, and you yourself can become an official ready to dunk a chicken, inspect a bag, I don't know, sniff the meat and fish and then whip out a pad and a big inspection stamp and bang it down. A kosher inspector or *mashgiah*—who need not be a rabbi, by the way—basically goes about scoping out eggs for offending blood spots, inspecting vegetables for insects, etc. but essentially his job consists of paying heed to three principles: (1) foods cannot contain a mixture of meat and dairy products; (2) foods cannot contain ingredients which are considered to be inherently unfit, like pork and shellfish; (3) foods cannot avoid specific Jewish laws, such as, animals must be killed with a minimum of pain. While some products state that they are kosher without also showing any identifying insignia, as do certain restaurants and catering establishments, kosher symbols differ not only from country to country but within each country have different organizations with different symbols! Check out KosherQuest! There are are more kosher symbols than belfry bats! It is a potpourri of stars, circles, acclamation points, interrobangs, sarc and snark marks, asterisms, doubt points, initials, octopuncts, percontation points.

Who can explain Jewish dietary laws? The Yoreh De'ah prohibits the drinking of water—I am not making this up—if the water had been left overnight and uncovered in an area where there might be "serpents," on the basis that a serpent might have somehow left its venom in the water! Eating meat and fish together may cause *tzaraath*, that is, things like bald patches, any disfigurative conditions of the skin, hair of the beard and head, clothing made of linen or wool, including unworked leather—excepting the hides of marine animals—even mildew on clothes and on houses! Classical rabbis have always prohibited any item of food that had been consecrated to an idol or had been used in the service of an idol. Fill in your own definition of an "idol." Because the Talmud views all non-Jews or Gentiles as potential idolaters, any food which has been cooked or prepared completely by non-Jews, with the exception of bread—go figure—is proscribed, even if it is sold by a non-Jewish baker! Gelatin, fish roe, blood-spotted eggs, all "flying creeping things," except locusts, bats, certain types of animal fat (*chelev*)—because fat remains the portion of the meat exclusively allocated to God (by burning it on the altar)—and fish-eating water-birds are all held in suspicion. Leviticus 3-17 it states, "All fat is the lord's. It is a law for you for all time throughout the ages, in all your settlements: you must not eat any fat or any blood."

Look up the "scandal of particularity." It is a theological phrase, referring to the resistance many people have to the idea that God, the creator of the universe, would enter human history in a biased, localized, or legalistic way. "Wherever there is a mystery," said Dr. Samuel Johnson, "roguery is not far off." I tend to find that any "law," especially a dietary one, is a *drogue infâme*!

20.

"PARSLEY IS GHARSLEY"

Comic writer S.J. Perelman who utterly condemned the entire spectrum of vegetables wrote in *Acres and Pains* (1947)

> I have no truck with lettuce, cabbage, and similar
> chlorophyll. Any dietician will tell you that a running
> foot of apple strudel contains four times the vitamins
> of a bushel of beans... Every time I crush a stalk of
> celery, there is a whirring crash, a shriek of tortured
> capillaries, and my metabolism goes to the boneyard.

In this list may finally be numbered the rapper, Jay-Z, who on his album, *Reasonable Doubt*, sings,

> Who wanna bet us that we don't touch lettuce,
> Stack cheddars forever,
> live treacherous, all the et ceteras.

In an endearing but serious way, M.F.K. Fisher goes to some length in *To Begin Again*, the last book she wrote, on the tastes—or lack thereof—of her Grandmother Holdbrook, an old woman who, among other faults, "did not believe in any form of seasoning." She had many vigorous dislikes. "We seldom ate cabbage: it did not agree with her, and small wonder, because it was always cooked according to her mid-Victorian recipes and would have made an elephant heave and hiccup. We ate carrots, always in a 'white sauce' in little dishes by our plates, and as soon as my grandmother died I headed for the raw ones and chewed at them after school and even in the dark of night while I was growing. But the flatter a thing tasted, the better it was for you, she fully believed, the more you should suffer to eat it, thus proving your innate worth as a Christian, a martyr to the flesh but a courageous one… she picked [religious] conventions where she could drink a glass of lukewarm seawater morning and night for her innards, and it made slight difference to her whether the water was of Pacific or Atlantic vintage."

Sen. John McCain (R-AZ)—the man looks it—refuses to eat any vegetables, whatever they may be. It is astonishing to hear that. One could almost guess that might be the case with him from the looks of his pasty, waxlike, insubstantial, toilet-paper-white complexion. A feature of those who suffer from lachanophobia, incidentally, is to have to endure in sad consequence, a dry, unwholesome, ineffectual, parchment-like skin. An ashen pallor virtually announces the curmudgeonly food refusal—and to a great degree the hidebound and often sniping way it is expressed—in the spiteful or negative anti-vegetable food crank. Dr. Samuel Johnson, scrofulous and "ruggedly" complected, told James Boswell who quoted him in his *Tour to the Hebrides* (1786), "A cucumber should be well sliced and dressed with pepper and vinegar, and then thrown out as good for nothing." Johnson did like fruit, however, and ate seven or eight large peaches in the morning before breakfast began, at least according to his friend, British diarist Mrs. Thrale (born Hesther Lynch Pizzi) in her *Anecdotes* (1826). I recall watching wide-waisted TV celebrity Rosie O'Donnell, a huge eater, anomalously making a tidy little cucumber dip on "The Martha Stewart Show." It seemed like such a tender gesture, even a sad one. O'Donnell, who suffered a life-threatening heart attack in 2012, confesses that eating right is still a daily struggle.

"It is said that the effect of eating too much lettuce is 'soporific'," wrote Beatrix Potter in *The Tale of the Flopsy Bunnies.* Does such an opinion seem somehow oddly thorny in such a mild book? You will be surprised to read in her *Merry Christmas, Peter Rabbit,* "All outward forms of religion are almost useless, and are the causes of endless strife… Believe there is a great power silently working all things for good, behave yourself and never mind the rest."

In Vladimir Nabokov's novel, *Pale Fire,* when the peculiar narrator/annotator Charles Kinbote meets the old poet John Shade at the faculty club, he writes, "His laconic suggestion that I 'try the pork' amused me. I am a strict vegetarian… Shade said that with him it was the other way around: he must make a definite effort to partake of a vegetable…" Curiously enough, soon enough, we find Shade at another point in the account loudly chewing a piece of celery.

We have alluded to the wide antipathy that is held for lima beans and my friend, the novelist William Vollmann's dislike of them. "Having eaten dog, cat, skewered scorpion shish kebab, and rat cooked in its furry jacket, I will say that the food I most hate is lima beans. My parents made me eat them.

Once they said I could get by with just one, so I kept it under my tongue all night, unable to bear the thought of chewing it, not wishing to be a bad little boy and spit it out—which in the morning they allowed me to do. I must have been about four." Disfavor for this vegetable, close to universal, includes chefs and cooks across the board. "One food that I find flavorless and unappealing is lima beans," declared Sandra Lee, the host of television's "Sandra's Money-Saving Meals," "I dislike all lima beans—canned, fresh or dried because of the starchy and grainy texture. Another food that I do not like is sweetbreads, which comes from the thymus gland or pancreas of a young calf, lamb or pig. Even when cooked properly, sweetbreads tend to be rubbery with a strong flavor and velvety texture. I find that when plated, the shape of the meat is unappealing and unappetizing."

Playboy model and reality-show celebrity, Kendra Wilkinson, hates cucumbers, fussily having made the point clear on one of the television episodes of "Sarah Palin's Alaska," where, in spite of themselves, the two divas of the day could not quite hide the fact that they also hated each other. "Cucumbers are vile," a friend of mine told me. "It's the *smell* for me, even cucumber-scented *toiletries* make me want to heave. I have managed to overcome many childhood dislikes of all sorts—mushrooms, radishes, kale, stinking cabbage—but I'm convinced that cucumbers caused the Black Death, and I will never ever look at one again." Talk-show host Rachel Maddow of MSNBC went on record the night of November 22, 2011, while inveighing against the brutal use by police of pepper spray on demonstrator, declared in passing that she also hugely dislikes bell peppers. It was an aggravation enough for her digression. I wonder if, in her pronounced dislike of them, Maddow was confusing bell peppers with something like those intensely hot *habañeros* or Scotch bonnets, chili peppers I remember from several of my trips to Mexico that, with their scorching bite, badly flooding your eyes, can run like electricity into your hair and feel more like an epilator than a pepper. I once tasted (and survived) the blast-oven-hot bite of Bhut or Naga Joloka pepper-powder in a goat stew in a native restaurant in Cape Town, South Africa, although I have heard that the scorching Trinidad Moruga Scorpion pepper is even hotter.

Who could hate parsley? Surely better to ask, who would bother? Is it not rather like fostering a dislike of the drifting motes of a dandelion? Poet Ogden Nash was one who called up such an animadversion. "Any dish that has either a taste or appearance that can be improved by parsley," he once snarkily wrote, "is *ipso facto* a dish unfit for human consumption." He reiterated this in his book, *Food*, with one of his memorable Nashian rhymes, "Parsley is gharsley." Yet is its "gharsliness" a value as an anti-corrosive? The ancient Romans ate parsley to prevent drunkenness. (It is the most commonly used herb in Italian cooking: *prezzemolo*. Slang in Italy *essere come il prezzemolo* means to turn up everywhere.) One might be reminded here not until as late as the mid 17th-century, on the then-celebrated occasion of famed chef Pierre François de la Varenne publishing his watershed *Pastissier Francois* in 1655, that vegetables as such were treated as a food in their own right, a fact that many a curmudgeonly anti-vegetarian might still contest.

Diligent respect for parsley, however, can be found in Juan Ramon Jimenez's *Platero and I*, his prose-poem about a writer and his donkey. The narrator's appreciation of his silver-grey donkey is such that at one point in his travels, he grants the beloved creature an ultimate honor, writing,

> Realizing that Platero has had his reward in his effort,
> as I have in my verses, I picked up a few sprigs of pars-
> ley from the house keeper's parsley bed, made them
> into a wreath and placed it on Platero's head, as on a
> Spartan's.

That is an apposite reference. The parsley leaf was the prize awarded winners at both the Isthmian games, held twice in each Olympiad at the Isthmus of Corinth, in honor of Poseidon, and at the Nemean games, celebrated at Nemea, in Argolis, in honor of Zeus. It was a tradition in ancient Greece that parsley—so-named because it grows near stones (Latin *petroselenum*, from Greek *petro-selinon*)—was strewn over graves or placed on the tombs of the dead.

I have previously mentioned that I find parsley, at best, irrelevant in food life, in spite of the fact that it is commodiously considered an herb, a spice, and a vegetable. I must admit that it is a storehouse of nutrients, one of the world's healthiest foods. Swiss-born chef Albert Stockli, the man who created the Four Seasons, the Mermaid Tavern, the Forum of the Twelve Caesars, Trattoria, Zum Zum, and other famous New York City restaurants, in his cookbook *Splendid Fare* refers to parsley as the "jewel of herbs, both in the pot and on the plate."

FDR hated broccoli. So does George H.W. Bush, who disliked virtually all vegetables. "The day he was 60, he said to me," reported his wife, Barbara, "'I am President of the United States, and I am never going to eat broccoli, Brussels sprouts, cauliflower or cabbage ever again.' And he hasn't!" He whined that he had never liked broccoli since he was a little boy when his mother made him eat it. As one response, covered by David Lauter of the LA Times, a positively huge broccoli shipment was delivered to the

White House. George Dunlop, president of the Washington-based United Fresh Fruit and Vegetable Assn., helpfully pointed out for the First Family all the virtues of the vegetable, and he cavalierly presented the First Lady with a vegetable bouquet. Broccoli is 'a green beam of light,' he said as he presented the First Lady with a beribboned vegetable bouquet. An extra 10 tons of the California-grown vegetable, which arrived in two truckloads, is being donated to a capital-area food bank. "Millie [the dog] and I thank you for the broccoli. We'll eat it," said Mrs. Bush, accepting the donated three boxes of veggies. But, as for the adamant husband, she said, "If his own blessed mother can't make him eat broccoli, I give up." No one was surprised to learn that #43's dim oldest son, George W. followed suit—same pedigree, same tastes, same kind of middling brain. (Does it not also say something about his unsophisticated son, George, that as one of his favorite foods he prefers his grilled cheese sandwiches made with Kraft Singles and white bread?) Barbara Bush, respectively wife and mother to the two Georges, is reportedly a terrible cook; that is, whenever she even went into the kitchen, reminding me of the old Henny Youngman joke: "My wife said she wanted to go someplace she had never been before. So I said, 'Try the kitchen.'" We all know the famous exchange in the cartoon in *The New Yorker* of December 8, 1928 (E.B. White's caption of a cartoon by Carl Rose):

> "It's broccoli, dear."
> "I say it's spinach, and I say the hell with it."

One of George H.W. Bush's favorite snacks? Pork rinds. Presidential taste has shown itself to be often peculiar. William Henry Harrison who subsisted on "raw beef and salt," as he put it, disliked vegetables. So did President Clinton who for the longest time thrived on fast food like Big Macs and Quarter Pounders, and there is no end of photographs show him stuffing his face with huge hamburgers virtually in both fists. Tubes of chubs! At one campaign stop in New Hampshire, the self-indulgent Clinton reportedly bought a dozen doughnuts and was working his way through the box until an aide stopped him. He eventually lost weight but like all true narcissists still loves to talk about his food, his diets. "To savor food, to conceive of a meal as an aesthetic experience, has been regarded as evidence of effeteness, a form of foreign foppery," wrote Michael Pollan in *In Defense of Food*, pointing out regarding political campaigns, "Few things have been more likely to get an American political candidate in hot water than a taste for fine food, as Martin Van Buren discovered during his failed 1840 re-election campaign." It had often been noted by visitors to the White House that Van Buren never ate pastries or puddings and avoided sweets, preferring instead a little fruit, but in 1840 had he dined out too elegantly and too often? Pollan offers that eating things like pork rinds and Big Macs were "politically astute tastes to show off."

An arbitrariness pertains to radishes regarding heat. Only the test of biting one reveals its flintiness. There are numerous varieties, varying in size, color, shape, and potency. The American poet Richard Armour addresses the dilemma in one of the entries in his poem, "Assorted Relishes:"

> Though pretty things, they likely as not
> Are either pithy or too hot,
> Nor do you know, till you have bitten
> If you've a tiger or a kitten."

I know people of a fastidious, squeamish cast who refuse to eat asparagus for its insistent after-smell in the urine. The vegetable—some call it a flower—contains sulfurous amino acids, which break down into sulfur-rich compounds on digestion, and the effect of eating asparagus on the urine has long been observed. Methyl mercaptan, the very same sulfur group that makes skunks so smelly, gives a peculiarly fetid odor to urine simply because certain compounds in it are metabolized to yield ammonia and sulfur-containing degradation products, including various thiols and thioesters, which impart to one's urine that characteristic pungent smell of this Spring delicacy. One British men's club is said to have put up a sign stating, "During the asparagus season, members are requested not to relieve themselves in the hat stand." Then who can forget in Proust's *La Recherche* that scene where Françoise, who is originally Aunt Léonie's cook at Combray and eventually Marcel's family cook—her arrogance, ignorance, and cruelty to all of the kitchen staff is legendary—orders the poor servant girl to peel the asparagus even though she is allergic to it? Did that possibly justify the wonderful asparagus and beef in aspic the stubborn cook produced? Maybe.

Asparagus has many virtues—some even hard to guess at. I marveled at the point when William Kuhn in his gossipy book, *Reading Jackie*, narrates a quaint and wonderful story to show an aspect of Ms. Onassis's quirkiness, one that John Loring told Caroline, recounting how when he and Jackie at Doubleday were editing a book, *The Tiffany Wedding*, Jackie had noticed a photograph of a thick bunch of wet asparagus tied together with a pink band. It struck her so forcefully—and whimsically—that Jackie exclaimed, "Oh isn't that beautiful? I just don't know why American brides can't carry bunches of asparagus at their weddings."

The food writer Elizabeth David who was born in 1913 to an upper-middle class family, rebelled against social norms of the day, later recalling with misery the plaguing boredom of nursery food in the 1920s. "We ate a lot of mutton and beef plainly cooked, with plain vegetables," she remembered. There were "odious puddings" of ground rice or tapioca "invented apparently solely to torment children." She "hated" the boiled watery vegetables she was given; green turnip tops, spinach, Jerusalem artichokes, parsnips. It was all burnt into her memory

What about leafy greens? While power-packed with nutrients and probably the healthiest foods you can eat, most of them *are* not always dark green in color—rough-hewn winter greens with a biting, unvarnished gritty taste like amaranth, arugula, Belgian endive, beet greens, broccoli rabe, chicory, cress, collard greens, curly endive, dandelion greens, dinosaur kale, escarole, mustard greens, nettles, puntarelle, radicchio, spinach, turnip greens, watercress, and rapini—they can be sharply bitter or nose-twistingly astringent and always rate high on food-aversion lists, and that includes the group of so-called "supertasters." Apparently, one in every four people is a special super-taster, a denomination applied to those few who possess a high number of taste buds, which results in a heightened sense of taste, at least according to Daniel Stone in *National Geographic* (December 2013). "The condition—seen more in women—can be bittersweet," he writes. "Supertasters eat fewer leafy greens, elevating the risk of colon cancer. They're also averse to fats. What they all have in common, says University of Florida's Linda Bartoshuk, is 'they're picky eaters.'"

Certain raw greens in many places and among many people connote "poor food." Truman Capote in his novel, *The Grass Harp*, depicts the young girl Middy "clutching a copy of *Screen Secrets*," making her brother, Appleseed, think Hollywood success will end their penury: "Middy's gonna be a big lady in the picture shows. They make lotsa money, the ladies in the picture shows do, and then we ain't gonna never eat another collard green as long as we live."

I suspect that the former Ugandan dictator, bullying Idi Amin Dada hated peas. There is a memorable scene in Giles Foden's 1998 novel, *The Last King of Scotland*, that strikes me as based on an actual food aversion, where (to give him his full title) "His Excellency President for Life, Field Marshal Al Hadji Doctor Idi Amin, VC, DSO, MC, Lord of All the Beasts of the Earth and Fishes of the Sea, and Conqueror of the British Empire in Africa in General and Uganda in Particular," in an unthinkably crude moment at a formal banquet in Kampala with tables filled with things like yam chips, fried groundnuts, and sweet potato rissoles, loudly calls out a warning to his guests. "'Watch out for this foods,' he bellowed, tapping a dish. 'There is an old Swahili proverb: if you give pigeon peas to a donkey, he will fart.' That is why I never eat this foods [sic].'" On the other hand, in contrast, Ninon de Lenclos, the 17th-century courtesan who was reported to have had more than 5000 sexual partners in the course of forty years, at least according to Norman Lewis in his essay, "Aphrodisiacs I Have Known," "attributed her successful amatory career partly to the assistance provided by pureed peas, to which she sometimes added a little sherry." Although I particularly like peas—to me, steamed and buttered just-picked peas may be among the greatest, if not the greatest, food treats on earth (except perhaps catfish in a Cajun butter-sauce with peppery batter-fried potato slices called "Jojos" in the Mississippi! Doo Dah!)—I wonder which of the two dishes I would have pushed away first, Ninon's slightly over-fussified puree or the unique breakfast munch.

A singular food aversion was the northen black-eyed peas, which were strictly fare for animals. When General William T. Sherman began his march to the sea on November 15, 1864 from the captured city of Atlanta to the seaport of Savannah, his soldiers, foraging for anything they could eat like livestock and grain, never once touched any of the stocks of black-eyed peas that they came across. At that time, in the northern states in general, the lowly black-eyed pea was not valued as food, not even close to it, so that the, to-them, strange little vegetables were left behind in great quantities as Union troops drove through the South in the assumption that such pig-fare would be of no use to the survivors either. (It was the same with possum, still thought of by some good ol' boys as the "other white.meat.") At the time, Southerners, grateful that they had anything to eat, made many a meal of black-eyed peas, which remain a staple there still, especially on New Year's Day, for good luck.

In Ian McEwan's children's book, *The Daydreamer*, a 10-year-old boy named Peter Fortune who lives somewhere between dream and reality selectively hates all vegetables but one. "Apart from all vegetables except potatoes, and fish, eggs, and cheese, there was nothing he would not eat." He loves chocolate—only for a while, mind you, for he even gets sick of that. I was surprised at the English boy's rejection of fish. In "The Language of Food," Anthony Burgess unhesitatingly contended, "Fish and chips is the finest dish in the world." It is a bias, of course, and a bit of an exaggeration, surely, but also understandable. He himself was a good cook. And as Simone Weil has noted, one is faithful to the food one was brought up on, and, as Burgess also suggests, "that probably constitutes patriotism." In his interview in the *Paris Review*, he stated, "I am sometimes mentally and physically ill for Lancashire food—hot pot, lobscouse, and so on—and I have to have these things. I'm loyal to Lancashire, I suppose, but not strongly enough to wish to go back and live there."

John Churchill, the first Duke of Marlborough, who never fought a battle he did not win, nevertheless met his match with cabbage—he was not only allergic to the vegetable but also detested it. Punk rocker Iggy Pop supposedly hates broccoli so much that whenever he performs anywhere, a "rider" put out by his publicist peevishly insists that both American Spirit cigarettes and a bunch of broccoli be placed in his dressing room. Questioned about this bizarre request, his response was that he wanted the broccoli—I am not making this up—so that he could throw it into a bin, obviously to express his hatred of it. You find that fussy? According to *The Blurb*, actress Jennifer Lopez in her riders petulantly demands "a trailer of substantial size, furnished all in white with flowers, tablecloths, drapes, candles, and couches, a VCR and CD player, and 43 music CDs selected by her covering all the latest R&B, hip-hop, and salsa. Oh, and she also demands that her coffee be stirred counter-clockwise only."

On October 6, 1809 a paper called "Of the Irritability of Vegetables" by the surgeon Robert Lyall was read in Manchester, England analyzing the properties of vegetables. Lyall advanced the theory that they bore within themselves a force parallel to the muscular power of the human body. The masterpiece of Vertumnus, Roman god of the seasons, posed as Rudolf II, Holy Roman Emperor by Arcimboldo, the ingenious—some say raving mad—16th-century painter to the court in Prague, seems to be making that very point in the flushed apple-cheeks, extra-strong cabbage shoulders, cornstalk ears, and full head of hair fashioned as bunches of grapes. Lyall had studied plants for years, of all sorts, examining how their leaves constrict, how they respond to insects, how they act under sun, wind, rain, heat, light, moisture, etc. I have actually read his full treatise. Among his many conjectures, he posits the theory that vegetable plants are both "sensible" and "irritable" and leaves us with the notion that, in their complexity, they have personalities. I have the distinct impression that he rates vegetables as basically censorious, if vital, and crotchety, if responsive, concluding that, as curmudgeons, they had best be left alone. It all seems humorously verified in "The Boy Who Hated Vegetables," a short story by the Indian writer Pareo Anand, in which a few anthropomorphized vegetables—Mr. Potato, Carrot Tops, etc.—who initially hate the boy, Balbir, turn the tables and eventually win him over. In the anti-vegetable department can be numbered singer Nat King Cole; multi-billionaire Donald Trump; writer Douglas Copeland ("I don't want any vegetables, thank you. I paid for the cow to eat them for me"); chef Dan Barber ("Vegetables deplete soil. They're extractive. If soil has a bank account, vegetables make the largest withdrawals"); actress Emma Roberts; the beautiful singer Rihanna ("I never eat salad. I make sure I don't put a lot of junk into my system, but I hate vegetables"); and, among others, the inquisitive four-year-old cartoon character who goes by the name Caillou. A quick visit here should also be made to the young pop-singer and actress, Miley Cyrus, who in her book *Miles to Go* (2009) professes repeatedly to an undisguised loathing for all vegetables.

A rude commonness has been ascribed to vegetables, a coarse and uncivil indelicacy. Rudimentary, vulgar. When the mistress of his dame school punished the disobedient young Edgar Allan Poe, she did so by hanging a vegetable around his neck and sending him home in disgrace.

"The earth yields nourishment to vegetables, sensible creatures feed on vegetables, and both are substitutes to reasonable souls," Robert Burton assured us in *The Anatomy of Melancholy* (1621)—as to the sanction of Holy Write, Proverbs 15:17 is a virtual advertisement for them—but the pre-industrial English, hearty beef eaters, were convinced that vegetables "ingender ylle humours and be oftetymes the cause of petrified fevers," melancholy, and flatulence, as Clifford Wright observes in his *Mediterranean Vegetables* where he notes that as a consequence laws were passed denying fruits and vegetables, which left the population living in a pre-scorbutic state. It was a disservice to that country, because, going back even to the days of ancient Rome, vegetables were at the center of Mediterranean cooking. "The hunger grows worse and worse. It seems to me an age since butcher's meat passed these lips; and, to add to my misery, I can hear every word the callous wretches are saying in the cabin," complains the traveler-by-boat (to Cadiz, Malta, Athens, Cairo, etc.) in "Wanderings of Our Fat Contributor" in William Makepeace Thackeray's hilarious but too little read *Contributions to Punch* (1845), a veritable hotcupboard of xenophobic snipes, wonderfully cheeky opinions, and boldly expressed food aversions, including fried sole, flabby raw mutton-chops, tasteless choky dried toast, port wine, sherry ("never worth the drinking"), and, yes, crocodile which he disesteems as "very fishy and tough."

Our Fat Contributor refers to Lord Byron losing weight by taking vinegar. He exclaims, "Vinegar?—nonsense—try Eastern travel." In light of its penchant for avoiding vegetables one may ask, is there a single national vegetable that can stand in the UK? Leeks are Welsh, as we know. Potatoes are inevitably associated with Ireland, and as to deathless, overcooked cabbage, cauliflower and Brussels sprouts there, they are usually associated with the drab fare of their public schools. "Asparagus is a strong contender for an

English vegetable, coming into season on St. George's Day," writes Nora Ryan, editor of the BBC Food website. But whether asparagus could be described as Britain's national vegetable is a moot point. The French have the green bean, garlic and onions, Eastern Europeans have the beetroot and cabbage, and Italians can pretty much lay claim to the tomato. Turnips are from Europe. Potatoes come from South America. The carrot supposedly hales from the Netherlands. Tell you what. I will have to go with Beatle John Lennon who sang, "Give peas a chance."

At one point at the Quebec Conference in 1943, according to James Thurber in a letter written to Harvey Breit on November 22, 1949, President Franklin Roosevelt, sitting next to Mrs. Winston Churchill, told her with tongue-in-cheek that the Brussels sprout was the great American vegetable. He convinced her that there were thirty-four interesting ways to cook them but added that, sadly, the English were not privy to the subtle secrets of its preparation. Clemmie was dubious, so Roosevelt decided to pull a practical joke on her. He told Mrs. Kermit Roosevelt—Edith—that he wanted to have a pamphlet privately printed titled, "Thirty-four Ways to Cook Brussels Sprouts" and said he wanted Thurber to draw the cover. Poor, half-blind Thurber admitted to having trouble drawing a good sprout and that all his attempts had came out looking variously like an apple, a squeezed baseball, or an electric light bulb, no surprise from a man who once tried to feed a nut to a faucet, thinking it was a squirrel. (Dorothy Parker once quipped that all of his drawings had the "semblance of unbaked cookies.") Thurber admits, "I did dozen of covers and finally solved the awkwardness by drawing my dog in front of the table on his hind legs with one paw reaching for the bowl." The pamphlet was printed, in any case, but only for members of the Roosevelt and Churchill families. Thurber dryly noted, "The artist did not receive a copy."

People with allergies, especially those suffering latex antipathies, avoid eating avocados. Avocado leaves contain a toxic fatty acid derivative, persin, which in sufficient quantity can also cause colic in horses, even death. Birds also seem to be particularly sensitive to this toxic compound. (Feeding avocados or guacamole to an animal should be avoided completely.) They are not always popular with humans, either. Charles Higham in *The Duchess of Windsor* gives an account of a Christmas when, to assuage his father, David, the Prince of Wales, got the Royal caterer, Frederic Corbitt, to scramble about to try to find—a task during a cold English winter—twelve avocados to give George V as a unique present. When they were served to him in a *vinaigrette*, the king snapped, "What in heaven's name is this?" David later telephoned Wallis, his consort, soon-to-be-wife, and was disconsolate.

Certain vegetables get a bad rap. Take what are called the "nightshade vegetables" or Solanaceae, a plant family that includes eggplant, peppers, potatoes and tomatoes. (The term "nightshade" seems to have been coined by Hollywood ass-clowns or diet ignoramuses simply because some of these plants prefer to grow in shady areas, and some flower at night.) Weirdly enough, an online search of "nightshade vegetables" yields results linking them to a host of health ailments from arthritis to migraines. Many naturopaths recommend that people with arthritis avoid nightshades. Patricia J, Wales, a naturopathic doctor from Calgary, Canada, says naturopaths often suggest that people with osteoarthritis eliminate nightshades. These vegetables are notably excluded from certain eating plans. *Dr. Joshi's Holistic Detox*—a book endorsed by Gwyneth Paltrow and Kate Moss—claims that nightshades are related to poison ivy and potentially poisonous! "But poison ivy isn't even in the same plant family," explains Barry Micallef, a plant biochemistry expert at the University of Guelph.

Kale is widely disliked. Garth Schnier, executive chef at the Sandton Sun Hotel, said, "Whoever decided that kale was good to use as a garnish has clearly never tasted it. I am a firm believer in garnishing a dish with edible ingredients that enhance it. So, while kale may look greenly bright in a garden, it should be kept well away from all plates!" A food that European peasants relied on for nutrition though hard winter months, kale is not only bitter when young (or when harvested after a frost) but stronger tasting than cabbage. When older, its leaves need to be steamed, boiled, or sautéed. "Our food is miserably poor. Dry bread and coffee substitute for breakfast. Dinner spinach or lettuce for 14 days on end," Anne Frank noted in her diary on April 27, 1943. "Potatoes twenty centimeters long and tasting sweet and rotten. Whoever wants to slim should stay in the 'Secret Annex,'" The eight Jews were eating potatoes at the Prinsengracht 263-267 Amsterdam at every meal a full year later. Young Anne's disgust for kale predominated. She wrote, "It's incredible how kale that is probably a few years old can stink! The smell is a mixture of W.C., bad plums, preservatives + 10 rotten eggs. Ugh! The mere thought of eating that muck makes me feel sick."

No, the Green Camp definitely has its solid detractors, including the sainted Anne Frank, modernism's living angel, a girl nevertheless whose entrepreneurial father, it turns out, fiddled with her private diary in order to make it jibe with some of his own opinions as well as to turn a penny.

Celery recently topped the list in a modern survey as the single most hated vegetable among adults in Japan. I have heard every complaint about it from the fact that one can have celery breath to its stringiness to the horror that its stink can pervade a house to the fact that it tastes like tap water.

Celery may be a building block of French cooking, but it has no place at the distinguished restaurant Chanterelle. "I don't use it in my stocks," says its chef, David Waltuck, whose loathing for it has become legend. "I don't use it in my mirepoix," he has complained. "It has no flavor. It is one-dimensional. It is an exercise in chewing. It is pointless." Greens are often abused and frequently given short shrift. In London Oscar Wilde once complained to a waiter about just having had the worst watercress sandwiches he had ever had. Apparently he had been served a "loaf with a field in the middle of it."

Okra seems to be a vegetable that is universally reviled, except in Louisiana and generally in Cajun country. Michael Holenstein, partner and chef at De Hoek in Magaliesburg, South Africa, hates okra. He asserts, "The slime and goo it produces is something one can't go into in a family newspaper. Also, I once had a nasty experience at a very snazzy five-star lodge—a combo of sweetbreads and mussels! Both were undercooked. The chef assured me that that's how they serve that dish. I couldn't believe the combination and the disgusting taste." Chef David Burke, the American chef and restaurateur, hates okra especially—along with anchovies and blue fish. So does talk- show host and media personality, Wendy Williams. Regarding okra, I am reminded of the lying compliment that the insincere bounder Jason Robards unconvincingly feeds to the truly incompetent would-be cook Jane Fonda in the awful movie *Any Wednesday* (1966), "I looooove your cooking. I mean that okra casserole with the poached egg in the middle and the cottage cheese was superb!"

Danny Meyer, proprietor of the Union Square Café and the Gramercy Tavern dislikes fiddlehead ferns, known down South as "ramps." "Let's be honest," Meyer has written. "A fiddle-head fern is not delicious, no matter how you prepare it. Blanched, sautéed, batter-fried, or raw, it is nothing more than a bland, oddly textured plant whose only redeeming virtue is that it doesn't poison you. (And I'm told it's even capable of doing that.) The best thing about ramps ('wild' leeks) is their name… A ramp is distinctive only if you eat one raw."

Pontificating on vegetables, for some reason—distinguishing facts and details and quirks, about them—seems to be a fascination for wealthy, over-advantaged people. As we have previously mentioned, novelist Truman Capote always insisted, comically to a degree, that the sole difference in the lives of the super-rich and the average person was the snobbish and ludicrous insistence by the former on very small vegetables. That was his social dividing wall. "Rich people," he explained, "always serve such marvelous vegetables." "Delicious little tiny vegetables," he mockingly wrote. "Little fresh-born things, scarcely out of the earth. Little baby corn, little baby peas.

Little lambs that have been ripped out of their mothers' wombs. That's the real difference. All of their vegetables are so incredibly fresh and unborn.

For most of his life Truman Capote insinuated himself into the lives of the super rich and moneyed classes, for it was a world he loved and one with which he was clearly obsessed. The diminutive author was correct, as a matter of fact. The fabulously wealthy,, whether they are "old money" or over-reaching parvenus, badly need distinctions of any kind to distinguish— to separate—themselves from the *hoi polloi*, anything to draw a sharp, discrete line between themselves and the people they often perceive as lower slobs and unsocialized stooges and bare-faced strivers. Baby vegetables they feel connote taste and the discerning qualities of a prim palate, like new potatoes, asparagus, delicate baby or "spring" ginger, the young, immature, more expensive kind with the pink blush, then only young broad beans, before they mature, which are even delicious when eaten raw, and of course sweet delicate petits pois (*Piselli novelli*), the sugars of which begin to turn to starch as soon as they're picked.

Not big gross heads of cauliflower, mind you, nothing huge, only a few tiny curds of it. Not fat regular green beans, but French *haricot verts*, which are more delicate. Not great fat walloping Vidalia onions, but sweet braised baby ones. It is the same with fruit for the rich. Not large Goa mangoes but the small, exquisitely scented, sweet Alfonsi mangoes. No huge bananas but smaller pisang mas or golden bananas. Not cheek-sized strawberries, but the intensely-sweet, robustly-flavored, day-neutral, thimble-sized Tristar strawberries developed from a wild strain in Utah. It is the same for them with seafood. Sweet baby clams, not big dumb plate-faced quahogs. Not Coquille St. Jacques-size oysters, but sweet miniature *pétoncle*. Not big dopey-headed pineapples, but tiny extra-sweet Queen Victorias from South Africa.

It is all about snobbery. Snootiness. Jim Harrison in *The Raw and the Cooked* preciously refers to lamb—this guy is a hearty hunter?—"braised with the smallest fresh April vegetables, including artichokes." The very idea suggests infanticide and such an overmastering craving is perverse. (The concept can even apply to clothes. The decadent Duchess of York, Wallis Simpson, particularly loved the fur of young or premature Karakul lambs and baby mink.)

The Irish poet/playwright Brendan Behan's mother, Kathleen, was a maid in the house owned by Maud Gonne MacBride and knew the poet W. B. Yeats quite well, according to Behan in his book, *Brendan Behan's Island*. Behan explains that Yeats was "absolutely impervious to what he ate, as he didn't know what he was eating half the time. He absent-mindedly would put sugar in the soup and salt in the coffee and all sorts of peculiar things like that." Behan goes on to say that the major dislike that he had in the way of food was basically parsnips. Once he was served parsnips by some mistake and the notoriously unfastidious Irishman remarked: "This is a very peculiar pudding." "After years of adventurous eating there are only a few things that I dislike," wrote the young macho writer Ernest Hemingway in a youthful piece in the *The Toronto Star Weekly* (November 24, 1923), who in a long lifetime of trial and travel ate virtually everything, including (his list) rhino meat, kudu, wolves, porcupine ("quill pig"), eels, sparrows, bird's nests, horse meat, even spiders. "One of them is parsnips. Another is the doughnut. Another is Yorkshire pudding. Another is boiled potatoes." Poetaster Ogden Nash in his antic poem, "The Parsnip" wrote,

> The parsnip, children, I repeat,
> Is simply an anemic beet.
> Some people call the parsnip edible.
> Myself, I find this claim incredible."

Speaking of doughnuts, H.L. Mencken actually found one thing to recommend in a taste-treat he despised. For some peculiar reason he disliked donuts, at one point declaring, "Anyhow, the hole in the doughnut is at least digestible." My brother Paul in several of his travel books goes on record, repeatedly, as disliking oatmeal, particularly lumpy oatmeal, which frankly my mother did make us eat—and refused to let us *refuse* it—especially on the kind of cold winter mornings that we woke up to in New England. He wrote, "It tasted like wallpaper paste." President James Garfield hated oatmeal. The reason? He was put on an oatmeal diet to recover from being shot. In her memoir of childhood, *Where the Wings Grow*, I love the uncompromising succinctness of Agnes DeMille's bold dismissal of the stuff: "I was never obliged to face up to oatmeal." Nor should this be forgotten: how did the man in the moon burn his mouth on the way to Norwich? Supping cold plum porridge!

Along with parsnips, let me add, Ernest Hemingway went out of his way to state that he also particularly disliked eating sea slugs, Chinese 100-year-old eggs, and mule meat. ("In ranking foods it should be placed somewhere between boiled moccasin and the more toothsome of the tallow candles.") A Francophile, he still chose to go on record as disliking snails, writing "But in Dijon you are no man if you don't eat escargots. So I ate them… The thing they remind you most of is an inner tube. Cross an inner tube with a live frog, and make the product slippery, and you have the texture." He also detested goat's milk. "Once upon a time I lived for almost three weeks on goat's milk," he wrote. "That was when my face was yellow as a Chinaman's with mountain jaundice, and they used to drive the goats up to the door of the hospital. I will never willingly take another drink of goat's milk." Strangely enough, Papa Hemingway praised as superb some of the more distinctly *outré* foods that he had eaten. "Muskrats are good eating, too, as any Indian can tell you," he declared. "The meat is as tender as chicken." "Beaver tail is another strictly Canadian delicacy... about the best thing I'd ever sunk a tooth into." He said, "Deer liver fried with back bacon is another wonderful article of food." "Octopus is a great article on the menu of all seaports of the Mediterranean." No, it was more common things like yams, boiled potatoes, Yorkshire pudding, and diner doughnuts, that he simply could not take.

If Hemingway disliked boiled potatoes, Leopold Bloom, one of the two memorable protagonists of James Joyce's *Ulysses*, had his own thoughts on them. In the wild "Sirens" episode, when Bloom sees young Dilly Dedalus, a girl from a large family, walk past, looking raggedy and underfed, his gloomy reflection on her condition is, "Potatoes and marge... Undermines the constitution." A Jew, Bloom feels contempt for priests who, having only their own mouths to feed, compel the faithful to increase and multiply in ever-larger families. Bloom has all kinds of food biases. We see him passing Lemon's sweetshop, reflecting on how the pastries and sweets damage the health of the poor. Seeing the mystic poet George Russell on the street causes Bloom to contrast the hearty diet of the carnivorous police with the vegetarian Theosophist who edited the *Irish Homestead*. One bit of advice in that journal against paralysis was its advice on how to improve the diet of ordinary families. Bloom is, however, skeptical of the vegetarianism and with satirical exaggeration mocks their extravagant admonitions, thinking: "Only weggebobbles and fruit. Don't eat beefsteak. If you do the eyes of that cow will pursue you through all eternity."

What we think of as veggie burgers—"nut-steaks" to Bloom—are fraudulent imitations. As he walks along, he is suspicious of the vague, cloudy poetry produced by the vegetarians of the Irish revival, while admitting that you could not squeeze a single line of poetry out of the over-fed police. Although he is disgusted by the rows of men guzzling meat in the Burton restaurant ("See the animals feed... men, men, men") which forms the thought in his mind, "Eat or be eaten. Kill! Kill!" we can see in the "Calypso" episode of *Ulysses*, that Bloom is nevertheless described as not at all put off by the unenticing exotica of certain foodstuffs:

> Mr Leopold Bloom ate with relish the inner organs
> of beasts and fowls. He liked thick giblet soup, nutty

gizzards, a stuffed roast heart, liverslices fried with crustcrumbs, fried hencods' roes. Most of all he liked grilled mutton kidneys which gave to his palate a fine tang of faintly scented urine.

As a sort of literary bookend here, Vera, the wife of the brilliant novelist, Vladimir Nabokov, in response to a projected book of celebrity recipes, wrote in reply,

Dear Miss Stephens,

My husband asks me to tell you, in reply to your kind letter of August 22, that he is fairly indifferent to gastronomic matters. However, he detests 1) underdone meat, 2) all inner organs, such as kidneys, brains, liver, tongue, sweetbread, etc., 3) sea food other than fish.

Sincerely yours,
Mrs. Vladimir Nabokov

Mrs. Nabokov fails to mention that her husband also disliked the taste of butterfly. Oh yes, the novelist, who refused to eat underdone meat, once ate a couple of butterflies—and found them disgusting. "When I was younger," Nabokov confided to a *Sports Illustrated* reporter in Switzerland,

I ate some butterflies in Vermont to see if they were poisonous. I didn't see any difference between a Monarch butterfly and a Viceroy. The taste of both was vile, but I had no ill effects. They tasted like almonds and perhaps a green cheese combination. I ate them raw. I held one in one hot little hand and one in the other. Will you eat some with me tomorrow for breakfast?

Nabokov's food dislikes are the virtual opposite of Mr. Leopold Bloom's, and I have been given to wonder often if this anti-menu of his was not a corrective to James Joyce, out of some deeply arcane competitive sense, because the man was pusillanimous and grudging to a fault and jealous of other great writers, among them Fyodor Dostoevsky, Henry James, and William Faulkner. He was vain, curmudgeonly, exotic, and cross-grained enough for that and not at all above envy, remaining fully convinced to the very end that he was above the common cut of all men.

As to Nabokov's authorial infallibility and eating, why would he have John Shade in *Pale Fire* say "We luncheoned"? It is the last thing a New England poet would say, a verbal implausibility—and a bit of a gaffe on Nabokov's part—more fitting for a wealthy dowager from Newport to say than an aging college professor from the town of New Wye in the Appalachian Mountains. Nabokov loved to pontificate on every fact and phase of life, making lordly pronouncements from on high. In one interview he wrote in high self-approval, "I have never been interested in what is called the literature of social comment (in journalistic and commercial parlance: 'great books'). I am not 'sincere,' I am not 'provocative,' I am not 'satirical.' I am neither a didacticist nor an allegorizer. Politics and economics, atomic bombs, primitive and abstract art forms, the entire Orient, symptoms of 'thaw' in Soviet Russia, the Future of Mankind, and so on, leave me supremely indifferent... My loathings are simple: stupidity, oppression, crime, cruelty, soft music." (I will leave it to the objective reader to evaluate the depth of insight of the infallible author of *Lolita* when—unasked and unsolicited—he affectionately judges himself "not provocative.")

In his book *Strong Opinions* (1973), as we have seen, the prissy self-regarding Nabokov stated," I don't belong to any club or group. I don't fish, cook, dance, endorse books, sign books, co-sign declarations, eat oysters, get drunk, go to church, go to analysts, or take part in demonstrations."

Loathings? *Try the entire Orient!*

How arrogant can you get?

What is remarkable is that offal, the entrails and innards of butchered animals—as an English mass noun, the term "offal" has no plural form—are considered a delicacy by some and by others sheer trash. "Variety meats" is the euphemistic term by which *haute cuisine* tries to push it onto you. The word shares its etymology with several German words: *abfall* (offall in some Western German dialects), *afval* in Dutch and Afrikaans, *avfall* in Norwegian and Swedish, and *affald* in Danish. These Germanic words all mean "garbage," or—literally—"off-fall," referring to what has fallen off during butchering. However, these words are not used to refer to food. For instance, the German word for offal is *Innereien*. Menu items include scrotum, brain, chitterlings (pig's small intestine), trotters (feet), heart, head (of pigs, calves, sheep and lamb), kidney, liver, spleen, "lights" (lung), sweetbreads (thymus or pancreas), fries (testicles), tongue, snout (nose), ears, tripe (reticulum), brains, and maws (stomach).

Much of our dislike of offal or innards or lights comes more or less from squeamishness rather than aversion to the taste or texture of it, but the fact remains that our word "garbage" was defined in the early 15th-century as "giblets of a fowl, waste parts of an animal." Its sense of "refuse" and/or "filth" is first attested to in the 1580s. "The fifth quarter," a delicate term for offal, still used in France and Italy, is also the name of an offal cookbook by the celebrated London-based cookbook author and teacher, Anissa Helou.

Enid Lambert's meals served to her husband and children in Jonathan Franzen's novel *The Corrections* are negatively memorable. But her revolting "Dinner of Revenge," conceived in her disappointment, is beyond grim. When her husband Alfred one morning forgets to say goodbye to her, she takes culinary revenge with a liver dinner which consists of "ferrous lobes of liver like corrosion" [all] dredged in "brown grease-soaked flakes of flour... impastoed on the ferrous, rust-colored bacon, boiled beet greens that "leaked something cupric, and mashed rutabaga that "expressed a clear yellowish liquid similar to plasma or the matter in a blister."

Strangely enough, the meal is full of health-bringing iron!

Novelist Henry Miller could not stand tripe (from French *tripes* which is from Italian *trippa*), which is a type of edible offal from the stomachs of various farm animals. It is one of those foods that, for weal or woe, has also become an eponym for worthless (see also "chopped liver"). Beef tripe is usually cobbled together to eat from only the first three chambers of a cow's stomach: the *rumen* (blanket/flat/smooth tripe), the *reticulum* (honeycomb and pocket tripe), and the *omasum* (book/bible/leaf tripe). *Abomasum* (reed) tripe is seen much less frequently, owing to its glandular tissue content. Tripe from pigs may also be referred to as—perfectly named—"paunch." Piled up in a market stall, tripe resembles a stack of discarded washcloths. Folks who say that they would never eat tripe probably have unknowingly consumed it in one form or another, say, in andouille sausage, potted meat, Scottish haggis, the Latin American soup called *mondongo*, Czech goulash soup, Serbian *skembisi*, Tripoux, and—hello!—a richly flavorful McRib, one of McDonald's barbecue-sauce-smothered boneless pork sandwiches, artfully molded to resemble a rack of ribs!

I recall in a grim recollection George Orwell's amazingly repulsive account in the pages of *The Road to Wigan Pier* of his lodging with the Brookers who sold tripe, "gray flocculent stuff," that was crawling with black beetles, and also the image of Mr. Brooker in particular who, with his grubby hands, insisted with smiling insistence on fussily and fixatedly doling out the bread for each lodger, one by one, leaving on each slice the imprint of his filthy thumb, which reminds me in its grubbiness of Edith Sitwell's lines from *A Book of Winter*,

> I thought I saw the wicked old witch in
> the richest gallipot in the kitchen!"

I might add here that Orwell, who defended English food, particularly loved clotted cream, sweet pickle, English breads, especially English cottage loaf and the "soft part of its crust," and, above all, cheese—he thought Stilton "the best cheese of its type in the world, with Wensleydale not far behind." One can contrast in the plastic food offered by the Ministry of Plenty in the dystopian Oceania in his novel *Nineteen Eighty-Four* which includes the ironically named Victory cigarettes, Victory gin, and Victory coffee, all of which are of extremely poor quality, but what else can one expect in a topsy-turvy world where individuality, even history as such, has vanished and "War is Peace," "Freedom is Slavery," and "Ignorance is Strength"?

I tend to recall the British Navy when I think of hard-tack, the crackers that also sufficed for much of the food the soldiers ate during the American Civil War and which one Union soldier said "required a very strong blow of the fist to break." It is said that to maximize the taste, the crackers—manufactured (and still made) by G. H. Bent Company of Milton, Mass., the largest suppliers to the Army of the Potomac throughout the war—should be soaked in water and fried in pork fat. Foot soldiers referred to this delicacy as "skillygalee." The crackers served well as naval rations, also, simply because, durable as linoleum flooring, they could weather storms at sea and stand up to the passage of time, at least to some degree. Served with grog, rum diluted with water, which was part of a sailor's daily allotment of British warships as late as 1970, although the U.S. Navy abolished its grog ration in 1862.

Former Massachusetts Governor Mitt Romney will not touch eggplant. Harry Golden also despised it. In his feuilleton, "How to Detect a Bad Cook" from the collection of comic essays, *You're Entitle'* (1956), he notes,

> Bad cooks are crazy about serving eggplant and invent
> every sort of excuse and plot and intrigue to make it
> a main course. Why bad cooks should have lighted
> upon eggplant, I don't know, but I do know they
> have an utterly strange attraction towards this bland
> and useless vegetable. If you meet a lady who serves
> you eggplant I recommend, if you love her, that you
> be nice and kind to her, but don't marry her. She's

> no one to whom to bring home the boss. My conclu-
> sion remains. Eggplant may be a dandy weapon for
> Neapolitans to hurl at tenors who sing flat, but it is
> no food for a growing boy or a grown man, as we say
> down heah [sic] in the South.

Nothing will appease him on the subject. A lady once sent Golden a recipe for eggplant cooked in tomato sauce with chopped beef. His reply? "Rat-atooey, if you will, was as bland a dish as ever I turned my back upon." Golden surely echoes what Robert Frost once said, "There is one thing more exasperating than a wife who can cook and won't, and that's a wife who can't cook and will."

Do you remember how in Gabriel García Márquez' novel, *Love in the Time of Cholera*, after she agrees to marry the town's most eligible bachelor, the beautiful Fermina inadvertently sends the real love of her life, Florentino, into a sad but inevitable downward spiral of romantic desperation and sexual debauch? Fermina's disheartening and baffling decision to wed Dr. Urbino largely hinges on one major condition, that being that the physician will never force her to eat eggplant, a food which she has feared and hated since childhood. The sad fact is Urbino does just that. Fermina's mother-in-law in fact serves up aubergine every day, "out of respect for her dead husband." The marriage does not end up being a very happy one.

"Eggplant is a waste not only of the chef's time, but [I] even wondered if the Creator could not have used the time to better result," wrote poetaster Maya Angelou, second-guessing God in her cookbook, *Great Food, All Day Long: Cook Splendidly, Eat Smart*. I suppose someone with so much experience has the right to question the Creator of the Universe, for Marguerite Ann Johnson (her real name) has been a calypso dancer, a bongo player, a hooker, a madame for prostitutes, a pro-Castro activist, a composer (or so she claims), a poet, a singer, an actress, and cranked out three spoken word albums, all the while taking the time, according to critic Mary Jane Lupton, to get married at least twice, although *Dr.* Angelou—as she insisted that she be called in public and always so introduced of course on celebrated occasions (she has been awarded over thirty honorary degrees!)—had never bothered to clarify the number of times that she has been married, "for fear of sounding frivolous." According to the six tortured autobiographies she wrote and to biographer Marcia Ann Gillespie, she married Tosh Angelos in 1951 and Paul du Feu in 1973 and began her relationship with Vusumzi Make in 1961, but never formally married him. She had a son Guy, one grandson, and two young great-grandchildren. Although she was one of the worst writers on earth, she was awarded the National Book Award, a Pulitzer Prize, the National Medal of Arts, the Lincoln Medal, and in 2011 the Presidential Medal of Freedom. "A national treasure," she was invariably called when she was introduced. She later appeared, full face on an official U.S. postage stamp, with a quotation cribbed from another writer.

Comedian and actor Jim Carrey cannot like carrots very much. On the television show *Late Night with Conan O'Brien*, he said in a skit, "In the year 2000, it is discovered that carrots do not actually improve your eyesight, but they are still number one for curing a deep rectal itch." That may have been the skit talking. In an interview, he once confessed, "Green eggs and ham was the story of my life. I wouldn't eat a thing when I was a kid, but Dr. Seuss inspired me to try to cauliflower." He is a vegetarian to this day. The curmudgeonly New York writer Fran Lebowitz said, "Large, naked, raw carrots are acceptable as food only to those who live in hutches eagerly awaiting Easter," a type that would disqualify the Jewish quipster on several counts. Actor Tom Selleck hates cooked carrots. Will Rogers disliked them, as well. He quipped, "Some guy invented Vitamin A out of a carrot. I'll bet he can't invent a good meal out of one." The argument for banning carrots bigger than your thumb is a bit more arbitrary. "I will serve baby carrots," said Alexandra Guarnaschelli, chef of Butter, as much a New York nightclub as a restaurant, which is located at 415 Lafayette Street (between 4th St & Astor Place) in New York. "But once it gets over two inches long I break into a cold sweat." Ms. Guarnaschelli, once the sous-chef at Guy Savoy's La Butte Chaillot in Paris, where julienne carrots had a permanent place on the menu, confessed with some alarm, "Now I have a panic attack when I see shredded carrot in a salad."

What is it about writers and carrots? Regarding food aversions, novelist Tom Wolfe holds carrots, as such, in low esteem. He once confided to me that he can only take "carrots with ginger genes; with ginger, in carrot ginger soup, they become what they were born to be." Boldly wrote Marian Keyes in *Lucy Sullivan Is Getting Married*, "I'd rather eat nothing than eat a carrot."

"I am not a fan of zucchini," Rosie O'Donnell told an interviewer on Warner Brothers online. Fattier foods she adores. Her weight has ballooned at times to 300 pounds. She told Regis Philbin on October 2, 1997, that after her son, Parker, got into an accident she scarfed down three boxes of Mallomars. On the other hand, she does not like mousse. When dietician Richard Simmons offered her a chocolate mousse cake on the Rosie O'Donnell Show on November 18, 1997, she would not touch it. His memorable response? Simmons picked it up and threw it on the floor. When a recent online survey asked people to write in, guessing what Rosie O' Donnell's favorite foods were, several people wrote, "Plankton and krill."

French philosopher Denis Diderot disliked potatoes. In his famous *Encyclopédie*, he dismissed the potato as tasteless, no matter how it was prepared, and Brillat Savarin who agreed stated, "None for me." Regarding the history of the potato, which was introduced into Europe by sixteenth-century explorers who had come upon it in Peru, it is a well-known fact that the poor at first resisted it as a dietary staple, although it gained a reputation as a curative and as an aphrodisiac by the end of the eighteenth century. To the Elizabethans, remember, the innocuous potato was not only sustaining but stimulating to lust. In *The Merry Wives of Windsor* that when the aging fat Sir John Falstaff—"gross wat'ry pompion [pumpkin]"—with the worst intentions, gets Mistress Ford and Mistress Page to come in to him, he cries out, "Let the sky rain potatoes; let it... hail kissing-comfits, and snow eringoes [candied root]" all aphrodisiac sweetmeats. "Jack" here is actually referring to candies, respectively made from sweet potatoes, anise and caraway seeds, and the roots of sea-holly, respectively, all breath-sweeteners and items to arouse sexual desire. It was such delicacies, rich tasty bon-bons, that blackened the teeth of the Virgin Queen, no doubt. Sir Walter Raleigh introduced the growing of potatoes into Ireland, and yet this particular tuber was slow to be adopted by distrustful European farmers, especially the French who regarded the tuber with suspicion, fare for pigs, the very worst of vegetables. In Burgundy, cultivation was forbidden by law," notes Claire Clifton in *The Art of Food*, "and in 1771 the French government directed the medical faculty in Paris to determine whether or not the potato was safe to eat." The root soon became a major crop throughout the continent, however, and put a significant end to repeated and widespread famines.

Sir Richard F. Burton disliked potatoes. The famous 19th-century explorer, enthusiastically preferred the African staple *fufu* to them and described it as playing a role equivalent to "...the part of European potatoes, only it is far more savoury than the vile tuber, which has already potatofied at least one nation." Fufu is often made with cassava and green plantain flour. Served along with soup, usually groundnut soup, Palm nut soup or Light Soup, fufu is the national dish of Ghana. It is nevertheless a food hated by the sad, bitter missionary in the Congo in Barbara Kingsolver's *The Poisonwood Bible* who laments, "What on God's earth did they eat...a gluey paste called fufu...It cooks up into the sort of tasteless mass one might induce an American child to try once, after a long round of pulled-up noses and double-dog dares."

"The potatoes were starch grenades," writes David Mitchell in his unique novel *Cloud Atlas*, so I gather he does not fancy them—or carrots, for he adds, "The canned carrots were revolting because that is their nature." There are all sorts of opinions about potatoes and no end of preferences not only as to the way they should be cooked but the quality of the end-product. "Really good mashed potatoes are as rare as virgins," said the novelist Raymond Chandler, whom I gather had many bad experiences with servings that way. The late columnist of the *New York Times* Russell Baker developed an overpowering loathing for French fries—or was it that he ate them so much that he became a fanatic of what the ideal one should be and hated greasy substitutes? "The French fried potato has become an inescapable horror in almost every public eating place in the country," he grizzled in one of his columns. "'French fries,' say the menus, but they are not French fries any longer. They are a furry-textured substance with the taste of plastic wood." James Beard is a co-religionist here. "Whoever invented the deep-fried potato surely didn't realize what a sin he was committing," grizzled the oft-disgruntled Beard. "Then to crown all other horrors, people drench them with cold catchup [sic] and eat them." Beard frankly liked potatoes well enough, but he could be picky about them. What he did find happily to derogate was the sweet potato. Not only did he never want sweet potatoes served at his Thanksgiving dinner table, he declared in *Delights and Prejudices*—and the chef and cookbook author was well-known for having something of a ferocious temper—"I have never had what I consider a good original Spanish potato recipe or a good original one from Scandinavia."

One wonders what he would have made of singer Julie Andrews' comment in her surprisingly dull memoir, *Home*, that predominant among her favorite food preferences are "American milk shakes and an occasional boiled potato sandwich." [sic!] What is a boiled potato sandwich and what other human being has ever eaten one? I suppose while we are on the subject we have to include here the madly intemperate rant against the fast-food hamburger and fries by Jean-Michel Chapereau in his *Un Hiver Americain* (1975): "We were taken to a fast food café where our order was fed into a computer. Our hamburgers, made from the flesh of chemically impregnated cattle, had been broiled over counterfeit charcoal, placed between slices of artificially flavored cardboard and served to us by recycled juvenile delinquents."

Julia Child would have taken Chapereau's side, for it was the famous "French Chef" who once queerly asserted, "I refuse to eat anything that is cooked in 30 minutes and contains no cholesterol."

Remember Owen Wister's jingle?

> Said Aristotle unto Plato,
> "Have another sweet potato?"

Said Plato unto Aristotle,
"Thank you, I prefer the bottle."

Los Angeles chef, Craig Thornton, the king of dinner-party-style cooking, will not eat fast food. With a growing reputation, this young avant-garde and frankly quite daring and intrepid 28-year-old chef dares to cook for selective groups of nine to twelve elaborately composed courses prepared in an open kitchen a few feet from the table—he has a reputation for never preparing a dish the same way twice—in his own apartment. The experiment is called Wolvesmouth. He who is the "Wolf" cooks, preps, and shops almost entirely by himself. He refuses to work in a professional kitchen, or even to open his own restaurant. "What I'm trying to do is strip down everything," he told Squid Ink food blog and added,

> As I keep going I try to strip down more and more. I
> try to take everything out. I guess my cooking is more
> of a study in psychology, and irony, and the essence
> of what something is. It's all these things smashed
> together... But sometimes [I like to cook with] a sense
> of humor. I want to get surgical trays, and serve raw
> meat on them, and have people eat it with surgical
> tweezers. And there's a dish called "primal," which
> is bone marrow, sweet breads, and broken bones on
> the plate. They're like smashed bones, obviously not
> edible. I'm actually not a fan of inedible garnishes, but
> with this one I was trying to make a statement.

Diners pay to have "insight into one very specific idea of what food should be," according to Kaitlyn Goalen, an editor at the food newsletter, *Tasting Table*. It is known as "underground" cooking and has become something of a fad in the United States. Zagat put Thornton in its first "30 Under 30" list for Los Angeles. I mention Thornton in the context of fast food simply because, as Dana Goodyear pointed out in a *New Yorker* article on him, "Toques from the Underground, "he once lost fifteen pounds driving across the country because he couldn't bring himself to eat road food. (At the end of the trip, he weighed a hundred and eighteen.)." For all his daring, I have to say that he is something of a food prig.

I have often wondered about that kind of bald intransigence in people, especially regarding food. To tell the truth, I cannot conceive of a person, out of gastronomic snobbery, relinquishing eating under any conditions, going to the extent, particularly, of losing fifteen pounds. I once broke up with an extraordinarily selfish, pretentious, and it goes without saying insecure, girlfriend of mine because, when I was once racing to meet a tight schedule, she stubbornly refused to settle for a quick bite to eat at a local Burger King. Are you surprised to hear that she was not only a fussy eater but also one of the worst cooks in the history of mankind? I frankly doubt it. I felt well rid of the affected and ostentatious oik, a tall, heartless, uneducated (and actually sexless) blonde with a man's first name whom I am convinced, like Françoise-Louise de Warens —one of Jean-Jacques Rousseau's "lovers" who supposedly only consummated their relationship to prevent him from misdeeds with other women—regarded the act of love as a matter of male hygiene. She ended up being married four (maybe more) times on a perpetual—and unsuccessful—search to avoid herself.

Chef Zak Pelaccio cannot stand sweet potatoes. "I find them a little too rich, a little too cloying, a little too overwhelming," he said. "I don't like to eat them." It isn't unusual for somebody to hold a deep dislike for a particular food, but Mr. Pelaccio is the chef of 5 Ninth, a very creative restaurant in Manhattan that is quite daring and inventive with its various ingredients. His veal breast is braised, topped with botarga, and served with green tomatoes, shishito pepper and ground ivy, for example. But never plain sweet potatoes? "I just have no desire to cook with them, ever," said the chef, "And sweet potato fries are the most disgusting things." Chef Alton Brown hastens to add that he dislikes sweet potatoes, as well. ("Botanically speaking, despite the name, they are not even related to potatoes," he explains, "but are in fact the root of the vine in the morning glory family!") By the way, the word sweet does not apply either—the misnomer was applied to the tuber by the Boston Irish a century ago. Brown dislikes fast food, canned soup, anything labeled "diet," and, although he loves Girl Scout cookies, he avoids them. "I can't have one," he confesses. "If you break the tube, you eat the tube. The second item I avoid? Milk. I cook with milk, I use milk in a lot of ways, but I don't drink milk because it made me eat Girl Scout cookies."

What Alton Brown passionately does love is good—perfect—coffee. This brings me to a primal consideration that must be raised. Excess in anything—extremism—can be a monster under any circumstances. A food addict, arguably, is in a sense as crackpated as a radical or severe aversionist. In his quirky book, *Gear For Your Kitchen*, Brown admits to being "obsessive" about coffee. I know that he is a perfectionist, something I admire, and I gather that he brews all sorts of exotic varieties—unusual and expensive robustas—such as Ethiopian Yirgacheffem, Sumatran Mandheling, and Guadeloupian Bonifieur. He confesses with honesty, "This may explain why

I own six coffee-making devices: two electric drop machines, one vacuum pot, one manual drip rig, and two French presses (one large, one small)... Although I've moved to a drip machine during the week, I like French press on weekend mornings and a vacuum pot for after dinners...when I'm trying to impress people."

What redeems Alton Brown for me is that he has—and greatly values—a spiritual life and is about the only chef I know or have heard of who takes the time with his family to say grace at table. "I live in Georgia, I am a Christian," he points out, "and I believe in the Bible, travel with the Bible, read the Bible every day. I don't hit people over the head with the Bible." In our secular age, this is a rare thing indeed. Brown goes on to say, "I still feel a funny little tinge in my stomach when I'm out to dinner with my wife and daughter in New York. We'll go to dinner and we'll be sitting around the table and we'll say Grace. You know what? People are going to stare at you. I used to feel really self-conscious. But I've gotten to a point where I think, nah, I'm not going to feel bad about that. I'm not going to apologize about that."

Along the lines of potatoes, the vegetable now can actually be synthesized into plastic-like materials! So if you do not like to *eat* vegetables, you can at least have them converted into vegetable-based products! The process for creating Plant Starch Material (PSM), as it is known, starts very much like making your favorite mashed potato recipe. Manufacturers start by washing, slicing, and smashing the potatoes into a slurry of sorts. They then take that substance, separate it, dry it, and cook down the starch, rendering it all rigid and therefore strong enough to create things like forks, knives and spoons. It has been found that PSM can tolerate heat better, but it does take longer to break down than PLA, or polylactic acid, 90 to 120 days in a commercial composting facility. There is some degree of waste produced when manufacturers process the potatoes; however, the pulpy side product is salubriously given to pig farmers to use as feed, thus rendering PSM an entirely green product.

If you're looking to replace plastic and Styrofoam with a more environmentally conscious option, also try corn—not on the cob, of course, but PLA, a decomposable plastic made from corn. PLA is made by converting corn into starch and then converting that starch into sugar. Microorganisms are then used to turn the sugar into polylactic acid, at which point the PLA is mixed with different starches and formed into Styrofoam-like food containers, cups and even "plastic" bags. PLA is freezer safe, allergen free and, best of all, compostable in just 30 to 45 days. Mike Centers, Executive Director of Biocor, a post-consumer products company, states, "Greater sustainability in plastic packaging depends on decreasing the carbon footprint of the plastics used and on recapturing and reusing a greater percentage of post-consumer packaging. Plastics made from renewable plant sources such as PLA, which is 100 percent bio-based, offer a means to achieve these goals."

Finally, we have the *pièce de résistance*. Dr. Kerry Kirwan, a researcher at Warwick Manufacturing Group, and Ben King, a student at Warwick University in England, have combined forces to create the Eco One, a one-seat sports car made almost entirely of vegetable products! Ninety-five percent of the materials used to build Eco One are completely biodegradable or recyclable including, yes, potatoes, cashew shells, rape seed oil, and hemp. The Eco One car can even run—motor!—on wheat and sugar beets. The steering wheel, seat, electrics and entire chassis are made from plain conventional materials, accounting for the five percent non-recyclable elements. The $41,000 sports car can hit speeds of up to 150 mph.

We will all remember what old Mr. Woodhouse, Emma's valetudinarian father in that Jane Austen novel, particularly hated: "Cake! Surely you're not serving cake at your wedding, Miss Taylor! Far too rich, you put us all at peril! Where is Mr. Perry, the apothecary? I'm sure he will support me!" Eleanor Roosevelt hated Brussels sprouts. So did Harry S. Truman, according to his daughter Margaret. Mamie Eisenhower disliked onions. Nathaniel Hawthorne and his wife, Sophia, hated eating cabbages, which they reluctantly outgrew however—out of a sense of duty?—when they first began living in the Old Manse in Concord, Mass., happily honeymooning. The beautiful gray old house still stands there. In the summer of 1816, when young Nathaniel was only 12, the entire Hawthorne family lived as boarders with farmers, so maybe growing things got into his blood. Maybe they were eating skunk cabbage. The *Peterson Field Guide to Wild Edible Plants* asserts that skunk cabbage has a few edible parts: if you peel the root into thin slices and dry them out a couple hours before cooking they are safe to eat. I have heard old Cape Codders made cordage from the fibers of Skunk Cabbage. Also, one is able to eat the young whitish green leaves that bloom in early Spring, that is, if you boil them in sets of water. Were you aware, by the way, that the word *Chicago* means "The Place of the Skunk Cabbage" (*Manhattan* means "The Place of the Great Drunkenness" or "The Place Where We All Got Drunk")

Fat, fussy, epicene drama critic Alexander Woollcott loathed even the very sight of green vegetables and anything like nourishing soup—he heartily consumed just about everything else and put away food by the truckload. "The immense amount of blubber perched atop his tiny feet still seemed an architectural incongruity," wrote his biographer, Howard Teichmann. "His pudgy little hands appeared out of character with a body, a head, and a pair of eyes so large." Poet W.H. Auden who weirdly, compulsively, always had to have potatoes with dinner, every dinner, every *single* dinner, never took salt with his eggs, and never ate sweets—never! On the other hand, pop singer La Toya Jackson, who by the way happens to be African-American, states that she cannot stand "white food like mashed potato and rice."

Speaking of salt, the late Jean-Louis Palladin, a fearless and passionate cook and owner of the restaurant in Washington, D.C., Jean-Louis at the Watergate, who helped to free French cuisine in the United States from a hidebound orthodoxy while influencing a generation of chefs and food lovers and who died so young, at 55, would not permit salt at any of his tables. At his restaurant Blue Ginger, Ming Tsai is gloomily surprised at how many diners indiscriminately use salt. It is a habit in casual diners that has always confounded chef Jacques Pépin.

Curiously, Mel Blanc, the classic voice of the character Bugs Bunny in the old cartoons, was, ironically enough, allergic to carrots! "They tried to give him turnips and celery and everything else [as the signature food prop]," legendary animator Chuck Jones explained to film-director Peter Bogdanovich, "but it turns out," as Bogdanovich wrote in his book, *Who the Devil Made It?* "nothing sounds like carrots except carrots. So all those years Mel was chomping for Bugs, they had to have a basket next to him [Blanc] so he could spit the carrots out as soon as he'd done the chewing noises." Who'da thunk it? The carrot, wonderfully apt as bunny food, is venerable—it is the only vegetable to have been detected in a Neolithic context.

Nevertheless, many a consumer hates carrots. Literary scholar Bliss Perry who grew up in Williamstown, Mass. in his autobiography, *And Gladly Teach* (1935), wrote, "But we boys thought there were too many vegetables in the world. It seemed to me that I weeded miles of carrots when I wanted to be chasing the butterflies, and I dislike the taste of that vegetable to this day." Another carrot-hater is Alex Guarnaschelli, the host of TV's "Alex's Day Off," who in one bold trifecta has managed to find three major vegetables that he dislikes, all of them major, but carrots are in the lead. "I cannot stand shredded carrots," he discloses. "There's nothing wrong with them; they never did anything to me, and yet if I see them, even one single shred, mixed into a salad, I can feel my heart rate quicken and my taste buds shrivel in disgust. I don't like green bell peppers, and I don't like raw onions. They are too abrasive and obliterate other flavors. They also linger on your breath." Can you seriously fathom a chef who dislikes raw onions? I myself find it inconceivable.

President Harry Truman hated onions so much that if he detected the smallest amount in a dish, he would shove the plate aside; his wife, Bess, said,

"I don't dare serve onions in any form!" Remember the forbidding portrait of "Mrs. Benjamin Pantier" in Edgar Lee Masters' *Spoon River Anthology*? In her blame-shifting monologue, replying in kind to her shiftless husband who preferred his dog to her, she said she loathed "the smell of whiskey and onions." One recalls the slapstick scene in Lubitsch's *Bluebeard's Eighth Wife* (1938) when Claudette Colbert, while being nuzzled on a sofa by Gary Cooper, in order to confound him, picks up a fistful of scallions, mouths the entire lot, and then begs him to kiss her. Cooper does just that, full on the mouth, pauses, stands up, and with a dark scowl, calls her—several times—an "animal." In a similar vein, and here we go back to carrots, Colbert hated crunching raw carrots for breakfast in *It Happened One Night*, while Clark Gable sits happily munching on them like a happy bunny. Colbert then gives in and deigns to eat one. In the film, Gable claims that he could write a book on the correct method of dunking donuts, and Colbert dutifully accepts that fact—what a masculine boast *(not!)*. What a deeply profound book idea, right? God bless the 1930s!

Gable must have especially loved crunchy vegetables. It is said that he was hugely passionate about raw onions, which is probably why it became *pro forma* for many of his female co-stars to complain about The King's bad breath. According to legend, Gable gobbled onions at just about every chance he had, with or without bread. Food aversions, in many instances, crop up by way of anxious people's fear of having bad breath. Bad breath irked Shakespeare, and it was one of his obsessions, not only in his plays—in Sonnet 130, the Dark Lady, a woman whom he saw as the soul of black treachery, is nevertheless accused of having halitosis.

We have had occasion already to quote from Thackeray's *Wandering Fat Contributor*. On his boat-trip, he finds to his delight that his "susceptible heart" has been given over to one of the passengers, Dolores, a Spaniard. "She always chooses the dishes with onions—she comes from the sunny South, where both onions and garlic are plentifully used—and yet somehow, in the depression on my spirits—I wish—I wish she hadn't a partiality for that particular vegetable." A measure of his new romantic feelings for her is that his ardor causes "a disinclination for food." At one point in the progression, however, we hear no more of lovely Dolores—could the woman being given that name have been a personification of the trip?—and El Rotundo goes on his merry way to continue his travels, eating more than ever.

What is it about green bell peppers, that staple of chili, shrimp creole, and so much New Orleans cooking, that so many people hate so much? In the movie *Adam's Rib* (1949), Katharine Hepburn playing Amanda Bonner squawks one order at her husband Adam (Spencer Tracy) who is futzing about with the salad in the kitchen, "Not any green peppers. Indigestible." Many chefs unambiguously abhor the vegetable. "They're headache-y," declares Anita Lo, chef at Annisa. "For some reason I've never gotten past the flavor." In an article on food aversions, "I'm the Boss, and I Say No Lentils," Oliver Schwaner-Albright documents a group of chefs all going on record as hating green peppers. Brian Bistrong, a chef at Botegga in Yountville, Cal., for example, cannot bear the way a green pepper lingers. "If you eat one, you're going to taste it the rest of the meal," Mr. Bistrong said. "I got rid of them when I finally had some authority. Now that I'm the boss, I cannot have them." Chef Dan Barber, who even goes so far as to prohibit green peppers in the kitchens of Blue Hill Restaurant in Manhattan or Blue Hill at Stone Barns in Pocantico Hills, NY, identified the problems with the vegetable "multi-tiered." "First, I don't like the flavor," he said. "And I've learned more about them. They are an immature pepper. You're eating a vegetable before it's supposed to be picked." Tasha Garcia, one of the chefs of Little Giant, recoils when she tastes anything that reminds her of a pepper. "We had a staff tasting and with this one cabernet franc it was like, oh, green peppers," grizzled Miss Garcia. She added that she was overwhelmed by the association. "I hated the wine, hated it, hated it."

"I don't eat in airports or on planes," chef Mario Batali told *Bon Appetit* (May 2013). "I consume Bloody Marys on flights. I consider them breakfast and lunch. It's the first thing I'll do on a plane."

Pretty and petulant Marie Bashkirtseff, the diarist, painter, and sculptor, makes it clear in several places in her *Journal of a Young Artist* (1889) that she hated onions. "At dinner a dish dressed with onions was served. I got up and left the dining room; the princess and Paul's wife were surprised," goes one diary entry in 1881. Four years earlier, she wrote, "My character has changed completely, and the change seems to be a permanent one. I no longer have need even of wealth; two black blouses a year, a change of linen that I could wash myself on Sundays, and the simplest food, provided it does not taste of onions..." Who can say why onions so nauseated the nubile striver, except that she was vain, privileged, and extremely flirtatious, a Lolita—at the age of 12 she falls deeply in love with the older Duke of H——and, beyond anything, she wanted to appear fresh, clean, available. Men thrilled her! Painting and romantic dreams of love were her all. At 15, she confidentally records in her diary her various opinions at the family table. "... I went on to give my views in regard to the advantages of good cooking, sustaining that it made men virtuous." By this, I gather that she meant that men who were well-fed would not stray. Bashkirsteff did not cook, of course; that was not a pastime for wealthy young ladies in the 19th-century. Did she mean that the habit of scorning food therefore constituted a vice? When she was 25—the last year of her life, 1884, when she died of consumption—she wistfully wrote,

> I wonder at people who can eat great pieces of raw fat mutton. I wonder at those fortunate people who can swallow raspberries whole, without minding the little insects that are always to be found in them. As for me, I must first examine them closely, so that the pleasure of eating them does not pay me for the trouble. I wonder at people who can eat all sorts of hashes and stews, without knowing what they are composed of. I wonder at, or rather I envy, simple, healthy, common-place natures, in short."

It was such details that gave Bashkirtseff her fascination.

The Old Testament reminds us that among the major sins of the Exodus was looking back with gluttony to the onions and leeks of Egypt. In the Vulgate version of the Psalms, moreover, according to Anthony Burgess, it also "alludes to the admirable Oriental mode of expressing satisfaction in repletion: *Cor meum eructavit laudem tuam* ('My heart hath belched forth thy praise')." Did you know that ancient Egyptians swore oaths with their right hand on an onion? Being round, the vegetable symbolized eternity. Still and all, round or straight, fat or thin, the enzymes and amino acid sulfoxides that are set free in a cut onion to mix with the sulfenic acids to produce pro-panethiol S-oxide, a volatile sulfur compound that wafts up toward your eyes to form tears, can be very strong, although the complaint usually involves neither taste nor smell.

Can you imagine the inability to perceive either and the terrible con-sequences of trying to so? It evokes a sad memory for me. One of my very brightest cousins, John Dittami, who for decades had been a highly esteemed professor of anthropology at the University of Vienna was set upon in the Austrian town of Tulln by a bunch of young thugs—*Berufsschläger*—and very badly hurt. As the result of being hammered on the head, he suffered a subdural hematoma. Added to the severe trauma—he was only 39—he com-pletely lost his sense of smell (*anosmia*). Thereafter, he could taste nothing (*ageusia*), since the ability to taste equals (and is influenced by) one's ability to smell an aroma. He had no way to determine what he was eating and could barely discern the texture of a given food. My cousin died last year.

Does it create food aversions? It can and does. Multiple nerves, including cranial nerves, transmit taste information from the mouth and pharynx to the brain by way of the brain stem. Although adaptive strategies have been employed to address the problem of taste deficit, in my cousin's case no otolaryngologist could correct the chemosensory impairment that he suffered or manage to increase the palatability of food for him. He used measuring devices when cooking, never "cooks by taste." "I have learned to eat things that make me feel good," he told me, explaining that he had to refashion the neurostructure in his brain by cognitive eating. Eating was relevant to him in a far different sense than it is to us. To see what others were eating and enjoy them by proxy and in limited quantities was one way he coped.

"I hate you, Swiss chard," wrote Eric Smith in a truly intemperate fulmination in *McSweeney's*. "Oh, how I hate you. I have hated you ever since I figured out why dumpsters smell like dumpsters. It's because of you. I always thought they took on that characteristic stench because long years of bad garbage odors combined together in an unholy stew that for some reason always smelled the same—kind of like how mixing lots of different paint colors ultimately always gives you brown. But no, it turns out that they smell exactly like you did two days after I brought you home from the grocery store. So it was you all along. Screw you, Swiss chard."

We would do well to understand the nature of such an attack. It speaks to the mystery of distaste—yet more. Notice in this particular rant the aspects of discovery. Facts have been unearthed. I have hated you ever since... it turns out that... So it was you all along... These are the locutions of exposure and address the suddenness that is at the heart of all disappointment. People like Smith may appear to be aberrant, nonsensical, and raving in their rebellion, granted. In a real way, however, they are implicitly making a plea for diversity. Self-assertion. Panfurious independence. ("I didn't write the rules—why should I follow them?") Personal force—felt force—can be liberating, a crucial part of self-identity. In his masterpiece, *Crowds and Power*, philosopher Elias Canetti insists, quite curiously, that a fire can sometimes unify a theater more than the play can! But isn't this also the major theme of Anthony Burgess's *A Clockwork Orange*? Is it better to be bad of one's own free will—as the protagonist Alex was—than to be good through scientific brainwashing (aversion therapy)?

It sharply applies to aporia about food. What good soul following the laws of right reason would not defend the few un-elected skeptics and scoffers who recognize the Bokanoskified world we inhabit or could fail to understand the healthy spirit of refusal and dissent of refusing anything fobbed off on us by the media where the "raucous stream of misinformation" (to borrow a phrase of Evelyn Waugh's) never ceases—and why should it not be a particular food? Why not indeed, the flat refusal—an option for the exclusivity of rejection—especially when the psychological occasions for mistrust in a forming mind, born of the thousand reasons a cynic can marshal in selecting to doubt, to question, to disbelieve, are legion? Freethinkers become rarer by the day. Who honestly believes we have options anymore?

We have only the "illusion of choice" in this country. Are you aware of the fact that as few as six corporations in the United States own 90% of the media—control almost 90% of what Americans see, hear, watch, and consider every day? These six giants dominate the national landscape enabled by FCC deregulation and decades-long orgies of mergers and manipulation. It is an oligopoly whose tentacles reach out everywhere and every way. Think of it! A group of 232 media executives control the completely closed information diet of 277 *million* American sheep. The total revenue of the Big Six for 2012 was almost 300 billion, $36 billion more than Finland's GDP. The Big Six own 70% of your cable. News Corp owns the top newspapers on three continents. (In 2010 they avoided $875 million in US taxes.) In 1995, the FCC forbade companies to own over 40 stations, yet Clear Channel owns 1,200 stations. The Big Six's box office sales hit $7 billion in 2010, two times the box office sales of the next 140 studios. (They are all major players in global holdings, as well.) Who are these corporate pigs and what are the names of their notable properties? GE (Comcast, Universal Pictures, NBC, Focus Features, etc.); Viacom (MTV, Paramount Pictures, BET, CMY, etc.); Newscorp (Fox, the *Wall Street Journal,* the *New York Post,* etc.); Disney (ABC, ESPN, Pixar, Miramax, Marvel Studios, etc.); Time Warner (CNN, HBO, Time, Warner Bros., etc.); CBS (Showtime, Jeopardy, 60 Minutes, the *Smithsonian* Channel, etc.)

Who can forget the Wall Street bailouts after the mid-September 2008 crash and how the government with the aid of Henry Paulson, treasury secretary under President George W. Bush and former head of Goldman Sachs, decided to allocate $85 billion to bail out the failing insurance and financing firm American International Group (AIG), when Goldman, the biggest, greediest, and most profitable of the Wall Street investment houses, stood to lose $13 billion in credit default swaps and other derivative contracts with AIG? In less than a year, Wall Street was back: the five largest remaining banks are today larger, their executives and traders richer, their strategies of placing large bets with other people's money no less bold than before the meltdown. In 2009, Goldman Sachs reported a record second-quarter profit of $3.44 billion and proceeded eventually to award its employees a record $22 billion in bonuses and salaries. Critic Matt Taibbi put it best in *Rolling*

Stone (July 2009) when he described Goldman Sachs as "a great vampire squid wrapped around the face of humanity, relentlessly jamming its blood funnel into anything that smells like money."

No, it is healthy to feel leery, unconvinced, suspicious, and questioning in a world where we feckless underlings are manipulated daily like poor, dopey, gullible Truman Burbank in the movie *The Truman Show* who unknowingly spends his entire benighted, and spied-upon life being duped and exploited by the media in a complete box-set built under a giant arcological dome, for in a real way ours is the same artificial alternatives and the same constructed reality. Eric Hoffer was correct when he wrote: "A successful social technique consists perhaps in finding unobjectionable means for individual self-assertion." But rejecting a food is often seen as objectionable. All food aversions are prime examples of low-level dissent. We are all rebels.

Nevertheless, rebellion, personal revolt and bold insurrection, can in the act turn a person into an isolato. In his brilliant *Crowds and Power*—"On the Psychology of Eating"—Canetti analyzes not only the social nature of community but also the intimidating sovereignty of being fatly full, writing, "The man who can eat more than anyone else lies back satisfied and heavy with food." His concept has to do with domination, control, and is about kingship, being a ruler, supremacy. Chiefdom. Aversionists, regarded as outcasts, are routinely seen as perversely *uncommunal*. To refuse a food is not unlike eating alone, for you have more or less indicated that you are a pariah. Canetti addresses the connection between power and digestion:

> "People like eating with others...It is a contest in
> repletion...The satisfaction of repletion, of the mo-
> ment when nothing more can be absorbed, is part
> of the goal and the pleasure of eating...Anyone who
> eats alone renounces the prestige which the process
> would bring him in the eyes of others. He bares his
> teeth simply for the sake of eating, and this impresses
> no one, for there is no one there to be impressed. But
> when people eat together, they can all see each other's
> mouths opening. Everyone can watch everyone else's
> teeth while his own are in action at the same time. To
> be without teeth is contemptible, and there is a touch
> of asceticism in refusing to show those that one has.
> The natural occasion on which to show off one's teeth
> is when eating with others."

A food aversionist shows his teeth, indeed—but strictly by way of refusal.
Renouncement.
Turndown.

21.

MAD ORNITHOPHAGES

We inevitably come to resent the familiar. But even worse, we all tend to dislike the idea that we all must proceed in lockstep. It is one of the paradoxes of the mystery of taste that arise when we talk about food aversions. Call it the "success of failure." Let us consider it at its extreme. There is a revolt and rebellion here that boils at the heart of it, a stance either cryptic or declared virtually conveying in an imperious way, "I am willful! I am willful!" It incorporates a kind of dark cynicism, a spiteful reverse of logic ("I have hated you ever since I figured out why... "), a flat-out unwillingness to cooperate or to play ball, in the way of the bitter, isolated, cross-grained unnamed narrator in Fyodor Dostoevsky's novella, *Notes from the Underground*, in which, as a harsh criticism of determinism and the intellectual attempt at dictating human action and behavior, he becomes intentionally irrational and spiteful to show in a kind of personal declaration of independence that one cannot avoid the simple fact that out of mere whim anyone at any time can decide to act in a way that is irked, obnoxious, or unpredictable simply to validate his existence and to protest that one (*moi-même!*) exists as an individual.

"I will not eat" is extremely close to the refusal "I will not serve," a protest of the victim against the world of executioners, victims whose opportunistic, hungry, resentful, and ego-wounded selves they cannot fathom and never could and so meet them (but never greet them) with the kind of questions that in Edward Arlington Robinson's "Flammonde," one of my favorite poems, the bewildered townsfolk dumbly ask of the poem's enigmatic protagonist,

> What was it that we never caught,
> What was he, and what was he not?

The "underground man" rejects fellowship. Recall how the Scribes and Pharisees or teachers of the law in Luke 15:1-3 angrily murmur, "This fellow welcomes sinners and eats with them" because Jesus, doing what they would not do—what they considered inappropriate for their class—was with a mystically conjoined and loving blessedness *welcoming* sinners by eating with them.

Like Franz Kafka's "hunger artist," the nonconformist clerk with his "pallid haughtiness" in Herman Melville's novella, *Bartleby the Scrivener* significantly rejects food and like the "underground man" stands in literature virtually as the arch-priest of oppositional deficit disorder in his refusal to perform any task asked of him. Readers often fail to see that the story is, more than anything, a parable of food-rejection.

We have previously alluded to Bartleby. The narrator, a settled New York lawyer with a comfortable business involved in helping wealthy men deal with mortgages, deeds, and bonds, optimistically bribes a turnkey to make sure that his dim, forlorn clerk, the jailed Bartleby, receives good and plentiful food. Upon visiting the fellow a few days later, however, he discovers with alarm that ther poor victim has died of starvation, having forgone all food to the very last. Although on a narrative level the defiant clerk obstinately rejects doing any of the kinds of writing demanded of him—during the spring of 1851, a self-conscious, lonely, and frustrated Herman Melville had very similar thoughts about his own situation as a writer—the short story rides on the repeatedly unrelenting theme at the Tombs of the renunciation of life-giving food right up to the end in a virtual suicide:

> He lives... on ginger-nuts, thought I; never eats a dinner, properly speaking; he must be a vegetarian then; but no; he never eats even vegetables, he eats nothing but ginger nuts. My mind then ran on in reveries concerning the probable effects upon the human constitution of living entirely on ginger-nuts.

A mélange of negation, nixes, and no's, this is a story of self-punition by way of food phobia. How interesting it is Bartleby would rather die than eat. The *will* will not! Notice the names of Bartleby's colleagues, Turkey, Ginger Nut (the office boy who has gotten his name from the little cakes that he brings the two scriveners), Nippers (he suffers from chronic indigestion—from too much "nipping" at food?), even Mr. Cutlets, the "grub man," who literally invites him to dinner, story-characters of nearly allegorical import revolving all around Bartleby almost as a nominal temptation for him to eat but only coming up against "his unalterableness." Non-acceptance, non-compliance becomes the one pathetic exercise of freedom poor Bartleby has. Bartleby had to starve himself to death in order to demonstrate his freedom.

"I would prefer not to," repeats the lonely scrivener in order to serve himself. Those who are at loggerheads battle for survival. A rivalry by definition pits one opponent against another. Who would deny that an eating preference—including the choice not to eat—becomes a matter of personal ethics? I can recall an astute observation made by Elliot Paul in *The Last Time I Saw Paris* (1942), his account of a venerable old city disappearing during the war years:

> In no totalitarian country is good eating encouraged,
> but only the kind of food that makes for soldierly
> stamina without mental health or elasticity. A restau-
> rant was a meeting place, and meetings are taboo.

Paul points out that the famous restaurants of Paris, which flourished before World War II were creative institutions, cafés, bistros and restaurants such as La Vachette, Bignon, Boulanger, Verdier, Les Frères Provenceaux, La Maison d'Or, Véry, Philippe, or Brébant where people met, discussed matters, played chess, sought a communal world to air ideas and fraternize over wine and food.

When we consider Bartleby's battle for survival, we cannot be surprised that nature itself is all about survival, that foods themselves compete for growth. Plants repel other plants. What is the transmogrifying science, if any, behind the strange fact that in the garden plants can be adversaries to each other and that onions are a major enemy of beans? Broccoli of peppers? Radishes of hyssop? Farmers and growers have believed for centuries that competing plants or vegetables, planted adjacently, can effect each other's growth, health, even taste. It has long been held that potatoes do not do well when planted near pumpkins, squash or cucumbers, and that sunflowers stunt their growth. Cabbages dislike tomatoes and pole beans, which, on the other hand, are helped by many-blossomed aromatic plants like celery and dill.

To some degree, the concept of "I-resent-friends-having-friends-I-would-not-have-for-friends" is involved. Tomatoes for example find allies in carrots, celery, chives, cucumber, garlic, and lettuce. Beets contend with runner beans. Cauliflower does not thrive with tomatoes or strawberries. Rue dislikes basil but thrives with raspberries and figs. ("Rue and the fig tree are in great league of amity," wrote Pliny two thousand years ago.) Most plants hate fennel. The plea for "companion" planting shows just how uncompanionable nature can be.

Trees in competition actually strive—mightily—against each other, as well, and always do. It is as if they have different personalities. (Thomas Hardy has assured us that every species of tree has a different *voice*—fir trees sob and moan, the holly whistles, ash trees hiss amid their quivering, etc.) A heterogeneous hostility definitely exists between cedar trees with their terebrinthic musk and the berbearing European mountain ash. Conventional wisdom says that you should never plant a Norway spruce or a silver maple within 50 feet of the drip-line of a walnut tree. Black walnut trees release a bio-chemical secretion called "juglone" that drips from the leaves onto plants below or leach into the roots. Its shade is even said to be harmful to other trees, and, according to centuries of popular wisdom, a person should never rest or sleep under a walnut tree. This type of adversarial relationship between plants is known as "allelopathy," where one tree or plant produces a chemical compound that inhibits the growth of one or more other species. A loblolly pine cannot grow near bluestem grass, also called broomsedge, simply because the action of the bacteria that fix nitrogen in the soil is prevented. Beech leaves contain a product that is detrimental to young spruces. While the black locust prevents the growth and development of certain pine trees, it favors the growth of several oak species.

Toxins produced by the roots of plants, such as heather, are harmful to mushrooms that are essential to the growth of various trees such as spruce, Norway pine, and white birch. Ash, spruce, and alder protect themselves by releasing in the ground products that repel certain mushrooms or pathogenic germs that make their roots rot. The black cherry in an allelopathic attack can give off a chemical that can immediately begin to inhibit the growth of red maples.

I love this subject. It is often within families—similar groupings—that contention most sharply announces itself. We resent the familiar.

In her splendid book *Carrots Love Tomatoes*, Louise Riotte warns against the folly of replacing a fallen tree by locating one of the same species in the same spot. She explains, offering the following example: "A young apple tree planted where an old apple tree was removed, withered, and died. Yet a young cherry put in exactly the same spot grew like a weed [meaning well]. Why? Root and leaf secretions left in the soil by the old apple tree worked poisonously against the young apple. On the other hand, for the cherry tree it was welcome nutrition." This is basically news about avoiding going shopping in the same bun shop day after day, so to speak, all of it recalling to a degree the avoidance of certain rare autosomal recessive genetic blood disorders that can arise from intermarriage among the same ethnic group, such as Tay Sachs disease among Jews and Sickle Cell disease among African-Americans.

Could it be that because such organisms can sense their environment, showing an aggressiveness or territoriality, in order to adjust their conditions to maintain some kind of optimality, that Michael Pollan, confusing acclimation with intelligence, believes that plants have intelligence? As a scientist, I would be far more interested in probing the possible colors of vegetation on the planets of other stars that might have different colored predominant light than our own sun's!

Composer and diarist Ned Rorem in *Facing the Night* specifically admits to hating mushrooms, Brussels sprouts, and bagels. "And liqueur in any sauce," he vigorously adds, although he says he loves *crème brulée*, key lime pie, "and anything chocolate with whipped cream." Bagels—the bagel was originally called a "*kipfel*," then a "*bügel*" after the riding stirrup, which in German is *steigbügel*; it is a German, not a Yiddish word—have only come into their own as a widely popular food in the last few decades. Brussels sprouts have been placed on American tables for a century but are widely hated. In an interview in *The Portable Curmudgeon Redux*, film director/writer John Waters sarcastically replied, "In a trough they might be good. On a plate I'm not too fond of them," to the question of whether it was true or not that he liked Brussels sprouts. He has referred to them elsewhere as "those little balls of hell." Waters' description of iceberg lettuce? "The polyester of greens," he says. Vegetables in general irk Waters. He disdainfully dismisses them all as "limp and wilted after a lifetime of being pissed on by birds and other contaminated creatures."

In his particularly silly hitchhiking-across-America book, *Carsick*, John Waters, the "Pope of Trash" at various times in his journey in which he more or less celebrates himself eats raw tofu, an uncooked turnip, Nutraloaf ("That crap is made from rotten tomatoes *kung pao*, week-old, moldy Wonder Bread, and the skin of tortured poultry! The opposite of free range!"), some pillow biter's trail mix, spoiled leftovers from a Chinese chicken dinner, mint Jujyfruits, and, if you can believe it—I prefer you read the account yourself—somewhere off Route 70 West someone's urine. I asked him once about any food aversions he had, but he replied that he was going to write his own book and maybe would save such stuff for that.

Jim Perdue, president of Perdue Farms, does not like olives. TV Sports broadcaster Al Michaels, according to a *Playboy* interview in 2002, cannot stand vegetables—any of them—and will not eat them. Filmmaker and writer Nora Ephron has stated that "nobody really likes capers no matter what you do with them. Some people pretend to like capers, but the truth is that any dish that tastes good with capers in it, tastes even better with capers not in it." Had the woman never even tried tasting a perfect chicken piccata or spaghetti puttanesca? I will file her blasphemous assertion against the positive line of lyrical advice raised in George and Ira Gershwin's hit song, "I'll Build a Stairway to Paradise," stating that "learning the steps of gladness...[is] the quickest way to paradise." Comedian Jack Benny, a significant part of whose persona was playing a notorious miser on his old radio show—it became the source of many a joke—always toadily invited over for dinner his elegant next-door British neighbors, the suave Ronald and Benita. Colman, invariably serving—to the the elegant and urbane Colman's private disgust—"baked beans under glass," and this became (a recurrent theme in the show) a food the couple particularly detested. The character Jack Twist is tired of—repudiates—beans in the Annie Proulx short story, "Brokeback Mountain," whereas his cowboy lover Ennis Del Mar does not like soup.

Beans, certainly not for the first time in literature, sum up in symbolic fashion the plain dull life—in movies and books—of many people, cowboys, prisoners, life in the military, especially the Navy. (A similar point is made in the musical *Gypsy* when Mama Rose sings "Goodbye, to blueberry pie" in the plaintive song, "Some People," to her dull and hopelessly settled Poppa, telling him that his unexciting kind of life is peachy for some people, but not for her or her kids.)

Beans can be dangerous. Raw kidney beans, and to a lesser extent some other beans (such as broad or fava beans), contain the toxin phytohaemagglutinin, which is destroyed by boiling, but not if slow-cooked at the lower temperature, so dry beans must be boiled at 100 °C/212 °F for 30 minutes before placed in a slow cooker or alternatively soaked in water overnight, and then, with the water replaced, boiled for at least 10 minutes. Merely a few beans can be toxic, and they can be as much as five times more toxic if cooked at 80 °C (175 °F) than if eaten raw, so adequate pre-boiling is vital. The fear of being poisoning by slow-cooked beans made an acquaintance of mine back in college give away his slow cooker. Try warning a passionate Dominican against eating beans, however. I have a friend who virtually lives for a native dish called "*La Bandera*" (A.K.A. "the Dominican Flag"), in which red kidney beans are cooked in a pungent herbed tomato sauce which is served with meat, either chicken or pork, along with a basic salad of lettuce and tomatoes. *A po' ta' bien*!

The cartoon character Bart Simpson, not only a 9-year old brat but something of a fussy foodist, has also gone on record in "Bart's Bottom 40" Simpsons *Comics Extravaganza* (1994) as hating Brussels sprouts. In that memorable but cranky list drawn up of general things he detests, he numbers, among foods, "creamed corn," "the hardened crust on the top of Mom's casseroles," "the gooey stuff underneath the hardened crust of Mom's casseroles," "the strawberry and vanilla parts of Neapolitan ice cream," and "sugarless anything." On the subject of strawberries, were you aware that the true, the actual fruit of the strawberry plant is in fact the plant's seed? In other words, each apparent "seed" (*achene*) on the outside of the fruit is actually one of the ovaries of the flower, with a seed inside that! In both culinary and botanical terms, the entire structure of the plant is considered a fruit.

Jane Austen ambiguously disquisits on strawberries with the comic character, Mrs. Elton, in her novel, *Emma*. At a strawberry party given by Mr. Knightley, fluty Mrs. Elton makes the following scattered remarks to no one in particular:

> The best fruit in England—everybody's favourite—
> always wholesome—These the finest beds and finest
> sorts—Delightful to gather for one's self—the only
> way of really enjoying them—Morning decidedly the
> best time—never tired—every sort good—hautboy
> infinitely superior—no comparison—the others hardly
> eatable—hautboys vey scarce—chili preferred—white
> wood finest flavour of all—price of strawberries in
> London—abundance about Bristol—Maple Grove—
> cultivation—beds when to be renewed—gardeners
> never to be put out of their way—delicious fruit—only
> too rich to be eaten much of—inferior to cherries—
> currants more refreshing.

Notice how her monologue dwindles down from high encomium into a small bias against the strawberry in favor of cherries and currants! A valid truism might go: there is a bias in every food opinion. Surely that truth lies at the core of the famous apothegm, "*De gustibus non disputandem est.*"

"I remember that during the Second World War my mother sometimes cooked Jerusalem artichokes or sunchokes, '*topinambour*,'" the matchless chef Jacques Pépin told me. "Their smell made me gag, and of course they were done '*au natural.*' Butter and cream do improve their taste greatly, yet even with those additions, I still can't get that vegetable past my nose." He added, "Otherwise, I am not crazy about coconut, and I certainly hate to drink water with my meats. I need wine for the food to be enjoyed properly and to be rightly digested." Chef Pépin declares that he dislikes any food that is "dry, overcooked, tortured and/or fussy." On one segment, "Rollin' in Dough" (Episode 117, September 10, 2011) of his cooking show, "Essential Pépin," this great chef, far and away the most distinguished of them all, declared as he put fresh butter on a baked loaf of *gros pain* and sampled it that if he had to choose one last meal on earth it would be simply fresh bread and butter. His exact words, written in a 2015 essay, were, "The greatest taste for me may be a perfect crunchy baguette slathered generously with the very best sweet butter." *The greatest taste!*

Although unpalatability is a common charge against artichokes, four centuries ago they—along with figs, onions, and lettuce—were thought to incite feelings of lechery. Catherine de Medici, making them famous, or infamous, is said to have introduced them to France when she married King Henry II in the mid-16th-century. She was quoted as saying, "If one of us had eaten artichokes, we would have been pointed out on the street. Today young women are more forward than pages at the court." A Paris street-vendors' cry back in that day went:

> Artichokes! Artichokes!
> Heats the body and the spirit
> Heats the genitals.
> Catherine de Medici was fond of artichokes."

As to artichokes, I should add here that in the heart of Rockefeller Center the executive chef at Del Frisco's Grille uses a popular ingredient that he does not hate so much as he hates what it does to the palate: artichokes. The main reason Scott Kroener dislikes this flowery vegetable is because of a particular enzyme in it that, depending on a person's internal chemistry, can create a bitter and metallic taste that comes out more when one is drinking wine. Given the extensive and well-thought-out wine list the restaurant has, this unsavory taste taints the experience for some, an issue Kroener takes into consideration when working with artichokes.

Other celebrity chefs hate certain other foods. Waverley Root hated tripe, for example, which surprised and somewhat shocked reporter—and gourmand—fat A. J. Liebling, who said of Root in his *Between Meals* (1962), "His insensibility to its charms seems to me odd in a New Englander, as he is by origin. Fried pickled honey-combed tripe used to be the most agreeable feature of a winter breakfast in New Hampshire and Fall River, Root's home town." French restaurateur Daniel Boulud dislikes bananas. New York chef Bobby Flay dislikes lentils. He claims to like just about everything in food but draws a line at only two: lentils and fiddlehead ferns. Dana Cowin, the editor-in-chief of *Food and Wine* magazine declared, "I don't like lots of organ meats that are dense and chewy and taste like blood—chicken heart, for example. But maybe that's more understandable than my next biggest pet peeve—wet scrambled eggs. I just hate the texture and flavor of soggy, curdly, squishy eggs." As an alternative he should give a try to what are still called "Guy Kibbee eggs," the name for a breakfast dish that consists of a hole cut out of the center of a slice of bread, with an egg cracked into it, all of which is then fried in a skillet. The cheery old 1930s actor prepared this dish in the film *Mary Jane's Pa*, hence the eponym.

Canadian pianist Glenn Gould, renowned interpreter of the keyboard music of Johann Sebastian Bach, would eat only scrambled eggs. When the now famous chef, Dione Lucas, was at The Egg Basket in Manhattan, Gould would always go there because she would make eggs the way that he loved them. Paul Myers, a friend, said, "He lived on his scrambles." A CBC profile noted that, "sometime between two and three every morning, the compulsive Gould would go to Fran's, a 24-hour diner a block away from his Toronto apartment, sit in the same booth, and order the same meal of scrambled eggs." It was to Fran's alone that Gould habitually repaired. There are theories that the piano prodigy might have been autistic, but this compulsion of his—fixing steadfastly on a repeated way of doing things—was shared by many another notable. The French chanteuse Edith Piaf would drink only white wine and with a besetting need obsessively tended to eat meals that consisted of the same dish for weeks at a time, such as chicken with *sauce suprême* (mushrooms, shallots, white wine, and cream). I have earlier referred to the strange and, needless to say, compulsive eating habits of Ludwig Wittgenstein.

"I don't care what I eat so long as it is always the same," the brilliant philosopher Wittgenstein declared. His *Tractatus Logico-Philosophicus* is itself a model of autistic cognition. He required sameness in routine—a repetitive style of dress, the same meal served again and again, insistence on a particular form of American detective story or Western tale. He was always compulsively focused. Over a lifetime, he displayed deep knowledge and ability in matters of narrowly defined interests—in engineering, in music, in mathematics, in logic, in architecture. He kept to favorite passages of literature or to a musical work that inspired him, but showed little interest in gaining a broad knowledge in any particular field, even in philosophy. Those who knew him, admirers and critics alike, describe him as atypical in manner, character, and behavior. Much of Wittgenstein's biography reads like the zigzagging journey of a man who both required and feared solitude. His intense and restless philosophizing, as much irritation as resulting pearl, comes across as an obsessive attempt to unearth the very root of mankind's connection to its universe—a challenge, it would seem, particularly irresistible to this driven autistic.

Alan Griswold has written quite brilliantly on the subject in *Autistic Symphony: The World as Wittgenstein Found It*. The economist John Maynard Keynes, after meeting Wittgenstein in Cambridge in 1929, wrote a very revealing letter in which he explained to a friend,

> My wife gave him some Swiss cheese and rye bread
> for lunch, which he greatly liked. Thereafter he
> more or less insisted on eating bread and cheese at
> all meals, largely ignoring the various dishes that my
> wife prepared. Wittgenstein declared that it did not
> much matter to him what he ate, so long as it always
> remained the same. When a dish that looked especial-
> ly appetizing was brought to the table, I sometimes
> exclaimed "Hot Ziggety!"—a slang phrase that I
> learned as a boy in Kansas. Wittgenstein picked up this
> expression from me. It was inconceivably droll to hear
> him exclaim "Hot Ziggety!" when my wife put the
> bread and cheese before him.

"One day Wittgenstein slept in late," Aberdeen professor Bob Plant wrote in *Philosophy Now* (December 2012). He added,

> When he arrived at the kitchen table (I think it was
> around 10 a.m.), I had already cleared away the break-
> fast things. I offered him some toast and tea but he
> asked only for two hard-boiled eggs. He seemed deep
> in thought and I wondered what he could be ponder-
> ing. "Wittgenstein." I finally asked, "are you thinking
> about logic?" "No," he curtly replied, "I was trying
> to imagine the form of life in which egg-laying caused
> neither shame nor embarrassment." He continued to
> eat his eggs and I reflected on his remarks. (I wonder
> whether he really liked poultry?)

Obsessions, repetitive behavior and routines, which can be a source of comfort, even delight, for people with an "autism spectrum disorder" (ASD), are of course a way of coping with everyday life. Such compulsions often show up in food choices and finickiness. One recollects that among the pals of Benny Profane in Thomas Pynchon's novel, *V.*—a member of the Whole Sick Crew—is Slab, an artist who cannot seem to paint anything other than cheese danishes. He belongs to the self-titled school of Catatonic Expressionism, "the ultimate in non-communication" and his studio is littered with canvases of cheese danish, symbols he startlingly declares will one day replace the cross in Western Civilization. One can imagine what Audrey Hepburn, who hated cheese danish, as we know, would have thought of Slab, aside from the fact that his only real ambition was to perfect the art of "schlemihlhood."

We have all read that the outlandish billionaire Howard Hughes over a lifetime developed debilitating symptoms of obsessive-compulsive disorder (OCD). The 1968 film *Ice Station Zebra* played on a continuous loop in his apartments or houses, a movie he is said to have watched about 175 times, doing so as he sat naked in his bedroom with a pink napkin placed over his genitals. Mormons were the only people that he considered trustworthy, although he was not a Mormon himself. Toward the end of his life he always had to be served exactly the same meal: steak, green peas, whipped potatoes. (He became even obsessed with the size of peas—one of his favorite foods—and used a special fork to sort them all out by size before he ate.) He became so exclusively and, needless to say, irrationally fond of Baskin Robbins' Banana Nut ice cream that his aides sought to secure by any means possible large bulk shipments for him, only to discover that the company had discontinued the flavor; they put in a request, however, for the smallest amount the company could provide for a special order, 350 gallons, and had it shipped from Los Angeles to Las Vegas. A few days after shipment, Hughes complained that he was tired of Banana Nut ice cream and now wanted only French Vanilla ice cream. The Desert Inn ended up distributing free Banana Nut ice cream to casino customers for a full year, until the entire 350 gallons were entirely gone.

"This preoccupation with his food and its preparation had begun decades earlier when, as a child," wrote Peter Harry Brown and Pat H. Broeske in *Howard Hughes: The Untold Story*, "he sat in his mother's kitchen and watched her scrub and scald and scour not just the pots and pans, but the meat and vegetables as well." Grim fears surfaced early. Brown and Broeske observe,

> The adult Howard feared that hordes of germs could
> attack him through ill-prepared nutrients. If Hughes
> had been a Renaissance prince instead of a mod-

ern-day tycoon, he would have undoubtedly pro-
cured a taster. Instead, he spent weeks devising ways
to insure that his meals were sanitary and cooked to
exact specifications... Howard's obsessive-compulsive
disorder produced full-blown food fetishes. Suddenly,
he was fixated on the minutes it took to open a can
in a sterile manner, the exact thickness of roast beef,
the shapes of stew vegetables, the precise number of
chocolate chips in a batch of the 'germ-free' cookies,
and the conditions of the vats that Kellogg's used to
prepare his favorite breakfast cereal...When he ordered
his special beef stew, the vegetables had to be pared
into perfect half-inch squares, with "each and every
corner cut off at a precise forty-five-degree angle." He
kept a slide-rule on his TV table to measure any suspiciously inexact pea or carrot. A plate of his chocolate
chip cookies had to have a precise number of chips
per dozen. And Hughes could gauge the amount just
by balancing the cookies in one hand. Too few or
too many chips and the cookies were rushed back to
the crestfallen chef. He even devised an exact way of
folding the chips into the batter "so that they would
not be bruised." ...There were distinct rules for preparation and delivery of room service orders, which were
prepared by Howard's staff of chefs, not the [Beverly
Hills] Hotel staff.

What is perhaps noteworthy in many cases of food aversion, certainly
as is evidenced with Hughes, many things are involved: hoarding, mental
illness; bi-polar disorder; germophobia, obsessive-compulsive disorder—he
used spoons with a protective covering that included two layers of tissue
paper and cellophane tape!—paranoia, physical pain, and, one might even
insist, reclusion.

A food aversion may be born of despair or scorn, as well. After she had
been brought to England as a newlywed, well-born Florence (neé Schieffelin)
Ismay of New York City, the wife of J. Bruce Ismay, the sole surviving White
Star high official (and some insist an infamous, self-serving coward) of the
doomed ship RMS *Titanic*, found it hard to adjust to drab Liverpool. (She
would later renounce her British subject status after her husband's death.)
Her granddaughter, Pauline Matarasso, in her memoir, *A Voyage Closed and*

Done (2005), wrote of the many wounding difficulties she faced in the long, complicated, and unhappy marriage of hers to a cold, joyless, forbidding, censorious, and emotionally unavailable husband who imperiously ruled over her and their family like a malign satrap. ("She released the bully in her husband who took pleasure in snubbing her at dinner parties, leaving her floundering and the guests confused.") "Florence retained a lasting nostalgia for her childhood home, which translated into a refusal to eat anything she hadn't eaten in her father's house: fifty years later this still ruled out a number of staples, notably sausages," writes Matarasso. In his splendid *How to Survive the Titanic: The Sinking of J. Bruce Ismay*, Frances Wilson portrays Ismay as a selfish, cynical, vain martinet with a cast-iron heart who also hated noise and kept his children confined to a specially-built wing of their house that was separated by two green baize doors and sees fit to explicate that man's own very odd food aversions—shedding further light on their personal pathologies—when he writes, "Because Ismay liked cold turkey, cold turkey was served every night." It is notable that the couple in strict compartmentalizing ways both attached their anxieties—hoping to allay them by way of tidy, marked reduction—to certain queer food habits and prandial quirks.

Russian lyrical poet/madman Sergei Yesenin, the wild, combative, alcoholic, polygamous husband (he was married twice before but never bothered getting divorced in either case) of the half-nude, reckless, audaciously expressionistic dancer Isadora Duncan ate nothing but cucumbers and sour cream. I love fresh sour cream. I had the occasion to visit Leningrad in 1969 back in the Soviet days and one snowy night after making a daring if not foolish but small-time money-swap on the black market, decided to go to the old Metropol Hotel and treat myself and my new-found friend to a dinner— happily slapping down the rubles on the table, "decorating the mahogany," I believe is the term for it—of rich Siberian black milk mushrooms with beef, onions and sour cream and pelmeni dumplings in saffron bouillon, all rounded off with some homemade Siberian pine vodka and, all the while creatively ignoring a be-hatted thug (NKVD agent?) eyeing me. I can still recall how delicious it all was.

Chefs can be pickier than you think. Liver, sea urchin, tofu, eggplant and oysters, of all things, top the list of foods chefs hate most, according to several national surveys. Only 15% of chefs that were recently surveyed said that they would eat absolutely anything. When eating out in other restaurants, chefs say they avoid pasta and chicken. Why? Simply, these dishes are often the most overpriced (and least interesting) on the menu. One temperate chef said, "I won't pay $24 for half a chicken breast." Said another, "I want something I cannot make myself." The reason that chef Steve Permaul from

Chelsea's Highpoint Bistro & Bar hates working with sea urchin is because it is an exhausting process to butcher for very little meat. First, he says, you meticulously have to clean the shells to get the iodine off, cut them and thoroughly rinse the insides. What is the result for all the effort?—a tiny lump of meat. Worthless. Instead of getting frustrated, Permaul makes the ingredient work by serving it poached in its shell with a lobster flan, or even simpler, he serves it raw with tuna sashimi. The sardonic Anthony Bourdain, known for eating some of the strangest foods in the world, claims that hakarl is the most nauseating thing he has ever eaten. Made by gutting a Greenland or Basking shark and then fermenting it for two to four months, hakarl is an Icelandic food that reeks with the smell of ammonia. It is available all year round in various shops in Iceland and is often served in cubes on toothpicks.

It was not chefs but general food critics who in the late '60s popularized the term "*nouvelle cuisine*," hardly a new phrase in culinary history, but it was Henri Gault, who picked up the phrase and with his colleagues André Gayot and Christian Millau ran with it in their restaurant guide, the Gault-Millau, or *Le Nouveau Guide*. But wasn't the gestalt of nouvelle cuisine food phobic? Chichi cooks suddenly became averse to complicated dishes, heavy sauces, flour-based roux, potent marinades, extravagant portions, large menus, and burp-inducing satiation.

Nouvelle cuisine, that dubious food trend in the 1960s and 1970s, seemed to be 90% presentation, 10% food. Close to the spa food or *cuisine minceur* ("thin cooking"), created—if you must insist on the word—by Michel Guérard, it was different only in that the latter was lighter and, if you can believe it, less filling. (I recall reading that the flim-flammer who came up with the concept of Miller Lite, a beer product using more water and less alcohol while costing more, was hugely rewarded.) It has been weakly argued that the outbreak of World War II gave a significant nod and impetus to the whole ideas of nouvelle cuisine—the scanty supply of any animal protein during the German occupation making it a natural development. It was novelty more than anything, one of those trendy flashes of pretense so common in society, a bit of legerdemain employed to get credulous patrons to believe that less is more. I have always secretly suspected that, with the spare servings it offered along with its tidy emphasis on presentation (on shorter, not larger menus) and its rejection of excessive complication, it bore the same severe, geometric functionalism—intentionally—of Bauhaus design, in many ways defining its program by defying its detractors.

Much of the food was steamed, with marinades and heavy sauces—no roux—all waived in favor of tiny, overly prim dishes seasoned with fresh herbs, high quality butter, lemon juice, and vinegar presented on large white platters—plates got bigger, portions smaller—all over-swirled in a final gesture of brainless theatricality with crazy, exotic drizzles and wavy, neo-geometric, Jackson Pollock-like spatters. Melodramatic revolving arm-and hand-flourishes were *de rigueur* by overweening waiters waving tongs when serving you, as they merely set down on a plate a single asparagus spear or a lonely plum or one dumb leek. I remember after one dinner at The Chanticleer, a high-end restaurant in the village of Siasconset on Nantucket—we were served braided fish, a potholder-size presentation fussily (and pointlessly) interwoven, with three shining baby carrots—I was so hungry on the way home I had to stop in the A&P to buy some onion rolls and cheese-sticks to stave off my hunger. Nouvelle cuisine has a lot to do with *legerdemain*. Waiters serve you large plates of tiny microscopic food with grand theatrical flourishes, lifting service plate covers as if to reverberations of a Handel-like chorus. It is all a joke. What previously was raw got cooked, what had been cooked was suddenly raw. Vegetables when brought to table were not so much served as fastidiously "placed," like rich gems into a tiara, often with impossible-to-explain creative pairings, tomato and turnip-tip, parsnip and pepper, a stalk of celery carved into a shillelagh, brainlessly ornate, fussily luxurious, and of course never filling.

It was more still-life arrangement than anything else. The chefs wanted to think of themselves as artists, their scrimp dinners paintings, including reflected light on glass and silver. Every meal was a would-be Chardin.

On the other hand, there was a rejection in nouvelle of excessive complication in cooking times for most fish, seafood, game birds, veal, and green vegetables, and pâtés were greatly reduced in an attempt to preserve the natural flavors. Steaming was an important trend from this characteristic.

Disguising food is a way of murdering it. I subscribe to the well-known truism of the illustrious Curnonsky, pen-name of Maurice Edmond Sailland who was the most celebrated writer on gastronomy in France in the 20th-century—he was dubbed the Prince of Gastronomy—when he said, "*La cuisine, c'est quand les choses ont le goût de ce qu'elles sont.*" (Good cooking is when things taste of what they are.) His motto was, "*Et surtout, faites simple!*" (And above all, keep it simple.)

I have mentioned previously that the noted Ferran Adrià, the "Salvador Dali of the kitchen," dislikes bell peppers, even though one of his signature dishes is pork loin with roasted peppers and parsley oil. *Dislikes bell peppers?* This from an extravagant chef whose unusual dishes include frozen whisky sour candy, white garlic and almond sorbet, tobacco-flavored blackberry crushed ice and Kellogg's paella (Rice Krispies, shrimp heads and vanilla-flavored mashed potatoes)? Cookbook author Rachael Ray of the Food

Network confesses that she does not like mayonnaise. "Mayo is a four-letter word to me," she says, "and I avoid using it when I can. It's all about that texture. I even make a no-mayonnaise potato salad that is perfect for picnics since you don't have to worry about spoiling." Celebrity party-planner Colin Cowie's food aversion is that he cannot stand to be served surf and turf on the same buffet or plate. Is that out of a kosheresque ideal or the result of some gross, off-putting picture printed on his brain? Chef Stanley Tucci expressly dislikes cilantro. Lidia Bastianich, author of the popular show Lidia's Italy on PBS, complains, "I just cannot stand cilantro—to me it is like having a mouth full of soap when I eat anything with cilantro. Another thing that I just cannot warm up to is sweet pickles. To me it seems like a contradiction. When I bite into a crunchy pickle, I expect it to be sour."

This is obviously the place to cite John Zacherle's novelty song from 1958 "Dinner with Drac" which goes in part,

> The waitress a vampire named Perkins
> Was so very fond of small gherkins
> While serving tea
> She ate 43
> Which pickled her internal workings

> and closes just as witlessly,
> For dessert there was batwing confetti
> And the veins of a mummy named Betty
> I first frowned upon it
> But with ketchup on it
> It tasted very much like spaghetti.

Touching on El Bulli, let me take a parenthetical moment to address the currently popular fad of exotic "tasting-menu" restaurants all over the world, where much of the cuisine coheres in a syntax outside of all logic or language, such as the very expensive Noma in Copenhagen, the French Laundry in the Napa Valley, Per Se in New York City, Senderens in Paris, Club Gascon in London, Alinea in Chicago, Quince in San Francisco, Samar in Dallas, and so, all of them rich places officially designated as the world's best restaurants where the balance of power has dramatically shifted from diner to chef, invariably a culinary (and often tyrannical) genius, and the pleasures of the grateful diners—devotees will pay as much as $500 or more a visit, waiting to sit in devotional knee-knocked states of hushed expectation, if not unconditional surrender, simply to get a bird's-eye view of what strangely devised or concocted food they will be served—are secondary to that magician's whims.

Grateful customers in most cases have to reserve seats months in advance, as if seeing the Pope, simply to experience meals or tastes of nine or ten to as many as fifty courses, offerings—forgive me, but in my mind I cannot help but picture these treats as tidbits, goodies, snacks or whatever, what Norwegians call *smakebit* (samples to taste), thrown as if to orcas—like *cuisse de grenouilles sur un bâton* or a foam of stinging-nettle spaetzle topped with a foam of spherificated grapes or knuckles of langouste in foamy wasabi-flavored cream sauce or antler-like "twigs" crafted from juniper-dusted malt flatbread with edible red flowers stuffed with escargot or steelhead trout roe with coconut and carrot *gelées*, young coconut slices, and micro cilantro on a bed of mild curry or an oyster leaf mignonette with calamari, sea urchin, and squid custard with four seafood bites (oyster mignonette, razor clam shiso, king crab with passionfruit, mussels with saffron and chorizo) served on driftwood on a bed of seaweed. Is it possible sci-fi writer Philip Dick was correct in *Valis* when he boldly remarked, "It is sometimes an appropriate response to reality to go insane?"

I find in these new deconstructed "tasting-menu" restaurants little but a dumb-show of posturing chefs, the real *maîtres cuisinier suprême*, intimidatingly bullying obsequious diners into assenting to their own—the chef's—importance, but surely we must understand that the diners are as culpable, as well, for as Ivan Karamazov makes clear in his "Legend of the Grand Inquisitor" in Dostoevsky's *The Brothers Karamazov*, all of those slavishly weak and cringing milquetoasts who willingly give up their freedom are every bit as culpable as those who are only too willing to take it. We read at the end of Saul Bellow's *Dangling Man*:

> I am no longer to be held accountable for myself; I
> am grateful for that. I am in other hands, relieved
> of self-determination, freedom canceled. Hurray for
> regular hours! And for supervision of the spirit! Long
> live regimentation!

True, the frustrated wimp, Joseph, having been drafted, is merely going into the Army, but his lame, slothful hope, an evasion, that the regimentation of military life will relieve his suffering, is quite sad.

It is a variation of deconstruction where the literary critic supersedes the author in assaying meaning, interpretation, and force and in its decadence suggests in a kind of surrealistic and somewhat disorienting way aspects of food aversions in several significant ways: one, especially touching on molecular gastronomy or what has been called "progressive cuisine," it implicitly argues in a highly decadent way that common food, indeed a customer's preferences, do not matter. Two, it asks us to reconsider taste itself which is nothing less than a repudiation of tested palates. Three, it turns away from food and looks pretentiously to art, which is not only a topsyturvification of dining but a blasphemy of the very act of eating. It transmogrifies food and to a degree mocks it. It does not celebrate food, it disguises it.

Hervé This (pron. *Tees*), a French chemistry professor who is known as the "father of molecular gastronomy" (he coined the term), actually *creates* foods from pure chemical compounds—cooking in a test-tube—basically abandoning all foods as we know them. Future kitchen shelves, he proclaims, will hold nothing but boxes of powder and bottles of liquid. Food waste will stop, world hunger end, and the world energy crisis abate. Were there any foods he disliked, I asked him? He replied, "For some time, milk and pears, but it was when I was a child." Invention certainly describes the work of Rirkrit Tiravanija, a contemporary chef of Thai extraction whose installations often take the form of stages or rooms for sharing meals, cooking, reading or playing music. Producing meals for gallery-goers, he also offers festive, large-scale, twelve-hour-plus banquets ingeniously composed of a single meal.

It is my sense that the effete novelist, Ronald Firbank was far ahead of his time, gastronomically speaking. When a London friend of his inquired what to order in one of the Lyons teashops, the dandy Firbank extravagantly replied, "Ask for heron's eggs whipped with wine into an amber foam." Eggs! They oddly seem to serve a decadent taste, as, for example, in the seventy-ninth perversion in the "Third Class of Criminal Passions" in the Marquis De Sade's *120 Days of Sodom*, which entails strapping a naked girl face down to a table and having "a piping hot omelette served upon her buttocks." (The engaged eater "uses an exceedingly sharp fork.")

Was that any different in degree, if not in kind, from some of the more *outré* creative offerings put out by Adrià and his jumped-up omnicompetents that include, among other orchidaceous delectables, Mentholated Pond ("the water vapor carries the flavor"); Gargouillou, a salad with more then fifty vegetables; Rose of Beet with Mandarin and Almond Sherbet; Semen of Fugu (a tempura dish); asparagus ice cream, and frozen polenta? A gastronomic Prospero, Adrià, like Hervé This, has by gastronomic legerdemain magically turned almonds into cheese, asparagus into bread, and mushrooms into blue foam, with nothing more than the aid of natural ingredients. With Houdini-like flourishes, he waves his arms and as if by magic produces foam of cod; gelatin noodles; foamy tomato-water sorbet; a liquid-filled one-bite ravioli of coconut milk encased in pasta-thin cuttlefish; calf's brains in sea-weed sauce with sesame-crusted turnips; knots of flash-cooked spinach and seaweed; and pickled sardines in raspberry oil. We read in *Gourmet* (October 1999),

> With a little gelatin to stabilize it, he discovered, any liquid can be transformed into a fluff—an *espuma*, as he called it. Truffle juice, asparagus, saffron, cheese, foie gras, mushroom. The list was endless. He could serve the resulting foam hot or cold. Foam provided a new perspective on old flavors. Stripped of its normal texture and puffed into a cloud, the pure taste of that asparagus or codfish could reach every part of a diner's tasting and smelling faculties. That's why Adrià boasts, "My basil jelly has more taste than basil does. My philosophy is to make with a carrot something more than a carrot."

I have often thought of such chefs as "Japanese Gardeners," you know, the kind of creative if manipulative, fiddling types who engage in the practice—Bonsai—of stunting a tree or silk plant, not for food or for medicine or for creating yard-size or park-size gardens or landscapes, but simply out of a kind of dimpled ingenuity. One comes across such untamed, corybantic meals in Boris Vian's novel, *Mood Indigo*, the American version of his 1946 classic, *L'Écume des jours*, except that with his invented mots, subtle wordplay, and surrealistic plots this is pure satire:

> Take a bunch of musk-antler bangers and skin them, taking no heed whatsoever of their screams. Carefully preserve their skins. Alternate rounds of the musk-antler bangers with sliced lobster claws that have previously been tossed in hot butter. Place them on ice in a pan. Heighten the flame and, in the space thereby gained, tastefully arrange little rings of coddled rice. When the bangers emit a continuous low note, take them swiftly from the flame and cover with rare old tawny port. Stir in with a platinum spatula. Grease a tin to prevent it rusting and then line it with the bangers. Just before serving, make a thick sauce of periwinkles, parsley, and a pint of pure cream. Sprinkle

> with valerian drops, garnish with the rice rings,
> serve… and disappear.

I have had the occasion to see Adrià cook, and it is a memorable sight to see his sleight-of-hand. Kenneth Tynan in his Hispanophiliac book, *Bull Fever* (1955), writes, "The genius of Spain is a manual affair, a matter of meticulous fingers: snapping in rhythm, flicking at castanets, stroking guitars, steering brushes over canvas, or guiding the course of the smooth notched sticks from which the red serge droops." Tynan is alluding here to the *torero*—the bull-fighter—prompting the bull forward as he waits with his sword and muleta, executing a few passes to slay the beast, but in a curious way it could apply to the subtly dexterous Adrià and, to quote Mercutio, his "antic, lisping, affecting fantasticoes, these new tuners of accents!"

Mercutio's disdain, in fact, becomes my question:

> Why, is not this a lamentable thing, grandsire, that we
> should be thus afflicted with these strange flies, these
> fashion-mongers, these *pardonnez moi*, who stand so
> much on the new form that they cannot sit at ease on
> the old bench?

Now I have nothing against the unique, the innovative, the distinctive, or the extravagant. Somehow there occurs in every generation, reaffirming and revising itself, a fascination for new colors, which in a way seems to parallel the current, adroit concept of experimenting with newer tastes in food. (When I was a youngster growing up, the colors of automobiles were proudly and singularly valued and all recognizably distinct, not the neutral catlap hues that we see today.) H.P. Lovecraft's 1927 story, "The Colour Out of Space," for example, mentions colors outside of the normal visual spectrum that are displayed by the alien entities from a meteorite landing on a New England farm. The concept of new colors outside of the normal human visual spectrum has been used by numerous fantasy and science-fiction authors. In his philosophical fantasy novel, *A Voyage to Arcturus* (1920), David Lindsay has his Earthman protagonist, "Maskull," bodily transported to the planet "Tormance" of Arcturus and finds not only that his human body has been endowed with a couple of new organs of perception but that he is suddenly able to experience with reinvigorated vision two new primary colors, "jale" and "ulfire." Then in *Three Worlds to Conquer* Poul Anderson depicted early contacts between Earthmen and the centaur-like quasi-humanoid inhabitants of Jupiter, with alternate chapters written from human and Jovian perspectives. The Jovians saw colors like "pirell," "lilla," "onsy," and "stawr."

No question that Adrià is a revolutionary. In his craft he recalls for me—exaggeration for emphasis—the late French lawyer, Jacques Vergès, who embraced anti- colonial causes and the role of devil's advocate on a world stage in order to defend war criminals, terrorists, dictators, and other notorious villains of the 20th-century. "I practice the '*defense de la rupture*,'" asserted Vergès, meaning his tactic of confrontation with the judicial system rather than one working within it. "My law is to be against all laws. My morality is to be against all morality."

Believe me, imagination in cooking is not new.

George Auguste Escoffier's famously elegant "*Cuisses de Nymphes à l'Aurore*" (Nymphs' Thighs at Dawn)—served to Edward VII at London's Savoy Hotel in 1901—was in fact frog's legs, but the French chef poached them in a white-wine court-bouillon, steeped them in a fragrant cream and fish sauce spiced with paprika, tinted them gold, then covered them with a champagne aspic-jelly to imitate water, to be served cold. This was the chef "who taught the English to eat frogs."

Chef Adrià and his minions work with the same devoted but much madder passion on their gastronomic creations, much of it, to me, a melodramatic faena of extemporaneous lunacy, however. It is a cuisine of new pathways, true. It is a fugue of audacity and adventure. But then, tell me, is it sane? I would compare it in the swirls and sensual shock to the insane doodles of a Jean Dubuffet *hourloupe*, the late-stage creative meanderings of the artist that abandoned the plane of the panel and ran back to supports freely opened into space. Overcerebral Adrià typically refers to the way that he handles food "deconstructivist," earnestly explaining, and unapologetically, that what he and his cooks are doing in the kitchen is not malicious tinkering or tampering at all but rather the creative act of "taking a dish that is well-known and transforming—transfiguring—its ingredients, all or in part, then modifying the dish's texture, form, and/or its temperature." So does his account sound solid and authentic, or is it merely—literally—culinary foam? As far as I am concerned, no matter what Adrià and his culinary ergopsychonauts do, however they try to explain it, they are altering the taste of foods, despite their repeated insistence that they are enhancing them.

Adrià *et cie* offer more shape-changing, taste-altering, food-camouflaging passes than the chromatophores on a cuttlefish. When are adaptations not alterations? Modifications, not redesigns? Transformations, not revisions? I come up with the word *substitutions* as a damning response.

I subscribe to the simple food theory that whatever a cook or chef does to a food that *disguises* the taste of it invariably disfigures or deforms that food, say what you will. This can be done in any number of ways, of course, by super-adding star anise to chicken or drowning a lobster in white sauce or suffocating a blueberry pie with too much lemon, too much heat here, too strong a spice there—you have killed it. Foods like fresh lobster, steak, tuna, and even spaghetti, say, are best prepared well, which often means simply and chastely unamplified. Adorning them with complicated sauces can be excessive and, distorting natural taste, even a kind of murder. The true taste of a food must not get lost by barmy over-inventiveness or the wild, histrionic transubstantiations of a vain chef's egotistical need to dress up a food looking "like the Pope's mother," as one wit described the daft 1970s costumes worn by the Swedish song group, Abba. Discomposing a food this way is disheveling it.

I tend to find far more credibility in the purposely anti-bourgeois, intentionally subversive, innovatively perverse, artfully seditious food drawings, prints, and paintings that the Pop Art painter Ed Ruscha did throughout the 1970s using the media of red wine, fruit and vegetable juices, maple syrup, tomato paste, Bolognese sauce, cherry pie, coffee, caviar, raw eggs and Nestle's chocolate, to say nothing of gunpowder, vinyl, blood, axle grease, daffodils, tulips, and grass stains. (For the April 1972 cover of *ARTnews*, he composed an Arcimboldo-like photograph that spelled out the magazine's title in a salad of squashed foods.) "Art has to be something that makes you scratch your head," said the revolutionary painter.

Still, must we insist that experimentation is imagination? It was John Ruskin's belief that the artist is an interpreter, a link between nature and men, where beauty resided in the "simplest of objects...in the most beloved sights that you see every summer evening along thousands of footpaths... of your old familiar countryside." It was a concept that delighted Marcel Proust, who claimed to have no imagination! The artist should only paint or describe what he sees; the painter Elstir presents the very same theory in *À la recherche du temps perdu*—it is the role of the artist as he sets out to explicate, clarify, and illuminate also to shed all preconceptions when he starts a painting in order to deliver only what he sees and not what he knows.

We live in a time—riddled with disguise, aliases, fakery, faux-food, imposters, sequels, duplicated movies, with the "virtual" perpetually reigning—when people cannot put their finger on what is real anymore.

I promise you that I am not a mindless and timid uniformitarian, conservatively insistent that new ways of cooking are dangerous or there should be no innovations in the kitchen or that any and all gastronomic experiments to search out and examine new tastes should be banned, as if I were stupidly and inflexibly fixed like all reactionaries to the gradualistic concept that "the present is the key to the past." It is simply that I personally dislike the idea that so many of these smug chefs, coming up with newer food tricks and radical transubstantiations, see themselves on the cutting edge of life, while the rest of us, slothful and unprogressive dolts, having just awakened with a yawn, groping about in our jim-jams in a slow hypnopompic haze, are too slow to understand, too lazy or too stupid to get out of the way—although Adrià's message, I gather, is pretty much that we *should* get out of the way.

I recall an observation of Sir Francis Bacon's in his *Novum Organum*, a treatise on the subject of heat and science, incidentally, a remark that had something of a distinct edge on it. The English philosopher, scientist, and essayist wrote, "The Chemists, again, have formed a fanciful philosophy with the most confined views, from a few experiments from the furnace." At the risk of sounding like an old stick-in-the-mud, it all makes one recall with some nostalgia, if not wish-fulfillment, the old Latin maxim that tells us to oppose beginning, "*Obsta principiis.*"

No, Ferran Adrià certainly has his critics. German food writer, Jörg Zipprick has gone so far as to accuse the Spanish Catalan chef of pretty much poisoning his customers with the very additives that he uses in his creative cuisine and has gone so far as to warn that his menus should carry health warnings, writing with admonition, "These colorants, gelling agents, emulsifiers, acidifiers and taste enhancers that Adrià has introduced massively into his dishes to obtain extraordinary textures, tastes and sensations do not have a neutral impact on health."

"God gave us intelligence to discover the wonders of nature," the self-absorbed and vainglorious scientist, Andre Delambre (played by David Hedison) tells his wife in *The Fly* (1958), his unnatural experiments in "transportation" leading to his death after he himself is fatally transmogrified into a fly. I have always thought that there is a sub-textual warning about their egotism in that their subservient maid Emma (Kathleen Freeman) has been told in a craven and demeaning way to have to call her middle-brow employers, "Master" and "Madame."

Adrià could not have produced his menu without a whole array of odd devices and paraphernalia. The kitchen tools used at El Bulli—centrifuges, dehydrators, sous-vide machines, Pacojets, homogenizers, gas-cartridge cream whippers (that is, a siphon or "charge") by which he aerates everything, liquid nitrogen canisters for making exotic espesantes and gelificación and "nano-emulsions," etc.—give the impression of a kind of "abracadabrante follies" and summon to mind the mad, exotic inventions that Lemuel

Gulliver discovers at the Grand Academy of Lagado when he visits the metropolis of Balnibarbi in Jonathan Swift's *Gulliver's Travels,* where in an atmosphere of learnéd arguments, logical debates, and no end of theoretical palaver all the scientists are constantly working on experiments, such as trying to extract sunlight from cucumbers or to turn excrement back into its original food it or to make gunpowder from ice, an ingenious experiment then being made at Laputa. (Professors there, fittingly, are also attempting to alter communication by doing away with language altogether.) How else do you think one can make potato foam, liquid olives, snail air, or spherified melon? The idea is, compulsively, to take experiments further and further—*plus ultra, plus ultra, plus ultra.* Deranged, demented or at least foolhardy and senseless experimentation and extravagant innovation, invariably an end in themselves, has often been the linchpin of decadence, corruption, and the desperate hunt for radical new sensations. Read the novels of Joris-Karl Huysmans. (But see, here you have an instance in living color of my own food aversions and intolerance, if you will.)

Are not Adrià's extravagant if exploratory acts of culinary *legerdemain* a great deal like John Cage's creation of his "prepared piano," where the idiosyncratic composer inserted or fitted onto the strings of the piano a variety of objects like wood, screws, or paper in order to produce a whole range of percussive sounds? How about the composer Morton Feldman, another experimentalist with indeterminate music, a development associated with the New York School of composers which included Cage, Christian Wolff, and Earle Brown? Feldman's works are characterized by sounds and rhythms that he sought to set free and floating, strangely unfocused pitch shadings, and recurring asymmetric patterns. His composition, "Projections," for example, was written out on squared paper with general instructions, allowing the performer almost limitless freedom of choice over pitch and not duration. Didn't Paul Hindemith in his opera, *Neues vom Tage,* call for—impishly, mischievously call for—a soprano while taking a bath on stage to sing about the wonders of modern plumbing?

A foodie of sorts, the odd, avant-garde Cage—a pioneer of indeterminacy in music, electroacoustic music, and the non-standard use of musical instruments—was also an expert on fungi and in 1968 won $5000 on an Italian TV quiz show, answering questions on that very subject. His most famous "musical" composition, *4'33"* (1952), requires a pianist to lift the lid of a piano and then not play anything for four minutes and thirty-three seconds. This blurring of the conventional separation of real life and the concert hall reached its extreme in certain notorious performances in which Cage would sit on stage frying mushrooms! Was it for the fizzling, sizzling sound? I would much prefer to hear any day of the week Johnny ("The Tan Canary") Adams—*repeatedly*—singing his masterpiece, "Reconsider Me"!

You can also find similar kinds of Swiftian apparatus on the second floor of Mejekawi, the lab and restaurant in Bali of Will Goldfarb, pastry chef extraordinaire—he once worked at El Bulli—a place described as a "murderer's row of culinary appliances," by journalist Howie Kahn in his article, "Chef Will Goldfarb's Dessert Laboratory in Bali." Goldfarb comes up with his original dishes, high-tech equipment like space-age climate manipulators, induction burners, a Heidolph rotary evaporator, and, among other things, an Irinox MultiFresh Blast Chiller, which, reaches 40 degrees Celsius, useful, writes Kahn, "for flash-freezing and therefore preserving the shapes of materials with unstable structures like bubbles and foams." Of this innovative expatriate chef in what seems a slightly dubious compliment, Kahn goes on to observe, "Goldfarb almost never speaks about food as something that's eaten. Rather, the discussion typically centers on process." Echoes of Trimalchio's feast!

Does this happen because chefs are not eaters? It is entirely possible. Chefs are characteristically no more gourmands than liquor store-owners are big drinkers or barbers particularly adore getting haircuts. As the critic and fabled editor of the old *Vanity Fair*, Frank Crowninshield, once declared, "Married men make very poor husbands," a line that was always quoted by the waspish but fey drama critic, Alexander Woollcott —a man of ambiguous sexuality—whenever he was questioned as to why he was not married.

Am I wrong or does not God himself manipulate, meddle with, or fool around with the universe? The fact is, matter and energy *distort* the geometry of the cosmos to produce the effect we call gravity. Is this tampering? Genius? Or must we conclude that God Himself works at cross-purposes?

While bold, there is something truly decadent, if not diabolical, in trying to devise something outside of nature in order to improve on it—not at all the same as inventing the automobile or discovering electricity, for those are classic examples of extending the possibilities of man's ingenuity, not perverting them like a vice-filled Roman emperor out of blind dissatisfaction with good food. The argument may be also made that it is a living insult to the desperately poor around the world who do not have enough to eat. It is not a cuisine, in a sense, but synthetic legerdemain that has no more chance of fixing in reality than the likelihood of Jesus Christ showing up in Jackson County, Missouri in the blossoming prairie outside of Independence where the Garden of Eden (hello, Joseph Smith!) supposedly had been located and where Adam has been predicted to return in the Last Days to visit his people.

Can one say with any finality that the gastronomic reach at El Bulli is strictly a case of serendipity, in the way of "All my pictures are accidents," as Francis Bacon once declared? Such mixtures, brews, preparations, hydrids, blends, potions—right out of an alchemist's workshop!

It is no different than the loonily numinous creations manufactured in the fictional factory of the manic candy-transubstantiating impresario Willy Wonka who, concocting swudge and everlasting gobstoppers and "invisible chocolate bars for eating in class," is also capable with his culinary magic to make marshmallows that taste of violets, and rich caramels that change color every ten seconds as you suck them, and little feathery sweets that melt away deliciously the moment you put them between your lips. (Surely they could not have been much of an improvement on Arnold's Candies, confected in Peru, Indiana—the shop closed in October 2005—for which Cole Porter had a standing order of five pounds a month, a sampling dish of which the great composer and lyricist always kept on top of his piano.) Stupendously, Wonka can make chewing gum that never loses its taste, and ingeniously fabricates candy balloons that you can blow up to enormous size before you pop them with a pin and gobble them up. Along with these astonishing prestidigitations, by a most secret method, he can also manufacture lovely blue birds' eggs with black spots on them, and when you put one of these eggs into your mouth, it gradually gets smaller, smaller, and smaller until suddenly there is nothing left except a tiny little pink sugary baby bird sitting on the tip of your tongue.

You can almost hear Adrià himself jumping up and screeching out with the zealous but often mumbo-jumboing Wonka, "Oh, you should never, never doubt what nobody is sure about," in mad delight over the scientific breakthrough of his stupendous chewing-gum meal, triumphantly exclaiming with him,

> There will be no more marketing to do! No more
> buying meat and groceries! There'll be no knives
> and forks at mealtimes! Just a little strip of Wonka's
> magic chewing gum—and that's all you'll ever need at
> breakfast, lunch, and supper! This piece of gum I've
> just made happens to be tomato soup, roast beef, and
> blueberry pie, but you can have almost anything you
> want!

Wonka's lordly (and tiresome) habit of megalomaniacally pronouncing upon everything—I have read that it was among the worst of Roald Dahl's own personal vices, the man who wrote the book—is nevertheless what we know him by, a goofy affectation rather like detective Philip Marlowe (Humphrey Bogart) pulling his ear in the frankly, to me, hypnagogic movie, *The Big Sleep*. But the madness of Wonka's experiments as ends in themselves border on comic witchcraft. (Did you know, by the way, that chewing gum, which was invented by a photographer named Thomas Adams, was originally planned to be used as a substitute for rubber?)

The madcap need for culinary alteration and upheaval—which is it, at bottom, exploration or exploitation?—must surely include Filippo Tommaso Marinetti, the Italian poet and editor who wrote *The Futurist Cookbook* (1932), part manifesto, part artistic joke, part subversive declaration of independence, in which one can find recipes for nocturnal love feasts; for sculpted meats; for making ice cream on the moon; and for "candied atmospheric electricities." It is a book expressly offering "brand-new food combinations in which experiment, intelligence and imagination will economically take the place of quantity, banality, repetition and expense." One experiment in this odd book documents the acts of Marinetti eating the same food while alternately resting his fingers lightly on velvet and then on sandpaper, where the perceived texture of the food, as he states, is quite different in the two cases. One of his more controversial caveats was for the outright abolition of pasta, as eating it caused lassitude, pessimism, lack of virility, and passion. He loathed pasta and at every chance denounced it as an example of a blind, pathetic Italian addiction to nostalgia and tradition, excess and dullsville. He pronounced, "Spaghetti is no food for fighters."

Marinetti sets other arguments against anything ill suited to modernity, while vigorously advocating a style of cuisine that would increase creativity. He pleaded that all of his Futurist meals combine the radical use of color, shape, music, lighting, and ideas, paradoxically leaving taste and nutrition off the list entirely. In fact, the modern vitamin supplement industry should make Signor Marinetti their patron saint, simply because the man argued that all of our sustenance should eventually come directly from pills, freeing up food to be the raw material of art—you figure it out—and helpfully he also buntily suggested that all pills preferably be consumed while one is listening to the soothing hum of an airplane engine!

The zealous Marinetti was a showman and dined his way from London to Prague to Budapest to Milan, staging ostentatious demonstrations with zany lectures provided as he consumed meals that included "Intuitive Antipasto," "Aerofood," "Cubist Vegetable Patch," and, among others, "Zoological Soup" ("Pastry in animal shapes, made of rice flour and eggs, filled with jam and served in a hot pink broth spiked with a few drops of Italian eau de Cologne [!]"). He tenders a striking recipe of "Raw Meat Torn Apart by Trumpet Blasts" and one that included chickpeas, capers, liqueur cherries, and fried potato chips, all eaten individually between carefully clocked stretches of silence. One of the more notable menus that he offers is for a "Tactile Dinner," a repast during which all invited guests must wear provided pajamas that have been prepared for the dinner—each one covered with a different material such as sponge, cork, sandpaper, or felt—the first course for which is a "polyrhythmic salad," which consists of a box containing a bowl of undressed lettuce leaves, dates and grapes. The box has a crank on the left side. Without using cutlery, the guests eat with their right hand while turning the crank with their left. This produces music to which the waiters dance until the course is finished. The Futurist Movement "disdained the example and admonition of tradition in order to invent at any cost something new which everyone considers crazy." Their aim was to shock. But the pressing question is, was it transformative and creative or valuable—or just sheer quirk? It was innovation by change and by revision and by violence. Remember, Marinetti was a militant fascist. Mussolini adored the man.

"To the conception of the imperishable, the immortal, we oppose, in art, that of becoming, the perishable, the transitory, and the ephemeral," he declared. "War is the world's only form of hygiene."

Marinetti wanted to abolish the fork. He wanted to employ perfumes to enhance the tasting experience. He insisted that certain foods on the table would not be eaten, but only experienced by the eyes and nose. No political discussion or speeches would be allowed, and all music and poetry was banned at table. He wanted Italians to stop eating foreign food and cease using its in-words: a bar should be called *quisibeve* (literally, "here one drinks" in Italian), a sandwich should be called a *traidue* ("between-two"), a *maître d'hôtel* a *guidopalato* ("palate-guide"), and so on. Old, dull traditional kitchen equipment would be replaced by scientific equipment, bringing modernity and science to the kitchen. Suggested equipment included autoclaves, colloidal mills, ultraviolet ray lamps, dialyzers and ozonizers. He was not so much a hater of European food as a modernist revisionary who was "infatuated by all things sleek, sharp, electronic, and shiny," as critic Tony Perottet points out. Oh yes, Marinetti was right up there with the chic Molecular Gastronomers we know today!

I wonder how many people regarding the matter of food, diet, health theories, nostrums, etc. end up in life's Casa del Wacko? Quite a few would be my guess. It is a world replete with moonstruck cuckoos!

We are long familiar with no end of insane procedures, from the fraudulent Wilhelm Reich's orgone box to Kevin Warick's cyborg to Michel

Persinger's God Helmet! Doesn't a caterer have to make daily visits to the museum exhibiting the Belgian neo-conceptual artist, Wim Delvoye's work, *Cloaca*? A unique work of art, *Cloaca*, which was unveiled at the Museum voor Hedendaagse Kunst, Antwerp, after eight years of consultation by Delvoye, with experts in fields ranging from plumbing to gastroenterology to internal medicine, is the first machine capable of reproducing the digestion-process from the ingestion of food to defecation! A caterer has to feed it every day. The work's excrement is then vacuum-packed and *sold*. As Robert Enright wrote in *Border Crossings*—and one is given to wonder if, tone-wise, any irony played in his aesthetic remark—"Delvoye is involved in a way of making art that reorients our understanding of how beauty can be created."

Critics insist that Delvoye's large installation that turns food into feces was created less to explore the digestive process than to make (satirical?) comment on the Belgians' love of fine dining. The food begins at a long, transparent mouth, travels through a number of machine-like assembly stations, and ends in hard matter, which is separated from liquid through a cylinder. As I say, Delvoye then collects and sells the realistically smelling output, suspended in small jars of resin at his Ghent studio. When asked about his inspiration, Delvoye stated that everything in modern life is pointless, that the most useless object he could create was a machine that serves no purpose at all except the reduction of food to waste. Cloaca has appeared in various incarnations including: Cloaca Original, Cloaca - New & Improved, Cloaca Turbo, Cloaca Quattro, Cloaca N° 5, and Personal Cloaca.

Is not Delvoye's fascination tangentially Adriàesque?

What exactly *are* beet embers? Celery notions? Vitello tomato cones presented in a rock? Bluefish rillettes? Noisettes of lapin with *parfum de farigule*? Air-filled foam of carrot? Pork confit with cotton candy? Squid ravioli in a lemon grass broth with goat cheese profiteroles? How about Arugula Caesar salad? Swordfish meatloaf with onion marmalade? Rare roasted partridge breast in raspberry coulis with a sorrel timbale? The last three of these are chef specials that are offered at the start of the film, *American Psycho*, from a novel that celebrates hedonism, in which food and drink are given especially great attention, often as a social weapon to intimidate the uninitiated and to overwhelm or keep away unwanted guests.

Coy, disguised food is not simply for the jaded palate. It is all of it a repudiation of normalcy, just as the fortress mentality and many of the anti-hospitality gestures in exclusive menu-tasting emporia are savage in the way that snobbishness is a kind of cruelty. Remember the scene when mad Patrick Bateman orders a Stoly on the rocks and the bartender charges him $25 for it and he responds by saying, although she cannot hear it because she is at the other end of the bar, "You're a fucking ugly bitch. I want to stab you to death, then play around with your blood"? That touches upon every note—each extreme—under consideration here. Brand names, so sacred to the perverted Bateman, are what squirrelly upstart diners seek to make themselves by their pilgrimages to rare restaurants. Do you happen to recall Bateman's favorite drink in *American Psycho*, both the film and the novel? The answer is J&B scotch. It also happened to be Truman Capote's favorite drink. His habit was to use its full name of Justerini & Brooks when ordering it at a shop. If the clerk did not know what he meant, Capote would bristle and simply flounce off the premises. Snobs, all.

"Some people think luxury is the opposite of poverty. It is not, it is the opposite of vulgarity," Coco Chanel once remarked. By her reasoning, if you cannot afford to pursue luxury, poverty is no defense against the humiliating charge that you are a vulgarian. How curious that Chanel loved the Nazis, sucked up to them, lived openly with a young Nazi lover—an officer in the SS—at the Ritz Hotel in Paris, and flourished mightily in her couture business during World War II, accumulating enormous sums in hard currency so that she was later able to piss off to Switzerland before the Allies retook Paris, and then gradually buy her way back to respectability by bribery. Nothing of vulgarity there, of course. No poverty certainly. And all the luxury a human being could want. So few today seem to care about that bad behavior. Chanel once gnomically gave voice to what I find to be an enigmatic, if not incomprehensible, remark, "Elegance is refusal." I wonder if she meant the refusal of the truth.

At one point in *American Psycho*, in extremis, Patrick Bateman has an upscale restaurant serve his date a urinal cake in a Godiva box instead of dessert. This is precisely the sort of humor a psychotic would have. Obsessive lifestyles based on name brands or accepted companies are status symbols, and worshiping them, which involves the aversion of hating anything generic in clothes or threads off-the-rack, is no different whatsoever than an aspect of food aversion. To insist loyally or snobbishly on buying one's suits at Huntsmen or Moss Bros or Alexandre in Savile Row invokes fixations of an unqualified kind. Status *qua* status, however, can be ignored or be re-jiggered, in an upside-down by way of what might call autoproletarianization. Multi-billionaire Donald Trump's favorite meal, hands down, for example, is common meatloaf, which he eats regularly, with gaudy ketchup, he says, and so this becomes a status symbol all on its own. (When Trump orders meatloaf, it must contain no vegetables, potatoes, rice, or anything else. Otherwise, the chef is *fired*!) He also thrives on pizza and eats whole buckets of KFC chicken with a knife and fork!

Aversions, as we know, are about obsessives and obsessions. Does not Bateman later murderously hack Paul Allen to death with an ax because Paul has nicer business cards than he does? It is all of it an arrogant display fusion, depraved, rich, and overripe. Patrick orders both a J&B straight and a Corona. Paul orders a double Absolut Martini. To soothe Paul, Patrick says the mud soup and charcoal arugula are "outrageous here," by which he means cool. Before murdering Paul, Patrick and his unsuspecting victim have dinner at a chi-chi restaurant called Texarkana. The overly fastidious Paul, a seriously obnoxious diner, is outraged that the restaurant has run out of its cilantro craw-fish gumbo, which Paul priggishly asserts is "the only excuse one could have for being in this restaurant, which is, by the way, almost completely empty." The level of soulless immorality can be seen in their gastronomic fussiness alone.

Oh, and Bateman's food aversion? When the psycho asks his girlfriend, "Why wasn't [billionaire mogul] Donald Trump invited to your party?" she responds with, "Oh god. Is that why you were acting like such a buffoon? This obsession has got to end!" An indication of his quaquaversal mind is the murderer's nutty response to this: "'It was the Waldorf salad, Evelyn,' I say, teeth clenched. 'It was the Waldorf salad that was making me act like an ass!'"

Did not Seneca, speaking out against elaborate Roman fare, once plaintively write, "I like food that a household of slaves has not prepared, watching it with envy"? Indeed. His was a much different world.

It is disheartening to look in on the decadent world upon which the ill and aged Emperor reflects with such desolation in Marguerite Yourcenar's *Hadrian's Memoirs* (1951) where we find the introspective man looking back with regret on a different world, wistfully recalling how in "official repasts" thrifty farmers and frugal soldiers formerly fed upon garlic and barley but "now suddenly enabled by our conquests to luxuriate in the culinary arts of Asia, [are] bolting down these complicated viands with the greed of hungry peasants." It was a different world for the Stoic. He writes to the young Marcus Aurelius who is his correspondent,

> We Romans cram ourselves with ortolans, drown ourselves in sauces, and poison ourselves with spices. An Apicius glories in the succession of courses and the sequence of sweet or sour, heavy or dainty foods which make up the exquisite order of his banquets; these dishes would perhaps be tolerable if each were served separately, and consumed for its own sake, learnedly

savored by an expert whose taste and appetite are both unspoiled. But presented pell-mell, in the midst of everyday vulgar profusion, they confound a man's palate and confuse his stomach with a detestable mixture of flavors, odors, and substances in which the true values are lost and the unique qualities disappear.

The aged Emperor's frequent reflections of tolerance for all religions, except for the politically disruptive "fanatics" like the followers of a Jewish prophet called Christ, all point to his major complaint, that "too many complications" have ruined "the simplest of our joys," and yet at the same time reveal, with a dramatic irony that perhaps I alone see, the blindness of the very man writing who reigned at a time (A.D. 117 to 138) when the straightforward Gospel of the Word in its utter simplicity, grace, and bold truth had by then been around and available—to a true seeker, to someone ready to listen—for more than a hundred years.

I wonder how he felt about ortolans. We certainly know the mindset on the subject of Vitellius (15–69 A.D.), the Roman emperor always described as lazy, self-indulgent, and obese, whose gluttonous fondness for eating and drinking four times a day—he often feasted on rare foods that he had sent the Roman navy to procure—led to his taste for decadent banquets, one of the more notorious in honor of the goddess Minerva at which the *pièce de résistance* ignobly called for the brains of a thousand peacocks and the tongues of a thousand flamingos—a hecatomb of rare birds for a single dish. Vitellius is reported to have starved his own mother to death in order to fulfill a prophecy that he would rule a long time if his mother died first. As to ortolans, composer and diarist Ned Rorem who is not a vegetarian—I have had the good fortune to dine with him several times—once alluded with disapproval to ortolan-eaters, gourmands who consume the plump little yellow buntings, songbirds, mind you, each about the size of a young girl's fist, which have been fattened on millet, drowned in armagnac, plucked, and stripped of its feet and a few other tiny parts, and then roasted in a ramekin for eight minutes, after which it is brought to the table while its pale yellow fat still sizzles, crisp-roasted and, rare to crunch, consumed whole, bones and all—all except the beak—"with napkins," according to Janet Flanner in her *Paris Journal,* "hoisted like tents over [the eaters'] heads to enclose the perfume, and maybe to hide their shame." Devouring the little songbirds at a single bite, bones and all, was a ritual established by Brillat-Savarin himself, including the use of a napkin over one's head.

Serving ortolans is now officially banned in France. Although a ban against killing and selling the bird, a member of the bunting family, has been in place in France since the late 1990s, many in the high-end restaurant business have been spoiling to override the ban, including such illustrious chefs as Michel Guérard, one of the inventors of "nouvelle cuisine," who has been plumping to serve the dish for at least one day or one weekend a year, and Alain Ducasse, who recently argued in a French food magazine that the prohibition "undermines centuries of tradition, customs, and promotes a black market with exorbitant prices."

The prized birds can fetch as much as $150 each, if and when sold (illegally) to restaurants. It is said that the decadent, sybaritic diners, who still seek to order them for their barbaric pleasure, in their nonchalant wastefulness savor not only this odd ritual of eating them but actual delight in the illicitness of doing so almost as much as enjoying the flavor. A degree of panache is attached to eating ortolans—it is mentioned in Proust's *Remembrances of Things Past*, and the pretty young nymphet, star of the musical *Gigi*, eats one. Chef Anthony Bourdain in a reechy, almost illicitly purple sentence, matching the act, gives us a true glutton's description of the experience, writing

> With every bite, as the thin bones and layers of fat,
> meat, skin and organs compact in on themselves, there
> are sublime dribbles of varied and wondrous ancient
> flavors: figs, Armagnac, dark flesh slightly infused
> with the salty taste of my own blood as my mouth is
> pricked by the sharp bones.

Part of the ignominy of eating ortolans is the way they are killed. "The method in which they are dispatched is savage. "Hunters catch the birds using traps set in fields during their migratory season (when they fly to Africa)," writes Harry Wallop in *The Telegraph* (UK); he goes on to explain,

> They are then kept in covered cages, encouraging
> them to gorge on grain in order to double their size.
> It is said that Roman Emperors stabbed out ortolans'
> eyes in order to make the birds think it was night,
> making them eat even more. They are then thrown
> alive into a vat of Armagnac, a trick that manages to
> both drown and marinade the animal at the same time.
> Killing two birds with one glug, as it were. French

chefs argue that "it's not a bad way to die." Indeed, it is probably no crueller than force-feeding a goose in order to fatten up its liver into foie gras, another dish that French gourmets refuse to give up despite mounting howls of horror around much of Europe.

François Mitterrand, the former president of France, notoriously feasted upon one at his "last supper," while terminally ill with prostate cancer, concealing his head beneath a napkin in the traditional manner. As Nathanael West writes in *The Day of the Locust*, "Few things are sadder than the truly monstrous."

Oscar Wilde had it right when it came to eating ortolans. "I want to taste one," a young fellow once said, dining with the great poet and playwright, who replied, "So young, and already so eager for disappointment! Why give up imagination? 'Ortolan,' the word, is far more beautiful than when it is made flesh. If you were wise you would learn life only by inexperience. That is what makes it always unexpected and delightful. Never to realize—that is the true ideal."

A would-be Apicius, Jim Harrison, novelist and poet, had an emperor-like appetite for food in every form and shape. He hunted, he grilled, he trapped, he loved the outdoors and the wild, he made stocks of shin bones, he invented sauces, he threw wild Lucullanesque parties by white moonlight, but, by far the biggest highlight, he ate like a grunting male water buffalo in green Spring, boasting (as he was prone to do) on how with one friend they together dispatched with "a half-pound of beluga with a bottle of Stolichnaya, a salmon in sorrel sauce, sweetbreads *en croûte*, a miniature leg of lamb (the whole thing) with five wines, desserts, cheeses, ports."

Quantity mattered to Harrison, in that it seemed to make him feel virile. "I have never eaten more than a gross of oysters a day," he boasted. In his book, *The Raw and the Cooked*, a celebration of himself, he pronounced on everything and quoted himself with wild abandon. "Wild turkey is the finest table bird on earth," "There is no substitute for Badia a Coltibuono olive oil," "Missouri, Iowa, and Minnesota... you doubtless know are not food states," "Bears love pork," "I can't abide buffet lines," "Sunlight generates a taste for tequila," and so on. Harrison's primal scream was, "We deserve pleasure, because we live nasty, brutish lives." The novelist had all the attributes of the classic sophomore, an irritating compound of someone simultaneously both clever (Greek σοφός [sophos] and stupid (μωρός [moros]), a man who had lots of factual knowledge but was oblivious to truth. His heartiness was tiresome and the arguments he put forth both to defend and extol it, at times with almost unparalleled opacity but always with the kind of ratty and self-admiring country logic that comes in quips and western aphorisms, the kind of thing I dislike in a man, were just short of bearable. He always kept to the sparsely populated regions of this country, maintained a living, active hatred for New York City, the Republican Party, the East, and, while he liked to claim that he had a strong identity with the poor, the disadvantaged, and the homeless, on the very same page of his food book where he seemed to find neither a particular nor bothersome conflict in spouting like Nero about truffled eggs and carpaccio and dreaming of putting away an elegant dinner of "stewed tripe at Locke-Ober's, the flavors married dizzily to a bottle or two of La Tache." I can easily imagine Big Jim Harrison munching rodents in the lines from Robert Browning's *The Pied Piper of Hamelin*:

> Oh rats, rejoice!
> The world is grown to one vast drysaltery!
> So munch on, crunch on, take your nuncheon,
> Breakfast, supper, diner, luncheon.

What is not surprising about Harrison is that he was not only "seriously overweight" (his own description) and had sinus trouble, goutish big toes, skin rashes, and, by his own count and assessment, but had gone through at least five major full-blown depressions—and, adding to the whole thing, he suffered from frequent headaches. Harrison became blind in one eye at the age of 7 after a childhood accident ("a little girl put out my eye with a broken bottle on a cinder heap at the edge of the woods in 1945"). He also smoked cigarettes. But that was all right, you see?

Trust me, the guy was very self-satisfied.

I never read a description of one of his extravagant if not excessive meals, when I do not think of Dr. Samuel Johnson's remark, "This was a good dinner enough, to be sure, but it was not a dinner to ask a man to."

Harrison of course had food aversions. Zinfandel for him is a "contemptible wine." Bacon and eggs is "another nasty food that had its inception in the dizzy thinking that followed shortly after World War I." He hated butter, carrot juice, skinless boneless chicken breasts, portobello mushrooms ("Those big domestic fungi are as sure a sign of mediocrity as skinless, boneless chicken breasts"), old bear meat, all snack foods, any *cuisine minceur*, desserts, and virtually all ham, explaining that "Ninety-five percent of the ham we are served [is] ham in name only... It is simple dead pig's ass, artificially smoked, steamed, or boiled, strictly what they call 'industrial food' in France, where it has also become prevalent." He loathed "fat-laden junk food" and "tasteless domestic cheeses." After eating two cans of Hormel chili in a rare populist moment, Harrison wrote, "I actually burst into tears, then walked exactly eleven miles to purge the whole experience." This lout who with his grizzled pretensions sounds like a perfect spokesman for the author, Michael, the middle-aged divorcee professor of Harrison's 1988 novel, *Dalva*, who is characterized by the eponymous heroine as "self-important" and "an expert at everything awful that ever happened in the history of the world"—he calls himself "a bit of a food snob"—who mocks proles. "We were seated fairly near the salad bar, with its ubiquitous Plexiglas sneeze shield—I noted bowls of Jell-O of every color of the rainbow, cottage cheese, pickles, three-bean salad... and I confess I've never felt so much like a real American since the Boy Scouts."

There was to be no common, run-of-the-mill fare for Harrison. In Hollywood, the novelist once visited Chasen's and "demanded Ronald Reagan's favorite meal, as he [Reagan] habitually ate in that particular restaurant." He condescendingly writes, "The maitre d' and waiter were amused and served me a boring 'pot roast,' which is braised beef and dark gravy. I was only able to eat it with a bottle of good Talbot." Notice how Harrison not only helpfully spells out for us what the dish called pot roast is but makes it clear that it is a navvy-like meal far too undistinguished for him, adding—in the very same paragraph—how once at a card game, "I ate five roasted deer hearts," superadding the muscular aside, "My favorite part, however, is the liver of a young female deer which might be called 'Lolita liver.'"

A mad ornithophage, Harrison who made no distinction ate wild ducks, doves, sage grouse, blue grouse, wood pigeons, pheasants, rock partridges, quail, waxwings, prairie chickens—on toast points, grilled, spitted, in stews, in casseroles, you name it. Avian hors d'oeuvres, for all I know. It is illegal to shoot robins, otherwise he would doubtless have been nailing them, as well. Same for seagulls. He has eaten parrot stew, he admitted. "In the South, some black people still eat starlings," he sagely informed us, but he died before he could manage to complete a successful avian dodecafecta. I should point out that barbecued starlings in Tanzania are in fact the equivalent of hot dogs in the USA. Harrison was one of those un-shut-up-able lore-masters who had personal access to such *deep* things like how to clean an owl's skull, where best to find pheasants in South Dakota, etc. He sagaciously lessons us that, while partridge is always brought to table and served without the head, woodcock is almost always brought to table with the head attached. Traditionally, by the way, the most prized part of eating woodcock is—grimly—the brain, scooped out. But, then, woodcock is shot, usually during a pheasant shoot; not trapped or drowned alive like ortolan.

Let me mention that, although the songbird ban in France prohibits the killing of woodcock, colloquially called the "timberdoodle," it is legal in both Britain and in the United States. The small, long-beaked bird can be found on menus, especially those known for "nose to tail" eating, where it is usually served with its head on, split down the middle.

"I have learned that it's not smart to eat a whole confit of goose thigh for breakfast," says the greedy, gouty glutton, but he apparently never stopped. Of another casual *agape*, he gluttonously writes, "I prepared the Blue Grouse in a casserole, browned and flambéed in Calvados, then simmered slowly with raisins, Juniper berries and small pieces of larding bacon, deglazed with cider and garnished with cabbage that had cooked in a stock of grouse and woodcock giblets and livers." His rodomontades were legion. Can you imagine this guy sitting next to you on a long bus ride and blabbing away across the endless miles? Hand me my Dramamine!

I wish him an eternity of—not rolling a boulder up a mountain, like doomed Sisyphus—but a tedious perpetuity of eating *coots!* A young newlywed, dancer Ginger Rogers, after her husband, actor Lew Ayres, returned from a hunting trip having bagged two birds, lovingly thought that she would surprise him, gave her cook the night off, and took over, soaking them with delectable spices and baking them in the oven. Soon the house began to reek with a burnt, foul odor. "I thought perhaps a polecat had left its love-note near our house," she wrote in her autobiography, *Ginger*, "Lew wiped my tears away and enjoyed a good, bridegroom's laugh, exclaiming, 'Don't you know coots aren't supposed to be eaten?'"

Many ducks are said to be inedible, such as the merganser and the spoon bill, simply because they are fish-eaters, but even those are tastier than the lowly coot. Waterfowl can really stink. The coot is a small swamp bird that is actually more closely related to sand hill cranes than it is to ducks. Coots are not very big, and there is not a whole lot of meat on them; their breasts weigh only about 2 ounces apiece, and the legs barely have enough meat on them to scrape off. Virtually anyone who knows what a coot is will tell you they taste dreadful, sickening, vile, something along the lines of muck or swamp mud. I have read that it helps to drench the birds in salad dressing and then grill them. Hunters with experience do claim that most of the atrocious flavor you get when eating any wild game comes from their fat. Trim away all the fat on a coot, and the real flavor of the bird will emerge, *maybe*.

It brings to mind when I read about this bird's gobbler's appetite the popular French Canadian children's song, "Alouette," which has rather macabre origins involving someone plucking the feathers from a harmless lark in retribution for being awakened by its song. It is a populist ditty reverting to the French fur trade, when "*voyageurs*" to pass the time and make work seem lighter sang to accompany the motion of paddles dipped in unison, when singing helped. French colonists loved eating horned larks, which back then were considered a game bird. "Alouette" as a lyrical apostrophe informs the lark that the singer will pluck its head, nose, eyes, wings and tail:

> *Alouette, gentille Alouette*
> *Alouette, je te plumerai*
> *Je te plumerai la tête*
> *Je te plumerai la tête*
> *Et la tête*
> *Et la tête*

> Lark, nice lark
> Lark, I shall pluck you
> I shall pluck your head
> I shall pluck your head
> And your head
> And your head

Harrison had publicly boasted that he once successfully ate a 37-course meal and repeatedly told of going on legendary binges in Key West during the 1980s from which he would return not remembering his own cat's name. A fat braggart, he was more than anything a gastronomical traffic-cop, cocky, pushy, loud with shirty advice and buttocky pontifications that explicitly implied that by following what he considered his exquisite diamond-pane taste we would all be much better off. The fact is the guy was 75 and in dicey health and should have been in church on his knees praying, instead of scarfing down interminable wrecking-ball dinners.

It only makes me think that Darwin was right. "Humans are different from animals, not in kind but by degree."

The fat cook "feeds his appetite as if he were stoking a furnace," observes John Thorne in *Simple Cooking*. It is clear that Harrison used the appetites of his projected readers as foils, fatuous fools and fan-butts, whom he metaphorically summoned to heed and to hearken to his pronouncements, only to amplify his own huge Grandgousier-like feedbag. Auguste Escoffier's adjuration, "Above all, make it simple!" was meaningless to him. I do not care how pious it may sound: no appetite should be pronouncedly larger, longer—or more rapacious—than our hunger.

An extreme fusser over food inexorably becomes worse than a man who dreams all day of Kobe beef briskets or Sevruga caviar omelets with rare bottles of Bernard Morey Batard Montrachet followed by cups of Kopi Luwak coffee. He is rather an intolerant and snobbish hog-slave to self-love, a cantankerous totalitarian who presides over his own realm in his almost exophthalmic hunt for the perfect food. A wind damage of ego empties his legs of strength, his mind of truth, but he wobbles on, an Ahasuerus on the stilts of craving in pursuit of excess. A gourmand wants you to find him benevolent, but he is merely a primitive with a great hump of savagery. It has been said that Satan's best trick is to prove that he does not exist. But in his malice he is far, far more subtle than that. The crafty, artful, and devious trick is his dissembling way of persuading us he is unimportant, merely casually at hand. The form of his illusive, insinuative affliction may be called the "noonday demon" (*daemon meridianus*)—a phrase taken from Psalm 91—which robs an individual of purpose and patience and time and replaces it with *acedia*, often called "the malady of monks."

In his poem, "Grub First, then Ethics," W.H. Auden singles out the glutton for the selfish, solely-food-focussed, timorous mouthbucket that he is, deaf to pity or care, fixed alone on his hunger, but more than anything unbrave, neither chivalrous or daring, essentially unmanly. They are basically eunuchs, "thin-lipped" in the way of being cunning, and are *beyond* condolence:

> The sin of Gluttony
> is ranked among the Deadly
> Seven, but in murder mysteries
> one can be sure the gourmet
> didn't do it: children, brave warriors out of a job,
> can weigh pounds more than they should
> and one can dislike having to kiss them yet,
> compared with the thin-lipped, they
> are seldom detestable.

The same sharpness of insight was conveyed as, if not more, powerfully three hundred years before Auden by the Scottish poet and dramatist, Joanna Baillie, a woman shrewd, observant of human nature, and persistent in her own views and opinions, when she wrote in her *Count Basil* (1798),

> Some men are born to feast and not to fight:
> Whose sluggish minds, e'en in fair honours field

Still on their dinner turn—
Let such pot-boiling varlets stay at home,
And wield a flesh-hook rather than a sword.

A food fussifier's blasphemy is false worship. It is invariably conveyed by the vice of boredom, also the subject of David Foster Wallace's *The Pale King*, about which David J. Michael in a splendid critique explains, "The root of acedia is the Greek word *kedos* which can be translated as 'to care about.'" We read about it in Athanasius's *Life of Anthony* and in the works of Origen, but it was not until the 4th-century that it developed in the writings of Evagrius (c. 345–399), a monk and desert hermit who was convinced that *acedia* was demonic and who helped articulate the monastic concept of the eight bad thoughts, which were thetaically related to the Platonic tripartite division of the soul and the forerunner to the seven deadly sins. Of these eight thoughts—gluttony, lust, greed, sadness, anger, *acedia*, vainglory, and pride—the most dangerous was *acedia*. It was to be especially feared because it could function as gateway to other bad thoughts, even as it recapitulates all of them, but also because it meant a rejection of the created world and the joy that a person was supposed to take in God. (Curiously, boredom is the one torment of Hell that Dante failed to include.)

It may be asked: but does not the glutton focus on the created world? The answer is, no, he doesn't, he does not. He *usurps* it. He exploits it. He reduces it to himself. It is the snatching ape that comes to mind, grabbing banana after banana. That is the point. Blasphemously, he does not "care about"—a *kedos*—anyone but himself. Jean Cocteau liked to quote an answer an Indian chief once gave, when accused of overeating at the White House: "a little too much is just enough for me."

I am quite certain that gourmands and wealthy consummate food inebriates of the recent past, eaters with an insatiable and likerish lust for exotic cuisine like Diamond Jim Brady, King Edward VII, J.P. Morgan, King Farouk, Lucius Beebe, A.J. Liebling, and even the avoirdupoiresque Gertrude Stein, and other inexhaustible beefeaters with vast, inflated bodies the size of astronaut's zoombags rarely if ever ate ortolans the way that ravenous gluttons did back in ancient Rome, consuming them, say, like the Emperor Elagabalus or the voluptuary Lucullus did while luxuriously dining within his aviary—for important feasts in the Ancient World it was not uncommon for an aggregate of up to 5,000 ortolans, thrushes and larks to be served at a single double-fisted banquet—but our greedy boys certainly did eat them, smugly, forks at the ready, privately, en-bibbed, at closed-to-the-public dinners and intemperate repasts that lasted whole days and even possibly weeks. These were great guys for eating birds of any and every stripe and in as many ingenious ways as they could devise: whole alouettes, little larks embedded in jelly; terrines of pheasant, *pâtés de grives* (thrushes) and *pâtés de bécasse* served in handmade oval crocks with the woodcock's head and long beak emerging at one end and the two clawed feet sticking out at the other.

It should not be overlooked that in *The Silence of the Lambs* Hannibal Lecter, the mad cannibal, was such a gourmand and was known not only for the excellence of his table (or the special oddity of his larder) but also for the numerous articles that he had contributed to various gourmet magazines. Courtly, erudite, punctilious in matters of grammar—he is deeply offended by rudeness and frequently kills people who simply have bad manners—he is a cook. He is a chef. He *prepares* food, not merely scarfs it like a common diner slob. No, Hannibal is not Goya's bestial pop-eyed Saturn devouring—madly gnawing the arms off—his son. This psychopath does not merely consume human brains as such but "dredges them lightly in seasoned flour, and then in fresh brioche crumbs, adding "shallots to his hot browned butter, and at the instant their perfume rises he puts in minced caper berries" and then "grates a fresh black truffle into his sauce and finishes it all with a squeeze of lemon juice."

Craig Claiborne, the *New York Times* food columnist, prissily dined on ortolan back in the 1970s on the occasion of his notoriously decadent repast at Chez Denis in Paris, where he dispatched more than thirty courses and drank extremely rare French wines, thanks to a successful bidding at an Amex auction for the right to eat in the restaurant of his choice anywhere on the planet (he won the prize with a bid of only $300). As I have said, many of the greedy, decadent, hyper-aesthetic diners—family *accipitridae* ("seizers") for they are not much different than hawks, kites, ospreys, or cinerous vultures who swoop down to clean up messes — followed the time-honored custom of draping their heads with a linen napkin in order to absorb the maximum odor with the flavor (and, some believe, to hide from God). You may recall how in the film *Gigi* (1958), the young girl attends a gala luncheon with her great aunt, Alicia, and is instructed how to eat ortolans as a main course. It was as late as 2007 that the French Government was moved to pass strict laws to protect the bird. Just for the record, the ortolan bunting sings sweetly, as does the pale, speckled mistle thrush. "We could have had thrush tonight," wrote humorist James Thurber, writing to Elliott Nugent from Aix-en-Province in 1937. "I don't eat warblers. I do a lot of things, but I don't eat warblers. Four and twenty blackbirds, yes, but not warblers. 'Please pass the nightingale' is something I shall never say."

Parsifal in that grand opera, remember, has defiled the castle by shooting a swan. (Some say that serious Wagnerians characteristically never forget this.) In 1860, in a letter to Mathilde Wesendonk, Wagner had written about the relationships between characters in *Lohengrin*, *Parsifal* and *Die Sieger*: "*Only the deeply wise idea of the transmigration of souls could show me the consoling point at which all creatures will finally reach the same level of redemption.*"

Novelist Jonathan Franzen should be numbered among such men of conscience. Film producer Roger Kass, with his brother Douglas, spent two full years making a documentary, "Emptying the Skies," a film that is based on one of Franzen's polemical *New Yorker* pieces, the subject of which was the illegal but profitable bird-trapping trade in Europe. The fact is that every year, as many as tens of millions of migrating songbirds are slaughtered in crude yet elaborate traps set by hunters and poachers in the European countries along the Mediterranean, unconscionable and greedy scofflaws who either kill for sport or plan to sell the delicate meat on the black market. For what he legitimately defends as an act of "journalistic integrity," an act of course that he had to steel himself to perform, Franzen, an executive producer of the film, at one point sat down to a traditional dish of *ambelopoulia*—cooked blackcap warblers or other songbirds—which is also known as "Cyprus caviar" and can go for $100 a plate. Forcing himself to take a bite, he described the tiny grilled birds as "a dozen little gleaming yellowish-gray turds." He wrote, "I couldn't tell if the meat's bitterness was real or the product of emotion, the killing of a blackcap's enchantment."

Passenger pigeons, also called "wild pigeons" and sometimes "the blue pigeon," for its color—they had blue wings and red tail plumes and were lovely and sang—have disappeared. It was once the most abundant bird on the North America continent and possibly the world but now is completely extinct. In the early 19th-century almost 50% of the birds in North America's were passenger pigeons (Ectopistes migratorius), which traveled in gigantic flocks that are described by naturalist Joel Greenberg in astutely observed, *A Feathered River Across the Sky* as "so massive as to block out the sun for hours or even days." He adds, "The down beats of their wings would chill the air beneath and create a thundering roar that would drown out all other sounds." Feeding flocks as they amassed in their glory would appear as, he says, "a blue wave four or five feet high rolling toward you." One flock in 1866 in southern Ontario was described as being literally a mile long, taking as long as 14 hours to pass and holding as a flock in excess of 3.5 billion birds. That number, if accurate, would likely represent a large fraction of the entire population at the time! The birds appear like jewels in the pages of American literature and inspired awe in the likes of Audubon, James Fenimore Cooper, and most notably Henry David Thoreau.

The pigeons were a cornucopia of food for hunters and food hustlers. A hundred thousand birds might be killed in one single night. Carcasses of the birds were carried away by the wagonload. The loud noises of the dying birds was so deafening, according to the British naturalist John James Audubon, having witnessed a Louisville pigeon shoot, "even the reports of the guns were seldom heard, and I was made aware of the firing only by seeing the shooters reloading."

Henry Thoreau wrote about them in his *Journals*. In June of 1861, he and one of his best friends, Horace Mann Jr., as Corinne Smith describes it in *The Year of the Pigeon*, "examined several wild pigeon nests that they had found in basswood, oak, and hop hornbeam trees in the prairie land near Minneapolis. When the men later steamed by riverboat up the Minnesota River, they passed through a remnant of the Big Woods, the noted old-growth stand that once covered 2000 square miles." Here the trees on either side of the water were "all alive with pigeons & flying across our course." As Thoreau passionately noted in his *Journals*,

> The pigeons on the trees looked like fabulous birds with their long tails and their pointed breasts. I could hardly believe they were alive and not some wooden birds used for decoys, they sat so still; and, even when they moved their necks, I thought it was the effect of art. As they were not catching then, I approached and scared away a dozen birds who were perched on the trees, and found that they were freshly baited there, though the net was carried away, perchance to some other bed. The smooth sandy bed was covered with buckwheat, wheat or rye, and acorns. Sometimes they use corn, shaved off the ear in its present state with a knife. There were left the sticks with which they fastened the nets. As I stood there, I heard a rushing sound and, looking up, saw a flock of thirty or forty pigeons dashing toward the trees, who suddenly whirled on seeing me and circled round and made a new dash toward the bed, as if they would fain alight if I had not been there, then steered off. I crawled into the bough house and lay awhile looking through the leave.

Thoreau, in a characteristically insightful passage in "Walking," his environmental masterpiece from 1862, which he considered "a sort of introduction to all that I may write hereafter," compares the then sadly diminishing numbers of this mast-eating pigeon in New England to the just-as-sadly dwindling number of thoughts in a man's head, "for the grove in our minds is laid waste."

The wild pigeons' propensity to nest, roost, and fly together in kits of vast numbers made them vulnerable to unremitting market and recreational hunting, according to Greenberg, who also explains that deforestation, the spread of railroads and telegraph lines created national markets that allowed the birds to be pursued relentlessly. It should be noted that pigeon meat as such was commercialized as a cheap food for slaves and the poor in the 19th century, just as lobster once was for the indigent, resulting in widespread hunting on a massive and indiscreet scale. A slow decline between about 1800 and 1870 was followed by a catastrophic decline between 1870 and 1890. Sadly, the last passenger pigeon disappeared in 1914.

In culinary terminology, squab is a young domestic pigeon, typically under four weeks old, and its meat—lean, easily digestible, rich in proteins, minerals, and vitamins with something like a mild berry flavor—is generally described as tasting like dark chicken, while the skin is fatty, like that of duck, and has a "silky" texture that is tender and fine-grained. It has a milder taste than other game. The term is probably of Scandinavian origin; the Swedish word *skvabb* means "loose, fat flesh." It formerly applied to all dove and pigeon species, such as the Wood Pigeon and Mourning Dove and the now completely extinct Passenger Pigeon. The modern squab industry uses "utility pigeons." Squabs are raised until they are roughly a month old, when they reach adult size but have not yet flown, before being slaughtered. Granted, more recently, squab meat comes almost entirely from domesticated pigeons. Although squab has been relished always and eaten throughout much of recorded western history, it is nowadays regarded as something of a rare and exotic food, it is not certainly a contemporary staple, and is largely consumed, not by the poor or working man but by the rich, the decadent, and the heedless with signal entrées like Ballotines de Pigeonneaux à la Madison and Chinese Lacquered Squab and Squab à l'Orange with Crystallised Tamarind and Chicklet or Royal Squab, an Asian specialty.

There was a time back in Old Colonial Days when blackbirds were pests, eating the corn of the Pilgrims—they were also seen as bad luck—and a law was passed that forbade a man to marry until he had killed his quota of blackbirds, at least according to Jeremiah Digges in his quaint book, *Cape Cod Pilot* (1937). ("Old men over 70 were excused from the consideration.")

Those days are gone, yet we have our human griffins and lammergeiers still, more janitors and undertakers than high-priests of food, ready to eat. At Cambridge, at least back in Lord Russell's and Ludwig Wittgenstein's days, dons luxuriated in eating pigeon pie while students, poor undergraduates, had to be satisfied with scrimp meals of tea and nut cutlets. I have gone on about the rough-hewn country squire and novelist, Jim Harrison. He chuntered on about his volucrine appetite and how he loved great walloping meals of squab, quail, partridge, roasted, toasted, spatchcocked, and crapaudined. Back in 2009 when the traveler, cook, wise-ass, and professional eater Anthony Bourdain visited him in Livingston, Montana, Harrison cooked him up an elk-and-antelope stew and grilled a few dozen doves, which they feefifofummingly washed down with several bottles of Côtes du Rhône.

Any dovecote in the Middle Ages was considered a "living pantry." Pigeon meat was even widely eaten in England when other food was rationed during World War Two. Pigeons are squab, and squab produced from specially raised utility pigeons continues to grace the menus of American *haute cuisine* restaurants such as Le Cirque and The French Laundry. "My good health is due to a soup made of white doves," Madame Chiang Kai-Shek once smarmily declared, who did not suffer rationing. She was a beady Republican zealot, a dogged advocate of Wendell Willkie. So what else would you expect? On the other hand, doves *are* described as food in the Holy Scriptures and were in fact eaten by the wandering Hebrews. So I guess that in one way I can—am obliged to?—forgive these gastronomic churls by way of Scriptural fiat.

Who will eat what and who won't constitutes the subject of this book and the discordant and refractory contrarians who people it. Intractability and nonconformism is our subject. "It must be the brook/Can trust itself to go by contraries," wrote Robert Frost in his poem, "West Running Brook."

It is fitting he wrote those lines. No one was more unruly, stubborn, insubordinate, dissident, perversely headstrong, non-conforming, or more flagrantly incompatible than this New England poet. One time Frost and Hyde Cox were walking in the woods up around Exeter, New Hampshire, and Frost bent down—yes—to lick a tree, saying, "Ahh, you can taste the salt. We're close to the sea."

Smelling the air would have happily sufficed for most individuals.

But trusting oneself to go by *contraries?*

Those are the people we are writing about.

22.

AYN RAND'S PRUNES

Horace mocks that kind of indulgence, the expense of the vanity of the "re-ligion of gastronomy" in his *Satire* II:2, when he writes, "If a peacock were served up, I should hardly be able to prevent your gratifying the palate with that, rather than a pullet, since you are prejudiced by the vanities of things, seduced by a rare bird that is bought with gold, with its ornate tail spec-tacularly spread: as if that mattered. Do you eat those feathers you admire? Has the bird the same beauty when it is cooked? There is no difference in the meat." "*Necdum omnis abacta pauperies epulis regum; nam vilibus ovis nigrisque est oleis hodie locus,*" writes Horace. ("Poor man's food not wholly absent from their feasts of kings: cheap eggs, black olives, hold their place.") "*Ergo si quis nunc mergos suavis edixerit assos, parebit pravi docilis Romana iuventus,*" he writes. ("If someone proclaimed roasted seagulls were tasty, the youth of Rome, so easily seduced, would acquiesce in it!") One finds the same attack on jaded palates and humorless food zealots in Horace's *Satire* II.8, at rich Nasidienus's dinner party which is attended by the best people, all named—among them, Maecenas, the poet's great patron—tucking into *recherché* delicacies like Lucanian wild-boar with water-parsnips, pickled fish, lamprey with prawns swimming about them, exotic fish sauce squeezed from Spanish mackerel, the best vinegar made from Methymnian grapes, jugs of rare Coan wine, and bright-red apples, only the best fruit that had been picked by the light of the waning moon. Although a canopy collapses, the banquet continues as they stuff themselves with crane's legs and the liver of white goose fatted on figs.

It could be any Hollywood party, where the fat, crass, dopey, and over-bloated can be seen ingurgitating food, with parties thrown in wretch-ed excess, as hustling Sammy Glicks are ambitiously working the rooms and pumping hands and falling all over themselves to make good. It is a con-demnation of Epicurianism, of course, and an implicit plea for simplicity.

(Suetonius tells us Horace came from humble origins, his father having been a slave for at least part of his life, and never forgot it.) I have always considered that for principles Horace's brilliant *Satires*, especially books I and II, shape the kind of sage advice that every father and mother should give their children—among other things they incorporate a perfect graduation speech, I mean *meaningful* words, not the kind of Polonius-like palaver that we constantly hear from politicians with their lame and sententious, pettifogging bullshit. A conclusive thought in *Ode III*: 6 is moral and quite beautiful in what it sums up:

> It is right, then, that I shrink from raising my head
> to be seen far and wide, dear Maecenas, glory of the
> Equestrians. The more that a man denies himself, then
> the more will flow from the gods: so naked, I seek the
> camp of those who ask for nothing, I'm a deserter,
> eager to abandon the rich.

Pretentiousness has been always been a trend, if that is not an oxymoron. What is the value of 50 food courses that you have not even seen yet? Surprise, of course. To be dazzled? Maybe dazed. Then there is novelty. Surely the weirdest movie moment in the *Spiderman* reboot is all that noisome chat at dinner about branzino. Strangest damn thing imagineable. It brings to mind by way of contrast certain lines of Walt Whitman celebrating the modest, unaffected food that he loved. He writes, "Or rude in my home in Dakota's woods, my diet meat, my drink from the spring... solitary, singing in the West, I strike up for a New World" and

> Sit a while dear son,
> Here are biscuits to eat and here is milk to drink,
> But as soon as you sleep and renew yourself in sweet
> clothes,
> I kiss you with a good-by kiss and open the gate for
> your egress hence.

Food fashions rise and fall, we know. Nearly all foods in New York were garnished with chervil in 1999. Remember quiche in the early 1980s—did anyone eat anything else? The Village Voice wit Michael Musto in one of his columns, "Blech! Spew! Things I Hate Food," subtitled, "40 dyspeptic reasons" (August 22, 2012), a fellow who probably will not be found any time soon eating expensive, lengthy, take-it-or-leave-it courses at Eleven Madison

Park or WD-50 or calling in reservations at the Chef's Table at Brooklyn Fare, even goes so far as to ask "Which trend-Nazi invented brunch? Give me breakfast or lunch, not some pretentious hybrid for hipsters with too much discretionary income." He grumps, "People who fetishize food really creep me out. ('Remember that giant cannoli we shared, honey?' 'Yes, darling-and my palate still gets moist when I think about the incredible sausage casserole we had for Valentine's Day.') Sublimate much?" Experimentation is often simply an end in itself.

Musto offers a sputtering great list of food aversions—and it is part of his personal thrill truly to gnaw at what bothers him:

> Mayonnaise makes me gag. So do butter and cream sauce. I'll find other ways to stay fat, thank you... WTF is imitation crabmeat made out of? No, don't tell me... You can never fully fold burritos. They should come with a roll of Scotch tape, especially at Chipotle... No one outside New York City has the faintest idea how to make pizza. It's like they lost the recipe at the border... Comfort food makes me nervous... Going to a restaurant with someone with dietary needs becomes an exercise in ritualized torture, whereby a minimum-wage server is put through an agonizing interrogation over whether there's any chicken stock in the broccoli soup and what the odds are that the Greek salad has pine nuts. You want to die, and you secretly pray they only spit in your friend's food... Growing up with meatloaf and Chef Boyardee, kids are always told: 'Finish your plate. Children are starving in China,' and they think, 'Lucky them'... I am so sick of salads... Everything does not taste like chicken. Ever try an ostrich burger... I can bike to Costco, but how do I ride 10 five-pound bags of quinoa home? And what is quinoa anyway?"

Too, he has his own snobberies, which in the matter of likes and dislikes on the subject of food ranks very high in the fulcrum department. Musto confesses, "The best ice cream in New York is at McDonald's. Alas, you have to hold your nose and head to the counter really quickly... Similarly, Dunkin' Donuts makes delightful smoothies, but it's career suicide to be spotted there. Maybe they deliver? 16 Handles has a cute selection of toppings-like pink animal cookies and sprinkly things, but you don't know how much it's going to cost until they weigh your creation. When did yogurt become a heart-pounding experience slash salad bar?"

One way of hating food is to make a list of what you abhor. Another way is simply to state what you like which is simply subtraction by addition. "My favorite sandwich is peanut butter, baloney, cheddar cheese, lettuce and mayonnaise on toasted bread with catsup on the side," blabby Senator Hubert Humphrey (D-MN) announced. You can't hate food more than that. It is a form, in words of "companion planting," so to speak. Just as beans and onions are natural enemies, to be kept at opposite ends of the garden, so Humphrey's declaration of what he prefers in food simultaneously oppugns it. Ignatius J. Reilly, the confused anti-hero of John Kennedy Toole's satire, *A Confederacy of Dunces*, a fat, flatulent, and sanctimonious eccentric whose mind is stuck in a medieval monastery but whose body—a big one—is stuck in 1960s New Orleans, while he calls canned food a "perversion," wolfs down hot dog after hot dog and, when his brain begins to reel, he simply says "I make an occasional cheese dip." The dear old lady from whom I bought my house on Cape Cod, built in 1895, moved into and then died in a nursing home, and whenever I went to visit her, as I did bi-weekly, the ghostly halls were always empty and dark and always seemed suffused with a kind of food sadness. "What is that odor, Olga?" I would ask. She would whisper, "Consommé." Technically speaking, the difference between stock and broth is that a stock is made from bones and a broth from meat—the French call both "*bouillon*"—while a consommé is a clear soup made from richly flavored stock that has been clarified, a process which uses egg whites to remove fat and sediment. It has been around a lot and reminds me of the middle ages and seems to be a favorite of ladies with hairnets.

I have referenced Musto and mayonnaise, along with his burrito problem, as well as Hubert Humphrey's loathsome sandwich combo. I am still trying to explain to myself how the bland actor, Cornel Wilde, in the movie *Leave Her to Heaven* (1945), possibly the *locus classicus* of demented jealousy movies, when handed half of a turkey sandwich by the lovely but cold and murderously neurotic socialite, Ellen (Gene Tierney), could preposterously ask after tasting it—blame the script-writers—"What kind of sandwich is this?" There are other disquieting revelations here. To one's amazement, the inept Wilde holds the sandwich like a motorman's glove and then takes a huge bite out of the center of it—a cartoon move! I cannot remember seeing that done before. (Maybe in a Mickey Mouse or Donald Duck movie?) Did they do such a thing in rural town of Prievidza, Hungary (now

Slovakia), where Wilde, a Jew, was born Kornél Lajos Weisz before going to Hollywood and appropriating that farcical name?

What about a fully unappeasable. unfettered, unapologetic hater of the sandwich itself? The insightful food writer John Thorne is that very man. His robust, and vigorous polemic, written in the splendor of all its genius and pure gall and fruitful generalizations, is pure oxyacetylene. "In my fantasy world, John Montagu, 4th Earl of Sandwich, would have been gored to death by a prescient bull before he ever came up with the idea of encasing his roast beef between two slices of bread," he writes. "As I see it, the world has never called out for the sandwich, and, on the whole, would be better off without it. Instead of sandwich shops, we would have fast food places that sold roast meat, each one specializing in an animal." Thorne continues,

> You would go into such a place, push your way up to the counter, and a carver would fill your plate with slices of the steer that rotated before you on a spit. If you asked for takeaway, he would look at you as if you were mad, then send you down the street to the dive that sold rotisserie chickens. If you were in the mood for fast food, you would just stop at the person on the side of the street who had a cart where he roasted a whole sheep or at another where several glistening piglets rotated. I apologize, but my fantasies don't spend much time accommodating vegetarians.
> Living in this world, which is far from my own devising, I have to make out as best I can. If I go into a deli, I just order a quarter pound of corned beef straight, and eat it with a little mustard and pickle. Believe me, it doesn't miss the rye. And there are few pleasures in life more profound than stopping in for a few slices of liverwurst, and then eating it as you walk down the sidewalk, pulling the casing between your teeth to get off the last little bits. And you simply haven't had a hot dog until you get one dressed with fried onions and wrapped up in a slice of prosciutto. Similarly, for my midnight snack, when I'm not simply having a piece of buttered toast (toast was discovered long before the sandwich was invented), I roll up thin slices of finocchiona, a salami containing ground wild fennel seeds, with equally thin slices of whatev-

er appropriate cheese I have in the fridge (a young *pecorino Tuscano* works spectacularly). Some of these and a glass of whatever cheap red wine I favor at the moment and to bed—with no lump of bread in the digestive tract to give me bad dreams.

This is not a rant, although I could write one at the drop of a hat about deli meats, especially those water-injected, suspiciously uniform slabs of beef, or ham, or chicken breast—it is simply a matter of appetite. At home, I do occasionally make and eat sandwiches, but they are not the usual suspects. For instance, if I have the right sort of bread, the sort that used to be called home-style before commercial bakeries destroyed any meaning in the phrase, I love a sandwich of butter and iceberg lettuce. In the summer, my wife, Matt, and I practically subsist on tomato sandwiches, either with that vegetable alone or with thin slices of fresh mozzarella. But the bottom line is that if I go into the kitchen to get some rations, it never occurs to me to make a sandwich, and I never do. As far as eating away from home, I haven't ordered a sandwich as such for over a decade, with two exceptions. The first is that I can't pass through Portland, Maine, without stopping at the original Amato's for an Italian sandwich. (I get it veggie style, which omits the cold cuts, but includes cheese, green pepper, onion, tomato, and dill pickle, a scattering of black olives, and good drenching with olive oil.) The second is a lobster roll on a grilled bun. (Since I live in New England, these are easy enough to come by, but usually I have to bring it home and grill the bun myself.) There would have been a time when I would have added a grilled cheese sandwich to this list, but nowadays I prefer to reduce a nice piece of cheddar to near molten consistency by means of some considered microwaving, and to then eat it with a spoon.

On reflection, I think that what kills the appeal of sandwiches for me is that second, top layer of bread, which, come to think of it, is really what separates a sandwich from other ways of eating things on bread.

Back in the seventies, I used to regularly visit a chee-
semonger in Boston's Quincy Market who smug-
gled in raw-milk cheeses from France. To catch the
attention of the flow of shoppers, he grilled tranches
of bread topped with recent arrivals. These were delicious, and I bought one every time I visited the place,
and never once thought of them as sandwiches, and
neither did he—he was tapping a culinary vein that ran
far deeper than that.

What that second piece of bread signals is: stuff your
face. It provides support for a heap of sliced meats,
cheese, condiments, whatever, that could never be
balanced on a single slice of bread. It's about gluttony, and, frankly, often cheapening of product. Not
all sandwiches are stuffed, of course, but they invite
careless eating. That's the whole idea. So there it is: to
hell with sandwiches. And what do you expect from a
creation named after a man who ordered one so that
he wouldn't get the cards greasy while he was playing
cribbage? It's hard to believe that once this feat had
been accomplished, he even noticed what he put into
his mouth.

The subtext of Thorne's dismissal of the sandwich is, in part, an implied
lament that in this modern world of short-cut accommodation it has too
often become a substitute for a balanced meal. One can only speculate what
Vladimir Nabokov had in mind when in one of his earlier novels, *Pnin*, he
mentions that on a walk to the college dining rooms and Faculty Club at fictional Wainsdell College, one encountered the "routine smell of potato chips
and *the sadness of balanced meals*" [my italics]. It is a taunt, a snobbish flout
by an aristocratic Russian who was not quite sure he approved of food eaten
by the common man. Lordly Nabokov is quite clearly mocking institutional
food, of course, its sameness, its predictability. But it also a jape at healthy
food, proletarian food, an arrogant sneer at the dreary, unrefined fare of
boring, unadventurous, common dullards, those of us doomed (unlike VN
himself, literature's most monstrous snob) to have to resort to such repasts—
his scornful contempt for the *hoi polloi*, unfit for imaginative dinners, never
mind rare and exotic cuisine.

23.

"IS IT OK TO FREEZE YOUR PERSIMMONS?"

("NO, YOU SHOULD DRESS WARMLY!")

Hating food, of course, is the ultimate food aversion—its absolute, needless to say, the most vivid example of its most neurotic extreme. It is ironic that St. Thomas Aquinas, a Dominican friar and one of the world's greatest philosophers and theologians, was not only a fellow hugely fat (he is described on a contemporary T-shirt as a "Deep Fat Friar") but the Doctor of the Church who most succinctly and intelligently—some might add joylessly—admonished us on the vile excesses of gluttony. It was his educated and conscientiously pious belief that the hideous vice (read *sin*) of self-indulgence could incorporate (pun intended), curiously, not only the obsessive anticipation of meals and the constant eating of delicacies but also of eating too well, eating too fast, too hastily, too passionately, and too expensively! This was the list of excesses in the matter of committing gluttony—*voracitas, gula, gastrimargia, gourmandise*—as compiled to the number of six by this burly saint affectionately called both by the pious, the "Angelic Doctor," and by his rude, unkind classmates, the "Dumb Ox:" *Praepropere*—eating too soon; Laute—eating too expensively; *Nimis*—eating too much; *Ardenter*—eating too eagerly; *Studiose*—eating too daintily or fussily; and *Forente*—eating too fervently. "The idea that eating can be a sin is prevalent in our society," writes Laura Moncur on her website on health and diet, "Starling Fitness." "Almost every disdainful look at a person because of his or her weight can be linked to the cold thought that gluttony is a sin. There is inarguably an innate human preference, a vain one, for a thinner, a more svelte, a slender appearance, but most of the aversion is simply because of the concept that being fat is sinful. This has not really helped our society, and in some cases, I believe it has made things worse." When in *Twelfth Night*, Sir Toby Belch tells Malvolio *et alii*,

"Dost thou think because thou art virtuous there shall be no more cakes and ale?" he is also thumbing his nose at Aquinas, the Dog of God.

Gluttony—*gula* (the word actually *sounds* like borborygmia!)—literally means to gulp down or swallow, and it is of course one of the Seven Deadly Sins. Paradoxically, gross overeating could actually be called a food aversion, for such intemperance, at least canonically, may constitute a sinner's pagan refusal to take food for what it actually *is*. Swallowing whole, so to speak, merely mimes—mocks—the true act of eating. It is difficult to follow one rubric for food consumption. St. Gregory the Great insisted that gluttony was a mortal sin, yet Pope Innocent XI said that it was not a fault to feel pleasure when eating, and the defect was only eating like a beast. The prophet Isaiah inveighed against the vain Israelites for ostentatiously, boastingly fasting when so much injustice surrounded them, crying out,

> No, this is the kind of fasting I want: Free those who
> are wrongly imprisoned; lighten the burden of those
> who work for you. Let the oppressed go free, and
> remove the chains that bind people. (58:6)

while the Torah scrupulously insists that one eat only when one is hungry and never to the point of being full.

Many people who hate certain herbs and other aromatics draw up wild associations in order to diss them. Oliver Schwaner Albright who surveyed chefs in New York City found many who have cultivated herbal hates. Gabrielle Hamilton of Prune thinks verbena "tastes like Lemon Pledge." That is exactly the phrase Michael Romano of Union Square Cafe used to describe lemon thyme. "I love lemon," Mr. Romano said. "I love thyme. I love them both together. I even like Lemon Pledge on my furniture." But he stops dead if lemon thyme sneaks into a dish. (I remember in the sixth grade earnest if loving Sister Mary Rupert told us with supreme confidence that thyme was in the hay of the manger in which the baby Jesus lay.) Shea Gallante of Cru insists cilantro tastes just like soap, and Wylie Dufresne of WD-50 makes the same grizzling claim of dill. "Not that I've eaten a lot of soap in my life," Mr. Dufresne explains. "I'm not phobic. I just think it's dreadful." Korean Chef David Chang of the Momofuku Noodle Bar and Milk Bar dessert shops in New York City also hates the taste of dill. (He also does not drink coffee and is not particularly fond of offal, which in an interview *Vanity Fair* magazine in 2014 he insists "puts him out of step with the prevailing offal-chic hegemony.") And Laurent Tourondel, the Executive Chef at Brasserie Ruhlmann in Rockefeller Center in Manhattan, habitually keeps the herb saffron away from all of his restaurants. "It reminds me of the dentist," he pronounces with disdain.

I can understand to a degree at least the mythic suspicion of basil, lovely though it is as a food additive, for this herb has for a long time carried a negative connotation. Salomé supposedly used basil leaves to conceal the severed head of John the Baptist. In Boccaccio's *Decameron*, one of the book's strangest tales (Fifth Tale) tells of Lisabetta, whose brothers slay her lover, who appears to her in a dream to show her where he is buried, whereupon she disinters the head in secret and sets it in a pot of basil which she waters with her daily tears. When her brothers take the pot, she dies of her grief soon after. Boccaccio's tale is the source of John Keats' poem "Isabella or The Pot of Basil," which in turn inspired the paintings by Millais, *Isabella* and *Isabella and the Pot of Basil*. A similar fable surrounds Rosamund, Queen of the Lombards, a story woven into a tragedy (verse play) by the English poet Algernon Swinburne in 1899. Finally, does actress Lisa Bonet dislike basil? Possibly not in real life, but at least the sentence and/or the concept has given us the cute palindrome, "Lisa Bonet ate no basil." Then, what about sorrel? Nobody ever seems to cook with it, or even mention the herb. It seems to be the most neglected or despised herbal of them all. Why is it that sorrel or spinach dock, as it often called, is never sold in supermarkets? Its leaves (and edible stems) have a flavor that is quite similar to kiwi fruit or sour wild strawberries. The plant's sharp taste is due to oxalic acid, which by the way is a poison. In small quantities sorrel is harmless; in large quantities it can be fatal.

I still swear by *Culpeper's Complete Herbal*, a standard in the field of herbal remedies for three centuries and for its comprehensiveness a book in my opinion that should be everybody's *vade mecum*. I am convinced its wealth of information, old and hoary as it may seem, could stem many a food aversion, never mind battle pretty much every illness from which we suffer, from the bloody flux to odd swellings to dry mouth to asthma to gippy tummy. Where else can you find read-outs on such rare herbs as Mouse-Ear, Toothcress, Duckweed, Black Cresses, Tansy Gum, Feverfew, Saxifrage, Thistle, and Orpine ("The moon owns this herb. It is seldom used in inward medicines. The distilled water is profitable for gnawings and excoriations in the stomach and bowels...")? Oh, by the way, Nicholas Culpeper explains how beets help to cure jaundice, work against dandruff, fight toothache, and anger up the blood, while its juices are efficacious for stemming noise in the ears and "if snuffed up the nose help [fight] a stinking breath."

Remember all those legendary Russian centenarians? Beets, frequently consumed either pickled or in borscht, the traditional Russian soup, may be one reason behind their long and healthy lives. Mr. Einstein, please take note.

A recent survey of South African chefs was highly revealing. Paul Anthony Finney, chef at The Elm Tree restaurant at The Syrene Hotel, Sandton, cannot bear the innards of chicken in virtually any form:

> I am originally from England. One of the first outlandish dishes I experienced here was *chicken livers peri-peri*. This brought back childhood memories of my mother preparing the chicken for our Sunday roast which entailed removing the giblets and boiling them off for the dogs to engulf... Imagine my surprise when I witnessed it offered to humans on a menu! The smell of that raw, slimy, putrid offal is enough to turn you vegetarian, never mind the appearance when it's raw! If ever chillies have been used to mask a dish, then it has to be with peri-peri chicken livers.

Marthinus Ferreira, chef at DW Eleven-13 restaurant in Dunkeld, Johannesburg, declares, "I tried frogs' legs once and did not find the texture appealing at all. The same goes for crocodile. And I will never eat on an airplane." Darren Roberts, executive chef at Grande Provence Heritage Wine Estate, dislikes "all forms of tripe." He expounded, "I cannot stand the smell, the texture or the taste. We were at a night market in Langkawi (in Malaysia) and they were boiling water buffalo tripe. They would cut off a chunk of the tripe and put it on to a stick like an ice cream. People would walk around eating it. I loved all the food up to that point." Jenny Morris, celebrity chef on The Food Network channel, says, "The one and only thing I will never eat is tripe cooked for me by a stranger. I imagine all kinds of things. How well was it cleaned? How many times was the water changed? Did it get a good scrub first? Just the thought of it makes me gag, especially if the person cooking it has dirty hair." Keith Frisley, executive chef at Fairlawns Boutique Hotel & Spa in Morningside, wholeheartedly agrees and says, "Tripe is another big no-no—the smell of it during preparation is enough to send me into the lavender bush!" Frisley also states, "I avoid garlic as much as possible and, luckily, most of our guests don't want to smell of it, which gets me off the hook. I once worked in a sushi bar and I still don't eat sashimi." (American comedian José Simon says, "In Mexico, we have a word for sushi: *bait*.") Adds Frisley, "I also can't stand the taste of tofu—it is awful and I cannot even bring myself to swallow it."

Tofu is one food that actor Robert Redford has gone public in dismissing as awful. Luke Dale Roberts, chef and owner of The Test Kitchen in Cape Town, said, "I particularly dislike sea cucumbers as they are really slimy and just plain gross. (Sea cucumbers are marine animals that look like worms.) I remember drinking snake wine in Vietnam as part of a group of 16 people sitting at an important table. I gagged a spray of fine mist of it at everyone."

A kind chef in Tesuque, New Mexico who became a fast friend of mine in my rambles around there once offered me rattlesnake hash which I refused, as I know severe strains of salmonella can grow in any snake's gut. Rattlesnake meat is often eaten in the Southwest, and popular recipes include rattlesnake chili, hash, and barbecued snake meat. Fat, we all know, is flavor. Reptiles with a very thin, tinny sort of flavor are missing it, however, and halfway through the chew the flavor evaporates and there's nothing left. But I wanted neither the chew, the flavor, the tinniness, the hash, nor the echoing *flikiflikiflik* sound of rattling terror in my nightmares.

Natasha Wray, partner and chef at 96 Winery Road Restaurant, Somerset West, Western Cape, will not eat Kalamata olives or blueberries. I wonder if she objected to them on the same grounds that Robert Frost did, who when he wrote in his poem, "Blueberries," "It must be on charcoal they fatten their fruit,/ I taste in them sometimes the flavor of soot" does not seem to endorse them. (It may be significant to recall here that the same poet pointed out in his poem, "After Apple Picking," that windfall apples "went surely to the cider-apple heap/ As of no worth.") "Unless they have been marinated in garlic, lemon and herbs, black olives just taste bitter and are pap with no texture," chef Wray offers. "Blueberries are so bland compared with other berries. They may be pretty to look at, but that is as far as it goes."

Reuben Riffel, chef and owner of Reuben's in Franschhoek, Western Cape, admits, "I recently had a taste of tempeh, much of a meal of it, and, I know a lot of vegetarians won't like this, but I would never eat it again. It tasted like I imagine cardboard would taste like." He adds, "Another pet hate is *haloumi*, a real good-for-nothing cheese, also with the texture of Styrofoam."

Margot Janse, the celebrity chef at Le Quartier Francais restaurant, Franschhoek, Western Cape, declared, "I simply can't do nutmeg. Just the thought of it creates a metallic taste in my mouth and I shiver. I grew up in the Netherlands and my mom used to put it on everything (or so I seem to remember), from cauliflower to Brussels sprouts and stewed endives… I taste it immediately, no matter how minuscule the amount added." Executive chef Robb Garceau would avoid nutmeg if he could, but since Great Performances, the catering company he works for, has an array of Indian-inspired dishes, it is impossible for him to not use it, he says. His catering company also puts nutmeg in their extra cheesy mac 'n'cheese, béchamel sauce, and it is not only included in many desserts and during the holidays but the ingredient seems to find its way into the spice-heavy menu across the board. Nutmeg (and mace), the seed of the evergreen tree indigenous to the Banda Islands in the Moluccas (or Spice Islands) of Indonesia, strangely enough, in its ground form, but even raw, contains "myristicin," a monoamine oxidase inhibitor, a psychoactive substance that can have hallucinogenic effects when taken in large doses. It is a strong enough deliriant to have been widely used as a substitute for marijuana by prisoners and convicts unable to lay their hands on cannabis products. Charlie "The Bird" Parker and his band-mates took it to get high. Nutmeg, along with comforters, soft cheese, homemade cookies, and some types of buttons, was on the "No List" at Capanne, the Italian prison where Amanda Knox spent four years for a crime that she never committed. "Apparently, when eaten in large quantities or smoked, it can make people drunk or high," she writes in her 2013 memoir, *Waiting to Be Heard*. But there is a long history of nutmeg's properties that way.

Hildegarde of Bingen (1098-1179), the German Benedictine abbess and mystic whose own advanced social and theological views were based on a series of visions that she had experienced as early as the age of 3, has been credited with providing one of the very earliest descriptions of its psychoactive effects, according to the *Dictionary of Hallucinations*. It has been reported to mediate visual, auditory, tactile, and kinaesthetic hallucinations (notably the sensation of floating), as well as body schema illusion.

Welcome to Connecticut, the "Nutmeg State"!

The Reverend Hugh Benson, a stutterer, lived in the early Evelyn Waugh era. "I observed him at dinner one day drinking champagne which he disliked and asked him why he had done so," wrote his brother, the writer E.F. Benson in his memoir *Final Edition* (1944). Hugh replied, "B-b-because I c-couldn't say c-claret." It reminds me of a parallel situation I once faced in my own life when I was about 16. I remember taking a pretty Italian girl to the movies, the then-elegant Paramount Theater on Washington St. in Boston, to see the movie of the musical, *South Pacific*. After I bought the tickets, as we entered the lobby, we stopped at the candy counter. I asked what she wanted, a box of popcorn, she said, which I proceeded to order. I knew what I wanted to order but felt awkward—I was unsocial and shy, especially because she was so beautiful—because she was standing right there next to me. I ordered a Hershey bar, and we walked into theater, she content with her popcorn, me less so with my candy bar and some regret. Regret?

The fact is I had badly wanted a box of sticky-sweet Jujyfruits but was too embarrassed to say the poncy-like brand-name out loud!

My memory is jogged here of Ford Madox Ford's occasionally grizzling entries in his memoir, *Joseph Conrad: A Personal Reminiscence*, about the bleak nature of English food and its baleful effect upon one's health. In an English pension in Bruges waiting for his friend, Joseph Conrad, "who liked to be amongst English people when abroad," Ford glumly makes this entry: "The diet of the English pension—thin slices of cold mutton, potatoes boiled in water, 'greens' boiled in water which remained with the greens—began seriously to deteriorate a digestion used to food more elaborate. The taste of greens was never out of the mouth."

Green beans were just about the only vegetable that Elvis Presley would eat. (A legitimate question is, did he like—and eat—poke salad?) As we all know, his favorite foods were uncomplicatedly hot dogs, cheeseburgers, bacon sandwiches, pork chops, chicken-fried steak, cured smoked ham, and peanut-butter-and-banana sandwiches. (A "killer" peanut butter and jelly sandwich called the "Fool's Gold Loaf" was a special of the Colorado Gold Mine Company, a restaurant in Denver, sandwiches Elvis craved and not a few times ordered his personal plane out from Memphis to bring back boxes of them.) He obviously never suffered from arachibutyrophobia, the fear of peanut butter sticking to the roof of the mouth, but many people do, and peanut butter is a specific and highly-to-be-avoided food among such sufferers. Elvis also loved cakes, fruit pies of all sorts, big brownies, and especially ice cream. When he was making all of those movies in the 1960s—usually three a year—Paramount studios saw fit to provide him with at least two large refrigerators for his luxuriant Hollywood dressing room, one of them used exclusively for ice cream. Sweets he positively loved.

Elvis of course loved comfort food—in short, "mommy" food. One of his favorite meals was roast beef, duck and dressing with string beans, creamed potatoes, mixed vegetables, and biscuits. In her book *Elvis: The Way I Knew Him*, Mary Jenkins discloses that she often spoke to Elvis in baby talk, which he loved, and that after he and Priscilla broke up, she often used to tuck him in at night. No, Elvis never got over his mother Glady's death nor the food she served him growing up. He was a creature of habit, and his habits were formed early and kept late.

The King's breakfast rarely varied all his life: a Spanish omelet, a pound of crisp bacon, toast, beefsteak tomatoes, coffee and orange juice. The doctors told Elvis to stay off chocolates when on meds, which was virtually all the time, but all of the drugs that he took, according to his pal, Sonny West, in *Elvis: Taking Care of Business*, "had given him a powerful sugar jones.

He ate Popsicles, Dreamsicles, Fudgsicles by the box." But no vegetables. Vegetables were out for Elvis. Bacon was his supreme fetish. It was for the King the *ne plus ultra* of foods. "Bacon is the candy of meat," says Dr. Kevin Taggart, and Elvis ate it by the pig slab.

Sweets can kill us. "She was my sugar. I needed her like sugar," wrote Russian poet Marina Tsvetaeva in "A Tale of Sonyechka" of her one-time Lesbian lover, Sonya Holliday, a woman who later cruelly betrayed her. "We all know sugar is not necessary and one can live without it, as we all did during the Revolution, replacing it with treacle or scraped beetroot or saccharin or nothing, drinking plain unsweetened tea. One doesn't die of that. But one doesn't live either." It was a crucial disappointment in her life. Plagued by such hurt and trapped by the NKVD Tsvetaiva, while living in Yelabuga she hanged herself on August 31, 1941.

What of fruits? Scientist Nikola Tesla once declared that just being near peaches gave him a bad fever. Winston Churchill rarely ate fruit, even when it was English fruit, and took the position even during World War II. I have mentioned that the eccentric chess-master Bobby Fischer particularly loathed (and feared!) maraschino cherries. "I hate watermelon, and I hate anyone who likes it," wrote Ned Rorem in *Lies, A Diary: 1986–1999* with his unflinching characteristic frankness.

The allure of fruit is such that to despise it seems to question a sacred blessing and forgo God-given luxuries. Its bounty seems more than any other food to grace the earth. In his books *Seeds* Thor Hanson writes,

> The bounty of the biblical Eden reflects a long tradi-
> tion of describing Paradise as a decidedly fruit-laden
> place. In the words of the poet Hesiod, those fortu-
> nate enough to reach Greece's famed Elysian Fields
> enjoyed "honey-sweet fruit flourishing thrice a year."
> Islamic texts allude to eternal gardens filled with ev-
> erything from dates, cucumbers, and watermelons to
> the quince of Paradise.

Contrarian man listens only to himself, however.

The date comes in for hard marks in Charles Doughty's masterpiece, *Arabia Deserta*, where under the most severe conditions imaginable (red hot sand, fetid air, harsh rocky terrain, freezing nights, fierce winds, a heat so intense "we seemed to breathe flames")—the explorer's health, even before his journey, was precarious—he was forced to depend on the scrimp

Bedouin diet, with its rude staples of camel's milk, dates, and occasional meat. Doughty observed,

> The Arabians inhabit a land of dearth and hunger, and
> there is no worse food than the date, which they must
> eat in their few irrigated valleys. This fruit is overheat-
> ing and inwardly fretting under a sultry climate; too
> much of cloying sweet, not ministering enough of
> brawn and bone; and therefore all the date-eaters are
> of a certain wearish visage, especially the poor Nejd
> villagers… though theirs be the best dates in the coun-
> try. What squalor of bones! The upper face is sunken
> and flattened, the jaw nearly brute-like and without
> beard!

An Estonian-American friend of mine, T. Peter Park, whose mother, worried about his constitution when he was a small boy, compulsively and repeatedly gave him pieces of fruit to eat to keep him healthy, confessed to me that for the rest of his life he has angrily associated all fruit with medicine and to this day flatly refuses to eat it—*any of it*—under any circumstances. (Actually, a banana is not a fruit, but rather a type of herb.) Nowadays, some fruits—indeed like some herbs (agrimony, betony, lemon verbena, feverfew, etc.)—seem to have gone out of fashion, like quince, loquats, whortleberries, gooseberries, etc.

Who goes huckleberrying anymore, as Henry Thoreau once did, a man who, claiming that he learned more in the local huckleberry fields of Concord than ever he did at school, virtually made a joyous outing of doing so? ("I served my apprenticeship and have since done considerable journey-work in the huckleberry field," he wrote.) Certain fruits from other countries seem rare to most Americans and rarely appear in our supermarkets, fruits like cocona; sweetsop, native to tropical America; mammee apples; platonia fruit, about the size of an orange with a thick yellow peel which oozes a yellow latex when pressed; pitaya, or dragon fruit; fragrant green feijoa; custard-tasting atemoya; breadfruit, duku or lungsat; Egg-shaped tamarillos or tree tomatoes; juicy longans, sweet like lychees but drier; safou or African pears; star apple; salak; and jabuticaba, a purplish-black grape from a tree found only in Brazil—and in that country, incidentally, it is commonly done to refer to anything odd, strange, or unique as a "*jabuticaba*," because that particular tree is native to Brazil and only grows there. It is commonly used in that country as a pejorative expression.

Then there is the Mangosteen. When Cole Porter took a world tour with his pals, Monty Woolley and Moss Hart, it was in Java that they had just been served that lovely eastern fruit, the mangosteen, a bright white fruit the size of a thumb, and were all greatly enjoying it. Hart said, "It's delightful!" then Porter piped up, "It's delicious!" but it was Woolley who exclaimed, "It's de-lovely!" And there was the title of the song for Porter, the origin of his classic, "It's De-Lovely" from *Red, Hot, and Blue*, the stage musical that appeared on Broadway in 1936.

How about the medlar? A fruit which is rotten before it is ripe, it has a dubious reputation. It is eccentric to eat medlars nowadays, even when it is considered strange even to grow quince, I believe, neither standard rations nor spectacular bearers of blossoms. "You'll be rotten 'ere you'll be half-ripe," notes Shakespeare of the fruit. The medlar is not ready for eating until it has been "bletted" by the frost, gone sleepy as they say, with incipient rottenness. Once bletted, the fruit can be eaten raw and is eaten as a dessert, for example with cheese and is sometimes used to make medlar jelly, even wine. Another dish is "medlar cheese," similar to lemon curd, being made with its fruit pulp, eggs, and butter. A medlar tea was once commonly drunk. Medlars have been often used figuratively in literature as a symbol of prostitution or dire poverty. In the Prologue to *The Reeve's Tale*, for example, Chaucer's character laments his old age, comparing himself to the medlar, which he names using the slang term "open-arse." In the 16th and 17th centuries, simply because of the shape of the fruit, medlars were bawdily referred to as "open-arses," inspiring often humorous and indecent puns in many Elizabethan and Jacobean plays. Slurs against the fruit are often found most notably in the Bard's plays, specifically, *Timon of Athens, Measure for Measure*, and *As You Like It*, where Rosalind makes a somewhat complicated pun involving "grafting" her interlocuter with a medlar and the trees around her which bear love letters: "I'll graff it with you, and then I shall graff it with a medlar. Then it will be the earliest fruit i' th' country; for you'll be rotten ere you be half ripe, and that's the right virtue of the medlar." (III.ii.116-119). Novelist D.H. Lawrence refers to medlars as "wineskins of brown morbidity, autumnal excrementa ... an exquisite odour of leave taking."

D*er Spiegel* editor Jan Fleischhauer, who grew up in a typical West German liberal family, has written that his parents would not let him eat oranges because they were grown in countries ruled by dictators. (He then grew up to become an extreme conservative.) How that would have displeased New York editor Diana Vreeland who craved oranges. The distinguished food writer M.F.K. Fisher, who spent her childhood in Whittier, California amid orange groves, would not agree. She was that unique thing, a Californian who disliked oranges. "By the time I was nearing my teens, I felt that orange trees were the dullest blob-like growths on the planet, tidy and stupid in shape and crawling with several kinds of lice," she surprisingly wrote in *To Begin Again: Stories and Memoirs 1908-1929* and goes on to say,

> I hated oranges because of years of surfeit and can still
> forgo them easily, except perhaps in a good marma-
> lade or tart. But the word ineffable was made for the
> perfume an orange tree in full bloom will give forth,
> especially in the moonlight—and especially if it is
> near a lime or lemon, when the blend with oxygen is
> dizzying.

Ugandan dictator Idi Amin Dada ate as many as 40 oranges a day, believing they were "nature's Viagra," earning him the nickname Mr Jaffa." (He had five wives, earlier claiming that a second woman then living with him was his sister—"*dada*." Thus, he was given his added surname.) An unstoppable eater, his favorite foods were roast goat, cassava, and millet bread. Later, when living in exile in Saudi Arabia, he reportedly loved to feast on pizza and buckets of Kentucky Fried Chicken.

I think of the faux-mystical references in poetry where, oddly, the images of oranges predominate—Leonard Cohen's poem "Suzanne," for example, with its lines, "And you know that she's half crazy/ But that's why you want to be there/ And she feeds you tea and oranges/ That come all the way from China" and James Merrill's "The Candid Decorator" with "I thought I would do over/ all of it. I was tired/ of scars and stains... Say, of a small tree,/ an orange or a pear . . . He listened dreamily/ Combing his golden hair" and the lines in Wallace Stevens's "Sunday Morning" with its "late coffee and oranges/ in a sunny chair," conjuring instead of the presence of Christ an aesthetic, a matinée exquise on an elegant porch in Newport or Hyannis or the Hamptons. I myself do not happen to go in for secular Eucharists.

As to the matter of renouncing oranges—and, by the way, store-bought 100% "real" orange juice is all artificially flavored—I remember reading a funny food bit in the *New York Times Magazine* by stand-up comic Jerry Seinfeld about those rock-hard cylinders of Birdseye concentrated frozen orange juice. "Orange juice was frozen years in advance. You had to hack away at it with a knife just to get a couple of drops of liquidity." He complained further, "Shredded wheat. It was wrapping your lips around a wood chipper. You had breakfast and then have to wait two days for the wounds to heal so you could speak again." Its tidy, familiar pillow-shaped form always seemed a bit of an anomaly to me and evoked the satirical nickname that we used in our household growing up, "baled hay."

After chocolate and vanilla—a fact perhaps worthy here to pass along—orange is considered the world's most favorite flavor. (On a personal note, I think I can say that I will never think of oranges or orange juice in quite the same way after I witnessed in *Pee-wee's Big Adventure* a Tyrannosaurus Rex use its mouth to juice oranges into a pitcher, as a life-sized figure of President Abraham Lincoln stands by, flipping pancakes onto the ceiling!) God bless America! Hypochondriac and ostentatious curmudgeon, the late Oscar Levant—and his dance partner—were laughed at and mockingly awarded a lemon at a junior high school dance, a public humiliation that he never got over. Consequence? In later years, Levant would never eat a lemon no matter which way it was served to him, its image conjuring up that moment of hideous abuse during adolescence. Sam Kashner and Nancy Schoenberger in their biography, *A Talent for Genius*, state of the grumpy Levant, "He would heap imprecations on any hapless waiter who ever served a wedge of lemon with a meal." Again, to bring in my hero Doughty, in *Travels in Arabia Deserta* he inveighs against the humble date.

While Sir Isaac Newton was notoriously restrained—from all I have read this seems, quirkily, to be a common condition of genius—and frequently never finished his dinner, he rather did like fruit, and could eat any quantity of it. Deprivation apparently sharpened his fierce mind, arguably one of the greatest minds if not the greatest mind in the history of all Christendom. "He kept neither dog nor cat in his chamber," said his secretary, Humphrey Newton, a distant relative, "which made well for the old woman, his bed-maker, she faring much better for it, for in a morning she has sometimes found both dinner and supper scarcely tasted of, which the old woman has very pleasantly and mumpingly gone away with." As a young lad, he can be found in his account-books spending his money on cherries, tarts, and marmalade, according to an article in *The [London] Times* (September 21, 1855).

Marmalade seems to have been a special delight of his, for he was always very fond of a small roasted quince for supper. Newton was also as fond of orange peel as was Dr. Samuel Johnson, and it was the Great Cham's inveterate habit to take it boiled in water for his breakfast instead of tea. "Apples, too," we read, "appear to have been a favorite fruit of his; one of his letters exhibits him longing after cider, and making great endeavors to secure some grafts of the genuine 'red streaks.' Perhaps it was one of those favored 'red streaks' that falling from the tree suggested the system of the world—the universality of the law of gravitation."

Tucking into delivered pizza was a big thing with MIT nerds during the early days of the personal computer, *circa* 1980-1985—I was teaching there at the time—which let them to work without pause and not have to stop to go out to eat. I believe it was the same with Newton. Eating fruits allowed him to continue working. His prescription for loneliness was work, work, and more work. Unlike prosaic Phillips Andover, M.I.T. was one of the schools where I taught for which I have enduring love and affection—two very different things, the second requiring respect.

"I Just Ate Fruit for the First Time and It Kind of Sucked" is an online article by Matthew J.X. Malady, a writer and editor who in May 2014 interviewed a guy named Joe. Malady gets to the point, asking "Joe! So what happened here?" Joe replies, "It's true, I've never eaten fruit. I've had avocados and tomatoes, but I've been told those "don't count." I've also never had juice, though I do drink red wine. That's technically juice, right?" Joe launches out splenetically,

> I just get nauseated about even thinking of eating fruit. I'm not sure why. I used to get sick a lot when I was younger, so my theory is that I probably attempted to eat fruit while ill and my brain associated those two things—like how if you get food poisoning after eating salmon rolls, for two and a half decades of your life you won't be able to stomach seafood or sail a boat or look at the ocean.
> "What about apples?" asked Malady.
> "No."
> "Oranges?"
> "No."
> "Jujubes?"
> "No!" Joe went on, "I've frequently been offered money in exchange for trying fruit—on one occasion as much as $500. But my dignity is not for sale!... I realize it's mostly psychosomatic, but the nausea is so bad that I sometimes get grossed out just by the scent of fruit. If someone starts peeling an orange on the subway I'll have to switch cars, or risk vomiting. Despite this, it was my New Year's resolution to try fruit."

He tried them—the big experiment. It turns out that, after tentatively tasting them, Joe liked peaches and kiwi. But not grapes (seedless, red). His response? "Eating it felt like chewing on grass that was wrapped around chilled mucus."

How about Champagne Mango?
Joe replies,
"My friend showed me her elaborate grid cutting system for mangos, while explaining that her mother used
to say that 'mangos are the apples of the Philippines.'
The analogy was lost on me. I excitedly took a bite,
and violently gagged. I somehow managed to choke
it down. It tasted like stomach acid. I don't remember anything else about it. It's possible I blacked out.
The whole thing was basically a core, too, like how
a potato chip bag is mostly air. What a huge rip-off.
Fuck mangos, man." And apples (Fuji)? "I ate a slice,"
responded Joe, "and it didn't taste like much—like
damp cardboard. Bland and crunchy. The juice kind of
grossed me out, but I didn't mind the taste and texture
overall. I could see myself enjoying it on a salad, or
maybe in a pie. Feeling empowered, I bit straight into
that sucker, which felt oddly satisfying."

Apparently, fruit, at least metaphorically, had a strangely ambiguous force for the Lithuanian/Polish Nobel Prize poet Czeslaw Milosz who had notably written in his 1955 poem "In Milan,"

I could compose, right now, a song
On the taste of peaches, on September in Europe.
No one can accuse me of being without joy
Or of not noticing girls who pass by.
I do not deny that I would like to gobble up
All existing flowers, to eat all the colors.
I have been devouring this world in vain
For forty years, a thousand would not be enough.
Yes, I would like to be a poet of the five senses,
That's why I don't allow myself to become one.
Yes, thought has less weight than the word lemon.
That's why in my words I do not reach for fruit."

Actor Cary Grant detested raspberries for some particular reason, hated any and all soft drinks, and refused ever to eat any food cooked by or prepared over charcoal, because, as he insisted, it "caused cancer," according to Maureen Donaldson—one of his romantic associates in the 1970s who met Grant when she was in her 20s and he was nearly 70—in her tell-all book, *An Affair to Remember*. "Only strangers eat tamarinds—but they only eat them once," wrote the predictably cynical Mark Twain in *Roughing It*. According to the undoubtedly reliable *Real Cheesy Facts about TV and Movies*, sexy Hollywood actress Lindsay Lohan is allergic to blueberries, which is particularly sad to relate, especially of a young beauty, because wild blueberries are said to have more antioxidants than any other fruit or vegetables. After discovering the late actress Donna Reed's entry in *The Dead Celebrity Cookbook*—a lemon Bundt cake recipe that calls for cake-mix and a box of pudding—I could only conclude that she could not only not cook but must have had the palate of a mud-hen.

The Nazarites mentioned in Numbers 6:1–4 are asked to abstain from everything that made a man drunk: "He must not drink grape juice or eat grapes or raisins. As long as he is a Nazarite, he must not eat anything that comes from the grapevine, not even the seeds or skins." A common end of the year custom in Spain is to eat one grape for each of the last twelve seconds of every year for good luck, a paradoxical event for anyone who dislikes grapes, an indisposition, I am told, that includes many recovering alcoholics.

Ayn Rand apparently disliked fruit. "The only fruit I ever saw her eat was Italian prunes. She called them 'manageable'—they were small, easy to hold, had a firm texture. She enjoyed certain Russian food—especially borscht and beef Stroganoff," wrote Mary Ann Sures who co-authored, with her husband Charles, *Facets of Ayn Rand*, memoirs of their longtime friendship with Ayn Rand and her dim husband Frank O'Connor. I assume the uncircumscribable girth of the simple pear, apple, or peach made them too hard to handle for Rand. Couldn't the woman grasp a banana? This selfish monster of a woman, who notoriously discouraged gift-giving, never refused fudge or discouraged anyone from giving it—or pretty much of anything—to her. (Self made men and women all seem to be piggish. "It's good to be selfish. But not so self-centered that you never listen to other people," Hugh Hefner has often repeated.) She adored chocolate and stuffed her face with it, especially the Godiva brand (she even saved the boxes), chunks of slot-machine chocolate, Woolworth scrambles, and even ice cream sundaes (at Trader Vic's, she enjoyed the ice cream ball rolled in coconut and served with chocolate sauce.) She gobbled chocolate by the box. Sures added, "She enjoyed the Godivas after dinner and before bedtime. When I stayed over with her, bringing out the box was a nightly ritual. She had sampled all the Godiva chocolates, and had her favorites. One was called 'open oyster'—a milk choc- olate shell filled with hazelnut praline." Rand also had a sweet tooth for miniature Danish pastries, always served with the coffee—black, diluted with cool water—but yet when coffee was served to guests, it was always accom- panied by heavy cream. She also liked Asian food and was fond of the small, dollar-size pancakes that were served at a restaurant in the Watergate Hotel, in DC. She liked eggs Benedict and often ordered it when she was out for a business lunch.

What she especially hated were salads—and anything connected to them, lettuce, tomatoes, carrots. "Whenever Eloise [her maid] prepared dinner, there was never a salad at Ayn's place," notes Sures. "She once referred to salads as 'grass'—which I've since learned is a Russian way of viewing salad." Tough, aggressive, Rand *would* want solids, not salads. This was a brass-as- sed woman, a person who once pontificated, "Until and unless you discover that money is the root of all good, you ask for your own destruction." The woman was an insufferable witch, a nag, a didactic shrew with an unhal- lowed hump of unidentified self-hatred on her back, and all of her writ- ing, even her gabby fiction, which supposedly celebrated human freedom, Whittaker Chambers called "shrillness without reprieve." She worshipped heroes, loathed the average man, or, as she called them, "members of the lit- tle street," "human herds," and literally despised ordinary people with a ven- geance. She was hammer-hearted enough to be said to have hated the sight of children's clothes on a wash-line. How interesting—and antithetical—that the Concord Transcendentalist Bronson Alcott considered children to be "A Type of the Divinity." No greater difference could be found between two people of "ideas," the latter an altruist, the former a mulish, ugly, and trucu- lent harridan, hateful to the core and fit company only for Stymphalian fowl.

One of Rand's favorite maxims was Nietzsche's, "The noble soul has reverence for itself." An irony remains that she herself was virtually the antithesis of the template she admired, just as the puny, club-footed Josef Goebbels was about as far-fetched an example of the golden Nazi ideal as could be imagined.

Ayn Rand was basically a *bednyak*, a Russian peasant. She and dull, word- less, empty-headed Frank usually ate dinner at a wonky bridge table, while watching TV. A favorite meal of theirs was a cheap casserole, patched togeth- er, that served as dinner for three nights—behind her back, Frank mocking- ly referred to it as the "*Atlas Shrugged* casserole"—one that without much intrepidity they had discovered on the back of a Mueller's macaroni box. It was quick, easy, and inexpensive, a combo of macaroni, onions, hamburger, and squeeze-cheese. "They ate simply," writes Sures, mistress of understatement. "They did something interesting with canned peas—they were served at room temperature, mixed with mayonnaise. Once in a while, we had hamburgers from Tailor Made. She would consult Frank and me, make up the order, call it in, and then Frank and I would walk over to pick it up." *They did something interesting with canned peas.* This from the lordly, insufferably priggish, intransigent money-elitist and author of *The Fountainhead*—lazily calling in grocery orders and hamburger orders like a prat while watching "Queen for a Day"! Clearly, she was three yards past the dock, as salty old Cape Cod fishermen like to put it.

I am not surprised that she doted on prunes. Contradictions do not exist. All concepts of God should be rejected. Facts should be derived from reason alone. Self-interest is moral, while altruism immoral. Selfishness is a virtue. Egotism alone makes a rational code of ethics. Give nothing. These were standard rules and regulation for her. She hated Beethoven, generosity, altruism, non-smokers, facial hair (though she herself was spiderishly hirsute), disagreement, Arabs, welfare, homosexuals, Karl Marx, Jesus Christ, and little children. She never put a child in her novels. "An embryo has no rights," declared the barren Mrs. Leptova, or "stone eggs," as I like to refer to Ms. Rosenbaum. "Nothing is more depressing than to see diapers on a clothesline" was another one of endearing remarks. She was dictatorial, thought she knew everything, and came on like dirt on a duck. I have often wondered if, in her awfulness, the woman was not following the formal Malāmatiyya technique of the Sufis, which is deliberately attracting disapproval. She was dwarfish, with a basin haircut, brutally chopped hair, toad hands, a bladed nose, bow-legged. A Raymond Chandler description in *The High Window* (1942) suited her to a T: "She had a lot of face and chin. She had pewter-colored hair set in a ruthless permanent, a hard beak, and large moist eyes with the sympathetic expression of wet stones." She was a walking, talking prune.

Mark Twain, who in all likelihood would have found Ayn Rand a borderline mental case, hated prunes. "When I sailed in the Batavia, I had a different opinion of the Cunard Line from that which I now entertain," he stated in an interview in the *New York Sun* ("Mark Twain Back Again," September 3, 1879) upon returning to the United States. "I objected to the prunes." He went on to say,

> I suppose you know that when the Cunarders changed
> from sailing to steam power, they maintained some of
> their old sailing ideas on the new steam propelled ship.

> Prunes was one of these old ideas...that was when
> they served out puddings, the same as they do sailors
> aboard a sailing ship. Then there were Tuesday beans,
> and Saturday beans, and prunes twenty-one times a
> week for dessert. They hunted the world for cooks and
> got the worst there were.

I have already mentioned that chef Daniel Boulud hates bananas. Apparently, so does the billionaire modern-living gadfly and demi-culture maven Martha Stewart. "Ugh! Why are bananas there? I hate bananas," she squawked at a recent photo shoot, according to Benjamin Wallace in his article called "When Martha Stewart Returned from Prison, the Future Looked Bright: The Comeback That Wasn't" (*New York*, August 8-15, 2011). Let me mention in passing that Stewart also greatly dislikes the innards, lights, and gubbins of animals, having once vented, not in a quiet way, "I will not eat anything that has brains in it."

"I cannot express how much I detested conkies," my friend Amber Bryan, born in Barbados, explained to me and went on to fill me in on her island likes and dislikes. "Crop-over, our name for harvest festival, meant conkies, OK? Everybody ate them. I could not abide them. Island pumpkin, *cou cou,* how we refer to sea eggs or what you call sea urchins—they walked across the sea bed at snail speed, but if you stepped on one the pain was excruciating—even sardines, canned mackerel in tomato sauce, I say, 'ugh' to all of them. I can admit that in the right hands, "sweet hands" as we would say, cou cou could be wonderful. However, one false note, and the lot was ruined for me. It had to be just perfect, OK? A mere whisper in the breeze, one false note, and I tell you I was having none of it! Far too many encounters with cold cou cou, a solid lump of concrete cornmeal covered with okra slime, would reduce me to tears every time I saw it on the plate. Sadly, to live on the island was to eat lots of cou cou. I myself liked fishcakes, pudding and souse, sour apples, English Red Rose tea every morning, real lemonade, breadfruit. I hated papaya. I hate papaya now, I hated it ten years ago, I shall always hate it. As God is my witness, I shall never eat papaya again," she joked. "I promise you that if there were a heaven (and I firmly believe there is not) and the cost of entry required a poor soul to consume a single bite of papaya, I would flatly decline! Ironic, isn't it, that I am a woman and the papaya, orange on the inside with a belly of pulp and little black seeds, is shaped like a female body without the arms, legs, and head? Still I will be honest with you. When I was growing up, I truly wished for hurricanes to knock every single papaya tree off the island!"

Although nobody loved eating more than Huck Finn did, he could draw the line. Do you recall the scene in Twain's *Adventures of Huckleberry Finn* where in Chapter 12 both he and Jim collude—by ingenious rationalization—to avoid eating crab-apples and persimmons? These are two fruits the runaways would never have stolen, so much did they dislike them. In the very same way, many Catholics during Lent piously devise ways sacrificially to "give up" eating the very foods that they actually hate in the first place. At the crack of dawn Huck and Jim are both great hands at sneaking into cornfields to "borrow" melons and pumpkins and other favorites. "Pap always said there wasn't any harm in borrowing things if you meant to pay them back at some point," the 13-year-old Huck confidentially explains.

> The widow, though, said borrowing was just a nicer
> way of saying stealing, which decent people didn't
> do. Jim said he figured that Pap and the widow were
> both right. He said it'd be best if we compromised by
> promising ourselves that we just wouldn't borrow cer-
> tain things anymore but continue borrowing others.
> So we talked about it one night while we were drifting
> down the river. We tried to decide whether we'd give
> up watermelon, cantaloupe, or mush-melons. By
> dawn, we'd decided to give up borrowing crab-ap-
> ples and persimmons. We'd been feeling a little guilty
> before, but now we felt much better about things. I
> was glad that we had settled this way, since crab-apples
> ain't ever good and persimmons wouldn't be ripe for
> another two or three months.

So it all worked out swell.

I love the brazenness of this over-rationalizing, self-absolving lie (don't all lies serve that function?)—young devious Huck clearly felt it to be his best ploy; for it to fail would be impossible (I am spending here two of my favorite grammatical constructions in honor of it: the infinitive as second object and the infinitive as object of preposition)—and am convinced that the self-absolving lie is, at least subjectively, probably among the best definitions of all for a food aversion.

Apples have irked certain eaters. The Delicious Apple, wrote curmudgeon A.J. Liebling, a polyphage incarnate, is "a triumph because it doesn't taste like an apple," and "the Golden Delicious… doesn't taste like anything." He declared, "The only test of a good breakfast place is its baked apple. (Possibly the major brief that the gluttonous Liebling held against apples—disappointing his omnivorous need for fat—are that they are 25% air.) "The Harvey girls never fail me," pronounced food writer M.F.K. Fisher's opinionated Uncle Evans, a character who now and again appears in the pages of her books, more often than not making pronouncements on food, but he didn't like apples. It was Uncle Evans who once scolded his niece on the occasion of her saying heedlessly, "I don't care" when as a teenager in a dining-car of a train she had been kindly asked by a solicitous waiter whether she would prefer a fresh mushroom omelet or an omelet with wild asparagus. In a classic moment of the avuncular, he upbraided the young girl, declaring in a bit of snit,

> You should never say that again, dear girl. It is stupid, which you are not. It implies that the attentions of your host are basically wasted on you. So make up your mind, before you open your mouth. Let him believe, even if it is a lie, that you would infinitely prefer the exotic wild asparagus to the banal mushrooms, or vice-versa. Let him feel that it matters to you... and even that he does.

Fisher would remember that admonition all of her life. "As Uncle Evans pointed out to me, I either care or I am a dolt, and dolts should not consort with caring people."

I remember reading once that Friedrich Schiller, the German poet, philosopher, historian, and playwright, for some reason, needed to have the scent of apples rotting in his desk in order to write well. My question: was this a fetish, a totem, or a psychological need? Yet how curious! The poet E.E. Cummings, on the other hand, in what was probably a more normal instance of a compulsion, claimed for the same reason that he needed to be able to see a tree from his window. Edgar Allan Poe wrote final drafts on seperate pieces of paper and attached them together with sealing wax. Mark Twain wrote lying down, Ernest Hemingway standing up. So did Virginia Woolf. Victor Hugo wrote without clothes, often stark naked, to fight the urge to go out. John Cheever wrote his pages stripped down to his underwear. Flannery O'Connor sat facing the blank surface of her wood dresser, which helpfully provided no visual distractions. Sir Walter Scott composed his poetry while on horseback.

Many apples that one finds stacked in the produce departments of supermarkets nowadays are shiny but bland and tasteless. Rarely can you find

Baldwin apples anymore, not in supermarket bins anyway, bright red winter apples, delicious tasting, perfect for pies, were once the most popular apple in New England, and New York—at one time America's most exported apple—ignored simply because held to be too homely, bumpy, unprepossessing, covered with knobs, along with a hectic red-yellow lack of color uniformity. American consumers feel that Baldwin apples don't quite measure up visually to their high fruit aesthetic.

The snobbery of physiognomy is involved here. What a pity.

Henry Thoreau in "Wild Apples" was characteristically an exception to the common run of men as apple fanciers, writing, "Almost all wild apples are handsome. They cannot be too gnarly and crabbed and rusty to look at. The gnarliest will have some redeeming traits even to the eye."

Food is often a fashion. I remember back in the 1970s people seemed to be eating only fondue and then in the 1980s quiche. Lobster, now so cherished, in Old Colony times—so unsightly as to be called "cockroaches of the sea"—was used for fertilizer, when not fed to prisoners, lackeys, apprentices, and even slaves as a way to save money. All that changed during the mid-1800s due to the innovations of canned food and railway transportation. Consumers could buy cheap canned lobster, which because it could now be shipped anywhere grew in popularity. After World War II, given a new status, lobster was soon considered a delicacy. Prices then began surging, incrementally. Trends rule. There is self-delusion in snobbery.

An appropriating mind works through trends or fads. It is as much about the need to belonging as not having an original soul.

A hundred years ago, when oysters were held to be the diet of the poor, they were of course undervalued, if valued at all. It is seafood, delicious in its own right, of course, but a food, as it were, "taken up" (as Henry James would say) as a special delight by the wealthy and the happily advantaged. Snobbery is a confusion of values. What you eat, how you eat, when you eat, where you eat are all gauges—litmus tests—for the snob who cannot take a chance on being found wanting, according to the ways of the world, so slim is his conception of self. "A snob's pursuits are sterile, and his satisfactions of a vicarious nature," wrote Arthur Koestler in *The Act of Creation,* a book in which he contrasts the inveterate snob's mind (borrowed light) with an actual creative mind (new light). "What the snob admires in public would bore him when alone, but he is unaware of it. When he reads Kierkegaard, he is not moved by what he reads, he is moved by himself reading Kierkegaard."

Cartoonist Roz Chast in an article in *The New Yorker* (November 8, 2010) declared that she wished "there wasn't such a fruit as the banana, or, more accurately, that people didn't eat bananas in public." She writes,

> I am disgusted by bananas' texture. Compare the tex-
> ture of a banana—mushy, baby-foodish, almost what
> you would feed a sick person—with the brisk, athletic
> crispness of an apple…. The main problem I have with
> the banana is its packaging… garbage of the worst
> sort, the kind you must get rid of right away.

Regarding fruits, of course, freshness is paramount. "There are only ten minutes in the life of a pear when it is perfect to eat," wrote Ralph Waldo Emerson whom one can imagine must have been fussy except in the orchard.

Such fussiness was surely thwarted when Roald Dahl has his spoiled little brat Veruca Salt suffering the fate of going headlong down the garbage chute at the eccentric chocolatier Willy Wonka's chocolate factory.

And then a little further down

> A mass of others gather round:
> A bacon rind, some rancid lard,
> A loaf of bread gone stale and hard,
> A steak that nobody could chew,
> An oyster from an oyster stew,
> Some liverwurst so old and gray,
> One smelled it from a mile away,
> A rotten nut, a reeky pear,
> A thing the cat left on the stair.

In "The Way of Eating Fried Sausages," one of Nobel Prize winner Kenzaburo Oe's better stories, he tells the tale of an older Japanese research associate and speaker at Berkeley whose reveries of an uncle lead to memories of deprivation during World War II. He draws a distinction between a long tradition of eating—and/or offering up—dried chestnuts and dried persimmons, which, in passing, highlights contrasting themes of self-control (in the East) and extravagant pleasure (in the West), regarding food. During the war in Japan, food was of course extremely scarce. The speaker in the story much prefers the persimmon to eat, contrasting its "resplendent sweetness"—"the sensation of biting into the dried persimmon, having it lie on your tongue, and letting it slip down your throat was such a sweet experience"—with the dried chestnut. "I clasped the small dried chestnut, hard as stone, and, trembling, prayed with a sad heart." Filled with regretful longing for the persimmon, he has to eat what he is given, however. "I would spit out the dry, coarse, outer skin and roughly peel and throw out the soft inner skin.

Then I would chew the tasteless cold lump of chestnut meat…" "According to the *World Book*, is it okay to freeze your persimmons?" asked host Peter Marshall on one of TV's Hollywood Squares episodes back in the 1960s. Center Square Paul Lynde wryly replied, "No. You should dress warmly."

Remember the sisters Lizzie and Laura gorging on fruit juice in Christina Rossetti's enigmatic poem, "Goblin Market"?

> "Lie close," Laura said,
> Pricking up her golden head:
> "We must not look at goblin men,
> We must not buy their fruits:
> Who knows upon what soil they fed
> Their hungry thirsty roots?"
> "Come buy," call the goblins
> Hobbling down the glen.

Surely there is a warning and something unholy in the lushness ("How fair the vine must grow/ those grapes are so luscious;/ How warm the wind must blow/ Through those fruit bushes") that tempts the two girls, the rich plums, the cherries, the melons, the "pellucid grapes without one seed," peaches, citron, dates. What is the nature of that fruit-call? The nature of those fruit-merchant men? The admonition against eating such Dionysian fruits offered by the lascivious, maleficent goblins. The eeriness recalls in Hawthorne's moral fable, "Rappaccini's Daughter:" "Give me thy breath, my sister," exclaimed Beatrice; "for I am faint with common air! And give me this flower of thine, which I separate with gentlest fingers from the stem, and place it close beside my heart." With these words, the beautiful girl in search of the food promised by the flower odors in the garden fatally plucks one of the richest blossoms of the shrub.

Fussiness is the *bête-noire* of many foodies. My brother Paul cannot seem to enjoy a meal without a bottle of McIlenny's Tabasco (hot sauce) at his elbow, which he splashes out as compulsively as vinegar is spattered on his own food by Fred Durkin, the literary gumshoe who is famous for being called in on many cases by Rex Stout's notable detective, Nero Wolfe, who for that very reason could not tolerate dining with the man. (Incidentally, Martha Stewart, American businesswoman, television personality, and quondam cook, has many times publicly declared that she will not *touch* hot sauce, while typically pandering, the fawning hustler Hillary Clinton told a black audience in 2016 that she always carries a bottle of it in her handbag.) What is it, by the way, with food snobbery and detectives? A proletarian lot, as portrayed, it seems that, as they less-than-glamorously plod through the grim cases they accept, they should settle for a burger and a simple piece of pie. Paradoxically, don't they all seem to be pompous asses about the food they eat —Wolfe, Philo Vance, Eugene Valmont, Homer Evans? Even unshowy Sam Spade could be fussy about his lamb chops.

No, fastidious and exacting eater can be found everywhere you turn, and habits are entrenched. Almost all French and Italian eaters enjoy bread with every meal. Most Koreans need a taste of lettuce to enjoy with Bulgogi, their grilled marinated beef. The French and Italians (I am proudly both by heritage) rarely sit down to a meal without the accompaniment of bread. Hungarians need paprika handy, and Rutabaga casseroles are common at just about every meal in Finland. In many households in Peru, *cena* is almost a repeat of breakfast *(desayuno)*, with bread accompanied by cheese, ham, eggs or olives. When eating a meal, the Inuit habitually place large slabs of meat, fish, or blubber, and other parts of whatever animal is theirs for the day on a piece of metal or cardboard on the floor, where anyone can cut off a piece of meat. (Inuit eat only when hungry.) Meals are often announced for a whole camp, with a woman—only a woman—shouting, "*Ujuk!*" which means "cooked meat." "Never eat in a place where you can't read your news-paper," pronounced Chicago poet and historian Carl Sandburg, rather pe-culiarly using that *sine qua non* as his litmus test for the quality of an eatery, dining room, or steak house. He was an odd little fellow, a compulsive reader while he ate, something of a provincial compulsion, to my mind.

People there are who will eat virtually anything. Lucullus, Dagwood Bumstead. Satch in the old Leo Gorcey movies. They all had hollow legs, deep appetites that were insatiable. Señor Diego Rivera several times almost literally ate himself to death. Nothing was off limits, everything was wel-come, just serve it up, keep it coming. Charlie Chaplin was astonished watch-ing Walter Matthau wolf down a meal when the actor and his wife Carol once visited with the family at Vevey. And tastes can be far-ranging. On the television show *Taxi*, the favorite lunch of the "Reverend" Jim Ignatowaski, a big eater, was SpaghettiO's and herring. Opie's best friend, Johnny Paul Jason (Richard Keith), on the Andy Griffith Show once ate tar. Wimpy in the *Popeye* comic strips—to you, J. Wellington Wimpy ("I'll gladly pay you Tuesday for a hamburger today")—ate nothing but cheeseburgers, well mostly. Once in while, Wimpy would tell someone, "I'd like to invite you over to my house for a duck dinner"—and then moving away quickly to a safe distance to yell, "You bring the ducks!" Cheeseburgers were also favored by short, bald, dim-witted Edgar Horace Jeffries, the actual name of the friend of Archibald J. Mutt, who went under the name Jeff in *Mutt and Jeff* comics. These little guys were all major eaters, indiscriminate ones, folks who could "put it away."

"What do people eat there?" was a predictably famous question—solely and exclusively—that the orotund, double-chinned, ingloriously fat radio announcer of the old *Jack Benny Show*, Don Wilson, always comically asked whenever one mentioned a foreign country or, say, showed him a postcard of other lands. The self-indulgent King Edward VII, he of the swollen girth, virtually never stopped eating. Sideboard spreads alone groaned the table. He habitually ate three breakfasts every morning, including, among other comestibles, venison, smoked fish, and frogs legs with the legs disguised in a pink paprika sauce prepared by Escoffier and cheekily called "*nymphs à la rose*" (after the dancer Vaslav Nijinsky's short ballet, "*Le Spectre de la Rose*," the legs being the *le spectre!*) At midnight, he invariably finished the day with guests—he could not bear to be alone—enjoying a cold buffet of plovers' eggs, ptarmigan, and salmon with every sort of liqueur and mineral water imaginable.

Oysters, it appears, are a passion for gluttons, who are as rabid for them as sea otters are, devouring them by the bag.

Diamond Jim Brady gobbled oysters all day. This turn-of-the-century billionaire and gastronome, the foremost eater of the Gilded Age, would dispatch three dozen of them as a mid-morning snack, and always the largest ones, always the giant Lynnhaven oysters, some of them as large as 6 inches long—it is said that their salty, sweet flavor comes from growing up in a river so close to the ocean—that had been sent up daily from Baltimore to Rector's, one of Brady's favorite restaurants. Oysters were always included in his rousing breakfasts of eggs, pancakes, pork chops, fried potatoes, cornbread, hominy, a large slab of beefsteak, and big fat muffins. He ate them at lunch and during his legendary fifteen-course meals which generally included a "deluge" of lobsters, clams, deviled crabs, tureens of turtle soup, terrapin, frogs' legs, rare steaks, canvasback ducks, pork chops, all served with rich buttery sauces, and even whole cakes, all of it always washed down, not with alcohol (he never drank the stuff) but with freshly-squeezed orange juice, to which, it may be noted, he was seriously addicted, swilling full gallons of the drink at breakfast and several beakers of it at every meal. He also loved and gulped no end of lemon soda.

"Jim liked his oysters sprinkled with clams," quipped the criminal hustler and Broadway scam-artist, Wilson Mizner, "and his sirloin steaks smothered in veal cutlets." "A napkin on his knee would have been as inadequate as a doily under a bass drum," said the voluble George Rector, restaurateur, raconteur, and food authority whose father, Charles, ran the famous Rector's

Oyster House in Chicago. When Brady suffered an attack of gallstones in 1912, surgeons opening the trencherman up found his stomach to be six times the normal size and covered in so many blanket layers of fat that they were unable to complete the surgery. The dogged Brady hung on living for another five years, all the while suffering from diabetes, bad kidneys, stomach ulcers, and serious heart problems and died of a heart attack at 61.

"Above all things," we read in *The Rule of St. Benedict*, a Trappist handbook, "gluttony must be avoided, so that a monk never be surprised by a surfeit; for there is nothing so unfitting for a Christian as surfeiting, according to our Lord's words in Luke XXI. 34." When I think of gluttony—the decadence of gluttony—I do not go back in mind to the slothful medieval monks of yore. My mind goes right to a remark that the singer Barbra Streisand once made: "Success to me is having ten honeydew melons and eating only the top half of each slice."

By the way, Streisand who is said to be almost pathologically averse to exercise was introduced to caviar by Gore Vidal who mentions this in his memoir—his last book, in fact—*Point to Point Navigation*. How did the singer start her day? "With five thousand eggs," she'd reply, meaning, of course, caviar. I had been told years ago that she was a pancake-maven and scarfed them at breakfast.

Remember Cold Duck? Poet John Ciardi biliously defined it as "a carbonated wine foisted upon Americans (who else would drink it) by winery ad agencies as a way of getting rid of inferior champagne by mixing it with inferior sparkling burgundy." Are you shocked at pedigree creeping into wine drinking? Hardly—it is its heart and soul! Recall James Thurber's much-loved cartoon showing two couples raising their glasses, as one wittily declares, "It's a naïve domestic Burgundy without any breeding, but I think you'll amused by its presumption." As I have said novelist James Joyce hated red wine. Preceding him of course was the unmistakable caveat in Proverbs 23:31–32: "Do not gaze at wine when it is red, when it sparkles in the cup, when it goes down smoothly! In the end it bites like a snake and poisons like a viper." Or so goes the *NIV Bible*. The Douay Version (Catholic) gives the same advice, however, with the one exception that there it warns against white ["yellow"] wine! Jean-Antoine in *Travels Amongst the Great Andes of the Equator* is quoted by the explorer Edward Whymper, a man who is best known for the first ascent of the Matterhorn in 1865, as declaring: "'White wine is bad; it cuts against the legs.'"

I have mentioned soup. Soups, whether starter, first course, entrée before a main meal, or the essential dinner, are traditionally classified into two main groups: clear soups—that is, a bouillon or a consommé—and thick soups, that is, purées or bisques, to use the French classifications. Chef Jacques Pépin has gone on record as stating—no small mouthful—"You can tell a good restaurant [solely] by its consommé." We all know that Andy Warhol painted soup cans. Certain people close to Warhol always claimed that the Pop-artist actually loved —purchased—Campbell's soup because it was what his mother back in Pittsburgh had served to him just about every day for lunch. Others, however, perversely claim that he hated the soup, possibly for the same reason. Warhol would have disagreed. In the main he said he loved Campbell's Soup. He loved it the passionate way a Cockney loves jellied eels.

Poet Arthur Rimbaud several times in his writings dwells disparagingly on the long yellow fingers and the grimy exposed breasts of the desolate old folks who frequented the town library in his hometown of Charleville, calling them "soup eaters," and he rejected them *en bloc*. (He despised his mother, and one feels inevitably that she served him soup once too many times.) Two beauties, whom I along with millions have always loved, struggle with soup, at least in the movies. The consummate beauty Louise Brooks in *Diary of a Lost Girl* (1929) in a reformatory for wayward girls can barely bring herself to eat its awful soup, which all the inmates have to sip by rote at the same time, as if they are part of an assembly line. The transcendent Greta Garbo, as well, in *Ninotchka* joylessly sips her fish soup as her Parisian seducer, Leon (Melvyn Douglas), plies her with clichéd jokes.

I have already mentioned that Samoans are not big for soups, of any kind. They do not like pea soup or any of the blends, admixtures, or composites that came to them in cans across the water from New Zealand. I gather it is just too comparatively insubstantial for a people who much prefer pork, *palusami*, taro root, *pilikaki, pisupo* (corned beef), all of those fattening dishes usually served with chopped onions in coconut milk, wrapped in taro leaves, then tin foil, and put into the *umu* for three or four hours—even whole pigs on special occasions. But aren't we told in Hebrews 5 13:14 that "solid food is for the mature" which pejoratively implies that milk, soup, liquids are for infants and amateurs and beginners and sucklings?

At "Firefly," his estate in Jamaica, Noël Coward loved to make iced soup (!) for his guests. By all accounts he was awful in the kitchen. "Oh my God, yes! We had a great time in Jamaica, but when he bought a house in Bermuda, there was a problem of domestic staff. You certainly couldn't get a cook, and he said, 'Oh, that's no problem at all, I'll do the cooking!'" explained Graham Payn at a memorial dinner for Coward at USC. Payn, the South African-born English actor and singer who was the life-partner of the playwright, went on to say,

Oh, God! His idea of cooking was to get every spice and every herb possible and throw it into whatever it was he was mixing up. Oh, it was a terrible time we went through! But he loved it. It was very hot, as you know, in Bermuda in the summer and when he was in the kitchen, he didn't wear any clothes at all, virtually nothing, except a little apron a plastic thing here in front was all. And one day he was busy in there and there was a knock on the kitchen door and he went and answered it and it was the vicar. And he said, "Oh! hello. Oh, how nice to see you. Do come in, do come in, but please, wait one minute. I'm about to see what's in the oven!" He went around, turned over. "Oh drat! Oh, it's all right. It's perfectly well, thank you. He's gone!" Frightened the hell out of the vicar. I hear he was a nice chap but we never saw him again. But also, he was a great speed merchant, you know. He drove his cars very fast and he bought a speedboat and this he loved. He used to zoom across the sound to Hamilton, go to the supermarket, buy more herbs and spices to come back and zoom back to make another awful dish for us to eat.

The mysterious death of Basil King, Canadian-born clergyman and novelist who died in Cambridge, Massachusetts, was due, or so some experts believe, to rat poison in the food he had been ingesting, giving rise to the once-familiar term "King's Soup," a phrase used for years to describe something poisonous or harmful. It was King who wrote the novel, *The Street Called Straight* (1912), a book with a beguilingly mysterious title—enough to intrigue me in junior high school—and which involved the loves of aristocratic and fetching but prideful Olivia Guion, a girl with a sculpted pretty face and chocolate-box prettiness, on whom in the process of writing a 9th-grade book report I developed a mad crush. ("St. Luke is careful not to commit himself," wittily wrote Mark Twain in *Innocents Abroad* of the famous ancient street in Damascus with which King's novel has nothing remotely to do. "He does not say it is the street which is straight, but 'the street which is called Straight.' It is the only facetious remark in the Bible.")

As to strange soup, on the day on which, notoriously, Andrew and Abby Borden were hatcheted to death in Fall River, Massachusetts, on August 4, 1892, the family ate one of the worst breakfasts imaginable—a three-day-old mutton soup with potatoes and cold leftover boiled mutton with johnny-cakes, bread, coffee, and cookies. Lizzie herself never—ever—ate breakfast, but they had all been eating roast mutton leftovers all week.

Bridget Sullivan, the maid, became ill in the backyard. The Borden family doctor, Dr. Bowen, blamed food left on the stove for use in meals over several days, but Abby had feared poisoning—Andrew Borden had not been a popular man. For several days before the murders, the entire household had been violently ill, excluding Lizzie who went on trial as the perpetrator of the crimes in a case that became a *cause célèbre* throughout the United States. It was a suffocatingly hot day. Had 32-year-old Lizzie Borden become discombobulated by the soup? Had that vile food played into the murders? Was slaying Mom and Dad the consequence of *agita*?

In history, soup, as we know it today, is a fairly recent innovation in the story of high cuisine. "*Le soupe* of old France—still a tasty if crude dish to linger over in the peasant backwaters of the provinces—was a meal in itself, with the meats and vegetables used in its preparation all thrown together and eaten at once," wrote Bernard Frizell in "Escoffier: God of the Gastronomes" (*Horizon*, May 1961). It took Georges Auguste Escoffier to refine soup as a kind of announcement to set the tone—provide the foundation—of the dinner. In his mind, the chef considered soup, not only as preliminary to a dinner, but an introduction, a prelude, that sets the theme of what is to come. He wrote, "After the manner of an overture in a light opera, soup should divulge what is to be the dominant phase of the melody throughout."

There have been some muscular enemies of soup, even the very idea of it. Sir Henry Marsh, Queen Victoria's physician, back in April, 1847, authored a ten-page pamphlet that was widely circulated animadverting against the notion of anyone, especially hard workers, relying on its value. He wrote,

> Our attention must not be too exclusively directed to soups and other semi-liquid articles of food. These pass away too rapidly from the stomach, are swallowed too hastily, and violate a natural law in superseding the necessity of mastication, and a proper admixture with the salivary secretion. Restricted to such food the carnivora cannot maintain life; nor can man, being half carniverous, if laboriously employed, long preserve health and strength of food of such characater...Food to be at once sustaining to the labourer, and preventive of disease, must have bulk—must possess solidity—must not be rapidly digestible, and must contain,

in varied proportions, all the staminal ingredients of
nutriment.

Soup can seem baleful and dull. Elsie de Wolfe, the formidable Lady
Mendl, among other things, nominal author of the book, *The House in
Good Taste* (1913), taught Ms.Wallis Simpson many things to suit British
requirements, such as how to speak more softly, by depending more on her
Southern (well, Baltimore) accent, to dress simply in order to accentuate the
angular lines of her strangely, almost incorporeally thin figure, to tone down
her personality, and, when entertaining, how to present her meals, and one
of her caveats was explicitly forbidding soup—her motto was, "Never build a
meal on a lake." There are of course soups more delicious than drinking lake-
water. How about a hot minestrone soup; Gulaschsuppe; Vietnamese *pho*; a
bowl of homemade tortellini; Korean Yukgaejung (spicy beef and vegetable);
old-fashioned chicken noodle soup? Poet Marianne Moore, when asked by
Harper's Bazaar (July 19, 1963) what foods she disliked, immediately answered, "Cold soup—vichysoisse or bean." What would she have thought of
rancid meat in soup, which is the very thing that caused the sailors to mutiny
on the Battleship Potemkin?

Many eaters distrust soup. It carries mysterious ingredients, orts and
sorts. There is a catalogue—a whole inventoiry—of cavils, quibbles, grous-
es, and grievances about soup. It smokes, it fogs up your glasses. Soup is a
fraud—is it even *food*? You cannot *eat* soup, therefore it is not even a meal. It
is a drink, face it. It is wet, too wet, wet through to the bottom. Old ladies,
spinsters, "auntie" types—the sort of old maids that Huck Finn and Tom
Sawyer fled—always serve it in tureens. It is lumpy and contains mysterious
quidnuncs. There is never a perfect temperature to soup; it is either too hot
or lukewarm like plap, and some misguided people even eat it cold. (The very
idea of cold soup is revolting.) There is, what, maybe a two-minute window
where a person can take actual mouthfuls of the stuff at an adequate temperature and still recognize what it is. You cannot take anything like a substantial,
satisfying "bite" of soup. You cannot chew it. It is always, only, eaten with
spoons, of the three the dumbest utensil. A person never knows which way
to row through soup in order to pick it up, forward or backward. It is never
ordered in a restaurant but something women concoct at home or slurp-slide
out of a small can and then ladle it with sloshing sounds into bowls where
it appears unrecognizably corduroy brown, gunmetal gray, gangrene, dog
jaundice yellow, ashen, or the famous beige color of the Macintosh computer.

I spent much my toddler life wondering why Shirley Temple sang
"Animal Crackers in My Soup"—making soup *un*attractive to me—when I

knew perfectly well that animal crackers more properly went into milk! Cold milk! Winston Churchill did not like creamed soups but preferred consommés; when served the former once on a visit to the United States he asked if they could not find some Bovril for him instead. (I wonder if he liked chicken soup. "The PM doesn't like his chicken 'messed about,'" complained his doctor, Lord Moran, when he was once offered it cut into bits and smothered in sauces.) I have never met a single Korean who disliked soup. Do you happen to recall what all the dwarves in Walt Disney's *Snow White and the Seven Dwarfs*—hungry little fellows, always ready to eat—literally scream for in that movie? "*Sooouup!*" No bigger endorsement for soup can be found than Lewis Carroll's poem, "Beautiful Soup," where his preference for it exceeds that for fish or meat:

> Beautiful Soup! Who cares for fish,
> Game, or any other dish?
> Who would not give all else for two
> Pennyworth only of Beautiful Soup?
> Pennyworth only of beautiful Soup?

But how many times do you come across characters slurping up soup in Honoré de Balzac's novels before you want to retch? French novels—Zola, Hugo, Verne, De Maupassant—are full of such soup guzzlers! German cherry soup, a dish of crushed cherries and ground-up pits, ferociously spiced, drowned in wine, and served cold, was singled out as being particularly hateful by Alexandre Dumas *père*, a hearty eater, author of *Count of Monte Cristo*, in his *Dictionary of Cuisine*. Actress Sarah Bernhardt when young was sent by her mother to Grandchamp, an Augustinian convent school near Versailles, and in her peculiar memoir, *My Double Life* (1907), much of it an anti-Christian polemic—she was widely known for her casual lies and facile exaggerations and extravagant personal claims—she complained constantly about victimhood and the bad soup that was forced on her to eat. I remember several cold nights in lonely bed-and-breakfast places up in rural Scotland being served bowls of thin soup—it went under the dubious name, I well remember, of Cullen skink—that seemed to have been dyed a lurid yellow. Dishwater! *La lavasse!* As "Tonight Show" host Jay Leno puts it, "Soup is just a way of screwing you out of a meal."

24.

WE INHABIT THE UNIVERSE OF MOM

Mothers: notice how frequently in these pages they figure, and in the matter of food, often how negatively. There is no small significance, regarding our mothers, to whatever we end up thinking or doing about *anything,* never mind one's food aversions or food obsessions. They are more often than not steadfast and unwavering. Only read Erik Erickson or Jean Piaget, however, on the many and various ways a mother can wrong-foot a child, even up to and into the twenties, and how crucially it can signify in later life. At the age of 18, the poet Harold Crane went so far as to change his Christian name to Hart simply because he could not bear to hear in echo the shrill "*Haaaarooold!*" that his mother employed all through his childhood calling him in from play. "Control of food across history and culture has often been a key source of power for women," state Carole Counihan and Penny Van Esterick in *Food and Culture: A Reader*, explaining how a woman's, a mother's, ability to prepare and serve food gives them direct influence over others, both material and magical." Food is a medium not only for gender definitions but is also linked to overall social hierarchies and power relations. I do not mean to suggest or even imply, obviously, that every food that disgusts us or that every memory attendant on that food reverts directly or symbolically to one's mother or to some be-mustachioed harridan or scold in an apron forcing us with a rolling-pin to sit at the table and, at the risk of death, eat our beets or finish our lumpy oatmeal or empty that bowl of peas. Nevertheless, there is no question that Dear Ol' Mom, under whatever conditions, is beyond any other consideration the "first and formal cause" of our food consumption or food fixations. Let's face it, half the time whatever we are eating we are tripping down mammary lane. To quote the signature lines of the late Jill Johnston's classic, *Lesbian Nation*, "On a clear day you can see your mother."

Mothers are, unquestionably, the First Cause in just about everything for a child as he or she is growing up. In his *Principles of Psychology*, William James perceptively wrote, "The first time we see light, we are it rather than see it. But all our later knowledge is about what this experience gives: the first sensation an infant gets, is for him the universe." James is perceptive in the experience mother's impart. It is nevertheless a benevolence not universally acknowledged, at least in terms of charity. Philip Wylie wrotes in *A Generation of Vipers*,

> Mom, however, is a great little guy. Pulling pants onto her by these words, let us look at mom. She is a middle-aged puffin with an eye like a hawk that has just seen a rabbit twitch far below. She is about twenty-five pounds overweight, with no sprint, but sharp heels and a hard back-hand which she does not regard as a foul but a womanly defense. In a thousand of her there is not sex appeal enough to budge a hermit ten paces off a rock ledge. She none the less spends several hundred dollars a year on permanents and transformations, pomades, cleansers, rouges, lipsticks, and the like—and fools nobody except herself. If a man kisses her with any earnestness, it is time for mom to feel for her pocketbook, and this occasionally does happen.

John Thorne, the best food writer in America, once told me, "An interviewer once asked me why a man would write about cooking. This answer popped unbidden from my subconscious: to tell his mother something."

You can always depend on mama's boys to have a strange, needy, always complicatedly intense relationship to just about everything, and among primary considerations is surely the subject of food. Smothering mothers, whether in the form of indulgent babas or bossy, fire-breathing matriarchal dragons—both variations commonly intertangle—have bequeathed the world some of its most convoluted, thorny, intricate, and tortured human beings: Adolf Hitler, Sigmund Freud, Ernest Hemingway, Harry Houdini, Maurice Utrillo, Liberace, Frank Sinatra, Elvis Presley, Norman Mailer, English comic actor and comedian Kenneth Williams, D-actor George Hamilton—who even admitted to having an affair with his stepmother, June Howard, when he was 12, shortly after she married his father—Woodrow Wilson, Noël Coward, Edgar A. Guest, Alexander Woollcott, Clifton Webb ("Cliftuary, Mabelle's ruined your life," the singer Libby Holman once told him of the woman who called him "little Webb" as an adult and whom he claimed had abused him as a child. "Why don't you chloroform the old cunt?"), Andrew Carnegie (who promised never to marry as long as his mother lived and kept his word), William Randolph Hearst, J. Edgar Hoover, FDR, General Douglas MacArthur, actor Peter Sellers, and, what the hell, why not throw in Arthur "Cody" Jarrett (James Cagney) in the movie, *White Heat*, scramble-brained Norman Bates, the beleaguered Bates Motel-keeper, and the Simpson's cartoon principal, Seymour Skinner?

Fastidiousness and persnickety both food-wise and in many other aspects of his profession, J. Edgar Hoover who lived with his mother until she died—he was 43 and would never marry—was, according to his niece, Margaret, "quite a tyrant about food."

Arguably, he had a deeply repressed sexual life, cohabiting with Mom until he was 40. His neuroses were likely rooted in childhood: He was ashamed of his mentally-ill father and was dependent on his morally righteous mother, Annie, of Swiss-German heritage, well into middle age. Until her death in 1938, he had no social life outside the office.

Hoover suffered from all sorts of phobias. He was a compulsive hand-washer, with a truly morbid fear of germs. "His home was equipped with an air-filtration system, which to his mind, allegedly 'electrocuted' poisonous particles, and he could become almost dementedly angry on seeing an unswatted fly." Superstitious, intense, he would insist that agents never step on his shadow. Cuckoo Hill!

J. Robert Oppenheimer, the neurotic theoretical physicist and "father of the atomic bomb," was an extremely emaciated neurotic with ravaged teeth—at six feet tall, he never weighed more than 130 pounds—had a pathological horror of the world and looked upon himself with revulsion. His powerful mother, Ella, whose formal, elegant demeanor struck many people as cold, ruled her son and cosseted him from birth with a

drive and discipline that was excessive. She suffered a congenitally unformed left hand, a deformity she was driven to hide by wearing long sleeves and a pair of chamois gloves. The glove covering her left hand contained a primitive prosthetic device with a spring attached to an artificial thumb. She passed on no end of semi-psychotic crotchets and neuroses to her son. In her case it was by means of the soft force of suasion rather than brute rule. Overly protective, she kept Robert apart from other children and, fearing germs and certain foods, strictly prohibited him buying food from street-vendors and instead of taking him to get a haircut in a barber shop ordered a barber come to the apartment to perform the task. To one of them, his high school English teacher, he once confessed, "I'm the loneliest man in the world."

A punitive rather than protective role is invariably more identifiable as a mother's position regarding food. In his cookbook, *Pickles, Pigs & Whiskey,* John Currence refers to a hearty soup that his mother made which he calls "my purgatory on Earth—I love to hate it, and I hate to love it." His term for it is "Punish Stew," the standard popular combination of meat, vegetables and potatoes, all of the ingredients of which in his critical, little mind, however, should never be served any other way but separately and never mixed up. It is the old story culled from the life of almost every person looking back ruefully to a childhood involving a food he hated. To Currence, soup was simply not dinner. "To me, soup was an appetizer," he confesses. "A meal comes on a plate!" His insistent mother, however, had other ideas. "One of her go-to recipes that my dad and my brother just loved and loved and loved over was this pot of beef stew." In his recollection it seemed as if every week, he would find this same stew waiting for him on the table, and every week he would became more and more adamant about refusing to eat it. The conflict led to a memorable confrontation.

Currence grew up in New Orleans, and his family had invited friends to dinner one February for a Mardi Gras celebration. What was served to them all—such is the way life goes—was of course the dreaded stew. Given the autocracy of mothers, permit me, I detect as much a bit of malice in the maneuver as an act of strategy. He wistfully recalls, "The little [feisty General Douglas] MacArthur that I was, I saw this as a battle and a place to really make a statement and fight the ultimate battle with my mom." Typically, hours passed, and the bowl remained untouched. Young John went to bed without dinner that night, but when he awoke the next morning, the stew was still waiting for him. Currence says his mother disputes what happened next, but he swears it is the truth: "She made me eat that cold soup for breakfast."

Is that small child a thankless monster, an untamed contrarian, a howling and ungrateful little mannerbereft who for whatever reason turns up his bowl or refuses to eat whatever an adult sticks in front of him? There is no question that any hectoring parent who tyrannizes a questioning youngster about food abuses him. A bowling pin needs only a tilt of 7.5 degrees in order to fall down. In *First Bite,* Bee Wilson draws what I consider a significant conclusion in the matter, noting,

> Genes do make a difference—to the foods we like, the way we taste them, and even how much we enjoy eating—but they turn out to be are much less significant than the environment in which we learn to eat those

foods. Contrary to our deepest beliefs about ourselves and our children, our likes and dislikes… are much more about nurture than nature.

Force, typically, refutes refusal. "There were seven children in my family, and the youngest kids—I was one of them—were not allowed to eat dinner with the adults and oldest children," Stephen Dixon told me. "We had to eat in the kitchen with the housekeeper. I wouldn't eat the mashed potatoes because they had lumps in them. She sat beside me holding a spatula and threatened to hit my hand with it unless I ate them. I refused because I thought I'd choke on them. Threats followed, and I was sent to my room." (Dictator Benito Mussolini claimed mashed potatoes gave him a headache and refused to eat them, as well. Although tempted by veal, he also hated meat in general.)

So no one would contest the influencing—and often balefully pressureful—power of a mother's force. It echoes through one's being and can last a lifetime. English author T.H. White at age 20 wrote,

> Contemporary photographs show a fat little boy in an Eton suit too tight for him, with rather thick lips. It was taken to send to my [domineering and sexually frigid] mother in India, and she wrote back that my lips were growing sensual. I was told to hold them in, with my teeth if necessary. Since then I have been ashamed of my lips and now wear them concealed by mustache and beard.

We inhabit the Universe of Mom. Her power is unrivaled. What she says, goes. She is a combination of virago, Vercingetorix, and Vesta, the goddess who disturbs. No, I believe a good many neuroses in kids are the result of matrogymnastic contrivance. "I hated oatmeal as a child," complained Martha Stewart, that modern doyenne of the hearth. She explains,

> We had six kids in the family, and oatmeal was one of the least expensive cereals to serve us. My parents served a lot of oatmeal, and always on oatmeal day we were required to eat cereal. So I would sit there, and my Mom would say, 'Sit there until you finish it.' And that was not a very pleasant experience.

The writer Upton Sinclair, whose martinet of a mother he felt badly damaged him for life with her many insistent food rules, grew up under circumstances even worse, at least so he ruefully felt. We have already considered Kafka's "The Hunger Artist" and how in that strange story, thematically, at least under the guise of fable or allegory, the author takes the measurement of parental abuse and the need to get out from his own oppression, even if by singular means.

The play and later film, *Brighton Beach Memoirs* (1986), begins with Neil Simon having his main character, Eugene Jerome, record in his diary the utter revulsion he felt over the liver-and-cabbage meals that his Jewish mother, Kate, always served him, calling it "Jewish medieval torture," with insult added to injury when he has to go shopping for her twice a day at Greenblatt's grocery store for more of it, reveries almost as revolting as the fat, cynical Uncle Abe shuffling around the house in Woody Allen's film, *Radio Days*, carrying great walloping—whole!—fish under his arm, only more Jewish horror-food. It is an incontestable fact that, if there is a universal culprit in the food aversion department, forgive me, I would point to dear ol' mom, a badgering mom, a hectoring mom, a nagging, ass-kicking, bullying mom, a mom with all her pennants flying, forcing you to sit there at that table until you have finished what is put in front of you, a mom who was always chuntering on about how all of the starving children in China would love that food! As novelist Henry Miller wrote, "Whatever needs to be maintained through force is doomed." Unfortunately, in too many if not most cases it is not the food that is doomed but the victims forced to eat it.

To me, Jewish horror-food meets force in the yearly ritual of Kapparot, where certain Jewish groups needlessly, anachronistically, and cruelly sacrifice chickens for "human sin" in the days preceding Yom Kippur, the Jewish Day of Atonement. Chickens are brutally swung overhead while still alive, after which they are slaughtered according to the laws of *shechita*, when their prayer goes, "This is my exchange, this is my substitute, this is my atonement. This chicken will go to its death, while I will enter and proceed to a good long life and to peace."

"For someone who's grown up eating snails, snakes, eel, shark fin, live shrimp, and all manner of exotic ingredients from around the world, my bad food experience is a simple one," says Christina Kuypers, a mixologist, in *Toronto Life*. "I was three, playing in the garden, and my mother gave me a handful of cubed pear. I found the texture of soft, sandy fruit to be so unpalatable, that I hid the little pieces of gritty sponge in flowerbeds and behind bushes and pretended I'd gobbled them all up. It was the first time I lied to my mother, and the last time I ate pear. *Bleh*."

Playwright George Kaufman was a lifetime "finicky food picker," according to Howard Teichmann in *Smart Aleck*, and was mocked by his obese, 300-pound fellow Algonquin Table mate and trencherman, critic Alexander Woollcott, who virtually lived to pack away heavy, indigestion-inducing, butter-drenched, cream-heavy, Luchow-like meals of steaks, fried fish, and boiled lobsters, which were often followed by quadruple orders of rich, sugary desserts. His extravagant at-home, all-day Sunday breakfasts of fat sausages, omelettes, French toast saturated in maple syrup, sugary doughnuts, and exotic pancakes stuffed or slathered with jellies and jams, as well as side-treats of salmon and kippers, along with bottomless pots of coffee, drew many acquaintances and became his favorite form of entertaining.

Alexander Woollcott once confided to Thornton Wilder,

> My theory about George Kaufman's [scrimp] eating habits in restaurants is that the boys in Jewish homes have devoted mothers who see to it that all nutrition is bound up with love. The mothers are martyrs to these special sons of theirs. Any dish in any restaurant therefore may be wonderfully prepared, marvelously served, but it doesn't have the element of love. It must taste like a glass of sand served off a shovel. There's a neurotic connection—the food and the mother.

The lavish dinners served to George and his friends by Kaufman's wife, Beatrice, were "triumphs of Teutonic cookery," as Teichmann notes, so that in what has often become a standard transferal she replaced her husband's mother in the coddling/domineering/overbearing department and soon grew fat herself. "George regularly nagged her to diet. He did not dare, however, make such a suggestion to his boss. Eventually the carbohydrates conquered." I daresay that psychiatrists can have a field day with a remark that the fey, homosexual, unappeasable food-freak Woollcott once made to Anita Loos, "All my life I have wanted to be a mother."

I tend to suspect that a lot of his eating choices, pro and con—he savored the exotic and the outré but perversely abhorred many conventional items—of Ernest Hemingway, a first son, second child, had to do with his supposedly overbearing mother, Grace Hall-Hemingway. As an adult, Hemingway professed to hate his mother. Her dogged insistence that he learn to play the cello became a "source of conflict," but her famous son never forgave her for imposing her will on a husband who never stood up to her. When Hemingway was a little boy, she dressed him as a little girl. "I hate her guts," he wrote in middle age, "and she hates mine. She forced my father to suicide." When she died, the novelist did not attend her funeral.

I found it revealing that the late feminist Shulamith Firestone, an angry person in whom self-repudiation and rage commingled in equal parts, was found dead on August 28, 2012, at 67, in the fifth-floor apartment of her tenement walkup on East Tenth St. without so much as a morsel of food in the place. Had the Canadian-born radical actually starved to death, and if she had, was it intentional? (No autopsy was ever conducted in deference to the family's religion.) So much of her work, the notoriously polemical *The Dialectic of Sex* (1970), especially, much of it toy Marxism and sheer codswollop, was nevertheless an explicit and implicit, coded and uncoded animadversion—all carried over from youth—not only against her Jewish Orthodox parents whom she resented as a domineering father and cunning, pushy mother, but also an attack against vitality and indeed the notion of fecundity itself. "Pregnancy is barbaric," childbirth is "like shitting a pump-kin," childhood is "a supervised nightmare" and "should be state-support-ed," "The best way to raise a child is to LAY OFF!" "She envisioned a world in which women might be liberated by artificial reproduction outside the womb," noted Susan Faludi in an astute *New Yorker* profile of the troubled feminist who notes that the longest chapter of her book is titled "Down with Childhood." In a "Last Letter to Mother," written in 1977, Firestone, who was then suffering from schizophrenia and chaotically revolving in and out of mental hospitals repeatedly, in the end angrily repudiated that domineer-ing woman for good, coldly writing, "I can offer no pity for the maternal sufferings you (continue to) bring on yourself. I DISSOLVE MY TIES OF BLOOD." It is notable she expressed her final fury by refusing food.

"The best way to raise a child is to LAY OFF!" In her fury, Shulamith Firestone recapitulates with her truism one of the caveats of Charles Fourier, a nagged and bedeviled counterpart of hers in having been abused by dom-ineering parents. Mothers acting professionally lorded it over them to their grief. Who is surprised that in her extremism Firestone became such a gender maniac or that Fourier is credited with having originated the word *feminism* in 1837? They were rioting within, probably from the very first sucks from the breasts.

Breaking free has much to do with food and its manipulations. Taste in a very real way is indeed selfdom, selfhood, selfness. An old Ugandan proverb goes, "If your mother is not there, your bowels ache while eating." It means not only that the presence of one's mother sweetens the food—something of a hamster wheel seems in play here—but that her absence both instills guilt in the experience and in an extreme sense invalidates the whole concept of eating as an existential act.

Anaïs Nin, diarist and author of erotic literature, falls into the category of food aversionist. In the 35,000 pages of the 150 volumes of her diary, which spans more than 60 years and from which she selectively harvested various of her novels and short stories—her life made a book—there is a glaring and darkly noteworthy omission of the subject of food. "No kitchen tastes or smells permeate her diaries or her fiction," notes Noël Riley Fitch in her biography, *The Erotic Life of Anais Nin*. "Two exceptions are burned food: the memory of a burned omelet made by her father [a cruel man who seduced the child, photographed her naked, and deserted the family when she was only ten] when her mother was in the hospital giving birth to Joaquinito, and, two, the memory of her own burning of a pan of noodles while she was busy reading." Fitch points out that Elisabeth Barillé, a French poet-novelist and Freudian critic, suggests Nin's was a case of anorexia nervosa, an unconscious fear of physical and sexual maturation, stating, "Only in the guise of a thin, girlish soubrette could Anaïs retain the slender form of the nude child whom daddy loved to photograph." Barillé goes on to analyse Nin's condition by observing that in her fiction "her characters never eat" and that the only smells in her creative work "come from night clubs, from bedrooms, [but] never from kitchens." Fitch concludes of Nin, "Her lack of interest in food and food preparation is also a rejection of her mother and her mother's nurturing role."

Gore Vidal who had an affair with Anaïs Nin in the mid 1940s (his love letters make for comic reading) later went on to write several malicious parodies of her in at least five of his novels, always unkindly stressing her narcissism and mocking her vainglorious attention to her body—he notoriously said "she gave self-love a bad name." He exuberantly skewered her in his memoir *Palimpsest*, because, as he insisted, she had lied about him repeatedly. Vidal had his own mother problems. He concurred with his grandmother who said of her own daughter that when Nina walked in a room, "it was like an evil spirit arriving." After a bitter divorce, she married Hugh D. Auchincloss who also divorced her and went on to marry Janet Bouvier, mother of Jackie Kennedy. "The thing is, she was just atrocious. Everybody who knew her hated her," The acidly observant Vidal explained to Robert Chalmers in *The New Review* (May 25, 2008). "You know what the problem was? It was racial. And I'll give you the race: Anglo-Irish. They are more vicious than most. She was a shit." He paused. "A drunken shit." Chalmers advanced, "It must be awkward, then, to contemplate the fact that, genetically, you are half her. Is there anything in your character that you recognize as inherited?" Vidal replied, "No. If I did, I would take an emetic."

An anecdote that makes the same point about the power of food and mothers refers to the sentimental and mother-loving, almost Oedipally fixated L.B. Mayer, the powerful MGM mogul who, watching the rushes of one of the early Andy Hardy movies, exploded in anger, horrified to see a distracted young Andy brusquely refuse his mother's cooking at dinner. "Did you ever throw your own mother's food back at her?" indignantly asked Mayer of the bewildered producer, Carey Wilson. "Did you ever tell her 'Take this junk away'? What kind of unnatural son would do that to his mother?" Mayer was virtually gibbering in fury. The entire scene was re-shot so that Andy was apologetic about his lack of appetite, according to Scott Eyman in *Lion of Hollywood: The Life and Legend of Louis B. Mayer.*

Could it possibly be that one's food aversions, by way of delayed revelation, are a resounding no to breast-feeding? "*Take that, Ma!*" The poet W. H. Auden, among notable others, held the rather uncommon theory that a person's particular ailments are often a subconscious manifestation of his own faults or vices and to a degree indicate his karma. A deformed person, for example, faces a struggle between instinct and will. Boils erupt when one is thwarted in love and the frustration is exuded in the form of pus. Cancer? A frustration of the creative urge. Constipation he put down to envy, and diabetes to the "sweets of sin." Biting one's tongue corrects the instrument of utterance by way of pre-emptive remorse. An exophthalmic person lives with the caveat not to snoop or ogle. (I think of pop-eyed John Keats goggling the Grecian urn!) Bad breath is emitted to keep others at a distance, a subconscious desire in a person to try to withdraw from society and to keep people at a far distance. A compulsive sneer is an act of warding off. If a person has rheumatism or is arthritic, Auden judged them to be stubborn or intractable. That sort of thing. The poet went so far as to suggest that tall people are all involved in some sort of attempt to reach up to heaven.

I myself have a distinct crease in my left-hand palm, a minor case of what is known as DuPuytren's Contracture—it has also been romantically called "Viking disease" or sometimes "Celtic hand." Does this mean I am therefore grabby or a thief? When told that Sigmund Freud had died of cancer of the jaw, Auden exclaimed, "Who would have thought he was a liar?" (Freud actually committed suicide, a fact that is often suppressed to make this overrated ikon look less cowardly—he took a fatal dose of morphine administered by a doctor at his request.) I suppose it could be worse. Nathaniel Benchley gloomily once remarked of Robert C. Benchley, "My father had a theory that everyone tends to become the type of person he hates most."

The Nietzschean idea in *The Gay Science* is that for a man or woman to love, he or she must "kill" God—must overcome dogma, habit, conformity, superstition, anxiety and fear. A necessary first stop is to fight family, church, school and not submit to rules and laws. Custom kills us. I can see no reason why Mom and her spatula, and saucy threats need be excluded from the list.

It all sounds deeply pessimistic, these remarks, no? Nietzsche, Benchley, Auden. Depressing. But, tell me, are you surprised? Ours is a fallen world. It is not lost on me that the three biggest country hits *of all time*—far and away the most valuable copyrights in all of country music—are the classics, "You Are My Sunshine, (1939), "Born to Lose" (1943), and "The Tennessee Waltz (1948). Every one of them is on the subject of lost dismal, disconsolate, heart-cracking love.

I believe that a case can be made, finally, that many thin or raddled people were often raised by mothers who trained rather than nurtured them, women who, more than resented, were hated. Such a figure may very well serve as a kind of ectomorphic sub-text, a soma-type of narrow, disobliging spirit with a touchy nervous system built from—shaped out of—rancor, acrimony, indignation, bad feelings, dissatisfaction, bitterness, irritation, pique, disgruntlement, animosity. I suggest thinness may be to a degree a harbinger of danger. No one would deny the prescience of the memorable lines in Julius Caesar, "Let me have men about me that are fat. Sleek-headed men and such as sleep a-nights. Yon Cassius has a lean and hungry look. He thinks too much. Such men are dangerous." Are the thin then thin-skinned? Johnny Carson, slim all of his life, hated his mother. Lucian Freud, the English painter, cut his mother out of his life ruthlessly and told his biographer, that he couldn't stand being near her. The eccentric poet Marianne Moore, chicken-scrawny and pale, who in the course of her long life was never known to fall in love, have an affair, or contemplate marriage, was almost pathologically mother-bound—the two of them actually slept in the same bed.

I have always thought her poetry was at best perplexing and that she was just an amiable crackpot, what the late scientist Carl Sagan referred to in another context as a "Fissured Ceramic." Marianne Moore never met or knew her father, a self-absolved but sincere religious fanatic. Her domineering mother, a lesbian, full of advice and finger-pointing directives, thought of her daughter as a son and often referred to her as "he." Suppressed, overruled, but compliant, Moore never traveled without her mother and lived with her for 60 years until that woman's death. Moore was a tiny, sharp, prickly, puckish, sometimes quarrelsome little bird and at best was almost always scarily close to being anorectic. At one point she weighed as little as 75 pounds. On one Thanksgiving dinner, she and her mother had leftover sardines. "What better food than apple seeds—the fruit within the fruit...?" she wrote in "Nevertheless."

There is a long list of slight, attenuated, insubstantial, and watery victims of cold, aloof, disapproving mothers: Nancy Cunard, Stephen Sondheim, Maria Callas, Arturo Toscanini, John Osborne ("A year in which my mother died can't be all bad," he wrote in 1983). Ted Kaczynski, the "Unabomber," hated his mother, Wanda, an atheist intellectual with an ego whom he accused of failing to nurture him. The frail poet Emily Dickinson, a rebellious creature who to a degree resented being female and severely tried to be unlike her mother by defying her father, wrote in 1874, "I never had a mother. I suppose a mother is one to whom you hurry when you are troubled. I always ran home to Awe [Austin, her brother] when a child, if anything befell me. He was an awful mother, but I liked him better then none."

It may be that a given food aversionist finds in rejecting a particular food a "break-out" of sorts, the need for self-assertion, a response to what Philip Wylie in that excoriating book of his we have already cited, *A Generation of Vipers*, referred to as "Momism." Might one say they fear "re-engulfment" and see there in their mothers' domination a kind of shackle that imprisons one? A point for that argument is that a food aversion is invariably an arbitrary or skewed one and the flat refusal of a selected particular food more often than not a tiny, fastidious, often very minor culinary demand—which is to say that the rejection speaks to some deep, subjective event playing out in the victim's mind, one that possibly reverts to some lost, hidden, secret-bonneted moment in one's early childhood.

We learn in Robert Bloch's novel, *Psycho,* that after the death of her husband John, Norma Bates raises her son, Norman—quoting her own name for him is eerie enough—with cruelty: she forbids the boy to have a life away from her and teaches him that sex is evil and that all women (except herself) are whores. The book also suggests that their relationship may have incestuous.

A food fear, like love—at least the love Ann Sheridan sings of in *Thank Your Lucky Stars*—is not born, but made. The vast and terrible reach of a mother's raw power, her sway on youth, in almost every significant way, was made in an especially vivid way in March of 1940 during a performance of Clemence Dane's play, *Cousin Muriel,* at the Globe Theatre in London, where Edith Evans was playing the title role and a young Alec Guinness her son. Cousin Muriel is a liar, a thief, and a cheat, and there is one scene called for where the son rebukes his mother for her crimes. On that evening, during the performance, Evans was so taken aback by the unparalleled venom and vituperation with which Guinness delivered his remorseless lines that, according to biographer Piers Paul Read in his biography, *Alec Guinness*, "she flung her arms in the air, screamed, 'Alec doesn't love me anymore! He doesn't love me! He hates me!' then fell onto the stage, kicked her feet, and began to chew the corner of a Persian rug." What the reader knows only too well at this point from reading Read's book is what a dread presence his mother was in the actor's life while he was growing up and indeed long after, beginning with the opening words of the book, when the biographer quotes Guinness as saying, "My mother was a whore." No early impression is too small to record, and one carries it through life.

Mary Jenkins who cooked for Elvis Presley at Graceland for many years often repeated that he liked banana pudding and that the recipe she used was exactly as his mother always made it. He often ate the same thing at every meal for several days, invariably food that Mama Gladys had made him when he was a boy. Decadent, shallow Hugh Hefner's favorite meal, according to reports, is still one his mother made, according to the chef William S. Bloxsom-Carter who has been catering for him and his parties for more than 25 years, serving about 100,000 guests annually. "He likes his mother's fried chicken with mashed potatoes. He's a Midwestern gentleman, so he enjoys those kinds of foods. He has two piles of mashed potatoes with a poached egg placed in each one. Pretty wild stuff but it's OK." I have read elsewhere that for his lunch Hefner sits in his plush bedroom, always alone, spooning up a bowl of Lipton's chicken-noodle soup, which he compulsively eats almost every day. One of Hefner's favorite hurt-dog stories, retailed over the years, as if he were Charles Dickens, is that his parents throughout his life rarely if ever hugged him. Did they create a compulsive food aversionist and disoriented crank? Chris Jones writes in *Esquire* (April 2013),

> There are very few things he will eat, most of them the same meals his mother made for him when he was a boy. Lately he has been calling down for the number 6 [on the *Playboy* Mansion menu]: "A BLT," he says. "With chips, milk, applesauce. And a blond." In the kitchen, there are photographs of each of his trays so that they can be replicated exactly each time out. The chips on the side are carefully selected by the chefs fully formed and unbroken. (If Hefner has crackers with his soup, they must all be uniformly white and sharp-cornered.) Today's blond is similarly flawless, twenty-six-year old Crystal Harris, a former Playmate

who, only a few weeks ago, on New Year's Eve, became the third Mrs. Hefner.

It is staggering to find that of all the gourmetish possibilities available
to the lord of that vast, empty-souled, hypersybaritic *Playboy* empire, the
sad founder's favorite dishes are still, wussishly, plain "mommy food." Who
knows, maybe even a bib and high-chair is involved. Memory is re-enacted
desire. There is no better proof of that than Hefner and his food. Baked
rice-pudding stirred on the stovetop, thick soups, mashed this and that,
milky bowls of comfort all warmed the cockles of Hefner's infantilized heart
and in his memory bank—what scientists call "images of desire"—had him
seek to acquire it over and over. Hefner's well-known if embarrassing breast
fetish is harmless enough. It is his balloon-headed delusions that bother me,
opinions, attitudes, pronouncements that only an over-cosseted and smug
ass-hat could hold. I mean, what else would one expect from a person who
once seriously declared, "I think the essence of Judaic/Christian teaching is
very similar to *Playboy*"? Hefner boasts of having been "involved with maybe
eleven out of twelve months' worth of Playmates during the late 1960s and
1970s, [of having] had affairs with twins—at times he was dating up to seven
girls at once—and he even admits to have "experimented with bisexuality."

He uniquely, conveniently, divides up his commitments to "Spouses"
and "Partners." In his eighties, he was commonly dating 20-year-olds, and
on December 31, 2012, at 86, he got married to Crystal Harris who was 26
years old. The idea that Hefner considers himself a trailblazing sexologist or
social reformer, never mind a cultural sage, teacher, or philosopher, is truly
comical.

The *Playboy* Forum? What a joke.

The *Playboy* Advisor? Puh-leazzze!

Elias Canetti points to a mother's "appetite for dominion," writing,
"Her passion is to give food, to watch the children eating and profiting by
the food it eats...Her behavior appears selfless...but what has really happened is that she now has two stomachs instead of one, and keeps control of
both...The mother's power over a young child is absolute."

An unsavory fact to disclose is that it is always mothers whom the greedy
industry focus groups of major corporations—Kraft, General Mills, Nabisco,
Proctor & Gamble, Coca-Cola, and Mars, to name the leading ones—see
as the most responsible person in each and every family for buying food,
for preparing breakfast, for providing lunch and dinner for everybody.
Companies have marketers and researchers who are "experts on cravings."
"Cohort studies" are developed with Mom in mind. (Nachos is officially the

single food most craved by pregnant women in the United States of America, according to statistics.) It does not matter that every other kid in this country is stuffing his face with salt, sugar, and fat and becoming as fat as a bread truck. The trick is to use the knight-move of mother-to-kid as a ploy to seduce both, and by way of pop design and advertising deceit, selling guile as a way of fobbing off such delightful child-friendly-spelled lunchables—ad writers get paid for such "creative writing"—as go-packs, fun mealz, lunch-kits, snak-paks to get as many kids as possible hooked on packaged and processed foods that are convenient and inexpensive. Farm fresh foods? Forget new peas or just-picked corn, never mind a *poulet fermier* or *pate de champagne* or a country flan! No smart Fauchon's for them nor elegant patisserie with its own-brand products, cakes and pastry, breads, and confectionary.

Add to that the pointless indolence of American kids sitting around for months doing nothing on ludicrously long summer vacations, with inane school boards still fecklessly following that 19th-century idea of students needing to be off a third of a year in order to help work fields and farms. The little goofballs are home finger-boarding away their afternoons on video games and mumping by the fistful Cow Tales, Ring Pops, Sour Watermelon Slices, Atomic Fireballs, Milk Duds, Skittles, Oh Henrys, Jolly Ranchers, and Butterscotch Discs!

Obesity in America is out of control. Nine million children and teenagers between 6 to 19 are badly overweight. Sixty million citizens or more, 20 years and older, are morbidly obese. One in three adults is also obese. Obesity rates have more than doubled in adults and children since the 1970s. Obesity-related conditions include heart disease, stroke, type 2 diabetes and certain types of cancer. As many as 24 million people in the United States are afflicted with diabetes. It is nothing less than a national epidemic. There is no responsibility, no guilt, no contrition, no codes. It is not merely that all of these corporations are diabolical, because covert; the mothers are blind, as well. We see the world as much through our sloth as through our senses and believe in what they mediate to us. Ludwig Wittgenstein was correct. The search is neither for a duck nor a rabbit, but for a curious hybrid that looks like nothing but itself. As the German savant wrote in his *Philosophical Investigations*, "We find certain things about seeing puzzling because we do not find the whole business of seeing puzzling enough."

It is common knowledge that the most iconic symbol of Prohibition was an angry, stern, intemperate, maniacal bulldog-faced giantess named Carrie A. Nation who was notorious for attacking saloons armed only with a hatchet and her unswerving belief (loony conviction?) that she was striking out at what Jesus "doesn't like" (*ipsissima verba*). Was her bellicosity based on the fact that Jesus was a fighter, as least according to Joshua 5:13–16 and Zechariah 14 3–5? Carrie was, at six feet tall and a hefty 180 pounds, no small hurricane, rather a censorious, moralistic, bustling busybody with a "wowser" ethos born of a lifetime of pain, divorce, abuse, rejection, and drunken husbands. Apparently whenever she saw anyone pissed out of his box, she went bonkers, I mean into a gibbering Caligula-like rage. Yet it was Nation's mentally ill mother who first experienced delusions and believed long and actively that she was Queen Victoria. Nation may never have thought she was a member of the royal family, but she did believe that her name was an assignment from God and that it was appropriate to attack people and property in the name of temperance with her chosen weapon. This God-haunted giantess confidently and somewhat exotically described herself in fact as "a bulldog running along at the feet of Jesus, barking at what He doesn't like" and claimed "a divine ordination to promote temperance by destroying bars." She began, in a comparatively mild way, greeting bartenders with pointed remarks, such as, "Good morning, destroyer of men's souls." Soon thereafter, hearing voices, God's among them, she claimed, she graduated to throwing rocks—"smashers," she called them—through tavern windows. It is not news then that Nation opposed drinking—her first husband, a severe alcoholic, died from drink—and all "rum-soaked, whiskey-swilled, saturn-faced rummies." Carrie Nation quite happily applauded the assassination of President William McKinley in 1901 simply because she believed that he secretly drank alcohol and that drinkers in the end always got what they deserved.)

Carrie Nation did not confine her polemics or any of her grievances to one vice, however. She fulminated as well against smoking—cigarettes, cigars, and pipes—short skirts, foreign goods, fraternal orders, European foods, any fine or soft clothing, which was an indulgence, echoing no doubt the sentiments of Matthew 11: "But what did you go out to see? A man dressed in soft clothing? Those who wear soft clothing are in kings' palaces!" She had something of the stagy applause-freak in her, a crude need for public appearance. But she was worse than a hectoring fishwife. She was a classic xenophobe, doctrinaire, sectarian, and prejudiced. In 1905 she proudly brought out an autobiography called *The Use and Need of the Life of Carry* [sic] *A. Nation*—her only book—in which she devoted substantial space to debunking the false myth that wine is food, then one of the core essential principles of great European cuisine. As Austin Cline points out in "Carry Nation: On a Mission from God to Fight Alcohol" in Atheism.about.com, "The science behind her assertion is an almost medieval vision of two 'classes' of food: 'flesh formers' and 'body warmers,' a rhyming distinction that we find both creepy and vague these days. By her frontier science, alcohol is neither a flesh former nor a body warmer, so it is not a food, and if it is not a food, it is therefore a toxin. Simple as pie, which of course is a food."

When you come right down to it, was not pretty much all American food, such as was available in 1902 and later, basically *foreign* food? Such simple fare as chicken pot pie, mashed potatoes, and plain chocolate pudding were exotic, "foreign," no? The thing is, it was usually European food transformed—or, if you want to be critical and even uncharitable—horridly transmogrified.

For centuries, for example, Americans had to settle for a dour yellow glop with bottles of available generic mustards. Charles E. "Chuck" Williams, who founded the highly successful company Williams-Sonoma, in a blog interview with Laura Martin Bacon explained, "In those early years, [back in the 1930s] Europeans were also eating different foods than we were here in America. Mustard is a good example. I like to say that we changed American's eating preference from French's Mustard to good French mustard. We brought in good olive oil from France, then Italy. There was French wine vinegar. And, of course, balsamic vinegar from Modena (which I mistook for hair tonic the first time I saw it in Milan)." I personally remember when common shoppers had to pay a small fortune for good olive oil, pasta made from real semolina, and even now easily available foreign cheeses.

No, look to Mom for early impressions! In P. Yogananda's "*Autobiography of a Yogi*" —Chapter 46 ("The Woman Yogi Who Never Eats")—the sage visits a woman in Bengal named Giri Bala, an ascetic, "the eighth wonder of the world," whose diet is thin air!" A breathanarian, she literally ate and drank nothing from age 12 to 68, explaining that her energy came from air, sunlight, and cosmic power passing through the medulla oblongata. Highly spiritual, right? *Not!* Giri explains, "My childhood was unremarkable save that I was possessed by an insatiable appetite...My mother shamed me morning, noon and night about my gluttonous habits." Warned that she would disgrace her future husband's family by her gluttony, she solemnly, desperately, vowed, "I shall never touch food again as long as I live!" Her body, she said, was blessedly free from "dependence on the gross food of mortals." TV's Oprah Winfrey's phobia of chewing gum stems from her childhood. The talk-show host, 63, is so anti-gum that she banned the substance from her studio in Chicago, Illinois. "Back in Mississippi, my grandmother used to chew gum, then stick it in the cabinet. There were rows and rows of Juicy Fruit and Spearmint. I was afraid of it. *I don't allow gum in the building!*" Such arrogance coming from anybody, never mind a woman the size of a dugong, raises my anarchist hackles. It is as cruelly unfair as

Rush Limbaugh's bald assertion that feminism was established so as to allow unattractive women access to the mainstream of society, but the final truth may be that what makes that mono-causal dunce attractive to listeners is, to some degree, what makes Winfrey popular: their obesity. Flawed people, with blemishes, which describes all of us, seek reinforcement in imperfection. Nothing elicits more pity than the defected and the damaged and the dopily determined. Limbaugh's constant boast, always the churl's, is how much money he makes. He claims he would never try being President of the United States because he would have to take a pay cut, exactly the way he sees things. A vicious, monstrously doubly-over-sized, fanatically right-wing college drop-out would of course be nominated, right? Ambrose Bierce in his *The Devil's Dictionary* defined politics as "The conduct of public affairs for private advantage."

The late King Farouk of Egypt, who usually devoured as much as a dozen eggs at a single breakfast sitting and often forty quail for lunch, at several points in his life went through a fetish of being concerned about his weight—he grew at one point to over 400 pounds—by altogether eschewing bread, which he isolated as the one food he believed was fattening. All of his life he compulsively gulped gallons of aranciata, a sweet fizzy orangeade made with lots of sugar, and he had it corked and chilled and bottled. He had many favorite foods and especially loved oysters, fruit, pigeons (which he felt were a great cure for impotence), voluptuous-tasting mangoes "by the grove," cold lobster with mayonnaise, steak and French fries, chocolate ice cream, white peaches, and pasta in all of its forms and styles. When Farouk's mother forced him to follow a strict diet as a teenager, he resorted out of hunger to eating cat food from a bowl that had been placed on the floor for one of the royal pets.

As an adult, Farouk's breakfast sometimes started with a tray of 30 boiled eggs from which he would select perhaps ten to eat. He would then move on to consume enormous plates of steak, quail, lobster, steak, and chicken. He was almost too fat to walk, his sugar quotient bolstered by drinking over thirty bottles of fizzy soft drinks every day. "He devoured mutton by the meadow," according to biographer William Stadiem in *Too Rich*. On March 17, 1965, shortly after his 45th birthday, Farouk took his latest playmate, a ravishing 22-year-old Italian blonde model named Annamaria Gatti, out to the Ile de France restaurant in Rome for a late-night supper. After consuming a dozen raw oysters drowned in Tabasco sauce, a rich lobster thermidor, followed by an *abbacchio al forno,* a treble portion of roast baby lamb with extra helpings of roast potato, plus a huge order of string beans drenched in butter, along with a thick creamy chestnut dessert of Monte Bianco, orange-flavored ice cream, two big bottles of Fiuggi water, and a sparkling Coca-Cola digestif, he triumphantly lit up one of the giant trademark Havana cigars he carrie—and dropped dead. *Levanta muertos!* A meal to raise the dead! Sadly, it was uniquely the opposite, a meal to die for. The obese royal actually died in the act of eating.

Omniverous, voracious, Farouk's predatory nature was not unlike Citizen Kane's need to amass. In his excesses, he belied the assertion that all animals feed but humans alone eat. Gluttony in the extreme is a kind of satyriasis for food, where the drive seems to be more important than—but actually becomes—the goal. He was as rapacious and unslakable as a black bear. I make that assertion simply because it is doubtful that any other creature on earth can boast an open food list as long and varied as that of a black bear, who relishes anything edible, animal, mineral, vegetable, or plant, anything whatsoever that he can scavenge—grass, sedge, ants, frogs, snakes, small mammals, peppery new leaves, flower horns of skunk cabbage, insects, grubs, honey, acorns, beechnuts, wild berries, mushrooms, mast of all kinds, bush pig, apples, fish of any kind, the inner sweet sapwood of trees, chestnuts, even its own species. One story about Farouk's lavish living in exile was that he refused to donate any money to relieve the poverty of his people on the cold, illogical premise that "If I donate my fortune to buy food, all of Egypt eats today, eats tomorrow, and the day after that they are starving once again," thus rationalizing his high living.

Ironically, the very name "*Farouk*" in Arabic means "one who distinguishes right from wrong." It is too paradoxical, too ironic, a concept to contemplate. As that tubby omnivore with the shapeless sort of misangled, flaccid, neo-geo body, Andrew Zimmern, King of Bizarre Foods, urges, "Don't eat till you're full, eat 'til you're tired." How about 'til you're dead? This is why Zimmern can never be the *chef de cuisine* that John Thorne is, who knows ten times about food what Zimmern does, for he studies to know, he cooks to test, he stays to care. Than a fat person swankily zugzwanging along through the world eating bull penises, raccoon feet, jellied moose nose, live sea squirt, cane rat with tilapia, cicada, snails in turmeric sauce, and fruit bat roasted in coconut husks as a form of show business—cultural benefit: zero—I never saw anything better calculated to excite disgust and scorn regarding a love of real food.

Adolf Frederick, who was King of Sweden from 1751-1771, qualifies here. On the night of his death, the king is reported to have gluttonized on lobster, caviar, kippers, sauerkraut and drunk champagne, with all of it topped off by fourteen helpings of *hetvägg*, the king's favorite dessert. *Hetvägg* or *semla* is a traditional Scandinavian pastry which consists of a cardamom-spiced wheat bun with a cut-off top—it serves as a lid and is dusted with powdered sugar—the insides of which are scooped out and filled generously with a mixture of bread crumbs, milk and almond paste, topped with whipped cream. *Fourteen helpings!* No Swedish meatballs? *God aptit!* Adolf died of digestive problems later that very same night, probably smiling. He was a chauvinist about his food. No herring from Norway.

Certainly no herring if poet William Carlos Williams had been dining. His poem "For Viola: De Gustibus" is not only a paean to caviar but a knock at herring:

> Beloved you are
> Caviar of Caviar
> Of all I love you best
> O my Japanese bird nest
>
> No herring from Norway
> Can touch you for flavor. Nay
> Pimento itself
> is flat as an empty shelf
> When compared to your piquancy
> O quince of my despondency.

I wonder how incandescent Williams's song to caviar would have been if he knew—as several friends of mine also do, who refuse to eat it—how brutally this luxury is "harvested." In "The Caviar Kings" in *Seed* magazine, looking at Russia's "black gold" which sells in New York for $2,500 a kilo, Simon Cooper gets right to the point in his study of the nature of heartless greed:

> The poacher selects a fat female. She is about four feet
> long and swollen with eggs. He hits her hard with a
> plank of wood—not hard enough to kill, but enough
> to stun. Blood trickles from her eyeballs, mouth, and
> gills. Quickly, the poacher rolls her over, slits open her
> belly, reaches inside, and carefully extracts a plump,
> gray-black sac about the size of a pillow. He puts the
> egg sac into a large plastic bucket and throws the
> eviscerated fish on the ground, where she flaps and
> thrashes, her abdomen gaping, until she succumbs and
> dies. Later he will butcher her for meat.

"Like nearly every other luxury in the world," Cooper goes on to explain, "caviar is tinged with hues of danger. It has the reek of gangsters and the taste of a dying species." But the savagery is not limited strictly to the ocean." The caviar mafia are thought to have been behind a terrorist bomb attack in the town of Kaspiysk that killed 67 people, including 21 children, and destroyed a nine-story apartment building. Most of the victims were Russian border guards and their families. The guards, who patrol Russia's new boundaries, had begun to produce results in regulating illegal traffic and, in doing so, made dangerous enemies. As Cicero told us, "If you would abolish avarice, you must abolish its mother, luxury." I have always mildly enjoyed the taste of caviar, but when I eat it, I am never unaware that it has long become, extravagantly, more fabulous as a metaphor for luxurious food than it is in reality. It brings to mind La Rochefoucauld's ironic remark about love, when he said that very few men would fall in love if they had never read about it.

As to bread, the mighty Confederate General Thomas Jonathan "Stonewall" Jackson, who was something of a health fanatic and self-denialist, virtually lived in order to study food. He preferred to eat it stale. He compulsively did not, and would not, eat butter. A dictatorial dieter, he wanted his wife to do exactly as he did in eating, mostly Spartan fare. He wrote to her,

> I have so strictly adhered to my wholesome diet of
> stale bread and plainly dressed meat (having nothing
> on it but salt) that I prefer it now to almost anything
> else. The other evening, I tasted a piece of bread with
> butter on it, and then the bread without it, and rather
> gave my preference to the unbuttered bread; and
> hence I may never taste any more of this once much
> relished seasoning.

Jackson's husbandly proscriptions seem to confirm Naomi Wolf's assertion in *The Beauty Myth: How Images of Beauty Are Used Against Women*, "A culture fixated on female thinness is not an obsession about female beauty, but an obsession about female obedience. Dieting is the most potent political sedative in women's history; a quietly mad population is a tractable one." It is curious. The beautifully exotic British model, Naomi Campbell, of Afro-Jamaican descent, as well as of Chinese-Jamaican ancestry through her paternal grandmother, is said never once to have dieted or worked out in a gym, and she supposedly smokes cigarettes in industrial quantities. If that is a dog dinner of genes, I will take a bowl of it, thank you.

Stonewall Jackson was a fan of mineral spas, water cures, sulphured water and was convinced that they could take care of the worst ailments. He consumed alum liquids but despised coffee, which is strange, because it was basically the staples of coffee and hardtack that kept both armies in the Civil War upright. Jackson sucked on lemons in battle, notably at Gaines' Mill, refused to eat pepper because he believed it weakened his left leg, and, another funny habit, frequently liked sleeping under wet sheets. As Mary Anna Jackson, his wife, was not healthy, the wiry, amazingly tough Stonewall felt obliged to give her all sorts of food directives, of his own devising. He wrote to her, "I regard green tea and coffee so injurious to the nerves that you should always prefer water to either." He was also of the belief that the white of an egg was worthless and told Mary by letter, "I think if you would adopt for your breakfast a cup of moderately strong black tea, stale wheat bread (wheat bread raised, and not less than twenty-four hours old), fresh meat—broiled or roasted is best—the yolk of one or two eggs—the white is hardly worth eating as it requires digestion and affords but little nutrition. For dinner the same kind of bread and meat, one vegetable only, say peas, beans, or this year's potatoes, and for drink, plain water."

In the matter of her illness, if she felt the need to complain or even reflect on it, the Spartan Jackson had a solution for that, as well. "You should try and forget that you are infirm, and pay no attention to your symptoms, as most any person can, by being less attentive to every little pain."

Not as fat as Farouk but just as self-indulgent was the gay snob and dedicated Boston voluptuary, Lucius, whom we have already encountered in these pages. An alcoholic, monied dandy, Beebe was a walking anachronism. (One friend observed that he cherished "a profound nostalgia for dead elegance.") He had his own column, "Along the Boulevard," in *Gourmet* magazine and wrote extensively for *Holiday* and *Playboy* about restaurants and dining experiences around the world. Restaurants he covered include The Colony, The Stork Club, The Pump Room, the 21 Club, Simpson's-in-the-Strand, and Chasen's. A noted boulevardier, Beebe always sported, preened with, an impressive and baroque wardrobe—only superior London tailoring for him—and lived a life of loud, highly opinionated, florid disdain for anything plebeian or smacking of the rube, the common, or the parvenu. It was Beebe who coined the phrase "Café Society." He spent a lifetime looking for a taste of what Sir Walter Raleigh called a "nectar's suckets."

He loved opera, four-Martini lunches, English manners, Partagas cigars, elegant old railway cars—he was as passionate about trains and general railroadiana as a hungry Dominican after *mangú*—the Cunard Line, top hats and tails. A shrinking violet he was not. While crafty and debonair, he was as cruel as broken glass. He was rude to people in service, spiteful to the common man. Worse, he had the *maladresse* to think himself important. Truly fastidious, he acted the royal. No true blue *feinschmecker*, for example, will eat soft-boiled eggs with a spoon made of anything but bone or ivory. Silver, they complain, imparts an unpleasant taste. So Beebe kept these treasured spoons handy. "If anything is worth doing, it is worth doing in style, and on your own terms, and nobody's Goddamned else's," he crowed. Once he confided to an interviewer, "I would like my obit to say, 'Everything he did was made-to-measure. He never got an idea off the rack.'" Overly refined and pointedly self-conscious *savoir faire* in a very real sense is always meretricious sophistication.

Toying at supper with his ortolans and flutes of Chambertin-Clos de Bèze, Beebe could always be found looking to make clever café cacklings always offered in super-fatted complacency, his most obvious characteristic, interrupted with occasional cockatoo-like screeches that some beleaguered waiter instantly appear to rectify some wrong his lordship suddenly discovered.

Beebe was the kind of fop who went in for those all-out, capacious Edwardian refections with courses like Fish Rissoles with Scalloped Potatoes, Mutton Pie, Fricassee of Lamb, and things like Golden Buck, a super, extra-rich Welsh Rabbit topped with a poached egg. His sartorial repertoire included 40 suits, at least two mink-lined overcoats, numerous top hats and London bowlers, a collection of doeskin gloves, walking sticks, and a substantial gold nugget watch-chain. While the vast majority of America was if not starving then at least mired in the miserable depths of the Great Depression, this master of meretricious sophistication publicly stated that he would do his part by limiting his food and drink allowance to $100 per day. This, during a lost period when in the West Virginia soft coal districts in the 1930s, miners and their families were often reduced to eating "bulldog gravy," a mixture of water, flour, and grease, and eaten with beans over a "water sandwich" (bread soaked in lard and water)—it is mentioned in the lyrics of the Appalachian lament, "Man of Constant Sorrow." It recalls in an untidy way Alexander Pushkin's play, "A Feast During the Plague," one of his four *Little Tragedies* (1830), in which we watch feasters and merrymakers eating well during a plague—in fact, after a good friend's death—where as a kind of doleful background music we hear the creaking sounds of a dead-cart passing by:

> But we are many left alive, so there's
> No reason to be sorrowful. And now,
> Let's raise a toast in memory of Jackson,
> Let glasses ring and lift our voices higher
> As if he were alive.

It was one of Beebe's fastidious claims—his fancy craving that such things be known—that he always brushed his teeth with good Chablis. (I am surprised that he did not use Billecart-Salmon, the house champagne of the 21 Club, or Perrier-Jouët, Cole Porter's favorite.) Still, by a strange, inexplicable quirk of the American psyche, a good many cast-down Depression-era readers were morbidly fascinated by the revelations and rants of the priggish rich, blowhards and blusterers like Beebe, even as half of the poor slobs were going belly up. In his chapter, "Gustatory Souvenirs" in his lush book, *Snoot If You Must* (1943), Beebe provides a gastronomic list of 35 or so of his favorite all-time dinners, providing the locations, often the chefs and hotels—English mutton chops at Frankie & Johnnie's, crabs Moro à la mode de Havana at Antoine's, tenderloin steak sandwiches at Jack Bleeck's, jugged saddle of hare at Luchow's, etc.—and what is revealed along with a hopelessly fastidious and unbearable personality is a mad, impatient love for a spectrum of creamed dishes, cream chipped beef, cheese fondue, pompano with mustard cream sauce, etc. I am certain, although he does not say so, that, like an oafish someone I once knew in the publishing world, he would have been meticulous in having the proper portion of Emmenthaler to Gruyère, with a hint of garlic, and the all important dollop of kirsch.

The ostentatious Beebe went roaming the globe to report on fabled restaurants, a glutton's pilgrimage, but his articles all blur and become little but a list of unending over-rich banquets: *le hommard Deauvillaise, poularde sautee au Champagne, croustarde de langouste,* and *soufflé Grand Marnier,* all washed down with Chateau Margaux '34 and topped off with snifters of Hine cognac and Cuban *belicoso fino.*

Who else in the early 1960s was dining like this?

What improvident, profligate, almost likerish excess!

"There was nothing in the whole world so dreadful as the power of riches wrongly used," wrote Gene Stratton-Porter, author of *The Girl of the Limberlost,* the nonpareil of book titles, in my opinion.

A snobbish throwback, a self-inflated windbag, Beebe boasted that he had never watched a television broadcast. He was a throwback, a consummate and sanctimonious egomaniac who railed against air travel, bemoaned the social decline of the derby, and, living in the past, once non-ironically asked in a column, "What Was So Wrong With 1905?" He would not so much as look in the direction of proletarian food. He was also a sour, crabby misogynist, among other things. Beebe often told the story that he once came upon a noted gastronome glaring with horror at a row of orchids on his table and screaming, "Throw wide the windows! Air the rooms! Is the bouquet of my wines to have to conflict with these stinking flowers?" The complainant very well could have been the decadent Beebe himself. It prompts a recollection of testy Joseph Alsop, art collector and wily political insider in Washington, D.C., whofor years refused to eat in certain Paris restaurants whose cellars were proximate to the Metro, because the vibrations might easily have disturbed the sediment in the wine bottles.

I never think of Lucius Beebe and his *amour-propre* without seeing in my mind's eye the famous Dorothea Lange photograph taken in Nipomo, California in February 1936 of that anxiety-ridden, weather-worn, dark-haired migrant-mother, Florence Owens Thompson in her ripped shirt, an anxious right hand to her face, her two children facing away from the camera. They were sitting in a lean-to tent. She would have been Beebe's age, about 34, as she sat there in the grip of apprehension. There was no work for her, their pea crop had frozen, and for days she and the children had been living on frozen vegetables and the few birds they could kill to eat.

Gourmands are worse than self-adoring, their bodies their shrines, their food consumption their altar offerings. Their rubric is food, their pledge of faith eating, and they themselves stand at the center, as God.

No gourmand is not also a pedant. R.W. Apple, Jr., an obese food writer, is a good example. He worked for the *New York Times* and supposedly knew every good place to eat in the entire world. He scurried from continent to continent not only eating everything in sight but obsessing with the goal, I swear, of tasting every food on earth. He was a belly traveler and his book *Far Flung and Well Fed* is basically a diary of everything he devoured. He was as fat as a distillery pig. Nothing didn't please him that he could stuff down his waiting gullet. As I say, like all lusty, true-to-his-code, belly-busters, he was a pedant—a dogmatist, a hairsplitter, a literalist, a pedagogue, a nit-picker, a squeam, a pettifogger, a precisian, a quibbler, and a merciless sophist. Brats should be pronounced *brots*. Alewives are properly called menhaden. Soft-shelled crabs should be eaten within four days of molting. *Pronunciamenti*—esoteric, cryptic, obscure—are the gospel texts of the professional gourmand.

Apple was word-perfect on where to eat the best morels and chanterelles. He would fly to Brazil to eat fritters with a base of bean pureé, ginger, and dried shrimp. To be good, water ice had to have the unmistakable tang of fresh fruit. Singapore has the best, and perhaps, safest street food. Food was his religion, eating his faith. He criss-crossed the country—nay, the world—on face-stuffing, pigging-out, gourmet safaris. He positively lived for Scottish breakfasts of scones, sausages, game pies, trout, roast beef, and sometimes haunches of venison on the sideboard. He knew mustards up and down, visited jelly factories, raced up to Wisconsin to scoff up Dutch apple pies ("Pie is to the Midwest as rice is to China"). It was as if every morning he woke up quivering to eat. He had to have the best *mozzarella di bufala,* the subtlest grappa, the crispiest soft-shell crabs "dipped in egg wash, dredged in plain bread crumbs and fried until the tops and the legs were crisp and the undersides rich and creamy" with tartar sauce house-made, of course. The pilgrimage—the pedantic hunt—was always to find the genuine article. The pedant's delight! Diners. Delicatessens. Dives. He hit them all looking for flawless meals. On October 4, 2006, Apple died from complications of thoracic cancer.

Reporter A.J. Liebling, who literally committed gastronomic suicide—his sole joy was shoving food in his face—swilling down food in gluttonous bouts year after year like an inflating Rabelaisian giant and living a life of hot, gut-bucket gluttony, often ordering five or six dozen oysters at a single sitting, along with endless martinis, unending meals of lobsters, osso bucco, piles of steaks. Moderation meant nothing to him, abstinence a mere word. Gluttony became his definition of freedom, fatal though it was. He died bloated at age 59. He literally scarfed his food, in deep sweats, burrowing in his food, making loud noises with plosives down the nose. Liebling's wholly unappeasable appetite reminds me of John Muir's comment on the grizzly bear: "To him almost everything is food, except granite."

It may be said that Liebling virtually ate with a copepod's fury. (Copepods, miniature monsters with a multitude of limbs, flattened at the tips like the blade of an oar—the name comes from the Greek "oar-footed"—are the world's biggest eaters. Each one consumes half its own weight in food every day. Some copepods in the ocean eat other small forms of animal life, but most feed on the only living things in the world more abundant than copepods themselves—phytoplankton.) It would not be too much of an exaggeration to say that Liebling, who was not a physically attractive man, had wabbling wattles, bulky and comic hamster-like cheek pouches, diplostomic flanges—"chops"—like Jonathan Swift's clever Brobdingnagian monkeys in *Gulliver's Travels* who stored their food in there. I always think of him with unmuffled laughter when I call to mind the famous remark of Mary I of England as recorded in Holinshed's *Chronicles* (1585)—I substitute one word—"When I am dead and opened you shall find a porkchop [not 'Calais'] lying in my heart."

In a sweat, the commodious Liebling could actually eat a full sheep's head "right down to the eyes," according to his biographer. One acquaintance of his saw him wolf down seven broiled chickens at a sitting. "There weren't any bones left," he said with shock. "He was so large," recalled the writer Ved Mehta, "it was impossible to walk next to him on the sidewalk."

I remember the silent film from 1916, *He Did and He Didn't*, in which Roscoe "Fatty" Arbuckle, as the result of eating too much, dreams his wife, played by Mabel Normand, is being unfaithful to him with an old friend, Jack. No one looks more at home at table than Arbuckle wearing a bib as he tucks into a plateful of several positively huge shiny lobsters. During the course of his lifetime, Liebling in high fettle must have lecherously dispatched literally thousands of lobsters, rattling shells included. Gorbellied, rubicund, lazy, he would have made for the perfect juror, at least according to Abraham Lincoln, who believed that fat men always made the best jurors because they were naturally jolly and easily swayed. (Chubby or heavy-set women especially intrigued our sixteenth president, as biographer David Herbert Donald notes in *Lincoln*, pointing out that size in any of the women he courted or favored was no disadvantage but rather a plus, "for all of the women he loved were plump," including the very mysterious Ann Rutledge and his wife, Mary Todd.)

It brings to mind the rich, evocative lines of Bayard Taylor's poem, "Angelo Orders his Dinner"—arguably the very best (and funniest) food poem in English—which begins, "I, Angelo, obese, black-garmented,/ Respectable, much in demand, well fed/ With mine own larder's dainties..." continues as Angelo cries out with irrepressible Dionysian gusto,

> Find me such a man
> As Lippo yonder, built upon the plan
> Of heavy storage, double-navelled, fat,
> From his own giblet's oils. An Ararat
> Uplift o'er water, sucking rosy draughts
> From Noah's vineyard—crisp, enticing wafts
> Yon kitchen now emits, which to your sense
> Somewhat abate the fear of old events,
> Qualms to the stomach,—I, you see, am slow
> Unnecessary duties to forgo,—
> You understand? A venison haunch, haut goût,
> Ducks that in Cimbrian olives mildly stew,

And sprigs of anise, might one's teeth provoke
To taste, and so we wear the complex yoke
Just as it suits my liking, I confess,
More to receive, and to partake no less,
Still more obese, while through thick adipose
Sensation shoots, from testing tongue to toes.

The Overweight Brigade is prodigious.

Oliver Hardy. Thomas Aquinas. Nikita Khrushchev. Herman Goering. Gustavus II Adolphus. Edward Gibbon.William the Conqueror (Suffering from peritonitis, a rugose bulk, he died a hugely fat man, and his obese corpse literally exploded at Rouen in 1087, throwing pus in every direction.) Pelagius, the British theologian (*"stolidissimus et Scotorum pultibus praegravatus,"* wrote St. Jerome). Antoine "Fats" Domino. Queen Victoria. King Louis XVIII. President William Howard Taft. (A morbidly obese 320 pounds when he came to office, Taft's sole dietary concession was to give up bacon because he said it gave him heartburn. He owned a special bathtub big enough for four average–sized men but got stuck in it on his Inauguration Day and had to be pried out.) Oprah Winfrey. Luciano Pavarotti. Babe Ruth. Edward VII. Colonel Harlan Sanders. G.K. Chesterton. Orson Welles. Henry VIII (At the end, "full of flesh and unwieldy," he was unable to lift his arms to sign Norfolk's death warrant by hand). John Belushi. The Big Bopper. Actors Eugene Pallette, Marlon Brando, Dom DeLuise, Fatty Arbuckle, and James Coco. Comedians Chris Farley and John Candy. Rappers like Biggie Smalls, Big Pun, and Heavy D. Legendary boogie-woogie piano player Aubrey ("Moon") Mullican (cf. "Cherokee Boogie," "I'll Sail My Ship Alone," etc.,) who weighed in at almost 300 pounds and while performing at the Kansas City Auditorium suffered a thunderous heart attack. On the last day of 1966, he had made a New Year's resolution to lay off pork chops. He died before the first day of 1967 ended. Even poor Elvis inflated at the end. I am prodded to recall, pondering that fulsome list, the singular cleverness— and possible truthfulness—of 19th-century Adam Sedgewick's quip, "No one has ever made a success in this world without a large bottom."

There was a heap o' livin' and a great lot of food in those gross bodies of heavy storage, double-navelled, fat, roasting in their own giblet's oils. (Most bore what the great chef Marie Antoine Carême declared was the distinctive mark of the big eater, a large lower lip.) It prompts a memory of the bleak, crowded churchyard in London to which the pinchpenny Ebenezer Scrooge is taken by the faceless Ghost of Christmas Yet To Come in *A Christmas Carol*, a desolate plot described by novelist Charles Dickens as "overrun by grass and weeds, the growth of vegetation's death, not life; choked up with too much burying; fat with repleted appetite."

Speaking of graveyards, I wonder if the fat actor, Charles Laughton, chatting with the just as fat actor Peter Ustinov in a scene in Stanley Kubrick's film *Spartacus*, was not, as they say, whistling past the graveyard when he said, "Corpulence makes a man reasonable, pleasant, and phlegmatic. Have you ever noticed that the nastiest of talents are invariably thin?"

George Balanchine, co-founder of the New York City ballet and its ballet-master for more than 35 years, was fussy about bodies. He who in his own waspish and Spartan way could be misogynistic had viewed with utter disdain the legendary Isadora Duncan perform in Russia in 1921. "I thought she was awful," he said. "I don't understand it when people say she was a great dancer. To me it was absolutely unbelievable—a drunken, fat woman who for hours was rolling around like a pig." He explained to an interviewer in *Horizon* (January 1961) how the mechanics of ballet depend on the music as well as the dancers, of course. It is not always a matter that is predictable or precise. "A long foot can compensate for the shortness of a leg," he said, "Bodies change, people are taller." He continued,

> In the Maryinsky Theatre, when I started, the girls stood in rows sixteen deep, and they were short and plump, with busts and corsets, and they wore their hair up. They were the ones who were the delight of the premier range. They were like those fat nudes on the balustrades of the Paris Opéra and painted on its ceilings—the place looks like a glorified whore house, you know, or at the very least a Turkish bath. But times have changed. Now we train our bodies to be bone, to be ascetic. Bone is personality, fat is pancake. You can dress a skeleton, make it sexy, anything. You can say, Ah, that person is so-and-so or such-and-such. But you never know what a fat man is.

You never *really* know what a fat man is.

It is an almost metaphysical indictment with its chubby focus, in a horribly undefined way, a kind of inscrutable quiddity that is subject to no strict identifying law of either becoming or being.

What we do know is a fat man is a big eater and in all probability, even in the widest sense of the term, a glutton.

What about gluttonous characters in novels? Major Joseph Bagstock in Charles Dickens' *Dombey and Son*; Lord Augustus Trefoil in Anthony Trollope's *The American Senator*; Somerset Maugham's Oliver Haddo in *The Magician*; Sancho Panza in Miguel de Cervantes' *Don Quixote*; Dr. Matthew-Mighty-grain-of-salt-Dante-O'Connor in Djuna Barnes' *Nightwood*; George Cole in Louisa May Alcott's *Little Men*; Ignatius J. Reilly in John Kennedy Toole's *A Confederacy of Dunces*; Piggy in William Golding's *Lord of the Flies*; Obelix, the best friend of Gaulish warrior Asterix in René Goscinny and Albert Uderzo's *Asterix the Gaul*, who can devour two whole roasted boars in one sitting; nine-year-old Augustus Gloop in *Charlie and the Chocolate Factory* whose "great flabby folds of fat bulged out from every part of his body, and his face was like a monstrous ball of dough with two small greedy curranty eyes;" and the heartless Judge Holden in Cormac McCarthy's raw novel, *Blood Meridian*, that overlarge, intelligent, menacing evil lunatic who is depicted as entirely devoid of body hair and philosophically emblematic of the eternal and all-encompassing nature of war ("War is God"). Fact, however, is usually stranger than fiction.

Take the voluptuary King George IV who was double-chinned even when he was the Prince of Wales, and by early middle age had a full 50-inch waist. He hosted one-hundred-course feasts and for his coronation banquet his sybaritic guests were treated to 7,462 pounds of beef; 7,163 pounds of veal; 2,474 pounds of mutton; and hillocks of lamb and poultry—an orgy of conspicuous consumption that in the end so offended his subjects that all coronation banquets were banned forthwith. It took several hours for George IV to be squeezed into the royal corset, and a pulley system had to be rigged up to allow him to mount his horse. In the end, suffering from arteriosclerosis, gout, peripheral edema ("dropsy"), and possible porphyria, he spent whole days in bed fighting off spasms of breathlessness that would leave him gasping and half-asphyxiated. On his deathbed, the King's appetite was still undiminished. Shortly before expiring from cardiac and respiratory problems at the age of 67, he ordered two pigeons, three steaks, a bottle of wine, a glass of champagne, two glasses of port, and a glass of brandy. After he died, in 1830, *The London Times* coldly dismissed the monarch, writing,

> There never was an individual less regretted by his fellow-creatures than this deceased king. What eye has wept for him? What heart has heaved one throb of non-mercenary sorrow?...If he ever had a friend—a devoted friend in any rank of life—we protest that the name of him or her never reached us.

I will mention here, only to condemn the book, that poor, desperate-for-attention, lonely Gore Vidal at the back end of his talent in one of his last execrable novels, *Live from Golgotha*—its style "too languid for fury," its plot "too silly to wound," as critic Mark Lawson asserts—feebly goes out of his way to give Jesus a glandular problem and blasphemously makes the Lord grossly fat. ("Wide as He was tall, Jesus waddled toward me... He spoke, His voice so high, so shrill that only the odd canine ever got the whole message.") I ask that the reader pray for poor Vidal. Incidentally, there can be seen at the Harvard University's Busch-Reisinger, a museum dedicated to the study of art from the German-speaking countries of Central and Northern Europe, a singular cross showing the crucified Christ as a large, overweight figure.

Last, but not least by any means, that great, fully fledged, boastful, loveable cockalorum, Shakespeare's fat knight, the *miles gloriosus* Sir John Falstaff, that "trunk of humours," "that bolting-hutch of beastliness," "that swoll'n parcel of dropsies," "that huge bombard of sack," "that roasted Manningtree ox with pudding in his belly," "that reverend vice, that grey iniquity, that father ruffian, that vanity in years," "that stuff'd cloak-bag of guts," "this bed-presser, this horse-back-breaker, this hill of flesh," a man who secretes sweat in such quantities that he "lards the lean earth as he walks along." Very few readers, even Shakespeareans, ever remember the most prominent characteristic of the man, at least according to his many commentators—ahh, yes, his "jubilant brain." Meet, if you will, Sir John Falstaff.

A jolly assemblage, to be sure!

How Ol' Abe would have loved a panel of sumo wrestlers, whose daily caloric intake can reach 8,000 kilocalories, more than twice that of an average Japanese adult male. Taiho, widely considered the greatest sumo wrestler of postwar Japan who retired in 1971 with a career record of 746-144-136, died of sudden heart failure in 2013, at 72. Scarcely over 300 pounds, he was one of the lightest of all. Weirdly, Sumo wrestlers—known in Japan as *rikishi*—are not normally allowed to eat breakfast, so that they will overeat later, and they are expected to have a form of siesta after a large lunch. What they traditionally eat is *Chankonabe*. It is a Japanese stew (a type of *nabemono* or one-pot dish) that is commonly eaten in vast quantities as part of a weight-gain diet. It contains a dashi or chicken broth soup-base with *sake* or *mirin* to add flavor. The bulk of *chankonabe* is made up of large quantities of protein sources, usually chicken (quartered, skin left on), fish (fried and made into balls), tofu (or sometimes beef), and vegetables (daikon, bok choy, etc.) The difference between regular and "*chanko*" *nabe*, is that *chankonabe* has lots of meat. There are all kinds of meat; beef, pork, chicken, you name it. And, after all that meat, they bring out noodles that you cook in the broth and eat. While considered a reasonably healthy dish in its own right, *chankonabe* is very protein-rich and usually served in massive quantities, with beer and rice to increase the caloric intake. Leftover *chankonabe* broth can also later be used as broth for *somen* or udon noodles. It is a dish, in short, that is not made according to a fixed recipe and often contains whatever is available to the cook. It is traditionally served according to seniority, with the senior *rikishi* and any guests of the *heya* receiving first choice, with the junior wrestlers getting whatever is left. It is also a popular restaurant food, often served in restaurants operated by retired sumo wrestlers who specialize in the dish; the first of these, Kawasaki Chanko, was started in 1937 in the Ryōgoku district of Tokyo, home to many prominent sumo stables. Note: *chankonabe* served during sumo tournaments is made exclusively with chicken, the idea being that a *rikishi* should always be on two legs like a chicken, not all fours.

There are no fast or hard-bound rules that dictate what goes into a classic chankonabe, in short. No fussiness. Nothing finicky. No caveats. No specific food prohibitions of any kind. Anything goes—pickles, chicken bones, salty red miso, sliced pork belly, burdock, chrysanthemum greens, eggs, sake, chives. Skip breakfast. Exercise on an empty stomach. (If a wrestler's body has no food, its metabolic thermostats are turned down even lower to conserve fuel.) The wrestlers nap after eating. Eat late in the day. Go to bed with full stomachs. An important rule for them is always eat with others in a social atmosphere. (According to leading researchers, a meal eaten with others can be at least 44 percent larger and with 30 percent more calories and fat.)

I would place former NBC weatherman, fat Willard Scott, in the hysterical food department. An article in *People* magazine (March 20, 1989) goes into his excesses. Scott is the kind of glutton who has actually memorized special meals and pig-outs that he has enjoyed from what has been apparently a lifetime of them, spreads and feasts of which even decades later he can literally savor each bite. We read of him in the magazine, "He also loves weddings, marching bands, Jaycees, the disabled (especially when they triumph over adversity) and Thanksgiving (which he likes even more than Christmas). And there is one thing that always commands his attention: food. 'When I'm eating breakfast, I'm thinking about dinner,' he admitted." Scott is a living Botero! His idea of a great meal is the next one, and any monologue of his or conversation with him, to which any inveterate *Today Show* watchers from years past will surely attest, cannot go more than a few seconds without some fond reminiscence or other of the foods and courses he has dispatched.

He spoke in *People* of his ancestors: "Our family settled in Wilkes County, North Carolina—yum, minced-barbecue country—in about 1750, and my father was the first to leave the farm." Pause. "You know, when I was working in Washington and I was in a barbecue mood, I'd go to the Dixie Pig in Alexandria and have six of those sandwiches with four long-necked Budweisers..." He says the Pioneer Club in Lake Charles, La., served him "the best meal I ever ate." It was 14 courses, which could account for his fondness. The first time he ever ate an oyster he ate 45 of them, and he fondly remembers devouring a whole box of Krispy Kreme donuts in eight minutes. On a visit to a Paris bistro last year, he demonstrated international flair, ordering 'mucho chocolata' for dessert. Out came four ice cream-filled, chocolate-covered profiteroles, each the size of a cannonball. He points out that he is not always to blame for his eating habits, that people see him coming and immediately start slaughtering livestock. "Nobody ever forces a lemon pie down a little guy," he complains. Willard's first memory is of a birthday cake. It came from a bakery in Alexandria, Va., where he was born 55 years ago, and he liked it so much he had cake from the same bakery at every birthday from age 1 through 40. Box 'em, fellers. Send 'em out! Serve 'em up!

Again, memory is re-enacted desire.

Singer Tiny Tim (Herbert Khaury in real life) was also a desperate and somewhat crazed over-eater. His first ex-wife, Victoria Mae Budinger, "Miss Vicky," confessed in a rather frank, detailed, truthful, but unloving article in the *Ladies Home Journal* (June 1972) that the unconventional singer literally had a fetish about food. With his long, dark, snarling bunch of frazzled hair and hovering, pear-shaped figure, he seemed at first glance, at least on television, to come across as fairly thin and scarecrowish, but he was in fact (I met the sweet man twice) all slob-fat and avocadine, and his wife who described him as "very large" and "heavy" wrote,

> He would spend $200 on a single meal. He would order everything on the menu—every flavor of ice cream. Maybe a psychiatrist could explain it. Maybe it was because he was poor as a child: but his mother said that when he was young, he did the same thing on a smaller scale. He prefers to eat alone, but he would eat meals with me because we were married. At first I thought it was because he has such poor table manners, but that's not it. He's just very interested in eating. When eating I could be dead at the table, and he wouldn't notice.

Although A.J. Liebling was born fat and called himself a "feeder"—he writes in *Between Meals* (1962) that even at 18, a student at the Sorbonne, "Eating soon developed into one of my major subjects"—he had many food aversions. "Sole doesn't taste much like fish," he nagged. "South African lobster tails… don't taste lobstery," he complained, "nor did synthetic vanilla extract taste vanilla-ry." He despised processed cheese. (Janette Rallison: "I don't care what you Yanks say, cheese should not *whiz.*") Like all food snobs he cultivated a taste for odd and exotic foods. He loved *truite au bleu*, for example, "a live trout," as he puts it, "simply done to death in hot water, like a Roman emperor in his bath." I have alluded previously to his dislike of Delicious and Golden Delicious apples as being tasteless. But he also dismissed turkey as being not worthy of eating. "Only in a civet is turkey good to eat," he wrote. (By civet, he meant what the French call *civet de lièvre*, a kind of rich hare stew whose sauce has been thickened with the animal's blood.)

It is not surprising to read that he pooh-poohed the classical ideal of *mens sana in corpore sano*, for in his mind he could not settle on how any sane man could govern his appetites or not be hedonistic. Liebling's principle: "No sane man can afford to dispense with debilitating pleasures." One of the very peculiar themes running through the pages of *Between Meals* is his attraction to women, repeated observations on them, which seems to fit snugly into his "pleasure principle," except that you never believe for a minute that he thinks of anything but food. An obese, terribly unattractive creature, homely as a winter pear—about that shape and not much bigger—poor tubby Liebling obviously yearned to convey to his readers that he was also virile and vital and attractive to the opposite sex when the fact is he was just a human swill bowl. (He married at age 30, but his schizophrenic wife was soon hospitalized.)

No better example presents itself, I think, than Liebling to justify George Orwell's famous remark in *The Road to Wigan Pier* that "A human being is primarily a bag for putting food into; the other functions and faculties may be more godlike, but in point of time they come afterwards."

Take the case, for example, of the once handsome, intemperate, madly excessive and vain, eventually bloated singer/actor of the 1950s, Mario Lanza. After he came to Hollywood, studio bosses, aghast, watched his weight balloon as he wolfed down spaghetti, ravioli, meatballs, always a steak and six eggs for breakfast, thirty and forty pieces of chicken at a sitting, often rounded off with a whole apple pie and a quart of eggnog. Even as a teenager, he was served breakfast in bed by his invalid father in Philadelphia. The 30 to 40 cups of coffee per day had a disastrous effect on his kidneys. A gigantic appetite, along with his huge consumption of alcohol, various drugs, and women chasing, led to an advanced case of phlebitis and eventually a blood clot in Lanza's coronary artery, which killed him at 38.

While food and coffee turned Lanza into something of a sexless barnyard gump, the great composer Giacomo Puccini's wife, Elvira, was so jealous of other women that she used to put bromide in her husband's coffee to reduce his sex drive. A heavy chain smoker of Toscano cigars and cigarettes, Puccini's complaints of a chronic sore throat toward the end of 1923 led to a diagnosis of throat cancer, and he died on November 29, 1924, from complications after the treatment: uncontrolled bleeding led to a heart attack the day after surgery.

It was of course no different with the operatic tenor, Luciano Pavarotti whose weight at times soared to as much as 350 pounds, if not more. A glutton, he rarely did any physical exercise—"Walking makes my teeth hurt," he once famously remarked—but virtually lived to eat, almost always consuming herculean dinners of cheese, pasta, tomatoes, arborio rice. He famously ordered beluga caviar by the kilo. In *The King and I* his agent, Herbert Breslin, recounts tales of Pavarotti consuming a full pound of caviar at a single sitting, bottle after bottle of Roederer Cristal champagne, and the most expensive salmon from Petrossian. (Still, when he died, the great operatic tenor left as much as $450 million in his will.) Pavarotti often shopped at Grace's Marketplace on Manhattan's Upper West Side, a shop which was always his first stop after flying in to this country. His favorite wine was Lambrusco, a light sparkling wine—he actually drank little else. Pavarotti, who in the end died of pancreatic cancer, grew increasingly worried that whenever or wherever he traveled he would fail to find all the foods he liked, and so he always voyaged abroad with an entire arsenal of kitchen supplies, espresso machines, prosciutto slicers, all sorts of pots and pans. When he went to China in 1988, carrying grave apprehensions about their cuisine—or (in his mind) lack of it—he brought an entire operation over on the plane. "There were crates of garlic, lemons, potatoes, onions, tomatoes, melons," wrote Breslin, adding,

> There were raw chickens and cuts of veal and sausages and Parma hams. There were wheels of Gorgonzola, Parmigiana, and Pecorino cheese. There were 1,500 bottles of mineral water and a comparable amount of Lambrusco (already starting to lose its fizz). There were hot plates to cook on, a refrigerator to preserve everything, and an oven to make bread. Pavarotti thought he might starve in China.

Although fussy, it seems that Pavarotti would try anything. I wonder if novelist William Faulkner was the opposite, I mean in the sense of being fussy or overly discriminate, for he once declared, almost as if a sort of anti-self were comforting him, he would like to be reincarnated as a buzzard, so that he could go anywhere, people would leave him alone and he'd be able to eat anything.

No one, I am convinced, for grossness and insatiable gluttony can beat out the Israeli politician, Ariel Sharon, whose freakazoidal appetite for chicken we've already mentioned. A xenophobic, expansionist fat-pants does not begin to describe the size of this war criminal, whose lust for food almost literally mimicked his thieving greed for land and the "depraved indifference" that informed his stealing West Bank hilltops from the Palestinians in direct defiance of a 1993 peace agreement, exactly like Hitler seizing Czechoslovakia and with the very same lies. He ed H was mortified by his size and, talking, cravenly always sought to sit behind a desk. In a *Salon* article (Oct. 22, 2011), Welsh novelist Matt Rees, who interviewed him, writes,

> I couldn't tell you exactly how heavy he was; the
> jacket of the light-gray business suit he usually wore
> disguised the extent of his belly and the dangling mass
> of his upper arms. Only when he walked could you
> make out the way he lifted his thighs around each oth-
> er instead of moving them directly forward. When I
> went to see him on his farm in southern-central Israel
> a few months before he became Israel's prime minister
> in February 2001, he wasn't wearing the business suit.
> His gargantuan form was revealed. In his casual shirt
> and jeans, he looked like Homer Simpson. His bulk
> was such that he seemed to lack all physical features.
> I could've drawn him as a single, smooth ellipse from
> forehead to toe.

Virtually ignored by the U.S. media, he was responsible—literally no one else—for the savage Sabra and Shatila massacre in Beirut of 3,500 civilians, mostly Palestinian and Lebanese Shiites. (The total of 2,977 victims in the World Trade Center disaster, on the other hand, is legend.) As Israeli Prime Minister, Sharon had the waking effrontery, the outrageous *chutzpah*, to declare on October 3, 2001, "We, the Jewish people, control America, and the Americans know it," a remark so volatile and so incendiary in its implications that it has been suppressed for two decades by the largely pro-Israeli, pro-Jewish media, both print and electronic, in this country, much of it Zionist-controlled. The all-consuming and undisguised hatred for Islam and for Muslims in American society, so casually expressed and born of such glaring ignorance, is a blasphemy and a nightmarish scandal. Long before 9/11, it has been sanctioned in this country, with impunity, for any loudmouth, callers on talk shows, pundits on cable, etc., to vilify Arabs with the same kind of names—and with the very same kind of hatred—that Jews had to put up with in Germany during the Nazi era.

One of Orson Welles' greatest feats was accomplished while filming *Citizen Kane*, where it is said that he regularly ate a dinner that consisted of two steaks, each with a baked potato, a whole pineapple, triple pistachio ice cream, and a bottle of scotch. "My doctor told me to stop having intimate dinners for four," he once declared. "Unless there are three other people." An oft-told story has it that on the way home from a Hollywood dinner, the actor had his driver stop at Pink's, the famous L.A. hot dog stand, to buy two dozen hot dogs for an after-dinner snack. Portly is not quite the word to describe the actor when he was at his fattest. In the film, *A Man for All Seasons*, playing Cardinal Wolsey, dressed all in red, he looked like a monstrous, auto-inflating tomato, actuating by way of the silver screen what is one of his most famous cinematic truisms, "Faces in color tend to look like meat, veal, beef, bologna."

Self-control was not Welles' forte. (Still, he knew everything and was a genius in conversation.) One particular food he hated was peanuts. "I hate television. I hate it as much as I hate peanuts. But I can't stop eating peanuts." It was a Zoroastrian war with him, eating (or not-eating) peanuts. Amazingly, as a food source, the peanut is one of the most concentrated sources of nourishment known to man. Pound for pound, the peanut provides more protein, minerals, and vitamins than beef liver, more fat than heavy cream, and—as Welles knew—more calories than sugar.

There is significance surely in reference to Welles's untrammelled appetite how in later life he steadfastly appeared to be indifferent to his great size—to push it, to be proud of it, marketing it, as it were, for the roles of John Falstaff and Cardinal Wolsey. (Johnny Carson once joked on the Tonight Show, "It was so hot today that Orson Welles was selling shade.") How unlike the suffering "campers" in Argentinean novelist Ana María Shua's *The Weight of Temptation*, the setting of which is a fat farm called The Reeds, a last resort for the overweight wealthy. There, regimented systems of public humiliation await the obese tenants whenever they cannot meet the impossible social demands for physical perfection. It makes a reader never want to ingest food again, never mind any foods extremely high in fat.

25.

FAT AND THIN, OR THE ANTI-GASTROLATERS

Marlon Brando would not eat *fafaru,* a dish of fermented raw fish. It not only has a horrible odor, but is usually eaten in a putrid state, although I am told that, if one controls one's breathing properly, it is possible to eat and can even taste quite good! A binge eater, in fact a desperate one, the famous actor ate just about everything else. Many stories of his food excesses are endlessly retailed about him. He was renowned for eating boxes of Mallomars and cinnamon buns, washing down his sweet treats by gulping quarts of milk. Although he would go on extreme crash diets, he would lose his willpower and subsequently gorge himself on inordinate breakfasts consisting of omelets, sausages, no end of eggs, bananas and cream, and monstrously tall stacks of hot pancakes that were drenched in maple syrup. (Interestingly, one of Brando's nicknames for himself was "Branflakes"). Karl Malden, a close friend, claimed that during the shooting of the movie *One Eyed Jacks* (1961) he would eat "two steaks, potatoes, two apple pies a la mode, and a quart of milk" for dinner, a diet that necessitated the constant altering of his costumes during filming. By the 1980s, one of Brando's girlfriends left him because he wouldn't keep his promise to lose weight. He always seemed to be dieting, and he swore up and down to her that he was doing so, but unknown to her, the wily actor was at the time having buddies of his throw full bags of Whoppers from Burger King over the gates of his Mulholland Drive estate. In the 1980s, Brando was routinely spotted at a Beverly Hills ice cream parlor, buying five gallons of ice cream, which he would down himself. During these years, the 5' 10" Marlon's weight would balloon up to an incredible 350 pounds. Reportedly, one of his last favorite "snacks" was a full pound of cooked bacon in—not and—an entire loaf of bread." In a 1949 issue of *Life* magazine, Brando's maternal grandmother, Elizabeth Myers, discusses the barbaric way that her grandson ate, and she is quoted as saying, somewhat apologetically, "Bud [Brando's nickname] doesn't bring the food to his face. He brings his face to the food."

As I have previously remarked, I am suspicious of raw fish. Agnes, Oskar Matzerath's mother, in Gunter Grass's novel, *The Tin Drum,* eats raw fish in a kind of consuming phantasmagoria until it kills her, an image of food that is hideously indelible in this caustic 1959 novel, a satire on Nazi Germany. At another point, everyone orders an onion the better to have a good cry. The notorious scene of the severed horse's head, gorging green eels, causes a revolted Agnes not only to regurgitate her breakfast but also, ironically— perversely—to go on those suicidal bouts of eating raw fish in a mystifying and paradoxical horror.

Gorging! To glut, to devour greedily, to stuff with food. It is a way of owning, actually, of possession, of taking custody, of being in charge, and to a degree it breaks almost all the 10 commandments at once. Lust, envy, greed, sloth. Writing about turkey vultures, Janet Lembke in *Dangerous Birds*, best to describe it, whimsically and most vividly uses the phrase "to vultch."

> They [vultures] are indeed so common, their feeding
> habits so well known, that they have given my family
> a verb, to vultch. It refers to the time before the
> appointed supper hour in which people, children es-
> pecially, circle the kitchen, perch on chairs, and vultch
> impatiently, waiting for their dinners to die [sic!] and
> be served.

Bernard Judge in *Waltzing with Brando* writes about time he spent with the actor during the 1970s working on projects, mainly architectural, on the small, sparsely populated atoll in the South Pacific called Tetioroa. It is Judge's claim that an immature Brando liked to "misbehave" not only to get attention but "to mask his fear of being thought inadequate or stupid." (His lack of formal schooling intimidated him.) "Having a meal with Marlon was always fascinating, whether at home, out with friends, or at a restaurant," notes Judge. One inevitably thinks of that raw eating scene in *Streetcar* where Stanley devours a chicken leg, licking each and every finger, while Blanche stares at him, fairly repulsed. Judge continues,

> While we ate together at his house in Punaauia, he
> would often comment on my table manners. "Bernie,
> why do you eat so delicately? Why do you sit up
> straight? Why don't you shove the food in your mouth

like me? Look, look what I'm doing," he'd say, as he
crammed food in his mouth, slobbering all over the
place. "Bernie, do it like me."... One night in Los
Angeles, Marlon came to dinner... We had all had a
good conversation before Dora [Judge's then wife]
brought out dinner and set it on the dining room
table. Marlon reached across and grabbed both ends
of the leg of lamb and, to the amazement of everyone
at the table, started chomping on it. Dora and I were
used to this sort of thing...

I have read elsewhere that on his private island Marlon liked to create his
own "real life mounds bars," cracking open a coconut, melting some chocolate in the sun, then stirring in the coconut for a tasty treat.

What many overweight people fail to understand is what I call the "fish-
flake" principle. Gorging—speed is involved—makes a person eat more. It is
a paradox at the heart of eating. Within seconds after being dropped into the
fish-tank, fish flakes absorb water, swelling to three or four times their original volume. All fish flakes should reach their full size before any fish reach
them and not later in the stomach, which is deleterious to them. (A few fish,
such as the Sumatra Barb, a species of striped, semi-aggressive tropical fresh-
water fish, feed even faster.) Curiously, aquarium fish can also be fed pure
crap, which covers terrible artificial foods like dried Daphnia, dried skimmed
milk, and yeast flakes. Fat is bad even for fish, and in fish food 6% is ideal.

Back in my college days, I had a highly loveable, roistering, red-nosed
hyper-gluttonous friend—he could burn through a dinner, turtle-snapping
every tidbit—whom we nicknamed "The Mole," after the notoriously hungry critter in nature, the Star-Nosed Mole, the marsh-dwelling burrower of
the earth who can detect, identify, and ingest its small prey (usually insect
larvae or earthworms) in an average of 227 milliseconds (less than a quarter
of a second). It takes a human being about 650 milliseconds, say, simply to
brake after seeing a traffic light turn red. The secret to this voracious mammal's foraging ability is the star-shaped set of 22 appendages that ring its
nose, helping it feel around in the dark for prey. Flexible fingers and twee-
zer-like incisors also help. Moles eat so fast that in their bumbling greed they
frequently make mistakes, skipping over edible food only to return later for
a second pass.

I fondly translate my old odd friend, The Mole, onto this page simply
because I believe that at bottom he actually *disliked* food, but, out of some
kind of non-specific, oddly inexplicable chronic anxiety, some driving, ma-

niacal, kinetic urge in his DNA, felt he had to dispatch it, getting it off the table, so to speak, in the same way that people with a sense of fate, accepting by dint of kismet a predetermined course of events, actually welcome with open arms any sudden accident in order to forfend the extra-burdensome worry of having to wait for it to happen. I used to view The Mole as a machine. He ate by rote, *burrowing* in his food. Charitably, I should perhaps have referenced the Bengal tiger instead, for it is generally agreed that no animal on earth is more fiercely omniverous. Franklin Russell in "The Last Tiger Hunt" (*Horizon*, Summer 1973) documents the range of that beast's highly catholic menu:

> He eats any deer or antelope, and the dainty, spotted chital, India's most common grazing animal, is his favorite. He attacks massive gaur, the ferocious wild pig (which sometimes kills him), bison, and the porcupine (which can cripple or kill him with spines in face and feet). He stalks birds, and grubs around in ponds and streams for frogs and crabs and fish. He eats snakes and bears, locusts and turtles, termites and nuts, berries and other fresh fruit.

Stephen King's character Annie Wilkes in *Misery* is a big bad bubble-butted psychotic dirigible—in a DVD forensic psychologist Reid Meloy has asserted that her stalking personality (as portrayed by Kathy Bates in the movie) is a virtual catalog of mental illness, covering everything from bipolar disorder, a severe personality disorder, and sadomasochism. A cunning, brutal, dangerously disturbed woman who hides her psychosis behind a cheery façade, Wilkes displays the kind of obsessive-compulsive personality disorder that would fixate—repellently or gluttonously—on food. It is the face of an eater, big-bodied, with a pig's upper lip. "That stony, obdurate look covered her face like a mask... Only her eyes, those tarnished dimes, were fully alive under the shelf of her brow," writes King. Frankly, I have always found Stephen King's *own* face, his loping head, to be much, much scarier than his books—that beetling brow, those thick spectacles that magnify his questioning—pinwheeling—eyes, made even loonier by corrective refractions, the hippo nostrils above a long baleful philtrum that is wider and longer than those of Josef Goebbels, Jackie Cooper, or Martin Sheen! Then there is that Humphrey Bogart-in-*High-Sierra* whitewall haircut of his, which in its extremity was last seen on Dr. Mabuse! It is an image altogether darkly minatory and Hallowe'enish—a barmy's persona. Anyway, I was disappointed in the last pages of *Misery*—a book I liked and in a very real way as a novelist I envied for the wonderful plot idea—to find that King had dropped the ball by virtually ignoring all of the novelistic possibilities in nutty Annie Wilkes of any extreme food lunacies.

Annie Wilkes is a near-Squidbillie. While not literally living in the Appalachian region of Georgia nor being a member of the ditzy Cuyler family, TV animations though they are, in her quacking opinions she does bear a resemblance to tubby Krystal. I think there is a great flaw in the novel, *Misery*: not a single food aversion of Annie's is ever mentioned in the book, not one menacing obsession that way, not a single weird crotchet of that "cockadoodie" fan, nope, not with Annie *who should have had tons of them*! It was surely blind of the imaginative King to fail so in this department, something akin to the gaffe it would have been for an otherwise blundering Shakespeare to have made the same mistake with his merry creation, big-bellied Jack Falstaff, except that the Bard comes through in style with that *miles gloriosus* having food on his mind all the time.

I would venture to say that no truly well delineated *character of excess* in a literary work of merit is not a maniac in the food department, at least in some way—by ignoring it or by indulging it. Check it out. After rabidly tearing into five or six big cutlets, I mean, the loony and cantankerous peckerwood Annie Wilkes should have been farting lightning and wheezing thunder with her huge earlobes flaming red! I see her earlobes wobbling scarlet, flaming, yes—a hideous alizarin crimson, totally abnormal! As M.F.K. Fisher writes in *The Art of Eating*, "After rare beef and wine, when the lobes turn red, was the time to ask favors or tell bad news."

A large segment of the American population seems ready for bariatric surgery. Bariatrics is that branch of medicine that deals with the causes, prevention, and treatment of obesity. (The term bariatrics was created around 1965, from the Greek root *bar-* ["weight," as in barometer], suffix *-iatr* ["treatment," as in pediatrics], a field that encompasses dieting, exercise and behavioral therapy approaches to weight loss, as well as pharmacotherapy and surgery.) I knew an older English couple who traveled across the United States in the 1980s as amiable tourists. Upon their return they were completely and utterly scandalized at the outsized helpings—the gigantic platters of food—served in our restaurants, so much so that at the end of their trip they almost breathlessly reported the situation to me not without small alarm—it was an excess that subsequently caused a slight aversion in them of eating "big." The couple had been through all the privations of Britain's World War II. They became in dire consequence of their American trip almost revolted by anything in the way of lavishness put before them. I tried to oblige them, all the while still encouraging them not to fade away. But it was a hard go. The very act of eating seemed to put them off. What Paul Brunton asserts in *The Notebooks of Paul Brunton* applies to the American dilemma: "Appetite has really become an artificial and abnormal thing, having taken the place of true hunger, which alone is natural. The one is a sign of bondage but the other, of freedom."

America's fat problem is out of hand. There are new treatments for obesity. That they are required shows just how extreme the matter is. Robert Paarlberg in *The United States of Excess*, cites several radical examples for those of us who simply have lost control of ourselves as to eating. A Boston-based firm, Gelesis 100, has been testing a product named Attiva, which is a capsule—a patented hydrogel—filled with super-absorbent particles to be taken with water before meals designed to trigger several important weight-loss mechanisms in the stomach and small intestine. A company named NAPILABS has introduced a unique $100 digital utensil—named the HAPIfork—that "reprimands overeaters with a vibrating buzz and a blinking red light if they lift the fork too soon between bites." No invention seems to be too dramatic or inventive. Paarlberg mentions GI Dynamics of Lexington, Mass., which has come up with an "EndoBarrier" sleeve for people who are obese or living with type 2 uncontrolled diabetes, a device to be inserted through the mouth and stomach, then placed at the upper portion of the small intestine, which emulates bariatric surgery.

I was reminded of a memorable passage that the Welsh actor Richard Burton, a habitual diarist, once confided to his journal, as recorded by Melvyn Bragg in his biography, *Richard Burton*: "Put some jaundice in your eyes and the act of walking is ludicrous and obscene, and swimming, and, above all, eating. All those muscles, in most people, 50 percent atrophied, sluggishly propelling people over land or through water or gulping oysters. Come off it." Burton seemed to harbor no food aversions and was not at all a snob about common fare. He loved American "short-order" cooking, as he put it. He made a note in one page, "I remember with watering mouth the soda fountain on 81st Street, one block west of the park in Manhattan, where in a blue of conjuring the cook would produce corned-beef hash with a fried egg on top and French fries on the side and a salad with a choice of about four or five dressings. All this magically produced and whipped onto the table piping hot." A poor Welsh boy from a large family—there were thirteen children—is surely speaking here. But the body for him, as Bragg puts it, was "a sham." The actor kept habitually thin, no doubt, from his wildly excessive smoking and boozing. "But his own [body] was pocked, banged about, a receptacle for abuse through alcohol and nicotine and a 'joke: strong men collapse in tears of laughter when they see me stripped for action'... His marvelous looks were a fluke." By all accounts, Burton was fascinated by cannibalism and one regret in his life, he said, was that he never witnessed it, although he did claim (falsely) to posh Londoners at dinner parties that he actually *had* tasted human flesh.

As to bodies, President William Howard Taft was a hugely obese fellow. A notorious gourmand, he weighed 340 pounds by the time he left the White House. His mere snacks became legendary. A big weakness was salted almonds. He nibbled on them whenever he had the chance. (Why not pistachios, for symmetry? They are the only nuts mentioned in the Bible. Gen 43:11) "On a visit to Savannah," notes Poppy Cannon and Patricia Brooks in *The Presidents' Cookbook*, "he once breakfasted on grapefruit, potted partridge, venison, grilled partridge, waffles with maple syrup and butter, hominy, hot rolls, bacon, and more venison." We have mentioned earlier that Taft despised eggs and could not look at them for breakfast. Cannon and Brooks go on to point out that "a typical Taft lunch might include bouillon, smelts with tartar sauce, lamb chops, Bermuda potatoes, green peas, and—for dessert—raspberry jelly with whipped cream, salted almonds, bonbons, and coffee. Like his predecessor and mentor, Teddy Roosevelt, Taft was a great coffee consumer." They do not mention steak, but steak was his favorite food. He always had a steak for his breakfast. Helen, his wife saw to it that a big steak appeared every morning. Toward the end of his life he had to modify his diet and so steak became more of a luxury. No meal passed the man by, however. We read in Cannon and Brooks, "Dinner some hours later would be, typically, lobster stew, salmon cutlets with peas, roast cold tenderloin with vegetable salad, cold tongue and ham, followed by frozen pudding, cake, fruit, and coffee." They go on to state, "At home, under the watchful eyes of a well-meaning wife, he might docilely nibble at his eight-ounce breakfast steak, his two oranges, several pieces of toast and butter, all washed down with quantities of coffee with cream and sugar."

I mention salmon. Rudolf Nureyev, the Soviet ballet dancer, who when dining invariably ordered a T-bone steak (bloody rare), always insisted on eating a piece of smoked salmon before cutting into it. His aversion was salt. Often he would throw the salmon at the waiter, screaming, "It is too salty. In Russia it is not salty." I can personally sympathize with Nureyev, since I myself find salt pretty much an unbearable condiment, headache-making, and always over-used, despite the fact the popular phrase "take it with a pinch of salt" in its original usage meant that, to make any food palatable, it should be taken with what was once considered pure white gold—a hugely valuable culinary commodity for both seasoning and food preservation. (We all know that soldiers were given a special stipend to make their food bearable, a commodity that was known as their salarium—thus our word salary.) So many of our words today are "salt" derivatives. The Romans *shook* salt into virtually every one of their sauces, of which there were many, and referred to them as *salsa*. Old French dropped the L, by which this became sauce. This word traveled through variations of *salsicus*, or salted meats, to transmogrify into *saucisses* eventually to give us our word sausages, which is cognate to the popular Italian and Spanish word *salami*. The word salad literally means "salted" and comes from the ancient Roman practice of salting leaf vegetables, for which their term became "*herba salata*," a phrase that we moderns have shortened and turned into the English word salad. I could go on: salary, salina, Salzburg. The taste of salt (saltiness) is one of the basic human tastes, but I still look to forgo it.

But what about anorexics, anti-gastrolaters, and congenital food haters in general—people that simply do not like to eat? A good example, the acerbic novelist Philip Wylie, echoing W.C. Fields, once complained, "During Prohibition I was forced to live for days on nothing but food and water." Spinoza and Epicurus were Spartan eaters. (An epicure is not an overeater, contrary to popular opinion, but one who eats simply with exquisite taste.) Henry Thoreau subsisted on bread, cheese, popcorn, and cold water. In a way, however, his tastes were quite delicate. No coffee, no tea, no wine—and no meat. (He could not bear to skin an animal. Still, one can question the nature of his sensibility, in light of his remark that a snowstorm meant more to him than Christ.) Tolstoy, Gandhi, and Kierkegaard all ate with pointed reservation, always sparely, and with elemental simplicity. John Calvin dined but once a day, on plain fare. For almost four years, John Wesley's diet consisted mainly of potatoes, partly to improve his health, but also to save money. He said, "What I save from my own meat will feed another that else would have none." As James Boswell notes, Dr. Samuel Johnson, even though in his habits he was not always personally proof of his preaching, spoke "with great contempt of people who were anxious to gratify their palates, and the 206th number of his *Rambler* is a masterly essay against gulosity." The Great Cham held up temperance as an ideal. Mother Ann Lee, founder of the Shakers, who cheerfully made up her meals strictly from the fragments left by others who were dining, remarked, "This is good enough for me, for it is the blessing of God, and must not be lost."

Lentils. Good for you. Healthy. And warming. But cocky, hip-swinging chef Bobby Flay despises lentils. "Whenever I tell somebody I hate lentils, they're shocked," said Flay, whose menu at Bar Americain initially had a beet and goat cheese salad with lentils listed, but then Flay rejected it before the restaurant opened. "When I go on vacation, they run specials on lentils," he said. "There are a lot of lentil fans out there. But lentils I cannot take."

It goes without saying—but must be mentioned—that times arise, hard, parlous times in war and famine, often both at the same time, when food of any sort is completely unavailable. The Siege of Leningrad. The Darfur Conflict in the Sudan, with 200,000 thousand dead from either direct combat or starvation. The continuing famine in the Horn of Africa: Somalia, Ethiopia, and neighboring countries. In many instances here, food aversions cede to having no food at all. I have read in several places that, out of some kind of psychological chiasmus, once being deprived of food, or certain foods, one can develop a revulsion of them. During World War II, Jews in Germany were prohibited from buying milk, eggs, fish, smoked goods, condensed milk, liquor, cheese, rice, cake or white bread, and from November 1942 on, no sugar or jam. The meager supplies still available to them—mostly cabbage, beets, potatoes, and coarse black bread—had to be purchased between 4 and 5 pm. Their telephones were disconnected; they were not allowed to buy newspapers or to have their shoes repaired except at two specially designated centers, and they were all required to register with a special Nazi labor office. The hideous irony is that these are the *very same policies* that the Jews of Israel ("an eye for an eye") have meted out to the Palestinians in Gaza and the West Bank, except that their thuggish occupation, restrictions, and food and medical blockades have been going on now for decades and show not a sign of ending.

Do you happen to remember the lines from the old children's story, "The History of Doctor Wango Tango" from Heinrich Hoffmann's *Slovenly Peter*? One of the couplets goes, "Old Doctor Wango Tango lived on a biscuit a day, and old Doctor Wango Tango got quite light this way." In the area of abstemiousness Old Doctor Wango Tango had plenty of company. Holy people legendarily eat very little. Jesus, Gandhi, Mother Teresa, St. Francis. These were not simply moderate. Self-denial, along with prayer, was a means of sacrifice, a means of humility and self-mastery to attempt to come close to Christ. St. Anthony of the Desert, one of the prominent leaders among the Desert Fathers, legendary anchorites who lived in Egypt—his feast day in January 30—famously ate nothing but black beans and drank water only—and that only after the sun went down. When he was about 18 years old, his parents died and left him with the care of his unmarried sister. Shortly thereafter, he decided to follow the words of Jesus who had preached, "If you want to be perfect, go, sell what you have and give to the poor, and you will have treasures in heaven; and come, follow me." In his monastic state, he only communicated with the outside world by a crevice through which food would be passed and he would say very few words, if any at all. He would prepare at times a quantity of bread that would sustain him for six months at a time. He did not allow anyone to enter his cell; whoever came to him stood outside and listened to his advice.

"Our society met today at the Duke of Beaufort's: a prodigious fine dinner, which I hate," wrote Jonathan Swift in Letter LXI in his *Journal to Stella*, the then 45-year-old prelate's nickname for the much younger woman, Esther Johnson, whom he first met when she was 8 years old and knew all his life—some think she was the Dean's secret wife. He added, "I have a sad vulgar appetite... I cannot endure above one dish; nor ever could since I was a boy and loved stuffing." I love the nomenclatural paradox of a sober, temperate boy who loves stuffing!

Photographer Eùgene Atget, who was said to be short-tempered and freakish, in his 50s stopped eating anything except bread, milk and sugar. Orphaned at a young age, he was raised by an uncle and went on to pursue a number of avocations. He was a sailor, a painter, a bit actor in a theater troupe, and, for a time, he studied to become a priest. He retained a lifelong sympathy for the working classes, and was given to quixotic habits, among them the adoption of the aforementioned diet. At the age of 41 and without formal training, Atget took up photography as an expressly commercial venture, selling his images of plants, animals and the natural world to artists for use as reference material. Upon recognizing the ruthless momentum of urbanization at the turn of the 20th century, the Bibliothèque nationale de France and the Bibliothèque historique de la ville de Paris wisely commissioned Atget to photograph old Paris—the project that would come to define his aesthetic legacy.

Fasting, virtually, was clearly part of Atget's anti-vision. Novelist Isak Dinesen, increasingly debilitated by syphilis, subsisted on little more than oysters, grapes, and white wine—and amphetamines. ("The greatest dishes are very simple dishes," said the great Auguste Escoffier. But this?) In all likelihood, she suffered from sitophobia, a morbid fear of eating, not generally, but usually in its specific forms—and I suggest in her case—anything remotely heavy or caloric.

Was it parsimony, paranoia, or prissiness that made vaudeville singer Eddie Cantor, as compulsively he always did, only eat cornflakes with milk for dinner, even when he went out to eat at a high-class restaurant? It was quite widely known that the comic was a notorious miser and skinflint. "I have eaten with [poet and writer] Allen Tate," observed my friend, scholar, and polymath, the late Guy Davenport in his *The Death of Picasso,* "whose sole gesture toward the meal was to stub out his cigarette in an otherwise untouched chef's salad [and] with [poet] Louis Zukofsky who was dining on a half piece of toast, crumb by crumb."

Alcoholics tend to eat little or nothing. Sinclair Lewis, William Faulkner, Dylan Thomas, Raymond Chandler, Truman Capote, Dorothy Parker, Charles Bukowski, to name but a few, found little interest at the table. Microbe hunter Paul de Kruif mentions in *The Sweeping Wind* reporter Frazier Hunt telling him: "Remember to eat plenty of hors d'oeuvres when you begin drinking, kid. Then you can go on forever." Crime novelist and eccentric Patricia Highsmith has gone on record as rejecting out of hand the whole idea of eating. She once uniquely declared, "I hate food." Highsmith wrote to a friend of hers, Alex Szogyi, a food writer, strangely enough, that food was her "*bête noire*" and that she had come to attach many personal confusions to the act of eating. When she got older and cranky, Mrs. Rose Kennedy, JFK's mother, unfailingly ate the same meager lunch over and over again, according to Frank Saunders in *Torn Lace Curtain*—"boiled chicken, white meat only, plain with no salt, pepper, or dressing of any kind, between two crust-less pieces of white bread; for dessert she liked a piece of angel-food cake, no frosting." Not quite "Cold Roast Boston," but close.

"My principal food aversion all my life has been boiled chicken, which my mother used to make all the time, and which I just hated (and still hate), almost to the point of literal physical disgust—there was and is something about the texture, and the occasional pieces of skin, bone, and gristle, that I just found and still find absolutely repulsive," says T. Peter Park, a friend from my University of Virginia days, whom I have previously cited regarding his dislike of fruit. He goes on,

> I have likewise never cared for fresh apples, although I do love apple pie, apple crumb cake, apple sauce, and apple cider! Strawberries and blueberries too for some reason turn me off, although I've tried hard to desensitize myself to my seemingly groundless and irrational aversion. Though I don't loathe fried chicken nearly as much as I do boiled chicken, I don't particularly care for it at all, either, but must say I have never understood why, as it is such a great Southern and African-American favorite. The same goes for buffalo wings—I've never been able to understand why macho American guys watching endless football games on television and guzzling Colt 45s in their living rooms or in bars find them such a treat. On the other hand,

while I'm no exactly wild about them, I've never been able to understand why so many people profess to hate spinach or broccoli.

A dislike or suspicion of the fruit curiously attaches to the notable chapter in the *Confessions* where St. Augustine explores the question of why he and his friends stole pears when he had many better pears of his own. (The great saint who hailed from a good family had never wanted for food.) He explains the feelings he experienced as he ate the pears and threw the rest away to the pigs, arguing that he most likely would not have stolen anything had he not been in the company of others who could share in his sin. Pears are oddly assigned a kind of Manichean gloss of both corruption and the perverse in this context. Wilhelm Stekel, the Austrian physician and psychologist who became one of Sigmund Freud's earliest followers, claimed that the pear symbolized the male organ. Janie has her first experience of sexual awakening under the blooming pear tree in Spring, just before her first kiss with Johnny Taylor in Zora Neale Hurston's novel, *Their Eyes Were Watching God*. Botanically, a pear tree can be regarded as bisexual by nature because of its self-fertilizing characteristics, as it has both female and male organs. So much of this is laughably overdetermined, and yet this is so very often the case with food and what in it may attracts or repulse us.

The pear tree is a sexual symbol in Katharine Mansfield's "Bliss," having to do with Bertha's bisexuality. There is a scene in Proust's *La Recherche* where the decadent Baron de Charlus, snobbishly wanting to show off his knowledge of food to Morel, a gifted violinist but a weak and corrupt associate, offers a disquisition on pears and cruelly berates an unfortunate waiter who is unable to distinguish them. Is there a fey subtext of pears and homosexuality in that particular scene? Count Robert de Montesquiou, the French aesthete and Symbolist poet, art collector, and dandy on whom Proust based his well-read, hyper-cultured homosexual, Charlus, was a well-known connoisseur of pears. In real life, he had no affairs with women, although in 1876 it is reported that he once slept with the tarty actress Sarah Bernhardt—she may very well have been a prostitute—after which he vomited for twenty-four hours. She supposedly remained a great friend!

As I say, Raymond Chandler was an alcoholic. If not an acid, bad-tempered, grouchy fellow, "like so many former alcoholics are," according to director Billy Wilder, who also happened to co-write the film-script with Chandler for *Double Indemnity*, he could be petulant and difficult. Prodded to finish the script of *The Blue Dahlia* at top speed so it could be immediately shot—the star of the movie, handsome Alan Ladd, was about to leave

Hollywood to join the US Army—Chandler came up with a desperate scheme of drinking and resorting to drugs. "He had a doctor who gave him such massive injections of glucose that he could last for weeks *with no solid food at all* (my italics). It was the sobering up that was perilous," wrote producer John Houseman of his friend in a posthumous essay, "Lost Fortnight." He explained, "During those last eight days of shooting Chandler did not draw one sober breath, nor did one speck of solid food pass his lips. He was polite and cheerful when I appeared, and his doctor came twice a day to give him intravenous injections… His long starvation seriously weakened him, and it took him almost a month to recover." This was not simply food aversion but rather food elimination all together.

The social ideals that led young Simone Weil to her insistence on body denial are surely strange to the layman, as was her sincere conviction—a born Jew's—that Hitler was no worse a would-be conquering figure than Napoleon, Richelieu, or Caesar. (She actually wrote that Hitler's mad racialism was nothing more than "a rather more romantic name for nationalism.") The *habitus* of a deep and abiding compassion for mankind nevertheless pervaded the life of this woman, and as the late critic Susan Sontag wrote, reviewing her *Selected Essays* in 1963, "we are moved by it, nourished by it." Sontag concluded,

> In the respect we pay to such lives, we acknowledge the presence of mystery in the world—and mystery is just what the secure possession of truth, an objective truth, denies. In this sense, all truth is superficial; and some (but not all) distortions of the truth, some (but not all) insanity, some (but not all) unhealthiness, some (but not all) denials of life are truth-giving, sanity-producing, health-creating, and life-enhancing.

A polar opposite of this saintly ascetic, both in wealth and temperament, was the close-fisted business tycoon, John D. Rockefeller, a true loner, a man who was thornily independent and never needed outside stimulus—he declared that he never experienced a craving for tea, coffee, or "for anything." A man who suffered from moderate digestive troubles, one of his favorite dishes was bread and milk, and it was his custom to keep a bag of apples on the sill outside of his bedroom window and eat one each time at bedtime. He preferred cold meals on Sundays, because to him it was a sin to cook on that day. Food meant nothing to Rockefeller; temperance was a glorious standard to live by.

Restrained, sober, and austere men and women rarely celebrate by the act of eating, which represents a wastrel's folly. To the great annoyance of his family, he declined to replace his shirts and suits until they became shiny from use. Much as he loved skating, he would not skate on the Sabbath or even direct workmen to flood his yard until 12:01 Monday a.m. He was a 1-ply toilet-paper man. Waste galled him, and all of his life he fought the specter of even moderate prodigality, until in the mid-1880s he met Swami Vivekananda, who urged him to take up philanthropy to help the poor and any distressed people. A committed Christian, he was something of an extreme and unbudging teetotaler. (To this day, a bottle of liquor is the one thing you cannot buy in Rockefeller Center.) Adjusting for inflation, his fortune upon his death in 1937 stood at $356 billion, accounting for more than 1.5% of the national economy, making him the richest person in US history.

Abstemious (but also niggardly), the Duchess of Windsor—she insisted on 25% discounts on her Dior, Balmain, and Mainbocher purchases but she supposedly never thanked a soul for anything in her whole life—ate virtually nothing, maybe lettuce, toast, an olive. When she arose at 1 p.m. and was dressed, a Cadillac would be waiting to take her to luncheon at some chic restaurant such as L'Espadon at the Ritz. She rarely lunched at home with the Duke (formerly Edward VIII) and is quoted as having said, "I married David for better or worse, but not for lunch." Rarely did the woman bother to eat, lunch or breakfast. Whenever she did, in order to maintain her size-six frame, the Duchess breakfasted on nothing but grapefruit juice and black Earl Grey tea and then only picked at lunch and dinner. She had a tropism for order. At dinner parties, she insisted that the food, whether it was lettuce leaves or pieces of fish, be trimmed to exactly the same size. She particularly—hugely—disliked soup, often repeating, according to her biographers, J. Bryan III and Charles J.V. Murphy in *The Windsor Story*, "Don't start a dinner with soup! It's an uninteresting liquid that gets you nowhere." "I am almost too fussy," she admitted. "She was always on a diet," says Anne Sebba in *That Woman: The Life of Wallis Simpson, Duchess of Windsor*. "In fact, she was quite obsessive about it. It was part of the way she controlled her life and her image."

Laura Charteris, the Duchess of Marlborough, who recalled Wallis, even at her calmest moods, as having a tropism for order, saw the woman as constantly on the move, aggressive, always jumping up to rearrange an ornament or to plump up a cushion on the sofa. One observer wrote about her in 1944: "The Duchess gives the impression of terrific neatness, not a hair out of place, not a line awry. Her nose never shines. Her slip never shows. She looks like a period room done by a furniture house, a room in which nobody lives comfortably." She had a grim, rachitic-looking body, at least to me, but then ultimately what is true beauty? Pieter Breughel's fleshy peasants. Giotto's ascetic saints. Choose whom you would.

In her obsessions and almost feral avidity, Wallis Simpson, an incorrigible control freak, pretty much embodied all of her life the asinine and disturbing remark one comes across in Margaret Atwood's shrill feminist novel, *The Edible Woman* (1969), a bit of fictional bollocks about an unstable woman who finds herself unable to eat, repelled by metaphorical cannibalism: "I always thought eating was a ridiculous activity anyway. I'd get out of it myself if I could, though you've got to do it to stay alive, they tell me." The problems with food that the loony narrator of the book, Marian McAlpin, undergoes begin when she finds herself empathizing with a steak that her boring boyfriend, Peter, is eating, imagining it "knocked her on the head as it stood in a queue like someone waiting for a streetcar." After this, she is unable to eat meat—anything with "bone or tendon or fiber." Neurotic, hand-wringing Marian, with her gerbil insight, concludes of course that Peter is metaphorically devouring her. To test him, she bakes him a pink cake in the shape of a woman and dares him to eat it. "This is what you really want," she says, offering the cake-woman as a substitute for him feeding upon her. Peter leaves, disturbed. Marian eats the cake herself. She returns to her first person narrative in the closing pages of the book. Duncan [a graduate student with whom Marian has an affair] shows up at her apartment; Marian offers him the remains of the cake, which he polishes off. "'Thank you,' he said, licking his lips. "It was delicious."

Actress Jennifer Aniston purportedly eats a 151-calorie lunch of cucumbers. (I wonder if in the process she understands that she is eating fruits, not vegetables, for the cucumber is in fact a fruit.) It is surely the case that the cucumber is about as close to bird-brained neutrality as a vegetable can get without ceasing to exist—it is 96 percent water. Dr. Samuel Johnson despised the things. "A cucumber should be well sliced, and dressed with pepper and vinegar, and then thrown out, as good for nothing," he once declared. An English proverb seems to support him: "Raw cucumber makes the churchyards prosperous." A cucumber diet seems to work for the svelte Aniston. Many actresses follow the same diet. Actress Gwyneth Paltrow swears by fasts and detoxes. Elizabeth Hurley swapped wine for vodka and, after the birth of her son, Damien, took to eating only one meal a day. Perhaps model Kate Moss is right when she counsels, "Nothing tastes as good as skinny feels."

I know several people, health zealots, who assiduously take gulping infusions of apple cider vinegar—the real raw, unpasteurized, organic, non-filtered "mother of vinegar"—as a strict regimen on a daily basis. It is their boast that as a panacea ACV cures virtually anything and everything that plagues the human species, managing to kill head lice, reverse aging, ease digestion, prevent flu, lower cholesterol and blood pressure, stem the onset of acne, arrest fungus, regulate PH balance, dissolve kidney stones, promote bowel irregularity, wash toxins from the body, and do just about everything short of the promise of immortality.

Sylvia Plath wrote cynically in her poem "The Thin People" of a "weedy race" that, in her words, have "found their talent to persevere in thinness," "unreal" people who "prop each other up,"

> Wrapped in flea-ridden donkey skins,
> Empty of complaint, forever
> Drinking vinegar from tin cups: they wore
> The insufferable nimbus of the lot-drawn
> Scapegoat.

Disgusted at the stagy violation of needy people walking about in "stiff battalions," Plath was writing with distaste bordering on loathing and even anger about what she saw as canny Jewish self-victimization after World War II, the almost professional shamelessness of masochists greedy "in their withering kingship" to display—to preserve—thinness. In her poem, the "menace" of such people in their desperate and gray but paradoxical self-spite is described in terms of their own mad wishes. The dark electricity of Plath's stark lines also comment on the anti-life world of fashion models as well as the savage fascination today among certain girls for anorexia, where starvation is seen as genocide against the self.

A tiny, fastidious person, Blanche Knopf, wife of the publisher Alfred Knopf—she was described by one wag as "seemingly held together by jewelry"—nourished herself daily on nothing but one martini, three shrimp, and a stick of asparagus. Virtually every table she sat down to was a Barmecide feast. Bone thin and queechy, she weighed little more than 90 pounds or so and could be summed-up in a word that Albert Einstein once used in describing Marie Curie, "*Haringseele*"—that is, lean, gaunt (in the sense of strained) with an added meaning of deathlessly humorless, meager in emotion. She could also be aggressive, even truculent, and had the irritable snap of a raw crowbite. Rebecca West, who was infamously uncharitable in her rash judgments, described Knopf, writing, "For lunch she would have a lettuce leaf, and then in the evening she would break out and have a lettuce leaf with dressing." Her strong aversion to food was well-known and often ridiculed. Stanley Olson in his biography *Elinor Wylie* writes, "At a luncheon (of all things) to honor her [Knopf] in 1940, Thomas Mann said, 'It seems rather paradoxical to honor with an excellent luncheon the merits of a lady who notoriously eats nothing.'" When she talked, I can picture her squeaking high or plinking like a fluorescent light. A funny little wound-up thing, seemingly, she was in fact tough as nails, hard as nacre, and cold as her massive and improbable jewelry.

When poet Marianne Moore faced any emotional stress, her habit was to stop eating. She confessed to a friend, "My stomach has been about as much use to me as a feather duster or a rim for spectacles without any glass in it." Refusing food became a paradoxical template for her survival. She associated food with invasion of her privacy. She was thin as a spindle. Her lack of body fat caused amenorrhea and loss of libido. She was often listless, inert, spiritless, and in poems, radically underweight, she portrayed her redheaded self as a carrot.

Cosmopolitan magazine editor Helen Gurley Brown whose raddled, slightly insane look was not merely thin—I am sure that when she was young she was a fat Arkansas hillbilly—but bloodless, etiolated, corpselike. She must have loathed food, in all of its phases. She was known for her celebrated "wine diet," the offering—brainless bird-piping—of a true simpleton: "Breakfast: 1 egg any style, no butter, one glass white wine. Lunch: 2 eggs any style, two glasses white wine. Dinner: 1 steak, finish the bottle of white wine." Her diet fit in with virtually every article (very few) I have ever read by her. The standard HGB template? Lewd, pragmatic advice with gamy pretensions in gummy alliance with small, amorphous ideas to gullible girls. It would figure that such guile would come from someone thin as a famished rat.

There was the Viennese architect, Adolf Loos, another "thinifer." After being diagnosed with cancer in 1918, the man had to have virtually all his stomach removed. For the rest of his life he could only eat—and try to digest—ham and cream. A Jewish nightmare! My question: how (and why) did he settle on those two items? Mrs. Knopf suffered in all probability from mageirocophobia, although many women who want to stay slim—Audrey Hepburn, Jackie Kennedy Onassis, and, indeed, Blanche Knopf—were chronic smokers all of their lives, which in terms of its comic and ironic lunacy and jittery lack of control is, as far as intemperance goes, actually no different than an obese kid in fat-pants roaring downhill after a runaway cheese-wheel.

Statistics tell us that most smokers tend to eat *more* sugar than non-smokers do. Ironically, many smokers feel a strong craving for sweet foods *after* quitting smoking, according to the American Heart Association. How unpleasant! This is what is called being on the horns of a dilemma.

It is no surprise to hear that the great dancer Fred Astaire ate lightly, and did so all his life. He ate a single boiled egg and one cup of bouillon which saw him *through the day*—and, until his last illness, he weighed a meager 134–136 pounds, just about what he weighed when he was dancing in top form! I am certain that food meant virtually nothing to him. John D. Rockefeller, Simone Weil, the Duchess of Windsor, Blanche Knopf, Fred Astaire. Eating for them was little more than a mechanical exercise, a dutiful act of rote done in a dogged, mindless, and disinterested fashion to preserve life. It was an anti-vital undertaking, in short, a sort of *anti*-agape, in its neutral severity almost a form of penance, Spartan, self-abnegating, a full and final repudiation, worse than austere, of the very concept of *joyously* nurturing the self.

The daily intake of the late heiress Barbara Hutton, toward the end, was 20 bottles of Coca-Cola, alcohol, vitamin pills, intravenous mega-vitamin shots (often mixed with amphetamines), a soybean compound, Metrecal, and a mixture of other drugs which included Empirin compound, codeine, valium, and morphine. She also smoked cigarettes, compulsively, heavily, one after another, gasping out smoke. Can anyone possibly hate food more than this? "I have wished many times I could do without eating altogether," said Henry Miller, the German-born California rancher and fanatical overachiever who in his day became the largest producer of cattle in all of California and one of the largest landowners in the United States, owning 1,400,000 acres and controlling nearly 22,000 square miles of cattle and farm land in California, Nevada, and Oregon. Driven, pushy, enterprising, ever on overdrive, he could not bear to stop work (or let his laborers) to fuel up, which he saw as a time-wasting bother meant only for layabouts, shirkers, sluggards, loungers, and ne'er-do-wells.

Upton Sinclair, author of the classic muckraking novel, *The Jungle* (1906), which exposed conditions in the U.S. meat packing industry, causing a public uproar that contributed in part to the passage a few months later of the 1906 Pure Food and Drug Act—actress Mary Pickford after reading *The Jungle* never ate meat or fish again—in his personal life, through a slow process of attrition stepped further and further away from the very idea of hearty food, stutterstepping down the long food ladder to pure fasting. Initially he became a vegetarian, forgoing meat, later he tried raw foods, a milk diet, followed by just nuts, then eventually he settled on a simple diet of rice and fruit. Fasting then became his fascination, which he wrote about in his book, *The Fasting Cure* (1911). There is no question that his autocratic mother, Priscilla Harden Sinclair, a strict Episcopalian who disliked alcohol, tea, and coffee, played a role in his growing self-restrain, public eccentricities, and a

lot of his later crackpated ideas. (He believed in sex solely for procreation.).
Sinclair struggled ferociously with his mother when he became older because
of her strict rules and refusal to allow him independence. He confessed to his
son David that around the age of 16 he decided to have nothing to do with
her and then willfully stayed away from her for 35 years in order to avoid the
inevitable fights that would start if they met.

There is a sort of reduced person. Designer Karl Lagerfeld is such a one.
He is a misanthrope in almost every way. It has been rumored that the once
grossly overweight fashion designer lost almost 90 pounds at the beginning
of the 1990 due to the consumption of only steamed vegetables and Diet
Coke, some say only tuna and blackberry mousse, still others insist he has
limited himself solely to horse meat and tomatoes. I have also read he eats
only sashimi and only from Nobu. "I never touch sugar, cheese, bread. I
only like what I'm allowed to like," he has stated. "I'm beyond temptation.
There is no weakness. When I see tons of food in the studio, for us and for
everybody, for me it's as if this stuff was made out of plastic. The idea doesn't
even enter my mind that a human being could put that into their mouth."
He told *Prestige* magazine in 2008. "I hate the smell of cooking. Some people love it, but I don't care for it. I don't eat sweet things. I don't eat greasy
things. And I like fish better than meat. In fact, I hate meat. My doctor calls
me to eat meat twice a week, as apparently we are cannibals." Pared-down
isn't quite the word for the designer who, along with a reputation for being
rude, is spare, bare, barely there. "I hate children—all children. For other
people, it is fine, but not for me. I was born not to be a family person... I
live in certain isolation. I never take appointments in the morning. I leave my
house only after lunch. I don't want to have a social life. I've had enough of
that in my life. It's *demodé*. It's another era. Perhaps people are still excited
by that era, but not me. It's uninteresting today. It says nothing. It's boring, pretentious and vulgar...Even for charity, people get paid. I try to avoid
charity. It doesn't happen for me. I'm rich enough not to have to do that.
Thank God I don't have to do that. I do a lot of unnecessary things for free,
but I'm very much against that. Money itself isn't interesting, the use of it is.
I imagine the world from my window. I am not a traveler. I hate it. I never
look at my watch. The good thing about private jets is that you go whenever
you're ready. That's the real luxury of today. In all my contracts it says, if you
want me, send a private jet."

It all brings to my mind the directness of Eileen Myles' poignant poem,
"To the Mountains," which I tender as an ironic counterpoint to Lagerfeld's
smug discriminations on his favorite beverage and private jet:

when I look out
at you
how absurd to think
of Diet Coke
killing me
I'm flying through
the air
and there you are
white and dangerous
who's kidding who

Lagerfeld declares with some kind of paranoia,

Also I cannot go on airlines because people stare at
me, you have to be touched by people. I hate that... I
hate bespoke because I hate to be touched by strangers. It bores me to death. I'm frustrated by nothing
at all, and frustration is the mother of all crimes.
Ambition? I have no ambition. I just want things in
a certain way... I don't want to be a teacher. I don't
want to inform others through myself. In that way,
it's all for myself. I'm the most selfish person in the
world. Being selfish, I take care of others. My mother
always used to say, "Don't sacrifice yourself too much,
because if you sacrifice too much there's nothing else
you can give and nobody will care for you."

Do forgive my need to quote this foppish zany to make a food point.
Pierre Bergé once said that Yves Saint Laurent, his long-time partner, was
"a man of exceptional intelligence practicing the trade of an imbecile." One
does wonder about that exceptional intelligence bit. One of YSL's models
recalls him pointing to her breasts and inquiring with disapproval, "What are
those?"

It is amazing how abstinent some people can be. Should one assert that
they are moderate, austere, frugal, sparing, restrained, self-denying, or is it
a combination, in changing flux, of all of these in some degree in one form
or another? Virginia Woolf on February 18, 1922—she was exactly 40—
found it worthwhile to confide to her diary, "I have an egg now every night
for dinner." One egg. For dinner. A jittery, tense woman, she drank lots of
coffee and smoked cigarettes, although in the instance above she was rather

parsimoniously toting up the cost of living. Leonard Woolf did not call his wife anorexic, but in his *Beginning Again: An Autobiography of the Years 1911–1918* he naively—almost comically—wrote, "There was always something strange, something slightly irrational in her attitude towards food."

Kate Middleton, the Duchess of Cambridge, smokes cigarettes, as well, and also has been criticized for being far too thin, scarily so, almost anorectic. Angelina Jolie who reportedly lives on a 600 calorie-a-day diet—anything under 800 calories a day is a starvation diet—is also a pack-a-day smoker. Although one does not think of him as a sparse eater, General Ulysses S. Grant who was inordinately thin during the Civil War, weighing only one hundred and thirty-five pounds, was a very sparse eater. He abhorred red meat of any kind, and the sight of blood made him ill. He insisted on his meat being cooked on the verge of being charred. He would not eat any kind of fowl, but was fond of pork and beans, fruit, and buckwheat cakes—basic fare, even for Gertrude Stein who, giving us a hint that it may be too common, once wrote, "I am feeding my friends beans with pork; I expect some will not stay for dinner."

The cadaverous novelist Joan Didion—physically, unprepossessingly, and visually probably the worst advertisement for food on the planet—seriously offers a "personal cookbook" of her own online, a bunch of astonishingly unoriginal recipes, menus of meals she has served while entertaining at home, some typed but most rendered in her own crabbed, hard-to-read handwriting—with cross-outs, inconsistent punctuation, ink stains, slapdash marginalia—including an unmemorable one for her parsley salad which is a dim *macédoine* of Parmesan cheese, oil and vinegar, and parsley, which is intended to suffice for—wait for it—35 to 40 guests! All of Didion's recipe directions, many of them scribbled off on hotel or business stationery, most written in standard dumbo, reflect her scrimp, punitively under-medicated prose style. There is a 40-word risotto recipe. One for borscht is a sloppy few lines scrawled on a *Life* magazine memo sheet. Shortcake is a fleeting, capsulized sketch. 'Nuff said.

A celery stick, Joan Didion looks like she exists on four blanched almonds and a glass of water a day. "She's so thin that if you touch her back you can feel the ribs, like ridges on a roll-top desk," as Leslie Garis observes. Her emaciated face with those cold, wet, unmoving eyes and thousand-yard stare, reflects disillusionment. She is in love with her disappointment and always has been with that driving need in her work to rain on parades. The sense of jittery ruin that emanates from both her fiction and non-fiction was actually summed up in Didion's last bleak book, *Blue Nights*, which Emma Brockes in *The Guardian* ("Joan Didion: Life after Death," Oct. 21, 2011) describes as a horrifying documentary of a writer observing herself in the moment of dissolution, when she can't remember how to write, can't wholly remember who she is." There Didion asks, "What if I can never again locate the words that work?"

I am reminded in the inane and insane circularity of Brockes's description of Didion's convoluted novel of the 1968 movie, *Symbiopsychotaxiplasm*, which has been laughably described—in all seriousnessness—as "a circular meta-documentary about a documentary, a documentary about a documentary, and a documentary documenting a documentary about a documentary."

The film, directed by William Greaves, which is shot and presented in the style of a *cinéma vérité* documentary, attempts to capture and examine pure reality unhindered by the presence of the running cameras all around! Metatextual storytelling was a perfect match for the raddled Didion.

A frail, querulous near-dwarf (5'2"), Joan Didion was a child in the Second World War when her father left the family to fulfill his army duties. Infuriated, abandoned or so she felt, the young girl vindictively and spitefully held her mother ransom by, suddenly, flatly refusing to eat all food. The woman who, as I say, is nearly malignantly attenuated, has always been slight, almost crazily pipe-cleaneresque, and, according to Brockes, "it annoys her when people comment on her frailty and interpret it as neurosis, instability, grief or an eating disorder." After Didion's early refusal conniptions, when her mother fearfully took her to a pediatrician, the doctor assured her that the ornery if despairing child would not put on weight until the family reunited with her father. When that did happen, the girl began to eat normally. Of every single book of hers that I have ever read, three pages were never turned, I noticed, before I was treated to a grim depiction of a woman unraveling. It was not just the pained face on the jacket, the wet wobbly eyes, the sparrow body ("Her arms are translucent river systems of veins," wrote someone), the pleading aura of deep need in her wide, duck-like mouth, but that faux-Hemingway prose and those bird-on-a-wire sentences so coy and so twee. It was as if I had entered some kind of Leperville.

But aren't all of her books—fiction and non-fiction—grief memoirs? The books themselves are filament-thin. Her persona has always been that of a brittle, nicotine-addicted, bird-small, migraine-ridden California intellectual, worrying away at the attrition, the atomization, of American society and the afflictions of being a writer ("I sit in a room literally papered with false starts and cannot put one word after another and imagine that I have suffered a small stroke"). Angela Carter despised Joan Didion, called her "an alien from another planet." It was no different with the female characters in her books. "Although I am a card-carrying and committed feminist," stated Carter with seemingly no exaggeration, "what I would like to see happen to Joan Didion's female characters is that a particularly hairy and repulsive chapter of Hells Angels descend upon their therapy group with a squeal of brakes and sweep these anorexic nutters behind them despite their squeaks of protest..." I have always taken Joan Didion to be the ultimate anorectic writer, scanty and dilute, from every angle. In Spanish art, a *bodegón* is a still-life painting, which depicts—bountifully displays—pantry items, such as game, victuals, and drink, all usually arranged on a simple stone slab, and also a painting with one or more figures, but always with significant still-life elements, typically set in a kitchen or tavern. Joan Didion in every way, shape, and form as a writer is the anti-*bodegón*.

Pop singer Prince (Rogers Nelson), a strict vegan, often went whole days without touching a morsel of food. A ceaseless worker, he is quoted in *Rolling Stone* 1985 as saying, "Do I have to eat? I wish I didn't have to eat." Prince hated mushrooms, feta cheese and onions although he could be induced to eat onions if they were "chopped up very finely to avoid the 'textural thing' that Prince had with the ingredient," according to Tamara Palmer in "What Did Prince Love to Eat? His Personal Chefs' Revelations Are Surprising and Funny" (*Bravo*, April 28, 2016). She explains that he tried a raw-foods diet for a month but gave up on it.

He loved spaghetti but would insist on eating it only when paired with orange juice. Mustard was one of his fanatical favorites. The magazine *Heavy Table*, allowed permission to look into the musician's refrigerator for an article (4/01/2011), reported that Prince kept as many as 18 different kinds of mustard sitting in his fridge, international, exotic brands from everywhere in the world. "I don't collect it, but LOL yeah there's a lot in there," the singer later explained. "U gotta love mustard. The raspberry kind is the best. You wouldn't expect it but that's how it goes."

I have alluded to physicist Paul Dirac. He frankly disliked eating anything, mainly because his parents martially insisted on his still eating even after his appetite had been sated, and he felt sick in having to consume every morsel of food on his plate. "Have you a tomato?" vegetarian George Bernard Shaw once asked his friend and neighbor, Stephen Winsten. "That is all I eat... with a piece of bread." Saintly Charles De Foucauld who lived among the Tuaregs took nothing but scraps of bread and water. I have read that wealthy film producer, Jean Doumanian, who bankrolled most if not all of Woody Allen's films until the two had a spiteful falling out, never eats anything other than lettuce, diet popcorn, and candy. She must hate all food, every category, you name it. Allen himself, who from all reports is particular about food, suspects the worst things about most of it, I would guess—

which is odd, because he orders lots of Chinese take-out, a cuisine of mixed mystery. Fastidiousness takes few chances. "I think shrimp dumplings and bruschetta are the only two things I've ever seen him eat," actress Scarlett Johansson told *Food and Wine* (February 2013).

Any creature solely bound to a single diet—pandas with bamboo, monarch caterpillars with milkwood, and koalas with eucalyptus plants, for example—is arguably the classic food phobic, the omniphage's opposite. One may legitimately ask how hyper- focused sticklers like Woody Allen are any different from the snail kite that eats apple snails almost exclusively or the black-footed ferret who eats only prairie dogs or the pen-tailed treeshrew of Indonesia which happily guzzles only the naturally fermented nectar of the bertam palm, source of palm wine, which has an alcohol content of 3.8 percent (the equivalent of a can of light lager), except that the little creature who drinks the equivalent of 10 to 12 cans of beer a night is much happier!

American intellectual Guy Davenport, writer, artist, and polymath, also claimed to live off Campbell's Soup, Snickers bars, and baloney exclusively, a diet I would recommend to anyone if it helped him or her think as brilliantly and originally as that man. Of Trappist fare I know personally first-hand: it is sparse, healthy, indeed, and of course strictly vegetarian. Yet there can be found no individuals more deeply grateful for the food before them as the monks pray before meals, "*Nos et ea quae sumus sumpturi benedicat dextera Christi in nomine Patris et Filii et Spiritus sancti. Amen.*" Temperance, as I have repeated, is part of Cistercian grace, moderation, and sanctity, a mode of self- restraint, nothing like the fanatical or neurotic food refusals of grouchballs or anything close to approaching peevish rejection of God's abundance. Catholic monks are among the healthiest lovers of good food on this earth. "When an animal laments, it is not a lament, it is merely the rasp of a poorly functioning mechanism," wrote Milan Kundera in *The Unbearable Lightness of Being*. To me, it all touches upon one of those roundabout situations described by the queer English cleric—and suicide—Charles Caleb Colton who so succinctly put it, "We hate some persons because we do not know them; and we will not know them, because we hate them"

An official government website once stated that the late pint-sized, tubby Kim Jong-il (1941–2011), Supreme Leader of the Democratic People's Republic of Korea, never needed to urinate or defecate. One therefore assumes that he never ate anything, a fact belied by another state report there in 2000 that he actually invented a new food which he called "*Gogigyeopbbang*"! It was described as "double bread with meat," although it took on the uncanny appearance of a conventional hamburger. (In 2006, another culinary revolution was introduced on Jong-il's orders in an attempt to alleviate food shortages—the breeding of giant rabbits.) An Italian chef, Ermanno Furlanis, who once worked for Kim Jong-il—further proof that the Supreme Leader in spite of the godhood he assumed in North Korea may have actually condescended to eat—wrote a book of his experiences and stated that he was ordered, among other things, to carve sashimi from a live fish and never to place anchovies on pizzas. He was also sent to Uzbekistan to buy caviar, Denmark to buy pork, China for grapes, and to Thailand for lush mangoes and papayas. Actually, Kim Jong-Il's favorite foods—a well-documented fact—were salo, shark-fin soup, and dog-meat soup, foods which he believed gave him immunity and virility. It was also widely reported in his lifetime that he had a team of women who made sure all the rice grains served to him were identical. A former personal physician also said that a team of as many as 200 scientists worked to cultivate the perfect diet for the dictator to ensure that he had a longer life. Like his father, the "Dear Leader" had a fear of flying and always traveled by private armored train for state visits to Russia and China. The BBC reported that Konstantin Pulikovsky, a Russian emissary who traveled with Kim across Russia by train, told reporters that Kim had live lobsters air-lifted to the train every day.

One comfort in Eternity for all of these sober and abstentious, self-denying individuals—that is, if they do get to Heaven—is that they are assured by Jesus in Luke 20:27-38 that different rules apply there and that the "children of the resurrection" who "do not belong to this age," by which he meant the Earth," are "children of God" and will be "like angels." He distinctly said, "Those who are considered worthy of a place in that age and in the resurrection from the dead neither marry nor are given in marriage." "They cannot die anymore," we are told, and so with the abrogation of all other earthly laws, say goodbye to the need for food!

An observation? Any gourmand in quest of ever new exciting renewals of taste sensations, restive, tense, greedy, unappeased in his perpetual searches, driven by his wandering appetite to what becomes an ontological dead-end by definition, shares a sort of ignoble symmetry with the equally restless person who walks those very paths in his equally unnatural drive to forego food.

Nevertheless, the existential question is not simple.

The fixation on food as a signifier of self involves an entire cartography of what we mean to say by what we must accept or refuse to eat. Almost like Prince Hamlet, we face situations sprouting with questions and quiddits we must answer. Jean-Paul Sartre writes in *Being and Nothingness*,

> The synthetic intuition of food is in itself an assimi-
> lative destruction. It reveals to me the being, which

I am going to make my flesh. Henceforth, what I
accept or what I reject with disgust is the very being
of that existent, or if you prefer, the totality of the
food proposes to me a certain mode of being of the
being which I accept or refuse…It is not a matter of
indifference whether we like oysters or clams, snails or
shrimp, if only we know how to unravel the existential
significance of these foods… Every human reality is a
passion in that it projects losing itself so as to found
being… Man is a useless passion.

Sartre never understood man's passion with transcendental goals ("the
idea of God is contradictory"). As Kant explained, we cannot comprehend
God, we can only believe in Him. Still, if Sartre failed to grasp the fulfillment
of that passion, at least he understood the nature of human lament.

26.

THE GREEDY OLD FAT MAN

A human lament, it may be argued, may be different in kind, but not in intent. It is my belief that in the matter of food aversions those laments, any such lament, at least proves that the mechanism is functioning, whether poorly or not. A thermostat is reading a wrong somewhere or somehow. Man is not only the master of his body, said Descartes, but also the proprietor of his soul. The mind controls the body, but the body can also influence the otherwise rational—and irrational—mind, such as when people act out of passion or speak out of swollen pride, an idea that in Descartes' day had previously been discounted regarding the relationship between mind and body when it had been taken strictly as unidirectional, mind solely to body. The two are often at loggerheads, it is true, and yet the seemingly irreconcilable tension between mind and body is as much blessed as it is bullish. There has been a great deal of philosophical ink spilled on the subject. Voluntary submission, nevertheless—*islam*—always has a touch of sanctity in it. I can never forget the reply by way of email that a former student of mine from Phillips Academy in Andover, the poet Revan Schendler, a gentle soul, wrote back when asked about food aversions, saying, "I will eat anything offered to me, even if it makes me gag, having lived in places where people who have nothing are offended when their guests reject something they may have worked a day to put on the table." This is the altruisic bookend to all food aversions.

One caveat in W.B. Yeats's *A Vision*, the esoteric system which he and his wife, Georgie, created around the gyres and phases of the moon and on which he based some of his best, if most abstruse, poems for which the cyclic vision provided both an historical and poetic metaphor, is that one cannot live at—or in or by or for or in relation to—the extremes. I believe this applies to the coordinates of facing food, as well. We have looked at both extremes, the indiscriminate polyphages (King Farouk, A.J. Liebling, Lucius Beebe, Diamond Jim Brady, Orson Welles, Adolf Frederick, Edward Gibbon,

King of Sweden, Alexander Woollcott, *et alii*) and their opposite counterparts, the over-deliberating oliphages (St. Anthony of the Desert, Simone
Weil, Èugene Atget, Patricia Highsmith, Blanche Knopf, Paul Dirac, Wallis
Simpson, the Duchess of Windsor, *et alii*). That anyone's scrupulous balance
is lost in acute immoderation is hardly a news bulletin, for it was something
taught—repeated here for emphasis—by both the ancient Romans (*ne quid
nimis*) and the ancient Greeks (μέδεν ἀγαν).

I find a farcical parallel, neither of them accurate while both of them
ludicrous, in the indefensible and outlandish cartoon pictures of small town
life portrayed, on the one hand, invariably negative, in the ironic novels of
Sinclair Lewis and, on the other hand, always mawkishly positive, on Garrison
Keillor's "A Prairie Home Companion." Lewis's fictional city of Zenith located in the equally fictitious Midwestern state of Winnemac, a rigid, conform-
ist, thrusting, vulgar world of social-climbing, shallow "boosterism," and
suffocating middle-brow standards with a lot of the folk monstrous, bawling,
and nasty, is no more honest or realizably coherent than is Keillor's senti-
mentalized Lake Wobegon, Minnesota, where "all the women are strong,
all the men are good looking, and all the children are above average," a settled, warm, neighborly world of pure-hearted bachelor Norwegian farmers,
Lutheran goodness, all of it far too cute and nauseating and unreal. These
alternately unheroic and heroic domestic vistas of American life, depressingly
and exaggeratedly oversimplified both, reveal that both writers, of fiddling
imagination, were caricaturists at best. There is no health to be found at the
far extreme of anything. No refuge ever resides in disproportion.

In Plato's *Symposium,* Socrates discusses the nature of love. In examining what Love desires, Socrates notes that "a thing that desires, desires
something of which it is in need" (200 b); whenever we say "I desire what
I have," we really mean to say, "I desire to have in the future what I have
now." Under these circumstances, desire arises from need. It is impossible to
desire what you already have.

In his *Enchiridion,* however, Epictetus tells us that desire, among those
things "in our power," is "by nature free, not subject to restraint or hindrance." To desire is to aim at something. Desire contrasts with aversion.
Epictetus tells us to "take away the aversion" to inevitable things (including
all that is immanent), because failure to avoid doing so leads to unhappiness.
Instead of seeking to make things happen as we desire them to, we should
settle for things as they happen. In other words, desire only what you already
have, which is to say be content.

An aversion is directly and vividly held. But a certain disease of consciousness is in attendance, objectifying the dislike that permits this "evil"

to mask and parade in the guise of good. J. Alfred Prufrock's simile in T.S. Eliot's famous poem, which begins with "the evening is spread out against the sky/ like a patient etherized upon a table," is a comment, not on the sky, but rather on Prufrock himself, a portentous line reflecting—confessing to—his anxiety. Contrast the depth and detail of any food aversions against the superficial and specious assumption of them. In other words, what food a person dislikes is a confession of a deeper truth, involving a much more complex epistemology than mere whim, arbitrary choice, what brought that aversion about. It is a signifier of a person's cognition, indeed of the person himself, in the same way that what makes a novel by Henry James the spiritual adventure it is is much less a matter of the objective and impersonal "facts of the case" than the accompanying prodigiously subjective side of the ongoing and complex experience.

What we eat is what we are, true. What we refuse to eat—like buckshot in meat, grit in clams, dirt in beets, sand in morels, etc.—tells us who we are. To seek, to find it, is up to you. I've always believed—and for decades told my students—that the sole purpose in living this life is to seek the *meaning* of it, always to be asking the ultimate questions, which are as important than the answers. What is required is to keep learning, whatever the subjects may be and from whatever teachers are available, from experiences good and bad, never failing the endless quest to know.

I suppose the all-accepting taste of normal people recapitulates the sentiments in Ogden Nash's poem, "Food," which goes,

Food,
Just food,
Just any old kind of food.
Let it be sour,
Or let it be sweet,
As long as you're sure it is
something to eat.
Go purloin a sirloin, my pet,
If you'd win a devotion
incredible;
and asparagus tips
vinaigrette,
Or anything else that is edible.
Bring salad or sausage
or scrapple,
A berry or even a beet.

Bring an oyster and egg or an apple
as long as it's something to
eat.
If it's food
it's food;
Never mind what kind of food.
When I ponder my mind
I consistently find
it is glued
on food.

But by no means all people!

Nothing is skewed when one has developed an intense hatred for a given food. It is merely another way at looking at something from a different angle. Perception is rarely other than relative. After all, moonlight is only sunshine, while the sky is black, not blue, for dust particles and droplets of moisture in the air reflect the sun's light and make it but appear that way. We see what we want, but we often imagine what we see. What food we come to hate, we cagily make devils of, finding in the thing a fetish, believing like a child that the object's power exists independently, in the very same way we fashion deities. In his dramatic poem, *Empedocles on Etna*, Matthew Arnold imagined false gods being worshiped (or hated) everywhere—as foils:

So, loath to suffer mute,
We, peopling the void air,
Make Gods to whom to impute
The ills we ought to bear;
With God and Fate to rail at, suffering easily. (II.
ii.278–82)

Why we single out a food to hate is as mysteriously deep as the fond of any given person's nature. Does it happen in part, at least philosophically, to exert our sense of choice? To reinforce our identity? To demand autonomy? There is in the arbitrariness of food aversions an unexplained specificity that seems in a certain sense to be insensitively discriminatory, unfair, prejudiced, even spiteful. It calls up the so-called "Scandal of Particularity," the impropriety that the Creator of the Universe would enter human history in a very localized way, such as choosing the Hebrews to be in a particularly covenanted relationship with him or, even more basically, the arguably discreditable fact of God entering into time. If the Supreme Being, as Catholics define him, is in a permanent state of *isness*, if he is indeed the eternal *I Am*, how is it possible for this God to operate within the finite terms of the *was, is,* and *will be*? Maybe this is one of theism's strengths in pointing out the immanence of God in time?

The metaphysics of food aversion is fascinating, whether we have taken our position from having been offered too much of a particular food or out of a particular history been deprived of it—even if in our furtive imaginations—that, raising our suspicion, it has come to represent something to offend us. I recall the song, "I Do Not Want What I Haven't Got," by Sinead O'Connor. You could say that the words are also an extension of "I do not want what has to be given or forced upon me," which is, along with being a fiat or a flat-out injunction, at least rhetorically an actual reversal of prayer, with the person involved seeking a kind of Kirillov-like autonomy from something he or she seeks to forfend before he or she is deprived of it—an attempt to "not need." It may be studied refusal, in short, in an attempt to make a personal assent.

It is almost to say, more than it is "an invitation to dinner reversed," as the great poet Oscar Wilde, who loved paradox, wittily viewed a prayer that is answered, it is the denial of something offered or available.

I cannot help thinking specifically of Wilde here. What is interesting is that in the very serious matter of prayer, Wilde, who knew about hurt, believed that a prayer should *not* be fulfilled. This goes back to a particular conversation that took place at the turn of the century. When Laurence Housman recalled a memorable exchange he had with Oscar Wilde and several others in Paris in an outdoor café in the fall of September 1899, he felt obliged to sit down in 1923 to reconstruct it and in doing so left us with a "*monologue d'outre tombe*" that, among other subjects, touched on prayer. It began when Wilde, always an enemy of the conventional and the bourgeois, satirically pointed out to his friends that people who want to say merely what is sensible should say it to themselves before they come down to breakfast in the morning, never after. (By this reasoning, one can avoid living by the logic of expectation.) Housman replied that this was exactly the time when "The White Queen" in *Alice's Adventures in Wonderland* practiced telling herself of all the things she knew to be impossible. The Queen lives backwards in time, one recalls, due to the fact that she lives through the eponymous looking-glass. All of this unreasoning strikes Alice as odd.

One recalls that the Queen offers Alice "jam tomorrow and jam yester-day—but never jam to-day," a sententious phrase now that has long since been taken in the language to become a proverbial expression standing for a promise that is never fulfilled. The Queen then speaks to Alice of all the things that she personally finds difficult to believe (one being that she is just over 101 years old), adding that in her youth she could believe "six impossible things before breakfast," and with high authority counsels Alice to practice the same rare skill.

"I always thought that meant saying her prayers," suggests one of the guests in that outdoor Paris café, regarding the Queen muttering of things she knew to be impossible. Driving home his personal message, Oscar Wilde proclaims,

> But saying prayers is always possible. It is only the *answer* to prayer that is impossible. Prayer must never be answered. If it is, it ceases to be prayer, and becomes a correspondence. If we ask for our daily bread and it is given to us as manna was given to the Israelites in the wilderness, it is merely an invitation to dinner reversed. How much more devotional the exercise becomes when we know that our food comes to us from quite mundane sources, irrespective of prayer.

"But your prayer then becomes merely a superstition," declared yet another guest, somewhat scandalized.

Counters Wilde, "Not at all: it is a compliment—a spiritual courtesy which one may surely hope is appreciated in the proper place."

A food aversion in the final analysis is no different than the person who holds the food in aversion, for is not the entire story, after all is said and done, a moral fable of those who, at least on this fussy food front, yearn to be in command as well as to be free? "On the outskirts of every agony sits some observant who points," wrote Virginia Woolf who, although she may have been thinking about God, but may very well have been pondering a person making a food complaint. In any caustic judgment, beyond that, there is almost always something cleansing and memorable. The dispute is to be distracted from a distraction. "Whoso would be a man must be a nonconformist," wrote Waldo Emerson. We are all of us incomplete and over a lifetime of difficult days face a chaos of contingencies. Is it any wonder that one looks to individuating instances to shore up a sense of self in the way of reinforcement and seeks any beacon toward which the unimpeded self might tend? On the other hand, is a person only his faults? Must he be said to equal his fancies as an identity? May not one argue there is no one-to-one correspondence between oneself and one's aversion; may not one legitimately say blame the aversion, if you will, but don't blame me?

In Sir Thomas Wyatt's song, "The Lover's Lute Cannot Be Blamed Though It Sing of His Lady's Unkindness," the narrator says

> Blame not my lute, for he must sound
> Of this and that as liketh me,
> For lack of wit the lute is bound
> To give such tunes as pleaseth me
> Though my songs be somewhat strange,
> And speak such words as touch thy change,
> Blame not my lute...
> My lute and strings may not deny
> But as I strike they must obey.

calling upon the audience not to hold his lute responsible for the sound that it makes. He explains that the instrument is controlled by him, it has no independent thought, and that its voice is dictated by the play. Don't blame me for my food aversions, although they be crotchets—they are but given me to express, be they born of neuroses or whim, choice or caprice, fancy or foible, impulse or inclination, although they can grip you for years tight as a tick or slowly or soon vanish like a baby's storkbite. *Don't blame me for my food aversions.* It seems a cop-out. Who after all's expressing them? The strangeness of the song is indeed that the song is being sung. What is the lute without the lutanist, however? Who can tell the dancer from the dance? as W.B. Yeats profoundly asked. Such questions have no easy or obvious answers.

Doubt, hindrance—and interrogation—are among mankind's natural modes. In the Gospels, Jesus Christ asks as many as 135 questions! Salvation *involves* queries and uncertainty. It is not just dissatisfaction, it is a seeker's desire, the doubter's need for reliance, the querulousness that keeps us moving, avoiding the stasis of the passive dolt. Be not afraid of moving slowly, only of standing still, as the old Chinese proverb goes. T.S. Eliot writes in "Choruses from the Rock,"

> Oh my soul, be prepared for the coming of the
> Stranger.
> Be prepared for him who knows how to ask questions.

I use the word hindrance. The food aversionist embodies the very notion of the concept of encumbrance, obstacle, interference. Impediment becomes a salient fact of his very existence. In his noble essay "Hindrance," published in the *Atlantic Monthly* in 1862, David Atwood Wasson, American minister and Transcendentalist author, essayist and poet, a man who is usually regarded as a disciple of Waldo Emerson, argued that "every definite action is conditioned upon a definite resistance, and is impossible without it." To Wasson, hindrance is a basic law of Nature. Hindrance to action, to him, in short, makes action possible. Professor Charles H. Foster in his preface to Wasson's selective writings, *Beyond Concord*, explains,

> The resistance of water is needed to keep the ship afloat; the tympanum of the ear must resist the sound waves to transmit their suggestion to the ear; objects must resist, that is reflect, the sun's rays to become visible; the marble, basalt, bronze must resist the sculptor to receive the impress of his thoughts. Inwardly and outwardly man needs resistance to evoke his insight, his wisdom, his art; the philosophers and saints were premature in lamenting the fact that body hampered spirit, for it was the very collision between them which struck out the spark of thought and kindled the sense of law.

Resistance, outward and inward, is nothing less than a whispering answer to our need. Observes Wasson, "Much that is in itself undesirable occurs in obedience to a general law, which is not only desirable, but of infinite necessity and benefit, mediating what it must master." The struggle is for freedom.

As to freedom in the matter, storybooks are filled with no end of intrepid and uncompromising questers seeking such freedom. Don't our most personal dreams, replete with the craziest wishes, ineluctably demand that life conform to our own ways? Dreams are about what is closest to us. Picasso often repeated that he wanted to make a sculpture that did not touch the ground. It reminds me of the old American folk-tale, "The Greedy Old Fat Man." In this tale, a fat man, greedy and old, consumes a hundred biscuits, a pot of mush, and drinks a barrel of milk. Still, after all, the old butter barrel is still hungry. He desperately sets out to find something more to eat and grows fatter and fatter as he eats a little boy, a little girl, a little dog, a little cat, a little fox, and, one by one, these characters disappear. It turns out, however, that a very clever squirrel refuses to be caught: he outsmarts the old fat man by going way out on a tree limb. When the greedy man tries to follow, he falls down, busting himself open, whereupon out jump all the creatures in his belly. The little boy cries, "I'm out." The little girl shouts, "I'm out."

The cat, the fox, and the rabbit all jump out and are free. The clever squirrel laughs but says, "I'm out too, because I wasn't in."

Because I wasn't in!

In a way, it seems somehow to sum up everything about food phobias, the loathed or avoided food, the active claimant involved, and his or her ringing if negative boast that, for whatever reason, he has side-stepped, if only for another day, a food he cannot bear to look at, never mind eat. Are our impressions illusions? So be it. Wrote Saul Bellow in *To Jerusalem and Back*, "A great deal of intelligence can be invested in ignorance when the need for illusion is deep."

In his Phi Beta Kappa oration at Harvard College in 1789 on the topic of "taste," some forty-eight years before his son Waldo's notable "The American Scholar" address, 20-year-old William Emerson exhorted his academic audience to renounce the notion of "universal taste" and to endorse the sanctity of *individual* expression by grasping "the powers of reason, and of the soul" and by acknowledging "not only the attributes of sound judgment, but all the warmth of imagination." Again, as Kant has assured us, it is the human mind that makes the material world knowable and predictable. Any and all categories of understanding that we intuit determine the very way we perceive what we call "reality." Knowledge begins with experience but does not come from experience. We all have our own compasses that fix the cardinal points or directions. Look to your own azimuths and bearings. Are they strange?

So be it.

The air is inhabited by sylphs, the wind by sprites, water by ondines, fire by salamanders, all dark, mysterious forests by elves, islands by sirens, mountains by trolls, the very loamy earth by gnomes, goblins, and halflings, indeed our dreams, both sleeping and waking, are populated by no end of pucks, antic imps, gremlins, succubi and incubi. Why can't food have its own devils?